Fagothey's

RIGHT & REASON

Ethics in Theory and Practice

Ninth Edition

Milton A. Gonsalves

Merrill Publishing Company
A Bell & Howell Information Company
Columbus   Toronto   London   Melbourne

Published by Merrill Publishing Company
A Bell & Howell Information Company
Columbus, Ohio 43216

This book was set in Garamond

Administrative Editor: Vicki Knight
Production Coordinator: Carol Driver
Cover Designer: Brian Deep

Photo Credits: American Honda, pp. 424, 438; John Bird Photography, pp. 15, 228, 548; Citicorp Savings, p. 410; Cobalt Productions/Merrill, p. 100; Paul Conklin, pp. 30, 80, 293, 521; Kevin Fitzsimons/Merrill, pp. 91, 265; Jean Greenwald/Merrill, p. 149; Jo Hall, p. 316; Peter Kresan, p. 475; Doug Martin/ Merrill, p. 48; New York Convention and Visitors Bureau, pp. 306, 360, 510; New York Stock Exchange, p. 456; Harvey R. Phillips, p. 213; Christopher B. Reddick, pp. 2, 173; Paul M. Schrock, p. 65; Michael Siluk, p. 120; Steve & Mary Skjold, pp. 131, 187; David Strickler/Strix Pix, pp. 161, 330, 497; Viscione, p. 198; Washington Area Convention & Visitors Bureau, p. 371; Hank Young/Merrill, p. 110; Allen Zals, p. 393; Gale Zucker, p. 245

Library of Congress Catalog Card Number: 88-80956
International Standard Book Number: 0-675-20914-5
Printed in the United States of America
1 2 3 4 5 6 7 8 9—92 91 90 89

Preface

Fagothey's Right and Reason introduces the reader to the living tradition of the Aristotelian-Thomistic ethical system, applying the wisdom of that tradition to the discoveries and problems of contemporary life. This text incorporates whatever seems worthwhile in later speculations as a genuine development, extension, clarification, or application of Aristotelian-Thomistic principles. In this ninth edition I have made every effort to be open to new insights and understandings while at the same time being aware that anyone's knowledge of the truth is always fragmentary. Newly discovered fragments of the truth is always fragmentary. Newly discovered fragments of the truth need to be fitted into one's grasp of the whole, perhaps adding to it a new perspective or bring out more clearly what is already known, and at times correcting a previous hasty judgment about what is currently being said or done.

We live in a pluralistic society in which any number of differing moral viewpoints coexist more or less peaceably with one another. That very pluralism has often prompted teachers to introduce their students to ethics by using anthologies of ethical writings. *Fagothey's Right and Reason* is for those students and teachers who have found this anthology approach unsatisfactory. This book provides the reader with one consistent point of view. Since everyone must begin somewhere to learn to think clearly and consistently about the moral problems we face daily at every level of our lives, the Aristotelian-Thomistic synthesis is an admirable base from which to make this start. Even in a pluralistic setting such as our own, moral positions are seen to be the result of a process of right reasoning and not the pure subjectivism of a "gut" reaction. Whether or not the reader is convinced by the Aristotelian-Thomistic synthesis as it is presented here, at the very least he or she has an excellent point of departure from which to discover something better or more adequate for life.

This book is designed for undergraduate courses in ethics. At the time of the first edition, such courses were commonly year-long or two-semester courses, the first semester devoted to ethical theory and the second to practical problems that arise in everyday life. Obviously, the teacher must adapt the material for the now more common one-semester or -quarter course. The book has been successfully used for introductory courses in ethics as well as for courses treating contemporary moral problems, business ethics, medical ethics, the ethics of war and peace, and various adult education courses. With the student in mind, every effort has been made to make the text readable and to provide discussion questions that are interesting and pertinent to everyday life.

MAJOR CHANGES IN THE NINTH EDITION

Since the publication of the eighth edition, ethics itself has often been the focus of national attention. At almost every turn we have been faced with ethical situations: the truthfulness in government, the confidentiality on Wall Street, the rights of genetic parents to raise their children, the just treatment of immigrants, the rights of journalists to report on the private lives of presidential candidates and nominees to the Supreme Court, the merits of arms-control agreements, the appropriateness of capital punishment, the handling and disposal of nuclear wastes, and so on. Public comment and debate on various issues has served to underscore the fact of pluralism in our society and has prompted some philosophers to search for a common moral ground that we can all agree on.

Accordingly, Chapter 1, "Ethics," has been revised. In place of the section on the possibility of a science of ethics, there are now two new sections, one on ethics as a scientifically objective discipline and the other on ethics in a pluralistic society. Pluralism is a fact of life in the United States and throughout the free world. Even so, one position on a moral question is not necessarily just as good as another. Students need to develop the capacity to articulate their own views and to listen carefully to others in order to understand alternative positions before engaging in criticism. They must learn to converse constructively with people who do not think as they do. Such dialogue is necessary in any pluralistic society, for it is the only way we can develop sound public policies that have the support of all and contribute to the common welfare of all.

The discussion of so-called animal rights in Chapter 18, "Rights," has been completely redone to take into account the views of animal rights activists and environmentalists and to stress our stewardship over the entire range of the earth's goods.

The discussion of abortion in Chapter 19, "Life," has been almost entirely redone by presenting the strongest arguments both for and against abortion currently in use.

Chapter 20, "Health," has been given a new section on the AIDS crisis with some suggestions for containing the epidemic; the section on the right to die has been expanded to include a discussion of the morality of withholding nutrition and hydration from hopelessly ill patients.

The statement of the problem for Chapter 24, "Sex," has been redone in the light of the AIDS crisis. An almost entirely new section on the virtue of chastity, a revised section on selective abortion, a complete revision and expansion of the discussion of artificial insemination, and a new section on surrogate motherhood have also been added.

"Government," Chapter 26, addresses some new and stronger arguments for and against capital punishment and offers a new conclusion that argues for abolishing the death penalty because of the current set of circumstances both here and abroad.

The discussion of employee stock ownership plans (ESOPs) in Chapter 31, "Capitalism," has been updated to take into account what corporations are doing with these plans in order to take advantage of incentives provided in the Tax Revision Act of 1986, one of those incentives being the conversion of ESOP into floor/offset ESOP pension plans.

ADDITIONAL CONTENT AND FORMAT CHANGES

1. The book is divided into seven parts, each having its own introduction to make it easier for the student to comprehend the book's structure. The order of the chapters is still the same, but the introductory matter for each of the seven parts is a brief prelection of what can be expected as the reader moves into the particular part.

2. The section on Heidegger and conscience has been omitted from Chapter 4.

3. The critique of Kant's moral philosophy in Chapter 12 has been simplified and clarified.

4. A nontheistic argument for the immorality of murder has been added to Chapter 19.

5. New information has been added on marijuana; the use of drugs in sports to enhance

performance is discussed; and the moral assessment of drug use has been redone in Chapter 20.

6. Some new reasons have been added to justify the gay liberation movement (Chapter 27).

7. The discussion of inflation has been omitted from Chapter 31.

8. New discussion questions have been added to 28 of the 36 chapters so that all the questions throughout the book now deal with specific contemporary moral problems.

PEDAGOGICAL FEATURES

Organization. The first half of the book, Chapter 1 through 18, deals with theoretical ethics and remains organized around 10 major theories covering the whole spectrum of ethical positions. Students do not come to ethics with much philosophical background. No one procedure can overcome that disadvantage, but the approach used in this text somewhat offsets lack of background. Law and duty cannot be omitted, but an appeal to them is kept toned down in favor of an emphasis on the dignity of the human person as rational and free. Natural law has a better chance of being understood and appreciated when it is seen as benefiting the lives of persons who live together in a shared culture and a world. Even though its first principles do not change, natural law extends and develops in the course of shifting historical and social experience.

The latter half of the book, Chapters 19 through 36, is devoted to practical ethics and continues to make incursions into the domains of sociology, medicine, economics, and political science, but always from a consistent philosophical point of view.

The problem method. The problem method has been kept: introducing one of the major problems of ethics, explaining how it arose

and why it is a problem, giving the main schools of thought on the subject with some historical background, stating the arguments for and against each proposed solution, weighing the arguments against one another, and finally, when possible, resolving the problem in light of the evidence and reasoning involved. Every effort has been made to avoid dogmatism and indoctrination. No apology is necessary either for expressing one's convictions or for being unable to resolve some thorny questions. Most problematic issues are treated by giving an equal number of arguments on each side, after which some ways of sifting out the truth are suggested. Traditional views are included, but they are countered with current criticisms.

Aids for the student. Like previous editions, this text offers the use of ordinary language rather than technical vocabulary, quotations from classical and modern philosophers, short summaries at the end of each chapter, questions for discussion, and reading lists that encourage the student to go to the sources. The bibliography has been thoroughly revised and updated.

ACKNOWLEDGMENTS

I am most grateful to those who have read and carefully critiqued my work and to my colleagues and friends who have encouraged me. Merrill Publishing Company obtained the experienced advice of the following excellent reviewers: Dr. Robert Hall, Niagara University; Dr. Joseph Lafaro, Gannon University; Dr. Thomas Baker, Gannon University; and Dr. Raphael Waters, Niagara University. Their suggestions and criticisms have had a marked influence on various aspects of this revision. Finally and most importantly, I am grateful for the time I had to know and work with Austin Fagothey.

Milton A. Gonsalves

Contents

PART I
The Subjective Factors in Moral Life

The human race was slow to pass from the concept of family and tribal guilt to that of personal responsibility. One of the fascinations of the *Oresteia* trilogy is to watch Aeschylus wrestle with the problem. Right and wrong, good and evil are not only characteristics of the deed done but also of the doer who commits him- or herself personally to the deed he or she chooses to do. We are not just playthings dangling on the strings of fate; we have a say in the shaping of our lives. This task is at the same time our most glorious personal prerogative and our most serious responsibility.

We begin our exploration of ourselves and our deeds with a discussion of ethics, the part of philosophy that studies the person and personal deeds from the point of view of the rightness or wrongness, the goodness or evilness, of the person and the deeds (Chapter 1). The next three chapters deal with the moral life from the point of view of the doer, the subjective side of the moral life. (The objective side of the moral life deals with the deed done by the doer, the moral agent or subject. It is discussed in Part II.) From the point of view of the subject (agent or doer), we shall examine the degrees of voluntariness of our personal acts (Chapter 2), the degrees of responsibility we can have for our personal choices (Chapter 3), and conscience as our personal guide to moral living (Chapter 4).

1
Ethics

ORIGIN OF ETHICS

In all our varied activities we see that not just any way of behaving will do, that there is a right and a wrong way to conduct ourselves. Early in human history people must have seen that this question could be asked of life as a whole: Is there a right and a wrong way of *living,* of gathering all these activities into the spending of one's life? Is there a pattern, a model, an ideal of the good human life? If so, where can people find it and how strictly *ought* they follow it?

While we have no record of any such primitive speculations, we do find in the dawn of history that people had already asked these questions and given them some sort of answer in the rather complex codes of conduct embedded in tribal customs and usage. Such knowledge of the good life is not a systematically organized body of knowledge based on constant and universal principles, though it often does involve some degree of reflective thought. Out of the material suggested by these primitive codes of conduct an awakened reflective intelligence could fashion a science of the good life. The standard and rules of conduct embedded in tribal customs and usage are called *customary morality;* here the individual behaves in accordance with social custom and usage. *Reflective morality* emerges when a person attempts to find general principles by which to direct and justify his or her personal behavior. The distinction between customary and reflective morality is relative rather than absolute, because even customary morality may involve some reflective thought. The distinction does point to a difference that is important for our purposes—the difference between outer conformity and inner conviction. Much of our conduct is simply and unreflectively accommodated to social usage. When we act in this way, we are conforming our behavior to an external standard, the social custom or usage of the day. We are engaged in reflective moral thinking when we begin to ask "Why ought I act in this way and not otherwise? Why is this right and that wrong? What is the reason why society frowns on this kind of activity and approves that?" Customary morality offers us definite rules and precepts to guide our conduct. Reflective morality leads us to search for constant and universal principles whereby we can decide for ourselves, from inner conviction, what the good life is and how we ought to live it.

The transition from customary to reflective morality began, in our Western culture, with the Greeks. By the sixth century before Christ they had reduced primitive speculations about the universe and our place in it to some sort of order or system and integrated these speculations into the general body of wisdom called *philosophy.* After a brilliant period of speculation on the structure of the universe, they began in the days of the Sophists and Socrates to turn their insatiable curiosity on themselves, on human life and society. Nothing was too sacred for their penetrating scrutiny. As seafarers and colonizers they had come into close contact with various surrounding peoples and were struck by the variety of customs, laws, and institutions that prevailed. They began to ask themselves whether their own were really so superior and, if so, why. In time their study led to an examination of all human conduct. This part of philosophy they called *ethics;* we call it by the same name and also use the terms *moral philosophy* and *moral theory* as well.

Ethics (moral philosophy, moral theory) grows out of life—situations in which we are confronted with some sort of perplexity or doubt about what is the right thing to do or the best course to follow, situations in which different desires strive for opposed goods or in which incompatible courses of action seem to be justifiable. Such conflict situations call forth personal inquiry into the reasons for deciding where the right really lies. This is the domain of moral philosophy, the domain of human intelligence reflecting in the face of moral conflict and doubt. When we already hold positive convictions as to what is right and wrong, we have no occasion for reflection and so moral theory cannot begin to emerge. But when a child questions the injunctions and prohibitions of his or her parents and teachers, moral theory begins to emerge because it is a generalized extension of what is involved in all reflective morality.

Ethics is concerned with human customs and usages, but from a particular point of view. Some customs and usages are mere conventions, such as table manners, modes of dress, forms of speech, and expressions of courtesy. These vary in different parts of the world and at different times; they can be changed as we please. Much of our lives, however, is regulated for us by custom and social usage. The roles we play in society are complex and intertwined with one another, regulated by societal standards, usages, and pressures. This regulation ranges from being very subtle to quite blatant. A woman, for example, may simultaneously be the daughter of her parents, the wife of her husband, the mother of her child, the teacher of her students, a voter in an election, a member of a church community, a patient of her physician, and so on. She plays a number of different roles in her relations with a number of other people. It is possible for her to accommodate her behavior to society's customary expectations of what any woman would do in these various capacities.

The complexity of any person's life leads to the perplexities and doubts we sometimes find ourselves having in given situations. This is the domain of reflective morality and of moral theory. Many fundamental customs such as telling the truth, paying our debts, honoring our parents, caring for our children, respecting the lives and property of others, and keeping our promised word are operative in our lives because we have been taught that they are right, they are what we ought to do. The woman of our example may be jolted into reflecting about what is the right thing to do when she leaves her home and enters into the stress of teaching her students at school. She may find that the moral standards which apply at home do not apply at all or do not apply in exactly the same way at school, for she is hired to teach her students, not mother them. We do not feel we are being arbitrary and whimsical when we expect teachers to teach students and mothers to care for and nurture their children. It is right for the teacher to be well prepared to conduct her class and help her students learn the subject she has been hired to teach them. This is the customary function of the teacher, but it is more than just customary. It is *right*. For the teacher to spend her time mothering the students would be *wrong*.

Ethics or moral theory is the study of the right and wrong in human conduct; it deals with societal custom and usage *from the point of view of their rightness and wrongness*. Society's acceptance of something as right or wrong is no guarantee of its rightness or wrongness. The reflective person will want to find personally the fundamental reason why something is right or wrong. Ethical theory (ethics, moral theory, moral philosophy) is the study which examines human conduct, social custom and usage, from the point of view of its rightness or wrongness, from the moral point of view, the point of view of what we *ought* to do to live a good (meaningful) life. The point of view of the ethical *ought* is the moral point of view.

PROBLEM

Humans have engaged themselves throughout history in asking questions about the good life. We have not only asked questions about the good life; we have also made judgments about what is the right and the wrong thing to do. This is part and parcel of our collective human experience, the *fact* that we make judgments about right and wrong. *From this fact of human experience ethics takes its start*. The development of ethics in the course of history shows us engaging in the persistent effort to account for this fact of human experience. We know that we do develop moral theory. What is it about us that accounts for this fact? Why do we keep returning to these questions about right and wrong?

Philosophy means "love of wisdom," the love that drives us to seek out answers to our questions about life and its meaning. Philosophy would not be what it is if it merely took for granted that life has a meaning or purpose and that there is a kind of life that can be called the good life. All philosophy begins as skeptical in the sense that it asks questions; it remains skeptical only if, after investigation, it decides no answers can be found. In all ages of human history we find confirmed skeptics who swept away all knowledge including that of morals, but this skepticism was not aimed more at ethics than anything else.

The first order of business for us is to look at the commonly held view of ethics, its nature as a scientifically objective study of the moral life, and its function and use in a pluralistic society. The following questions will guide our discussion:

1. What is ethics as commonly understood?
2. Is ethics a scientifically objective discipline in its own right?
3. How does ethics function in a pluralistic society?

ETHICS AS COMMONLY UNDERSTOOD

Subject Matter and Point of View

Ethics as the history of philosophy portrays it has for its purpose the interpretation of this *fact* of human life: the acknowledgement of right and wrong in human conduct. We find throughout the human race a tendency to judge that there are three kinds of acts:

1. Those that a person ought to do
2. Those that a person ought not to do
3. Those that a person may either do or not do

At this point in our study we do not yet determine whether this judgment is correct or mistaken; we simply note that it is a *fact of experience* that people do judge in this way. So important are these judgments considered that people will regulate their whole lives in accordance with them and will even sacrifice life itself rather than diverge from them. We apply these judgments not only to our own conduct but to the conduct of others: we punish people and even put them to death for doing what we think they ought not to do or for not doing what we think they ought to do. The person who does whatever he or she

wants, with no regard for what he or she *ought,* is outlawed from society and hunted down like a wild beast.

This fact, that people do make judgments of right and wrong, is the basic fact of experience from which ethics takes its start. Philosophy, as an interpretation of human life, cannot afford to overlook so widespread an experience but must investigate it and explore all that it involves. If people are correct in distinguishing right from wrong, we need to know why and on what grounds this judgment is justified. If they are mistaken in distinguishing right from wrong, we also want to know why, and how such wholesale error can be accounted for. Without prejudging the case in either way, we can see that ethics is a necessary study with a large and legitimate field of inquiry.

Every distinct branch of learning must have a subject matter that it studies from a more or less definite aspect or point of view. The subject matter of ethics is human conduct, those actions that a person performs consciously and willfully and for which he or she is held accountable. The aspect or point of view from which ethics studies human conduct is that of its rightness or wrongness, its *oughtness,* if we may manufacture a noun corresponding to the ethical verb *ought*. Ethics is not interested in what a person *does,* except to compare it with what he or she *ought* to do. We call those actions *right* that a person ought to do, and those *wrong* that a person ought not to do. Ethical writers of almost all shades of opinion agree that the investigation of the *ought* is the distinctive feature of ethics, the one that separates it from every other study.

Finally, the point of view of the *ought* is the *moral* point of view. *Moral* cannot be defined in the sense that something else could that is a species or instance of some more generic reality. *Moral* and *morality* can only be described. Moral means human in the sense of *ought,* the sense of being normative, so we can say that moral means "normatively human" or "what the human being ought to be." True, we use "human" descriptively when we say "It is human to err," but we also use "human" normatively when we say

"It is inhuman (not human) to demand a severely retarded person to function and behave as well as one who is not retarded." Here we mean that we *ought not* to make impossible demands of anyone, that it is wrong to do so. What humans ought not to do is immoral; what they ought to do is moral. The moral domain is the domain of the normatively human.

Relation to Other Studies

Besides its relation to the other branches of philosophy, of which it forms a part, ethics is also related to the other human and social sciences. These latter sciences all have the same broad subject matter, but ethics differs from them by its distinctive point of view.

Anthropology and ethics both deal with human customs on various levels of culture and civilization. Anthropology studies the origin and development of human customs without passing any judgment on their moral rightness or wrongness, but it is this rightness or wrongness alone that interests ethics. Anthropology testifies to the existence of moral notions among primitive peoples; ethics borrows such data from anthropology but goes on to examine the moral value of these concepts and customs.

Psychology and ethics both deal with human behavior, with the abilities people have and the acts they perform. Psychology studies how humans actually do behave, ethics how they ought to behave. Sanity and sanctity, a well-adjusted personality and a morally good character, despite the relationship between them, are essentially different things; so too are their opposites, madness and sin, psychic eccentricity and moral depravity. What psychologically motivates a person to a deed, good or bad, is different from the goodness or badness of the deed he or she does. Ethics is dependent on psychology for much information on how the human mind works, but it always passes on from how people do act to how they ought to act.

Sociology, economics, and *political science* study human social life, and so also does ethics but with the same difference of viewpoint. These three sciences deal with actual social, economic, and political institutions—what they are and how they function; ethics determines what they ought to be and how they ought to function. A hard and fast line between these three sciences, and between them and ethics, would render all four studies impractical. The endeavor to remedy the social, economic, and political ills of mankind involves an application of ethics to these three fields. Such a combination is sometimes called *social, economic,* or *political philosophy*. But ethics, precisely as ethics, always preserves its distinctive point of view, the *ought*.

The study of *law* is closely related to ethics. Yet, though both deal with the *ought,* the civil law and the moral law do not always perfectly correspond. The study of civil law deals only with those acts permitted or prohibited by civil law, ethics with the tribunal of conscience judging all of our acts. There is a difference between crime and sin, legal rectitude and moral worth, being law-abiding and having true virtue of soul. A mingling of ethics and the civil law on a wider field gives us the *philosophy of law,* the study of how laws *ought* to be framed and interpreted, a study some writers call *jurisprudence*.

ETHICS: A PRACTICAL SCIENCE

Ethics, it has been said, may be an interesting study, but it can never be a science. According to this view, the scientific method is one of exact mathematical measurement, unsuitable for evaluating virtue and vice. Science proceeds by prediction based on hypothesis and follows with experimental verification. In contrast, personal conduct, especially if regarded as free, is seen as too unpredictable for hypothesis. Science deals with facts and the laws governing them, whereas ethics deals only with opinions about what ought to be and never wholly is. And finally, science engages in the hardheaded pursuit of wresting from nature her secrets, while ethics is lost in a nebulous quest for ever-beckoning yet ever-elusive ideals and aspirations.

The difficulty is partly semantic and dependent on one's definition of science. The scientific world is still largely under the spell of the nineteenth-century mode of thinking, originated by Auguste Comte, known as *positivism,* which eliminates all speculation from philosophy and restricts scientific knowledge to facts and relations between facts. If science is defined so as to apply only to the physical or experimental sciences, then ethics will not qualify as a science. However, current usage defines science as any body of systematized knowledge about an object, and ethics is surely this. Among philosophers, science has traditionally been defined as *the certain knowledge of things in their causes.* Ethics preeminently fulfills this definition, for it studies the purpose or final *cause* of interpersonal life; that is, the final end or goal that is the moral good for all persons, their highest good. Ethics has its own proper object and method of procedure; it studies the purpose of personal life, the principles and laws governing the means to achieve the person's highest good, and, like any other science, tries to establish its conclusions with demonstrative thoroughness. Aristotle warned that ethics cannot be an exact science in the same sense that physics, for example, is exact; and that we must look for no more precision than the subject admits.[1]

Though not exactly like the physical and experimental sciences, ethics is a science; it is a body of systematized knowledge. Like any other science, ethics weighs, assesses, analyzes, and studies relationships of empirical data. The moral rights and wrongs, goods and evils, have a definite reference to the physical universe where the persons engaged in these activities live. Like any scientist, the ethicist engages in inductive fact gathering and analysis with completeness and objectivity as the goals. And, like any other scientist, the ethicist also knows that absolute objectivity and precision are ideals we strive for but never completely achieve. Like every other science, ethics will have its disputed points, but these will be shown to revolve around a solid core of established truth. The physical and experimental scientists have no right to rule ethics out of court. Ethics is a science, the science of

the *ought.* The *ought* itself is a fact demanding explanation as insistently as any other fact in the universe.

Sciences can be considered either theoretical or practical: *theoretical,* if their purpose is the mere contemplation of truth; *practical,* if they not only contemplate the truth but also are directed to action. Since the aim of ethics is to enable the person to act and live right, it is a practical science, standing somewhere between a purely theoretical science and its corresponding art. A science that gives rules or norms for acting is called *normative,* especially if these norms have to do with a person's inner goodness and perfection rather than with the making of external objects. Since ethics sets down the norms for right living, it is a *normative* science, the science of the moral *ought.*

Ethics, then, is both a practical and a normative science that discovers, explains, and demonstrates the principles and rules of right conduct. A further point should also be clear: it is one thing to be a student of morals and quite another thing to live a moral life. The study of ethics is no guarantee that the one who studies will live morally. Something more is required; namely, a conviction and resolve to live and act morally and actually choosing to do so. A person gradually develops a practical skill, not unlike an art, for right living by making the right moral choices in order to live a good life day by day. For this reason, ethics has also been called an art (practical skill). It is certainly like an art in focusing on moral beauty and involving emotion, imagination, intuition, and taste. The moral good cannot be effectively captured by intellectual processes alone. Ethics by its nature must also be immersed in emotion and feeling, in a sense of fittingness, contrast, and even in the grisly and gruesome. Ethics is *like art,* but it is not strictly speaking *an art.* Morals are not aesthetics, and yet a sensitivity similar to aesthetic sensitivity is required to appreciate morality. A morally good life is like the creation of a work of art, for the whole person is involved in living it and develops by living it. Moral theory (ethics) is indeed an intellectual endeavor, but it draws its data from

---

[1] Aristotle, *Nicomachean Ethics,* bk. I, ch. 3, 1094 b 12, 25.

life as it is lived, charged with emotion and feeling.

Ethics and Metaethics

Current ethical writing distinguishes between *normative ethics,* that is, ethics as the study of what humans ought and ought not to do, and *metaethics* or *analytic ethics,* that is, the inquiry into the presuppositions of normative ethics. Metaethics is then the study of ethical theory itself; it is ethics' own reflection on itself judging the success or failure of itself as moral theory. In general, metaethics has two aims: (1) to analyze the meaning of the terms used in moral argumentation and (2) to examine the rules of reasoning and methods of knowing by which moral beliefs can be shown to be true or false.

The first aim is to explain precisely how such terms as "good" and "evil," "right" and "wrong," "duty," "ought," and "moral obligation" function in moral language. We express our moral convictions, judge our conduct, appraise our own and others' character and motives, reflect and deliberate about what we ought or ought not to do, and evaluate what we and others have done. In all these activities we are using moral language, carrying on moral discourse. The task of metaethics is to make a careful and thorough analysis of the meaning of the words and statements that make up moral discourse so that we can understand fully our moral concepts and how they function in moral discourse.

Metaethics' second aim is to make explicit the logical principles that are followed (or intended to be followed) when we give moral reasons for or against doing something or when we try to justify our acceptance or rejection of a moral judgment or argument. What philosophy of science does for the natural sciences, metaethics does for ethics, that is, try to show the logical structure underlying the method whereby statements are verified and theories are supported by appeal to evidence. So metaethics tries to show how moral beliefs or convictions can be established as true or false and on what grounds a person can claim to know that they are true or false. There is a great deal of dispute among philosophers doing metaethics about what methods of reasoning are to be used and even about whether any method is possible at all. This second aim of metaethics then is itself twofold: (1) to determine whether there is any such thing as moral truth or moral knowledge and (2) if so, to discover the method or methods for attaining it.

While it may be argued that metaethical questions must first be answered before we can succeed in developing a system of normative ethics, we should note that these two branches were not distinguished until the middle of the twentieth century. Prior to that time, moral philosophers tended to cover the problems of both branches or phases of ethics in their writings without making the distinction explicit. In studying the writings of earlier philosophers it is then helpful to ask oneself whether the philosopher is doing normative ethics or metaethics. Is the philosopher making moral judgments and attempting to show that they are justified? If so, normative ethics is being done. Is the philosopher examining what it means to claim that a moral judgment can be justified? If so, metaethics (analytic ethics) is being done. The clearer we can be about what questions the philosopher is trying to answer, the better we shall be able to judge the soundness of the philosopher's arguments.

For our own purposes in this book it would be too artificial to maintain a consistent separation between these two phases of ethics, between ethics talking about human conduct and ethics talking about itself. We shall try to justify ethical concepts, principles, and conclusions as we come to them.

ETHICS IN A PLURALISTIC SOCIETY

Some nations today, including our own, are pluralistic societies, societies comprised of many subgroups or subcommunities, each of which has its own view of the morally good life. Living peacefully side by side in pluralistic societies are Jews, Christians of many denominations, Moslems, Buddhists, atheists, agnostics, and several other groups. Each has its own moral tradition, its own vision of what constitutes the moral good for people. Among the various groupings or subcommunities we find some agreement but also much disagreement about what is morally good or bad, right or wrong. Differences in opinions are expected in life; they cannot be avoided, ignored, or dissipated. Diverse moral views are an inexpungeable characteristic of life in any pluralistic society. We must give serious attention to this difficult and often confusing fact, for it has ethical implications for each of us personally and for us as a nation.

Whatever the diversity and disagreement we find, we also find general (all but universal) agreement that mature persons are free to articulate and choose for themselves the lifestyle, religious beliefs, moral convictions, and sentiments they want *as long as they do no harm to any other person*. That last phrase is a key to understanding the shared general desire we as a society (nation) have to continue in existence, to stay alive and share the benefits of living in a group as a nation. This desire has led and continues to lead us to condemn murder, robbery, arson, assault, and pollution of the environment. On these matters we have general agreement that not even one person be allowed to go about freely doing any of these things, because the ultimate result would be the destruction of the entire society. We also agree that a number of other actions must also be condemned: no one may be allowed to bear false witness against another, no judge or legislator may accept a bribe, every violator must be punished in a suitable manner, and the innocent must not be interfered with. We agree about these basics because in doing so we all have a better chance of staying alive.

These matters of general agreement are moral matters just as shared general desires and condemnations are moral matters. However, we must ask: are they moral because of the *general* agreement and *shared general* desire or condemnation; *or* do we agree on and desire or condemn

them because they *are* right and good (or wrong and evil)? Our very intelligence enables us to answer that we agree on and desire those things because they are right and good (and condemn others because they are wrong and evil). Morality is not a matter of public opinion or public consensus. As rational beings, we conform our opinions and form our consensus on the basis of the *known* morality or immorality of those matters. This point is important to remember in discussing moral issues in a pluralistic society. As rational and free beings, we are always concerned with concrete historical situations that give rise to facts that need to be judged by the light of reason so that we can pursue the goods that accord with and avoid the evils that would degrade our rationality and freedom.

Mutual respect and esteem of all persons for one another is a further positive side of the coin that makes living in a group not merely tolerable but a genuine human good. It is the only safeguard the nation as a whole has against false self-righteousness and unjust intolerance. This awareness of the difference between right and wrong, good and evil, together with the mutual respect and esteem of all for all, forms the firm basis for the moral values, ideals, goals, and commitments that hold the nation together as a moral community whose aim is the common good of all its members. This same mutual respect and esteem of all for all in freedom and peace also safeguard the existence of the many moral subgroups.

Each person in a pluralistic society is not only a citizen participating in and contributing to the common good of the nation but also is a member of one or more subgroups or subcommunities. The moral life of each person is then lived on at least two levels: (1) on the national level as a citizen, and (2) on the subgroup or subcommunity level as a member, for example, of a particular church. As a citizen, each person cooperates with all other citizens to achieve the common good, which consists in maintaining justice and peace as well as providing an equal opportunity for all to share in the temporal welfare of the nation in proportion to each one's contribution to the national well-being. As a member of a subgroup or subcommunity, each person further shares in the moral tradition of the group and pursues the moral good as envisioned by the group. Because the moral vision of the good differs at least somewhat from subgroup to subgroup, it is easy to see how the formulation of national public policy on some issues may be difficult to achieve. However, without resorting to force we manage at times to forge a consensus on some issues affecting the common good. For example, we agree generally that perjury and fraud are moral evils that ought not to be tolerated; that every citizen over a certain age has an equal right to vote; that discrimination on the basis of race or religion is morally wrong. On other issues that also affect the common good, such as capital punishment, homosexuality, abortion, in vitro fertilization, and surrogate motherhood, to name but a few, we find no consensus and so no general satisfaction throughout the nation with the public policies on these issues and the moral values involved.

The common good, considered abstractly, is always the same: the general welfare of all. In the concrete circumstances of any particular time in its history, the nation as a whole must decide which specific goods to pursue for the public weal and how to make them realities. Each person as a moral agent undertakes, as a loyal citizen, the obligation to pursue the common good and also undertakes the further obligation of pursuing the moral good as envisioned by the subgroup(s) of which he or she is a member. This task requires a further loyalty on the part of each person. One group's moral vision of the good sometimes conflicts with another group's vision, as is all too obvious when persons of different subgroups come together to discuss the morality of a controverted issue such as abortion. On such occasions we begin to see the need each of us has to be free to hold and live by one's own moral convictions, and the right each of us has to that freedom. Not only must each one be *free from* being forced to agree with someone else's view, but also each of us must be *free to*

pursue the good of which he or she is convinced. Mutual respect and esteem for one another is a necessary bulwark of our personal freedom and so of the common good. In any society, freedom is an all-or-nothing affair. As long as one person is not free to hold the moral convictions of his or her choice and live by those same convictions, then no one else can be free to do so. The mutual respect and esteem make for tolerance and create an atmosphere in which peaceable discussion of a controverted issue may lead to a clearer understanding and appreciation of the concepts, principles, and values at the core of the issue. We are all limited beings; none of us is perfect. Our grasp of the truth about any complex issue is, at best, limited. We need to share one another's insight and understanding if we are to create reasonable public policies satisfactory to all, for only in this way can we be loyal both to the nation and to the subgroup(s) of which we are members.

Does this mean that any public policy, once formulated, becomes the final arbiter of what is right and good or wrong and evil? Not at all. The purpose of public discussion of controverted issues is to find what is in accord with human reason, for this is the right and the good. Each of us is rational and free. The good we seek and the evil we avoid are in accord with our rationality and freedom. Since most controverted issues are complex, we need to reflect carefully together and to listen to the voices of the wisest among us in order to discover and learn what is in accord with our rationality and freedom. We do not seek the least but rather the full-blown right and good, here and now. This task requires time and care to reflect, think, study, and listen. In the long run, we find that the dictates of reason eventually prevail even though the road to consensus may be long and at times tortuous. The all-but-universal agreements and the shared general desires stem from and are rooted solidly in what is in accord with our rationality and freedom. This fact is also the basis of our loyalty, for loyalty is nothing more nor less than our striving to be true to ourselves as rational and free in our search for what is right and good.

A Purely Philosophical Ethics

Philosophers are more and more willing to address themselves to current issues and have been aided in their task by the data and insights of the social sciences. Religious persons are sometimes unwilling to turn to philosophers for help with these issues, because religious faith should be sufficient to guide them through any issue, no matter how thorny, to a genuinely moral conclusion. All the religions of the world are concerned with morals and take on the task of showing people how to be good. Theology, the intellectual study of religion, investigates the moral aspect of life as well as the other phases of religious living and should, so some religious people think, make any purely philosophical study of morals redundant.

The Judeo-Christian religious tradition, which is too conspicuous a fact of our society to be overlooked, is especially rich in moral teaching and has developed an elaborate code of morality. Does the religious person need a double study of morals, one from a purely philosophical standpoint and another from that of divine revelation? How does religious faith relate to moral reasoning? Does religious faith add material content to what is in principle knowable by human reason? These questions may seem academic, touching only the periphery of real life, but the answer we give to them affects not only philosophical ethics but public policy as well, because public policy, even though not identical with sound morality, draws on and builds upon people's moral convictions. If religious faith adds new material content to morality, then the formulation of public policy is even more complex than it seems. For example, if Catholics precisely as Catholics know something about abortion that others cannot know unless they believe it as Catholics, then in our pluralistic society we shall have problems with discussion of the abortion issue in the public

forum. The very methods we use or do not use to judge the moral rightness or wrongness of issues like apartheid, artificial insemination, warfare, and poverty programs can be affected by the way we answer these seemingly academic questions.

We offer here a tentative view. The Judeo-Christian tradition does not and cannot add to human ethical self-understanding as such any material content that is, in principle, new or foreign to humans as they exist and experience themselves. The Judeo-Christian tradition provides, or ought to provide, an outlook on what it means to be a person, and the Judeo-Christian community ought to be one of privileged access to personhood. This tradition, anchored as it is in faith in the meaning of God's covenant with persons, provides a way of viewing and being in the world, of interpreting its meaning, of ranking its values, of responding to its conflicts and perplexities. In our view the Judeo-Christian tradition only illumines human values, supports them, and provides a context for discerning them at any point of history. It helps us to stay human and personal by underlining the truly human and personal against all popular cultural efforts to distort it.

The Judeo-Christian moral tradition is much more a conserver of values than it is a giver of answers. We do not find in revelation concrete answers to the complex moral problems of our day. We do find a world view that informs our reasoning in terms of the basic human and personal values. This world view checks and challenges our tendency to make policies and choices in the light of cultural enthusiasms that can reduce the good of personal life to mere therapeutic adjustment, collapse the individual person into a function of business or society or both, exalt personal uniqueness into isolated individuality, or suffocate it in collectivism.

The Judeo-Christian tradition admits that the human reasoning processes are "darkened" by original sin and that divine revelation is necessary for us so that we can know about God with certainty and no admixture of error. Human reason, however, is not so corrupted by original sin that it is incapable of functioning. The tradition refuses to allow the members of its community to avoid rational deliberation and hard work in developing a normative ethics informed by faith. So the normative ethics of this tradition is developed by philosophical reasoning that is informed by faith, not replaced by that faith.

Not everyone will agree with this view of religious ethics. Some Christians and Jews will insist that philosophical ethics cannot achieve its own purpose by its own methods independently of divine revelation and that the principles it uses and the conclusions it draws are at best only partially true for humans as they concretely exist and actually live in the world today. This is not the view taken in this book. Why not take such a view? Because there are millions of people who have not had the benefit of the Judeo-Christian revelation, who do not know that they actually live in the supernatural order of redemption, who do not perceive the working of divine grace within them, and who must trust entirely to their unaided natural powers to construct for themselves a moral way of living. It seems monstrous to say that they have the obligation to live morally, as all people have, and yet they cannot find out what the moral life is or how to live it.

Philosophical ethics is a purely natural and rational study. To try to absorb it into religion would be to destroy it. As a discipline in its own right, philosophical ethics admits of and allows no regulation of it by theology; it neither enters the field of theology nor uses theology's material. As a matter of fact, religious ethicists (moral theologians) make abundant use of purely philosophical ethics in their work, which, however, is always informed by their religious faith. Philosophical ethics abstracts from religious faith and makes no pretensions of being more than it is, namely, a valuable study of what human reason can show to be the morally good life for all persons.

Philosophy aims at wisdom that is a lucid commitment both to our world and to the realization and development of our personal dignity and self-esteem. Wisdom is a kind of harmony that is nothing more than an identity between our established emotions and an optimal set of reflective judgments that sees the emotions most to our advantage, those that maximize the possibility of personal intimacy and friendship together with mutual respect and self-esteem. The task we give ourselves when we reflect honestly is to force our choices and preferences into the open where we can examine them for what they are and confront them with whatever contrary evidence exists, compare them with their alternatives, and finally, if they are worthy of us, take hold of them as our own fully deliberate and chosen commitments, but if they are unworthy, to liberate ourselves from what is destructive of us and others as persons.

The need for reflective morality and for moral theory grows out of the various conflict situations we find ourselves faced with. This realization defines the service moral theory can provide and protects us from false conceptions of it as well. Moral philosophy studies human customs and helps us to reflect critically on the definite precepts and rules, the definitive injunctions and prohibitions, the values embedded in customary morality. However, moral theory is not a substitute for custom; it does not offer a table of commandments. It can help us to make our personal choices more intelligently, but it cannot make those choices for us any more than it can set up ready-made conclusions about how we ought to act in the concrete situations we face.

Moral philosophy can do three things for us: (1) generalize the kinds of moral conflicts that do arise, and in this way help a perplexed and doubtful person clarify his or her own particular problem or question by placing it in a larger context; (2) state the principal ways such problems and questions have been handled by others who have thought about such matters; and (3) help us to reflect more systematically and consistently by suggesting values that might otherwise be overlooked. Moral theory then is no substitute for customary morality; it can help each of us to develop the capacity to reason about (reflect on) our society's moral code and so develop a critical, reflective morality of our own.

SUMMARY

Philosophy has its origin in the human effort to understand the meaning of our life in this world. *Ethics,* also called *moral philosophy* or *moral theory,* originated in philosophical speculation about the good life and was systematized into a part of philosophy by the Greeks.

Customary morality is the standards and rules of conduct embedded in social customs and usage; *reflective morality* is reasoning about or reflecting on customary morality in order to find for oneself general principles by which to direct and justify one's own conduct. Ethics or moral theory emerges from and is a generalized extension of what is involved in all reflective morality. Ethics is concerned with human customs and usages from the point of view of their rightness or wrongness, and this is what is called the *moral* point of view. The concern of ethics is with what we *ought* to do or not do in order to live a good life, a meaningful life.

As traditionally conceived, the purpose of ethics is to study a *fact* of experience, that people distinguish right conduct from wrong and have some awareness of what *ought* to be done or avoided. The *subject matter* of ethics is then human conduct; its *point of view* is that of rightness and wrongness, of *oughtness.*

Ethics is related to all the human and social sciences but is always distinguished from them by its unique point of view, its concern with what ought to be done.

If ethics is called a *science,* it is not in exactly the same sense as the experimental sciences but in the sense of its being a body of systematized knowledge. It is like the experimental sciences in weighing, assessing, analyzing, and studying relationships of empirical data. It is like art in focusing on moral beauty and in involving emotion, imagination, intuition, and taste, but it is not an art. Ethics is a practical science.

Today we distinguish *normative ethics,* the study of what humans ought and ought not to do, from *metaethics,* an examination of (1) the language and concepts used in moral discourse and (2) the rules of reasoning and the methods of knowing by which moral convictions can be shown to be true or false. An adequate study needs both, and they need not always be kept separate.

A pluralistic society is one composed of several subgroups or subcommunities, each of which has its own moral tradition and vision of the moral good. Each member of a pluralistic society lives the moral life on at least two levels: (1) as a citizen participating in and contributing to the common good, and (2) as a loyal member of one or more of the subgroups. Mutual respect and esteem for one another are a necessary bulwark of each member's personal freedom and of the common good; they also create an atmosphere in which peaceable discussion of a controverted issue may lead to a clearer understanding and appreciation of the concepts, principles, and values at the core of the issue.

Some think that the study of morals so belongs to religion that no purely philosophical ethics is possible. If this were so, the people of the world who have no contact with religious revelation would be doomed to live a moral life without the knowledge of how to do so.

The *wisdom* philosophy seeks is a lucid commitment both to our world and to the realization and development of our mutual personal dignity and self-esteem.

Questions for Discussion

1. Ethics takes as its starting point the fact that people make judgments about the rightness and wrongness of human conduct. Are there any presuppositions ethicists must make to be able to work out an explanation of this fact? What are they? Would you make the same presuppositions? Why?

2. You are a candidate for one of your state's

seats in the United States Senate and have to prepare positions on a number of controversial issues such as capital punishment, abortion, care for critically ill newborns, and immigration. How can you accomplish this task without compromising your own moral integrity and yet be able to appeal to a large enough number of voters to win the election?

3. Down through history it has been said that error has no rights. You and your entire subgroup (e.g., church membership) are convinced that another subgroup's (e.g., a different church) beliefs about how to develop a sound public policy regarding pornography and sodomy are simply wrong. How would you go about engaging the other group in meaningful discussion? Would it be moral to force the other group to change its position? After all, you are certain the group is wrong.

4. We have a high regard for telling the truth,

keeping our promises, meeting our financial obligations, being polite to others, doing no harm to others, playing fair in games, and so on. The list could obviously be made longer, for these are just some of the items that can be labeled matters of customary morality. You are a parent with two children in their early teens. How would you go about helping them to reflect on the rightness or wrongness of these matters?

5. You are a medical doctor specializing in gynecology and obstetrics. Your religious faith is important to you, and your church is adamantly opposed to abortion on demand. While you agree with your church's teaching, you do, at times, deal with women who are carrying defective fetuses and want to have abortions. How do you handle such situations? Why?

Readings

Aristotle's preface to his *Nicomachean Ethics,* bk. I, ch. 1–3, is the best start. There are many translations and editions. J.L. Akrill's *Aristotle's Ethics* has an excellent introduction and provides good notes on the text. Aristotle's *Ethics* and *Politics* are continuous, forming one large treatise of human living.

St. Thomas Aquinas, *Commentary on Aristotle's Ethics and Politics,* follows Aristotle section by section; each subsequent reference to Aristotle's *Ethics* or *Politics* can be understood to include a reference to St. Thomas's *Commentary.*

Part II, ch. 1, of Dewey and Tuft's *Ethics* is an excellent discussion of moral theory. Part II is published separately under John Dewey's name as *Theory of the Moral Life.* Daniel C. Maguire, *The Moral Choice,* argues for the scientific character of ethics as does Henry Margenau in his *Ethics and Science.*

For an appreciation of Anglo-American ethical theory in the twentieth century, good resources include A.J. Ayer, *Language, Truth and Logic,* 2nd ed.; C.L. Stevenson, *Ethics and Language;* A.C. Ewing, *Ethics;* D.J. Mabbott, *Introduction to Ethics;* W.H. Werkmeister, *Theories of Ethics;* W.D. Hudson, *Modern Moral Philosophy;* Jonathan Harrison, *Our Knowledge of Right and Wrong;* J.O. Urmson, *The Emotive Theory of Ethics;* G.J. Warnock, *Contemporary Moral Philosophy;* Alasdair Macintyre, *A Short History of Ethics;* R.M. Hare, *The Language of Morals;* P.H. Nowell-Smith, *Ethics;* and Stephen Toulmin, *An Examination of the Place of Reason in Ethics.*

For a lucid and interesting discussion of ethics in a pluralistic society, consult the opening chapters of H. Tristram Engelhardt, Jr.'s *The Foundations of Bioethics* and John Courtney Murray's insightful essay, "Natural Law and Public Consensus" in *Natural Law and Modern Society.*

Volume 3 of *Encyclopedia of Philosophy* (Paul Edwards, editor-in-chief) has Kai Nielsen's article, "Ethics, Problems of," which presents a good survey of Anglo-American ethics from the point of view of the early 1960s. As we move into the 1970s we find more and more detailed descriptions of various aspects of the moral life given with great care for clear conceptual distinctions. See writers like John Rawls, *A Theory of Justice;* the essays of Philippa Foot, Kai Nielsen, Marcus George Singer; Georg von Wright, *Varieties of Goodness;* and Bernard Gert, *The Moral Rules: A New Rational Foundation for Morality.*

For further discussion of the relation between philosophical ethics and religion see Richard A. McCormick, "The Insights of the Judeo-Christian Tradition and the Development of an Ethical Code," in Eugene C. Kennedy (editor), *Human Rights and Psychological Research;* Charles E. Curran, *Ongoing Revision: Studies in Moral Theology;* and James M. Gustafson, *Protestant and Roman Catholic Ethics: Prospects for Rapprochement.*

D.J.B. Hawkins, *Man and Morals,* has an original starting point.

Alfons Deeken, *Process and Permanence in Ethics: Max Scheler's Moral Philosophy,* provides a good discussion of the role emotions play in our moral life.

2
Conduct

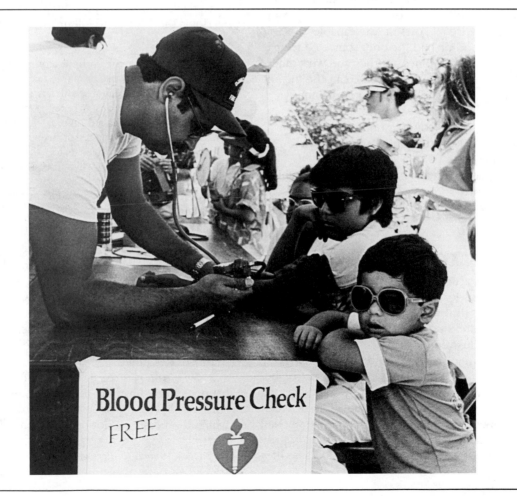

PROBLEM

Babies are not born morally good or bad, and yet we find grown men and women who are morally good or morally bad. How does it happen that each of us in the course of growing to adulthood becomes morally good or bad? Human beings have no moral character to begin with; they build one for themselves by the way they live. Our conduct, the way we live, shapes our moral character; the kinds of things we do are either good or bad, and by doing them we ourselves become good or bad. Before we can determine what moral goodness and badness are and how our actions can be good or bad and so shape our moral character, we should look at human conduct in which moral goodness or badness can dwell. What sorts of acts can a person engage in? Are all sorts of acts capable of being morally good or bad, or only some of them? If only some, which ones are they and what differentiates them from the rest? We can use the following questions to guide us in our inquiry:

1. What is human conduct?
2. How is this conduct under our control?
3. Can we control only our will or also our physical acts?
4. What qualities of the human act have ethical import?
5. How is responsibility entailed in the human act?

HUMAN ACTS

A person's actions taken collectively make up his or her behavior or conduct. *Behavior* is more of a psychological word and is applied even to animals, whereas *conduct* has an ethical meaning and is exclusively human.

We distinguish between the parts of our body we can control and those we cannot control, between those we can move more or less as we want and those that move in spite of us, between the striped, or voluntary, muscles and the smooth, or involuntary, muscles. The words *voluntary* and *involuntary* are interesting here because they are ethical rather than biological words and refer to the fact that certain actions are or are not subject to our will. In ethics we are not concerned with the muscles we use but with the actions we choose to do with or without them, and especially with the governing factor in us, whatever it may be, that we call the *will*. For the moment we can speak of the will as our ability to control ourselves, to be masters of ourselves, to do what we want to do rather than have it forced on us, so that as a result we are held responsible for what we do. Two main things that would prevent our acts from being voluntary, from being willed by us, are ignorance and external force, and therefore a voluntary act is said to be knowingly or deliberately willed. We do not say yet whether it must also be free, and for the present we may overlook the hint of freedom in the following classic statement:

> Of actions done by man those alone are properly called human which are proper to man as man. Now man differs from irrational animals in this that he is master of his actions. Wherefore those actions alone are properly called human of which man is master. Now man is master of his actions through his reason and will, whence too the free will is defined as the faculty of will and reason. Therefore those actions are properly called human which proceed from a deliberate will. And if any other actions are found in man, they can be called actions of a man, but not properly human actions, since they are not proper to man as man.[1]

From the foregoing passage we can validly distinguish two main kinds of acts:

1. *Voluntary acts* or *human acts:* those acts that we consciously control and deliberately will and for which we are held responsible. These acts constitute human conduct and form the subject matter of ethics.

2. *Involuntary acts:* those acts that a person happens to perform but that he or she does not consciously control or deliberately will and for which the person is not held responsible. Such

---

[1]St. Thomas, *Summa Theologica,* I–II, q. 1, a. 1.

are the acts done in infancy, for example, and in sleep, delirium, or insanity. They do not constitute human conduct and have no ethical significance.

Note carefully that this distinction between voluntary and involuntary acts is not a distinction between mental and physical acts. It is true that mental acts such as thinking and willing are proper to human beings in the sense that they alone can do such acts, whereas physical acts such as eating, sleeping, walking, and growing are actions that humans have in common with other beings.

Humans are the only beings in this world who can think, but if a person's thoughts simply run along by association without his or her conscious direction and control, such thoughts are only *involuntary acts,* not *voluntary* or *human acts,* even though they are mental. On the other hand, eating and sleeping are physical acts that humans do in common with brute animals, but they become *voluntary* or *human acts* if the person does them knowingly and willingly. To put food in one's mouth while in a distracted state of mind is an *involuntary act,* but to determine deliberately to eat this food is a *voluntary* or *human act.* To be overcome by drowsiness and fall asleep is an *involuntary act,* but to go to bed intentionally for the purpose of sleeping is a *voluntary* or *human act.* Although it is impossible to have a *human act* unless it is guided by intellect and will, the act itself can be of any sort. A human act can be either physical or mental provided it is deliberately willed.

BACKGROUND OF CHOICE

What do I do when I make a choice? What is the exact point at which an involuntary act may turn into a voluntary or human act and so pass from being ethically indifferent to being ethically significant? A human act is the result of an interplay of intellect and will. We know and want. Our ability to know beyond what is immediately present to our senses is intellect; our ability to want what we know intellectually and to seek it is will.

Strictly speaking, intellect and will do not perform any act at all; they are but abilities by which the whole *person* acts. Such abilities are not independent agents, little persons within the larger human person doing things on their own, nor are they geared like the wheels and levers of a machine. The act of choice is the result of an interplay of functions, for to know and to want are not the same kind of doing even though they are done by the same person who is the only doer in the whole process. If we speak of the intellect or will as doing anything, we are speaking in a loose way to mean that the *person* does something by using his or her intellectual and will powers (abilities).

For us to act we must first be attracted by some good. When we perceive something as good, we find it attractive in some way. If we see that it is not only good in itself but also good for us, our attraction to it becomes a desire or wish. The wish may remain ineffectual, but if we further understand the good as something we can attain, this intellectual insight moves us to tend toward the good. We strive with our will to gain the object without yet counting the cost in effort and possible loss of other goods. Now we turn to the task of intellectually weighing the reasons for and against striving for this good and the various sets of means by which we can attain it. This intellectual activity is called *deliberating,* the outcome of which is to arrive at one of two practical judgments: "This is to be done here and now," or "This is not to be done here and now." The matter has now been laid out for a personal choice. We know thoroughly what we want to do and the reasons why. The stage is set for a verdict, the supreme act of expression of one's being as a self-directed person. We accept one or the other of the alternative practical judgments by making a choice, by willing an act of commitment. The practical judgment immediately preceding the choice and expressing the chosen alternative is called the *last practical judgment.* The yielding to one alternative rather than the other, after deliberation, is the deliberate act of the will. It has two elements: (1) taken absolutely, as a yielding to the attraction of the object and an acquiescence in the judgment of the intellect, it is called *consent;* (2) taken comparatively, as a preference for one alternative over the other, it is called *choice.* Then using our intelligence, we direct our striving in the use of the means to carry out our personal choice. Finally, when the good is attained, we enjoy it.

The striving for the good that precedes deliberation is a spontaneous movement of our emotions and will toward embracing the perceived good. We have no control over whether we shall feel the attraction and the preliminary stirring of desire. Our recognition of this attraction is what starts our deliberating, a kind of debate with ourselves whether to yield to the attractive object or to resist it. If after deliberating we yield, the striving persists until the choice is made and carried out. Then we say the act was done with deliberate intent, and the act is voluntary or a human act. The initial stirrings we feel before our deliberating and choosing are not voluntary or human acts but only movements of our spontaneous tendency to strive for good.

Deliberation itself is not a human act unless we reflect on it and initiate a secondary deliberation. We begin to weigh motives for and against our contemplated course of action spontaneously without recognizing that we are doing so. But if our attention is turned to the fact that we are deliberating, the question arises whether we should continue or break it off. If we choose to continue, our act of deliberating becomes a human act, but the original attraction to the perceived good is not yet a human act because we have not yet consented to *it* but have consented only to deliberate about it. Such reflections on our own acts can become quite complex.

The important point in all of this is the distinction between deliberate and indeliberate acts of willing. The acts preceding the deliberation process are indeliberate (involuntary) and those following upon the process are deliberate (voluntary or human acts). The most important part of the process is the choice made, for this is what we consent to and what makes the act ours in

the sense that it is chargeable to us. Prior to choice the act is not a human act; afterward it is.

So far in our discussion of the background of the voluntary or human act we have looked at the functions of intellect and will. Both are powers of human consciousness or reason. Now we must turn to a third very important element—our emotions. They too are integral powers of our consciousness or reason and enter strongly into any choice we make. Reason in the sense of consciousness is not only intellectual and volitional, it is emotional as well.

True, we can distinguish the various ways we have of being conscious of someone or something, and we do this for purposes of talking about those ways of being conscious. But those very ways of being conscious do not exist and operate in separation from one another; they mix and mingle continuously in our conscious life, the life we live and experience. We constantly have emotions with our thoughts, and these emotions are accompanied with images and thoughts.

Without our emotions, we would find the world simply a set of facts where nothing is more important or worthwhile than anything else. The value, importance, or worth we recognize in our concrete experience is first picked up by the emotional side of our consciousness. The original attraction to the perceived good is a response by our emotions to the attractiveness we felt in what we perceived. Our emotions put us in touch with value (goodness or badness) in someone or something, and those same emotions respond to that value by being attracted or repulsed. Without emotions we would have no way of knowing values and responding to them and certainly no way of forming ideas about values.

The emotions are operative at the level of our preconceptual awareness of value. They are the ultimate basis for the intellectual judgment that something is good and ought to be done or that something else is bad and ought not to be done. The goodness is first felt affectively by the emotions and responded to with a simple attraction, and likewise badness or evil is first felt by the emotions and responded to with revulsion. The emotions, constantly mixed and mingled with our sensations, pick up the goodness or badness to be found in things and in interpersonal situations.

Choice always involves values. If we are to be self-determining moral agents, then we must be in touch with values by way of our own emotions. We need to have our own affective grasp of the world. We cannot afford to leave to others the determination of the values we shall choose to pursue in life. Our emotions are much involved in the deliberative process not only as the original perceivers, so to speak, of the values involved but also as strengthening the reasons for and against; in this way they exert great pressure on the will to consent or refuse consent.

COMMANDED ACTS

We think of the will as the controlling factor in us, but we never accomplish anything by merely willing it. By the will we decide to walk, but the will cannot do the walking; it commands the legs to carry out the decision. By the will we decide to think, but the will cannot do the thinking; it commands the intellect to turn its attention to this thought rather than that. The will can command itself, as when it decides to reach a decision now or to put it off until later. The will can command, then, both bodily acts and mental acts. I decide to study, and this decision is the act of the will itself. I take out my book, turn to the lesson, bend my eyes on the page; these are bodily acts commanded by the will. I focus my mind on the matter, try to understand what I am reading, and fix it in my memory; these are mental acts commanded by the will. Thus study is an act involving the use of the eyes in reading and of the intellect in understanding, both under command of the will.

Which of these acts is the *human act?* It might seem that only the act of the will itself is the *human act*. In one sense this is true, for it is in the will that choice and consent reside and give an act its specifically human character. If a person chooses to do something with clear consent of will but is prevented by circumstances from carrying out the choice, he or she is responsible for this consent. A man, for example, can be guilty of murder in intent even though he never gets the chance to carry out his intent.

Commanded acts share in the consent of the will that commands them. We are held responsible for all that we control by the use of will, both for the acts of the will itself and for the acts of other abilities that the will commands.

VOLUNTARINESS

After this brief survey of the background of the *human act* we must take a closer look at that property which characterizes it from the ethical standpoint—the property of voluntariness.

It should be evident that there can be no voluntariness without knowledge. We cannot strive for what we do not know. The will can make no choice without the intellect, whose business it is to conceptualize the good we are aware of by means of our emotions, to propose it to the will as something desirable, and to pass judgment on the suitability of the means to be used in its attainment. The work of the intellect is especially apparent in the process of deliberation, where the motives for and against cannot be weighed unless they are known. There must also be an awareness of what one is doing, a focusing of attention on the acts being done so that we are conscious or aware of our own acts. This awareness is impossible without a certain amount of reflection by which the mind turns back and looks at itself acting. We have a need *both* to know that we know *and* to know that we will.

Awareness and reflection occur in varying degrees, and so they affect the human character of the act according to the degree that they are present. An act is a *human* act only insofar as it is known and reflected on. Any part or circumstance of the act that the doer is unaware of is not attributable to the person as the doer of the act. This works both ways: a man who knowingly and willfully kills another without knowing that the victim is already dying of cancer commits murder nonetheless; a woman who steals money not knowing that it is counterfeit is guilty of theft even though she gets no profit out of it.

For a human act to be performed, it is not sufficient that it be guided only by knowledge; it must also be *willed*. We point to this union of knowledge and will when we call an act *voluntary,* and we can then define it this way: *A voluntary act is one that proceeds from the will with a knowledge of the end or goal to which the act leads.*

Voluntariness is one of our simplest and most familiar notions. We should not take the impression that there is anything recondite or mysterious about it. A voluntary act is simply a *willed act,* one in which the agent knows what he is about to do and wills to do it. The difficulty is that some of the words we commonly use to indicate this kind of act have certain connotations we do not wish to stress. We say that a person acts willingly, willfully, intentionally, deliberately, or voluntarily; these words all mean the same in the present context. To act willingly one does not have to act gladly and eagerly; to act willfully it is not necessary to be wayward or obstinate; to act intentionally does not require that one act vigorously or ostentatiously; to act deliberately there is no need of acting slowly and painstakingly; to act voluntarily it is not necessary to volunteer or freely offer oneself for some work. The English words often have these shades of meaning, but we use them simply in the sense that persons *knowingly will* what they do.

A voluntary act, as the product of one's own will guided by one's own intellect, is the actual exercise of personal control over one's conduct. Even when the act is done and finished, it is still referable to the person as *his* or *her act*. The basic explanation of why it was done rather than not done is that *this person willed it,* and so it remains forever related to the doer. We call this relation *responsibility* and *attributability*. These two terms express the same relation between agent and act, but they look at the relation from different sides. Responsibility looks to the *agent* who is responsible, answerable, accountable for the act; attributability looks to the *act* as it relates to the agent who is chargeable or gets the credit for the act.

Voluntariness then is the measure of the degree of responsibility and attributability.

Besides the relation between agent and act there may be a further relation of both to praise and blame. An act is transitory, lasting only so long as it is being done, but praise and blame are not always given immediately on the doing of a deed. A person murders someone but is apprehended only years later; we feel justified in blaming the murderer now, even though the evil act lasted only a moment years ago. A soldier receives a medal for bravery long after the battle is over; we feel that, even though his deed is only a memory, something of it remains in him and calls for praise. Some kind of moral reality must be produced in the doer by the act done to connect the doer with the praise or blame to come. This moral reality or property relating the human act done to the doer is called *praiseworthiness* or *blameworthiness* and is an important consequence of voluntariness.

We should note at this point that if voluntariness is the measure of the degree of responsibility and attributability as well as of the degree of praiseworthiness and blameworthiness, then voluntariness itself is a matter of degree, as we shall see in the next chapter. Since this fact is the case, the human act is human by degrees also, and the degree to which a human act is human turns upon the degree to which intellect and will are present.

EMOTIONS, MOODS, DESIRES

Earlier in this chapter, we said that our emotions provide us with the original awareness of value we have, and that they are intimately involved in our deliberations. Since this is so, we need to understand our emotions along with the moods and desires that arise from them. They are all integral to our conduct and form the essential structures or patterns of meaning in our lives. Only when we are in touch with our own emotions do we in any sense understand ourselves, for our emotions provide the subject matter for our thinking and the motivation to carry on that thinking. What gives our lives meaning is not something beyond our lives, but rather the richness intrinsic to our lives. We ourselves produce that richness by means of our emotions. Philosophy's purpose is to help us illuminate our lives so we can see the patterns of meaning that are already there as well as some meanings that can yet be put there by our own personal choices.

Before we proceed any further, we had best give at least some descriptive definitions of emotion, mood, and desire. An *emotion* is an immediate appreciation of the value and significance of persons, things, and situations; it is *not* a reaction to stimuli, but an activity that we do. This immediate appreciation of value is an evaluation that in part structures or sets up the world as *my* world. It is almost always about someone or something particular. For example, love, hate, joy, sorrow, shame, and guilt are all emotions—immediate appreciations of the value of persons, things, or situations. As personal appreciations, they are our responses to what we have found there in our world—value or disvalue.

A *mood* is generalized emotion; it too is an immediate appreciation of value, but a mood tends to focus on the world as a whole rather than on a particular person, thing, or situation. Some emotion or set of emotions is what precipitates and forms the mood. We are attuned or "tuned in" to the world by the moods we have. Depression, for example, focuses on the world as a whole and not on anyone or anything in particular. It is precipitated by some particular emotion or set of emotions, residing visibly but indistinctly at its core; for example, being depressed may result from having a set of emotions one finds debilitating but is unable to let go of.

Desire is a wanting or striving for someone or something valuable to me; it is not always based on emotions. We are interested in those that are. Primitive desires like hunger and thirst more often than not precede all emotions and moods. Our interest is in the desires we form on the basis of our emotions, the desires that structure

our lives, like concern for personal reputation, desire for friendship and love, the need for self-esteem, the ultimate desire for happiness. Such desires are built upon a base or structure provided by our emotions.

Emotion as Judgment

Now that we have these descriptive definitions to work with, we can fill out that description of emotion and give it more precision. First of all, we must see what emotion is not. Emotion is neither sensation nor feeling, although sensations and feelings are nearly always associated with our emotions. Some feelings are just sensations, like feeling nausea, feeling a cramp in the stomach, or feeling tense in the back or neck. Emotion is none of these sensations. Nor are emotions feelings of a special kind, even though we speak of feeling angry, feeling love for someone, having our feelings hurt, or feeling embarrassed, shamed, anxious, tired, bored, envious, upset, proud, and so on. None of our sensations or special feelings defines an emotion.

Once we understand what our emotions are and how they function in our lives, we shall also better understand our moods and desires. Emotions are *about* someone or something. I am never simply angry. I am angry *at* someone *for* something. What an emotion is *about* is called its object, and the object defines the emotion. Every emotion has its particular object, and that object is what structures, "makes" or "sets up," the emotion. The emotion is not simply in my mind, because its object is in the world. I am angry at someone for something he did. An emotion always has a subjective and objective aspect. The subjective aspect is due to the emotion's being mine. I am the one who is angry. The anger is my doing, not something that just happens to me. The objective aspect is due to the fact that I am angry *at someone for something*. The object defining my anger is in the world, but it is there *as I perceive it to be there, as I experience it there* in terms of my concerns and values. I interpret what someone does in terms of how I am affected, how it fits in with my concerns and values. The someone-doing-something is of great importance to me, affects me and my world, and so my response is one of anger. Whatever the object's status in the real world, it is subjectively experienced by me as deserving a response of anger.

An emotion is not separable from its object. As an object of this emotion, it has no existence apart from this emotion. This emotion itself has no existence apart from its object; there is nothing to the emotion but its object. Once I realize that the person did not do what I thought he did, there can be no more anger at him for doing that particular thing. I may feel upset at being angry with him for what I think he did, but the "feeling upset" is not the anger. Feelings are simply insufficient to differentiate one emotion from another. Even when I speak of myself as feeling angry, what I mean is that I recognize my anger as being about his doing something specific.

If an emotion is identifiable only in terms of its object, what is an emotion? An emotion is an unarticulated, undeliberated, and unreflective immediate appreciation or evaluation that we make *in active response* to the object as we perceive that object. In short, an emotion is a judgment, but one that is unarticulated, that is, not formulated and expressed in words. My anger at someone for something is my judgment that I have been wronged or offended by what-that-person-did-to-me. An emotion is always an evaluation, an evaluative judgment about my situation and about myself or about another person or persons. My emotion is my personal evaluation of the significance of a particular incident; it is my interpretation and evaluation of what happened. It is not a simple reaction to what I have observed. Emotions are always self-involved and relatively intense evaluations or appreciations. An emotion is set up or "made" by the evaluation of the object as especially important to me, meaningful to me, concerning matters in which I have invested myself. What makes emotions so special in our lives is not so much *what* they value as *that* they value and endow our lives with meaning. A person whose life is meaningless is a person who is not emotionally committed to anyone or anything or whose commitments are not all they seem.

Emotions are self-involved in the sense that they are important to me; they are about me as well as the immediate object, whether explicitly or not. Every emotion involves a judgment about me and my world. It is through my emotions that I make myself the self that I am. The *ultimate* object of my emotions as judgments is always my own sense of personal dignity and self-esteem, my sense of myself as a self.

Emotions are not just judgments about my *present* situation. They are also judgments about my *past,* editing and organizing the countless incidents and acts of my previous years into coherent meaningful patterns depending on my judgment of the present situation. And, even more importantly, emotions include intentions for the *future,* to do something, to change the world and myself in some particular way.

Emotion as a judgment is different from a reflective judgment about any emotion I may have. My being angry, for example, is my making a judgment about someone for doing something; my recognition that I am angry is a reflective judgment about my anger; my further recognition that my anger is not justified because the person I am angry at did not do what I thought he did is an additional reflective judgment. The idea of emotion as judgment may seem suspect because it does not conform to our usual idea of a judgment as an explicitly intellectual, publicly expressed, deliberated pronouncement such as one finds in a courtroom or in other public written or spoken discourse. But not all judgments are explicit. We make many judgments every day that are never articulated, deliberated, or thought about, for example, reaching for the light switch, turning off the alarm clock, putting on water for coffee or tea, walking to class or to the store, and so on. Emotions are such undeliberated, unarticulated, and unreflective judgments. They can become deliberate; they can be articulated in words; they can become reflective in the sense of being aware of themselves, their purposes, and their objects. Not all emotions can stand the scrutiny of reflection and survive; for example, unreasonable anger will wilt in the light of reflection.

Emotions as Constitutive Judgments

Emotions are all evaluative judgments, but of a peculiar kind. They constitute or set up the evaluations they make; they supply the standards or norms of interpretation and evaluation. The way the world is for me is never simply the way the world is. My emotions set up or constitute the world I live in; they "make" the framework within which my knowledge of the factual world has some meaning, some importance, some relevance *for me*. Emotions may at times seem unwarranted, absurd, or foolish, but they are never right or wrong. They are not descriptive judgments that must correspond to the facts to be right; they are constitutive judgments. Take my anger once again as an example; it is not a report of or a reaction to the fact of an offense. My anger *declares* what someone did to be offensive, and it *pronounces* that person guilty of doing that. I do not become angry because the person in fact says something offensive. What the person says is offensive by reason of its being an object for anger in my world. The object of my anger is as it is constituted or set up by me.

We do not create the forms of interpretation and standards of evaluation that we use in our emotional judgments. We learn them from our parents, our peers, our teachers, and from examples. The problem for us is that we are taught any number of alternative and conflicting sets of evaluative forms and standards, and so we must always choose among alternatives. Our emotions, from our slightest angers to our most impassioned romances, are legislative decisions; they are decisions about the way our world will be. An emotion puts together a set of rules and guidelines for itself.

An emotion is anything but open-minded, disinterested, or merely curious. We do not live with open minds and disinterested curiosity, accepting whatever comes our way. We live and survive on certain predeterminations and expectations; we live, for example, on the resoluteness to treat cruelty as wrong rather than as a fact of life, to be grateful for kindness rather than take it for granted, to esteem and respect other people as persons rather than use them as mere means for our own gratification, and to take every opportunity to act according to our predetermined ideals. There is no room for being lukewarm or wishy-washy in such matters. Without a passionate commitment to a set of ideals, we cannot live a meaningful life nor take a moral stance in the world. Without such commitment, what goes on in the world is just a set of facts; nothing is more important than anything else.

Every emotion lays down a set of standards to which the world, other people, and ourselves are expected to comply. When through reflection our emotions are themselves rendered consistent and free of arbitrariness, their very resoluteness stands at the foundation of all love and respect, all ideals and values, all relationships and senses of community. The collective system of all our emotions constitutes the way we are and the way our world is. My anger at someone for doing something constitutes his action as offensive and pronounces him guilty for doing that. With my anger I am somewhat like a dignitary christening a ship. The ship is named "Ariel," we might say constituted as "Ariel." Whether someone else likes the name "Ariel" or not, that ship upon being christened is "Ariel." Just as before the christening the ship had no name, so my friend's action is just another fact in the world until I am angered at him for doing that.

FREE WILL AND DETERMINISM

It may seem that we have settled the question of free will, for is not a voluntary act the same as a free act? No; the problem is not that simple. The notion of freedom adds to the notion of voluntariness the possibility of choice between two or more eligible alternatives, at a minimum the alternatives of acting or not acting. Whatever a person deliberately and willfully does is voluntary, whereas for freedom it is commonly thought that one must have been able at the moment to have chosen otherwise. In our description of the voluntary act we left open the relation between the last practical judgment and the consent. If the last practical judgment does not determine the will but becomes the last in the series of practical judgments merely by the fact that the will consents to it and thus cuts off deliberation, then we have freedom or a free will. But if the last practical judgment is determined to be the last in the series by some cause other than the will itself so that it necessitates the will to embrace it, then we have a kind of determinism.

Full study of this problem belongs to metaphysics and philosophical anthropology, but we must see enough of it for our purpose. We can begin by looking at some forms of determinism that are incompatible with freedom and responsibility in an ethical sense. Generally speaking, determinism is any theory of human conduct which holds that there is no such thing as free choice, for any choice that we ever make is already settled prior to our very act of choosing. All of our conduct, including the choices we make, is determined, fixed, settled by factors prior to the acts we perform, factors external to our wills.

1. *Fatalism* supposes that the future is prescribed for each person by some outside power, whether it be an impersonal force, the decrees of the gods, or something called fate, whether it overpower a person's will or use free personal choices as the very means of reaching its inexorable goal. Now humans are surely not accountable for events that they can in no way prevent.

2. Not very different from fatalism is *theological determinism*. Based on God's omniscience, this view would hold that if God knows everything, he knows the future, including the so-called free choices we make, and so our whole future is viewed as inevitably laid out for us. Theologians and metaphysicians have wrestled with the problem of God's omniscience for ages, but most hold that it arises from too anthropomorphic an interpretation of God's knowledge, from a mistaken idea that knowledge produces its object instead of discovering it, from the difficulty of imagining a timeless knowledge portraying time-bound events, and from a confusion between predestination and predetermination. Predestination merely means that God accepts and ratifies his created universe with all that is in it, including human free choices and their consequences. Predetermination would mean that God caused human beings to choose the way they do, thus interfering with their freedom. So, the position we are calling "theological determinism" interprets predestination as predetermination. The problem with this view has to do more with the idea of God than with how human beings act and choose.

3. Another form of determinism that also is incompatible with free will is often called *hard determinism*. It is based on the rigid causality that is apparent in the physical universe. Though it recognizes a distinction in concept between causation, determination, unavoidability, and predictability, in practice it makes all four of them imply one another. Not only must every effect (anything that happens) have a determinate cause (which may be a complex of many causal factors), but every cause must produce a single determinate and therefore predictable effect. The physical sciences are committed by their subject matter to this type of predictability. To admit freedom is to admit an element of unpredictableness in the universe and to put the highly successful scientific method in jeopardy. What we call free choice is thought to be nothing more than our own ignorance; that is, we cannot predict our own or others' future behavior because we do not know all the elements affecting the situation. While we cannot help engaging in the process of deliberation, the choice we make is determined, according to hard determinism, by whichever set of motives is stronger. There can never be any possible proof that we could have acted otherwise, since this, it is held, is precisely what never did and never will take place. A life of crime is predetermined for the criminal by genetic inheritance and environment; such persons are not really responsible for what they do, and society is also predetermined to hold them guilty and to punish them, using punishment for its corrective and deterrent values as part of the general predetermining environment. Of course,

according to this view, determinists cannot help being determinists nor libertarians being libertarians. Both are predetermined to exhort to the good life, and the hearers are predetermined to accept or reject the exhortation according as they have been conditioned. Thus ethics itself becomes a process in which we have to engage and whose results are already predetermined.

4. The absolute opposite of this hard determinism is *indeterminism,* the view that humans are an exception to the rigid determinism that occurs in nature. It admits that the law of causality may apply to everything else in nature, thus agreeing with the meaning of causality as accepted by the hard determinists, but insists that such causality does not apply to our free choices. There are no causes for our free choices. Our free acts are uncaused events that simply happen without being brought about by anything. Some appeal to Heisenberg's Principle of Indeterminacy to show that randomness in the universe is compatible with science. It is worth noting that this principle has nothing at all to do with choice or free will and for this reason has no bearing on the argument. Indeterminism gets into some insoluble difficulties. An uncaused act might perhaps be called free in some sense, but it could not be free as the result of a free choice, for if the free choice were the cause of the act, the act would not be uncaused. It could not be the kind of act for which one would be morally responsible, for if the act is uncaused, the doer of the act did not cause it and is therefore not accountable for it.

Besides these four views, each of which leaves much about human action unexplained, two others deserve serious consideration.

5. *Soft determinism* is an effort to reconcile freedom with determinism. It does this by limiting both concepts to the point where the apparent incompatibility between them becomes unnoticeable. Soft determinism admits that humans are free agents in the sense that they are often free from outside compulsion and thus conduct themselves unhindered in doing what they choose; but it claims humans are determined in the sense that they cannot choose to act against

their individual characters. Thus a person must submit to what attracts him or her more, and that is why one who knows someone well can reasonably predict what that person will do. However, our characters are not wholly the product of outside forces; we ourselves have helped shape them by our previous personal choices, so that we have freely made ourselves the kinds of people we are. Since we are responsible for our individual characters, it follows that we are responsible for the choices we now make according to our characters. Thus our every choice is caused, not by something outside us, but by the kind of being each of us has become by reason of our previous personal choices. This view, it is thought, avoids the mistakes of indeterminism which admits of causeless acts, and the mistakes of hard determinism, which leaves responsibility a baseless fiction.

Despite the conciliatory tone of soft determinism, however, many who study human action carefully are unhappy with it. What is the use, they say, of freedom to do what one chooses if one is not free to choose what one wants? What is the point of freedom from external compulsion if one is subject to an irresistible movement of one's already formed character? In neither case can one at the present moment do otherwise than he or she does. The opposite may be both logically and physically possible, but it is not psychologically possible. Nor is it much help to say that one's character, which determines one's present act, has been freely molded by the person's former free choices, for each of these was in turn determined by the state of one's character at that previous moment, and so on back to the beginning in childhood, when no deliberate free choices were possible. Thus say the critics of soft determinism. While this view admits of freedom, freedom from external compulsion, that is not the kind of freedom meant by free choice or free will. While in this theory there can be a kind of responsibility, for no one else but the individual person can be blamed or praised for the act that is determined by that person's character shaped by his or her own former acts, this is only the kind of responsibility that anyone has to repair the damage he or she has caused in an unavoidable accident. But such an accident could hardly be called freely chosen. This theory succeeds in fusing the two elements of determinism and freedom, but it also does away with something worthwhile in each of them.

6. The theory that we shall call *self-determinism* is an alternate mediating proposal that does not commit the mistakes of soft determinism. Self-determinism insists on the fact that nothing can happen without a cause, and therefore our free acts are definitely *caused* acts. But it rejects the claim that all causes necessarily produce only one determined effect. There are necessary causes and free causes, and a person when acting as a free agent is a free cause. When a person chooses, the choice is not made by something else either outside or inside the person but is the act of the very person. This is what it means to be a *person*. We cause our own acts; within limits we freely choose what acts we shall be the cause of. An act of free choice requires motives, which are conditions making choice possible, and in fact motives on both sides, for and against the contemplated course of action. But, says the self-determinist, though we humans are strongly influenced by the motives and must deliberate between them, still we are not necessitated by them either way; we make our own choices. Should it be said that we must be necessitated by the subjectively stronger set of motives, those that made the greater appeal at the time, then the self-determinist asks how they became subjectively stronger. The answer is that we as individuals make them so by freely attending to them, dwelling on them, and building them up within ourselves as part of a consciously controlled deliberation. The point that self-determinism stresses is that in an act of free choice there is nothing else in the person that chooses for the person, but rather it is the very person who makes his or her own choice. The ability of a person to do this is one mark of the dignity or worth of personality. An act so chosen as the free expression of one's personality obviously entails moral

responsibility and is of ethical significance.

Self-determinism seems to account most completely for the way we experience our own actions. Our future discussions will proceed on the basis of self-determinism, and the reader who holds other views can make the proper adjustments. As a final word, we can observe that soft determinism, though open to serious criticism, does leave room for freedom and responsibility of a type. By holding that we are at least remotely responsible for the development of our individual characters from which our acts flow, it accepts conclusions on which an ethical system can be based. Ethics is chiefly interested, not in how a person arrives at an acceptance of freedom and responsibility, but in the fact that he or she does accept them. The answer that we give to the free-will problem will color our interpretation of responsibility.

The importance of personal freedom can best be seen when we take the time to reflect on the kind of world we would like to live in and the *quality of life* we want for ourselves and for all people in that world. Sometimes we fall into a pattern of thinking that blames the social, economic, and political structures of our world for whatever is wrong with the quality of our personal lives. We need to recognize that the structures of this world are made by human beings who desire them for particular purposes, to achieve certain values. The frustrations, disappointments, hassles, desperation, and pressures we experience will not automatically disappear if the structures are changed. Why not? Because the economic structures, for example, do not teach greed and alienation. We ourselves are greedy and alienated, and so we use the economic structures to feed our greed and increase our alienation. Our emotions set up the basic structures of our lives; they support the social, economic, and political structures of our world. All of us together are responsible for the kind of world we have, and each of us individually is responsible for the quality of his or her personal life. If the world needs changing, then the work for change will have to begin at home with the individual life of each of us. If the world is cold and loveless, it is because we are that way ourselves. The self each of us creates by our conduct (by our free choices) contributes to the kind of world we share together.

Our emotions keep us in touch with our own lives and in touch with the world as well. We are integral parts of the world, and the world is an integral part of us. We cannot afford to ignore the traditions, customs, and usages of our society and civilization, but we must understand that the values embodied in our world are values that were discovered and appreciated by other human beings down through history. If we are in touch with our own emotions, we can use them to test the validity of the values handed on to us by our parents and our civilization. Those we find to be genuine we can make our own; those we find to be disvalues we can leave aside. Unless we learn to discover and test values for ourselves, we shall always be dependent on others to show us the values we ought to integrate into our lives, and we ourselves shall never be truly free. Freedom depends on value; our personal freedom depends directly on the range of values we can discover and appreciate for ourselves.

SUMMARY

What precisely is conduct? It consists of *voluntary* or *human acts*. In contrast to *involuntary* acts, *human acts* are those of which a person is master by consciously controlling and deliberately willing them.

The *human act* is the result of a complex psychological process in which the decisive point is the *consent* of the will after the deliberation of the intellect. It is here that the person yields to the attractiveness of the object, the attractiveness being first picked up by his or her emotions, and makes a commitment to it.

Our *emotions, moods,* and *desires* acted upon provide the essential structures of our experience and so provide the subject matter for our philosophical reflections on the meaning of our lives.

An *emotion* is an unarticulated, undeliberated, unreflective judgment, an immediate appreciation of the value and significance of persons, things, and situations. Emotions as judgments are both evaluative and constitutive.

A *mood* is generalized emotion; it too is evaluative and constitutive.

A *desire* is a wanting or striving for someone or something valuable; some desires are formed on the basis of our emotions.

The aim of philosophical reflection is to discover the emotions, moods, and desires that enhance our *personal dignity* and *self-esteem* and those that do not.

Reflection is an activity of intellectual reason judging our emotions, moods, and desires to discriminate those that are successful (rational) from those that are not (irrational). Our emotions, moods, and desires are integral to reason in the sense of consciousness just as intelligence and willing are. The emotional side of consciousness is the source of our *awareness of value,* and it provides the content for our value concepts. Without emotion we could make no intellectual value judgments at all.

Commanded acts are those mental and physical acts that the will commands. They share in the consent of the will that commands them, and so we are responsible for all acts we control through the use of our will.

Voluntariness is the most important characteristic of a human act. It means that the act is really willed, that it proceeds from the will with a knowledge of the end or goal to which it leads. The agent knows what he or she is doing and wills to do it. *Intellect* points out the end or goal and the means to achieve it, guides deliberation, and provides awareness and reflection, without which there can be no consent of the will.

Voluntariness is the measure of the degree of *responsibility* in the agent, the *attributability* of the act, and *praiseworthiness* or *blameworthiness* of both agent and act.

The controversy about *freedom* and *determinism* is metaphysical in nature with important implications for ethics, because the side one takes in this controversy affects the notion of voluntariness and so of free choice and responsibility. *Determinism* is a general term used to describe any theory of human conduct which holds that there is no such thing as free choice since any choice that we ever make is already settled prior to our act of choosing. Of the forms of determinism examined in this chapter, *fatalism* and *theological determinism* have little appeal today. *Hard determinism* makes a person's every act rigidly conform to the law of causality operative in the physical universe and reduces free choice to an illusion. *Indeterminism,* the opposite extreme, explains free choice by exempting a person's free acts from all causal influence. *Soft determinism* compromises by admitting that a person is free from outer compulsion but necessarily follows the bent of his or her character; a person is determined not physically but psychologically. *Self-determinism* holds that a person's free acts are caused, but caused by the very person as a self-governing agent, so that he or she could have acted otherwise and freely chose not to do so.

One's position on the free-will question will obviously color his or her interpretation of responsibility.

Personal *freedom* depends on our awareness of values that we can discover and appreciate for ourselves. The scope of our freedom is as wide as the values we have available for our choices.

Questions for Discussion

1. The scene is a federal courtroom. The case before the court is veterans versus the United States. The veterans maintain that, as a result of radiation exposure while on active duty in the military services from 1946 to 1962, they are suffering variously from cancers, blood disorders, nerve problems, and defects in their offspring. The government's defense, based on information provided by the Pentagon, is that 99 percent of the veterans received less than 5 rems of radiation during their tours of duty either in Japan, in the Pacific (Bikini and Eniwetok), or in Nevada and Utah, an amount less than the safety standard for workers in a normally operating nuclear plant. Attorneys for the plaintiff have to prove the government responsible for the veterans' problems, whereas the attorneys for the government must show that it was not negligent. If you were the plaintiffs' attorney, how would you go about establishing responsibility? If you were the attorney for the defense, how would you go about constructing the best defense?

2. You are a *soft* determinist engaged in a discussion with a *self*-determinist on how the government can best respond to global terrorism. Each of you is an official of the government with the task of making concrete suggestions to the president's adviser for national security; how would you both go about coming to some agreement on a policy to recommend?

3. The local TV news program director employs you as a reporter and gives you wide discretion over the stories you choose to pursue and the issues you choose to investigate in depth. Naturally, you want to keep your viewers' interest, but you also have a choice to make. Must you keep the public good in mind as you make your choices, or must you have only your employer's good in mind? Do you have a right to influence public opinion, or must you report only facts and leave the viewing public to form its own opinions?

4. Working in the highly competitive advertising industry, you own and operate one of the largest and most successful agencies. The national TV advertising you have done for some large companies has been both engaging and effective. One soap manufacturer has just come to you with a proposal that you use subliminal techniques in your advertising campaign for

that company. How would you respond to the client's proposal in such a way as to avoid questionable techniques without losing the client's business?

5. When you encounter bigotry and prejudice, what do you do? Do you think fear is at the root of much of it? If so, what is the object of the fear? Do you think such fear is reasonable? If you do not think fear is at the root, what emotional causes can there be for bigotry and prejudice? Does the bigoted and/or prejudiced person have any choice in the matter? If so, why? If not, why not?

Readings

Aristotle, *Nicomachean Ethics,* bk. III, ch. 1–5, treats of voluntariness; he is feeling his way toward clarifying the concept. We have tried to reduce to a small space what St. Thomas says in the *Summa Theologica,* I–II, qq. 6, 8, 11–17. In q. 9 he discusses what moves (motivates) the will, and in q. 10 he shows that the will is not moved of necessity (not necessitated). This follows up what he had said in pt. I, qq. 82 and 83, on free will. Walter Farrell's *Companion to the Summa,* four volumes, is a readable popularization of St. Thomas's *Summa Theologica,* following St. Thomas's order. We need not refer to it again, since the appropriate place is easily found.

Etienne Gilson, *Moral Values and Moral Life,* ch. 2, and his *The Christian Philosophy of St. Thomas Aquinas,* pp. 251–256; Vernon Bourke, *Ethics,* ch. 3; and George Klubertanz, *Philosophy of Human Nature,* ch. 10, all give excellent summaries of the process of choice and the making of a human act.

John Macmurray's *Freedom in the Modern World,* pp. 105–115 and 145–166, and his *Reason and Emotion,* pp. 13–32, are excellent for his discussions showing that the capacity for reason belongs to our emotional nature just as much as to intellect.

Robert C. Solomon's *The Passions: The Myth and Nature of Human Emotion,* pp. 1–49 and 172–213, reinforces and clarifies Macmurray's thesis and provides a moving treatment of the need for philosophical reflection and for an understanding of our emotional life. Alexius Meinong's *On Emotional Presentation* is also important.

Alfons Deeken's *Process and Permanence in Ethics: Max Scheler's Moral Philosophy,* pp. 30–44, discusses the role of emotion in ethics according to Max Scheler. Dietrich von Hildebrand, *Ethics,* has a lengthy discussion of emotion as apprehending value and goes so far as to maintain that emotion "perceives" value in somewhat the same way our external senses perceive color, sound, odor, and so forth. Von Hildebrand was influenced by Max Scheler's work on value, especially Scheler's *Formalism in Ethics and Non-Formal Ethics of Values.*

Willard Gaylin's *Feelings: Our Vital Signs* is a psychiatrist's effort to call our attention to the importance of the subjective aspect of our emotions.

For presentations of divergent viewpoints on free will see Sidney Hook, *Determinism and Freedom in the Age of Modern Science,* Bernard Berofsky, *Free Will and Determinism,* and Willard F. Enteman, *The Problem of Free Will,* three anthologies containing many well-known articles. See also William James, "The Dilemma of Determinism," in *The Will to Believe,* pp. 145–183; Jean-Paul Sartre, *Being and Nothingness,* pt. IV, ch. 1, §III; John Hospers, *Human Conduct,* ch. 10; C.A. Campbell, *On Selfhood and Godhood,* lecture 9, and *In Defense of Free Will;* P.H. Nowell-Smith, *Ethics,* ch. 20; Moritz Schlick, *Problems of Ethics,* pp. 143–158; Yves Simon, *Freedom of Choice;* R.L. Franklin, *Freewill and Determinism.*

Joseph M. Boyle, Jr., Germain Grisez, and Olaf Tollefsen, *Free Choice: A Self-Referential Argument,* clarify and examine the controversy over free choice and develop a self-referential argument for the thesis that humans can make free choices.

3
Responsibility

PROBLEM

From the acts humans perform we have separated out those over which a person has control or mastery. We have fixed the point of control in the consent of the will, prepared for by the deliberation of the intellect on the basis of the value perceived. If the consent can be given to any available alternative, the individual person is the cause of his or her own choice and is therefore responsible for the act chosen. The only reason why this act was done rather than not done or why this act was done rather than some other possible act is that the person, by a personal choice under the guiding light of his or her own intellect, made the act to *be*. The act is that *person's* own act precisely because and insofar as that *person* did it.

Is a person equally responsible for all the acts over which he or she has control, that is to say, for all his or her human acts? Not all knowledge is equally clear, nor does the will always consent with total decisiveness. In addition, what proceeds from the will may be closely or remotely connected with the willed act itself and may share in its voluntariness in varying degrees. We must now examine the factors that enhance or limit a person's responsibility by increasing or diminishing his or her control, making the act more or less *human,* more or less that *person's.* The following questions will guide us in understanding these factors:

1. What are the main kinds of voluntariness?
2. What precludes or weakens our responsibility?
3. Are unwanted but foreseen consequences voluntary?
4. When may one permit foreseen evil consequences?
5. Must we avoid contributing to others' moral harm?

LEVELS OF WILLING AND NOT WILLING

There is a difference between *not willing* to do something and willing *not to do* something. In the first case there is no act of the will and there-fore no voluntariness. In the second case there is an act of the will, an act of deliberate omission or refusal, and this is quite voluntary. Hence voluntariness can be positive or negative, according as we will to do something or to omit something, and both of these kinds of voluntariness are different from a state of nonvoluntariness, which is an absence of willing. Some writers reserve the word *involuntary* for what happens against our will and use *nonvoluntary* for what we have no attitude toward, but this usage is not consistently observed.

The state of *not willing* is often psychologically impossible to maintain. We *do not will* so long as the doing of an act does not even cross our mind. Once we think of it, and especially after we have reflected on it and deliberated about it, we must do one of two things: either take it or leave it, either will to do it or will not to do it. One course is as voluntary as the other. Thus negative voluntariness is not the same as no voluntariness, much as a negative number is not the same as zero.

For my act to be voluntary I must will it knowingly. But must my mind be focused on the act at the very moment I am doing it? Can I be responsible for an act done in a state of complete distraction? For any responsibility to remain, must a previous decision to act still influence my behavior, or may it have entirely ceased its influence? Can I be responsible for something that I never did will but presumably would have willed if I ever thought of it?

To answer such questions it is customary to distinguish four levels of intention with which an act is performed, representing a progressive diminution of voluntariness.

An *actual* or *active* intention is one that a person is conscious of at the moment he or she performs the intended action. The person pays attention not merely to what he or she is doing but also to the fact of here and now willing it.

A *virtual* intention is one that was once made and continues to influence the act now being done, but it is not present in the person's consciousness at the moment of performing the act. Thus a woman walks to a definite destination;

her intention was actual on starting out but soon becomes virtual as her mind drifts onto other subjects while she takes the right turns and arrives at where she wanted to go. What she willed was the whole series of acts that would bring her there, but she need not be thinking of her destination every step of the way. After her first decision the subsequent acts could be carried out while her mind is completely distracted from its original purpose.

An *unrevoked* intention is one that was once made and not retracted, but it does not influence the performance of the act intended at present. For example, a man fully resolves to kill his enemy but is prevented by circumstances from carrying out his intent, though he never revokes it; later, while hunting, he shoots at what he thinks is an animal but finds that he has accidentally shot his enemy. He is responsible for intending to kill an animal, not for killing his enemy. In this instance he had no intention of killing his enemy.

An *interpretative* or *presumed* intention is one that has not been made but presumably would have been made if the person were aware of the circumstances. If, for example, the literal application of a law would cause more harm than good, one might interpret the intention of the lawgiver and relax the law in this particular case.

For an act to be voluntary an actual intention is not necessary; a virtual intention suffices. The unrevoked and interpretative intentions have much less importance. They indicate that the person's will (either once actually had or merely presumed) is objectively carried out, but not by the person's own voluntary act.

MODIFIERS OF RESPONSIBILITY

Voluntariness is said to be *complete* or *perfect* if the agent has full knowledge and full consent. It is *diminished* or *imperfect* if there is something wanting in the agent's knowledge or consent or both, provided he or she has both in some significant degree. If either the knowledge were wholly lacking or the consent were wholly lacking, there could be no voluntariness at all. The question now arises: What sorts of things render voluntariness imperfect, reducing the specifically human character of the act and making the agent less responsible? Since we are not interested here in the psychological strength of the act but in the degree of the agent's self-control, we shall call them *modifiers of responsibility*. There are five main modifiers:

1. Ignorance, affecting the knowledge
2. Strong emotion, affecting the consent of the will
3. Intellectual fear, opposing to the will a contrary wish
4. Force, actual use of physical compulsion
5. Habit, a tendency acquired by repetition

Ignorance

We are interested in ignorance only to the degree that lack of knowledge affects the voluntariness of a human act so as to make the act less a human act. Since voluntariness is the measure of the degree of responsibility, the less voluntary the act, the less responsible the agent is for that act. The only ignorance that has ethical import is ignorance an agent ought not to have, an *ignorance that ought not to exist*. There are three kinds of such ignorance:

1. Ignorance that can be overcome by acquiring the requisite knowledge is called *vincible* ignorance.
2. Ignorance that cannot be overcome because the requisite knowledge cannot be acquired is called *invincible* ignorance.
3. Ignorance deliberately cultivated in order to avoid knowing what ought to be known is called *affected* or studied ignorance.

These three kinds of ignorance can be looked at as three degrees of lack of knowledge thereby affecting the agent's voluntariness and so his or her responsibility.

1. *Invincible ignorance precludes responsibility*. Knowledge is requisite for voluntariness, and in the case of invincible ignorance this knowledge is simply unobtainable. A person can be invincibly ignorant for one of two reasons: (1) being unaware of his or her ignorance, the per-

son does not know there is any knowledge to be acquired or (2) being aware of his or her ignorance, the person's efforts to obtain the knowledge are of no avail. Since in either case the knowledge is unobtainable and since no one can be held to do the impossible, what is done in invincible ignorance is not voluntary, and so the agent is not responsible. A woman, for example, who pays for something with counterfeit money, not even suspecting that the money is counterfeit, does no wrong. The act of paying is voluntary, but not her paying in counterfeit money.

2. *Vincible ignorance does not preclude responsibility, but lessens it.* The person knows that he or she is ignorant and that the knowledge is obtainable. If such a person deliberately fails to make sufficient effort to overcome the ignorance and so allows the ignorance to remain, the effects that follow from such ignorance are indirectly voluntary. By willing to remain in ignorance, the person is responsible for the consequences that he or she foresees will or may follow from that ignorance. If a surgeon, knowing that he or she does not have sufficient knowledge for a difficult operation that can be postponed, performs the operation anyway and the patient dies as a result, then even though the surgeon did not want the patient to die, we must say that he or she deliberately exposed the patient to serious and unnecessary danger and is therefore responsible for the death. Still, though the surgeon is aware of being ignorant, he or she is not sure of the effects of such ignorance. Consequently we can say that the surgeon is less responsible than one who would deliberately plan to kill a patient in this way.

The blameworthiness of vincible ignorance depends on the amount of effort put forth to overcome it, and the amount of effort called for depends on the importance of the matter and the obligation of the agent to possess such knowledge. The person who makes a little effort, but not enough, shows some goodwill but insufficient perseverance. One may know that the knowledge can be obtained but is too lazy or careless to search for it. Another may doubt whether the knowledge can be obtained and,

after a little effort, may hastily but wrongly judge that the knowledge is unobtainable. Still another may make no effort at all, either with full knowledge that the ignorance is vincible or not caring whether it is or not.

3. *Affected ignorance in a way lessens, in a way increases, responsibility.* Such ignorance lessens responsibility, as does all lack of knowledge, since the person does not see clearly the full import of what he or she is doing. The ignorance, deliberately cultivated, increases the responsibility if the person intends to use the ignorance as an excuse, for example, to lessen the risk of punishment or to avoid having to carry out a known duty. Here the person is not only willing the act but also willing the ignorance as a means of facilitating the act. The increase of voluntariness and therefore of responsibility in this latter respect is usually more important than the lessening of voluntariness in the former respect.

Strong Emotion

Emotion, if felt very strongly, may make us will something more intensely than we otherwise would and will it with less self-control than we would have when our emotions were more calm. Strong emotion increases the force of the willed act, but to the degree such emotion lessens voluntariness it also lessens responsibility, and so the act is to that degree less a *human act*.

Our emotions may arise quite spontaneously before the will has acted. Remember that our emotions mix and mingle with our senses constantly. When an object is sensed, our emotions are operating along with the senses and pick up the beauty or ugliness, for example, in what we are sensing. We stir emotionally in the very process of sensing something and respond almost automatically with a sudden feeling of joy or disgust. We are simply responding with our emotions to what we have come in contact with in the sensed object. Sudden feelings of joy, anger, hatred, grief, shame, pity, disgust, and the like are the emotions we are talking about. If they are very strong or violent, they can modify the responsibility we have for what we will when we generate such strong emotions. And, when such emotion is generated *before* the will can act, we call emotion of this kind *antecedent* emotion.

We can also deliberately choose to generate very strong emotions, for example, by brooding or focusing on the objects that arouse them. We can actually make ourselves angry by rehearsing insults in our imagination or frightened by recalling the details of a particularly frightening experience from the past. This kind of deliberately aroused emotion is called *consequent* because we generate it *after* and as a result of our own choice. Antecedent emotion is *involuntary,* whereas consequent emotion is *voluntary* and so is a human act. Antecedent emotion becomes consequent when it is recognized for what it is and then deliberately retained or fostered.

1. *Very strong or violent antecedent emotion may preclude responsibility.* If the emotion is so sudden or violent as wholly to block the use of our intelligence, it makes deliberation impossible, and the act performed under the influence of such emotion is then neither free nor voluntary. If the act is not voluntary at all, then the person is not responsible for the act. Such complete loss of control happens rarely.

2. *Very strong or violent antecedent emotion usually lessens responsibility.* In most cases even when moved strongly by emotion, we remain in control of our acts. Enough knowledge and consent remain for the act to be both voluntary and free, and so the person is held responsible for his or her act. Calm, intellectual deliberation becomes more difficult, the motives on each side cannot be weighed with careful impartiality, the will is predisposed more strongly toward one side rather than the other, and thus the person's freedom of action is hampered. As a consequence an act done under the influence of strong or violent emotion, when free, is less free than one done knowingly and with no disturbing emotions. Without calm judgment on the part of the intellect the choice of the will cannot be as voluntary and free. Responsibility is therefore lessened to the degree that voluntariness is lessened.

3. *Strong or violent consequent emotion does*

not lessen responsibility but may increase it. When the strong or violent emotion is deliberately aroused or fostered, we voluntarily put ourselves in that emotional state. The acts we perform under the influence of such deliberately aroused or fostered emotion are either directly voluntary or voluntary only indirectly (indirectly voluntary acts will be examined and explained later in this chapter). For example, a person intentionally (deliberately) broods over an insult in order to work up to an act of revenge; the person is using the emotion as a means to accomplish the goal of revenge, and so both the emotion deliberately worked up and the revenge taken are directly voluntary. An indirectly voluntary act, however, is quite different. Take a man, for example, who does not want to kill but foresees that his continual brooding over supposed wrongs done to him will get himself into such a frenzy that he will very likely kill; yet he deliberately continues to nurse his anger and, as a result, becomes insane with rage and kills his enemy. His emotional state is directly voluntary, for he deliberately put himself into that very state by brooding on the supposed wrongs; his act of killing is indirectly voluntary, because he foresaw what very likely would happen and did nothing to keep from falling into the insane rage. He is responsible for the death of the person, and the rage, having been deliberately fostered, increases his responsibility for the killing.

Obviously we do not mean to give emotion a bad name by what we have said above. Our emotions are very important because they are the basic powers we have to get in contact with what is valuable or worthwhile in ourselves and in our world. Human consciousness is an emotional consciousness as well as being a consciousness that senses, conceptualizes, deliberates, and wills. Reflective deliberation does not have to be emotionless intellect aloofly observing the whirl of our emotions, nor does it have to govern those emotions as a tyrant who is afraid of being overthrown. Reflection is a conscious act that we as persons perform. Our emotions are intimately involved in the reflection along with the intellect. Our intellectual powers share in the activity of our emotions, which constitute the importances (values) in our lives, by giving our emotions advice and direction that they often would not have on their own just because of their immediacy and impatience. Since whatever emotions we do have are our emotions, we must acknowledge them as ours and take responsibility for the way we choose to integrate them into our self-image and attitude toward the world, ourselves, and other persons.

Fear

Fear is the emotion that apprehends impending evil and manifests itself in the desire to get away, avoid, or escape as far as possible from the impending threat. The aim of fear is to protect the self from the anticipated evil. We can also have an *intellectual fear,* comprising an understanding of a threatened evil and a movement of the will to avoid this evil by rationally devised means. This intellectual kind of fear may have no easily discernible emotional component. Someone may coldly decide to steal, for example, because of fear of living in poverty, to lie because of being afraid to be disgraced, to murder because of fear of being blackmailed. This kind of fear deserves attention as a separate modifier of responsibility.

To estimate its effect on responsibility, we must consider intellectual fear relatively to the person and his or her circumstances. What would produce a slight fear in one person may produce grave fear in another; some people are naturally cautious, whereas others are bold; some have little aversion to a condition that others would find intolerable. A lesser evil threatening us now may produce more fear than a greater evil still far off.

What we are calling intellectual fear is a modifier of responsibility only when we act *from* fear as a motive for acting and not merely *with* fear as an accompaniment of our act. A soldier deserting his post in battle because of cowardice is motivated by fear and acts *from* fear; if he stays at his post despite the danger, he may have just as much fear, but even though he acts *with* fear, he does not let that fear influence his conduct.

1. *Intellectual fear does not preclude responsibility*. This kind of fear does not produce panic and loss of self-control. The person calmly looks about for an escape from the threatening evil and makes a deliberate choice. He or she could choose to face the evil but chooses instead to yield to the fear rather than resist it and therefore wills what he or she does. Fear of this sort thus does not necessarily preclude responsibility.

2. *Intellectual fear lessens responsibility*. An act motivated by intellectual fear is one that we deliberately will; however, we would not will it except for the fear we experience. This reluctance weakens the consent of the will, leaving us with a divided mind and a hankering after alternatives the situation does not have. This reluctance and hankering lessen our self-control.

If my choice is clear-cut and straightforward so that I act without regret or reluctance, my act is voluntary and I am responsible. But when I act regretfully and reluctantly, when I choose something I would rather not be obliged to do, there is a conflict, so to speak, between my *will* and my *wish*. My will is what I deliberately choose; my wish is what I would like if circumstances permitted.

A time-honored example is that of the sea captain who throws his cargo overboard to save his ship in a storm. The act contains both a voluntary and an involuntary aspect: voluntary in the sense that he jettisons his cargo deliberately and intentionally with sufficient knowledge and consent, for he could refuse to do so and try to weather the storm or even let the ship sink; involuntary in the sense that he would rather not have to do this and, if there were no storm, certainly would not do it. He *wills* to jettison his cargo, *wishing* that he did not need to do so. Despite the contrary wish the captain is held responsible for this act of jettisoning the cargo but not as responsible as he would be were there no contrary wish present.

Acts done under *duress* and *intimidation* have what we are calling intellectual fear as a motive. These acts are extorted under threat of evil to be inflicted by another human will. Unless the person becomes so upset as to become temporarily unable to control his or her acts, acts done under duress and intimidation are responsible acts, for the person could have refused and taken the consequences. Contracts unjustly extorted through fear can be nullified by positive law, not because the parties are never responsible but because the common good requires that extortion be made unprofitable. These points can be looked at more carefully if we examine the relation of force to responsibility.

Force

Force, violence, or compulsion is physical power used to make someone do something against his or her will. In common language, one who yields to a threat of violence is said to be *forced,* yet this is not really force but *fear,* and the person's voluntariness and therefore responsibility is to be judged by the criteria for fear. Now we must consider *force* in its strictest sense as not merely a threat but as *the actual use of physical might.* If I hand over my money to a thug because he thrusts a gun at me, that is fear; if he physically overpowers me and rifles my pockets, that is force.

Force in this physical sense cannot reach the will directly, for physical action cannot touch the act of the will. We can continue to will the opposite, no matter how violently we are forced to do the act. Hence the act we are forced to do is involuntary, so long as we do not will it. Someone may have the physical strength to make us *do* something, but he cannot make us *will* it.

The act a violent aggressor is trying to make us do may or may not be evil in itself. If it is not, we may yield to it and comply with the aggressor's demands; our rights are outraged and injustice is done against us, but we ourselves are not doing wrong, only saving ourselves further harm. One who is kidnapped, for example, need not struggle (and this is true of acting from fear as well as force), for there is no moral wrong in merely going off to another place. But in a case such as rape, where consent would involve moral wrong, resistance is required.

What counts as resistance and how much is required? At least internal resistance, withholding

the consent of the will, and passive external resistance, noncooperation with the aggressor, is required. Active external resistance, consisting in positively fighting the aggressor, is also necessary when without it the withholding of consent would be too difficult to maintain. This is not required when it would be useless or when there is no danger of consent.

The victim of force has no responsibility if he or she does not consent. If the victim consents reluctantly, he or she has reduced responsibility because of the contrary wish. If a person actually wants to do what he or she is being forced to do and, for example, pretends to resist, he or she is not truly a victim of force and has complete responsibility, or if he or she would not have done the act without being forced, nearly complete responsibility.

Habit

The nature and kinds of habit will be discussed later in the chapter on habit; here we are interested only in the way habit may affect our responsibility for an act. For our present purpose we may define a habit as a constant way of acting acquired by repetition of the same act. When a habit has been acquired, the actions follow from it spontaneously, almost automatically, so that deliberate guidance becomes unnecessary and, in a sense, even difficult.

1. We may set out *deliberately to acquire* a habit, as when we try to learn how to play a game or how to pick pockets. Then the habit is directly voluntary, and the acts resulting from it are either directly voluntary if performed with the intention of acquiring the habit or at least indirectly voluntary if they are the unintended but foreseen consequences of the habit. We are completely responsible for the habit and the acts resulting from it.

2. We may not intend to acquire a habit for its own sake but *voluntarily* perform acts that we know are *habit-forming,* as when a person takes up smoking or drugs. Here the acts done are directly voluntary, and the forming of the habit is indirectly voluntary, since we know that we

cannot do habit-forming acts without getting the habit. After the habit has been acquired, acts unintentionally following from it are also indirectly voluntary. We are completely responsible for the habit and the acts resulting from it.

3. We may discover that we have *unintentionally* acquired a habit, either because we did not realize that we had done the same thing in the same way so often, or because it did not occur to us that such actions were habit-forming. Most of our habits of speech and gesture are of this type. In this case we are not responsible for the existence of the habit or for the acts that unintentionally follow from it, so long as we remain ignorant that we have the habit. A rather gross lack of reflectiveness may cause this condition to remain about a great many patterns of action even over a long time.

In whatever way we may have acquired the habit, as soon as we fully recognize that we have it, we face the choice of either keeping the habit or trying to get rid of it. In either case a new act of the will is called for; the act of getting a habit and the act of keeping it are two distinct acts, and each may be voluntary.

If we decide to *let the habit remain,* our possession of the habit now becomes directly voluntary, and the acts that unintentionally follow from the habit are indirectly voluntary. The habit, however acquired, is now deliberately kept, and we are completely responsible both for the habit itself and for its effects.

If we decide to *get rid of the habit,* we are now the victim of two opposite pulls, the voluntary decision of our will to suppress or get rid of the habit and the involuntary persistence of the habit itself. Long-standing habits of some types are not overcome in a day or by a few days' effort and when our vigilance is relaxed, will inadvertently reappear in the corresponding act. Success in this struggle is bought only by constant watchfulness and effort. If we let down our guard, we shall soon find ourselves drifting back to the old familiar way. Our responsibility for these particular acts depends on the amount of advertence at the moment when the act is performed and also on the amount of effort expended to get rid

of the habit. Here, just as in the dispelling of vincible ignorance, we are obliged to put in an amount of effort proportional to the importance of the matter. Depending on these factors and on our sincerity in the particular instance, we may have complete responsibility for acts done from habit, or only some, or even none at all.

Additional Modifiers

To these five modifiers of responsibility it is possible to add others, such as sleepiness, sickness, pain, alcohol, drugs, and other conditions that reduce awareness and self-control. They are very important, but since they produce their effect on voluntariness by involving one or more of the five modifiers already discussed, no new principles need be added to those explained above.

Abnormal mental states will, of course, seriously affect the capacity of a person to perform human acts. The lighter neuroses will probably only lessen voluntariness, whereas the deeper psychoses may preclude it entirely. The mentally disturbed may have complete self-control at times or along certain lines and little or none at other times or in other forms of behavior. A kleptomaniac may be a very rational person except when under the spell of this particular compulsion; these acts are involuntary but not the other acts the person performs. Each case is different and must be judged by itself. In order to make a judgment in a particular case we have to know how the individual abnormal state affects voluntariness, because the degree of voluntariness is the measure of the degree of responsibility.

The same principles seem applicable also to the refined methods of physical, mental, and social torture used for political purposes, beginning with "brainwashing" and aiming at total "thought control." It is said that in such a long, drawn-out process everyone has his or her breaking point. If so, the victim has full responsibility at the start, suffers a gradual diminution of it as the inhuman routine continues, and after the breaking point, if there really is one, the victim ceases to be a responsible person. A person need not be reduced to insanity. It is sufficient that one cannot control one's moral judgments or the actions resulting from them. Whether any moral responsibility is left only the victim really knows, though a psychologist might be able to make a good inference.

Nothing has been said about the unconscious, about the drives, complexes, and motivations sunk beneath the threshold of our awareness, which are such powerful influences affecting our behavior. They are indeed of the greatest importance in the development of our personality and have much to do with our ethical life, especially with our moral principles and attitudes. They may explain why some have such a keen, and others such a blunted, sense of moral values. Since such urges are unconscious, however, they exist in us involuntarily and do not make the act human by what they contribute. They are much like habits inadvertently developed. We cannot be responsible for them until we recognize them, and by that time they have been dredged up from the unconscious to a condition of conscious awareness. Then we are faced with the problem of what we shall choose to do about them. They may supply the real motivation of acts that we attribute to other motives, but since at the time we choose the act as we see it, we are responsible for the act as seen and chosen, and not in terms of the hidden motives from which it may actually stem.

Neither Freud nor the psychoanalytic movement has strengthened the force of traditional morality. By showing the weakness of consciousness before the unconscious, the psychoanalytic movement has left us less able to believe in our moral freedom. We find ourselves perhaps talking more in terms of neuroses and complexes than in terms of virtues and vices. But we still go about our everyday lives guided by moral will, and we make judgments in its terms. We do distinguish among people we know in terms of their virtues and vices; for example, we speak of the almost scrupulous honesty of one, of another as well nigh incapable of telling the truth, and of another as being the very embodiment of kind-

ness and understanding. And we deal with people in these terms. We forgive people for occasional failings, but almost never do we find ourselves excusing them because they are neurotic about something or have such and such a complex over which they have no control. If we do discover some neurosis or complex in ourselves, we have become conscious of it and can begin to understand how it affects our behavior. The point is that the neurosis or complex is no longer unconscious but is now a part of our conscious awareness. Now we are responsible for what we do about it, for how we integrate it into our lives, for the impact we let it have on our behavior. As long as we do not know something, we cannot be responsible in regard to it.

THE INDIRECT VOLUNTARY

There is a difference between the way in which the act itself is voluntary and the way in which its consequences are voluntary. Something is *directly voluntary* when it is the thing willed, whether it be willed as an end or as means to an end. Something is *indirectly voluntary* when it is the unintended but foreseen consequence of something else that is directly voluntary; the agent does not will this consequence either as end or as means but sees that he cannot get something else without getting it. The agent wills the cause of which this is a necessary effect. Thus one who throws a bomb at a king to assassinate him, knowing that he will kill the king's attendants also, directly wills the throwing of the bomb (as means), also directly wills the death of the king (as end), and indirectly wills the death of the attendants (as consequence) though their death gives him no profit. A consequence, however, that is neither intended nor foreseen is involuntary, such as the death of one who unexpectedly rushes up to the king after the bomb has left the thrower's hand.

Note that what we are concerned with here are *physical* actions that we directly will to do and that have physical consequences or effects that we do not directly will but foresee and accept or permit because of the physical effect we want to achieve with our action. Now there seems to be some significant difference between a person's directly intending something and that person's foreseeing and accepting something else that will happen along with the effect directly willed. In our example we have been dealing with several physical evils that result from the assassin's physical action. Of these we must say that as a killer he is more willing to have the king die than he is to have the attendants die and even less willing to have innocent bystanders die. Note further that insofar as there is moral evil in the situation, the moral evil lies in the assassin's will, for he intends (directly wills) to kill the king, foresees and accepts the deaths of the attendants (indirectly wills these deaths), and accepts, though he does not necessarily foresee, the deaths of possible innocent bystanders (indirectly wills these deaths).

Having examined the voluntariness of the assassin's action with regard to the deaths of the king, the attendants, and the possible innocent bystanders, we are now in a position to assess his responsibility for these various deaths. Note once again that the voluntariness of one's action is the measure of the degree of responsibility that the person has for that action. The distinction between the directly and the indirectly voluntary acts helps us to articulate what is happening psychologically, namely, that the assassin by his act directly intends the death of the king and is willing to accept the foreseen deaths of the attendants and possibly those of innocent bystanders. All the other deaths apart from the king's are indirectly willed and so are indirectly voluntary, and these deaths are willingly accepted precisely because the death of the king is sufficiently important to the assassin to justify, in his own mind, his acceptance. The assassin must be assigned complete responsibility for the king's death, but how much responsibility does he have for all the other deaths? Even if he is reluctant to accept the other deaths, must he accept complete responsibility

for them? He is completely responsible because he is perfectly willing to accept any other deaths as long as he succeeds in killing the king. Those deaths may be an unfortunate side effect of the killing of the king, but his foreseeing them was not sufficient to deter him from killing the king, and so he has complete responsibility for them.

Good or indifferent actions also may have evil physical consequences that can be foreseen. How responsible are we for these physical evils? Must we always refuse to do a good act if we foresee that it will or can have some physical evil as one of its effects? While we have not yet established the existence or nature of moral good and evil, much less separated out the particular factors from which these moral qualities arise, for our present purpose we can take them on the commonsense level on which we began our study: that humans judge some actions to be good, others bad (evil), and still others indifferent. Our business here is to determine how responsible one is for the physical consequences of one's actions, whatever their moral quality, and our examples are mere commonsense illustrations.

If we were obliged to avoid every action that will result in physical evil, life in this world would soon become unlivable, impossible to bear. Human beings are limited beings. Physical evil attends our life in this world. True, some of it merely happens to us as when we are beset with violent disruptions of nature such as hurricanes, earthquakes, floods, and the like, but some are also caused by us. The human situation is such that it gives rise to value conflicts and to particular situations in which we have to act to achieve some important good but in so doing we bring about some sort of evil as well. Our situation is also permeated with human limitations that are not merely physical but psychological, sociological, pedagogical, and aesthetic as well. In addition, most situations are very complex. Nevertheless we must try to do the right thing in spite of the complexities. One who accepts a job when jobs are scarce cuts someone else out of a livelihood; a doctor who tends the sick during a plague exposes himself to catching the disease; a lawyer who must present this bit of evidence to win her case may put an innocent person under suspicion; or a teacher who gives a competent examination knows that some will probably fail. The world in which we live is a mixture of good and evil that affects each of us as we try to live an upright moral life. We seem to be caught on the horns of a dilemma: either human life cannot be lived as it actually is, or we are compelled to do evil and to do it voluntarily.

There is a solution to the dilemma in the principle of the *indirect voluntary,* commonly known as the principle of the *double effect*. This principle has a long history and helps resolve some of the moral complexity of our lives. The first part of this principle is that no evil must ever be willed simply for its own sake either as end (goal) or as means, for if the evil were willed in either of these ways, it would be the direct object intended by our willing and would necessarily render our entire action evil, even if there were good, morally correct consequences that flow from the act. Briefly stated, evil must never be *directly* willed, for such an act is *directly voluntary*. The second part of the principle is that evil may be willed *indirectly,* that is to say, as a foreseen but unwanted consequence; such an act is *indirectly voluntary* and may be willed *only if* it can somehow be reduced to an incidental and unavoidable by-product or side effect in the achievement of some good the person is rightly seeking.

Though I am never allowed to will evil directly, I am not always bound to prevent the existence of evil. Just as I may tolerate the existence of evils in the world at large, since I could not cure them all without bringing other evils on myself or my neighbor, so I may sometimes tolerate evil consequences from my own actions if to abstain from such actions would bring a proportionate evil on myself or others. Sometimes I cannot will a good without at the same time permitting the existence of an evil that in the very nature of things is inseparably bound up with the good I will. But I must not do so indiscriminately. Sometimes I am bound to prevent evil, and in these cases it

would be wrong for me to permit it. How can we determine these cases?

The *principle of double effect* says that it is morally allowable to perform an act that has an evil effect under the following conditions:

1. *The act to be done must be good in itself or at least indifferent*. This is evident, for if the act is evil of itself, evil would be chosen directly, either as an end or as a means to an end, and there could be no question of merely permitting or tolerating it.

2. *The good intended must not be obtained by means of the evil effect*. The evil must be only an incidental by-product and not an actual factor in the accomplishment of the good. If the act has two effects, one good and the other bad, the good effect must not be accomplished by means of the bad, for then the evil would be directly voluntary as a means. We may never do evil in order that good may come of it. A good end does not justify the use of bad means. Hence the good effect must follow at least as immediately and directly from the original act as the evil effect. It is sometimes said that the evil must not come before the good, but this may be misunderstood. It is not a question of time but of causality; the good must not come *through* or *by means* of the evil.

3. *The evil effect must not be intended for itself but only permitted*. The bad effect may be of its own nature merely a by-product of the act performed, but if the agent wants this bad effect, he or she makes it directly voluntary by willing it.

4. *There must be a proportionately grave reason for permitting the evil effect*. Though we are not always obliged to prevent evil, we are obliged to prevent a serious evil by a small sacrifice of our own good. Hence some proportion between the good and evil is required. How to estimate the proportion may be difficult in practice. For the present we can say that the good and the evil should be at least nearly equivalent. If the good is slight and the evil great, the evil could be called incidental only in a technical sense, and the obligation to avoid it would be overwhelming. Also, if there is any other way of getting the good effect without the bad effect, this other way must be

taken; otherwise there is no proportionate reason for permitting the evil.

Does the principle of the double effect do away with responsibility for the evil effect that is merely permitted but not directly intended? Responsibility is measured by voluntariness. The evil effect is, according to the principle of double effect, indirectly voluntary, that is to say, not directly willed but foreseen as a consequence of something else that is directly willed. I get the evil effect and cannot avoid getting it because I want the good that I rightly intend. I am therefore completely responsible for the good as well as for the evil. The principle of the double effect neither does away with responsibility nor was it intended to do away with it. Its purpose is, in some conflict situations, to do away with moral blame for permitting the existence of an evil that cannot be avoided if the good is to be obtained.

The act is not morally allowable unless all four conditions are fulfilled. If any one of them is not satisfied, even though the other three are, the act is morally wrong. There is no question here of telling people that in the conditions specified they can go ahead and do wrong. Rather, it is a way of showing that the action in question is not wrong. The bad effect spoken of is a physical evil of some kind. The double-effect principle expresses the conditions under which one is not morally blameworthy for permitting a physical evil to happen.

An example will help to illustrate the application of the principle. A man passing by a burning building dashes in to save a child trapped there, though he may be severely burned and even lose his life. We recognize his deed as heroic, but its justification is found in the principle of double effect:

1. The act itself apart from its consequences is merely an act of entering a building. It is surely an indifferent act and morally allowable.

2. This act has two effects: one good (saving the child) and the other bad (being burned or even death for the rescuer). However, he does not save the child by means of dying or being burned but by means of reaching the child and carrying it or throwing it to safety. If he can do

so without harm to himself, so much the better. The good effect is accomplished in spite of, rather than by means of, the bad effect, which is thus made only an incidental accompaniment in the rescue of the child.

3. If the rescuer were using this chance as an excuse for suicide, he would intend the evil for itself rather than merely permit it.

4. There is a sufficient proportion: at a minimum, a life for a life. To enter a burning building merely to rescue some trifling possession could not be morally justified.

A few more cases will show how one or another of these four conditions can be violated:

1. An employee of a bank embezzles money to pay for the care of his sick child, hoping to pay it back later. Here the act itself of embezzlement (taking money belonging to another and falsifying the accounts) is neither good nor indifferent but wrong, and it cannot be justified by any good intentions or good effects that might follow. He must try to raise the money in some other way, and for the purposes of this example we stipulate that it is possible for him to do so. The first condition is violated, and the evil is *directly voluntary*.

2. A man living with an alcoholic rich uncle stocks the house with liquor, knowing that he will inherit a fortune when the uncle has drunk himself to death. For purposes of this example we stipulate that the uncle simply has no control over himself in the presence of alcohol. The act of stocking the house with liquor is indifferent in itself. It has two effects, bad for the uncle by occasioning his death, and good for the heir by bringing him his inheritance sooner. But the money cannot be inherited except through the uncle's death. The good effect (obtaining the money sooner) is accomplished by means of the bad effect (the uncle's death), and thus the second condition is violated.

3. A political boss distributes money to poor people to get them to vote for an unworthy candidate. Here the giving of money to the poor is a good act. The good effect (relieving poverty) is not accomplished by means of the bad effect (electing an unworthy candidate) but rather the

other way round, the bad effect through the good. But here the third condition is violated because the evil effect, the election of the unworthy candidate, is directly intended as the end.

4. The owner of a private plane has his pilot fly him through exceedingly dangerous weather to complete a business deal that will net him a small profit. To fly a plane is an indifferent act; the danger has to do with the possible effect rather than with the act itself. The good effect (completing the business deal) is not obtained by means of the bad effect (possible loss of life). The bad effect is not intended for its own sake, for neither wants to die. But the fourth condition can easily be violated here, for there does not seem to be a sufficient proportion between the risk to their lives and the rather slight financial advantage to be gained. There is always a risk in flying, of course, and financial advantage can be great enough to justify it, but for the sake of an example we presuppose an excessive risk.

Though the foregoing examples show how the principle of double effect can be violated, many of the ordinary actions of life find their justification in a correct application of the principle. Thus people may take dangerous occupations to earn a livelihood, firemen and policemen can risk their lives to save others, a surgeon can operate even though he may cause pain, a man can vindicate his honor or rectify past wrongs even though other people's reputations suffer from his disclosures, or the people may be subjected to great sacrifices to defend their country. If a person were obliged to avoid every deed to which evil could be incidental, we could do so little that we might as well stop living.

RESPONSIBILITY FOR THE ACTS OF OTHERS

Only the person who knowingly and willingly does an act can be responsible for it. In this sense no one can be responsible for the acts of another person. But we are responsible each for our own acts insofar as we knowingly and willingly intend to permit them to affect another person as incentives to good or evil. The ways in which we can help our neighbor to good or ill are so numerous that it would be impossible to list them. It will be useful here, since we have just discussed the double-effect principle, to consider two ways in which we must try to avoid doing moral harm to other people, and how far this avoidance is possible.

Occasion of Evil

The word *scandal* originally meant a stumbling block, and metaphorically something we trip on and fall over in our moral career. Now the word has lost its force and means only shocking conduct and juicy gossip. To regain the old meaning we shall call it *occasion of evil*. It is any word or deed tending to lead, entice, or allure another person into wrongdoing. It may be only *given,* or only *taken,* or both *given* and *taken,* so that the question of responsibility may arise on either side or on both.

We *give* occasion of evil to another *directly* if we intend his or her evil act either as an end or as a means. To intend it as an end would signify a truly diabolical hatred, for such an intention looks to the moral destruction of the other person. The usual motive for inducing others to evil, however, is to use the other's evil doing as a means to one's own profit, as do those who make their living by selling addictive drugs. The direct voluntariness of this direct giving of occasion of evil makes for complete responsibility for the evil on the part of the giver. The taker's responsibility is also complete if the evil is done knowingly and willingly; his or her responsibility may be diminished by any of the modifiers of responsibility discussed above.

We *give* occasion of evil to another *indirectly* if we do not intend the other person's evil act either as end or as means but foresee it as a consequence of something else we do. Care for our neighbor's moral welfare obliges us to avoid even this as far as possible, but life would be intolerably difficult if we had to avoid all actions in which others might find an occasion to do evil. Here the principle of double effect applies: the act we do must not be wrong in itself though we foresee it will be a temptation to another; the good effect we intend must not be accomplished by means of the other's evil act; we must not want but only permit the other's temptation; and there must be a proportionate reason for permitting it.

Occasion of evil is *taken but not given* when someone with peculiar subjective dispositions is led to evil by another person's innocent words or deeds. It may be due to the taker's *malice,* and then is wholly the taker's responsibility. Or it may be due to the taker's *weakness,* to his ignorance, youth, inexperience, prejudices, violent emotions, or unconquered habits. Love of other human beings requires us to avoid words and actions, otherwise harmless, that might be a source of moral danger to the innocent or the weak. But sometimes such situations cannot be avoided, and it is here that the principle of double effect comes into play.

Cooperation in Evil

Cooperation in another's evil deed may occur by joining that person in the actual performance of the act or by supplying him or her with the means for performing it. If two men plan a robbery, one may hold the gun while the other relieves the victim of his valuables, or one may lend the other a gun to enable him to carry out the robbery alone. In either case one not only helps another to do evil but also knowingly and willingly joins in his evil intention. This is known as *formal* cooperation and all the cooperators share completely in the responsibility for the act.

A lesser variety of cooperation occurs when without approving another's wrongdoing one helps him perform his evil act by an action of one's own that is not of its nature evil. Thus an employee is forced by robbers to open the safe, or the driver of a car is compelled by gangsters to drive them to the scene of intended murder. This is known as *material* cooperation. There is nothing wrong in what I do or in what I intend, but there is the bad circumstance that my otherwise innocent act aids others in their wrongdoing. Consequently, if there is a proportionately

grave reason for permitting this evil circumstance, material cooperation can be justified by the principle of double effect. Since the act I do is not wrong in itself, since I do not use the other's evil deed as a means to any end of my own, and since I have no wrong intention and so no moral responsibility for the other's evil act, the only remaining difficulty is that of the proportion. This proportion must be estimated by the following:

1. The amount of evil my cooperation helps others to do
2. The amount of evil that will happen to me if I refuse to cooperate
3. The closeness of my cooperative act to the other's evil act

The first two points are only common sense and are formally justified in a later chapter by the principles bearing on a conflict of rights. My duty to my fellowman does not oblige me to suffer an injury greater than or equal to that which I am trying to ward off from him, but it does oblige me to suffer a small loss to prevent a great loss from happening to another, and it may even oblige me to sacrifice my life to prevent a huge public calamity. The third point, however, needs some further explanation.

Cooperation may be *proximate* or *remote,* depending on how close it comes to the actual evil deed of the principal agent. The more proximate the cooperation, the greater the proportionate reason needed to allow material cooperation.

If no one else could be substituted to help in the evil act, I have a greater obligation because I can actually prevent the act from happening, and I should have a proportionately greater reason. Also, greater reason is required to justify material cooperation by persons who have an *explicit* duty to prevent that particular kind of evil from happening. This would occur if a soldier were forced to cooperate with the enemy, a policeman with criminals, a watchman with burglars, a customs officer with smugglers.

The forms that cooperation can take are too numerous to mention, for it is possible to cooperate with almost any act, at least by encouragement and support. Hired workers, because they engage their services to a company whose policy they do not determine, are particularly open to the danger of material cooperation. One should not keep a job with a company that continually and habitually does a morally objectionable business. If it does so only occasionally, employees need not be disturbed so long as their material cooperation is kept remote but if they find that proximate material cooperation is demanded of them fairly frequently, they should have a grave reason for continuing in their job and should meanwhile make an earnest effort to obtain other work.

SUMMARY

Responsibility is the relation between the act and the agent as doer of the act, as answerable or accountable for that act. The agent willed the act knowingly, and so the act done is the agent's act. The *voluntariness* of the agent in doing the act is the measure of the degree of responsibility the agent has for the act.

Voluntariness is *positive* when one knowingly and willingly does something and *negative* if one knowingly and willingly omits doing something. Four levels of *intention,* what a person knowingly and willingly aims to do, represent a progressive lessening of voluntariness: (1) an *actual* or *active* intention is one now present to one's consciousness at the moment the act is performed; one who acts with such an intention acts with complete voluntariness and so has complete responsibility for the act; (2) a *virtual* intention is one that was once made and continues to influence the act now being done, but the person is not consciously aware of the intention at the moment of performing the act; since the voluntariness is lessened by the lack of awareness of the intent, the responsibility is likewise lessened; (3) an *unrevoked* intention is one that was once made and not retracted but does not influence the performance of the act intended at present; since this kind of intention does not influence the voluntariness of the act, the agent is not responsible for the act done by reason of an unrevoked in-

tention; (4) an *interpretative* or *presumed* intention is one that has not been made but presumably would have been made if the person were aware of the circumstances; since the agent has not acted, he or she has no voluntariness and so no responsibility.

Voluntariness is said to be *complete* or *perfect* if the agent has full knowledge and full consent; with such voluntariness, responsibility is also said to be *complete*. Voluntariness is said to be *diminished* (lessened) or *imperfect* if something is lacking in the agent's knowledge or consent or both, provided he or she has both in some significant degree; with diminished voluntariness, responsibility is also said to be *diminished*.

The degree of the agent's control over his or her act can be lessened by what we have called *modifiers of responsibility*. Following are five main modifiers:

1. *Ignorance,* a lack of knowledge that the agent ought to have, is called (a) *invincible* if it cannot be overcome; such ignorance precludes responsibility; (b) *vincible* if it can be overcome; such ignorance lessens but does not preclude responsibility; (c) *affected* or deliberately cultivated ignorance increases responsibility because the ignorance is deliberately willed as a means of facilitating the act.

2. *Strong emotion,* (a) if prior to the act, is called *antecedent* and may preclude responsibility by making deliberation and therefore voluntariness impossible; usually such emotion lessens voluntariness and so lessens responsibility; (b) if generated after and as a result of our own deliberate choice, is called *consequent* and does not lessen responsibility but may increase it.

3. *Intellectual fear,* consisting of an understanding of a threatened evil and a movement of the will to avoid this evil by rationally devised means, affects voluntariness only when it is the motive for acting and does not preclude responsibility but lessens it because of the contrary wish mingled with our actual will.

4. *Force* is the actual use of physical might to

make us act against our will. The act is involuntary if we withhold consent, and then we have no responsibility.

5. *Habit* is a constant way of acting and is acquired by the repetition of the same act. The acquisition of a habit may be (a) directly voluntary, and if so, the agent has complete responsibility not only for the habit but for the acts that result from it; (b) indirectly voluntary, and because the habit is formed by deliberately doing acts we know to be habit forming, the agent has complete responsibility for the habit, which was foreseen, and for the acts resulting from the habit; (c) involuntary, and as long as the agent remains unaware of his or her habit, the agent is not responsible for the habit or for the acts resulting from the habit. Once the agent is aware of having the habit, the agent is faced with the choice of keeping or getting rid of it. If the habit is kept, the agent has complete responsibility for it and the resulting acts; if the agent chooses to get rid of the habit and deliberately works at countering it, the acts that inadvertently reappear would be less voluntary and so the agent would be less responsible or, in some cases, not responsible at all.

An act is *directly* voluntary if it is willed either as an end or as a means; it is *indirectly* voluntary if it is the unintended but foreseen consequence of something else that is directly voluntary. Unforeseen consequences are involuntary. Responsibility for indirectly voluntary acts is dependent on the consequences that are foreseen even if they are unintended in themselves. To the degree that such consequences are foreseen and accepted the agent is responsible.

To try to avoid every act from which some evil effect might follow would make life impossible. We are never allowed to will evil directly, but we are not always bound to prevent the existence of evil.

The *principle of double effect* summarizes the conditions under which we may perform an act from which we foresee that an evil consequence will follow:

1. The act must be good or indifferent in itself.
2. The good that the agent intends must not be obtained by means of the evil.
3. The evil effect must not be intended for itself but only permitted.
4. There must be a proportionately grave reason for permitting the evil effect to occur.

All four conditions must be fulfilled. Violation of any one of them makes the evil a directly willed effect and not merely permitted as an incidental by-product. The agent, even though not directly willing the evil effect, is nevertheless responsible for it. Responsibility may be diminished by a contrary wish that the good be obtainable without the concomitant evil. The principle of the double effect does not do away with responsibility, but it does make it possible for a person to act in some conflict situations without incurring moral guilt or blame for the evil effect that is permitted.

We can be responsible for another's misdeed by inciting that person to do wrong or by helping the person to do wrong.

1. We are an *occasion of evil* for another when we use our words or actions to lead that person to do wrong. To intend the other's evil act as means or as end is always to incur responsibility along with the other for the other's act. To permit another's evil act only as an indirect consequence is allowed when the principle of the double effect is satisfied, for then we incur no guilt even though we must accept responsibility for the evil we foresee.

2. *Cooperation in evil* is helping another to do wrong by joining in the other's act or by supplying the other person with the means to do wrong. Cooperation is (a) *formal* if we intend the evil directly; this kind of cooperation, being completely voluntary, brings with it complete responsibility for the evil the other does; (b) *material* if without intending the evil we actually assist in its performance by an act of our own that is not itself evil. We are responsible to some extent for the evil, because while we do not intend it, we do permit it. We incur no guilt when we limit our material cooperation according to

the principle of the double effect. We must consider not only the balance of evil to ourselves and to others but also how close our cooperation comes to the evil. Strong reasons are needed to justify *proximate* material cooperation; lesser reasons suffice for *remote* material cooperation.

Questions for Discussion

1. You have been selected as a jury member for a murder trial. The defendant has entered a plea of "not guilty." After you and the other jurors have listened to day after day of testimony, the time has come for the final summation by the prosecution and defense counsels. The prosecutor goes over the evidence with you and shows that the defendant did "with malice aforethought" and "without provocation" willfully shoot and kill the victim. The defense counsel, however, maintains that the defendant was in a state of passion and that the gun fired accidentally, resulting in the death of the victim. The jury now retires to consider the evidence. What do you look for to determine whether the prosecutor has proved his case? And what to determine whether the defense has proved her case?

2. A moderately wealthy woman owns a number of rental properties throughout the city in areas that are largely white and middle- to upper-class. Because she fears the devaluation of her properties, she chooses not to rent to any racial minorities. She does in fact discriminate. Recently in court she has been formally accused of illegal discrimination by the district attorney. She entered a plea of "not guilty." Her defense is fear of poverty. Is her defense plausible? Why? Does she have a better defense? How would you defend her if she retained you as her attorney?

3. Recently an agent of the U.S. Drug Enforcement Administration was doing some investigating in another country where some of the police are in collusion with drug dealers. The police took the agent into custody for questioning in an effort to discover how much was known about their drug operation. In the course of the interrogation, the agent was submitted to torture and when he could stand no more pain, he gave the desired information. Was his act voluntary? To what degree? Is he also responsible for betraying secret information?

4. You are a heroin addict and have just been apprehended by the police for stealing in order to maintain your habit. You have been stealing regularly, but this is the first time you have been caught in the act. The district attorney decides not to prosecute provided you enter a drug-rehabilitation program. The district attorney believes that more good would be accomplished by rehabilitation than by prosecution. How do you look at your own responsibility in the matters of the thefts? Why?

5. In wartime it is considered legitimate for military personnel on one side to kill military personnel of the enemy. Both sides, however, are morally obliged to avoid killing civilians because they are noncombatants. You are a battalion commander and have been assigned the task of knocking out an enemy weapons depot located in an area where a significant number of civilians live. You know that the destruction of the depot will also result in the death of many of the civilians. How would you justify carrying out the operation? Can you make a reasonable argument against undertaking the operation? On what grounds?

Readings

Plato in the *Laws*, bk. IX, talks about voluntary and involuntary crimes. In the *Lesser Hippias*, a work of doubtful genuineness, he discusses the question whether it is worse to do wrong voluntarily or involuntarily; the argument is inconclusive but illuminates the question.

Aristotle, *Ethics*, bk. III, ch. 1–5, makes the first serious study of voluntariness.

Read St. Thomas, *Summa Theologica*, I–II, q. 6, on voluntariness; q. 76, on ignorance; q. 77, on passion; q. 78, on malice and habit. In I–II, qq. 22–48, St. Thomas gives a lengthy treatment of the passions, what we have called the "strong" emotions. This matter is summarized in Etienne Gilson, *Moral Values and Moral Life*, ch. 4, and in his *Christian Philosophy of St. Thomas Aquinas*, pp. 282–286. One of the first express uses of the double-effect principle is found, though by no means clearly expressed, in St. Thomas's *Summa Theologica*, II–II, q. 64, a. 7, where he deals with self-defense. Richard A. McCormick, *Ambiguity in Moral Choice*, and Charles E. Curran, *Ongoing Revision*, make significant contributions to the ongoing discussion of the double-effect principle. An excellent summary of the discussion may be found in William E. May, "Double Effect," *Encyclopedia of Bioethics*, vol. 1, pp. 316–319.

Read Albert Jonsen, *Responsibility in Modern Religious Ethics*, especially ch. 1, 3, and 5. See also Nicolai Hartmann, *Ethics*, vol. III, ch. 13; H. Richard Niebuhr, *The Responsible Self*; Moira Roberts, *Responsibility and Practical Freedom*.

William James, *Principles of Psychology*, ch. 4, presents his famous essay on habits, which is well worth reading and can be inserted in any philosophical background. Arthur Koestler's *Darkness at Noon* and George Orwell's *1984* are novels dealing with the systematic breakdown of personality and responsibility; one can examine them in the light of the principles we have given.

4
Conscience

PROBLEM

We make two kinds of judgments about ourselves and our actions: (1) I judge whether and how far I am responsible for my acts and so for my very self and (2) I also judge whether these acts are good or bad and whether I as a person deserve praise or blame as a result of doing these actions. As we said earlier, ethics takes as its starting point a fact of human experience: the conviction that some acts are right and ought to be done, that others are wrong and ought not to be done, and that still others are indifferent and may either be done or not. Whether such evaluative judgments are correct or not is another matter, but the fact we are interested in is that people do make them. They also judge themselves and one another as persons. The power to do this kind of evaluative judging is called *conscience,* the conscious self attuned to moral values and disvalues (right and wrong, good and evil) in the concrete and judging the self and its personal actions in terms of those values and disvalues.

How far we as individuals are responsible for our acts only the individual person can know. The act I do has its source in me; it is my act. Because this is so the quality of my act reveals the quality of my own personhood. I am the kind of person who does this kind of act, and so to the degree that I am responsible for the quality of my acts I am also responsible for the kind of person I am. Others may judge me, but without my help they can see only the externals. I usually know when I have been misjudged by others, and I can know this only by comparing their judgment with my own and passing a further judgment on both these judgments. Reflecting on my act in this way, I can usually find the degree of my own responsibility for the act I have done and for the further determination I have given my own personal character by doing that act. The judgment of responsibility as such is different from the judgment of conscience. The two are certainly connected with one another, because we normally judge the goodness or badness, rightness or wrongness, of only the acts we are responsible for. The judgment about responsi-

bility is a *factual* judgment about the degree of voluntariness; the judgment of conscience is an *evaluative* judgment about the moral value or disvalue of my act and so of myself as a person.

Since we have been dealing up to this point with the subjective aspects of the human act such as voluntariness and responsibility and since morality first presents itself to our experience as a personal reflective judgment on our acts and ourselves as being good or bad, right or wrong, moral or immoral long before we have begun to articulate the principles on which such judgments rest or should rest, it will be convenient to continue with the subjective aspects of morality. All people, no matter what their system of morals might be, make the kind of evaluative judgments associated with conscience and admit that they make them. It is when we try to find an objective basis for the judgments of conscience that ideas about values, about what is good or bad, right or wrong, moral or immoral begin to diverge.

The differences of approach that people take in these matters cannot be understood, compared, and examined until we make the effort to justify our own personal judgments of conscience. Embedded in all the differences is something common to them all—the need to be true to oneself as a person. Apart from what others may think and do, I must in the last analysis make my own informed judgments, so I am ultimately dependent on my own judgments of good and bad, right and wrong, moral and immoral. This personal judgment in these terms about my own actions and about myself as a person is what we mean in this chapter by the judgment of *conscience*.

We shall use the following points to guide us in our discussion:

1. What do we mean by morality?
2. What is conscience?
3. How is the judgment of conscience formed?
4. What part do our emotions play in forming the judgment of conscience?
5. Must we always follow the judgment of conscience?

6. May we act with a doubtful conscience?
7. How can doubts of conscience be solved?

MEANING OF MORALITY

Morality is the quality or value human acts have by which we call them right or wrong, good or evil. It is a general term covering the goodness or badness of a human act without specifying which of the two moral values is meant. The term *moral* is also used at times as a general term covering both good and bad qualities or values in the same way that morality is used, that is, without specifying whether good or bad or both good and bad are meant. We speak of the moral character of a person's acts or personality and say, for instance, "Harry is a mature adult capable of moral discrimination," meaning that Harry can differentiate between good and bad; "Jane's moral character is an unknown quantity to me," meaning that Jane may be good or bad; "George's motivation in helping the poor seems morally ambiguous," meaning that George seems to have a mixture of good and bad motives.

The terms *moral* and *immoral* mark the extremes of good and bad within morality, the field of morals, when moral is used as the opposite of immoral. The term *moral* means "morally good" *only when it is clearly opposed to immoral,* which always means "morally bad." When moral and immoral are used in opposition to one another to describe human acts, each indicates that the act has a definite moral quality or value. An act is moral when it has the quality or value of being good; an act is immoral when it has the quality or value of being bad. For instance, "John's decision not to have the operation was moral" or "Jane did the moral thing in telling Harry how she feels about George." Usually the context will make the meaning of *moral* clear. The word *amoral* is sometimes used in the sense of "nonmoral," but more often it is applied to persons deficient in moral concern or responsibility.

Moral, beyond being used to designate the good or bad quality of human *acts,* is also used to designate the quality of a *person* as good or evil, as upright or despicable. The field of morals, that is, morality, is possible because of the kind of beings human beings are, namely, beings who have the power to do both good and evil. Such are our possibilities. We can do good but we can also *not* do it. That "not" points to the limitedness or finiteness that is integral to our being as persons and affects our relations with the rest of the world. Because there is this negativity or limitedness about our being, we as personal beings *can fail* to live always in accord with our potentialities and our vision of the good. To some extent we are all closed and indifferent to others. We cannot love enough to be completely open to all others and concerned with their lives and what happens to them; we are imperfect and weak at times even when we would like to be more perfect and strong. Because of our limitedness as persons, we have the possibility of doing evil rather than good.

In judging the morality of a human act, we take into consideration the subjective peculiarities of the agent (the doer of the act) and look at the act as conditioned by the agent's knowledge and consent, background, training, prejudices, emotional maturity and stability, value orientation, and other personal traits. We ask whether this individual person did right or wrong in this particular situation, whether this particular act was good or bad *for him or her to do in the particular circumstances.* Considered in this way, morality is *subjective,* the goodness or badness being determined by whether the act agrees or disagrees with the agent's own judgment of conscience.

We may also abstract from such subjective conditions which, though always present in any individual act, can be known directly only by the agent's personal judgment of conscience. We can simply look at the kind of act performed and at the outward circumstances apparent to any observer. Then we ask not whether this individual is excused from responsibility for the act because of strong emotion, ignorance, or any other modifier of responsibility, but whether, if any normal person with full command of his or her own powers deliberately willed that kind of act, the result would be a morally good act. We would be judging the objective nature of the act done, not the subjective state of the doer. Morality considered in this way is *objective* morality.

If we ask, "Is murder wrong?" "Is truthfulness right?" we are asking about objective morality. If we ask, "Did this man fully realize what he was doing when he killed that child?" "Did this woman intend to tell the truth when she blurted out that remark?" we are asking about subjective morality.

Morality in its completeness includes both its subjective and its objective aspects. Neither aspect is more important than the other. Unless acts have a rightness or wrongness of their own with which a person's judgment of conscience can and should be in agreement, anybody's judgment is as good as anybody else's, and ethics becomes a mere listing of personal opinions. The study of ethics generally stresses objective morality. But each person has a life to live, must personally account for his or her deeds as he or she saw them, and will be judged morally good or bad in terms of the sincerity in following his or her conscience even if his or her moral judgments turn out to have been objectively incorrect. In this sense, subjective morality is paramount for each person; but at the same time, each of us tries to conform his or her judgment of conscience to what is objectively right, and in that sense, objective morality is paramount.

MEANING OF CONSCIENCE

In the popular mind, conscience is often thought of as an "inner voice," sometimes as the "voice of God," telling us what to do or avoid, but this is metaphor. If conscience speaks with a voice, it is our own. Doubtless, most people do experience a kind of subconscious reaction based on their childhood environment and training, a tendency to approve or disapprove of things for which approval or disapproval was shown in childhood. Such a tendency will often give correct moral estimates or evaluations if one has been brought up well. As a result of such early childhood experiences I may have a vague, unidentifiable feeling, a sense of unease and even of "guilt" in departing from the established pattern, even when I recognize the feeling as un-

reasonable. This is not what is meant by conscience in the traditional sense, nor is it to be identified with Freud's "super-ego," though they are somewhat related.

In the traditional sense, conscience is not a special power distinct from our intellect. Otherwise our judgments about the rightness or wrongness of our individual acts would be non-intellectual, nonrational, the product of something other than our own consciousness. Conscience is only the intellect itself exercising a special function, the function of judging the rightness or wrongness, the moral value, of our own individual acts according to the set of moral values and principles the person holds with conviction.

Conscience is a function of intellect concerned with actions that can be good or bad. It does not deal with theoretical questions of right and wrong in general, such as "Why is lying wrong?" "Why must justice be done?" but with the practical question: "What ought I to do here and now in this concrete situation?" "If I do this act I am thinking of, will I be lying, will I be unjust?" Conscience is the same practical intelligence I use to judge what to do or avoid in other affairs of life: how shall I run my business, invest my money, protect my health, design my house, plant my farm, raise my family? Like other human judgments, conscience can go wrong, can make mistaken moral judgments. As a person can make mistakes in these other spheres of human activity, so he or she can make mistakes about what is the right thing to do here and now. In making any such practical judgment, however, a person has no guide other than his or her intelligence desiring to do what is right and good and what that intelligence reveals about what it is right and good to do in the situation here and now.

Conscience, in this traditional sense, can then be defined as the intellect's practical judgment about an individual act as good and to be done, or as evil and to be avoided. The term *conscience* can actually be applied to any of the three distinct aspects of this judgment process:

1. The intellect as a person's ability, under the influence of a desire to do the right and the

good, to form judgments about the right and wrong of individual acts

2. The process of reasoning that we go through, under the influence of that desire, to reach such a judgment
3. The conclusion of this reasoning process, which is called the evaluative judgment of conscience

The reasoning process we go through in arriving at a judgment of conscience is the same as in any logical deductive argument, even though we rarely spell out the steps for ourselves. Usually we draw the conclusions so quickly that we are not aware that we have been engaging in a process of deductive reasoning. We arrive at the judgment of conscience by a kind of "shortcut" that seems to conceal the deductive process. For example:

1. "Should I say this? No, that would be a lie."
2. "Must I correct this mistake? Yes, it may hurt someone."
3. "May I keep this? Of course, no one else owns it."

These are all examples of a shortened form of deductive reasoning used to form a judgment of conscience. If we were to formulate explicitly each of the deductions in these examples, this is what we would have:

1. Lies are immoral. This explanation of my conduct is a lie. This explanation of my conduct is immoral.
2. Mistakes that may endanger someone must be corrected. The mistake I just made may endanger someone. I must correct the mistake I just made.
3. What belongs to no one may be kept. This object I just picked up belongs to no one. I may keep this object I just picked up.

Deductive reasoning supposes a major premise or general principle, a minor premise or application of the principle to a particular case, and a conclusion necessarily following from the two premises. The major premise employed in forming the judgment of conscience is a moral value or a general moral principle known by means of our rational predisposition to appreciate moral values and formulate such principles so as to have them in mind ready for use as the basis of our conduct. The major premise may be either a principle I have directly formulated as a result of this predisposition such as "Do good and avoid evil," "Respect the rights of others," and "Do to others as you would have them do to you" or a conclusion derived from such a principle and held as a general rule of conduct for myself. The minor premise brings the particular act here and now to be done under the scope of the general principle stated in the major premise. The conclusion that logically follows is the judgment of conscience itself.

EMOTION AND CONSCIENCE

The judgment of conscience is an evaluative judgment made in terms of the goodness or badness of the act I did or am thinking of doing. Say, for example, my "conscience bothers me" because I feel guilt or remorse for speaking harshly to one of my closest friends when he criticized me for the way I voted in the last election. I am reflecting on a past act, speaking harshly to my friend, an act done in a situation that obviously involved a great deal more than intellectual activity. I was in conversation with a close friend whom I love, and it was in that context that he criticized me for voting as I did. I had voted the way I judged that I ought, given my own moral and political convictions. I was trying to be true to myself in voting as I did. My friend could not allow the incident to pass without criticizing my view because he loves me and cared enough to try to help me see something I did not see before. I became angry with him because of his criticism of my views and expressed that anger in harsh words. Now I am experiencing guilt or remorse for having responded to his love and care in that way. Why? Because I find, on reflection, that anger and harsh words were an inappropriate response on my part. My anger at the moment blocked out the fact of our mutual love and my response was one of taking offense where none was meant.

Note the interplay of emotion as evaluative on both sides in this situation. If emotion was not at all involved, there would be no judgment of conscience in the first place, because I would have been aware of no values either to form my convictions about how to vote or to respond to my friend's love and care. My moral awareness in terms of forming personal convictions about how to vote and how to deal with a friend simply would not have been there. The evaluational elements that I use in living my life have their beginnings in my emotions, the affective side of my being. Conscience is not so much a part of ethics as it is *the morally evaluating self* that ethics as a study seeks to serve. This morally evaluating self that my conscience is grows out of my appreciation of myself and of other persons as valuable, intrinsically worthwhile, and important just because we are all persons. My moral awareness, my conscience, has its roots in this appreciation of self and others and grows and develops in the process of experiencing myself and others in our interrelatedness. Just as no two persons are ever absolutely identical, so no two consciences will ever be identical.

My conscience bears the unique markings of my moral journey through life. It is conditioned by my personal history and is developed as my history develops. What my conscience has in common with other consciences is its rootedness in that moral experience of self and others as interrelated and valuable. My conscience is like a housing that I myself build and carry around with me through life. I look out at the world and other persons through the windows in this housing. Another way of speaking of this housing is to call it my personal value orientation, my set of moral values and principles that I hold with conviction, the values and principles I have found for myself and tested out with my own emotions and then integrated into my own moral approach to life.

Conscience is not developed by critical thought alone. Emotion also enters into its development along with imagination, for conscience is not merely our power to judge the past in moral terms but is also our ability to see alternatives in moral situations that have implications for the future. All moral knowledge has an emotional dimension, and our emotions draw the values we experience into the interior of our personality. These values enter into our intellectual framework for use in making our evaluative judgments of conscience. The values and principles we accept and hold with conviction become so much a part of the moral self that we use them in making our judgments of conscience without reformulating them as we go along. We use the rules of grammar when we speak, but we do not reformulate those rules explicitly as we speak. So too, in working out a judgment of conscience, we use the values and principles we have found for ourselves and integrated into our moral stance toward others and to our life itself without explicitly reformulating those moral values and principles when we act. They are enfleshed in us and at our service even if we do not think of them explicitly.

The person who is morally good is one who loves the good and is sensitive to its presence. Love enables us to discover the value of others by guiding us to those values and revealing them for our understanding and appreciation. A love-informed conscience has a special keenness for discerning the good that exists and a creative impulse to bring about an increase of good in our lives and the lives of others.

Another way we can see how much emotion is involved in conscience is to realize that our most profound interpersonal relationships are precisely relationships in which one moral consciousness meets another at the level and in the intimacy of conscience. To love another person is to give one's deepest self to that other to cherish and, in turn, to accept and cherish that other's deepest self. This is the same as moral conscience meeting and cherishing another moral conscience. The encounter of self with another self is total. Certainly it is not a mere meeting of intellects; it is a meeting of persons with all that this means in terms of emotion, intellect, will, imagination, and inclination. Since conscience is the total moral personality, conscience is also more than intellect and includes emotion, willing, imagination, and natural inclination as well.

In the opening chapter of this book we spoke of the difference between *customary morality* and *reflective morality*. Customary morality enters into the formation of the conscious moral self each of us is by teaching us the moral tradition of our society and civilization. We also learn about moral values and principles from our parents and other persons of authority. Our awareness of moral values and truths has a social dimension, for we depend on one another in knowing ourselves and our world. Conscience, just because it is personal and unique, need not be closed-minded but can be realistically open to embrace the truth wherever it is discovered. What we must not do is allow ourselves to be engulfed and dominated by others. A good conscience is both individual and social at the same time. We, as persons, are not atomistic centers of moral judgment; we live our lives in dialogue with others, and so the moral self that I am mirrors my social nature. Conscience is not a matter of me against them; it is an affair of me distinct from them but together with them. If I am to follow my own conscience, then I must also question my own conscience and test it. I can do this only with the help of others, being emotionally sincere and intellectually honest with them. From those around us we need love and respect as persons, conscious moral selves, and then we can explore the depth and dynamics of our moral awareness but only if we respond to that love and respect in a creative way.

KINDS OF CONSCIENCE

Conscience may be a guide to future actions, prompting us to do them or avoid them, or a judge of our past actions, the source of our self-approval or remorse. For the purpose of ethics, conscience as a guide to future actions is more important. Its acts are chiefly four: commanding or forbidding, when the act must either be done or avoided; persuading or permitting, when there is question of the better or worse course of action without a strict obligation.

Since the judgment of conscience is an intellectual judgment and the intellect can err, either by adopting false premises or by drawing an illogical conclusion, conscience can be either correct or erroneous. A *correct* conscience judges

as good what is really good, and as evil what is really evil. In this case, subjective and objective morality correspond. An *erroneous* conscience judges as good what is really evil, or as evil what is really good. All error involves ignorance, because a person cannot make a false judgment unless he or she lacks knowledge of the truth. The ignorance involved in error is either *vincible,* if the error can be overcome and the judgment corrected, or *invincible,* if the error cannot be overcome and the judgment cannot be corrected, at least by means any normally prudent person would be expected to use.

A person's judgment of conscience may also be certain or doubtful. We are *certain* when we judge without fear that the opposite may be true in fact. We are *doubtful* when we either hesitate to make any judgment at all or make a judgment but with misgivings that the opposite may be true. If we make the judgment with fear that the opposite may be true, we assent to one side, but *our judgment is only a probable opinion.* There are varying degrees of probability, running all the way from slight suspicion to the fringes of certainty.

The fact that people differ in their levels of sensitivity to moral values gives habitual characteristics to their judgments of conscience. We call their judgments of conscience *strict* or *lax,* tender or tough, fine or blunt, delicate or gross, according as they are inclined to perceive or habitually overlook various moral values. A *perplexed* person is one who cannot make up his or her mind and remains in a state of indecisive anguish, especially if he or she thinks that whatever alternative he or she chooses will be wrong. A *scrupulous* person torments himself or herself by rehearsing over and over again doubts that were once settled, finding new sources of guilt in old deeds that were best forgotten, striving for a kind of certainty about one's moral state that one simply cannot have in this life. Scrupulosity can be a serious form of self-torture, mounting to neurotic anxiety that is more of a psychological than an ethical condition. Such a person needs to learn, not the distinction between right and wrong, which he or she may know very well, but how to stop worrying over groundless fears, how to end ceaseless self-examination and face life in a more confident spirit.

FOLLOWING THE JUDGMENT OF CONSCIENCE

Having seen what conscience is and the forms it takes, we must now discuss our obligation to follow what conscience approves and disapproves. There are two chief rules, but each of them involves a problem. The two rules are:

1. Always follow a certain conscience
2. Never act with a doubtful conscience

Always Follow a Certain Conscience

First, notice the difference in meaning between a certain and a correct conscience. The term *correct* points to the objective truth of the person's judgment; the person's judgment of conscience represents the real state of things. The term *certain* refers to the subjective state of the person judging, namely, how firmly assent to the judgment has been given, how thoroughly fear of the opposite has been excluded. Obviously, the kind of certainty meant here is a subjective certainty, which can exist along with objective error. We have two possibilities that need to be examined:

1. A certain and correct conscience
2. A certain but erroneous conscience

1. *A certain and correct judgment of conscience* really offers no difficulty. Our obligation is clear. The person judges what conduct is required here and now. The judgment is correct, and the person is certain of its correctness.

What degree of certainty is required to call our judgment certain? Traditionally it has been said that *prudential certainty* is sufficient. Prudential certainty is not something absolute. It is still a matter of degree. This kind of certainty excludes all *prudent* fear that the opposite may be true, but it does not require us to rule out imprudent fears based on bare possibilities. That is, the reasons are strong enough to satisfy a normally prudent person on an important matter, so that the

person would feel safe in practice even though there is theoretically a chance of being wrong. He or she has taken every reasonable precaution but cannot guarantee against rare contingencies and freaks of nature. When there is a question of action, of something to be done here and now, but often something involving future consequences some of which are dependent on the wills of other people, the absolute possibility of error can never be wholly excluded; but it can be so reduced that no prudent person who is free from neurotic anxiety would be deterred from acting through fear of it. A prudent person, having investigated the case, can then say with *prudential certainty* that this business venture is safe, that this person is guilty of a crime, that this employee is honest. This degree of certainty, since it excludes all reasonable fear of error, is much stronger than high probability, which does not exclude such reasonable fear.

2. What happens when I have an *erroneous conscience,* that is, when I make a mistaken or *incorrect moral judgment?* If I know my judgment may be wrong and I am able to correct the possible error, then I have an obligation to do so before acting. Otherwise, I run the risk of doing moral evil. Obviously, if I make an error and do not know about the error, I have no means of correcting it. Since my error and ignorance are unavoidable because they are unknown to me, I act morally when I go ahead and follow my judgment of conscience. My judgment is certain and correct as far as I am able to know here and now, so even if I do something objectively wrong, I am responsible for what I do but am not morally blameworthy for having done it. Conscience is the only guide a person has for acting here and now. If I were not obliged to follow my conscience when my judgment is certain even though mistaken but not known to be mistaken, then I would be forced to the absurd conclusion that I am not obliged to follow my judgment of conscience when it is certain and correct.

A person's willing the good depends on his or her understanding of that good. Whether the judgment about the good is correct or not, the willed act is good if it consents to what the intellect understands and presents as good, and the act is bad if it consents to what the intellect understands and presents as evil under the guise of good. A person firmly convinced that an action is right is in fact choosing the good as far as possible; a person firmly convinced that an action is wrong is choosing what is thought to be evil whether it really is so or not. Such persons are not responsible for the unknown error of judgment, but they are praiseworthy or blameworthy for their choices of what they judged was good or evil.

Never Act with a Doubtful Conscience

We have seen that a person acting with a certain but unavoidably mistaken conscience is avoiding moral evil as far as possible. The mistaken judgment is not the person's fault, for the person has no reason to believe that the judgment is mistaken. But the same cannot be said of one who acts with a *doubtful* conscience. This person has reason to believe that the intended act may actually be wrong and yet is willing to go ahead and do it anyway. True, the person is not certain about the wrongness, but such a person is not willing to take the means to avoid this probable wrongdoing by determining the true nature of the act, if that is possible. This type of person acts without care for the rightness or wrongness of acts. Even if the act turns out to be objectively right, this is only accidental. Therefore, we may conclude that one must never act with a doubtful conscience.

But, then, what should a person with a doubtful conscience do? The person's first obligation is to try to solve the doubt, to find out the true nature of the act. If I am a person with a doubtful conscience, I must reason over the matter more carefully to see whether I can arrive at certainty. I must inquire and seek advice, even the advice of experts if the matter is important enough and there are experts available who can help me. I must investigate the facts of the problem and make certain of them, if this is possible. I must use all the means that normally prudent people

are accustomed to use, in proportion to the importance of the problem. Before deciding on an important course of action, business and professional people, for example, take a great deal of trouble to investigate a case, to secure all the data, to seek expert advice, besides thinking over the matter carefully themselves. The same degree of seriousness and care is demanded in moral affairs.

What if a prudentially certain conclusion cannot be reached by doing all of this? For example, it may happen that the required information cannot be obtained because the facts are not recorded, the records are lost, the obligation remains obscure, the opinions of the learned differ, or the matter does not admit of delay for further research. If one should never act with a doubtful conscience, what can one do who is still in doubt? It may seem that the answer is easy: do nothing. But often this approach will not help, for doing nothing can often have as many and as important consequences as doing something. Surely omissions can be voluntary, and the doubt may concern precisely the question of whether we may morally refrain from acting in this case.

The answer to the difficulty is that every doubtful conscience can in actual practice be turned into a certain conscience. That is, no one need ever remain in doubt about what he or she must do. To see this, we must distinguish between the *direct method* of inquiry and investigation, which has just been described, and the *indirect method* of forming our conscience by the use of reflex principles. Note first, however, that we are not offered a choice between using the direct or the indirect method. We *must* use the direct method *first*. Only when the direct method yields no result may we use the indirect method.

FORMING ONE'S CONSCIENCE

The doubting person who has exhausted the *direct method* described above without obtaining the knowledge he or she needs has a double doubt:

1. What is the actual truth about the matter in hand?

2. What is one obliged to do in such a situation?

The first question is a *theoretical* doubt, and it cannot be answered if the direct method was used and failed to yield results. But the second question is a *practical* doubt, and this question can be answered in every instance by use of the *indirect method,* which we shall now describe.

Though many doubts are theoretically insoluble, every doubt is capable of being solved practically. Any person can become certain of what he or she is obliged to do, how he or she is morally required to act, even while remaining in a state of unsolved theoretical doubt. Thus, though the rightness or wrongness of the action may not be settled in the abstract, a person can become prudentially certain of what he or she in these actual circumstances is obliged or allowed to do and can therefore act with a certain conscience. What he or she determines is the kind of conduct that is *certainly* right for a *doubting* person in this situation. This process of solving a practical doubt without touching the theoretical doubt is called the *indirect method* or *forming one's conscience*.

The process of forming one's conscience is accomplished by the use of *reflex principles,* so called because we use them while reflecting on the state of doubt and ignorance in which we now find ourselves. We have only two possible courses of action open to us: "play it safe" or "take the easier way." Since these two courses of action are almost always opposite courses, may we take whichever we please in any case? No. Forming one's conscience by use of the indirect method consists in determining when to "play it safe" and when to "take the easier way." The two reflex principles we use are (1) the morally safer course is preferable and (2) a doubtful obligation does not bind. We must now examine each of these principles to determine when to use the one or the other.

The Morally Safer Course

By the *morally safer course* is meant the course of action that more surely preserves moral goodness and more clearly avoids moral wrongdoing.

One is always *allowed* to choose the morally safer course of action. If I am not obliged to act and simply am in doubt about whether I am allowed to act, the morally safer course is to omit the act. For example, if I doubt whether this money is justly mine, I can simply refuse it. If a person is certainly allowed to act but doubts whether he or she has an obligation to act, the morally safer course is to do the act. If I doubt, for example, whether I have paid a bill, I can offer the money and risk paying it twice. Sometimes neither alternative appears morally safer and the obligation on each side seems equal; then we may do either.

We have an *obligation* to follow the morally safer course whenever we have a known moral obligation to fulfill or an end (goal) that we ought to achieve to the best of our power. The only doubt we have is about the effectiveness of the means to be used for this purpose. The obligation we must fulfill or the end we ought to strive for places a further obligation on us to use certainly effective means. A lawyer, for example, who has agreed to take on a client and defend that client in court has a clear obligation to fulfill his or her agreement to defend that client. That clear obligation places a further moral obligation on the lawyer to use the most certainly effective means at his or her disposal to defend the client. The lawyer must take the morally safer course when it comes to choosing the means to fulfill his or her moral obligation to defend the client. In such cases, the doubt is solely about a *matter of fact,* namely, which means will certainly fulfill the moral obligation incurred in agreeing to defend the client.

A Doubtful Obligation

There are other cases in which the *obligation itself* is the thing in doubt. Here we have a different question. The morally safer course (our first reflex principle), though always allowable, is often costly and inconvenient, sometimes physically more dangerous and even heroic. Out of a desire to do the better thing we often follow the morally safer course without question, but if we were to have an obligation to follow it in *all* cases of doubt, life would become intolerably difficult. To be safe morally, we should have to yield every doubtful claim to others who have no better right than we do, and so we would become the victims of every cheat and swindler whose conscience is less delicate than ours. Such difficulties are avoided by the use of the *second reflex principle:* a doubtful obligation does not bind.

This second principle is applicable only when I doubt whether I am bound by a moral obligation. My doubt of conscience concerns whether the act I am thinking of doing is one I am obliged to do or obliged to avoid doing. The principle that *a doubtful obligation does not bind* may be used in both of the following situations:

1. I doubt whether such an obligation exists or is genuine.
2. I doubt about how to interpret the obligation, that is, I doubt whether the existing obligation binds me here and now.

I may doubt, for example, whether the fruit on my neighbor's tree hanging over my fence belongs to my neighbor or me, whether I am sick enough to be excused from going to work today, whether the damage I caused was purely accidental or due to my own carelessness. We are assuming that there are in the examples questions of fact that cannot be settled, but they still bring up questions of what is morally allowed: Am I allowed to pick the fruit, to stay home from work, to refuse to pay for the damage? Is there any known moral obligation that is applicable to my case and that certainly forbids my doing what I am thinking of doing? If the direct method fails to prove any moral obligation, then I am justified in going ahead and doing these things on the principle that *a doubtful obligation does not bind*. The reason behind this principle is that an obligation must be certain in order to have binding force, and a doubtful obligation is not sufficiently certain to bind the person about to act here and now. It is important to remember that we are talking about situations here in which the person is sincerely doubtful whether there is a moral

obligation (principle or rule) that covers the case. If the person is not doubtful, then this second reflex principle does not apply.

We must be careful to distinguish these doubtful obligation cases from those that fall under the first reflex principle. If the obligation itself is the thing in doubt, then I am not obliged. If the obligation is certain and only the means of carrying it out are doubtful, I must follow the morally safer course and not use doubtful means if certainly effective ones are available. I may not roll boulders down a hill in the mere hope that they may not hit anyone on the road below, but I may cart off boulders from property that is only probably mine. I may not leave poisoned food lying about on the chance that no one will care to eat it, but I may manufacture clearly labeled poison if such manufacture is only probably forbidden. In the first instances there is no doubt about the obligation: I am not morally allowed to jeopardize human life unnecessarily. It may happen that no harm results from my acts but those acts are certainly dangerous, and so *the morally safer course must be chosen*. In the second instances, the obligation not to seize others' property or not to manufacture dangerous products is of doubtful application to my case, and I may morally go ahead and do the thing, for *a doubtful obligation does not bind*. However, if the manufacture of poison turns out to be forbidden by civil law, I would be legally liable even though not morally at fault.

How doubtful does the moral obligation have to be to lose its binding force? Must the existence or application of the obligation be more doubtful than its nonexistence or nonapplication, or equally so, or will any doubt suffice to exempt a person from the obligation? Such questions were hotly debated during the seventeenth and eighteenth centuries, though more by moral theologians than by philosophical ethicians. The view that survived this debate as the most tenable in theory and the only one workable in practice is called *probabilism*. It does not refer to a weighing of probabilities on either side of the case but rather requires me to have a *solidly probable* reason for thinking that a moral obligation does not exist or does not apply to my case for me to be morally allowed to go ahead and do the act. Solid probability means that the reasons against the obligation's existence or application are not frivolous or fictitious but genuine and weighty, even though they may be somewhat less so than the reasons in favor of the obligation. No judgment can be certain if there are genuine and weighty reasons against it. If it is not certain, it is doubtful, and if it is doubtful, it does not bind. To list all the reasons on both sides and weigh their relative merits is often a hopeless task, baffling the best experts. The average person has neither time nor knowledge nor ability for such a complete comparison. In practice, choices must be made promptly and yet be made with a certain conscience. The theory of probabilism enables a person to do so by saying that a moral rule does not oblige when there are solid reasons for thinking that it either does not exist or does not apply to the person's case here and now.

One final caution is in order: we have been dealing with moral obligation and not with obligations that stem from civil law. The second reflex principle that a doubtful obligation does not bind *does not apply to cases of civil law*. Ignorance may be an excuse in some cases of civil law, but *ignorance of the law* is almost never an excusing condition before the civil law. Once a civil law has been passed and put on the books, the presumption is that the citizens know the law as it applies to them. We have a moral obligation to obey civil laws that are just. We shall discuss this matter in the chapter on government.

CONCLUSION

The whole matter of forming one's conscience may seem to involve a great deal of subtlety, as if we were whittling down moral obligation to its lowest terms. Is this not contrary to moral virtue and personal honor, straightforward simplicity and sincerity? In answer, the first thing to note is that we can always follow the morally safer course. But in ethics we must study not only what is the virtuous and better, the nobler and more heroic thing to do, but also exactly what a person is strictly obliged to do. A generous person will not haggle over good works, but a reasonable person will want to know when he or she is doing something that is strictly a duty (carrying out a clear moral obligation) and when he or she is being generous.

Accurate moral discrimination is also important in judging the conduct of others. In our own personal lives we may be willing to waive our strict rights and to go beyond the call of duty, but we have no business imposing on others an obligation to do so. The borderline between right and wrong is often difficult to determine. It is certainly foolish to skirt it too closely; but we are not allowed to accuse another person of wrongdoing if he or she has not truly done wrong. This is another reason why we need to detail these principles very carefully.

SUMMARY

Morality refers to *the rightness or wrongness of human acts*. We speak of *objective* or *subjective* morality accordingly as it overlooks the particular characteristics of the doer of the act and his or her circumstances or else takes them into consideration. *The norm of subjective morality is the evaluative judgment of conscience.*

Conscience is not a special faculty but a practical function of the intellect, under the impulse of the desire to do the right and good, that judges the concrete act of an individual person as morally good or evil. The reasoning used by the intellect in doing this is a form of deduction. The major premise is an accepted moral value or principle, the minor premise is an application of the value or principle to the case at hand, and the conclusion is the evaluative judgment of conscience itself.

Conscience functions both as a guide to future acts and as a judge of past acts. A *correct* conscience judges good as good and evil as evil; an *erroneous* conscience judges good as evil or evil as good. A *certain* conscience judges without doubt or fear that the opposite is true. A *doubtful* conscience either makes no judgment or judges with fear that the opposite is true. Conscience is said to be *strict* or *lax* according as it tends to perceive or overlook various moral values.

Always obey a certain conscience even when it is unknowingly or unavoidably mistaken. A *certain and correct* conscience is the clear and proper judgment about one's moral duty or obligations. Prudential certainty, the exclusion of any *prudent* fear of the opposite, is all that can be expected in moral matters. A *certain but erroneous* conscience must also be followed because the agent cannot distinguish it from a correct conscience and has no other guide; the act is subjectively right even if objectively wrong.

Never act with a doubtful conscience. A person who acts with a doubtful conscience is willing to do an act whether it is wrong or not, refusing to take the means to avoid doing moral evil.

A person in doubt must first use the *direct method* of inquiry and investigation to dispel the doubt. That is, the person must reason over the matter more carefully, inquire and seek advice of experts if possible, and investigate the facts of the problem to make certain of them if possible—in short, use all the means a normally prudent person would use in proportion to the importance of the problem. If the direct method yields no results, the *indirect method* of forming

one's conscience may be used. This consists in solving not the *theoretical doubt* (what is the actual truth?), for that is what cannot be solved if the direct method fails, but in solving the *practical doubt* alone (how should a doubting person act in this case?). The practical doubt can always be solved by using one of two reflex principles:

1. *The morally safer course is preferable.* This course is always allowable but sometimes is very burdensome. It *must* be used if the case concerns not the existence or application of an obligation but the effectiveness of the means used to fulfill a certain moral obligation or attain an end that must certainly be attained.

2. *A doubtful obligation does not bind.* This principle may be used only when there is question of the obligation itself, when either the existence or application of an obligation is genuinely in doubt.

Probabilism is the name given the claim that to bind, an obligation must be certain, and no obligation can be certain if there are solidly probable reasons against it no matter how strong the probability, that is, the reasons for it, may also be. It is practically impossible to weigh the degrees of probability on every side completely, so probabilism holds that such a comparison is really unnecessary.

The purpose of this practical study of conscience is not to whittle down moral obligation but to help us make accurate moral discriminations both about ourselves and about others.

Questions for Discussion

1. The Library of Congress each year since 1970 has paid to have three dozen magazines produced in Braille so they can be read by the blind. One of these magazines is *Playboy* without the pictures and advertising. This year Congress cut the library's budget by the exact amount it costs to produce the Braille edition of *Playboy.* The librarian then dropped the Braille edition of *Playboy,* and was promptly sued by *Playboy* and several organizations for

the blind. The U.S. District Judge ruled that the librarian had acted unconstitutionally and the decision to halt the Braille edition constituted viewpoint discrimination in violation of the First Amendment. Reconstruct the judgments of conscience that seem to be operative here and the reasoning that apparently led to those judgments.

2. The President of the United States is responsible for the nation's foreign policy and has

an obligation to safeguard the nation's interests around the world. At this point in time he is working quietly to provide significant aid in terms of money and arms to a group of insurgents who are seeking to overthrow the existing legitimate government of a central American nation with whose policies he is in fundamental disagreement. How would you define his moral obligations in this matter? Are those obligations certain or doubtful? Does he have any goal(s) which must certainly be attained? If so, what are they and why must they be attained? What means are at his disposal to attain the goal(s)?

3. For months prior to the death of a prominent fashion designer there were rumors throughout the fashion industry that he had AIDS (acquired immune deficiency syndrome). When he died, reporters throughout the country were divided about whether or not to mention the rumor in the designer's obituary. The vast majority of newspapers chose not to mention the rumor, but a few did mention it. All the journalists, we may suppose, were trying to behave responsibly, and yet they took two different approaches to a very sensitive subject. Argue the case that can be made both for and against mentioning the rumor. In each case, it is a matter of the journalist either taking the safer course or deciding that he or she has an obligation to cover the story fully. Do you think the obligation could have been doubtful? Why? What would you have done? Why?

4. You have inherited 500 shares of common stock in an electronics company that manufactures, among other things, police surveillance equipment. From the annual report to the stockholders you discover that the company has been selling to and maintaining its surveillance equipment for a totalitarian government that uses the equipment to prevent its people from exercising some of their natural rights such as freedom of speech. The company pays regular quarterly dividends on your stock. If you do not agree with the company's policy of doing business with such a government, because you consider such business as cooperating in immoral activity, what can you do? What ought you to do? If you are in doubt about the proper course of action for you to take, how can you solve your doubt?

5. Political terrorism has struck often enough throughout the world to make every affected government study why terrorists act as they do. If we can understand them, we should be able to stop them. Terrorists are persons committed to some particular cause and have a vision of the good they are trying to achieve. They also have consciences and make the same kinds of practical moral judgments every other person makes. Put yourself "in the shoes" of a terrorist of your choice and, in your own imagination, study the conscience of that terrorist. Do you find a vision of the good, doubts, opinions, certainties, and so forth? Does the terrorist have to form his or her conscience in order to make the commitments he or she makes? Do you find that you and the terrorist share some of the same emotions, and have the same need for personal esteem, self-respect, and freedom from oppression? Do you find the terrorist's conscience erroneous? If so, is there anything you can do to help that person?

Readings

St. Thomas Aquinas, *Summa Theologica*, I, q. 79, aa. 12–13, on synderesis (the rational predisposition to formulate first moral principles) and conscience. The matter treated in this chapter was not very thoroughly developed by St. Thomas, because his treatment of moral virtue did not require a theory of conscience. For him, as for Aristotle, the moral life was more a matter of virtuous living rather than one of determining when conscience was right or wrong. In his treatise on moral virtue in *Summa Theologica*, I–II, he wrote in terms of prudence and the moral virtues rather than in terms of conscience, because practical moral judgments are judgments of prudence seeking the means to achieve the right and good ends desired by the other moral virtues. The theory of conscience was developed when moral theologians and philosophical ethicians began to downplay prudence and the moral virtues as central to the moral life and to consider more what a person's strict obligations were in terms of living a moral, but not necessarily morally virtuous, life.

Cardinal Newman's treatment in his *Grammar of Assent,* pp. 105–112, is well worth reading.

Eric D'Arcy, *Conscience and Its Right to Freedom,* is recommended as a whole; Parts I and II are pertinent here.

John Donnelly and Leonard Lyons (editors), *Conscience,* presents a philosophical analysis of conscience by contemporary authors. Freud's contention that the phenomenon of moral conscience is explained by his theory of the superego is examined, pp. 85–114.

A modern personalist approach to the subject is found in Ignace Lepp, *The Authentic Morality,* and in Louis Monden, *Sin, Liberty, and Law.* The treatment in both is psychological and somewhat theological, but they put it in the language of phenomenological and existential philosophy. An excellent treatment of conscience and guilt is found in Daniel C. Maguire, *The Moral Choice,* ch. 12; Andrew Varga, *On Being Human,* ch. 13; and Bernard Häring, *Free and Faithful in Christ,* vol. 1, "General Moral Theology," ch. 6. Häring also provides an illuminating discussion of the social context in which probabilism was developed.

Martin Heidegger has a long treatment of conscience from his own phenomenological point of view in *Being and Time.* J. Glenn Gray, *The Warriors: Reflections on Men in Battle,* pp. 171–213, presents a view of guilt and conscience that is Heideggerian in inspiration and very readable.

PART II
The Objective Good in Moral Life

The subjective factor of personal choice and responsibility is of utmost importance in ethics, as we have just seen. Almost no one maintains, however, that anything I choose is moral merely by the fact that it is my choice. Some of my choices are good and some are bad, and I am responsible for both. The business of ethics is to help us see which choices are good, which bad, and why. Now it is time to begin our investigation of the good (Chapter 5), the objective side of the moral life.

One group of ethical theories holds that nothing is good or bad in itself but only in terms of the consequences to which it leads. Chapter 6 deals with such consequences conceived of as *pleasure* to the individual or to the group or to the whole human race. In Chapter 7 we examine *social convention* as a possible standard for determining what is good. Pragmatism (Chapter 8) judges acts as good or bad insofar as they are more or less useful in satisfying felt needs, a kind of consequence. These theories are efforts to derive moral goodness from something that is not moral, something extrinsic to the act itself.

Yet another group finds this approach deficient. If an act is good or bad only in terms of its consequences, how do we determine good and bad consequences; if because it produces pleasure, how do we determine good and bad pleasures; if because it conforms to custom, how do we determine good and bad customs? Not all good can be instrumental good, good only because it leads to some other good; ultimately something has to be *intrinsically* good, good in itself. G.E. Moore has shown that all definition is analysis of a concept into its components. The starting points of all reasoning are primitive, unanalyzable, indefinable notions that simply are what they are, and of them we have direct *intuition* (Chapter 9). Both intuitionism and *rationalism* result from pushing knowledge back to its immediately known and indemonstrable principles (Chapter 10). We examine St. Thomas's theory of *natural law* (Chapter 11) and Kant's theory of the moral law manifesting itself as *absolute duty* (Chapter 12).

Next we turn to those theories that claim that it is a mistake to seek some objective foundation on which to base our moral judgments, whether that foundation be extrinsic or intrinsic to the moral act. The whole value of the moral act lies in its subjectivity, the fact that the self is the doer of the act. It matters little what one does so long as it is a *free* expression of personality (Chapter 13). The very concepts of law and duty are to be discarded as restrictions hampering the autonomy of the authentic person who must decide the loving thing to do in a particular *situation* (Chapter 14).

Freedom and love, two of the greatest values that can characterize a person, are severely limited as focal points for ethical theory. Freedom does not tell us what a person should be free to do, nor does love tell us what makes a person worthy of love. We do not, however, discard freedom and love for this reason. In Chapter 15 we analyze the subject (moral agent) as subsistent and therefore as person to illuminate subjectivity and intersubjectivity, and we find that *love* is the only way we have of penetrating another person precisely as subject. Good *habits* (moral virtues) are viewed as the means to attain happiness (Chapter 16), and what I wish most for myself and the people I love is precisely that *happiness* (Chapter 17).

5
Good

PROBLEM

I, as an individual person, rely on my own moral awareness to determine the degree of responsibility I have for my acts, and on my own conscience to judge the good or evil, the rightness or wrongness, of these acts I have done in concrete circumstances. There is no more ultimate court of appeal in this world than the testimony of conscience. But subjective morality alone is insufficient. If it were all we had, there would be as many judges of morality as there are persons, and sincerity would be the same as truth in moral matters. Conscience can be erroneous as well as correct; error can be vincible as well as invincible. When objective truth is attainable, conscience cannot rest satisfied with a subjective opinion that it knows may be false. Our next endeavor, therefore, must be to find whether there is an objective morality with which the judgment of conscience should be in agreement, and, if so, what that morality is. Henceforth the whole of our study will be devoted to this pursuit. We begin by asking:

1. Is the good definable?
2. Is the good an end to be sought?
3. Are we obliged to seek the good?
4. Is the good a value simply in itself?
5. What distinguishes moral values from other values?

DEFINABILITY OF GOOD

What is the good? How do we define goodness? It seems that we must settle this question at the outset, for if we do not know what *good* means, how will we recognize it when we come across it? On the other hand, no one has succeeded in giving a good definition of *good*. In fact, would not a good definition of *good* require that one already know *good* before defining it? And, if so, why define it?

The question of the definability of good was made acute around the turn of the century by George Edward Moore.[1] His reasoning is that all definition is analysis of a concept into its components, that good is a simple concept unanalyzable into anything simpler, and that therefore the concept of good is indefinable. We can, of course, point to certain properties in objects because of which we call these objects good, but that does not tell us what is good about these properties or why it is good to have them. In a sense we can define *the* good, the object which is good, but not the predicate *good* itself. That we cannot define good does not mean that we cannot know what it is. Not all knowledge is by definition. We cannot define yellow but can only point to yellow objects; the wavelength of the light tells us nothing about the color we see. To try to define good in terms of something else that is not good is not to define it but to lose it. The reduction of good, the simplest of ethical ideas, to something nonethical involves what Moore calls the *naturalistic fallacy,* as if good were a sort of natural property that some things possess and others lack. Good is just good, irreducible, unanalyzable, and indefinable.

One might criticize this argument by pointing out that the dictionary contains a definition of good and that rules for the use of the word *good* in language can be formulated. Linguistic analysts spend much time at this task, but Moore anticipated them by noting that the subject matter of ethics is the concept of good itself and not correctness in speaking about it. Others solve the problem of the definability of good by actually defining it, for example, as pleasure, desirability, evolution, life according to nature, and similar concepts. We shall have to examine these claims, but they are examples of precisely what Moore means by the naturalistic fallacy. Another objection is that, if good cannot be defined, it will have to be known by some sort of direct intuition. This Moore admits, despite the unpopularity of intuitionism. How much intuition must be admitted in ethics is discussed in a later chapter.

Whether or not good is indefinable in principle, we have to begin our study of it without a definition, since we could achieve one only by committing ourselves in advance to a philosophy we have not yet examined. Even without a def-

---

[1]G.E. Moore, *Principia Ethica,* ch. 1; also reprinted separately as "The Indefinability of Good."

inition much has been written about the good. The ancients developed one of its most fruitful aspects, the good as end, and we may well begin with this traditional approach.

THE GOOD AS END

Aristotle begins his *Ethics* with the statement: "The good is that at which all things aim."[1] This is not to be taken as a definition of the good, but only as a recognition of the relationship between *good* and *end* or *aim, goal.* An end he declares to be "That for the sake of which a thing is done."[2] For him all change is a process whereby some given underlying substrate (the matter) acquires a new specification or determination (the form) through the action of an efficient operator (the agent) moved to act by the attraction of some good (the end). Such a view of the universe with its constant changes supposes *teleology,* or purposiveness, a directed world in which all things have an aim, as opposed to the *mechanistic* theory that all changes come about by chance. A directed world needs a principle of direction, and the name for that principle is the *nature* of each being. Each being is so structured that it acts only along certain definite lines. The nature of a being is not some kind of driver, whether outside or inside the being, not something distinct from the being that acts, but its very self. It is the *essence* of each being considered as the principle or source of its activity. Direction supposes not only a nature, a moving principle to make a thing go, but also a target toward which to move. So nature and end are correlative terms. Natural activity is teleological activity.

Human beings also have a nature, the source of the inner dynamism of their being, making it *natural* for them to seek the good as their *end.* That the nature of a being structures it to act along definite lines is not a bar to freedom. Human beings have a free nature, are built to act freely; they naturally guide themselves to their end by free choice. Other beings lack freedom

and automatically run along tracks their nature has laid. In either case they tend to ends.

Every end is a good and every good is an end. An end would not be sought unless it were somehow good for the seeker, and the good by being sought is the end or purpose of the seeker's striving. No activity is possible except for the attainment of some end, for the sake of some good. This is the *principle of finality* or *teleology,* which St. Thomas explains as follows:

> Every agent of necessity acts for an end. For if in a number of causes ordained to one another the first be removed, the others must of necessity be removed also. Now the first of all causes is the final cause. The reason of which is that matter does not receive form save in so far as it is moved by an agent; for nothing reduces itself from potentiality to act. But an agent does not move except out of intention for an end. For if the agent were not determinate to some particular effect, it would not do one thing rather than another: consequently in order that it produce a determinate effect, it must of necessity be determined to some certain one, which has the nature of an end.[3]

In other words, before it acts, a being with potentiality or ability for acting is in an indeterminate condition, and can either act or not act, act in this way or in that way. No action will ever take place unless something removes this indetermination, stirs the being to act, and points its action in a certain direction. Hence the principle of finality, "every agent acts for an end," is implicit in the concepts of potency and act, and in the whole notion of causality. If every agent acts for an end, the human agent certainly does too.

The foregoing description is based on Aristotle, who gave to teleology its classical expression. But our interest is in human beings. Whatever one may think of teleology in the world at large, no sane person can deny that human beings act for ends. Even one who tried to prove that they do not would have this as the end or purpose of the argument. Failure to adapt one's conduct to rational ends is the accepted sign of mental de-

---

[1] Aristotle, *Nicomachean Ethics,* bk. I, ch. 1, 1094a 3.
[2] Aristotle, *Physics,* bk. II, ch. 3, 194b 33; *Metaphysics,* bk. V, ch. 2, 1013a 33.

[3] St. Thomas, *Summa Theologica,* I–II, q. 1, a. 2; see also *Summa Contra Gentiles,* bk. III, ch. 2, 3, 16.

rangement. The very admission, therefore, that there are such things as rational human acts is an admission that human beings do act for ends.

The question arises: If all things, including humans, inevitably seek an end that is also the good, how can any act fail to be good, how can human conduct go wrong? The good as end, as perfective, as good *for,* has various meanings among which we must sort out the moral good.

The thesis that "every being is good" refers only to the goodness of *existence*. It means only that every being, by the very fact that it *is* a being, has some goodness about it and is good for something, contributing in some way to the harmony and perfection of the universe. Every being also has a certain amount of *physical* goodness, which consists in a completeness of parts and competence of activity. Though some things are physically defective, they are good insofar as they have being, defective insofar as they lack being. From the fact that every being is good for *something,* however, it does not follow that every being is good for *everything*. What is good for one thing may not be good for another, and what is good for a thing under these circumstances or from this aspect may not be good for the same thing under different conditions or from another standpoint. The branch of philosophy called metaphysics considers the good in its broadest scope and so can find good in everything in some way; ethics considers the good in the limited line of voluntary and responsible human conduct. The murderer levels his gun and fells his victim. It is a good shot but an evil deed. As a piece of marksmanship it is admirable, but as human conduct it is damnable. There is some good in all things, but it need not be the ethical or *moral* good.

Because not everything is good for everything, it is up to a person's judgment to determine what things are good *for him or her*. Human judgments are open to error, and therefore one may mistake an *apparent* good for a *genuine* good. Unless a thing at least appears to be good we could not seek it at all, for it could make no appeal to our emotions, the affective side of our consciousness; but we can easily confuse what is good for some-

thing else with what is good for us, or what would be good for us in other circumstances with what is good for us here and now. If some lesser good makes impossible the attainment of the absolutely necessary good, this lesser good is not the true or genuine good for us. The moral good must always be a genuine good, but not every genuine good is a moral good.

Thus there are degrees of goodness. We may seek a good not for its own sake but as a means to some further good; it is desirable only because it leads to something more desirable. This is the *useful* or *instrumental* good, and it is good only in a qualified and analogous sense; such are all tools and instruments. We may seek a good for the satisfaction or enjoyment it gives without considering whether it will be beneficial to our whole being; it delights us now and may be harmless, but it offers us no guarantee that it may not hurt us in the long run and render us unfit for the greater good. This is the *pleasant* good, and it attracts us most vividly. Lastly, we may seek a good because it contributes toward the perfection of our being as a whole, because it fits a human being as such. This is the *befitting* good, the upright and honorable, the noble and righteous, and it is good in the fullest sense. It is not only good for us, as the term *befitting* implies, but good in itself as an independent value apart from its effect on others; under this aspect it is called the *intrinsic* good. The moral good, while it may also be useful and pleasant, is always and necessarily the befitting good.

This analysis of the kinds of good shows that human conduct must always be directed toward the good in some sense, but that this is not always the moral good. To strive for the moral good is life's purpose and our obligation.

THE GOOD AS OUGHT

The good, we have just seen, is our constant quest. We are not born possessors of it but are born seekers of it. Our existence is a passage from capacity to fulfillment, from potentiality to actuality, from perfectibility to perfection. Our emptiness clamors to be filled, and whatever satisfies our hunger is called a good. Thus the good appears to us as an end.

But what obliges us to engage in this quest? As an end the good is attractive and invites us to itself. It calls for being, it deserves to be, it should be realized, it ought to exist. But the bare recognition that a thing ought to be does not of itself imply that I am the one who should make it be. We say that a work of art ought to be, in the sense that it is a noble conception worthy of production and it would be a shame not to bring it to light; yet no particular artist is strictly obliged to create it. We tell someone that she ought to invest her money in this enterprise, that it ought to bring her a better return than she can hope for from any other investments; yet no one thinks of this ought as a strict obligation.

Here we see two different senses of the *ought,* which the good always implies, the nonmoral and the moral ought. Every good except the moral good is optional, but the moral good is necessary. There is no getting away from the demands of morality, from the requirement of living a good life and thus being a good person.

This obligatory character of the moral good is what impresses itself on those who see ethics chiefly in terms of duty. It is not so much the loveliness of the good that invites them as the stern voice of duty that calls them. Often the choice is between a moral good and some other kind of good, and the other kind of good seems at the moment by far the more attractive. If we consider the good merely as an object of desire, as an end to be sought, the apparent good can beckon with alluring smiles while the genuine good gravely points to the harder path. Yet one is obliged to follow genuine good and not merely apparent good.

What is the nature of this moral *ought* that commands with such authority? It is a kind of necessity that is unique and irreducible to any other. It is not a logical necessity based on the impossibility of thinking contradictions. It is not a metaphysical necessity stemming from the identity of being with itself: what is, is. It is not a physical necessity, a *must* that compels us from without, destroying our freedom. Nor is it a bio-

logical or a psychological necessity, an internal impossibility of acting differently built into our nature, likewise destroying our freedom. It is a *moral* necessity, that of the *ought,* guiding us in what we recognize as the fitting use of our freedom. It is a freedom that is a necessity and a necessity that is a freedom. The requirement is absolute, and thus it is a necessity, but it can also be refused, though to our loss, and thus it is a freedom.

Moral necessity affects me, the acting subject, but it comes from the object, the kind of act I the subject am performing. The act in its real being is something contingent that may or may not be, but in its ideal being as held up to my reason and will for deliberation and choice, it assumes a practical necessity demanding decision. The demand is absolute. Bad use of artistic, economic, scientific, and other particular abilities is penalized by failure, not by fault, because I had no obligation to pursue these endeavors and hence no absolute obligation to succeed in them. But I cannot help being human and absolutely have to succeed as a human being. If I am a failure at it, it is my fault because the failure was willfully chosen. I do not become bad in a certain line, but become a *bad person.* Everything I do expresses my personality in some way, but the use of my freedom is the actual exertion of my unique personality as constituting my inmost self.

Take the case of a man offered a huge fortune for one act of murdering his best friend. Minimize the dangers and enhance the advantages as much as possible. Make the act absolutely foolproof. Yet it *ought not* to be done. Why not?

1. Eliminate the *legal* sanction. Suppose that the man is not only certain of not being caught but also finds some loophole by which he does not even break any existing civil law and could not be prosecuted for any crime. Yet he sees himself a murderer and cannot approve his act.

2. Eliminate the *social* sanction. Since no one will know, there is no one's disapproval to be feared. Yet he deserves that disapproval even if he does not receive it. How different when social sanctions are not deserved! We do not blame

ourselves when we are innocent but blame society for condemning us unjustly.

3. Eliminate the *psychological* sanction. The feelings of depression, disgust, and shame, the inability to eat or sleep with the twinge of remorse and guilt, may disturb him, but others can be immune to such feelings, and even in him they can come from other sources. The moral element remains. If somehow the guilty *feelings* could be removed so that he no longer felt any psychological disturbance over his deed, still in all sincerity he would judge his act wrong and would *know* that he is guilty, despite the absence of feelings. Guilt is not a subjective feeling; it is the objective quality of evil that accrues to the person who does the evil deed. Whether one feels guilty or not, the guilt belongs to the person who is the source of the evil deed.

4. Eliminate the *religious* sanction. Were God not to punish it and were we certain that he would not, even in this absurd hypothesis the act ought not to be done. The doer might feel glad to escape but would know that he did not deserve to escape. The act is of the kind that God ought to condemn, and we would be disappointed in him if he did not. We would begin to question God's justice, so that God himself would no longer measure up to the ideal. This is perhaps the clearest indication of the absoluteness of the moral order.

5. What remains is the *moral* sanction. It is intrinsic to the very act itself, identical with the deliberate choice of the will, the relationship between the doer and the deed.

In despising the moral good I despise myself. As I accept or reject the moral good, I accordingly rise or fall in my own worth as a person. The moral good provides the scale by which I necessarily rate myself, unavoidably judge myself. This judgment is not merely a subjective opinion but an objective estimate of my true worth as a person in the scheme of things. This rise or fall is not something optional; I am not allowed to fall. It is not a question of whether I am interested in my own betterment; I am not allowed not to be. It is not a disjunctive necessity: Do this or take the consequences. It is simply: Do this. I am not allowed to expose myself to the conse-

quences of not doing it. In fact, whatever consequences there are must themselves be judged by this moral criterion, and ultimate consequences must contain their own moral worth.

Some writers[1] prefer to express this *ought* aspect by the terms *right* and *wrong* rather than *good* and *bad*. It is true that the first pair have a more obligatory flavor than the second, but it is impossible to get people to use such simple terms with consistency, especially if they are taken as indefinables. We can use them as synonyms and rely on the context to make them clear.

As we emphasize the good as end or the good as ought, we have two main varieties of ethics: the *teleological*[2] and the *deontological*.[3] An unfortunate opposition between these two views has infected the whole study, as if one must opt either for an ethics of ends and consequences or for an ethics of law and obligation, in a word, for an ethics of *happiness* or for an ethics of *duty*. Is it possible to go beyond such a dichotomy and to show that these two aspects are not opposed but supplementary? Should not the good be done for its own sake, purely and simply because it is good, independently of what consequences it may lead to or what authority may impose it as a duty? This may appear from a third and fairly modern approach to the good, the *axiological*,[4] the consideration of the good as a *value*.

THE GOOD AS VALUE
Value in General

The term *value* or *worth* seems to have its origin in economics, but long before the rise of axiology as a formal study it was applied analogously to other aspects of life. There is no more agreement on the definition of value than there is on the definition of good, but in practice we all know what a value is, and our discussion can begin on this commonsense level.

One thing appeals to us in some way, whereas something else does not. What appeals may sup-

---

[1] Ross, *The Right and the Good.*
[2] From the Greek *telos,* end.
[3] From the Greek participle *deon* of the verb *dei,* it ought.
[4] From the Greek *axios,* worthy.

ply a need, satisfy a desire, arouse an interest, stimulate an emotion, provoke a response, motivate a deed, or merely draw an approval. The existence of subjective values—valuations or evaluations or value judgments, as some prefer to call them—is a matter of experience. We do make value judgments, whether these judgments are justified or not, and whether they have any real content to them or not. Some of these judgments are noncomparative, in which we merely express our approval or disapproval; others are comparative, and by putting them in order we can construct a scale of values. A full scale would be too complex for anyone to complete, but we all have some constant preferences that represent known points on our scale.

Some general characteristics of value immediately appear.

1. Values are *bipolar,* with a positive and a negative pole: pleasant, painful; easy, difficult; strong, weak; rich, poor; beautiful, ugly; true, false; good, bad. The positive pole is the one preferred; the negative pole is better not called a value at all but a disvalue.

2. Values are *not homogeneous* but of many kinds, some quite unrelated, and this is why the construction of a complete scale of values is so difficult; there are too many crosscuts.

3. Values *transcend facts* in the sense that nothing ever wholly comes up to our expectations; even if anything should, it only shows that our expectations were pitched too low and we want something further.

4. Values, though not wholly realizable, *clamor for realization.* They should exist, they deserve to be, even if we have no way of bringing them into existence.

Existence of Value

Do values really exist or do they belong wholly to the domain of thought? Do we call a thing valuable because it possesses some real property in itself or because we clothe it with a value by our attitude toward it? The subjectivist philosopher, to be consistent, must adopt the latter view. But even objectivist philosophers, who in their theory of knowledge admit the existence of real being that is there independently of our thinking, can be subjectivist on the question of value. Things exist, they say, but whatever value they have is conferred on them by us; there is objective being, but no objective value. What evidence is there on this question?

That there are values is evident from the fact that we have preferences. That some values are wholly subjective is attested by the arbitrariness of some of our preferences. The thing has no intrinsic worth, at least for us, but we give it a value because of our peculiar prejudices, our psychological conditioning, our unaccountable tastes and fancies. Social as well as personal values can be subjective. Polls, popular vote, and other forms of opinion gathering are only a summary of the personal values of individuals and do not prove that there is an objective basis for the widespread preference.

Other values are subjective in nature, but their lack of complete arbitrariness shows that they have some objective basis. Many values, such as the value of paper money, of credit, of reputation, of academic degrees, or of artistic masterpieces, are created by human convention. That these conventions are not wholly subjective is seen in the fact that, if they have no backing in reality, they are considered fraudulent and their value vanishes.

Besides both of these varieties of subjective value, we find others that we can properly call objective. Not that any value can be so absolutely objective that it does not contain a subjective component. All values have relation to a valuer; they are values for somebody. When we call a value objective, we do not deny this relation to a valuing subject but assert the existence of an objective reason for this relation in the valued object. There is something about the thing that makes it suitable for this person, so that the personal preference is not arbitrary. Thus a person's taste in foods is subjective and arbitrary, but the need for food in general is objective and rooted in the person's biological requirements.

How extensive objective values are can be seen from a partial list of them. That life is a value and death a disvalue, health a value and sickness a disvalue, pleasure a value and pain a disvalue, prosperity a value and poverty a disvalue, beauty a value and ugliness a disvalue, intelligence a value and stupidity a disvalue—carry the list as far as you want—is too evident to need comment. The reason is not merely the fact that most people prefer one to the other, but its fittingness or unfittingness for the kind of beings we are.

How do we come to recognize these values? That depends on the stance we take toward ourselves and the world. If we simply take an *objective stance,* then we presuppose the existence of a value-neutral, factual world independent of our consciousness of it. We presuppose further that our experiences are common to every other person who has "normal" sense perception, that there is common evidence and common observations, that there are common objects and a common world which we all share. None of us has anything like a privileged role in this common universe; neither we nor any of the objects and events are intrinsically valuable. On the other hand, if we take a *personal stance,* we view ourselves and the world personally and *self*-consciously. We find ourselves emotionally involved, not in reality as a whole, but in those portions of reality that matter to us, that are important to us. The world from this standpoint is substantially identical to the world as viewed from the objective stance, but there is a difference, the difference my emotional involvement makes. The objects of the world are not just heavy or light, made of iron, wood, or canvas; they are also beautiful or ugly, pleasing or displeasing. The people are not merely other human beings with such and such physical characteristics; they are also beautiful or ugly, attractive or repulsive, lovable or unlovable. Actions are more than mere events with such and such causes; they are also important or trivial, admirable or blameworthy. The world from this subjective or personal standpoint includes objective value; it is not value-neutral and simply factual.

Our emotional involvement is what makes the difference. Why? We have not stopped our processes of thinking and willing, the very processes we have been using in taking our objective stance. What we have done is allow our emotions to operate, and they have shown us that reality is much more than just a set of facts. They have shown us the value that is there in the world, and we have initiated certain responses to the values that our emotions have revealed to us. If we do not repress our emotions but rather allow them the freedom to operate, we find on reflection that they are a further way we have of being conscious of ourselves and our world. In fact, by way of our emotions we take whatever stance we do within reality, even the so-called completely objective stance. Even the very desire to know in an objective manner by screening out personal attitudes and preferences is rooted in emotion. We are more than just sensing, thinking, and willing beings; we are also capable of experiencing by way of our emotions. We sometimes use the term *feeling* to mean our emotional life, our life of hoping, enjoying, loving, hating, appreciating, esteeming, sorrowing, and so forth. Emotion is as fundamental for experiencing as are sensing, thinking, and willing.

Emotion is our way of orienting ourselves toward a person, situation, event, or thing to which we already stand in, or now come into, fundamental relation. Take, for example, being excited about someone or something. That someone or something is being experienced as valuable and the "being excited" arises out of or is centered in an awareness of value. The "being excited" is an immediate and direct awareness of objective value; it is an opening of oneself out toward another person or thing, and value reveals itself in that very "being excited." The emotion is not merely directed toward something or someone other than myself but also reveals *objective reasons* for the "being excited." Thus our original, personal experience of objective value is through conscious emotion as immediate and direct appreciation of value.

Between emotion and its object there is no medium such as an act of imagination, understanding, or judgment. Emotion arises spontaneously and uniquely as a directedness toward an object, person, event, or even reality as a whole in its value dimension; the object, person, event, or reality as a whole in its turn reveals itself as value. Emotion is our way of being beyond ourselves in relation to and involved in what is other than ourselves and precisely in terms of its value, worth, or importance. Emotion is our way of actively receiving the objective value that is there to be perceived. Through emotion we are active in relation to reality so that reality reveals itself as it is, namely, as having a value dimension that is knowable and can be responded to. What is known through emotion is irreducible to what is known through sense and intellect.

Emotion, as value appreciation, is insightful and preconceptual. The value discovered at the level of emotion is the content that is preserved and transformed at the levels of forming intellectual value concepts and making intellectual value judgments that utilize such concepts. Value appreciation is immediate and direct involvement with reality; it is an open involvement in which one sees, as it were, for the first time and something new is revealed, to wit, objective value. Emotion also grounds all will activity, because all ethical willing is based on some value appreciation. The will is not activated by a judgment concerning what is good or by a concept of a good. The will's motives are concrete goods, and what is good *is* in fact good by virtue of a value that reveals itself concretely through emotion. In the absence of value, the will cannot move. Unless emotion makes value insightfully present, the will cannot be actualized in the ethical sense.

Some derivative values can be arrived at by logical reasoning from other values, but the primary values are not reasoned. They simply present themselves. We experience the attraction of the good by way of our emotions. When we ask ourselves why the thing is attractive to us, either we find that there is no reason but our own psychological conditioning or the passing fads of the group, and these values we label *subjective;* or we find an objective reason in a real suitability of the thing to ourselves, a suitability that we do not create but find already existing, and these values we call *objective.*

The difficulty can be raised that all values are only abstractions and therefore subjective because they exist only in the mind that conceives them. This objection rests on the theory of knowledge called *nominalism,* which underlies most forms of empiricism and positivism. Nominalism admits no basis in reality for abstractions and universal ideas but considers them as mere names that facilitate our way of speaking. Hence it is not surprising that nominalists have trouble with value, which is an abstract concept and a universal idea. The difficulty here is not with values but with nominalism, which is an inadequate theory of knowledge. None but extreme Platonists wish to give to abstractions independent existence as real things, and thus abstractions exist formally as such only in the mind. Most abstractions, however, are not formed arbitrarily and therefore have their basis or foundation in the way things really are. Those who admit a realistic basis to universal ideas will accord the same realism to values, that is, to those values we called objective. As there is no universal without a knower to make the abstraction, so there is no value without a valuer to do the valuing. Values, like other universals, are drawn from the data of experience and have their concrete fulfillment in existing persons, things, and actions. It is a fact that we evaluate goods to buy, persons to employ, students to reward, candidates to vote for, and friends to live with. We do so because we see some objective qualities in them that make them deserving.

The foregoing is meant to be introductory to the question of moral values. Are there moral values distinct from other values such as those we have been describing, and are these moral values objective?

Moral Values

The common estimate of mankind separates moral values from other values. We say that a man is a good scholar, athlete, businessman, politician, scientist, artist, soldier, worker, speaker, entertainer, companion, and yet that he is not a good man. We say that someone else is a failure at some or perhaps even all of these, and yet that he is a good man. On what do we base such judgments? Why do we separate out this last value? Because we recognize that it is distinct from the others and more fundamental, more valuable than the other values.

Moral values are understood to be those that *make a person good purely and simply as a person*. They are not external objects that, though they may help a person to become the kind of being he or she ought to be, are not the very person. Nor are they qualities or attributes of the person but outside his or her control, such as having good health or long life or family status or bodily beauty or mental acumen or artistic talent or a magnetic personality. These are all values, but no one can command them. Moral values are personal, not only because a person has them, but because they are the expression of each one's unique personality in the innermost center of one's being, as shown in the act of choice. Moral values, therefore, reside both in the acts a person chooses to do and in the results of those acts on the character of the person. There are morally good or bad human acts and morally good or bad persons.

A shark attacks one of two young men swimming at the beach. The other comes to his rescue and, braving the danger, wards off the shark and brings the wounded companion to shore. We feel pity for the one who was attacked but pass no moral judgment on him. He did not act but was acted on. Toward the rescuer our attitude is quite different. His swimming may have been awkward, his lifesaving technique faulty, his approach to the shark unscientific, his act unseen and unpublicized, and the whole venture useless because the victim died. Even one whose feelings are not aroused to admiration cannot help judging the act to be fine and noble and worthy of approval. It has no value but one, and that is its *moral* value. Suppose an opposite case. The shark attacks both swimmers. To save himself, one of them deliberately kicks his companion into the path of the shark's mouth, thus gaining time to scramble onshore while the shark is occupied

with its morsel. As an act of self-saving it has value, for it was done quickly, efficiently, cleverly, and resourcefully. But we cannot approve. The only excuse for such an act would be instinct or panic. As a willful, deliberate act it merits condemnation.

Two husbands have wives afflicted with a lingering and incapacitating disease. Both families are alike: five children, moderate income, no hope of remedy. One husband does his best to be both father and mother to the children, works overtime to pay for his wife's care, and spends what time he can with her to brighten her days. The other man decides that he has had enough, deserts wife and children, gets work in a distant city under an assumed name, and is not heard of again. Our emotional attitude toward the wives and children is one of congratulations in one case and compassion in the other, but they are only passive figures in the case. Toward the husbands also our emotional responses differ: the one we admire and the other we scorn. When we make our intellectual judgment, we have to approve of the first husband and disapprove of the second. It is not a question of consequences. Suppose that the deserted dependents are better taken care of by public charity than the husband could have done for them. Still we must condemn his action as morally wrong. The moral value and disvalue remain in these two cases as irreducible elements.

Examples of this type could be multiplied indefinitely. But these are sufficient for our purpose: to isolate the characteristics of moral value as distinct from any other value.

1. Moral value can exist only in a *free* personal being and in that person's *voluntary* or *human* acts. By willing moral good a person becomes good. It cannot happen accidentally. It makes no difference whether the act is successful or not. It is done intelligently in the sense that the agent knows what he or she is doing and wills to do it, but it need not be brilliantly planned and executed.

2. Moral value is *universal* in the sense that

what holds for one holds for all in the same conditions. The reason is that it shows the worth of a person *as a person*. Even when no one else could duplicate one person's circumstances, all would approve of his or her action as the right thing to do in the case, whether they would have the strength to do it or not.

3. Moral value is *self-justifying*. Thus at least it appears on the surface, though we shall have to delve deeper into this matter in a later chapter. We suspect that any further justification of moral value will be found to be part of the moral order itself and not some extrinsic reason. Even the truth must be pursued morally, though it be the truth about morals.

4. Moral value has a *preeminence* over every other value. A moral value can be compared only with another moral value. If a moral value conflicts with another type of value, this other must take a subordinate place. We think that a person simply must be true to himself or herself as a person, no matter how much else might be lost in the effort.

5. Moral value implies *obligation*. We just discussed this in our section on the good as ought and will say more on it later. Someone may disregard all other values, and we shall call that person foolish, stupid, clumsy, crude, dull, ignorant, impractical, and many other names, but we can still respect the individual as a person. Not so if he or she loses personal moral integrity.

The Moral Ideal

The foregoing discussion brings out the fact that we do form for ourselves an ideal of human conduct and an ideal of personhood. These are not two ideals, for a person's conduct is that person's life. It is only good conduct that can make a good person, and a person is called good because that person's past acts show him or her to be the kind of person from whom good acts are expected.

We find it impossible not to form such an ideal, since it is implied in every moral judgment, and we do make moral judgments. The word *ideal* should not be understood here as some romantic fancy, a knight in shining armor, some sort of superman or bionic woman with unearthly powers, the kind of being that could not happen in real life. What we use in moral judgment is not an idealized figment of the imagination nor an esthetic ideal, but a *moral* ideal. It is true that no one ever perfectly lives up to it, but it must mean the ideal a person *could* live up to because one *ought* to. The ideal as an ideal does not exist in reality, but it is not subjective in the sense of being arbitrary. It is an ideal image or model constructed out of the core of values we have recognized in the persons we have encountered in life. Our initial recognition of our parents was not simply to see them as two factual human beings. Through our emotions we found in them a core of values against which we measured other persons present. This initial value recognition, made possible by our own emotional value appreciation, is the source of the ideal moral model we develop for ourselves. Our acts of willing presuppose the value content of the model and are grounded in our love for the model. We follow and strive to be like the person we love as our model. We form an image of our parents, relatives, and friends and determine their significance for us on the basis of the core of values we find in them. What we find on reflection is an ideal image of the moral person that is formed as a result of the values we have encountered in others and projected for ourselves as our ideal of the moral person.

This ideal image or model exerts an effectiveness on one's moral judgments and choices; it lies in the depths of our consciousness, moving, growing, and transforming itself and us in a mysterious manner. The model is a kind of exemplar of personal value accessible to our emotional insight and love; it is a person, though not necessarily one actually existing, who exhibits a unique value structure in his or her behavior. The model's effectiveness as a moral ideal is grounded in his or her value structure, and we experience it as the moral demand of an ideal ought, not a duty ought. The model attracts, draws, invites, allures us in the sense of being a person who already is most nearly what he or she ought to be. We experience the demand as a task, namely, as a demand to become what only each of us as individuals can become. The model is not the goal toward which we strive, and yet for each of us our individual model is goal-determining.

How do we discover our own personal model? Only in the performance of our practical every-day actions is our ideal model localized and available for reflection. If we never take the time to reflect on our actions and our experiences of ourselves acting in various situations, we shall never become conscious of our model as a model. Prior to reflection, however, we do have the experience of knowing that our actions are or are not measuring up to our ideal, or that they are in conflict with or in violation of our ideal. In such experiences we are recognizing the model in practice without making a special act of recognition. The moral model is regulating each of our experiences without our becoming expressly aware of the model as a model. Only in reflection can we begin to bring our ideal moral model into focus.

The moral model is effective not only in our individual actions; it also effects a moral transformation in us. We give ourselves freely to the attractiveness (values) of the model to become *as* the model is, not what the model is. We learn to will and act *as* the model wills and acts. This is neither a case of slavish imitation nor of simple obedience to the commands of another person. No, this is a free response to recognized value. We grow morally by striving to be and live *as* the model is and lives. Primarily it is a matter of loving *what* the model loves and *as* the model loves, for only in this way can each of us grow as a person and so gradually become what each of us in our own individuality can become.

To become the person we can become requires something more than intellectual keenness. One must have a love of self and a love for others that generates the energy and enthusiasm needed to seek to become the person each of us as individuals can become. If we are ever to understand this, it will be thanks to love. Love seeks so that understanding may find. We do not seek what we already possess and yet to seek is to assume in some way the thing sought and so to know it already but not with perfect clarity. Once love for the moral ideal is awakened, that same love provides a favorable atmosphere and beams forth a light that illumines the values, the moral qualities and perfections, of our moral model. Love reveals to us what we would not see without it and love inspires us to go beyond ourselves as we are now in order to become what we can yet be. Love for the moral model's value is the energizing force of the entire moral life.

As the artist has an ideal of the perfectly proportioned human body, as the scholar has an ideal of the perfectly intelligent human mind—and, being human, these are not beyond the possibility of realization—so we all have an ideal of the perfectly living human being. So far as a person approaches this ideal, he or she has moral value and is good. So far as one admits into his or her life that which degrades this ideal, that person has moral disvalue and is bad.

The notion of the good as expressed here is that of the intrinsic, or perfect, good as opposed to the instrumental, or perfective, good. The ideal is good, not as leading to something else, not as a means useful to something further, but in itself. It has value because it has what it ought to have to be itself in the fullest expression of itself. This is the good in the highest sense, for what is good for another ultimately supposes something for which others are good, and this last must be good in itself.

This conception of the good, especially this latter part dealing with the moral ideal, derives from Plato and Max Scheler. The unacceptability of Plato's interpretation of ideals should not prejudice us against what is true in his thought. We need not accept his theory of a direct vision of the ideal as Ideas or Forms recalled from a former life in which we saw them more clearly. Our concepts, including our concept of the ideal good, can be manufactured by the process of abstraction and intellectual refinement from the data of experience. How we do this and what standards we use in judging our moral ideas and ideals will be our occupation throughout the next several chapters.

CONCLUSION

We have looked at the good under three aspects: as value, as ought, and as end. A more learned way of saying it is that we have seen axiological, deontological, and teleological ethics. The good as *value* stresses the intrinsic good, the perfect good, that which is good in itself irrespective of any goodness it may have for anything else. This must be the most fundamental aspect of the good. The good as *ought* stresses the fact that each thing ought to be as perfect as it can be, that the ideal is not merely something to be contemplated but to be put into act, and that this demand is laid on a free being in the form of moral obligation. The good as *end* emphasizes the obligation of any being, if it is not yet perfect, to strive toward perfection as its end and to seek other goods as means to this end. These are not three kinds of good, but three ways of looking at the same good. The absolute good is the ultimate *end* that *ought* to be sought because of its supreme *value*.

SUMMARY

The good can best be taken as a primary notion, irreducible and indefinable. It can be considered as end, as ought, and as value.

As *end,* the good is that at which all things aim. An end is that for the sake of which a thing is done. Every good is an end, and every end is a good. A means is good insofar as it leads to the end.

All human conduct is for an end and a good, according to the principle of finality: "Every agent acts for an end." Since no agent can produce an undetermined effect, something must determine the agent to act rather than not, to produce this effect rather than that; what removes this inde-

termination is the end. A free agent determines his or her own end.

The good may be *ontological,* the good of mere being; or *physical,* the good of completeness; or *moral,* the good of right living, of rightly directing free conduct to its due end. The *genuine* good really *is* good; the *apparent* good only seems so. The *useful* good leads to something else that is good; the *pleasant* good satisfies a particular appetite; the *befitting* good perfects the whole person as such. Though every being is ontologically good and has some physical goodness, not every being is always morally good. The moral good is always a genuine and befitting good.

As *ought,* the moral good is seen not as optional but as necessary. This necessity is of a unique kind called *moral* necessity, not a *must,* but an *ought,* not physically compelling but morally demanding, leaving us able but not allowed to refuse. It is a human being's absolute obligation to succeed *as a person* because humans are personal beings. Hence it is derived from the human being's value as a being and as a person.

As *value,* the good displays its deepest meaning. Value or worth is a term used for anything that appeals to us in any way. At least subjective values exist, for we do make value judgments and have preferences. Values are bipolar, heterogeneous, idealized, yet calling for realization.

Some values may be purely subjective, but others are *objective*. We cannot be wholly arbitrary about them. As ideals they exist in the mind but are formed by the mind's abstractive power from the data of experience.

Moral values are those that make a human being good simply as a personal being. They can exist only in a *free* being and in voluntary acts, are *universal* since they pertain to human beings as personal beings, are *self-justifying* and independent of other values, are *preeminent* over every other value, and imply *obligation*.

It is impossible not to form a scale of values in which there is some top value or highest good. In such a scale, moral value claims the highest place. The ideal human life ideally lived is the *moral ideal*.

Questions for Discussion

1. Advertising in magazines and newspapers as well as on television is geared to motivate the public to some action. Choose some examples from any of the media and examine them to find the good the advertiser presents to motivate the public. By what criterion does the advertiser guide his or her composition of the ad? By what criterion do you guide yourself in responding to the ad?

2. G.E. Moore has argued forcefully that good is indefinable. Others have argued that good has a very precise definition: what is morally good is an act in keeping with an ultimate and all-but-universal guide to action. Is this in fact a definition? Why?

3. You are a senior in high school and have smoked marijuana since you were in the ninth grade. You started because you wanted to meet new friends, and you did meet them. In the course of your high-school career you have put everything up your nose from crystal (methamphetamine) to cocaine. You even tried LSD a few times without bad results. Now you find yourself "hooked," smoking at least three joints of marijuana a day and snorting cocaine whenever you can get it. You escaped boredom for a while, met new people, and got some attention. Now you find your grades have steadily slipped downward, and you are becoming more of a "loner" because smoking and snorting cost less when you do not have

to share with anyone. What can you do to help yourself? What ought you do? Are they the same? Why?

4. Someone recently said that the ultimate and all-but-universal guide to action is the desire that not everything be destroyed. Beyond this desire there is literally nothing, no talk, no writing, no criterion, no desire, no moral theory, nothing at all. If an act will lead to the destruction of everything, then we are at the end of the line and the act must not be done. It would be an immoral act. Has the ultimate criterion of morality been found? Is this the good of question #2 above? Can this criterion be used meaningfully in making the choices we are daily faced with? Why?

5. In a large eastern city, hospitals have treated at least 23 airline crew members for medical crises related to drug abuse, including a pilot near death from a cocaine overdose. These airline people in all probability constitute a threat to public safety, but neither the doctors nor the hospitals involved reported these people to the Federal Aviation Administration, which is responsible for the safety of air travel. The reason given is doctor-patient confidentiality, an obvious good that, according to the doctors, not only must be respected but ought to be preserved. If you were one of the doctors involved, what would you do? Why?

Readings

Read Aristotle's *Nicomachean Ethics*, bk. I, ch. 1–6. Henry Veatch, *Rational Man*, gives a modern interpretation of Aristotle's *Ethics*.

Our present chapter is an adaptation of St. Thomas's *Summa Theologica*, I–II, q. 1, and his alternative presentation of the same matter in the *Summa Contra Gentiles*, bk. III, ch. 1–3, 16, 22, and 24. Some of St. Thomas's illustrations are drawn from antiquated physics and astronomy; they are not essential to his argument and can be judiciously bypassed. St. Thomas's metaphysical development of the good is found in the *Summa Theologica*, I, q. 5.

The following modern writers have matter pertinent to this

chapter: Etienne Gilson, *Moral Values and Moral Life*, pp. 15–26; Mortimer Adler, *A Dialectic of Morals*, pp. 74–97; William R. O'Connor, *The Eternal Quest*, ch. 5–6; and Leo Ward, *Values and Reality*, ch. 1–4.

A study of the good is found in A.C. Ewing, *The Definition of the Good*, and in W.D. Ross, *The Right and the Good* and *Foundations of Ethics*. Ross makes obligation a characteristic of the right rather than of the good, as he defines them. G.E. Moore's essays on "The Indefinability of the Good" and "The Naturalistic Fallacy," the first two chapters of his *Principia Ethica*, are the source of much modern philosophizing on the ethical good. Timothy J. Cooney, in

Telling Right From Wrong: What is Moral, What is Immoral, and What is Neither One Nor the Other, argues against G.E. Moore on the indefinability of good and is very worth looking into. G.H. von Wright, *The Varieties of Goodness,* examines all the meanings of good.

A classical work on value theory is Ralph Barton Perry, *General Theory of Value,* supplemented by his later work, *Realms of Value;* John Dewey, *Theory of Valuation;* Nicolai Hartmann, *Ethics,* vol. I, sec. V, and Vol. II; C.I. Lewis, *Analysis of Knowledge and Valuation;* and Stephen Pepper, *Sources of Value,* present value theory from various philosophical backgrounds. Ray Lepley edits two symposia, *Value, a Cooperative Inquiry,* and *The Language of Value,* by contemporary American philosophers on value theory, treated more from a behavioral than from an ethical standpoint. A.H. Maslow, *Toward a Psychology of Being,* pt. V, has a psychological-moral treatment of values.

Dietrich von Hildebrand, *Christian Ethics,* centers his whole book on values, treated in an original, phenomenological manner. See especially ch. 5–19. See Robert C. Solomon, *The Passions: The Myth and Nature of Human Emotion,* ch. 2 and 3, on subjectivity and surrealism, respectively. Max Scheler, *Formalism in Ethics and Non-formal Ethics of Values: A New Attempt toward the Foundation of an Ethical Personalism,* pp. 572–594, has an excellent discussion of moral models.

6
Pleasure

PROBLEM

The good life might accidentally happen to someone, but the odds are strongly against it. Even if a person were in ideal circumstances, he or she can so misuse the opportunities that failure and frustration are the results. Philosophy, as organized human wisdom, is supposed to show us how to avoid falling into any such unhappy state and to give us positive help toward making this life as satisfying as it can be.

In this chapter and the four immediately following, we discuss theories which ask what the norm or standard of the good act is:

Chapter 6—Is it *pleasure?*
Chapter 7—Is it social *convention?*
Chapter 8—Is it the *consequences* of the act?
Chapter 9—Is it *intuition?*
Chapter 10—Is it *right reason?*

In the search for something that might make life satisfying, the most obvious candidate is pleasure. We can distinguish two descriptive meanings of pleasure: (1) the whole range of sensations or feelings that we get through the stimulation of our bodily organs and nerve endings; its opposite is bodily pain; and (2) the entire class of experiences that any person enjoys, likes, or finds satisfying; its opposite is a painful or unenjoyable experience. Whichever of these two meanings is adopted makes no difference, for in both cases the pleasure is explicitly or implicitly apprehended by the person as worthy of being desired. No one objects to enjoyment though not all will enjoy the same thing. One who enjoys nothing is in a sad condition indeed, except those abnormal persons who paradoxically enjoy being miserable, and they at least seem to enjoy that. So there is a place for pleasure in the good life. Many think that it is the only element in the good life, and this view expressed philosophically is called *hedonism,* from the Greek word for pleasure.

Hedonism assumes two chief forms, according to whose pleasure is sought. Egoistic hedonism concentrates on the personal pleasure of the individual. Altruistic hedonism seeks the pleasure of others; if it embraces that of the whole human race, it is often called universalistic hedonism. We shall follow general practice in reserving the word *hedonism* for the egoistic variety and calling the altruistic and universalistic variety *utilitarianism.*

We consider the following questions:

1. What are the reasons for and against egoistic hedonism?
2. What are the reasons for and against altruistic hedonism or utilitarianism?
3. What is the proper place of pleasure in the good life?

HEDONISM

Hedonism is one of the oldest, simplest, and most earthy of ethical theories. It has persisted throughout all ages, and many people who have never consciously formulated for themselves any philosophy of life live according to its principles.

We find hedonism first proposed by Aristippus, leader of the Cyrenaic school, who identified happiness with pleasure. He held that pleasure results from gentle motion, and pain from rough motion. Anything is good that produces pleasure, and that is best that produces the most vivid and intense pleasure. Virtue is useful as restraining us from excessive passion, which is rough motion and unpleasant.

Hedonism was refined by Epicurus, who joined it to the physical theories of Democritus. It is the ethics most consistent with mechanistic materialism. For Epicurus the end of life is not intense pleasure, but an abiding peace of mind, a state of cheerful tranquility. Above all we must avoid fear of the gods and fear of death. Intellectual pleasures are better because they are more lasting, but we cannot do without sense pleasures. The wise man so regulates his life as to get into it the greatest amount of pleasure and the least amount of pain. Moderation is counseled to enable one to enjoy future pleasures. We must learn to restrict our desires within the bounds in which we think we can satisfy them. Whatever will increase our pleasure or our general peace of mind is good, and anything that decreases it is bad.

We call pleasure the beginning and end of the blessed life. For we recognize pleasure as the first good innate in us, and from pleasure we begin every act of choice and avoidance, and to pleasure we return again, using the feeling as the standard by which we judge every good. And since pleasure is the first good and natural to us, for this very reason we do not choose every pleasure, but sometimes we pass over many pleasures, when greater discomfort accrues to us as the result of them . . . . Every pleasure then because of its natural kinship to us is good, yet not every pleasure is to be chosen: even as every pain also is an evil, yet not all are always of a nature to be avoided. Yet by a scale of comparison and by the consideration of advantages and disadvantages we must form our judgment on all of these matters . . . . When, therefore, we maintain that pleasure is the end, we do not mean the pleasures of profligates and those that consist in sensuality . . . but freedom from pain in the body and from trouble in the mind.[1]

Thomas Hobbes would hardly be classed as an Epicurean, but he does subscribe to a hedonistic view with a strong strain of egoism. He thinks that nothing is by itself good or evil, but that these are names we give to what we desire or detest. We desire what will give us pleasure, either of body or mind, and we detest what gives us displeasure.[2] He does not think that the tranquility lauded by the Epicureans is possible in this struggling world, but the formation of the political state is our only means of controlling the struggle and making life bearable. Society is formed not for the benefit of other people or of humankind as such but for the peace and safety of each particular person looking out primarily for himself or herself.

Though Jeremy Bentham did not limit his hedonism to the egoistic type and is commonly regarded as the founder of utilitarianism, his statement of the hedonistic principle is classic:

Nature has placed mankind under the governance of two sovereign masters, *pain* and *pleasure*. It is for them alone to point out what we ought to do, as to determine what we shall do. On the one hand the standard of right and wrong, on the other the chain of causes and effects, are fastened to their throne. They govern us in all we do, in all we say, in all we think: every effort we can make to throw off our subjection will serve but to demonstrate and confirm it. In words a man may pretend to abjure their empire: but in reality he will remain subject to it all the while. The *principle of utility* recognizes this subjection, and assumes it for the foundation of that system, the object of which is to rear the fabric of felicity by the hands of reason and law.[3]

In Bentham we have hedonism with the egoistic aspect toned down. In our day several varieties of egoism have appeared with the pleasure aspect deemphasized. Robert Olson[4] argues for a naturalistic pursuit of both personal and social well-being, in which rational self-interest is the supreme moral criterion, and health, friendship, contentment, and pleasure are the chief goods. Ayn Rand[5] carries self-interest still further and makes a virtue of selfishness. The ultimate value is a person's survival, without which there would be no people to have other values, and each one is responsible for working out the means to survival. This must be done by reason, not by whim. She is confident that individual codes of values, if rationally constructed, will not conflict, for we deal with one another as traders, giving value for value. No sacrifice for another's sake is ever necessary, for the compromises we must make are in our own self-interest. Thus an economic system of laissez-faire capitalism and a hands-off policy by government are essential. Working egotistically but rationally for self will automatically bring about the best for all.

These samples of the hedonistic view are sufficient for our purpose. We may sum up the case for hedonism as follows:

---

[1]Epicurus' "Letter to Menoeceus" in Diogenes Laertius' *Lives and Opinions of Eminent Philosophers,* bk. X, 27. Whether the letter is genuine or not, it is a good summary of Epicurean thought.
[2]Hobbes, *Leviathan,* bk. I, ch. 6.

[3]Bentham, *Introduction to the Principles of Morals and Legislation,* beginning.
[4]Olson, *The Morality of Self-Interest.*
[5]Rand, *The Virtue of Selfishness.*

1. The basic assumption, that everything we do is for pleasure, is an evident fact. Why should a person do anything except to fulfill a desire, and what is a desire if not a striving for something I want, and why should I want anything unless it affords me some satisfaction? Some think that we cannot act except for pleasure, or for the avoidance of pain, which is a kind of negative pleasure. Others do not insist on the impossibility of acting otherwise but state that we do not act otherwise. Still others will admit that we do often act otherwise, but we ought not, for to deprive ourselves of pleasure is an unwise wasting of life's opportunities.

2. Few hedonists would limit people to sense pleasures alone. By including pleasures of intellect, imagination, and emotion, hedonists have no difficulty in explaining why people readily forego sense pleasure for the fulfillment of duty, because they acknowledge the satisfaction we experience in a duty well done. There is something intellectually satisfying in a harmonious life, even if it costs us something to live it. Self-sacrifice for others, if we want to call it that, stimulates our imagination, especially when we imaginatively put ourselves in another's place. Even heroism under the most tragic circumstances can be so emotionally appealing that we choose it rather than live in ignoble comfort.

3. Willingness to curb our appetites for the common good of society is explained by the fact that we ourselves are members of that society and share in this common good. Thus there is always a self-regarding interest in what seems to be the most altruistic behavior. Why not frankly admit it, instead of trying to disguise it under a puritanical hypocrisy? Even love has its self-regarding aspect and is unfulfilled unless it is returned.

4. Those who seek a reward in a next life are likewise motivated by hedonism. They are willing to wait longer for the enjoyment they hope for, but it is this expectation of future happiness that motivates them to endure their present sufferings. Christianity has thus been called "egoism with a spyglass." The bliss of heaven is made appealing by fostering the belief that it will exceed anything we can now imagine, and its secure possession forever is worth a temporary price.

Nonhedonists do not find these arguments convincing:

1. Mere statement of the hedonistic principle does not make it true. That many people pursue pleasure all the time and that all of us pursue it some of the time can be readily granted, but there are too many glaring exceptions for it to be a universal rule. Though I cannot willfully act except for something I want in some sense of the word *want,* and achieving it will be a satisfaction of that want, yet it does not follow that the want and the satisfaction must be of the type properly called *pleasure.* That we always act for pleasure can be refuted by deliberately refusing a pleasure; if we are told that we did it for the pleasure of showing our opponent wrong, then pleasure is made to mean any kind of acting; to hold that we always do what we do is hardly distinctive of hedonism.

2. Duty, generosity, self-sacrifice, and heroism have their attendant satisfaction; otherwise they could not be motives for acting. But to call every such satisfaction by the name of pleasure is a misuse of words. On what is the mind fixed, the duty itself or the pleasure attending it, the person helped or the glow felt in helping that person, the sacrifice made or the joy in making it, the heroic act or the emotional uplift in dying nobly? It seems here that the accompanying pleasure can be absent and, even when it is present, it is too paltry to be the main motive. Even if it were uppermost, what constitutes the act as a *moral* act—the fact that it is an act of duty, generosity, self-sacrifice, or heroism, or the fact that I enjoy it? If only the latter, wisdom dictates that I should pick less painful enjoyments.

3. The good of society does redound to the good of the individual. But what happens when the good of society does not redound to the good of *this* individual, as when someone is called on to make the supreme sacrifice for the benefit of

others? Hedonism requires that the person co-operate with society only so far as he or she can share in its benefits. Enlightened self-interest has its place, but is society possible on these terms? To use society for one's own benefit alone seems to be the source from which most of the ills of society spring. And though there is a self-regarding aspect in all love, hedonists are not logical unless they make it the only aspect.

4. To live the moral life *exclusively* for the sake of pleasurable rewards, even in the life to come, would be a form of hedonism. There is surely nothing wrong in hoping for the happiness of heaven, just as there is nothing wrong in seeking legitimate pleasure on earth; hedonism occurs only when pleasure is made the exclusive end. The true hedonist would not do good or avoid evil unless there were a reward for it. In the hedonist's mind, there is no good or evil except in the reward. Thus the one to be rewarded becomes the last end and the highest good. Most believers in a future life also believe that this would be the surest way of losing the reward.

UTILITARIANISM

The extension of hedonism beyond the pleasure of the individual to the pleasure of the group, and then to the pleasure of all humankind, is called *utilitarianism*. Jeremy Bentham[1] starts, as we have seen, with the idea that pleasure and pain are the only motives governing human activity; and goes on to show that personal pleasure and pain depend on the general happiness and prosperity of the whole community. Therefore in framing a hedonistic calculus, the calculation of pleasures and pains inseparable from any hedonistic system, we must consider, among the other criteria of intensity, duration, certainty, propinquity, fecundity, and purity, also the *extent* of pleasure and pain, the number of people affected by our policy of conduct. The moral goodness of an act is to be judged by its *utility* in promoting the common welfare of all as well as the personal

advantage of each. The aim of human life is expressed in the *Greatest Happiness Principle:* "The greatest happiness of the greatest number." However, since Bentham wishes to promote the interests of the community at large chiefly because doing so will redound to oneself as a member of that community, his system is still more egoistic than altruistic.

In John Stuart Mill, utilitarianism reached its full development. He recognized its strong roots in hedonism:

> The creed which accepts as the foundation of morals, utility, or the *greatest happiness principle,* holds that actions are right in proportion as they tend to promote happiness, wrong as they tend to produce the reverse of happiness. By happiness is intended pleasure, and the absence of pain; by unhappiness, pain, and the privation of pleasure.[2]

Whereas Bentham thought that units of pleasure and pain can be calculated arithmetically and that ethics can be made into an exact science, Mill recognized that pleasures differ in *quality* as well as in quantity, that there are higher and lower pleasures, so that a lesser amount of a higher pleasure is better than a greater amount of a lower pleasure, the determination to be made by a person of culture who can experience both.

> It is better to be a human being dissatisfied than a pig satisfied; better to be Socrates dissatisfied than a fool satisfied.[3]

An existence as free from pain and as rich in enjoyments as possible, both in quantity and quality to be secured to all people, is the end of human action and the standard of morality. His proof is often quoted in logic books as an example of a fallacy, since "desirable" does not mean "able to be desired" but "worthy of being desired:"

> The only proof capable of being given that an object is visible, is that people actually see it. The only proof that a sound is audible, is that people hear it: and so of the other sources of our experience. In like manner, I apprehend, the sole evidence it is

[1]Bentham, *Introduction to the Principles of Morals and Legislation,* ch. 1–4.

[2]Mill, *Utilitarianism,* ch. 2.
[3]*Ibid.*

possible to produce that anything is desirable, is that people do actually desire it . . . . No reason can be given why the general happiness is desirable except that each person, so far as he believes it to be attainable, desires his own happiness. This, however, being a fact, we have not only all the proof which the case admits of, but all which it is possible to require, that happiness is a good: that each person's happiness is a good to that person, and the general happiness, therefore, a good to the aggregate of all persons.[1]

He goes on to show that virtue, far from being opposed to happiness, is one of the elements that make up happiness: the feeling of self-satisfaction in contributing to the common welfare even at personal expense.

Utilitarianism was given a new turn by Henry Sidgwick,[2] who united it with intuitionism. He has done us the service of putting utilitarianism to a most searching scholarly examination but can find no unassailable proofs for it. The greatest happiness principle is not an empirical induction, as Mill thought. The only way to save it as an ethical principle is to make it a rational intuition, like the axioms of mathematics. Sidgwick was convinced that there is no practical incompatibility between utilitarianism and intuitionism, though he could find no positive theory to explain their union.

G.E. Moore[3] combines utilitarianism and intuitionism in a different way. He calls his theory *ideal utilitarianism*. All actions are to be judged by their consequences, that is, their usefulness in producing the ideal good for all people, which includes but is not limited to pleasure, and is an irreducible and indefinable nonnaturalistic property cognizable by us in some intuitive way.

Much is made today of a distinction between *act* utilitarianism and *rule* utilitarianism.[4] The former asks which act has the greatest utility, the latter which rule has. For the act utilitarian "telling the truth" may be a good general rule, but

one should tell a lie if in this particular case the general good would certainly be advanced more thereby. For the rule utilitarian, "telling the truth" may be found to be so necessary a rule for the general good that no exception may be allowed, that one ought to observe it even in cases in which it may be fraught with adverse results; the permission of exceptions would in the long run have more disastrous consequences than all the particular advantages that could be gained from breaking the rule. Both, however, are forms of utilitarianism, for neither the acts nor the rules have any value in themselves apart from the consequences to which they lead. The same critique can be used, with proper reservations, of both.

Since utilitarianism has always had trouble with its own logic, it can perhaps make out the best case for itself by pointing out its own useful consequences:

1. Utilitarianism seeks a happiness in which all will be happy rather than only the fortunate few. The individual sacrifice required for this contribution to the general good is a small enough price to pay for the happiness of so many. Individual pleasure tends to restrict itself, for no one should feel happy knowing that his or her happiness is bought by other's misery.

2. As a wise combination of egoism and altruism, utilitarianism is an expression of the kind of life most of us lead. It recognizes that humans are social, that we are all in this enterprise of life together, and that like passengers in a boat, the safety of each is tied up with the safety of all. Avoidable pain should be eliminated. Unavoidable pain can be made tolerable by ensuring that no one has to bear more than his or her share. Thus utilitarianism is a great stimulus to social improvement, for it takes people's egoistic tendencies and harnesses them to social needs, since each sees his or her own happiness integrated in that of the group.

3. Those charged with the public welfare can hardly use any other than utilitarian principles, since they must seek the common good and at the same time protect individual rights. Utilitarianism gives each person the right to seek his or her own pleasure and places limits on this only

---

[1] *Op. cit.,* ch. 4.
[2] Sidgwick, *The Methods of Ethics.* Summarized and criticized in C.D. Broad, *Five Types of Ethical Theory,* ch. 6.
[3] Moore, *Principia Ethica.*
[4] See Frankena, *Ethics,* 2nd ed., pp. 34–43 for a lucid summary.

when the person would encroach on another's equal right. Utilitarianism thus seeks the greatest amount of individual liberty compatible with the greatest amount of public liberty.

4. Utilitarianism eliminates the grossness of egoistic hedonism by a qualitative discrimination of pleasures, and thus makes a place for culture, taste, and beauty in human life. It relies greatly on education as a means of enabling more people to appreciate the higher pleasures, and on economic and social reform as a way of bringing the better life within their grasp.

5. Utilitarianism is contrary neither to virtue nor to religion. It demands the social virtues needed for community living and restrains only those few whose fanatical or distorted interpretation of virtue might issue in antisocial acts. The principle of utility itself encourages the religious believer to store up treasures in heaven, if he or she is convinced of a future life, and prohibits only the forceful imposition of such a belief on others, as destructive of freedom and incapable anyway of producing internal conviction.

For these and other reasons we see that there is a great deal of truth to utilitarianism, for in any system of ethics, one must consider the consequences of one's actions and social consequences are important. When the question is merely one of public welfare and the means suggested to achieve it are all moral as determined by some other standard, those means should be chosen that will best promote the public welfare, as far as enlightened foresight can determine it. But it will not function as the basic, and certainly not as the only, standard of morality. Among others, there are the following criticisms:

1. Egoistic hedonism is at least logical in proposing that, if pleasure is the highest good, each person should seek as much of it as possible. But why should anyone forego pleasure for the sake of others? If a person enjoys self-sacrificing for others, that is still egoistic hedonism and not utilitarianism. If one feels that such sacrifice is some kind of duty, the duty will have to be established by a firmer argument than a mere announcement of the greatest happiness principle.

2. How is the pleasure of the group, and es-

pecially of all humanity, to be determined? Hardly by vote. Thus the common pleasure will be decided by each person according to what it pleases each one to think the common pleasure should be. We are back to egoistic hedonism. Also, how far into the future must we look? The greatest happiness of the greatest number must include, not only the present generation, but all future generations. Any action taken now may have an indefinitely long train of consequences, and there is nothing in utilitarianism to limit us to immediately foreseeable consequences.

3. One of the simplest ways of eliminating pain from the world is to eliminate the sufferers. Infanticide for defective children, painless execution for hardened criminals, and euthanasia for the incurably sick would surely minimize pain throughout the world and increase the general level of happiness over unhappiness. How, apart from some intolerable despotism, could such a program be carried out? Utilitarians in general would repudiate any such drastic measures as immoral, but then they are using some other standard of morality than the utilitarian one.

4. The altruistic component in utilitarianism is not justified by the system. Unless there is something in another person that makes that person worthy of the sacrifices I am called on to make, I am losing my personal pleasure in vain. If we say that it is the dignity of the human person, then that dignity is measured by some standard other than utility, especially if the person contributes nothing to my good or to the common good. The only kind of love utilitarianism can admit is a love based on usefulness, which is so poor a kind of love as hardly to deserve the name.

5. Virtue and religion can have only a peripheral place in utilitarianism. Virtue is recommended, not because it is virtue, but only because it has useful consequences. The possibility of a future life is tolerated as a harmless eccentricity, for the only morally good acts acknowledged in the theory are those that maximize the pleasures of this life, and there is no way of knowing an act's worth for a future life without using some other criterion. Utilitarianism remains typical of the bourgeois ideal of middle-class comfort and

reduces to that level all aspirations toward nobility and heroism.

THE PLACE OF PLEASURE IN THE GOOD LIFE

The attempt to make pleasure, either of the individual or of the group, the main purpose of life and the standard of morality results in failure. That does not mean that pleasure is not important in human experience or that it has no ethical significance. If the extreme of hedonism is to make pleasure everything, the opposite extreme, which we may call the puritanical spirit, is to consider pleasure bad, as if there were something not only frivolous but defiling about it. The proper attitude must be somewhere between these extremes.[1]

There is no sense in trying to define pleasure, but it can be described. We know what it is by experiencing it, and there is no doubt about the experience. Psychologists have written extensively on pleasure, but what they say has little ethical import, except for the *hedonistic paradox*—the fact that intense mental concentration on the pleasure one is now experiencing rather than on the pleasurable object causes the pleasure to disappear. This confirms the following analysis.

We have no special faculty of pleasure. We cannot just simply *enjoy*. We enjoy *this* or *that,* which means that we enjoy doing something or experiencing something. The doing or experiencing must occur by the use of some ability we possess, the main purpose of which is something else besides enjoyment. The fact that we distinguish between sensuous and intellectual pleasure shows that pleasure is an accompaniment of the use of these powers.

Electrical stimulation of an area of the brain can give us pure pleasure without any other accompanying activity. Even so, this could hardly be called normal life, and few people could afford to spend most of their time at it. The only thing that might be immoral about such stimulation would be that people might be tempted to overdo it and substitute it for real living.

Since, in the process of normal living, no one of our abilities has as its purpose pleasure and nothing else, pleasure is but the accompaniment of the normal exercise of abilities that exist for the accomplishment of some other purpose. We eat primarily to keep ourselves alive, though eating is also pleasant. We have eyes to perceive what we need and to guide our movements, though many sights also give delight. Sex is the biological means for the reproduction of the race, though it also has its pleasure. Intellect enables us to live a civilized life, and there is also satisfaction in a problem successfully solved. The same can be said of our other abilities. Pleasure finds its place in the scheme of things by alluring a person to exercise a natural function that is otherwise beneficial to the individual or the race. We might not take the trouble to eat unless we felt hunger and food had a taste. We keep our eyes open because we enjoy looking. People would not shoulder the responsibilities of matrimony were it not for the pleasures of married life. We would give up hard thinking if we did not find problems an attractive challenge.

It would be a mistake to think of pleasure merely as a means to an end. This is what it is *objectively,* in the way human nature is structured, and people also use pleasure as a means when they offer it to others as an incentive. But pleasure considered *subjectively,* as a personal experience of the enjoyer, is sought for its own sake and is its own end. It is foolish to ask someone why he or she wants enjoyment. We want it because we enjoy it.

Failure to distinguish these two aspects of pleasure, the subjective and the objective, lies behind the two extreme attitudes we have mentioned. It is not possible to reduce pleasure to a mere means, at least for the person enjoying it, and one cannot help seeking it for its own sake, since that is the kind of thing it is. In this respect one

---

[1]Plato and Aristotle give us a very balanced analysis for their day. See Plato, *Philebus;* Aristotle, *Nicomachean Ethics,* bk. VII, ch. 11–14; bk. X, ch. 1–5.

may agree with the view[1] that pleasure taken precisely as pleasure is always good and never bad. If a pleasure can ever be called bad, it is not because the pleasing object is pleasant but because it has other features connected with it that are harmful or unworthy, such as violating others' rights or stunting one's personality. Thus there is nothing wrong in seeking pleasure for its own sake, since it cannot be sought otherwise, but it must be done in a fitting manner. It is when we so center on the subjective aspect of pleasure to the exclusion of the objective, by making pleasure the only end or the chief end in life, that we thereby exclude the end for which pleasure is adapted by nature as a means. By acting thus we contradict our own nature and make ourselves incapable of fulfilling the purpose for which we exist. So pleasure is an end and a good, but it is not the last end and the highest good, though there could hardly be a last end or a highest good unaccompanied by a corresponding degree of pleasure.

Also, we must not forget the partial character of pleasure compared with the all-embracing nature of happiness. The pleasures of this life are not attainable by all people at all times. To have some pleasures we must forego others. Pleasure is not lasting, for none of our faculties can stand ceaseless exercise. Too much indulgence makes pleasure cloying and often brings with it its own punishment. Old age diminishes the possibility of pleasure, and death ends it. Hence, though there is nothing wrong with pleasure, it cannot fully satisfy.

Altruistic pleasure, though on a higher plane than egoistic, is also unsatisfying. The joy we feel in kindness, in giving gifts, in helping others, in relieving distress, in social uplift, in works of charity and benevolence, is among the purest and best we can experience. The many who devote their lives to these activities are worthy of praise, but again, not all have the time and means for such works, the joy taken in them is often marred by ingratitude, and many schemes for the bet-

terment of humanity grind to a halt in disillusionment. The philanthropist is by all means to be encouraged, but such a person had better keep in mind those being helped and not expect too much personal satisfaction. Besides, there is something incoherent in the altruistic ideal unbuttressed by other aims. If we exist for the sake of other people what are the other people for? If everybody exists for the sake of everybody else, then, when the process is brought round full circle, what is all humanity for?

This last is the question that egoism and altruism, hedonism and utilitarianism, indeed all other forms of naturalistic humanism, remain unable to answer. Despite many useful contributions to the study of human life, pleasure ethics has some problems that must be overcome if such an ethics is to be helpful to us in living a meaningful life.

SUMMARY

Hedonism picks egoistic pleasure as our highest good. It need not be the pleasure of the moment or sensuous pleasure only, but can be a wise blend of enjoyments spread out over one's probable lifetime.

Arguments *for:* We do in fact seek pleasure and shun pain; even duty affords a kind of intellectual satisfaction, altruistic behavior has a self-regarding aspect, and those who seek a reward in the next world expect to enjoy it.

Arguments *against:* We often refuse pleasure for higher motives; satisfaction in doing one's duty is not the same as pleasure, enlightened self-interest is not our only motive, and those who would not do good unless it were rewarded are unworthy of the reward.

Utilitarianism prefers the altruistic pleasure of seeking the greatest happiness of the greatest number, and measures the morality of an act by its utility in promoting the common welfare.

Arguments *for:* It seeks others' happiness as well as one's own, recognizes our social needs, curbs our selfish greed, accepts qualitative differences in pleasures, and is open both to virtue and to religion.

Arguments *against:* It gives no reason why one

---

[1]Hinted at by Aristotle, *Nicomachean Ethics,* bk. VII, ch. 13; bk. X, ch. 5.

should consider others, cannot determine what makes for the general happiness, should logically eliminate sufferers, has no place for real love, and makes the noblest acts not good in themselves but only useful means.

Conclusion. Pleasure cannot be the highest good; yet it is a very important good. It is a natural stimulus that allures us to the proper use of our abilities. It is also a subjective experience sought for its own sake. There is nothing wrong in seeking pleasure for itself, so long as it is kept within proper bounds and not too much is expected of it. A puritanical attitude toward pleasure is not praiseworthy. Pleasure is *a* good, but not *the* good.

Questions for Discussion

1. If, according to Ayn Rand, the ultimate value is a person's survival and each person is responsible for working out the means to survival, government ought not interfere in any way in people's lives. Nevertheless, we find the federal, state, and local governments fostering welfare programs of various types to help people who seem unable to help themselves. Could Ayn Rand on her own principles justify welfare programs? How?

2. Develop a critique of the following criticism of utilitarianism: The trouble with utilitarianism is that it lays the groundwork for wiping out one group of innocent people after another, for example, the old because they are not producing anything, the young because they are a nuisance, cripples because they are too much trouble, and racial minorities because they are hated. The greatest pleasure for the greatest number really means "the greater pleasure for the greater number."

3. Take either the position of an act utilitarian or a rule utilitarian and show how the principle of utility applies to such questions as homosexual acts between consenting adults,

divorce, capital punishment, gambling, the use of alcohol by adults, premarital sex, and the manufacture and sale of pornographic materials to adults.

4. When individual persons tell lies, those acts are called "lies," but when the government tells a lie, that act is called "giving disinformation." The "disinformation" is given in order to deceive the public about government intentions and actions that are either ongoing or contemplated, for example, covert bombing raids in Cambodia during the Vietnam War or the preparations to rescue the American hostages in Teheran. Imagine that you are a convinced utilitarian and have been called upon by the government to justify to the press corps the use of "disinformation" in both instances. How would you go about your task without compromising your utilitarianism?

5. Derive the principle "all life must be preserved whenever possible" from the principle of utility and then show how that principle leads to a specific position on abortion, capital punishment, vivisection, meat and fish eating, and the eradication of insects.

Readings

Read Plato's *Philebus,* the dialogue on pleasure, and the part of the *Gorgias,* §492–500, where Plato argues that pleasure is not *the* good; and Aristotle's two sections on pleasure in the *Nicomachean Ethics,* bk. VII, ch. 11–14, and bk. X, ch. 1–5.

Lucretius' poem *De Rerum Natura* (On the Nature of Things) proclaims the philosophy of Epicurus. Cicero discusses Epicureanism together with other ancient philosophies in his *Tusculan Disputations* and other philosophical writings. Diogenes Laertius' *Lives and Opinions of Eminent*

Philosophers gives a summary of Epicureanism, with some notice of the Cyrenaics.

Read Hobbes, *Leviathan,* pt. I, ch. 6, 11; Robert Olson, *The Morality of Self-Interest;* and Ayn Rand, *The Virtue of Selfishness,* for varieties of egoism.

Jeremy Bentham, *Introduction to the Principles of Morals and Legislation,* ch. 1–5; and John Stuart Mill, *Utilitarianism,* offer the classic exposition of utilitarianism.

Many books and articles give detailed criticisms of hedonism and utilitarianism, among them G.E. Moore, *Principia Eth-*

ica and Marcus George Singer, *Generalization in Ethics*.

John Rawls, "Two Concepts of Rules," in *Philosophical Review*, vol. 64, no. 2(1955), reprinted in various collections, distinguishes act and rule utilitarianism. His *Theory of Justice*, written using utilitarianism as a contrast to his own contract theory of justice as fairness, has a criticism of hedonism as a method of choice, pp. 554–560.

7
Convention

PROBLEM

Despite the large part that pleasure plays in life and despite the moral acceptability of many of the pleasures we may enjoy, pleasure itself cannot be the standard of moral good and evil. It affords no reason why we are morally bound to do some things we find unpleasant and to refrain from other things to which we are strongly attracted. The ought is not always what we like, either as individuals or as a group. If the ought does not come from our likes and dislikes, from where does it come?

The later utilitarians had already gone beyond pleasure as that which constitutes the good of society. If we pursue the topic along these lines and provisionally take the good of society as the goal toward which we should strive in moral living, the next question would be: Who is to decide what that good is? The simplest answer is to let society itself decide what is good for it. The history of the human race is the history of our constant quest for self-improvement. With long and often painful experience various groups of human beings have organized themselves for the pursuit of their common good and have embodied the results in their various laws and customs. They have not all arrived at the same formula for their common happiness, but each individual must live in the group, tribe, city, or nation to which he or she belongs, and must adapt to its way of living. Why not say, then, that morality is that which the group decrees and which it enforces by the strong sanctions of social approval and disapproval? Thus morality would not be something that humans find already existing in the world, but something created to make living possible, something artificial and fictitious in itself but a historical fact avoidable only by the outlaw and outcast. Morality would be reducible to the conventions of society, whether those conventions be enacted into law or informally recognized as approved customary behavior. We shall discuss the following points:

1. What is the meaning of conventional and natural morality?
2. Does all morality come from the civil law?

3. Does all morality come from custom and social pressure?
4. What is the place of convention in morals?

CONVENTIONAL AND NATURAL MORALITY

To set the question, we must define two important kinds of morality. An act that is neither good nor bad of its own nature but becomes so only because it is commanded or forbidden by some law or custom is said to have *conventional* or *extrinsic* morality. An act that is good or bad of its own nature independently of any command or prohibition is said to have *natural* or *intrinsic* morality. Note that both are varieties of objective morality, since they do not ask about the state of the doer's conscience but about what makes that kind of act, whoever does it, right or wrong.

That conventional morality exists is evident, for no one can deny the existence of laws, such as the laws of the state or the unwritten law of custom, which issue abundant commands and prohibitions, rendering good or bad many actions that would otherwise be morally indifferent. Hence the question is not one of choosing between conventional and natural morality, but whether *besides* conventional morality there is *also* natural morality. To sum up the question:

1. Are all acts good only because they are commanded, bad only because they are forbidden?
2. Or are some acts commanded because they are good, forbidden because they are bad in themselves?

To accept the first alternative is to say that all morality is determined by convention, that it is the result of some human will commanding or forbidding certain kinds of acts, that it is not based on something intrinsic in the human act itself or in human nature. Thus it makes all morality a creation of human society. The theory takes two main forms, according as the convention or decision to consider some acts right and others wrong is the result of the following:

1. The laws of the state—*social contract theories*

2. The human customs—*social pressure theories*

SOCIAL CONTRACT THEORIES

Some think that no act is wrong unless there is a law against it, and the only law they acknowledge is the civil law. Where the arm of the law cannot reach, anything goes. Morality is thus the product of civilized life, which necessarily entails political organization. Morality is made the same as legality. This popular conception has had few philosophical defenders, but there are two of great influence.

Thomas Hobbes and probably Jean Jacques Rousseau maintain that before people organized themselves into political communities there was no right and wrong. The state itself is not a natural society but the result of the social contract, a purely conventional agreement whereby people give up part of their natural rights (liberty to do anything they please) to preserve the rest. Once civil society is formed, it commands and forbids certain actions for the common good, and this is the beginning of right and wrong. Therefore no acts are right or wrong of their very nature but only because commanded or forbidden by the political state.

Hobbes and Rousseau differ greatly in their views on the state of nature, on the form of the social contract, on the mode of transferring rights, and on the seat of sovereignty, but these views belong rather to their theories on the state. Here we are interested only in the fact that they deny natural or intrinsic morality. One may wonder what value morals can have if they are merely arbitrary human conventions, but Hobbes and Rousseau both insist on the validity of morality once the state has been established.

A few key passages will show Hobbes' view:

During the time men live without a common power to keep them all in awe, they are in that condition which is called war; and such a war as is of every man against every man....

To this war of every man against every man, this also is consequent: *that nothing can be unjust.* The notions of right and wrong, justice and injustice, have there no place. Where there is no common power, there is no law; where no law, no injustice. Force and fraud are in war the two cardinal virtues .... It is consequent also to the same condition, that there be not propriety,[1] no dominion, no *mine* and *thine* distinct; but only that to be every man's that he can get; and for so long as he can keep it....[2]

Where no covenant hath preceded, there hath no right been transferred, and every man has a right to everything and consequently, no action can be unjust .... Before the names of just and unjust can have place, there must be some coercive power, to compel men equally to the performance of their covenants, by the terror of some punishment greater than the benefit they expect by the breach of their covenant ... and such power there is none before the erection of a commonwealth.[3]

It may be unfair to class Rousseau with Hobbes. Rousseau seems rather to think that in their primitive state of innocence humans naturally did what is right without the formulation of any moral rules. Whatever his general theory, he lays himself open to the charge of conventionalism by the opening words of his *Social Contract:*

Man is born free, and everywhere he is in chains. Many a one believes himself the master of others, and yet he is a greater slave than they. How has this change come about? I do not know. What can render it legitimate? I believe that I can settle this question .... The social order is a sacred right which serves as a foundation for all others. This right, however, does not come from nature. It is therefore based on conventions. The question is to know what these conventions are....[4]

Since no man has any natural authority over his fellow-man, and since force is not the source of right, conventions remain as the basis of all lawful authority among men....[5]

The passage from the state of nature to the civil state produces in man a very remarkable change, by substituting in his conduct justice for instinct, and by giving his actions the moral quality they previously lacked.[6]

---

[1] *Propriety* here is but the old form of the word *property.*
[2] Hobbes, *Leviathan,* ch. 13.
[3] *Op. cit.,* ch. 15.
[4] Rousseau, *Social Contract,* bk. I, ch. 1.
[5] *Op. cit.,* bk. I, ch. 4.
[6] *Op. cit.,* bk. I, ch. 8.

All readily admit that the state can pass laws on indifferent matters and make them binding under moral obligation. As guardian of public order and safety, the state decrees that we shall drive on the right side of the road, though either side might have been chosen. This law does not change the intrinsic nature of the road, but it does make a deliberate act of driving on the wrong side unsafe, antisocial, and to that extent immoral. Thus the state gives extrinsic morality to an act intrinsically indifferent.

Can all acts be of this kind? There are some acts the state cannot command and others the state cannot forbid. No state could survive that commanded murder, theft, perjury, and treason, or that forbade kindliness, honesty, truthfulness, and loyalty. Such actions were good or bad before there was any state. They are not good or bad because the laws of the state command or forbid them, but the state is obliged to command or forbid them because they are good or bad in themselves.

SOCIAL PRESSURE THEORIES

The theory that morality is mere custom has always been widespread since the days of the Sophists and Skeptics of ancient Greece. Some give legitimacy to the custom after it has been introduced, whereas others advocate its abolition. One who wishes to do away with morality must adopt some such theory to explain how people ever became deceived into thinking that right and wrong exist.

Some think that morality was imposed by clever and influential persons to keep the common people in subjection; by the force of public opinion and the weight of tradition the ordinary person accepts the moral code and wears the chains forged for him or her; only a few bold spirits assert and achieve freedom. This is the philosophy of the world's moral rebels. Bernard de Mandeville[1] gives the idea expression but thinks it a providential arrangement.

The opinion of Friedrich Nietzsche[2] is not very different. In the beginning there were no good and bad, only the strong and the weak. The strong, with their masculine virtues of power, cunning, and ruthlessness, despised the weak, with their feminine virtues of patience, obedience, and kindliness; and the weak feared the strong. Each class admired its own qualities and condemned the opposite; thus arose the distinction between master morality and slave morality. By weight of numbers, assisted by the influence of Christianity, slave morality triumphed. This outcome was, in Nietzsche's eyes, a disaster. The common herd does not count, and it is the duty of society to produce an aristocracy of people who go beyond what the world's moral heroes have yet attained and who will be superior to any and all of them. Nietzsche used the word *Übermensch* to denote this kind of aristocratic person, and the word has been misleadingly translated as "Superman." He seems to mean a person who goes *beyond* what humans have yet achieved and who is *superior* to all who have yet achieved anything. Such a person is joyous, guiltless, free, the master and not the slave of his or her instinctual drives, and so such a person will be the embodiment of the masculine virtues and will restore the master morality. This person will be beyond good and evil as they are conceived by the herd and so will be in a position to make something of himself or herself rather than simply being the product of instinctual discharges and the overcoming of external obstacles. Nietzsche has tried to present an ideal that is attainable by humans; he would have us seek the higher fulfillment of ourselves as human beings by filling us with a sense of mission and of value yet to be attained.

Karl Marx and Friedrich Engels[3] with their communist followers hold the materialistic conception of history, according to which moral, political, artistic, social, and philosophical ideas are determined by the economic conditions of so-

---

[1]Mandeville, *Enquiry into the Origin of Moral Virtue.*

[2]Nietzsche, *Genealogy of Morals, Beyond Good and Evil,* and other works.
[3]Marx and Engels, *Communist Manifesto.*

ciety; each age, people, and class forms its ideas to suit its own peculiar economic situations; the economic changes to be brought about by the downfall of capitalism will require the formation of a new morality to supplant the present outmoded "bourgeois" morality.

Social evolutionists, of whom Herbert Spencer[1] is typical, trace the first beginning of moral ideas in animals. As humans gradually evolved from a brutish condition, these moral ideas underwent a parallel evolution. Ways of acting that were found profitable developed into primitive tribal customs, which with the progress of civilization were gradually purified into our present system of morals. This will give way to a still higher system as the evolutionary process continues.

Positivism, founded by Auguste Comte,[2] is a general philosophical attitude holding that metaphysics is useless and that philosophy is limited to the facts and laws discovered by the *positive* or experimental sciences. The last science to become positive is the science of society, for which Comte invented the name *sociology*. Ethics is a part of sociology, for moral customs grew out of social customs and fluctuate with changes in society.

John Dewey[3] holds that customs, folkways, and established collective habits so form the texture of our lives that there is no escaping from them. More will be said of his ethical views in the next chapter.

All such views received new cogency from a nonphilosophical source, the rise of cultural anthropology and Freudian psychology. These studies are not necessarily committed to a definite ethical view, but in the hands of some have been used to bolster the social pressure theory of moral obligation. Tribal taboos, however artificial and fictitious they may seem, often serve a purpose in the culture in which they flourish, though advanced peoples have outgrown them. Civilized mores are merely a lingering remnant of the same thing in a more advanced style. Both have the same obligatory force: social pressure. It is easier to conform than to push against the demands of the crowd, and what is really only expediency becomes invested with an aura of duty.

We recognize that morality differs in every society, and is a convenient term for socially approved habits. Mankind has always preferred to say, "It is morally good," rather than, "It is habitual," and the fact of this preference is matter enough for a critical science of ethics. But historically the two phrases are synonymous.[4]

While some thus reduce ethics to anthropology, others make it a form of psychology, so that the sense of moral obligation is identified with submerged psychic feelings of guilt. The person vaguely feels bound but is unable to account for this inner sense of obligation until his or her early life is dredged up from the depths of the unconscious, and the feelings of guilt are seen as stemming from repressed infantile encounters with social, especially parental, disapproval. Doubtless, anthropological and psychological facts have strongly influenced the development of ethics. Whether they are the total explanation is another question.

All the foregoing opinions are but samples of this type of theory. They agree in trying to reduce morality to social pressure and differ in their way of trying to account for the existence and influence of social pressure. They all deny that there is any intrinsic morality, that there is any basis in the nature of things for the distinction people commonly make between right and wrong. To

---

[1]Spencer, *Principles of Ethics,* of which the *Data of Ethics,* sometimes published separately, forms the first part.

[2]Comte, *Cours de philosophie positive.* A convenient exposition of his philosophy in English is Harriet Martineau's *Positivist Philosophy of Auguste Comte.* Positivism in general and logical positivism are named from the positive or experimental sciences, whereas moral positivism and legal positivism are named from positive law as opposed to natural law. The two meanings of positivism are not related, except incidentally.

[3]Dewey, *Human Nature and Conduct,* pt. I, sec. V.

[4]Ruth Benedict, "The Concept of the Normal," taken from Mandelbaum, Gramlich, Anderson, and Schneewind, *Philosophic Problems,* 2nd ed., p. 596.

assess this view we must see what is meant by custom.

What is Custom?

Custom arises by repetition of the same kind of act in the same way. It is the external result of habit. Why do people repeat acts? Because the first time they did a certain act they found it pleasant or useful, and they want to obtain the same good again. In the beginning people do not repeat acts merely because they have done them once or twice before, but for the sake of some advantage. Until the custom has been formed, custom itself is not the source of action. Customs and traditions have their value as passing on to future generations in readymade form the profitable experiences of our elders. As historical connections with the past, as the cement of cultural continuity, they are the mainstay of every civilization.

Custom can also act as a drawback. Over a long period circumstances may change radically, and acts that were formerly advantageous may now in the new conditions become useless or even harmful; yet people by force of habit continue to perform them without reflecting on why they do so. Thus people continue to observe certain rites and ceremonies long after they have forgotten their meaning. Traditions can so pile up that a whole people will persist in doing a thing in a wasteful or illogical manner, even after they recognize its absurdity, because they find it easier to conform to prejudice than to try to make themselves abandon familiar patterns of behavior. Our clumsy calendar, our irregular English spelling, and our clumsy system of measurement are instances.

As we noted in the very beginning of ethics, there are two kinds of customs: *manners* which are mere customs in the sense that they are repeated solely because they have been done before, and *morals,* which are customary patterns of behavior but are based on something deeper in us than arbitrary usage. Manners can be changed by lapse of time, by powerful authority, by con-

tinual propaganda, and by popular reeducation. This change may be difficult to accomplish, but history shows that even the most deeply lodged traditions, if they are mere traditions, can be broken. This is not true of all customs, not of the kind called *morals,* for there are:

1. Some customs that cannot be abolished and
2. Some kinds of acts that can never be made customary

Some Customs Never Abolished

Eating and bathing are customs, but people cannot be reeducated to do without them. Conversation and exchange of ideas are customs, but only a fool would try to prohibit them. Music and artistic expression are customs, but there is no prospect of ever eradicating them wholly from any people. The reason is that, though customary, they are not mere customs but are founded on human physical, mental, and emotional needs.

These instances are drawn from outside the field of morality, but the same conclusion holds true of the moral life. It is customary for people to respect the lives and property of others in peacetime, to love their children, to pay their debts, to tell the truth, to be faithful to their friends, to fulfill their promises, to help others in distress. But these are not mere customs. If they were, they could be abolished and the opposite customs introduced. Not only would people refuse to accept the opposite customs, but there would be an end to human life and society. There would be no property, no children, no commerce, no talking, no friends, no promises, and no human would live to maturity, much less produce a second generation. Here we are using only a few obvious examples and not trying to set up a full code of morality. We say only that some customs cannot be abolished, and the reader can take what examples he or she wishes.

We may call such acts customs in the broad sense of something done over and over again, but they are not mere customs in the sense that the only reason they are done is that they have been done before. They represent the way we must live if we are to have a human life at all. Therefore such acts are good, not because they are customary, but because of their very nature. They are good in themselves, and were so before they became customary.

Some Acts Never Customary

We cannot make it customary for a person to walk down a street shooting people indiscriminately, for witnesses in a law court to lie, for soldiers to desert in battle, for hosts to poison their guests, for every person to slander a neighbor's character. There must be some reason why such acts could not be established as customary. It is because such acts are evil in themselves and of their very nature. They are destructive of the fundamental human capacities and requirements and hence of human nature itself.

Of course, there are people who do these things, but that is not the point. The point is that this kind of conduct is branded as wrong, and we are trying to find out why. Such conduct must ever be the exception, not the rule; the isolated instance, not the practice of the group; a blot on humanity, not the accepted ideal. If it becomes too widespread, it threatens the very existence of the society within which it grows. In our tolerance of human behavior, customary or otherwise, there is a limit beyond which, if we are to survive, we cannot go. There is a vast difference between antisocial conduct that people view with an amused or annoyed forbearance and the life of the outlaw, whom society is forced for its own protection to hunt down like a beast. This latter kind of conduct can never become so prevalent as to be the accepted custom of the race, and even if it should, nothing could make it moral. Morality, therefore, is based on something deeper than custom.

We do not deny that some evil customs may be adopted even by a whole people or nation, but history shows that no block of humanity can thus deteriorate without paying the price. Nations as well as individuals can be guilty of immoral conduct and can become outlaws from the family of nations. We are experiencing in the world today the results of international immorality, and the lesson to be drawn from it is this: People ought not to live that way!

PLACE OF CONVENTION IN MORALS

In the earliest stages of human development, both of the individual and of the race, probably little discrimination is made between physical and moral necessity, between legality and morality. As the child grows up and as primitive people arrive by self-examination at a more sophisticated attitude, the confusion disappears and the distinction is recognized. Compulsion from without is seen to be not the same as obligation from within. There is a difference between what I *must* do or suffer the penalty and what I *ought* to do whether there is a penalty or not.

Thus a person emancipates himself or herself from sole dependence on social and political pressure, from the laws and customs of the tribe or city or nation with their sanctions, and recognizes those ways of life that are proper to a human being as human. Such a person is still a member of the group and strongly influenced by its approval, but he or she has grown critical of it and has found some norm for the criticism. Even those who attack all moral obligation do so in the name of sincerity, authenticity, and freedom, as liberating people from the weight of superstition, prejudice, and conformity. Thus they attack existing moral values and obligations for the sake of other moral values and obligations, rejecting the socially accepted code for one of their own making. Since we are not saying here what the correct moral values are but only that there are *some,* we could hardly find a better instance of the impossibility of reducing moral obligation to social approval than in those who criticize society itself in the name of morals. Nor is total social rebellion necessary to perceive this. No mature person is wholly satisfied with his or her society. Where someone's approval does not correspond with society's, he or she is using some standard other than political or social convention.

CONCLUSIONS

Some actions are right or wrong merely because someone in authority has commanded or forbidden them. These actions are determined by positive law. The state has the right to forbid some actions not otherwise wrong for the sake of good order, and human customs may sometimes have the force of law.

There are other actions so good of their very nature that no human law or custom could make them bad, as well as actions so bad of their very nature that no human law or custom could make them good. Besides, no human law or custom can make acts that are good or bad in themselves become indifferent acts, but they can, by command or prohibition, make acts that are indifferent in themselves become extrinsically good or bad.

We insist that diversity of opinion on morals does not affect the present question. However much opinions may differ, there is a common denominator of moral action among people, and the arguments are drawn from this alone. People may dispute whether this particular act is murder, theft, or lying, but there is no dispute that all sane persons condemn murder, theft and lying in general, and recognize that such acts cannot be made the standard of good conduct by any law or custom. If not, there must be some reason why not, and this can be found only in the very nature of such acts.

We may tie all these strands together in one argument. If all morality were conventional, all actions would be right or wrong because commanded or forbidden, approved or disapproved, either by the state or by society, by law or by custom. But some actions are such that the command or prohibition, the approval or disapproval of the state and its laws, of society and its customs, could not be otherwise, for any other mode of behavior would be destructive of the state, society, and humanity itself. Therefore not all morality is conventional, but there is also a natural morality.

SUMMARY

Is all morality conventional, or is some morality natural?

Many hold the theory that all morality is conventional, resulting from the command or prohibition of the state and its laws or from the approval or disapproval of society and its customs, but that there are no acts good or bad of their very nature. The theory takes two forms:

1. *Social contract theories.* Hobbes and Rousseau say that there was no morality before the formation of the state, and that morality now consists of obedience or disobedience to the civil laws. The argument against this theory is that the state can give conventional morality to indifferent acts, but no state can be completely arbitrary in its laws; there are acts every state must command and other acts every state must forbid, because human life itself demands it; these acts were moral or immoral before there was any state.

2. *Social pressure theories.* These theories are held by philosophers as widely separated as Spencer and Nietzsche, Comte and Marx. Custom can attain the force of law and give conventional morality to indifferent acts, but not all morality can be based on custom, for some customs cannot be abolished, and some kinds of acts can never be made customary. The only reason is that these acts are good or bad independently of any custom, and custom is not the source of all morality.

Such theories fail to distinguish the *must* from the *ought,* compulsion from without and obligation from within. Why obey the law or custom? Force and fear are physical, not moral necessity.

Conclusion. Some acts have only a conventional morality; of themselves indifferent, they become good or bad only because someone in authority has commanded or forbidden them. There are other acts that have natural morality; they are good or bad of their very nature, and no human law or custom, no form of social approval or disapproval, can make them otherwise.

Questions for Discussion

1. Take another look at Nietzsche's approach to morality and cast it in terms of leaders and followers, with the leaders setting the moral pace towards the development of values not yet achieved and the followers working to achieve the value goals set by the leaders. Must we not still ask by what criterion or standard a leader is a good leader, capable of determining the value goals for the followers to achieve? Do you think Nietzsche's view of Christian morality is justified? Why?

2. Karl Marx and Friedrich Engels believed that the economic system of a society determines the kind of morality that society adheres to. Take the capitalist economy that is currently operative in this society and show what moral positions and/or questions arise from it. Is it possible to question the goodness or badness of those positions? Why? Is it possible to argue that morality itself determines the quality of socioeconomic structures and forces in a society? Why?

3. Moral thinking has developed over the years; it has never been a static affair. Can a case be made for the evolutionist position? After all, we used to allow slavery and have now abolished it; we once prohibited charging interest on loans but now allow it. Make a list of other matters on which we have seen moral change and/or development. Do those changes and developments bolster the evolutionist position? Why?

4. Both genetics and moral opinion are lined up against incest, and there is currently no serious discussion about allowing it for those who wish. The basic reasons are that over a long period it might lead to the destruction of the social group and in the short term it is destructive of the family. Is the prohibition of incest no more than a social convention and therefore a proof that morality is nothing more than society's way of protecting itself from extinction? Why?

5. Some acts we can never allow even one person to do, because such tolerance would lead to the destruction of society. For example, if we allow the killer of one person to go about freely killing anyone else he or she pleases, then we are doomed. The Nazi persecution began with one Jew. Moral prohibitions seem clearer and easier to formulate than positive moral values to be pursued if society is to survive and survive well. Create a list of positive values that are not only good for society but also morally necessary and justify them.

Readings

Plato's *Gorgias,* §481 to the end, and *Republic,* bk. I, §338, to bk. II, §368, are pertinent to the subject. Also Cicero, *De Legibus* (On Laws), bk. I, xiv–xvi.

St. Thomas has one short chapter on the subject in the *Summa Contra Gentiles,* bk. III, ch. 129, and some background material in the *Summa Theologica,* I–II, q. 18, a. 1. Natural morality was taken for granted in his day and is not given extended treatment.

Read Hobbes' *Leviathan,* bk. I; Rousseau's *Social Contract,* bk. I; Nietzsche's *Genealogy of Morals* and *Beyond Good and Evil;* on Nietzsche's moral views, read Arthur C. Danto, *Nietzsche as Philosopher,* ch. 5; Spencer's *Data of Ethics;* Dewey's *Human Nature and Conduct,* pt. I, sec. V.

8
Consequences

PROBLEM

The common mark of the ethical theories we have seen so far is that they are all forms of relativism. To these we may now add the variety of relativism called *pragmatism* because of its stress on the practical, on what works, on results or consequences. Pragmatism is closely associated with utilitarianism, the main difference being that pragmatism is a theory of knowledge, holding the *true* to be that which works, so that the truth of propositions is to be tested by their consequences in producing more satisfaction for the individual or the group; whereas utilitarianism is an ethical theory, holding the *good* to be that which works, so that moral goodness is judged by its consequences for society in obtaining the greatest happiness of the greatest number. When there is question of the truth about the good, the two theories fairly coincide.

Utilitarianism is bound up with the pleasure principle because of its historical roots in hedonism. The later utilitarians, however, went beyond the narrow view of restricting consequences to pleasurable ones only, and included the overriding value of consequences generally beneficial to mankind, pleasurable or not. Such a broader view is pragmatism.

Ethical relativism means that there is nothing good or bad absolutely, but that all morality is relative to the individual or to the society to which one belongs. Utilitarianism and pragmatism, and also conventionalism in its way, talk about consequences. Consequences *to whom?* What may have good consequences to one person may be disastrous to another, what may work in one part of the world or in one age may not work in another, what may be beneficial to one form of society or culture may be harmful in another. Hence, relativists say, there is no common morality for the whole human race throughout all history, but we must be content with a morality relative to our time and place.

None of these ways of thinking need be regarded as subjectivism. They do not say that any act is moral merely because I think it moral, that I construct my own code of morals out of my own subjective whim. Rather, they are seeking the objective good, what is truly beneficial to the individual or to society. Individuals and societies differ, and so do their wants and needs. Hence for them ethics is not arbitrary, even though it is not uniform.

Conventionalism is a form of relativism, but there are other forms of relativism that are not conventionalism. Pragmatism, for instance, would not be happy with a wholly extrinsic morality. It does not consider an act good or bad because it is commanded or forbidden by someone in authority, but rather tries to find what it is that authority ought to command or forbid. It is highly critical of existing society and recommends getting rid of outworn customs. Pragmatism is one of the strongest foes of traditionalism and is constantly calling for new social experiments to discover more beneficial ways of living. Society is constantly evolving, and the ways of the past may no longer serve the present or the future.

Relativism in the form of pragmatism is chiefly concerned with the ends or purposes of human living. It rejects any absolute good, any supreme purpose in life. In answering the question, "Has life any meaning?" it says yes, if you are willing to restrict yourself to relatively limited and immediate objectives that can differ for different times and places; but it says no, if you are asking for one absolutely ultimate end and supreme good for all people. This latter would be an absolute, the kind of thing relativism rejects.

Having thus set the stage, we may proceed to our questions:

1. Is it possible to have no aim in life?
2. Are we limited to short-range, relative ends?
3. Are there reasons for an absolutely last end?
4. Can the relative and the absolute be reconciled?

OPPORTUNISM

The problem of the meaning or purpose of life gradually grows on one. At first the child's life lies on the sensuous plane with no intellectually understood goals. As its consciousness develops, the child begins to see some short-term objectives and plans for them with a rudimentary use of means and ends. But to every normal person the time must come when the problem of life's meaning becomes acutely insistent, the irrationality of haphazard living grows glaringly evident, and the former excuse of ignorance and immaturity vanishes before the clear light of developed reason. From then on an intelligent organization of life is imperative.

While this development is going on, the child is not left to drift aimlessly. So long as it cannot steer itself, it is steered by others. It is born into a family and is led by its nature to accept parental direction, to be guided by the rules of the society it cannot yet criticize, and to rely on the primitive observations it can form from its growing stock of experience. Eventually it will have to go through some process of self-searching and reflection to arrive at a reasoned plan of life with consciously formed aims.

As one can arrive at physical maturity without mental maturity, so one can attain to both without moral maturity. The unconsciously adopted philosophy of the child can be rationalized and protracted into adulthood. We call this widely practiced way of life *moral opportunism*. It is not merely a willingness to use opportunities as they arise and to adapt to sudden windfalls of fortune, a useful trait for anybody, but rather it is a refusal to have any principles. It is a contentment to live on a day-to-day or year-to-year basis, looking only to the immediate prospect and letting the distant future take care of itself. It is a deliberate intention to remain open and uncommitted. Not so much a reasoned conviction as an attitude of emotional, intellectual, and moral sloth, it merits the Socratic rebuff, "The unexamined life is not worth living."[1]

One may indeed consciously choose to float with the tide rather than set a course, to shun any fixed program so as to be free to reshape life as the main chance offers, and above all to avoid encumbrance by embarrassing principles and responsibilities. This is a form of life that can be chosen quite deliberately. A person who takes to it does not avoid having a goal in life; such a person mistakenly takes wandering itself for life's chief aim by the very fact that he or she seeks nothing beyond. One may aim at aimlessness, rationally choose to live irrationally, but such conduct must be branded as unworthy of a human being. As the vagrant is an economic anomaly and a social liability, so is the opportunist an ethical misfit and a human failure.

RELATIVISM AND PRAGMATISM

For the opportunist, there is too much trouble in finding out life's meaning if it has one. For the relativist, especially of the pragmatist type, life can be somewhat meaningful in retrospect and in immediate prospect, but its total and ultimate meaning is undiscoverable by us now and unnecessary for relatively successful living.

John Dewey's[2] form of pragmatism, which he calls *instrumentalism,* is ethical relativism with a strong evolutionary bent. His basic assumption is that each human being develops in and through interaction with the world. No individual human being and no society of humans exists except in a definite situation, with a definite history and culture and with some definite desires, strivings, and ideals. There is in each of us a drive to achieve fulfillment, and the fulfillment of human personality is not merely a passive process, for the individual person is not entirely formed by reacting to the environment. Neither is human personhood something static, simply given, already there; rather it is dynamic, changing, initiating, and creative, assuming responsibility in choice of belief and conduct. The individual person has a distinctive way of feeling the impacts of the world and of showing a preference in response to these impacts; it develops into itself only through interaction with actual conditions. The vocation of the person is to grow intellectually and morally and so to rise above monotony and routine to find enlargement and refreshment of spirit.

Because of these concerns, Dewey rejects any

---

[1] Plato, *Apology,* §38.

[2] Dewey, *Human Nature and Conduct,* pt. IV, I; *The Quest for Certainty,* ch. 10.

moral theory that departs from our concrete human condition and seeks to give us a separate set of moral rules and ultimate standards of right and wrong deduced from speculations about the final end proper to us as human beings. Such ethical theorizing confronts us with directives for action that are impossible because they do not take sufficiently into account the concrete human condition in which each of us is living and developing. Since the personal self is achieved by inner striving and creative initiative under the impulse of desire for the enrichment of the individual as well as the members of the community, the task of morals is to organize our desires and impulses so that each of us can use his or her own initiative and creativity to develop and shape the self each of us can become. The personal self develops through interest in values shared by the community, the pursuit of which will contribute to the enrichment of the lives of all. The moral ideal is that we as individuals should be ready to use our intelligence and exert our emotional energies unselfishly for the enrichment of all.

Thinking, he says, is functional, instrumental to action, not done for the sake of finding truth but of making life more satisfactory. A value is whatever a person finds satisfaction in doing in this world of experience. An ethical question arises when one must choose between values. The good is always the better; an evil is only a rejected good. Selection is made by considering one's capacities, satisfactions, and the demands of the social situation, and by taking that which embodies the most foreseen possibilities of future satisfaction. A want arises only when a need is felt, that is, in a particular situation. Only felt wants demand satisfaction, and a satisfied want automatically creates a new want. When we have finished one stage, we experimentally cast about for means to the next stage in the ongoing process. Evolution is continuity of change, readjustment, and redirection. Each stage is a new experimental adventure, which includes the setting of new goals as well as the choice of new means. Thus there is no need of an absolutely fixed goal to give meaning to human life.

The general case for a relativistic pragmatism of this type can be argued in the following way.

1. Acute sensitivity to our limitations and to the folly of being ambitious beyond our known possibilities should cause us to reject all absolutes. If such an assertion seems too absolute, it can be softened into the observation that no supreme purpose for humans has yet been identified with certainty. We do not see far enough into the future to be able to make assertions about it with absolute confidence and thus cannot put before us an absolute goal without serious danger of deception and disillusionment. We have had to correct too many overconfident philosophers of the past. Intellectual humility requires that we lower our sights and probe cautiously into the unknown.

2. There is no need of absolutes to keep us from drifting with the tide, like the opportunist, not caring where. The shorter-range goals that experience puts before us are a sufficient guide toward improving our own condition and working earnestly toward universal betterment. Like a sailor in a fog, we steer in what seems the most likely direction at the moment, with a memory for the course we have traveled and with our eyes open for any clearing ahead. We have to be ready for continual readjustment and change of course.

3. We work chiefly by the trial-and-error method, experimenting with the data at hand. Absolutes have been used to rule out certain possible fields of experimentation until some bold innovator defied the taboo and was thus able to expand immeasurably our mental horizon. As we progressively adapt ourselves to a constantly changing environment, we find our theories on morals, though lagging far behind, gradually changing into more enlightened and humane judgments on human behavior. These have rarely been set as fixed goals to be achieved but were usually the practical result of wise experimentation.

4. To many the very idea of an absolutely last end or ultimate goal appears too rigid and stifling. What would we do when we had reached such an end? Would there be no further growth or

progress? How could there be if the last is the absolutely last in the sense that there is nothing further? Such stagnation holds no hope for anyone. Without novelty the adventure of existence would lose all its zest. There is more joy in the excitement of the chase than in bagging the quarry, and when the journey is interesting it is better to travel than to arrive.

5. According to Dewey's theory of the *continuity of means-ends,*[1] as there is no means that is not a means to an end, so there is no end that is not a means to a further end. The chain of means and ends is thus necessarily indefinite in length, and the notion of an absolutely last end is essentially incoherent. Anything like an ultimate fixed goal is both impossible as breaking off the continuity of means-ends, and undesirable as curtailing flexibility and freedom of human progress.

These samples of argumentation should make the theory clear enough. Nonrelativists are ready with replies:

1. It is well to remind philosophers of intellectual humility and the limitations of the human mind, but should we be so humble as to refuse to look at the truth when it stares us in the face? Genuine humility shows itself in the acceptance of the evident truth more than in refusal to submit to evidence. If the real motive is intellectual fear of being deceived or disillusioned, and if there is no further reason why relativists adopt relativism, they make this a last end and an absolute, whether they care to call it so or not. Thus a proximate end is lifted to the status of an ultimate end without deserving the honor.

2. Life does require continual adjustments, not of ends, however, but of means. We must be ready to alter our course only if there is some port for which we are making and some reason for trying to arrive there, but there is no sense in cruising about a foggy sea on a voyage to nowhere. How do we know we are bettering our condition unless there is some fixed standard of goodness by which we can measure our approach to it?

3. The trial-and-error method is the normal way of experiment when we are searching for means to a known end. If there is no end, why make the trial and how tell success from error? The pragmatists are correct in criticizing those who set up their pet notions as absolutes not to be questioned and thus block off possible avenues of fruitful experimentation, but the fact that it is possible to adopt false absolutes does not prove that there are none. Relativism is likewise open to abuse. Logically it reduces to Protagoras'[2] view that only that is true that the perceiver perceives here and now and only as long as he perceives it. No science is possible on these skeptical terms.

4. Why must a last end or goal of life be something static that would freeze all further growth instead of a condition of perpetually assured growth? Here imagination can play one false. The fulfillment of the human person would have to be something corresponding to human nature, not some stifling suppression of it. If death is the end of all, as many relativists are willing to accept relatively, it is the most static and rigid of all last ends, nothingness. There the excitement of the chase has ended, and all along there never was a quarry to bag.

5. There is no proof for Dewey's theory of the continuity of means-ends. There is nothing in the nature of an end that must necessarily make it a means to a further end. Perhaps only felt wants demand satisfaction, but it is false to assume that wants arise only in an immediate situation. To find some answer to the riddle of life and to seek some meaning or purpose in existence as a whole are unquenchable wants felt in every human being, and to try to satisfy them has been the business of philosophy from the beginning. An ethics that strives to answer them but fails can be respected for its effort, but it is hard to excuse an ethics that dismisses them as nugatory.

ABSOLUTELY LAST END

Those who are not satisfied with relativism have the burden of proving the impossibility of an endless series of means and ends. Some are will-

---

[1]Dewey, *Theory of Valuation*.

[2]Plato, *Theaetetus*, §152 *ff.*

ing to take this as self-evident: if there must be an end or purpose for each one of the parts, there must also be one for the whole; it is non-sensical to think that, whereas each single thing in life is seen to have a meaning, no meaning can be found for the whole of life that these acts are meant to constitute. Others consider the matter important enough to be put into a formal argument. One of the best has been proposed by St. Thomas Aquinas. A review of some simple definitions is helpful in understanding it.

A thing is intended either for its own sake or for the sake of something else. The former is an *end,* the latter a *means.* A means always supposes an end; it is called a means precisely because it lies in a mean, or middle, position between the agent and the end, and its use brings the agent to the end. The same thing may be both means and end in different respects, for it may be sought both for its own sake and for the sake of some-thing further. This is called an *intermediate* end, and there may be a long series of such inter-mediate ends, as when we want A in order to get B, B in order to get C, C in order to get D, and so on.

That which is sought for its own sake and not for the sake of anything further is what is meant by a *last end* or *ultimate end.* It closes the series of means and ends. It may be a last end only in a relative sense, meaning that it closes a particular series but that the whole series is directed to some further end; thus the reception of an aca-demic degree terminates one's education, but education itself has the further purpose of fitting one for life. In the full sense of the word, the last end means the *absolutely last end,* which is directed to no further end at all, but to it every-thing else is directed. Since the end and the good are identified, a being's absolutely last end must also be its highest good.

In a series of means and ends we must distin-guish the order of *intention* from the order of *execution.* The first thing that comes to mind (the order of intention) is the end, and the means are chosen with a view to accomplishing the end; but in the actual carrying out of the work (the order of execution), the means must be used

first, and the last thing that is obtained is the end. This is the key to the argument, for whatever may be thought of the possibility of an infinite series in other matters, an infinite series of means and ends is quite impossible; thus there must be an *absolutely last end* to which the whole of human life is directed.

> That which is first in the order of intention is the principle as it were moving the appetite; conse-quently if you remove this principle there will be nothing to move the appetite. On the other hand, the principle in execution is that wherein operation has its beginning; and if this principle be taken away no one will begin to work. Now the principle in the intention is the last end; while the principle in ex-ecution is the first of the things which are ordained to the end. Consequently on neither side is it pos-sible to go on to infinity; since, if there were no last end, nothing would be desired nor would any action have its term nor would the intention of the agent be at rest; while, if there is no first thing among those that are ordained to the end, none would begin to work at anything and counsel would have no term but would continue indefinitely.[1]

When a man uses A to get B, B to get C, C to get D, he must (unless he is acting at random and irrationally) first desire D, and then find out that to get D he needs C, to get C he needs B, to get B he needs A. Thus his planning (intention) is in inverse order to his acting (execution). That which is first in intention is last in execution, and vice versa. Thus the steps are as follows, starting with D:

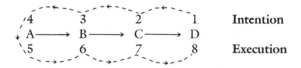

They are first planned out in the mind and then transferred to execution. If the planning went on forever, nothing would ever be done, for in ra-tional action the execution cannot begin until the planning is complete. There must then be a point A (the proximate means) at which planning ends

---

[1] St. Thomas, *Summa Theologica,* I–II, q. 1, a. 4.

and execution begins. This closes the series on one side, but to arrive at point A in the planning, it was also necessary to begin somewhere. Neither A nor B nor C is wanted for itself. Unless there is some point D that is wanted for itself, neither A nor B nor C would be thought of, and no plan would be formed. Hence there must be some point D (the last end) that starts the whole process going. This closes the series on the other side. Hence in any intelligent procedure apart from fitful and random behavior one must already have the last end in mind before beginning the first act. Humans therefore not only act for an end but for a last end.

But, one might say, this argument merely proves that there must be some end that is the last in a series, a relatively last end, not that there must be an absolutely last end to which all series of means and ends are directed and beyond which there can be nothing further. To this objection it is answered that the necessary logic of the argument carries it to all series of means and ends, and to all series of series. The same reason that requires that a single series of means lead to an end requires that any series of series lead to an ultimate series, the last member of which is the absolutely last end, since neither a single means nor a series of means nor a series of series of means, no matter how extended, would be chosen except for the sake of some end to which they all lead.

Another objection is that this argument proves too much and therefore nothing. A child would have to fix upon its last end and formulate a whole plan of life before it could even perform its first act, a supposition that flouts all experience. The answer is that what we described was the *rational* activity of a *mature* person, the use of means to end as directed by intellect in adult human behavior. The child comes only gradually to an understanding of life's purpose and is at first restricted to relative ends, but sometime between adolescence and maturity he or she must decide on the purpose of life as a whole or, as happens with the opportunist, find the question decided

for him or her by default. In either case a person is responsible, whether it be for choosing as he or she did or for choosing not to choose.

Does this mean that, once I have chosen such a supreme goal in life, I am forever stuck with it? It seems that I should be, if it is an absolute; if I can change it, does that not show that it was merely provisional and relative? No. Even in the choosing of an absolutely ultimate goal, human error is possible. The possibility of error about the goal does not make the goal itself any less absolute, nor do I commit myself to it only tentatively or provisionally. Certainty does not exclude the possibility but only the prudent fear of error; otherwise one could be certain of hardly anything. A man, for example, can commit himself wholeheartedly to a definite goal that he has chosen on mature reflection and thus be quite certain, without thereby closing his mind to all future knowledge. Succeeding periods of self-examination can bring greater maturity and enlightenment. If further experience and reflection show that he has made a mistake, he will correct the error and reform his decision. One can never be so stuck with an erroneous goal in life that the error cannot be corrected. On the other hand, no one should be afraid of being stuck with the truth, so to speak. The truth does cling to anyone who has found it, and that was why he or she sought it.

Supposing that there is an absolutely ultimate end for all humans, is there any reason it must be one and the same for all persons? To grant various ultimate ends to different individuals, groups, and historical eras might satisfy the claims of some cultural relativists. It is difficult to answer this question without determining just what the absolutely last end of all humans is, and we have not yet laid all the groundwork. For the moment we can say that, whereas subordinate ends may differ, the absolutely last end, whatever it is, would have to be something that is proper to *human beings as humans,* and therefore would not be something different for various persons, races, classes, epochs, or cultures. We differ subjectively in our judgments on what constitutes the ultimate goal of life, but we are dealing with the objective truth these judgments are groping to discover and express. Nor is each person faced with a number of possible last ends among which to choose. None of us chose to be a human being; we find ourselves human whether we like it or not. Only one last end or highest good is offered to us. We may take it or leave it, but we have no more option for a substitute than we have for becoming something other than human.

THE RELATIVE AND THE ABSOLUTE

The controversy between relativists and absolutists involves the whole of one's philosophical outlook. We cannot take up this larger issue but must restrict ourselves to the way in which these two attitudes affect our subject, ethics.

Much can be said in favor of relativism, especially if one is content to accept a relative form of relativism. The relativist who denies all absolutes contradicts himself or herself by holding at least one absolute: the proposition that everything is relative. If absolutely everything is relative, relativity itself becomes the absolute, and the distinction between relativity and absoluteness disappears. If only relatively everything is relative, the absoluteness of relativity could be diluted only by the introduction of some non-relative element, some absolute. Relativism does not go wrong by the admission of relativity but by the exclusion of any absolute to which all relatives could be relative.

Certainly there is no thing that is not related to some other thing, in fact, to all other things. Knowledge and truth are relations; the mere fact that we know a thing establishes a relation between it and us. Desire and goodness are relations; that a thing is good for us merely expresses a kind of relation it has to us. In the present chapter we said much about means and ends; these terms make no sense except in relation to each other. This last pair is useful to illustrate

the fact that not all relatives are equally relative. There is less relativity in ends than in means. The means, taken precisely as means, exist wholly for the sake of the ends they serve, whereas the ends do not exist for the sake of the means that lead to them. The end, besides its relative aspect toward the means, also has an independent and absolute aspect.

This may give us our key to the solution. Relative and absolute are not things but ways of looking at things. If we look at the way a thing is toward something else, we stress its relative aspect; if we consider it merely as it is in itself, without denying but only disregarding its bearing on others, we stress its absolute aspect. In this way the same thing can be both absolute and relative at once, though not in the same respect. The saying, then, that everything is relative is true in the sense that everything has a relative aspect; false, in the sense that nothing has any absolute aspect.

When we speak of an absolutely last end, we do not mean that this end has no relation to us. It is absolute because there is no further end, relative because it is *our* end, one that *we* must achieve. To put before us an endless series of ends implies that, when all is said and done, there is no end to which we are related, and this is to make an absolute of ourselves. Some relativists may wish to do this and are merely saying so in a disguised fashion. We shall take up later the question of whether we can be our own absolutely last end.

In ethics, everything else but the absolutely last end is relative, and even this, as we just said, is relative to us, though not relative to a further end. All the means of living the moral life are relative to the end of moral living and thus to the person whose life it is. Only a few propositions in ethics will be announced absolutely, and these will turn out to be variants of a single proposition of such transcending generality that no more all-embracing proposition could be found to which it might be subordinated.

Pragmatism affords a very important *secondary*

criterion of morality, for many acts are indifferent in themselves but become good or bad because of their consequences. Remove or modify these consequences and the acts change their moral significance. The difficulty with pragmatism is its insistence that every act is of this type and its failure to provide any moral criterion for judging the consequences except by further and further consequences forever.

These remarks have been made to show the importance of the relative and the pragmatic in ethics. They also have been made to show that the relative is inherently unintelligible except in terms of some absolute and that the pragmatic must be judged in terms of some theory by which good and bad consequences can be discerned.

SUMMARY

Ethical *relativism* holds that there is nothing good or bad absolutely, but all morality is relative to the individual or to society.

Opportunism refuses to have a goal in life so as to remain open and uncommitted. But this aimlessness is itself an aim.

Pragmatism is a relativism that judges the moral value of acts by their consequences, not limiting itself, as utilitarianism does, to pleasurable ones. Dewey's *instrumentalism* is a form of pragmatism that admits proximate goals but no ultimate goal for human life, according to his theory of the continuity of means-ends.

Reasons *for:* We have been disillusioned too often, must be ready for continual readjustments, work by trial-and-error, find an absolute goal too rigid and stifling, and must be open for future progress.

Reasons *against:* We are not wholly deceived, use trial-and-error and make readjustments only to a known end, see no reason why an ultimate end must be static, and fail to see how progress is progress if it goes nowhere.

That all human conduct is for a last end and a highest good is argued thus: There cannot be an infinite series of means and ends, since ends are known before means can be chosen toward them, but the means must be used first before the end is achieved; intention and execution being thus in inverse order, the last end is the first thing desired and the last attained; if there is no last end, nothing is desired and no activity can be started.

The relative is intelligible only if there is some absolute to which all relatives are relative. Even an absolutely last end is relative to us but not relative to any further end. If everything is judged on its consequences, and these on their consequences, and so on, there is really no criterion of consequences or of anything.

Consequences, when we are dealing with acts indifferent in themselves, provide a *secondary criterion of morality,* for such acts become good or bad because of their consequences.

Questions for Discussion

1. You have, from time to time, met a person who resists committing himself or herself decisively to a date for dinner or a show on a definite night one week hence. When pressed, Mr. or Ms. Indecisive will admit that he or she will surely keep the date unless something more promising comes along. While this attitude of "keeping all options open" can play havoc with a friendship or love relationship, is it not a species of opportunism? Does that make it immoral? Why?

2. According to Dewey, the personal self devel-

ops through an interest in and pursuit of values shared by the community so that the enrichment of the person goes hand in hand with the enrichment of the community. Our community is a pluralistic society in which we find a number of shared values and desires. Make as complete a list of those shared values and desires as possible, and then show how each contributes to the enrichment of the individual as well as the community. How would Dewey handle values and desires not universally shared? Why?

3. Recently Robert Jay Lifton published *The Nazi Doctors: Medical Killing and the Psychology of Genocide,* and in an interview he admitted that he ran a risk in doing such a study, the risk of replacing condemnation with insight. In the course of researching his book, Lifton interviewed 28 former Nazi doctors, including 5 who had worked in the death camps; he further interviewed some 80 survivors of Auschwitz, including a number who had worked as prisoner-doctors together with the German medical staff. One of the survivors asked Lifton what kind of people he found the Nazi doctors to be. Lifton responded that they were neither brilliant nor stupid, neither inherently evil nor very insensitive ethically, certainly not the demonic figures people have thought them to be. The survivor replied that it is *demonic* that they were *not* demonic. How would Dewey analyze the consequences of the doctors' acts, the final remark of the survivor, and Lifton's project?

4. The constant quest for well-being and happiness can generate in us a feeling of excitement and a sense of adventure. We can set goals for ourselves and take the means to achieve those goals, and yet we are never completely satisfied. Experience, as Dewey has stated, shows us to be involved in a continuity of means-ends. The rational argument given in this chapter against the continuity of means-ends really flies in the face of human experience, does it not? Why?

5. A story is told about Gertrude Stein. Once she was asked what she would do if, by pulling a switch, she killed her brother but simultaneously saved the lives of 500 Chinese. She was so upset by the question that she went to bed for a week! What would you do? What do you think Dewey would do? Why?

Readings

Plato in the *Protagoras* and the *Theaetetus* discusses the relativity of knowledge without limiting it to ethical knowledge.

St. Thomas's arguments on man's last end are in the *Summa Theologica,* I–II, q. 1, aa. 1–2, 4–7; and *Summa Contra Gentiles,* bk. III, ch. 2–3.

William James argues against absolutes in his *Pragmatism.* For John Dewey's thought see *Human Nature and Conduct, The Quest for Certainty,* and *Reconstruction in Philosophy.* See also James Gouinlock (ed.), *The Moral Writings of John Dewey: A Selection.* Eliseo Vivas, *The Moral Life and the Ethical Life,* ch. 6–8, is strongly critical of Dewey. For a sympathetic treatment of John Dewey's thought, see Robert J. Roth, S. J., *John Dewey and Self-Realization,* ch. 1.

Edward Westermarck's two books, *The Origin and Development of the Moral Ideas* and *Ethical Relativity,* are classical statements of relativism. See also Moritz Schlick, *Problems of Ethics,* ch. 5; two articles from the *Journal of Philosophy:* Paul Taylor, "Social Science and Ethical Relativism," LV, 1 (1958); and Carl Wellman, "The Ethical Implications of Cultural Relativity," LX, 7 (1963).

9
Intuition

PROBLEM

All the ethical theories discussed so far imply some norm or standard of morality. They not only proclaim the fact that morality exists but also that there is some way of distinguishing the good from the evil, the right from the wrong. Ethical theories do not differ greatly in the actual codes of morality they adopt. The list of approved and disapproved acts, despite some glaring exceptions, is in general much the same. Where they differ most is in their reasons for the approval or disapproval, in the principles on which they base their judgment about morality, that is to say, in the norm or standard by which they judge morality.

This agreement about the facts and disagreement about the reasons is explained, say some moralists, by the hypothesis that we just know directly what is right and what is wrong. They think that we have a feel, a sense, an instinct, whatever one wants to call it, that immediately manifests to us what is good and what is evil in the moral sphere, and this is basically the same in all of us. It is when we come to explanations, to study, reasoning, and proof, that we begin to diverge in our views because we now are committing ourselves to some particular ethical theory.

The view that moral knowledge is direct, immediate, or intuitive, though out of favor with philosophers today, has always had a popular appeal. It gives one a sense of infallibility without having to give any reasons, for all moral problems are solved by placing them before the scrutiny of the internal moral faculty, which then delivers its oracular verdict. That this would be an easy solution to our moral difficulties is hardly an argument against it, and we cannot afford to pass it by unexamined. The following questions will guide us in our discussion:

1. What is meant by a norm or standard of morality?
2. What are the reasons for and against a special moral faculty?
3. Is there intuition without a special faculty?
4. How is our first moral knowledge obtained?
5. How much truth, if any, is there in intuitionism?

MEANING OF A NORM

A norm is a rule, standard, or measure; it is something fixed with which we can compare something else whose nature, size, or qualities we doubt. Thus a norm of *morality* will be a rule, standard, or measure by which we can gauge the morality of an act, its goodness or badness. It will be something with which an act must positively agree to be morally good, with which it must positively disagree to be morally bad, and toward which it must be neutral to be morally indifferent.

A norm may be proximate or ultimate. To find out whether a space is a yard long, we apply a yardstick to it. But how do the makers of yardsticks determine what a true yard is? They measure their yardsticks by some officially recognized yard beyond which there is no appeal, such as the metal yard bar kept in London or a definite mathematical fraction of the metal meter bar kept in Paris. In general, a *proximate* or *derived* norm is one directly applicable to the thing to be measured and is here at hand ready for use; an *ultimate* or *original* norm is the last reason why the proximate norm is what it is. Theoretically, the same thing can fulfill the functions of both ultimate and proximate norms. It is possible to carry a thing to London or Paris and measure it by the metal bar there, but in practice this is inconvenient, and it is usual to have two concrete embodiments of the same abstract measure, one for practical use and one for ultimate reference.

That there must be some norm of morality is evident, if one admits the existence of morality at all. It would be nonsensical to suppose that one is expected to do the good and avoid the evil while being unable to distinguish one class of acts from the other. There must be a proximate norm, for otherwise the measure would be useless, inapplicable to individual concrete acts, which are the only kind that can actually exist. There must be an ultimate norm, for otherwise there would be nothing to guarantee the validity of the proximate norm.

THE MORAL SENSE THEORY

That the perception of moral good and evil is the work of some faculty distinct from the intellect or reason was held by a group of British moralists in the late seventeenth and throughout the eighteenth century. This special faculty they called the *moral instinct* or *moral intuition* or *moral sense*.

1. Shaftesbury,[1] who was much taken up with speculations on the beautiful, recognized that besides its other forms there is also moral beauty, that a moral life is really a beautiful life. The sense of beauty he considered a special faculty of the mind, and when applied to moral beauty it becomes the moral sense. Moral beauty consists of a proper balancing of public and private affections, of selfish and social impulses, resulting in a well-rounded and harmonious life. This theory is called *moral aestheticism*.

2. Francis Hutcheson[2] developed Shaftesbury's views by separating the moral sense from the aesthetic sense, giving to the former the specific function of distinguishing right from wrong. Joseph Butler[3] took the rather obvious step of identifying the moral sense with conscience, which he seems to consider a faculty distinct from the intellect. Thomas Reid, representative of the Scottish School of Common Sense philosophy, sums up the *moral sense theory* as follows:

> The abstract notion of moral good and ill would be of no use to direct our life, if we had not the power of applying it to particular actions, and determining what is morally good, and what is morally ill.
>
> Some philosophers, with whom I agree, ascribe this to an original power or faculty in man, which they call the *Moral Sense*, the *Moral Faculty, Conscience* . . . .
>
> In its dignity it is, without doubt, far superior to every other power of the mind; but there is this analogy between it and the external senses, that, as

by them we have not only the original conceptions of the various qualities of bodies, but the original judgment that this body has such a quality, that such another; so by our moral faculty, we have both the original conceptions of right and wrong in conduct, of merit and demerit, and the original judgments that this conduct is right, that is wrong; that this character has worth, that demerit.[4]

3. Adam Smith, the economist, approaches ethics from the standpoint of psychological analysis. The moral faculty or conscience is an instinctive sentiment of sympathy, which he explains in a novel way:

> We either approve or disapprove of our own conduct, according as we feel that, when we place ourselves in the situation of another man, and view it, as it were, with his eyes, and from his station, we either can or cannot enter into and sympathize with the sentiments and motives which influence it . . . .
>
> When I endeavor to examine my own conduct, when I endeavor to pass sentence upon it, and either to approve or condemn it, it is evident that, in all such cases, I divide myself, as it were, into two persons; and that I, the examiner and judge, represent a different character from that other I, the person whose conduct is examined into and judged of.[5]

These theories all demand some faculty distinct from the intellect to judge of right and wrong, either making this its sole function or identifying it with the aesthetic sense or with conscience or with the sentiment of sympathy. David Hume,[6] though not interested in any special faculty, agrees with Smith in reducing morality to feeling, especially to the sentiment of humanity, benevolence, or sympathy, and insists that moral distinctions are not derived from reason. The moral intuitionism of Ralph Cudworth[7] and Samuel Clarke[8] belongs in the same class of opinions, for though they make the intellect the faculty of

---

[1] Shaftesbury (Anthony Ashley Cooper, third Earl of Shaftesbury), *Characteristics of Men, Manners, Opinions, and Times,* bk. I, pt. II, §3; bk. II, pt. I, §1.

[2] Hutcheson, *Inquiry into the Original of Our Ideas of Beauty and Virtue,* Treatise II, sec. I.

[3] Butler, *Fifteen Sermons upon Human Nature,* Sermons II and III.

[4] Reid, *Essays on the Active Powers of Man,* Essay III, pt. III, ch. 6.

[5] Smith, *Theory of Moral Sentiments,* pt. III, ch. 1.

[6] Hume, *Treatise on Human Nature,* bk. III; also *Inquiry Concerning the Principles of Morals.*

[7] Cudworth, *Treatise Concerning Eternal and Immutable Morality,* bk. IV, ch. 6.

[8] Clarke, *Discourse upon Natural Religion,* I.

judging right from wrong, they have it do so, not by any process of reasoning, but by an immediate intellectual intuition of the eternal fitness of things, which is an expression of the Divine Ideas.

Critics of these views reject any need for a special moral faculty distinct from the intellect. Moral judgments are not of an essentially different nature from other judgments. To understand is the function of the intellect. Any faculty other than the intellect would not understand why certain actions are good or bad. To make any such other faculty the norm would lower moral life to the instinctive and brutish. Why should we expect humans to use their reason in the fields of science, business, law, and politics but not in the realm of morals and on the goal of life itself? In particular:

1. To identify the moral sense with the aesthetic sense solves no problem, for we need no special faculty for the perception of the beautiful. It is true that there is moral beauty, that virtue is beautiful and vice is ugly, but this judgment comes from intellectual reflection and not from immediate perception. It is not always their goodness that attracts us to good people, and we often have a sneaking admiration for splendid vices.

2. Conscience is the norm of subjective, not of objective, morality. It is not a special faculty but only the name for the intellect in its judgment of the morality of a particular concrete act here and now. The judgment of conscience is the conclusion of a process of intellectual reasoning. Conscience criticizes our actions according to the norms we have but does not set up those norms.

3. Sentiments, even the noblest, such as sympathy, cannot by themselves alone be a reliable guide to right and wrong. They are constantly varying, depending on our physical condition and emotional mood. The same act would be good or bad, according to one's feelings. Even if acts be classified by the feelings they commonly evoke rather than by the passing feeling of the moment, some objective reason must be assigned why they commonly evoke such feelings, and this objective reason will be the norm.

INTUITIONISM IN GENERAL

The postulating of a special faculty for the perception of right and wrong has now become almost obsolete together with the general trend away from faculty psychology. It is still quite possible, however, to hold for some direct, immediate, intuitive knowledge of morality without attributing such knowledge to any special faculty. The following are some general reasons for moral intuitionism.

1. Any well-meaning person seems to have an immediate sense of what is right and what is wrong. Many who have had hardly any opportunity for moral instruction do nevertheless have a basic moral awareness. The great value of moral instruction is to settle doubtful details, to supply one with cogent reasons, and to bring consistency into one's moral convictions, but all this is not necessary for the first formation of those convictions.

2. People had moral ideas and convictions long before philosophers developed a formal study of ethics. This prephilosophical knowledge of right and wrong was not reasoned out and logically criticized. It was therefore a spontaneous knowledge occurring to the mind without consciously directed reasoning, and hence it must come from some intuitive or insightful activity of the mind in recognizing the right and the wrong and discriminating between them.

3. Our reasoning on moral matters, when we do use it, is subsequent and confirmatory to an initial direct perception of rightness and wrongness. We first see that the course of action is right or wrong, as the case may be, and then look for reasons. If our reasoning leads to an answer contradictory to our spontaneous moral judgment, we tend to let the reasoning go and stick to our simple moral intuition, which we consider a surer guide than our elaborate arguments, whose very elaborateness can arouse a suspicion of rationalization.

4. Our reasoning can go wrong on moral matters as easily as on other matters. Though invincible ignorance excuses, we cannot allow it to govern so large a share of our lives that our moral

responsibility is on the verge of vanishing. We must have some way of deciding basic moral issues. That we cannot do so by reasoning, studying, and philosophizing is evident from the many contradictory schools of ethical thought. Therefore we have to rely on some kind of moral instinct, insight, or intuition, which can act as a sure guide.

On the other hand there are serious difficulties against any form of intuitionism:

1. The word *intuition* has fallen on bad days and stirs up so much misunderstanding that it can hardly be used. Intuition is Latin for insight, a looking in, and therefore a very appropriate word for the direct activity of the intellect in grasping self-evident truths. But it has become associated with hunches, wild guesses, irrational inspirations, clairvoyance, and other fancies so lacking in scientific respectability as to give utterly the wrong impression. It should be clear that guesses and hunches are of no more value in the ethical sphere than in any other sphere.

2. We have no inborn set of moral rules with which we might compare our acts to see whether they are moral or not. There is no evidence for the existence of any innate ideas in the human mind, including ethical ideas. All our knowledge comes from experience, and our moral ideas are likewise derived from experience. We do not have any faculty, not even conscience, that automatically flashes a warning signal as soon as we think of doing something wrong. If conscience seems to act in this way, it is nothing but habit, by which we have become accustomed through training to avoid actions of a certain kind and to judge them to be wrong. Such habitual action is quite different from instinctive action, and such judgments need not be intuitive.

3. An appeal to intuition has the disadvantage of being immune to objective criticism. One claims to see it, and no one can prove that he or she does not; another claims not to see it, and no one can prove that he or she does. The two claims are not contradictory, for each reports only his or her own experience. Such intuitive

knowledge, if it exists, can be of benefit only to the possessor and cannot be used to convince anyone else. Unless most people testify to having the same intuition (as does happen, for example, regarding sense experience), this sort of private knowledge lacks the universal character of scientific knowledge. Since there is no common agreement on moral intuitions, an appeal to intuition in morals can result only in subjectivism, each one following a personal moral code privately discovered by personal insights.

4. Those who find that they do not experience moral intuitions are either left without any ethics while obliged to live ethically or are obliged to develop an ethical theory on other grounds. They have to judge both their own ethical theory and the intuitionist theory on some basis other than intuition, which by hypothesis they themselves do not possess. The intuitionists, however, must either appeal to intuition to establish the truth of their own theory, thus convincing only themselves, or they must abandon intuition and resort to rational argument when it comes to establishing their theory. Either way shows the weakness of the method.

Despite these and similar criticisms of an intuitionist ethics, we can still ask whether it is possible to remove all intuition from ethics. Certainly we shall remove intuition in the sense of hunches and guesses, in the sense of a special faculty for the perception of morals, and in the sense of a direct apprehension of moral rules immediately applicable to particular actions. These illegitimate uses of intuition have tended to ruin the whole concept.

However, there remains a legitimate use. Not all knowledge can be derived from previous knowledge. There must be some original knowledge, some primitive experience, some immediate apprehension from which derived knowledge can originate. Thus not all knowledge can be the result of a reasoning process. Premises are proved by previous premises and these by others still more previous, but the process cannot go on forever or nothing will ever be proved.

Somewhere one must come to direct experience (and this is intuition in the original meaning of the term) or to some principle that cannot be proved and needs no proof because it is self-evident.[1]

In ethics there are two particular areas in which we must appeal to such direct and underived knowledge: one is the kind of knowledge of morals people had before developing a scientific ethics, and the other is the first or basic moral principle on which scientific ethics rests. In other words, the development of ethics in history must have been preceded by an era in which people had ethical ideas that were not the result of reasoned proof, and even after they developed a scientific ethics they still had to trace it back logically to some immediately known and underived principles. The first of these principles is called connatural knowledge, our next topic.

CONNATURAL KNOWLEDGE

A person need not have studied ethics to know right from wrong. Humans are valuing beings as spontaneously and naturally as they are breathing beings; even among the most primitive cultures that we can find, humans are ever and always value-seeking and value-driven beings. The moral dimensions of a person's life have a thoroughly natural basis not reducible either to infantile origins or social custom. Ethics makes a formal and sophisticated investigation into the moral notions we already have, confirming or correcting our more primitive knowledge. How did we obtain this primitive knowledge, and how accurate is it? A child of today will receive it from his or her parents, teachers, and companions, and from religious instruction, social custom, and civil law. But how did they get it? Furthermore, the child turned youth will begin to criticize what has been told him or her, thus showing some source of knowledge besides tradition.

---

[1] See Aristotle, *Posterior Analytics,* bk. II, ch. 19; *Metaphysics,* bk. IV, ch. 4.

This primitive way of knowing is called *knowledge through connaturality, through union, through inclination* or *through congeniality.* Such knowledge is not innate as the term *connatural* might suggest; it is called *connatural* because we are the kind of beings who easily pick up such knowledge just by the experience of living. It is sometimes called knowledge *through union* in the sense that we have a knowledge of what bravery means if we already are brave, or we know what loving means simply because we love someone; this kind of knowing is a result of our already embodying in ourselves bravery or love. We live in accordance with the bravery or the love and so know through our being united with the bravery or the love. When it is called knowledge *by inclination* or *congeniality,* it is knowledge that is arrived at by simply looking at and observing the kind of being we are with such and such inner bents or propensities. This knowledge is a self-awareness that reveals our own natures to ourselves; it is a direct and immediate perception of the powers we possess, of their clamor for exercise, and of the appropriate objects on which they are to be exercised. We do not have to reason the matter out to know what our eyes and hands and legs are for, what our minds and wills are for, what our emotions and moods are for. We use them without question, knowing without argument that it is right to use them. Human beings sought food before they studied the science of nutrition, reproduced without benefit of genetics, trained their children before child psychology, formed families and cities without sociology, spoke without linguistics, claimed their due without law courts, and lived moral lives without a formal study of ethics.

This knowledge is an act not of intellect alone but of the intellect plus the affections and natural inclinations, the emotions and the dispositions of the will, and the intellect is *guided and directed by* them to an immediate and direct awareness of value. It is nonlogical, nondiscursive knowledge, nonconceptual in its lack of clearly defined concepts, rational in the sense that it is consciously known, and nonrational in the sense that it is not argumentative or demonstrative or scientific. In it the head consults the heart, is directed and guided by the heart to a preconceptual grasp of particular singular values.

It is through connaturality that moral consciousness attains a kind of knowing—inexpressible in words and notions—of the deepest dispositions—longings, fears, hopes or despairs, primeval loves and options—involved in the night of the subjectivity. When a man makes a free decision, he takes into account not only all that he possesses of moral science and factual information, and which is manifested to him in concepts and notions, but also all the secret elements of evaluation which depend on what he is, and which are known to him through inclination, through his own actual propensities and his own virtues, if he has any.[1]

We began our study of ethics with the recognition of a fact, that people do have an awareness of right and wrong, that they do make moral judgments. Our study would be incomplete if we made no effort to isolate the kind of knowledge that accounts for this fact. We should not be disturbed at being unable to describe it more clearly, for it is the nature of prescientific knowledge to be obscure, unformulated, and unreflective. When we reflect on it, conceptualize it, define its terms, catalogue its contents, pose its problems, and prove its theorems, it ceases to be connatural knowledge and becomes moral philosophy or ethics. Connatural knowledge is not immune from error and needs the criticism, correction, and development ethics can give it. In practical living the two continue side by side, for a reflective study does not eliminate the very thing it is studying.

Is this connatural knowledge intuitive? Since it is nonlogical, nondiscursive, nonargumentative, it can be called intuitive in the best sense of that misused term, in the sense of a directly perceptive and insightful experience. Notice that it makes no claim to infallibility, that it offers itself for critical examination, that it is quite willing to step down and yield to rationally investi-

[1] Maritain, *The Range of Reason,* ch. 3, p. 26.

gated knowledge. Yet it is through this connatural knowledge that people first recognize moral value and form their moral ideal, that they have their first glimmering of moral obligation and their first thoughts of law, that they begin organizing their lives purposively for the attainment of a meaningful end.

THE FIRST MORAL PRINCIPLE

The second area in ethics in which a direct insightful or intuitive knowledge is unavoidable is that of first principles, from which all other moral principles and directing norms are logically derived. Even a philosophically developed and fully sophisticated theory of morals will have to rest on some basic bedrock that accounts for itself and requires no further support beneath it. Ethics is not the kind of subject that can be based on a postulational system, logically drawing consistent conclusions from unverified assumptions, so that the whole theory achieves only a hypothetical truth. Ethics deals with real life, with the way we must regulate our conduct in the actual world of experience, and since we cannot go through the experience of life again, failure in the enterprise is irremediable disaster. Hence we must have some way of knowing with certainty the basic principles from which all the rest of our ethical knowledge is derived.

By reflecting on our connatural knowledge of moral values, our moral ideal, and our awareness of moral obligation (the moral *ought*), we come to understand that the basic principle of the moral life and the presupposition of all moral living is "Do good and avoid evil." The principle enunciates that good is what *ought* to be done, while evil is what *ought* not to be done. How does the *ought,* the moral obligation or moral necessity, come to be expressed in the principle itself? We have already seen that, in the moral sphere, our connatural knowledge is a primitive awareness of moral value. Our primitive awareness of moral obligation, of the moral *ought,* is found on reflection to be based on this connatural awareness of moral value. To say, for example, "This particular good action *ought* to be done," is already to have comprehended a *relation* between the value in the intention of the particular action to be performed and the actual action eventually performed. The moral *ought* is not itself the relation between the moral value and the action eventually to bear that moral value, but the *ought* is always essentially based on such a relation. The *ought* is related immediately to the sphere of real existence and is experienced by us as a "being obliged" to do something morally valuable that has not yet been done, to do away with a moral disvalue, or to avoid doing moral evil.

One of the continually controverted ethical questions since the time of David Hume is whether the moral *ought* can be derived simply from our knowledge of facts, of what *is.* If it can, then it could be said that ethics needs no self-evident principles, since its basic principle can be derived from other sciences, and ultimately from metaphysics, which is preeminently the science of being as being, of the *is.* Since Hume[1] emphatically stated the impossibility of deriving the *ought* from the *is,* mainly on the obvious ground that you cannot get an *ought* in the conclusion of a syllogism when there was none in its premises, many have considered the question settled. Some analysts, however, have resurrected the problem and find it a stimulating linguistic exercise.[2]

Hume and Thomas Aquinas have little in common in their general philosophical outlook; yet they seem to agree, though for different reasons, on the underivability of the *ought* from the *is.* On first principles St. Thomas says:

> That which falls first under apprehension is *being,* the understanding of which is included in all things whatsoever a man apprehends. Therefore the first indemonstrable principle is that *the same thing cannot be affirmed and denied at the same time,* which is based on the notion of *being* and *not-being:* and on this principle all others are based, as is stated in

Metaphysics iv.[3] Now as *being* is the first thing that falls under the apprehension absolutely, so *good* is the first thing that falls under the apprehension of the practical reason, which is directed to action (since every agent acts for an end, which has the nature of good). Consequently, the first principle in the practical reason is one founded on the nature of good, namely, that *good is that which all things seek after.* Hence this is the first precept of law, that *good is to be done and promoted, and evil is to be avoided.* All other precepts of the natural law are based upon this; so that all the things which the practical reason naturally apprehends as man's good belong to the natural law under the form of things to be done or avoided.[4]

It is clear that St. Thomas is speaking in terms of natural law, a subject we are not yet ready to discuss, but what he says about the first principle of morals can be understood independently of the conclusions that can be drawn from it and whether they assume the form of law or not. Before any law is possible there is logically presupposed such a thing as obligation, by which the subjects of the law are morally enjoined to keep it, and an infinite series of laws and obligations would solve nothing. Thus the first principle of the moral life, which can be stated in various ways: "Do good and avoid evil," "Lead a life of virtue," "Be the kind of person you ought to be," "To yourself be true," is not so much a precept of the natural law as a first principle and presupposition of all moral living. One may ask intelligently, "Why should I be moral?" but not, "Should I be moral?" just as in metaphysics one may ask, "What am I?" but there is no point in arguing the question, "Am I?"

To conclude this discussion, we may note that we have the following options:

1. We may admit moral intuition, with or without a special faculty for it, to which we can appeal for obtaining immediate insight into the moral quality of each particular act. There is no objective evidence for any such intuition.

2. We may deny moral intuition altogether. In this way we get rid of unverifiable subjective claims

---

[1] Hume, *Treatise of Human Nature,* bk. III, pt. I, section 1, end.

[2] See for example Searle, John R., "How to Derive 'Ought' from 'Is,'" *Philosophical Review* vol. 73, 1964, pp. 43–58. The author argues ingeniously from the *fact* of making a promise to the *obligation* of keeping it, but one may ask whether the *ought* is not already surreptitiously contained in the meaning of the word *promise.*

[3] Aristotle, *Metaphysics,* bk. IV, ch. 3, 1005b 29.

[4] St. Thomas, *Summa Theologica,* I–II, q. 94, a. 2.

but are unable to explain the historically primitive and logically underived knowledge from which our moral reasoning can proceed.

3. We may reduce moral intuition to its narrowest scope, admitting it only where we cannot do without it. Intuition is thus confined to the intellect's grasp of self-evident truths and first indemonstrable principles under the guidance of the affective side of our consciousness, namely, the affections and appetites, the emotions and the dispositions of the will.

The first two alternatives beget such unresolvable difficulties that any other alternative is preferable. The third option remains as the only tenable one. It does not give us a whole philosophy of intuitive ethics any more than a list of axioms gives us a geometry or stargazing gives us an astronomy. It only supplies us with the beginnings from which a science of ethics must be developed by further exercise of our intelligence.

SUMMARY

A *norm of morality* is a standard to which we can compare human acts to determine their goodness or badness. A *proximate* norm is immediately applicable to the acts; an *ultimate* norm guarantees the validity of the proximate norm. There must be a norm of morality, or one would be obliged to do good and avoid evil without being able to distinguish them.

The *moral sense theory* appeals to a faculty distinct from the intellect for judging right from wrong. Most ethicians see no need for such a faculty; it would make moral conduct nonrational and unworthy of an intelligent human being.

Intuitionism in general holds that humans have direct, immediate, or intuitive knowledge of morality, with or without a special faculty.

Reasons *for:* People can tell right from wrong without giving reasons, know right and wrong without studying ethics, use reasoning to confirm their spontaneous judgments, and reject arguments that contradict their basic moral convictions.

Reasons *against:* Intuition is too vague a word to be of much use, we have no innate moral ideas or principles, intuition would be a purely subjective experience and scientifically useless, and the intuitionist can convince no one but himself or herself.

There is a legitimate use for *intuition* in the sense of an intellectual acceptance of self-evident truths.

Connatural knowledge is the name for prescientific knowledge that is neither innate nor instinctive but comes from the use of intellect under the direction and guidance of emotion and our natural inclinations. It is knowledge in the intellect, but it is unformulated, unreflective, nonconceptual, and nondiscursive, because it has not been clearly defined and argued out. Ethics is the endeavor to formulate, criticize, correct, develop, and prove these primitive moral judgments.

If the first moral principle, such as "Do good and avoid evil," is not intuitively known, it must be derived from some other knowledge. It is debated whether the *ought* can be derived syllogistically from the *is,* but so far no one seems to have done it convincingly. Thus for all practical purposes we must take the first moral principle as intuitively known and self-evident.

Questions for Discussion

1. Intuitionism maintains that we have direct insight into the rightness or wrongness of actions. Such knowledge is gained by simply "looking at" the actions themselves without considering their consequences. No reasoning process is required. Everyone simply sees quite clearly that murder, kidnapping, rape, forced sodomy, arson, and pollution of the environment are utterly wrong. If intuition is the ultimate source of our moral knowledge, then how can we account for the fact that apart from the actions just mentioned we do find

people disagreeing about the rightness or wrongness of other acts such as direct euthanasia, abortion, and capital punishment? If intuition is always correct, it deserves to be the ultimate foundation of morality; if it is sometimes wrong, then it is worthless and belongs on the scrapheap of failed moral theories. What do you think? Why?

2. We have argued in this chapter that "Do good; avoid evil" is not so much a precept of the moral law as it is a first principle and presupposition of all moral living. But is this principle not based on the human community's shared desire to live as a group and to continue to live as a group, the shared desire being ultimately based on the realization that one cannot survive alone? If your answer is "yes," then how would you describe the first principle of moral living? If, on the other hand, your answer is "no," how can you account for the shared desire and the realization on which it is based?

3. Poll your classmates to see which acts are universally agreed to be always and everywhere right and which wrong from among the following: murder, arson, kidnapping, abortion, capital punishment, keeping your promises, lying, cheating, and homosexual acts. Concerning the acts on which you are in agreement, do you also agree on the reasons why those acts are right or wrong? Concerning the acts on which you are in disagreement, can you account for the disagreement? How? Has intuition played a part in any of this? What part and why?

4. Intuition has been described as a very dangerous business when it is called on to be the foundation of certain general rules for moral living, rules on which no compromise is possible because they are morality itself: return what you borrow, keep your promises, pay the debts you owe, tell the truth, and do not cheat. This list of rules is not meant to be exhaustive, merely illustrative, and we know intuitively that these examples are moral, do we not? Nevertheless, any one of these rules must be set aside when following it would lead to disaster either to oneself or to the group; for example, following the rule of returning another's property could lead to disaster if you return a machine gun to a mad killer just because it happens to be his. Does this mean that intuition is useless? Would you not agree that adherence to the rules even if it would cause death and destruction would be immoral? Why?

5. Is it possible to argue from a set of known facts to the existence of moral obligation, i.e., from "is" to "ought?" Can "ought" legitimately appear in the conclusion of an argument if it is not somehow included in the premises? If "ought" must already be in the premises, how do you arrive at the primitive or ultimate "ought" on which all other "oughts" logically depend? Take some of the moral rules mentioned in question #4, express them as "ought" statements, and construct arguments that justify the rules. Do you find that you have to fall back to some extent on intuition? Explain.

Readings

The eighteenth-century British moralists and their main works are mentioned in the footnotes to the text. Selections can be found in convenient form in L.A. Selby-Bigge, *The British Moralists;* D.D. Raphael, *British Moralists;* Benjamin Rand, *The Classical Moralists;* and other collections.

Evaluation of Spinoza, Butler, Hume, Kant, and Sidgwick, all of whom contain some intuitionism, is found in C.D. Broad's *Five Types of Ethical Theory.*

W.D. Ross, *The Right and the Good* and *Foundations of Ethics;* A.C. Ewing, *Ethics,* ch. 1 and 7; and H.A. Prichard, *Moral Obligation,* advocate a limited intuitionism.

W.D. Hudson, *The Is/Ought Question,* has a whole book of modern articles on both sides of this vexed problem. See also his *Ethical Intuitionism,* which concludes with a critique of intuitionism.

On connatural knowledge read St. Thomas, *Summa Theologica,* I–II, q. 94, a. 2; II–II, q. 45, a. 2. Also read Jacques Maritain's explanation of it in *The Range of Reason,* ch. 3. Max Scheler's discussion of value-cognition or value-intuition in his *Formalism in Ethics and Non-Formal Ethics of Values,* pp. 30–44 and 68–69, may provide a way of corroborating the discussions of Aquinas and Maritain.

10
Reason

PROBLEM

Our discussion of connatural knowledge shows our most basic knowledge of good and evil to be a nonconceptual awareness that is neither innate nor instinctive but a kind of knowledge we develop by letting our intellects be directed and guided by our emotions and natural inclinations. By connatural knowledge, we acquire our primitive knowledge of value and disvalue, of good and evil. We find ourselves making moral value judgments, discriminating between moral good and evil. This is the basic moral fact.

Now we want to move beyond this basic moral fact to ask ourselves whether there is an objective norm or standard we can use to provide us with objective reasons why our moral judgments are justified or not. We already know that we have no special moral sense or instinct that immediately points out to us what is right and wrong. We know too that moral judgment in the full sense of the word is an intellectual act that preserves and at the same time goes beyond the content of sensory and emotional awareness. If no one of our ways of knowing is sufficient in and of itself to render a reliable judgment about what is right and wrong in the moral sphere, what can we use as a norm of morality? Even though the first moral principle, "Do good and avoid evil," immediately apprehended by intellect under the direction and guidance of natural inclination and emotion, is the bedrock of all thinking about morals, it cannot be a norm for it gives no further indication of exactly what good is to be done and what evil is to be avoided.

One source still left to us is the proper use of our intellectual capacity operating in harmony with our external and internal senses and with our emotions and natural inclinations. This looks promising as long as intellectual reasoning does not tyrannize our emotions and as long as emotion is illumined by intellectual reasoning. Throughout this chapter we use the term *reason* in a wider sense than intellect alone. Why? If reason is what distinguishes human beings from all the rest of organic life on earth, then it is the characteristic of personal life that gives rise not only to science but to art and religion as well. All three—science, art, and religion—are persistent cultural expressions of human nature at its best. This means that whatever is a characteristic and essential expression of human nature must be an expression of reason. A conception of reason that is applicable to science but not to art and religion as well is at least inadequate and at worst false. The obvious difference between science on the one hand and art and religion on the other is that science is primarily intellectual while art and religion are more emotional than intellectual. Human reason, we conclude, must have an emotional as well as an intellectual expression. Intellectual reasoning is obviously not our only rational capacity that is characteristically human and personal.

In the wide sense of the word, reason means human consciousness including all its ways of operating. Basically, reason is our capacity to behave consciously in terms of the nature of what is not ourselves, to behave in terms of the nature of objects and persons in the world. Just as we desire to know the truth and know that this means we must subordinate our wishes and desires to the nature of the world, so we know that morality demands that we should act in terms of things and people as they really are and not simply in terms of our subjective desires, inclinations, and private sympathies. The difficulty of morality is that of overcoming our own subjective bias in favor of ourselves and those we love, asking special consideration for them and us. We should not be surprised to find that moral knowledge develops into an intellectual awareness only under the direction and guidance of our natural inclinations and conscious emotions; neither should we be surprised that the truth of our moral knowledge is established in the same way as all other truth. If we have been using the judgment of reason (in its wider sense) all along in our evaluation of various ethical theories, that same capacity of reason can judge the moral value of the actions the theories are constructed to explain.

That the good life is the life of reason was a commonplace among the Greek philosophers.

What this meant varied from philosopher to philosopher, depending on how the relation between intellect and emotion was viewed. For Plato, the philosopher is a person in whom the rational is predominant, but this rationality includes a passionate love for the highest good because that good is beauty itself. The kind of rational thinking sponsored by Plato and Socrates includes the worth and meaning of a person's desire to live a better life, so that the truly profound thinker must be a lover of truth, goodness, and beauty. For Aristotle, the intellectual virtue of practical wisdom or prudence, under the impulse of a desire for the good, seeks the midpoint between excess and defect in appetite and emotion and thus acts as the norm regulating the practice of the other virtues of which the moral life consists. The Stoics call reason the *hegemonikon,* the ruling power, by which one conforms to the law of nature, frees oneself from being the plaything of one's emotions, and lives the life of a wise person. The Stoic tradition insists on the opposition of intellect to emotion; its ideal makes intellect dominant and emotion subservient or even the source of all evil, while it glorifies the life of sheer intellect and will with an emphasis on law and principle, plan and policy. In succeeding ages, reason in the sense of intellect has played an honored part in nearly all ethical theories while emotion is held in a subordinate position. We cannot afford to ignore the importance of emotion, however, for it is the creative force in human experience, providing the impetus that motivates us to further growth and development.

The problem arises from the fact that human reason, in its wider sense, though a trustworthy instrument in itself, is not immune from abuse. The philosopher has the task, not only of determining as exactly as possible the critical sensitivity of this instrument, but also of learning how to use it so that it actually does yield the desired results. When and how can reason go wrong and if it does, what is the corrective? We have the following questions to guide us:

1. When is human reason right?

2. How does right reason act as an ethical norm?
3. How is right reason applied to human nature?
4. How practical is right reason as a norm?

MEANING OF RIGHT REASON

Human reason does not function in a vacuum but needs some data to go on, some findings from which the reasoning process can take its start. It derives them from experience. Consciousness in all its ways of being aware is what we mean by experience. In the ethical field our conscious awareness, our experience, provides the material on which to work. We examine our own conduct and also observe human life around us and the actions we see others doing. Certain patterns in human behavior begin to emerge, and we group human actions into various classes according to their common traits. We ask ourselves why we group them the way we do and state our reasons in the form of principles, expressing in general terms the characteristics that acts must have to deserve inclusion in one group rather than another. We turn to an examination of the principles themselves, rejecting some as inadequate, correcting others, and accepting those that survive our scrutiny. We then attempt the task of ordering the accepted principles into a scheme or system that will give intelligibility to the whole.

The *inductive* use of intellectual reasoning is this finding of general principles in the particular human actions observed. It defines and compares concepts, and states and establishes rules, organizing both into wider and wider formulations, and more and more comprehensive generalizations, until it finally subsumes the whole under the universal embrace of the good. It sees, not only that they can be organized in this way, but also that their intelligibility demands that they be so organized, since they are logically interdependent. The *deductive* use of intellectual reasoning applies these principles to new specific acts a person is thinking of doing, pointing out why this mode of conduct is good or bad because of the relationship it has to him or her as a human being and to those among whom he or she must live. All this is an endeavor to *understand* what is good or bad about one's conduct, and why. Understanding, as we should expect, is done by the intellect.

The goal of intellect in thus trying to work out a systematization of ethics would be a luminously intelligible concatenation of moral values and principles from the most general down to the most particular, hierarchically grading the whole ethical life. Intellect, being what it is, would delight in such an arrangement, just as it delights in a mathematical problem elegantly and brilliantly solved. The prospect looks chilling. Who would want to live in such a framework of icy logic? We need have no fear. The matter is far too complex and the human being too full of surprises for us ever to work out a complete system of human living. We will never be able to give people a rule book listing the goodness or badness of every possible form of human act, so that all they need do is look it up.

Intellectual reasoning and rationality have assumed a connotation today that need not be associated with these words. Perhaps the computer world in which we are beginning to live is responsible for our thinking of reason as behaving in a cold, impersonal, unfeeling, and loveless manner. We tend to forget that intellect is not something separate from the rest of the person and functioning on its own. Rather it is an integral part of a human being and has its place within consciousness, reason in its wider sense. Thus reason includes all the feelings, emotions, and sensibilities, as well as the moods and desires, along with intellect. A person who failed to integrate feelings, emotions, and sensibilities along with the moods and desires into whatever program of life he or she is devising would be a very unreasonable person. The truly reasonable person is the total personal being, not one who lives by intellect alone.

But in our totality as personal beings, a certain preeminence is given to reason's intellectual, crit-

ical ability. The various other aspects or features of personal consciousness, important as they are, are incapable of sitting in judgment on themselves. Intellect judges not only itself but also the other constituent aspects of personal consciousness and, what is particularly important, the various relations between all these constituents. An inability to construct a completely ordered system of ethical principles expressing the full gamut of moral values is not a result of reason's intellectual incompetence or of the matter's unintelligibility but of the slow pace of our intellectual and emotional growth. Meanwhile, reason has explored and ordered a fairly large part of the field and guides us through some very difficult terrain. Thus intellectual reason functions as a norm.

But how sure a norm? How are we to know when intellect is right? Intellect has to be its own critic. To determine when intellect is right and when it is wrong, there is nothing else to appeal to but intellect itself. Only when intellect reflects on itself can knowledge be known precisely as knowledge. By use of our intellect, we discover truth and, by use of that same intellect, we are capable of error; in practical matters of moral living, we use intellect to discover the right thing to do, but that same intellect is also capable of making mistakes. What kind of mistake can intellect make? It can judge as genuinely good what is only an apparent good. How can this happen? We, as humans, are conscious personal beings with the power to know other things and persons as they really are and we also have the ability to value them at their true value.

As soon as the term *value* arises we know immediately that we are in the realm of emotion for, when we are dealing with good and evil and their significance for our lives, we know that intellect depends on emotion for the *content* of such concepts. Emotion, when it is indeed real emotion, is what enables us to grasp the worth or value of persons and things. Without emotion, nothing would be more worthwhile to us than anything else, and in that case we could not choose one thing rather than another. In matters of what is good and bad, emotion that is confirmed by intellectual reflection as real is the proper guide for intellectual reason. We have already seen this in our discussion of connatural knowledge. Real emotion directing and guiding intellect is our way of grasping the genuine value of what is other than ourselves. *The moment that emotion ceases to be directed outwards to appreciate the thing or person with which it is connected in fact it becomes unreal and intellect ceases to be right about value*. Hence, intellect is right *when it is rectified by emotions and desires that are right,* for intellect is then in touch with genuine moral value and can engage in selecting the means to adopt in making those values real in one's life. Intellect and intellectual reasoning can be right if, and only if, they are rectified by real emotion apprehending genuine moral value.

All thinking about how to act morally in any situation is hopeless in the absence of real emotion to guide us. This means that right intellectual reasoning is primarily but not exclusively an affair of emotion because if right intellectual reasoning is our capacity to act in terms of genuine moral value, it is right emotion that stands directly behind such activity determining its substance and direction. Intellect is related to action only indirectly and through emotion. Intellect determines the form of the action, but emotion determines its substance and direction.

By using our intellect we discover truth, and by using our intellect under the guidance of real emotion we discover concrete moral value. Just as we can make a mistake when we use our intellect and miss the truth, so too can we miss genuine moral value even when our intellect is under the guidance and direction of emotion. By using our will we seek the good, but by that same will we can also do evil by seeking the merely apparent good. The will seeks anything that intellect proposes to it as good, so the will needs a norm but cannot be one. Intellect also needs a norm and must be one, for it can find none but itself. This seems paradoxical.

We can resolve the paradox by distinguishing two uses of intellect: (1) intellect can be used

rationally when it is consistent with itself and faithful to its own law and function; and (2) intellect can be used *irrationally* by contradicting itself, subjecting it to a law foreign to it, and functioning to its own destruction. Intellectual reason used to plot a crime, for instance, is intellect used irrationally because only the means are rational and not the end or goal; intellect thwarts itself by its own cleverness in using its capacity to order parts into an irrational whole. When intellect is enslaved to serve irrational ends and when it is free to be fully itself, intellect alone can know.

RIGHT REASON: INTELLECT AS A NORM

Does intellectual reason in and of itself have any guidelines for determining when it is right and when it is not? Since making such a determination is part of intellect's own critical function, it will have to find the guidelines within itself. Let us see how intellect works out an ethical judgment.

1. Any moral choice is preceded by an awareness of moral values about which intellect deliberates. The deliberation itself is motivated by emotional awareness of the values and a desire for a good based on the value awareness. The intellect, under the guidance of desire for the good, weighs the reasons for and against the contemplated course of action. These reasons are expressed in or based on evaluative judgments, practical judgments that are, in conjunction with desire, directive of action. They present to the will for its acceptance the good apprehended by intellect under the direction and guidance of emotion, the arguments in its favor, the strength of the moral obligation involved, the general moral principle of which this act is an instance, and therefore the reasonableness of choosing this form of action. Such a process issues in a *dictate* of practical reasoning that takes the form: I ought (or ought not) to do this act. So the first checkup on the rightness of intellect consists of making sure that this particular action does verify in itself a moral principle and value that I already hold.

2. There is as yet no guarantee that the moral principles I hold are correct and the moral values genuine. The next point in intellect's self-examination is to see why I hold these principles and values. Except for my earliest actions, based on my parents' or others' principles and values rather than my own, my moral principles and values are habitual possessions. A habit is necessary because, when the moment of decision has arrived, it is too late to examine the quality of my moral principles and values; I must now have them ready for use. The habitual possession of rationally and correctly derived principles and values is sometimes called *right reason,* and the person who lives according to them is both upright and reasonable. Such a habit of right reasoning lies between two other habits, the habit of first moral principles and the habit or virtue of prudence, which applies principles and values to individual acts. But my moral principles are not necessarily correct nor my moral values genuine from the mere fact that I happen to hold them. A periodic checking on them is needed, especially in times of calm self-examination or when they are challenged. Since habits can be bad as well as good, wrong as well as right, they must be examined and certified before they can be cleared as the habits of *right* reasoning.

3. Habit is said to be second nature. If we want to find out whether habits are good or bad, we should compare them with the nature they are supposed to enhance. Intellectual reason, reflecting on the human nature of which it is a part, sees the congruity of some actions and the incongruity of others with that nature, pronouncing the former good and the latter bad. Conformity of action with nature is the rule all over the universe. Since a human being is a natural being within the scope of total nature, human actions are good if they conform to human nature, bad if they go counter to it. But this is only a test of ordinary natural goodness, rating a human being as an efficiently performing being of a definite type. In a determination of moral goodness, something more than mere human nature must be considered. Many actions are natural in the sense that we feel inclined to perform them; yet they are immoral because they are unfitting for a rational and free being. Thus human nature, if it is to be a norm of *morality,* is not to be taken merely as one nature among other natures, one type of being among other types, explaining how people *do* in fact behave in their own characteristically human way. No, a norm of morality must exhibit how we *ought* to behave, for morality deals with the *ought* rooted in genuine moral value. Thus the emphasis here is not on human nature *as nature,* nor even on human nature *as human* in a general way, but on human nature *as rational and free,* the attributes we share with no other nature on earth. These two connected attributes make morality possible, the first in harmony with emotion discerning the good and the second pursuing it. Nature in us does not work automatically, infallibly leading us in the right direction, but supplies us with intellect and will, with emotions and inclinations, with rationality and freedom, by which we can govern ourselves with responsibility for what we do. It is this that makes a human being a *person* and explains why only a person has morality.

4. It is characteristic of intellectual reason to select the means to achieve a desired end. Aimless or random conduct is called *irrational,* even when a human being does it. Can we then say that intellect is right when it clearly and certainly points out to us those actions that enhance personal life and those that degrade it, those that will lead us to our final goal and those that will hinder us from it, labeling the first good and the second bad? Surely intellect is right when it does this. But we continue to ask: Why should this be so? Is the act good because it leads to the end, or does it lead to the end because it is good? Is the moral good merely instrumental to some final good, or is the final good itself included within the moral good? Only the second alternative is acceptable. Intellectual reason can perceive the inner dynamism of the human being, the capacities craving fulfillment, and the suitability of certain acts and objects to contribute to the human being's fulfillment of his or her personal being. But the good as instrumental, as perfective, as completing natural tendencies, appeals only to

the nature *as nature* and does not specify the moral good as such. The end itself must be good if it is good to strive for it. Thus right intellectual reasoning judges not only the means to good living but good living itself, not only what brings about fulfillment but also why fulfillment should be good for a being and why this being deserves fulfillment.

5. We have been gradually pushing ourselves back into the realm of the self-evident. If something is good, not because it leads to something else but because it is good in itself, its goodness will shine out of itself into the eye of intellect, which must necessarily acknowledge the evident truth it beholds when it is in harmony with real emotion. Some values are seen to be nobler in intrinsic worth, more inclusive in scope, more compatible with other values, and more productive of order and harmony in us and in our relations with the universe. Intellect, reasoning under the guidance and direction of emotion, sees that such values must have a higher place in any order of things that enhances personal life and that any effort to arrange them otherwise can be done only by flying in the face of intellectual reason and willfully acting irrationally. Only if intellect were to say to itself: I see clearly that this is the higher value in the objective order of things, the order disclosed by real emotion, and this other value is subordinate to it, but I am going to overturn this order and subject the higher value to the lower—only if intellect were to act in this way could it fail to be right, for then it would no longer be rectified by real emotion. Obviously intellect cannot thus deny its own truth under its own power, but it is not the only power we have at our disposal. Intellect, to be sure, cannot only be disregarded, in which case it may be right but not used, but it can also be interfered with, can be enslaved by prejudice and degrading emotion and willfullness, can abdicate its position of illuminating and discriminating among values and principles and thus deny its own value in the scheme of things. Then intellect is not right. Nothing can correct intellect but intellect itself. Intellectual reasoning about moral matters is right when intellect is faithful to its own law. Then it

declares that whatever is inconsistent with the ideal good or would prevent its realization must be rejected as merely an apparent good, and whatever harmonizes with the ideal good and promotes its realization is a genuine good. The genuine good in the sphere of human conduct is the moral good.

Thus the norm of morality is found in right intellectual reasoning—but it must be taken in its full scope. No one of the five aspects just discussed is to be taken in isolation, but they must all be fitted together. Then we can know that intellect is right. In the deliberation preceding an act:

1. We advert to the *dictate* of the intellect reasoning about moral matters and pointing out the right path under the guidance and direction of real emotion.

2. We check this dictate against our *habitually* possessed code of moral principles and hierarchy of moral values.

3. We examine the principles and values to see that they express the logical consequence of our *nature as rational and free*.

4. We see that the act we are contemplating will bring us to the attainment of the *end* to which our inner dynamism, that is to say, our emotions and natural inclinations, motivates us.

5. We perceive the end itself as not merely a good for us but as verifying in itself the *ideal* of the moral good.

HUMAN NATURE TAKEN COMPLETELY

We determine the useful or the pleasant good by noting its suitability to some partial aspect or particular craving of our being. It may be suitable in one way and harmful in another, but we are dealing here with the moral good, the befitting good, which must be good simply and without qualification. Hence right reason, intellect rectified by real emotion, must look to the whole, to human nature taken adequately or completely.

1. *Human nature must be taken with all its parts*. These comprise its metaphysical aspects

(organic vitality and rationality), its physical components (body and psyche), and all the integral parts (bodily members and powers) that happen to be present in any individual human being. We are obliged to manage our complex nature and keep these parts working in harmony.

By nature we are animate and bodily beings. Each must take care of his or her body and minister to its needs. We must not attempt to live like angels or disembodied spirits. Our nature is such that we could not live this way and to try to do so would not befit us. Our bodily needs are so vivid and insistent that there is little danger in this direction, though at times some have tried.

By nature we are not merely animate but rational as well, and we must also live as rational beings. The life of a brute is not suitable for a being of reason in the wide sense of that word. Our rational and nonrational sides must be kept in harmony or a split develops in our nature.

2. *Human nature must be taken with all its relations.* There must be not only inner harmony between the parts and powers that make up a person but also outer harmony between the person and his or her surroundings. Humans are not solitary beings but parts of the universe; we must fit ourselves into the total scheme of the universe and occupy the place destined for us by the kind of nature we have. There are three essential relations and a number of accidental relations that may arise from circumstances or the fulfillment of certain conditions, such as marriage, parenthood, profession, employment, and the like. We need consider here only the essential relations that make up our nature:

1. A contingent, i.e., nonnecessary, being in regard to the uncaused source of all that exists
2. A social being in regard to our fellow human beings
3. A caring being in regard to the goods of the earth

Toward the source of all that exists, human nature is *contingent,* totally dependent, existentially not necessary. For those who acknowledge the existence of God as the uncaused source of all that exists here and now, the relation is one of total dependence. For those who do not acknowledge the existence of God, the relation is not explicitly acknowledged, although the contingent, nonnecessary character of human existence is known and expressed variously as radical finitude, thrownness, and so on. To claim for oneself absolute independence and/or necessary existence is to refuse to accept one's contingency and thus to go against one's rational and free nature, which is at its core finite and nonnecessary in the order of existence.

Toward beings on the same level, human nature is *social*. We are born into the society of the family and are made for companionship with our fellow humans, on whom we depend to supply our needs and develop our abilities. Hence what promotes a well-functioning social life among us is good for us; what tends to disrupt human society and to hinder this mutual helpfulness and cooperation is bad for us.

Toward nonhuman beings, human nature is *caring*. By our very nature we need to care for and use material things: food, water, air, and sunlight for the maintenance of life itself and so many other less necessary goods for the development of our abilities and the living of a decent and cultured life, to which our rational consciousness entitles us.

To sum up: That conduct is morally good that right reasoning shows to be fitting for a rational and free bodily being, with all its components, dependent for its existence here and now on the uncaused source of all existence, living with other humans, and caring for the goods and products of this earth. That conduct is morally bad that right reasoning shows to be unfitting for such a being. In any conflict between the three essential relations, the relation to the source of our existence (for theists, God) comes first, to fellow human beings second, to the goods of this world third. This hierarchy is arranged according to the intrinsic worth and excellence of these two main parts of humans and of these three orders of beings.

Humans are no exception to the general rule that every being must act according to its nature. But if we humans are no exception to the rule and we do not set up a norm of goodness for other beings, why do we do so for ourselves? Because we are rational and free, whereas other beings in this world are not. Nonfree beings must act according to their natures, and thus they necessarily fulfill their purpose in the universe. We alone, being free, can act either according to or against our nature. In all things the nature of the being is the norm of its activity. Since nonfree beings must necessarily act naturally, in them the norm is automatically applied and need not be definitely expressed. Since we ought to act naturally but can act otherwise by abusing our freedom, we need rational formulation and conscious application of the norm of morality in our conduct.

PRACTICALITY OF THE NORM

How practical is such a norm? Can we actually use it to guide our moral lives and apply it directly to definite human acts? There are the following affirmative reasons:

1. The norm must be such that from it the same rules of morality can be derived for all human beings. By its nature a standard must be applicable to all the objects of a class. To say that each person has his or her own standard of conduct is the same as saying that there is no standard at all. Human nature, as rational and free, is common to all of us, and the rules derived from it by the exercise of right reasoning will be applicable to all human beings.

2. The norm must be such that from it all the rules of morality can be derived. Otherwise it would not be the complete norm, but it plus something else would be the norm. The personal agent, the doer of the act, is taken with all his or her parts, so that the act must be befitting to him or her as a whole, and the relations connect him or her with every possible object on which or toward which it is possible to act, or that can in any way circumstance or condition the act. The intellect with its reflective power can embrace the totality of our parts and relations.

3. The norm must be immutable yet flexible enough to admit of varying applications according to circumstances. If the norm is not immutable, it is no standard at all; yet it will be useless if it is not applicable to every possible circumstance of human conduct, for this is what it is supposed to measure. Hence the norm must be flexible without being elastic, like a tape measure that is fixed in length but can conform to any surface. Human nature is immutable in essentials but accidentally variable, specifically the same but individually diversified, and human reason with its abstractive power can separate the essential from the accidental.

4. The norm must be constantly present and manifest to all human beings. Human acts entail responsibility, and if we could perform them without being able to find the norm of morality, we would be responsible for conduct, the morality of which we could not determine. We must therefore, whenever confronted with a rational choice, always be able to compare our conduct with the norm. But the only thing always present to a person in all possible circumstances is his or her own rational and free nature. Wrecked on a desert island, a person still has the norm of morality available.

No other conceivable standard has these qualifications. An external object distinct from the human being could be lost or left behind and not available when needed. Something internal but only accidental to a person would not be present in all people, even though all people must live morally. Something essential to human nature but only a part of that nature could not function as a measure of conduct suitable to the other parts. Therefore, the norm of morality must be the whole of human nature.

The norm of morality is not only a standard or measure, but also a director and guide. In this last function, the concept of norm leads into that of law.

SUMMARY

The moral life is above all a conscious and intelligent life. Intellect alone has had an honored place in all traditional ethics because it is our critical and reflective ability, the only power we have capable of passing judgment on itself and everything else. But since intellectual reasoning can fall into error, it must be *right reasoning,* not just any intellectual reasoning, that guides us in living the moral life.

How do we know when intellect is right in moral matters? Intellect itself must be the judge. It is right when it is rationally exercised, consistent with itself, faithful to its own law. In moral matters, this rational exercise of intellect is guided and directed by real emotion, emotion directed outward to persons and things to reveal their intrinsic value. The substance and direction for our moral reasoning is provided by real emotion, while intellect in harmony with such emotion works out the means to achieve the moral good desired. Intellect is right when it is rectified by real emotion, emotion that is right because it is an immediate appreciation of genuine moral value. Only intellect is capable of the reflection and criticism needed to know whether it is in harmony with real emotion or not. As a norm, right reasoning issues in a practical dictate of intellect directing the person to the ideal good for him or her as a rational and free being by choosing the moral good in this particular instance.

Right reasoning is concerned with human nature taken completely in all its parts and relations.

Parts {
Metaphysical:
  organic vitality and rationality
Physical:
  body and psyche
Integral:
  bodily members and powers
}

Relations {
Contingent:
  toward the uncaused source of our existence
Social:
  toward fellow human beings
Caring:
  toward the goods of the earth
}

Argument for *right reason* (intellect in harmony with and under the guidance and direction of real emotion) as the norm of morality: Everything is intended to act according to its nature, since a nature is the essence of a thing as the inner directing principle of its activity. Reason's intellectual capacity is part of human nature and is the directing principle of free beings in moral matters when it seeks out the means to achieve a *desired* moral good. Intellect can reflect on and criticize itself and so know when it is right. Hence, *intellect rectified by real emotion and examining human nature taken completely in all its parts and relations* is what we call *right reason* and is held to be the norm of morality.

That this is a proximate and practical norm follows from the inability of anything else to fulfill the functions essential to a norm:
1. It gives the same rules of morality to all people.
2. It gives all the rules of morality to each person.
3. It is immutable yet applicable to all cases.
4. It is always present and manifest to all people.

Questions for Discussion

1. If human nature taken completely as rational and free is *the* norm of morality present to everyone always and everywhere, why is there so much mayhem in the world and so little peace? Are some of us mistaken about our personhood? Or are some of us mistaken about which actions are fitting for us to do and which unfitting? Or is it possible that we just have not yet discovered the ultimate norm of morality? What do you think? Why?

2. G.E. Moore, whom we discussed in the chapter on the good, has argued that it is always

possible to ask a philosopher one telling question about his or her norm of morality, namely, by which norm have you chosen your norm? If the chosen norm truly is the ultimate norm, then it will never make sense to say, "This act does not square with the norm, but even more importantly it will lead to such and such consequences." Take the norm we have argued for in this chapter and apply Moore's test question. Do you think it makes sense to say, "This act is fitting (or unfitting) for a rational and free being (person) to do, but even more importantly it will lead to x consequences"? Why?

3. Using the norm of morality set forth in this chapter, apply it to the question of a minimum wage to be set by Congress for all workers in this nation. As of this writing, the minimum wage is $3.35 per hour, set in 1981. A recent editorial in the *Los Angeles Times* argued that while the question obviously has an economic side, it is above all a moral issue. How would you go about lobbying Congress to raise the minimum wage? Ask some members of your class to assess the morality of your argument.

4. Some critics of the norm of morality set forth in this chapter argue that it is too complicated to be readily workable. One alternative suggested is this: the desire that not everything be destroyed. Why is this so? Because this desire is the end of the line. Beyond it and its demands there is literally nothing. Check out this suggestion for its workability and its universality. Apply G.E. Moore's test question (see #2 above). Can this norm be used as a universal guide to morally good action?

5. You are the chairperson of the board of directors and the chief executive officer of a large multinational corporation that has a very profitable investment in a nation whose government pursues a strict and unrelenting policy of racial discrimination and separation for the benefit of the white minority over the nonwhite majority. The board of directors has just decided that the corporation's involvement in such a society is immoral and has voted almost unanimously in favor of disengaging from that country and selling its holdings to nonwhites currently involved in managing the operation. Using both (a) human nature completely considered and (b) the desire that not everything be destroyed, construct two justifications to the corporation shareholders of the board's actions. Is one argument superior to the other? Why?

Readings

All of Plato's writings emphasize the role of reason in governing man's moral life. It is the whole theme of his *Republic*. Eros is, however, the driving force of that rational life that is, at its best, a life in which the love of beauty drives a person to seek the good, which is also the highest beauty.

Aristotle's *Nicomachean Ethics,* bk. VI, deals with the intellectual virtues and the special impact of prudence on morals. Note Aristotle's view of appetite as setting the goals or ends for reason, which selects the means to arrive at the ends.

Marcus Aurelius' *Meditations* and Epictetus' *Discourses* stress the reigning position of reason in the Stoic ethical theory.

The concepts of *reason* and *nature* run throughout the whole Aristotelian-Thomistic philosophy. See the *Summa Theologica,* I–II, q. 19, aa. 3–4; q. 21, a. 1; q. 59, a. 5; q. 71, aa.

1–2; and the *Summa Contra Gentiles,* bk. III, ch. 129. Read Michael Cronin, *Science of Ethics,* vol. I., ch. 5; also Leo Ward, *Values and Reality,* ch. 11, and *Christian Ethics,* ch. 6–8.

John Macmurray, *Reason and Emotion,* pp. 13–65, provides an excellent counterbalance to the Aristotelian-Thomistic discussion of reason. Robert C. Solomon, *The Passions,* pp. 126–128, discusses the function of reason in relation to the emotions. John Findlay, *Values and Intentions,* pp. 166–178, discusses the role of feeling and emotion in our actions and endeavors.

Stephen Toulmin, *An Examination into the Place of Reason in Ethics,* and Kurt Baier, *The Moral Point of View,* take a new viewpoint on reason's place in ethics. The latter is an example of the "good reasons" school of moral thinking.

11
Law

PROBLEM

Those who give a large place to intellect in the determination of morality usually hold that *right reason* expresses itself in the form of law. Since there is question of intellect directing moral action, the judgment of right reason assumes the form of a command prescribing as moral or forbidding as immoral a certain kind of conduct, and this is what is commonly understood as a law. A law is closely related to a norm or standard, the main difference being that a norm appeals to the intellect, enabling it to distinguish one thing from another, whereas a law imposes an obligation on the will to conform to the standard. Since norm and law are not contradictory but supplementary, it is not always necessary to keep a sharp distinction between them.

Law is a highly controversial topic in morals today. Some will not hear of the word. It is bad enough, they say, to have to endure laws in the state as a necessary evil needed to restrain the refractory and uncooperative elements in society, but let us hear nothing about laws governing our moral life. Surely the good life should appeal to us without any form of coercion, and how is it possible to coerce a moral life, whose dwelling place is in the interior of each person's soul?

We are faced with a difficult problem. Shall we throw away a good word because it has come to be perversely misunderstood, or engage in the task of educating people in the proper understanding of what law really is? If the word *law* had irretrievably picked up such disastrous connotations as to be beyond rehabilitation, we should drop it and use other expressions, but the case does not seem that desperate, and we would lose too much. The word *law* is so fixed in the tradition of ethical writing that students would have to learn its meaning anyway if they want to do any serious reading in the great ethical writers. They will have to keep an open mind and not look exclusively at the coercive aspect of law.

The following questions can guide our discussion:

1. What is the meaning of law?
2. How did the idea of natural law develop in history?
3. What are the arguments for and against a natural law?
4. How do we come to know the natural law?
5. What is the content of natural law?
6. Is natural law invariable?
7. Is there an eternal law beyond the natural law?

MEANING OF LAW

When we say the word *law,* what comes to mind first of all is human law, the law of the state. This is what St. Thomas seems to have in mind when he gives us his classical definition of law, though the definition is also applicable to law in a wider sense:

> Law is nothing else than an ordinance of reason for the common good, promulgated by him who has care of the community.[1]

1. It is called an *ordinance* because it is no mere advice, counsel, or suggestion but an order, a command, a mandate imposing the legislator's will on the citizens and binding with moral necessity.

2. A law is said to be of *reason* because it must be no arbitrary whim but intelligent direction, imposed by the superior's will but planned and formulated by right reason. To be reasonable a law must be consistent with other laws and rights, just in distributing benefits and burdens, observable as not being too harsh or difficult, enforceable so that proper observation is actually secured, and useful in that the good it aims at is worth the price.

3. A law is for the *common good,* for the welfare of the community as a whole, and not for the benefit of individuals as such. A command authoritatively given to an individual about a private matter can require that person's obedience but is not a law.

4. A law must be *promulgated,* or made known to those whom it binds. It must be published in

---

[1] St. Thomas, *Summa Theologica,* I–II, q. 90, a. 4.

such a manner that it can be known readily, though each subject need not be given personal notice.

5. A law must come from one who has *care of the community,* from a legislator having authority or jurisdiction, who may be a single individual or a body passing laws by joint action. Not anyone who pleases may pass a law. What sets the lawgiver off from the rest with the right to command is the lawgiver's authority.

So a law must be mandatory, reasonable, community-serving, promulgated, and authoritative. Without these characteristics it is not a genuine law and has no binding force. Law in this primary and strict sense directs *free* beings by imposing on their freedom the restraint of obligation, duty, or oughtness, the type of necessity we have called *moral necessity,* which does not consist of physical compulsion, though the threat of it may be used as enforcement. Such laws can be disobeyed and often are, but they ought not to be, and it is in this *ought not* that moral necessity consists. Governance by law is the only way of regulating human acts that is consistent with the dignity of a person.

In an extended and analogous sense the term *law* is applied to *nonfree* beings to express an observed uniformity or regularity in their behavior. The laws of physics, chemistry, biology, and allied sciences may be considered as mere formulas, and then they are laws in only a metaphorical sense. If it is thought that this observed uniformity does not happen accidentally but that there is something in the very nature of the bodies and the structure of the universe that sets their pattern of activity for them, then this *physical necessity* constitutes *physical law.*

Metaphorical uses of the term *law* go beyond scientific formulas to express observed uniformities less closely connected with the nature of things, such as the law of diminishing returns in economics or Grimm's law in philology, or to express entrenched social customs such as the laws of etiquette and diplomatic protocol.

It was necessary to describe these various meanings of the term *law* to bring out its analogous character. The meanings are related but not wholly the same. Nothing but untold confusion will result if we try to talk about the *moral law* or the *natural law* by applying to it the modes of legislation and promulgation proper to the civil law, or on the other hand if we think of it in the merely figurative sense of observed regularities of behavior. It will be law in the strict sense and not in a figurative one, but with marked differences from the law of the state and physical law. To make much sense of the controversy on natural law we should first see something of its history.

HISTORY OF NATURAL LAW

The term *natural law* has had its ups and downs and has not been understood in the same sense in every age. It is important to see some of these swings in meaning, for an argument or a criticism that is valid in one period will not apply to the term as understood in a different historical context.

The early Greeks contrasted *physis* (nature) and *nomos* (law), the latter being understood in the sense of human convention and contrivance, so that a union of the two words in a phrase such as *natural law* seemed contradictory. Yet they had a feeling for what is right and just beyond human laws. Plato is unintelligible without the ideas of law and justice in which all human law and justice participate. Aristotle is more explicit:

> Particular law is that which each community lays down and applies to its own members: this is partly written and partly unwritten. Universal law is the law of nature. For there really is, as every one to some extent divines, a natural justice and injustice that is binding on all men, even on those who have no association or covenant with each other. It is this that Sophocles' Antigone clearly means when she says that the burial of Polyneices was a just act in spite of the prohibition: she means that it was just by nature.
> Not of today or yesterday it is,
> But lives of eternal: none can date its birth.[1]

The Stoics were the first to make wide use of

---

[1] Aristotle, *Rhetoric,* bk. I, ch. 13, 1373b 4. Aristotle quotes from Sophocles' *Antigone,* lines 456–457. See also Aristotle, *Nicomachean Ethics,* bk. V., ch. 7, 1134b 18.

the term *natural law*. For them it is the absolutely necessary course that nature fatalistically follows, with no distinction made between physical and moral law. Reason urges us to obey it willingly rather than have it forced on us, since thus we intelligently comply with the inevitable law of our being. Cicero's remarkable passages are probably to be understood in a Stoic sense:

> There is a law, judges, not written but inborn, not learned or passed on by tradition but sucked from nature's breast . . . .[1]
>
> There is truly a law, which is right reason, fitted to our nature, proclaimed to all men, constant, everlasting. It calls to duty by commanding and deters from wrong by forbidding, neither commanding nor forbidding the good man in vain even when it fails to move the wicked. It can neither be evaded nor amended nor wholly abolished. No decree of Senate or people can free us from it. No explainer or interpreter of it need be sought but itself. There will not be found one law at Rome and another at Athens, one now and another later, but one law, everlasting and unchangeable, extending to all nations and all times, with one common teacher and ruler of all, God, this law's founder, promulgator, and enforcer. The man who does not obey him flees from himself and, even if he escapes other punishments normally incurred, pays the supreme penalty by the very fact that he despises the nature of man in himself.[2]

On the whole, the natural law as conceived by the Greeks is a rising beyond the particular and contingent to a universal and necessary ideal of conduct, describing how one must behave to be truly human, giving a rule of life that we transgress at the peril of unhappiness in the frustration of our powers and the stultification of our being. It is not a law imposed and enforced authoritatively by a human legislator. With the Romans came the distinction between *jus,* or right, and *lex,* or law, between what is just (*jus*) and the command to do it (*lex*). For the natural law the only legislator could be God, as Cicero says, but he is not yet clearly portrayed as a personal God.

The Judeo-Christian tradition introduced a new turn into this speculation by regarding nature as the product of God's creative act. God acting as a lawgiver sets the law for his creation by his wisdom and enforces it by his will. His providence constitutes him governor of the universe, which he directs to its appointed end. Here we have the concept of the *eternal law* developed by St. Augustine, which is the old natural law of the Greeks but seen from the side of God the creator and lawgiver. The codification of Roman law brought the civil law into contact with the natural law; the law of nations (*jus gentium*) lies in the area where the two meet and partly overlap. By the thirteenth century, studies in Roman and Canon Law, in ethics and politics, had laid the ground for an adequate philosophy of law, which first appeared in St. Thomas's *Summa Theologica* as the Treatise on Law,[3] with his fourfold distinction of eternal law, natural law, human law, and divine (revealed) law. But some unsolved difficulties remained. The medieval Church asserted her position as guardian of faith and morals. Are natural morals included too? Can there be an authoritative interpreter of natural law? If so, how does the law remain *natural*? These questions clouded an understanding of the natural law for some centuries and are not yet wholly dispelled.

Early Protestantism continued the medieval tradition, looking on nature as God's creation and on God as supreme lawgiver. But further difficulties arise. Any claims of the Church to be an interpreter of the natural law are rejected in favor of private individual conscience. But how shall it decide? The theory of total depravity, emphasized by Luther and still more by Calvin, seems incompatible with a natural law. Human nature, if totally depraved, offers no sure guidance for our moral life. Nothing is left but the political state. An established religion, national rather than international, modeled on the union of nation and religion in the Old Testament, seemed to them the best refuge. A theocracy like that of Geneva or Massachusetts, minutely regulating people's private lives, was the logical outcome.

---

[1] Cicero, *Pro Milone,* iv, 10.

[2] Cicero, *De Republica,* bk. III, xxii, 33. Quoted by Lactantius, *De Institutionibus Divinis,* bk. VI, ch. 8, 6–9.

[3] St. Thomas, *Summa Theologica,* I–II, qq. 90–108.

In such a view the moral law is stressed, but its natural character seems to have disappeared.

It should be expected that the Enlightenment of the Age of Reason would carry us back to pre-Christian concepts. Natural law returns but in a new guise. God as lawgiver drops out. If he is acknowledged at all, he is conceived in deist fashion, unconcerned with the world and not governing it by his providence. Again we have natural law without an eternal law, without a lawgiver, without any really binding obligation. Again it is *jus* rather than *lex,* natural right or justice rather than a natural law in the strict sense. But the *natural* aspect of it, far from being abandoned, is reinforced and reinterpreted. In that rationalistic age human nature is regarded as eminently knowable by human reason. The method that reason pursued, however, is not a search for what is essential to human nature but for what is primitive in it, or if it seeks the essential, it endeavors to find it in the primitive. The distinction between the essential and the accidental is confused with the distinction between the natural and the artificial. The way to find human nature, it was thought, is by stripping from human nature the artificial accretions of civilization so that it may be seen in its native state, in the so-called *state of nature*. The natural is understood to be the native, original, or primeval, and "natural man" is the human being before or without the social contract that established human society. Human nature is not so much the abstract essence as the unspoiled savage. Thus the Age of Enlightenment passes into the Age of Romanticism.

In the nineteenth century, trust in rationalist procedures waned. Kant's separation of morality and legality put rights in the sphere of legality and made them a function of the civil law. He leaves no place for natural rights. He affirmed the moral law but had it known intuitively and not by reasoning from human nature; thus understood, it is a moral law, but is it a natural law? The rise of the historical school of jurisprudence and the influence of evolutionary theories in Hegel and Darwin brought in the view of human nature as something constantly developing and progressing. Laws and morals, rights and duties change as human nature changes; they are products of human custom, relics of traditional folkways, variable for each focus of culture and for each stage of social evolution. Legal positivism and legal pragmatism appear on the scene and relegate natural law and natural rights to the museum of discarded superstitions. The names may be kept because of the aura of veneration surrounding them, but all their substance is interpreted away. The legal profession especially is suspicious of any appeal to a higher law beyond the written law. And with good reason, if we remember the interpretations read into the "due process" clause of the Fourteenth Amendment canonizing the status quo as the only natural one and protecting vested interests. On the other hand, what guarantee have we of our rights with a judge who goes beyond the written law to decide a case by some private intuition he or she may have of a higher law?

The twentieth century, despite the persistence of legal positivism and pragmatism, is witnessing a tentative revival of natural law. There may have been abuses of the higher law theory, but what else do we have? The old question returns. Without natural law, what guide have our lawmakers but utility and expediency, trial and error? How can they determine what ideally ought to be the laws of states and of human conduct? The dilemma is a serious one. Either there is no law beyond the civil law, and hence no natural rights, no court of appeal, no recourse from tyranny, and I am subject to the arbitrary will of anyone who can control me by force; or there is beyond the civil law a higher law, but then I am my own judge and, though it is evident to me that this higher law objectively embodies natural right and justice, my associates have no assurance that my judgment is correct. The first horn of the dilemma causes the appeal to a higher law, to which the founders of our country turned against the arbitrary decrees of Parliament. The second horn causes the qualm of the legal positivists, who see citizens setting aside a civil law because it disagrees with their personal interpretation of a higher law. We are back again to Antigone's problem. It is not solved by putting the matter to vote and accepting majority rule, for that would mean no rights for minorities. The tyranny of the monarch would be exchanged for the tyranny of the mob.

The problem is insoluble for any society so based on skepticism and relativism as to maintain that human nature is unknowable, that rights and duties cannot be determined, that justice is an empty abstraction, that in morals there is nothing but opinion and anybody's opinion is as good as anybody else's. Society can flourish only in some commonly breathed atmosphere of thought and principle and must rest on some public philosophy. That the natural law seems to be the only possible one is the reason for its revival in our time.

THE NATURAL LAW THEORY

That there is a natural law, at least in the sense in which the Greeks took it, without explicit reference to a divine lawgiver, is implied in much that has been said so far: the existence of values and their objective basis; the preeminence and self-justification of moral value; its irreducibility to any other value, and its absolutely imperative but noncompulsory necessity; the inner drive of each being toward the attainment of its end, which is the fulfillment of its function in the universe; the ability of humans to use reason to reflect on their nature to distinguish moral good from moral evil in living their lives. What remains is to point out that all this material put together adds up to a *law,* and, since it is rooted in human nature as rational and free, to a *natural* law.

That there are physical laws governing the activity of beings in the universe is claimed as evident from the very existence of scientific knowledge. An utterly haphazard world could not be studied. Formulas expressing the observed regularities of natural phenomena are in many cases also rules of action carried out with remarkable constancy. Living beings, especially, direct their activity toward their self-preservation, growth, and reproduction, following the definite pattern of living prescribed for them by the kind of beings they are, by their structure and function, which is what is meant by their nature. Departure from nature's pattern does not happen spontaneously. A mild deviation imposed from the outside usually results in maladjustment and debility, an extreme one in death. To fulfill their function they *must* live according to their natures, and this is the *physical law* of their life.

The same physical law of nature that applies to inanimate, vegetable, and animal nature applies likewise to human nature. As it applies to each of the other three levels with a *difference,* so also it applies to human nature with a *difference.* Human beings are unique in being rational and free. Though subject to physical law like any other chemically composed body having mass and energy, to the biological drives and urges that control the world of living organisms, to the sensitive reactions and appetites characteristic of brain- and nerve-equipped animals, yet beyond all these we can intellectually *know* what is good for us and can willfully *choose* to follow it. We are subject to a moral law, the natural law. By examining the kind of being I am, my nature, I can find the kind of conduct suitable to me and can see how this conduct alone can lead me to what is good for me. I see that modes of conduct that are inhuman or antisocial, abusive of myself or of my fellows, while conferring a temporary advantage, must be destructive of me and of my race in the long run. I also see that I cannot renounce my rational and free nature and the responsibility bound up with it. Come what may, I must maintain my human dignity or become intolerable to myself. I must demand that others treat me as a person, even when they refuse to, and I must deserve my own and their respect by behaving as a person.

Natural law, it is said, tests itself in the laboratory of history. Superficial observation may seem to show such differences of detail in various cultures as to eliminate any universal pattern of human living, but more careful scrutiny detects a highest common factor in all moral codes. Even the most degraded savages are recognizable as human beings, not merely by the shape of their bodies but chiefly by the way they live and act. Too great a departure from the normal mode of human behavior leads only to frustration and extinction. Individuals here and there, as well as tribes and nations here and there, may flourish though they have adopted a form of life contrary to the natural law, but they are the exceptions that prove the rule. History itself catches up with them and eventually punishes the folly of such living because it violates our very nature. This is what is meant by the natural law.

To sum up the argument: The only means both effective and suitable to direct human beings to their proper good, to the fulfillment of their function in the universe, and to the attainment of their end is the natural moral law.

1. It must be a *law*. A mere wish, counsel, hint, or suggestion would not be effective, for it would lack binding force and could be disregarded without fault or penalty. It would be an insufficient motive in the face of difficulties. It would work when it is not needed, when the path is clear and the going pleasant; but it would not work when it is needed, when we must be goaded forward over the dark and rough spots of life. Nothing less than a law will do.

2. It must be a *moral* law. Physical laws are suitable only to nonrational beings. An internal determination or necessity of our nature such as is found in nonrational beings would destroy human freedom and make us a living contradiction, beings made free but not able to exercise their freedom. External compulsion would mean that we must accomplish our end despite our freedom, and thus would do violence to both our freedom and our rationality.

3. It must be a *natural* law. Every creature tends to its end by its activity guided by its nature, for a being's nature means nothing else but its essence considered as the principle of its activity. Humans are no exception; we too have a nature, and in us it fulfills the same function. Humankind cannot be the only being in nature designed by its nature to go against its nature. Therefore hu-

man beings also can find that their nature is the means that will guide them to their end, and this is what is understood as the *natural law*.

CASE FOR AND AGAINST NATURAL LAW

Many moralists, chiefly those of the last century and the present, oppose the basing of morals on nature or on law, and especially on the combination of the two. We take up the objections first and then the replies.

1. Natural law stems from the Aristotelian concept of a fixed essence or nature in human beings and from the Stoic notion of universal nature. These concepts of nature have been invalidated by the experimental method of modern science, which fails to discover any such hard and fast categories among things, and the theory of evolution, which shows that there are no invariable classes of living things. Process philosophies see everything on the move, becoming something quite new, with no static patterns of behavior to be forever repeated. If there is no fixed human nature, there can be no obligation arising from it.

2. There is not as much uniformity in human behavior as natural law theorists assume. It is not the person who conforms who is the best example of the human race, but the one who has the courage to break out of the narrow circle of conformity and to initiate new ways. As the thinker and creator, he or she pushes beyond the dictates of nature and expresses the uniqueness of his or her personality. Natural law with its static ideals is actually contrary to our rationality and freedom and a drawback to self-development.

3. What regularity we observe in human behavior does not come from any law in human nature. The general tendencies are simply there, urging us to certain kinds of behavior, chiefly of the physical kind, but imposing no obligation to act in a definite way. To see a law in this behavior is the fallacy of mistaking the figurative for the literal. The state governs us by law; to see us as

also governed by our nature is a mere figurative expression personifying human nature as a lawgiver and represents no real government or real law.

4. A natural law should be easily known by those in whose nature such a law is supposed to reside. People disagree not only on how to fulfill their obligations but also on what their obligations are and whether they have any. Even those who admit a natural law do not agree on its content, interpretation, or application. Hence, even if a natural law existed, it would be practically useless as a guide to moral living.

5. The natural law is a useless figure of speech unless it is imposed by some superior who has the power of enforcement. The most logical thinkers, therefore, are those who deduce a natural law from an eternal law in God. But not all people accept a theistic philosophy. Those who admit a direct governance over them by God need to have something by which God manifests to them the divine decrees. If there are no such decrees, no manifestation of God's will need be written in our nature.

6. Christian revelation sees human nature infected with the evil of sin, especially that sin inherited from the original fall of humankind, however interpreted. Some consider that human nature is so essentially depraved in its fallen state that it can be no trustworthy guide to human living; in fact, the important thing is to rise above human nature by the help of grace, and unless one does so, one has not even begun the ethical life. Thus natural law, which is of no value to nontheists, is also of little value to a large group of theists.

7. Natural law has been used to justify any kind of act one wants to impose on all people. All one has to do is to refer glibly to what one declares to be a natural law precept. Likewise, it has been used to excuse any kind of conduct. One merely says that the act, though perhaps not very laudatory, is not forbidden by any natural law precept. Thus natural law is a device for having and proving any kind of conduct one wants. Though

abuse does not destroy the use of a thing, anything that is set down as the absolute standard of morality should not be capable of such ready and frequent abuse.

8. Natural law is the source of the legalism, casuistry, pharisaism, and bourgeois smugness that have characterized so much ethical thought. The human person is made to serve some abstract formulation, as if the person is for law rather than the law for the person. Instead of burdening ourselves with more and more rules, adding to civil law and social custom still more hidden laws behind the obvious laws, we ought to declare our independence, exert our freedom, and express the uniqueness of our personalities.

9. Law and love are so opposed that it is difficult to reconcile them. It is true that they may both coincide in such a way that the law commands what love prompts. But the motives are so different that it is psychologically disrupting to try to act from both motives at once. Love is so far superior to law that it is better to trust to love alone and to disregard the motive of law. The fear of transgressing a law should be wholly overcome in following the inspiration of love.

These and similar arguments are of sufficient weight to require serious consideration, so much so that several succeeding chapters will be needed to explore them. Only a word on each is possible now. Natural law theorists claim that they are based on a misunderstanding of what natural law purports to mean. They answer:

1. Aristotelianism and Stoicism both logically lead to some kind of natural law, but the converse does not follow. One can accept natural law without interpreting nature either in an Aristotelian or in a Stoic sense. Modern science may have blurred the edges of hard and fast categories, but we can still tell humans from other kinds of beings. It is true that evolution of species held no place in historical Aristotelianism, but the two need not be totally irreconcilable. In Aristotle, nature itself is a principle of development, of process, of passage from potentiality to actuality; its extension from the individual to the species, from the on-

togenetic to the phylogenetic, might be judged a legitimate modification of Aristotelianism to suit modern discoveries. However, there is no necessity of holding to a strictly Aristotelian interpretation of nature to have a natural law.

2. There is no need to consider the nature of a being as absolutely static. Especially, a rational and free being could not be static and also faithful to its own rationality and freedom. It is because we are by nature rational and free that we are thinkers and creators. In developing the arts and sciences, in establishing and furthering civilization, we are acting most in accord with our nature. In particular, it is by our rational and free nature that we develop our morals and advance to clearer formulations of the ideals of conduct to which we ought to aspire. Besides, humans are by nature personal beings and they act most naturally when they provide for the fullest expression of their personalities.

3. The extension of the term *law* beyond the civil law to analogous modes of directing human life is a perfectly legitimate usage quite consonant with our normal mode of thought and speech. Deception should occur only if we fail to separate out the connected meanings or confuse one for the other. The natural law lacks many features of the civil law and has some features that the civil law lacks, but there are fundamental resemblances as important as the differences and justifying the use of a common if analogous concept.

4. If the natural law were known intuitively by a simple inspection of human nature and no careful study of this nature were required, then there should be no disputes about natural law. But it is not according to our nature to know difficult and complex matters in such a simple way. We are made to think, to reason, to argue matters out for ourselves, and it is in this way that we arrive at the content, interpretation, and application of natural law.

5. It is no accident that the natural law will appeal more to theists and that they will recognize its counterpart in the eternal law. But our historical sketch showed that the Greeks recognized natural law centuries before St. Augustine developed the concept of eternal law. Eternal law would not have much meaning without its promulgation in the natural law, but natural law can be recognized even by those who in their philosophy made no direct reference to God. The argument given previously made no appeal to the eternal law, though it certainly did not deny it.

6. Ethics as a philosophical discipline must be developed independently of such theological concepts as original sin. The weaknesses of human nature are plain to all, and there is no conflict between a philosophical ethics and original sin, but there is no philosophical evidence for a theory of total depravity, and, in the opinion of most, no theological evidence for it either. The natural law can still be a good guide even if not an infallible one, especially when there is no other.

7. One purpose of a study of natural law is to purge it of the errors and abuses that have been committed in its name. Some of its friends by overworking it have been its worst enemies. One common abuse is to give it an absoluteness it cannot have. This is not to deny that the natural law has an absolute foundation, but to recognize that a natural law must be as relative as human nature. The readiness and frequency of the abuse is hardly a valid argument; civil laws are readily and frequently abused, yet we cannot on that account deny that there are any or that we need them.

8. Legalism, casuistry, hypocrisy, and externalism can be called occupational hazards of law, of any kind of law. People tend to follow the letter rather than the spirit, especially when the letter favors them. Since the natural law is wholly unformulated, it has no letter and is all spirit. For this reason natural law is the best corrective for an overliteral interpretation of positive law and has been so since Antigone was portrayed as appealing to a higher law against the cruelty of her uncle the king. Since anyone possessing human nature is a person, he or she cannot live according to that nature without expressing the unique-

ness of his or her personality; this is perhaps the main thing the natural law demands.

9. An opposition between law and love is artificially contrived and vanishes with a proper understanding of both. The human person is by nature a loving being. To suppress all love in oneself would be to make of that self a kind of monster that the natural law could not approve. However, it would be unrealistic to say that one's love is in no need of illumination and guidance by reflective reason. When a man, for example, feels the urgent thrust of passionate desire toward a woman he is not allowed to have, he has to keep his eye both on the quality of his love and on the law, whether he finds it psychologically disrupting or not. No one can avoid all moral crisis in this life. Love is indeed the higher motive, but law is often a needed safeguard.

The summary character of both these questions and answers is readily granted, but there is an advantage in placing them in immediate confrontation. Several of them will become clearer from our next discussion.

KNOWLEDGE OF NATURAL LAW

We tend to think of a law as a written decree or spoken command, but nothing of this sort is found in the natural law. Failure to understand that the natural law of itself is not formulated has led believers in innate ideas and other intuitionists to imagine that we have moral concepts and judgments ready made in our minds at birth or that we easily form them by the use of some infallible special faculty. Critics of such views have hastily jumped to the conclusion that, if the natural law can be known only in this way and since there is no such knowledge, there can be no such thing as a natural law. The fallacy is in the first premise; the natural law is not known in this way.

How, then, is it known? Natural law is an unwritten law. Our knowledge of it has grown and developed little by little along with the growth and development of our moral awareness. To understand this process of growth in moral consciousness, we have to appreciate the work of the anthropologists who show us the primitive structures of tribal life and the aura of magic within which this consciousness began to form. Some philosophers (and theologians) have failed to appreciate the history of our moral development, which has passed through many diverse stages and forms. Humans did not always know what we know today about moral values and moral principles. Our own knowledge of the natural law is, to be sure, still in the process of further development and will likely become more and more refined as long as humanity continues to exist. Without an appreciation of our history with regard to moral development, we cannot begin to appreciate how our awareness of the natural law began to develop nor can we appreciate its roots in our own awareness of it.

Our awareness of the natural law begins with connatural knowledge. Without study or reflection, humans in a prescientific and prephilosophical condition simply follow their inclinations and emotions in using their powers for the purposes they obviously can serve. Such persons are following the natural law when, for example, they see that taking a human life is not the same as taking an animal's life. Human reason has not discovered this regulation of the natural law in an abstract and theoretical manner. Nor was it discovered through the conceptualizing power of the intellect alone. Human reason discovers the regulations of the natural law through the guidance of the inclinations and emotions of human nature. This is knowledge *through inclination,* not knowledge through concepts and conceptual judgments. It is at first an obscure, unsystematic, lived awareness by connaturality or congeniality in which human consciousness consults and listens to the stirrings and vibrations of one's own abiding tendencies and emotions. Human beings have consulted and listened to these inclinations and emotions throughout history, and the human knowledge of the natural law has been progressively shaped and molded by those inclinations and emotions, starting from the most basic ones. These inclinations and emotions are rooted in our very being, which is vitally permeated with the preconceptual life of our reason. Those genuine inclinations and emotions were either developed or released as human development progressed. They are shown by the very history of our developing moral awareness. Starting from the most ancient and primitive social communities, those inclinations and emotions were genuine that guided human reason in becoming gradually aware of the regulations that have most definitely and generally been recognized by the human race. Our awareness of the primordial aspects of natural law was at first expressed in social patterns rather than in personal judgments. Throughout history our knowledge of natural law has developed within the double protective housing of individual human inclinations and emotions and human society.

Knowledge through inclination and emotion shows us the fundamental dynamic schemes of natural law. Some examples of this kind of knowledge might help us to see the difference between it and moral regulations conceptually discovered and rationally deduced. For instance, to take a human life is not the same as taking an animal's life; the family as a group has to comply with some fixed pattern or order; sexual intercourse has to be contained within given limits; human beings are bound to live together under certain rules and regulations. Understood in their still undetermined meaning, these general tendentious forms or dynamic schemes of moral regulations are found everywhere and in every time. Neither the individual in his or her growth to maturity nor the human race in its development toward civilization can remain always in this primitive condition. Nevertheless, we must appreciate fully this kind of knowledge because our moral lives have their roots right here in knowledge through inclination and emotion, connatural knowledge.

Knowledge of the natural law grows slowly. Ours is a rational and free nature, and we find the natural law by the use of reason in drawing conclusions about our own nature. We have no moral judgments formed at birth and ready for use but must form them for ourselves. We are equipped by our very nature with the ability to form such judgments and have a natural tendency to use this ability, and our own nature is the object from which we draw our moral ideas and concerning which we frame our moral judgments.

People have a natural interest in and facility for forming rules of conduct. I can reflect on myself and, finding myself interesting, am stimulated to self-observation. I can evaluate and criticize my own actions and the actions of others like me. I can understand the needs of my own nature and suitability of my deeds to these needs. I can compare my conduct with my nature and understand the conformity or nonconformity between them. I can therefore draw up rules of conduct that will preserve and enhance this conformity. If a person becomes a legislator in human society, he or she formulates such rules and promulgates them to the citizens by some external sign; the law now becomes positive law. Such rules, before formulation and external promulgation, were already natural law.

All law is promulgated through reason because it is reason alone that can understand a law. This statement is true both of the natural law and of positive law. But positive law is manifested to reason by the help of some external decree or announcement intimating the intention of the lawgiver. The natural law is manifested to reason not by any external sign but by a rationally conducted examination of human nature taken together with all its parts and relations.

The natural law exists in a *virtual* condition in every rational and free being even before that person's reason is sufficiently developed to form actual moral judgments. An infant possesses the natural law in the same way as it has intelligence, that is, as an undeveloped power. As the person advances in the use of reason and *forms* moral principles, either with the help of moral training or by his or her own efforts, the natural moral law passes from the *virtual* to the *formal* state. A similar advance occurs in the passage of the race from a primitive to a cultured society. To aid people in this process of moral growth is the aim of ethics as a practical science.

CONTENT OF NATURAL LAW

How do we come to know the content of the natural law—what it actually prescribes? Though people by the use of reason are able to develop the natural law into a formal and explicit code of moral conduct, how many actually succeed in doing so? Anyone invincibly ignorant of the prescriptions of the natural law is excused from keeping them, but if most of those possessing human *nature* were in this condition, how could it be called a *natural* law? On the one hand, the natural law must be sufficiently known to the generality of humankind. On the other hand, there is much controversy and disagreement of opinion on matters of morality, betokening a widespread ignorance. Many of these disagreements can be discounted as dealing not with principles of morality but with their application; the law itself is clear, and the argument is only about cases. Other controversies are not so readily disposed of and concern the very principles of morality. If these principles can be unknown, how is the natural law sufficiently promulgated?

The way out of this dilemma is to recognize that the natural law consists of precepts of varying degrees of importance for the welfare of humanity, that the more fundamental principles of the natural law cannot be invincibly unknown by normal mature persons, whereas reasoned conclusions derived from them can be. St. Thomas says:

> There belong to the natural law, first, certain most common precepts that are known to all; and secondly, certain secondary and more particular precepts, which are, as it were, conclusions following closely from first principles. As to the common principles, the natural law, in its universal meaning, cannot in any way be blotted out from men's hearts. But it is blotted out in the case of a particular action, in so far as reason is hindered from applying the

common principle to the particular action because of concupiscence or some other passion . . . . But as to the other, the secondary precepts, the natural law can be blotted out from the human heart, either by evil persuasions, just as in speculative matters errors occur in respect of necessary conclusions; or by vicious customs and corrupt habits, as, among some men, theft, and even unnatural vices . . . were not esteemed sinful.[1]

Levels in the Knowledge of Natural Law

A more precise discrimination of these principles is needed. The more general the principles, the more impossible it is for them to be unknown, whereas the more particular and determinate they become, the more possibility there is for ignorance and deception. We may distinguish:

1. The first moral principle
2. Commonly known general principles
3. Reasoned conclusions
4. Particular applications

1. *There is one principle of the natural law,* which in the practical field corresponds to the principle of contradiction in the speculative field. We have already discussed this first moral principle,[2] "Do good and avoid evil," and now expressly refer it to natural law. It cannot be invincibly unknown to anyone who has the use of reason at all.

2. *There are other common or general principles based on the first principle,* following from it by inference so simple and easy that no *normal, mature* person can fail to make it. These moral axioms express the natural inclinations we have in common with all substances, such as "Preserve your own being," or in common with other animate beings, such as "Care for your offspring," or the inclinations clearly springing from our rationality and freedom, such as "Avoid offending those among whom you must live."[3] One could hardly know the first principle, "Do good and avoid evil," and fail to see what is good and what

---

[1] St. Thomas, *Summa Theologica,* I–II, q. 94, a. 6.
[2] See pp. 116–118.
[3] St. Thomas, *Summa Theologica,* I–II, q. 94, a. 2.

is evil in such obvious cases. These common principles cannot be invincibly unknown to persons whose reason is developed, that is, to persons of normal intelligence who have arrived at mental maturity and who have received an adequate moral education. It is to be expected that the feebleminded through incapacity and children through immaturity will be deficient in this knowledge. An adequate *moral* education is a very important factor. It need not run parallel with mental education. One may have no book learning at all and yet have received an excellent moral training; on the other hand, highly educated people of brilliant talents may be victims of defective or perverted moral training. The latter cannot be considered morally normal, for their moral reason is undeveloped. One brought up in an atmosphere of cynical misanthropy, one trained from youth in crime and degeneracy, one encouraged to rebellion against all authority, has had the moral side of his or her nature artificially blinded and starved. This cannot be called the normal human condition.

3. *There are remote conclusions derived by a complicated process of reasoning*. There is nothing doubtful about these conclusions; the conclusion is certain and the logic perfect, but the reasoning is long and involved, as in a difficult theorem in geometry. Untrained minds cannot follow it, and trained minds can become sidetracked through confusion or prejudice. Such moral questions as suicide, mercy killing, dueling, divorce, polygamy, slavery, and racism are examples in point. These remote conclusions can be invincibly unknown even by intelligent people living in a cultivated moral atmosphere. Since even educated people can be mistaken in other fields, such as science, history, and politics, they can likewise be mistaken in moral matters when the argumentation becomes difficult and contradictory conclusions seem equally plausible.

4. *There are applications of the principles of the natural law to particular cases*. Normal, mature people may err in their application of any principles to a concrete case. The resulting misjudgment does not mean that they do not know the principles themselves or that they are igno-

rant of the natural law, but only that they are inexpert in applying principles to practice, like one who knows mathematics but gets bogged down in working problems.

Thus there emerge four levels in our knowledge of the natural law. The first principle and the simplest inferences from it cannot be invincibly unknown to normal and mature persons, whereas the remote conclusions and applications can be. Ignorance of the general principles, since they ramify into all fields of conduct and are the mainstay of all law and order on earth, would make moral life and human society utterly unlivable. Ignorance of the remote conclusions, though these are important enough, is not nearly so devastating; moral life and human society can still go on, however lamely. For example, promiscuity and polygamy are not equal in their effects. Polygamous societies have functioned and flourished, though not as well as monogamous ones, but no human society has ever been totally promiscuous or could be.

Invincible ignorance of any moral duty excuses from its observance, thus taking care of the individual's conscience. But we are concerned here with objective morality. Widespread ignorance of the general principles of morality would be disastrous to the human race, and our nature itself through the natural law ensures that such widespread ignorance does not occur. However, the remote conclusions are such that invincible ignorance of them can be tolerated without wrecking humanity, and we are left to draw these conclusions for ourselves. Just as raw materials and necessities of life are scattered throughout nature and do not fail, but we are left to our own ingenuity in developing science, culture, and civilization, so we cannot fail to know the general principles of morality but must use our own reason (in the wide sense of that word) in working out the details of a complete moral system. And just as people depend on experts in other fields of knowledge, so those who have less ability or opportunity to study difficult matters in ethics can be guided by the teaching and example of persons whose intelligence and character they respect. Even here mistakes will occur, as they do in all things human, but we are not responsible for them if we act in good faith.

The terms *normal* and *mature,* used in the foregoing discussion, may seem too inexact, but greater preciseness in this matter is not possible because of the gradual way in which human reason develops. It depends on ability, age, opportunity, effort, habit, and environment, all of which shape the moral character of the person. There will be many borderline cases, but ethical theory must start with what is clear and normal before proceeding to the indistinct and abnormal.

Apparent Exceptions

Many difficulties can be brought up from the customs of primitive tribes and even from some civilized practices. To cover these in detail would be too long an excursion into anthropology and sociology, but a few norms can be laid down for handling them. About any alleged practice one should ask:

1. Are the facts certain?
2. Are the moral implications properly interpreted?
3. Is this a general principle or a remote conclusion?
4. Is this a moral precept itself or its application?
5. Are these people normal and mature?
6. Is their ignorance really invincible?

The first thing is to verify the facts. The accounts of early explorers are full of fanciful tales uncritically lumped with true observations, and even modern anthropologists can draw hasty conclusions. Reports of tribes with no moral notions whatever were later disproved; primitive peoples jealously guard their traditions from strangers and share them only with proved friends. The acts of savages must be interpreted, not by the conventional standards of civilization, but against their simple geographic and cultural background. To enter a house and pick up anything they see may not be theft for them, for they have no privacy as we know it and no idea that a

family's home is its castle. Their cruelty and revengefulness can be exaggerated manifestations of courage and justice. In general, they learn more vices from contact with civilization and from mistreatment by colonists than they ever practiced in their native condition.

Some practices are the result of inability to resolve an apparent conflict of moral principles. Human sacrifices were made on the principle that the best thing should be offered to God, and a person's dearest possession is his or her child. Cannibalism was done as a religious rite, to acquire a warrior's courage by eating his heart, rather than as an ordinary source of food. Suicide, too, is sometimes done as an act of religion, as was also the custom of burning a man's wives and slaves on his funeral pyre. Killing deformed children, incurable sufferers, and the aged was thought an act of mercy, as some consider euthanasia today. Prolonged social injustice may cause one to think it right to take from the rich to help the poor. Dueling was regarded as an obligation of honor and to refuse a challenge as a manifestation of cowardice. Feuding and lynching are mistaken forms of family or public justice where organized law is not in force. These practices are not defended here but only cited to show how an apparent conflict of moral principles may result in a faulty application of them or in conclusions wrongly reasoned from them.

It is possible also for people to become victims of moral depravity introduced in previous generations. Those who introduced the immoral customs may have done so with conscious knowledge of their immorality, but succeeding generations now come to take them as a matter of course, having grown up not in a normal but in a perverted moral environment. Tribes reduced to brigandage for a living may cease to see anything wrong in theft, at least from strangers. Slaves threatened with death for bringing bad news may come to feel justified in lying. The constant tolerance of concubinage by public opinion may dull the consciences of unreflecting persons. Public apathy toward political graft and unfair

patronage may cause some to view them as per-
quisites of office. Ignorance in all such matters
is not usually invincible, but it may be, especially
in extreme cases.

NATURAL LAW, ABSOLUTE OR RELATIVE

Some view natural law as a rigid and stifling box
put around their lives and cramping them into
an unrelieved round of prescribed duties. Others
may find natural law to be so vague and fluid as
to be practically useless. In answer to such exaggerations it is said that natural law is as absolute
and relative as human nature. Even in his day St.
Thomas saw this:

> To the natural law belong those things to which a
> man is inclined naturally; and among these it is
> proper to man to be inclined to act according to
> reason. Now it belongs to the reason to proceed
> from what is common to what is proper.... The
> practical reason is concerned with contingent mat-
> ters, which is the domain of human actions; and
> consequently, although there is necessity in the
> common principles, the more we descend toward
> the particular, the more frequently we encounter
> defects.... In matters of action, truth or practical
> rectitude is not the same for all as to what is par-
> ticular, but only as to the common principles; and
> where there is the same rectitude in relation to
> particulars, it is not equally known to all.[1]

Some modern legal writers speak of a "natural
law with a variable content,"[2] looking toward a
compromise that will give them both the needed
higher law on which human law should be modeled, and an adjustibility of this law to fit human
progress. But the whole content cannot be variable, since human nature is variable only within
limits, outside which the being could no longer
be regarded as human. Human beings are essentially and invariably rational and free beings,
but they are adjustable to circumstances and ca-

pable of growth. The human develops by exercise, human reason by education, and personal
character by habits. Likewise the race, while remaining essentially the same, grows in the course
of history.

A change of essence or nature is implied in
fitting humans into the general scheme of biological evolution. The change is too slow to make
much difference for ethics, which is strictly a
human study. Prehumans were not yet human,
and they followed the law of their own nature.
There could be morals only when the beings
passed the threshold into the human state, however gradual that transition might be. If humans
in the far future should evolve into some being
so superior or so different that they are no longer
human, they would no longer be guided by the
laws of human nature but of the new nature into
which they have evolved. Such a law could still
be called natural law, inasmuch as a being's conduct ought to correspond with the nature it has.
Since it would not be human nature, its natural
law would not have wholly the same content as
ours.

Although the core of the natural law for human
beings has absolute moral necessity, there are
peripheral areas that have a conditional moral
necessity. We have some natural duties that are
consequent on certain conditions of life, such as
marriage, employment, wealth, or leadership.
They flow from our social nature and are therefore natural, provided society has taken a certain
form and we have a particular position in it. Since
society itself, though natural, develops its institutions gradually, some conclusions of the natural
law will not have application until a certain degree of cultural sophistication has been reached.
Thus the natural law may permit to savages some
forms of seizure and violence that could be only
brutality or revenge in a civilized person. The
former has no institutions for securing justice;
the latter must use those society has established.
The moral law of justice remains the same; only
the mode of administering it is different. Here,
to use St. Thomas's language in the foregoing

---

[1] St. Thomas, *Summa Theologica,* I–II, q. 94, a. 4.
[2] Rudolf Stammler, mentioned in Rommen, *The Natural Law,*
p. 229, and Haines, *Revival of Natural Law Concepts,* p. 249.

quotation, practical rectitude in particular actions is different because of different conditions. In other matters there is the same rectitude concerning particulars, but it is not known to all, as with the evils of predatory warfare, slavery, or race prejudice. These evils were always contrary to human nature, but only lately have we become conscious of our duty to eliminate them. That we have not yet fully done so is proof of our need of further moral development.

What is said here is by no means an adoption of relativistic morals. The relativist has no anchor at all and drifts anywhere on the tide of fickle human desire, giving morals no more stability than fads and fashions. On the contrary, experience shows that human nature has stability without rigidity. It is like a fixed anchor with some slack in the line, permitting a circle of swing around the center. It is the business of moralists to pull the line taut and fix the position close to the center, but they should not try to abolish entirely the leeway nature itself gives them. By striving for absolute strictness and mathematical certainty in morals, they would not be following the law of their own nature.

THE ETERNAL LAW

Can the human being as rational and free, who is at least the proximate basis of the moral order, also be the ultimate basis, or must we look for something beyond? Naturalists and humanists make the human person supreme and, if they admit any moral law at all, could not admit one imposed on humans from above them. They could, as the ancient Greeks did, have a natural law without an eternal law. The theist, who views the universe with humans in it as created by God, understands that there can be no morals and no law independently of God. Such a theist therefore accepts the natural law as "the rational creature's participation of the eternal law."[1]

What is called the *natural law* from the standpoint of the human subject is called the *eternal law* from the standpoint of God the lawgiver. In a sense it is the same law looked at from the two sides. It is given different names to emphasize its double aspect: as actively proceeding from God the creator and passively received in the creature. The eternal law expresses the necessary relation of creation to its creator. It is defined by St. Augustine as: "That law by which it is just that all things be most perfectly in order"[2] and also as "The divine reason or the will of God commanding that the natural order of things be preserved and forbidding that it be disturbed."[3] St. Thomas, after agreeing with St. Augustine, defines the eternal law as: "The exemplar of divine wisdom, as directing all actions and movements."[4] The eternal law includes both the physical laws and the moral law. God directs all his creatures to their ends, nonfree beings by the physical laws inherent in their natures and free beings by the moral law to which they are expected freely to conform their conduct. Ethics emphasizes the eternal law insofar as it contains the moral law.

St. Thomas argues to the existence of the eternal law as follows:

Law is nothing else but a dictate of practical reason emanating from the ruler who governs a perfect community. Now it is evident, granted that the world is ruled by divine providence, ... that the whole community of the universe is governed by the divine reason. Therefore the very notion of the government of things in God, the ruler of the universe, has the nature of a law. And since the divine reason's conception of things is not subject to time, but is eternal ... therefore it is that this kind of law must be called eternal.[5]

If the premises are accepted, the argument hardly needs explanation. It contains these three steps:

1. God rules the world. Being supremely intelligent, he has a plan in creating the world and cannot be indifferent whether this plan is carried out.

2. God rules the world by law. The plan of his

---

[1] St. Thomas, *Summa Theologica,* I–II, q. 91, a. 2.

[2] St. Augustine, *De Libero Arbitrio,* bk. I, ch. 6.

[3] St. Augustine, *Contra Faustum Manichaeum,* bk. XXII, ch. 27.

[4] St. Thomas, *Summa Theologica,* I–II, q. 93, a. 1.

[5] St. Thomas, *Summa Theologica,* I–II, q. 91, a. 1.

intellect carried out by his will is truly a law. It is an *ordinance* of divine *reason,* establishing order and harmony in creation for the *common good* of all creatures, *promulgated* by being embedded in the natures of the creatures governed by it, and emanating from supreme *authority.*

3. This law is an eternal law. God is eternal, and whatever he knows and wills is as eternal as himself. But human participation in it, the natural law, is not eternal but as temporal as the persons in which it exists.

Thus the eternal law is also called the ultimate norm of morality.[1] The ultimate reason why a human act is good is that it shares through the eternal law in the goodness of God, and the ultimate reason why a human act is evil is that by flouting the eternal law it contradicts the source of all goodness.

SUMMARY

What obliges us to conform our conduct to a norm or standard is *law.* Law in general is a rule and measure of acts directing them to the proper ends. St. Thomas gives us the classical definition: *An ordinance of reason for the common good promulgated by him who has care of the community.* It must be mandatory in form, reasonable in content, community-serving in purpose, knowable in manifestation, and authoritative in source.

Law directing nonfree beings to their ends by the necessitation of their nature is *physical* law. Law directing free beings toward their ends by imposing moral obligation on their freedom is *moral* law. Law can also be used in a figurative sense to mean observed uniformity and regularity without the idea of necessitation.

The *natural law* theory has had a long history in ethics: as natural justice for the Greeks and Romans, as participation in the eternal law for medieval Christians, as moral law imposed on corrupt human nature in early Protestantism, as the native and primitive in the Age of Enlightenment, as almost extinct in the positivistic out-

look of the nineteenth century, and as staging a fairly vigorous revival at present.

General argument for the natural law theory: Humans must be guided to their end by means that are effective and suited to their nature. Such means must be a *law* with binding force, for advice is not always heeded; a *moral* law, for inner necessity or outer compulsion would destroy human freedom; and a *natural* law, for humans are no exception to the general direction of every being toward its end by its nature.

Natural law is objected to as being outworn Aristotelianism and Stoicism, as repressing creativity for the sake of conformity, as being unknown by most people, as having no method of enforcement, as justifying any kind of conduct one wants, as the source of legalism and pharisaism, as opposed to the higher motive of love. Natural law theorists think that such difficulties are based on misinterpretation of the theory and merely shoot down a caricature of the natural law, leaving the real thing intact.

Natural law is said to be *promulgated* to us through our *reason,* and its *content* to be sufficiently *knowable.* Its *general principles* cannot be invincibly unknown by normal and mature persons, though its *remote conclusions* can be. The first moral principle, *Do good and avoid evil,* is known to all. Simple and obvious deductions escape only the abnormal or the immature or those with defective moral training. Difficult conclusions and applications can be invincibly unknown even by the learned, just as error occurs in any field of knowledge. Hence the diversity of opinion in morals.

Natural law should be as variable and invariable as human nature. The human being remains human though his or her abilities develop. Natural law should be absolute only in its core but admit of relativity in details and applications. Since it is our nature to live in history, it is natural for us to undergo moral growth.

Beyond natural law must there be a further law, an eternal law? Naturalists and humanists say no. Theists argue thus: God cannot without contradiction be indifferent to the carrying out of his plan of creation. The plan of his intellect and

---

[1] St. Thomas, *Summa Theologica,* I–II, q. 21, a. 1.

decree of his will that creatures attain their ends are the *eternal law*. It fulfills the definition of a *law,* and it is an *eternal* law, for whatever is in God is eternal and identified with him. Temporal participation in it by human beings is the natural law.

Questions for Discussion

Since the natural law is the judgment of right reason based on the norm of morality (see the previous chapter) expressed in terms of a command or prohibition (the "ought" or moral necessity), try your hand at fashioning some natural law arguments concerning the following issues:

1. All persons, no matter what their race or creed, are equal so that prejudice against another person or group of persons on either basis is immoral.

2. Women are not second-class citizens; they are equal to men and are owed the same rights men have.

3. Terrorism, even if it is a protest against injustice, is immoral.

4. Both violent and nonviolent means may be used to depose a tyrant, even if that tyrant holds political power legitimately.

5. The internment of Japanese-American citizens during World War II was unjust and the government has a moral obligation to compensate them for the property they lost as a result of their internment.

Readings

As instances of the recognition of the natural law among the ancients, see Sophocles' *Antigone,* especially lines 450–460; Cicero's *Pro Milone* (For Milo), iv; *De Republica* (On the State), bk. III, xxii; *De Legibus* (On Laws), bk. I, v, to bk. II, vii. Cicero probably understood the natural law in a Stoic sense.

St. Augustine's notions on the eternal law are found in *De Libero Arbitrio* (On Free Choice) and in *Contra Faustum Manichaeum* (Reply to Faustus the Manichaean); there are several English translations.

St. Thomas, *Summa Theologica,* I–II, qq. 90–97, is known as his Treatise on Law. See also Suarez, *De Legibus* (On Laws), bk. II, ch. 1–15, translated in J.B. Scott, *The Classics of International Law: Selections from Three Works of Francisco Suarez.*

Modern philosophical treatments of the natural law include: Yves Simon, *The Tradition of the Natural Law;* Heinrich Rommen, *The Natural Law,* all-inclusive, and his *The State in Catholic Thought,* ch. 5–8, mainly political; A.P. d'Entrèves, *Natural Law,* stressing the historical and legal side; and Johannes Messner, *Social Ethics,* bk. I, pt. I. Jacques Maritain's *Rights of Man and Natural Law* is a very valuable little book, to be read with his essay "Natural Law and

Moral Law," the latter found in Ruth Nanda Anshen's *Moral Principles of Action,* ch. 4; *Man and the State,* pp. 84–94, is also recommended. John Wild's *Plato's Modern Enemies and the Theory of Natural Law* is a modern defense of natural law. See also H.L.A. Hart, *The Concept of Law,* ch. 9. D.J. O'Connor's *Aquinas and Natural Law* presents an interesting critical assessment of natural law thinking from the standpoint of contemporary analytical philosophy.

The legal profession has recently written much on the natural law. Charles G. Haines's *Revival of Natural Law Concepts* is the chief work in this field. The *Natural Law Institute Proceedings,* published over some years at Notre Dame, contains many fine articles. Arthur L. Harding edited the results of similar conferences at Southern Methodist University in *Natural Law and Natural Rights.* There are many good articles in *Law and Philosophy,* edited by Sidney Hook, and in *Natural Law and Modern Society,* edited by the Center for the Study of Democratic Institutions. The Natural Law Forum is a periodical devoted wholly to the subject.

Attack against the natural law is presented in Hans Kelsen's *What is Justice?* and in the writings of Reinhold Niebuhr.

12
Duty

PROBLEM

Some philosophers believe in the existence of a moral law without conceiving it in terms of a natural law. Usually they do not deny that it is a natural law, but the idea of each thing having its own nature is not emphasized in their philosophy. They may not be sure whether the natures of things can be clearly known, but they are quite sure of the existence and force of moral obligation. It speaks to them with the stern voice of duty, and it is in the concept of duty rather than in that of nature that they would locate the foundations of ethics.

The connection between law and duty is obvious. If there is a law, there is a duty to observe it. If there is a duty, it can only be because some law imposes it. But the moral law binds without the use of physical force and without any inner determination necessitating observance. What is this duty or obligation or oughtness that the moral law imposes? How does it accomplish its effect? Where does it obtain and how does it exert its binding force?

The theory of duty for duty's sake, of obeying the moral law purely and simply because it is the law, has been made famous by Immanuel Kant. His aim is the laudable one of keeping morality free from the taint of self-interest, from the lure of reward and the fear of punishment, from the reduction of morality to a mere means instead of an end in itself, from the mercenary motive of living the moral life only if it pays off in some good other than the moral good. There is the further aim of safeguarding human freedom, autonomy, and personal dignity so that the person is under orders from no one, of solving the dilemma of how a person can be governed by law and yet not be the slave of the lawgiver. Then, too, there is the case of the person who does good accidentally and how such a person differs from the morally good person. The outward effects are the same, but the former, not intending or foreseeing the good, accomplishes only a physical good by a morally indifferent act; the latter differs from the former by intending the good, acting from the motive of duty and out of respect for the law, thus performing a morally good act.

We shall first outline a sketch of Kant's moral theory with some difficulties connected with it, then expose an alternative theory, and finally propose some recommendations on the place of duty in an ethical system. We can use these questions to guide our discussion:

1. Can moral obligation be self-imposed?
2. Can there be moral obligation without a lawgiver?
3. Does all moral obligation come through the moral law?
4. Is the moral law enforced by sanction?

KANT'S AUTONOMOUS MORALITY

Kant never tired of saying that two things ever filled him with admiration, "the starry sky above and the moral law within." On the moral law he based the whole structure of his philosophy, for after he had devoted his *Critique of Pure Reason* to denying the ability of speculative human reason to penetrate beyond appearances, he tried to build up philosophy on a practical and moral foundation. His ethical views are found chiefly in his *Critique of Practical Reason* and in his *Fundamental Principles of the Metaphysic of Morals.*

Exposition

He begins by stating that the good taken purely and simply is found only in a *good will,* and a good will is one that acts, not from natural inclination and emotions, but from *duty.* Only acts done from duty have moral worth. Even acts done in the line of duty but not from the motive of duty have no moral value. They lack the *form* of morality, that which precisely gives them their moral quality, and this can be nothing else but *respect for the law,* which is what he means by duty. Thus an act is not good because of the end to which it leads, but solely because of the motive of duty from which it is performed.

The moral worth of an action does not lie in the

effect which is expected from it or in any principle of action which has to borrow its motive from this expected effect. For all these effects (agreeableness of condition, indeed even the promotion of the happiness of others) could be brought about through other causes and would not require the will of a rational being, while the highest and unconditional good can be found only in such a will. Therefore the pre-eminent good can consist only in the conception of the law itself (which can be present only in a rational being) so far as this conception and not the hoped-for effect is the determining ground of the will. This pre-eminent good, which we call moral, is already present in the person who acts according to this conception and we do not have to expect it first in the result.[1]

What is this law, respect for which must be the motive of an act to make that act moral? It must be the pure concept of law as such. If any act I do is to be moral, I must ask myself: Can I make the maxim or principle on which this act rests into a universal law binding all?

The shortest but most infallible way to find the answer to the question as to whether a deceitful promise is consistent with duty is to ask myself: Would I be content that my maxim (of extricating myself from difficulty by a false promise) should hold as a universal law for myself as well as for others? And could I say to myself that everyone may make a false promise when he is in a difficulty from which he otherwise cannot escape? I immediately see that I could will the lie but not a universal law to lie. For with such a law there would be no promises at all inasmuch as it would be futile to make a pretense of my intention in regard to future actions to those who would not believe this pretense or—if they overhastily did so—who would pay me back in my own coin. Thus my maxim would necessarily destroy itself as soon as it was made a universal law.[2]

Kant goes on to say that, whereas everything in nature works according to laws, only rational beings can have an idea of law and consciously conform their conduct to principles. This capacity is *will,* which is the same as *practical reason.* An objective principle of law binding the will is a

command, stated as an *imperative* expressing the *ought.* An imperative may be *hypothetical* (if you want this end, you must use these means) or *categorical* (you must do this absolutely).

If the action is good only as a means to something else, the imperative is hypothetical; but if it is thought of as good in itself, and hence is necessary in a will which of itself conforms to reason as the principle of this will, the imperative is categorical . . . .

It concerns not the material of the action and its intended result but the form and principle from which it results. What is essentially good in it consists in the intention, the result being what it may. This imperative may be called the imperative of morality . . . .

There is . . . only one categorical imperative. It is: Act only according to that maxim by which you can at the same time will that it should become a universal law.[3]

This statement of the categorical imperative is repeated often by Kant, sometimes with a slightly different wording and emphasis, but the underlying meaning is always the same. What in Kant's view makes an act morally wrong? It is in making an exception for myself while, at the same time, asserting the universality of the law for everybody, including myself. Thus I try to make myself an exception and not an exception. No one can reasonably will such a contradiction.

When we observe ourselves in any transgression of duty, we find that we do not actually will that our maxim should become a universal law. That is impossible for us; rather, the contrary of this maxim should remain as a law generally, and we only take the liberty of making an exception to it for ourselves or for the sake of our inclination, and for this one occasion.[4]

The fundamental reason why such conduct is wrong is that it subjects other persons (as means) to myself (as end), perverting the whole *realm of ends,* according to which each rational being, each *person* must be treated never merely as a means but always as an end. The dignity of the rational being, the nobility of a person as such,

---

[1] Kant, *Fundamental Principles of the Metaphysic of Morals,* sec. I.
[2] *Ibid.*

[3] *Op. cit.,* sec. II.
[4] *Ibid.*

is therefore the fundamental reason why I must be moral. But this principle involves a further and startling conclusion. If I must not subject other persons as means to myself as end, I myself am not subjected as means to another as end.

Who, then, imposes the moral law on me? I impose it on myself. This is what Kant calls the *autonomy* of the will.

> Reason, therefore, relates every maxim of the will as giving universal laws to every other will and also to every action toward itself; it does not do so for the sake of any other practical motive or future advantage but rather from the idea of the dignity of a rational being, which obeys no law except that which he himself also gives . . . .
>
> He is thus fitted to be a member in a possible realm of ends to which his own nature already destined him. For, as an end in himself, he is destined to be legislative in the realm of ends, free from all laws of nature and obedient only to those which he himself gives. Accordingly, his maxims can belong to a universal legislation to which he is at the same time also subject. . . . Autonomy is thus the basis of the dignity of both human nature and every rational nature.[1]

Kant goes on to derive from the moral law the three truths that he thought could not be established by speculative reason: the freedom of the will, the immortality of the soul, and the existence of God. Unless we are free, we can neither legislate the moral law for ourselves nor observe it. We can never reach but only approximate a perfect fulfillment of the moral law, but since our function in existence is always to tend to realize it more perfectly, we must be immortal. The one who does realize it perfectly, who is the absolute fulfillment of holiness and the ideal of all goodness, is God.

> Granted that the pure moral law inexorably binds every man as a command (not as a rule of prudence), the righteous man may say: I will that there be a God, that my existence in this world be also an existence in a pure world of the understanding outside the system of natural connections,[2] and finally

that my duration be endless. I stand by this and will not give up this belief.[3]

Thus these truths are neither mere hypotheses nor rational convictions, but practical postulates demanded by our moral needs, which we accept on *belief,* an attitude Kant calls *pure rational faith*.

Criticism

Kant's vigorous assertion of the moral law, his stern preachment of the claims of duty, the paramount importance he attached to the ethical issue, and the high seriousness with which he approached the fundamental problems of philosophy acted as a powerful antidote to the materialism and hedonism of a shallower age. All this was to the good, but his critics pick out certain difficulties in his theory, especially concerning four points:

1. The motive of duty
2. The categorical imperative
3. The autonomy of the will
4. Values and freedom

1. To rest all morality on the motive of *duty* is unnatural and inhuman. Kant nowhere says that an act not done from duty is immoral, only that it is nonmoral; nor does he say that to be moral it must be done from pure duty alone. All he says is that unless the motive of duty is present it cannot be moral, and, if it is done from both duty and inclination, it is the motive of duty that gives it its morality. But even this statement overplays the role of duty. Is it only her sense of duty and not her love for her child that gives morality to a mother's devotion? Is it only cold obligation and not large-hearted generosity that makes relief of the poor a moral act? Certainly a sense of duty will be present in such cases, but love and generosity are always esteemed as higher motives than mere duty and give the act a greater moral worth. We fall back on duty only when other motives fail. Duty is rather the last bulwark against wrong acting than the highest motive for right acting.

---

[1] *Ibid.*

[2] By "outside the system of natural connections," Kant means that which is *not causally predetermined, as physical nature seems to be, but possessing free will.*

[3] Kant, *Critique of Practical Reason,* pt. I, bk. II, ch. II, § viii. See also § v.

How could Kant explain heroic acts, such as giving one's life for one's friend? These acts are always thought the noblest and best precisely because they go beyond the call of duty. Kant is then faced with this dilemma: either he must deny that heroic acts are moral, thus putting the best of human acts outside the pale of moral goodness; or he must make heroic acts a duty, thus putting a burden on human nature that it cannot bear and robbing these acts of the very quality that makes them heroic.

2. That the moral law commands us with a *categorical imperative* is undoubtedly true, and Kant emphasizes it well, but his formulation of it is faulty. The moral imperative is properly "do good and avoid evil," plus the more definite principles derived from this, rather than Kant's formula, "So act that the maxim from which you act can be made a universal law," which is only a negative rule. Evil ways of acting could never become universal laws, for they are self-destructive; but there are also good ways of acting that can never become universal laws, such as a life of working to alleviate poverty. Hence the reason for the moral goodness of an act is not the fact that it can be made a universal law. Kant might answer that we can will the alleviation of poverty to be a universal law for a definite type of person in definite circumstances; but this answer is no help, for if we start making exceptions of this sort, the term *universal law* loses all meaning. It finally narrows down to just one single case. To use Kant's own example of a lying promise, I might will that anyone in my peculiar predicament could get out of it by lying, and still have the law universal for that class of people.

To determine the goodness of an act wholly from the motive that governs it and not at all from the end to which it naturally leads is to adopt a purely subjective norm of morality. It is difficult to square Kant's view not only with objective morality but also with intrinsic morality, since in his view no acts are good or bad in themselves but only because of the motive of the doer.

3. Kant's recognition of the dignity of the human person is one of the most admired parts of his philosophy, but he carries it so far as to make a *created* person impossible. We must never use each other merely as means, but God may do with us what he pleases, short of contradicting his own attributes. To make the human will absolutely *autonomous* does violence to the relationship between the creature and God the creator. Kant is forced to this position by his rejection of the traditional proofs for God's existence. In Kant's system our reason for accepting God's existence is ultimately that we will his existence, for we need him to justify morality to ourselves. As Kant says, this is a practical faith rather than a reasoned conviction. Here his critics see a dilemma. God either does or does not exist; if he does not exist, we cannot will him into existence simply because we feel a need of him; if he does exist, the human will cannot be wholly autonomous but is subject to the law God imposes on us.

Kant sees clearly that there can be no morality without freedom, but in his discussion of freedom there is always a confusion between freedom of choice (positive freedom) and freedom of independence (negative freedom), as if one could not retain freedom and still be under the command of another's law. To save freedom he demands autonomy, but by demanding autonomy he destroys all real obligation and therefore all real law.

The obligation an autonomous will imposes on itself is an obligation only in name. A will that binds itself is no more bound than a man, for instance, who locks himself in but still holds the key in his hand. Kant does not think that we may either make or not make the moral law for ourselves as we please, or that we frame its provisions arbitrarily. We cannot escape from the categorical imperative, and the maxims that we will into universal laws cannot be otherwise than they are. Why not? If this necessity is founded on the very nature of things (and Kant thinks that it is, for it is our one grasp of the *noumenon,* the thing-in-itself), then it is determined for us by something other than our own will unless we want to set ourselves up as creators of the universe. Either there is no obligation or it is imposed on us from outside our own will. The only other alternative is an identification of the human will with the divine, the pantheistic trend taken by Kant's followers.

4. Insight into objective values is impossible in Kant's system, for this would mean that we could find values in abstraction from reason and would have a basis in human sensibility for our moral activity. To have such insight would mean, for Kant, that we would be acting only on our inclinations and emotions, which are necessarily egoistic, individual, and chaotic. He makes a rigid separation between reason and the inclinations and emotions of human beings. A notion of connatural knowledge would never be allowed, for this would be tantamount to destroying the autonomy of reason. And yet, without an ability to know the value of what is other than oneself and to know it as it is in itself, we have no range of choices available on which to exercise our positive freedom. Kant would restrict our consciousness of our positive freedom to an awareness of our duty; he would never have us ask ourselves what lies in our power so as to determine within the limits of our power what we ought or ought not do. He would have us listen first to the voice of practical reason, which categorically obliges us to an action, and only then to come to an awareness that we *can* also do what we ought. To postulate positive freedom on the basis of the prior discovery of the categorical imperative is not justifiable. It is senseless to impose commands or prohibitions that do not lie within the scope of the freedom of the person on whom they are imposed. We are not dependent on the moral law for a knowledge of our positive freedom.

TELEOLOGICAL CONCEPT OF DUTY

Kant's is the most famous expression of pure deontology, or the theory of duty for duty's sake. He sought to liberalize duty by making it autonomous, or self-imposed, but had difficulty in explaining why the self should impose it and why

it should be binding. Is there any other way of having duty as stringent as Kant would make it, yet without having recourse to an external legislator?

An effort in this direction had been made by the medieval followers of Aristotle—not by Aristotle himself or by any of the ancient Greeks, whose sense of duty was limited to means and hypothetical imperatives. For them the end itself was happiness, and the living of the moral life sprang from the love of wisdom; they would think it odd to call the pursuit of happiness a duty, since happiness is so eminently desirable in itself. The medieval writers wanted something more than a hypothetical imperative and found it in God, the supreme ruler of the universe and legislator of the moral law. Since few of them wished to conceive of God as an arbitrary dictator, they cast around for some reason that the moral law ought to be followed even if it were not imposed by God. Up to a point they were able to derive moral obligation from the teleological, or purposive, character of the universe, a concept that pervades the Aristotelian outlook.

St. Thomas[1] noted that necessity arises from the causes of a thing. The external physical necessity of compulsion comes from the efficient cause. The internal physical necessity of determination by a being's nature comes from the material and formal causes constituting that nature. Moral necessity, which binds a free will without destroying its freedom, must come from the final cause, for only an end or good known by the intellect can move the will. But one cannot will an end and at the same time refuse to will the means necessary to the end; otherwise he or she would have a mere ineffectual wish, not a free choice made by the will. Four possibilities occur:

1. Neither the end nor the means are necessary.
2. The end is necessary but not the means.
3. The means are necessary but not the end.
4. Both the end and the means are necessary.

---

[1]St. Thomas, *Summa Theologica*, I. q. 82, a. 1.

1. Obviously there is no obligation when both end and means are optional.

2. If there are several alternative means to the same end, there is no necessity of willing these means rather than those. Even if the end is absolutely necessary, other means can be used and the end can still be reached.

3. If the end is not absolutely necessary, there is no necessity of using the means even when they are the only possible means. This is always the case when the end is not an absolutely last end, for every intermediate end is also a means to a further end and is not necessary unless this further end is necessary.

4. The end is one that absolutely must be obtained at all costs, and there is but one means to it, with no substitute possible. The means are necessary *if* they are the only means and *if* the end is necessary. By fulfilling both conditions, we pass beyond hypothetical necessity to categorical necessity and arrive at the absolute *ought* of moral obligation.

Applying this analysis to our moral life, we find both requirements fulfilled:

1. A necessary end absolutely to be obtained
2. One necessary means with no substitute possible

1. We have an absolutely last end, attainment of which is absolutely necessary for us. The human will is not free to seek or not seek the ultimate good but must of its very nature seek it. It is the sole purpose for which we exist, the only reason why we have any being at all. The intellect perceives this design impressed on our very nature as the objective order inherent in the universe and exacted by our being the kind of beings we are.

2. We have only one means of fulfilling our nature and reaching our last end, morally good human acts, and only one means of perverting our nature and losing our last end, morally bad human acts. Our nature as free beings who must earn their own moral worth and incur their own moral guilt makes any substitute means impossible.

Can, then, genuine moral obligation arise merely from the necessary connection of necessary means with a necessary end, independently of any commanding authority? In a sense, yes. Before any authority can command there must already exist the freedom and the moral obligation of obeying the command. Moral obligation is entailed in the very idea of the highest moral value. Just as the evidence of the truth imposes itself on theoretical reasoning and demands assent, so the moral ideal imposes itself on practical reasoning and commands consent. Moral obligation is but the clear manifestation of the intrinsic connection between an act to be done, as the necessary means, and the love of the good, as the necessary end. One cannot love the good and refuse that act.

Only the good can be of obligation, yet not every good is of obligation. Does not this show that obligation adds to the good the notion of some authority's imposing it? Not for this reason alone. Good acts are of two kinds: those that *may* be done and those that *must* be done. The kind of good that *may* be done but is not of obligation affords an option, since the end can be obtained in another way and the necessity is not absolute. The kind of good that *must* be done is the kind whose omission would render the necessary end impossible and thus is as necessary as the end itself. Hence even without an external legislator and simply by reason of its necessary and indispensable relation to the ideal of goodness, the living of the moral life is a moral obligation.

The explanation given so far shows how it is possible for one to recognize and accept moral obligation without a clear and certain knowledge of anyone's imposing the obligation. We can see that there is no need of trying to have ourselves impose the obligation on ourselves, as Kant thought, but that it comes from the very way things are; from the kind of being we find ourselves possessing without our choosing; from the structure of the universe about us, which we did not produce; and from the requirements of social life, which inevitably must emerge from our contact with one another by the very nature of group living.

It is because the order of knowing does not always parallel the order of being—since in the order of being cause comes before effect, but in the order of knowing the effect is often perceived first and then its cause is sought—that we can have a sufficiently workable notion of moral obligation and acknowledge its binding force without arriving at a personal lawgiver. In our way of knowing, starting with connatural knowledge, we rise from the actual concrete values we experience to the formation of purer and higher ideals of value until we come to the ideal of the good as such, the abstract notion of absolute perfection, which has to be the highest good and the moral ideal.

Is such an ideal verified in any existing reality? So far the theist and the nontheist can agree, but here they part company. Nontheists have to leave the moral ideal in this abstract condition, since they can find no concrete reality with which to identify it. Though the ideal can never be reached, it remains an inspiring vision of what ought to be and thus engenders the moral obligation of coming as close to it as time and effort allow. Experience shows that such an abstract ideal is capable of motivating a noble and even a heroic life. Theists agree but think that it can be carried a step farther. They identify the ideal with a concrete, really existing being, a personal God who is absolute goodness in himself and the source of goodness in us. Thus moral obligation, though founded in the nature of things, comes ultimately from the founder of the nature of things, from a personal legislator with commanding authority, the one who established the end and the means and their necessary connection, and who uses his authority, not arbitrarily, but to ensure the carrying out of the objective order of the universe. Thus for the theist, moral obligation is in a truncated condition until God is put at the apex.

Our purpose here has been not to establish the theistic outlook but to see how far moral obligation can stand on its own merits. We have seen it from both the deontological and the teleological standpoints. These are often regarded as opposites, though they might be better viewed as complementary parts of the one whole truth.

Both agree in seeking a firm basis for moral obligation.

IMPORTANCE OF DUTY IN THE MORAL LIFE

We have arrived at the following alternatives. Either there is no such thing as moral obligation or it does exist. If it exists, it is either imposed on us by a legislator or it is not. If not, it springs out of human nature and its place in the universe. If it is imposed, either we impose it on ourselves or it is imposed on us from outside us. In the latter case it must come either from God or from our fellow human beings, for nothing beneath us can bind us. If it comes from our fellow human beings, it must be from them as politically organized into the state or from the customs their society has developed. These alternatives cover a broad spectrum of ethical theories. A word on each by way of summary:

1. Moral obligation cannot be denied. It is passed over in such ethical viewpoints as hedonism and opportunism, but their inability to account for moral obligation is a deficiency that renders them untenable.

2. Moral obligation does not come from oneself. Kant's valiant and ingenious attempt to make it do so will not stand up. One cannot have authority over oneself and be subject to oneself in the same respect, be one's own superior and inferior. Lawmakers can repeal their own laws. If human beings made the moral law for themselves they could never violate it, for they cannot will both its observance and its violation simultaneously and any act of violation would be an act of repeal. Such a law could impose no obligation.

3. Moral obligation cannot come from our fellow human beings. Moral positivism and the various social pressure theories eliminate rather than explain moral obligation. As persons all of us are equal. No person or group of persons has original jurisdiction over another so as to bind that person under moral guilt, under pain of losing his or

her intrinsic worth as a person. What obligation have we to obey the state? Of itself the state can exert only physical compulsion or the threat of it, unless it can appeal to the authority it receives from a source beyond itself that enjoins obedience to the state as part of the moral law, unless it can appeal to the consciences of people to do their duty as citizens. Lesser groups have even less authority. Hence moral obligation cannot come from our fellow human beings, whether taken individually or as organized into society.

4. Moral obligation does spring out of human nature and its place in the universe, but this source is proximate rather than ultimate. It is the kind of grounding given to moral obligation by the natural law considered in isolation from the eternal law. Many stop here and find the abstract concept of the ideal good a morally compelling force sufficient to constitute a categorical imperative absolutely commanding the moral life. Others acknowledge that this is so but ask further why it should be so.

5. Moral obligation, though stemming proximately from human nature and the individual's value as a person, finds its ultimate justification in God. This gives the answer to the previous question. We need to see just what there is about the good that constitutes its overwhelming necessitating power yet at the same time leaves us freedom of choice, so that the obligation is absolute, yet a moral one. We can do so only by tracing the good to a really existing source of goodness, to the one who is goodness in person, from whom goodness descends to everything else that is good, and who wills the goodness of all other things even as he wills his own goodness. The source of all being is likewise the source of all good.

The philosopher is obliged to trace the origin of moral obligation as far back as possible. Yet, whatever be our theory on the ultimate justification of the *ought,* we cannot overestimate its importance in the moral life. Duty is hardly an attractive concept in itself. It is often made more unattractive by the harsh way in which it is first

encountered. A parent's arbitrary decree obliging the child to do something disagreeable with no instruction on the reasonableness of the command naturally provokes resentment in one whose intelligence is awakening. "Do it because I say so," accompanied with an appropriate threat of punishment, may get the desired result but at the expense of lasting inner scars. A psychological prejudice against duty can harden into a habitual feeling of rebelliousness at the confrontation with any duty, so that one will refuse to do even what he or she most wants to do merely because he or she has been told to do it. One so conditioned can become incapable of acting with mature responsibility, which is nothing else but the assumption of the duties of adult life. The union of duty and responsibility is clear. Anyone with a duty is responsible for fulfilling it, and anyone with responsibility for anything, whether it be that person's own conduct or some affair put under his or her charge, has the duty of carrying out this responsibility.

All government of humans on earth finds its ethical basis in moral obligation. All human laws, which are the only instruments by which humans can be governed consistently with their rational and free nature, derive their binding force from the moral law. There are only three reasons why a person obeys a law:

1. The law commands what is personally advantageous.
2. Threat of punishment makes it expedient to obey.
3. The citizen feels a sense of duty or moral obligation.

The first two reasons cannot guarantee obedience to the law. It will be kept as long as it seems advantageous or the vigilance of the police cannot be eluded. Since the citizens experience no moral obligation to keep the law, they will break it as soon as it becomes more expedient to break it than to keep it. In these cases it is not the law itself that binds the human will but the attractiveness of what the law prescribes or the fear of the punishment threatened. A law, as a law, can bind the human will only by imposing moral obligation. Positive laws can impose no moral obligation on their own account but can do so only if the moral law commands that just laws enacted by legitimate authority are to be obeyed. Therefore positive laws derive what binding force they have from the moral law.

SANCTION

Obligation is moral necessity, a necessity resulting from the final cause, which is a motive urging a person to act but not destroying freedom. The only way that a lawgiver can have the law obeyed is by proposing a motive sufficiently strong to attract the citizens to free acts of obedience. Such a motive, such a means a lawgiver uses to enforce the law, is called a *sanction*. Sanction means the promise of reward for keeping the law or the threat of punishment for breaking the law, or both; it also means the rewards or punishments themselves. Its function is *both* to induce people to keep the law and dissuade them from breaking it, *and* to restore the objective order of justice after the law has been kept or broken.

A *natural* sanction follows from the very nature of the act performed, as when sickness follows from intemperance or loss of business from dishonesty to customers. A *positive* sanction is imposed by the lawmaker and has no natural connection with the act, as when a fine is levied for speeding or tax evasion is punished by imprisonment. A *perfect* sanction is one that is both *strong,* in that it provides a reasonable person with a sufficient motive for keeping the law, and *just,* in that it sets up equality between merit and reward, demerit and punishment. An *imperfect* sanction is in some measure either weak, unjust, or both.

Is there a sanction attached to the moral law? Observance of the moral law brings about the harmony between our acts and our nature, between our physical and rational tendencies, between our creatural, social, and proprietary relations. Barring accidents, there should result peace of mind, friendship, honor, prosperity, health, and a long life, as the result of the virtues of prudence, justice, fortitude, and temperance. Frequent violation of the moral law should result in remorse of conscience, loss of friendship, dishonor, poverty, disease, and an early death, as the expected consequences of folly, dishonesty, cowardice, and debauchery.

As life is actually lived, this sanction is imperfect. Too often the good suffer and the wicked prosper all life long. Unforeseen calamities play a large part in life, and they are not distributed according to one's moral worth. Few violate the whole moral law, and the punishments for breaking part of it are offset by the rewards for keeping the rest. Crimes are concealed and the punishments avoided. It may be true in general that "Crime does not pay," but in many particular instances it pays well. One may find a bad conscience easy to live with for a million dollars dishonestly gained. One may be put to the supreme test, to choose between gross moral evil and death.

The theist holds that God, being a wise and just lawgiver, must assign a perfect sanction to the moral law. Since the sanction in the present life is not perfect, the perfect sanction must be applied in the life to come. It must be the gain or loss of our last end and highest good. Those who deliberately refuse to use the means deprive themselves of the end, and those who deliberately choose evil deprive themselves of the good. If even this threat does not always prevent wrongdoing, and experience shows that it does not, surely nothing less would do so. God is unable to provide a stronger sanction without encroaching on human freedom, for he cannot offer a greater reward or threaten a greater punishment than the gain or loss of the highest good achieved through one's own free choices.

SUMMARY

How does moral necessity, which is the same as oughtness, obligation, or duty, accomplish its effect?

Immanuel Kant held that we impose obligation on ourselves. Nothing, he says, is simply good except a good will. A good will is one that acts from the motive of duty. Duty is the necessity of acting from respect for law. The moral law commands with a categorical imperative: So act that the maxim from which you act can by your will be made into a universal law. The basis for the categorical imperative is human personhood. A person is never to be used as a mere means, always to be regarded as an end. The human will is an end in itself, autonomously imposing the moral law on itself.

Kant is criticized for refusing to admit a basic experience of positive freedom, overstressing the idea of duty, incorrectly formulating the moral imperative, and making the human will supreme while emptying obligation of all meaning.

Moral obligation is inherent in the very idea of the absolute moral good and should be conceived as logically prior to any commanding authority, which presupposes an obligation to obey the command. Yet without a lawgiver it is incomplete, for there is no one to whom one is obliged. Nontheists can and do admit moral obligation but have difficulty finding a secure basis for it.

Moral obligation cannot come from *oneself,* for any lawmaker can repeal his or her own laws, nor from a *fellow human* for, as persons, all of us are equal and no one has original jurisdiction over another. Theists trace moral obligation to *God,* who determines the necessary connection between the observance of the moral law and our last end and makes the attainment of the last end absolutely mandatory. This determination he manifests to us through the *moral law,* which is the proximate source of all obligation; from it alone *human laws* derive their binding force.

Sanction is the promise of reward or threat of punishment added to a law to secure obedience. There is an *imperfect* sanction to the moral law in the present life, but a *perfect* sanction must be looked for in the life to come. This perfect sanction, the strongest possible without destroying human freedom, must consist in the gain or loss of our last end and highest good.

Questions for Discussion

1. Kant's categorical imperative, "Act only according to that maxim by which you can at the same time will that it should become a universal law," is essentially the same question parents ask their children, "What would happen if everyone did that?" Or are they the same? Why? Obviously, if we allowed people to kill anyone they wanted to, we would have disaster. If we make a general rule *and* it leads to disaster (because everyone follows the rule), we can only conclude that the act is wrong and we ought not to do it. Is not the avoidance of disaster our ultimate guide and the categorical imperative only a striking way of finding what leads to disaster? Why?

2. The categorical imperative has been criticized as dangerous when used indiscriminately, because it leads to the banning of far too many acts. It is certainly true that enormous numbers of people all doing the same thing could lead to disaster: for example, if almost everyone decided to become a priest or nun and live a celibate life, that would be the end of society, for no more children would be born. The odds against this happening are rather enormous and so we continue to allow people to live celibate lives. Why does the categorical imperative not work in this instance?

3. The categorical imperative has been invoked to support the prohibition of certain acts such as gambling, drinking alcohol, smoking marijuana, and homosexual acts. The argument runs that enormous numbers of people will engage in these acts unless they are morally prohibited from doing so and disaster would be the result. If none of these acts is prohibited, we set a dangerous precedent because we could end up with everyone doing them, which would be the end of the group. We would become a society of drunken, homo-

sexual gamblers high on "pot," an unmitigated disaster for any society. Do you agree or disagree? Why?

4. Using both the natural law and the categorical imperative, compare the approaches that must be taken on the following three matters: (a) killing others, (b) avoiding jury duty, (c) having sex with someone of the same sex. The possibilities concerning any one of these acts are the following: (a) if one person is allowed to do it, that could destroy the society; (b) if anyone is allowed to do it, everyone will do it; (c) if anyone is allowed to do it, only some will do it. What differences do you find in the approaches to these acts? Are all three genuine moral concerns of equal importance or are they really three quite different matters that must each be considered separately? Why?

5. The proliferation of nuclear weapons is a moral question to which morality demands an answer but to which morality itself compels no *one* answer. Relate both the natural law and the categorical imperative to this question. What does right reason say? What duty does the categorical imperative impose? Do both demand an answer? Does either have an answer for us? Does one approach serve morality better than the other? Why?

Readings

Aristotle, *Ethics,* bk. VII, ch. 2–3; St. Thomas, *Summa Theologica,* I, q. 13, aa. 3, 6; *Summa Contra Gentiles,* bk. III, ch. 10; Suarez, *De Legibus* On Laws), bk. II, ch. 9. These writers give background material rather than matter directly on the subject of this chapter.

Immanuel Kant's *Fundamental Principles of the Metaphysic of Morals* and his *Critique of Practical Reason* present his ethical views. His *Lectures on Ethics* are a simpler but less famous statement of the same thing. A well-nigh definitive commentary is Lewis White Beck's *A Commentary on Kant's Critique of Practical Reason.* H.J. Paton's *The Categorical Imperative* is a well-known commentary on *The Fundamental Principles of the Metaphysic of Morals.* Robert Paul Wolff's *The Autonomy of Reason: A Commentary on Kant's Groundwork of the Metaphysic of Morals* deserves careful attention. C.D. Broad's *Five Types of Ethical Theory* has a good critique of Kant. A.C. Ewing in *Ethics,* ch. 4, comments on Kant and in ch. 8 discusses deserts and responsibility, or sanctions.

H.A. Prichard's *Moral Obligation* is a classic study. See also W.D. Ross, *The Right and the Good* and *Foundations of Ethics.* F.H. Bradley, "My Station and Its Duties" in his *Ethical Studies,* interprets duty in terms of self-realization.

13
Freedom

PROBLEM

The history of philosophy is a history of pendulum swings from one extreme of thought to the other. The pendulum spends twice as much time near the middle as it does near either extreme, and the amplitude of its oscillation varies, but without extremes no oscillations could occur. The overemphasis of the last few centuries on rationalism and legalism is being balanced in our time by an emphasis, some would say overemphasis, on voluntarism and anarchism. Our three chapters on reason, law, and duty presented these subjects from a fairly moderate standpoint, but there are those who think them irrelevant to a treatment of morals. What is needed is a declaration of independence against all three, and this can best be done by a proclamation of freedom.

Freedom is hardly a new idea in our history. Any primitive hunter caught in a trap set for animals or any tribal warrior captured by his enemies longed for escape from his bonds. As life became more complex, so did the forms of freedom. Older philosophers, though recognizing the value of freedom, have not much to say about it. They seem to take it as a condition necessary for the pursuit of other goods but do not put much emphasis on it as a good in itself. The reason may be that, though freedom looks so positive, its only definite meaning, as they see it, is negative. Freedom enables us to do what we want, but it does not tell us what to want. Freedom is not a virtue. It does not make a person good. Rather, it is a condition necessary for the exercise of virtue, and good acts remain mere good intentions unless one is free to do them.

The modern emphasis on human rights and the dignity of the human person has probably had much to do with the conception of freedom as one of our chief values. From the political sphere the idea entered the moral sphere. That state is thought best that best guarantees the freedom of its citizens. Thus freedom becomes thought of as a value in itself, one that a state ought to protect and that its citizens ought even

to fight for, and hence a moral value concerned with the ought. In this sense freedom, far from being opposed to law, is quite consonant with it. We shall begin with some of these older views and then take up the modern ethics of freedom. The following questions will serve to guide our discussion:

1. What is the relation between law and freedom?
2. What is the existentialist view of freedom?
3. What is the case for and against existentialist ethics?
4. What is the proper place of freedom in ethics?

LAW AND FREEDOM

Freedom in its negative sense means absence of bonds, ties, or restraints. Law is said to *bind* those subject to it, and whoever is bound finds his or her freedom curtailed to some extent. But not all freedom is necessarily good; in its negative sense the word can mean both a vicious license as well as true liberty. The purpose of law is to eliminate the first and promote the second. How does it produce this effect? One can be bound by various kinds of bonds, and those imposed by law are of a special nature. There are three kinds of negative freedom corresponding to three kinds of bonds:

1. When we think of bonds there immediately come to mind such things as chains, ropes, bars, prison walls. The one bound is subjected to force, violence, coercion, applied externally. Such bonds impose *external physical necessity,* which compels or restrains bodily actions only and cannot touch the inner act of willing. Freedom from such external compulsion is called freedom of *spontaneity.* In this sense a man turned out of prison is set *free,* or an uncaged animal roams about *freely.*

There is not much point for a human being to have this kind of freedom without its positive counterpart, for a person must know some values he or she wants to pursue and so needs freedom of spontaneity in the sense of not being bound or hindered from this pursuit. However, some positive freedom in the sense of personal power is also necessary if a person is going to do something freely.

2. Less obvious but more rigorous bonds are imposed by the inner determination of a being's own nature. A being lacking free will is utterly subject to its own natural tendencies and instincts and must act in the way its nature prescribes for it. The nature of a being imposes on it *internal physical necessity;* this is the domain of the physical laws, which are not the kind of laws we deal with in ethics. Freedom from such inner determination of one's nature is what is meant by freedom of *choice* or *free will,* the prerogative of a rational being. It is in this sense that a human act is said to be done voluntarily and *freely.*

Freedom of choice is not simply our independence of some degree of internal physical necessity. The independence is a negative freedom, a freedom *from,* but the freedom of choice is something quite positive over and above this negative freedom. Choice presupposes a range of options, two or more values, that I can actualize in my life. I am not determined necessarily to select one rather than another. In accordance with my own preference, I choose one value or set of values from the range of values I know and actualize it *by* and *through* my own personal power. This is an exercise of my positive freedom that is made possible by my negative freedom, my freedom from both external coercion and the internal necessity of my human nature.

3. In contrast to the two kinds of physical bonds, outer and inner, just mentioned, there are also moral bonds, which are ways of restraining the free will of rational beings by the authority of a commanding will. Moral bonds are *laws* in the strictest sense, moral laws as opposed to physical laws, and the necessity they impose is *moral necessity,* which is the same as oughtness, obligation, or duty. Freedom from law, from dictation by a commanding will, is called freedom of *independence*. In this sense Americans by the War

of Independence became *free* from the laws of England, a husband whose wife has died is *free* to marry again, a person who has paid a bill in full is *free* from that debt.

Because the bonds are different, one kind of freedom may exist without the other. Hence a person can retain free will and yet be bound by a law. The person may be physically free to do an act, since he or she is able to do it, but that person may not be morally free, since he or she ought not to do it.

Here we see the difference between the last type of freedom, freedom of independence, and the other two types. It is a perfection to be free from the compulsion of external force and from the determinism of a rigidly necessitating principle of action in one's nature, but it is no perfection in a creature to be free from *all* law. Freedom of independence has meaning only with regard to human laws, which are not passed universally for all people but for certain political divisions or classes of people. A person is free from the laws of other jurisdictions to which he or she does not belong, but as a citizen of some country a person cannot have complete freedom of independence from all human law. We can have no independence at all from the moral law conceived as rooted in universal human nature.

The freedom we have been considering is *freedom from;* more important is *freedom for*. The only reason why it is good for a person to be free *from* various restrictions and hindrances is that he or she may be free *for* the kind of life a person is meant is live, for the attainment of his or her end. Freedom *from* is merely negative, but this does not mean it is unimportant. In relation to the universe, the person is free *from* his or her own body and environment in the sense of not being held fast by them. Only because of this negative freedom can the finite person use his or her positive freedom to decide *what* to do and *how* to live. This negative freedom is the necessary requisite for the person's being positively free to make choices. Our negative freedom is our freedom from the kind of causality our psychic and biophysical structures can exert on us, but it is possible for us by this same freedom to live in varying degrees of dependence on those structures. It is possible for a person to live "in his or her stomach" or to live "in his or her spirit." Our personal mode of existence makes it possible for us to move in either direction precisely because this negative freedom is co-constitutive of what it means to be a person.

Freedom *for* is the positive complement of negative freedom and is revealed to us in our consciousness of power, personal power. First of all, this consciousness of personal power designates the awareness we have of our power to choose one way or another and to carry out that choice. This is the basic meaning of positive freedom. The second meaning revealed in the consciousness of power is the power to do otherwise, that is, it is a consciousness of *that over which* we have the power. The essence of freedom is the power of the will to come to a decision within the scope of the options one sees available. It is experienced as not being forced, but this does not mean that the essence of positive freedom is a lack of coercion. The positive content in the experience of positive freedom consists precisely in the performance of the act itself that I experience as an act performed by "me" and through "me." The only basis for an awareness of coercion is this very consciousness of one's positive freedom, one's personal power. The experience of coercion is impossible in the absence of positive freedom. The source of our freedom of choice is our personal power to effect what we will, and the source of the content of the decision is ultimately our emotional awareness of the value(s) to be brought into existence by the choice. The moral law curtails freedom *from* because it imposes obligations a person would otherwise be free from, but it enhances freedom *for* because it enables a person to live the kind of life that befits a rational and free being. The most profound consciousness of positive freedom is not the consciousness of our power to act otherwise than we actually do choose to act, a consciousness

that accompanies every choice. Neither is it the consciousness of the power to choose that accompanies every act setting forth a purpose selected from a plurality of possible projects. The most profound consciousness of positive freedom considered as power is the consciousness of the power to transform oneself either in the sense of moral conversion or in the religious sense of spiritual rebirth.

The purpose of the moral law, then, is not to impose undue hardship or needless restriction on people but to protect and promote true liberty. The moral law tends to make people good, directing them to their last end and pointing out to them the means necessary to this end. Even in the lesser sphere of our temporal welfare, human law fulfills the same function, that of pointing out means to end and the obligatory character of both. Law makes us free to attain our goal by directing us to the right course and keeping us on it, at the same time leaving us physically free to take or refuse this direction, since it does not destroy our inner freedom. Thus the moral law and good (just) human law free us from bondage to ignorance and error without lessening our responsibility and self-control.

A man lost in a forest is not free to reach his destination because he does not know in what direction to go or what means to take. A signpost and a pathway do not destroy his freedom but rather free him from the necessity of staying in the forest. He is still free to follow the sign and path or not, but if he refuses, the penalty is that he remains lost. In like manner laws point out how we must act to attain our goal; we retain our freedom to obey or disobey them, but the penalty for disobedience is that we cannot reach our end. True liberty, positive *freedom for,* therefore, is not license to do anything at all however evil it might be, the freedom of outlaws, but the ability to direct ourselves to the good with the help of both the moral and human laws. In this sense it is correct to say that true freedom is the right and power to do what we *ought,* and law shows us where the *ought* lies. But neither law nor freedom irresistibly compels us to choose as we *ought;* we are free to comply or not.

EXISTENTIALISM

We might think first of the *anarchists* as the main opponents of law and advocates of unlimited freedom, but theirs is a superficial opposition, a dislike for governments and authority. Of the twin concepts, law and order, they will take the order without the law, thinking this possible because humans by nature are so good in themselves that all they need is to be left alone and their reason will guide them aright. Anarchists are not necessarily opposed to a moral law, which operates without legislators, judges, and police.

The real opponents of law are the *existentialists,* especially those who espouse the philosophy of the absurd. Their opposition is implicit, for they make no attack on governments or civil laws and strongly insist on our responsibility for the society in which we live. But they assert freedom in such a way as to remove all basis for any law. They deny that there is a human nature that could be either good or bad and, in their abhorrence of the excesses of rationalism, put no trust in human reason.

Existentialism is an attitude rather than a school of thought, for its proponents resist being lumped together and tagged with a label, and much less is it a system, since they have nothing but scorn for system building. Since they do not take kindly to definitions, we have to gather their meaning in many cases indirectly from their dramas, novels, journals, and autobiographies—modes of expression they find congenial. Even their strictly philosophical works proceed more by way of description than by strict philosophical argument. What we have to say will be taken mostly from Søren Kierkegaard and Jean-Paul Sartre, as representing the theistic and atheistic wings of existentialist thought.

The initial picture they present may seem a gloomy one. We find ourselves in this world, confronted with the bare fact of existence. We did not ask for it, but the fact is that we are here, thrown into existence. The world that we live in makes no sense in and of itself. It is often hostile to us and, worst of all, indifferent. We look around and see that most people live an animal life, some almost a vegetable life, that is barren and empty. They are faceless ciphers going through the motions of living. The few who reflect on this meaningless existence become uneasy and restless. Life fills them with a sense of futility and despair, of anguish and nausea. What should we do? What should we believe? These are agonizing questions, but there seems to be no answer. Not only are our minds too weak to work out an answer, but even if we found one, it would be absurd. Yet we must decide because we are free. Freedom is the undefined and unproved basic datum.

Kierkegaard solves the problem by faith. He sees life in three stages. The *aesthetic* man lives the life of the senses to the full and finds it empty. Sensations are fleeting, sterile, buried in memory, an ever-hungry filling up of a bottomless appetite. The *ethical* man sees the claims of abstract duty, fitting his life into the rational grooves laid for him by the system. This is the moral life in the usual sense and better than a mere aesthetic life, but it is not an authentic existence, not a creation of one's own unique self, not an expression of one's subjectivity, but a smug and presumptuous self-sufficiency. The only authentic life is the religious life lived by the man of *faith*. Faith is a leap in the dark, into infinity, into absurdity. Nothing can prepare one for it. It is an acceptance of something supremely unreasonable: for Abraham the command to kill his son, ethically a detestable crime; for the Christian the commitment to the Incarnation, that God becomes Man, the Infinite finite, the impossible a fact, with all the scandal of the cross. To commit oneself to an authentic Christian life is to transcend the aesthetic and the ethical for something far higher, but we know there is this higher only by faith, and faith is a commitment to what seems to our reason to be absurd. The act of faith is not a rational act. Before deciding to believe as a pure act of our freedom, we have no way of knowing that it is the right decision, whether it is better to leap or not. For our choice we bear the full responsibility, for each man's faith is his own. Our decision is made in the midst of despair, but faith is the only way of conquering despair, transcending the absurd, and finding God's will in the calm serenity of silence. For reason life is meaningless, but faith gives it meaning and hope.

Sartre and the atheistic wing of existentialists can find no comfort in faith, for they have already postulated that there is no God and no future life. We are thrown back on our own resources. The world is absurd, but the brute fact is that we are here, and we cannot avoid the necessity of choice. If the absurd cannot be transcended, it must be confronted and accepted for what it is—absurd.

> If existence really does precede essence, there is no explaining things away by reference to a fixed and given human nature. In other words, there is no determinism, man is free, man is freedom. On the other hand, if God does not exist, we find no values or commands to turn to which legitimize our conduct. So, in the bright realm of values, we have no excuse behind us, nor justification before us. We are alone, with no excuses.
>
> That is the idea I shall try to convey when I say that man is condemned to be free. Condemned, because he did not create himself, yet in other respects is free; because, once thrown into the world, he is responsible for everything he does. . . .
>
> The existentialist does not think that man is going to help himself by finding in the world some omen by which to orient himself. Because he thinks that man will interpret the omen to suit himself. Therefore he thinks that man, with no support and no aid, is condemned every moment to invent man . . . . "Man is the future of man."[1]

We begin with existence but no essence. My essence, *what* I shall be, I make for myself by every free choice. By each decision, taken in absolute freedom, we become *authentic* individ-

uals, not meaningless stereotypes or lifeless props on the fantastic stage of life, but meaningful characters in that drama of our own composition which is our life. By each decision we create ourselves and determine what we shall become. This is why each choice is such a dreadful but inescapable responsibility, molding both oneself and one's world into the kind of thing one has chosen it to be. Each person is responsible not only for himself or herself but also for all people, for they, too, are conditioned by their commitments. Each of us is not only being-for-itself but being-for-others. Each must engage in the work of society and must not shirk social responsibilities. But ultimately and finally, for what? All our commitments come to a head in death. No sooner have I made myself, created my essence, achieved my authenticity by the full use of my freedom, than the whole structure is swept away in death, the ultimate and tragic absurdity, the final irrationality in all this meaningless existence. Only by freely accepting my own as well as the world's absurdity can I rise above the nausea of despair, live with my constant quest to become the God I never can be, and embrace the fact that "man is a useless passion."

CASE FOR AND AGAINST EXISTENTIALIST ETHICS

The following are some of the reasons that can be presented for existentialist ethics, especially of the Sartrean variety:

1. Freedom must be the basis of any moral theory, for only a free act can have any morality. Since one is responsible for all his or her free acts and only for those free acts, any other basis would be superfluous. Nor can freedom be demonstrated. One must accept freedom by an original act of commitment to it, and such a commitment must be free, thus presupposing any freedom one might be trying to demonstrate.

2. A human being has no nature, no essence. The most we can say is that we exist in the human condition. Existence is simple presence and beyond explanation. Of course, a human being is human and not something else, but that is given

---

[1] Used by permission of Philosophical Library, Inc., from *Existentialism* by Jean-Paul Sartre, copyright, 1947, by Philosophical Library, Inc., New York, pp. 22–23.

and unimportant. It is not what the human being as such is or can become that is important, but what *this* human being is and can become, what I am and can make of myself. Each individual must live his or her own life, and there is no person-in-general. In this sense the human being has no essence and must create it by every act he or she does.

3. Morality is creativity, and creativity done according to rules would not truly be creativity. If what I am to make of myself must be something wholly unique, how can I have prescribed to me ahead of time what I am to make of myself? It would not be myself but something other than myself I make myself into, thus losing myself.

4. Each one chooses his or her own moral principles. Values have value only if we have chosen them as valuable. There are no universally valid absolute moral values. We can change our values only by our own decision, and no omens will tell us that we have decided rightly. The approval of others or of society cannot justify our actions, nor is there any transcendent self or moral ideal to which we can look. Our transcendence is a function of our present choice, which we freely make on our own responsibility.

5. I as a person am in "bad faith," as Sartre calls it, if I decline to accept the fact that I am what I am, namely my past actions, my present decisions, and my projected future. I am "sincere," in the pejorative sense, if I refuse to admit that I am not what I am, thus denying my freedom to become what I am not yet. In both cases I am trying to live some other person's life, to be a personality with a given role in society that has been imposed on me from the outside.

6. The ethics of ambiguity is the acceptance of this division in my being, my "is" and my "is not," my being-in-itself and my being-for-itself, my facticity and my consciousness. I am constantly outside myself, projecting myself, losing myself outside myself, making my own existence. This is the supreme exercise of my freedom.

7. Authenticity is this realistic grasp of the ambiguous nature of human reality. It is honesty and courage, a facing of what the inauthentic individual is afraid to face: the pursuit of tran-

scendent goals that are of one's own choosing and for which one is responsible both for the choice of the goals and for what one does in their pursuit.

8. There is not only the subjective commitment, by which my choice becomes relevant to myself, but also the objective commitment to society, which is all-important. Our being is also a being-for-others. We live in a world of intersubjectivity. Other people are indispensable to my own existence as well as to my knowledge about myself, and I am responsibly involved in their lives. There will always be a conflict here, between my project and others' projects, and this is part of the ambiguity I must accept as implied in life's absurdity.

Much can be learned from the existentialist viewpoint. It has brought philosophy down from the clouds of abstraction and impersonality by an eloquent probing of each one's deepest and most vital concerns. Many find fault with existentialism, not for its affirmations, but for its denials. We need to stress existence, freedom, subjectivity, meaningfulness, relevance, authenticity, commitment, and involvement. But need we go at them by way of irrationalism and absurdity?

1. There is no question of the value of freedom, whether it can be demonstrated or not, and it is true that only free acts can have morality. Many free acts, however, are morally indifferent; for them the doer is responsible but not morally responsible. Also, morality is of two kinds: good and bad. The mere fact that an act is done freely does not necessarily make it morally good. Freedom is one of the requirements of a morally good act, but it should also be the kind of act one *ought* freely to perform.

2. It is misleading to say that I have no nature or essence, when all that is meant is that I have not yet completed the living of my life and fully made myself the being I am to become. Though I am a unique person, I exist as a member of the human race. Besides my uniqueness, I have a commonness with the rest of the human species, and this commonness can be as important as my uniqueness. The impossibility of resigning from

the human race shows that I have an essence and that it is only within the limits of a morally decent human life that I may express the uniqueness of my person.

3. The accent on creativity is one of the best fruits of existentialist thinking. No rules can be prescribed to creativity, it is true, but that does not prevent creativity from working within rules and norms. The artist does it all the time. As in much modern art, the norms may be reduced and relaxed, but they are never wholly abandoned, or one could never judge a daub or a ditty to be bad art or no art. Pure unregulated creativity in the moral life could just as well issue in criminality or futility as in a life worth living.

4. Each one does choose his or her own moral principles, values, and ideals, but it is the business of ethics to guide people in this choice and not to shirk this responsibility. To choose moral principles, values, and ideals one need not originate them but only make them one's own; it is not necessary to refuse help from reason and experience. One who makes such a refusal is in no condition to find any universally valid absolute moral values (except that of freedom), but whose fault is it if not the refuser's own? What if one freely chooses to have moral absolutes? Who can outlaw this free choice as invalid if freedom is the only norm?

5. I must surely both be what I am and be free to develop myself meaningfully. If my whole life is nothing but playing a role, I deserve the contempt Sartre has for me. But this does not mean that no one can do the normal work of society without falling into "bad faith." Must everyone express his or her uniqueness by exhibitionism and eccentricity, which seem to be the worst kinds of role playing? Or may one play a normal role in life but do it with a correct existentialist attitude? If so, who or what makes any attitude correct?

6. That humanity is an enigma and full of ambiguity is recognized in most philosophies. That the ambiguity is unresolvable is part of Sartre's irrationalism and hopelessness. If one antecedently denies anything on which a solution could be based, one will have to accept the ambiguity. But then it is an absurd world only because one has chosen to have it absurd.

7. Authenticity is a valid and valuable concept in ethics. I cannot be leading the moral life unless I am an authentic person, really myself and responsible for myself and all I do. Since no one but I can judge my authenticity, we have here an affirmation that the individual conscience is the subjective norm of morality. There does not seem to be any contradiction between authenticity and objective morality if the person is firmly convinced that his or her objective norms are true. Even if the person did not invent them, he or she has adopted them and made them his or her own. The person would not be authentic unless he or she lived by them.

8. Existentialists have been at pains to include society in their ethics, but critics are not convinced that they can do so successfully. That one is responsible for one's own free choices is clear, but not that one is responsible for others' choices and for the social ills that surround us. Nor does one become responsible for them by refusing suicide as a way out. A moral obligation to participate in social reform would logically follow from our social nature, but the existentialists do not admit a human nature that could be social. If we are free to choose our own values, what gives us a moral obligation to choose social values? Being-for-others seems to be only pasted on to being-for-oneself, with no reason why the paste sticks. Hence the appeal to ambiguity and absurdity. But then why spend such an enormous flow of words trying to put meaning into the meaningless?

PLACE OF FREEDOM IN ETHICS

Freedom has no less a place in a rational than in an irrational ethics, in a meaningful view of the world than in a philosophy of the absurd. The latter takes freedom as an indefinable and unprovable basic datum, which without further examination may be only groundless assumption, but the former after investigation fits freedom into the total scheme of a rationally ordered universe, where it finds its very important but proper place.

Freedom and responsibility necessarily entail each other, as the existentialists are not alone in emphasizing. We are indeed responsible for the free choices we make, but not everything in the world is of our choosing. To make us responsible for our whole environment, physical and social, over which we have no control, is carrying responsibility beyond any accepted usage of the term. One can argue that someone must be responsible and, if there is no God, responsibility for these things must be assumed by the only responsible being we know, that is, a human being. But the logical answer should be that no one is responsible, since we did not create the universe, did not freely put ourselves in it, did not even freely choose to be free. A coherent view of responsibility makes it just as extensive as freedom and no more. Since we have not freely willed our environment, we cannot be responsible for it, but only for our attitudes toward it. And this is held by any philosophy that admits freedom.

The concept of God as a supernatural stalkinghorse on whom we can throw our responsibility and shed our blame is not uncommon among believers. No wonder they reject such a God. Believers, too, can treat God in this fashion, for the ways of superstition are manifold and can include psychological projection. But this is not at all what knowledgeable believers mean by faith and religion. Rather than lower their responsibility by throwing it off on another, their acceptance of God increases their responsibility and makes it meaningful. With God, they are responsible to someone, they must answer to someone, they must give an account to someone. This is surely more than responsibility to oneself, which seems synonymous with no responsibility.

There is a temptation to pass from some of life's more galling absurdities to a castigation of the whole of life as one grand absurdity. Then we have the existentialist dilemma of either accepting the absurdity and defying it, as Sartre and Camus do, or of seeking deliverance by a nonrational act of faith, as Kierkegaard and Marcel do. In both cases philosophy as a work of reason is bankrupt. In the first case it stays bankrupt and hugs its own absurdity; in the second it is bailed out by God, who plays *Deus ex machina* in a serious sense. But there is no need for philosophy to go bankrupt, if it holds on to its treasure of wisdom and manages it with the guidance of reason, judgment, and prudence. Philosophies that do so make a great deal of sense out of our harmoniously ordered and beautiful universe, taking with a sense of humor its occasional absurdities and facing with courage the challenges it offers.

Why stir up an artificial conflict between being a free person and having a rational human nature? Trying to free us from our nature is trying to free us from ourselves. We are free because we have a nature of which freedom is an essential attribute. Existentialists implicitly agree by attributing freedom to humans alone. Freedom is a natural consequence of intelligence. Rational beings can be free because they have within themselves a natural guide to the use of their freedom, their right reason. Existentialists say that each one of us must have a project in life, what each one will make of himself or herself. Such a project can exist nowhere but in the mind of a person directing his or her free choice of actions to bring about the project's fulfillment. As existing in a person's mind, such a project cannot be some wild fantasy detached from life's possibilities but must be some rational aim both worthy and capable of accomplishment. How would it differ from the moral ideal we spoke of earlier? Either such an ideal is constructed and criticized by right reason, or else it has to be some blind stab in the dark. If the former, we have a rational ethics including the benefits of the existentialist outlook; if the latter, we have an absurd philosophy fit only for an absurd world it is absurd to try to live in.

Let us by all means have freedom, both positive and negative, and as much of it as we can, while recognizing that even freedom has its limits. Of itself, freedom has no judgment. As mere freedom, it is open to anything and everything and calls for guidance. As mere freedom, it is open to good and evil and is willing to take either. It must be steered to the good and away from the evil, and we have nothing to steer it with but the light of right reason. Right reason and freedom, intellect and will, knowledge and desire work together as a team, not as separate things within us, but as concurrent emphases of our one human nature, enabling us to fulfill the project we ought to accomplish, the embodiment of the moral ideal in each of us.

The upshot of all this is that the most valuable part of the existentialist philosophy is quite compatible with other ways of thinking and need not be taken in an exclusively existentialist sense. We should be very grateful, however, to the existentialists for emphasizing and eloquently presenting an extremely important but hitherto neglected aspect of ethics.

SUMMARY

Freedom is one of our most cherished values. On it some wish to build the whole of ethics.

Many see no opposition between freedom and law. They say that the purpose of law is to make the exercise of freedom possible, that the function of law is not to impose needless restraint but to direct people to their ultimate goal without destroying their freedom.

There are various kinds of negative freedom corresponding to various kinds of bonds from which one may be free; freedom of *spontaneity,* opposed to external physical necessity (compulsion); freedom of *choice* (free will), opposed to internal physical necessity (determinism); freedom of *independence,* opposed to moral necessity (law). Law, being a moral bond, is a restraint only of the last kind of freedom and, even in this case, only of the abuse of freedom. Without the guidance of law, liberty becomes license.

Positive freedom, freedom *for,* is our personal power to accomplish something by and through oneself. In relation to the moral law, this positive freedom is presented with the good for our rational and free nature, the good known through connatural knowledge, our emotional awareness of objective value, and our reflective reason. We have the power to pursue this good and so to comply with the natural moral law, and we have the power to pursue apparent goods to the detriment of our true good and so not to comply with the natural moral law. Our positive freedom can move in either direction precisely because we have negative freedom as co-constitutive of our very being along with our positive freedom. The moral law commands us with a moral necessity from which we are not morally independent but to which we must freely comply if we are to succeed as human beings. Without the guidance of the moral law, our positive freedom becomes license instead of the true liberty it can be.

Existentialism is hostile to all law. It stresses the primacy of freedom as a basic datum, the unavoidability of commitment, the dreadful responsibility of each decision, the confrontation of death, the purifying value of anguish and despair, issuing in a free act either of blind faith in God (theistic) or of accepting the ultimate absurdity of nothingness (atheistic). The latter variety especially is the philosophy of the absurd.

Many think that the positive contributions of existentialism, the values of freedom, subjectivity, authenticity, creativity, relevance, commitment, and involvement, should be stressed in any ethics, but that this can be done without the negative attitudes of nausea, despair, absurdity, alienation, ambiguity, and lawlessness that pervade existentialist thinking.

Questions for Discussion

1. Kierkegaard deplored rationalism for its propensity to build systems that explain the world and define the good for us. For him, only the "leap of faith" in freedom conquers the despair of living a life without meaning and hope. Are the evangelical crusaders of our own time correct in urging us to turn to faith in God if we wish to live a meaningful life? Human rea-

son has not been notoriously successful in showing us the way to lead a good life. The crusaders urge us to go beyond a life immersed in the pleasures of the senses and beyond the ethics of this world to embrace a life of religious faith. Here, they say, is true freedom to become the person each of us can become. Is this freedom in both its negative and positive senses? Explain your answer. Does a Kierkegaardian leap of faith free you from the moral law? From human law? From God's law? Explain your answers.

2. Sartre calls us among other things useless passions, vain desires to be God. Unlike Kierkegaard, he has no use for organized religion and more than likely would say that the person who makes the "leap of faith" is just opting out of the absurd world and choosing to live in "bad faith." How would Sartre confront the evangelical crusaders of our day and what would he have to say to them? Explain your answers. Is an existentialist ethics, or any other ethical theory for that matter, simply superfluous for the person of faith or does it supplement the message of faith? Why?

3. The minute virus that causes AIDS (acquired immune deficiency syndrome) is spreading in near epidemic proportions. So far we have not found a cure for what it does, and the development of a vaccine to protect us from its ravages is as yet only a remote possibility. Is this not the latest absurdity in an already absurd world which we can face only with despair? Life is cut short by AIDS; death is the only certainty at the moment. Construct a response to this situation as Kierkegaard might have done and then as Sartre might have done.

4. In the Declaration of Independence Thomas Jefferson called "liberty" a God-given, unalienable right necessary for the pursuit of happiness. Each of us has this right and certainly each of us pursues happiness according to his or her understanding and scheme of values. Do not the existentialists promote this very thing? Are there any constraints on our freedom today? What are they and what can we do about them? Are some of the constraints actually forms of oppression from which we need to be liberated in order to be truly free to become our authentic selves? Explain.

5. You are the fond parent of three children, aged 10, 15, and 18, respectively. In this scenario, have them be all boys, then all girls, and then a mix of boys and girls. You have recently learned about AIDS. You do not want your children to risk getting it; you want to protect them. What can you do? Obviously, some education about sex is going to be necessary, for ignorance is too dangerous. What do you teach them at home? What do you want them taught at school? What part do you want the government to play in this—local, state, and federal? How much freedom can you allow your children? How much freedom do you want and need to educate them properly not just to avoid catastrophe but to ensure as far as possible their future happiness?

Readings

On freedom in general see Mortimer Adler, *The Idea of Freedom,* with extensive reference to the whole literature of the topic.

All the existentialist writers treat moral matters at least obliquely. It might be well to begin with Kierkegaard's *Fear and Trembling* and its sequel, *Sickness unto Death,* and then his treatment of the subjective in his *Concluding Unscientific Postscript,* pt. II, ch. 1–3, pp. 115–224, 267–322. Josiah Thompson (ed.), *Kierkegaard: A Collection of Critical Essays,* provides helpful discussions on aspects of Kierkegaard's thought.

The philosophy of the absurd is clearly expressed in Jean-

Paul Sartre's essay *Existentialism.* He has a long treatment of freedom in *Being and Nothingness,* pt. IV, ch. 1, and draws ethical implications at the end of the whole work. Albert Camus's *The Myth of Sysyphus* and *The Rebel* also expound the philosophy of the absurd. See also Joseph S. Catalano, *A Commentary on Jean-Paul Sartre's "Being and Nothingness";* Arthur C. Danto, *Jean-Paul Sartre,* an excellent study; Maurice Cranston, *The Quintessence of Sartrism;* Germain Brée, *Camus and Sartre: Crisis and Commitment;* Mary Warnok (ed.), *Sartre: A Collection of Critical Essays.*

About existentialism see Kurt Reinhardt, *The Existentialist*

Revolt; James Collins, *The Existentialists;* William Barrett, *Irrational Man;* Norman Greene, *Jean-Paul Sartre: the Existentialist Ethic;* George Alfred Schrader, Jr. (ed.), *Existential Philosophers: Kierkegaard to Merleau-Ponty;* John Macquarrie, *Existentialism;* Patricia F. Sanborn, *Existentialism;* Calvin O. Schrag, *Existence and Freedom: Towards an Ontology of Human Finitude;* Hazel E. Barnes, *An Existentialist Ethics.*

14
Situation

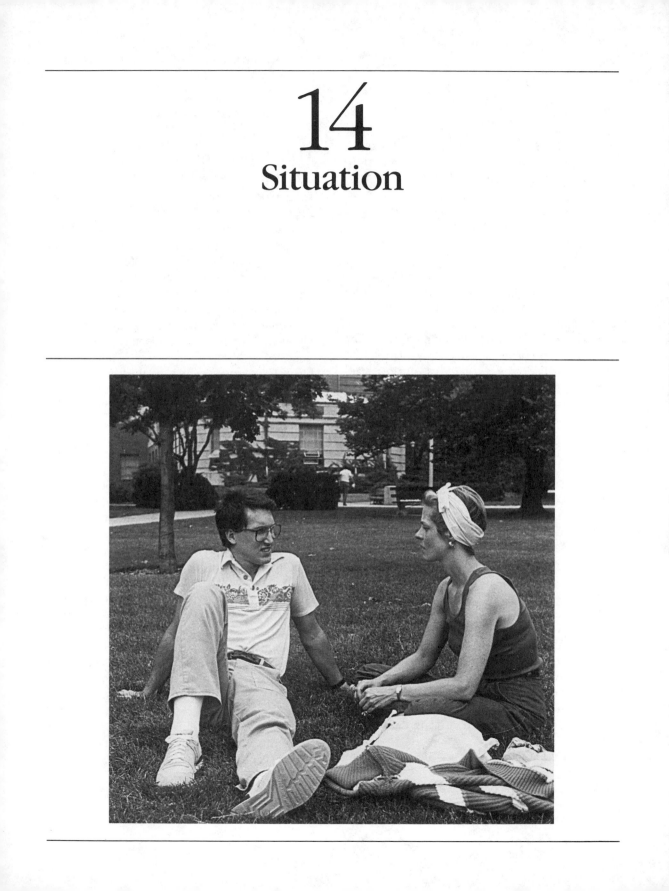

PROBLEM

Everyone knows that when we act we cannot just *do;* we have to do *something,* and that something must be a definite act done in a concrete situation. This is too true to need saying, but some philosophers think that not enough has been made of it. The situation, they say, is all important. In fact, they make it so overwhelmingly important that, in the opinion of many, it seems to have swallowed up whatever was supposed to be in the situation. Because of its strong roots in existentialism and its outspoken opposition to legalism, this view logically comes up next for consideration.

Situationists are distinguished not so much by the affirmation of the situation as by the negation of universals, essences, natures, norms, standards, rules, laws, and absolutes. The negation is indeed not absolute but enough to result in a fairly drastic deflation. They argue that every situation is unique. No act considered in its totality with all its context of surrounding circumstances can ever be repeated. It has some resemblance to other acts, but we cannot judge it on its resemblances only; we must also take into account the differences, which may be crucial. What, then, is the value of laws, norms, and rules, since they must be applied to individual acts done under concrete conditions and the application will be different every time? Why not simply say that there are no moral rules and every act must be judged in its concrete situation?

Our procedure will be to discuss, first, the way traditional philosophies view the situation of an act, then the theory of situation ethics as popularly proposed, and finally the philosophical assessment of situation ethics. These questions can guide our discussion:

1. What do motives and circumstances add to an act?
2. What are the reasons for and against situation ethics?
3. What is the place of the situation in ethics?

4. What does the uniqueness of each person contribute to the situation?

THE THREE MORAL DETERMINANTS

Those who hold to an objective norm of morality, whatever it be, have the problem of applying the norm to concrete cases. Just in what way and how far does the act agree or disagree with the norm? What must we look for in the act to see whether it is in agreement or disagreement? There is the act itself with its very own nature as an act, and there are the circumstances in which the act is performed. Among the circumstances, one, the motive or intention of the agent, may be singled out as of such importance as to be put in a class by itself. Two persons may do the same thing but from different motives, or different things from the same motive, or the same thing from the same motive but in different circumstances. In each case the act can have a different morality because of a different combination of these three elements.

The accepted terminology since St. Thomas's time is to call these three sources or determinants of morality the *object,* the *end,* and the *circumstances.*[1] By *object* is meant the object of the willed act, that which the will chooses to do, and this is nothing else but the act itself, which is deliberately willed. By *end* is meant the purpose for which the act is willed, and it may mean either the purpose the act is naturally fitted to achieve or the purpose the agent personally wishes to accomplish by willing that act; here the latter meaning is taken, since the former is implied in the nature of the act. By *circumstances* are meant the various accidental surroundings of the act. In the interest of clarity we shall call these three:

1. The act itself, or what a person chooses to do (the object)

---

[1] St. Thomas, *Summa Theologica,* I–II, q. 18, aa. 2–7.

2. The motive, or why the person does it (the end)
3. The circumstances, or how, where, when, etc., the person does it

The Act Itself

Morality resides in the will, in the will's consent to what is presented to it as morally good or evil. But we cannot just *will;* we must will *something,* to do or omit some *act,* which is therefore the *object* of the will's consent. The consent of the will derives its morality first and foremost from the kind of act to which the will consents. This is *what* the will wills; if the act willed is a bad kind of act, the willing of it must be bad; if the act willed is a good kind of act, and if there is nothing else about it to render it evil, the willing of it must be good. This point is so obvious that it hardly needs expression.

How do we know that an act is a good or a bad kind of act? The existence of verbs in any language shows that acts can be classified. No two performances of the act are exactly alike, but they are sufficiently alike to afford a basis for a universal concept. We can make a classification in the *physical* order, regarding only the muscles used and the material objects displaced, as when we speak of sitting, standing, walking, talking, grasping, hitting, throwing. Such acts are morally indifferent in their nature; whatever morality they have must come from the motive and circumstances. We can also make a classification in the *moral* order by putting certain moral characteristics in our definition. When we speak of hating, envying, murdering, stealing, lying, or slandering, moral evil enters into the very definition of the concepts indicated by the words and thus belongs to the kind or nature of the acts described. Verbs indicative of good acts, such as loving, honoring, helping, protecting, or benefiting, do not always have such a clear moral connotation, but in some contexts it is quite evident. Acts that thus have morality included in

their definition are good or bad of their very kind or nature.

What may seem to be mere circumstances in the physical order can belong to the very nature of the act in the moral order. We distinguish seizure and theft, killing and murder, speaking and lying. The first of each pair indicates only the physical act, which may be right or wrong; the second means an act that is morally wrong in its nature. Theft is not mere seizure, but the seizure of another's rightfully owned property against the owner's will; murder is not mere killing, but the direct killing of an innocent person; lying is not mere speaking, but the saying of what one knows to be untrue. At first sight these added qualifications may seem to be mere circumstances, whether what I take is mine or another's property, whether the man I kill has lost his right to life or not, whether the words I utter express my thought or contradict it. But in the moral order these points are essential. The moral order is the order of *willing,* and some features cannot be detached from the act willed. You cannot will merely to kill but must will to kill some definite person; you cannot will merely to take but must will to take some definite thing; you cannot will merely to say but must will to say some definite words. Thus from the moral standpoint the innocence of the victim killed, the ownership of the goods taken, the truth of the words said are not accidental or circumstantial but essential. They do not merely add to a morality already present but give the act its first moral quality and go to make up the very essence of the act in the moral order.

Here one might ask whether this traditional explanation is more than a linguistic front. It may be convenient to have words indicating acts with their morality built into them by including their moral circumstances, but how valuable is an argument drawn from a way of speaking? Are these qualifications *really* part of the act itself or added circumstances?

In a sense these are not circumstances. The

moral order, we repeat, is the order of will. What did that man *will* when he did that act? He whips out his gun, takes aim, fires, and kills his enemy. Would it be correct to describe this act as a mere movement of his fingers? Can we say that it is a mere circumstance that his finger moved against the trigger, which exploded the powder, which drove the bullet, which entered the victim's heart, which then stopped beating and left the man dead? In the physical order it might be described in this way, but in the moral order we can hardly say that all the man *willed* was a movement of his finger and the rest was mere circumstance. What he willed was the murder of his enemy and, especially if he was an expert marksman, the movement of his finger squeezing the trigger would be habitual and almost automatic once he had made up his mind to kill.

But in another sense these *are* circumstances. It does not make a great deal of difference whether one adopts the explanation just given or whether one says that the act itself, considered physically, is morally indifferent but surrounded by circumstances, some of which are so bound up with the act as to be the main object of the will and to give the act its first moral character.

In either of these two explanations the act receives a moral character, whether from the nature of the thing done or from some necessary circumstance known to be present and willed with the willing of the act. Thus it seems unnecessary to ask whether perjury is an essentially different act from lying or whether it is lying accompanied by additional immoral circumstances. The important thing for ethics is that perjury is morally evil and the perjurer is guilty of all the immoral parts and aspects of his or her act, whether they constitute the essence of the act or are its willed accompaniments.

The reason for discussing this matter at such length is to lay the ground for our inquiry into situationism, lest it become too much a dispute on words. One such dispute concerns actions said to be intrinsically good or evil.[1]

---

[1]See pp. 179 and 180, point 2, on each page.

The Motive

The motive is that which the agent has in mind when he or she acts, that which he or she consciously sets out to achieve by the act. If a person has no further reason for acting than the act itself, then the act and motive coincide, but more often a person uses his or her act as a means to something further. This further reason distinct from the act itself is what we are considering here. It is called by many names with subtle differences between them that are not important here: value, end, purpose, intent, intention, aim, goal, object, objective. The least ambiguous name in the present context is *motive,* which stresses the influence it has on the will in moving the agent to act.

In a murder the police look for the motive of the crime, knowing that one hardly ever kills for killing's sake, but to have revenge, to remove a rival, to seize the victim's money, to be rid of a blackmailer. The proverb "No one is a liar for nothing" recognizes the need for a motive in lying, to get out of a difficulty or obtain an advantage. That this motive influences the morality of the act prompted by it is obvious.

When I direct my act to some consciously intended purpose, I deliberately will this purpose together with the act, and both are voluntary. When I deliberately use a means to an end, in the one same act I will both the use of the means and the attainment of the end. As the act itself can be morally good, bad, or indifferent, so can the reason why the agent does it. Therefore, in addition to the morality that the act has by its own nature, the act also derives morality from the motive with which it is performed.

The motive may give an indifferent act its first moral quality, either good or bad. Thus one who borrows money with the firm intention of never returning it is not a borrower but a thief; one who refuses to testify in court because he or she wants the innocent enemy to be convicted turns the negative act of silence into one of hatred and injustice. The motive may only increase or decrease the same kind of morality the act already has; thus one may lie that he or she is lying so that the first lie will be believed; a clerk who pilfers a little money each day to build up to a predetermined sum cannot use as an excuse the smallness of each single theft. The motive may also add to a moral act quite a new kind of morality; thus one who gives money to the poor for the sole purpose of being praised turns such an act of kindness into one of vanity, and a man who steals money to have the means of seducing his neighbor's wife is, as Aristotle[1] observed, more of an adulterer than a thief.

Would it be correct to say with Abelard[2] that morality is found wholly in the intention, or with Kant[3] that morality consists solely in a good will and the motive of duty, so that the external act is quite outside the scope of morals? Such statements can be true only in the sense that without intention and will, no act can be moral or immoral, for a voluntary act requires knowledge and consent. But if there are some acts that one is never allowed to intend or will, and if there are circumstances in which we are not allowed to intend or will an otherwise good act, morality is not entirely dependent on our good intentions or good will.

The Circumstances

The circumstances are the various surroundings of the act, including everything affecting the act, except the motive just discussed. The motive, as we said, is a circumstance but was separated out for special treatment; we mean here all the other circumstances. A convenient way of listing the circumstances is to ask the familiar questions: *who? where? when? how? to whom? by what means? how often?* and the like. But not *what?* or *why?* since these questions ask for the act itself and its motive.

Some circumstances have nothing to do with

morality: whether one poisons with strychnine or cyanide, slanders in English or French, steals with his right or left hand. Other circumstances do affect morality: whether one robs a rich or a poor person; murders a stranger, a friend, or a parent; has sexual relations with a married or an unmarried person; damages another's character in private or public; charges exorbitant prices for food in normal times or when people are starving. These latter circumstances are the only kind we consider.

Like motives, circumstances can so affect the act as to make it a different *kind* of act from the moral standpoint. Dishonor to parents is not ordinary dishonor but also a breach of filial respect. Intimate relations between persons married but not to each other are violations of justice as well as of chastity. Perjury in a law court is not merely lying but also a violation of religion and justice. Other circumstances only change the *degree* of goodness or badness the act already has. It is still theft, whether one steals a large or a small sum of money; it is still drunkenness, whether one has had five or fifteen too many; it is still slander, whether one has partly or wholly ruined another's reputation. Such differences, though only in degree and not in kind, can be of the utmost importance.

It is evident that a human act can have its morality colored by the circumstances in which it is done. No act can be done in the abstract; every act actually performed is surrounded by a number of concrete circumstances involving persons, quantity, quality, place, time, manner, means, frequency, and relations of all sorts. These circumstances can be foreseen and willed in the willing of the act, and thus contribute to the morality of the act.

The fact that these are called circumstances should not lead us to think that they are negligible or unimportant. Sometimes they are made more of than the act itself, and to them the will is chiefly directed. There are some people who will lie but not to their mothers, others who will steal but not from their friends, still others who will kill but not a baby. Many otherwise indifferent acts

---

[1] Aristotle, *Nicomachean Ethics,* bk. V. ch. 2, 1130a 24; as quoted by St. Thomas, *Summa Theologica,* I–II, q. 18, a. 6.
[2] Peter Abelard, *Ethica seu Scito Te Ipsum* (Ethics or Know Thyself). This is what he seems to say in ch. 7 and 11; but he modifies his statements in ch. 12 and 13.
[3] Kant, *Fundamental Principles of the Metaphysic of Morals,* sec. II.

receive their whole morality from circumstances, because they are done at the right or wrong time, in the right or wrong place, by the right or wrong means, in the right or wrong manner.

Practical Application

To be morally good a human act must agree with the norm of morality on all three counts: in its kind, its motive, and its circumstances. Disconformity in any one of them makes the act morally wrong. Just as to be physically healthy one must have all one's organs functioning rightly, and if only one organ is deranged the person is unwell, so to be morally healthy no element of immorality must be present in any of one's acts.

An *evil* act cannot become good or indifferent by a good motive or good circumstances, and much less by indifferent ones. It is wrong to begin with, and no additions to it can get the evil out. No person is ever allowed voluntarily to will that kind of act in any circumstances or for any motive. That is why we must reject the principle, "the end justifies the means," in its usual acceptation. Though a good end renders good the use of indifferent means, a good end cannot justify the use of evil means. We are never allowed to do evil that good may come of it. A good motive and good circumstances may somewhat lessen the badness of the act, but it remains bad. Each bad motive or circumstance added to a bad act makes it worse.

A *good* act becomes better by each good motive and good circumstance added to it, but any seriously bad motive or circumstance is sufficient to render the act wholly and seriously bad, no matter how good it may otherwise seem. If there is only one motive and it is slightly bad, it will make the whole act slightly bad, for the whole act is for this one purpose only. When there are several motives or circumstances, a slightly bad motive or circumstance will not render the act wholly bad but only less good. Thus a person may give alms out of benevolence touched with vanity, may obey legitimate superiors but discourteously, may work at his or her job but lazily or negligently, may tell the truth but with a little

exaggeration. Such defects, commonly called *imperfections,* even though intended, cannot wholly ruin an otherwise good act, for the act retains its natural goodness in a somewhat tarnished form.

An *indifferent* act, since it has no moral quality of its own, must derive all its moral goodness or badness from the motive and circumstances. They must be all good or at least indifferent if the act is to be morally acceptable. Simply speaking, any bad motive or circumstance will make an indifferent act morally wrong. This matter can become quite complicated. How shall we judge cases in which an indifferent act is surrounded by a mixture of good and bad motives or good and bad circumstances? When the act itself is indifferent, and each motive or circumstance can be separately willed, it is easier to consider such acts as virtually multiple, that is, as compounded of a good and a bad act. Here we really have two moral acts and can judge each on its own merits. A lawyer in defending an innocent person may win the case by bribing the jury; the act of vindicating justice for the client is good, but the act of violating justice by bribery is evil. The two parts of the total act do not necessarily imply each other and can be separately willed, for the case might be won without bribery, and bribery can be used for other purposes. However, if this be considered one whole act, it must be judged evil.

SITUATION ETHICS

Situation ethics had a religious rather than a philosophical beginning. It seems to have sprung up in Germany between the two World Wars as a protest against overlegalistic interpretations of the Christian life, both Catholic and Protestant. It has been popularized by Bishop John A. T. Robinson[1] in England and by Joseph Fletcher[2] in the United States. It is sometimes called "the New Morality," though the newness is recognized as relative. It can be considered apart from any religious background as a form of a larger movement known as *contextualism.*

---

[1] Robinson, *Honest to God* and *Christian Morals Today.*
[2] Fletcher, *Situation Ethics* and *Moral Responsibility.*

Situation ethics is proposed as a middle ground between two extremes, *legalism* on the one side and *antinomianism* on the other.

Legalism is understood to be an abuse of law, making prefabricated rules and abstract prescriptions of the law into such absolutes that the real human good is to be sacrificed to them. It results in a hair-splitting and logic-chopping study of the letter of the law, either to free people from its toils or to use it sadistically to hurt rather than help them. It can result in a straightlaced, sour-faced, unloving life of meticulous duties, what Mark Twain called "a good man in the worst sense of the word."

Antinomianism, on the other hand, fares no better. It supposes no principles or maxims, let alone rules and laws. It is spontaneous and extempore, resulting in a kind of moral anarchy. Those who wait for the inspiration of the Holy Spirit to tell them what to do in each particular case exemplify a religious variety of this attitude. Extreme application of the existentialist ethics of ambiguity could have similar results from a philosophical point of view.

The situationists claim to be at the proper balancing point between these extremes. They approach every decision armed with maxims and principles, but use them as enlighteners and guides. They obtain from them all the good possible, but they will not be bound by them when they will lead to harm rather than good. Situationists consider no law or principle absolute. The situation alters rules, and it is part of moral responsibility to have the courage to discard the rule for a greater good.

Situation ethics acknowledges its affinity with pragmatism, relativism, positivism, and personalism. Fletcher tells us that for the situationist there are no rules, none at all, but then proceeds to give us six principles, as he calls them: Love only is always good, is the only norm, is the same as justice, is not the same as liking, is the end justifying the means, and decides in the situational there and then. The bulk of his work consists of case histories, vividly and dramatically told, portraying crucial moral situations. Many of them even hard-bound legalists could solve as

sympathetically as Fletcher, though few would be as latitudinarian in all cases.

Fletcher's popular style does not lend itself easily to the presentation of sustained argument. The following seem to be his main contentions:

1. Situationism accepts the nominalistic interpretation of universals, that is, they are mere names, conveniences of language. There is therefore nothing real about classes of things, types of actions, kinds of conduct, so that a general rule could be formed about them. Only the individual act with all its situational concreteness can have any reality. Ethics, the organized knowledge of such acts, can give only concrete description, not universal prescription.

2. Morality is not intrinsic to acts, but an extrinsic addition they acquire from the situation. Goodness is not a property of actions but only a predicate of some of them. It is not in the act but happens to it. There are therefore no kinds of acts that are intrinsically or of their own nature good or evil. If they become good or evil, it must come from the circumstances in which the act is situated. Since these are different in every case, no universal judgments or rules are possible.

3. Morality is relative, not absolute. The goodness or badness of the act that is done is relative to the situation, which alone gives it its goodness or badness. No law can be formed that could take in all varieties of all possible situations, and thus no law can be absolute. All it can do is describe what is the best course of action in most cases, but there is always room for exceptions.

4. Laws are but illuminating guides, not authoritative commands. Laws are for people, not people for laws. Laws are to be respected for the wisdom they embody and the help they give, but not to be worshiped and idolized as unbreakable and unbendable absolutes. This is no irresponsible antinomianism but a recognition of the true place and function of law.

5. If there must be an absolute, it is love. But love does not command, it invites. Love is not a law but a lure. Love makes its decisions situationally, not prescriptively. Love is not a thing, a being, a reality apart from people, not something we *have* or *are*, but something we *do*. In meaning

it is not a noun but a verb. Without love even the most legalistically correct actions are immoral. With love no legalistic prescriptions are needed for a full moral life.

Nonsituationists, while not denying the partial truth contained here, think that on the whole it is an inadequate account of the moral life. In particular:

1. Nominalism is a very shaky theory of knowledge that, when applied to ethics, results in disaster. Universals as such are not things but abstractions, it is true. The only reality about a class of objects is the objects that make up the class. But the objects do have the properties or attributes because of which they were grouped into a common class, and thus universal class concepts have a basis in the really existing objects comprehended under them. Thus the only kind of organized knowledge we can have, conceptual knowledge, refers to things and is true of them. There is no way of intellectually organizing discrete singulars, and situationism, which cannot get beyond the singular situation, makes ethics as an organized body of knowledge impossible.

2. Extrinsicalism merely transfers goodness and badness from acts to the situations in which they occur. Then we ask: Is goodness or badness intrinsic to the situations? Are there certain common situations in which a certain act will always be good or will always be bad? If so, we can express such situations in a general rule. If not, how can we recognize whether any act is good or bad, intrinsically or extrinsically? If moral goodness or badness does not reside intrinsically in anything, but is always attributed extrinsically from something else, how can there be any objectivity in ethics? Situationism does not want to be sheer subjectivism, but how does it escape?

3. That there is a great deal of relativity in morals should be obvious to all. That there cannot be absolute relativity is implicitly granted by the situationists when they make love into their one absolute. There is probably no law that does not admit of some exceptions, except such general formulations as "Do good, be upright, live the moral life," even "Do the loving thing." But the fact that laws have exceptions does not mean that they do not command with authority in those matters that do not come under the exceptions.

4. There is no contradiction in a law's being both a guide and a command. Certainly, laws are for people, not people for laws; but people are not only for themselves but also for other people, and the laws merely state how they should act toward other people. To worship the dead letter of the law is the kind of idolatry called legalism, but to avoid legalism there is no need of emasculating the law by denying its commanding authority and making it into something less than law. This *is* antinomianism.

5. Let us endorse all the beautiful things said in favor of love. But is it clear enough to be a reliable guide? How do I know that this is the loving thing to do, and not that? The love the situationists mean is not romantic love, passionate love, or even the love of friendship, all of which are exclusive, but that love of good will to all people called by the Greeks *agapē*. Since it is no subjective feeling, it must be judged by its results, that is, by the good it does to others. We are back in utilitarianism, as Fletcher admits.[1] If acts are neither good nor bad, how do we know the goodness or badness of consequences? Are they good consequences because they are the loving thing, and the loving thing because they have good consequences?

PLACE OF THE SITUATION IN ETHICS

Situationism has produced strong reactions, some hailing it as the long-awaited deliverer from the narrow confines of legalism, others dismissing it as a shallow attempt to justify the doing of anything you want and calling it moral. The proponents of situationism, because of their exaggerations, must bear the blame for its ambivalent image. At the risk of some repetition we

[1] Fletcher, *Situation Ethics*, pp. 95, 115.

shall try to disentangle its useful aspects from its rather glaring inadequacies.

That every act is concrete and done in a situation is no news. Traditional ethics always recognized the importance of motives and circumstances, which make up the situation or context of an act. The virtue of prudence, indispensable in moral living, is simply the habit of properly applying general principles to concrete cases. There are no rules for prudence, precisely because it deals with individually situated acts. The trouble with legalism is a failure of prudence, a stupidly wooden application of the letter of the law, rather than a failure in the law itself. But prudence has laws to apply and recognizes exceptions intelligently, whereas situationism wants no laws and makes every act exceptional.

Whether any acts of their very nature are good or bad depends on how they are defined. If they are taken in the physical order only, with no moral quality entering into their definition, they must receive morality from outside themselves, from the situation. Situationists regard all acts in this way, but if some act is defined to include morality or immorality in its concept, then such an act is already good or bad in itself. This is the view of those who hold for intrinsic morality, and they have good grounds in the common use of language, which is full of morally tinged, even morally soaked, words. Situationists may prefer their own explanation but are hardly the ones to lay down rigid laws on the use of language.

Situationism does not like any laws but is willing to admit principles, so long as they are not absolute. Natural law is out, because they think there is no discoverable human nature. One may ask, then, whether humans may live in any manner? If not, there is something that forbids them, and this is what is meant by law. May we make for ourselves any kind of law we want? If not, we must find the law already existing, and where else but in the kind of being we have with relation to all the kinds of situations we can get into? To consider the natural law as wholly nonsituational is to caricature it. To be sure, the law can consider only *types* of situations, not this concrete situation here and now; but this is the place of prudence in the application of the law, and that laws should be applied prudently is part of the natural law itself.

Condemnation of rigid legalism is situationism's best feature. Textbook morality, with its often glib statement of rigid rules, was bound to provoke a reaction. Traditional principles, some of them resting on false facts and outworn science, some not universal to humankind but only customs of Western culture, some taken for granted without the periodic reexamination to which even the most sacred truths must be subjected, have been asserted as absolute and immutable precepts of the natural law. Situation ethics issued the necessary dramatic challenge to this complacent dogmatism, but by its reckless exaggeration it jeopardizes its own case. There is no need of throwing away law to correct law's abuses.

Even situationists cannot do without an absolute. Natural law advocates are accused of making the whole natural law absolute, but this is a misconception. It is absolute only in the center, in its most general principle: Do good and avoid evil. As one passes from the center to the periphery, from the general to the specific, the situation comes in more and more. The more specific a precept is, the more relative it is, the more it suffers exceptions, the more careful we must be in its application lest we contradict a more general principle. Thus the natural law takes in the human situation, all of it, but does not become so situational that it ceases to be human.

Situationism balances off law against person. Laws are for persons, not persons for laws. True enough when we are talking about the abuse of law, of subordinating living people to empty abstractions, but the opposition is a false one when we are talking about law itself. Situationists quote Kant with approval when he says that we must treat each human being as a person and not as a thing, as an end and not as a mere means; but for Kant this is one way of stating the categorical imperative, which is an expression of the moral *law*. The dignity of a person does not come from the person's situation but from the kind of being a person is, a rational and free *nature*. Respect for the person and respect for the moral law are but phases of the same thing, not opposed and not even separable. The reason behind natural law principles is respect for the dignity of persons.

Another questionable opposition in situationism is that between law and love. Here the two notions are quite different, and it is possible to have one without the other. But it is also possible and usual to have both together. When the situationists insist that we must always do the loving thing, they admit no exceptions and lay it down as a law as absolute as any law could be. Of course, one does not legislate love, that is, pass laws regulating emotional love, but when the love is *agapē,* good will to all people, and is not distinguished from justice and prudence or any other form of good living, then the law of love becomes merely the law to be good, to be moral, to do the right thing—the first principle of the natural law.

If the situationists want to reduce everything to one principle, they do well to choose love. Nothing is more inspiring, more ennobling— and nothing is more difficult. How does one decide what is the loving thing to do in the situation? Some critics are unloving enough to say that situationism encourages a kind of infantilism. St. Augustine's often quoted remark, "Love and do what you will,"[1] has been called the worst possible slogan for youth and a safe guide only for a saint in the autumn of life. For if you know that you do truly love, then you can do what you wish, for you will not wish to do anything unloving. But how do you know that you truly love? It is to the situationists' credit that they do not trust to any fuzzy inner feeling, to a warm glow of self-approbation, or to a complacent judgment that it must be the loving thing to do because I, the

lover, choose to do it. No, love is proved in deeds. But the question remains unsettled. What deeds?

The situation has a very important place in ethics, but the situationists have no monopoly on it. It is important not only to have the right situation in which to act but also to do the right thing in whatever situation.

THE HUMAN SITUATION AND HISTORY

Even as spiritual beings, we humans breathe only in history and society. Our nature as rational and free is at the same time historical and social. We are historically situated at a particular place and time in relation to all the other human beings existing as we exist. All our knowledge of ethics, our awareness of moral values and the natural law, is historically situated in our social context and is thus relative, though not absolutely so, to the history and society within and from which anything is known. The historical character of our being is not limited to our existing at a definite particular place and time, but it also includes the history of the moral thinking, the moral tradition, of the people among whom we dwell at our time of life. This history and tradition is an essential part of our present situation, an unavoidable aspect of our own approach to morality and moral living.

Historical events are the medium within which we discover something about moral values and our need of them as well as the demands some values make on us to be realized in our present world. Since historical events have some novel value elements, and since historical developments foreclose some possibilities and create the conditions for others, we must be open to reform and revise our thinking about moral questions in every time. Our particular historical time and space is the arena of our moral action. Actions are by persons and to a large extent they are actions on other persons; we act with the moral insight we presently have and these actions are relative to the particular historic conditions and so require of us human responses relative to

---

[1] St. Augustine, *In Epistolam Joannis ad Parthos,* Tractatus VII, 8.

those conditions. Furthermore, the present human community to which you and I belong is in the process of developing moral insights through our historical experience, insights that will influence our future moral attitudes, judgments, choices, and actions. Changing experience allows the community to develop new insight into its moral tradition or to see new implications in that tradition. For example, the community in which we live and act and have our being as rational and free is presently in the process of wrestling with questions such as the justifiability of abortion, capital punishment, and waging nuclear war. If what *is* is at the same time what *ought* to be, we could stop our ethical endeavors right now, but we are not content to do this. We are still in the process of learning about ourselves and what we might yet become; we are developing further insights into human values and making further determinations about how to act in relation to our particular historical situation.

Another way of looking at our historical situation and its social context is to ask the question: "What particular demand is being made of me, the unique person I am, at this hour of my human and historical being and life?" Sheer rationalism in ethics, such as Kant's, looks only for universality and tends to ignore the modifying aspects of history and time. We need a composite view of the total human situation in which each of us keeps in mind universal values for the totality of his or her life even while each watches for the unique demand of the hour. We need in each of our lives a balance between universalism and individualism, a balance between cultivating the values universally valid for all people and those values comprehensible and available to one person alone (or family, people, nation). All the universally valid values for persons represent, in relation to the supreme and final good of the person, only a minimum of values without which the individual person cannot reach the perfection due his or her nature as rational and free. But these values do not in themselves embody all the possible moral values this individual person needs to actualize in his or her life to reach moral perfection as *this* particular person. Each person must, without neglecting the values universally valid for all persons, cultivate those values that he or she alone can bring into actual existence because those values call only to that person at that particular hour with the demand for actualization. This is the only way each person can achieve the good-in-itself that each of us must achieve to become fully the person each of us can uniquely become.

The moral demand of the present hour is an essential aspect of a person's whole moral "ought," and a matter of signal importance for the individual's moral life and growth. Every hour in a person's historical development offers the possibility of insights into unique values and so calls that individual to certain moral projects and actions. The moral content contained in the demand and the call is the good-in-itself "for me," not in the completely subjective sense, but in the sense of an objective good that is independent of me for its goodness but dependent on me for bringing it into being in this particular hour, an existence that it otherwise would never have. As a good that ought to be, it is a call to me to give it effective existence in the world at this particular hour. For me to miss the opportunity thus offered is to impoverish the world to that extent, for without me the value will not be given concrete existence in the world and I shall have failed to fulfill myself to that same extent.

The controversy over situation ethics would be illumined and enriched if the parties to the discussion were to study Scheler's idea of "the demand of the hour"[1] before they began their usual discussions of law, norm, and context or circumstance. Besides the extremes of legalism and situationism, there is the historicity of each personal human nature with its awareness of universal values and the demand of the hour pointing to individually valid values as well.

---

[1] Max Scheler, *Formalism in Ethics and Non-Formal Ethics of Values: A New Attempt toward the Foundation of an Ethical Personalism* II, 6B, pp. 489–494.

SUMMARY

To apply the norm of morality to concrete cases we must find out what there is in the act that can bring it into agreement or disagreement with the norm. We find three such sources or determinants of morality: the act itself, the motive, and the circumstances.

The *act itself* is simply what the agent wills, considering it not in the physical but in the moral order. An act receives its first morality from the kind of act it is.

The *motive,* or intention, is what the agent personally wills to achieve by the act over and above what the act naturally tends toward. The motive, being consciously willed, contributes to the morality of the act, sometimes giving it a new kind of morality.

The *circumstances* are the accidental surroundings of the act. Some have no effect on morality; others have an effect, changing the act either in kind or in degree. Circumstances can be foreseen and, if so, are willed in the willing of the act, thus contributing to its morality.

An *evil* act cannot be made good or indifferent by motives or circumstances, though the degree of badness may be somewhat modified. A *good* act is ruined by any gravely bad motive or circumstance; slightly bad ones weaken the act's goodness but do not destroy it. An *indifferent* act receives all its morality from motives and circumstances: if any one of them is bad, the rest being indifferent, the act becomes bad; if some are good and others bad, it may be possible to resolve the physical act into two moral acts.

Situation ethics holds that there is no intrinsic morality, no acts good or bad of their very nature, but every act must be judged in the situation. It admits laws, but they are only illuminating guides, not prescriptive commands, and none of them is absolute. It has one absolute principle (not law), that of agapeic love, and the only rule is: Always do the loving thing.

Situationism is criticized for its nominalistic theory of knowledge, for merely transferring morality from acts to situations, for overemphasizing the relativity of morals, for actually being antinomian while protesting that it is not, and for insisting on the doing of the loving thing while reducing the loving thing to utilitarian consequences.

The good points of situationism, the importance of seeing each act in its concrete setting, the condemnation of rigid legalism, the place of the relative in morals, the preeminence of the human person, and the primacy of love in the moral life, can be separated from the exaggerations of the situationist writers and incorporated into other ethical theories.

The excesses of situationism and legalism can be avoided if we remember the historical and social character of our being and keep a balance in our lives between cultivating the values universally valid for all people and those values demanded by the hour and experienced as a call to the individual person (or family, people, nation, or other group), values comprehensible and available only to that individual.

Questions for Discussion

1. Nell, Franny, and Tom are three friends, all young. Nell is from a wealthy and influential family. Franny is a struggling artist. Both are interested in Tom and he in them. Franny has long desired to continue her art studies in Paris and has applied for a scholarship there, but she is torn between her desire to go to Paris and her growing interest in Tom. Nell, through family connections, secures the scholarship for Franny. Excitedly she brings Franny the news, telling her how hard she worked to get Franny the scholarship. Franny receives the news coolly and does not seem very grateful. Feeling angry and hurt, Nell confides all this to her friend Grace, who suggests that Franny is just feeling sad at having to leave

her friends, especially Tom of whom she has been growing very fond. Nell replies that that could not be the reason, for Franny would never allow anything to interfere with her art. In any case, it is good for Tom that she go, because Tom is very sensitive and Franny's artistic temperament plays havoc with his nerves. Nell has often noticed this. In fact, when she was working to get Franny the scholarship, she had Tom's well-being in mind too. So whether Franny is grateful or not, she really does not mind. She has done something good for both her friends.

Analyze the morality of this situation from both a situationist point of view and that of another ethical theory. What do you think Nell's real motive was? Put yourself in her situation. What would you have done? Why?

2. Your mother, whom you love dearly, is suffering through the final stages of cancer of the esophagus. Once the cancer had been diagnosed as inoperable, you brought her home from the hospital to make her as comfortable as possible. Though she does not complain, you can hear her moaning with pain. Her physician has prescribed morphine tablets to ease the pain. They helped at first, but as the cancer has progressed the pain has become more acute and constant in spite of the morphine. Seeing her suffer is tearing you apart. Finally, you decide to crush all the morphine tablets and dissolve them in hot chocolate, which you give your mother to drink. The overdose works quickly and well. Her suffering has ended.

Analyze your action as a situationist and then as a natural law theorist. What differences do you find? Is one approach superior to the other? Why?

3. You are a member of the 99th Congress and sit on the Foreign Relations committee of the Senate. You and your colleagues have been struggling with the question of what to do about apartheid in South Africa. The President is opposed to stronger sanctions than those already in place, but throughout the country the sentiment is growing that something must be done to help the suffering Blacks of South Africa. Your constituents expect you to do something meaningful, and you and the other committee members want to do something too. The immorality of the situation must not be allowed to go unchallenged by the other nations of the world any longer. You feel obliged to propose legislation enforcing severe sanctions. The bill passes both houses of Congress, the President vetoes the bill, and Congress then overrides the veto. Were you morally obliged to do something in the first place? Is apartheid clearly immoral? Compare Fletcher's approach to such a question with a natural law approach. Do you find one more satisfactory than the other? Why?

4. The House Energy and Commerce subcommittee has obtained documents from the Department of Energy that detail a series of radiation exposure experiments on human subjects over a 30-year period from the mid-1940s through the mid-1970s. The purpose of the experiments was to measure the biological effects of radioactive material injected, ingested, or inhaled. The subjects included prisoners, the elderly, and the terminally ill. Some were willing subjects, but there is no record of informed consent for others. The government has made no attempt to find those still living to look for increased incidence of radiation-associated diseases and to compensate them for suspected damages. Analyze the nature of the act, the motives, and the circumstances. What is your assessment? How would Fletcher handle this situation?

5. AIDS (acquired immune deficiency syndrome), tragic as it is, must be faced by all people now, for all are at some risk. The Surgeon General of the United States has called for an end to silence about sexuality and for the start of a sex-education program for everyone. In the past we have been reticent in dealing with subjects of sex, sexual practices, and homosexuality. The silence must end. This may very well be a "demand of the hour" that is being made on all of us, for our very lives are at stake. Both medical and moral information are required. Create a panel to

discuss what to teach, when to teach it, and how to teach it. How do you think Fletcher would go about creating a curriculum for sex education in the light of AIDS? How would a natural law theorist go about it? Would you expect to find any significant differences between the two approaches? Why?

Readings

St. Thomas, *Summa Theologica,* I–II, qq. 18–21, treats of the goodness and badness of human actions, and of their objects, ends, and circumstances.

Eric D'Arcy, *Human Acts,* discusses the same thing from a modern point of view.

Situationism is defended by Joseph Fletcher in *Situation Ethics* and *Moral Responsibility.* A volume of reactions to the first book is published as the *Situation Ethics Debate,* in which well-known critics participate. An able criticism is found in Paul Ramsey, *Deeds and Rules in Christian Ethics,* ch. 7. Robert Cunningham edits a book of readings entitled *Situationism and the New Morality.*

Outka and Ramsey edited *Norm and Context in Christian Ethics,* a book of readings on both situation ethics and natural law, with some excellent articles.

Ignace Lepp, *The Authentic Morality,* and Louis Monden, *Sin, Liberty, and Law,* write perceptively on the new morality with a well-balanced judgment toward situationism.

Daniel C. Maguire, *The Moral Choice,* especially ch. 4 and 5, discusses circumstances and touches on situationism; James M. Gustafson, *Protestant and Roman Catholic Ethics: Prospects for Rapprochement,* discusses the historical situation of ethics; Alfons Deeken, *Process and Permanence in Ethics: Max Scheler's Moral Philosophy,* ch. 4, discusses "the demand of the hour," but Max Scheler, *Formalism in Ethics and Non-Formal Ethics of Values: A New Attempt toward the Foundation of an Ethical Personalism,* II, 6B, pp. 489–494 should be pondered carefully.

15
Love

PROBLEM

The situationists, as we saw in the previous chapter, make ample use of the idea of love. Love is too important a reality in human life to allow us to rest satisfied with what was said in Chapter 14. A human life without love can hardly be thought of as human, but love can be praised in such a way as to leave us with the impression that it is blind and incapable of functioning meaningfully in the moral life. This is what happens when critics of situationism, even while admitting that love is surely the noblest inspiration and the most dynamic force we have to drive us on toward whatever good we know, tell us that love is too uncritical a norm and too blind a guide to show us what is good.

We are sometimes given the choice of having an ethics of law or an ethics of love. Situationism has made such a choice and has opted for the ethics of love. Legalism is hardly a distinct ethical theory, but strict deontologies such as Stoicism or Kantianism opt for an ethics of law without paying much attention to love. We can ask whether any such option is necessary. Are love and law so opposed that we cannot have both?

Since we have given a fairly full exposition of law, and in our study of situationism may have seemed to short-change love, the time has come for a more thorough treatment of love. An important concept in connection with love is that of person, since love can exist only between persons. We have these questions to consider:

1. What is a person?
2. Why are persons intersubjective?
3. Why is intersubjectivity shown as love?
4. How can we love all people?
5. What is the place of love in ethics?

PERSON AND PERSONALITY
History of Person

The Greeks began philosophy as a study of the external world with only scanty reflections on the self. They did not even have a word for *person* but had to express the idea indirectly. It was not until the Christians speculated on the Trinity and

the Incarnation that a distinction was made between nature and person, and the word *person*[1] came into common use. The classical definition of person was given by Boethius: "A person is an individual substance of a rational nature."[2] This definition, repeated and commented on through the whole medieval period, is so explained as to mean that the person is not a *what?* but a *who?*, not an object but a subject, not a thing but a self, who has the mastery of his or her own acts, self-owned, self-possessed, self-controlled, with a uniqueness that is incommunicable to anything or anyone else.

Study along these lines is true enough as far as it goes, but it conceptualizes *person* and universalizes it like any other concept. Every human being is a person, just as every human being is human in the sense of being rational and free, but these are not stated in quite the same way. Humanity expresses what is common to us, but personality expresses what is unique in each of us. We are all persons, but no one else can be the person I am. This I cannot share with any other member of the same species. Though it is important to know what makes a person a person, and to know how this person verifies intrinsically the general concept of personality, what modern thinkers are more interested in is the uniqueness of this single person in his or her absolute unrepeatableness.

Descartes's meditations on the "I" of "I think, therefore I am" begins the modern trend toward subjectivity. Unfortunately, he identifies the "I" with the mind, which is only part of the person, though he does see that a person is a center of consciousness. Kant spoke well when he said:

> Beings whose existence does not depend on our will but on nature, if they are not rational beings, have only a relative worth as means and are therefore called "things"; on the other hand, rational beings are designated "persons," because their nature in-

---

[1] The Greeks used *prosopon* (face) and the Latins *persona* (mask).
[2] Boethius, "A Treatise against Eutyches and Nestorius," in *The Theological Tractates,* The Loeb Classical Library. Quoted by St. Thomas, *Summa Theologica,* I, q. 29, a. 1.

dicates that they are ends in themselves, i.e., things which may not be used merely as means.[1]

This emphasis on the dignity of the person went a long way to set up the person as *the* fundamental value in the center of ethics. But in both Descartes and Kant the person is still regarded as an object to be studied or dealt with, and not as the experiencing subject in its unique selfhood.

The personalist movement in philosophy began around the turn of the century. Borden Parker Browne in the United States founded *personalism,* a philosophy centering all knowledge about the Self, both the human and the divine personality, as an antidote to naturalism and positivism, without particularly developing the ethical side of personality or the aspect of love. A stronger movement of personalism came to the fore about 1913 in Germany with Max Scheler and about 1930 in France with Emmanuel Mounier, both of whom relate person and love. Some incitement toward this way of thinking may be traced to Henri Bergson, whose distinction between closed and open morality, the closed morality of laws and duties as against the open morality of inspiration from the teaching and example of noble men, led to an ethics of personal response. Martin Buber's "I-Thou" relationship helped to dramatize the intersubjectivity and interpersonality of human life and to show that the connecting link between persons is one of love.

Meaning of Person

The following exposition puts together the thoughts of a number of modern thinkers, trying to extract some common elements. Much of the writing on this subject is imprecise and capable of various interpretations.

Person is not to be understood as opposed to nature, even though the two are often balanced against each other. Rather, we should say that a human being is a being whose nature is rational and free, and every being with human nature is necessarily a person. Nature and person are not two things in a human being, nor are they two parts of that being; they are two distinct concepts representing two aspects of one and the same being. It is possible to have an ethics so centered about human *nature* that only the general requirements of humanity are considered, with no thought taken as to how this individual human being is to apply these general requirements to his or her own life. It is likewise possible to have an ethics so centered on this particular *person* as to disregard all other beings in existence, and what is left is a self-centered subject immured within the self, a kind of solipsism. Thus neither nature nor person alone will suffice. One can, however, admit that in human beings there are both nature and person and yet say that the aspect of the human being that is more important for ethics is not the nature but the person. We are obliged to live morally, not because each of us has a nature, since everything has a nature; nor because our nature happens to be human nature, since that merely names our nature among all other natures; but because our nature comes in the form of personality, and it is this personality that makes the moral life the appropriate life for each of us.[1]

Person is not to be understood as opposed to *individual,* even if we distinguish between the person and the individual in the same human being. Those who hold the Aristotelian theory on individuation[2] say that by matter, that is, body, a human being is this individual, since the form is repeatable only by being received in a different piece of quantified matter. But the form of a human being, the soul, is rational and free, and this it is that enables the human being to be a self-guiding, freely choosing, responsible person.[3] One can see in this explanation why there can be individual animals, plants, and inorganic particles, without their being persons. But in a human being the individual is the person and

---

[1] Kant, *Fundamental Principles of the Metaphysic of Morals,* sec. II.

[1] See pp. 126–128.
[2] Aristotle, *Metaphysics,* bk. VII, ch. 8, 1034a 5; bk. XII, ch. 8, 1074a 33. See also St. Thomas, *Being and Essence,* ch. 2, 4; *Summa Theologica,* I, q. 47, a. 2; I–II, q. 63, a.1.
[3] Maritain, *The Person and the Common Good,* ch. 3.

the person is the individual. The kind of individuality a human has is personal individuality. Hence, though the idea of person and the idea of individual partly overlap and partly coincide, in any individual human person they are the same thing. Thus we do not deny individuality of a human being because he or she is a person, and any difference between these concepts should not be overdone. But in talking of a human being we must choose the right word. Individuality says: "I am myself and no other." To go no farther would be to imprison oneself forever in one's own poverty. Personality says: "I am myself but open to others." The person, being an embodied consciousness that is rational and free, is responsive intellectually and emotionally to the whole universe and especially to other persons.

What distinguishes a person is not his or her spirituality or mentality. This was Descartes's mistake. The person is a center of consciousness, but in humans this consciousness is linked to the body and works through the body. The person is the whole human being, not a part, even if it be the better part. Popular language speaks correctly when it says, "He laid hands on my person," for the person includes the body. The person, therefore, is not only a unified memory or a stream of consciousness, so that it would be possible to have a split personality or successive personalities in the same body. When psychology speaks in this way, it is focusing on the integration of clusters of experienced personality traits. These clusters make up only the phenomenal personality, which psychology has explored with great ingenuity and success as part of its proper field. We are treating here the self, which underlies all such manifestations as their subject.

What does distinguish the person is *subjectivity*. The person is a subject, not an object. All attempts to form an objective notion of the subject are bound to fail. In a sense the only things that exist in the real world are subjects. They become objects by our knowing them. The object is something of the subject transferred by the process of knowledge into the knowing mind.

Since we know only the partial aspects they present to the mind, we never finish discovering them. The peculiar thing about a person is that it is a subject that cannot become an object. We try to make it one when we form the universal concept of person, but the result is that we nowise get at the person but only at an abstract concept of personality, which is not itself a person.

It seems that we can know only our own person, since we are subjects to ourselves. But how far can we know even this? Each of us is situated at the center of our world, in the observation tower of our own personality, from which we survey the landscape of the universe. We can look only through our own eyes, be aware only through our consciousness. For me all the landscape consists of objects, and in the midst of it I alone am the subject. My intuition of subjectivity is existential and presents no essence to be understood in a concept. Subjectivity is thus an unknowable abyss, an impenetrable night. In this sense one can agree with the existentialists[1] who say that we have a hole in the midst of our being, a radical nothing in the center of our consciousness, if this is taken to mean that all our knowledge is of objects, and we cannot be an object to ourselves. But we have a vague knowledge of ourselves simply by being ourselves, by existing as subjects. This knowledge is nonconceptual, more like the connatural knowledge that presents our early moral inclinations or like the creative intuition of the artist who is aware of having hit on the right color or the right word without being able to explain why.

I am the center of the world, subjectively. Objectively I do not count, for objectively I am only a thing among things and have lost myself. What happens to others is a mere incident to me; what happens to me is of absolute importance to me. I oscillate miserably between the subjective and objective perspective. If I slide into an object, I am false to my uniqueness. If I absorb everything into myself, I am selfish and proud. I want to

---

[1] Sartre, *Being and Nothingness,* pt. 1, ch. 1, sec. 5.

know myself as I really am and cannot do so without making an object of myself, which is the very thing I can never do. I know myself as I am to myself, which gives me only a subjective awareness of myself, whose objective reality I cannot certify. Others know me as object, not as subject, in the same way I know them. What they know is the I-in-them, a poor substitute for the I-in-myself. Thus I am severed from myself and wounded in my identity. From such reflections the existentialists can take off into alienation and anguish. Not all of them have discovered love.

INTERSUBJECTIVITY

We have been speaking of subjectivity. Care must be taken to distinguish it from subjectivism. Subjectivity is the condition of being a subject and the distinctive mark of personality; subjectivism is the theory that I exist, and whatever else seems to exist is but a state of myself. The student, hearing of the ethics of the person or of personal morality, may think of it as *my* morality, that is, any morality I personally want to adopt for my own living, and thus equate personalism with subjectivism. Nothing could be farther removed from the dignity of the human person than such an egoistic subjectivism. Any morality I happen to adopt does not become true or good by the mere fact that I adopt it. It may be wholly uninterested in the good of other persons and quite content to treat other persons as things. This would be entirely contrary to personalism as an ethics of the person.

We said that we can know others, even other persons, only as objects. Such objectification, conceptualization, or universalization is not false to essences, for that is the way they are made present to the mind and the only way we can know them intellectually. But it is false to subjectivity as subjectivity and is the reason that we cannot know it. In other words, the only way to know the other precisely as other is to *be* that other, which I can never be. Knowledge is not the only kind of communication, however. There

is also the communication of love. Before discussing love, we must see what makes love possible.

The person is not wholly a person if completely isolated and alone. Being includes both subject and object. Being itself is neither interior nor exterior to the knowing self. It *is*, purely and simply. I am not being itself, but I am within being and sharing in being. I do not affirm being without affirming myself, and I do not affirm myself without affirming opposite me an object, since this too is given to me in consciousness. With some of these objects I find I can communicate by means of signs, objective but meaningful symbols, a poor substitute for subjective experience but sufficient to let me know that the other is a person, a center of consciousness, like myself. Though I know the other only as an object, I know objectively that the other is a subject. Just as I am taking the other into myself and absorbing the other's thoughts and feelings insofar as he or she can communicate them, so the other at the same moment is taking me into himself or herself in the same way. The other contributes to my growth by what he or she shares with me, and I contribute to the other. This is intercommunication, but it is not intersubjectivity, because each is still only an object to the other, and the means of communication are objective. But this intercommunication is far more fulfilling than being alone.

We have here a transition from the I-It to the I-He/She relation. The other is recognized as a person like myself, though this recognition is on the objective and conceptualized plane. The other is not to be treated as an It, a thing; neither is the other to be used or consumed as a means to my end, but to be respected as an end and value in himself or herself. The other is the subject of rights, and toward him or her I have duties. Our relation is one of justice and quite sufficient to establish a working social order. Conceptually I can put myself in the other's place and I can rationally argue that I must treat the other as I would want the other to treat me. Between us an ethical order can be established of a high type, but not of the highest type. What is wanting is love.

PERSONAL LOVE

Human love in its fullest sense is an experience of intersubjectivity. It passes beyond the I-It and the I-He/She relation to an I-Thou relation. *It* is a thing to be used as a means. *He* or *she* is someone else standing over there about whom we are talking; we communicate about but not with him or her. But to me you are *Thou,* and I am *Thou* to you. Why not say *You?* We use the archaic English form to emphasize that it has to be singular. It signifies the relationship between one center of consciousness (I) and one other center of consciousness (Thou). If love is for a person, it is focused on that one person, and if the love is returned, it is focused back on me. Three people can love each other, but if the love is reciprocal and thus truly personal, there are six acts of love.

Love is silent. Why do I love you? Because you are you. There is no reason and it is futile to search for one. If one could be found, it would show the love to be of the lesser sort, a love for various desirable qualities you may have, and this could be more a love for the advantage those qualities may bring to me than a love for you. This lesser love of desire is genuine love and by no means to be despised, but it contains more of an element of self-love and does not rise as high as love in its fullest perfection, which goes beyond all desirable qualities of the beloved directly to the beloved as a person. It bypasses the beloved's suchness to reach his or her selfhood, a Self subsisting in its own goodness, not as perfective of the lover but as loved for itself in its own person.

Love is communion. Lovers love themselves but do not remain wholly within themselves. Love in a sense is one, and in another sense is two. As *one,* it is a uniting, a union, based on likeness. Because the beloved is like the lover, the lover can love the other, since he or she sees in the other some image of the lover's own self, and in

the best love an idealized image of what the lover would want both of them to be. Communion in love demands community in goodness. Love is *two* in the sense that the union does not do away with the lovers. The term of love is the selfhood of the other, the unique, irreplaceable, incommunicable subsistence as a person. The other, retaining his or her uniqueness as a person, which is the very reason that he or she is loved, still somehow becomes one with the lover. Thus that I-Thou relation remains. Love makes the other a Thou, but the Thou never loses its identity to fuse with the I.

Love is presence. Lover and beloved share in a common value that must be present in both. I as subject am present to myself as the secret and profound source of all the activity that constitutes my life, the consciousness of myself as I. This is no abstract concept, but a living experience. The subject is present to the other and the other to the subject, not as a universal concept, not as an existing nature like other natures, not even in the abstract recognition of his or her subjectivity and personality, not as an It and not as a He or She, but in that indescribable presence, so like my own presence to myself, that is designated by the Thou. To me, the Thou becomes a second self as a subject, and open to me in the same sense in which I am open to myself.

Love is self-giving. Only insofar as I love another do I really love myself. I find that what I love in myself is not confined to myself but extends out to a Thou. By my love I make myself a gift to the Thou. This self-giving is essential to the completion of my personality, but it is not consciously directed to the completion of myself but of the Thou. My goal is to make the other infinitely lovable—but not by shaping or twisting the other into anything else but the other's self. I appreciate his or her freedom as I appreciate my own. Far from subjecting the other to myself, I help him or her to become himself or herself in the full exercise of his or her self-directing freedom. Because this gift of myself is never total, love can increase forever.

Love is creative. It is not a dreamy feeling or a lazy repose, but a vigorous commitment toward the fulfillment of the Thou. It influences another center of consciousness and helps that center grow in the presence of the lover. Love does not create the original personality of the other but finds it. The beloved exists in the world, displays his or her personality there, and merely by being a self has made his or her being shine into my own. I will the continued existence of the other as developing autonomously in harmony with the ideal he or she is striving for and I anticipate in him or her. Thus love is creative by cooperating with the beloved's work of creating his or her own fulfilled personality.

Love is reciprocal. Loving implies both the desire and the fact of being loved. It is possible to have love that is not returned, but its unsatisfactoriness is evident. This desire to be loved manifests the inevitable component of self-love in all love, a self-love that in no sense need be selfish but is a simple regard of the worth of oneself as a person even as one regards the worth of the other as a person. Thus love links persons into a community. The reciprocal journey of the I to the Thou and of the Thou to the I results in a We. The We of love is the meeting of two subjects whose being is in each's self but whose having is in the other's self, and the awareness of this communion. It is a heterogeneous identity of the I and the Thou, not absorbing the I or the Thou, but expressing their mutuality. There can be a lesser We consisting of a mere crowd or a loose class-conscious group or an organized society of cooperating members, but the We of love is the personal I-Thou relation.

Love is the supreme value. We may question this statement, but on reflection we see that love must be all or nothing—although not in its actual exercise, for we may love more or less and never love perfectly any more than we do anything else perfectly. In its thrust and goal, however, love is limitless and can take second place to nothing else. Love does not oppose any existing realities but animates them while respecting them. Love is its own value, which is the value of the person. But is not God the supreme value? Certainly, but God is Love. All that was said here about love between two human persons is verified on an infinitely higher plane in God, in our love for God and God's love for us, and in God's own love for himself. Even love between human persons is unfinished unless their union is seen as a participation in the love of God, who is the very acme of personality and lovableness.

LOVE FOR ALL HUMANKIND

The intense personal love we have been talking about cannot be extended to all humanity. One can be friendly toward all but a friend to only a few. We can will to exclude no one from our friendship, but we can include positively only those with whom we can establish an I-Thou relation. Here we are victims of the narrowness of our experience and the limitations of our powers.

When we talk about love of the neighbor, and by neighbor mean everybody, this love has to be on another plane. It extends to those we have never seen or heard of, those we cannot like, even those who have done us harm. With them we can have no experienced intimacy and no sharing in their very subjectivity. Our love for them is grounded in sympathy, which sees and appreciates all other persons precisely as other than oneself and yet as *like* oneself in being intrinsically worthwhile. Each and every other person is unique in his or her way of being present in the world and is therefore an absolute value just as I am an absolute value. As uniquely lived, the life of each and every person has profound value. This is not a matter of mere appreciation and understanding; it is that, but is coupled with an awareness that each individual person in his or her value dimension is unique and that each person lives his or her life uniquely. Sympathy thus overcomes egocentrism and opens us to all human beings as unique persons in all their lived uniqueness as absolutely valuable. This openness to all humans as persons, that is, as absolute values, is the basis for authentic love of all humankind. This love does not depend on prior distinctions, for example, between citizens and foreigners, the law-abiding and the criminals, educated and illiterate, good and bad. Sympathy and love of humankind are directed toward all persons simply because they are persons.

The specific directedness of genuine love of humankind arises spontaneously, grounded as it is in the relational unity made concrete in sympathy. Love of humankind takes sympathy's openness to all others' likeness to oneself in their absolute and unique value, and in its movement this love penetrates that relation of likeness more profoundly. As long as we remain divided into friends and enemies, high and low born, as long as love is encouraged toward friends and hatred toward enemies, recognition is given the high born and not the low, and all this is given moral sanction, the unique personal presence of another person can be disclosed only in the case of the friend and the high born. As long as this situation prevails, genuine love of humankind and all the more so personal love is impossible, for the penetration operative in genuine love of humankind brings to light the fullness of unique persons participating in humanity and so opens us to the possibility of personal love itself.

The love of humankind is thus a true love; it is not unemotional and simply reasoned, at least not at its outset. This love is directed to others in response to the values our emotions disclose in them as persons. The directedness of all our loves, even this love of humankind, discloses the whole value presence of a person in its potential for fullness. What is thus disclosed could be disclosed only in that very love. Such a love is not only possible for each of us but is ethically demanded of us. Each person in the world is a call to me to love him or her with this kind of love we call love of humankind or love of neighbor.

The fact that our fellow human is a person gives him or her a dignity worthy of our esteem beyond mere respect for his or her minimum rights. Our social nature makes us see in another a companion on life's journey, one with whom we share common burdens and hopes, one destined to pursue in common with us the fulfillment of his or her being. As we seek for ourselves all good and no evil, we must seek the same for our fellow humans. This is love, not of the deep and intense form that binds lovers into one heart, but of the wide and all-embracing type that takes in the whole of humanity as our brothers and sisters.

Love of this kind includes justice but goes far beyond. Love and justice are often contrasted, and yet they spring from the same root. Justice is love limited to the absolute requirements of basic human equality. Love is justice expanded to the fullest scope of the human person's dignity. Justice is minimizing and negative in emphasis: do not take or keep from another what is rightfully that other's. Love is maximizing and positive: go as far as you can in giving to another what will help that other. Justice and love spring from different motives. Justice is connected with law, obligation, rights, and duties and measures out its awards according to equality or merit. Love is large-hearted and generous, giving its gifts without measure or stint, rejoicing that it has something to give. Justice and love are the two great social virtues that govern people who are living together. Since there can be no love without justice, the requirements of justice must be fulfilled first. Then, when justice is established, love urges on as far as human ability can go.

A theistic philosophy can give to love of the neighbor a dimension necessarily lacking in the various secular humanisms. Though *we* cannot establish an I-Thou relation with each and every human being in existence, God does so. He is intimately present to the subjectivity of each of his creatures, and his infinity enables him to embrace them all. Thus we can love all humanity, even those who can never enter our experience, because God, whom we love, loves them. They are persons because they are likenesses of the most personal of all beings. Our openness to God, to whom they are also open, enables our love to pass through him to them. This is why it can be said that we love our neighbor in God. Our love for each other is thus a mirror of God's love for himself and for us.

PLACE OF LOVE IN ETHICS

The ethical theory presented here may be regarded as a rather eclectic form of *personalism* and, as far as the love part is concerned, could be called *agapism,* from *agapē,* the Greek word for charity, or the highest kind of love. We did not oppose *agapē* to *erōs,* as some do. All disordered love would be *erōs* without *agapē,* and the love for the neighbor could be *agapē* without *erōs.* But the two can occur combined and ought to in the highest type of love. One's love for God can be consumingly passionate, as the history of mysticism shows. Whether or not *erōs* is present, what gives love its moral value is the element of *agapē.*

Morality, the field of ethics, is a demand on us humans for rational behavior, that is, a demand that we conduct ourselves in terms of things and of persons as they really are in themselves. The motives for our conduct are rooted in our emotional life, for our original contact with value that is independent of us, objective value, is by and through our emotional awareness of those values. The moral life consists largely of our response to those values, and once again the response is emotional in its roots or at its core. Rational behavior, then, consists of our allowing our emotions and desires to be fashioned by things and persons outside us so that we can respond to them as they are in themselves. When our emotions operate objectively, they are not a mere reaction to a stimulus; they are our immediate appreciation of the value and significance of real persons and things. By and through our emotions, reason is able to apprehend objective values and formulate ideas about these values.

In our relations with one another, our interpersonal relations, love is the fundamental, positive emotion characteristic of human beings. Like any of the other emotions of which we are capable, love too can be either purely subjective and so irrational, or it can be objective and so rational. When I have a feeling of love for another person, I can be experiencing either a pleasurable emotion that that person stimulates in me, or I can love that person. The feeling of love is completely subjective and irrational if I am just enjoying myself in being with that person who is just an instrument for keeping me pleased with myself and enjoying merely the feelings I am

feeling. My love is objective and rational, on the other hand, when it is really the other person that I love and enjoy precisely as a person whose existence and uniqueness are important in themselves. The capacity to love objectively is what makes us persons. This same capacity to love is the ultimate source of our capacity to behave in terms of things and persons as they are in themselves, our capacity to behave objectively. Love then is at the very roots of morality just as it is at the core of our rational consciousness.

Love is the guide to a person's discovery of value, both value that already exists concretely and value that is not yet real but ought to be real. Whatever consciousness of objective values we have is a result ultimately of love. Our development and growth in value consciousness is always a love-guided growth and development that begins at birth and need never stop. Each of us develops a stance with regard to value, called our fundamental value orientation. This orientation determines each person's approach to the world in terms of value, and it is therefore what ultimately determines our sphere of choices and so also the scope of our positive freedom. This fundamental value orientation is the order of our loves, our own individual system of value preferences. This system of preferences is based on and grows out of our own emotional acts that alone give us access to objective values; its content is objective, and its uniqueness is a result of each individual person's own ordering of the given values. Since a person's fundamental value orientation is, so to speak, the basic moral intention or stance of that person, it is absolutely basic for all levels of moral activity and is an absolute requisite for there being any moral value at all at any of the levels of willing—aim, intention, choice, or realization. Love is then not only one of the greatest moral values, it is also our guide to all the others. The moral life can accurately be characterized as a love affair with goodness and beauty.

There was no mention of sex in our treatment of love, and by design. Even *erōs* is not limited to sex but is any kind of desire. There can be love without sex and sex without love; they are two different things. There can, of course, be sex with love, and that is surely the way sex ought to be, but that is a problem for sex, not a problem for love.

Missing from this chapter is a balancing off of opposing theories. One may quarrel with details presented here, but among philosophers there is no systematic opposition to love. Would anyone claim that love is not good? The ethics of love seems to be quite compatible with all and any of the philosophical viewpoints we have described and is rather in addition than in opposition to them. There are ethical theories that neglect love, but that is a sign of their inadequacy. What theory of morals can afford to overlook the greatest of moral values?

SUMMARY

Person was defined by Boethius as "an individual substance of a rational nature." *Personalism* is any philosophy based on the central importance and outstanding dignity of the person.

Person is not opposed to *nature* in the human being, even if the person be thought the more important aspect for ethics; nor to *individual,* despite the reference of individual to matter and of person to form. Though chiefly regarded as a center of consciousness, the person is the whole being, not merely the mind.

The distinguishing mark of person is *subjec-tivity.* We can define person only by conceptualizing it and making it an object. The subject is known only by direct experience. I have direct experience only of myself as a subject, for I am the only one I can ever be. The person is a subject that cannot become an object.

Intersubjectivity is possible, not by knowledge, but by love. We pass beyond the I-It and the I-He/She relation to the I-Thou relation.

Love is *silent,* for it can give no reason for itself; *communion,* because it unites two with no destruction of their identity; *presence,* by which the Thou as subject becomes a second self to the I as subject; *self-giving,* not directed to the completion of myself but of the other; *creative,* by helping the other in the creative work of fulfilling his or her personality; *reciprocal,* in that the meeting of the I and the Thou results in a We; *supreme value,* inasmuch as love pervades all other values, and God is Love.

Love for all humankind is a less intimate love, not based on direct experience of others' personalities but on the emotional awareness that they are persons. It includes justice but extends beyond it. It is raised to its highest plane when suffused with the love of God, who created persons in the likeness of his own personality.

The ethics of love is not opposed to other ethical theories but is compatible with what is good in all of them.

Questions for Discussion

1. We are born helpless. As soon as we are conscious, we discover others and we also discover loneliness. We discover that we are needy—we need others physically, emotionally, and intellectually. An awareness of the personal self gradually emerges from these needs and their satisfaction. We go on to discover that we not only need love but that we have a need to give love to others and that within that gift of love is an appreciation and admiration of the other. We find further that we are giving the very thing we need and that we have a need to do this. Take some time to reflect on your own history to see if you can discover a direct experience of yourself as a person, as a subject involved in intersubjectivity. Can you share this experience with others?

2. We use the one word "love" to describe many different relationships, for example, love of mother, father, sisters, brothers, and other family members, as well as friends, nature, country, and pets. We also use the word to describe the relationship of "sweethearts" and husband and wife. All of these relationships are important to us; they contribute to the

fullness and meaningfulness in our lives. Love obviously has more than one meaning, and yet there must be some common thread that runs through all these loves. What is it? Is it concerned only with the one who loves or also with the one who is loved? Do the loves in your life tell you anything about yourself? If so, what?

3. Aristotle once said that no one would want to live without friends. Do you find this true of yourself? Can what was said in this chapter about love be applied to that unique love we call friendship? Do you find you love your friends in this way? In your opinion, what are the marks of a true friend? Do you find that you are truly free only in and through the reality of your friendships? If so, why? If not, why not?

4. "Love of neighbor" or "love for all human-kind" on our part can be manifested in many ways that go beyond matters of justice. If the members of the entire class were to engage in a session of collective "brainstorming," they might all be surprised at what they would discover about this love and how it manifests itself to the world in deeds. Does not the very desire to work for social justice grow out of a love for the neighbor?

5. Denis de Rougemont holds that any of our loves becomes a demon the moment it becomes a god. This is another way of saying that any love can go bad on us, for example, the very friendship that can be a school of virtue can become a school of vice. If that is true, how do you prevent any of your loves from going bad? If love is the greatest value, the most important thing in life, how can it possibly go bad?

Readings

On person read Emmanuel Mounier's *Personalism,* and Jacques Maritain's *The Person and the Common Good* and *Existence and the Existent*.

Anders Nygren started a stream of writing on love with his *Agapē and Erōs*. Martin D'Arcy in *The Mind and Heart of Love* and Gene Outka in *Agapē: An Ethical Analysis* respond to Nygren and each adds his own development. Denis de Rougement has a well-known work, *Love in the Western World*.

Read Maurice Nédoncelle, *Love and the Person,* and Robert Johann, *The Meaning of Love*. From these, together with Maritain, much of our material was taken. See also A.R. Luther, *Persons in Love: A Study of Max Scheler's Wesen und Formen der Sympathie;* and Max Scheler, *Formalism in Ethics and Non-Formal Ethics of Values;* John Macmurray, *Reason and Emotion*.

Also Martin Buber, *I and Thou;* Erich Fromm, *The Art of Loving;* C.S. Lewis, *The Four Loves;* Frederick Wilhelmsen, *The Metaphysics of Love;* Robert Hazo, *The Idea of Love;* and Rollo May, *Love and Will*.

16
Habit

PROBLEM

The good life does not consist of choosing to do unrelated good acts. In the chapter just completed, we have seen that love is its own value and indeed the greatest of the moral values because it discloses the value of the person as a person. When we realize that the objective norm of morality is the person considered in all his or her parts and essential relationships, we can easily see that the value that love reveals, the person, is the supreme value in terms of which all other values in this world are judged and ranked. As this world's supreme value, the person taken completely in all his or her parts and essential relationships is the ideal or moral model clamoring in each of us for full realization and development. The demand that the value places on us is the basis for the moral ought. What good ought to be done and what evil avoided to bring about my full realization and development as a person comes to first awareness through connatural knowledge and becomes conceptualized through reflection as the natural law.

The good life then consists of living according to the precepts of the natural law. The obligation is one of absolute moral necessity for I have an absolute obligation to succeed as a human being. As each person lives his or her life in a definite situation and makes moral decisions in particular circumstances, he or she is always faced with the need to apply the precepts of the natural law in individual instances when something definite must be done. To bridge the gap between the general or universal principle and its application to a particular instance, we need good habits of moral thinking and desiring. The moral virtues and prudence (or practical wisdom) are developed precisely to bridge that gap by disposing us to choose with ease the moral good that befits our personal nature in all its essential relationships.

Our acts of choice lead into one another, reinforce one another, and form chains of good conduct. The good life would be harrowingly difficult if each good act had to be done on its own without any influence from one's past behavior. The only way of assuring ourselves that our acts will be morally good is by turning them into a habit. Virtue and vice are only names for morally good and morally bad habits. Virtue testifies to good acts done, for there is no other way of acquiring a virtue, but it is also and chiefly the spring of further and better moral acts in the future. Virtue stands somewhere between a single good deed and a whole good life.

This chapter is mainly descriptive, but it does contain some problems. One is the paradox that the choice of good acts produces virtue, and virtue itself is the source of choosing to do good acts. Another is the Socratic concept of virtue as knowledge, from which it might seem that virtue can be acquired by study rather than by choosing to do good acts. Another is the Stoic concept of virtue as the end itself rather than a means. A last problem is to determine which among the almost innumerable virtues exert the chief influence on our moral choices. We ask:

1. What is the moral significance of habit?
2. Does virtue consist of knowing?
3. Is virtue its own reward?
4. How does virtue stand in the middle?
5. Which virtues are basic to all the rest?

MORAL HABITS

By derivation *habit* means a *having,* and on this score anything we have is a habit. But over the centuries the word has become narrower in its meaning. Aristotle calls habit a lasting disposition,[1] a holding oneself in readiness to act in certain ways, and gives this definition, often quoted by St. Thomas:[2]

> Habit means a disposition according to which that which is disposed is either well or ill disposed, and either in itself or with reference to something else.[3]

So vague a definition made it necessary to distinguish *entitative* habits, or habits of being, from *operative* habits, or habits of acting. The former would be such qualities as health or strength or

---

[1] Aristotle, *Categories,* ch. 8, 8b 27.
[2] St. Thomas, *Summa Theologica,* I–II, q. 49. a. 1, ff.
[3] Aristotle, *Metaphysics,* bk. V, ch. 20, 1022b 10.

beauty, which we hardly call habits today. Modern language recognizes only operative habits, the tendencies we *have* developed in ourselves from repeated acts.

We are born with a nature endowed with certain powers of acting. We begin to exercise these powers, and each time we do a thing we find it easier to repeat the action in the same way. Habit is beginning to take shape. It is an actualization of our potencies or capabilities but has the peculiar position of being somewhere between bare capability and full act. Take the example of a carpenter. As a child he was only a potential carpenter, having an undeveloped natural ability. Now that he has developed the skill and learned the trade, got the habit, he is an actual carpenter, one actually expert in this kind of work. But he happens at the moment to be asleep. Though he actually has the habit, he is not exercising it and is in a state of potency toward that exercise. When he awakes and starts plying his trade, he not only is an actual carpenter but is actually carpentering. Thus the habit is a sort of midway stage between undeveloped ability and expert operation.

Habit does not give us the power to *do* something; this we must have from our nature. Rather, habit enables us to do something *more easily and readily*. If the habit is good, it turns our originally fitful and clumsy efforts into quick, smooth, and masterful action. If the habit is bad, it makes us fall more easily and readily into the undesirable course of action. Habit has therefore been called a "second nature,"[1] for just as nature is the principle or source of action itself, so habit is the source of facility in action. The habit comes from the acts, and the acts come from the habit, but in different ways: by acting repeatedly in a certain way we acquire the habit, and the habit now acquired tends to manifest itself in habitual acts.

Habits are typically *human* things. God can have no habits because he has no potentiality and does all things with perfect ease. Animals cannot have habits in the proper sense because their potentialities are too narrow and their lines of

action are laid out for them by their nature through their instincts; people can train animals to quasi-habits, but they are imposed from without and not developed by the animal alone. Humans have a nature plastic enough to be molded in various ways. By free choice we can do the molding ourselves to some extent, and our environment will do the rest. People cannot spread their abilities over the whole field of action possible to them but must channel them along definite lines. Habits are these channels, cut deeper with each repetition for better or for worse, until the person's native temperament is carved out into the thing we call character.

Though all habits are acquired in the sense that we are not born with any fully formed, they differ greatly in the amount of effort needed for their development. The intellectual habit of first principles, the understanding and use of such truths as the principle of noncontradiction in the speculative order and the first moral truths in the practical order, is virtually in the mind from the start. Other habits grow only by painstaking and persistent practice and need constant exercise to keep them at the peak of efficiency, such as the arts, skills, and sports. Bad habits may result from defective development of our abilities, so that instead of ease and smoothness we beget a wasteful and bungling style of operation. Other habits develop no ability in us but only create a tendency to repetition; the acts are not done better but only more often until we fall into them inadvertently, as with swearing. Still other habits come from building up in oneself an organic craving, whether wholly acquired or the ripening of a predisposition, as in the use of drugs and stimulants. Finally, there are those forms of routine more properly called customs than habits, which, however often repeated, normally require a voluntary act each time, such as attendance at class.

Habits are destroyed either by disuse or by contrary acts. Disuse starves out the habit, and contrary acts replace it with the opposite habit. In rooting out a bad habit it is important never to allow a single slip back into the habit, for one fall can undo the work of a long and painful

---

[1] Aristotle, *Nicomachean Ethics,* bk. VII, ch. 10, 1152a 30.

conquest. Habits are useful servants created in us by our own acts, but they have a subtle tendency to enslave their masters; they must be kept in their place.

VIRTUE AND VICE

Some habits perfect us only physically, mentally, or socially, but if they perfect our nature taken completely, they are good habits of living or conduct and are called virtues. Originally the word *virtue,* from the Latin *vir,* meant manliness, and the Greek ἀρετή had a similar sense. From excellence in battle it came to mean any kind of excellence, and that is how ancient writers use it. Only in modern times has it become restricted to an ethical sense. *Vice* likewise meant any kind of flaw, but it now means only an ethically bad habit.

Socrates taught that virtue is knowledge and vice is ignorance. This doctrine runs throughout the writings of Plato, appearing in two often recurring questions: "Is virtue one or many?" and "Can virtue be taught?" Plato explains how knowledge is the common element in all virtues, the courageous man knowing what to do in danger, the temperate man knowing how to restrain his passions, the just man knowing what rightly belongs to himself and to others. Virtue is therefore one, and since it is knowledge it can be taught, though not in the way the Sophists tried to teach it.[1] He says that the philosopher alone has true virtue because only the philosopher has true wisdom, and insists on the importance of attaining that wisdom.[2] Because of this conviction Socrates and Plato took their teaching mission seriously.

The sublimity of Plato's thought should not blind us to its defects. If virtue is knowledge and vice ignorance, no one does wrong voluntarily; at most a person could be censured for neglecting to acquire the proper knowledge. Plato admits this:

No man voluntarily pursues evil, or that which he thinks to be evil. To prefer evil to good is not in human nature; and when a man is compelled to choose one of two evils, no one will choose the greater when he may have the less.[3]

In his discussion of voluntariness, Aristotle directly argues against Plato's opinion:

The end being what we wish for, the means what we deliberate about and choose, actions concerning means must be according to choice and voluntary. Now the exercise of the virtues is concerned with means. Therefore virtue also is in our power, and so too vice . . . . Now if it is in our power to do noble or base acts, and likewise in our power not to do them, and this is what being good or bad meant, then it is in our power to be virtuous or vicious.[4]

If our knowledge were perfect and if our appetites and emotions were under the full control of reason, Plato's theory would be correct, but in this life our knowledge is not perfect nor are our appetites and emotions always illumined by right reason. A vicious act requires some voluntary clouding of knowledge, a willful refusal at the moment of acting to use the knowledge we have. We seek evil not for itself but for some good found with it or through it. We try to concentrate on the good and overlook the evil; yet we know the evil is there and choose it voluntarily. Also, our control over our appetites and emotions is not the same as our control over our muscles. When we command our hand or foot, it obeys, but when we command our appetites and emotions they can and sometimes do rebel.

The soul rules the body with a despotical rule, whereas the intellect rules the appetites with a constitutional and royal rule.[5]

Hence the necessity of training the other parts of our being to be subject to right reason. Such training results in good habits, and these are virtues. In a virtuous person the emotions and appetites are habitually illumined by right reason like the free citizens of a well-governed state, but

---

[1] Plato, *Protagoras,* §359–361; *Republic,* bk. IV, §441–445.
[2] Plato, *Phaedo,* §68–69, 107–108; *Phaedrus,* §246–256.

[3] Plato, *Protagoras,* §358; see also *Laws,* bk. V, §371, and bk. IX, §860.
[4] Aristotle, *Nicomachean Ethics,* bk. III, ch. 5, 1113b 3; see also bk. VII, ch. 2–3, 1145b 22–1147b 19, regarding continence.
[5] Aristotle, *Politics,* bk. I, ch. 5, 1254b 3.

in the vicious person they are an unruly mob. In any single act a person can keep them in line and is responsible for failure to do so, but by and large a person will find the effort too great, will relax his or her control, be caught unawares, and act contrary to right reason. Thus, though there is some knowledge in all virtue and some ignorance in all vice, knowledge alone will not suffice to make people good because intellect alone cannot move us to do anything. Appetite and emotion are the motives or sources of action.

STOICISM

Though both Plato and Aristotle center their ethics on the concept of virtue, the Stoics were the ones who carried virtue to the extreme. Just when the Epicureans were promoting pleasure as the greatest good, the Stoics were opposing them with the unyielding claims of virtue. Stoicism grew out of the Cynic school of thought, which taught that virtue is no mere means to happiness but is happiness itself. Virtue is the only good, vice the only evil, and everything else is indifferent. The essence of virtue is self-sufficiency, independence from everything and everybody. The Cynics despised riches, pleasure, comfort, family, society, culture, and sometimes even common decency.

Stoicism dropped the grossness of this attitude and made it respectable by joining it to pantheism. The world, they said, is composed of the world body, consisting of coarse matter apparent to our senses, and the world soul, fine matter that blows as a wind through the world, giving it motion and making it a huge animal. Our body and soul are only limited portions of the world body and the world soul. The whole world itself is God or Nature, for these are the same. Nature develops itself according to inexorable law, so that the universe can be called not only Nature and God but also Fate and Destiny, Reason and Law. Hence Stoicism is a form of *materialism, pantheism,* and *fatalism.*

> Our individual natures are all parts of universal nature; on which account the chief good is to live in a manner corresponding to nature, and that means

corresponding to one's own nature and to universal nature.[1]

Nothing else, they say, could ever happen except what does happen. Everything that will befall me is decreed by Fate; I can accept these decrees graciously or rebelliously, but accept them I must. Rebellion is only an emotional reaction against Nature, a childish pouting that can change nothing and only makes me miserable. Nature stands serene though I rail against it. The reasonable thing to do is to develop *apathy,* a state of indifference to all things, of complete control over my emotions, the only thing I can control. Emotion is irrational and bad; action according to reason, which shows me the inexorable law of Nature, alone is good—and it is *virtue.* Virtue is the only good. It is not a means to an end but the end itself. "Virtue is its own reward."

> Virtue is a disposition of the mind always consistent and always harmonious; one ought to seek it out for its own sake, without being influenced by fear or hope or any external influence.[2]

The virtuous person stands firm though the world crashes down in ruins; realizing one's identity with Nature, one is beyond good and evil. There are no degrees in virtue, and a person who has one virtue has all, for either one lives according to Nature or one does not; the former is wise or a philosopher, the latter a fool.

The modern philosopher Baruch Spinoza gives us a moral system that is fundamentally Stoic in tone, though based on the physical and psychological doctrines of Descartes rather than on those of the ancient Stoics. His great work, though entitled *Ethics,* is more of a metaphysical treatise embodying a complete pantheistic philosophy, culminating in the way we can reach "blessed immortality" by deliverance from bondage to our passions (emotions) and by realization of our identity with Nature, which is God.

The Stoics argued vigorously in favor of their view, especially with their rivals, the Epicureans. The following are a few of their arguments:

---

[1] Diogenes Laertius, *Lives and Opinions of Eminent Philosophers,* bk. VII, 53.
[2] *Ibid.*

1. Stoicism sincerely faces the facts of life, that nature is hard and inexorable, neither favoring nor disfavoring us but rolling on its relentless way with utter indifference to us. It is foolish to read into nature aspects that are merely the reflection of our own emotions. If nature is indifferent to us, the only reasonable attitude on our part is indifference to it.

2. In this attitude of apathy we are really the gainers. It is a fact that we are a part of nature, and by conforming ourselves to nature we fulfill our role in the great cosmic scheme, whatever it is. To act unnaturally brings pain, and we ourselves are the only losers by this behavior. To act naturally will not necessarily bring us pleasure, but such action will be at least as painless as possible. Surely to act thus is wisdom, and failure to do so is folly.

3. There are no rewards or punishments in nature, only natural consequences of the way we act. There is something mean and despicable about refusing to do good unless we are rewarded for it or shunning evil only for fear of punishment. Stoic ethics is as pure and disinterested as can be, for virtue is its own reward and needs no meretricious accouterments to make it attractive.

4. Since human nature is part of Nature (the world or God), the law that governs Nature is itself the law to which human action ought to be conformed. Human beings as rational beings can become conscious of the laws to which they necessarily conform. Virtue consists of conscious assent to the inevitable order of things; vice is dissent from this order. Passion, emotional impulse, and desire give rise to the vice of rebellion against Nature. Reason must dominate the emotional side of our nature so that we can live according to Nature whether we want to or not. To live according to reason alone is to act by will, by rational decision alone, in conformity to the inexorable law of Nature.

5. The greatest tribute we can give a person is to love him or her without looking for the favors he or she may give us. Likewise, Nature, which the Stoics identify with God, is to be loved because it is what it is and not because of any favors it might give us. Otherwise we love the favors rather than Nature or God.

6. Stoicism enables us to adopt the best attitude toward the three important philosophical questions: freedom, immortality, and God. It leaves room for the rigid determinism of natural science and yet gives us some inner freedom to control our emotions and attitudes. It encourages apathy toward a future life: if there is one, we will have it, want it or not; if there is none, we have no way of producing it. It admits the omnipotence of God as Nature, the sum total of all that is, without trying to construct some transcendent God beyond nature, for whom it sees no evidence.

Opponents find their chief objection to Stoicism in the fatalism, materialism, antiemotionalism, and pantheism implied in the system. More specifically:

1. It is indeed foolish to be upset by those aspects of nature that we cannot control. We have to take them, like them or not. There are some things we can control, however, and we are foolish if we do not better our condition. Nature does have kindly aspects that we can use, as well as harsh aspects that we have to endure.

2. We are indeed part of nature, but we should use our *rational* nature to bring the blind forces of irrational nature under our control, insofar as we can do so to our benefit. To have a rational nature and yet to stifle it by unnatural apathy does not seem to be conformity to nature at all. Our whole being cries out for fulfillment, not for absorption and extinction in an impersonal universe.

3. It would be wrong to do good merely for reward and to avoid evil merely for fear of punishment, but it is quite possible to do the good for its own sake and also to accept the reward that naturally comes with it. The phrase "Virtue is its own reward," is another way of saying that virtue has no reward. But by its very notion, virtue is a means, not an end. Virtue consists of morally good habits, and these habits are called good precisely because they lead us more easily and readily to the accomplishment of some purpose in life. Virtue is a straight way, a right direction,

a true aiming at the highest good, but no one takes a way to a way or directs himself or herself to a direction or aims at aiming. Unless some goal, mark, or target is set up, virtue has no meaning.

4. The Stoic tradition in moral thinking has gone very deeply into Western civilization. Its insistence on the distinction between and separation of reason and emotion, its idealization of reason as the master of emotion, and its glorification of the rational life, the life of will with its emphasis on law and principle, makes us blind to emotion as the creative force in human experience, the only source of living growth, progress, and development. Reason, it is true, can organize what is given, order and stabilize what we already know, and so prepare for new advances in knowledge and living, but only emotion can give the impetus for us to move forward to further growth and progress. By suppressing the emotional basis of conduct in the interest of rational principles, we have developed intellectually while we remain emotionally vulgar and primitive. A morality based solely on reason and will tends to make us insensitive to our emotions and ends by destroying both their integrity and our own personal integrity as well.

5. Spinoza writes sublimely on the "intellectual love of God," an unemotional approval of Nature the way it is, without expecting God to love us in return. This attitude is disinterested indeed, so disinterested as to be inhuman. Love to be perfect must be reciprocal. The only God worthy of the name is a personal God who loves us infinitely more than we can love him, not impersonal nature incapable of love.

6. The three basic philosophical topics are here bargained away. The freedom is not real freedom but slavery to the omnipotent universe of matter. An immortality so problematic cannot stir up in us the slightest glimmering of hope. The God is not a God, but only Nature, for good and evil are denied all objective reality and reduced entirely to our purely subjective emotional attitudes toward things. Conformity to a universe that is not good cannot make us good, and thus the Stoic ethical ideal fails. The Stoics accuse the Epicu-

reans of frivolity, with some justice, but there can be a stern futility as well as a frivolous one. Stoic virtue leads nowhere else and in itself offers only hopeless resignation to an indifferent and basically cruel universe.

INTELLECTUAL AND MORAL VIRTUES

We shall take leave of the Stoics and the Stoic tradition to enter into the realm of the Aristotelian and Thomistic theory of the virtues. Just as we abhor the Stoic subordination of emotion to reason, so we abhor the subordination of reason to emotion. The theory of virtue that we will now examine is based on the view that reason and emotion can operate in harmony and so contribute to the full development of the person. The so-called cardinal virtues of prudence, temperance, fortitude, and justice are the perfection of that harmony.

Good habits of the intellect, enabling it to be a more efficient instrument of knowledge, are virtues in the broad sense. Their effect on one's moral life is quite remote, for they may make one a better student of ethics but not a better living person. Failure to exercise them results rather in involuntary mistakes than in morally wrong conduct. However, though less important for ethics, they are very valuable in themselves.

Aristotle[1] distinguishes three virtues of the theoretical or speculative intellect concerned with the contemplation of the true:

1. *Understanding:* the habit of first principles, the habitual knowledge of primary self-evident truths that lie at the root of all knowledge

2. *Science:* the habit of conclusions drawn by

---

[1] Aristotle, *Nicomachean Ethics,* bk. VI; St. Thomas, *Summa Theologica,* I–II, q. 57. Different translations of Aristotle use different names to indicate these virtues; the following list may help to avoid confusion:

νοῦς = understanding = intuitive reason
ἐπιστήμη = science = scientific knowledge
σοφία = wisdom = philosophic wisdom
τέχνη = art = craftsmanship
φρόνησις = prudence = practical wisdom

demonstrations from first principles, the habitual knowledge of the particular sciences

3. *Wisdom:* the habit of knowing things in their highest causes, an ordering of all principles and conclusions into one vast body of truth

Then there are two virtues of the practical intellect, concerned with making and doing, the two forms of action:

4. *Art:* the habit of knowing how to make things, how to produce some external object; it includes the mechanical, the liberal, and the fine arts

5. *Prudence:* the habit of knowing how to act well, how to direct activity that does not result in tangible products, how to live a good human life

Though all the intellectual virtues have some reference to the moral life, prudence is the most directly concerned because it enters into and illumines every act of the moral virtues. When we speak of the practical intellect, we are using a shorthand expression for intellect when it is acting on the basis of our desire for some end or good. Prudence is *the* virtue of the practical intellect in moral matters, for every virtuous act is going to be an act stemming from both prudence and one of the moral virtues. Prudence is a perfection of intellect operating in harmony with right appetite or desire, while the moral virtue is a perfection of the appetite itself that prudence illumines. The moral virtues are good habits in the appetitive side of our consciousness, directing the activity of the will and moderating the sensory appetites and emotions to aim for the good things that are befitting our nature in all its essential relationships. They provide prudence with the goals at which to aim, and prudence, on the basis of our desire for the goal, chooses the means to attain the goal. Prudence and the moral virtues, operating together harmoniously, enable us not merely to know what to do and how to do it, but they actually assist us in the very doing of it. Doing a thing well is opposed to overdoing and to underdoing it and consists of hitting the mean between excess and defect. This is Aristotle's famous doctrine of the *mean,* which he expresses thus:

Virtue [that is, moral virtue] is a state of character concerned with choice, lying in a mean, i.e. the mean relative to us, this being determined by a rational principle and by that principle by which the man of practical wisdom would determine it. Now it is a mean between two vices, that which depends on excess and that which depends on defect; and again it is a mean because the vices respectively fall short of or exceed what is right in both passions and actions, while virtue both finds and chooses that which is intermediate. Hence in respect of its substance and the definition which states its essence virtue is a mean; with regard to what is best and right, an extreme.[1]

In other words, moral virtue is a habit of choosing the mean between the extremes of excess and defect in action, and this mean is determined by right reason, that is, reason under the impulse of desire for the end and guided by the intellectual virtue of prudence. As too much or too little food, sleep, or exercise hurts the body but just the right amount promotes its health, so excess or defect in the habits of the soul hurts its health and "virtue stands in the middle." Moral virtue aims us at our end and must neither overshoot nor fall short of the mark. Courage is a mean between cowardice and rashness, temperance between gluttony and abstinence, generosity between stinginess and prodigality, friendliness between surliness and flattery.

The mean is not absolute but "relative to us," for what is the right amount for one would be too much or too little for another. A brave deed for a soldier under arms would be foolhardy for an unarmed civilian, a temperate meal for a wrestler would be overindulgence for a dyspeptic, a generous gift from a poor person would be a stingy one from a rich person. Thus the intellectual virtue of prudence is the guide by which the mean of the moral virtues is to be decided.

Criticism of Aristotle's doctrine of the mean is

---

[1] Aristotle, *Nicomachean Ethics,* bk. II, ch. 6, 1106b 36. The translation uses some unusual expressions: "state of character" is *habit,* "rational principle" is *reason,* "practical wisdom" is *prudence.* The English edition of St. Thomas shortens the definition thus: "Virtue is a habit of choosing the mean appointed by reason as a prudent man would appoint it" (*Summa Theologica,* I–II, q. 59, a. 1).

often vitiated by a careless reading of his text, as if he meant that we should not be too good or too moral but only moderately so. Nothing could be farther from his mind. To say that you must neither overshoot nor undershoot the mark is not the same as saying that you should aim carelessly or lackadaisically. He carefully notes that, though the virtue itself is a mean between extremes, the virtue is not to be practiced moderately but fully. The judge must go all out for justice, but justice itself is a mean between lenience and severity; the witness must be exactly truthful, but truthfulness itself is a mean between exaggeration and understatement. In acts that are bad in themselves there is no virtuous mean. It is not good to be moderately murderous or adulterous; we must simply not be so at all.

CARDINAL VIRTUES

Four virtues have been traditionally picked out as the most important in the ethical order. They are called *cardinal* virtues from the Latin *cardo,* a hinge, because they are the four hinges on which the other virtues swing. Plato, though he probably did not invent them, makes his whole theory of the human soul and of the political state dependent on them. Aristotle centers his *Ethics* on them, and they have been universally adopted by Christian writers. St. Thomas divides the cardinal virtues as follows:

> The formal principle of the virtue of which we speak now is the good as defined by reason. This good can be considered in two ways. First, as existing in the consideration itself of reason, and thus we have one principal virtue called *prudence.* Secondly, according as the reason puts its order into something else, and this either into operations, and then we have *justice,* or into passions, and then we need two virtues. For the need of putting the order of reason into the passions is due to their thwarting reason; and this occurs in two ways. First when the passions incite to something against reason, and then they need a curb, which we thus call *temperance;* secondly, when the passions withdraw us from following the dictate of reason, e.g., through fear of danger or toil, then man needs to be strengthened for that which reason dictates, lest he turn back, and to this end there is *fortitude.*

In like manner we find the same number if we consider the subjects of virtue. For there are four subjects of the virtue of which we now speak, viz., the power which is rational in its essence, and this is perfected by *prudence;* and that which is rational by participation, and is threefold, the will, subject of *justice,* the concupiscible power, subject of *temperance,* and the irascible power, subject of *fortitude.*[1]

Prudence

Prudence is an intellectual virtue by essence, but it enters into the field of the moral virtues by pointing out the mean and suggesting ways of attaining it. Without prudence, fortitude becomes boldness, temperance becomes moroseness, justice becomes harshness. Prudence chooses the right means toward worthy ends; the choice of good means toward bad ends is mere cleverness or shrewdness, but not true prudence.

The reason it is impossible to have a morally virtuous act without prudence and likewise impossible to make a morally good judgment about how to act without moral virtue is that moral choice is always a complex act of intellect and appetite, of reason and emotion. Thought and desire are both necessary to effect an act of choice. By means of moral virtue we desire the good with a desire that will be the source of action. Prior to the desire, prudence causes us to know the particular action well, but knowledge without the interjection of desire does not move us to act. Given the good known by prudence and desired by moral virtue, prudence deliberates about and decides on the means to achieve the desired good. By including the means determined by its judgment within the desire for the good end, prudence causes us to desire the means efficaciously. This is really only one action. The morally good end-by-these-means is achieved, because the desire of moral virtue (the motive force of the action) and the judgment of prudence (the light of reason within the act) collaborate harmoniously so that the judgment of prudence is transformed on contact with the desire of moral virtue into an imperative, the moral choice that

[1] St. Thomas, *Summa Theologica,* I–II, q. 61, a. 2.

this ought to be done. Our morally virtuous deeds are always complex acts of prudence and one or more of the moral virtues.

The importance of prudence in the ethical life cannot be overestimated. Whenever a general rule of conduct, such as ethics devises, must be applied to a concrete case, prudence is needed. Rules cannot be given for prudence itself, because all rules must have some universality, and prudence deals with the single instance. How to break bad news gently, when to ask one's employer for a raise, whether to punish a fault or to let it pass this time, whom to pick out as the right person for the right job, how to arrange the troops for battle in a particular terrain, what legislation will best promote the common good and conciliate all interests—all such matters, great and small, are governed by prudence. The widest possible observation and experience of human behavior are the only teachers of prudence. It has little correlation with book learning. Some pick it up readily, some otherwise intelligent persons are slow to catch on, some geniuses are deficient in it. It is hard to correct imprudence, for imprudence itself largely consists of refusing to accept advice or learn from experience. Imprudent people may commit few sins, for one does not consciously will to be imprudent, but their lives are a series of blunders. The virtue of prudence does not consist of a single prudent decision but is the acquired habit of always or nearly always using the right means to achieve the particular good ends we desire.

There are a number of lesser virtues implied in prudence, such as foresight, care, docility, caution, and circumspection. Negligence, precipitation, inconsideration, recklessness, headstrongness, and the like indicate a defect of prudence. Craftiness, deceit, timidity, and pusillanimity may result from an excess of prudence not balanced by other virtues.

Temperance

Temperance regulates the appetite in the use of sensible pleasure. It moderates our two main inclinations or drives, toward self-preservation and race preservation, and thus acts as a curb on excessive indulgence in food and drink and in the use of sex. Its opposed vices are gluttony and lust. Temperance as a virtue, perhaps better called temperateness, moderation, or self-control, does not mean total abstinence. Some persons find that any indulgence leads to temptations they cannot overcome, and for them total abstinence is the only cure; others, for higher motives and for their spiritual perfection, voluntarily give up some otherwise legitimate pleasures. But no pleasure is bad in itself, and natural morality merely requires that pleasures be indulged in with moderation and insofar as they help to worthy ends. The habit of doing this is temperance illumined by prudence. Since most persons are inclined to excess in pleasure, the mean is usually short of one's desire and closer to the side of restraint. People differ greatly in the strength of their sensuous cravings, and so the mean varies with different persons.

Temperance contains the subordinate virtues of abstinence and sobriety, chastity and continence. By analogy temperance also regulates cravings that are less bodily in nature and puts a proper curb on our self-esteem; in which cases it is called humility, modesty, gentleness, mildness, and docility. Lack of temperance appears in gluttony, drunkenness, lust, pride, cruelty, and vanity. Too much restraint, which is intemperance in the opposite direction, may produce insensibility, stolidity, sullenness, moroseness and fanatical austerity.

Courage

Courage, fortitude, or bravery inclines one to face danger and toil without flinching. As temperance is a bridle, so courage is a spur. Most people are inclined to quail before danger, and courage drives us into it. But not everything that looks like a brave act is a manifestation of the virtue of courage. It does not consist of one brave act but is a habit of self-mastery. To rush into peril out of anger, ignorance, or stupidity is no sign of courage; the truly courageous person acts from a rational motive, whereby through prudence he or she appreciated the danger while counting it the lesser evil. To our instincts death is the most dreadful of all things, but reason tells us that there are some things better than life and others worse than death. Courage enables us to overcome our abhorrence of death, and still more of lesser evils, when it is reasonable to do so. It frees us from slavery to fear, though it need not take away fear itself. The brave person may act with fear but, in spite of it, faces the danger.

Courage is the primary requisite of the soldier, who is useless without it, but in some way it enters into all fields of life. *Active* courage consists of attacking the threatening evil, fighting against it, and overcoming it. *Passive* courage is endurance of an evil that cannot be overcome, holding one's ground and not yielding, no matter what the cost. Thus courage can exist on both sides, in the victor and the vanquished. Besides these two types of *physical* courage, there is also *moral* courage, which is the same two attitudes but toward evils and dangers that do not involve bodily harm. Everyone is expected to stand up to life's troubles and misfortunes, to put in the effort to overcome them when possible, and when not possible to bear them with honor. Moral courage, in the sense of refusing to do anything morally dishonorable no matter what the consequences, is essential to any moral living.

Courage implies patience, perseverance, and constancy. Aristotle adds two unusual virtues; magnificence, to dare wisely in the matter of expense and magnanimity, to dare wisely in the matter of honor. His often quoted picture of the magnanimous man,[1] the highminded or superior man, which seems to be his ideal, has been criticized as a model of priggishness and stuffiness; perhaps each one must make up his own ideal. Lack of courage is shown in cowardice, weakness, timidity, impatience, and irresoluteness. Boldness, presumption, stubbornness, quarrelsomeness, and ruthlessness are faults of the overbrave.

---

[1] Aristotle, *Nicomachean Ethics,* bk. IV, ch. 3, 1122a 33; the Oxford translation calls him "proud," a term that can easily be misinterpreted.

Justice

Justice inclines us to give to each one his or her own. It supposes at least two persons between whom there can be some sort of equality, so that each person receives what really belongs to him or her. Temperance and courage regulate our control over our appetites, but justice regulates the will's government over itself where dealings with another person are involved. Justice, illumined by prudence, grants each person what really belongs to him or her and takes the properly moral means to do so.

Justice is divided by Aristotle into general and particular. *General* justice is so broad as to cover all virtue that has any social significance and is therefore not the specific cardinal virtue of justice. *Particular* justice, which is the cardinal virtue, he divides into *distributive* and *corrective*. The latter is now more commonly called *commutative,* a name derived from the commutation or exchange of goods. We shall take them in inverse order.

Commutative justice exists between equals, that is, between one person and another or between groups acting as if they were private persons negotiating on equal terms. Commutative justice is the basis of contracts. In a contract, such as barter or hire, the two persons start equal; when one has fulfilled his or her part of the contract the equality is unbalanced; then justice demands the restoration of equality by the other's fulfillment of his or her part. The same holds outside the field of voluntary contracts in those situations in which nature itself demands the balance of equality. One who has injured another by depriving that person of something rightfully his or hers is obliged in justice to restore it to that person. Commutative justice, when violated, carries with it the obligation of restitution. Justice remains outraged until proper compensation has been made to reestablish the balance of equality.

Distributive justice is a relation between the community and its members. As its name indicates, it requires a fair and proper distribution of public benefits and burdens among the members of the community. Though existing in some way in all organizations, distributive justice applies chiefly to the state. It is the particular obligation of public officials and is violated by favoritism and partiality. It does not exist between equals, but between a superior and his or her subordinates; the equality, implied in all justice, here means that each subordinate should get a proportionate or fair share, a share equal to his or her just deserts. Distributive justice has its converse, the obligation of the members to contribute to the common good. In this aspect it might be called *contributive* justice.

Social justice is a modern term that has been given various meanings by various writers. The tendency now is to identify it with St. Thomas' *legal* justice, so called because it shows itself in law-abiding conduct; it is the same as Aristotle's *general* justice. Social justice refers to the organization of society in such a way that the common good, to which all are expected to contribute in proportion to their ability and opportunity, is available to all the members for their ready use and enjoyment. It shows itself more in economic, industrial, racial, and political relations but is by no means restricted to them. It involves everything connected with being a good citizen or a good member of society and reaping what ought to be the reward of upright and cooperative social conduct, one's proper share of the benefits of social living. Any arrangement of society that excludes or hinders certain classes or groups within it from their fair share of the common good is a violation of social justice. Nearly the whole of social ethics is a study of social justice.

GROWTH IN VIRTUE

We can see from our discussion of prudence and the moral virtues that our human consciousness is never an affair of intellect alone when we bring it to bear on the moral life. The virtue of prudence perfects the intellect in such a way that intellect can illumine the affective side of our consciousness about how to achieve the goods we desire. The particular goods we desire, however, are first intuited by our emotions, drives, and inclinations. These latter, the affective side of our conscious-

ness, are our capacity to apprehend objective values, those already existing in the world and those that can yet be brought into existence by our own activity. Our emotions, drives, and inclinations are rooted in love, the fundamental positive emotion characteristic of human beings. Love is the source of all our activity that takes us beyond ourselves to live and deal with the persons and things in our world. This love, as we have already seen, can be either subjective and irrational or objective and rational. For example, take the desire to be benevolent to others. In doing what appears to be a benevolent act, I can either do it only because it makes me feel good or I can do it because such acts are good in themselves. The difference between these two kinds of love is the difference between irrational and rational love, respectively. The capacity to love objectively is the capacity that makes us persons and is the basis for the moral life. This capacity to love objectively is then the root and source of genuine objective morality, for it is ultimately the source of our capacity to behave in terms of the object, of what is other than ourselves.

The moral tenor of a person's life grows out of what one loves and hates. I find myself in a vast world of sensible and spiritual objects and persons that move my heart and passions, that receive my active responses of love and/or hate and revulsion. My inclination and disinclination to act, my many-sided interest in the persons and things of this world, depends for its morality on the order of my loves and hates. This is why prudence and the moral virtues are so important. Those virtues grow out of my personal loves and hates when those loves are truly worthy loves, and when those hates are truly worthy hates. The objective norm of morality is the standard or measure against which I must hold up my loves and hates to see if they are fitting for me as a human and personal being or not.

All of us as persons are obliged to develop and train our abilities to make them fit instruments for the attainment of our own individual ultimate goods. Love for that good is the motivating force of all our actions. We all have a general obligation to make good use of our talents, as gifts entrusted to our stewardship, though no one has a particular duty to develop any one of them rather than another. Each one should choose some sphere of action proportional to his or her gifts and educate himself or herself in it to the point of expertness and competence. This cannot be done without a fair degree of the intellectual virtues.

Far more important in our development as persons are the moral virtues and prudence. Each person must develop his or her emotional and affective life as well as learn self-mastery. Since evil acts must be avoided, each person must keep himself or herself clear of the evil habits or vices that are the source of such acts, and learn to love as much as possible what will develop the contrary virtues and so ensure his or her ability to cope with the ordinary difficulties and seductions of life. No one can succeed as a human being without a good grounding in prudence and the moral virtues, without loving the goods to which those virtues tend.

No one is born with virtues, and they do not come to one by chance but only by long and arduous training. Parents are the ones charged with the responsibility of beginning the training of their children to give them a moral start in life. Human life is so arranged that each succeeding generation fits into the preceding one, so that the virtues of parents, by instruction but much more by example, are passed on to their children. Parents must have what they are to transmit. Moral discipline must begin long before the child is old enough to appreciate its value or even its meaning. The exercise of parental authority should gradually dwindle until it vanishes with the coming of adulthood, which is not the time to forge the weapons for life's battle but to hold them ready for use.

Exaggeration of the so-called "generation gap" does no service to either generation. The gap has always existed, but its exaggeration is a phenomenon of our time. The prevailing atmosphere is one in which respect, honor, courtesy, and loyalty are held in small esteem. Young people, being strict conformists to the pattern of their peer group, are confirmed in their adolescent attitude by their parents' own permissiveness. Youth has always had to cut the apron strings sometime, to test its newly developed strength, and to branch out on its own. One should sympathize with this feeling of expanding powers, increasing maturity, and solidifying responsibility. But to think that such growth can be accomplished with no help from one's elders, that parents have nothing to tell one, that it is impossible even to communicate with them, is to engage in an initial folly that bids fair to wreck young lives. The time will have passed in which young people can come back to repair the mistake. Some things must be done at the right time, or they cannot be done at all. The time for parental direction is before and not after the young person has left home, and when that time has passed it cannot be made up. How to discharge their parental responsibility in these days calls for the utmost in prudence as well as in love.

Our treatment of virtue may seem too cursory for so important a topic, but it is meant only as a summary and an introduction. Most of the following chapters will consist of a more detailed examination of the various virtues. Some will be treated at greater length because of the problems they raise, but the length of a discussion does not always indicate the importance of the topic.

SUMMARY

Habit is a quality difficult to change, disposing a being well or ill, either in itself or in its relation to others. Habit is a partial actualization of our natural capacities, adding to nature by giving it ease in performance, the acts intensifying the habit and the habit facilitating the acts. Habits of acting are acquired by constant repetition, lost by disuse or contrary acts.

Good moral habits are *virtues,* evil ones *vices.* The Socratic doctrine that virtue is knowledge and vice is ignorance is countered by the Aristotelian teaching that the control of right reason over the passions is not despotic but political. The appetites can rebel against right reason, but they ought not and must be trained not to do so.

Stoicism holds that virtue is its own reward. It

controls emotion by *apathy* and cultivates resignation to inexorable fate in a pantheistic universe. The main difficulty is that virtue is a means, not an end.

Intellectual virtues make the intellect a better instrument of knowledge. They are understanding, science, and wisdom in the speculative intellect, and art and prudence in the practical intellect.

Moral virtues in conjunction with prudence moderate the appetites, both rational (*will*) and sensitive (*concupiscible* and *irascible*). According to Aristotle, they consist of the habit of choosing the *mean* between extremes, directed thereto by the intellectual virtue of prudence.

The *cardinal* virtues are the hinges on which the other virtues swing. They are *prudence* in the intellect, choosing right means toward worthy ends; *temperance* in the concupiscible appetite, restraining it from overindulgence; *courage* in the irascible appetite, spurring it on to face necessary danger; and *justice* in the will, giving each one his or her due.

Justice is particular or general. *Particular* justice is either *commutative,* from person to person, restoring the balance of equality, or *distributive,* between the community and its members. These two comprise the cardinal virtue. *General* or *legal* or *social* justice regulates the whole of social living, comprising both the acquisition and apportionment of the common good.

Questions for Discussion

1. You are an Associate Justice of the Supreme Court of the United States. You and your fellow justices have decided to hear a case involving the use of state funds to provide abortions for women on welfare. You personally do not approve of abortions for any reason, but the Supreme Court has in the past (*Roe* vs. *Wade*) ruled that some abortions are legitimate. This ruling was made before you joined the court. Now you must apply the law of the land to the case at hand. What ought you to do: abstain from ruling on the case, dissent and write a separate dissenting opinion, or sit on the case, hear the arguments, and give the best ruling you can in the light of the law involved? Explain your answer and describe the virtues involved.

2. You are now a parent for the second time. Your first child is almost five. She is getting to be a chubby little girl. You and your wife (or husband) are becoming concerned about the child's weight and even more concerned about how to teach the child not to overeat. You are concerned that the child learn moderation not only in the pleasures of eating but in all sensual pleasures, and you are also concerned about not being tyrannical parents. How can you achieve your aims?

3. You are now a sophomore in college, living in a very congenial dorm, and are beginning to enjoy college life much more than you did last year. Some of your friends, of whom your roommate is one, have begun to try a little marijuana. What was a once-a-week affair has become a nightly routine, and you have been joining in regularly. Smoking marijuana is fun and your friends would think less of you if you did not join in. In short, you are afraid not to continue. Tonight, one of the group has brought some cocaine to snort. Now what do you do? You not only like the marijuana, but have come to depend on that nightly relaxation. Can you afford the risk of escalating to cocaine?

4. Doctor-patient confidentiality is a great value in the medical profession and an ingrained habit with doctors. You as a physician have always taken great pains to reveal absolutely nothing of what your patients discuss with you. Lately you have encountered AIDS (acquired immune deficiency syndrome) in some of your patients. One in particular has caused

you greater concern than usual, because she does not want to tell her husband that she has AIDS. You have counselled her to tell her husband in order to protect him if he does not have the disease and to help him if he does. The woman refuses and will not give you permission to speak to her husband. Moreover, now that she knows she is going to die, she wants to become pregnant so that she can leave him something of herself, a child. She does not believe that she can give her husband AIDS even though you have carefully explained to her that the disease is transmitted sexually. What is the virtuous thing for you to do? Explain your answer.

5. The local school board plans to offer birth-control counseling and contraceptives at high-school clinics throughout the city. The board

members have come in for a great deal of criticism and are being severely pressured to abandon their plan by groups that emphasize the family's obligations in such matters. The fear of those opposed is that the presence of clinics that offer birth-control services is going to send a message to the students legitimizing behavior that contradicts the traditional Judeo-Christian ethic. Furthermore, it is going to undermine parents' rights by allowing teenagers to make serious decisions involving their health concerning oral contraceptives, abortion, and treatment of venereal diseases. If you were a parent, what would you want? If you were a student? If you were a teacher? If you were a member of the counseling staff? If you were the local bishop or rabbi? What does prudence counsel or command?

Readings

Plato has written little that does not deal with virtue in some respect. The *Protagoras, Phaedo, Phaedrus,* and bk. IV of the *Republic* are recommended. The *Charmides* discusses temperance, and the *Laches* courage.

Aristotle's treatment of virtue in the *Nicomachean Ethics* runs from bk. I, ch. 13, to bk. VII, ch. 10. This is the original source of most of the matter in this chapter. Henry Veatch, *Rational Man,* ch. 3–4, discusses Aristotle's theory of virtue. Two other helpful studies are D.J. Allan, *The Philosophy of Aristotle,* and J.D. Monan, *Moral Knowledge and its Methodology in Aristotle.*

The classical Stoic writings are Seneca's *Letters* and *Moral Essays,* Marcus Aurelius' *Meditations,* Epictetus' *Discourses,* and the philosophical writings of Cicero. See also Diogenes Laertius' *Lives and Opinions of Eminent Philosophers,* bk. VII.

St. Thomas follows Aristotle, omitting some points, developing others more thoroughly, and adding the theological virtues. His discussion of habits and virtues is found in the

Summa Theologica, I–II, qq. 49–61; qq. 63 and 64; q. 65, a. 1; q. 66, aa. 1–5; q. 71, aa. 1–4. The Second Part of the Second Part (II–II) takes up each cardinal virtue in detail. Into this framework St. Thomas puts most of his writing on morals. Charles J. O'Neil, *Imprudence in St. Thomas,* is helpful for understanding why prudence is *the* virtue of the practical intellect.

Spinoza's *Ethics* is a whole philosophy in itself. Books IV and V are pertinent here.

George Klubertanz, *Habits and Virtues,* gives a full modern treatment of this subject with an extensive bibliography. Josef Pieper has three little books, one entitled *Justice,* another *Prudence,* and a third *Fortitude and Temperance,* now all put together into one, *The Four Cardinal Virtues.* Etienne Gilson, *Moral Values and Moral Life,* ch. 5, 8–11, treats the cardinal virtues in general and each one in detail. See also his *Christian Philosophy of St. Thomas Aquinas,* pp. 256–264, 271–332.

17
Happiness

PROBLEM

The conflicting claims of happiness and duty, like those of love and law, run all through the history of ethics. The *deontologists,* champions of duty, have had their say through Immanuel Kant. Few of them would deny the claim of happiness, but they want to keep it secondary, as an added bonus for faithfulness to duty rather than an aim consciously to be pursued. This view appeals to people of sterner stuff and to the puritanical-minded, who equate happiness with enjoyment and have never learned to enjoy themselves with a comfortable conscience. The *eudaemonists,* champions of happiness, have also been vocal. We could have begun ethics with happiness, as Aristotle does, but postponed it for the sake of a more disinterested approach, wishing to show that the good is worthy of pursuit just because it is good in itself apart from its benefit to us.

It is time now to hear the case for happiness, but not to contrast it with duty. The dichotomy is a false one. To achieve happiness is our duty if happiness is our end, and the fulfillment of such a duty necessarily results in happiness. Both duty and happiness are united in the good, for the ought and the end are good only if they have intrinsic value.

That we seek happiness in the abstract is shown in all we do. The more important question is whether we can reach it. Can our pursuit of it be successful, or are we doomed to be ever chasing a will-o'-the-wisp that constantly lures us on but ever eludes our grasp? We have a choice between ethical *optimism* and *pessimism,* according as we engage in the inevitable pursuit of happiness with hope or despair. The following points sum up our study:

1. What is the meaning of happiness?
2. Do all people seek happiness?
3. Do all people think happiness attainable?
4. Is happiness really attainable somewhere?
5. Where is happiness found, if anywhere?

MEANING OF HAPPINESS

The root meaning of *happy* is that of being favored by fortune; a happy person is one to whom good things *happen*. The equivalent word in other languages usually has the same basic meaning. Hence one may wonder, as Aristotle[1] does, whether we should be called happy until we are dead, since misfortune may befall us in old age. We carry the word *happiness* beyond its linguistic origin and the uses of common speech. Those of us who are fortunate, lucky, successful, satisfied, cheerful, glad, or joyous may be comparatively happy in the sense that we have come closer to happiness than most, or have done so in some particular line, but we are not necessarily happy in the way the philosopher speaks of happiness. Thus *happiness* is an analogous term, applying to various signs of, approaches to, and contributions toward happiness. The philosopher is not interested in these diminished manifestations but in the full concept of happiness as such.

Happiness is not a passing feeling or emotion, such as joy or gladness, but is a lasting state of being. One may be generally happy though suffering a temporary grief, just as another's chronic unhappiness may be punctuated by moments of joy. Nor is happiness a permanent quality of a person's character, a sunny disposition, a cheerful outlook on life, however much this may help to happiness; some people can maintain such a disposition in the face of disappointment, whereas happiness is satisfaction. The immature and feebleminded can have a cheerful outlook, but it is a result of lack of appreciation, not of fulfillment.

Animals are incapable of happiness. They tend instinctively toward ends and have appetites that can be satisfied by things good for them. Having sense knowledge, they can *feel* satisfied and are capable of a kind of contentment. The animal that has eaten all it needs is content for the moment, though it will soon be hungry again. Only rational and free beings are strictly capable of happiness. They alone can reflect on their state and *consciously* appreciate the satisfaction they enjoy. Happiness is a subjective condition entailing the existence of desire in oneself, the consciousness of the existence of the desire, the actual satisfaction of the desire, and the consciousness that this

---

[1]Aristotle, *Nicomachean Ethics,* bk. I, ch. 10, 1100a 1 to 1100b 10.

desire is being or has been satisfied. Such a state can exist only in a being capable of reflection and self-consciousness, a rational and free being.

Even in human beings contentment is not happiness. We can be content if we limit our desires by a judicious compromise, being willing to forego some desires so that we may attain others. In this life such an attitude is often necessary, but no one is ever *fully satisfied* with a compromise; it is the best we can have in the circumstances, but we wish the circumstances would allow us more. If the existing desires are based on real emotion, they want to be satisfied, not sacrificed for the benefit of other desires.

What, then, is happiness? From our observations it follows that happiness is the conscious state of satisfaction or fulfillment accompanying the possession of, or being in communion with, the good.

Perfect happiness comes from the complete possession of, or participation in and communion with, the perfect good, from that which *fully* satisfies *all* our desires. Boethius defines it as "a state made perfect by the aggregate of all good things,"[1] and St. Thomas as "the perfect good which lulls the appetite altogether."[2] *Imperfect* happiness falls off from the perfect by leaving some of our desires wholly or partially unsatisfied. One who is imperfectly happy is happy insofar as his or her desires are fulfilled and unhappy insofar as they are not. Resignation to this state of affairs, to a partial happiness mingled with unhappiness, is what we have called contentment; thus it is evident that contentment is not happiness itself. Perfect happiness may be taken absolutely or relatively. *Absolutely* perfect happiness is happiness to an infinite degree and pertains to God alone. *Relatively* perfect happiness is all that a finite being can have; its capacity is limited, and it is perfectly happy when that limited capacity is filled.

OUR NEED FOR HAPPINESS

That all people seek happiness in general, in the abstract, without specifying the object supposed to produce it, is evident from the very definition of happiness. We cannot desire something without at the same time wanting our desire to be satisfied; otherwise, we both do and do not desire it. But happiness is only a name for our self-conscious realization that our desires have been or are being satisfied; therefore we cannot desire anything without desiring happiness. One who would not crave happiness must have no emotions and so no desires, and such a one could not be human. St. Thomas put this with his usual clearness:

> Happiness can be considered in two ways. First, according to the general notion of happiness; and thus of necessity every man desires happiness. For the general notion of happiness consists in the perfect good. But since good is the object of the will, the perfect good of a man is that which entirely satisfies his will. Consequently to desire happiness is nothing else than to desire that one's will be satisfied. And this everyone desires. Secondly, we may speak of happiness according to its specific notion, as to that in which it consists. And thus all do not know happiness, because they know not in what thing the general notion of happiness is found. And consequently in this respect not all desire it.[3]

We humans are not free with regard to happiness in general. We are so made that we must seek it. But we are free in the choice of concrete objects by whose possession we hope to obtain happiness. All want to be happy, but not all know how to find happiness.

It is a psychological impossibility to desire misery for its own sake. Those who seem to take a morbid delight in making themselves miserable manifest a perverted condition, an exception that proves the rule by showing how unnatural such behavior is; what they really seek, subconsciously perhaps, is some form of sadistic or masochistic gratification they receive from it, as the crank probably does from being mean. While yearning for happiness in the abstract, one may judge that

---

[1] Boethius, *Consolation of Philosophy,* bk. III, prose 2.
[2] St. Thomas, *Summa Theologica,* I–II, q. 2, a. 8. Plato, in *The Symposium,* 205E, shows that possession of the perfect good does *not* lull appetite or desire completely, for we desire the continual possession of the good.

[3] *Op. cit.,* I–II, q. 5, a. 8.

happiness in the concrete has become impossible through lack of means to reach it; the person in the throes of despair wants happiness so badly that he or she cannot face the idea of its loss. One may feel that it is better to endure present misery than the worse misery of making an effort to escape from it; thus the lazy abide in a filth and squalor they do not enjoy, and the timid let opportunities for self-betterment pass them by. Introverted visionaries may find the dream of happiness too engrossing to be shattered by the prosaic reality of hard work; they want happiness now in the only way they can get it now. A person who deliberately chooses an evil does so because of the good seen to be bound up in it. At least we think it the lesser of two evils; because we want to be less unhappy. We choose what appears to be a relative or comparative happiness; thus the suicide seeks relief from life's wretchedness. All these examples are only seeming exceptions to the universal law that all humans seek happiness.

Happiness is the basic motive in everything we do. Our every act is motivated by some desire, satisfaction of which is intended as at least a partial ingredient in the sum total of happiness. We often have to sacrifice some goods for the sake of others, we may mistakenly choose the apparent good in the place of the genuine good, we may foolishly prefer some temporary enjoyment here and now to lasting bliss in a better world, but we do all this for happiness. It goes to show, not that we do not want happiness, but rather that we want it so much that we cannot stand the delay in waiting for it, and impatiently snatch at its partial and imperfect forms that vividly appeal to us now.

We need not be *explicitly* thinking of happiness in all that we do. We do not pause before each action and say to ourselves, "I am doing this to become happier." Now and then, when we reflect on the meaning of life, we may explicitly form this intention, and it remains in the back of our minds governing the rest of our deeds. Even one who never reflects on the purpose of life is acting

implicitly for happiness; otherwise that person would not be able to act at all.

ETHICAL PESSIMISM

Is happiness attainable? No one will deny the possibility of imperfect happiness, the leading of a fairly satisfactory life of partial fulfillment, at least for the more fortunate people, but by definition this state is not wholly satisfactory. We want to know whether we can attain *perfect* happiness, perfect not absolutely but relatively to us.

A negative answer represents the pervading attitude of the philosophies of India. It is not pessimistic in the sense of encouraging a gloomy or cynical outlook. Rather, it is productive of a remarkable serenity that is the admiration of other peoples. But it must be judged pessimistic in its theoretical conclusions, in its resignation to a state of irremediable negativity.

The many systems of Hindu thought have this in common: that the only thing that really exists is Brahma; that all else is illusion; that the illusion is full of pain and sorrow, that human desires are part of the illusion and human thirsts are unquenchable; that since the desires cannot be filled, the thing to do is not to try to satisfy them but to extinguish them so that they are no longer felt; that unless we arrive at this state, the desire itself will reincarnate us into another round of painful existence. Therefore by asceticism and contemplation rid yourself of all longings, even to be yourself, and you will escape from the wheel of birth and sink back into the undifferentiated background of Brahma, which is all there really is anyway. Buddhism accepts most of this view, without Brahma. Despite its beautiful teachings on kindness and compassion, in its extreme form it is a sort of nihilism: nothing really exists. The soul is only what it thinks, and it thinks illusion. Again, the counsel is to stifle all desire, thus escaping the cycle of rebirth and sinking into the blessed state of Nirvana, the utter peace of nonbeing. Nirvana is hardly a future heaven but a state of mind, or perhaps a nonstate of nonmind, in which there are no disappointments because there are no expectations.

Interest in oriental thought was awakened in Europe by Arthur Schopenhauer,[1] the prince of pessimists. He thought that life is so full of miseries that it is better not to live. The whole universe is but the manifestation of a primeval force, the *will-to-live,* which is the source of all the struggle and misery in life. The worst thing we can do is to propagate the race, because it only brings into existence more sufferers. The chief virtue is sympathy, by which we substitute the *will-to-let-live* for the *will-to-live* and thus obtain some rest from the constant struggle. This wan glimmer of relief is all the happiness we can hope for.

Western thought in general is too hardheaded to clothe what pessimism it has in mystical garments and too activist to sit and wait in passive resignation. The atheists and materialists among us see that a denial of God and of a future life must necessarily limit human destiny to whatever temporary happiness is possible in the present life. Some bettering of our condition in an imperfect world and some contented moments in a fleeting existence are about the best we can hope for. We must toughen ourselves to face the fact that the quest for real happiness is futile. The following passage from Bertrand Russell eloquently states this view:

> That man is the product of causes which had no prevision of the end they were achieving; that his origin, his growth, his hopes and fears, his loves and his beliefs, are but the outcome of accidental collocations of atoms; that no fire, no heroism, no intensity of thought and feeling, can preserve an individual life beyond the grave; that all the labors of the ages, all the devotion, all the inspiration, all the noonday brightness of human genius, are destined to extinction in the vast death of the solar system, and that the whole temple of Man's achievement must inevitably be buried beneath the debris of a universe in ruins—all these things, if not quite beyond dispute, are yet so nearly certain, that no

philosophy which rejects them can hope to stand. Only within the scaffolding of these truths, only on the firm foundation of unyielding despair, can the soul's habitation henceforth be safely built.[2]

Even if in his later days Russell dismissed this essay as youthful rhetoric, it remains a vivid picture of the naturalist's substitute for the last judgment. Even should we succeed in our constant efforts to create utopia on earth, the relentless course of entropy will overtake us and bring all our works to naught. But, they say, enjoy the brief day and live as well as you can in it. The ethical life is still possible, but it has no ultimate goal and no meaning beyond itself.

ETHICAL OPTIMISM

Optimism rather than pessimism has characterized the Western tradition. Plato[3] recognized that happiness in the possession of the very Idea of the Good is the goal of human living. It is to be sought in the present life but cannot be experienced here. In a former existence, before being steeped in the river of forgetfulness and imprisoned in the body, we once had it. Our purpose now is to strive through the practice of virtue in successive lives to escape from the body, from this sensible world of becoming and decay, and to return to the intelligible world of Ideas, the world of true and lasting being, in which we shall eternally contemplate the Ideas in their full perfection. To this we are led by fleeting glimpses of the Ideas awakened in our memory by their imperfect copies in this shadowy sense world. Happiness, though the road to it be long and arduous, is ultimately attainable.

Aristotle in his masterly analysis of happiness, though never expressly denying a future life, restricts his consideration to the present world. Happiness, he says,[4] is the end or goal of all

---

[1]Schopenhauer's main work is *The World as Will and Idea.*

[2]Russell, "A Free Man's Worship," in *Mysticism and Logic,* ch. III.
[3]Plato, *Phaedo; Phaedrus,* §§245–257; *Republic,* bk. VII, etc.
[4]Aristotle, *Nicomachean Ethics,* bk. I, ch. 4–13; and bk. X, ch. 6–9.

human beings. It is not inactivity but action, or else one could be happy while asleep. It must be the highest kind of action, not done for something else but desirable for its own sake. It is not amusement, which is only relaxation between work. It is not found in producing things, since such actions are for the sake of the product, and happiness is for its own sake. It is not action of the body or senses but of what is noblest and best in us, our reason. It is not activity of the practical reason, for this is full of care and trouble, but of the speculative or theoretical reason, which acts in quiet and leisure, for we work to have leisure. Hence it is not the activity of the soldier and statesman but of the sage and scholar.

Because it is the good life, it is the life of virtue, and of the highest virtue, not merely of courage and temperance, which fit a man for practical life, but of the intellectual virtues, the chief of which is philosophic wisdom, which fit a man for contemplation, the contemplation of the highest truth and good. The contemplative life is the most pleasant, leisurely, continuous, enduring, and self-sufficing. This is the life of God, and it is the best.

Such a life is too high for people on earth. We must interrupt our contemplation of the true and the good to take care of our bodily needs, but we should devote ourselves not to what is mortal but to what is most godlike in us and cherish the periods of contemplation to which we can attain. Happiness of a sort is possible even in the practical life. For it we need a sufficiency of health, maturity, education, friends, worldly goods, and length of days—all of which should be made subordinate aids to the truly happy life, a life most like that of God.

These two strains of thought, one from Plato and one from Aristotle, elevated to the supernatural plane by the teaching of Christian revelation, find their full flowering in the medieval thinkers such as St. Thomas.[1] But St. Thomas is primarily a theologian and only secondarily a philosopher. He nowhere makes a complete study of the human end explicitly undertaken from the standpoint of pure reason alone. He gives the

groundwork for such a study, however. We can sift out the data of Christian revelation and, putting them aside as beyond the philosopher's scope, see what is left. There remains the hypothetical natural human being. The whole question of our natural destiny rests on the question of the immortality of the human soul. If immortality cannot be proved on rational or philosophical grounds, our natural destiny could be to achieve only such happiness as is possible in this world. If immortality can be proved on rational or philosophical grounds, our destiny even in the natural order lies beyond the bounds of the present life. Only on the second hypothesis is the problem of our ultimate happiness open for further philosophical investigation.

State of the Question

The preceding material leaves us with five options:

1. To abandon the quest for happiness by extinguishing the desire for it and the emotions on which that desire is based, and to make this extinction our chief ethical aim. This is the answer of oriental pantheism and nihilism.

2. To deny the existence of God and of a future life, and therefore to settle for the imperfect happiness of this world. This is the answer of atheism and materialism.

3. To bypass the question as unanswerable and to put all consideration of it outside the scope of philosophical ethics. This is the answer of practical agnosticism.

4. To hand over the whole question to theology, admitting philosophy's inadequacy to cope with it. This is the answer of supernaturalism, which some would call theologism.

5. To take the metaphysical position that there are philosophically valid arguments for God's existence and for immortality, and then to draw the logical conclusion regarding our destiny. This is the answer of philosophical theism.

The first two views have been discussed, and the next two put themselves outside philosophical consideration. It remains to be seen what the last opinion has to say for itself.

---

[1]St. Thomas, *Summa Theologica*, I–II, qq. 3–4.

The Argument for Ethical Optimism

To some theists, especially those whose theism rests on nonrational grounds or whose approach to philosophy is nonmetaphysical, the following argument will have little appeal. To nontheists, of course, it can have none, but others see it as the only logical conclusion to be drawn from the existence of God and the immortality of the human soul, taken as philosophical positions established in metaphysics. Whether one finds it convincing or not, it is worth serious consideration. The argument is stated in the form of five logically connected assertions:

1. *All humans seek happiness to the fullness of their capacity*. We have already seen that we have a desire for some kind of happiness, and that this is the basic desire penetrating all our other desires. But we are not satisfied with only some degree of happiness. The slightest suspicion that more can be obtained will start a craving for that more. Our intelligence reaches out to truth indefinitely and cannot rest so long as there is anything more to know. Our willing reaches out to good indefinitely and cannot rest so long as there is anything more to seek. In like manner all our abilities demand complete satisfaction. Thus we want happiness as such, and all the happiness we can have.

2. *Our seeking for happiness is a natural tendency, one that springs from human nature itself*. Though we have no innate ideas, we have certain native drives and urges that spring into action as soon as the requisite concepts have been gathered from experience. On the sense level both humans and animals have the drives popularly called instincts. On the rational level humans have similar devices peculiar to themselves, and the basic one is this tendency for happiness. Among all our tendencies, the one for happiness is unique. It is *universal,* for it is found in all of us without exception, appearing even in morbid and abnormal persons though with some distortion; one person may refuse to seek happiness here, another there, but no one can refuse to seek it somewhere. It is *inescapable,* for it lasts through-

out life and cannot be eradicated; no one can quench the desire for happiness, and no matter how hard we may try not to feed it, the hunger grows in spite of us. It is *irresistible,* for it insistently demands satisfaction; our ceaseless unrest shown in our constant activity is only an expression of this basic impulse in varying forms; one who is not happy wants to be happy, and one who is happy wants to be happier.

3. *Such a natural tendency must have been implanted in human nature by its author, God*. There must be an adequate explanation for the existence of such a basic urge. Since it is not accidental to us or casually acquired, but rooted in the very constitution of our rational and free nature, the only possible reason is that God made human nature that way. We seek happiness because God made us for happiness. Therefore responsibility for the existence of this natural tendency in us must be placed on God Himself.

4. *A tendency implanted in human nature by God must be intended not for frustration but for fulfillment*. Here we must suppose that God has the attributes without which he could not be God, especially that he is truthful, wise, and good. His *truthfulness* will not let God mislead us into thinking that happiness is possible if it is not. His *wisdom* will not permit God to place in our very nature an inescapable urge that serves no purpose. His *goodness* will not allow God to put into our nature a basic craving whose sole function would be to tantalize and torment us. Truthfulness, wisdom, and goodness are found in God; lying, folly, and cruelty are not. Therefore, once God has implanted in us a drive toward happiness, he must provide *some* attainable object by which this urge can be satisfied. We are not yet concerned with what that object is, but only that there must be *something*.

5. *The fulfillment of this tendency, or the attainment of happiness, is our last end*. From the preceding analysis it follows that God has destined us for happiness and has made it possible for us to attain it. Happiness, therefore, forms at least part of our last end. But the happiness we naturally seek is all-inclusive, the full satisfaction of all the desires rooted in real emotion that

spring from human nature itself. We have no natural capacity for anything above, beyond, or beside it. Therefore it is no mere part but the whole of our last end, so far as human reason can discover it.

Discussion For and Against Ethical Optimism

Those who object to this argument by denying the metaphysical premises on which it rests are referred to metaphysics, where these premises are investigated. There can be no discussion where there is no common ground. Others have the following difficulties drawn from the structure of the argument itself:

1. The mere fact of having a desire is no guarantee of its fulfillment. The construction of fantasies and the wishing that they might come true result from the kind of creative imagination we have. Any mature person has long ago given up the illusion that they may someday be verified, and such a person does not blame God that those dreams are only dreams.

2. Even granting that the desire for happiness is a natural desire does not prove that it must be fulfilled. We naturally desire health, wealth, knowledge, and other goods but cannot always obtain them. How, then, can we be sure that the natural tendency for happiness is on a different level and cannot be destined for frustration?

3. Why should human beings alone have natural tendencies that must be destined for fulfillment? Animals have natural needs that we often see frustrated, and we do not think that God is obliged to provide them with a future life in which to recompense them for their present disappointments. How can we be sure that God must provide special care to satisfy our natural tendencies?

4. The argument can hardly be taken to suppose that unrepentant, evil-living people will actually attain perfect happiness in the world to come, since they make themselves unworthy of it. Yet they must desire it as much as anyone, since this desire is rooted in human nature, which all possess. Does this not show that the tendency

to happiness not only can be but also sometimes actually is frustrated?

5. If our natural destiny consists of seeking our own happiness, how do we avoid the charge of being naturally and essentially selfish, a very unethical trait? It is a far nobler thing to spend oneself in helping other people on earth than to spend an eternity merely resting in the enjoyment of one's own happiness.

To these and similar objections the following answers are offered:

1. The argument was so stated as to avoid the charge of mere wish-fulfillment. It is not the case of mere imaginative desires that any adult can recognize as illusory, but of the most deep-seated urges and emotions of human nature. We can give up our wistful dreams but not ourselves. Our whole nature cries out against our becoming hopeless futilities, and we cannot believe that God has made us such.

2. The word *natural* may mean anything that is not unnatural, or it may mean something positively demanded by our nature. Health, wealth, and the other lesser tendencies are natural in the first sense, happiness in the second. The lesser goods perfect us in a partial way but must sometimes be sacrificed for the all-inclusive tendency, which is love for the highest good.

3. Animals have needs, but not for happiness, of which they cannot even form an idea. Not being persons, they are subordinate to the utility of each other and of humans. Nature is so arranged that one of the purposes animals are naturally destined to serve is to be food for one another. Thus they always fulfill one of the alternative purposes for which they exist: either to grow to full maturity or to be consumed in assisting others to do so. A human personal being is not a mere means to another's end.

4. The argument does not say that all of us *will* attain happiness but only that all of us *can* attain it. It must be possible for all to reach it. If someone loses it, the loss must be that person's own fault. God must offer it, but we are free to take or refuse the offer. We are destined to happiness conditionally, and the condition is that we voluntarily do our part to earn it.

5. Self-seeking is selfishness only when one seeks self inordinately, in the wrong way or measure, to others' loss. Happiness does not come in limited quantities, so that if I have more, you must have less. Every person can attain all the happiness he or she can enjoy without depriving anyone else of the least. Ethics requires of us the proper kind and amount of self-love. We are responsible for seeking our own self-development and for bringing our life to its appointed goal. It makes sense to help others if they, too, have some meaning to their lives and are not destined to futility. The greatest love one can show other people is to help them to their ultimate happiness.

PURSUIT OF HAPPINESS

Those who accept the foregoing argument, that there must be *something* in which we can find our ultimate happiness, are faced with the next question: Where can we find this happiness? Since we are not born perfectly happy, with all our desires fully satisfied, we must achieve happiness by coming into possession of, or into union with, some object we previously lacked. What is this object?

Those who have followed the argument so far will have little difficulty in suspecting the answer. For the sake of method and as a kind of summary, it will be helpful to look at the various candidates suggested for this position. A process of elimination will ensure that we have examined all claims, and then we can verify the credentials of the successful claimant.

Process of Elimination

The object that can make us happy must be either ourselves or something that is not human but either subhuman, equal to us, or above us. It cannot be a being that is not human but equal to us, for we know of no such being and cannot seek something we do not know. Three alternatives remain:

1. Something below us
2. Our own self

3. Something above us

1. *The first main point is that subhuman things cannot make us happy.* The good things of this world, such as wealth, family, honor, fame, position, power, and influence, not only can be possessed with unhappiness, but also can cause unhappiness by the care and burden they impose. We have desires they cannot satisfy, such as the craving for knowledge and love. Some chance on them without forethought or labor, whereas others cannot secure them even with the greatest effort, and they often come to the most unworthy. When obtained they have an uncertain existence, and they must all be left at death. These goods of fortune are means, not ends. They are for us, we are not for them.

2. *The second main point is that we cannot make ourselves happy.* We cannot find our last end either in the possession of ourselves or in the possession of certain qualities of ourselves. There are three possibilities:

a. *Goods of body.* Health, strength, beauty, physical skills, and other bodily endowments are all subject to the imperfections of the goods of fortune. Without gifts of fortune that afford them scope for their proper exercise, they are often useless. They are not lasting; the art of growing old gracefully consists of intelligently adapting oneself to their loss.

b. *Goods of soul.* Though happiness, as a subjective state experienced within the consciousness, is a good of the soul, it must be produced in the soul by the acquisition of or union with something else, since no one is born happy. By goods of the soul are meant such things as knowledge, the good of the intellect, and virtue, the good of the will. These are both highly estimable, and a life dedicated to their pursuit is truly noble. No one could be really happy without them. But knowledge as such and virtue as such can give only partial happiness at most, since they are means to the end and not the end itself.

i. *Knowledge.* The person who devotes himself or herself to the life of learning has chosen wisely among the good things of this world, and such a person will probably be happier than most people, but this person is chasing a phantom if he or she expects from it perfect happiness. The knowledge we can obtain in the present life is acquired by hard and toilsome study, is never fully clear, cannot be completed in the longest lifetime, and disappoints by confronting the undiscovered and inaccessible. That learning can be devoted to the service of evil shows that it is only a means that can be abused, and that of itself it is not *the* good.

ii. *Virtue*. Though accompanied by peace of conscience and spiritual exaltation, the practice of virtue demands self-control, self-sacrifice, and at times even heroism. However admirable this may be, nothing painful or difficult is compatible with complete happiness, since one would be happier who could attain the same good without the pain and difficulty. Virtue is an indispensable means to happiness, as making us worthy of it, but it is not that happiness itself.

c. *Goods of body and soul together*. If the goods of neither body nor soul taken separately can make us happy, perhaps happiness should be sought in the satisfaction of the whole person, of both body and soul taken together. Here again two possibilities arise, according as one seeks this satisfaction in enjoying a good already attained or in the very process of striving to attain it. Pleasure is the enjoyment of a good attained, and progress is the process of attainment.

i. *Pleasure*. The possession of the goods discussed so far results in pleasure of some kind, either sensuous or intellectual. Most hedonists, when they propose pleasure as the aim of life, mean both sensuous and intellectual pleasure combined into one object and seek happiness in a wise blend of physical and mental delights. Pleasure must be admitted as an ingredient in happiness, for it is actually desired and we could not be satisfied without it. But those who propose pleasure as the highest good are referring to the pleasures of this life only, to be derived with our present abilities from the objects surrounding us. We have already examined the hedonist theory and seen its limitations.

ii. *Progress*. By progress is meant the actualization of all our potentialities, either of the individual or of the race. There is indeed a moral obligation to actualize the potentialities with which our nature has endowed us, but it will not make us completely happy. It is *one* of the ends of human life but not the last end.

Self-development results in the fully developed person, but we cannot be satisfied with ourselves. We are not satisfied with the mediocre abilities we have to begin with, and much less with the imperfect development we can give them. The self-development possible in this life would consist of a combination of goods of soul, body, and fortune. Few of us can succeed in acquiring them in sufficient proportion, and no one can keep them forever.

Social progress, development of the whole human race, is a favorite view of evolutionary humanism. The end of the individual is to contribute toward the future good of humanity, and we, who are now capable of little happiness, must evolve into a higher race capable of more. But this answer is no solution. The future happiness of the race cannot benefit the individual now living, who wants to be personally happy as well as to make others happy. This happiness could only be a greater material prosperity and a higher level of culture, an increase in the goods of body, soul, and fortune, which, however increased, can never be fully satisfying. If the individual is for the whole race, then what is the whole race for? To devote oneself to the advancement of civilization is a worthy and high-minded enterprise, but it is not enough. We cannot be completely satisfied even with our civilized selves.

3. *The third main point is that our happiness must be sought in something above us*. From our whole discussion so far it follows that neither subhuman things nor we ourselves can make us perfectly happy. None of these things taken separately can satisfy, nor can the combination of them all taken together, because no one can secure all these goods in one lifetime; some of them are mutually exclusive, and any choice

among them will leave other desires unsatisfied. They are all fleeting and insecure, and over the whole of them is flung the shadow of death. The fact of death alone is sufficient argument to show that none of these transitory things could be the purpose for which we live.

Above us we have *God*. No one ever suggested that we exist for the sake of some superhuman creatures to be used or consumed for their well-being in the same way as animals are for our sake; the fact that each of us is a person makes this impossible. It follows, then, by the process of elimination that the only object that can make us perfectly happy, and thus is our absolutely last end, is God.

The validity of a process of elimination depends on the completeness of the disjunction, that is, on the assurance that no possible alternative has been overlooked. Though ethical systems have an infinite possibility of variation in detail, and as the history of philosophy progresses, future theories will be proposed to supplant their predecessors, it can be safely said that no theory is conceivable that cannot be classified under one of the headings just given. Any such system that does not make God our last end must, if it is to be taken seriously, fall into the category of those that make *us* our own last end. But we are inherently incapable of satisfying ourselves or of being our own happiness.

Positive Argument

The following argument is independent of the process of elimination just given, but the two arguments reinforce each other. For our happiness God is both required and sufficient. If he is required, we cannot be happy without him. If he is sufficient, nothing else is necessary.

God is *required,* for no lesser being will do. We are by nature rational and free, and rationality and freedom are the bases of two main tendencies: the tendency of the intellect to know all truth, and the tendency of our willing and emotions to love and commune with all good. But

God is perfect truth and goodness. Without him our intellect, willing, and emotions cannot be satisfied.

God is *sufficient* for one who is intimately united with God. Such a person may also enjoy creatures, but have no strict need of them. There can be no desire in us that God cannot satisfy to the full. There can be no truth that is not found in truth itself, no good that is not found in goodness itself.

The upshot of all this argumentation is that, even on the purely natural plane, we must be destined to a last end that is also our highest good, that this last end subjectively is perfect happiness and objectively is God. Does this mean the beatific vision that theology speaks of? No. Philosophy knows nothing about that. All that pure reason can discuss and try to establish is a knowledge and love of God fully proportioned to our natural powers and capacities, so that they are not left frustrated but given thorough satisfaction. This is all to which we can *naturally* aspire.

Would such a happiness be a static condition incapable of growth or progress? Only in the sense that God does not change and there is nothing beyond God to attain to. But there is no reason for happiness to be static on the part of the creature. There is no inherent impossibility in the supposition that the knowledge and love of God would be a continuously expanding knowledge and a continuously deepening love, at each moment perfectly corresponding to the proximate capacity of the soul at that particular stage, and thus satisfying it, but with a remote capacity of indefinite growth because God is the inexhaustible source of everlasting new manifestations of his infinite perfections.

SUMMARY

Happiness is desire satisfied by the conscious possession of, or participation in and communion with, the good. It is a lasting subjective state that can exist only in a rational and free being. It is neither mere contentment, passing emotion, nor sunny disposition.

All of us seek happiness in general, since we all want our desires satisfied, but we differ in what we judge will make us happy. Those who appear to desire misery or choose evils are only seeming exceptions. Happiness is the basic motive in all we do, though we may seek it only implicitly.

Perfect happiness fully satisfies all our desires; *imperfect* happiness has flaws in it. Because of our finite capacities, our happiness cannot be *absolutely* but at most *relatively* perfect.

Is such relatively perfect happiness attainable? Pessimism says no. Oriental pessimists seek relief from suffering in the extinction of individual consciousness. Atheists and materialists counsel contentment with this life and the acceptance of death as the end of all. The optimistic Western tradition holds that happiness is our last end and is attainable. The argument, presupposing God's existence and the soul's immortality, includes these steps:

1. We seek all the happiness of which we are capable.
2. This is a natural tendency springing from our rational and free nature.
3. Such a tendency is implanted in human nature by God.
4. God cannot intend a natural tendency for frustration.
5. He intends it for fulfillment as our last end.

It is objected that this is mere wish fulfillment,

that animals' natural needs are left unfulfilled, that evil-living people do not deserve happiness, and that seeking one's own happiness is selfish.

It is answered that our natural desire for happiness is our basic tendency and unique, that animals have no idea of happiness, that attainment of happiness requires our cooperation, and that legitimate self-seeking is not selfishness but the very purpose of our being.

Where can one find the happiness to which he or she is destined? What is our objective last end? The argument is twofold:

1. *Process of elimination.* Nothing subhuman can make us happy, nor can we make ourselves happy; therefore, only something above us can do so, and this is God. Goods of fortune and goods of body are given to few, held with anxiety, and lost in the end. Knowledge is toilsome, incomplete, and unsatisfying. Virtue, besides being hard to practice, is but a means to the end and not the end itself. Pleasure cannot be constantly enjoyed. Service of others supposes that these others have some last end. Personal progress results only in a fully developed person who cannot be satisfied with himself or herself. Progress of the human race does no good to the individual now and leaves unanswered what the race is for.

2. *Positive argument.* God is *required* to satisfy all our desires, because our intelligence tends to all Truth and our willing and emotions to all Good. God is *sufficient,* because all perfection is found in the Infinite.

Questions for Discussion

1. Check back in Chapter 6 on the Utilitarians, who want the greatest happiness for the greatest number, and compare their desire with the view expressed in this present chapter that all persons desire to be happy. When you discount the misers, cranks, sadists, masochists, and the depressed, do you not have the same thing the Utilitarians want, namely, the greatest happiness for the greatest number? Do you find any significant differences be-

tween Utilitarianism and ethical optimism? Explain.

2. When you were 12 years old, you decided to be a fighter pilot when you grew up. This became an overriding desire. Everything you did for the next nine years focused on that goal. Now you are a Marine at an air base in flight training. Earlier this year you suffered a minor injury (a flight embolism) that left you physically unqualified for military flight

school. The sense of loss was tremendous, but you did not give up that easily. You had to experience flying a fighter at least once, so during the early morning hours you climbed aboard a fighter that was scheduled to be flown the next morning, started it up, taxied out on the runway, and took off without benefit of runway lights or tower clearance. As soon as you pushed the throttle to go down the runway, your head snapped back against the ejection seat, and you were happy. You did not want to go through the rest of your life frustrated because you had not flown a jet fighter. Is it true that we cannot desire anything without desiring happiness? If a person did not desire happiness, would he or she ever do anything at all? Explain.

3. Happiness is said to be desire satisfied by the conscious possession of, or participation in and communion with, the good. Psychologically, to satisfy a desire or an emotion is to "be rid of it." But our emotions give meaning to our lives and keep us going. The total satisfaction of all our emotions and desires would be in effect to leave our lives devoid of meaning, like the Nirvana of Buddhism. An ambition satisfied is an ambition no more. Ethical optimism may not be Buddhism in disguise, but in the long run does it not end in Nirvana? Is not the definition of happiness merely a recipe for an overwhelming sense of depression and meaninglessness? Would we not all be happier with some of our desires and emotions dissatisfied? Explain.

4. We work for many reasons, and among those reasons are money, satisfaction, and leisure. Most people work in order to have the money for the things they need to enjoy life. However, we have a large number of workaholics in our midst, people who work almost constantly and are unhappy when they are not working. What would Aristotle think of such people? Do they not give the lie to his theory that contemplation is our highest and best activity? Is the marijuana smoker not more in tune with Aristotelian contemplation than the workaholic? Explain.

5. Ethical optimism argues that only God can satisfy our desire for happiness and that only God is required. Atheists, agnostics, and other nontheists seem condemned to unhappiness by this theory. To those for whom there is no God, they themselves must be their last end and are thus doomed to frustration for we are each inherently incapable of satisfying ourselves or of being our own happiness. Is the nontheist therefore incapable of being optimistic about the world and its people? Do only theists have reason to be ethical optimists? If this is so, is philosophy then nothing more than a sham or does it still have something to offer everyone, both theists and nontheists?

Readings

In the oriental vein: The *Bhagavadgita* is a sublime poetic expression of Hindu thought. It would be well to read some of the Buddhist *Sutras*. Of both, there are many translations and editions. Schopenhauer's attitude can be seen in his essays, edited from *Parerga and Paralipomena,* especially bk. V.

Plato's writings are full of reflections on man's purpose in life and on happiness. The *Phaedo, Phaedrus, Symposium,* and bk. X of the *Republic* give Plato's idea of human destiny.

Aristotle's *Nicomachean Ethics,* bk. I, ch. 4–13, and bk. X, ch. 6–9, provide the basic reading material here.

St. Augustine, *De Vita Beata* (The Happy Life), *De Moribus Ecclesiae Catholicae* (Of the Morals of the Catholic Church), and *De Doctrina Christiana* (On Christian Doctrine), does not separate philosophy and religion.

St. Thomas's *Summa Theologica,* I–II, qq. 2–5, presents the views of a theologian. Hence he treats of supernatural rather than natural happiness. This is why he says that we cannot attain ultimate happiness, by which he means the supernatural beatific vision, by our natural powers. What he says is useful for philosophy with the proper reservations. The same holds true of his treatment of happiness in the *Summa Contra Gentiles,* bk. III, ch. 25–63.

Leibniz' *Principles of Nature and Grace* treats of what most modern philosophers prefer to overlook.

Etienne Gilson's *Moral Values and Moral Life,* pp. 26–51, and his *Christian Philosophy of St. Thomas Aquinas,* pp. 351–356; Leo Ward's *Values and Reality,* ch. 5–6; Mortimer Adler's *Dialectic of Morals;* and William R. O'Connor's *The Eternal Quest* have good material.

PART III
Practical Ethics

Applying general ethical theory to the various areas of human life is our next concern. We distinguish between the individual and society, but the distinction is mainly for the sake of emphasis. As individuals we do little that involves no one else or has no social dimension. Society consists of individuals, so that anything a person does as a social being is also done as an individual, and each person is responsible for his or her social acts. Whether society itself has a corporate moral responsibility is debata-

ble. If it is not an entity distinct from the persons who constitute it, responsibility for what society does comes down to the personal responsibility of those who control society's acts.

We look first at *personal life* and discuss questions concerning natural and legal rights (Chapter 18), the right to life and our duty to preserve it (Chapter 19), the nature and care of health (Chapter 20), and truthfulness in communication (Chapter 21).

18
Rights

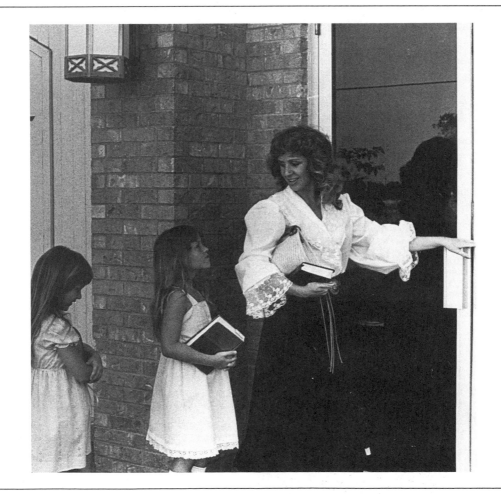

PROBLEM

We have considered happiness as the end of the moral life and have already seen the meaning of natural law and its place in the moral life. Now we take up the fundamental question of the duties imposed on us and the fundamental rights assigned to us by the natural law. Because we are human and personal beings, we are or can be conscious of what is fitting our nature in all its essential relationships and conscious of the needs we have to grow and be fulfilled through our moral choices. Human nature, taken completely in all its essential relationships, requires that human beings have certain things such as life, work, and freedom from coercion as their due. We can claim life, work and such freedom as our due because we need them to pursue our final end with genuine inner freedom. We have a right to them as persons; we have a duty to respect others' rights to them by reason of their intrinsic value and dignity as persons. Human society striving for the common good of its members implies and requires recognition of the fundamental rights of persons, rights based on the intrinsic value and dignity of those persons. Rights imply society and have an intrinsic connection with the common good, with the ultimate value of society and the means to achieve that value. Rights and duties have an intrinsic connection with our final end as personal beings, which is also the end toward which living in society is a means.

Finally, rights and duties are specifications of the relative kind of positive freedom that is ours as persons. By this we mean, for example, that we have a right not to have certain of our external movements hindered or forced because we need some freedom of movement to carry out our own moral choices, the choices for which we must take responsibility. Because my personal being is an inner free being, a being that is free in the positive sense of that word, I need freedom *from* external interference (negative freedom) to exercise my positive freedom. As a personal, free (in the positive sense) being my need for negative freedom is the basis or foundation for my right to some external freedom of movement. My positive freedom gives rise to my need for some negative freedom; my inner freedom or power to determine the quality of my personhood by my own free choices gives rise ultimately to the natural rights I have by reason of the kind of being I am.

We come back to a further consideration of the means to happiness. The common good consists of maintaining peace, affording equal opportunity for all persons, and giving to others and receiving from them powers, resources, and values that as individuals none would possess. The pursuit of the common good requires the idea of law and the virtue of justice that in turn imply the existence of such things as rights and duties. They logically form the next topic in our study, especially since the remaining part of ethics consists chiefly of determining what our rights and duties are. The natural law requires that whatever it leaves undetermined shall subsequently be determined either as (1) a right or a duty existing for all humans and made known to them by right reason or (2) a right or duty existing for a certain group of people and made known to them by positive law. Our right to existence, to personal freedom, and to pursue the perfection of moral life derive from natural law; the right to vote and to hold private property in certain ways derive from the positive law of the state.

Some people not interested in a natural law still claim what they call natural rights. They may not even use the term natural rights but speak of human rights, rights that belong to any and every human being simply because he or she is human. We shall have to examine the logic of this attitude. What is the source of such rights, and what obliges anybody to respect them? There are also those who clamor for their own rights but are unwilling to acknowledge that they have duties, or perhaps they will admit some duties but only those they voluntarily accept. Can any sense be made of such an attitude? What happens when I assert my right and others refuse to recognize it, or when others impose on me a duty I refuse to accept? We can discuss the matter using the following questions to guide us:

1. What are rights?
2. What are the components of a right?
3. Are there natural rights?
4. How is right related to might?
5. What are duties?
6. What if rights and duties conflict?
7. What excuses one from duty?

MEANING OF A RIGHT

The English word *right* has two main meanings, as illustrated in the following sentence: "It is right (morally good, worthwhile, important, valuable) for us to demand our rights (things owed to us either as valuable in themselves or as means to achieve a further value)." The two meanings stem from the same root idea, the ethical concept of *oughtness:* how I ought to act, and how others ought to act toward me. As we have already seen in Chapter 5, the moral good for human beings demands that we use our positive freedom to realize (make actual in our lives) the values necessary for us to become or develop into the persons we can be. By our very nature as conscious rational beings, we know and experience ourselves needing to have certain values just to be the kind of beings we are. Our nature clamors to have certain values such as life, work, and freedom from external coercion just for us to succeed as persons. In our actions we must, with moral necessity, realize moral values, for everything we do expresses the unique personality each of us is. The use each of us makes of his or her individual positive freedom is the actual exertion and further development of the inmost self each of us is. As a personal self, I ought to act in ways consonant with the moral development of that self, and others ought to act toward me in ways consonant with both me and themselves as morally developing persons. Hence we have:

1. Right as opposed to wrong
2. Right as correlative to duty

Right originally means something that is straight, not crooked, in opposition to *wrong,* which is wrung or twisted from the straight. Right is something that squares with a rule or norm, such as a right line or a right angle. In ethics *right* means

that which squares with the norm of morality and thus is morally good. Up to now we have dealt only with this meaning of the word *right,* and we have by no means finished with it.

Right is also used to mean that which is just: a just law, just deed, just debt, just claim, that which is owed. This is *right* as correlative to *duty,* and it is this sense of *right* that we must now study.

We cannot be obliged to keep the moral law and at the same time be deprived of the means necessary to this end. This obligation requires that we have the positive freedom, the *power,* both to do the things necessary for keeping the moral law ourselves and to restrain others from interfering with our freedom to observe the moral law. In the language of freedom, this power is our own inner freedom to observe the moral law, to fulfill our moral obligations. No one can be obliged to do the impossible; hence, if it is a fact that we are obliged, we must be *empowered,* have the inner freedom, to fulfill our obligation. Power is of two kinds:

1. Physical power, or might
2. Moral power (freedom for), or right

Might, or physical power, is the bodily strength needed to secure an end. It comprises not only our own skeleton and muscles, together with all the tools, weapons, and machinery we can use, but also the bodily strength of all other persons under our command and the force of all the instruments they can use to help us accomplish our end. Thus a whole army can be at the disposal of a single officer's will and is an enormous extension of that officer's personal might. Though applied by a will or even by many wills cooperating, physical power accomplishes its purpose by mere force which is indifferent to the claims of justice and can be used to help or hinder the observance of the moral law. Hence might in itself is neither good nor evil, and becomes either by the will that directs it.

Right, moral power, or *freedom for,* on the other hand, works by appeal to another's inner freedom through his or her intelligence. When I claim something as mine by right, I demand respect from others for my claim, a respect that others must grant if they are to attain their own purpose in life. I am claiming a value that is either intrinsic to my very existence as a human person or instrumental for me to maintain my personal dignity. In urging a right I equivalently say, "This good or value is mine, a means given me to help me fulfill my moral function as a person; if you try to interfere with my freedom, you can do so only by doing wrong, incurring moral guilt, violating the moral *ought,* thus damaging your own moral worth as a person." A right thus puts a moral bond on the inner freedom of another so that, even if the other person can infringe my right physically, he or she cannot do so without committing an evil deed and incurring moral guilt, with its corresponding sanctions. Hence a right is said to be morally inviolable even when it is physically violable, because the right is needed to guarantee the intrinsic dignity of the person. If it were the case that any action whatsoever is permitted in certain circumstances, no good or value intrinsic to the person or instrumental for maintaining personal dignity would be safe from invasion and suppression. This would mean that in certain circumstances the person could be sacrificed to the attainment of ulterior ends, and the human person would become simply one more item in the world with a relative value, inviolable up to a point but expendable after that.

1. Right is defined as moral power over what is one's own, or more expressly, *moral power or inner freedom to do, omit, hold, or exact something of value.* Right as thus defined exists in the person possessing the right; it is right in the primary sense of the word.

2. By a figure of speech we transfer the word *right* from the person who has the right (the moral power) and apply it to the thing or object over which he or she has the right. We say, "I will get my rights," and "This woman is deprived of her rights," meaning some object due the person in question. *Object* as used here is not necessarily a physical substance but may be actions, goods, services, or omissions. If I were deprived of my right in the sense of moral power (inner freedom *for*), I would have no right to the thing at all and could not legitimately claim it; what we mean in saying I am deprived of my right is that I am deprived of some object to which I retain a right.

3. Rights are founded on law, and law supposes rights. They imply each other. For this reason *law* itself is sometimes called *right,* a usage common in other languages but infrequent in English. Since all right comes from law, rights are called natural or positive, divine or human, ecclesiastical or civil, according to the kind of law that confers the right.

These three meanings of right are illustrated in the following sentence: A man is unjustly deprived of his rights (an object due him); recourse is made to the code of civil rights (the law); the man is given a fair trial to which he has a right (moral power to do, omit, hold, or exact something; in this case to exact).

COMPONENTS OF A RIGHT

A right involves a system of relations in which there are three terms and a basis or foundation on which the relations are grounded. In the example of a workman having a right to his wages, we may separate four elements, or components: the workman who has earned the wages, the employer who is bound to pay the wages, the wages the workman has earned, and the work done whereby the workman has earned the wages. In general, in every right we distinguish the following:

1. Subject: the person possessing a right
2. Term: those persons bound to respect or fulfill a right
3. Matter: that to which one has a right
4. Title: the reason why this person, that is, the subject, has a right to this matter

1. The *subject* of a right can only be a *person.* Rights exist because we are obliged to guard the moral value of our being and fulfill ourselves by voluntary observance of the moral law and thus to reach our last end. To this kind of action rights are essential, because if we must guide ourselves by use of our inner freedom, we must be guaranteed immunity from hindrance (freedom *from*) in our choice of the necessary means. Since only

persons have free choice and are obliged by the moral law, only persons can have rights. Other creatures, acting spontaneously and without inner freedom or responsibility, need no such guarantee.

The subject of a right may be not only a *physical,* or *natural,* person, an individual rational being, but also a *moral,* or *juridical,* person (sometimes called a corporate, conventional, fictitious, or artificial person), such as a society, firm, corporation, or government. People may act singly or in groups, by themselves or through representatives, and group action is in accordance with our social nature. We attain our end by social as well as by individual activity, but a society would be useless if it could not command the means necessary to achieve its purpose; therefore societies as well as individuals can have rights.

2. The *term* of a right must also be a *person.* This proposition is evident from the definition. The term is the one or ones morally obliged to respect or fulfill the rights of another, and only a person can have moral obligations.

3. The *matter* of a right can *never* be another *person.* As we saw previously, a person cannot be subordinated to the interests of another to be used and consumed as a mere means for another's benefit. Since in the exercise of any right the subject always subordinates the matter to himself or herself and uses it as a means to his or her own end, it follows that the matter of a right can never be another person. This conclusion does not mean that one person can never do a service for another. Social life is a constant interchange of goods and services, and we were made by nature to be helpful to one another. When we hire people to work for us, we buy their labor, not their persons, and labor can be the matter of a right.

4. The *title* of a right is the reason this particular concrete right exists. Its purpose is to establish a connection between the subject and the matter of a right. For example, a person has a right to own property in general, but this right is abstract, not specifying any particular piece of property. Something is necessary to give this particular person rather than someone else the right

to this particular piece of property to change the abstract into a concrete right. The contract of sale does so, and this fact is the person's title.

According to title, rights are congenital or acquired. *Congenital,* or native, rights come with birth or even before birth; the title to these rights is the bare fact of existence as a human being. *Acquired* rights have as their title some contingent historical fact, such as purchase, inheritance, or arriving at the age of majority. In either case, the title is always some fact connecting this subject with this matter, this person with this thing.

Three important questions arise in connection with the subject, the matter, and the title of a right:

1. Since the *subject* of a right is always and only a person, how can we respond to those who claim that animals and other nonpersonal beings also have rights?

2. If a person may never be the *matter* of a right, is there any moral justification for either voluntary or penal servitude?

3. Do humans have absolutely inalienable rights, or may a person's *title* to a right ever be given up or taken away?

SO-CALLED ANIMAL RIGHTS

From the above explanations it follows that animals, not being persons, have no rights. Persons have rights; nonpersons do not. Nevertheless, the issue of animal rights is receiving increased attention today. All animals are living beings that together with us form the chain of life in the world as we know it. Among all those living beings, we designate ourselves alone as the ones who have rights based on our personhood. This is by no means the equivalent of saying that animals have no intrinsic value or that they have only the value that persons assign to them. As living beings they individually and collectively have intrinsic value, and we as personal beings owe them respect for their well-being and have a duty not to harm them. Toward both animate and inanimate beings we rational and free beings have a relationship of caring. Were we to admit that animals have rights, we would also have to admit that they have corresponding duties and hold them responsible for the exercise of rights and the fulfillment of duties they could never understand.

Much of what we have seen and are seeing of animal treatment today constitutes a perversion of the caring relationship that we ought to have in regard to animals. They are raised, sometimes in abominable conditions, and slaughtered for food. Captured animals are kept and used in wild animal parks, circuses, zoos, and even petting zoos. They are used in the classroom and laboratory for experiments. Commercially, they are used to test the toxicity of chemicals and drugs. Sports enthusiasts hunt and fish for the thrill of it. Some species have been hunted or fished to extinction and others well nigh to extinction. For the endangered species we have placed a moratorium on hunting and fishing. Use and abuse are both deprecated by animal rights advocates.

Certainly all abuse of animals is contrary to the natural law, because any such activity is unfitting for rational and free beings and clearly a violation of our duty to be caring in regard to all forms of life, both human and nonhuman. Does the natural law preclude all use of animals? It does not seem so, but there may be a telling argument still to be made. Until then, prudence would counsel avoidance of all abuse and the exercise of great care in our use of animals for human purposes. Any use can easily become wrong through circumstances, for example, by using them in inhumane or cruel ways. Certainly, wanton and wasteful destruction of any of the goods of the earth is immoral, and animals are certainly among the goods of the earth we have a duty to respect and care for.

SLAVERY

Slavery is wrong because it comes so close to treating a person as a thing, a mere object to be used. It is impossible to own a person, if we understand *person* in the philosophical sense of the word. To own a slave's person would be to own not merely that person's body but his or her spirit as well, the slave's innermost self. That self or personality always remains under the slave's control and is the source of the voluntary and free acts for which the slave, like any other human being, is responsible. Precisely because they are rational and free beings capable of voluntary and free acts, persons cannot be owned. Though the slaveholder does not, and cannot, deprive a person of his or her inner freedom, he does deprive the slave of external freedom, one of the most precious attributes and fundamental rights of a person.

Slavery might be imposed as punishment for crime. If the state can, with moral justification, put criminals to death (a position yet to be argued), it should be able to impose lesser punishments. Imprisonment for crime is used in all societies, and the distinction between it and slavery is rather nominal. When a man, for example, hires out his labor, he can always quit and thus save his personal dignity; the slave and the prisoner cannot. Under desperate conditions a man might sell himself into slavery. If he can hire out his services for pay, why not for mere maintenance; if he can do it for a time, why not for life? One would hardly condemn a desperate man for saving himself in this way, but one would condemn a society for allowing such intolerable conditions to exist. For the public good, the state should forbid such a contract. These two forms of servitude, the penal and the voluntary, are the only ones for which even a semblance of moral justification can be found.

Slavery as a historical institution looked on slaves as property, as animated tools, to be bought and sold. There can hardly be anything more degrading to personal dignity or more destructive of human rights than this revolting practice. There can be no possible moral defense for slave hunting, nor for letting children be born into slavery, and what begins unjustly and in bad faith cannot be righted by the mere passage of time. That the civilized world accepted this institution for so long illustrates the slow growth of moral social consciousness and the difficulty of seeing remote conclusions of the natural law.

INALIENABLE RIGHTS

The terms *alienable* and *inalienable* rights cause so much confusion as to be practically unusable in ethics. To alienate is to give away or to take away. No right, if it is a genuine right, can be taken away except by the one who has granted it. Positive rights can be taken away by the grantor and given up by the possessor. Natural rights, since they are granted by God through the natural law, cannot be taken away by human authority and are in this sense inalienable. Can they be given up, waived, or renounced by free choice of the possessor? Some of them can, for though granted by nature, they are not strictly necessary in all possible conditions of life. For example, a person may decide not to own property or not to marry because these goods are not strictly necessary for the kind of life this person decides to live. Other rights, however, are so indispensable to a person that their exercise is also a duty; such rights may not be arbitrarily taken away by human authority nor voluntarily renounced by the possessor and so are in this sense inalienable. Parents, for example, have a natural right to rear their children but may be deprived of this right because of their incompetence or cruelty to their children. The parents' right to rear their children has come in conflict with the right of the children to be well cared for, and the civil authority of the state settles the conflict by depriving such parents of their right to protect the children's more fundamental right.

Not every natural right is therefore of its very nature inalienable, but the most basic rights are absolutely inalienable in every sense. The right to life is such a right. It has been granted by God through the natural law and cannot be taken away by human authority. Some people argue that a criminal can be justly condemned to die, not because he or she has lost the right to live by reason of the crime committed, but because he or she, by committing the crime, has renounced the possibility of justly asserting this right. To explain the loss of rights by saying that the person keeps the right itself while losing the right to its exercise seems a meaningless subtlety. Moral power that *cannot* or *must not* be exercised is not moral power. It is better to say that the right itself is lost.

A further reflection on this question of the absolute inalienability of one's right to life should lead to the conclusion that capital punishment is never justifiable and so should be abolished wherever it is practiced. Those who argue in favor of capital punishment must ultimately be able to show that the right to life is not absolutely inalienable by reason of its being granted to each human being by God through the natural law. If the right to lead a moral life is absolutely inalienable in all senses, it is clear that the right to life is even more fundamental and so is also absolutely inalienable in all senses. Perhaps some of our confusion with regard to the right to life comes from moral positions we wish to take in regard to questions such as capital punishment, abortion, personal self-defense, national self-defense, and heroic acts of self-sacrifice for the life of another. Our philosophical reasoning demands of itself a self-consistency in our approach to and solution of these questions.

NATURAL RIGHTS

In much of the literature, the term *inalienable right* simply stands for *natural right*. We need not prove that there are such things as rights, for no one denies it. To deny all rights, one would have to deny all law, and even the most extreme anarchists would admit some form of customary law. All law supposes rights, and all rights suppose law. The concepts are inseparable. There cannot be a right unless all others are bound to respect that right, and that which binds them is law. There cannot be a law unless someone is charged with moral power to exact obedience to the law, that is, with the right to enforce it, and law exists for the purpose of protecting someone's rights. Hence the saying, "No law, no rights," and vice versa.

Unanimity ceases when we ask: Which law is the origin of rights? Since no one denies that there are positive laws, no one denies that there are positive rights. The problem then, centers on the existence of the natural law. If there is a natural law, there should be natural rights; if not, there can be none. So the main cleavage of thought is as follows:

1. Are there no rights but positive rights?
2. Besides positive rights are there also natural rights?

Positivist View of Rights

Moral and *legal positivists* are logically compelled to adopt the first position. If there is no natural law, there can be no natural rights, because there would be nothing to oblige people to respect such rights. Some moral positivists use the term *natural rights,* but by it Hobbes[1] means only that in the state of nature a person had a right to do whatever he or she was able to do, and Spinoza,[2] consistently with his pantheistic determinism, cannot distinguish between natural moral law and natural physical law, so that a person's natural rights are on the same plane as that of a rose to bloom or of a cat to purr. Such uses of the word *right* make it but an empty name, as Rousseau[3] correctly observes. Moral positivists must either deny that the commonly accepted natural rights are really rights or reduce them somehow to positive rights.

There is also a group of compromisers who will not go so far as to deny a natural moral law but think that civil law should be studied independently of it. They make a complete separation between the juridical order of rights founded on the civil law and the ethical order of moral rights founded on the natural law. Hence they are not strictly *moral* positivists (no natural morality) nor *legal* positivists (no natural law), but *juridical* positivists (no natural rights). All moral and legal positivists must also be juridical positivists, but not vice versa. Of course, if one defines the word *right* in such a way that it can apply only to positive rights, there would be merely a dispute on words, but these writers do not admit natural rights un-

der any other name and thus are denying not the word but the thing. Because of these differences and the importance of the matter, it is worth risking some repetition to outline these views briefly. The chief sources suggested by moral, legal, and juridical positivists for all the rights they admit are:

1. The state, by its constitution and statutes
2. A contract, expressed or implied
3. The concept of freedom, universal for all people
4. Custom manifesting the spirit of the people

1. *The state.* The notion that no one has any rights except those given by the state has always been widespread in practice, if not in philosophical theory, throughout all ages from the ancient oriental despotisms to their modern counterparts. Tyrants have acted as if their groveling subjects' right to live and breathe were their own graciously granted favor. Even today some otherwise enlightened states declare in their constitutions that the citizens have no rights except those expressly granted them by the state. Hobbes[4] gave this doctrine, that all true rights come from the state, its first clear philosophical expression; in it he is followed by others, such as Spinoza,[5] whose total system is of quite a different cast. Among American jurists Justice Oliver Wendell Holmes[6] said that a right is only a prophecy that the state will use its courts and its might to sustain someone's claim.

Criticism of this view may be summed up as follows. The state cannot be the source of its own right to existence, for it would have already to exist before it could confer this right on itself. Either the state has no right to exist, or there is some source of rights prior to the state. Apart from force and fear, the state can bind its citizens to respect the positive rights it confers only by appeal to its own natural right to exist and function as a state. If the state were the source of all rights, it could give itself and withhold from its

---

[1] Hobbes, *Leviathan,* ch. 14.
[2] Spinoza, *Theologico-Political Treatise,* ch. 16; *Political Treatise,* ch. 2.
[3] Rousseau, *Social Contract,* bk. I, ch. 3–4.

[4] Hobbes, *loc. cit.*
[5] Spinoza, *loc. cit.*
[6] Holmes, *Collected Legal Papers,* "The Path of the Law," "Natural Law."

subjects any right it wished, it could do no wrong, tyranny would be impossible, individuals could have no rights against the state, one state could have no rights against another state, and since a state can rule only its own subjects, there would be an end to all international rights.

2. *Contract*. Hobbes and Rousseau, holding that the state originated by the social contract, trace the origin of rights both to the state and to a contract. But they differ in emphasis, Hobbes stressing the state more than the contract, and Rousseau the contract more than the state.

Critics of this theory say that though many rights originate in contracts, not all rights can result from contracts, and no right can be wholly grounded on contract alone. Before making a contract, the contracting parties must first have the right to enter into such a contract, which might come from a previous contract, but the series cannot be infinite. Contracts receive their binding force from something existing prior to all contracts, the moral law, which requires the observance of just pledges and agreements. The right to life and other nonrenounceable rights cannot result from a contract freely made, since such a contract would be voidable at will, and such rights cannot be contracted away. One cannot by contract acquire a right to commit a wrong, as another's murder, for the person to be murdered already has a right to life and did not obtain it by contract.

3. *Concept of freedom*. Kant separates legality from morality, the juridical order from the ethical order, saying that right, or legality, has to do with external action and comes from the state; ethics, or morality, has to do with the inner motive of duty and comes from the moral law. Both are derived from the absolute freedom of the person, which is twofold: freedom from inner compulsion, the basis of morals, and freedom from outer compulsion, the basis of rights. Kant says:

> There is only one innate right. Freedom (independence from the constraint of another's will), insofar as it is compatible with the freedom of everyone else in accordance with a universal law, is the one

and sole original right that belongs to every human being by virtue of his humanity.[1]

All people have equal shares in the external goods of the world and the right to use as much of them as is consonant with the equal right of every other person. Right pertains only to this external use; the motive from which a person acts, whether the moral motive of duty or any other, pertains to the private sphere of ethics. This system of equal shares of free external action is the system of rights.

This view is criticized for the following reasons. Both the internal act and the external act, the inner motive and the outward deed, form one voluntary human act. The legal order is part of the moral order, and hence there can be no complete separation of legality from morality. Apart from morals the word *right* has no real meaning, for all rights suppose obligation somewhere, and obligation belongs to morality. Not all rights are deducible from the concept of freedom limited only by the equal freedom of all others, but they are specifications of the kinds of freedom that are ours by reason of our being persons. Even a child's right to support from its parents is a result of its natural needs to grow and develop to mature personhood, which entails the fullness of both negative and positive freedom. If human freedom were limited only by the equal freedom of all other persons and all rights were based on such freedom, we should have the right to freely give up any right, even those that we are not morally allowed to surrender. To say that we have a *right* to do anything we wish, so long as it hurts no one else, would give us a right to practice private vices, provided we allow others to do likewise. No amount of equally shared freedom among people can create a right to do what there is a moral duty not to do.

4. *Custom*. The historical school of jurispru-

---

[1]Kant, *The Metaphysics of Morals,* pt. I, The Metaphysical Elements of Justice, Division of the Theory of Justice, B. [LLA ed., p. 43].

dence, a reaction against Kant, grew out of the philosophy of Hegel and found its juristic expression in the writings of Friedrich Karl von Savigny. It holds that every people unconsciously develops its own speech, manners, art, and culture much as an individual develops his or her own mannerisms and personality. Rights are part of this development and are grounded in immemorial customs, which are the outward expression and unconscious product of the spirit of a people. The state is not the origin of rights but can and should assist in their development, since the people show their spirit in their political institutions as well as in every other feature of their national life.

Critics grant that some rights do originate in custom, for some laws originate in custom and rights come from law, but deny that this can be true of all rights or be the basic source of any right. The people must already have a right to originate and follow such a custom. With this theory how could one obtain a right to do anything new? There would be no rights until a custom had been sufficiently established; by what right, then, were the first acts performed? Customs, even national customs, can be evil as well as good. By doing bad acts often enough a people could secure a right to do them. Rights customarily violated could not be vindicated, since it would then become the custom, and therefore a right, to violate them. We are not so wholly absorbed in our tribe, race, or state that we have no rights but those they are accustomed to give us.

Argument for Natural Rights

The foregoing criticism of the various forms of juridical positivism can be taken as a negative argument for natural rights. Having seen something of the historical background of this controversy, we are now ready to see how the natural law theorists view the problem. On the premises they accept, their positive argument is very simple:

There is a natural moral law that imposes obligations on all human beings to achieve the purpose for which they exist as human persons and to conform their conduct to the norm of morality as the only means to achieve this purpose. But human beings cannot have such obligations unless they have a right to fulfill them and a consequent right to prevent others from interfering with the fulfillment of these obligations. All rights that I have suppose in others the obligation not to interfere with my exercise of my rights, that is, the obligation to respect my outer freedom (freedom *from*) as well as my inner freedom (freedom *for*). The right I have to fulfill the obligations imposed by the natural moral law presupposes both my freedom *from* external force and my inner freedom *for* fulfilling the purpose for which I exist. Therefore there are rights that stem from the natural law, and they by definition are natural rights.

RIGHT AND MIGHT

The separation of the legal and juridical order from the ethical order, that is, the separation of rights from morals, is practically equivalent to identifying right with might, for if rights do not rest on moral obligation, they rest on physical force or the threat of it. Right was defined as moral power and might as physical power, but now it is necessary to examine more thoroughly the relation between these two.

1. *Right and might are not the same*. An interesting discussion of the claims of right and might occurs in Plato's *Republic,*[1] where Thrasymachus defends the proposition that right is might, or justice is the interest of the stronger, claiming that all laws and rights are framed by men in power for their own advantage and to keep the rest in subjection. In the *Gorgias*[2] Callicles maintains the contrary proposition, that justice is the interest of the weaker, who by sheer

---

[1]See bk. I, from §336 on.
[2]From §481 on.

force of numbers are able to extort concessions from the few strong, and these concessions become the people's rights bulwarked by laws and conventions; such is conventional justice only, for by natural justice the stronger ought to prevail simply because they are stronger. Plato agrees with neither of these views on justice but has Socrates define it as "the having and doing what is a man's own"[1] whether he be strong or weak.

Right and might are two different things because there can be right without might and might without right. By natural right each one is entitled to the means necessary for living the moral life, but each one is not granted the physical force necessary for securing and defending these means. The child depends on its parents, the sick and the aged on those who care for them. In fact, no one, however strong physically, is wholly independent of others. Since all persons are equal in their ultimate destiny and in their common moral obligations, but unequal in physical strength and also in wealth and authority by which they can command the physical strength of others, some safeguard must be provided against the encroachments of physical force. This safeguard is provided in the form of rights, natural rights from the natural law and positive rights from positive law. Therefore, since right and might do not always correspond, they cannot be the same thing.

2. *Some rights, but not all, imply the right to use might.* Though right and might are not the same thing, there is evidently some connection between them, because some violated rights can seemingly be redressed only by the use of force. What is this connection? Hegel holds that not all might is right, but all right is might or at least implies might. He says:

> Abstract right is a right to coerce, because the wrong which transgresses it is an exercise of force against the existence of my freedom in an external thing. The maintenance of this existent against the exercise of force therefore itself takes the form of an external

act and an exercise of force annulling the force originally brought against it.[2]

Since the first use of force against a free being is a crime, not all might is right; right implies a second use of force, repelling the first, unjustified use of it.

Two objections can be brought against this view: it restricts rights to external physical objects and acts only, and it confuses the essence of a right with a property of some rights.

a. One could limit the word *right* to external matters, but both English usage and the concept of a right as *moral power* counsel otherwise. We speak of a mother's right to her children's love, of a benefactor's right to gratitude, of a person's right to his or her friends' loyalty. The subject imposes a duty on the term, even though there is no way of physically compelling fulfillment of the duty; violation of the duty produces moral guilt, which is the proper effect of the exercise of moral power. Here there seems to be everything needed to constitute a genuine right.

b. Other rights can be enforced by the use of might. Physical actions can be exerted or restrained, and physical objects can be defended or recovered by the use of physical force. Rights to such matters would be useless unless we were morally allowed to use physical force in protecting and securing them. Even here the ability to resort to force is not the essence of the right. The right must already be a right before it can be vindicated by might. There is really a double right: the original right, such as the right to life or property, and a secondary right annexed to it, the right to use might in defense of life or property.

Rights that may thus be upheld by recourse to might, force, or coercion are *coercive* rights; they are also *juridical* rights, because they can be sued for in a law court that enforces its verdict by appeal to the executive arm or might of the state. In contrast to rights founded on loyalty, gratitude, friendship, benevolence, and similar virtues, all

---

[1] Plato, *Republic,* bk. IV, §433.

[2] Hegel, *Philosophy of Right,* §94.

coercive or juridical rights are founded on *justice*. Their enforcement should normally be entrusted to the civil government, since the maintenance of justice, the adjudication of disputes, and the protection of citizens' rights is the chief function of the state.

DUTIES

Limitation is a property of rights just as limitation is a property of our positive freedom (freedom *for*). Limitation is that point beyond which a right cannot be exercised without violating the right of another. Moral laws make up one organic system much like the physical organism. The functions of one organ are limited by the other organs of the body, each being apportioned its share of nutriment and having its sphere of exercise, but not to the detriment of other organs. No one organ is the whole organism, which is the complex of all organs working harmoniously. If any organ encroaches on another, it works harm to the whole body. Thus each person has an end to fulfill and is endowed with rights for this purpose, but the whole of creation also has an end to fulfill, and no one may seek his or her own end in such a way as to frustrate the end of the whole.

Right is limited by duty. I may exercise my right up to the point where my duty to others supersedes my right. A right ceases to be a right when it injures others' rights. I have a right to build a bonfire on my own property, but not when it endangers the property of my neighbors. Parents have a right to their children's obedience, but not in choosing their state of life.

Duty is *the moral necessity to do or omit something;* it is the absolute demand for realization that some value makes on one's inner freedom. Though compulsion may be used to enforce a duty, the duty exists and obliges independently of enforcement. This *moral* necessity laid on a person is duty in the primary sense. In a transferred sense duty also means the thing that must be done or omitted.

Rights and duties, as we have defined them, are correlative and complementary. That they are so follows from the moral inviolability of a right. If I have a right, everyone else has the duty to respect my right; thus the term of a right becomes the subject of a duty. If I have a duty, someone else has a right to the thing I must do or omit; if no other human appears to have such a right, then at least God has it, as in my duty to preserve my life. If I have a duty, I have also the right to fulfill that duty and do all the things necessary for its fulfillment; otherwise it could not be a genuine duty. But if I have a right, I have not necessarily a duty to exercise that right; in fact, no one can exercise all his or her rights simultaneously but must choose among them, for some of them are simultaneously incompatible, such as the right to stand and the right to sit.

All duties, like all rights, come from law. Duties are divided in the same way as the corresponding rights and thus are natural or positive, divine or human, ecclesiastical or civil. Another classification is also of importance here: into affirmative and negative duties.

Affirmative duties follow from affirmative laws (commands) and require the performance of an act. *Negative* duties follow from negative laws (prohibitions) and require the omission or avoidance of an act. Care should be taken not to call affirmative laws and duties *positive,* for the word *positive* is already used in another sense, as the opposite of *natural*. Affirmative duties may connote negative duties, as "Honor your parents" connotes "Do not dishonor your parents." The importance of the distinction between affirmative and negative duties is that they impose a different type of obligation. Negative laws and duties require constant fulfillment every moment; one must never be doing the thing forbidden. Affirmative laws and duties impose a lasting obligation, in the sense that one is never exempt from it, but the obligation does not require constant fulfillment every moment: a property owner is *always obliged* to pay taxes by reason of his or her permanent status of property-owning or money-earning taxpayer; yet such a person is not obliged to be *always paying* taxes but only when they are due.

CONFLICT OF RIGHTS AND DUTIES

The conflict between rights and duties is a very practical problem, for it sometimes happens that one person has moral power to do a thing and another has moral power to prevent his or her doing it, two persons each have moral power to do, hold, or exact the same individual thing simultaneously, the same person has two incompatible duties to discharge for two different people at the same time, or the same individual has a duty to one person to do a thing and also a duty to another person to refrain from doing it. What is to be done when a right conflicts with a right, a duty with a duty, or a right with a duty?

This question is easy enough to answer in theory. There can be no real conflict of rights and duties, either with one another or among themselves. All rights and duties are derived from law, and all law is a reasonable ordinance that cannot both command and forbid the same thing. Therefore the conflict is only apparent. The stronger right or duty prevails; the weaker simply ceases to be a right or duty at all. In other circumstances it would be an existing right or duty, but in these circumstances it vanishes in the face of a higher claim. The stronger right or duty does not conflict with lesser ones but extinguishes them.

How can we determine which is the stronger right or duty? In practice such determinations can become exceedingly intricate and beyond the competence of the ordinary person. One of the chief functions of positive law, drawn up by professional legislators and applied through the courts of justice, is to settle disputed claims. Both reason and experience prescribe that we shall set up such means for determining just which right or duty prevails, and in most of the matters that come under this jurisdiction the decisions of the courts, unless manifestly unjust, are binding in conscience. But not all matters are subject to the civil law and its courts; often the decision must be made on the basis of natural ethics. We can lay down only a few general norms. Other things being equal, the stronger right or duty can be determined from the following scheme:

The subject
1. *The higher-ranking person:* God before humans
2. *The closer relationship:* relatives and friends before strangers

The term
3. *The more common good:* world peace before personal comfort
4. *The wider social order:* the country before the family

The matter
5. *The graver matter:* life before property
6. *The greater urgency:* fighting a fire before reading a book

The title
7. *The higher law:* natural law before positive law
8. *The clearer title:* a certain claim before a doubtful one

What makes these norms hard to apply is that in concrete cases other things are not equal. One right or duty may appear stronger according to one of the headings just listed, and the opposite right or duty according to another heading. The main use of the scheme is to show us what to look for, not to give us automatic rules.

1. A doctor is about to attend divine worship on Sunday when an emergency call comes for an urgent case; God comes before humans, but if the case is postponed, the person may die.

2. A young man wants to take a college education but has no funds; the mind comes before the body, but if he does not eat, he cannot study.

3. A son has been disinherited in a civilly valid will but for dubiously just reasons; the natural

law prevails over the positive, but the positive title is clear and the natural one doubtful.

4. In time of war a man is torn between duty to his country and to his family; the common good prevails over a private good, but his family is related to him more closely than the bulk of the citizens.

For a solution to these and similar apparent conflicts of rights and duties, no hard-and-fast rules can be drawn up. Each case must be taken in its concrete setting and every circumstance carefully weighed. In these matters there is no substitute for good moral sense, which is another name for the cardinal virtue of prudence, *the* virtue of practical reason. Most cases are settled by working out some proportion or compromise between the various factors and claims, except that the negative duty of never doing anything inherently evil prevails over everything else. In the foregoing cases:

1. It would be wrong for a doctor to be so engrossed in his profession as to have no time at all for the worship of God, but in this instance God can be served later and the sick person cannot; the doctor should tend to the patient.

2. A person must live before he or she can live well; the student must first provide for himself the minimum requirements of life, and thereafter he does well to devote himself to the things of the mind rather than to the things of the body.

3. The disinherited son may contest the will, but if the will is upheld in the civil courts, he has no choice but to accept this decision; the parent may have done a private wrong in disinheriting him, but the son would commit a public crime if he attempted to seize the property by force.

4. A country at war can require its citizens to come to its defense, yet defer or exempt those who can least easily be spared by their dependents; this policy balances the claims of private and public good, and brings in the element of urgency.

It may happen that after the most careful investigation two rights or two duties or a right

and a duty seem equally valid and equally certain. In this case one may do either, or, if the matter is divisible, do part of both. The bankruptcy laws are an instance of the latter, where no creditor can be satisfied in full but as equitable a distribution is made as the matter allows.

EXCUSES FROM DUTY

Duty is imposed by law, which by definition is reasonable and for the common good. The purpose is not to crush us with unreasonable burdens out of proportion to the good aimed at. According to the principle of double effect, the physical evils (burdens, losses, restrictions, inconveniences, dangers) sometimes unavoidable in the fulfillment of duty are to be incidental to the accomplishment of good and not disproportionate to it. Hence there are causes that can excuse from duty, because in these cases the duty really invades our right.

No one can do the impossible, and all excuses from duty can be reduced to impossibility of fulfillment taken in a broad and relative sense; we shall call it *hardship*. Some norms can be established by putting together four elements:

1. The kind of hardship, inherent or incidental
2. The amount of hardship, normal or excessive
3. The kind of duty, affirmative or negative
4. The kind of law, natural or positive

1. Only incidental and excessive hardship excuses from a duty. *Incidental* hardship arises from the particular circumstances of the person concerned, such as being sick, disabled, captive, or destitute. If hardship essential to or inherent in the duty itself could excuse, there would be no duties; thus workmen are not excused from their work because it makes them sweat nor soldiers from battle in a just war because it endangers their lives. Hardship may run from practical impossibility through extreme, grave, and moderate difficulty to slight inconvenience. To be an excuse it must be *excessive,* out of proportion to the importance of the duty. A duty can be so nec-

essary as not to admit of excuse, even in the face of death.

2. A *negative* duty arising from the *natural* law admits of no excuse whatever. Such a duty concerns matters so evil in themselves or in their situation that nothing could justify them. We are obliged to choose death rather than commit them. There is question here of the worst possible evil, moral evil, to which no other evil can be proportioned. Even here subjective excuses can arise from the modifiers of responsibility, such as ignorance or violent emotion, but we are speaking now of objective morality and fully responsible agents.

3. An *affirmative* duty arising from the *natural* law admits of excuse because of impossibility or excessive hardship. There must, however, be no violation of negative natural duty involved; for instance, the omission of an act of honor toward someone must not give the impression of contempt. Since affirmative duties do not require constant fulfillment every moment, the acts can often be postponed for more favorable circumstances when the hardship will not be present, and then they must be done; if they cannot be postponed, the obligation ceases entirely.

4. A duty arising from *human positive* law, whether *affirmative* or *negative,* admits of excuse because of impossibility or excessive hardship. Here also no violation of negative natural duty must be involved. Merely human duties, even the negative ones, concern matter that is morally indifferent in itself, and the human laws that impose them are meant to be a help rather than a hindrance to human living.

SUMMARY

We have seen *right* as opposed to *wrong;* now we take up *right* as correlative to *duty.* In the latter sense *right* is moral power, appealing to another's inner freedom and intelligence, as opposed to *might,* which is physical power or force. Right is defined as moral power (freedom *for*) to do, omit, hold, or exact something. Things to which we have a right are often called our *rights.*

A right has four components: *subject,* the one

possessing the right; *term,* the one bound to respect the right; *matter,* that to which one has a right; and *title,* the reason why this person has a right to this thing. The subject and term must always be persons; hence animals have no rights. The matter can never be a person; even slavery, one of the world's most flagrant violations of human rights, supposed a right only to the slave's services, not to his or her person.

All rights come from law, *natural* rights from natural law, *positive* rights from positive law. All admit positive rights, but are there natural rights? Moral and legal positivists deny the natural law; they admit no natural rights. Juridical positivists deny natural rights, though they may admit a natural law. Both these groups derive all rights from one or more of the following sources:

1. *The state.* If so, the state itself has no right to exist, has no basis for the positive rights it grants, can withhold from its subjects any right it wishes, and can have no rights against another state.

2. *Contract.* If so, the first contract was made without any right to do so, contracts have no binding power but force, nonrenounceable rights are subjected to contract, and one can by contract obtain a right to anything, however evil.

3. *Equal freedom for all.* If so, rights are limited to external acts, legality is separated from morality, which alone gives it meaning, all rights can be freely surrendered, and we can have a right to immoral acts provided they hurt no one else.

4. *Custom.* If so, mere repetition of acts begets a right to them, there were no rights until the custom was established, evil customs can create rights, and people become the victims of the customs their race unconsciously develops.

Natural rights are deduced from the natural law. The natural law imposes obligations on humans, who must therefore have moral power or inner freedom to fulfill them and prevent others from interfering with this fulfillment; such rights coming from the natural law are natural rights.

Right and *might* are different because they can exist separately. All people have equal moral obligations but differ greatly in physical strength.

Rights are our moral safeguard against the encroachment of superior might. Rights concerning external matters due in justice imply the right to use might in their defense or recovery. This right of coercion is not the essence of any right, but a property of some rights.

Right is limited by *duty,* which is the moral necessity to do or omit something. Every right supposes a duty, and vice versa. *Negative* duties require constant fulfillment, *affirmative* do not.

There can be no real conflict of rights and duties; the stronger extinguishes the weaker. In practice it can be very difficult to determine which is the stronger right. The subject, term, matter, and title must be considered together with the factor of urgency.

Impossibility and excessive hardship are excuses from duty. Hardship inherent in the duty never excuses from it. Disproportionate hardship, depending on the importance of the matter, excuses from *affirmative* duty under *natural* law, and from both *affirmative* and *negative* duty under *human positive* law. *Negative* duty under *natural* law admits of no excuse whatever.

Questions for Discussion

1. Among the many rights we claim for ourselves is a right to privacy in our homes. We expect that others will not eavesdrop on our private conversations, enter our homes without our permission, spread rumors about us, and so forth. By what title do we claim this right of privacy? Who are the people who have a duty to respect this right? Friends, parents, police, neighbors? Do you have the right to tell anyone about what you have heard regarding another person whether or not you know what you have heard to be true? Suppose you do not know if what you heard is true; do you have a right to repeat it?

2. You are an active member of a group who has set out to protect the world's remaining whales. Iceland, along with some other nations, continues to hunt whales and does not recognize any need to protect them. Your group considers this position immoral in the extreme and, in the still of the night, you secretly scuttle a number of whaling vessels in Reykjavik harbor. Describe the rights and duties involved in this episode and the titles to those rights.

3. In this chapter we have argued that the right to life is an inalienable right. Is it inalienable absolutely or only relatively? Consider the case of the specialist in fetal medicine who is visited by a pregnant woman who says that she wants to know if her fetus is developing normally. The doctor does a sonar scan to see if he can discover any abnormalities, finds none, and tells the woman so. She seems relieved and asks offhandedly what the fetus' sex is. The doctor tells her it is a girl. Immediately the woman becomes upset and tells the doctor she will terminate the pregnancy, because she and her husband do not want a girl. The doctor then feels that he has been deceived. He would not have done the sonar scan if the only information wanted was a knowledge of the sex of the fetus with a view to abortion if the fetus was not a male. Did the woman have a right to do what she did? Were any of the doctor's rights violated? Does the fetus have any rights? Then describe the rights in this case in terms of Subject, Term, Matter, and Title. Do you find any conflicts of right with right and/or right with duty? Explain.

4. In keeping with his right to defend himself and his property with might, a shopkeeper has wired his store not only with a burglar alarm but also had the wiring done in such a way that any thief entering the property after business hours would get a good electric shock. Of course, the shopkeeper has posted the fact of the burglar alarm but does not have any warning signs about the shock factor. Late one night, a thief manages to enter the property through the attic and is electrocuted. Has the shopkeeper violated any rights of the thief?

Could he be prosecuted for manslaughter? Explain your answer.

5. Consider the following argument of an opponent of natural rights: The so-called basic or fundamental rights such as the right not to be murdered, robbed, set afire, or assaulted are really proscriptions of acts that any society must forbid if it is going to survive. Beyond that any so-called rights are merely a matter of opinion as to how a group should conduct itself and have nothing at all to do with morality. Millions of people throughout the world get along very well without freedom of speech and the press, the right to vote, the right to bear arms, freedom of assembly, and right to form labor unions. To call another government immoral because it does not guarantee these so-called rights is monstrous and will inevitably lead to bloodshed. Leave aside God and the natural law, and these so-called rights seem to derive their sanction from two sources: (1) we who have them like them very much and (2) they restrain would-be tyrants and allow our system of government to adjust to wants, grievances, and injustices without always resorting to revolution. Does this argument have merit? Explain.

Readings

Read Plato's *Republic,* bk. I, §336, to bk. II, §368, on the relative merits of justice and injustice, right and might. Read Aristotle's defense of natural slavery in his *Politics,* bk. I, ch. 4–7, to see how disappointing a great man can sometimes be. One might hope for a correction in St. Thomas' *Commentary,* but he merely expounds Aristotle. Cicero's *De Officiis* (On Duties) is rather a treatise on morals in general and runs through man's chief duties as connected with the cardinal virtues and one's state in life.

The little that St. Thomas has to say on rights is found in the *Summa Theologica,* II–II, q. 57. A discussion of the term *jus* (right) as related to *lex* (law) in the usage of Roman law is found in Suarez, *De Legibus* (On Laws), bk. I, Ch. 2, translated in J.B. Scott, *Classics of International Law: Suarez.*

Immanuel Kant, *The Metaphysics of Morals,* is published in two small volumes by the Library of Liberal Arts, part I as *The Metaphysical Elements of Justice,* and part II as *The Metaphysical Principles of Virtue.* The whole is a different work from Kant's *Fundamental Principles of the Metaphysic of Morals.*

W.D. Ross, *The Right and the Good,* pp. 48–56, has some objections against the correlativity of rights and duties, partly because of his admitting that we have duties to animals, though animals have no rights. Counter to the view concerning animal rights presented in this chapter is Tom Regan's *The Case for Animal Rights,* especially cc. 8 and 9.

There have been numerous attempts to codify fundamental human rights. That of UNESCO, published in its own symposium entitled *Human Rights,* is worth considering and that suggested by Jacques Maritain in *The Rights of Man and Natural Law.* Le Buffe and Hayes, *The American Philosophy of Law,* ch. 5, lists various codifications; it also contains an appendix by John C. Ford, criticizing Justice Holmes' legal philosophy. Holmes' views are found in his *Collected Legal Papers,* especially "The Path of the Law" and "Natural Law," and in the *Holmes-Pollock Letters.* Rubin Gotesky and Ervin Laszlo have edited *Human Dignity This Century and the Next: An Interdisciplinary Inquiry Into Human Rights, Technology, War, The Ideal Society,* which opens with an interesting discussion of inalienable and natural rights and an effort to give a phenomenological description of human dignity. David Lyons (ed.), *Rights,* discusses rights central to our social practices as well as to our moral and political principles.

David Ritchies's *Natural Rights* and Leo Strauss' *Natural Rights and History* are well-known studies. See also Heinrich Rommen's *Natural Law,* ch. 12: and Arthur Harding's *Natural Law and Natural Rights.*

19
Life

PROBLEM

Since ethics is not only a normative but also a practical science, it cannot be satisfied to give only the general norms of morally good conduct but must try to apply these norms to the chief types of human conduct. Though human acts taken individually are indefinitely variable so that no two are ever exactly alike, they can be classified under certain headings, and the general norms can be made more specific so as to bring out more clearly the goodness or badness of each class of acts.

Earlier writers, such as St. Thomas, built their whole treatment of applied ethics around the classification of the virtues and opposed vices. Some modern writers prefer to make a specific investigation of the rights conferred and the duties imposed by the moral law. The first method, unless used skillfully, tends to become a sterile process of naming and cataloging. The second method gives the impression that ethics is restricted to the minimum of goodness imposed by law. Our method will consist of mapping out certain *areas of concern* in our moral life, involving rights and duties, habits and virtues, aspirations and ideals, that pertain to each area.

First in dignity comes our relation to God. The whole moral life is the fulfillment of our duty and the expression of our love toward God. On this problem the findings of philosophical ethics appear so thin, compared with the rich offerings of religion and theology, that we will hand over this whole topic to these studies.

Among our rights the right to life is fundamental, for there can be no further rights or duties unless there is someone there to have them. That this is a natural right is evident. The only way I can fulfill my function as a person, reach the goal of my existence, and achieve my highest good is by performing morally good acts. To perform such acts I must live. My very nature as a human person, therefore, demands that I have the right to life.

Is this right a nonrenounceable one, so that not only may no human lawfully take it away from me but also even I myself may not give it up? Is

it a right that is also a duty? Is it always wrong to deprive another of his or her life, even incurable sufferers, even unborn babies? What about self-defense, when one can save his or her own life only at the expense of another's? Here we deal only with deliberate destruction of human life, saving marginal questions for the next chapter. Our questions are:

1. May one kill oneself?
2. May one kill another person?
3. May one kill the incurable?
4. May one kill the unborn?
5. May one kill in self-defense?

SUICIDE

Suicide is here taken in the strict sense as *the direct killing of oneself on one's own authority*.

Direct killing is an act of killing that is directly voluntary; that is, death is intended either as an end or as a means to an end. Either the action is capable of only one effect and that effect is death, or the action is capable of several effects, including death, and among these death is the effect intended, either for its own sake or as a means to something else.

Indirect killing is an act of killing that is indirectly voluntary; death is not intended, either as an end or as a means to an end, but is only permitted as an unavoidable consequence. The action is capable of at least two effects, one of which is death, and the agent intends, not death, but the other effect. To avoid misunderstanding it is better not to speak of the indirect killing of oneself as killing at all, but as the deliberate exposure of one's life to serious danger. Such exposure is not what is meant by suicide.

The killing is not suicide unless it is done *on one's own authority*. Two others might be thought of as having authority in the matter: God and the state. God, having a supreme dominion over human life, could order a woman to kill herself, but to know God's will in such a case, a special revelation would be needed, for which there is no provision in philosophical ethics. The state, supposing that it has the right of capital punishment, might appoint a man condemned to death to be his own executioner. Whatever be the morality of such an uncommon and questionable practice, it is not suicide according to the accepted definition.

Suicide can be committed positively, by the performance of some death-dealing act against oneself; or negatively, by omitting to use the ordinary means of preserving one's life. It is suicide to starve oneself to death, to refuse to avoid an oncoming train, to neglect to use the ordinary remedies against an otherwise fatal disease.

Among the arguments proposed in favor of the moral permissibility of suicide are the following:

1. It is understood that no one should commit suicide for whom life holds out some hope or promise, and that people suffering from temporary despondency should be prevented from harming themselves, but there are always some for whom life has become an intolerable and irremediable burden. They are useless to society and to themselves. It is better for all concerned that they retire from the scene of life through the ever open door.

2. It is an act of supreme personal self-determination to summon death when life's value has been spent. A person is expected to manage his or her life intelligently and not to be merely passive in the face of inexorable nature. When reason shows that life has no more to offer, it is folly to drag out life to its last bitter breath. The person preserves dignity and self-mastery by ending his or her life at the moment when all its worth and meaning are exhausted.

3. A person is allowed to choose a lesser evil to avoid a greater. Since there are worse evils than death, why cannot death be chosen as the lesser evil? There is nothing unnatural about it. If it is not wrong to interfere with nature to prolong life, as medical science does, why should it be wrong to interfere with nature to shorten life? In both cases it is done for the benefit of the person concerned and by his or her own consent.

4. Even admitting that God has given us our life, yet it is truly a gift. A gift belongs to the receiver, who may now do whatever he or she wills with it. No gift is expected to be retained indefinitely at the expense and to the harm of the receiver. When its possession becomes more injurious than its surrender, it should be in accordance with the will of a good God and a wise use of his gift to relinquish it.

5. To suppose that suicide in any way defrauds God of his supreme right is to have a very naive idea of God. No creature could possibly defraud God of anything. In giving us the gift of life, God knew how we would use it and expected us to use our intelligence and freedom in managing it. He allows us to destroy animals and plants, other life, for our purposes. Why should our own life be withdrawn from our control?

6. In the case of self-defense we have the right to destroy other human lives for our own safety. The state claims the same right in war and capital punishment. It seems, then, that God can and sometimes does give us direct ownership over human life. Why must it be only over others' lives? The reasons for suicide are often stronger than for self-defense, either personal or national. Why not kill ourselves when we have become our own greatest enemy?

These rather persuasive arguments are countered by opposing arguments:

1. Suicide is often regarded as an act of cowardice and a refusal to face life courageously. We take the easy way out when we thrust the burdens we cannot bear onto the shoulders of our dependents. But not all are in this case; rather, they themselves are a burden on others. Yet they must not forget the worth of their own person. Who can be called useless? Suffering has no earthly value and might be called the worst of earthly disvalues, but its moral and spiritual value can be tremendous. Courage and patience cannot be discounted in any moral appraisal of human life.

2. It is a natural prompting of well-ordered self-love to keep one's person in being against all destructive forces. There are times when one must face death without flinching, but there is something inordinate in willfully acting as that destructive force oneself. Everything naturally seeks its own being and tends to keep itself in being as long as possible. Intelligence is meant to promote, not counteract, that natural urge.

3. The lesser of two physical evils may be chosen when there is no moral evil involved, but

moral evil may never be chosen to avoid a physical evil. Medical science is an intelligent use and development of the remedies nature provides to preserve life. To use them to destroy life is not wise management but a wrecking of what has been entrusted to our care. I would be free to wreck myself if I were responsible only to myself, but this is not so if there is a God to whom I am ultimately responsible.

4. Life is a gift from God, but some gifts are given outright and others have strings attached. All God's gifts are restricted, not because of any lack in his generosity, but because he has to make us responsible for their use when he entrusts them to our freedom. Freedom itself is perhaps his greatest gift, but we are not allowed, though we are able, to misuse it. Life has been given, and its allotted span goes with the gift. It is not ours to decide when we have had enough of it and to tell God that we are quitting.

5. We can never actually defraud God, but we are not allowed even to *try* or to be willing to do what would defraud God were he not infinitely beyond all possible harm. God allows us to destroy animals and plants because they are not persons and are provided for our use and consumption. Human life is not on the same level as other life; personhood makes the difference.

6. In self-defense the defender kills the attacker not on his or her own authority but on God's authority implicit in the defender's own natural right to life. The defender has no ownership over the attacker's life but only repels force by force, a situation the attacker brought on by the crime. The state also acts on authority given to it by God as a natural society, authority not to be used in any way the state pleases but only in defense against the nation's internal and external destroyers. The suicide is both attacker and attacked, and there is no defense. Crime and punishment are here simultaneous and extreme. The suicide is simultaneously executioner and murderer.

It can be readily seen that from a nontheistic viewpoint there is no argument against suicide. A person who acknowledges no being higher than himself or herself assumes supreme dominion over his or her life and can do away with it at pleasure. The fact that a theistic philosophy sees life as a gift from God does not of itself make suicide wrong, for an outright gift may be used or abandoned in any way the recipient wishes. The case against suicide, then, requires proof that God's gift of life to us is not an outright but a restricted gift, that he has not given us full ownership and control over our person with the right to consume and destroy it at our discretion, but he has given us only the use of ourselves, the right of stewardship and management, for which he will demand an account. Since philosophy cannot ask God what he willed to do, its only recourse is to show that God not only did not but *could not* give us full ownership over ourselves as persons.

The reason that God must reserve to himself full mastership over human life is the peculiar nature of a rational and free being, such as the human being is. We can attain the end for which we have been created only by freely choosing to do morally good acts. These acts take time, and the length of each person's life is the opportunity allotted for doing them. It is for God and not for us to say when we have done enough well enough to deserve the end. The suicide equivalently tells God that He will have to take the deeds performed and virtues developed so far, and that He will simply get no more. The creature thus tries to dictate what God will have to be satisfied with, in contradiction to what God in creating has a right to demand from His creature. God cannot give such authority to a creature without making the creature supreme over Him. The suicide by making further works of his or her own impossible, invades God's exclusive right, is a rebel against the creator, and commits moral wrong.

MURDER

In ethics we find the civil law's distinction between murder and manslaughter of little help. Murder supposes malice aforethought and thus full voluntariness, but the civil law can judge only by external criteria. Morality, which resides chiefly in the act of inner freedom preceded by knowledge, does not always correspond with the amount and kind of evidence presentable in court. So long as the act of killing another is both directly voluntary and unjust, we shall call it *murder,* following the usage of common language rather than the technical terms of the civil law.

Murder is defined as *the direct killing of an innocent person.* It is *direct* killing, directly voluntary, so that death is intended as end or as means. Indirect killing, or the exposure of life to serious danger, is discussed later; it does not come under the heading of murder.

An *innocent* person is one who has not forfeited his or her right to life. Murder is *unjust* killing, done without legitimate authority. This excludes killing another on the authority of God or the state, as mentioned before under suicide. The soldier killing the enemy in a just war and the executioner putting criminals to death are acting on the state's authority, presuming the state has that authority. The state, however, can commit murder by acting outside the scope of its legitimate authority. Killing in self-defense is not murder because the defender acts by authority of his or her natural right to life, as will be discussed later. The word *innocent* must be understood as objectively innocent, for it is not murder to kill a maniac in self-defense.

That murder is morally wrong hardly needs a separate proof if the argument against suicide is already admitted, for if a person is not allowed to take even his or her own life, much less would a person be allowed to take the life of another. Murder is morally wrong because it violates the right of God, who has exclusive full ownership over human life, the right of use ownership that each person has over his or her own life, and the right of the state to administer justice and preserve public order.

From a nontheist point of view murder is immoral, because the murderer violates the rights of both the person murdered and the state of which the murdered person was a member. The murderer commits a double injustice: (1) against the individual by depriving another of the life to which he or she has an absolutely inalienable right as a rational and free being, and (2) against

the state as a society that exists to foster the common good of all its members and cannot long continue to do so if even one of its members is allowed to go about freely killing other members.

Murder can be treated briefly because no one of sound mind, not even a philosopher, has ventured to defend it. It has always been recognized as one of the worst of crimes and as the most glaring example of a morally evil act. But some are not convinced of the injustice contained in certain types of direct killing, and these must be examined further.

MERCY KILLING

Mercy killing, or *euthanasia,* is the giving of an easy, painless death to one suffering from an incurable or agonizing ailment. Its advocates argue that the person will die anyway, that the purpose is not to invade the person's right to life but only to substitute a painless for a painful death, that the shortening of the person's life merely deprives him or her of a bit of existence that is not only useless but unbearable, that the person can do no more good for anyone, himself or herself included. Some would leave the decision to a qualified physician; most would require the subject's consent.

Although one can sympathize with the sentiments of compassion and mercy inspiring this proposal, moral judgment on it falls into the two categories of action just described. If administered by oneself, euthanasia is suicide. If administered by another without the victim's consent, it is murder. If administered by another, with the victim's consent or cooperation, it is suicide and murder combined. Nontheistic ethics has no solid argument against it, unless it were done without the victim's consent. Theistic ethics has to condemn it, and say that, even if it should be made permissible by civil law, for which there is strong propaganda in some quarters, it still remains an immoral act.

Until recently, *euthanasia* had only this meaning. It is still the only meaning appropriate to the term *mercy killing,* where *killing* has an active sense. However, *euthanasia* is now being used in an extended sense, and a distinction is being made between *active* euthanasia, which is killing the person, and *passive* euthanasia, which is letting the person die. Passive euthanasia is an indirectly voluntary act and, among other risks to life, will be considered on pp. 283–285.

ABORTION

Abortion is a hotly controverted issue in American society today and has polarized us into proabortion and antiabortion forces with both sides at times using dishonest and immoral tactics to carry their point. We need less heat and better manners if we are going to communicate successfully with one another. Most of us are weary of the continued debate and might be inclined to yield to fatigue rather than to grapple with the problem. We shall try for a dispassionate and philosophical discussion of the topic by observing some guidelines[1] for our discussion:

1. Identify, if possible, areas of agreement such as the tragic nature and undesirability of abortion because this might lead us all to cooperate in supporting policies aimed at eliminating the personal and social causes of abortion or seeking alternatives to abortion.
2. Avoid the use of slogans because they hinder or stop effective discussion and often depend on highly questionable assumptions.
3. Represent the opposing positions accurately and fairly.
4. Distinguish carefully the objective right and wrong from the subjective good or bad intention. In this way we can disagree with one another without imputing moral evil to one another.
5. Identify, if possible, the central issue at stake in the argument and separate other issues

that cluster around abortion without demeaning those other issues. That issue is the evaluation of nascent human life and the moral claims the nascent human being makes on us.
6. Admit doubts, difficulties, and weaknesses in our own position and not extend clarity and certainty beyond what the facts warrant.
7. Remember that the verbal formulation of a moral conviction is not necessarily an accurate reflection of the substance of that very conviction.
8. Take care not to confuse morality with public policy, because legality does not necessarily always coincide with morality. We shall remark on this matter later.
9. Be careful to incorporate women's perspectives as an important ingredient in any discussion of abortion.

Morality of Abortion

Abortion is the expulsion of a fetus from the womb before it is viable, that is, before it can live outside the mother. It is not the premature delivery of a viable fetus. To hasten birth is not wrong if the child can be kept alive, but it presents such a serious risk that grave reasons are required to make it permissible. It can be justified by the principle of double effect, the proportionate reasons being the danger to the health of the mother, child, or both, if the gestation be allowed to reach its natural term.

A spontaneous *miscarriage* is nobody's fault. Our discussion is about *induced* abortion, which is voluntarily brought about. If the death of the fetus is intended as end or as means, it is a *direct killing,* and no mere exposure of the fetus to danger, for by this act it is taken from the only place where it can live and is put in a place where it cannot live; there is no more efficient way of killing a person. No one can seriously say that the fetus dies from natural causes after it has been born; it has not been allowed to be born properly. All killing consists of interfering with nature in such a way that a person dies of it.

[1] We follow here the suggestions of Richard A. McCormick, "Abortion: Rules for Debate," *America* **139**(2): 26–30, July 22, 1978.

Applying the Principle of Double Effect

Today we are no longer living in a world that commonly rejects abortion and judges it as always immoral. The tradition we have inherited focused on cases of indirect abortion that ethicists could justify according to the principle of double effect. The following discussion illustrates how such argumentation proceeds.

The principle of double effect is of no value in cases of direct abortion. The act itself is directly destructive to the fetus, and the bad effect, death to the fetus, is no merely permitted side effect but is the means used for the accomplishment of whatever good effect may accrue to the mother. Since the first two conditions of the double-effect principle are not verified, it makes no difference whether there is a good intention and a sufficient proportion. Thus it is futile to attempt any moral justification for direct abortion on the basis of the double-effect principle. Any justification, if possible, would have to be based on other principles.

It is a different situation if the death of an unborn child is only indirect, so that it is merely permitted and not willed as a means or an end. This situation of *indirect abortion* arises when the mother has some serious illness (pregnancy itself is not an illness but a natural condition), and the only workable treatment, whether medical or surgical, will have two effects: the cure of the mother's disease and the death of the fetus. This is the type of case to which the principle of double effect readily applies. The fetus is not directly attacked, and its death, even if certain to follow, is an incidental and unavoidable by-product in the performance of a legitimate act. The mother herself needs the treatment no matter what effect it may have on the fetus, and the death of the fetus is not the means by which she is cured. She has a right to take such treatment and is morally allowed to do so. The doctor has the responsibility of deciding whether the mother's condition is truly pathological and whether the treatment contemplated is the only effective remedy.

The More Recent Discussion

The rapid development and advances in medical knowledge and technology have created not only new possibilities for caring for pregnant women and the children conceived, but those very advances and developments have also given rise to new ethical questions as well, questions or issues where the direct-indirect distinction used in double-effect reasoning does not seem applicable. For example, when a woman and her physician are confronted with a fetus that is developing either without all or a major part of the brain (anencephaly) and therefore clearly lacks the biological substrate for *any* expression of truly personal life, is it absolutely clear and certain that the woman must preserve that life or may she opt to abort without moral evil being imputed to her? Would this be abortion in the full moral sense of that word? If such a fetus is allowed to come to term and is delivered, it will surely die shortly after birth.

Opinion is divided, as you may expect, given the pluralistic society in which we live. Many of the people involved in discussing these issues are convinced more by good reasons and keen discernment than by applications of the direct-indirect distinction used in double-effect reasoning. No one denies the value of the traditional formulation of the double-effect principle and its application, for it does help us see our way through cases such as a pathological pregnancy in the Fallopian tube or in a cancerous uterus. Something more is needed to handle certain extreme cases of fetal abnormality such as anencephaly.

The discussion of these cases of extreme fetal abnormality centers on questions about "the sanctity of life" and "the quality of life" that such fetuses may be expected to have after birth. At times people seem to treat "sanctity of life" and "quality of life" as though the two expressions are opposing moral principles. In fact, both are values, and the principles correlative to them are "life is to be preserved" and "do no harm to another." Based on the principle that life is to be preserved, life is valued as sacred. On the basis of the principle of doing no harm to another, a life of extremely poor quality is valued negatively, since it is injurious or painful to the person experiencing it, whereas life of an acceptable quality is valued positively, since it benefits the person experiencing it. Depending on which principle predominates in the discussion, the corresponding value will predominate also.

While current discussion seems to suggest a dichotomy between "sacredness of life" and "quality of life," in actuality they are not. The dichotomy seems to be false. One way to see this is to think of personal life in terms of its integrity, and then the ethical issue becomes one of respect for life and its integrity. Such respect involves an appreciation of the fact that physical existence alone has little meaning and value in and of itself. The integrity of personal life demands a certain richness consisting of a modicum of self-awareness, interaction with the environment, interpersonal relatedness and love, and autonomy, coupled with the capacity to experience joy and sorrow, pleasure and pain.

The principle of respect for personal life and its integrity recognizes the preciousness of life, which the "sanctity of life" position stresses, and emphasizes the importance of interpersonal life as distinct from mere existence, which the "quality of life" position stresses. This may be the principle we need to help us see our way through cases of extreme fetal abnormality such as anencephaly in which we do not have the physical basis for personhood in the full sense of that word. We shall see more of this in the chapter on sex when we discuss "Genetics and Sexual Reproduction" (see pages 340–341).

Some Distinctions and Arguments, Pro and Con

We give here some distinctions necessary for an understanding of the arguments: Abortion can be *spontaneous,* a miscarriage that is no one's fault, or *induced,* voluntarily brought about. Induced abortion can be *indirect,* the foreseen but unwanted consequence of doing something else, or *direct,* the expulsion of the fetus intended as end or means. These distinctions have relevance for ethics because they separate the voluntary from the involuntary and the indirectly voluntary from the directly voluntary.

Some of the following arguments favor abortion on demand, whereas others would allow it only under certain conditions. Since the notion of *person* is crucial for understanding what is to follow, we shall first look at some further distinctions currently being proposed by some pro-abortionists before we proceed to the arguments themselves.

A person, in the strict sense of that term, is an adult moral agent having the three characteristics of self-consciousness, rationality, and moral awareness. The same term is also used in speaking of *young children, infants,* the *newly born,* the *senile,* the *severely* and *profoundly retarded,* and the *demented,* none of whom is a full moral agent able to engage in moral discourse. Rights are also accorded to all of these "persons," but not the rights of full moral agents. The term *person* has various meanings derived from the social standing that each has in the community of moral agents who are persons in the strict sense. The rights and the moral standing of young children, infants, and so on are imputed to them not by reason of their developing personhood but *by reason of duties and obligations the moral community of adults accepts in regard to them.* When it comes to the consideration of fetuses, embryos, and zygotes, these are seen as having an even lesser standing in the moral community than the newly born and infants. The moral standing of each "person" is then a matter of degree, the adult moral agents having full moral standing and the zygote having the least, with the degrees lessening as we proceed from young children through infants to newly borns, fetuses, embryos, and zygotes. In terms of rights, young children have stronger ones and so a stronger moral claim on the moral agents of the community than do fetuses, embryos, and zygotes.

With these distinctions in mind, let us look at some of the arguments in favor of abortion:

1. To speak of abortion as murder is nonsense because the human fetus is not a person in the

strict sense of the word. To deny a distinction between a conceptus and a newborn baby is absurd. Either the fetus (conceptus) is a part of the mother to be treated as any other appendage, or it is a separate living being within the mother but not yet arrived at the moral status of full personhood. In the first case it belongs to the mother and may be removed from the mother's body as an undesirable excrescence. In the second case it also belongs to the mother and may be put out of the way for a good reason just as we kill animals and other forms of nonpersonal life for our own benefit.

2. To say that the fetus is inviolable from the moment of conception (zygote stage) is to fly in the face of certain phenomena in the preimplantation period, namely, the twinning process, spontaneous abortions (miscarriages), and the rare process of recombination of two fertilized ova into one. We have no solid evidence as to the moment when the fetus receives a human soul. Many modern thinkers hold to the moment of conception, but an honorable ancient and medieval theory said several weeks later. Since certainty is not possible on this question, we must have recourse to probability. Recent research shows that only 40%–50% of zygotes survive to become persons in the full sense. At the moment of ensoulment, the zygote has less than a 50% chance of reaching full personhood. We can therefore act on the probability that the fetus is not a person and for good reason terminate the pregnancy.

3. Even if the fetus, because of biological continuity and chromosomal inheritance, is regarded not merely as a potential but as an actual human being, it has not yet become an actual person. Only an actual person has rights, including the right to life. The fetus is at most a potential person. So, if the fetus is a potential person, it follows that the fetus is not a person. Consequently, the fetus does not have the actual rights of a person, but only potentially has those rights. That being the case, the fetus does not yet possess the right to life. As a consequence, its life may be terminated for a good reason without any breach of good morals.

4. Even if the fetus be granted a right to life, in any collision of rights the fetus' right yields to that of the mother. On all possible counts the mother's right takes precedence, because she is a person in the strict sense of the word and has higher moral standing in the moral community than does the fetus. She is an adult person, a full moral agent exercising her intelligence and freely controlling her life, with already assumed responsibilities toward her family and others. For the fetus all this is in the future. It barely lives, is not conscious, and is wholly dependent. The mother can live without it, but it cannot live without the mother. To argue that the fetus ought to be protected at the expense of the mother is, for now at least, absurd. Until such time as artificial wombs are available, the fetus must yield to the rights of the mother.

5. In some cases the fetus can be considered an unjust aggressor against the physical or mental health of the mother. Danger to the mother's physical health in certain pregnancies is the reason why most states allow therapeutic abortion. But mental health is every bit as important as physical health. To make the rest of the mother's life an intolerable torture of psychic derangement is too high a price to ask. The mother is allowed an adequate defense against such a prospect, and the only defense is the elimination of the cause.

6. At least in those cases, now fortunately rare, in which both mother and child will certainly die unless the fetus is aborted, only a benighted legalism could oblige the obstetrician to let both die rather than save one. No fine distinctions between direct and indirect actions, principal and incidental effects, wanted and permitted consequences, and similar rules should be adored as fetishes while a life is at stake. Necessity knows no law.

7. No unwanted child should be brought into this world. A child needs love and cannot live a normal life without it. Some parents can learn to love it later, but even the child can detect the strained feeling behind the show of love. In many instances there is not even the show of love, and the child grows up rejected and resentful, to take

out his or her spite later on against society or all humanity. Such misfits should not be allowed to be born. Those most closely involved with the fetus, the mother and father who conceived it and especially the mother who is bearing it, have first claim on evaluating the fetus. They produced it; it is theirs; they do not love it. The fetus, therefore, having no value, may be terminated.

8. No pregnant woman who wants an abortion should be denied one. The continued presence of the fetus within the womb is completely dependent on the discretion of the pregnant woman, for a woman has the right to determine her own life. Since no one knows with certainty when human life begins, the matter should be left to the pregnant woman. Very few men concern themselves with the consequences of sexual intercourse or determine their sexual behavior in the light of possible undesirable aftereffects. Since this is the case, why should women bother about it? The prejudice against abortion has been made by men and should be removed by women. A woman has the right to control her own sexual activity including procreation and, because of the callousness of many men, needs the freedom to choose an abortion as the final means of preventing unwanted children.

9. The population must be controlled. So urgent is this need that some individual rights will probably have to be submerged for the greater good, the very survival of the human race. Contraception and sterilization would be better methods than abortion, but human beings are too unpredictable and uncontrollable to eliminate the need for abortion entirely. Rather than forbid abortions we should promote them and should be gratified that they are being done voluntarily, thus putting off the time when we may have to make them compulsory. We have come to the point of global ethics, in which lesser issues are transcended.

Those opposing abortion find these arguments unconvincing, especially in that they do not provide for the interests of the fetus. The concept of personhood espoused in the following argument differs from that of the proabortionists in that the value of the person does not depend on its being recognized by any particular society. Each adult person in the moral community is a knowing subject (has self-consciousness), is rational and free, capable of entering into personal relationships and of engaging in moral discourse with others. This is approximately what the proabortionists have said about the adult moral agent. The two sides part company on the foundation of the moral standing the person has. The antiabortionist holds that from the moment of conception all the way to adulthood the person is intrinsically unique in its own right, an end in him- or herself, and has the same right to life as any other person. As the process of development from conception progresses, the personhood becomes more and more recognizable and perceivable. For theists, the person is an embodied subject who is also ensouled by the Creator at the moment of conception. The conceptus carries the genetic code derived from its parents and the soul created by God, the giver of life. This is not an effort to restrict personhood only to humans, but rather to highlight the personhood of the only persons known to us by reason alone. Whether there are other personal beings in the universe we do not know. Further, this notion of personhood does not depend either on society or on developmental biology for its moral status. The very existence of the person entails its moral status and its right to life.

The arguments that follow seek to provide for the interests of the fetus as an objective value in the world:

1. All biological evidence confirms the fact that the fertilized ovum has the human chromosome pattern containing all the inheritable factors, and it can never grow into anything but a human person. Biologists are also unanimous in testifying that fetal life is distinct from the mother's life, even though the two are connected during the period of gestation. Therefore any analogy with the surgical removal of tumors or with the killing of animals is inapplicable to the case of abortion. Direct abortion is the killing of an innocent person, and that is murder, even if the mother has stewardship over the fetus. As a matter of fact, the mother's very stewardship calls for

her beneficence toward and care for the well-being of the fetus, while abortion is the greatest harm she could do the fetus.

2. Aristotle[1] thought that the embryo does not become human until some time after conception, and this may be why he saw no wrong in early abortion. St. Thomas[2] accepted Aristotle's opinion as probable physical theory but drew no such ethical conclusion. We do not know and may never know the exact moment when the human soul comes to the body to make a human person, and so for all practical purposes we must consider it a person from the moment of conception. Probabilism is of no use here, for we have no doubt about the moral law or the moral obligation to do no harm to another person. The doubt is about a matter of fact. Just as we may not bury a person who is probably dead, so we may not kill a fetus if it is only probably a person. In such matters we must take the morally safer course, which is to treat the embryo as a living person.

3. The language of potentiality is misleading, because it sounds as if one is saying that a potential person already possesses in some mysterious fashion the being and significance of personhood. We have enough mystery already concerning ensoulment and do not need more. Clearly, if the fetus is not a person, it has no right to life and can be killed with moral impunity. But what criterion shall we take for personhood? If we take the actual use of intelligence and freedom, then we could kill the newly born, infants, and young children for some years after birth. Whether the child is inside or outside the mother can hardly constitute the essence of personhood. The only way to deal with this matter is to consider the human embryo or fetus as a human person with all the rights, including the right to life, that go with being a person. In this consideration the child is not a potential person but an actual person, though full use of its personality will have to wait on the gradual attainment of maturity.

4. All persons are equal in their right to life, and age gives no priority. If there is question only of indirectly permitting the death of one or the other, that one should be chosen who has the better chance of survival. A collision of rights cannot be settled by appealing to a higher moral standing for the mother. Both fetus and mother are intrinsically valuable as persons, and the fetus has done nothing to lose its right to life. In this case the mother's right yields to her duty to do no harm to another person, in this case her fetus, and neither may be killed. The mother may not kill any of her born children to be free of her various responsibilities; why the unborn?

5. To consider an unborn child as an aggressor against its parents, who by their own voluntary act caused its presence in the mother's womb, seems absurd. Aggression does not consist in merely being present but in *doing* something; *there must be an actual attack* or at least the start of an attack. If the pregnancy is not developing normally, this is one of those accidents that is no one's fault, surely no more the fetus' than the parents'. The abnormally developing fetus is not attacking the mother. The mental-health angle is different. Here the mother is the one who needs therapy, and the killing of the fetus is no moral solution, any more than the remedy for paranoia is the slaughter of all the imagined persecutors.

6. No ethicist wants doctors to be remiss in their professional duty of saving human life. They must use all legitimate means, but they must not use means that are morally evil. Their duty obliges them above all to do no harm. They have no more right than anyone else to put innocent persons to death. The fact that the unborn child cannot protect itself does not mean that its right can be invaded at anyone's discretion. Protection of the child's right to life is not legalism but the correct use of law. That necessity knows no law may be a popular proverb, but it has little standing as a moral guideline. Some kind of necessity could be thought up for anything.

7. All recognize the importance of love in the

---

[1] Aristotle, *On the Generation of Animals,* bk. II, ch. 3, 736a 24–737a 17. See also *Politics,* bk. VII, ch. 16, 1335b 24.
[2] St. Thomas, *Summa Theologica,* I, q. 118, a. 2, reply to obj. 2; *Summa Contra Gentiles,* bk. II, ch. 89.

child's life. But shall we say that if the child is not loved, the thing to do is to kill it? Let us put the blame for the unwanted child on the right parties, on those who conceived it. They took the chance of conception and are responsible for the result. Whether or not they can learn to love the child, they have the obligation of caring for it and not harming it. Even unloved children would rather live than be put to death. Who has the right to make this decision for them before they are born? Furthermore, the fetus as a person with the right to life has an intrinsic value that does not depend on its being valued by the parents. That the parents do not recognize its objective value is no excuse for terminating the child's life.

8. Abortion may solve the problem of unwanted children in individual cases, but it surely is no answer to the general callousness in human relationships that makes abortion "necessary" in the first place. Psychologically a woman can never be free of the memory of someone who was inside her at the wrong moment. Pregnancy can be an expression of many things besides mutual love, but no matter what pregnancy expresses it is always an expression of a need more complicated than the needs abortion can satisfy. The quality of a woman's life is at stake when she enters into a sexual relationship with a man and becomes pregnant. Life exists for her, inside her. To choose abortion may free her from the fetus but not from her state of mind. Abortion may give women greater control over their own bodies, but it also lessens their sense of relationship to their bodies and leaves unresolved all the questions they have in relation to themselves as women. That a man can be coward enough to abandon a woman he has mistreated is the man's moral crime. Abortion is a woman's more difficult way of seeking equality in iniquity. A second wrong is not the way of righting the first one.

Furthermore, no fine philosophical distinctions about freedom and rights can quiet the minds and hearts of the enormous number of women who have had abortions and now regret their decisions. Many women feel "forced" into

the abortion procedure by external circumstances and would keep their child under better circumstances, that is to say, with emotional and/or financial support from husbands, boyfriends, parents, doctors, and social workers. Once the abortion has been performed, it is the woman who has to contend with the emotional and psychological stress of hallucinations, nightmares, memories of the abortion experience, and thoughts of the aborted child. Some women after their abortions feel uncomfortable around children, are less able to experience emotions, feel victimized, see themselves as less worthwhile, fear that others will learn of their abortion, and feel grief, sadness, regret, and loss.

9. We are all conscious of the population problem and know that something must be done about it. Whatever solution we arrive at, if there is one, will have to accord with morality. Widespread abortion is not the answer. Compulsory abortion would be so flagrant a violation of human rights that any people would have the right to resist it violently. We do need global ethics, but if it consists of global immorality, there are no ethics left.

The arguments just concluded propose a view of personhood that does not depend on community recognition for its moral standing. It is intended to provide for the protection of the weak, the innocent, and the disvalued of our own kind. The history of humankind should serve to remind us that the weak and powerless are easily exploited and abused by the strong. This view of personhood is further intended to cultivate the virtues of compassion, sympathy, courage, patience, and trustworthiness in regard to one another, especially in times of weakness and powerlessness when we are most vulnerable. Theists hold that human life is a God-given gift over which we have stewardship. Even while they affirm the duty to care for and guard that life, they do not deny that there are at times difficult decisions to be made in regard to the care and protection of fetuses, newly borns, and infants. In the light of this known obligation, they choose to take the safer course even when faced with difficult probabilities. If a mistake is to be made, and mistakes inevitably are made, the theist wants to operate with a clear bias for life while at the same time knowing that the quality of that life is also important and a value to be considered.

There are many viewpoints and interpretations on the question of abortion, and each has its ethical, legal, social, and medical implications. The position one takes on abortion depends on one's ranking of the values involved. To arrive at agreement as to which value belongs where on the scale of importance is not a simple matter. Each person must decide how to rank at least the following values: the life of the fetus, the woman's freedom of self-determination, the common good of society. Over and above these values, there is a series of rights designed to protect these values: the right of the fetus to life, the right of the woman to determine what she will do with her body, the right of society to make laws restricting freedom, the right of doctors and other health care personnel to participate in abortions or not. If we can agree on the values at stake and the rights we want to guarantee to protect those values, perhaps we can cut through some of the side issues in the debate to address ourselves to the main issues. The debate itself will probably continue until we can determine exactly when life begins and come to a consensus about whether we want to protect that life and, if we do, to what extent we will protect it. Thus far in the debate no one seems satisfied because neither the antiabortion nor the proabortion forces have come to any agreement with one another. Certainly neither side has managed to convince the other of the rightness of its position.

We conclude this presentation of the arguments with some thoughts about the social dimension of abortion and its implications for us as a society. Generally, abortion is examined in terms of private, personal morality, but when we see the large number of abortions performed each year we should also ask ourselves: what is happening to us as a society? The sheer number of abortions points not to a simple accumulation of homogeneous cases but to a qualitatively different moral reality. We cannot find that reality's meaning for our society by asking about the purpose of an individual abortion or about what the law permits, but we can and must ask ourselves: what is happening to our society and what is a fitting response for us to make to this social phenomenon? The movement toward abortion on demand points to something that has happened and continues to happen to us as a society.

Pregnancy has become an entirely private affair; it is not seen as an event having social implications. A woman's body even while she is pregnant is regarded as an entirely private possession of the woman. The women's movement, born of a desire for freedom from male oppression, in espousing abortion on demand as a right for all women has created a class of women who now gain their freedom at the expense of the nascent human life in their wombs. Have they accepted abortion as a technological solution to human problems? Has abortion technology settled us into a cultural mind-set so powerful that we now accept easily what was previously unacceptable? Are we as a society giving up on the protection of human life? Are we decivilizing ourselves by legalizing abortion and by further making no appropriate response to the rising number of abortions? Are we corroding the very values we hoped to pursue? We need to look at what is happening with new eyes, the eyes of human responders to a situation of our own making. To fail to ask ourselves these questions is to miss a very significant dimension of the entire abortion controversy—the dimension of social justice.

The author and the reviser of this book conclude from this debate that there is no moral justification for direct abortion, because no one has a right to engage in the direct killing of the innocent, and if anyone is innocent, it is the fetus. The only line of investigation open to those who wish to make a moral case for abortion on demand is to establish somehow that the fetus in question is not a human person and so has no right to life. Efforts along this line have been made, but these demonstrations have not been made successfully. The only other possible course we see is to demonstrate that in some cases of extreme fetal abnormality there is no bodily basis for personhood at all, so that the termination of such a pregnancy would not at all be abortion in the moral sense. As fetology, perinatology, and neonatology develop further, we may finally come to the point when cases of extreme fetal abnormality can be corrected and then the question would once again become one of the morality of abortion on demand.

Legalization of Abortion

A further question arises on the control of abortion by the civil law. It is one thing to hold an action immoral and another thing to forbid and punish it by civil legislation. It is not the business of the state to regulate the whole private life of its citizens, and many immoral practices must be tolerated by the civil law as being outside its scope.[1] Can we say that abortion belongs wholly to the moral sphere and that civil law should not attempt to deal with it?

Most such cases deal with victimless crimes and consenting adults, such as prostitution, homosexuality, and such matters. Though many proabortionists try to reduce abortion to this category, it will not fit. Abortion invades the fetus' right to life, and the protection of its people's rights is the chief business of the state. No state can overlook killing as not its business; abortion, whether called murder or not, involves the same right to life. Even when the state does not define the unborn as a citizen, the question remains whether the state can get rid of an obligation merely by defining it away. Abortion concerns not only the consenting adults, mother, doctor, and father, but also the nonconsenting nonadult, the fetus, whose stake in the matter is crucial but whose interest is often wholly overlooked. Is not the state obliged to protect the life of the otherwise defenseless fetus? This is a strong argument for severe, even rigorous, abortion laws.

On the other side there is the nature of the political state itself and what can be accomplished by its laws. A state, especially the pluralistic state of today, must operate within a framework of popular consensus. The argument for the immorality of abortion, the theory of rights on which it rests, and the philosophy of the person underlying the ethics of rights are not admitted by a large part of the population. There is popular consensus on the wrongness of murder, theft, and similar crimes; the defense is never that the act was not wrong but that the accused did not do it. Abortions, however, are readily admitted, and the defense is that it is not a wrong act but one within the rights of the mother. Does one group of citizens (whether majority or minority) have the right to impose its opinions and the philosophical backing for those opinions on another group that disagrees? A democratic and pluralistic state will say no.

Hence there are many who think that there should be no laws on abortion. Some do not want abortion to be legalized, since that may be interpreted as approving of it, but rather decriminalized. Without approval, the state simply does not punish such acts and turns them over to the individual consciences of its citizens. Would not the state, then, fail in its duty to protect the rights of the innocent? Every antiabortionist will say yes. But such failure is inherent in the limited function and power of the state. The state cannot force all its citizens to adopt the same philosophy of rights, the same respect for human rights, and the same judgment on the personhood of the human fetus. To attempt it would involve a grave violation of the freedom of its citizens. On the other hand, no doctor should be obliged to perform an abortion, no nurse to assist at one, and no private hospital board to allow one to be done with the hospital facilities. These persons also should not be pressured to act against their consciences.

As can be seen from balancing both sides of this debate, there is a conflict between two very basic moral principles: that of the right to life and that of the right to freedom. Is the right to life so great that we can force our fellow citizens to accept our view of it against their conviction,

---

[1]See St. Thomas, *Summa Theologica,* I–II, q. 96, a. 2.

or is the freedom of the citizen to think and act according to his or her convictions strong enough that to defend it we are allowed to entrust unborn children to the tender mercy of their mothers? Many think that the best solution would be to spend less effort on legislation and more effort on moral persuasion of the mothers.

SELF-DEFENSE

Our right to life implies a right to the means necessary to preserve our life. The right to life is a coercive or juridical right, one that may be protected by the use of physical force. It is often impossible, when one's life is attacked, to appeal to the civil government, the normal guardian of our rights. After the attack is over, punishment of the offender belongs to the civil government alone, because the factor of urgency is not present, but at the moment of the attack the victim must often use *self*-defense or there will be no defense. On what principles is self-defense morally justified, and how far may one go in defending one's own right to life?

The act of violating or attempting to violate another's right is *aggression*. As we use the term, it always means an *unjust* attack. Mere intention to attack without any external attempt is not aggression, but there may be aggression without deliberate intention, as in an assault by a maniac. The distinction between an intentional and an unintentional aggressor describes the guilt or innocence of the person attacking, but we are interested here in what the person who is attacked may do. He or she needs to repel the threat to life, whether the assailant means it or not.

Conditions of a Blameless Self-defense

Each of us has a right of self-defense, but only under certain conditions. There are four of them, and they stem from the very notion of defense:

1. *The motive must be self-defense alone.* If self-defense is only a mask for hatred or revenge, the act becomes evil because of evil intent.

2. *Force may be used only at the time of the attack.* The danger to one's life must be actual,

not merely prospective. The mere fact that someone sends me a threatening letter does not allow me to go out and kill that person, for many threats are never followed up. There would be an end to public order if anyone could use force to repel merely imagined attacks.

3. *Force may be used only when there is no other way of repelling the attack.* Recourse must be made to the police and public authority when possible. One need not run away from every fight but should try not to provoke one. Persuasion or other nonforceful methods should be used if there is any reasonable hope of success.

4. *No more injury may be inflicted than is necessary to avert actual danger.* If I can save my life by injury less than death, I must not proceed further. If the assailant is knocked unconscious, there is no need for killing. More harm than necessary may not be inflicted for defense.

The second of these conditions has the most difficult application. In concrete cases it is often hard to determine just when preparation for attack turns into actual aggression. Mere purchase of a gun by my enemy with a declaration of intent to shoot me is not aggression, but I do not have to wait until the person has actually shot at me, for then no further defense may be possible. Defense may begin as soon as the aggressor lifts the gun or even approaches the oncoming fray, depending on the circumstances. Here the common estimate of sensible people must be taken into consideration. In a matter so crucial, when the action to be efficient must be swift, it is impossible to draw fine lines and make delicate discriminations, and it is better to favor the defender of life than the attacker. Individual conscience will decide subjective guilt or innocence in concrete cases; we are trying to discover objective principles for any act of self-defense.

Morality of Self-defense

Self-defense seems to be merely an application of the principle of double effect, and so St. Thomas appears to consider it. He says:

Nothing hinders one act from having two effects, only one of which is intended, while the other is beside the intention. Now moral acts take their species according to what is intended, and not according to what is beside the intention, since this is accidental . . . . Accordingly the act of self-defense may have two effects, one is the saving of one's own life, the other is the slaying of the aggressor. Therefore this act, since one's intention is to save one's own life, is not unlawful, seeing that it is natural to everything to keep itself in *being,* as far as possible. And yet, though proceeding from a good intention, an act may be rendered unlawful, if it be out of proportion to the end. Wherefore if a man, in self-defense, uses more than necessary violence, it will be unlawful: whereas if he repel force with moderation his defense will be lawful, because according to the jurists, *it is lawful to repel force by force, provided one does not exceed the limits of a blameless defense* . . . . It is not lawful for a man to intend killing a man in self-defense, except for such as have public authority, who while intending to kill a man in self-defense, refer this to the public good, as in the case of a soldier fighting against the foe, and in the minister of the judge struggling with robbers, although even these sin if they be moved by private animosity.[1]

It should be easy to recognize in this passage the source from which the principle of double effect was derived, by broadening it to suit other questions besides that of self-defense. However, in applying the principle of double effect to self-defense a crucial problem about the first two conditions arises: Is not the killing of an assailant a *direct* killing, so that in defending my life I am using an evil as means to a good? On this matter there are two opinions:

One opinion holds that legitimate self-defense is always only an *indirect* killing. Though more fully expressed by his commentator Cajetan,[2] this opinion seems to be that of St. Thomas. Only one in public authority may *intend* killing another, even in self-defense. According to this opinion, all that I as a private person may do in defending myself is to produce a state of quiet or nonactivity in the assailant so that he or she cannot continue the attack. If my attempts to produce this nonactivity, a thing that is morally indifferent, result in death, that is incidental and regrettable. But I must not *intend* anything more than the quieting of the adversary, not the death.

The other opinion holds that in self-defense the killing may be *direct.* John de Lugo puts it as follows:

> We may intend whatever is necessary for the defense of our life. Sometimes the striking of blows alone is insufficient for this purpose, but the death of the adversary is necessary. His stubbornness is such that he will not cease from attacking you, either by himself or others, unless he dies. Therefore you can intend his death, not merely as the striking of a blow [from which death may follow] but as death, because it is useful to your safety not otherwise than as death . . . . The death of the aggressor is not merely connected with another means that is intended, but it itself, and as death, is useful and judged necessary to your defense.[3]

This latter opinion falls back on a *collision of rights.* By the very fact that the assailant's attack is unjust, his or her right to life yields to that of the person attacked. The right to life of the two parties is no longer equal, but the aggressor temporarily loses the right to life by the unjust act of aggression. Killing in itself is not wrong, but what makes it wrong is its *injustice,* the invasion of another person's right. If that right is extinguished, there is no injustice present to make the act of killing wrong. This second opinion has the double advantage of eliminating the subtle distinction between killing and quieting and of permitting both direct and indirect killing in self-defense.

Whichever of these explanations is preferred, there is no doubt about the existence of the right of self-defense. The use of force is not in itself wrong. It is so only when one has no right to use it. We must have a natural right to self-defense for the following reasons:

1. The assailant who breaks the moral law cannot thereby acquire a better right to life than the

---

[1] St. Thomas, *Summa Theologica,* II–II, q. 64, a. 7.

[2] Cajetan, *Commentaria* (Commentaries on the Works of St. Thomas), on the above passage. This is found in the Leonine Edition of St. Thomas, vol. IX.

[3] De Lugo, *De Justitia et Jure* (On Justice and Right), Disputation X, sec. VI, §149.

innocent person who keeps the moral law, so that on being unjustly attacked one finds that his or her right to life becomes a duty to die.

2. The good and upright members of the population cannot have the duty to let the criminal element, by their indiscriminate and unchecked use of force, seize control of human society and thus pervert it into an instrument of evil.

Therefore our natural right to life would defeat itself unless, under proper conditions, it carried with it authorization to use force even to killing in self-defense.

The argument proves that each person has a *right* to self-defense. Is it also a *duty*? No. As we shall see, I have the duty to use ordinary means to preserve my life, but the killing of a human being, even if he or she is an aggressor, is surely an extraordinary means. Therefore nothing prevents me from choosing the heroic course of giving up my own life rather than taking another's. Only in unusual circumstances could self-defense become a duty, for example, in the case of a public personage indispensable to the community's welfare.

One may come to the assistance of another whose life is unjustly attacked. Such assistance becomes a duty for custodians of public order because of their office and for others who have a natural duty to protect their charges. The casual bystander has a general duty in common humanity to come to another's assistance in distress; if this action goes so far as to require the killing of an assailant, it usually entails serious risk to one's own life, a risk one is allowed but not obliged to take.

Unintentional Aggression

The preceding argument is expressly directed at *intentional* aggression but applies with proper reservations to *unintentional* aggression. A person who has lost the use of reason, either permanently or temporarily, cannot perform a voluntary act and cannot incur moral guilt, but such a person can be just as serious a threat to other people's lives. The same is true of someone who has the use of reason but does not realize that the act he or she is doing at the moment will kill someone; for such a person the act is voluntary only as far as he or she sees it, and its unforeseen consequences, though involuntary, can be fatal to others who have a right to protect themselves against them.

Such acts are unjust aggression from the standpoint of the person attacked, because his or her right is actually, though unintentionally, violated. Such persons may protect themselves even to the killing of the assailant under the four conditions of a blameless self-defense. The unintentional aggressor's right yields to the defender's, not because of the former's fault, but because of his or her misfortune. Human lives cannot be placed at the mercy of the insane, however blameless they may be, nor are we obliged to give up our lives in deference to another's ignorance. Most assailants are malicious, but it is not necessary that they be so in order that we may exercise our right of self-defense against them.

Goods Equivalent to Life

Each of us has a right not only to life itself but to a human life, a normal and decent life fit for a rational and free being. My right to defend my life would be of small value if I could not also defend my right to live that life in a manner befitting a personal being. This right entails the possession of certain goods that make life worth living, goods that some writers call equivalent to life. Force may be used to defend such goods even to the killing of the unjust aggressor, under the same conditions that apply to the defense of life itself. Personal goods considered equivalent to life are liberty, sanity, chastity, and bodily completeness. Many would rather die than submit to such evils as rape, insanity, blindness, or enslavement, and, whether they would or not, why should anyone have to yield to a fiend who tries to inflict them?

Material goods, even of great value, may seem so disproportionate to human life that we may never kill to defend them. On the other hand, the social as well as the personal aspect must be considered, and the good of society requires that people be secure in their possessions, especially those on which their whole livelihood depends. Acts of violence, whether against one's person or against one's property, cannot be allowed to go unchecked in society, and in the last resort they can be checked only by opposed violence. The attacker can easily save his or her life simply by desisting from aggression.

Honor and *reputation* have been deliberately omitted here. They are as important as any of the goods just listed, for their loss can mean utter ruin, but they are not the kind of thing that can be defended by force. Self-defense is the repelling of force by force. Lies and slander are words and cannot be beaten back by fists or swords or hand guns. The only weapon against them is the truth. The use of physical force against a liar would only prove me physically stronger but would not restore my reputation; if I use physical force to coerce a recantation, it would not be generally believed under the circumstances. However, force short of killing may be the only way of closing the mouth of a reviler or slanderer who refuses to stop. Here physical force can be effective.

SUMMARY

Our right to life is based on the fact that each of us must achieve his or her goal and fulfillment as a person by morally good acts, and to do so each must live.

Suicide is the direct killing of oneself on one's own authority. Arguments favoring suicide are that life can become intolerable and a worse evil than death, that God's gift of life is to be used intelligently and surrendered when useless, and that God gives us rights over others' lives and why not over our own?

Theistic arguments against suicide are that God gives us only *indirect* dominion over ourselves, the stewardship of our person, but no *direct* dominion, no right to destroy that person, for this is so exclusively God's that He cannot give it away; it is for God to decide that each of us has had sufficient opportunity for a good life; by suicide we arrogate this privilege to ourselves and invade God's exclusive right.

Nontheists have no arguments against suicide.

Murder, the direct killing of an innocent person, is morally wrong because it violates the right of God over all human life, of an innocent person to his or her life, and of the state to public order and safety.

Mercy killing, or active euthanasia, is suicide if done by oneself, murder if done by another with or without the victim's consent.

Abortion is the expulsion of the fetus from the mother before it is viable. If the mother has a serious illness, she may be given necessary treatment even though the death of the child *indirectly* results. But the double-effect principle cannot be applied to *direct* abortion in the full moral sense of that word.

Some recent discussion of the abortion issue relates to cases of extreme fetal abnormality, focusing on the seemingly opposed values of "the quality of life" vs. "the sanctity of life," which correlate, respectively, with the moral principles "do no harm to another" and "human life is to be preserved." Neither the values nor the moral principles are opposites but rather are seen as complementary when we think in terms of "respect for personal life and its integrity." The use of this latter principle may help all parties engage one another more meaningfully in discussion of the issues at stake.

Arguments favoring direct abortion, based on a concept of person that applies fully only to adult moral agents who impute some degree of moral standing to fetuses only by reason of whatever duties the moral community of adults accepts in regard to them, are that the fetus (1) is either only a part of the mother or at least not yet a person and so has no rights; (2) is probably not a person and for good reason may be terminated; (3) is at most a potential person with only potential rights; (4) in a collision of rights, by reason of its lesser moral standing must yield to the right of the mother who has full moral standing; (5) can be considered an unjust aggressor against the mother; (6) may be terminated whenever necessary, for necessity knows no law; (7) may be terminated when it is not wanted by the parents who establish its value; (8) is protected by men, who are responsible for the prejudice against abortion, at the expense of the women who are unfairly penalized for having an active sex life; (9) given the problem of overpopulation, may have to be aborted whether the parents agree or not.

Arguments against direct abortion, based on a concept of person that applies fully both to fetuses and adults who have moral standing by reason of their very existence, deny both the alleged facts and the conclusions. Though we do not know just when the human soul enters the embryo or when it becomes a human person, we cannot use probabilities here but must follow the morally safer course. From the moment of conception the fetus must be considered ensouled and, given its chromosomal inheritance, can never be anything else but a developing person; it must be treated as a person with the full right to life. The mother, who has stewardship over her fetus, has a duty to protect and care for the developing person in her womb. No possible reason, even the convenience of the mother, can justify putting an innocent person to death.

How far the civil law should go in protecting the fetus involves almost insoluble difficulties in a pluralistic society. There are good reasons for strong abortion laws and also for no laws on abortion.

Self-defense, the repelling of force by force, should ordinarily be entrusted to the civil government but sometimes must be done personally. There are four conditions of a blameless self-defense:

1. The motive must be self-defense alone.
2. Force must be used only at the time of attack.
3. There must be no other way of repelling the attack.
4. No more injury may be inflicted than necessary.

Some say that self-defense must aim only at the quieting of the assailant, and death must be indirect. Others think that even a direct killing is allowable because of a collision of rights.

The natural right to life implies the right to protect that life, even by the killing of the assailant if necessary. Otherwise, criminals have a better right to life than the innocent, and the criminal element get a free hand in the control of society.

Self-defense is a right but normally not a duty. We may defend others who are attacked, but we are not obliged to risk our lives for those not under our charge.

We may defend ourselves against *unintentional* aggressors, because they are actually though unwittingly invading our right.

We may also defend goods equivalent to life: limbs and faculties, sanity, liberty, chastity, material goods of great value. But honor cannot be defended by force.

Questions for Discussion

1. You are a special agent of the Central Intelligence Agency assigned to do undercover work in a country that does not have diplomatic relations with the United States. You are the CIA's liaison with a revolutionary underground organization engaged in subverting that country's government, the overall aim of the subversion being the creation of a democratic and therefore friendlier government. If you are captured and tortured, you might not be able to sustain the pain and so give away vital secret information. To be on the safe side, you have been given a dose of cyanide to use as a last resort. All you have to do is bite down and the torture is over. Is this not suicide? Does the argument given against suicide cover this case? Why?

2. The social dimension of abortion requires us to look once again at what personal life means, what respect we owe ourselves and others, and what constitutes moral standing in our society. The respect for and integrity of per-

sonal life is what is at stake. Are the arguments given against direct abortion in this chapter simply wrongheaded in regarding the fetus as a person instead of a potential person? Explain why you give the answer you do.

3. The perspective of women is very important in looking at the abortion issue. They need the right to abortion on demand because of the callousness of men who "love them and leave them." Do you agree? Why?

4. Suppose the government were to decriminalize abortion and abrogate all laws regulating it. What do you think would happen to our society? Would such a policy by the government lead ultimately to the destruction of the family and of our society? Or would enough people still have children so that society would continue? Explain your reasons for answering as you do.

5. Life in some of our large cities has been likened to life in a jungle. At times it is kill or be killed. You have taken up the practice of carrying a handgun for use against attackers. No one is going to mug and rob you and get away with it! You also keep a gun in the nightstand by your bed in case of attempted robbery. Take another look at the section on self-defense. Are you justified in carrying and/or keeping the gun and using it in self-defense? Explain.

Readings

Read Plato's *Phaedo,* §61–62, which shows that Socrates, whatever we may think of his drinking the hemlock, certainly did not intend to commit suicide; the famous death scene is at the end of the *Phaedo.* Plato in the *Laws,* bk. IX, proposed what he thinks are the best laws on homicide and assault.

St. Augustine, *City of God,* bk. I, ch. 17–27, treats of suicide. David Hume and Arthur Schopenhauer each have short essays on suicide; they can be read in Abelson, *Ethics and Metaethics,* pp. 108–121. Emile Durkheim's work, *Suicide,* is a classic. Albert Camus' *The Myth of Sisyphus* and *The Rebel* contain an existentialist's views, the first on suicide and the second on murder, with many other reflections.

St. Thomas treats of all kinds of killing in the *Summa Theologica,* II–II, q. 64. There is no English translation of Cajetan or de Lugo to make accessible their views on self-defense. Michael Cronin, *The Science of Ethics,* vol. II, pp. 93–110, and Joseph Rickaby, *Moral Philosophy,* pp. 202–224, argue for Cajetan's position.

The legal as well as the moral angle is developed by Norman St. John-Stevas in *The Right to Life; Life, Death, and the Law;* and *Law and Morals.* Other more recent studies include: Peter Steinfels and Robert M. Veatch (eds.), *Death Inside Out;* John A. Behnke and Sissela Bok (eds.), *The Dilemmas of Euthanasia;* O. Ruth Russell, *Freedom To Die: Moral and Legal Aspects of Euthanasia.*

On abortion: H. Tristram Engelhardt, Jr., *The Foundations of Bioethics;* Earl E. Shelp, *Born To Die? Deciding the Fate of Critically Ill Newborns;* and Rasa Gustaitis and Ernle W.D. Young, *A Time to Be Born, A Time to Die: Conflicts and Ethics in an Intensive Care Nursery* have each had a significant impact in the restructuring of the abortion arguments in this chapter. Robert E. Cooke and others edit a symposium entitled *The Terrible Choice: the Abortion Dilemma.* See also David Granfield, *The Abortion Decision;* Daniel Callahan, *Abortion: Law, Choice, and Morality;* Germain Grisez, *Abortion, the Myths, the Realities, and the Arguments;* John T. Noonan, *The Morality of Abortion: Legal and Historical Perspectives* and *A Private Choice: Abortion in America in the Seventies;* Bernard Häring, *Medical Ethics;* George H. Kieffer, *Bioethics: A Textbook of Issues. The Hastings Center Report* carries articles regularly that reflect the current status of the abortion debate. Other writings that illuminate both sides of the question include: James B. Nelson, *Human Medicine;* Harmon L. Smith, *Ethics and the New Medicine;* Thomas W. Hilgers and Dennis J. Horan (eds.), *Abortion and Social Justice;* Leonard J. Weber, *Who Shall Live?;* William E. May, *Human Existence, Medicine and Ethics;* Charles E. Curran, *Politics, Medicine, and Christian Ethics;* Thomas J. O'Donnell, *Medicine and Christian Morality;* H. Tristram Engelhardt, "The Ontology of Abortion," *Ethics* **84** (April 1974), 217–234.

20
Health

PROBLEM

Millions of Americans have taken their health into their own hands. Daily exercise has become a way of life for many; jogging and the intricate movements of T'ai Chi are among the favorites. Diet has also assumed an importance it did not have previously. Whole bran, herbal teas, and assorted other "natural" foods and vitamins are consumed in unprecedented amounts. So many people have a daily regimen they pursue with a seriousness and intensity that one wonders whether a healthy, vigorous body has become an end in itself instead of a means to pursue other life goals. This new health consciousness shows itself in forms that range from the sensible to the bizarre. We are told in a variety of ways, "Take care of your health. The life you save may be your own!"

Reflection on this current situation raises a number of questions about health, professional health care, risks to life, the obligation we have to guard our health and the extent of that obligation, the right we may or may not have to professional health care, the meaning of disease and illness, and so on. Many of these concepts have ancient roots, but in our pluralistic society we find it difficult to agree on definitions and goals. One central guiding principle, however, does appear to be generally agreed on: the individual adult person is responsible for developing and maintaining his or her health. But what does "responsible" mean? What does "health" mean? To what extent must a person go to preserve life and health? May I expose myself to serious danger or even to certain death in a good cause? Must I keep myself whole as well as alive, and what if I cannot do both?

We shall use the following questions as a guide to our discussion of some of these issues:

1. What exactly do we mean by "health?"
2. When may a person risk his or her life?
3. How much care ought to be given to one's health? to defective infants?
4. Does each person have a right to health care?
5. What ought to be our moral response to the AIDS epidemic?
6. Ought any limits to be placed on the use of new medical techniques and psychotropic drugs to control one's own or others' behavior?
7. Does each of us have a right to die?
8. Are mutilation and sterilization justifiable?
9. Is medical experimentation on humans justifiable?
10. What can be done for radiation victims?

DEFINITION OF HEALTH

The World Health Organization defines health as " . . . a state of complete physical, mental and social well-being and not merely the absence of disease or infirmity."[1] The negative part of this definition seems relatively clear in stating that health is " . . . not merely the absence of disease or infirmity," but the positive side of the definition tells us little. We can still ask, What is " . . . a state of complete physical, mental and social well-being?" In fact, what is well-being?

The definition points to both problems and possibilities in our common conceptions of and attitudes about health. The definition tells us that health is at least the absence of disease and infirmity, and it also tells us that, while we are speaking of the individual, our understanding of health is not individualistic. Health is, at least for the World Health Organization, also a social and relational phenomenon. Even though it concerns individuals, it is intimately bound up with the nature and quality of the individual's interpersonal relationships at all levels. Beyond whatever problems we as individuals may have with our heart, kidneys, and so on, health also has something to do with our wholeness both as integral and as interrelated persons. If I have a malfunctioning kidney or heart, my emotions and spirit are also affected. If only my kidney or heart is treated, my health as a whole person is still in jeopardy.

We think of health in various ways: (1) in a *mechanical-physical* sense, health is the adequate

---

[1]Preamble to the Constitution of the World Health Organization, *World Health Organization: Basic Documents,* ed. 26 (Geneva, World Health Organization, 1976), p. 1.

functioning of the parts of our bodies; (2) in a *chemical* sense, health is an appropriate balance of the chemical substances and processes within us; (3) in a *biological* sense, health is the appropriate interaction of the self as an organism with its total environment and this includes work, rest, movement, food, and so on; (4) in a *psychological* sense, health is a good balance between a secure sense of personal identity and an ability to care for and be involved with others; (5) in a *social and historical* sense, health is the creation of a society's traditional style in the art of living, celebrating, suffering, and dying, so that the understanding of personal health depends in some measure on the ideology of one's society and its culture; and (6) in a *spiritual* sense, health is an awareness of and a capacity to relate to the source and meaning of life that transcends us and yet is immanent to our inmost being.

The dimensions of our lives that these various senses of health point to are interrelated because they are the dimensions of a single personal life. Each person is a multidimensional unity and so the person's health is also a multidimensional wholeness. We can define health, tentatively at least, as *the person's capacity to maintain a favorable, self-regulated state of being that is a prerequisite for the effective performance of an indefinitely wide range of functions both within the person's anatomical-physiological system and in relation to the person's physical, psychological, sociocultural, and spiritual environment*.

This definition of health can focus on any dimension of a person's health without losing sight of all the other dimensions. It can focus on the organic level of the person without being narrowly physical. At the same time it is broad enough to include the whole range of bioethical concerns from birth through death together with the person's functioning in between these two extremes. Our view of health will have important consequences for our view of health care and the goals of the health care professions. Too broad a definition might lead us to expect the health care professions to aim at bettering any state of non-well-being, for example, poverty or ignorance. Too narrow a definition might limit health care

strictly to the body as a mechanism to be repaired. The definition offered above avoids both of these extremes.

Personal health, according to our suggested definition, is a process of adapting to reality by the person's culturally shaped yet autonomous response to it. We say that health is culturally shaped because culture gives a unique form to our notion of health and to a large extent shapes our attitudes to pain, disease, impairment, and death. Health is also an autonomous response because successful adaptation within one's social environment is in large part the result of the self-awareness, self-discipline, and inner resources by which each person regulates his or her own daily rhythm and actions. The ability to cope with pain, sickness, impairment, and death is fundamental to personal health and can never be replaced by professional and/or governmental intervention. In fact, the more an individual can do personally, the less society will have to do by way of health management.

Given our tentative definition of health, we must now attempt to define disease and illness as well. To begin with, we can distinguish illness from disease by saying that *illness* is used to identify the group of signs and symptoms that the individual who is not well feels and/or recognizes as disrupting in some degree his or her capacity to function as usual. A person may be ill without having a particular disease and, conversely, may have a particular disease without feeling ill. A *disease* is a disorder or cause of a disorder of a certain kind within the range of ongoing life functions; it is used to explain (where applicable) the illness the person experiences.

We humans generally subscribe to sets of values that we want as means to other ends, values such as staying alive, prolonging life, limiting pain, gratifying desires, ensuring the security of our bodily and personal being along with our property and associates, and so on. These values might be called enabling interests, for they are means to attain something else, or they might be called general conditions requisite for attaining other values. The medical profession in any society by providing care and cure ensures the individual person's wholeness sufficient for that person to exercise his or her enabling interests. Notice, moreover, that the medical profession always serves a particular society that has a determinate ideology and a set of long-range goals so that the profession's concept of illness and disease cannot help but reflect the state of technology, the social expectations, the division of labor, and the environmental condition of the society it serves.

RISK TO LIFE

Suicide, or the direct killing of oneself on one's own authority, meets with rather general moral disapproval, but the indirect killing of oneself or the deliberate endangering of one's life, even when the danger may be so great that death is certain, can be a praiseworthy act. When we say that life is a nonrenounceable right and its preservation a duty, we do not mean that a person may never sacrifice it under any conditions, but only that he or she may not give it up at pleasure. When a person may rightfully risk his or her life is determined by the four conditions of the principle of double effect:

1. The act involving the risk must be allowable in itself apart from its consequences.
2. Death must be an incidental by-product and not the means by which the good is attained.
3. Death, even though foreseen, must be merely permitted and not intended for itself.
4. There must be some proportionate reason why the risk is worth taking.

Cases frequently arise in which all the conditions are fulfilled. In this event, provided any other evil circumstances arising from other possible sources are excluded, the deliberate exposure of oneself to the risk of death is not morally wrong.

This we all know through ordinary experience in the hazards of life. If we could never risk our lives, no one could nurse the plague-stricken or undergo a serious operation or mine coal or build a skyscraper or fly an airplane or even drive on the highways. Human life as we know it would come to a standstill.

The fourth condition, the proportionate reason, requires some additional remarks. How is it to be estimated? Except in cases in which death is certain, we must not balance the good we seek against death itself but against the *risk* of death. Is the good proportioned to the danger?

The danger may be:

1. *Ordinary* or *extraordinary*
2. *Proximate* or *remote*
3. *Certain, probable,* or barely *possible*

The greater the risk, the greater must be the desired good that can justify such a risk. There is an ordinary, remote, and possible hazard in driving a car or flying a plane, and yet one may do so for mere pleasure. To drive on sleety streets or fly in bad weather is much more dangerous and requires a better reason. Conditions can become so bad that no driving or flying is allowable, except perhaps to save a life, and then we must see how much that life is endangered.

To save another from certain death, we may expose ourselves to certain death. Such an act is usually allowable but becomes obligatory only under special conditions. Those who, either by nature or by contract, have charge over the lives of others may and sometimes must take greater risks to protect their charges. Parents will sacrifice themselves for their children. Soldiers, sailors, police officers, firemen, doctors, nurses, and others are obliged by the contract implicit in their occupation to fulfill their duties even in the most serious danger.

The greater benefit an action or occupation is to society, the more dangerous it may be without overbalancing the proportion. Columbus could take chances not otherwise permitted because of the enormous boon to all people a successful voyage would bring, and so may astronauts of the present and space travelers of the future. Dangerous work with radiation is justified when truly directed to the advancement of science or to national welfare, under proper precautions both for the investigators and the public. A person may do right in facing the ordinary risks of a hazardous occupation such as coal mining or dynamite manufacturing and at the same time do wrong by creating extraordinary dangers for self and others in his or her way of working, especially by willfully neglecting the usual safety precautions.

Is mere entertainment sufficient reason for risking one's life or health? It can be, if the proportion is kept. Acrobats and daredevils are morally allowed to ply their trade because their skill renders the danger remote; when age blunts their skill, they must lower their pitch and finally bow out. Auto racing, because of increased speeds over courses not made to take them, may in some contests have already passed the morally tolerable point. Injuries in football and other body-contact sports are accidents outside the game's structure and presumably outside the players' intention and thus come under the indirect voluntary and the double-effect principles. The same cannot be said for prizefighting, which lacks its climax unless it ends in a knockout; the knockout is the direct intention of each contestant and shouted for by the spectators. We now know more about the effect of the knockout blow on the human brain than we formerly did; each one produces some irreparable lesion, adding up to a progressive brain deterioration known as the "punch-drunk" condition. Promoters and backers of the sport, perhaps more than the participants, therefore have a serious moral problem on their hands. Some moralists would ban the sport entirely, most would require at least firmer regulation, and only few would see no moral problem at all in it.

The infinite variety of possibilities in this whole question of risk to life and health rules out the setting of any hard-and-fast norms. Positive law and custom, crystallizing the human race's age-old experience with danger, are helpful guides but are not infallible. We must ultimately fall back on the intellectual virtue of prudence; this we sometimes call common sense, and for it there is no substitute.

CARE OF HEALTH

Health is a good that requires reasonable care. It is a good each of us needs if we are going to be able to pursue our goals in life. If among our life goals there is one or more that we have a moral obligation to achieve, we also have a moral obligation to maintain our health because it is one of the necessary means to achieve the goal we are obliged to achieve. Our obligation to care for our health then would derive from our obligation to achieve the goal(s) we are obliged to achieve. But we can also ask whether our health is something we have an obligation to maintain for its own sake. Is health good in itself over and above the goodness it may have as a necessary means for implementing other goals? We may consider these two questions from a (1) theistic and (2) nontheistic or secular humanist point of view.

1. A theistic ethics takes the position that a person's life is a God-given gift to be used, not just in any way the person sees fit but in such a way as to achieve the divine purpose for which life was given in the first place. We are given stewardship, not the absolute right of disposal, over our lives and consequently have a moral obligation to care for our health so that we can achieve the goal for which we were created. The obligation we have rests on our relation of dependence on our creator as to our final goal. We have no moral obligation to maintain our health simply for its own sake. Our health is a means necessary for carrying on our activities in such a way as to achieve our ultimate goal, the end for which we were created.

2. A secular humanist or nontheistic ethics does not admit of making a case for a person's having a moral obligation to care for his or her health for its own sake. The secular humanist may well be able to justify the existence of other moral obligations by reason of which a person may then have an obligation to care for his or her health precisely to fulfill the other moral obligations. From the secular humanist point of view, can a person be said to have an obligation to himself or herself to maintain his or her health? The most that can be said from this point of view is that I owe it to myself to care for my health so that I can advance my interests and objectives. This statement is a prudential maxim, not a moral rule or precept. If I have the desire or need to pursue

my interests and objectives in life, then I would be well advised to maintain my good health. If I do not take care of myself, I can be said to be foolish but I cannot be said to have violated any moral obligation.

Finally, whether it be the theist or the secular humanist who has a moral obligation to care for his or her health, health is often beyond the person's capacity to achieve or maintain. The obligation is to take the available means and do what is reasonably conducive to the state of health. We are not obliged to become health cranks; we are obliged to use the ordinary means to keep healthy. Not to make use of the ordinary means would be to needlessly expose one's life to danger, for life itself is dependent on health. By ordinary means we refer to proper food, clothing, and shelter, due moderation in work and exercise, avoidance of foolish risks and dangers, taking the usual remedies in illness and seeking and following medical advice when necessary; all such care supposes rather normal conditions and does not contradict what was said earlier about exposing one's life to danger.

We have no obligation to preserve life and health by extraordinary means, for no one is obliged to do what is practically impossible or disproportionately difficult. A person in ordinary circumstances is not obliged to undergo a serious and costly operation, to break up his or her home and move to another climate, or to adopt some regimen that would prevent earning a living and make the person a burden on others. Health must be preserved but not at all costs. Whether a means is extraordinary or not must be judged, not absolutely, but *relatively to the condition of the patient*. A form of life tolerable to one person would be unbearable to another. The terms *ordinary* and *extraordinary* are to be taken in their moral sense, which need not correspond with their meaning in the medical (technological) sense. In the medical sense, installing a heart pacemaker, for example, is quite ordinary nowadays because it is a commonly followed procedure and readily available, whereas in the moral sense, it might be senseless and constitute a brutal prolongation of life depending on the age and condition of the patient. Medically speaking, extraordinary means would be what is new, experimental, rare, or complex; morally speaking, extraordinary means is defined not by reference to the mode of treatment but the effects of the treatment on the patient.

Two questions will be useful to determine whether the mode of treatment is extraordinary or not. First of all, we want to know: Does the use of this means offer reasonable hope of benefit to the patient? If the answer is no, then we have no reason to consider this mode of treatment. If the answer is yes, then we want to know: Will the use of this means involve excessive expense, pain, or other inconvenience? If the answer to this further question is also yes, then we have an *extraordinary* means being proposed and have no obligation to use that means. If the answer to the second question is no, then the means is, morally speaking, *ordinary* and we have an obligation to use ordinary means to preserve our health. The patient has no obligation to submit to the use of extraordinary measures nor does the attending physician have an obligation to use such measures. The physician does have an obligation to inform the patient fully about the available treatments for the patient's disability, but the choice must be left to the patient.

CARE OF DEFECTIVE INFANTS

Modern medical technology can sustain an infant's life often only in an impaired or defective condition without being able to cure or substantially improve the basic defect. With our attention being focused on the infant's unremedied (even if alleviated) condition, some ethicians are arguing that life need not be sustained if the *quality of life* that can be foreseen for the infant is not humanly satisfactory. They conclude that the best treatment is no treatment at all—the infant should be allowed to die.

In the section immediately preceding this one, we made a distinction between ordinary and extraordinary means of preserving life and health. Life is a value, precious and good, but it is not an absolute value to be saved at all costs. Only ordinary means, i.e., means relative to the condition of the patient, must be used to preserve life and health. Life then is a relative value, but relative to what? The perspective we have taken in this book is that life is a value for each human being insofar as it is a requisite for living the personal life, a life in relation to other persons whom we love and who love us. Surrounding those relationships are other values such as justice, respect, affection, care, concern, understanding, fidelity, and support. Since life is a relative good, the duty to sustain it is limited by the possibility of living in meaningful relationship with other persons, enjoying them and the values surrounding those relationships. This is what is meant by a humanly satisfactory life.

The problems parents and physicians face in dealing with malformed and/or defective infants can be agonizingly difficult to solve. The ethician's concern is to provide some guidelines that can be used in making a decision to treat the infant or let it die. Obviously, we are not talking about embracing infanticide. What we are seeking here is the infant's good. This matter is not simply a private family affair. The public (society at large) also has an interest and concern here, for the infant has been born into society and is now one of its members. Every infant, even the malformed and otherwise defective, has a right to life *equal* to that of every other member of society. Care for the infant ought not to be omitted or withdrawn because the hospital finds it difficult or because the parents are unwilling or unable to undertake the necessary care. Society has an obligation to care for such infants if the parents are unable to do so. Neither ought retarded infants be left to die but ought to be given the care they need either by their parents or by society. Retardation alone can never be a justifiable reason for omitting or withdrawing needed care, because even retarded children are capable of giving and enjoying love.

Nevertheless, we do have to consider cases of extremely malformed infants and some with severe internal defects. Parents, physicians, and other health care professionals have been involved in decisions about whether to give whatever treatment is possible or to withhold such treatment and thus let the infant die. The public has been involved more and more in this kind of discussion since the late fall of 1963, when a baby boy born prematurely and mongoloid (Down syndrome), with an intestinal blockage (duodenal atresia) that could have been corrected surgically, was not given treatment and was left to die in the nursery of The Johns Hopkins Hospital. The decision to withhold treatment was made by the parents in consultation with their physician. Much of the public discussion that followed was, to put the matter mildly, in basic disagreement with the parents' decision. The point being made here is that, while the decision ultimately must be made by the parents in consultation with whatever experts are available to them, they must be prepared to justify the reasons for their decision to the satisfaction of the public. The parents make the decision because the infant is incapable of doing so. Society is concerned because the infant is one of its members and has a right to be treated as an equal along with all the other members of society. The parents have a duty to articulate their position carefully and to defend that position against counterarguments. How else can society know that justice was done to one of its own?

The decision is not about the infant's humanity and so about its value. We know the infant is human and therefore valuable in its own right. The question in situations like this concerns the *quality of life* the infant is going to have. The parents are being called on to make a prudential judgment about how to bring about the good of the infant. Prudence is concerned with the means to achieve the good desired. Are the available means adequate to correct or ameliorate the infant's difficulty sufficiently so as to assure the infant the possibility of a life that is humanly satisfactory?

The people involved in making the decision for the infant's good need guidelines of two kinds: (1) concerning the *available means* to correct or ameliorate the defect, and (2) concerning the *quality of life* the infant is going to have if the means are used. In making any judgments of this type, there is always going to be margin for error. We want to narrow down that margin by making sure that, if an error is made, we err on the side of life for the infant. This is why we said that neither institutional nor managerial reasons should count nor should retardation alone count. We want the good of the infant.

In the light of the infant's potential for human relationships, with the possibility of enjoying the further values attendant upon those relationships, the available treatments must be considered. The guidelines within the limits stated so far are the following: It seems morally justifiable to omit or withdraw treatment when we have an infant whose malformation or defect places it somewhere between such extremes as anencephaly on the very severe side and mongolism on the less severe side *and* (1) when the convalescence is going to be long, painful, and oppressive and the prognosis is poor; and/or (2) when the infant's life expectancy will be brief and possible only with the use of artificial feeding. If the infant is in either or both of these two situations, its potential for human relationships is more than likely going to be lost in the very effort to survive and the infant can be said to have already achieved its human potential. When that is the case, the best method of care is to forego treatment, make certain it is as comfortable as possible, and allow it to die as painlessly as possible. One final caution is in order, namely, that judgments such as we have been discussing do not admit of mathematical exactness. We can judge someone's potential for human relationships only with humility and a clear bias for life.

RIGHT TO HEALTH CARE

The first important ethical concern associated with the delivery of health care services is respect for persons and the provision of services that reflect that respect. The second ethical concern is the distribution of those services in an equitable manner to every member of society. In the light of distributive justice, we ask whether or not health services can be provided in a way that benefits and burdens fairly all persons and classes in the society. Given these two important concerns, we address the question of whether or not each person has a right to health care such that either individuals, local communities, or the state and federal governments have an obligation to make such care available.

A right, as defined in Chapter 18, is *the moral power or inner freedom to do, omit, hold, or exact something of value*. The right to health belongs among our natural moral rights as an implication of our right to life and to preservation of our lives. Corresponding to the citizens' right is the obligation of the governmental authorities to protect them from recognized dangers to health that individuals cannot ward off by their own unaided efforts. All citizens should be secured against assaults that could damage their health or destroy their lives. Having a right to health in this sense does *not* prove that each person therefore has a right to health care, i.e., medical diagnosis and treatment of illness and disease.

In recent years we have been hearing a great deal of discussion about whether we as persons have a right to medical care. The person who is ill or disabled would be the *subject* of the right; federal, state, and local governments would be the *term* of the right, that is, the agencies bound to fulfill the right; medical treatment or other form of health care would be the *matter* of the right; and having an illness, disease, or some form of disability would be the subject's *title* or reason why the subject has a right to this medical care or treatment. To assert such a right implies that neither money, charity, nor poverty is the moral basis for medical care. If each person has a right to medical care, no person should lack medical care because of inability to pay for it. There should not be two systems of medical care, each differing in quality and quantity, for those who can pay and those who cannot. No one should be deprived of care because the social, cultural, and geographical organization of medical care makes access to health services difficult. Ability to pay cannot be a necessary condition for treatment, because we have no justification for distinguishing among ill persons on that basis. Illness and/or disease is the sole reason for medical treatment and so would be the sole title by reason of which we can be said to have a right to health care. All who are ill deserve equally to be treated, precisely because they are ill persons.

As the public discussion of this question has proceeded, a number of arguments have been proposed against our having a right to health care. The principal arguments against it appear to be the following:

1. Physicians, surgeons, and other health care professionals may argue that their skills are personal accomplishments and so those who have the skills have the right to determine how, where, and when they shall be put to use. Since they cannot treat everyone who is ill, they have a right to choose who shall receive treatment.

2. Illness and/or disease cannot be the sole basis for treatment. Some diseases are more serious than others, and some diseases do not affect individuals and society as seriously as others. Some grounds other than illness itself may be needed to distribute care fairly.

3. Medical care does not always effect a cure nor is it always successful in preserving health. This makes the existence of a right to health care seriously doubtful, because we cannot have a claim on something whose existence is dubious.

4. Many illnesses and diseases, like the current AIDS (acquired immune deficiency syndrome) epidemic, are the result of voluntary persistence in harmful habits. Such illnesses and diseases can hardly be a title to medical treatment at public expense.

Granted that these arguments against the right to medical care have some merit, we might argue in favor of a right to medical care as follows:

1. A person's health is an important ingredient in his or her self-regard as an autonomous (self-determining, free) agent and is also a significant reason for others to respect that autonomy and freedom. The autonomous person is one who controls or governs his or her own actions. Such a person is able to reflect on his or her decisions, motives, desires, habits, and so on. Autonomy allows a person the freedom to develop precisely as a self-governing agent, to improve his or her skills, to lead his or her own life, and to choose among alternative courses of action. Such a person is more socially competent and valuable than one who is not autonomous.

2. Each person's health is an important ingredient or component of the entire society's well-being, because the healthy person contributes to the cultural and political vitality of society and to the support of its economy. The more autonomous a person is, the more socially competent and valuable he or she is. If health differs significantly from class to class in a society, this difference can reinforce other inequities and seriously undermine the well-being of society.

3. All persons have a moral right to medical care to the extent that (a) medical care can be provided and (b) the social institutions can be arranged so that care is available to all in equal need and can be provided in a way that is conducive to self-respect. The federal, state, and local governments in cooperation with one another have the moral obligation to provide the medical care. This obligation arises from the basic moral obligations of governmental authority to respect the autonomy of persons and to promote equal justice for all.

4. Whether an illness or disease is the result of voluntary persistence in harmful habits such as the sharing of needles among intravenous drug users, or the result of activities generally regarded as morally reprehensible such as engaging in homosexual sex and having sex with prostitutes, society at large is still put at risk and the government has an obligation to protect everyone from the ravages of illnesses and diseases, especially those which threaten to wipe out large numbers of people as AIDS is presently doing. Since the health of society is at stake, those stricken with an illness or disease that threatens society have a title to medical treatment, which ought to be provided at public expense if the individuals so stricken cannot afford to pay for the needed medicines and treatments.

The right to health care, if the argument offered is sound, is a *moral right* because personal autonomy and freedom along with the conditions for their security and enhancement should be respected. This right is *general,* for it does not arise from a particular transaction or special re-lationship; it is prior in importance to these and provides them with their moral quality. The right to health or medical care is *conditional* because its implementation in social institutions is limited by the existing states of these institutions, the quantity of existing material resources, and the continuing reassessment of the effectiveness of the medical and health services provided. The right to health or medical care does not pertain to the person in the same way that civic rights do. This is clearly seen in the matter of imple-mentation. One cannot, for example, be given the right of due process gradually. If full due process is not given each individual in every for-mal and public consideration of his or her case, then that person's right has been violated. The right to health or medical care is more like the right a person has to education, because it is conditioned by the individual's need, the avail-ability of doctors and other health professionals, the availability of materials, and so on. By reason of their right to health or medical care, persons can demand that the government provide for suf-ficient trained professionals with adequate re-sources to meet a range of needs and to deal with many of the most debilitating and difficult problems as these are seen from the perspective of the particular culture. The citizens of any coun-try have the right to demand that the institutions providing health and medical care do so in such a way that the major health needs of their society are met by the most effective use of available medical science and technology for this purpose.

THE AIDS CRISIS

Since 1981 we have gradually come to face AIDS (acquired immune deficiency syndrome) for what it is, an epidemic of a life-threatening disease and so a major public health issue for all of society. Its impact is already devastating. In the United States alone about 1.5 to 2 million people are estimated to be infected by the AIDS virus, named variously by the scientific community HIV (hu-man immunodeficiency virus), HTLV-III (human T-lymphotropic virus type III), or LAV (lemphad-

enopathy associated virus), denoting a virus that attacks white blood cells (T-lymphocytes) in hu-man blood. The AIDS virus attacks the person's immune system, damaging the person's ability to fight off other diseases and/or infections. More than 40,000 persons have already contracted full-blown AIDS, and about half that number have already died because at present there is neither a known cure for nor a vaccine to prevent AIDS. By the end of 1991 an estimated 270,000 cases will have occurred and the death toll will have mounted to an estimated 179,000 persons.[1]

The epidemic is not limited to the continental United States; it is spreading through other coun-tries as well. It is expected to become *the* major international concern during the next ten years. Once a person's immune system has been dis-abled by the virus, that person becomes vulner-able to infection by bacteria, protozoa, fungi, as well as other viruses and malignancies that may cause life-threatening illnesses such as pneu-monia, meningitis, and cancer. The virus may also attack the central nervous system, causing dam-age to the brain. The AIDS virus is not the killer, but the other infections and diseases kill once the immune system has been destroyed or sig-nificantly weakened by the AIDS virus.

For reasons not yet clearly understood, some people remain apparently well after infection with the AIDS virus. They show no obvious symptoms of illness, but they can spread the virus to others through intimate sexual contact and/or sharing hypodermic needles for intravenous drug use. The AIDS virus is not transmitted by everyday casual contact. People living with individuals who have the AIDS virus do not become infected, even though they may embrace, kiss, and share food, towels, cups, razors, and even toothbrushes. The virus is transmitted either through the sharing of blood-contaminated hypodermic needles or dur-ing intimate sexual contact with the infected per-

---

[1]These statistics have been taken from *The Surgeon General's Report on Acquired Immune Deficiency Syndrome*. The sta-tistics are going to change, probably for the worse, as sci-entists and public health officials become more knowledgeable about the extent of the infection and its modes of spreading.

son's blood or semen and possibly vaginal secretions. In such sexual contact the virus enters the bloodstream through the rectum, vagina, or penis. Infected blood donors have also passed AIDS on to others who have received blood transfusions.

What can be done to stop the spread of AIDS? Each person, in keeping with his or her degree of maturity and place in society, must know the facts about AIDS and the types of behavior that place one "at risk." This is something each person can do. You are "at risk" if you engage in "high risk" activities with people who have been infected. "High risk" activities include intimate sexual contact or sharing needles to inject intravenous drugs. Each person has a moral obligation not to engage in "high risk" activities. The AIDS virus has infected people of all ages, races, sexual orientations, and social groups. The only people not "at risk" are couples, both heterosexual and homosexual, who have maintained a monogamous relationship and have been *absolutely* faithful to one another for at least eight years. If either member of such a relationship has used illegal intravenous drugs or had a blood transfusion during that time, that person is "at risk," which also puts his or her partner "at risk." Unless you know with absolute certainty that neither you nor your partner is carrying the AIDS virus, you must take protective measures for your own sake and that of your partner. Complete abstinence is the safest and in some cases the most virtuous course to follow. Should that for whatever reason be impossible or impractical the Surgeon General recommends the following:

1. If you have engaged in any "high risk" activities, you should have a blood test to determine whether you have been infected with the AIDS virus.
2. If your blood test is positive, you should tell your sexual partner and, if you jointly decide to have sex, protect your partner by using a rubber (condom) during sexual intercourse. It should be used from start to finish in both vaginal and rectal (anal) intercourse.
3. If you or your partner is "at high risk," avoid

all mouth contact with the penis, vagina, and rectum.
4. Avoid all sexual activities that can cause cuts or tears in the tissue of the penis, vagina, and rectum.
5. Avoid sex with prostitutes of either sex.
6. If you are an intravenous drug user, use only a clean, previously unused needle to inject the drug solution.
7. If you have engaged in any "high risk" activity, do not donate blood.

The Surgeon General's recommendations are not meant to be a set of moral guidelines; they are factual statements about how the individual can personally reduce the risk of contracting AIDS. Remember that at present there is neither a cure for nor a vaccine to prevent AIDS. Ethics is concerned with the facts only in terms of what morally ought to be done. Society is faced with a health problem of pandemic proportions. That is the fact. What moral obligations does society have in the face of this fact? Our obligation is to stop the spread of AIDS and to find, if possible, a cure for it and a vaccine to prevent it.

The goal we aim at, the common good we seek, is an AIDS-free society and compassionate care for those already stricken with AIDS. Without a cure or a vaccine, we must endeavor to contain the epidemic. What means are available at this time to achieve the goal? Three good means are available: (1) education of the public, (2) voluntary antibody testing coupled with comprehensive counseling, and (3) adequately funded, well-coordinated research to discover a cure and/or vaccine.

Since the goal undoubtedly must be attained, the morally safer course must be taken by using the available good means to attain the goal. First of all, education of the public is necessary because it can help save lives. Informing the public can help ensure that individuals "at risk" will stop engaging in "high risk" activities themselves and make it possible for all of us to deal humanely with those who have AIDS. Fear and ignorance are the greatest threats to society. Accurate information and careful education overcome ignorance and the fear arising from it. Furthermore, individuals "at risk" have a moral obligation to stop engaging in "high risk" activities. Complete abstinence is the safest course these individuals can take to protect their own health and the health of their partners. This is the moral "high road," which some will take and some will not. Those who do not would be well advised at least to follow the Surgeon General's recommendations most carefully.

Secondly, widespread testing for the AIDS antibody must be made available to all who wish to be tested. Testing should be done only with the informed consent of those tested, and comprehensive counseling must also be made available to those tested to help them deal with the serious psychological consequences of a positive test and to help them adopt the behavioral changes mandated by a positive test. Counseling is also important to those who test negative so that they will not be lulled into a false sense of security about their own behavior. Test results can be a valuable tool in educating people only if those tested take the right message from the results. Any testing program must be voluntary, not mandatory, and where possible anonymous or with the strongest guarantees of confidentiality. Informed consent must be obtained from every participant before testing, and antidiscrimination protections must be provided by the government for all who undergo testing or who have AIDS or an AIDS-related condition.

Compulsory blood testing of the general population or of "at risk" individuals is not an ethically acceptable means to reduce the transmission of the infection. Public health officials are almost unanimous in warning against legislation that requires testing. Not only is it not necessary, it would be unmanageable and prohibitively expensive. AIDS is uniformly fatal and leads to great grief and suffering. Mandatory testing would create a climate of distrust and fear, and it would drive into hiding many who are "at risk" for fear of losing jobs, insurance, and their positions of respect within the community. Large sums of money that ought to be spent on general prevention, education, treatment, and research would be diverted into a counterproductive program.

In an open and free society, the real solution to this medical crisis depends on the cooperative spirit of those who may be infected and those who engage in activities which cause them to be "at risk" of infection. The crisis itself must not be used to try to justify unnecessary invasions of privacy when there is no demonstrable impact on the health of the public at large.

Finally, the government in cooperation with public health agencies and the pharmaceutical industry must see that research is funded and coordinated in the most adequate and efficient manner. Much has already been done, but as always much more must be done to fund research adequately and to see that time and effort is not wasted or duplicated but properly coordinated. In the matter of legislation, the government must not only seek to protect the rights of the healthy majority but must also secure the rights of those who are infected and in need of treatment. AIDS must never be used as an excuse to discriminate against any group or individual. Fear and ignorance on the part of the majority can play havoc in any society, especially during an epidemic. Government has a particularly strong obligation to provide the public with accurate information as it becomes available and to educate the public about how to protect against the disease. Government has a further obligation to ensure that providers of health insurance do not discriminate against anyone and at the same time assure those same providers that they will not go bankrupt if they agree to provide health insurance to those "at risk" or who already have AIDS or AIDS-related complex (ARC).

BEHAVIOR CONTROL

Behavior control is the modification of other people's behavior by means other than motivational appeal to their personal freedom. Control is power, and behavior control is the exercise of some kind of power over another so as to get that person to do one's bidding. The moral issue, in the face of the techniques available for behavior control, is the problem of how to use the power justly if it is to be used at all. Without the requirements of justice, which restricts the use of these techniques to benefit the patient, personal freedom is, or could be, endangered by evil manipulators.

Some of the current popular literature may mislead us into believing that more is known about the human brain and its functions than is actually known. It is unlikely that in the foreseeable future we shall acquire the capability to control specific behavior, for example, to administer a drug or to implant an electrode in the brain that can modify neural activity to elicit discrete, fine behavior of a particular kind. Research to date seems to indicate that few areas of the brain are concerned with the regulation of one and only one behavior. No single area in the brain has complete control over any single behavior. Many brain functions are distributed throughout most brain regions. Every thought process involves vast areas of the brain, though some regions may contribute more than others to certain functions.

The age of psychotechnology has *not* arrived. Mass behavior control is *not* imminent. Research is being done on various techniques to control human behavior, and some techniques are already being used. Direct manipulation of the brain is now being done by three methods listed here in the order of least to most severity relative to their direct physical intrusion into the brain: (1) electroshock, also known as electroconvulsive treatment (ECT) or simply shock treatments, (2) electrostimulation of the brain (ESB) by implanting electrodes in specific regions of the brain, and (3) psychosurgery or brain surgery in which part of the brain is surgically removed or destroyed. Each of these methods is used to alter some function of the person's subjective experience—the mind. The assumption is that the brain is at least the neurophysiological basis for all our sensations, emotions, thoughts, and willing, in short, all our mental activity by which we control our behavior. A further assumption of those using these methods is that predictable and therapeutically useful changes in mind function can be gotten by directly altering activity in the brain.

Electroshock therapy has been used to treat severe depression, schizophrenia, and other acute psychoses. The medical community is not in general agreement about how it works, nor is it in general agreement about its desirability. Some doctors are calling for its complete ban, because of the serious side effects such as temporary, long-term, or even permanent memory loss and possible brain damage. More practitioners, however, are supportive of this form of therapy than are against it.

Electrostimulation of the brain is used to prevent responses by disrupting neural circuitry or by activating inhibitory circuits, for example, to overcome chronic insomnia, block epileptic convulsions, suppress aggressiveness, or relieve severe physical or psychological pain. This method triggers or modifies only what is already in the brain; it does not insert new experiences, for example, it does not teach mathematics. Although its usefulness as a therapy is limited, its potential for misuse is rather enormous.

Psychosurgery has aroused the most divisive controversy because it is the most drastic of the behavior control techniques. Different areas of the brain are removed or destroyed in an effort to modify certain sorts of behavior. Among the long list of such behaviors, we find emotional stress, hallucinations, impulsive aggressive behavior, drug addiction, homosexuality, and pain. Schizophrenia, paranoid psychoses, epilepsy, and movement disorders such as Parkinson's disease have at various times been subjected to psychosurgery. At present, neurosurgeons have no way of predicting exactly the short- or long-term consequences of such surgery. The consequences range from complete relief through some or little amelioration to no effect whatever on the symptoms. Side effects such as obliteration of personality have been devastating. Within the medical community, the debate goes on without seeming to come to any general agreement one way or another.

A great deal of care is being given by moralists to assess the values and disvalues in this whole area of behavior control by direct manipulation of the brain. The person's right to autonomy and freedom is to be protected and encouraged insofar as possible with that person. Techniques of behavior control that deny personal autonomy are morally repugnant. Direct manipulation of the brain should be undertaken only when a person's abnormal behavior can be traced to organic brain disease. Certainly none of these methods should be used to treat moral, social, and political problems. In the last resort, however, we have to trust the moral sensitivity and the diagnostic skill of the neurosurgeon in each particular case to determine whether or not one of these methods is indicated.

Obtaining informed consent from the patient for the surgery or other procedure can be a problem. If the patient is unable to make a rational decision, the nearest relatives or someone else will have to give permission. The patient must be protected against others making the decision in their own best interests rather than the patient's. Review committees have been suggested as a guard against this latter difficulty.

All other types of surgery are designed to benefit the overall functioning of the patient, and they are justified for this reason. If the overall functioning is made worse, the surgery is unjustified. Psychosurgery sometimes worsens the overall functioning of the patient, but we never know this until after the fact. Psychosurgery, most moderate opponents would argue, should be a last resort after other methods of treatment have failed. This does not mean, however, that such surgery is to be only a final heroic effort at a cure. Sometimes it is dangerous to wait too long.

Drug Use and Abuse

The indirect control of behavior by the use of *psychotropic* drugs is already widespread, and the science of *psychopharmacology* is growing rapidly. Psychotropic drugs are chemicals that influence the mind and alter behavior, mood, and mental functioning. They are sometimes called *psychoactive* drugs. Depending on the purpose for which they are used, these drugs fall into three main groups: (1) therapeutic drugs of which there are three main classes, (a) the antipsychotic (the major tranquilizers), (b) the antidepression (including the psychomotor stimulants), and (c) the antianxiety (the minor tranquilizers); (2) nontherapeutic drugs for recreation or personal enjoyment: alcohol, hashish, marijuana, psychedelics, and various opiates; and (3) drugs to enhance performance and capabilities (caffeine and amphetamines to counter fatigue and anabolic-androgenic steroids to increase lean body mass and strength).

Therapeutic Drugs

The *antipsychotic* drugs can provide sedative, hypnotic, and mood-elevating effects and are used to treat the major mental illnesses such as schizophrenia, paranoia, and mania by suppressing the symptoms. Note that they do not cure the illness, but by suppressing the symptoms they reduce the period of necessary hospitalization and help ease the patient's return into the community. Maintenance therapy is required over an extended period, often at lesser dosage. These drugs are relatively safe but appear to have a fairly wide range of side effects such as slurred speech, hand tremors, uncontrollable restlessness, jerkiness, and tiredness. These side effects are serious enough to warrant their use only under the direction of a doctor. They should never be used simply to calm minor anxieties.

Antidepressant drugs are not tranquilizers. They tend to stimulate rather than depress the central nervous system and are used for depressed patients. Amphetamine is the most widely known but has little clinical value in treating depression because the changes it induces are of such short duration; it tends to produce psychic dependence and toxic states. As a whole these drugs are generally effective in relieving endogenous depression, but they seem ineffective in relieving the minor ups and downs of everyday life or in relieving the sadness from some emotional setback such as the death of a loved one. They do produce numerous side effects but most are mild.

Many children diagnosed as hyperactive are treated with Ritalin, Dexedrine, or Cylert, which are psychomotor stimulants. Hyperactivity is a behavioral disorder manifesting itself in purposeless physical activity and a significantly impaired span of focused attention. The source of the disorder is not known; it may be some kind of minimal brain dysfunction in about half the cases. Between 500,000 and 2 million school children between 5 and 12 years of age take one of these drugs regularly to control their hyperactivity. The stimulant drug serves to heighten attention focus and so accounts for the paradox that stimulant drugs can reduce overactive behavior. Considerable controversy has arisen over this practice of prescribing psychoactive drugs to achieve social control over children.

The most commonly prescribed groups of psychotropic drugs are the *antianxiety* group, the minor tranquilizers. The oldest and least effective of the group are the barbiturates, the second most widely used means of suicide in the United States. They are effective in the treatment of epilepsy, but they have a high tendency to produce dependence and addiction. Once addicted, a person can die after total withdrawal. Librium, Valium, and Serax are the best of the antianxiety group for the treatment of anxiety, tension, and related states. There are less frequent addictions to these, and they are much less dangerous than barbiturates. Valium is the most frequently prescribed drug in the world. It has been called the poor person's psychiatry. A study by the National Council on Drug Abuse estimates that four-fifths of the soft drug users and one-fourth of hard drug users chronically abuse Valium.

Nontherapeutic Drugs

Nontherapeutic drugs are used for purposes of recreation, pleasure, self-transcendence, and religion. What is sought is a transient feeling of gladness, joy, elation, or simply a relaxation of the day's tensions. While alcohol, tobacco, and caffeinated beverages are culturally accepted and widely used, they pose certain dangers for those who use them. Alcohol provokes aggression more than all psychochemicals. Lesser amounts of alcohol may bring relaxation and a sense of group well-being; higher intake levels, however, can result in physical dependence as well as a number of other disastrous personal, social, and economic effects. Tobacco is hardly a rewarding activity either to those who smoke or to those in their vicinity. We hear and see often enough the warning that cigarette smoking may be hazardous to the smoker's health, and yet people persist in cigarette smoking. The connection between cigarette smoking and lung cancer as well as other respiratory ailments seems clear. Caffeinated beverages such as coffee and tea taken in moderation do not appear to be dangerous.

When we examine the drugs used for pleasure under other than legal conditions, we find a number of odd things. The achievement of a euphoric feeling, a "high," occurs not only with stimulants but also with depressants. Efforts to stay "high" continuously are never successful. The initial period of use may be enjoyable, but continued substantial use can lead to feeling terribly unwell or unhappy, a "downer." Most heroin addicts do not use the drug to get "high;" they need it just to avoid the withdrawal sickness. What initially was an experience of euphoria turns into a losing battle to feel normal.

"Snorting" cocaine, smoking it in the form of "crack," or injecting it intravenously gives a "rush" within moments. The stimulation is intense and the effects dissipate quickly. The various amphetamines are like a longacting cocaine. Amphetamine users are the "speed freaks" of the 1960s and early 1970s. These stimulants are used because of their mood-elevating and energizing properties.

The hallucinogens and psychedelics, including LSD and mescaline, have a way of altering the normal mood state in a way that users find pleasurable. In average doses LSD induces an intensification of sensory awareness, particularly visual awareness. Colors appear more saturated. The object perceived seems to have greater depth and luminosity; it seems enormously meaningful. Immobile objects move. Time is slowed down. Synesthesias are experienced such as the scent of music and the flavor of color. The ego's boundaries along with its critical function are obliterated. Thought, sensation, and emotion seem to fuse into some primordial mental process. The LSD "trip" is an intense, novel, aesthetic experience that seems more novel and intense precisely because the user is unable to be critical of its effects. The controversy over LSD and other hallucinogens and psychedelics arose because of the toxicity associated with them, which led to so many bad "trips" for so many users.

Marijuana *(Cannabis sativa)* as a pleasure-producing drug is second only to alcohol in worldwide popularity. It has been used for both pleasure and self-transcendence and has been used by a number of cultures as a religious ceremonial drug. Marijuana was once thought to have a rather trivial effect on consciousness and behavior, but further research has revealed that it has impairing effects on the lungs, the heart, sex organs, the reproductive system, the brain, and the immune system, as well as on babies born to women who use marijuana. Studies show that the damage done by the active ingredient THC (delta-9-tetrahydrocannabinol) through its affinity for the body's lipoproteins reaches from the molecular structures of life all the way to the mind and personality.

Drugs to Enhance Performance and Capabilities

Developments in this area are mostly as yet in the experimental stage. Whatever drugs emerge from the laboratories into this group will probably represent the most significant advances in psychopharmacology. We shall yet see drugs to enhance learning and improve memory, intellectual functioning, and sexual ability. The development of learning-enhancing drugs is said to be proceeding very rapidly.

In sports, performance aids are used either as an adjunct to training, e.g., anabolic-androgenic steroids, or during competition, e.g., amphetamines. Research in this area has not been extensive. Some benefits have been noted, for example, the use of anabolic-androgenic steroids together with proper diet during training does increase lean body mass and strength and so enhances performance. However, some adverse effects have

also been noted in the use of these drugs: in the liver, along with metabolism changes blood-filled cysts and tumors sometimes develop; development of glucose intolerance and increased blood pressure; frequent mood swings, increased aggressiveness, and changes in libido; males suffer decreased sperm production, testicular atrophy, impotence, and prostatic hyperplasia; and females experience masculinization and menstrual changes. Some of these adverse effects are reversible with discontinued usage of the drug, but some are not.

Moral Assessment

The use of psychotropic drugs is controversial. There are two opposing attitudes toward control of access to these drugs: (1) Many people think the government ought to regulate the pharmaceutical industry more stringently to ensure the safety, efficacy, and purpose of the drugs developed. They fear that serious harm can be done in the course of unregulated medical treatment, and they are also convinced that the public at large needs protection from error and/or excessive greed on the part of both the industry and physicians. (2) Many other people want increased freedom to use whatever drugs they wish for personal, nontherapeutic purposes. These are the people involved in the debate over the legalization of marijuana.

The fundamental moral problem is to determine the values by which behavior ought to be controlled. Certainly self-control of one's behavior is to be preferred to having others control one's behavior. Respect for the freedom and autonomy of each person is basic. However, not everyone is capable of self-control. We have instances of severe psychoses such as schizophrenia that have been helped by treatment with *antipsychotic* drugs. While these drugs do not cure the psychoses, they control the symptoms and facilitate the patient's remission of the symptoms and social readjustment within the larger social community. Drug therapy makes the patient better but not well, sufficiently improved to be out of the mental hospital but not well enough to be fully self-sufficient. Are such patients better off living in the larger society, or should they be kept institutionalized? What is best for the patients? If they can be given the care they need outside the institution, this is what should be done. The opportunities for individual freedom are greatest in a social setting where we can choose those we will interrelate with and in what manner.

The *antidepressant* drugs have sharply reduced the need for hospitalization to care for affective disorders, especially depression. They have also dramatically reduced the need to use electroconvulsive therapy. Perhaps the most controversial aspect of the use of these drugs comes from treating hyperactivity in children. The difficulty appears to be diagnostic, since it is difficult to distinguish children whose learning difficulties are a result of social deprivation or of the limitations in the educational system from those whose difficulties are a result of some kind of minimal brain dysfunction. Too often in the past, both types have been treated indiscriminately with a drug such as Ritalin. The child with the biological abnormality does benefit from being able to focus his or her attention and so to learn. The child who is not abnormal is simply drugged to make him or her easier to handle at home and/ or in school, a situation obviously not for the benefit of the child.

The *antianxiety* drugs are said to be both so overused and abused that many people are concerned that we are becoming an overmedicated society. If we are indeed relying on the use of psychoactive drugs to deal with our everyday anxieties, tensions, disappointments, and frustrations, we are risking physical harm to our bodies along with the possibility of addiction. There is the further fear of moral degeneration, for excessive use of drugs is said to undermine moral fiber. However, actual research contradicts the assumption of overuse and abuse. Most physicians are conservative in prescribing the minor tranquilizers as regards indications, dosage, and duration. Civilizations down through history have used substances to alter mood and behavior. Remember that moods are generalized emotions.

In this area, the individual must decide *whether* to cope with moods on his or her own *or* to seek the help of physician-prescribed drugs. The ideal of self-reliance based on the power of personal freedom and autonomy is a valid human value and better suited to be used in solving personal problems and social dilemmas than are drugs, but at times the drugs can also be a help.

With the *nontherapeutic* use of drugs, we pass from strict medico-moral problems to the larger issues of ethics and social values. Careful distinction must be made between *use* and *abuse*. The use of drugs for pleasure and recreation is a personal choice to control behavior, mood, and experience. Such use is not in and of itself drug abuse. The *antidrug point of view* is that such drug use is a form of weakness and in fact an abuse, because drugs are to be used only for therapeutic purposes. To have everyone abstain from all nontherapeutic use of drugs is the ideal of this group. Many mental-health professionals promote the value of self-restraint in the use of drugs, because they see drug use as a crutch and a refusal to use one's personal powers for securing genuine insight into one's personal life and problems. The *prodrug point of view* sees the exemption of alcohol, caffeine, and nicotine from inclusion among the taboo drugs as an inconsistency in society's values. Many people abuse these exempt drugs and have become addicts, so the prodrug people think that alcohol and tobacco abusers are not to be trusted when they condemn other drugs such as marijuana and cocaine. There is, from the prodrug point of view, nothing wrong with using drugs for pleasure unless we want to be so foolish as to say that pleasure is wrong.

Keeping in mind the distinction between *responsible use* and *compulsive, addictive abuse*, we still have to deal with toxic and other harmful side effects that drugs produce. Until such time as the pharmaceutical industry can produce drugs without toxic or other harmful side effects, we have no right to use nontherapeutically any substance that will damage our health. On the other hand, assume that drugs became available that could induce euphoria, pleasantness, expanded states of awareness, and feelings of well-being without producing the bad effects associated with psychedelics such as LSD or the dependence and addiction associated with heroin and the other opiates. Would we be willing to condone the use of such drugs purely for purposes of recreation and pleasures as we have done for alcohol and tobacco? Before we answer this question, we would do well to reflect on the fact that the capacity for pleasure is also the capacity for pain; they are the very same capacity. That is the dilemma of human life. The technological advances we anticipate with the production of pleasure-giving and learning-enhancing drugs may well heighten our sensitivity to pain and ignorance along with enhancing our abilities to enjoy and to learn. Such advances are bound to have a profound impact on our values and our ideals concerning the nature of the good life.

Narcotic and psychedelic drugs are not evil in themselves and are to be judged from their effects. Under a doctor's supervision, *narcotics* are merciful means for the alleviation of pain. The doctor must balance their desirable and undesirable effects and judge by the principle of double effect that the good they will do outweighs the harm that must be tolerated. The chief danger is that of addiction, but even this danger may sometimes be chanced for a proportionately great good.

People who voluntarily take addictive drugs for the thrill of it ought to know what they are letting themselves in for. No one is morally allowed to bring on the physical deterioration and personality collapse that results from addiction to opium derivatives such as morphine and heroin. From an individual evil it branches out into a social evil, since addicts easily resort to crime to sustain the increasing expense of greater supplies of the dwindlingly effective drug. No individual is allowed, along with accomplishing his or her personal ruin, to burden society the way nearly all addicts do.

Apart from being a menace to him- or herself, the addict who shares the use of needles or syringes with other addicts runs the risk of becoming infected with the AIDS virus and in turn passing on the virus to others. At present, users of intravenous drugs make up 25 percent of the cases of AIDS throughout the country. The AIDS virus is carried in contaminated blood left in the needle, syringe, or other implements, and the virus enters the bloodstream of the new victim who uses the implement. Even the smallest amount of blood left in a used needle or syringe can contain live AIDS virus to be passed on to the next user. For addicts who have not changed their behavior, the only way not to get AIDS is to use a clean, previously unused needle or syringe for the injection of the drug solution.

The *psychedelic* drugs have not yet been sufficiently explored to warrant a firm categorical judgment about them. Their liberating and mind-clarifying effects on some are paralleled by suicidal and dangerous tendencies in others, and in the same person at different times. Since the effects are so uncertain and since no one can predict how he or she will react at a particular time, one who takes these drugs is chancing what may happen and is indirectly responsible for any untoward consequences. No one is allowed to play fast and loose with his or her body, mind, and character for no better justifying reason than the thrill of a "trip." Adolescents are the least qualified to experiment intelligently with these mind-blowing chemicals, and yet they are the ones who find them most appealing. Further knowledge may lead to a revised opinion, and we may find that under proper supervision the heightening of our perceptual powers may lead to marvelously beneficial results, but that is still problematic, and we can make moral decisions only in the light of what we know now.

A final word should be said about the right of access to these new drugs. True, we are responsible to use in a civilized manner the available drugs as well as those being developed. But this is also the point at which fear seems to take over and the desire to regulate drug development and use becomes paramount in people's minds. The problem created by this fear and desire is that those who need behavior control of some sort can be deprived of the drugs they need to achieve control. Our society ought to formulate and guarantee the right to access to new technology as an essential counterbalance to the right to be protected from the abuse of it. People who need the help of these drugs should not be deprived of the benefits such drugs offer.

THE RIGHT TO DIE

Much is still being written and discussed about a person's right to die, especially to die in peace with dignity. A theist approaches this matter with humility, realizing that if errors are made, the safer course morally is to err on the side of life, and knowing that life is a God-given trust over which we have stewardship but not absolute dominion. Both theists and nontheists share in common a respect for the dignity of the person who is seriously ill and possibly dying. Most doctors take seriously the Hippocratic oath and feel a strong obligation to keep the patient alive to the last possible breath with the use of all the means that medical science can provide. This attitude is much to be praised, and we could have no trust in the medical profession if it adopted the opposite attitude. However, even the best of attitudes can become exaggerated, and with the advance of medical technology, the more human aspects of the science have sometimes been lost.

Traditionally, religious leaders, lawyers, and moralists have left to physicians the burden of defining death and clarifying the criteria for determining when death has occurred. The traditional signs are the cessation of spontaneous respiration, heartbeat, and the central nervous system's functions. If any of these three stops for very long, the other two stop shortly thereafter and we then have death. The cessation of these three functions has been, and still is, accurate enough to identify death. However, modern techniques of intensive care loosen the connection between these three vital functions. A brain damaged to the point that the patient will never regain consciousness can still function enough to control some nonconscious functions such as breathing. If the breathing continues, the heart can continue to beat, pumping oxygenated blood to the brain. When the patient cannot eat or drink by himself or herself, nutrients and hydration can be supplied intravenously and so the person can be maintained in coma for a long time. This was the case with Karen Ann Quinlan.

If the coma is irreversible and if the patient also needs to be connected to a respirator to breathe, is the patient already dead or would death occur only when the respirator is turned off? If respiration can be taken over by the patient but the heart can be kept beating only by mechanical means, is the patient alive or dead? In the small percentage of cases where death is uncertain because the traditional criteria are obscured due to the intervention of resuscitation machinery or where irreversible brain damage or permanent coma are suspected, the following criteria have been offered by the Harvard Medical School's Ad Hoc Committee to Examine the Definition of Brain Death:

1. Total unawareness of externally applied stimuli and complete unresponsiveness to even the most painful stimuli.

2. No spontaneous muscular movements and no spontaneous breathing. After the patient is on the mechanical respirator, the total absence of spontaneous breathing is tested by turning off the respirator for three minutes to observe whether any effort is made to breathe spontaneously.

3. No reflexes except those mediated by the spinal cord (pupils fixed and dilated and do not respond to bright light; no ocular movements; no evidence of postural activity; no oral activity; no motor reflexes).

4. An isoelectric or flat electroencephalogram (EEG) for at least a full ten minutes is to be used to *confirm* the three tests above. This is not diagnostic but only confirmatory.[1]

If all the above tests, upon being repeated 24 hours later, reveal no change, the person is to be considered dead on the basis of irreversible brain damage. Note that there are two exceptions to these criteria: (1) patients whose internal body temperature is below 90°F (hypothermia) and (2) patients suffering from administration of central

---

[1] Paraphrased from "A Definition of Irreversible Coma," J.A.M.A. 205: 337–340, 1968.

nervous system depressants (for example, barbiturates).

Apart from the two exceptions just noted, these criteria were offered as a way of determining death only in cases where death cannot otherwise easily or readily be determined by the traditional criteria. Not everyone agrees that the Harvard Committee's criteria are satisfactory. They are regarded as a good test of serious brain damage but not adequate to establish positive brain death. One further criterion has been suggested: the nonconsumption of oxygen by the brain. This can be determined in various ways that we need not detail here.

We should also note that the discussion of criteria for death and the definition of death continue. The only acceptable criteria for death are those that will not falsely consider someone dead. In favor of the Harvard criteria, it can be said that no person known to have met those criteria has survived.

Moralists have been able to preserve a balanced attitude on the question of passive euthanasia precisely because of their distinction between ordinary and extraordinary means. They see that means and techniques have value not in themselves, but in the end to which they lead, that mere biological life is not human life in any valuable sense, and that the death of the person is to be determined by the absence of consciousness and self-control rather than by the impossibility of mechanically stimulating certain organs to function. Hence the distinction between ordinary and extraordinary means is to be measured *humanly* rather than scientifically. A treatment may be common medical practice or involve standard hospital equipment; yet for a particular person the cure may be worse than the disease. If the patient, or the family speaking for the patient, wishes, all the treatment medical science can offer should be given, but there is no moral obligation to ask for it. The doctor should not urge it but clearly explain the alternatives. Especially in terminal cases, there is no point in prolonging life, regardless of trouble and expense, for a few more days, weeks, or even years of torment or coma. It is often better to let

nature take its course so that the patient can die in peace. This is what is meant by passive euthanasia, and from the moral standpoint, supposing the proper conditions present, it seems justified.

Even food and liquids (nutrition and hydration), while not usually considered to be medical therapy or treatment, can at times be considered extraordinary or aggressive care depending on the circumstances. Food and liquids are necessary to sustain life and are generally considered aspects of ordinary care. But for a person in a permanent coma that, as far as can be predicted, is irreversible, are food and liquids ordinary means to sustain life or can they be considered extraordinary? How can something as fundamental as food and drink be considered extraordinary in the medical setting? Does the denial of nutrition and hydration deserve to be called immoral?

If the nutrition can be delivered only by means of a tube inserted into a patient's esophagus, a tube that causes continuous discomfort, and if hydration can be delivered only intravenously, the burden of receiving nutrition and hydration may begin to outweigh the benefits to the patient of continued life. If the purpose of the tube feeding and intravenous hydration is to sustain life and if the procedures only prolong the process of dying, then the provision of nutrition and hydration in such circumstances deserves to be called extraordinary and may morally be omitted in hopeless cases. The decision to discontinue giving nutrition and hydration is not a scientific judgment but rather a human judgment based on the scientific facts known in the particular case. If nothing more can be done medically for the person and, in fact, the person is in the process of dying, the decision to withhold nutrition and hydration is made so that the person can be allowed to die.

Physicians, of course, have their legal and professional responsibilities to consider and must protect themselves against malpractice suits. They should secure written permission from the patient or the patient's representative. Some doctors have no trouble about not using extraordinary techniques in the beginning but cannot bring themselves to turn off a machine that has already been functioning, to "pull the plug." The first is letting nature take its course, but the second looks like direct intervention. Most moralists think that they may be spared such scruples. The initial decision to use or not use the machine is not significantly different from the decision to continue or not continue using the machine now that the case has turned hopeless, and there is no moral obligation to continue doing something useless. The main thrust of the doctor's will here is toward helping the patient, not toward running a machine.

More is being written nowadays on preparing the patient for death. As a rule the medical profession has in the past been unsympathetic in this regard, perhaps because the aim of the whole profession has been the preservation of life and the loss of a patient has therefore been regarded as somehow a medical failure. The profession itself is now seeing more clearly that death is part of life and that the time comes when a particular human life just cannot be saved any longer. Not to save a patient who can be saved for further profitable living is medical failure, though often no one's fault, but the goal of the profession cannot be to make everyone live forever. Rather, it should be part of the purpose of the medical profession to assist people to die well when it has exhausted its resources to help them live well, and physicians should cooperate with nurses, family, friends, social workers, and others to help the patient die with peace and dignity.

MUTILATION

Mutilation is an action by which some part or function of the body is injured or destroyed. To paralyze a part of the body by cutting the nerves is mutilation, but a mere wounding or incision that will heal and leave no disability is not.

The same argument that proves that suicide is wrong also proves that unnecessary mutilation is wrong, whether we inflict it on ourselves or allow others to do it to us. If we have only stewardship or use of our person, we are obliged to keep intact what has been entrusted to our care. We may therefore not part with our members or carve up our bodies on our own authority.

Surgery

We are also obliged to preserve life and health, which is sometimes impossible without surgery. Must we undergo it? If the operation involves great pain or risk or reduces one to a condition in which life would not be worth living, it would be an extraordinary means of preserving life, and one would not be morally obliged to submit to it. But this is not always the case.

What makes mutilation allowable? It is not a mere permitting of a physical evil, such as can be justified by the principle of double effect, but a direct attack on the wholeness of the body, an action directly voluntary, and therefore the accomplishment of a good *by means of an evil*. It is true that it is only a physical evil, but it is morally wrong to inflict physical evil unless one has a right to do so. We do have this right. The principle involved here is the *principle of totality: The part is for the sake of the whole*. By the natural order of things a part of the human body is subordinated to the good of the whole, the various organs, members, and functions existing not for their own sakes but for the purpose of maintaining life in the whole organism. Hence it is a legitimate act of care for one's life and health to sacrifice, when necessary, the part for the sake of the whole.

Well-founded hope of notable improvement in health, efficiency, or appearance can be proportionate reasons for lesser operations.

Organ Transplants

Organ transplantation is a highly technical matter, on which we can make only a few remarks. Blood transfusions, skin and bone grafts, and transplants from animals and from human cadavers are legitimate. The moral difficulty about transplants from other living humans is the unavoidable disability left in the one from whom the organ is taken. If the disability is not disproportionate to the good accomplished, some allow the operation, not on the principle of totality, which does not apply, but on the grounds of love for the neighbor, of which it is a most noble and generous instance.

Heart transplants offer no particular moral difficulty except that it must be certain that the donor is already dead and not killed for the purpose. In this case death cannot be determined by the ceasing of the heartbeat, for a person can be kept alive with an artificial heart, and a heart can be kept going outside the person. It seems safe in practice to conclude that a person is dead when the brain has so deteriorated that no restoration of consciousness will ever be possible. Medical science, whose business it is to make such judgments, follows the criteria mentioned earlier in connection with the right to die. Until further research discovers more, we do well to follow the best information available.

Sterilization

Sterilization is a form of mutilation, for, though it can be done simply by ligature without depriving the body of a physical part, it renders impossible one of the body's natural functions, the power of reproduction. Because this power is for the race rather than the individual, it involves a special problem.

1. *Indirect* sterilization, when sterility is but the foreseen effect of something else that is done, is allowable by the double-effect principle. *Direct* sterilization is the production of sterility itself as an end or a means. It follows the principles set down for mutilation: it is allowable if required for the life or health of the whole body. Mere sterilization is not at present the remedy for any disease, but should it become so it may be done. This form might be called *therapeutic* sterilization.

2. May the state impose sterilization as a punishment for crime, especially for sex crimes? On the one hand, if the state has the authority to put criminals to death, a question that is disputed and discussed in the chapter on government, it *may* have the authority to decree sterilization as

a punishment, and for sex offenders it is a punishment that seemingly fits the crime. On the other hand, sterilization is useless because it destroys neither the desire nor the possibility of sex satisfaction, but only renders it unfruitful, a situation sex criminals would not resent. Hence *punitive* sterilization, despite a questionable theoretical justifiability, is practically ineffective and immoral because it neither saves the life nor the health of the sex offender.

3. Some people wish to undergo sterilization to avoid parenthood, and some doctors wish to produce it when they foresee danger in future pregnancy. It is being advocated as a means of controlling overpopulation, especially in underdeveloped countries. Such *contraceptive* sterilization has the same morality as that of contraception, with the added effect of making it a permanent condition. Contraception is discussed later in the chapter on sex.

4. Sterilization is proposed also as a *eugenic* measure. The study of eugenics deals with the development of a better breed of human beings by methods commonly used in the breeding of animals. Eugenists are alarmed by the low birth rate among the more successful classes of society, and by the high birth rate among the less gifted groups, especially the mentally deficient. They see the best families dying off, while the diseased, feeble-minded, shiftless, and criminal elements are multiplying apace, thus bringing about a gradual deterioration in the general level of human excellence. Therefore they argue that defective strains must be eliminated from the race.

The factual case for eugenics is very shaky. Most scientists agree that there is no real evidence that the human race is deteriorating and that, even if it were, sterilization is not the remedy. Even if sterilization were effective, is it a means that is morally permissible? Though surgically only a minor operation, sterilization is a major mutilation because it deprives one of a very important natural function. No one is allowed to submit to a major mutilation unless it is necessary to save one's life or health. Eugenic sterilization is not done for the sake of the individual's life or health but solely for some problematic effect it may have on the future of the race. Therefore in eugenic sterilization the reasons that alone can justify mutilation are not present, and this act is morally wrong.

If *voluntary* sterilization is thus morally wrong, the state has no right to order *compulsory* sterilization. Eugenic sterilization is not inflicted in punishment of crime, since it deals with disabilities that are presumably only hereditary. The state has the obligation to protect its citizens in their rights and not to maim them for something not their fault. The good of the society may require the segregation of harmful defectives, which adequately prevents any damage they can cause. The main reasons that the state favors sterilization is that it can then turn defectives loose on society without fear that they will burden the state with families they cannot care for. This financial argument has no moral value whatever.

It may be objected that just as the members of the individual body exist for the sake of the whole and may be sacrificed for the good of the whole, so may the members of the social body; defectives may be called on to sacrifice the possibility of offspring for the benefit of society. Only in a totalitarian state could such an argument be admitted. The citizen is not wholly for the state and has natural rights the state must protect, among which is the right to bodily completeness. According to this argument the state could kill them just as readily. No matter how much it would help the public welfare, the state has no right to kill or mutilate its citizens.

HUMAN EXPERIMENTATION

The development and expansion of medical knowledge depends on research, and sound medical research ultimately must resort to experimentation on human beings. Scientific knowledge is neither the only value nor the highest value to which all other values are subordinate. The human person has an intrinsic value and dignity and may not be used as a mere means to some higher good or to the greater good of society.

When science takes up human beings as its experimental subject, two values immediately come into conflict: the freedom of scientific inquiry and the individual inviolability of the person. If this primary inviolability of the person is to be infringed on by experimentation, some justification in terms of values and needs must be offered. What values are being gained to compensate for the values surrendered?

In a certain sense every medical procedure is experimental. Administering an antibiotic to see if it will lower a fever or doing a barium X-ray to determine the condition of the stomach or intestines is experimental because the outcome is not absolutely certain. Furthermore, every common medical and surgical procedure entails some risk. All the same, most commonly used procedures have been well tested and established so we can be fairly certain of their results. They are therapeutic rather than experimental even though there is always the possibility that they will not work on this particular case or will be harmful to this particular patient. A truly experimental procedure is one that has not been thoroughly tested and established and so its outcome is as yet problematic.

Experimentation on the patient for the direct benefit of the patient is justifiable when established procedures either do not work or do not exist, because the physician is trying to cure the patient. The experimental procedure may be used as long as the risk involved is not disproportionate to the benefit desired. There is little danger in a situation such as this, because a conscientious physician will take no unnecessary risks but only those warranted by the needs of the patient.

The danger of abuse lies much more clearly in experimentation done on the patient but not for the specific benefit of the patient. Such experimentation is done on that patient for the expansion of medical knowledge that, it is hoped, will benefit others. Here is where the conflict arises between the scientist's freedom of inquiry and the rights, dignity, and security of the patient. Such experimentation requires the explicit consent of the *informed* patient. The knottiest problems are here. When is the subject fully informed? How can the researcher explain risks that often are unknown? What constitutes an adequate explanation for a person not trained in medicine? When is the patient's consent truly voluntary and free? How free is a patient who is dependent on his or her physician?

The Department of Health, Education, and Welfare (DHEW) in 1974 issued regulations in this matter of informed consent:

1. A fair explanation of the procedures to be followed and their purposes, including identification of any procedures that are experimental
2. A description of the attendant discomforts and risks reasonably to be expected
3. A description of the benefits reasonably to be expected
4. A disclosure of appropriate alternative procedures that might be advantageous for the subject
5. An offer to answer any inquiries concerning the procedures
6. An instruction that the person is free to withdraw his/her consent and to discontinue participation in the project or activity at any time without prejudice to the subject

Clearly, DHEW recognizes in these guidelines the near impossibility of attaining fully informed consent and appears to settle for *reasonably informed consent*. This may be all that is possible in such a situation.

Because of the problems with getting even reasonably informed consent, some doctors and moralists argue that no experiments should be performed on children, mental incompetents, or prisoners. The only exception to this rule would be for experiments involving no risk at all. The rationale for strict limits to medical experimentation is that it is better to set limits than risk experimenting on someone without his or her informed and free consent. In the final analysis, the burden of the responsibility for ethical experimentation lies with the researcher who must see to it that the experiment is ethical from beginning to end.

HEALTH CARE FOR RADIATION VICTIMS

Nuclear experimentation and weapons testing by the government have created health problems for the subjects of those experiments and tests, and these programs pose a moral problem for the government. Radiation exposure constitutes a definite hazard to a person's health; the higher the level of radiation, the greater the hazard. This we now know and have known for a long time. In the early days of nuclear testing many a serviceman served without protective clothing at nuclear test sites in Nevada, New Mexico, Bikini, and Eniwetok. These men were placed dangerously close to the point of detonation. In Nevada servicemen were put in trenches during the actual blasts, and then were sent into the immediate area devastated by the nuclear explosion to determine how combat troops would function in a nuclear battlefield. Near Bikini and Eniwetok servicemen were ordered to stand in the open during the blasts, again without protective clothing. During all of these experiments and tests, the men were exposed to dangerous levels of radiation and are now suffering and dying from the effects of that radiation in the forms of leukemia, bone cancer, and other radiation-related illnesses.

The responsible authorities obviously did not know at the time just how dangerous to these servicemen their orders were. At least this is the presumption we must make in order not to regard those responsible as simply monstrous and totally immoral. Each new test yielded further knowledge and some fearful surprises such as the extent of harmful fallout from a nuclear blast. All the same, it is difficult to comprehend how military commanders could place their men in such grave danger, especially in view of the fact that the nation was not at war. The ignorance of the commanders, if that is what it was, may have been inculpable although it gives every appearance of having been culpable.

We have argued earlier in this chapter that everyone has a right to medical care and, to the credit of the government, civilian victims of radioactive fallout in Japan and the Marshall Islands have received the care to which they were entitled. To the everlasting shame of administration after administration of the United States government, our own service veterans have been denied medical help and yet they are suffering and dying from radiation-related illnesses stemming from their time in the service. The government steadfastly refuses to recognize them as radiation victims. The government, furthermore, failed to warn them of the potentially harmful effects of radiation exposure when they were discharged from active military service.

Clearly the government has a *moral obligation* to seek out the people who under orders participated in these tests and a *moral obligation* to see that each and every one of them receives the medical help necessary. If anyone has a right to medical care, these veterans certainly do. A great injustice was done them, and they continue to be treated unjustly. We need legislation to provide uniform compensation and medical care for all radiation victims.

CONCLUSION

This and the preceding chapter deal with the dignity of the human person as a living being. The exercise of the right to life can be looked down on as "mere survival" and rated low on the scale of values as something brutish rather than ennobling. So it may appear if we overdo the contrast between it and the heroic sacrifice of one's life in a great cause. But we are not always faced with such sharp alternatives, and it is in the calm flow of our everyday life that the pattern of right living appears. We have to respect our own persons and the person of others. We may not tamper irresponsibly with our own bodies or neglect proper care of our bodies. We may not subject other persons to ourselves by treating them as things to be destroyed for our own advantage. We may assert our right when attacked and defend ourselves against aggression, since we are not made to be misused by others. Life itself is beset with many risks, and we cannot shrink from all of them without losing our per-

sonhood, but if we must live dangerously, the danger must be such as to be humanly worthy. Life is entrusted to each of us to be used responsibly as befits one endowed with the dignity of being a person.

SUMMARY

Health is tentatively defined as the person's capacity to maintain a favorable, self-regulated state of being that is a prerequisite for the effective performance of an indefinitely wide range of functions both within the person's anatomical-physiological system and in relation to the person's physical, psychological, sociocultural, and spiritual environment. *Illness* is the group of signs or symptoms that the person feels and/or recognizes as disrupting in some degree his or her capacity to function as usual. *Disease* is a disorder or cause of a disorder of a certain kind within the range of ongoing life functions.

Deliberate exposure of life to risk is allowable when the four conditions of the *principle of double effect* are satisfied. To estimate the proportion, note that danger may be ordinary or extraordinary, proximate or remote, certain or probable, or barely possible. Even when we are allowed to risk our lives, we are not obliged to do so, except under special conditions.

We have no moral obligation to maintain our health simply for its own sake, but by reason of other moral obligations we must take reasonable care of it. We are not obliged to take *extraordinary means* to preserve our health, such means being judged *relatively to the condition of the person*.

Malformed and/or defective infants have an equal right to life and care along with all other members of society, but it seems morally justifiable to omit or withdraw treatment when an infant is somewhere between anencephaly and mongolism *and* (1) when convalescence is going to be long, painful, and oppressive and the prognosis is poor; and/or (2) when the infant's life expectancy will be brief and possible only with the use of artificial feeding. If an infant is in either or both of these situations, its potential for human relationships is more than likely going to be lost in the very effort to survive and the infant can be said to have already achieved its human potential.

The *right to health* is a natural moral right based on our right to life and our right to preserve that life. The *right to health care* is a moral right that is both general and conditional—*moral,* because personal autonomy and freedom along with the conditions for their security and enhancement should be respected; *general,* because it does not arise from a particular transaction or relationship but is prior in importance to these and provides them with their moral quality; and *conditional,* because its implementation in social institutions is limited by the existing states of these institutions, the quantity of existing material resources, and the continuing reassessment of the effectiveness of the medical and health services provided. A person's illness and/or disease is that person's entitlement to the health care.

AIDS (acquired immune deficiency syndrome) is caused by a virus that attacks white blood cells (T-lymphocytes) in human blood, damaging the person's ability to fight off other diseases and infections. Each person who has had intimate sexual contact with or shared drug syringes with an infected person is "at risk" of contracting AIDS and has a moral obligation to avoid intimate sexual contact with others and/or sharing needles to inject intravenous drugs. Society as a whole has a moral obligation to contain the epidemic even though there is as yet neither a known cure nor a vaccine to prevent AIDS. The goal of containing the epidemic must be attained, hence the safer course of using the available good means must be taken, namely (1) education of the public, (2) voluntary antibody testing coupled with comprehensive counseling, and (3) adequately funded, well-coordinated research to discover a cure and/or vaccine.

Behavioral control is the modification of other people's behavior by means other than motivational appeal to their personal freedom. Techniques for exerting this control involve either *direct* manipulation of the brain by (1) electroshock or electroconvulsive treatment, (2) electro-stimulation of the brain by implanting electrodes, and (3) psychosurgery or *indirect* manipulation of the brain by use of psychotropic (psychoactive) drugs. The person's right to autonomy and freedom is to be protected and encouraged insofar as possible with that person. Direct manipulation of the brain should be undertaken only when a person's abnormal behavior can be traced to organic brain disease. If the patient is capable of giving informed consent, that consent must be obtained before treatment is begun. The best interests of the patient must always be primary, even when someone else must take the responsibility for giving consent for treatment.

Psychotropic drugs fall into three main groups: (1) therapeutic drugs of which there are three main classes, (a) the antipsychotic (major tranquilizers), (b) the antidepression, and (c) the antianxiety (minor tranquilizers); (2) nontherapeutic drugs for recreation or personal enjoyment, including alcohol, marijuana, cocaine, the psychedelics, and the opiates; and (3) drugs to enhance performance and capabilities, which are mostly as yet in the experimental stages. Therapeutic use of psychotropic drugs is allowable under the direction of properly licensed medical doctors when the drug has some value for the patient. Nontherapeutic use of psychoactive drugs is allowable if the drugs produce no toxic or other harmful side effects such as addiction.

Each person has a *right to die* in peace and dignity. In terminal cases there is no need to prolong life uselessly by extraordinary means. This is *passive euthanasia.*

Mutilation is the destruction of some member or function of the body. Since we have only use ownership over ourselves, mutilation is not allowable at will. Mutilation, since it is a direct attack on the wholeness of the body, is justified on the principle that *the part is for the sake of the whole,* and is allowable only to save life or, in lesser mutilations, to obtain a proportionate improvement in well-being. Organ transplants can be justified within limits.

Sterilization is depriving a person of the reproductive function. Like other mutilations it is moral when necessary for life or health. As a punishment for sex crimes, its morality would be questionable even if it were effective, but it is not. As a contraceptive measure, its morality must be judged by the same standards as that of contraception. As a eugenic measure, it can neither be justified if done voluntarily, because it is not required to save the life or health of the individual, nor if done compulsorily by the state, because the victim is guilty of no crime which could conceivably justify such a procedure.

Sound medical research ultimately depends on *human experimentation*. Two values come in conflict when the research is done not for the direct benefit of the subject but to advance medical knowledge for the benefit of others: (1) the freedom of scientific inquiry and (2) the individual inviolability of the person. In every case, informed consent of the patient or the patient's

representative is required. Experimentation for the direct benefit of the subject is justifiable when established procedures either do not help or are not available and when the risk involved is not disproportionate to the benefit desired. Experimentation not for the direct benefit of the subject is justifiable with the informed consent of the subject and when the attendant discomfort and risks are not disproportionate. Research on children, mental incompetents, and prisoners is probably unjustifiable because of the near impossibility of getting informed consent. Military personnel present a peculiar problem when it comes to getting truly informed consent. Commanders are grossly immoral when they order their troops into experimental situations without asking for volunteers and explaining clearly the hazards involved.

Questions for Discussion

1. The right to privacy on the part of an individual can be in relational tension with the rights of all other persons who are members of the same society. Does George, who has just tested positive for antibodies to the AIDS virus and is engaged to be married, have a moral obligation to tell his fiancée? George chooses to remain silent because he does not want to ruin his marriage plans. As George's physician, how would you advise him?

2. You are chairperson of the U.S. Senate's Health committee, which is presently holding hearings to determine the need for health insurance for the poor. They obviously cannot afford to pay for their own health coverage. Does the committee have any moral obligations to recommend legislation in this matter? If so, what are those obligations? If not, why not?

3. Given the rapid advances being made in fetal medicine and in neonatology, it is possible to transplant hearts, kidneys, and other organs from unborn fetuses. Would it be possible to work out some kind of arrangement with an abortion clinic to harvest needed organs while

the fetuses destined for abortion are still alive? Would this be advisable? Do we need some sort of public policy in this regard? What sort of policy would you recommend?

4. Driving violations by alcoholics under the influence are on the increase. Clearly this is behavior that ought to be controlled for the good of society. You are a mayoral candidate in a large western city that has a high incidence of alcoholism and of related driving violations. Part of your platform is a proposal to commit all alcoholics who drive while drunk either to treatment in a special medical clinic or to jail. Can you make such a law palatable to enough civil libertarians to get yourself elected? How would you go about your task?

5. The AIDS crisis is growing more acute with each passing day and we still do not have a vaccine to counter the killer virus. Normally, the development of a new medicine or vaccine for human use is subjected to long periods of animal tests before it is ever used on humans. But AIDS patients are dying every day. Can the government condone using AIDS

patients in place of laboratory animals to test these new medicines and vaccines? If so, how would you argue the case?

Readings

The problems treated in this chapter are given extensive treatment in several sources, one of the best being Warren T. Reich (editor-in-chief), *Encyclopedia of Bioethics,* 4 vols.

Books devoted to medical ethics are more than plentiful. From the Catholic point of view, we have John F. Dedek *Contemporary Medical Ethics;* Bernard Häring, *Medical Ethics* and *Ethics of Manipulation: Issues in Medicine, Behavior Control and Genetics;* Richard McCormick, *How Brave a New World? Dilemmas in Bioethics;* Thomas J. O'Donnell, *Medicine and Christian Morality,* a third revision of his *Morals and Medicine;* William E. May, *Human Existence, Medicine and Ethics;* Benedict M. Ashley and Kevin D. O'Rourke, *Health Care Ethics: A Theological Analysis.* Other works in this area are also excellent and to be recommended highly: Paul Ramsey, *The Patient as Person;* Tom L. Beauchamp and James F. Childress, *Principles of Biomedical Ethics;* Robert M. Veatch, *A Theory of Medical Ethics;* Stanley Hauerwas with Richard Bondi and David B. Burrell, *Truthfulness and Tragedy: Further Investigations into Christian Ethics;* George H. Kieffer, *Bioethics: A Textbook of Issues;* James B. Nelson, *Human Medicine: Ethical Perspectives on New Medical Issues;* Harmon L. Smith, *Ethics and the New Medicine;* Bernard Vaux, *Biomedical Ethics: Morality for the New Medicine;* Ruth Macklin, *Mortal Choices: Bioethics in Today's World.* H. Tristram Engelhardt's *The Foundations of Bioethics* is particularly challenging to natural law ethics.

Care of defective newborns is given in-depth treatment in Earl E. Shelp's *Born to Die? Deciding the Fate of Critically Ill Newborns* and in Rasa Gustaitis and Ernlé W.D. Young's *A Time to Be Born, A Time to Die: Conflicts and Ethics in an Intensive Care Nursery.*

Books of readings in medical ethics are too numerous and diverse to be mentioned in detail, but two collections are extraordinary in the range of topics treated and the importance of the material included. They are Stanley Joel Reiser, Arthur J. Dyck, and William J. Curran (eds.), *Ethics in Medicine: Historical Perspectives and Contemporary Concerns* and H. Tristram Engelhardt and Daniel Callahan (eds), *The Foundations of Ethics and Its Relationship to Science,* 4 vols.

Special mention should be given to Ivan Illich's *Medical Nemesis: The Expropriation of Health,* which documents the thesis that modern medicine is itself a major threat to our health; and to Germain Grisez and Joseph M. Boyle's *Life and Death with Liberty and Justice: A Contribution to the Euthanasia Debate,* which sorts out the ethical issues and discusses most of the pertinent literature on the topic. Karen Grandstrand Gervais gives a thorough analysis of problems and questions about definitions of death in her *Redefining Death.*

On drug use and abuse, the following are helpful: Peggy Mann's *Marijuana Alert,* which presents hard scientific evidence on the damaging effects of marijuana, and Arnold S. Trebach's *The Great Drug War: And Radical Proposals That Could Make America Safe Again.* On performance-enhancing drugs in sports, consult *1985 Yearbook of Sports Medicine* and *1986 Yearbook of Sports Medicine* as well as Tom Donohoe and Neil Johnson's *Foul Play: Drug Abuse in Sports.*

On the AIDS epidemic, one of the most important pieces of imformation is *Surgeon General's Report on Acquired Immune Deficiency Syndrome,* available free of charge from U.S. Department of Health and Human Services. Dennis Altman's *AIDS in the Mind of America: The Social, Political, and Psychological Impact of a New Epidemic,* David Black's *The Plague Years: A Chronicle of AIDS, The Epidemic of Our Times,* George Jacobs and Joseph Kerrins's *The AIDS File: What We Need to Know About AIDS Now!,* Randy Shilts's *And the Band Played On* all provide important information on the history and implications of the epidemic. Two special supplements of *The Hastings Center Report,* "AIDS: The Emerging Ethical Dilemmas" (Vol.15, no.4, August, 1985) and "AIDS: Public Health and Civil Liberties" (Vol. 16, No. 6, December, 1986) deal directly with many ethical issues.

Much of the writing on bioethical issues is currently being published in periodicals, among which we should mention *The Hastings Center Report,* published by the Institute of Society, Ethics and the Life Sciences and devoted entirely to bioethical issues; *The Journal of Medicine and Philosophy,* which is excellent; and *The American Journal of Law and Medicine,* which is very helpful. The National Academy of Sciences publishes periodic reports of bioethical interest.

Atomic veterans and their plight are ably discussed by Thomas H. Saffer and Orville E. Kelly, *Countdown Zero,* and by Michael Uhl and Tod Ensign, *GI Guinea Pigs: How the Pentagon Exposed Our Troops To Dangers More Deadly Than War, Agent Orange and Atomic Radiation.* See also Howard Ball, *Justice Downwind: America's Atomic Testing Program in the 1950s,* and Richard L. Miller, *Under The Cloud: The Decades of Nuclear Testing.*

For bibliography on health, health care, and related topics see *The Hastings Center Bibliography of Society, Ethics and the Life Sciences,* which is published annually with annotations. Bioethics Digest provides summaries of literature on medical ethics.

21
Truthfulness

PROBLEM

Now that we have examined questions relating to health, we turn to one of the most important areas of the personal life, interpersonal communication. We take care of our health precisely so that we can live in meaningful relationships with others and enjoy the values surrounding our relationships. Among those values is truthfulness. All of us claim respect for our own personhood as conscious rational subjects and must show similar respect for our neighbor's personhood by putting right order in the communications between our own minds and feelings and the minds and feelings of others. Whoever speaks is expected to speak truthfully, but we can still ask whether we are always obliged to speak truthfully. Is truth-telling an absolute value in any and every circumstance?

When we think about truthfulness, we usually think first of all about intellectual honesty and almost never give a thought to emotional sincerity, which is another name for emotional honesty. We are very sensitive to the virtues and vices of the mind; we admire a truthful person and are repelled by a liar. Lying is despicable, shameful, and immoral; it is intellectual dishonesty, intellectual insincerity. Our emotional life has its parallel to this, for we can express emotions we do not feel and deceive others about the emotions we actually do feel. We can lie not only about the truth we know but about the emotions we have as well.

The problem of truth-telling arises from the fact that a person may also have a right or a duty to conceal the truth about what he or she thinks or feels. Each of us has a right to privacy. We may be entrusted with a secret that must not be divulged. There might not be much trouble on this point if people did not have the habit of asking questions, but then the privilege of inquiring goes with the gift of speech. What can we do when questioned point blank on a matter we must keep secret? How can we veil our speech to guard the truth as well as to communicate it? Does a phy-

sician, for example, have a duty to tell the patient the whole truth and nothing but the truth? Are there occasions when the substance of our humanity is too frail to bear the full burden of the truth? Certainly our social world cannot endure without the truth and yet if the absolute truth were always to prevail in human affairs, we could not endure it. We need to explain:

1. What is a lie?
2. Are all deceptions lies?
3. Why and how far is lying wrong?
4. Why must secrets be kept?
5. How can secrets be kept without lying?

MEANING OF A LIE

What is a lie? The literal-minded person may define a lie as any statement not in strict literal accord with actual facts. But no one with the faintest spark of imagination or the most primitive inkling of courtesy could confine his or her speech within such narrow bounds. Speech not only exchanges information but also contributes to the amenities of life. Candor has its place, but the outspoken telling of the unvarnished truth on every occasion would lose us all our friends and make us unfit for society. Speech need not always be used thus, and this literal-minded definition would require a distinction between lies that are allowable and those that are not, between so-called white lies and black lies. A better procedure is to reserve the word *lie* for the misuse of speech that is morally wrong and to define it accordingly. To distinguish it from the looser usages of everyday speech, we may call it a *strict* or *formal* lie. We are concerned with it alone.

Commenting on St. Augustine's[1] definition of a lie as "a false statement uttered with intent to deceive," St. Thomas[2] says that it contains three things:

1. The falsity of the statement. This provides the material for a lie, for it is not a lie to say what

---

[1]St. Augustine, *De Mendacio* (On Lying), ch. 4; *Contra Mendacium* (Against Lying), ch. 12.
[2]St. Thomas, *Summa Theologica,* II–II, q. 110, a. 1.

is actually false while thinking it true, though it is a lie to say something is actually true while knowing it to be false.

2. The will to tell the falsity. The essential element of a lie as a human act is the willful disconformity between one's thought and one's speech, so that it is "speech contrary to one's mind."[1]

3. The intention to deceive. This is the usual motive for lying and indicates its normal effect on the one lied to. The intent need not be efficacious, as when a liar knows that he or she will not be believed.

Some add a fourth, that a lie must be:

4. Told to one who has a right to the truth. If this addition is properly understood, it will make the explanation of lying much simpler and clearer. It should not mean that we can say anything and everything we want to a person merely because that particular person has no strict right to demand the truth of us. It must be presumed that anyone to whom we speak has the right to be spoken to truthfully if we speak to him or her seriously on any matter at all. Respect for the person as a person requires that we speak truthfully. Someone loses this right only when we have the greater right to withhold the truth and cannot do so by silence. In this case speech must be used to conceal rather than reveal the truth, and what we are really communicating to the person is the fact that we are not communicating. Such a person should be able to take the hint that he or she is not being lied to but is being put off.

The person who has the right to the truth about what we think may also have a right to know the truth about what emotions we feel. If it is to this person's advantage or to someone else's advantage that he or she know what I feel, if it makes a real difference to this person or to another, then to express an emotion I do not feel and/or to conceal emotions I actually do feel is a failure to be honest. To express an emotion I do not

feel is, in this context, emotional insincerity, a kind of emotional untruthfulness; to fail to express what I actually do feel is, in this same context, a suppression of the truth, an act of dissimulation. To express love for a person when I do not feel it is one of the most cruel forms of emotional insincerity, just as it is equally insincere to conceal my true feelings from someone to whom the knowledge would make a real difference. Other examples of this kind of dishonesty are pretending to like things or persons we do not like or pretending to feel sympathy or joy for a person when we do not. Just as a person who habitually trifles with the truth tends to lose the ability to distinguish between truth and falsity, so a person who habitually cheats others about his or her emotions soon becomes unable to know what he or she really feels. The end result is not only deception of others but self-deception as well. When we tamper with the sincerity of our emotional life we destroy our own inner integrity, we become unreal for ourselves and for others, and we lose the ability to know what we actually feel.

The problem comes down to the nature of speech as a medium of communication and its function in human society. For a strict lie there must be an indication, at least in the circumstances, that:

1. Serious communication is going on.
2. It is meant to be taken as true.
3. It is being accepted by the hearer as true.
4. Yet it is known by the speaker to be false.

Conventionality of Speech

It is natural for us to speak, but apart from a few obvious gestures and imitative sounds, there is no natural language. The so-called natural languages are merely those that were never consciously invented but grew up historically. Language is *conventional,* the symbols used being developed by human artifice and dictated by custom. Hardly any word has a single univocal meaning whenever used, like the symbols of

---

[1] A commonly accepted definition of lying, but embodying only the first two elements.

mathematics. Language is a peculiar mixture of logic and tradition, in which the conventions are undergoing subtle but continual change. By convention we distinguish fact and fiction, literal and figurative expressions, jokes and serious statements, emotional outbursts and sober information, ironical allusions and scientific data, polite compliments and solemn testimony. Often nothing but circumstances indicates the difference.

1. Communication is not limited to words but is *any sign used to convey thought*. Looks, gestures, nods, winks, shrugs, facial expressions, tones of voice, and even the circumstances in which something is said are all signs capable of telling another what we think and, if used for this purpose, are communication. Lying is possible by any of these means.

2. The sign must be *intended* by the speaker *to convey a meaning*. Involuntary looks and gestures are not communication. It is not always lying to conceal our emotions under outward calm nor to appear cheerful when we are sad, but only when we are intentionally using our appearance to express our real feelings.

3. The sign must be made *to another person*, for communication is between personal selves. It is impossible to lie to oneself, nor would it be lying to confide untruths to one's dog. Talk in other people's presence, when it is clearly not directed to them, is not communication to them. Eavesdroppers listen at their own peril.

4. The sign must be such as to *express the speaker's own judgment*, what he or she believes to be true. To lie, therefore, the speaker must express as true something thought to be untrue, or as certain something not known for certain. If I mistakenly think that what I say is true, though in fact it is not, I do not lie; my speech is untrue but not untruthful.

5. *Fiction* is not lying, for the story is used as an expression of one's creative imagination and entertaining ability, not of one's factual judgment. Jokes and exaggerations are not lies if there is any circumstance to indicate that they are not to be taken seriously.

6. *Figures of speech* are not lies. When a word has several meanings, its sense in this particular statement must be judged by the context and the meaning of the whole statement by the total situation. Sometimes we speak literally, sometimes figuratively, and the figurative meaning can be just as genuine as the literal.

7. Many *polite expressions* and *stereotyped formulas* have lost old meanings and acquired new ones through convention. "Not guilty" in a law court is a legal plea by which the accused does not confess but demands that the case be proved. "Good morning," "goodbye," "how do you do," "see you later" once meant something but are now mere forms of greeting and parting. How far one can go in the use of polite excuses depends on convention. "Not at home," "in conference," "occupied," "too busy," "previous engagement" are recognized as urbane ways of putting one off, depending on the circumstances. Once these probably were lies, but use has softened their import.

8. *Circumstances* can be such that, though words are used, there is no formal speech because no communication is intended nor should it be expected. A captured soldier, for instance, may regale his captors with tall stories about the disposition of his own troops. Even if they are foolish enough to believe him, he is not lying because circumstances show that he is entertaining and not communicating. The case is different if a prisoner is put on parole and seriously accepts the conditions.

Lying and Deception

Deception is the usual motive for lying, but we must not confuse these two concepts. Feints, disguises, impersonations, fictitious names, and other such pretenses are deceptions but not lies. The difference is in the lack of communication in the sense just explained. Deception is not wrong in itself but can become wrong from motives and circumstances if intended or foreseen as a cause of harm. The wrong comes not from the act done, which is indifferent, but from the consequences, the harm that follows.

Most games are built on harmless deception. Even harmful deception may be permitted in the protection or vindication of one's rights, according to the principle of double effect. Thus stratagems and military maneuvers in war may be designed deliberately to mislead the enemy. Such deceptions are not lies because nothing is *said,* no judgment is expressed, no statement is made by the usual symbols of communication. Actions are done, it is true, but if the enemy takes a meaning out of them, he does so at his own peril. The intent to deceive may be justified on the grounds that one is defending one's own rights and merely permitting the enemy to harm himself. Some even classify the presentation of forged passports and other documents to elude an unjust government as deceptions but not lies, because circumstances show that they are not communications but only an external compliance with demands the officials have no right to make.

Hugo Grotius[1] correctly distinguishes between lies and stratagems, but his application is poor; he classes among stratagems some actions that really are lies: to tell a falsehood to do someone a service, to use false intelligence to encourage troops, and his approbation of Plato's "noble lie"[2] told for the public welfare. These are not stratagems, actions capable of a deceptive interpretation, but lies. A free hand cannot be given to one of the worst forms of lying yet invented, mass propaganda of militant nationalism.

ARGUMENTS ON LYING

We have shaved down a lie to the minimum because people use speech loosely and give it other social functions besides that of communicating thought. There remains an irreducible residue: speech meant and taken in all seriousness as communication from person to person. The hearer trusts the speaker and has a right to be told the truth if he or she is told anything. Hence lying in the sense defined and explained, which we have called a *strict* or *formal* lie, is a morally evil act. St. Thomas's argument cites Aristotle and St. Augustine:

As words are naturally signs of intellectual acts, it is unnatural and undue for anyone to signify by words something that is not in his mind. Hence the Philosopher[3] says that lying is in itself evil and to be shunned, while truthfulness is good and worthy of praise. Therefore every lie is a sin, as also Augustine[4] declares[5].

The first of the following arguments is an expansion of St. Thomas's argument, and the other two are additions to it.

1. *Argument from the abuse of a natural ability.* It is natural to intelligent beings to have some means of communicating their thoughts to win assent from others. To communicate as thought what is not thought, to convey seriously to another as true what one knows to be untrue, is to abuse this means of communication and to render it unfit for its purpose. Hence lying is an act against our nature and a violation of the natural law.

2. *Argument from our social nature.* Human society is built on mutual trust and faith among people. If lying were morally allowed, we could never tell when a person is lying and when not, whether the next statement will be a lie or the truth; we could not even accept a person's assurance that the statement he or she is now making is the truth. Such speech would cease to have any meaning for us, and if this practice became widespread, there would be an end to human communication and thus to human society.

3. *Argument from the dignity of the human person.* No one's intelligence ought to be insulted by being fed falsehood instead of truth under the assurance that it is truth. This is precisely what the liar does. By subjecting another's intelligence to a lie for the liar's own advantage, he or she degrades the person of a fellow human being and in so doing degrades his or her own person.

No moralist advocates lying as a normal practice or thinks that we may play fast and loose with the truth as we please, but some, and not only relativists, object to the rigidity and absoluteness of the arguments just given. There are

---

[1]Grotius, *Rights of War and Peace,* bk. III, ch. 1.
[2]Plato, *Republic,* bk. III, §389–414.

[3]Aristotle, *Nicomachean Ethics,* bk. IV, ch. 7, 1127a 28.
[4]St. Augustine, *Contra Mendacium* (Against Lying), ch. 1.
[5]St. Thomas, *Summa Theologica,* II–II, q. 110, a. 3.

occasions, they think, when lying is allowed and perhaps even required.

1. Words are a means to an end and have no sacredness in themselves. They may be used for communicating or for withholding the truth. There is no reason why one should be a natural use and the other an unnatural abuse. We use other abilities for purposes not directly intended by nature, as when an acrobat stands on her hands, without considering it an abuse. Why should speech be treated differently?

2. Everyone recognizes the social value of speech and the need for trust among people. But the good for society may sometimes be promoted more by a lie than by the truth, for instance, to save an innocent person's life or to avert war. Kant thought that if I were hiding a friend from a pursuing murderer, I could not save him by telling the lie that he is not here.[1] Such idolatry of principle would be more antisocial than social. It would destroy the fugitive's trust in men, and even the pursuer, while accepting my betrayal, would despise me for it.

3. A person should be morally allowed to lie, not arbitrarily, but only in limited social situations. The person would be using the lie for protection, and the greater the lie the more extreme would have to be the peril to justify it. The rest of us can usually recognize when someone is cornered and can make due allowances for the truth value of his or her speech. We actually do so anyway; yet the social value of communication is not thereby destroyed.

4. If self-defense allows us to go so far as to kill an attacker, why may we not save ourselves at much less cost by telling a lie when lying would get us out of the situation? Why should physical force be an allowable means of self-defense and the spoken word an immoral one? To let someone be deceived is a far less evil than to kill him or her.

5. In self-defense the means of defense are to be proportioned to the means of attack. If we may repel force by force, why should we not repel a lie with a lie? Force cannot defend against speech, it is true, but speech can defend against speech. One who slanders my good name can be deterred by knowing that he or she will receive the same treatment from me.

6. The difference between a lie and other kinds of deception is that a lie uses the common symbols of communication called speech, whereas other forms of deception use actions capable of misinterpretation. Why make so much of this difference? Why not consider a lie as any other feint or stratagem, and treat it on the same terms?

There is value to some of these objections. Others have already been considered in determining the factors necessary for a lie to be a lie in the strict sense.

1. Many prefer not to use the argument from the abuse of a natural ability, not as denying that such abilities can be abused, but as questioning how we decide what uses are unnatural abuses, since many things in nature have several alternative uses. Standing on one's hands does not make them unfit for their normal use, but to drive nails by punching them in with one's bare fist would soon do so. The boy in the fable who cried "Wolf!" so ruined his speech that he could no longer communicate when it became necessary. Does such a result come from a lie or two, or from the reputation of being a habitual liar?

2. The telling of a lie seems a small price to pay for saving life or averting war. But where does one stop? Murder or any other crime could be done for similar reasons. Not the size of the evil but the kind is what counts. Moral evil may not be done to avert even the greatest of physical evils. All this makes sense only if the lie is really a lie in the full meaning of the term. Murderers have no right to know where their intended victim is, and nothing said to them has the character of communication. This is not an example of a real lie, and there is no need to follow Kant's rigid interpretation of duty.

3. The same answer is applicable to a person in extreme difficulty. We do not expect literal truth from such a person because we know that he or she is not communicating. The case is dif-

---

[1]Kant, "On a Supposed Right to Tell Lies from Benevolent Motives," in Abbott, *Kant's Theory of Ethics,* Appendix I, pp. 361–365.

ferent when this person is put under oath in court, for then what he or she says is taken seriously by those who have a right to know, unless the court itself is corrupt and a vehicle of injustice, a fact to be proved and not presumed.

4. One may summon all one's powers to aid in defense against an unjust attack, but one must not misuse these powers so that they become evil means to a good end. We should certainly defend ourselves by speech rather than by killing, if the speech can be morally justified in any legitimate way, but not if it is a real lie in the strict and formal sense previously discussed. Physical force can be a moral or immoral means of self-defense, depending on how it is used, and so can speech. A strict lie is an immoral means by definition. If in most such cases the adversary would not have a right to the truth, what is said would not be a strict lie.

5. We have here a different case from the preceding. It is not a case of warding off physical attack by speech rather than by force, but of trading off lie for lie. To answer a lie by telling another lie is returning evil for evil and not a repelling of the first evil. A lie against me is a wrong use of speech and is properly repelled by my own right use of speech, which is telling the truth.

6. The value of our examination into the factors that make up a lie in the strict sense here becomes apparent. Speech may often be used as a means of deception, as we have seen partly and will see more clearly. Feints, stratagems, and other forms of deception may not be used indiscriminately, and neither may speech. A lie in the strict sense is always an immoral use of speech and not just any form of deception.

TRUTHFULNESS IN THE DOCTOR-PATIENT RELATIONSHIP

Does the physician have the duty to tell his or her patient the truth and nothing but the truth in any and all circumstances? The patient obviously has a right to know the physician's diagnosis of his or her case. Is the right to know absolute, that is, unqualified, in any sense? Today we are concerned that each patient have the ultimate decision as to the care and medical treatment to be given. Only an informed consent will suffice. If the patient does not have sufficient information, including a knowledge of the viable alternatives available for choice, how can such a person make an informed decision? On the other hand, the physician has agreed to care for and treat the patient so as to heal, restore to health, a person who asked for help in the first place. An attitude of trust on the part of the patient is essential if the healing process is to begin. Competence on the part of the physician usually must be presumed on the part of the patient, and this competence is guaranteed by the government in licensing the physician to practice.

Traditionally, the judgment of the physician has been held paramount in the area of truthtelling, and the early oaths and codes of medical practice are all silent on what physicians should tell patients. The general principle that seems to emerge from our tradition is that the main concern of the physician and others attending the sick is to maintain the good spirits of the sick person. If telling the whole, unvarnished truth will harm the patient, then the tradition would sanction withholding the truth or even bending it.

Clearly the tradition is paternalistic and needs further nuancing for the contemporary physician. No casuistic solution can be advanced here to govern all cases. The personal dignity of the patient must be upheld by the physician, for the patient always has the right to know the seriousness of his or her condition to the extent that this knowledge is required for the patient's decisive response. The physician has a duty to reveal the gravity of the patient's situation step by step in accord with the patient's ability to cope with it and in accord with the time left for the patient to deal with this knowledge. The greatest insult to the patient's intelligence is to lie to the patient. Most patients desire to be told frankly but gently about their condition as they approach death. Unless the patient indicates clearly, either explicitly or implicitly, that he or she does not want the whole truth, the physician ought to inform the patient gradually but fully as a way of befriending the patient and helping him or her search for the ultimate truth of his or her life. For the physician to indulge in deception is to destroy the mutual respect and trust that may well be the physician's most valuable therapeutic asset.

SECRETS

If our speech is such that it is serious communication, what we say must be true, but there are times when we may and times when we must refuse to speak. We must reveal the truth when the other party has a right to it. Such would be a lawful superior, a judge in court, or a party to a contract. We must not reveal the truth when it is a strict secret. A secret is knowledge that the possessor has the right or the duty to conceal. For want of a better term we shall call a truth that one has a *duty* to conceal a *strict* secret. A person may be obliged to keep a secret because:

1. The knowledge of its very nature is private
2. He or she has promised not to reveal it

The first is a *natural* secret, because the matter it deals with is private. What belongs to a person's private life, to the closed circle of the family, to the status of business firms and corporations, to military and diplomatic affairs of governments, cannot be aired in public without injury to the parties concerned. Those who share in such matters are bound to keep them secret. Others who happen to find out about them are also bound to keep them secret, but not to the jeopardy of their own rightful interests.

The second comprises secrets of *promise,* when one already has the knowledge and then promises not to divulge it; and secrets of *trust,* when the knowledge is confided to one only under the condition, expressed or implied, that the matter is confidential and not to be revealed. Both of these may also be natural secrets or not, depending on the nature of the matter. Professional secrets are typical examples of secrets of trust and are usually natural secrets also. A secret of trust is the strictest kind of secret and binds in justice, because it is based on a contract expressed or implied.

That we are at times *permitted* to conceal the truth should be evident from our nature. Besides being a member of society, each of us is also an individual. I have not only social and public relations but also private and personal affairs of my own. I have a right to my own personal dignity and independence, to freedom from meddling and prying into my private affairs.

Furthermore, we are at times *obliged* to conceal the truth. One of the purposes of speech and of human society itself is that we can get help from our fellow human beings, that we can get advice from our friends and consult experts without danger of making private affairs public, that when we organize with others for the pursuit of a common goal, we can exchange information without fear of betrayal to a hostile group. One of the main purposes of speech would be lost unless we can also control how far the knowledge we communicate will spread.

How far does the duty of keeping a secret extend? This question concerns a conflict of rights, when the right of one party to have a certain matter kept secret conflicts with the difficulties the other party experiences in trying to keep it secret. In general, one is no longer bound to secrecy:

1. If the matter has otherwise been divulged
2. If the other party's consent can rightly be supposed

The first of these conditions is evident, since the secret no longer exists, but the second needs some explanation. One may be expressly released from the obligation of secrecy and then is no longer bound. Even if this release is not expressly given, conditions may be such that it can reasonably be presumed, for no one has the right to expect a person to keep a rather ordinary secret at the expense of his or her life. The laws on excuses from duty, as previously explained, apply to natural secrets and secrets of promise; one is no longer held to keep the secret when doing so would cause disproportionate hardship. However, one who has expressly promised to keep the secret even under grave or extreme hardship must keep the promise, unless it were morally wrong to have made such a promise.

Greater reasons are required to release one from a secret of trust, but even such a strict secret may cease to bind if the holding of the secret would cause serious damage, not merely hardship, to the parties concerned, to a third party, or to the community. Sometimes however, the revealing of a secret, such as a military secret, would cause such damage to the community that it must be guarded even at the expense of one's life.

What means can one use to keep a secret when directly questioned about it? The following four are customarily noted:

1. *Silence.* The normal way to treat an impertinent question is to refuse to answer. A courteous statement that one is not free to talk of such matters usually ends the subject. Persistent pryers are not put off, however, and silence is often interpreted as consent.

2. *Evasion.* The use of evasion distracts the questioner without giving the information he or she wants, by changing the conversation, answering a question with a question, passing it off as a joke, or assuming an injured air. Evasion requires more ready wit than some people can command.

3. *Equivocation.* By the use of double-meaning expressions the speaker says what is true, though the words are capable of another meaning that is false; if the incautious hearer takes the wrong meaning, that is not the speaker's problem. Thus a man may speak of his child without saying whether it is his child by birth or adoption; the hearer who assumes one rather than the other is making a hasty judgment. For equivocation to be legitimate, both meanings must be discoverable by the hearer, even though one meaning is much more obvious.

4. *Mental reservation.* Mental reservation is the limiting of the obvious sense of words to some particular meaning intended by the speaker. It is the truth but not the whole truth. Part of the truth is reserved in the speaker's mind, lending a possibly deceptive coloring to the part that is expressed. For mental reservation to be legitimate, some outward clue to the limited meaning must be objectively present, though the speaker hopes that it will not be noticed by the listener. The clue may be nothing else but the circumstances in which the words are said. A doctor is asked whether his patient has a certain disease and answers, "I don't know," meaning, "I don't know, secrets apart and in my nonprofessional capacity." He may even answer, "No," meaning, "No, not insofar as I can tell you." The very fact of his profession is sufficient clue to the meaning, for the questioner ought to know that the doctor cannot speak in his or her professional capacity. Thus this example can be taken as a mental reservation but is better interpreted as an instance of noncommunication.

May a person use evasions, equivocations, and mental reservations at any time and for any reason? No. They are not lies and not wrong in themselves, but an act can become wrong by its motive or its circumstances. An unrestricted use of these means of concealment would have ruinous social effects and would break down mutual trust among people. It is not the normal mode of speech, and we cannot be constantly combing over every sentence uttered to us to find possible hidden meanings. We expect our neighbor to speak to us with candor and sincerity, and we take his or her words in their obvious sense in the ordinary transactions of life. These combinations of speech and nonspeech are to be used only as a refuge to guard a secret from prying questioners who have no right to the information they seek. With this motive and in these circumstances they are morally allowable.

Finally, in circumstances in which the questioner not only has no right to the information but would use it to do evil *and* the necessary concealment can be accomplished by neither equivocation nor mental reservation, what is morally allowable? We must avoid cooperating in evil and so cannot take a chance of giving the questioner some outward clue to the information. Given the duty to maintain the secret, the further duty to avoid cooperation in evil, and the fact that the questioner has no right to the information, we may tell the questioner anything that sounds reasonable. In this way we succeed in deceiving the questioner and so deflecting him or her from doing evil without telling a strict lie.

The world we live in is an imperfect one. Duplicity and deceit are a real part of that world and cannot be wiped out altogether. At the same time, we know that personal integrity demands truthfulness from each of us and that trust and integrity are precious values that are difficult to regain once they have been squandered. Only on the basis of respect for truthfulness can trust and integrity flourish in society. For this reason we have insisted that concealment be kept at a minimum and that in the use of mental reservation there be some outward clue to the meaning objectively present.

Legitimate as these subterfuges may be, they should not be overstressed. Most cases of allowable verbal deception can be explained simply by the fact that speech is not being used in its function of serious communication.

CONCLUSION

By nature we are social beings, and the ability to speak is perhaps the chief means by which our social life is carried on. Like all other gifts, speech may be used or abused. Thus truthfulness is good and lying is wrong.

Speech can be abused in two ways: by seriously communicating as true what one knows to be untrue or by revealing truths one has no right to reveal. We are never allowed to do the former, since the hearer has a right to the truth. We would have no difficulty about the latter were it not for other people's prying minds and impertinent questions; against them we have a right to protect ourselves, a right that often becomes a duty when other people are involved. In such a difficult situation we are allowed, sometimes obliged, to summon all our ingenuity to extricate ourselves from the difficulty and to guard the trust others have placed in us. Apart from such situations, sincerity and candor should rule our speech.

SUMMARY

A lie in the strict sense is speech contrary to what one knows with intent to deceive someone who has a right to the truth. Speech is any sign used to communicate thought, including language, gestures, tones of voice, and even circumstances. To lie a speaker must outwardly show that he or she seriously intends to express to another person as true a judgment that he or she knows is untrue. Deception is the normal motive for lying, but not all deceptions are lies. Fiction, jokes, figures of speech, and expressions of politeness are not lies, since speech must be interpreted according to convention. The important thing about a strict lie is that it has all the appearance of serious communication of truth when the speaker knows it is not.

Lying is *morally wrong* because it is an abuse of the natural ability of communication, because it is contrary to our social nature, which requires mutual trust among people, and because it debases the dignity of the human person, whose mind is made for truth.

It is argued that a lie is not always wrong, because it is merely a use of words to conceal rather than reveal, it can sometimes help society more than the truth, it can be less harmful than force as self-defense, and should be classed among the legitimate stratagems.

It is answered that lying is not mere use of speech for a secondary end, leaving the primary end intact. It may promote a particular good, but by evil means and at the expense of a greater good, mutual trust. There is no parallel between killing in self-defense and lying in self-defense, for one is a right use of force, the other a wrong use of speech.

The *doctor-patient relationship* has traditionally been regarded paternalistically as requiring of the doctor only as much truth as the doctor judges the patient can sustain. More recent discussion of the patient's right to know the whole truth about his or her condition would require the doctor to reveal to the patient the gravity of the patient's condition step by step in accord with the patient's ability to cope with this knowledge and in accord with the time left for the patient to deal with the whole truth. Only if the patient indicates clearly, either explicitly or implicitly, that he or she does not want the whole truth, may the doctor withhold it.

A *secret* is knowledge the possessor has a right or a duty to conceal. A *natural* secret deals with matter that is private, a secret of *promise* with matter one has promised to conceal after finding it out, and a secret of *trust* with matter confided after exacting a promise of secrecy.

Concealment of the truth is often permitted, sometimes required. Each of us has a right to personal dignity, freedom from meddlers, and the right to seek advice without betrayal of our private affairs.

We are excused from secrecy if the matter has otherwise been divulged, or with the other party's expressed or presumed consent. Even a secret of trust ceases to bind if serious damage would result from keeping it.

The ways of keeping a secret are *silence, evasion, equivocation,* and *mental reservation*. The last two require that there be some outward clue to the speaker's meaning, though the hearer may fail to take it.

Questions for Discussion

1. You are an investigative journalist who suspects the President of the United States of lying to the public about his own and his subordinates' wrongdoing. You have tried to corroborate your suspicion by every moral means available to you, but without success. Now you decide to lie to each of the subordinates in turn about what you know and the extent of that knowledge so as to get at the truth. Your motive? To inform the public about the "cancer" surrounding the presidency. To deceive wrongdoers into incriminating themselves by lying to them is certainly no worse than what the wrongdoers have done. Are you justified in using this method?

2. The mayor of a large city is running for re-election and once elected, fully intends to do away with rent controls. During the campaign, however, he avoids mentioning rent controls, because he knows he will lose votes if his intention becomes known. Just prior to the election a reporter asks him point blank about his intentions in this matter. The mayor denies any intention to do away with rent controls and even reaffirms his strong support of such controls. He is convinced he can do a good job for the city. What do you think? Why?

3. A 35-year-old woman goes to a clinic for a routine physical check-up and is diagnosed as having a form of cancer likely to cause death within 6 months. No known cure is available. Chemotherapy could prolong her life a few extra months, but the side effects for the woman would be severe. The physician is convinced that such therapy should be reserved for patients with some hope of recovery or remission. The patient has no symptoms to alert her to the cancerous condition and is about to leave on a short vacation. What ought the physician do?

4. A large corporation sells heavy electrical machinery. For some years, lower level management practiced illegal price-fixing involving sales valued at more than one billion dollars a year. These managers worked together to fix prices, rig bids, and split markets. They held secret meetings, used misleading code words, and falsified expense accounts. All these activities were covered up and the responsibilities for continuing them were passed on to new management as the older moved up the corporate ladder. All the time this was going on, top management sent around strict prohibitions against price-fixing while at the same time demanding increased sales from the lower level managers. How would you analyze this situation morally?

5. It has been said that control over secrecy and openness gives the one in control power. In government there is obvious need for some secrecy, but how much openness ought democratic government to strive for? Does secrecy tend to minimize accountability and openness maximize it?

Readings

Despite the fact that he allowed the "noble lie" in the *Republic,* bk. II, §382, and bk. III, §414, Plato really has not much use for lying. Read the *Republic,* bk. II, §381–383, and bk. V, §484–490. See Aristotle's *Nicomachean Ethics,* bk. IV, ch. 7.

St. Augustine in *De Mendacio* (On Lying) and *Contra Mendacium* (Against Lying), both translated into English, is treating a special aspect of the subject and later expressed dissatisfaction with his work.

St. Thomas deals with lying in the *Summa Theologica,* II–II, qq. 109–110. In the following three questions he continues with a discussion of hypocrisy, boasting, and irony, which are subjects kindred to truthfulness and lying.

Sissela Bok examines the quandries we face today in two masterful works: *Lying: Moral Choice in Public and Private Life* and *Secrets: On the Ethics of Concealment and Revelation.*

Hugo Grotius explains his view in *The Rights of War and Peace,* bk. III, ch. 1.

Kant's views on lying are found in the *Fundamental Principles of the Metaphysic of Morals* and in the monograph "On a Supposed Right to Tell Lies from Benevolent Motives," both in Abbott, *Kant's Theory of Ethics.*

Cardinal Newman's *Apologia pro Vita Sua,* note G, contains his reflections on equivocation. See Joseph Rickaby's *Moral Philosophy,* pp. 224–237.

J.A. Dorszynski, *Catholic Teaching About the Morality of Falsehood,* accepts the broader view.

Daniel C. Maguire in *The Moral Choice* treats of the connection between truthfulness and our emotions. John Macmurray's *Reason and Emotion* discusses explicitly the notion of emotional sincerity as emotional honesty or truthfulness.

Joseph Fletcher's *Morals and Medicine,* ch. 2, treats of the right of the sick to know their condition. Bernard Häring's *Medical Ethics* discusses the patient's right to truth in a very engaging manner and receives support from the work of Elizabeth Kübler-Ross. George J. Annas's *The Rights of Hospital Patients: The Basic ACLU Guide to a Hospital Patient's Rights* is an interesting and helpful book to consult. Ronald Munson's *Intervention and Reflection: Basic Issues in Medical Ethics* treats of both paternalism and truth-telling in medical and health care.

PART IV
Social Life

After looking at some of the significant areas of our lives as individuals we can easily see that the moral issues involved in those areas have a social dimension as well. We live and act out our lives in the company of many other persons. What we do as individuals often affects others as well, so the responsibility we must accept for our own actions has a social dimension that we must examine. We turn our attention at this point to the social dimension of our lives and discuss questions concerning the naturalness of our propensity and need to live with other persons (Chapter 22); marriage as the commitment of two people to live their lives together out of love and so form a family, the basic unit of society (Chapter 23); and finally our natural tendency to use our sexual powers for both pleasure and the generation of new life (Chapter 24).

22
Society

PROBLEM

We start with the easily observable fact that each human being is not alone in the world but lives in company with other human beings. Each of us is more than an isolated individual. We are personal beings as well; we live in more or less close communion with other humans in what we call a personal life. Many living beings thrive in groups, clusters, colonies, or herds in which there may be some degree of cooperation and even a primitive form of leadership. Such groupings are sometimes called "societies," but we reserve the term *society* in its primary sense for those uniquely human groupings that consist of something more than mere togetherness, be it of place or activity.

Each of us as unique and absolutely distinct personal beings is situated somewhere and somehow in this world with other personal beings. The fact of situatedness points to the relational dimension of our being. We are unique, individual persons who live in this world with other persons. Such personal being is never isolated being, for we find our primary experience to be that of living in relation with one another, sharing in a whole set of values, perceptions, ideas, and emotions. Being born into and living with our family, race, and nation is a fact of our human existence. We come to an awareness of ourselves as individual persons only from out of this primary experience of the *we* of our life community. Given the fact that humans do live in society, we ask why they do so and what there is about human society that makes it different from other ways of living together. We formulated our questions as follows:

1. Why do humans live in society?
2. What is society?
3. What is the common good?
4. Must there be authority in society?
5. What are the main kinds of society?

NATURALNESS OF SOCIETY

The moralist's problem about society is different from the sociologist's. The moralist wants to know whether humans live in society by their own choice, so that society itself is but a product of human invention, or whether humans are so fitted by their rational and free being for social living that any other form of living would be unnatural for them. Since society imposes serious obligations on people, are those obligations only such as people have created for themselves, so that they may extricate themselves from them at will, or do they stem from our very nature as rational and free, so that they become unavoidable moral obligations? This question is basic to any treatment of the moral aspects of human social life.

Throughout ancient and medieval times, except for a flurry of dissent among the Greek Sophists, it was taken for granted that humans are social by nature. This view is implicit in Plato and expressly formulated by Aristotle in the beginning of his *Politics,* where he declares: "Man is by nature a political animal."[1]

In the seventeenth and eighteenth centuries this view was challenged by Hobbes and Rousseau. Both envision a primitive condition called the *state of nature,* of human beings without society. Hobbes, who makes people antisocial, pictures the state of nature as one of constant predatory warfare. Rousseau, who thinks the human being only extrasocial, describes it as an era of blithe and carefree innocence. According to both, our gift of intellect enabled us to see the advantages of cooperative action, to frame the social contract, and thus to pass from the state of nature to that of society. Having given up our liberties by the social contract we need never have made, we are now the slave of the monster we have created. Society is not natural to us but only conventional; its undoubted advantages are counterbalanced by its unnatural restrictions. Since it is impossible to return to the state of nature, we must make the best of the situation. Hobbes counsels complete submission to the all-powerful *Leviathan;* Rousseau, a fight for a recovery of at least some of our lost liberties. The "back to nature" movement with its hatred for the artificialities and conventionalities of civili-

---

[1]Aristotle, *Politics,* bk. I, ch. 2, 1253a 2.

zation found its inspiration in Rousseau, the great Romanticist.

The nineteenth century gave a new turn to the philosophy of *evolutionism*. The theory of biological evolution, which is almost universally accepted today, was eagerly seized on by materialists of the last century as a way in which mind can be reduced to matter and our specifically human characteristics leveled to mere continuations of ancestral animal traits. Since we evolved from animal ancestors of the herding type, we are naturally social, but our sociality is only a more developed form of our instinctual gregariousness rather than a product of our *intelligent and free* conformity to our moral requirements. The tendency today is to recognize the evolutionary aspect of this view without necessarily interpreting it in a materialistic sense.

The view that people are not naturally social has some plausibility to it:

1. There is much truth in Hobbes's oversimplified description. Think away the products of human convention, and what is left is our natural condition. Each of us would compete for food, protect himself or herself against wild beasts and hoard against all comers what he or she could wrest from niggardly nature. Our greatest enemy is other humans, the only ones with intelligence like ourselves to outwit us. To stop the wasteful war of all against all, the natural human condition, we fashion the social contract by agreement with other humans and thus create society by our own intellect and will. Society is thus a conventional and artificial product of human ingenuity.

2. One can discount Rousseau's romantic picture of the natural human condition, but even in those regions in which struggle for survival was less acute, people would see the advantages of cooperation, with cooperation would come quarrels, and again the need of a social contract as a means of living peacefully and safely with others. Here also society is something to which nature is indifferent, something that people have introduced, something conventional and artificial that we pay for by the loss of much that was natural.

3. Society would not have arisen until humans were sufficiently evolved to reflect on them-

selves, to set their own purposes and choose the means to achieve them. If we distinguish the social tendency from the herding instinct, we see that humans are naturally gregarious and have lifted this instinct to the social level by their own intelligence. Society is thus something that we humans have added to our nature, a human contrivance that we must constantly modify to suit our continuing cultural development.

4. The growth of our social consciousness over the ages shows the artificiality of human society. It took us ages to emerge from the tribal condition to political organization. Only recently have we become conscious of such global troubles as war, racism, poverty, and ecology. They are problems we have artificially created, to which we have not yet found the solution. Since the problems are not natural, neither is the society from which they spring.

Opponents admit most of the facts here cited but say that they have to do only with the form society took in particular instances and do not show that we humans are not meant by our nature to live in some kind of society. Their arguments:

1. People abhor solitude and crave companionship. Some solitude is good for us, perhaps more than most of us have, but excessive solitude can go so far as to unhinge reason. We spontaneously seek others and enjoy their company, whereas loneliness sets up a veritable hunger in the soul. Hobbes's picture fits some miserable outcast from the tribe, not the normal situation. Even primitive people have relatives and friends, without whom survival must have been nearly impossible. The more primitive the society, the more immediately dependent the human being is on it.

2. We cannot take care of ourselves alone. The child must be reared by its parents for many years. Even in adult life a solitary person cannot supply the bare means of subsistence, not to speak of the goods required for living a decent life befitting a human being. Without the family no children grow up, and living in the family implies cooperation right from the beginning of each one's life. The mode of cooperation may be by convention or agreement, but the fact of coop-

eration is a requirement of our rational and free nature for any kind of life at all.

3. The gift of language fits us to communicate with one another, to discuss projects of common interest, to agree on means and ends for cooperative effort. Thus the ability of speech indicates that we are meant to live a social life. Speech itself is natural to us though each particular language is a construction of human art. Likewise our social tendencies are the form gregariousness naturally takes in an intelligent being, though capable of development by human ingenuity. Any particular culture is a work of human art and to this extent artificial, but to tend toward the development of some culture, although not natural to unintelligent animals, is natural to us, given our intelligence. Only we have human nature, not our prehuman forebears, and only our nature is claimed to be social.

4. Intellectual and moral development require constant communication of ideas and values among people, an exchange possible only in society. If small, isolated communities stagnate because they are out of touch with new ideas and values, how much more would this condition be true of single individuals? That our social consciousness has grown over the ages hardly shows that society is not natural. What is more natural than growth? That we are now becoming more conscious of global social problems is a hopeful sign that we are gradually edging closer to social maturity.

What emerges from this discussion is the conclusion that we humans are social by nature and that society is natural to us. But socialization is no automatically operating instinct. Rather, it is a value demanding or clamoring for realization, a demand made on our full consciousness to set up for ourselves a mode of living with other people that will satisfy our needs as human beings for safety and fulfillment, and that will extend these benefits to all people. The methods are largely left to our own ingenuity, and the actual societies that we form, this particular family and this particular state, are human products. The imperfections of society come from the fact that we are only partially successful in this effort, just as we are only partially successful in our private lives. As we have the moral obligation to seek constantly our own individual personal improvement, so we have the moral obligation to work with others for the social betterment of all people.

It is not enough for society that people live together and haphazardly give one another occasional assistance when the mood strikes them. Mere communal living is not necessarily society. For society some organization is required, whereby people at least implicitly bind themselves to cooperate for common ends by the use of common means, each guaranteeing personal help to the rest so that all can depend on it. When people bind themselves together in this fashion, they have formed a society in the strict sense. Since we act this way by the prompting of our rational and free nature, society is natural to us. Insofar as the means to be used and the mode of organization are not determined by our nature but freely chosen, society can be regarded as a work of human artifice and contrivance.

Society is essential to humans in general. Not every individual must live in society, nor is a hermit's life wrong in itself. Society can get along without the few who count themselves out by renouncing both its burdens and benefits, so long as they do nothing to impede its functioning. A solitary life can be good or bad depending on its motive, but it cannot be the life of most people. Aristotle is right in saying that the life of solitude is fit only for a beast or a god.[1]

DEFINITION OF SOCIETY

What sort of thing is society as it emerges from the foregoing discussion? We notice that several elements are necessary:

1. There can be no actually existing society without *members*. Only rational and free beings can form a society, since it is a union based on agreement about goals. The number of persons is not specified, but there must be at least two; otherwise there can be no togetherness or commonness of interests and activity.

---

[1] Aristotle, *Politics,* bk. I, ch. 2, 1253a 29.

2. The members must be united in a *stable,* or *enduring,* way. A single act of working together may be only a haphazard occurrence. The union need not last forever or for life but must last for some considerable time.

3. The members must *cooperate,* or work together for the attainment of some *end.* This end will be some *common good* that all the members will share in and that no member could accomplish singly. The end differs for each kind of society and determines the nature of the society more than any other factor.

4. Society is held together by bonds, *moral bonds* of means and end. Either the members bind themselves by contract, pledge or agreement, or else the bonds are imposed on them by some law, natural or positive. It is this moral bond that distinguishes a society from a crowd, makes the individuals committed members, and obliges them to their commitment.

5. To guide the cooperative effort to the common good, society must be equipped with that moral power called *authority.* Authority is the right to determine the means and direct the members in their use.

Hence society may be defined as an *enduring union of a number of persons morally bound under authority to cooperate for a common good.*

Society is not a physical thing. The only thing physical about it is the members and their actions. But it would be a mistake to say that society is not real. Of course, it is not a separate substance, for it has no existence of its own separate from the individuals who compose it; it is not a kind of superperson built out of people, as the living body is made up of cells. Society is a kind of *relation,* not a single relation but a number of relations unified and systematized into an *order.* These relations link people together in a definite way. An order is not a physical substance distinct from the things that are ordered, but this does not mean that the order and the relations constituting it are not real. The order is real if there are real beings ordered in that way.

If society is not a physical being, what kind of being is it? It has more than ideal or mental being, for that would only make it an idea or thought in the mind of some thinker. Perhaps it is best called a *moral being.* Not every relation, but only a unified system of relations, is an order. Not every order, but only an order resulting from a human act, a rational choice relating means to end, is a moral being. Not every moral being, but only a moral being resulting from the simultaneous free choices of many people to cooperate toward a common end and achieve a common good, is a society.

THE COMMON GOOD

The common good is the end for which society exists. The common good is an intermediate end, an end that is also a means toward the ultimate end of each member. To say that the common good is *the* end of society means that it is the end that is distinctive of society as such. Society is a temporal thing, and it exists for a good realizable in this world.

The common good is the temporal welfare of the community, taken both collectively and distributively. The collectivist stresses the first element only, making the common good an entity over and above the individual good, the former absorbing the latter. The individualist sees only the second element, making the common good a mere sum of individual goods. An adequate view of society and the common good must find a place between these extremes. The common good is realized only in the individuals who make up society, but it is a good that they could achieve only by the cooperative interaction of the many.

To have a common good that can be the end of society, it is not enough that it concern several persons. That might give us two interdependent private goods, such as we find in contracts of exchange. If an employer is interested only in profits from business and an employee only in wages from his or her labor, each benefits the other, but they have no common good in the strict sense. To have a common good as the end of their joint effort, the employer must be genuinely interested in the welfare of the employee, the employee must have at heart the success of the business, and these two interests must be merged into one common enterprise. They must help each other not only accidentally, because their private goods are entangled, but essentially, because they share in the one same good. For lack of this common good, the employer-employee relation normally found today is not a society.

Negatively, the common good consists of the establishment and maintenance of *order*. Each one has a place, his or her relations to others, his or her rights and duties as compared with others' rights and duties toward him or her. Each can rely on the other not to interfere; each is guaranteed a wide enough scope for private action and development as a person. There result peace, harmony, security, opportunity, and freedom. Cooperation for the maintenance of order must be done by all for the benefit of all and is thus a truly common good. But alone it is not enough.

Positively, the common good consists of giving to others and receiving from them powers, resources, and values that as individuals none would possess. It is both active and passive, both supplementation and participation; a single word for it is *union,* or better, *communion.* Scattered raindrops over a wide enough area may, if added together, equal the force of a waterfall, but they cannot do the work of a waterfall harnessed to a turbine. The common good is not an arithmetical sum of each individual's contribution but something new resulting from the channeling of human energy and the mobilization of nature's resources. The economic products of an advanced civilization depend on the genius and labor of thousands of people who invented the machines, developed the processes, and continue to work them. The literature and art of a culture must be built up over the centuries and stored in books, monuments, libraries, and museums that we may now enjoy them and absorb the knowledge and inspiration of the great minds of the past into our own. A family depends on the two sexes and the love between them; mutual protection and support exemplify the negative common good of order, but the begetting and rearing of children is the best illustration of the positive common good of communion.

The means society uses to develop and share the common good are often called *institutions,* such as schools, libraries, laboratories, hospitals, police, military forces, public utilities, corporations, banks, stock exchanges, law courts, and countless others. Some of them are also societies in their own right, but as institutions they are regarded as instrumental agencies used by society for developing, storing and distributing the common good.

The common good is to be shared in by all. The negative aspect of the common good should be shared in *equally,* for it consists of the absence of interference and the affording of opportunity. Even if nature does not give equal opportunity to all, there should be no artificial human restrictions on such opportunities as nature does offer. The positive aspect of the common good should be shared in not equally but *proportionately.* The proportion is a blend of equal and unequal elements. There should be equality between one's contribution to society and one's share in the distribution of society's benefits, but since not all contribute equally, neither should all receive equally. This establishment of social justice, the foremost task of society, is so difficult that in this imperfect world we can hope for no more than an approximation.

The dynamic character of the common good becomes apparent here. It is the end of society, but, since it is never perfectly attained, society is never static. Temporal welfare is a thing that can be constantly bettered. Even if a society should once achieve a condition of perfect social justice, new conditions would arise with new difficulties to be met, and the problem of adjustment would have to be faced anew. The common good is thus the driving force in social progress.

If the common good is constantly changing, how can people agree on it to will it together? The common good taken abstractly (the general welfare as such, without specifying anything definite) always remains the same abstract ideal and must be willed by all the members of society. Thus society always has an end and the same end. But the common good taken concretely (the specific good to be achieved here and now and the means to it) varies with circumstances and need not be willed or even known by each and every member; it is sufficient that each accomplish his or her part. Each soldier wills victory, the abstract common good, but only the high command plans the precise steps by which the battle is won, the concrete common good. Each nation in the world wills or ought to will peace, the abstract common good, but how to achieve it, the concrete common good, has so far eluded us. How the parts the members play fit together is determined and willed by the leaders of society in their exercise of authority.

AUTHORITY IN SOCIETY

Authority is the moral power or right of a society to direct and control the members so that they cooperate toward the attainment of the common good of that society. It should be evident that no society can function without authority, but this proposition is denied by the *anarchists*. They argue that social life and the absence of all restraint are compatible, that authority is necessary now only because of the imperfect condition of society. They say that society has evolved from despotic to monarchic, from monarchic to aristocratic, from aristocratic to democratic, and that the next step should be from democratic to anarchic. There is a gradual lessening of authority as humankind rises to a higher degree of development. Communists, despite their differences with the anarchists, have the same idea of the fully developed communist society, when "the state will have withered away." The difference is rather about the means of accomplishing this end than about the character of the goal itself.

Anarchism is understandable as a reaction against the abuse of authority in an overly regimented society, but it takes an exaggeratedly optimistic view of human nature. We must take human nature as it is, untinted with any rosy colors supplied by our imagination. A realistic appraisal shows that no society could endure without authority. Authority is needed:

1. *To remedy ignorance*. Only the more general principles of good living are evident to all; the remote conclusions about what the good life really is are not easily grasped and must be enforced by one having the moral power or authority to do so for the common good and public order.

2. *To enforce justice*. People are eager to claim benefits but prone to shirk duties; someone must see to it that both are distributed fairly, and that the greedy are restrained and the slothful stimulated. Besides direction, enforcement with the right to use penalties is necessary.

3. *To provide leadership*. Though all may agree on the end of human society as the common good, there may be many disputes on the means to be used in attaining the end; someone must be empowered to choose the means and to insist on the cooperative use of the means chosen. Cooperation is impossible without direction and control.

Authority is therefore essential to every society, since without it the society cannot exist or fulfill its function. The first two points mentioned stress the *substitutional* function of authority, by which it remedies human deficiencies either of intellect or of will. This kind of authority tends to diminish and become unnecessary the more it fulfills its function; thus paternal authority disappears when the child reaches adulthood, and corrective authority ceases when the delinquent has been reformed. A chief difficulty of the anarchists is that they consider this function of authority alone. Leadership, the third point mentioned, brings out the *essential* function of authority, which would exist even in a society of perfect human beings. Because there could be several sets of equally effective means to the end, yet only one set can be used cooperatively, someone would have to choose between them and prescribe the one to use.

NATURAL AND CONVENTIONAL SOCIETIES

When it is said that human beings are naturally social, that they live in society, and that society is natural to them, no reference is made to any specific grouping. Society in this sense is the abstract concept of people living together in interdependence and interaction for the sake of some unspecified common good. This is *society* but not *a society*. It is society-at-large, so to speak, the whole community of humans, but not a definite social entity. In concrete fact people break up into numerous overlapping divisions, each of which is a society in the definite sense.

Some of these societies are informal and unorganized *groups:* ethnic, linguistic, geographical, neighborhood, class, and cultural. They are united by the fact of their common location or interest rather than by any deliberate decision. They find themselves together rather than gather together. Opposed to these are *associations* or *organizations,* which are deliberately instituted with a determinate structure for specified ends under a definite authority. These groups are societies in the strictest sense. There are many kinds, but for our purpose we classify them under two main headings: conventional and natural.

Conventional societies are artificial products of human contrivance, founded by the free agreement of people who set the end and choose the means. Clubs, fraternities, athletic leagues, business firms, labor unions—all such organizations are conventional. They may be established or abolished without affecting human nature as such. If some of them are necessary to life as we know it, their necessity is not absolute but dependent on historical contingencies that are not universal, and for them other arrangements could be substituted.

Natural societies, on the other hand, are those conceived of as required by human nature and having their end set by that nature. Human beings, reasoning on their own rational and free nature

and its needs, perceive that they are morally obliged to form those societies without which they would be unable to live in a way consonant with their human dignity. Are there any such natural societies? The mere fact that it is natural to us to live in society does not lead to the conclusion that nature specifies any definite societies to which we must belong. This question must therefore be settled independently for each society for which this claim is made. For the time being we can note that the commonly held specific natural societies are two: the family and the state.

Before taking up each of these societies in turn, it will be helpful to see the different ways in which authority manifests itself in conventional and in natural societies, and thus bring out the ethical importance of this social topic.

In a *conventional* society, authority comes from the members contracting to organize themselves, who vest the authority in a head or leader of their choosing, either a single person or some type of governing board. With no authority there would be no society; but since the authority is wholly conferred by the members, they can withdraw it, limit it, or extend it as they please. In such a society the right of direction and control is hypothetical, for it affects a person only so long as he or she is a member; the extreme penalty for disobedience is expulsion from the society. Any member is free to repudiate the authority by resigning from the organization. Hence, if the family and the state were only conventional societies, they could have no more authority than the contracting parties in marriage or the founding fathers of the state possessed as individual persons, and association with these societies would be terminable at pleasure. A person would have no more obligation to them than is contained in the voluntary contract of membership.

In a *natural* society, supposing for the time being that the family and the state are such, a very different situation prevails. People enter into natural societies by the prompting of their human nature and remain members by the continuing demand of their nature. Fulfillment of their duty as members of a natural society is enjoined on them by the very requirements of human living and cannot be extinguished by expulsion or resignation from the society. A natural society supposes a scope of authority, an extent of direction and control, a right to inject itself into the lives of its members and demand of them the utmost in loyalty and dedication, which the members as individuals never had or can have. Hence authority in a natural society cannot come from the individuals composing the society, since they do not have it to give, but has to come from some higher source.

What could such a higher source be? The natural law theorists find it in natural law. For them a natural society is one that is required by natural law and has its authority conferred on it by natural law. But just as there are some who find natural law objectionable but accept natural rights, which they may prefer to name human rights, so there are those, mostly the same ones, who disapprove of natural law but see the necessity of natural societies or, as they may prefer to call them, natural institutions. If they do not wish to appeal to natural law, they may find a satisfactory basis in the dignity of the human person. What is important here is that such societies or institutions are required by the kind of being a human person is; because of the dignity of the human person, which no one can renounce, they are equipped with authority to confer moral rights and impose moral duties of a type more stringent than can result from mere human agreement.

Here the theist is in a better position than the nontheist. On the theist's premises, a natural society is ultimately traced to the author of human nature. Authority in a natural society is conferred by God, who created us with a social nature and is thus the ultimate founder of natural societies, which he equips with all they need for their proper functioning. Not that he dictates the exact structure of the society or picks out the persons to lead it, but through the natural law embedded in our rational and free nature he gives authority to the society and its leaders as soon as people, by the prompting of their own human nature, bring the society into being.

SUMMARY

Is society natural to humans?

That humans are not naturally social, but that all society results from convention, is claimed: a human being is a natural predator and wars against all, we passed from a natural to a social state by forming a social contract, we had to evolve intellectually before we could become social, and our work of socializing ourselves is not yet finished.

That humans are naturally social is argued from these properties of human nature: people abhor solitude and crave companionship, they cannot supply even their basic needs alone, language fits them for communication and cooperation, and progress in culture is impossible outside society.

The conclusion that emerges is that humans are obliged by their nature to form society and live in it, but the detailed shape society takes is the work of the people's own art.

Society may be *defined* as an enduring union of a number of persons morally bound under authority to cooperate for a common good. Society is not a physical thing distinct from the members but a moral being consisting of a system of real relations coordinating the members' activities among themselves and toward a common end.

The *common good* consists negatively in *order,* a maintenance of peace and affording of opportunity, and positively in *communion,* an increase of powers by their mutual supplementation. Institutions are means established for the developing, storing, and distribution of the common good. Social justice is the equal or proportionate sharing by the members in the common good.

Anarchists think that society can get along without authority. This opinion is too optimistic, for what is socially good for us is not known equally by all, benefits and burdens must be distributed fairly to all, and someone must choose among various means the ones to be cooperatively used.

Besides society-at-large, there are particular societies existing as unorganized *groups* or organized *associations*. Societies are *natural* or *conventional,* according as they are requirements of human nature itself or have no other basis than the free agreement of people. Two natural societies are recognized: the family and the state.

Authority in a conventional society comes from the members, and one may quit at will. Authority in a natural society must come from a higher source, since it binds individual members more strongly than they can bind themselves. Even apart from natural law, it can be deduced from the dignity and requirements of the human person. Most logically it is derived from the natural law proximately and from God ultimately.

Questions for Discussion

1. If we have a moral obligation to work with others for the social betterment of all, how does this obligation fit with the obligation each of us has to care for his or her well-being? Even if we do not want to be totally selfish and greedy, do we not have to be both selfish and greedy part of the time just to be able to take care of ourselves?
2. The abstract formulation of the common good sounds very noble, but that lofty formulation needs to be translated into a set of concrete goals that we as a society can achieve. When a politician runs for president as the candidate of his or her party, are the planks of the party platform a set of means to make the common good concrete? If so, does the abstract formulation of the common good provide us with a standard or norm against which to measure each of the planks of a political party's platform?
3. The establishment of social justice is said to be the foremost task of society. If each member of society is free to pursue his or her own opportunities without hindrance, is that not social justice? Is this any different from a free marketplace where each one takes advantage of his or her opportunities? If social justice is more than this, spell out what that "more" ought to be.
4. In this age of the AIDS epidemic, more than ever before, we can see the functions of authority to be (a) to remedy ignorance, (b) to enforce justice, and (c) to provide leadership. Explain why you agree or disagree.
5. Science, art, and religion are elements of any human culture. They are also integral to the institutions involved in the transmission of culture from age to age. Look at our own civilization today. Science is certainly playing its role, but do you find art and religion also playing vital roles today? Why or why not? What other institutions are part of contemporary culture? Would our society be what it is without them?

Readings

The ancients did not treat of society apart from its specific forms, such as the family and the state.

The following modern authors have matter pertinent to this chapter: Johannes Messner, *Social Ethics,* bk. I, pt. II, but the whole is a monumental work on all phases of society; Heinrich Rommen, *The State in Catholic Thought,* ch. 1 on social being and ch. 13 on the common good; Yves Simon, *The Nature and Functions of Authority,* a lecture expanded and developed in *The Philosophy of Democratic Government,* ch. 1; Frank Sheed, *Society and Sanity;* and Robert Paul Wolff writes of his failure to find any theoretical justification for the authority of the state and entitles his work *In Defense of Anarchism.*

All books on sociology necessarily treat of society, but not all from a philosophical or ethical standpoint. The following have interesting chapters on most of the forms of society and social disorders to be discussed later: Walter Lippman, *The Good Society;* Pitrim Sorokin, *The Crisis of Our Age,* and other works; Gabriel Marcel, *Man Against Mass Society;* David Riesman, *The Lonely Crowd;* Harvey Cox, *The Secular City;* and many other popular works.

23
Family

PROBLEM

In the past many philosophers have argued that if any group has the right to be called a society, that group is the family. Some philosophers went even further and maintained that if any society can call itself a natural society, the family has the best claim to that title. In every group of human beings, from the most primitive to the most cultivated, we find the family immemorially entrenched, and this is true even in societies that are permissive of homosexual unions. Human sexuality by and large inclines to a union of man and woman, and this inclination leads the two to have children, whose care further cements the union of husband and wife. It is no wonder that marriage has been considered a natural institution.

Neither philosophers nor anyone else can take anything for granted. Today we find the very institution of marriage and its traditional functions widely questioned. The divorce rate alone shows people's attitudes are changing. Traditionally, the family functioned as an institution (1) to control sexual activity and relations, (2) to provide a stable setting for the reproduction of offspring and so for the continuation of society, (3) to nurture and integrate the children into society, (4) to nourish and develop the adults emotionally, (5) to furnish a setting for economic activity, and (6) to assign social status to its members. Each and every one of these functions is being challenged and subjected to changes as a result of the impact of society's high mobility, questioning of sex roles, the move to the cities, industrialization, and technological developments that provide reliable contraceptives and promote increased longevity.

Recent sociological studies show that we are moving toward a variety of family types with no single form being statistically normative. For example, we have families in which both parents and their children live in the same household; single adults without children; single parents, either divorced or separated but living with their children; remarried couples with children; childless couples; experimental family forms such as two families sharing the same household. These are the main variations to be found today, and while none is statistically normative this is not the same as to say that none of these forms is ethically or morally normative. Such variations show that some significant changes in the perception of marriage are occurring. Marriage is more and more becoming a choice rather than a societal imperative. The search is on for alternatives to the traditional image of monogamous marriage and the nuclear family. More and more women as well as men are choosing to postpone marriage or to remain single. Many young adults live together prior to or instead of marrying. We can see a trend toward having fewer children as well as a trend toward deliberately child-free marriages. Some couples reject sexual exclusiveness as essential to marriage and seek intimate sexual relationships within a limited group as positively supporting both their marriage and personal growth.

To write all this off as mistaken hedonism, wishful thinking, or an unrealistic fear of permanent personal commitments would be a mistake. These things may well be present, but also present is a desire for more meaningful personal relationships and sexual bonds. We would be making a further mistake if we were to suppose that the moral form of marriage and the family is eternal and unchanging in the history of human experience. History is an ongoing process that includes institutional changes wrought by human decisions in response to differing human needs. Change does not automatically mean progress. Our contemporary search for new understandings and forms of marriage and the forms of marriage and the family must be evaluated carefully. Since we are historical beings we ought not to fear change as long as it is fitting for the kind of beings we are.

We have to ask whether marriage is a natural institution and, if it is, why it is so. Ever since the beginning of ethics and the Greeks' first probing into human customs, the question was raised whether marriage is a natural institution necessary for the human race or only the prevailing convention we have grown to accept as a matter of course. If the former, it would seem that marriage is the only morally allowable arrangement between the sexes; if the latter, marriage may still be the most desirable arrangement but not the only possible one even from the ethical standpoint. If marriage is a natural institution, the family is a natural society; otherwise it is not. The importance of this question for ethics is obvious.

Other questions immediately follow. Who can marry, why do they marry, how do they marry, how many wives or husbands may one have, how long does the marriage last, what happens when a marriage goes bad? We have space in this survey for only the most basic questions. We ask:

1. What is marriage?
2. Is marriage a natural institution?
3. What are the conditions of the marriage contract? Of the marriage convenant?
4. Must all marriage be monogamous?
5. What about divorce?

MARRIAGE AND THE FAMILY

We begin with a description of the family as existing today and through most of history. In former times the word *family* was extended in two different ways: it included all blood relatives, whether they lived together or not; on the other hand, it also meant all who lived together in the same household, including servants, retainers, and other nonrelated persons. We take the more restricted meaning of the word: the family is a society consisting of husband or father, wife or mother, and their children.

The family, or domestic society, consists of two components, or subsocieties: a horizontal component, the union of husband and wife, called *conjugal* society; and a vertical component, the union of parents and children, called *parental* society. These are not really two distinct societies, but two aspects of the family. Accidentally a family may have one component only, but this is not the usual case. The bond between husband and wife is a moral one consisting of definite rights and duties guaranteed by a free and binding formal agreement for the good of all concerned. This good is achieved by their living together in mutual love.

Marriage may be considered as the act of getting married (wedding) or as the state of being married (wedlock). The first is the marriage agreement in which the man and woman on the basis of their personal love relationship exchange vows or promises publicly and formally to love, honor, and cherish one another exclusively and permanently. Traditionally, this public and formal agreement has been spoken of as the marriage contract in which the man and woman give and receive rights and duties toward each other concerning cohabitation and sexual intercourse. In more recent discussion, the term *covenant* has been proposed as preferable to contract because of cultural changes that have occurred. Marriage today is not usually arranged by parents to support political and/or economic considerations, but is rather arranged by the couple and based primarily on their mutual love. By their covenant they commit themselves to one another to grow in their union of love. Viewed as a contract, marriage is an agreement based on justice; viewed as a covenant, it is one based on love but clearly involving justice. As a state, marriage is a society or lasting union of a man and a woman resulting from such a contract or covenant. We shall consider the state of marriage first, for people get married to live in the married state; hence the nature and conditions of the contract or covenant are determined from the state that the contract or covenant aims to produce.

The state of marriage traditionally implies four chief conditions:

1. There must be a union of *opposite sexes*. Since marriage has to do with the reproduction of the human race, this requirement is obvious. Marriage is not necessarily between only one man and only one woman, though monogamy is considered the ideal.

2. Marriage is a *permanent* union. It must last at least as long as is necessary for the fulfillment of its purpose and the discharge of its obligations, and hence until the last child is capable of living an independent life. Thus marriage differs from promiscuity. Marriage, at least when contracted, is intended to involve lifelong permanence. When covenanted, it is more fragile but is nonetheless

a commitment to one another to grow in their union of love throughout their lifetime.

3. It is an *exclusive* union. The partners agree to share sexual relations only with each other, so that extramarital acts of sex are a violation of justice and/or of mutual love. Whether we think in terms of contract or covenant, adultery is then a moral violation against marriage.

4. Both *contract* and *covenant* guarantee its permanence and exclusiveness. Mere living together without a free and binding agreement to do so does not constitute marriage, even though the partners actually remain together for life. The contract or covenant makes the difference between marriage and concubinage.

MARRIAGE: NATURAL OR CONVENTIONAL?

Some moralists favor the view that humans gradually developed from primitive promiscuity through various forms of polygamy to the monogamous marriage, the stage corresponding to our present development; future evolution will probably lead on to some more advanced arrangement; hence, though we may be naturally social in a broad sense, marriage is a purely human institution that may be abandoned for something better. Those moral positivists who hold that we are not naturally social should logically deny that the family is a natural society, but they seem to be thinking rather of the political state than of the family in this connection; at any rate Rousseau[1] says that the family is the only natural society. Those who hold that marriage is merely conventional may advocate the abolition of the convention in favor of freer relations between the sexes, or they may think that on utilitarian grounds it is an excellent convention by all means to be maintained.

On the other hand, the prevailing and traditional conviction is that marriage is no mere convention but a natural institution. Aristotle's sagacious words deserve quoting because they contain the germ of the argument as well as a penetrating insight into human nature:

> Between man and wife friendship seems to exist by nature; for man is naturally inclined to form couples—even more than to form cities, inasmuch as the household is earlier and more necessary than the city, and reproduction is more common to man with the animals.[2] With the other animals the union extends only to this point, but human beings live together not only for the sake of reproduction but also for the various purposes of life; from the start the functions are divided, and those of man and woman are different; so they help each by throwing their peculiar gifts into the common stock. It is for these reasons that both utility and pleasure seem to be found in this kind of friendship. But this friendship may be based also on virtue, if the parties are good; for each has its own virtue and they will delight in the fact. And children seem to be a bond of union (which is the reason why childless people part more easily); for children are a common good to both and what is common holds them together.[3]

The Thomistic statement is built on this passage but casts the idea into a more formal type of argument:

> That is said to be natural to which nature inclines, although it comes to pass through the intervention of the free will; thus acts of virtue and the virtues themselves are called natural; and in this matrimony is natural, because natural reason inclines thereto in two ways. First, in relation to the principal end of matrimony, namely the good of the offspring. For nature intends not only the begetting of offspring, but also its education and development until it reach the perfect state of man as man, and that is the state of virtue. Hence, according to the Philosopher[4] we derive three things from our parents, namely existence, nourishment, and education. Now a child cannot be brought up and instructed unless it have certain and definite parents, and this would not be the case unless there were a tie between the man and a definite woman, and it is in this way that

[1]Rousseau, *Social Contract* bk. I, ch. 2.

[2]"Reproduction is more common to man with the animals" than forming cities is common to man with the animals. Reproduction is common to man and *all* animals, but political or quasi-political organization is common to man and *some* animals only, such as bees and ants.
[3]Aristotle, *Nicomachean Ethics,* bk. VIII, ch. 12, 1162a 16–28.
[4]*Ibid.,* ch. 11, 1161a 17.

matrimony consists. Secondly, in relation to the secondary end of matrimony, which is the mutual services which married persons render one another in household matters. For just as natural reason dictates that men should live together, since one is not self-sufficient in all things concerning life, for which reason man is described as being naturally inclined to political society, so too among those works that are necessary for human life some are becoming to men, others to women. Wherefore nature inculcated that society of man and woman which consists in matrimony.[1]

The argument may be restated in the following fashion, carrying it along by steps and bringing out each point expressly:

1. Our human nature inclines us toward the continuance of the human race, because by our very nature we have the sexual power and inclination for reproduction. Our sexuality inclines us among other things to a union of man and woman to reproduce in a sexual manner. People may marry for a variety of motives, for love, for companionship, for money, for position. The idea of begetting children may be very subordinate, perhaps only tolerated rather than desired, in the minds of marrying couples; it need not be psychologically uppermost in their minds. People eat mostly for the pleasure of it and rarely think of its necessity for sustaining life; yet they recognize on reflection that sustaining life is the objective purpose of eating. The same may be said for sexual intercourse; it may be done for a number of subjective reasons, such as pleasure or attraction or love, but its objective, natural purpose is to sustain the race. Our sexuality inclines us very strongly to reproduce, so strongly that most humans follow their inclination without reasoning logically about the need for us to reproduce if the human race is to continue.

2. The duty of caring for the child devolves on the parents. The parents are the cause of the child's existence and therefore are charged with caring for its welfare. There is nothing so helpless as the human infant. Some animals can fend for themselves shortly after birth, and none requires

a long period of care. Natural instinct prompts the parent animals, when both are necessary, to remain together until the offspring are sufficiently reared to care for themselves. In no case does this last until the next mating season, and therefore promiscuous mating does no harm to the offspring of animals and allows well for the preservation of the species. The same cannot be said of human beings. The human child cannot live at all without intense care for several years, and on the whole needs from 15 to 20 years of rearing and educating before it is really able to live a fully independent human life. The ones equipped with the means for rearing and educating the child and normally impelled to it by natural inclination and love are the parents. Other agencies are poor makeshifts in this regard. Therefore the parents are the child's proper guardians.

3. The duty of rearing and educating the child belongs to both parents, not to one alone. That this duty belongs to the mother is clear from the fact that she must bear the child. But the father is equally the cause of the child's existence and therefore is equally responsible for the child's welfare. Together they gave the child life and together they must care for it, not in lives apart and independent, but in that joint life that makes up the society of the family.

From these three points it follows that the nature of the family demands a permanent and exclusive union between the sexes, and one guaranteed by contract or covenant, in other words, that marriage is a natural institution. The father and mother have different but complementary capacities, and the influence of both parents is necessary for the adequate training and education of the child.

Those who are convinced that marriage is not a natural but only a conventional institution do not usually deny the facts cited in the argument given but deny that they warrant the conclusion drawn from them. In particular:

1. We must give some explanation why marriage is so widespread a phenomenon, but the fact that it has been universal up to now does not prove that it is necessary for all time. Children

---

[1]St. Thomas, *Summa Theologica,* III, Supplement, q. 41, a. 1.

must be taken care of and provided with a home, but communal care in state nurseries might accomplish the same end as well or better. Parents had to care for them when no one else could, but we have now arrived at a condition of social organization when parents can be relieved of this obligation and can pursue their independent careers free of this all-absorbing hindrance.

2. When a man and a woman remain together, either for the sake of the child or for the sake of each other, why should they have to bind themselves by contract or covenant? Their actual love for each other or their duty to the child should be enough to hold them together; when it is not, no mere ceremony will make much difference. The marriage contract or covenant should be optional for those who want it, but it should not be necessary for all who intend to live together.

3. If the argument for marriage as a natural institution is drawn from the parent's obligation to the child, it would seem that childless marriages are not really marriages but only attempts at marriage. When it becomes evident that no children will be forthcoming, the parties should be free to separate and seek fruitful unions elsewhere.

4. The argument supposes that the help of both mother and father working together is necessary for the upbringing of the child, but human nature sometimes allows the child to be deprived of father or mother or both. Why should human beings be morally obliged to accomplish an end set by their nature, when human nature itself often fails to keep its own law? If marriage is regarded as a mere human convention, not so much is expected of it.

5. If marriage is a natural institution, then it should be contrary to human nature not to marry. What is natural for humans pertains to all who have human nature. Those who uphold marriage as a natural institution should agree with those who condemn voluntary celibacy as a failure to fulfill a natural duty. Yet some want illogically to approve both states as natural.

6. A natural institution should not be capable of so much mismanagement and unhappiness. Marriage cannot be regarded as particularly suc-

cessful among human endeavors. That there have been happy marriages goes without saying, but one of the greatest sources of human misery is a brace of mismatched partners whose home is a den of spite and strife. How can one say that it is natural for them to remain together? If marriage is conventional, a bad marriage is but a human mistake that the partners can rectify by agreeing to disband.

7. Marriage contains too much of human contrivance to be called natural. Human nature does not tell whether one should marry, does not select the partners, does not teach married couples how to get along with each other, does not prescribe just how to raise the children, does not automatically supply the family with its needs. All these things must be discovered by human ingenuity. Why not say that the whole institution is only a human device and one that humans seem to be rapidly outgrowing?

Those who hold that marriage is a natural institution find these objections unconvincing.

1. Modern psychology reinforces what has always been known: the child's need for love. If state-operated institutions can take care of some children, as they do, enough of them could take care of all, but this institutional upbringing is a poor makeshift for the home. We have to resort to it when necessary but recognize that it is far from the ideal. There is no substitute for the child's experience of its parents' personal love. Events over which they have no control excuse parents from their obligation, but they are not allowed to shed it voluntarily.

2. Parental society requires no contract or covenant, since the infant cannot make one, and later on it finds itself already a member of parental society by disposition of human nature itself. The same is not true of conjugal society, which is entered into freely by adults. Each must be assured of the other partner's faithfulness before assuming the heavy burdens that marriage entails. An implicit understanding might do for the partners themselves, but marriage is a public and social affair, not solely a private and personal one. Public order requires that it be publicly known who is married to whom and where responsi-

bility for the family lies. Thus society has a right to insist on the registration of marriages and other formalities.

3. There is no marriage unless the partners transfer rights and assume duties toward one another, which in the normal course of events should issue in the existence of children. Human nature tends toward the end but does not guarantee that it will be attained in every case. Childless couples form a family in its conjugal relation, even though the parental relation never becomes actualized. They have the same duties toward one another as any other married couple, but their duties as parents are in abeyance so long as they have no child.

4. The design of human nature must be judged from the normal instance. Loss of a parent, and much more of both, is a great misfortune in a child's life. Nothing in our nature ensures against misfortune, and a parent's early death is one. Those who are alive and able to fulfill their obligations are not excused because of other people's death or inability. Adoption into another family is the best way of caring for orphans, but this supposes that there should be families. If the family is natural, human nature here supplies its own remedy.

5. Procreative marriage is a duty for the race but not for the individual. The individual's good can be obtained only by the individual's effort; thus no person can live by getting others to eat for him or her, but the good of the race can be obtained if a sufficient number tend toward it. Marriage would be a duty for each individual only if the human race were in danger of dying out, but there is little need to fear on this score.

6. Humans can mismanage anything. The blame is not to be put on human nature but on the mismanagers. We can ruin our health, stultify our mind, pervert our will, squander nature's bounty, pollute the earth's surface, and even blow ourselves off the map. Abuse of these natural things does not render them not natural. That we reserve some of our most exquisite follies for the mismanagement of marriage does not make marriage any less natural.

7. What is natural to humans does not pre-clude the use of human ingenuity but requires it. Since our nature is rational and free, we are expected to use our rationality and freedom even in the exercise of those things that are most natural to us. Thus we follow the prompting of our nature in entering into marriage and approving the existence of marriage in society, but most of the details of marriage and family life are left to our ingenuity.

THE MARRIAGE CONTRACT

Whether we speak of the marriage contract or the marriage covenant, we are dealing with the question of marriage as an institution of society. The traditional term is that of a contract, which highlights the justice aspect of the agreement between the man and the woman. More recent discussion of the marriage agreement shows a dislike for the word contract as too businesslike and a preference for speaking of the agreement as a covenant. The Judeo-Christian inspiration is more obvious in the use of covenant than in the use of contract. We shall treat each separately so that the differences can be clearly discerned before deciding which term better expresses the reality of the state of marriage, the reality that the marriage agreement aims to produce and foster.

The married state of individuals begins by a contract entered into by the mutual free consent of the man and the woman. People are not born married and may remain unmarried throughout their lives. The right to marry is a natural right, but one that need not necessarily be exercised. Clearly then, no one has a duty to marry. Since our human nature does not select the partners for marriage, we ourselves must determine *whether* we shall marry and *whom* we shall marry. We do this by arranging the marriage contract.

Contract is a general word for any voluntary meeting of minds concerning the transfer of rights and the assumption of duties or obligations. Marriage is a contract in the full sense of the word and, as such, must fulfill all the conditions requisite for a contract in general, as well as some peculiar to itself.[1] By it the parties transfer to each other strict rights and incur toward each other strict duties, which they henceforth owe to each other in justice. The essential right transferred is the right to perform the generative act of sexual intercourse exclusively with the other. Cohabitation, support, sharing of goods, and the like are consequent rights. The transference of the essential right is permanent and exclusive; failure to make it so invalidates the contract.

By its very nature as a contract, marriage requires mutual free consent and the absence of error and fear. Freedom of consent is particularly important in marriage, because marriage supposes love, and love cannot be extorted, besides the fact that marriage imposes heavy burdens that no one is obliged to assume, much less to assume in company with a particular person.

An impediment to marriage is some inability in the contracting party that makes the marriage contract (covenant) either invalid or illicit. The first kind renders the contract null and void from the beginning, so that the parties never were actually married. The second kind simply makes it wrong for a person to marry under such conditions, but if he or she does so, the marriage contract (covenant) holds. The chief invalidating impediments from human nature itself are impotence, too close kinship, and being already married. The church, because of the religious and sacramental aspect of marriage, and the state, for the sake of the common good, can establish additional impediments of either grade.

The ban of kinship may need a few remarks. The crime of incest has always been regarded with particular horror. Any marriage between parent and child is absolutely outlawed by human nature as utterly opposed to the parental relation already existing. Marriage between brother and sister is not absolutely contrary to human nature, but the only condition under which it could be considered allowable would be that otherwise the race could not propagate. The reason for banning marriage between brother and sister is the fact that they grow up in the same home and develop during their immaturity a kind of love free from all erotic passion; anything else would mean the utter ruin of the family and make the home an unlivable place.

MARRIAGE AS COVENANT

In introducing this chapter, we saw that marriage is taking some forms different from the traditional one thought of as a contract. One thing that differing forms means is differing forms of fidelity. Marriage as contract is designed to ensure the sexual exclusivity and permanence of the marital or conjugal relationship. Sociological facts and estimates about what is or what will be should not be confused with moral judgments about what ought to be. While we should give serious attention to all the relevant facts, still we must strive to arrive at an ethical conclusion for ourselves. We must also remember that changes have occurred in the past and that they will continue to occur in the future. The forms that marriage takes ought all to be fitting with the authentic needs of persons. Short-term and/or short-sighted superficial desires are not necessarily the same as authentic human needs, the needs we have as persons in the process of becoming fully personal beings. Marital forms in which the persons are trivialized cannot be morally acceptable forms. Each form is also a symbol of our fidelity or faithfulness to other persons.

Marriage today is based primarily on the mutual love of the man and the woman. To speak of their free and binding agreement as a contract seems to trivialize their love and their mutual commitment. The Judeo-Christian inspiration of the covenant, which God makes out of love for his people and in which he calls them to intimate friendship with him and guarantees his fidelity and love as perpetual, provides a richer understanding of marriage than does the notion of contract. The covenant will be a pledge of enduring and ongoing fidelity to the well-being and growth of each partner in their union of love. It is a covenant of intimacy between the two persons, an intimacy that is both emotional and physical. There is a mutual

---

[1]See pp. 426–428 on contracts in general.

caring for the growth and fulfillment of each as a person that requires openness, honesty, and trust as well as a willingness to explore ways of opening the self to the partner at the deepest level possible and accept the risk of the pains that may come. Their erotic love is supported, infused, and transformed by their free and mutual self-giving love. Self-giving love present with sexual desire, erotic aspiration, and mutuality releases the couple from self-centeredness and possessiveness into a relationship that is humanly enriching and creative. The marriage as covenant genuinely enlarges the couple's capacity for communion with others and expands their willingness to participate in the creative work of giving new life and renewal to the world.

We said earlier in this chapter that marriage as covenant is more fragile than the contractual form, because the marriage might break down when the loving relationship is no longer present or possible. No individual choice, however important, can ever be totally identified with the person who always remains something of a mystery. The solemn covenantal commitment requires a most mature and well thought-out decision, but there is always the possibility that a mistake is being made that might become apparent only in the years ahead. All the same, marriage as covenant involves a great act of faith and of hope on the part of the couple. The future is unknown; it will include joy and laughter as well as sorrow and tears. But on the basis of their mutual love they give one another support and the hope necessary to face the future.

MONOGAMY OR POLYGAMY

That marriage must be between man and woman follows from its nature and purpose. Between how many men or women? The marriage of only one man with only one woman at the same time is *monogamy;* marriage to two at the same time is *bigamy;* marriage to more than one at the same time without specifying the number is *polygamy*. Polygamy is general to either sex; it is:

1. Polygyny, when one husband has more than one wife
2. Polyandry, when one wife has more than one husband

Polygyny does not wholly subvert the purpose of marriage. It places no hindrance to the birth of children and allows at least the essentials of the child's rearing. Each mother can devote herself to the rearing of her own children while supported by the father. Unless the number of wives is extremely large, the father also should be able to assist somewhat in the training of the children.

But polygyny falls far short of realizing the ideal of marriage. The father cannot give the same attention to the training of the children of several wives that he could give to those of one wife. The mutual love and help that should exist between husband and wife are weakened by being single in one direction and divided in the other. There can be no equality between husband and wife when she is only one among several, and there is little wonder that in polygamous countries the position of woman is not far above that of a slave. Jealousy among the wives is to be expected when each vies for the husband's favor and each is ambitious for her own children. Almost superhuman ingenuity is required of the husband to be perfectly fair to the wives and the children, and this kind of society seems possible only when the woman's condition is so degraded that her will does not count. Though such evils may occur in a monogamous family, they occur there only accidentally, through the fault of the parties concerned and not through the nature of the institution; but in a polygynous family these evils spring from the system and can be avoided only accidentally. Hence polygyny should not be approved as a morally acceptable form of marriage.

Polyandry wholly subverts the purpose of marriage. The only alleviating factor is that the several husbands would all be pledged to the support of one wife and all the children she would have. But material support is not the main element in marriage. The excuse of polygyny, quicker propagation of the race, is absent in polyandry, for a woman cannot bear more children to many husbands than to one. The rearing of the children as nature intends becomes impossible, because the father cannot be determined with certainty and is thus unable to perform his function of giving help and guidance to his children. The children would naturally quarrel over which husband is the father of which child. All the fathers might try to fulfill these duties to all the children or divide them arbitrarily, but the resulting relation cannot be truly parental.

STABILITY OR DIVORCE

We said before that marriage must be lasting, but we did not say for how long. Can it be dissolved, or must it last until the death of one of the partners? Married persons may break up their home in either of two ways:

1. By separation from bed and board
2. By attempted dissolution of the marriage bond

A *separation* means that the two parties cease to live together and to discharge marital functions but remain married; the marriage bond remains intact so that neither party is free to marry again. It is easy to see that such a separation is sometimes necessary, but it should be undertaken only for the gravest of reasons. People who intend only a separation may sometimes have to obtain a civil divorce to protect themselves from the other party, to gain support for and custody of the children, or to effect a civilly valid distribution of property. Divorce in such cases touches only the civil effects of marriage and need not be intended to dissolve the marriage bond.

The term *divorce* is usually understood to mean an attempt to dissolve the marriage bond itself, so that the parties are free to marry with other persons. Divorce, like the marriage contract or covenant that it tries to dissolve, is regulated by ecclesiastical and civil law. We are obliged to consider the matter from the standpoint of natural morality alone, a limitation that necessarily makes our treatment incomplete.

Parents' duties to their children require that the marriage endure until the family is fully reared.

Marriage, as we saw, has as its aim not only the begetting but also the rearing of children. Human nature itself requires that marriage last until this end is accomplished, until the child is fully reared and able to live an independent life of its own. To rear one child normally takes from 15 to 20 years, but if the parents must live together for that time, other children are ordinarily to be expected. Hence marriage must last for at least 15 years after the birth of the youngest child. The woman is capable of bearing children up to about 45 years of age. Normally, therefore marriage must last until husband and wife are 60 years of age.

Love between the married couple requires that the marriage last until the death of one of the partners. When married people have reached advanced age, hardly any reason could justify a separation. Life together could not have been too intolerable. Most separations occur in the early years of marriage, in the difficult period of mutual adjustment, when the romantic mist has blown away to reveal each to the other in the hard light of reality. It would be absurd to think that this has not already happened to an elderly couple who have shared all the joys and sorrows of life together for so long.

The chief reason against divorce is the havoc it works in the life of the child. The child is the one who pays for parents' failure. Parents who break up the home deprive the child of the environment in which it should grow up. Cases happen in which the child profits by being removed from a bad home, but natural law looks to what is normal, not what is accidental. The new husband or wife of a divorced person can often do quite well in rearing the children but in too many cases is bitterly resented. The children may love both their real parents and become confused as to which side to take or why they should have to take sides. The situation is anything but ideal.

Even the strongest proponents of divorce recognize it as a serious social evil and a breakdown in social morality. Those who consider marriage a mere human convention should logically allow divorce for the asking. In their view there should be nothing binding in the contract but the parties' continued will, even if they originally meant it for life. If marriage is a natural institution, the case is different. Then marriage is a free contract or covenant in the sense that one may either marry or not, but the conditions of marriage are laid down by human nature itself and not by the parties marrying, and the term for marriage is until the death of one of the partners.

How inexorable is human nature? Take the case of a marriage that for some reason, whether it involves moral fault in either or both of the parties concerned or whether it is one of those situations that is nobody's fault, has gone so bad that there is no chance whatever of rehabilitating it. Must the parties, since they cannot live together, spend the rest of their lives in continent singleness until one of them dies? What is the reasonableness of demanding any such thing?

From the standpoint of pure reason it is hard to see any reasonableness in it. The marriage does not fulfill any of the purposes of marriage. Love is dead, the home is broken up, the children are not being reared by both parents together, and there will be no more children. Much stress has been placed on the wedge argument: that the granting of divorce for the gravest reasons gradually leads to a letting down of the bars until trifling excuses are accepted. History shows that there is a great deal of truth to this argument. However, we do not apply it with such absolute stringency to other affairs in life, and why should we do so here? It seems unjust to punish people who have genuinely valid reasons because others make the same demands under flimsy pretenses. Also, one can sermonize on how important a step marriage is and how those who enter it hastily or with little sense of its serious obligations must pay the price of their folly. But not all divorced persons entered marriage hastily or foolishly, and those who did are now paying the price. In all the other affairs of life one can get out of an irredeemably bad bargain and start over. Against this it is argued that laws are made for the common good, and since divorce is ruinous to society generally, individuals will have to uphold the common good of marital stability at personal sac-

rifice. Any law, however, admits exceptions, especially where failure to do so would circumvent the purpose of the law itself. We have such a case here.

Thus the voice of reason seems to speak. But marriage has its religious as well as its natural aspect. Proof that no valid marriage can ever be dissolved will have to be sought from theological sources, and even here most religious bodies admit at least a few specified exceptions.

Nothing said here was meant to impugn the stability of marriage or to advocate divorce as a general remedy for marital unhappiness. There was question only of certain hopeless cases. Looking at the divorce record in most countries of the world today, one is forced to the conclusion that most divorces are morally unjustified. What is particularly noxious is the bad example of many prominent people who never intended their marriage to be stable and are willing to shuck husband or wife whenever a more desirable person comes in view. This form of successive polygamy has perhaps done most to make a mockery of marriage as a social institution. The antidote is to point to the many happy homes in which a healthy family life is actually flourishing.

CONCLUSION

Without doubt the statistics on divorce and other forms of family breakup indicate that all is not well with the family. As long as there are humans, there will be problems. Nevertheless, the family as an ideal lives on exemplified more or less well in millions of homes everywhere. High praise and moral support are due to all those men and women who pass on to their children some three thousand years of civilization and without whose nurturing care and love progress would come to a halt. The family today has to its credit considerable accomplishments in the economic, political, and moral-cultural spheres.

1. The economic sphere. Whether economic theory chooses to recognize it or not, economic self-interest includes the family. Each of us has his or her economic starting place in life given by the family. The isolated individual can never be the sufficient unit of economic analysis. Many families place a high priority on education, for parents know that their children must use their intelligence well not only to survive but to be able one day to give their own children even greater benefits than they themselves have received. In many families, the economic welfare of each individual depends in large part on the immediate family as well as on the extended network of blood relatives. These families aim to enable each succeeding generation to begin at a higher financial level than the preceding one. Parents work and sacrifice, struggle and save, invest if possible, all with an eye to the future well-being of their children. Through this regard for family, the individual avoids mere self-interest and human sociality arrives at its normal full development. In fact, the sociality of the family counteracts exaggerated individualism in the economic sphere and the freedom of the family counteracts excessive intervention by government in the lives of the individual citizens.

2. The political sphere. The right of the family to own and transmit property to its children sets an effective barrier to totalitarianism and provides a space within which the children can be taught effective self-government. The family holds the primary right in the education of the children. The state has lesser rights and may require certain areas and levels of competency, but it may not take over the right of parents to direct the education of their own children. The state has no right to infringe on the intellectual and moral traditions of the family. The family then is the social space the child needs for physical, emotional, intellectual, and moral nurturing on its way to adulthood and the full exercise of citizenship. In the family he or she learns the habits and virtues of mind and will necessary for the practice of a republic form of self-government.

3. The moral-cultural sphere. First and foremost the family is nature's own school for virtue. One of the first lessons it teaches husband and wife with each other and with their children is humble acceptance of human frailty. All of us have feet of clay and need no illusions about our goodness, virtue, and attractiveness. Honesty and sincerity are absolute requirements for the virtuous citizen, and it is in the bosom of the family that we learn them. Acts of self-denial and self-sacrifice are routine for parents during the years they are rearing their children, and so the children gradually learn what heroism is. They also learn about independence, the rule of law, liberty, and obedience, while the parents learn how to exercise authority and apply discipline. The family is a school of practical wisdom, for all the members learn to reflect critically and clearly about the world of experience, to make practical judgments about it, and to act. The quality of family life will always be reflected in the life of the state, for the family as a natural society is the basic unit of the state, which is also a natural society. Last, but by no means least, the children learn about God and the practices of their parents' religion.

SUMMARY

The family, the most primitive society, consists of two subsocieties: *conjugal,* the husband-wife relation, and *parental,* the parent-child relation. Marriage, which creates and maintains the family, means both the contract or covenant and the resulting state. The married state supposes a man and a woman united by contract or covenant in a permanent and exclusive union of shared life and love.

Is marriage merely a human convention or a natural institution? That it is a natural institution is argued thus:

1. Human sexuality inclines us to the propagation of the race.
2. The parents' duty of caring for the child lasts for many years.
3. The rearing of the child belongs to both parents jointly.

Therefore our human nature demands a permanent and exclusive union guaranteed by contract or covenant—that is, marriage.

Objections: Children can be brought up in state-operated nurseries, a ceremonial contract or covenant is but an empty rite, sterile unions would not be marriages, death often leaves orphans, all would have a natural duty to marry, a natural institution should not be open to so much abuse, and married life has to be run by human ingenuity.

Replies: Institutions cannot supply parental love, public order requires external formalities, childless couples have the conjugal relation, orphanhood is an unfortunate exception, marriage is a duty for the race but not for the individual, possibility of abuse does not make a thing not natural, and humans are expected to use their rationality and freedom in natural matters.

By the marriage *contract* each transfers to the other the right to intercourse and cohabitation. It must fulfill all the requisites for contracts in general and be free of error and fear. Any fault in the essentials of the contract renders it invalid. Impotence, too close kinship, and being already married are natural impediments. Church and state may add others, rendering the contract either invalid or illicit.

Marriage as *covenant* is inspired by the Judeo-Christian understanding of God's covenant with His people as a call to intimate friendship with Him with His guarantee of perpetual fidelity to His people. The covenantal marriage commitment is a mutual promise to love one another and to help one another grow in that union of love no matter what happens. It guarantees sexual exclusivity as well as permanence, but with a realization that human fragility may be causing them to make a mistake. Nevertheless, the couple strives to give one another a love that includes self-giving, friendship, a proper love of self, sexual desire, and erotic aspiration.

Polygamy has two forms. *Polygyny,* one husband with several wives, makes the rearing of the children difficult, degrades the status of woman, fosters jealousy, and is divisive of the husband's love. *Polyandry,* one wife with several husbands, wholly subverts the purpose of marriage.

Divorce means not a mere separation but an attempted dissolution of the marriage bond to leave the partners free to remarry. Marriage requires the partners to remain together until the last child is reared; since they are then 60 years of age, almost no justifying reason can be found for breaking the marriage. Divorce may not be harmful in individual cases, but its widespread practice is a serious social and moral evil.

Questions for Discussion

1. Since the family is the basic unit of any society, does the quality of life in the society testify to the quality of life of its individual family units? Consider the divorce statistics in your state. Do those statistics point to anything more than a rearranging of the households involved? Is society as a whole adversely affected by divorce? Explain your answer.

2. Imagine yourself married for five years. You now have two children, one three years old and the other almost two. You have gradually come to the realization that your mate is bisexual and is having affairs on the side one after another. Is your marriage a natural society that ought to be held together? Explain your answer.

3. You are the national director of the Immigra-

tion and Naturalization Service called upon to administer the new law providing amnesty for some illegal immigrants. According to the provisions of the law, some families must be broken up because one or other of the spouses does not qualify for amnesty. You decide to return to Congress to ask for enough latitude in the law to keep from breaking up families. How would you argue your case before the lawmakers?

4. The nuclear family is undergoing some changes today. Make a list of the changes you are aware of and show which changes are accidental modifications and which are in fact essential, that is to say, changes which have created a new reality that is no longer a family. Justify your answer.

5. Marriage is an institution that serves the common good of society. It is also described as a contract and as a covenant. Does one or the other description fit the notion of institution better? Explain your answer. Is the institution meant to serve the people involved or must the people involved serve the good of the institution? Explain your answer.

Readings

Plato's dissolution of the family for the guardians in his ideal state, *Republic,* bk. V, is well known. Aristotle's refutation is in the *Politics,* bk. II, ch. 1–4; otherwise he has only passing remarks on the family in the *Nicomachean Ethics,* bk. VIII, ch. 10–12, and in the *Politics,* bk. I, ch. 2.

The treatise on marriage in the *Summa Theologica,* pt. III, Supplement, qq. 41–68, added by St. Thomas's followers from his other writings, is mainly theological but discusses some philosophical aspects in qq. 41, 44–48, 51, 54, 65, 67.

The *Pastoral Constitution on the Church in the Modern World* of the Second Vatican Council is an important document that should be read; the theological viewpoint rests on a philosophical basis. John Ford and Gerald Kelly's *Contemporary Moral Theology,* vol. II, treats the whole of marriage and is one of the best expressions of the conservative attitude. Bertrand Russell, *Marriage and Morals,* represents the radical view.

Cardinal Suenen's *Love and Control* is excellent. See also: T.G. Wayne, *Morals and Marriage,* a little book for those contemplating marriage; Dietrich von Hildebrand's two short books, *Marriage* and *In Defense of Purity;* Jacques Leclercq, *Marriage and the Family;* Wingfield Hope, *Life Together;* and Gustave Thibon, *What God Has Joined Together.*

For the more recent discussion of variant marital forms as well as a development of the notion of marriage as covenant, the following will be especially helpful: Charles E. Curran, *Issues in Sexual and Medical Ethics;* Anthony Kosnick *et al., Human Sexuality: New Directions in American Catholic Thought;* James B. Nelson, *Embodiment: An Approach to Sexuality and Christian Theology.* Of course, the philosophical basis of the theological argumentation is what is of interest in each of these works.

24
Sex

PROBLEM

Although we have seen marked changes in sexual attitudes and practices since the 1960s, nothing has sparked a more intense interest in them than the AIDS epidemic. We are all keenly aware that AIDS is transmitted most often through intimate sexual contact and is, as far as we know, always fatal. People are worried and often fearful. What we cannot afford is ignorance about our sexuality. We are sexual beings by our very nature, and we have a natural curiosity about sex. We need to develop a balanced view of our sexuality and learn to behave morally as the sexual beings we are. To focus our discussion, we ask the following questions:

1. What is the meaning and place of sex in a person's life?
2. How do we evaluate sexual behavior morally?
3. Is the virtue of chastity for everyone?
4. What is the place of love and sex in marriage?
5. May married people have sex without conceiving children?
6. Given the new discoveries in genetics, is it moral to tamper with human reproduction?
7. What is the place of sex in the lives of the unmarried?
8. What rights do the mentally retarded have in sexual matters?
9. What can be said of homosexual sex?

MEANING AND PURPOSE OF SEXUALITY

We make a distinction between sex and sexuality. *Sex* is a biologically based need oriented toward generation of new life and toward pleasure and release of tension as well. The aim or goal of sex is genital activity culminating in orgasm. *Sexuality,* a very basic dimension of our personhood, is our self-understanding and self-expression, our way of being in the world, as male or female. Obviously, sexuality is a broader term than sex, although it includes sex and relates to our genital organ systems. Sexuality permeates and affects to some extent all our emotions, thoughts, and actions; it includes the culturally defined attitudes and characteristics that we make our own as masculine and feminine. It also involves our affections toward and appreciations of those of the opposite and/or same sex. Our attitudes toward our own bodies and those of others is rooted in our sexuality. We are embodied consciousnesses, body-selves.

Sexuality is a sign of our incompleteness as individuals and a means of calling us to interrelate with other humans, to communicate and commune with them. Not everything about our sexuality is clear. It is mysterious too. The mystery of our sexuality is the mystery of our need and yearning to reach out to other persons, to embrace them both physically and spiritually. In this way, sexuality serves to *create* and develop our personality by *integrating* us as persons into human society.

THE MORAL EVALUATION OF SEXUAL CONDUCT

In Chapters 3, 4, and 9, we discussed the subjective and objective norms of morality and showed that *both* must be used in making moral evaluations. The moral evaluation of genital conduct, difficult enough for uninvolved bystanders, is peculiarly difficult but not impossible for the person who is trying to judge his or her own behavior. Sound moral evaluation involves at least these factors:

1. A recognition of both the subjective and objective aspects of human conduct as indispensable to any genuine moral judgment
2. An awareness of the complexity and the unity of the person's sexuality
3. An effort to avoid overemphasis of *either* the creation of personality *or* the integration of the person into society so as to keep both aspects of human sexuality in balance
4. A keen awareness of the interpersonal dimension of the sexual experience as constituting an integral part of any moral standard or judgment

Inevitably we find it impossible to measure

and evaluate any specific act in a way that is totally adequate to all the intricacies of human genital experience. Yet we must ask what can be known in order to act in as enlightened a manner as possible. We offer here a tentative series of criteria in terms of which such sexual conduct may be evaluated. Since the total human person is committed to foster by his or her conduct *both* creative growth as a person *and* integration into society, it is meaningful to ask whether and to what extent genital conduct realizes the following particularly important values: personal love and freedom, respect and reverence for the other as a person, honesty, fidelity, social responsibility, service to life, and joy. We shall consider each of these values in turn.

Personal Love and Freedom

Human sexuality functions as an important source and means of personal growth toward maturity. Sexual expression in a genital manner is meant to serve and satisfy a wholesome self-interest and self-fulfillment; it is not exclusively an altruistic and loving self-giving to another person. Loving another person satisfies a deep need each of us has; it is fulfilling for us at the same time that it is a self-giving. The loving expression of the self to the other person is also liberating, for the authentic self needs to express itself fully without hindrance just to be itself. Any sexual expression that closes the self off from the other person is then inappropriate, whereas any loving self-expression that is liberating is not for that reason alone appropriate.

Respect and Reverence for the Other as a Person

Does one's sexual expression of self to another contribute positively to the personal growth of the other person? If so, then that expression shows a genuine interest in and concern for the well-being of the other. It calls forth the best from the other without being demeaning or domineering. One's behavior toward the other is guided by the other's needs and capacities for growth as a person.

Honesty and Sincerity

What one feels for the other is expressed as openly and truthfully as possible. No feeling is expressed that is not sincerely felt; all that one feels about the relationship is expressed because it is important for the other to know.

Fidelity

The sexual expression shows a consistent pattern of interest and concern that grows deeper and richer as the partners grow and develop in their mutual love. Being true to one another contributes to the stability and strength of the relationship. While the mutual fidelity grows, it does not isolate either person from all other personal but nongenital relationships.

Social Responsibility

The pair's sexual relationship reflects both their interpersonal relationship and their relatedness to the larger community of family, nation, and world. With the awareness of their interrelatedness to the larger community they know that the quality of their life as a pair affects the quality of life of the larger community. The bond of their relationship enables them to use their sexuality in a way that truly builds and enhances the human community.

Service to Life

Sexual expression must respect the intimate relationship between the creative and integrative aspects of human sexuality. Every life-style provides means for giving expression to this life-serving quality. The vowed and promised celibate, the unmarried, and the married lives all have a way of serving life creatively and in an integrated manner appropriate to each. Through entering into the relationship with another person or set of persons, each of us is able to express his or her sexual creativity and to move toward integration both as a person and as a member of society.

Joy

Sexual expression, whether it be genital or not, is not merely pleasurable but, when done appropriately, gives rise to sheer joy and exuberant appreciation. Feelings of guilt and remorse have no place in appropriate sexual expression.

LEVELS OF MORAL EVALUATION

Over and above the factors we have just looked at and the particularly important values to be kept in mind, there are four levels of moral evaluation to be aware of as we move from abstract principle to concrete decision:

1. Universal principle
2. The particularly important values associated with human sexuality
3. Concrete norms, rules, precepts, or guidelines
4. Individual conscience making its concrete decision

We shall examine each level more closely.

The Level of Universal Principle

This is the level of the objective norm of morality that we found to be the nature of the human person taken completely in all its parts and essential relations (Chapter 9). The implications of this basic evaluative norm for the area of human sexuality are highlighted by expressing it in terms of creativity and integration. Creative growth as a person toward integration as a self into society expresses in a very fundamental manner how sexuality is to serve the human person and be consonant with human freedom and dignity. The principle is absolute and universal; it provides the overall purpose or goal toward which all wholesome sexual activity ought to tend.

The Level of the Particularly Important Values

Personal love and freedom, respect and reverence for the other as a person, honesty and sincerity, fidelity, social responsibility, service to life, and joy all serve to further unfold the meaning of the universal principle of creative growth as a person toward integration as a self into society. No one specific sexual expression will equally serve and protect all these values simultaneously, but the substantial violation of any of these values raises serious questions about the ability of that particular sexual expression to enhance the creative and integrative growth of the person.

The Level of Concrete Norms, Rules, Precepts, or Guidelines

These are formulations distilled down through history from the experience of the human community. They serve to enlighten us about what patterns or forms of sexual behavior have proven generally to aid or to be destructive of creativity and integration. This is what moral tradition is all about. The presumption should be in favor of the guidelines of tradition even though they may not be universal and absolute moral norms. While none of us ought to be the unthinking slave of any tradition, the burden of proof that departure from the guideline will be creative and integrative not only for the individuals involved but also for the larger community rests with those who make the exception.

The Level of Personal Conscience

The moral life is not simply a matter of conformity to predetermined rules and guidelines. The well-formed conscience will be well aware of the universal principle of creative growth as a person toward integration as a self into society. It will be open and responsive to the complex of values involved in wholesome sexual expression. Further, it will be attentive to the wisdom of human experience expressed in the traditional concrete guidelines. But when all is said and done, the person must exercise his or her own freedom to choose and take full responsibility for the choice made. The ultimate norm of morality is the subjective one, the well-formed individual conscience.

THE VIRTUE OF CHASTITY

In Chapter 15 we discussed habit and virtue to show that we need good moral habits (moral virtues) to lead the good life. We saw further that virtuous acts are complex acts that proceed from prudence (right reason) and some moral virtue. The end or goal intended is set by the moral virtue and the means to attain the goal is determined by prudence (right reason in moral matters). The virtuous act is then the moral goal-achieved-by-these-means, a complex act of both prudence and moral virtue. Now, to live morally as the sexual beings we are, we need to develop by positive acts the moral virtue of chastity. The purpose of this particular moral virtue is to help us use our sexuality to grow as persons and to integrate ourselves as male or female in every area of our lives, not just in situations in which we express ourselves in a genital manner. *Chastity is the moral virtue that enables us to live our sexuality in its fullness in keeping with our particular state in life.* It concerns the whole personality with its capacity for love and warmth and human relationships; it facilitates the fullest realization of one's self as male or female and fosters the integration of one's self with others in the human community. Chastity is an inner reality enabling us to express properly the truth of our sexuality in our attitudes and actions. It grows and develops through our making the right moral choices in keeping with our state in life and, as it grows and develops, it makes easier the right moral choices we need to make as sexual beings. As such, chastity is not the denial, repression, or submersion of our sexuality outside of marriage. Chastity is very positive and concerns our whole personality as it is open to and conscious of reaching out as male or female to other embodied persons. No matter what our state of life—vowed or promised celibates, married, or unmarried—chastity is the moral virtue that enables us to transform the power of our sexuality into a creative and integrative force in our lives.

To develop the virtue of chastity is impossible unless we acknowledge and frankly integrate into our consciousness the sexual movement toward other persons that is in our bodily existence. As males and females we are attracted to one another and should delight in this receptivity and allurement. To be chaste is impossible in the absence of our joyfully embracing our sexuality, our masculinity or femininity, in full consciousness. We have a constant challenge to develop our sexuality into a creative and integrative force in our lives, no matter what state of life we have chosen. To be chaste we need:

1. Clear and accurate knowledge of the basic facts and meaning of our sexuality
2. Positive acceptance of our sexuality as fundamentally good
3. Proper respect and reverence for our sexuality as a means of interpersonal communication, that is, as more than a biological, physical, genital, or emotional fact
4. To recognize that chastity can be developed only by being open to the challenges and risks involved in living as the sexual beings we are
5. To know clearly that to be sexually sensitive and responsive requires self-control, especially in moments that call for restraint and/or nonexpression as the most effective means of achieving creativity and integration
6. To call on our religious faith, if we have one, for the needed strength and motivation to live chastely

LOVE AND SEX IN MARRIAGE

In treating marriage as an institution, stress is placed on its objective, external, legal, and juridical aspect. This is unavoidable, for marriage is a social fact and a social institution. Every government in the world finds it necessary to regulate marriage and to include domestic relations in its civil law; primitive tribes enforce with social sanctions their traditional marriage customs, and nearly every religion makes the wedding ceremony a religious rite. It is the business of the moralist to evaluate these practices and thus consider the institutional side of marriage.

Marriage is not only an institution; it is also a personal experience, one of the most profound a human being can have. Marriage cannot mean to the detached outsider what it means to the married couple, an intersubjective union, a love relationship unique to the two who share it and incommunicable to anyone else. Any discussion of marriage that omits the love of husband and wife is like an interpretation of a poem limited to the grammar of the sentences.

The traditional distinction between the primary and the secondary ends of marriage is out of favor today. It looked on marriage wholly from its institutional aspect as a contract. The primary end was seen as the perpetuation of the human race through the begetting and rearing of children. Begetting implies the moral obligation of rearing or education, which is to be understood in the broadest sense as full physical, mental, and moral development, fitting the children to face life, to pursue their ultimate goal, and to work with their fellows for the common good. This is the public task married people take on themselves, for which they are responsible, and for which they bind themselves into the permanent contractual union called marriage rather than meet in a temporary, indiscriminate union.

In this older, contractual view the secondary ends of marriage were summed up in the mutual love and help exchanged between husband and wife. Chief among these would undoubtedly be the fulfillment of true human love, directed to the other as a person with qualities of mind, heart, and soul, and the intertwining of their lives in the mutual gift of each to the other. Included also were the goods of cohabitation; the companionship resulting from the fact that the two sexes are ideally suited to each other; the legitimation of sexual desire, which most people are unable to forego but cannot satisfy in a moral way outside marriage; and the urge toward self-perpetuation, by which one leaves behind an image of oneself

and sets one's mark on the universe by carrying on the family strain. These ends, though called secondary, were never meant to be incidental or unimportant. They were called secondary because they take second place in a legal or juridical consideration of marriage as an institution, which could continue to exist without them.

The tendency today is to play down the distinction between primary and secondary ends of marriage because of misplaced emphasis. It is thought that marriage should not be looked at from the outside only, but more from the standpoint of the married couple who covenant their mutual love. For them the legal and juridical aspect takes second place to the interpersonal love and intimacy that has changed their whole way of life. Hence it is suggested that there is but one overriding end of marriage, and that is *love*. Love is here to be taken in its widest possible scope and on all possible levels.

1. On the highest level love is between persons who are attracted to each other as persons. It is simultaneously self-fulfillment and fulfillment of the beloved. Each gives himself or herself to the other, so that in a sense the two lives are merged into one greater life. Together they share life's joys and bear up one another in life's sorrows. Love does not always require the intensity of romantic passion but shows itself more enduringly in quiet devotion. Marriage at its least, as an institution, can exist without love, but at its best, as an ideal, it cannot. It should be a seeking of a life situation or environment in which love can flourish and grow, for love is a developing thing that the lovers themselves must foster.

2. Human love involves not only the spirit but also the body, and hence married love includes genital sex. Married people are not supposed to use each other merely as means of sexual satisfaction, which would be love of self rather than of the other, but sexual union is a normal expression of married love and a means toward mutual growth in personal love. Since it is naturally fruitful, it should result in the creation of new life, in that permanent mingling of the qualities of

the two wedded lovers in a new person who mirrors both. Actual fruitfulness cannot be guaranteed in any marriage.

3. Living together results in constant companionship, which is mutually beneficial in a practical way apart from personal love and sexual passion. The psychological temperament of each person needs its complement. There results a love of friendship and affection on a more prosaic level that acquires greater significance in old age. Some marriages have been successful almost on this level alone, though it hardly represents the ideal.

If love is taken as the one essential end of marriage, it must be taken in all three of the aspects just mentioned: personal, genitally sexual, and companionate. The first is undoubtedly the noblest and most important, but it is the least subject to external regulation. Love in its highest sense is attracted, not commanded, and cannot be reduced to a contract. Rights and duties based on justice belong to the contractual aspect of marriage, but love alone can inspire the ideal of marriage as a covenant and make it what it ought to be. In this sense love is the essential end of marriage.

It is essential also in this sense, that no marriage could be successful that was consciously limited by the married couple to its legal and juridical aspects, to the insisting on rights and the fulfilling of duties. Love is generous, and love in marriage is subject to the paradox of generosity—that it requires one to do more than one is strictly required to do. There is no better illustration of the continuity of justice and love and of the fact that the mere fulfillment of duty is not enough for the good life.

BIRTH CONTROL

Can there be immoral uses of genital sex within marriage? Any use of sex between husband and wife is right and good, unless it is done in some unfitting way. The main point of interest here is the issue of birth control. Is it immoral?

Birth control ought to mean any way of controlling births, including abstinence from intercourse and its limitation to sterile periods. But it is usually taken to mean *artificial contraception,* the use of mechanical, physical, or chemical means to make the sexual act possible without a resulting conception. This is the sense in which the term is taken in the present discussion.

Some such methods have been used from the earliest times, but they were crude and ineffective and overlaid with superstition. The advance in medical knowledge and the widespread marketing of perfected devices have brought contraception within the reach of most and have made it a social as well as a moral issue. It is propagandized as a method of counteracting overpopulation, reducing the breeding of subnormals, relieving economic distress in overlarge families, and obtaining the optimum number and spacing of children in normal families. Few would oppose these ends, but the use of contraception as a means to these ends has long met with moral opposition. The moral condemnation of contraception is traditional; its widespread acceptance is new. Today the immorality of contraception continues to be maintained by large sections of society, especially by those who hold a natural law ethic, and the reasons alleged reduce to the *unnaturalness* of the practice. The chief reasons seem to be the following:

1. The primary end of marriage, regarded as an institution, is the begetting and rearing of children. Even those who no longer speak of primary and secondary ends admit that responsible procreation is an essential end. Marriage is a natural institution, and to take advantage of this natural institution contrary to its primary or essential purpose is to subvert human nature and thus to act immorally. Contraception is such a subversion and therefore against the natural law.

2. The sex faculty, as everyone knows and biologists know scientifically, is obviously meant for reproduction. There is nothing wrong in abstaining from its use, but if it is used, it must not be deliberately frustrated of its natural issue. To frustrate a natural power of its primary and essential purpose is to go against human nature, to act in a manner directly contrary to the norm of morality, and to do something intrinsically wrong. There is a natural goal in the reproductive

process by which the whole of it is directed to the child. Our personal goal must accord with our natural power, not contradict it.

3. Artificial contraception is wrong for the reason that it is an unnatural vice of the same sort as homosexuality and masturbation. It has been described as mutual masturbation, a using of each other for mere sexual pleasure rather than for the expression of true human love, which is creative of new life. To turn our sexual powers away from their natural purpose, the good of the race, to a mere means of individual satisfaction is what is meant by perversion. This is precisely what artificial contraception does.

4. Contraception is seeking the pleasure while at the same time avoiding the responsibility. The strong desire that we feel for sex gratification is our nature's way of alluring us to breed. Since our nature attaches the pleasure as an inducement to accept the responsibility, the acceptance of the pleasure together with a deliberate repudiation of the responsibility is acting against our nature. It has been likened to deliberately vomiting after eating, to have the pleasure of additional eating while preventing the natural consequence of nourishment. If we want the pleasure, we must take the natural consequence attached to it.

5. Contraception is a contamination of one's bodily temple. Married couples are privileged to cooperate with the Creator in the noble work of creation, and it is for this reason that they are fruitful. Thus there is something sacred about our reproductive power. It is not one's own in the same sense as other abilities but is consecrated to the good of the race. Hence it may not be withdrawn from the fulfillment of its natural purpose and devoted to some secondary purpose of one's own.

6. Contraception cannot be engaged in without necessarily having an evil intention. One who performs the sex act is seeking the procreative good, for it is not possible to use our procreative powers otherwise. By contraceptive intent the person is intending the hindrance of the procreative good at the same moment and in the same act in which he or she is intending the

seeking of the procreative good. Since both intentions are unavoidable in contraception and contradictory in purpose, contraception is necessarily evil in intent and therefore immoral.

7. Contraceptive intercourse is psychologically unsatisfactory. The barrier put between husband and wife to prevent conception means that neither can derive full sexual satisfaction. But human nature obviously tends to this satisfaction by attaching it to the normal and unimpeded use of sex, thus teaching us how this power is to be used. An unsatisfactory sex life leads not only to psychological disturbances but also to loss of love, and hence it attacks the nature of marriage itself.

8. The marriage act should be the perfect expression of conjugal love. There should be no reserve in the surrender of each to the other. Mature sexuality is a complete self-fulfilling and other-fulfilling interpersonal relationship. The use of contraception is a reserve in the surrender, a withholding of what ought to be given, a defrauding of what is due to the other, an acceptance of the other's affection but a refusal of the other's substance. Hence contraception prevents marriage from being the perfect expression of conjugal love.

These arguments overlap greatly, but each lights up a different side of the question. They are a strong presentation of the traditional view, but the publicity given to contraception, its ready acceptance by so many well-meaning people, the medical and economic problems families face, the unsatisfactoriness of continence and rhythm for some, the hopelessness in underprivileged areas, and especially the zooming population explosion, all force on us a rethinking of the whole question. Even some adherents of the natural law ethic challenge the foregoing arguments, and on two main counts:

1. Biological knowledge requires that we revise some of our opinions on the exact natural character of the reproductive process.
2. Ethical sincerity requires that we reconsider some of our assumptions concerning the proper interpretation of the natural law.

Specifically, the following sort of counterarguments have been proposed:

1. The begetting and rearing of children certainly constitute an essential end of marriage (call it primary or not), which no marriage can wholly exclude. But must it be sought every time the sex act is used? Other human powers have no such restriction. Also, the rearing of children is a part of the primary end as much as the begetting of children. One of the chief reasons given by people for practicing contraception is that any more children would render difficult or impossible the proper rearing of the children they already have. Hence the primary end of marriage may require family limitation as well as family expansion.

2. There is a natural goal in the reproductive process, but that does not mean that we may never interfere with it. In a way many applications of human science or art are frustrations of nature, making nature accomplish human ends rather than the ends their own nature drives them to. The design of God must be respected, but just what is that design? It includes the fact that we use our intelligence and modify nature to suit our legitimate aims. Should we not also intellectually govern our sexuality and moderate our fertility by responsible parenthood? That contraception is an evil way of doing so is assumed but not proved in the argument.

3. Analogies drawn from homosexuality and masturbation are beside the point. These acts are not between married people, who have to live together and express a proper love for each other, who have done their duty to the race by generating enough family but happen to be overfertile. Married people can use each other for selfish indulgence, which is wrong, but they can also love each other too strongly for abstinence, even periodic, and yet cannot afford to have more children.

4. One must take a responsibility that necessarily comes, but is it necessary to create that responsibility? One must care for the child one has, but must one conceive it? Why must the responsibility for procreation prevail over the responsibility for education? The old notion that sex pleasure is somehow wrong unless justified by an excuse, and the only excuse is children, is challenged today as having Manichaean (matter is evil) overtones. Sex is good in itself as the expression of love between husband and wife, and it needs no excuse. It can be overused, just as eating can be overdone, and in both cases the virtue of temperance must be exercised.

5. That there is something more sacred about the reproductive ability than about other abilities does not seem to have any standing in philosophical ethics. Parents cooperate with the Creator in the starting of new life and also in its continuance, so that every act parents do for their child later on should also be sacred, together with the powers they use in doing it. Is not the love aspect of sexuality as much the Creator's purpose as its fertility aspect? We must avoid an undue preoccupation with the biological side of sex to the exclusion of its human significance.

6. Married couples must seek the procreative good, but must they seek it in every single act of intercourse? Mutual love and parenthood, sexuality and fertility, seem to be two separable moral intentions. Human nature itself separates them most of the time, since the sterile part of the woman's period is longer than the fertile part, and in periodic continence one is deliberately sought without the other. Why cannot they separate these intentions also in a contraceptive act? Because contraception is forbidden? But this is the point to be proved, not assumed.

7. Whether or not contraceptive intercourse is psychologically unsatisfactory, psychological satisfaction is not a matter of obligation so that it must be obtained in every act. There is far more psychological dissatisfaction, even neurotic anxiety, in the prospect of an overabundant family with all the worries of providing for it. For many the rhythm method is psychologically most unsatisfactory, forbidding intercourse when it is desired and allowing it when it is not wanted. The "pill" puts no barrier in the performance of the sex act and solves at least this aspect of the question. Furthermore, Nature as such does not teach anything. Humans reflect on their nature to discover what is fitting and what is not.

8. A contraceptive act is certainly not the perfect expression of conjugal love and is by no

means the ideal. This is readily granted. But the ideal can never be perfectly realized. More children might make ideal family life impossible. Continence and rhythm can play havoc with the proper expression of love and can divert conjugal love even farther from the ideal. Though we should always strive for the ideal, we must realize that an ideal is by its very nature never perfectly attainable.

This balancing off of arguments represents the state of the question as it is today. Many find the traditional arguments thoroughly convincing, others find them unsatisfactory, and still others hold to the traditional conclusion but seek new arguments or a reformulation of the old ones. The question is complicated by some other factors: traditional views are not lightly to be set aside, since they are our heritage, yet serious and difficult obligations are not to be imposed unless they are certain; the widespread practice of abortion on demand is a much more serious matter for both the individual and society than the issue of contraception; such intimate matters should be entirely a family matter and withdrawn from public discussion, yet the size of families has social effects that are the concern of all.

The idea of *responsible parenthood* is commonly admitted today. Parents are not obliged to have as many children as possible and should determine their number and spacing for the good of the whole family. The only controversy is about the morality of the means. Opponents of contraception offer two means: continence and rhythm.

Marital *continence* is refraining from genital relations with mutual consent. Marriage as a contract transfers rights, and it is a violation of the marriage contract to refuse them to the spouse who reasonably demands them, but there is no obligation to demand them. Both must agree to abstain and must be able to do so without proximate danger of being unfaithful. Marital continence is not easy, but it is not impossible.

Rhythm, or periodic continence, is the limitation of relations to the sterile period that nature itself provides. Since there is no obligation to demand marriage rights at all, there is no obligation to demand them at one time rather than another. It is known that the act will be unfruitful, but nature itself has made it so. There is no question here of using artificial means, and thus rhythm is not a form of artificial contraception. The intention may be the same, but unless it is an intention of never having any children at all, it is a legitimate exercise of responsible parenthood. That it be responsible, some justifying reason, medical, eugenic, economic, or social, should be present.

The contraceptive *pill* remains problematic. It is still too soon to observe all its effects. This uncertain state of affairs leaves us without the facts on which to make a solid judgment. However, the undesirable side effects belong under the question of risk to health and are irrelevant to the contraception issue. Even if all the side effects were eliminated, that would not of itself legitimize the use of the pill, if contraception itself is morally wrong.

There should be no objection to a pill that would merely regularize a woman's cycle to make the use of rhythm surer. It is hard to interpret any existing pills as working in precisely this way. Some consider the existing pills as destructive of a possibly fertilized ovum and thus as abortive. Others consider them as delaying ovulation, which may be direct temporary sterilization and wrong on that count (if anything so temporary really should be called sterilization at all). Others think of the pill as merely prolonging nature's sterile period and thus as assisting nature rather than opposing it; they find nothing wrong in it. The pill has the advantage over mechanical and physical contraceptives in that it does not interfere with the ordinary performance of the sex act and commends itself to those who distinguish between sexuality and fertility as two possibly separable intentions. At all events, future developments of the pill seem to offer the best hope of finding some sure means of family limitation that can be accepted by people of all moral persuasions.

Contraception is a makeshift and far from the ideal solution to the problems we have been discussing. Our personal choices ought not to be in opposition to the natural goal-directedness of a human process like sexual intercourse. We need further intensive study of the human reproductive system to discover how it can be controlled, regulated, and developed by right reasoning in such a way that our reproductive capacity need not be turned off in the interest of family planning or personal fulfillment. Nevertheless, when all is said and done, increased knowledge of human fertility and a more human use of the genital aspect of our sexuality will always require us to govern ourselves morally. In such a complex matter we need not rest satisfied with philosophical reasoning alone; we, who are theists, will want the guidance of our religious faith and the interpretation of the natural law in the official pronouncements of the church to which we have given our adherence.

GENETICS AND SEXUAL REPRODUCTION

One of the reasons why married people sometimes choose to remain childless is that genetic dangers make it unwise for them to have children. The science of genetics studies the events and processes of heredity and development. Scientists have long used genetic knowledge in tampering with plants and animals through selective breeding and have succeeded in producing a great number of new plants and animals. Geneticists are now in the process of discovering more and more about the factors that control the characteristics we inherit from our parents and that to an extent control our development as human beings.

Along with rapidly developing genetic knowledge, technologies are being developed to enable us to predict the sex of a fetus, to determine whether the fetus is afflicted with a hereditary disease such as hemophilia or some serious defect, to fertilize an ovum in a test tube (in vitro fertilization) with either the husband's or a donor's sperm and implant the fertilized ovum in either the wife's or another woman's uterus, to use sonar scanning to discover fetal abnormalities such as anencephaly, and to abort unwanted fetuses. Someone has said that whatever *can* be done *will* be done by some people. A good number of people believe that in genetic matters what *can* be done *ought* to be done; that is, if we *can* participate in the evolutionary process, we *ought* to do so for the benefit of the human race.

To argue from the fact that we *can* participate in the evolutionary process to a moral obligation *(ought)* to do so is not at all compelling. On the other hand, if we have a genuine moral obligation to do something, we can readily argue that we *can* do it. The moral ought always implies our capacity to fulfill the moral obligation, whereas the capacity to do something never in and of itself implies a moral obligation to do it.

The great strides made by medical science since 1910 have enabled people carrying genetically inherited diseases such as diabetes to produce children who will grow up to reproduce and so pass on that inheritance. In earlier times, a diabetic person probably would have died before reaching reproductive age. Natural processes still take care of many of the worst genetic defects; about 25% of all conceptions fail to reach the stage of viability and are naturally aborted in miscarriages. The cells of each of us carry between three to ten potentially harmful genes. One out of every five persons has a genetic defect that will be passed on to or through offspring. Most people are completely unaware that they have defective genes until deformed, diseased, or retarded children are born to them.

What if anything can be done about all this? Does society have the right to submit its members to a program of genetic screening to prevent couples from producing genetically defective children? If so, then the right of couples to produce offspring is not an absolute and inalienable right. Society certainly has, as we have already seen, a duty to protect the health of its citizens. Does this duty provide the foundation for a right on the part of the state to try to prevent the most seriously crippling genetic diseases from being transmitted? We already admit the propriety of blood tests prior to marriage for the control of venereal disease. Ought we to have a premarital genetic test not to stop people from marrying, but rather to help them be more responsible in using their capacity to reproduce children? No public policy has as yet been formulated, but the discussion of these issues is underway with a view to formulating some sort of public policy.

Meanwhile life continues. Defective children are being born. What can be done at present when a couple produces an affected child or knows that an affected child has probably been conceived? At the present time, we have basically three choices.

1. We can choose to do nothing to modify the conditions of the genetic pool and continue to treat affected individuals without regard for the wider social genetic picture. This is the choice of people who are convinced that we should not tamper with our genes for whatever purposes.

2. We can prevent those who carry defective genes from passing them on to their offspring by offering such people prenatal diagnosis in conjunction with genetic counseling. Those who take this second option have at least four further alternatives open to them once they have the information that the fetus is positively affected or is at risk of being affected by some genetic abnormality: (a) to treat the fetus if this is one of the rare cases when prenatal therapy is possible, (b) to allow the pregnancy to go to term and treat the handicap as best they can now that they know what to expect, (c) to allow the pregnancy to go to term and make arrangements to put the child up for adoption or to place the child in a foster home, and (d) to abort. The use of selective abortion in connection with prenatal diagnosis is highly controversial.

3. We can eliminate defects by controlling reproduction by means of artificial insemination using either the husband's or a donor's sperm depending on which would result in a better offspring. The use of artificial insemination is also highly controversial. We shall limit our discussion to the issues of selective abortion and artificial insemination.

Selective Abortion

The number of known genetic disorders determined by single genes of large effect is almost 2,000 and continues to grow with further research. Add to this the number of conditions determined by two or more genes and the number becomes even more impressive. One important goal of genetic diagnosis and counseling is to prevent genetic disease in individuals or families. The usual approach to this problem has been to identify moderate- to high-risk families (those with a 25% or greater recurrence risk) through the birth of an affected child and then to do comprehensive genetic counseling with such families. In such counseling, one or more specially skilled and trained professionals tries to communicate to the counselee (individual and/or family) the diagnosis, genetic mechanism, prognosis, and alternative courses of action available to manage the genetically determined disorder. The counselee is then able to choose a course of action consistent with the medical, economic, and psychological nature of the disorder, the short and long-range goals, together with the ethical and religious values that will lead to the best possible adjustment for all involved.

When a child or adult is found to have some kind of genetically determined disorder, the affected person, the parents, and other family members have emotional reactions that vary according to the nature and seriousness of the disorder and the expectations of the family. The strong emotions and emotional conflicts almost always interfere with the educational aspect of the counseling. The tension, anxiety, possible guilt feelings, depression, denial, grief, and hostility all make the counselor's work more difficult, because these emotions must be dealt with along with the genetically determined disorder.

Marital stress and sexual maladjustment frequently result from the diagnostic process. Right now the options for couples at risk who wish to avoid having affected children are mostly negative. These options include: (1) the avoidance of having any more children, (2) adoption, (3) artificial insemination of a noncarrier surrogate mother by the husband's sperm, (4) artificial insemination of the wife by a noncarrier donor, and (5) waiting for a medical breakthrough that will provide effective treatment of the disorder. If the couple at risk still wishes to express their mutual love sexually while at the same time avoiding conception, they must adopt some contraceptive procedure. Should the chosen contraceptive method fail for some reason and conception occur, the couple will want to know whether *this* fetus is affected.

The most commonly used diagnostic process used to detect genetic defects in the fetus while it is yet in the womb is *amniocentesis*. This is the process of drawing off some of the fluid surrounding the fetus. Fetal cells from the fluid are then either directly examined or grown in a nutrient solution for later examination. By means of amniocentesis, chromosomal irregularities as well as sixty or so biochemical or metabolic disorders can be detected.

The alpha-fetoprotein (AFP) test is done on amniotic fluid to check for excessive levels of alpha-fetoprotein, which is manufactured by the fetal liver in the first 15 weeks of gestation. This test is effective in detecting almost all cases of anencephaly, the absence of all or a major part of the brain. Excessive amounts of AFP after the fifteenth week indicate the possibility of faulty development that has left open the spinal column (spina bifida). The results of this test are verified by ultrasound scanning and sometimes by amniocentesis as well.

Ultrasound scanning, originally developed for military purposes to detect the presence of ships and submarines, is used to create a picture of the fetus showing size, position, formation, age, and condition. It reveals some defects.

Chorionic villi sampling can be used in the first trimester of pregnancy to detect Down syndrome and chromosomal abnormalities. Guided by ultrasound, a very thin plastic catheter is inserted through the vagina and cervix into the chorion, a layer of tissue that develops into the placenta. A sample is taken from the villi (tiny projections from the chorion), which transfer oxygen, nutrients, and wastes between mother and embryo. This test is considered an alternative to amniocentesis. However, the use of this technique can bring about a miscarriage in some cases.

The couple can then decide what to do if the fetus is affected. They can choose to allow the pregnancy to continue to term, have an abortion, or treat the defect if the technology is available.

The moral issues: The genetic counselor is responsible for maintaining confidentiality. Only if a serious and forseeable danger to others exists ought the rule of confidentiality be set aside and then only after the counselor has failed to persuade the parents to share the information themselves and after the counselor has indicated to them why and to whom the information must be disclosed.

The couple has a right to know that the counselor has their welfare at heart and that their welfare and interests will not be sacrificed for some long-term social interests. Ordinarily, the genetic counselor's obligation should never extend beyond the family, since the prime responsibility is always the welfare of the immediate counselees. When there is a conflict between the interests of the counselees and the interests of society at large, the burden of the justification is on the counselor who will have to help the counselees grasp the social implications and costs along with their own.

The issue of truth-telling is important, and the general rule that seems to be followed is that the counselees should be told the whole truth except when, in the counselor's judgment, it will do more harm than good. When some truth is withheld by the counselor, then he or she must be prepared to justify the reason or reasons for this.

The controversy arose not with the techniques used in prenatal diagnosis nor with the notion of genetic counseling but when couples chose abortion as the means to solve the problem of how to avoid bringing into the world a child with a genetically determined disease or defect. Abortion in such a situation is called selective abortion.

The proponents of prenatal diagnosis with selective abortion argue that we have an obligation to reduce or prevent suffering for the affected family, the fetus in question, and society, and we also have an obligation to prevent genetic diseases and their impact on future generations until such time as we have successful genetic therapies available. Their particular arguments are:

1. Not only does a seriously affected fetus not have a right to be born, it has a right *not* to be born when the only outcome will be intense suffering and certain death. The right to life is not absolute; it is conditional on the rights of others and dependent on the ability of the individual, with the help of others, to live a human life. When such a human life is impossible, then that fetus has a right *not* to be born.

2. With the birth of an infant having a serious genetic disease or defect, the entire family suffers and not just the infant. The emotional impact of such a birth can be devastating to the parents' self-understanding and alters their sexual activity significantly. When the handicap also involves serious mental retardation, the demands for care to protect the child from harm increase greatly and the other children in the family do not receive as much attention and care as they need. Prenatal diagnosis with selective therapeutic abortion can assure parents that they will have unaffected offspring and so avoid the suffering that an affected child would have and the suffering that would be inflicted on the family.

3. Since the decision to abort a seriously affected fetus is made by the parents who are the ones who would have to live with and care for the child were the pregnancy allowed to continue to term, there is no way that other individuals or society as a whole ought to restrict their freedom and rights in such a matter. The physician does not necessarily and certainly ought not to exercise undue influence on the parents to decide one way rather than another. At times, the good of the race should override the good of the individual and, in cases in which defective offspring grow up to reproduce, society itself is endangered because such individuals increase the number of deleterious genes in the gene pool. Prenatal diagnosis with selective abortion ought

to be used to control humanity's genetic destiny to ensure the well-being of future generations. We cannot afford to be sentimental about the victims of birth defects such as Tay-Sachs disease and Down syndrome, for such individuals would have been better off if they had not been born. To concentrate all our energies on caring for defective individuals would divert us from the more important task of trying to prevent such births in the first place.

4. Parents have an obligation to control the consequences of reproduction. No couple has a right to bring defective children into the world, children who will suffer a great deal and simply be burdens on the family and society. If they are a moderate- to high-risk couple, they have an obligation to seek out prenatal diagnosis and genetic counseling with selective abortion.

Its critics develop two themes in their writings: (1) abortion violates a basic purpose of medicine, namely, to save life; and (2) even though some abortions may be justified, to use prenatal diagnosis to set apart certain fetuses as deserving abortion is to treat such fetuses unequally and unjustly. The particular arguments of the critics are:

1. The right to life is fundamental to all persons, for all are born with impulses to self-preservation. A defective physical condition does not provide any reason not to respect that right to life. Care, not killing, is due the defective fetus in the same way it is due any ailing person. To single out defective fetuses for abortion on the basis of arbitrary and changeable social and personal reasons threatens the moral equality of all persons who, by reason of their personhood, have a right to life.

2. No one denies that genetically defective children sometimes suffer terribly nor does anyone deny that the family of such a child also suffers a great deal. However, to call selective abortion therapeutic is not only euphemistic but illogical as well. Abortion is killing and cannot logically be called therapeutic for the fetus. Therapy has to do with care and healing, not killing. Therapeutic abortion is a contradiction in terms.

3. The reasoning in favor of selective abortion

is flawed on the grounds of (a) inappropriate line-drawing concerning the types of fetuses to be aborted, because any determination of categories of fetuses to be considered destructible is subject to the caprices of social opinion; (b) unequal treatment of the innocent and unconsenting fetus, because we open ourselves to the risk of treating all weak, defenseless, and socially undesirable people as deserving destruction and also place ourselves at risk in the very process; (c) putting the physician in the role of a technician who fulfills the desires of society rather than leaving the physician in the role of healer, and (d) giving unwarranted power to physicians to decide who shall live or die, because as physicians they have no special training or competence to make such decisions.

4. Just because we *can* perform selective abortions is no justification for concluding that they *ought* to be done, especially in view of the fact that selective abortion contradicts the equal right to life. A technology that introduces such a moral contradiction into the social body must be drastically restricted and used only for therapeutic intentions within the practice of fetology. The desire for a selective abortion can never be a sufficient reason to sacrifice the greater good of respect for the moral principles of equality and justice that protect life and nurture social existence.

Among ethicians who have looked into this controversy, we find some who try to find a mediating position between the two extremes. They try to retain as many of the contending values, rights, and situational factors as possible while, at the same time, not absolutizing a particular value to the exclusion of other values, for example, the right of the fetus to live as opposed to the right of the mother to choose to terminate her pregnancy. These ethicians would favor selective abortion in medically severe cases as long as society adopts a policy of providing financial assistance for families who choose to accept a defective infant and financial support for the research required to perfect genetic therapies; they would support freedom for parents who object to selective abortion on moral or religious

grounds and would claim malpractice on the part of genetic counselors who withhold abortion information in connection with prenatal diagnosis because of the counselor's own convictions on abortion.

To theists holding a natural law ethics, neither the argument of the proponents of selective abortion nor the middle position just described is satisfactory. We simply may never do evil that good may come of it. There is no moral justification for direct abortion even in the difficult circumstances described above. We have no right to engage in the direct killing of the innocent. The only line of reasoning open to those who wish to make a case for selective abortion is the same as that open to those who wish to make a case for abortion on demand, namely, to establish that the fetus is not an incipient human person and so has no right to life, or to demonstrate that the fetus is actually an unwitting aggressor against the mother and so forfeits its right to life. So far this has not been successfully done.

Artificial Insemination

A good deal has already been written about the issues involved in artificial insemination. Whether it involves the sperm of the husband (AIH) or that of a donor (AID), this issue raises difficult questions for those whose cultural roots are Judeo-Christian. Why? Because artificial insemination seems to be totally opposed to the very meaning of human sexuality and parenthood. Through our bodily sexuality, we realize our human power both to love and to create other beings like ourselves. To separate in principle the realm of human love from the realm of human procreation strikes very profoundly at the human in all of us.

The reasons for making use of this reproductive technology can be either individual and personal or for the good of society. For example, AIH can be used to fertilize a surrogate mother when the wife is known to be the carrier of a serious genetic disease. The couple want children, but if they copulate they are at serious risk of producing a defective child. If the husband is the carrier, AID could be used for the same individual and personal reason. On the other hand, this technique could be used in a program of positive eugenics, the preferential breeding of so-called superior individuals to improve the genetic stock of a larger society. We shall limit our discussion to the individual and personal reasons, since the question of positive eugenics was discussed in Chapter 20.

Ethicians can be divided into two groups on the question of AID: (1) those who maintain it is morally justifiable and (2) those who argue on the basis of natural law that it is not at all justifiable.

The presuppositions of those who think that it can be fully justified are: (1) an act or practice is right and just if, on balance, it does more good than harm and helps minimize human suffering; (2) sexual love and the generation of human life are two quite disparate activities; (3) parenthood as a relationship is essentially and primarily defined by acts of nurturing, not by acts of sexual intercourse. Those favoring AID present the following arguments:

1. Donor insemination does not of itself violate the marriage covenant, because marriage is not exclusively a physical notion concerned with sexual intercourse. The mutual consent by husband and wife protects the couple who use a donor from the accusation of infidelity to one another.

2. AID makes parenthood possible for couples who love one another deeply but are incapable of producing a healthy child without the help of this reproductive technology. As long as the consent is mutual, the child conceived by means of AID can be loved and nurtured as well as any child conceived without the help of medical technology. To make parenthood take its roots exclusively in sexual intercourse within marriage is to biologicize marriage needlessly.

3. At present, the practice is to keep the relationship between the donor and the wife completely impersonal, but this need not and probably ought not to be the case. The child ought eventually to know his or her father. Deception is never a healthy thing for any relationship and

certainly not for the parent-child relationship. The name of the donor ought to be a matter of record. Since the husband has agreed to the use of the donor, there is no reason why the wife should not know his name and certainly no reason why the husband and wife should not tell their child at the proper time. The act of nurturing is what constitutes parenthood, not simply the act of generating. The donor, by providing the needed sperm, simply cooperates in the generation of the child. The husband and wife have the responsibility for nurturing the child. The donor cannot be faulted for not accepting that responsibility, because it is not his in the first place.

4. Masturbation for purposes of artificial insemination is just one way of acquiring the needed sperm. Other methods are available. Nevertheless, masturbation does no physiological harm to the donor; it is emotionally and relationally damaging only if and when the donor's intentions and attitudes make it so. In the case of donor insemination, the donor could have a procreative purpose for his masturbatory act, but more than likely he will be motivated by the fees he receives. If he is prostituting his sex function, he still cannot be accused of damaging a marriage since he is, at least at present, anonymous and the mutual consent of husband and wife protects their marriage from such damage.

Those opposed to AID base their arguments on the following points: (1) factors other than consequences must be taken into account in making a valid ethical evaluation of any human act; (2) the relationship between sexual love and the generation of new human life is meaningful and reciprocal, that is, one act both expresses that love and generates new life; (3) every procreation of a child must be the result of sexual intercourse within the unity of marriage; (4) the act of generating life is parental in nature and carries with it the obligation to nurture the life generated; (5) the child is the living image of the spouses' mutual love and self-giving, the concrete living expression of their paternity and maternity. They reject AID as immoral with the following arguments:

1. AID is a violation of the marriage covenant in which husband and wife have mutually agreed to perform generative sex acts only with one another. To use AID, even in an extreme case and by mutual consent, is to break this bond of covenantal fidelity to one another.

2. Since the child is the embodiment of the abiding and unitive love of husband and wife, AID takes procreation out from the intimacy of this loving union and isolates it in a sphere beyond this intimacy. Parenthood ought not to be separated from the act of generation, for parenthood is a natural consequence of the act of generative love.

3. AID violates the rights of the child by depriving it of its filial relationship with its father and can hinder the process of the child's maturing personal identity. The donor remains anonymous and, in doing so, violates the right of the child to know him and his love. The donor exercises his fatherhood without accepting the obligation to nurture the child. AID brings about a rupture between genetic parenthood, gestational parenthood, and responsibility for upbringing. Such damage to the personal relationships within the family threatens the unity and stability of the family and so harms society, for the family is the basic unit of society.

4. Even if all the other reasons for using AID were good reasons, the means for obtaining the sperm makes it immoral. The donor masturbates to produce the sperm. Even when done with a good intent, masturbation is immoral because it drives a wedge between the unitive and procreative meanings of human sexual intercourse.

Ethicians who oppose AID do not oppose AIH as long as the act of intercourse is carried on in the normal fashion *and* the technical help of the physician is used only to facilitate the act and help it reach its natural objectives. If the technical procedure were to replace the act of sexual intercourse altogether, these ethicians would regard the procedure as immoral.

The ethicians who oppose AID and restrict AIH represent the natural law tradition that affirms the inseparable connection between the unitive and procreative meanings of the act of sexual intercourse within the unity of marriage. The connection between the two meanings of intercourse is based on the link between the goods of marriage, the mutual love of husband and wife, and their capacity for fatherhood and motherhood. Both the link between the goods of marriage and the link between the meanings of the act of sexual intercourse are based on the unity of the human person, a unity that is spiritual and bodily at the same time. Procreation must conform to the dignity of the person, the dignity of the persons involved in the procreative act and the dignity of the person generated in that act. The child conceived must be the result of its parents' love. To desire and conceive the child as the product of technical intervention, be it medical or biological or both, is to reduce that child to being an object of scientific technology. Because we *can* do something does not mean necessarily that we have either the *right* or the *obligation* to do it.

Surrogate Motherhood

Surrogacy is a method assisting couples to have children without the wife's having to become pregnant. The term "surrogate mother" is currently being used to name a woman who conceives, bears, and delivers a baby for others. The name is misleading, because a surrogate normally means a substitute for the real thing. In this context, however, the "surrogate mother" is actually the child's real mother, who has agreed prior to insemination to give up the child to the father and his wife.

Surrogacy programs are currently being used mostly by affluent couples with a fertile husband and a wife who is either infertile, or has a genetic disease that she does not want to transmit or a medical problem that makes pregnancy impossible or inadvisable. The "surrogate mother" enters into a contractual agreement with the couple for money; the contract calls for the "surrogate mother" to give up to the couple the child that is born through insemination with the husband's sperm. This is really a form of AID with the further complication that the "surrogate mother" may herself be married. The net result of carrying out the contractual agreement is this: (1) the husband within the couple that wants a child gives his sperm to a woman who is not his wife, and (2) a woman who may be the wife of another man is inseminated with sperm that is not her husband's. A third party has entered into the motherhood and fatherhood spheres, disrupting the unity of the family. The man who has given his sperm receives the child to exercise his fatherhood in loving and raising the child with his wife. The "surrogate mother" exercises her motherhood only during the period of gestation and then by the terms of the contract must give up the child and so deny her motherhood thereafter. For any surrogacy program to succeed, the "surrogate mother" must be prepared not to love the child and not to want to keep it.

The child of surrogacy, conceived and born through a surrogate arrangement, enters the world unable to establish and maintain a substantial relationship with his or her genetic mother. The contract precludes such a relationship in advance. The child is a product of a commercial transaction (when the "surrogate mother" is paid a fee). The consequences for the child can become more and more devastating as he or she grows to maturity should he or she ever learn of the circumstances surrounding his or her conception and birth. The child is not the creation of the love between his or her father and genetic mother. Love between father and mother has had nothing to do with producing this child.

Surrogacy is wrong not merely because of the effects it has on the child. It is also wrong because it disrupts the unity of a marriage by introducing a third party into the marriage relationship to assume the mother's procreative role and is a threat to the stability of that family. A child born of a "surrogate mother" is not a bond between the father and his wife and can easily be a divisive force. If the "surrogate mother" herself has a family, her other children are going to react negatively to the fact that their baby brother or sister has been given away. The entire program, however well-intentioned, harms the unity and stability of marriage and the family and so harms

society as well, because the family is the basic unit of society.

SINGLE PERSONS

The case of the single person deserves attention because, apart from the divorced or widowed, more and more men and women are remaining single for a number of reasons. Some choose to remain single to pursue a career or profession; others see so many marriages end in divorce that they are reluctant to marry; still others are convinced that the population problem would be aggravated if every single person married; finally, some want to satisfy their sexual desires without marrying and having to accept the responsibility of caring for children. The attitude of society is becoming more accepting of those who remain unmarried, and properly so because the individual has no moral obligation to marry.

Nevertheless, the single person is a sexual being who must live in a way that will contribute to his or her personal growth and integration as well as that of others. The value of interpersonal growth and development is so great that it is worth the risk of entering into close personal relationship with another person of the same or opposite sex. A healthy relationship between single individuals will foster the same values mentioned earlier: personal love and freedom, respect and reverence for the other as a person, honesty, fidelity, service to life, social responsibility, and joy.

Interpersonal relations between responsible persons need not and ought not be lacking in signs of warmth, affection, love, and friendship. The signs, however, ought to be in proportion to the nature of the relationship. The casual sex of the so-called "swinging singles," sex for fun or recreation, is self-destructive, exploitative, unstable, and consistently not life-serving. This is not our concern here. We are concerned for responsible persons who may be drawn to give one another intimate expressions of love, even genital expression. Is such genital expression moral or not?

The following reasons have been put forth in favor of the moral allowability of nonmarital sex.

1. Aside from cases of prostitution and seduction, where sex is bought and sold like a commodity or where undue advantage is taken of another's innocence, it is hard to see any wrong in a sex act guarded against possible pregnancy. The sex act itself is purely natural, neither right nor wrong. The idea that it is bad in itself or that it needs some excuse, such as procreation, for its performance is an old, irrational taboo, from which we are now emancipated.

2. It is false that sex is cheapened and degraded unless severe restrictions are put on it. Married persons might want to protect and rationalize their situation by interdicting sex to the unmarried, but they should have no right to impose their prejudices on the unmarried.

3. Sexual relations between the unmarried do not in any way harm the marriage possibilities of the two involved, whether they marry one another or not. Virginity in one's spouse can still be honored as a desirable trait for those who esteem it, but because some prefer it is no reason for making it a universal law. Nonmarital sex neither attacks the institution of marriage as such nor renders difficult any of its aims.

4. What is so important about a ceremony and a certificate? How can a few words and a piece of paper change an act from immoral to moral? Those who seriously love each other should be able to satisfy their love without asking anyone's permission or going through an empty ritual. At least those whose intimacy is not casual but serious have from nature itself the right to sexual relations. If society insists on it, they can go through the formalities later.

Those who maintain the immorality of nonmarital sex consider these arguments irrelevant and focus their attention on the persons of the two involved rather than on any harmful effects.

1. The sex act in itself is natural and morally neutral, but motives and circumstances must be considered in any act. If the two parties are merely using each other as means of gratification with no real love between them, they are guilty of seriously wronging each other's person, of degrading a person to the level of a thing. No one is morally allowed to do this to another or let it be done to oneself. If the relationship involves a genuine mutual commitment that preserves the important values already mentioned, then why not marry?

2. Nonmarital sex is not wrong because of any supposed monopoly of sex by the married. Only if they commit themselves unreservedly to one another for a lifelong union of shared love can they preserve their dignity as persons and respect the person of the other. This is what married people do and what the unmarried, as long as they are unmarried, fail to do.

3. Nonmarital sexual relations seem to have no effect on subsequent marriage, and those who indulge in them can make just as good husbands or wives as those who come to marriage with their virginity intact. Thus the prevalence of nonmarital sex is not a danger to the institution of marriage, which continues to flourish anyway. No argument against nonmarital sex should be drawn from these sources. Its wrongness does not stem from its effects but from itself, from a failure of a complete and wholehearted giving of each self to the other, in which love consists.

4. If a man and woman really do love each other with total commitment and seriously intend to share their lives together, than as far as nature, philosophy, and right reason are concerned, they are married. If they seal their commitment by intercourse, their use of genital sex is not so much nonmarital as preceremonial. It is true that the state and the church have the right to regulate the public and social condition of marriage with certain formalities, even to making a marriage invalid unless they are complied with. However, it is not a certificate or a ceremony that marries them but their declaration of total commitment to each other. It is this that the marriage ceremony solemnizes and celebrates.

It follows that the only case of nonmarital sex that is morally allowable, a total, lifelong, exclusive commitment of love, turns out to be not nonmarital at all. If the two persons have felt this way about each other for sufficient time to know that they are serious, there seems to be no reason why they should refuse to go through a marriage ceremony.

MENTALLY RETARDED PERSONS

Special mention should be made of mentally retarded persons, for they too relate to the world as male or female. Their sexuality must not be denied them. They need special care and protection, special guidance and education, but they cannot be expected to live as nonsexual beings. They must be informed as much as possible about the nature of their sexuality and their inner feelings and urges. They have a right in this matter that must not be denied them, but that right has limitations. The limiting factor is the degree of responsibility the retarded person can personally assume for his or her behavior. Parents and counselors have a special responsibility to help the retarded person understand the degree of the handicap and to find the appropriate means of expressing his or her sexuality, that is to say, to find a means of expression that is truly proportionate with his or her ability to accept responsibility. Mentally retarded persons need to learn to express the sexual dimension of their personhood to achieve the degree of personal growth and integration into society of which they are capable. The public at large needs to rectify its stance toward mentally retarded persons.

HOMOSEXUALITY

Homosexuality or inversion is the erotic, sexual attraction of a person toward members of the same sex and the absence of attraction toward members of the opposite sex, at times to the extent of positive disgust at the very thought of genital relations with the opposite sex. Research to date suggests that it is impossible to categorize all persons simply as either heterosexual or homosexual, but that most persons are both with more of an emphasis on one rather than the other. Statistics seem to indicate that about 5% of the men and women in this country are *exclusively* homosexual through their entire lives. This means that some twelve million American men and women are exclusively homosexual.

Our concern here is with the *exclusively* homosexual person.

Society seems to be more willing to accept homosexuals than previously, but there is still a good deal of prejudice and misunderstanding. Many myths about homosexuals are still passing as facts with large segments of the public. The following are some examples:

1. Every homosexual is attracted to children and adolescents and wishes to have genital sex with them.
2. Male homosexuals look and act effeminate, while female homosexuals look and act masculine.
3. Homosexuals can recognize one another easily.
4. Homosexuals invariably tend toward particular professions, for example, music, theatre, other fine arts, interior decorating.
5. All homosexuals are promiscuous and unable to form enduring relationships.
6. Homosexuals, having deliberately chosen their sexual orientation, can correct their situation by an act of will or by getting to know some member of the opposite sex intimately.

It goes without saying that these myths are just that—myths. A person's sexual orientation, as far as we know, is not set by a deliberate act of will. The homosexual person finds himself or herself with an orientation to the same sex just as a heterosexual does to the opposite sex. The orientation is a felt sexual attraction or preference over which we have no control once it is formed. Much scientific research has been done but with inconclusive results as to the causes of homosexuality. The homosexual orientation is not a confusion about one's maleness or femaleness but rather a preference for persons of one's own sex as erotic partners. While we have no control over the orientation or preference itself, we have control over our behavior that stems from our sexual orientation.

Homosexuals have the same needs and rights to love, intimacy, and relationships as heterosexuals, and they are bound to strive for the same ideals of human wholeness and integration into society. The norms governing the morality of homosexual activity are those that govern all sexual activity. The homosexual must judge his or her relationships and actions in terms of whether or not they are loving and self-liberating, enriching to the other person by reason of the respect and reverence for him or her as a person, honest, faithful, life-serving, and joyous. All of us, homosexuals and heterosexuals alike, are bound to avoid depersonalizing ourselves and others because selfishness, dishonesty, and promiscuity are harmful both to the individual and to society.

Although homosexuality is more openly and sympathetically regarded today than in the past, large segments of our society still consider it morally wrong and they base their position either on religious views or on traditional natural law arguments. We are not concerned here with theological but rather with philosophical arguments that point to the immorality of the practice of genital sex between homosexuals. The chief reasons seem to be the following:

1. The Judeo-Christian tradition has constantly regarded genital sex between homosexuals as unnatural, a perversion of the meaning of human sexuality, and therefore immoral. The argument runs as follows: (a) The objective meaning of sexual acts is to be an expression of a loving relationship, one that is totally self-giving and creative of new human life. Acts of genital sex derive their *human* meaning from such a loving relationship. (b) Any act of genital sex that does not express this interpersonal relationship is a use of sex without human meaning, because it withdraws from the values that nourish this relationship. Such acts are a misuse of a symbol that tends of its own nature to strengthen within marriage the love uniting a husband and wife *and* to engender a child. (c) Homosexual genital sex represents a withdrawal from and a rejection of this relationship and a rejection of at least the value of engendering a new human life. (d) Hence the practice of homosexual genital sex is a refusal to grow in one's own intersubjectivity and heterosexuality, a rejection of one's own personal growth. (e) Since the distinction between male and female is part of the natural order willed by

the Creator, heterosexual genital sex must be normative in the matter of generating new human life. Homosexual intercourse can never be generative or creative in this sense. Consequently, any kind of genital sexual expression between two partners of the same sex, even though it may be loving and said to strengthen the union between them, will always be contrary to the order of nature by reason of its failure to be open to procreation and therefore immoral.

2. The fundamental order of nature and the existence of the male and female sexes justify speaking of homosexuality as unnatural, as not in accord with the order of nature. Homosexuality as a sexual orientation must be placed on the same level with abnormal personality structure, mental illness, and psychological aberration. The very orientation of the homosexual is abnormal, an objective disorder, and the genital behavior flowing from such an orientation must be regarded as sick, in need of healing. Neither the orientation nor the genital behavior based on the orientation can be placed on the same level with the normal natural order of the sexes. From this it follows that the homosexual is called on to regard and recognize his or her condition as something questionable. The homosexual must therefore be willing to be treated or healed as far as this is possible so that he or she can be brought back into the right order of things.

The truly human sexual orientation is heterosexual; the homosexual orientation is less than human. Each of us has a moral obligation to care for our health, both psychic and physical. If we find ourselves with a homosexual orientation that is influencing our behavior in such a way as to hamper our full development as persons, and this is what genital homosexual behavior does, then we have a moral obligation to seek healing, seek a cure. If psychotherapy is possible, then it should be tried so that the person can change his or her orientation or at least learn to act and behave heterosexually. This is the only way to protect the very important values of unitive and procreative love. While a person's sexual orientation is usually not freely chosen and is therefore not morally reprehensible, the person is usually free and in control of his or her actual behavior. Since homosexual behavior flows from the homosexual orientation and is unnatural, the homosexual should seek to change or shift his or her orientation if this is at all possible. This is the only way to avoid depreciating and making a mockery of the full human meaning of sex.

3. To be human means to be a sexual being, a being who has at the core of his or her being the urge to relate to members of both sexes to form interpersonal relationships. While these relationships can develop into warm affective friendships, the relationship between a man and a woman who love one another and are married is the only one in which genital sexual expression can ever be appropriate according to the right order of nature. To use genital sex to express one's love in any other interpersonal relationship is a violation of that right order of nature. The only responsible way for homosexuals to behave is for them to live celibate lives, for they are bound by the same moral law that binds unmarried heterosexuals to live celibate lives.

4. While it is possible for two persons of the same sex to love one another in the deepest sense of the word and to establish a permanent relationship based on that genuine mutual love, such a relationship can never be enough to justify the use of genital sex. Homosexuals do use genital sex to express mutual love and affection, but such use always falls short of the human meaning of sexual communion. Genital sex is ideally for us humans an act of creative love; it does express the mutual love and affection, but it always goes further in its being open to the generation of a new human being who is like the two partners, a concrete image of their mutual love. This ideal will always elude homosexuals, for genital sex between homosexuals can never be creative of a new human being because it is not even open to such creativity in the first place. Homosexual genital sex is essentially incomplete as an expression of fully human love and full sexual communion.

5. Homosexuals frequently engage in casual sexual encounters with little or no regard for love. Genital sex is used for sheer pleasure and recreation. Even though the homosexual orientation is not in and of itself morally reprehensible, such casually promiscuous behavior is always immoral because it depersonalizes both parties to the act. Such sexual activity is neither open to the creation of a new human being nor is it, in any sense of the word, love-making. It depreciates the meaning of human sexuality by indulging in the selfish taking of sexual pleasure through the use of another person's body. Mutual consent to such activity does not make it any the less damaging and immoral, because each person consents to an impersonal act and, in so doing, depersonalizes both himself or herself and the consenting partner. Such an act of depersonalized sex totally negates the human symbol that sexual intercourse is ideally meant to be, a sign of total, unreserved mutual self-giving. Genital sex is meant to be expressive of oneself as a person. To be completely sincere and not a lie, the sexual communion must grow out of the existing relationship between the persons. In the absence of all emotional contact and responsible pledge, the act of genital sex is the ultimate insincerity, nothing more than impersonal self-gratification.

These arguments against the practice of genital sex between homosexuals overlap to some extent, but each highlights a different side of the question. They are a strong presentation of the natural law ethic, but the publicity given to homosexuality, its growing acceptance by well-meaning people, and the unsatisfactoriness of continence for some homosexuals invite us to rethink the whole question. Some adherents of the natural law ethic challenge the foregoing arguments on two main counts:

1. A deeper understanding of human sexuality requires that we revise some of our opinions on the exact natural character of the reproductive process.
2. Ethical honesty and sincerity require that we reconsider some of our views concerning the proper interpretation of the natural law.

The following counterarguments have been proposed:

1. The Judeo-Christian tradition assumes—it does not prove—that the order of nature demands human genital expressions of love be heterosexual. In actual fact, we are sexual beings who are quite capable of giving genital expression of our love to persons of either sex. There is nothing artificial or unnatural about either homosexual or heterosexual sex. Each is an expression of our sexuality, though the heterosexual expression is more common than the homosexual. The true purpose of the genital organs is said to be the reproduction of our own kind. No other organ in the human body is capable of performing this function. The natural order of things demands that our genital organs be used for this purpose. To use them for any other purposes is said to be unnatural, abusive, potentially harmful, and therefore wrong.

Our sexual organs seem to be uniquely adapted for other purposes also. They are well adapted, with their great concentration of nerve endings, to give their owners and others intense pleasure. Since they are naturally so designed, to use them for pleasure does not appear to be unnatural. The sex organs are also uniquely adapted to express the deepest and most intimate of emotions, the mutual love of one person for another. Human beings are very complex and adaptable creatures. The generalization that a given organ has one and only one proper function does not hold up, for the function or purpose of a given organ may vary according to the needs and/or desires of its owner.

The assumption of the natural law argument is that what is natural is good, what is unnatural is bad. Homosexual sex is said to be unnatural, having some quality objectively identifiable as unnatural and therefore detrimental to those who engage in such behavior or to those around them. Because of this detrimental characteristic of the behavior, it must be considered wrong, immoral, something to be discouraged by society. The argument fails to identify the objectively detrimental quality. Furthermore, the concepts "unnatural" and "bad" are not synonyms; they are different

concepts. The natural law argument must be rejected.

2. It is at best questionable and at worst manipulative to assume that homosexuality must always be regarded as an abnormality and sickness (illness). The presently established order of things institutionalizes heterosexuality as normative of what a sexual orientation ought to be. The Judeo-Christian tradition of our culture is precisely what does that institutionalizing. If our society can get the homosexual to regard himself or herself as abnormal and ill in a physical and/or psychological sense, then the homosexual will want to be cured so as to be able to function within the established order of society as a normal heterosexual.

No one knows definitively as yet the physical causes of the human sexual orientation. The natural sciences are not in a position to back up society's view with irrefutable facts. The psychiatrists and psychologists are far from unanimous in calling homosexuality a mental illness or mental disorder. Society exerts a great deal of pressure on homosexuals to change, but it has very little ground thus far for exerting such pressure. Other cultures such as the Polynesians of Bora Bora, the Melanesian, the Koniag of Alaska, the Lango of East Africa, and the Tanala of Madagascar are either more tolerant of homosexuality or accord the homosexual special, respected status in the community. Each of us needs to be comfortable with his or her sexual orientation. If the heterosexual majority continues to segregate the homosexual minority and reject it, this may induce some homosexuals to try to change their orientation for a heterosexual self-identity. Psychotherapy and intensive psychological counseling are not notably successful and the reason may be that it is impossible for the definitive homosexual to change.

3. The heterosexual majority expects the exclusively and irreversibly homosexual person to live a celibate life. Why? What legitimate expectation can the heterosexual majority have for the homosexual minority? No one's sexual orienta-

tion gives him or her any special privileges except the call to be himself or herself. Each of us is a sexual being with a capacity for relating to others as persons and so for loving others as persons. Sexuality is what is essentially human, not the particular orientation. It is possible to misuse both the homosexual and heterosexual orientation depending on how the other person is approached. The capacity for love, caring, and fellowship can be misused and has been misused by persons of both orientations. This constitutes a violation of our personhood in both cases, not just in the case of the homosexual. How we use our sexuality is much more important than what particular orientation one has.

4. Biologically speaking, the only genital sex act that can create new human life is that between a man and a woman. Genital sex between persons of the same sex is said, for this reason, to be unnatural and therefore immoral or, to put the matter more leniently, essentially incomplete, not the fullness of human sexual expression, not normative for full sexual communion, one that can never be ideal. This view of human sexuality is taken from the heterosexual point of view, which is assumed to be normative, the ideal, fully complete, the fullness of the meaning of sexual communion. Philosophically speaking, the assumption remains unproven but is used as though it were an absolute truth. The preponderance of the evidence seems to favor heterosexuality as the ideal for human sexual expression, but this does not warrant the conclusion that is drawn from it. The biological basis of the argument is also suspect, for if we are speaking of a law of nature we are speaking of something that is simply descriptive. Such a law imposes no obligation on anyone or anything. All it does is state a matter of fact, namely, that when new human life is produced it is the result of the genital coupling of a man and a woman. The law of nature enables us to predict what will be the case, not what morally ought to be the case.

5. Genital sex between heterosexuals is also often not an expression of love in addition to being closed to the creation of new human life. Such activity on the part of heterosexuals depreciates the meaning of human sexuality just as much as the same kind of activity on the part of homosexuals does. The argument fails to show that all genital expression between homosexuals is depersonalizing.

Range of Conviction

There is no consensus among ethicians on this question. As far as these arguments are concerned, some find the natural law arguments thoroughly convincing, others hold to the natural law conclusions with some reservations, and still others find them unsatisfactory. They are also divided concerning the orientation itself: some hold that the orientation is unnatural and therefore immoral; others hold that the orientation, not being a matter of choice, cannot be regarded as intrinsically immoral but as morally neutral. Among those regarding the orientation as morally neutral, some hold that genital sex among homosexuals is always immoral, and others maintain that genital sex for homosexuals in the context of a loving union striving for permanence is objectively good. The entire question is further complicated for two reasons: (1) traditional views, since they are our moral heritage, are not lightly to be set aside, and (2) serious and difficult obligations are not to be imposed unless they are certain.

On the question of the morality of genital sex for the exclusively homosexual person, the range of current conviction can be expressed as follows:

1. Orientation unnatural, acts unnatural. Ethicians who find the natural law arguments thoroughly convincing admit doubts about some of the facts connected with homosexuality, but they find no doubt about what the natural law prescribes. Since there is no doubt about the law, probabilism cannot be invoked in favor of countenancing genital sex for exclusively homosexual persons even if such acts are done in the context of a loving relationship with both parties striving for a permanent union. No person of whatever sexual orientation is ever allowed to engage in genital sex acts that sever the procreative aspect of the act from its unitive aspect. Each act of genital sex ought to be open to the possibility of generating new life. This is the moral norm that the natural law holds out to each person, and each person must measure his or her sexual activity by this norm or standard. Genital sex between homosexual persons will always be objectively immoral no matter what the subjective attitudes of the sexual partners may be. Morality is not a matter of statistics. Philosophically speaking, it is a matter of right reasoning. As in all complex matters, but especially in one so important to us as persons and as a race, each person must take particular care to avoid doing objective evil.

2. Orientation illness, acts unnatural. Some ethicians agree with the natural law arguments in maintaining the unnaturalness of the homosexual orientation. Furthermore, they hold that the orientation is an illness comparable to alcoholism. Without being condemnatory toward the homosexual person, they urge him or her to try to change orientation with the help of psychotherapy, because the orientation is a psychic disorder. The person is not blameworthy because of the orientation but only because of the genital sex acts which stem from the orientation. The homosexual person is counseled to abstain altogether from genital sex activity just as an alcoholic is counseled to refrain from taking even one drink, because the consequences are bad in each case. Furthermore, the consequences of accepting homosexual relationships as good would have unacceptable implications for the institution of marriage, the limitations appropriate to genital sex activity, the rearing of children, and the family as a natural society.

3. Orientation unnatural, acts sometimes acceptable. This group also holds the conclusions of the natural law argument but with some reservations. The homosexual orientation, while it is unnatural and cannot be regarded otherwise, is not in itself immoral. Since that is the case and since the ideal form of intercourse is

heterosexual, the better thing for the homosexual person is to abstain altogether from acts of genital sex and sublimate his or her sexual desires. Some homosexual persons, however, are unable to practice such abstinence and, when that is the case, they should try to give genital expression to their love in the only morally responsible way open to them, namely, in a fully committed relationship of love.

4. Orientation acceptable, acts acceptable. This group of ethicians bases its position on the premise that the homosexual orientation is a given, not a free choice, and on the conviction that homosexual relationships can be the vehicle for interpersonal love, growth, and development. While the use of genital sex ought not to be separated from responsible love, genital sex and the procreative possibility need not be irrevocably joined together. Even for heterosexuals it is moral for two people to marry and engage in acts of genital sex with one another although one of them is known to be irrevocably sterile.

Concluding thoughts. The discussion from these various points of view continues. The sheer quantity of books and articles published in recent years points to the complexity of the matter. No textbook can hope to deal definitively with such a vast question. From what has been said, the reader can see to some extent the depth and makeup of the discussion as it goes on. The last word has not yet been written on homosexuality. A thoughtful look at a very complex matter has been attempted here in the hope that it may help others begin to understand. As persons we have to find truth for ourselves. We have the right to make the search and to accept the results we sincerely arrive at and, if our search is inconclusive, we have the right to reserve judgment until further investigation convinces us one way or another.

SUMMARY

This chapter continues the previous one.

To be human is to be a sexual being. *Sex* is a biologically based need oriented toward generation of new life and toward pleasure and release of tension as well. The aim of sex is genital activity culminating in orgasm. *Sexuality* is our self-understanding and self-expression, our way of being in the world, as male or female. It is a sign of our incompleteness as individuals and a means of calling us to interrelate with other human beings, to communicate and commune with them. Interpersonal encounter is always sexual, whether it be genital or not, and shows the *purpose of sexuality* to be both creative and integrative of the personal self as an individual and as a member of society.

The *moral evaluation of sexual conduct* involves a recognition of both the subjective and objective aspects of human conduct, an awareness of the complexity and unity of the person's sexuality, an effort to keep the creative and integrative aspects of sexuality in balance, and a keen awareness of the interpersonal dimension of the sexual experience. Since the ultimate judge is the well-formed individual conscience, it will keep in mind the universal principle of creative growth as a person toward integration as a self into society, the particularly important values associated with human sexuality, and the concrete precepts and guidelines of tradition.

Chastity is the virtue that enables us to transform the power of our sexuality into a creative and integrative force in our lives whether we are vowed or promised celibates, married, or unmarried.

Marriage regarded legally as an institution was said to have as its *primary end* the begetting and rearing of children and as its *secondary end* the mutual love and help between the spouses. But marriage regarded as an ideal and as a personal experience can be said to have only one end, and that is *love* in its widest scope and on all levels, personal, sexual, and companionate.

Birth control, in the sense of artificial *contraception,* has been traditionally regarded as an immoral use of sex within marriage. Its immorality is now being challenged.

Arguments against contraception: Contraception frustrates the primary end of marriage, interferes with nature's design, is a form of unnatural perversion, seeks the pleasure while avoiding the responsibility, contaminates the temple of one's body, seeks and simultaneously hinders the procreative good, is psychologically unsatisfying, and impugns the totality of the surrender in marriage.

Replies: The rearing of children is as primary as their begetting, all human art and science interfere with nature, not fertility itself but overfertility is controlled, responsibilities need not be created, reproduction is not more sacred than other acts, the procreative good need not be sought in every act, an overlarge family is psychologically frustrating, and the ideal can never be perfectly realized.

Continence and *rhythm,* not being forms of *artificial* contraception, are morally acceptable means of family limitation.

Genetic diagnosis and counseling aim at preventing genetic disease in individuals or families. Moderate- to high-risk families are identified through the birth of an affected child. Specially skilled and trained professionals make the diagnosis and then educate the family concerning the genetic mechanism, prognosis, and alternative courses of action available to manage the genetically determined disorder.

Selective abortion is the use of abortion to avoid bringing into the world a child with a genetically determined disease or defect. *Proponents* of the procedure argue that seriously affected fetuses have a right not to be born; it saves the child and its family from needless suffering; the parents have the freedom and right to make such a decision; it protects society from an increasing number of deleterious genes in the gene pool; it ensures the well-being of future generations; and parents who use this procedure are simply being responsible about their reproduction. A *mediating position* favors selective abortion in medically severe cases as long as society (1) provides financial assistance to families who accept the defective children born to them and (2) supports research to perfect genetic therapies. *Critics* of this procedure, among them the author and the reviser of this book, argue that it is immoral on grounds that it violates the fetus's right to life, is not therapeutic for the fetus, opens society to the possibility of killing anyone considered undesirable, treats defective fetuses unequally and unjustly, removes the physician from the role of healer, gives physicians unwarranted power to decide who shall live or die, and sacrifices respect for the moral principles of equality and justice, which protect life and nurture social existence.

Artificial insemination, whether it uses the sperm of the husband (AIH) or that of a donor (AID), is problematic because it seems to separate in principle the realm of human love from the realm of human procreation. The *proponents* presuppose (1) an act or practice is right and just if, on balance, it does more good than harm and helps minimize human suffering, (2) sexual love and the generation of human life are two quite disparate activities, and (3) parenthood as a relationship is essentially and primarily defined by acts of nurturing, not by acts of sexual intercourse. They argue AID is fully justified because it does not violate the marriage covenant when both husband and wife agree to use it, it makes parenthood possible for couples who would otherwise remain childless, it is not an act of parenthood on the part of the donor, and other means besides masturbation are available for obtaining the sperm. *Opponents* of AID, among them the author and the reviser of this book, presuppose (1) factors other than consequences must be taken into account in making a valid ethical evaluation of any human act, (2) the relationship between sexual love and the generation of new human life is meaningful and reciprocal, (3) the act of generating new life is parental in nature and carries with it the obligation to nurture the life generated. They argue AID is immoral because it is a violation of the marriage covenant, removes procreation from the sphere of intimate love, is an irresponsible exercise of the donor's fatherhood, and uses an immoral means to obtain the sperm.

Surrogacy is a method of assisting a couple to have a child without the wife becoming pregnant. "Surrogate mother" is the term used of a woman who agrees, by entering into a contract with the couple, to conceive by artificial insemination with the sperm of the husband, carry the child until

birth, and give it over to the couple shortly after birth, renouncing all rights to the baby as her own. Surrogacy is wrong because (1) the child will never know its genetic mother, (2) the child may find out later that it is the result of a commercial transaction and technological intervention rather than the result of procreative love between its father and mother, a fact which could be devastating for the child, (3) the contractual arrangement disrupts the unity of the couple's marriage by introducing a third party to assume the wife's procreative role, (4) the child can easily become a divisive factor between the father and his wife, and (5) if the "surrogate mother" is herself married with a family, the unity of her own marriage is disrupted by the introduction of a third party into the procreative process, and her other children may well react negatively to the fact of her giving away their baby brother or sister.

Nonmarital sex is being defended today, for if contraceptives are used, it causes harm to no one. But it is necessary to look not only for harmful effects but also at the persons involved. If it is meant as a serious and permanent commitment of love with all its responsibilities, it amounts to a common-law marriage and is not really nonmarital. Common-law marriages have an anti-social aspect about them and do not deserve moral approval.

Mentally retarded persons are sexual beings who, within the limits of the responsibility they can assume for their behavior, have a right to express their sexuality and so to achieve the degree of personal growth and integration into society of which they are capable.

Homosexuality is the erotic, sexual attraction of a person toward members of the same sex and the absence of attraction toward members of the opposite sex. This is a sexual orientation that the Judeo-Christian tradition has long regarded as unnatural and the behavior stemming from it as immoral. The immorality of the behavior and the unnaturalness of the orientation are now being challenged.

Arguments against homosexual genital behavior: Such behavior is a perversion of the order of nature willed by God, because it can never be procreative of a new human being; the truly human sexual orientation is heterosexual, while the homosexual orientation is abnormal and sick and, consequently, the behavior flowing from an abnormal and sick orientation must also be abnormal and sick; the use of genital sex to express mutual love in any interpersonal relationship other than in marriage is a violation of the right order of nature; homosexual genital sex is essentially incomplete and falls hopelessly short of the ideal of full human love and full sexual communion; frequently homosexuals engage in casual sexual encounters with no regard for love and thus depreciate the meaning of human sexuality while they demean both themselves and their partners as persons.

Replies: The tradition assumes, but does not prove, that the order of nature demands human genital expressions of love be heterosexual because only heterosexual intercourse is open to the creation of a new human being; sex organs can have more than one purpose other than procreation; the Judeo-Christian tradition has institutionalized heterosexuality as the only normal sexual orientation, but other cultures have accepted both orientations as good and valuable; to expect homosexuals to live celibate lives is a kind of persecution carried on by the heterosexual majority, but no one's sexual orientation gives him or her any special privileges; the law of nature merely enables us to predict what will be the case, not what morally ought to be the case; impersonal sex between heterosexuals is also immoral.

Questions for Discussion

1. Each one's sex life seems to be so private that it should hardly be discussed in ethics. Here, if anywhere, personal conscience should reign supreme. So long as no one is hurt, what a person does in private with another is his or her own business. What of this argument?

2. No laws can be laid down to regulate love and its genital manifestation. Human beings are sexual beings who have the personal responsibility for regulating their own genital behavior. Attempts by busybodies throughout history to regulate it have all been unsuccessful, for we have always had adultery, fornication, and homosexual behavior as long as there have been humans to do these things. Why continue this futile interference?

3. Whatever increases human freedom is morally good. Do you agree that contraception has been one of the greatest steps in the liberation of women, freeing them from the slavery of childbearing and rearing? Is contraception not preferable to abortion?

4. Do you have any reason not to approve of adultery? Should the frigid approve of it? If variety can be said to add to the spice of life, should you not approve of spouse-swapping and marital communes composed of congenial people who want more variety in their sex lives?

5. Take the arguments for and against artificial insemination by a donor as well as by a husband and apply them to *in vitro* fertilization (fertilization of ova in a test tube or laboratory dish using the sperm of either a donor or a husband). Go a step further and consider the case of a married couple that contributes its own ova and sperm for *in vitro* fertilization and has the fertilized egg implanted in the womb of a surrogate mother. Evaluate philosophically the natural law arguments against these procedures. What is your own reasoned position on these matters?

Readings

On love and sex in general see Ignace Lepp, *The Psychology of Loving;* Marc Oraison, *The Human Mystery of Sexuality;* Erich Fromm, *The Art of Loving;* C.S. Lewis, *The Four Loves;* Peter Bertocci, *Sex, Love and the Person;* John Wilson, *Logic and Sexual Morality;* Helmut Thielecke, *The Ethics of Sex;* John F. Dedek, *Contemporary Sexual Morality;* Charles E. Curran, *Issues in Sexual and Medical Ethics;* Anthony Kosnik, et al., *Human Sexuality: New Directions in American Catholic Thought;* Joseph and Lois Bird, *The Freedom of Sexual Love* is an excellent discussion of human sexuality; and James B. Nelson, *Embodiment: An Approach to Sexuality and Christian Theology.*

On birth control: John T. Noonan's *Contraception* is a thorough scholarly study; Louis Dupré, *Contraception and Catholics,* questions traditional views, whereas Germain Grisez, *Contraception and the Natural Law,* upholds them in a new way; John L. Thomas, *Marriage and Rhythm,* explores that particular subject; John Rock, *The Time Has Come,* argues for the "pill" he helped to discover. Dorothy Bromley, *Catholics and Birth Control,* offers a well-balanced short study by a non-Catholic. Archbishop T.D. Roberts, *Contraception and Holiness;* William Birmingham, *What Modern Catholics Think about Birth Control;* and Michael Novak, *The Experience of Marriage,* are collections of essays airing both sides of the question.

Read Pius XI's encyclical *Casti Connubii* (Christian Marriage) and Paul VI's *Humanae Vitae* (Of Human Life).

On genetics and reproduction: Consider the philosophical principles of the March 10, 1987, Vatican "Instruction on Respect for Human Life in its Origin and on the Dignity of Procreation," which is a careful statement in terms of natural law reasoning; Richard McCormick, "Reproductive Technologies: Ethical Issues," *Encyclopedia of Bioethics,* vol. 4, pp. 1454–1463; Robert F. Murray, "Genetic Diagnosis and Counseling," *Encyclopedia of Bioethics,* Vol. 2, 555–566; John C. Fletcher, "Prenatal Diagnosis: Ethical Issues," *Encyclopedia of Bioethics,* vol. 3, 1336–1345; William E.

May, *Human Existence, Medicine and Ethics;* George H. Kieffer, *Bioethics: A Textbook of Issues;* Joseph Fletcher, *The Ethics of Genetic Control: Ending Reproductive Roulette;* Paul Ramsey, *Fabricated Man: The Ethics of Genetic Control;* Bernard Häring, *Ethics of Manipulation: Issues in Medicine, Behavior Control and Genetics;* and James B. Nelson, *Human Medicine: Ethical Perspectives on New Medical Issues.*

On homosexuality: W. Dwight Oberholtzer, ed., *Is Gay Good? Ethics, Theology and Homosexuality,* presents an interesting discussion of the pros and cons by several authors among whom Henry J.M. Nouwen's "The Self-Availability of the Homosexual" deserves special attention; John F. Dedek, *Contemporary Medical Ethics,* has an interesting chapter on "Transsexualism and Homosexuality;" Anthony Kosnik, et al., *Human Sexuality: New Directions in American Catholic Thought,* James B. Nelson, *Embodiment: An Approach to Sexuality and Christian Theology,* and John J. McNeill, *The Church and the Homosexual* have influenced the discussion in the present chapter; Hendrik M. Ruitenbeek, *Homosexuality: A Changing Picture, A Contemporary Study and Interpretation,* discusses changes in psychiatric and clinical thinking; Burton Leiser, *Liberty, Justice, and Morals,* examines the unnaturalness argument; Wainwright Churchill, *Homosexual Behavior Among Males: A Cross-cultural and Cross-species Investigation,* has an excellent discussion of the acquisition of sexual preferences (orientations) together with an effort to discuss the morality of homosexual behavior; Peter Fisher, *The Gay Mystique: The Myth and Reality of Male Homosexuality,* gives a serious look at male homosexuality from a homosexual point of view; Del Martin and Phyllis Lyon, *Lesbian/Woman* discuss female homosexuality from the lesbian perspective; Joseph A. McCaffrey, ed., *The Homosexual Dialectic,* offers enlightening discussions from both the heterosexual and homosexual points of view.

PART V
Political Life

The political state is one social organization we cannot avoid. In the next three chapters we examine (1) the nature of the political state as a natural outgrowth of the family (Chapter 25), (2) the functioning of the state, or what we call the government (Chapter 26), and (3) the means available to us to protect our rights both natural and civil (Chapter 27).

25
State

PROBLEM

This part of ethics is sometimes called *political philosophy,* a study somewhere between political science and pure ethical theory. We need to be aware of the consciousness that dominates our perceptions of our social world; we dare not leave philosophy's critical, normative, and systematic task to the social scientists. For the sake of our lives both as personal beings and as citizens of some state, we must make the effort to frame for ourselves the genesis and historical development of the ideas and institutions of the state we live in, the liberal and democratic state. Political reflection is absolutely essential for every citizen, and such reflection presupposes critical moral principles that may be rationally grounded. We want to understand "what is" in terms of "what ought to be," that is, in terms of clear and defensible moral ideals.

In this chapter we shall deal with the state itself, its origin, properties, purpose, and structures. In the following chapter we shall discuss the functioning of the state, or government, and the moral means at our disposal to bring about needed changes. The matter for the present chapter can be arranged under the following headings:

1. Is the state a natural outgrowth of the family?
2. To what extent does the state depend on a contract?
3. To what extent is the state sovereign?
4. Is the state for the citizens or the citizens for the state?
5. How is the state built up out of its elements?

Our first problem deals with the origin of the state itself as a political entity, the transition of a people from a nonorganized to a politically organized condition. On this point there are two main opinions:

1. The state is a natural society because it arose as a natural outgrowth of the family.
2. The state is a merely conventional society because it arose from a social contract freely entered into.

NATURAL ORIGIN THEORY

The Greeks took it for granted that the state is a natural society, although they do not call it that, perhaps because they have no word for *society* in general but use the word *polis,* city, to stand for both state and society.

Plato derives the state from our economic needs, which of course are natural needs. He says:

> A state, I said, arises, as I conceive, out of the needs of mankind; no one is self-sufficing, but all of us have many wants. Can any other origin of a State be imagined?
>
> There can be no other.
>
> Then, as we have many wants, and many persons are needed to supply them, one takes a helper for one purpose and another for another; and when these partners and helpers are gathered together in one habitation the body of inhabitants is termed a State.
>
> True, he said.
>
> And they exchange with one another, and one gives, and another receives, under the idea that the exchange will be for their good.
>
> Very true.
>
> Then, I said, let us begin and create in idea a State; and yet the true creator is necessity, who is the mother of our invention.[1]

Aristotle derives the state from the family, but not without due consideration for our economic needs. Plato could hardly have stressed the family when he was going to abolish it among the rulers and guardians, but Aristotle is strong for the family. Here are his words:

> He who thus considers things in their first growth and origin, whether a state or anything else, will obtain the clearest view of them . . . .
>
> Out of these two relationships between man and woman, master and slave, the first thing to arise is the family . . . . The family is an association established by nature for the supply of men's everyday wants . . . . But when several families are united, and the association aims at something more than the supply of daily needs, the first society to be formed is the village. And the most natural form of the village

---

[1]Plato, *Republic,* bk. II, §369.

appears to be that of a colony from the family, composed of children and grandchildren . . . .

When several villages are united in a single complete community, large enough to be nearly or quite self-sufficing, the state comes into existence, originating in the bare needs of life, and continuing in existence for the sake of a good life. And therefore, if the earlier forms of society are natural, so is the state, for it is the end of them, and the nature of a thing is its end. For what each thing is when fully developed, we call its nature, whether we are speaking of a man, a horse, or a family. Besides, the final cause and end of a thing is the best, and to be self-sufficing is the end and the best.

Hence it is evident that the state is a creature of nature, and that man is by nature a political animal . . . . And it is characteristic of man that he alone has any sense of good and evil, of just and unjust, and the like, and the association of living beings who have this sense makes a family and a state.[1]

The foregoing passage from Aristotle was quoted at such length because of its fundamental importance. Before examining his argument, we have three preliminary remarks to make:

First, we have to speculate on the origin of the state by observing the forms of primitive society in existence today and by examining the traditions handed down among people now civilized. Of particular value are the Greeks, whose literature developed so early as to reflect both tribal and political life.

Second, we are interested in the passage of people from nonpolitical to political existence, the formation of the state as such, not of this or that particular state. The states in existence today came into being by colonization, conquest, revolution, or similar causes, in which we see only the patterning of new states on the ready-made framework of old ones, not the original formation of political society.

Third, the first formation of the state must have been gradual. As a rule people do not consciously aim at things of which they have had no experience. As various needs arose and better solutions to them were devised, people were unconsciously forming the self-sufficient state. It

was spontaneous but also guided by reason as a product of many converging acts of human thought. The first states were not vast empires but, rather, slight though real improvements on tribal organization.

In the light of these remarks Aristotle's theory can be expressed under the following points:

1. *The most elementary form of society is the family*. The family is here taken in the extended sense to mean all blood relatives living together and any servants or others adopted into the household. It can provide for its own welfare in mere daily wants, but it cannot provide for a broader human life. The arts and appliances of civilization could never be developed within one family; for these there is needed the cooperation of many minds and many hands through accumulated generations.

2. *As the family grows, the end it can attain also grows*. The children reach maturity and found new families, usually nearby. In several generations a group of families all interrelated live close to one another. Division of labor comes in; people begin to specialize in different kinds of work and to exchange their products.

3. *The interrelated group has become a clan or tribe*. A clan is a smaller group with a tradition of descent from a common ancestor. A tribe is a larger group and may be an amalgamation of several clans; at least the blood relationship is not so clear. Some tribes never get beyond the tribal condition, either because of nomadic habits, because they are wholly occupied in war, or because they show no ingenuity in developing the earth's resources. In forming a state a peaceful, industrious settlement—a central village where the people trade—is necessary.

4. *The village community can supply more of its wants than a single family, but it is not yet self-sufficient*. Military organization against enemies from without, economic organization against famine and want, and legal organization for settling internal disputes are still wanting. These things are handled rather arbitrarily by the tribal chief with the council of elders. This chief may be the patriarch or matriarch of the whole family, or the eldest son or daughter, or a descendant

---

[1]Aristotle, *Politics*, bk. I, ch. 2, 1252a 24 to 1253a 18.

appointed by him or her, or one elected by the tribe to be their leader, or one who simply assumes leadership and keeps it by his or her ability.

5. *From the village community or an aggregate of such villages the state is formed.* One village composed of people all descended from a common ancestor may expand to such a size in such a favorable location that it is now able to take care of all its needs and has become self-sufficient. More probably several such villages would aggregate and organize for common defense, mutual trade, and a common legal system. As soon as these things have been determined and an authority has been established to enforce them, the state has come into existence.

The argument can be summarized as follows: The family is demanded by human nature and is a natural society, but the state is a natural outgrowth of the family and becomes necessary for human living when a number of families realize the need of cooperation for their common good under authoritative leadership. Therefore in these circumstances the state is demanded by our human nature and is a natural society.

SOCIAL CONTRACT THEORY

The theory opposed to the natural origin of the state is the contractual theory. Since it is the only theory consistent with moral, legal, and juridical positivism, we must expect the names familiar to us from those movements to recur.

To what we said previously about *Thomas Hobbes's* description of the state of nature we may add his description of the formation of political society:

The only way to erect such a common power, as may be able to defend them from the invasion of foreigners and the injuries of one another, and thereby to secure them in such sort as that, by their own industry, and by the fruits of the earth, they may nourish themselves and live contentedly, is, to confer all their power and strength upon one man, or upon one assembly of men, that may reduce all their wills, by plurality of voices, unto one will; which is as much as to say, to appoint one man, or

assembly of men, to bear their person, and everyone to own and acknowledge himself to be the author of whatsoever he, that so beareth their person, shall act or cause to be acted in those things which concern the common peace and safety, and therein to submit their wills, everyone to his will, and their judgments to his judgment. This is more than consent, or concord; it is a real unity of them all, in one and the same person, made by covenant of every man with every man, in such manner as if every man should say to every man, *"I authorize and give up my right of governing myself to this man, or to this assembly of men, on this condition, that thou give up thy right to him, and authorize all his actions in like manner."* This done, the multitude so united in one person, is called a *commonwealth,* in Latin *civitas.* This is the generation of that great *Leviathan,* or rather, to speak more reverently, of that *mortal god,* to whom we owe under the *immortal God,* our peace and defense.[1]

Since Hobbes's view cannot be gathered from one paragraph, however long, we append the following summary. Humans by nature are not social but antisocial. In the state of nature, before the founding of the commonwealth, "man was a wolf to man," there was a "war of all against all," there was no right or wrong, no justice and injustice, for there was no law. Force and fraud governed people's actions. This condition was intolerable, and one powerful impulse, self-preservation, drove people to seek a remedy for constant warfare. The remedy was the *social contract,* by which people agreed to hand over all their liberties to some individual or group, provided everyone else did likewise. Thus they created authority, to which all are now subject and which directs the destinies of all. The power of the ruler is the aggregate of the powers of the individuals. The social contract, once effected, is irrevocable. The sovereignty of the ruler is absolute within the terms of the contract, and rebellion can never be lawful; only if the ruler can no longer protect the subjects does their obligation to obey cease. We have no rights except those granted back to us by the sovereign of the all-powerful state.

Jean Jacques Rousseau is as strong a propo-

---

[1] Hobbes, *Leviathan,* ch. 17.

nent of the contractual theory as Hobbes, though the two differ in their interpretation of the social contract. Rousseau says:

> To find a form of association which may defend and protect with the whole force of the community the person and property of every associate, and by means of which, coalescing with all, each may nevertheless obey only himself, and remain as free as before. Such is the fundamental problem of which the social contract furnishes the solution . . . .
>
> In short, each giving himself to all, gives himself to nobody; and as there is not one associate over whom we do not acquire the same rights which we concede to him over ourselves, we gain the equivalent of all that we lose, and more power to preserve what we have.
>
> If, then, we set aside what is not of the essence of the social contract, we shall find that it is reducible to the following terms: "Each of us puts in common his person and his whole power under the supreme direction of the general will; and in return we receive every member as an indivisible part of the whole."
>
> Forthwith, instead of the individual personalities of all the contracting parties, this act of association produces a moral and collective body, which is composed of as many members as the assembly has voices, and which receives from this same act its unity, its common self, its life, and its will. This public person, which is thus formed by the union of all the individual members, formerly took the name of *City,* and now takes that of *Republic* or *Body Politic,* which is called by its members *State* when it is passive, *sovereign* when it is active, *power* when it is compared to similar bodies.[1]

The following supplies the background for the passages quoted. People are not naturally antisocial but only extrasocial. In the state of nature people lived a carefree life in the forests, sufficient for themselves, bound by no obligations, subordinate to no one. People are naturally good, and there was no war of all against all, but the establishment of private property, as a result of our natural inventiveness, brought with it frauds, disputes, and conflict. Then the state had to be established as a necessary evil to keep the peace. The state was set up by the *social contract,* by which each person handed over all power of self-rule to a sort of universal person, the *general will,* provided all the rest did the same. Thus the individual will becomes part of this general personality, the right of the state the accumulation of all individual rights. In obeying the general will I really obey myself as part of the general will, because in the social contract itself I have willed that the general will shall be my will and shall prevail over any particular decision I make. The general will is always sovereign and, even if it appoints representatives, cannot transfer sovereignty to them. Especially in this last point Rousseau parts company with Hobbes.

A combination of the natural and contractual origin of the state is found in *John Locke.* He believes that people are naturally social, that there is a natural law conferring natural rights, but he thinks that political society could begin only by the social contract, which however, we are impelled to make by the demands of our nature. He says:

> Men being, as has been said, by nature all free, equal, and independent, no one can be put out of this estate and subjected to the political power of another without his own consent. The only way whereby any one divests himself of his natural liberty, and puts on the bonds of civil society, is by agreeing with other men to join and unite into a community for their comfortable, safe, and peaceable living one amongst another . . . .
>
> And thus that which begins and actually constitutes any political society is nothing but the consent of any number of freemen capable of a majority to unite and incorporate into such a society. And this is that, and that only, which did or could give beginning to any lawful government in the world.[2]

There seems to be no warranted objection to placing an implicit contract as the actual instrument by which many particular states were founded. Locke's critics point to his making such

---

[1] Rousseau, *Social Contract,* bk. I, ch. 6.

[2] Locke, *Second Treatise of Civil Government,* ch. 8, §95, 99.

a contract a universal requirement for the origin of all states, to his basing every state on majority rule, to his requiring implicit renewal of the contract by each citizen on reaching adulthood, and to his making the chief function of the state the protection of property. But these important details are not our present concern, which is not to prove or disprove a contract but to ask whether the state is a natural society or an arbitrary creation of merely human deciding, and whether, if there was a contract, people were impelled to make it by the requirements of human nature and the dictate of the moral law.

The *case for* the social contract theory of the state has just been presented in the authors' own words. The *case against* consists mainly of criticisms of Hobbes and Rousseau, who deny that the state is a natural society, rather than against Locke, who does not:

1. People are naturally social, not antisocial or extrasocial. They are neither utterly depraved nor thoroughly upright in nature, but inclined both to good and evil. There is no evidence that people have ever lived in this state of nature, and it is probably not intended to be historical, but it does not give a correct view of human nature.

2. There never was a state of nonmorality, without rights, duties, justice, or law. There was always the natural law, and from it rights and duties immediately flow. The first child would set up a whole system of rights and duties. There never was an utter absence of private property, for anything occupied becomes such, and ownership immediately involves justice and injustice.

3. The function of the family in preparing for the state cannot be overlooked. Human beings had to live at least temporarily in some society to be able to survive as a race. A mere animal life, whether predatory or carefree, is impossible for us, for no one can supply his or her needs unaided. Family life naturally develops into the clan or tribe, and from there into the state.

4. There are certain rights of the individual and of the family that it is immoral to transfer to another, for they belong to the dignity of the human person and to the very nature of the family. A social contract that requires the transference of all rights is contrary to human nature.

5. A social contract that is not a requirement of human nature as such but a mere convention could not bind posterity. The unborn were not parties to the contract and might refuse to enter into it. No one would become a citizen of the state by birth, and anyone could resign from the state at will.

6. The social contract cannot have greater authority than the contracting parties give it. There are rights of the state that no individual can possess, because they concern the common good. In the contract theory there is no way in which the state can legitimately obtain them.

SELF-SUFFICIENCY AND SOVEREIGNTY

The state is said to be a natural society, which the family is also, and a self-sufficient society, which the family is not. A *self-sufficient* society is one that is independent, autonomous, and sovereign. As a society, whether it function well or ill, the state is not tributary to, or dependent on, another society for the attainment of its end. It is because the family is not self-sufficient, is unable to protect itself and to provide its members with all they need for the good life, that the state is necessary. If the state itself were not self-sufficient, it would require a higher society on which it could depend. Such a series could not be infinite, and by the name *state* we mean precisely that society that is self-sufficient and independent.

Self-sufficiency here does not mean *autarky,* or economic isolation. The state need not grow all its own food or produce all its own manufactures if it can obtain them by trade from other countries. It need not have an army that can stand off any other army in the world if it can secure its own protection by treaties and alliances. It must be independent in the sense that it acknowledges no dictation from other nations in its internal affairs and negotiates with them as an equal in external affairs. Such a state is self-governing, a law to itself, autonomous. Considered as a quality in the will of a people and their rulers, this autonomy is called *sovereignty,* the independent power of self-rule by which a state controls its citizens and its territory in such a way that there is no higher appeal in the political order. Sovereignty in the state corresponds somewhat to personality in the individual.

Such qualities cannot be absolute or unlimited. As there are restrictions on the freedom and independence of the individual person, so also are there on the state. Its right to do what it pleases is limited by the natural rights of people, by the existence of other states with equal sovereignty. All nations form the world community to which they belong, like it or not, by the fact that they all exist on this same earth and cannot avoid each other. A League of Nations or United Nations does not form a superstate or destroy the sovereignty of individual states. Nor would a tighter federation of states destroy sovereignty, though it might limit it still further. A union of all peoples into a single world state would so absorb the sovereignty of individual states as practically to reduce them to mere provinces. Whether this would be desirable is a debatable question. What we are saying here is that it would not mean the end of political society but the substitution of one political state for many. And this one state would have to be self-sufficient, independent, autonomous, and sovereign.

THE STATE AND THE PERSON

The fact that the state is sovereign and in a sense supreme brings up the question of its relation to its members. How can the autonomy of the individual person be reconciled with the supremacy of the state? Aristotle touches this question in a passage immediately following the one quoted earlier:

> Further, the state is by nature clearly prior to the family and to the individual, since the whole is of necessity prior to the part . . . . The proof that the

state is a creation of nature and prior to the individual is that the individual, when isolated, is not self-sufficient; and therefore he is like a part in relation to the whole. But he who is unable to live in society, or who has no need because he is sufficient for himself, must be either a beast or a god; he is no part of the state. A social instinct is implanted in all men by nature, and yet he who first founded the state was the greatest of benefactors. For man, when perfected, is the best of animals, but, when separated from law and justice, he is the worst of all.[1]

Contrast this quotation with the one cited in the chapter on the family:

> Man is naturally inclined to form couples—even more so than to form cities, inasmuch as the household is earlier and more necessary than the city.[2]

The individual and the family are prior to the state in *time,* as being earlier, but the state is prior to the individual and the family in *nature,* as being their end and purpose. Does this mean that the individual and the family exist for the sake of the state? So it would seem, but it would be an anachronism to make Aristotle a totalitarian. He is only mirroring his own Greek society, where ethical life was inconceivable apart from the civic life of the *polis,* and all citizens took a more active part in civic affairs than is customary in modern life. Besides, no Greek developed the theory of the human person, which is one of Christianity's historical contributions to philosophy; thus Aristotle failed to see that the dignity of the human person does not admit of the person's being subordinated as a means to an end, even if that end be the collective good manifested in the state.

Whatever Aristotle himself may have thought, we are interested in his problem:

1. Is the state for the people?
2. Are the people for the state?

If we must choose one or the other of these

---

[1] Aristotle, *Politics,* bk. I, ch. 2, 1253a 19 to 1253a 39. See p. 362.

[2] Aristotle, *Nicomachean Ethics,* bk. VIII, ch. 12, 1162a 17, quoted on p. 319.

alternatives without qualification, we ought unhesitatingly to choose the first: The state is for the people; the people are not for the state. But an unqualified answer is too superficial. Individuals and families are often obliged to subordinate their private good to the common good, as is evident from the very idea of the state. Nor is it sufficient answer to say that the common good redounds to the benefit of all the individuals making up the community. An individual is sometimes obliged to sacrifice his or her life for the state, as in a just war, and receives no personal good from it at all. If the state is for the person, why must the person die for it? There is, then, a qualified sense in which the individual is subordinate to the state. We must still say that the state is for the people, but not for any single member of the state to the detriment of all.

A solution that gets at the roots of this problem is developed by Jacques Maritain.[1] He argues from two apparently opposed passages in St. Thomas: "Every individual person is compared to the whole community, as part to whole"[2] and: "Man is not ordained to the body politic according to all that he is and has."[3] The whole person is a part of the state, but not a part of the state by reason of all that is in him or her. When a man runs, the whole man runs, but by reason of his muscles and not by reason of his knowledge of astronomy. Thus the whole human being is an individual person, a member of the family, and a citizen of the state, but something different in the person sets up each of these relations.

The human being is a person but not the highest type of person. As a person I am for myself and cannot be subordinated to a greater whole, but because my self-sufficiency is so limited I must band with other humans to supply my needs.

Because I am a *person,* I transcend all temporal societies, for I have a destiny beyond this life and in my immortality will outlast all the empires of this world. There is nothing above human personality but God, and herein lies its high dignity. In this sense human society exists for each person and is subordinate to each. The state must not compromise our natural rights, because they are given by a higher law than the state's. The state itself is only one of the means granted to us by the natural law to help us achieve our last end, and we cast it aside as an outworn instrument when we pass out of earthly society into the kingdom of heaven.

However, because we humans are such a *lowly type* of person, subject indeed to no being but God, utterly dependent on our equals for every kind of service and abounding in needs and wants, both physical and intellectual, that only our fellow humans can supply, we, during our earthly life, become a part of a larger whole whose common temporal good is greater than the individual temporal good of each member taken separately. In this sense the common welfare takes precedence over private comfort and security. Since the state exists to protect the life, liberty, and property of all, the individual may be called on to play a part in the common defense even at the expense of his or her own life, liberty, and property.

The theory continues with an exploration of the concepts of personality and individuality as verified in the selfsame individual person. The whole human being is a person, and the whole human being is an individual; personality and individuality are only mentally distinguished aspects of the one human being. According to the Aristotelian theory that quantified matter is the principle of individuation, a human being is an individual because each human being is an embodied being, a bodily being. But a human being is a person by reason of spirit or soul, which is the form of the body. By spirit we mean consciousness in all its modes: sensory, intellectual, emotional, volitional. By reason of spirit or soul, each of us is a conscious person. So by reason of our embodied individuality founded on our

---

[1]Maritain, *Scholasticism and Politics,* ch. 3; *The Rights of Man and the Natural Law,* ch. 1; *The Person and the Common Good.*

[2]St. Thomas, *Summa Theologica,* II–II, q. 64, a. 2.

[3]*Op. cit.,* I–II, q. 21, a. 4, obj. 3.

temporal needs each of us is a member of the political community and subordinate to it, but by reason of personality based on our eternal destiny each of us transcends the political community and subordinates it to the personal self each of us is.

STRUCTURE OF THE STATE

The building blocks of the state are the members, the individual human beings of whom the state is composed. How is the state built up out of these materials? Is it composed directly of individuals with no structures or subgroups in between, or is it made up of families, which in turn are made up of individuals? Should we include other groupings larger than the family but smaller than the state? Are such groups essential to the state or only incidentally found in some states? There are three main views:

1. The *atomistic* concept of the state holds that the state is made up directly and proximately of individuals. Each citizen is like an atom in a homogeneous mass. Each counts for one and no more than one, not representing others who are subordinate. No intermediate groups such as the family, the business firm, or the labor union are recognized as structural units in the state. They exist, of course, and the state must deal with them extensively, but they are not regarded as part of the state's essential makeup. In the state each individual is expected to act for himself or herself alone, banding with others only for mutual self-interest in a contractual relation. The atomistic view is characteristic of laissez-faire individualism.

2. The *biological* concept of the state gives the state not merely a moral unity but a physical being over and above the members that compose it. It overdoes the analogy between a society and a living organism. Just as the organs and members of the living body have no life of their own but live with the life of the whole, so also the individual person and the family are thought to be as completely submerged in the state as a cell or organ in the living body. There are various interpretations of this view, but the most extreme as

well as the most logical is the *totalitarian* concept, in which the individual counts for nothing. There is just a global mass of social humanity in which the individual has not even the independence of an atom.

3. The *hierarchical* concept of the state stands between these extremes. The state is seen as a complex structure of individuals and families, so that the family is an essential ingredient in the state's composition. Some individuals live singly outside families, and members of families have some relations to the state independently of their family status, but the very existence of the state depends on a healthy flourishing of family life among its people. Within modern states there are also a number of voluntary associations with semipolitical functions, carrying on work for the common good that the state would otherwise have to do by itself. These voluntary associations are not essential to the state in the same way as the family but are sort of properties pertaining to a well-developed state. This structure of individuals, families, voluntary associations, and the state forms a hierarchical arrangement. Some writers call this the *organic* theory and contrast it with the biological theory, which they call *organismic,* but the similarity of names is confusing, especially since other writers call organic any theory opposed to the atomistic. Care must be taken to stress that the state is not a physical organism but a moral organization in which individuals and families retain their identity, rights, functions, and relative autonomy.

Of these three views the hierarchical one alone contains a proper balance of the individual and the social. It insists on the *principle of subsidiarity:* that no higher organization should take over work that a lower organization can do satisfactorily. The higher does not exist to absorb or extinguish the lower but to supplement and extend it. Otherwise the rights given by nature to the individual and to the family, and our freedom to organize for lesser pursuits within the state, are rendered meaningless. On the other hand, the state should provide a favorable environment in which individuals, families, and voluntary associations can fulfill their functions properly. It has the right and duty to intervene when they fail to function as they ought or cannot harmonize their activities for the common good.

SUMMARY

The state is held to be a *natural* society and not merely a conventional society, because the family naturally broadens out into the tribe with a central village and becomes a state when it achieves self-sufficiency under a common authority. Any group arriving at this condition is bound by the demands of nature to organize itself into political society.

Opposed to this theory is the *contractual theory* of Hobbes and Rousseau, according to which the state is an artificial product of human agreement. The *social contract* supposes a nonsocial and nonmoral state of nature, overlooks the natural expansion of the family, requires the alienation of inalienable rights, cannot logically bind posterity, and does not account for all the rights the state claims.

The state is a *self-sufficient* society, independent, autonomous, and sovereign. It has all it needs to fulfill its end and depends on no higher society. But its sovereignty is not absolute, for it is limited by the moral law and the equal rights of other states.

The state is for people, not people for the state. This cannot be said without qualification, because a person must sometimes sacrifice himself or herself for the state. Maritain explains it thus: The whole person is part of the state, but not by reason of all that is in him or her. Because each of us is a *person,* we transcend all temporal societies and are subordinate only to God. Because we are a *lowly type* of person, poor in self-sufficiency, each of us is dependent on others for temporal welfare and must be ready to sacrifice personal good for the common good. The state itself, however, is not for itself as a state but for all its people.

The *structure* of the state is the arrangement of its components. The *atomistic* view has the state built up proximately of individuals, like atoms in a homogeneous mass. The *biological* view submerges the individual in the whole, like a cell in the living body. The *hierarchical* view sees the state as a structure of individuals, families, and voluntary associations that retain their identity, rights, and functions while directed to the common good by the state according to the *principle of subsidiarity*.

Questions for Discussion

1. We have accepted Aristotle's account of the origin of the state, but perhaps we have been somewhat hasty and ill-advised to do so. Many of the existing states are more the product of revolution than evolution. Our own state is an example in point. Can Aristotle's view be reconciled with the reasons our founding fathers gave for founding this nation of ours? Explain your answer.

2. A number of totalitarian states exist around the world at present. Do you find any in which the *biological* concept of the state is exemplified? Are there any in which the *hierarchical* concept is embodied? Is one better than the other?

3. In discussing the hierarchical concept of the state, we mentioned "voluntary associations with semipolitical functions." List and describe some of these associations as they function in our state. Are any of them essential to the state in the sense that they are needed for the realization of the common good? Explain the reasons for your answer.

4. The Iran-Contra affair that has occupied so much attention nationally raises some questions about state sovereignty. What are those questions? What are the moral implications?

5. Do the citizens of a state have any moral obligations toward the state? Conversely, does the state have any moral obligations toward the individual citizens? Enumerate and justify those moral obligations.

Readings

The great classics of political philosophy include such works as Plato's *Republic,* Aristotle's *Politics,* Cicero's *De Republica* and *De Legibus,* St. Thomas's *De Regimine Principum,* Niccolò Machiavelli's *The Prince* and *Discourses,* Jean Bodin's *De la République,* Robert Bellarmine's *De Laicis,* Francis Suarez's *De Legibus,* Thomas Hobbes's *Leviathan,* John Locke's *Two Treatises on Government,* Montesquieu's *Spirit of the Laws,* Jean Jacques Rousseau's *Social Contract,* Hamilton, Madison, and Jay's *Federalist Papers,* and John Stuart Mill's *Representative Government.* From this formidable array the student should find something of interest.

On the matter of this chapter read Plato's *Republic,* bk. II, §369–374, and *Laws,* bk. III, §676–682; Aristotle's *Politics,* bk. I, ch. 1–2; Hobbes's *Leviathan,* pt. I and II; Locke's *Second Treatise on Government,* ch. 1–4, 7–10; and Rousseau's *Social Contract,* bk. I–III.

Read Jacques Maritain's *Man and the State,* which sums up the results of his important work in political philosophy. Two earlier booklets of his are recommended: *The Person and the Common Good* and *The Rights of Man and Natural Law.* Yves Simon's *Philosophy of Democratic Government* is a unique and rewarding work; see ch. 1. Read Heinrich Rommen's *The State in Catholic Thought,* ch. 4, 9–12, 17–18; Johannes Messner's *Social Ethics,* revised ed., bk. III, pt. I and II; and George Catlin's *Story of Political Philosophers,* ch. 3, 5–9, 14. See Reinhold Niebuhr's *Moral Man and Immoral Society* for a different approach; Peter T. Manicas in his *The Death of the State* challenges some of our most deeply ingrained beliefs regarding man, power, authority, the liberal state, and the democratic state. The student will find Manicas a very stimulating thinker.

26
Government

PROBLEM

A state is said to rule, or govern. Government primarily means the actual exercise of the state's function, its direction of its citizens to their common good. To accomplish this purpose a state can be organized in various ways. The particular organization used in a certain state is called its constitution. It determines the number of officers, how they are chosen, their coordination and subordination, their powers and duties, and the apportionment of authority among them. Government often means the constitution, especially when we speak of the form of government. We tend to concretize abstractions and refer to the body of legislative and administrative officers, the group of persons officially exercising government, as *the government* of that particular state. Thus government means the act of governing, the constitution, and the persons holding political power.

There can be no society without authority. It is evident that if authority exists anywhere in a state, it must exist in the government. How do the government officials obtain it? How should they use it? We shall discuss the following topics:

1. How is the recipient of authority designated?
2. Is there any best form of government?
3. How much should the state interfere in private life?
4. Why must the moral law be supplemented by positive law?
5. Is there a law between natural law and positive law?
6. Are we morally obliged to obey the civil law?
7. Why and to what extent does the state have the right to punish?

RECIPIENT OF AUTHORITY

In a conventional society the same convention or agreement that establishes the society determines the mode of selecting its officials. How authority in *political* society begins to reside in one person or group of persons is a controverted matter. Among those who accept the state as a natural society, rather than as a merely conventional one, three main explanations have been devised:

1. The theory of the divine right of kings
2. The theory of popular consent
3. The patriarchal theory

1. The theory of the *divine right of kings,* defended by King James I of England and by Sir Robert Filmer, held that the actual rulers have their authority by an immediate personal grant from God, who not only gives authority to the state but even selects the rulers, either by positive intervention as in the case of King Saul in the Jewish theocracy, or by tacit approval of the ruler selected by appointment, election, hereditary succession, or some other traditionally recognized manner. Most is made of the title of hereditary succession. The kings were not loath to have their thrones bolstered by this theory, which would make it immoral to unseat them no matter how badly they governed.

2. The endeavor of kings to bend philosophy to their service provoked an immediate reaction. The formerly prevailing view, that of popular consent, also called the *translation* or *transmission* theory, implicit and undeveloped in medieval writers, was more expressly formulated by St. Robert Bellarmine in his *De Laicis* (On the Laity) and by Francis Suarez in his *De Legibus* (On Laws) and *Defensio Fidei Catholicae* (Defense of the Catholic Faith). John Locke wrote his *Two Treatises of Government* against Filmer's *Patriarcha.*

Bellarmine and Suarez, whose opinions are substantially the same on this point, hold that the state is a natural society, that people are not free to form the state or not as they please but are obliged to do so by their natural needs and inclinations, and that all authority comes from God and is no mere product of human convention. Nevertheless, though the people themselves do not give authority to the state, they are the ones who select the ruler who is to bear that authority. God immediately confers authority on the whole people civilly united; the people then determine the form of government and transfer

Hobbes-Rousseau	Bellarmine-Suarez
People are not naturally social and form the state only out of expediency.	People are naturally social and are obliged by the natural law to form the state.
The state is an artificial institution and a purely human invention.	The state is a natural society based on natural human needs and inclinations.
The social contract establishes political society itself as an institution.	The contract determines only the form of government and the ruler.
Authority is but an aggregate of individual human wills.	Authority comes from God to the people, who transfer it to the ruler.
The ruler somehow acquires rights the people have no power to give.	The state receives its superior powers from God through the natural law.
The contracting parties bind posterity but with no valid authority to do so.	The natural law binds posterity to honor the state's just commitments.

the authority to an individual or a group for its actual use.

That families are descended from a common ancestor, live near one another, have common needs and interests, and have organized themselves into a tribe with a central village are all causes disposing groups of people toward statehood and making the formation of a state naturally imperative. But the formation of an actual concrete state with a definite ruler and a definite type of organization requires the consent of the people. The consent of the people may be either express or tacit, either direct or indirect, but in all cases it is the ruler's original title to authority. Though neither Bellarmine nor Suarez uses the exact words of Jefferson's phrase, "Governments derive their just powers from the consent of the governed," it aptly summarizes their opinion.

The difference between this theory and the contractualism of Hobbes and Rousseau should be apparent at a glance (see box above).

3. Some antiliberals of the nineteenth century, alarmed by the excesses of the French Revolution, tried to steer between the divine right of kings and the basically democratic theory of Bellarmine and Suarez. The *patriarchal,* or *desig-*

nation, theory, stemming from the work of Joseph de Maistre,[1] Donoso-Cortés,[2] Karl von Haller,[3] and Aloysius Taparelli,[4] holds that when civil society is first formed, some person or group may be so outstanding in fitness and leadership as to receive an immediate grant of authority through the natural law independently of the consent of the people. Some natural fact indicates this person or group. It may be the patriarch himself, or the eldest son of the eldest branch of the family, or the tribal chieftain, or a victorious military leader, or a person who by gifts of intellect and will has done most to weld the people into a body politic. Such a person is granted authority immediately from God, independently of the consent of the people, for they are obliged by the natural law not to refuse this leader. Even when no such person appears and the people choose their leader, that person receives au-

---

[1] de Maistre, *Du Pape* (On the Pope).
[2] Donoso-Cortés, *Ensayo sobre el Catholicismo, el Liberalismo y el Socialismo* (Essay on Catholicism, Liberalism, and Socialism).
[3] von Haller, *Restauration der Staatswissenschaften* (Restoration of Political Sciences).
[4] Taparelli, *Saggio teoretico di diritto naturale* (Theoretical Essay on Natural Right).

thority so directly from God that it does not pass through the people.

The theory of the *divine right of kings* is easily disposed of. Except in the Jewish theocracy, no act of divine intervention designating the form of government and the person of the ruler has occurred in history.

The *patriarchal theory* argues against the popular consent theory thus:

1. The patriarch or chieftain already had some sort of authority in the tribe before it passed into statehood, and it is natural that he should keep it.

2. Authority is essentially an attribute of a ruler, whether an individual or a group, and cannot dwell in the community as such. The whole people are too unwieldy to exercise authority.

3. Popular consent, though one of the titles, is not the only title to political power. It cannot be proved historically that all original rulers were elected by the people.

The *popular consent theory* answers these arguments as follows:

1. The patriarch or chieftain probably would become the ruler of a newly formed state, but not without the people's consent, at least tacit, if the state is not to start as a tyranny instead of a just government. There is no need of express consent in the form of a vote.

2. Formal authority ready for immediate use resides in the ruler, but basic authority resides in the whole community. Because they are too unwieldy a body, the people transfer the exercise of authority to an individual or group charged with the task of governing.

3. There are many titles to political power, but they are all derivative except the one basic title of popular consent. No other title is valid by itself but becomes so only when confirmed by at least tacit consent of the people. Rule against the people's will, maintained chiefly by force, is the perversion of government.

Besides, during an interregnum there is no person in the state holding supreme authority; if authority vanishes, the state itself vanishes. The patriarchal theory cannot solve this difficulty, but the popular consent theory simply has the au-thority revert to the people. Also, natural law must provide some remedy for tyranny. Tyrants can be removed only by revolution, but no one can authorize a revolution except the people themselves, and to do so some form of authority must already dwell in them. By its very nature all government must be *for* the people, since its purpose is the common good. The popular consent theory says that it should also be *of* the people, arising from their consent and with their authorization; whether it should be *by* the people, so that they do the governing themselves, depends on the adoption of a democratic form. The popular consent theory does not require this last element but finds it congenial.

FORMS OF GOVERNMENT

From the earliest times political writers have tried to classify the forms of government. Plato[1] has a fivefold division based on a gradual falling off from the ideal (aristocracy, timocracy, oligarchy, democracy, tyranny). Aristotle[2] has a sixfold division based on a double principle, the number of rulers and the quality of their rule; he lists three good forms (monarchy, aristocracy, polity) and three perversions (tyranny, oligarchy, democracy). These ancient divisions have yielded in the popular mind to the threefold classification into monarchy, which may be absolute or limited; aristocracy, which may be of birth or wealth; and democracy, which may be pure or representative. These forms may be combined in so many ways that no two governments are exactly alike.

There is nothing ethically wrong with any of these forms or their combinations. Moralists think that the way a government functions is more important than the way it is constituted. Government is a means to the end of the state, the common good, the temporal welfare of the people. Any government that actually fulfills this end to the satisfaction of human expectation is good;

---

[1]Plato, *Republic,* bk. VIII.
[2]Aristotle, *Politics,* bk. III, ch. 7, 1279a 22 to 1279b 10. For the ancients democracy meant mob rule; hence it is listed among the perversions.

any that does not, but governs for the benefit of the few at the expense of the many, is not good.

There have been efforts to prove that representative democracy is the best form of government. A distinction must be made between the relatively best, the best for this people in these circumstances with these traditions and in this stage of its historical development, and the absolutely best, the best for an enlightened and mature people in almost ideal conditions. In the first case one type of government will be best for one people, another for another; which to adopt or maintain is a matter of political prudence. In the second case one can make out a good argument for democracy, since, other things being equal, it is more fitting for a free people not only to be ruled but also to share in the act of ruling. In actual fact, however, other things hardly ever are equal, and for democracy to work a people must have had a long apprenticeship in self-government.

In structure, all forms of government are ethically acceptable. In function, only those forms can be approved that actually succeed in realizing the end of the state. It is wrong to force on a people a type of government they do not want. Tyranny, the misuse of government, is perhaps the worst moral crime that can be committed, because it hurts so many. Leaders of the state, and to some extent the people, have a serious moral obligation in justice to do what they can to correct the defects in their government.

GOVERNMENT CONTROL

Having seen how authority comes to reside in the governing body of a state, and the chief forms it takes, we now ask how far the government should go in the exercise of its authority, in controlling the lives of its citizens. Including untenable extremes, we can list five possible views, grading them from the least to the most interference. Government should:

1. Be abolished as unnecessary
2. Be mostly negative and limited to mere policing
3. Positively assist private initiative for the common good
4. Assume direction and control of all public affairs
5. Absorb the whole of human life

We shall discuss these opinions, beginning with the extremes and working toward the center. Nothing further need be said about the first opinion, *anarchism,* and the fifth opinion, *totalitarianism.* Both are clearly contrary to human nature, since the first denies the rights of society and the other the rights of the person.

The second opinion is *individualism.* The nineteenth century called it *liberalism;* today it would be regarded as reactionary conservatism. It is a theory of economics as well as of politics. It was advocated by the Physiocrats in France,[1] who coined the phrase "laissez faire," and by the Economic Liberals and the Manchester School in England.[2] It is resentful of all government interference in business and wants no more government interference elsewhere than is strictly necessary. The activity of the state should be limited to keeping public order, protecting property, punishing criminals, and defending against foreign attack. Because its functions would be mainly negative, it is sometimes called the *watchman state.* It is also known as the *minimizing* theory, since it can be summed up in the statement: "The best government is the least government."

The fourth opinion, so far as it falls short of totalitarianism, is called *statism* and *paternalism.* Its corresponding economic theory is socialism, but it can exist without socialism, as in the mercantilist monarchies before the French Revolution. If not socialistic, it allows private property but leaves little scope for private enterprise in its use. Paternalism imposes the minutest regulations on all business and makes the undertaking of nearly all public works a state monopoly. Although free from theoretical convictions that the individual and the family are mere cogs in the state machine, in practice it interferes unduly in the personal and family lives of its people and

---

[1]Francois Quesnay, Anne Robert Turgot.
[2]Adam Smith, David Ricardo, Richard Cobden, John Bright.

infringes on their natural rights. As the name *paternalism* indicates, it looks on its subjects as incapable children rather than as responsible citizens.

The third opinion seems to gravitate to the center and to maintain the proper balance between the claims of the individual and the state. It does not want any more government interference than necessary but is willing to admit it when necessary. It leaves the way open for private initiative but is ready to come to its assistance when private initiative fails. It not only protects but positively promotes all enterprises undertaken for the common good. It carefully respects the rights of the individual and of the family, does not try to usurp their duties, and helps them rather by offering opportunities than by regimenting their behavior. On the other hand, it does not hesitate to correct abuses, by legislation if necessary, when it becomes apparent that private influences cannot cope with them. No government has ever put this theory into practice perfectly, but it represents the ideal of many governments, including our own. No term unequivocally designates this ideal, and we shall simply call it the *middle way*. It can still be the middle way even if it has leanings to one side or the other, as in the conservative and liberal elements of our own country.

Individualism may work successfully for a while, especially in a land of unlimited opportunity, such as in the early days of our own country, but sooner or later proves inadequate to cope with the social stresses and strains of an advanced society. Paternalism may be necessary in colonial administration and among backward peoples not yet fit for self-rule, but even here should assume the role of a temporary educator rather than that of a permanent dictator. Whatever be the form of government or type of constitution in a state, the middle way represents the only way in which a government can exercise its powers consistently with the dignity of a mature and free people.

NEED FOR POSITIVE LAW

If we are already governed by the moral law,

whether conceived precisely as natural law or generally as whatever source of moral obligation there is, it may seem that other laws are superfluous. However, we have seen that the natural law is clear to all only in its most general principles; it is unequally known because knowledge of it must be gradually developed, and in any case it lacks statement in an expressed formula. This formulation human legislators supply by enacting positive laws.

Human positive laws may assume two forms. *Declarative* positive laws simply declare in so many words what the moral law prescribes or draw conclusions deducible from it. Such would be laws forbidding murder, theft, perjury, and the like. These laws differ from the moral law only in the way they are promulgated. *Determinative* positive laws determine or fix ways of acting in accordance with the moral law but not deducible from it. Such would be traffic laws, ways of collecting taxes, times and methods of electing magistrates, the conditions for contracts, and the like.

The moral law needs to be supplemented by positive law, both declarative and determinative, for these main reasons:

1. *The dictates of right reason may be obscured in some persons*. In every community there are some with defective or perverted moral education. Against such individuals society must be protected by a code of laws drawn up by the more responsible members of society, expressly stating what right reason demands and setting up some mode of enforcement.

2. *There is no definite natural penalty for wrongdoing*. Many are willing to live with a reproachful conscience, if only they can satisfy their selfish will, but these people cannot be allowed to destroy society. Hence society has the duty to compile a code of criminal law, specifying definite and just punishments for definite crimes.

3. *There is often a choice of means to the end*. In merely individual action each one may pursue his or her own method, but sometimes the end must be achieved by concerted social action. Where teamwork is necessary, individual pref-

erences must be sacrificed. Hence some social authority must decide among all these legitimate means and possible methods just which one is to be used in a given case.

4. *Complex social life continually changes.* To these changed conditions human society must be harmoniously adjusted, and new applications must be made to fit the new situation. Thus the industrial revolution brought up problems undreamed of before, and though the principles of justice remain the same, they must now be applied to this new form of social organization. To prevent untold confusion positive laws providing a social and cooperative solution of these problems must be passed.

THE LAW OF NATIONS

The great lawgivers of antiquity were the Romans, whose legal system is the basis of nearly all modern law in the European tradition. The Romans developed their law in the early days of their Republic, but when they began to expand and incorporate other nations into their empire, they left a good deal of autonomy to their subject nations, allowing them to run most of their internal affairs according to their own laws. Difficulties arose when cases were to be decided between a Roman citizen and an individual of a subject nation or between individuals of different subject nations. They solved the problem by extracting the common elements from the laws and customs of all their subject peoples. This highest common factor they developed into the *jus gentium,* or *law of nations.* It was a gradual growth, but at the height of the Roman Empire it had become an impressive body of customary law. The new nations that resulted from the breakup of the Roman Empire continued to use this law of nations with which they were familiar, and on it they built the structure of their own laws.

The other source of European law is the customs of the Germanic tribes, but on the Continent these customs were grafted onto Roman law. The only comparable rival to the Roman law of nations is the English *common law,* which is the basis of English and American law. The common law consists of unwritten precedents and decisions of the common courts handed down through the centuries, as distinguished from statute law, or acts of Parliament. The English common law is independent of the Roman law of nations but has been greatly influenced by it.

The *jus gentium* is not the same as natural law. The *jus gentium* is positive law, for it is a sifting out of the common elements in the legal codes and customs of various peoples. However, since it abstracts from the peculiarities of different peoples, it is in great part an embodiment of natural law. The first clear distinction between natural law and the law of nations is found in St. Isidore of Seville.

> Natural law is common to all peoples in that it is had by an instinct of nature, not by any human agreement, as the marriage of man and woman, the begetting and rearing of children, the common possession of all, the one freedom of all, the acquisition of those things that are taken in the air or sea or on land; likewise the restoring of property entrusted or lent, the repelling of violence by force. For this or whatever is like this could never constitute an injustice but must be considered in accord with natural equity.[1]
>
> The law of nations is the occupation of territory, the building and fortification of cities and castles, wars, captivities, enslavements, the recovery of rights of postliminy, treaties of peace and others, the scruple which protects ambassadors from violence, and prohibitions of marriage between persons of different nationality. This is therefore called the law of nations because nearly all nations have made such things their custom.[2]

The law of nations in the sense of the *jus gentium* is not the same as international law. International law aims to regulate the mutual relations of states as states. The *jus gentium* was a general law within all nations, not between nations, and dealt with activities of individuals without considering their nationality; it was supranational

---

[1]St. Isidore of Seville (570–636), *Etymologiae,* bk. V, ch. 4.
[2]*Ibid.,* ch. 6. (Translation of both passages taken from Le Buffe and Hayes, *Jurisprudence,* pp. 64–65.)

rather than international. The term *law of nations* is used by most modern writers to mean international law, thus causing much unfortunate ambiguity.

From this brief survey it can be seen that the *jus gentium* holds somewhat of a middle place between natural law and civil law. The *jus gentium* is limited both in space and time. It is derived only from Western peoples and at a particular era of their history. It does not represent the whole natural law, and it contains some things not required by natural law. Despite these limitations, it is of great help to the moralist.

MORAL OBLIGATION OF CIVIL LAW

Besides the law of nations, there are also the civil laws of particular states. What sort of obligation do they impose—a mere civil obligation of outward conformity or also a moral obligation binding on the moral conscience? The answer is implicit in what we have seen. If the state is a natural society required by the moral law for directing our social life, is endowed by nature with authority for this purpose, and is the institution entrusted with the task of enacting and enforcing the positive laws needed to supplement the moral law, then the moral law itself imposes obedience to the civil law.

The argument, put this way, is general. Each of us is morally obliged to be a law-abiding citizen. Some points come up regarding the extent and seriousness of this moral obligation:

1. *Is the individual obliged or only the group?* One might argue that the state will not be destroyed by occasional disobedience of individual citizens, and therefore only the citizenry taken collectively and not the individual is morally obliged to obey the civil law. We see that the state continues despite individual acts of disobedience, but general disobedience would overthrow the state and make it futile. No one citizen has a better right to disobey than another; it is a case of all or none. To allow all to disobey would be to allow general disobedience. Therefore no one is allowed to disobey. We must not overlook the fact that the citizens as citizens are united into one body demanding cooperative action; each must contribute to the common good and does so by keeping the laws.

2. *Must the lawmaker intend to bind in conscience?* Some argue that many modern lawmakers no longer believe in genuine moral obligation and hence cannot intend civil laws to be morally binding. A formal and explicit intention of making the law binding in conscience is not necessary. Whatever be the theoretical beliefs of these lawmakers, they often have the practical intention of giving to their laws full authority, of making them bind as thoroughly as laws can bind. This is an implicit intention and is sufficient to constitute a real law. Even when the legislator's authority does not demand their observance, the common good may.

3. *Is popular acceptance necessary for civil laws?* Not unless the nature of the state or of the law requires it. In a pure democracy, and in laws requiring a popular referendum, the people themselves are the lawmakers, and the law becomes valid only by their consent. Ordinarily legislative authority is handed over to one person or a group, who has authority while in office to pass laws without referring them back to the direct vote of the people. Such laws should be changed by petitioning the lawmakers or electing new ones, not by disobedience. The refusal of the people to accept a law or general disobedience to it does not of itself nullify a law. At most it may arouse suspicion of some radical defect in the law, that it may be unreasonable or unjust or against the common good, and therefore not really a law; investigation can then verify or dissipate such a suspicion. Sometimes a legislator does not expressly repeal a law but tacitly lets it become a dead letter; this may be equivalent to repeal by the legislator, and if so, the law ceases to bind. A true law cannot be got rid of except by repeal, express or tacit, by the authoritative legislator, and until this happens it continues to bind morally.

4. *How are laws to be interpreted?* Interpretation of a law is its genuine explanation according to the intention of the lawgiver. Laws may be

interpreted by the lawgiver personally, or by lawyers and jurists of standing, or by custom that has the tacit approval of the lawgiver. Custom has been called the best interpreter of law. The custom must not be reprobated by the lawgiver but must receive at least the lawgiver's tolerance and silent approval. It is this attitude of the lawgiver toward the custom that gives it authority as an interpreter of law and prevents it from being an illegitimate assumption of authority by those subject to the law. With the tacit approval of the lawgiver, custom may not only interpret but also establish or abolish laws. A too rigid interpretation of the letter of the law may go contrary to its spirit and do more harm than good. Hence most governments admit the principle of *equity,* a tempering of the rigor of the law in the interest of reasonableness and natural justice.

Purely Penal Laws

There are certain civil laws that many good people feel no qualm in violating. They know their conduct is illegal, but they do not consider it immoral. A person who breaks traffic laws when there is no danger, gets something through the customs office without paying duty, or operates a business without a license, does not feel he or she has committed a morally evil act. A penal law is any law provided with a penalty, and a *purely penal law* means one that imposes no obligation in conscience but has a penalty attached for violation.

Purely penal laws pose a problem. They are commonly regarded by the people as genuine law; yet a law that would impose no obligation whatever does not seem to have what the idea of a law demands. We seem to be faced with the dilemma that either these so-called laws are not really laws or that they do bind in conscience. In either case we go against the widespread opinion of well-meaning and conscientious persons.

Many writers of the intellectualist tradition, that law is mainly an act of reason guiding people to the good, will not admit the concept of purely penal law. They argue that a law is a work of reason and meant for the common good; if, there-

fore, lawmakers intend a law at all, they must intend its full observance. Some say that all civil laws, unless manifestly unjust, bind in conscience, and their violation is a moral fault measured by the seriousness of the matter. Others require that a true law be really *necessary* for the common good and admit that certain so-called laws are only rules and regulations for civil decorum and public good order, whose violation does not imply a breach of morals unless accompanied by contempt for authority. This group, then, either will not hear of purely penal laws at all or, if they use the term, mean so-called laws that are not really laws.

Those of the voluntarist tradition, that law is mainly an imposition of another's will, generally accept purely penal laws. Law is essentially a free will act of the lawmaker who may choose not to bind the people to obey in conscience. A common explanation of this theory is that a purely penal law imposes a disjunctive obligation: either obey the law literally or be willing to pay the penalty if caught breaking it. Thus the law is really a law because it does impose moral obligation, though a disjunctive one. The legislator, it is said, can intend to make the obligation disjunctive, with an option for fulfilling it in one way or the other, even though literal observance is preferred. By assessing heavy penalties out of all proportion to the crime, the legislator seems not to be averse to allowing the act if one will pay the price. Some laws, especially those designed to raise revenue, may attain their end in this way, for the fines collected for breaking the law may exceed what the law would have brought in had it been kept by all. The fact that modern states rely so heavily on police machinery to enforce such laws, rather than on an appeal to duty, is considered an indication of the lawmaker's intention.

In summary, there are three possible views on the moral obligation of the civil law: all bind in conscience, none do, or some do and some do not. The first view, though it has its defenders, is too severe and contrary to common opinion and practice. The second view is too lax and plainly false, for some civil laws are evidently necessary for the common good. The third view seems the only reasonable solution, but it brings up the problem of distinguishing which laws bind in conscience and which do not. Those that do not can be called purely penal laws with a disjunctive obligation, according to the voluntarist theory; or it can be said that they are mere directives and not really laws, according to the intellectualist theory. In either case civil laws that are thought not to bind in conscience can be recognized if their main purpose is raising revenue, if the penalty is much too severe for the offense, if police methods are exclusively resorted to, or if they involve mere technicalities of procedure.

Taxation

The state's right to exist and to pursue its end implies the right to the necessary means. Since no state can get along without revenue, the state has a right to tax its citizens. Since no right is unlimited, legislators are morally obliged in justice to keep taxes within reasonable limits, to account for the use of public funds, and to distribute the tax load as equitably as possible. How taxes ought to be arranged to preserve distributive justice is the business of political and economic experts. Ethics can only point out to them their obligation.

If the state has the right to impose taxes, the citizen has the duty to pay taxes. One who is not too poor to pay some taxes yet pays none whatever is plainly failing in an important duty concerning the common good. Indirect taxes now make this condition almost impossible. Is one morally obliged to pay all the taxes imposed? If the tax is clearly unjust, there can be no moral obligation. The judgment that taxes are unjust must not be made hastily; people are always complaining about taxes even when there is no doubt of their necessity. Yet is there an obligation to support the waste, graft, and inefficiency that are rampant in almost all government? Some distinguish between the duty of paying taxes in general, a clear moral obligation, and the duty of paying this or that particular tax, a controverted issue.

Can the latter, that is, certain particular tax laws, be regarded as purely penal law? For those who admit that there are purely penal laws, there is some probability to this opinion, especially when one considers the previously mentioned four criteria for discerning which laws might be purely penal. In financial matters even idealists tend to cut corners and find it hard to break away from a narrowly legalistic interpretation of moral duty.

PUNISHMENT

Laws are useless without enforcement, and enforcement supposes the right to punish. Punishment is a harm inflicted by the executive power of the state on a person who is judged to have violated a rule or law. To harm a person means to take away what the person has or to deprive that person of what he or she otherwise has a right to have, do, or enjoy. For example, a fine as punishment for exceeding the speed limit deprives the speeder of money he or she would otherwise have the right to keep; imprisonment as punishment for embezzling deprives a person of freedom he or she would otherwise have the right to expect to enjoy. Punishment is applied by the executive power of the state, but the judgment that punishment is deserved is rendered by the judicial power. Punitive justice involves distributive and legal justice (sometimes also commutative) in the function of restoring the balance of equality upset by crime.

The following discussion has no reference to the punishment of animals, children, maniacs, or others who cannot be guilty of moral evil. This is not punishment in the strict sense but a figurative extension of the term. There is a resemblance in the means used, but the purpose is quite different: not to repay for crime committed but only to train or restrain irresponsible beings.

Punishment in the strict sense has three functions, one looking to the past and two to the future. As looking to the past, punishment is *retributive,* because it pays the criminal back by giving him or her the crime's just deserts, reestablishes the equal balance of justice that has been outraged, and reasserts the authority of the lawgiver that the criminal has flouted. As looking to the future, punishment may take two forms. If directed to the offender's improvement and rehabilitation as a member of society, it is *corrective*. If directed to preventing similar crimes by others, showing by example what happens to offenders, it is *deterrent*. An ideal punishment should fulfill all three functions and thus serve all parties concerned. It should be:

1. Retributive, vindicating the rights of the offended
2. Corrective, rehabilitating the offender
3. Deterrent, forewarning the community at large

In most acts of wrongdoing punishable by society three things are usually involved: an injury against the individual, a crime against the state, and a sin against God. For the *injury* done to the individual the offender is obliged to make restitution or compensation for the loss inflicted. This is only part of what is demanded by justice, for it merely restores things the way they were before the offense. It involves no payment for the crime as a crime and therefore is not punishment. The offender simply did not get away with it this time and may try again later. The individual offended, as an individual, is not entitled to more than compensation and has no right to wreak private vengeance, but the offense is a *crime* against the state as well as an injury to the individual. The government of the state is responsible for maintaining the order of society and for restoring that order when it has been disrupted. This is a highly important aspect of the common good, the very reason for the existence of the state. The root of the state's right to punish someone who violates the legal order is the state's duty toward the common good of the citizens. Hence, besides receiving compensation, the offended party can turn the criminal over to the state for punishment. The state has the right to exact retribution for the breach of public order and the assault on the majesty of the law, as well as the duty of trying to reform its wayward citizen and deter others from like crimes. A theistic ethics will look on the evil act as also a *sin* against God. Neither the individual

offended nor the state can do anything about this. Forgiveness and punishment must be left to God, who is both merciful and just.

Basis of Punishment

There is no difficulty about the corrective and deterrent aspects of punishment. Everyone sees that without them human society is impossible. But much has been written on retributive punishment in modern times, and some have thrown it out as a relic of benighted barbarism. They argue that it is mere revenge and is therefore immoral in itself, that it only adds one evil to another and does not overcome evil by good. This is not a new idea—it is found in Plato:

> No one punishes the evil-doer under the notion, or for the reason, that he has done wrong; only the unreasonable fury of the beast acts in that manner. But he who desires to inflict rational punishment does not retaliate for a past wrong which cannot be undone; he has regard to the future, and is desirous that the man who is punished, and he who sees him punished, may be deterred from doing wrong again. He punishes for the sake of prevention.[1]

Plato, as logic requires, connects his theory of punishment with his view that no one does wrong voluntarily. He also expresses the very modern notion that crime is a disease and should be treated as such. Many modern writers adopt Plato's theory on other grounds; they are determinists in psychology and utilitarians in ethics; no one can be guilty of crime if there is no free will, and there is nothing useful to the public welfare about merely retributive punishment.

It is well to pay tribute to the humanity of these well-meaning people, but we must not so emphasize mercy as to destroy justice. They are right in condemning revenge but revenge and retributive punishment are not the same. Revenge aims at the emotional pleasure one receives from hurting an enemy, retributive punishment at securing justice simply. This is one reason that jus-

---

[1] Plato, *Protagoras,* §324. See also *Laws,* bk. XI, §934; *Gorgias,* §525.

tice is best administered by a neutral party. Retribution is not merely adding one evil to another, unless one were to hold that justice itself is not a good. Many of the punishments used in former times were unjust and cruel, but that is an abuse and no argument against punishment itself. Some criminals are mentally ill, and they should be restrained, not punished; but to call *all* criminals mentally ill is to adopt an a priori theory that contradicts the evidence.

The reason we cannot abolish the retributive function of punishment, and limit ourselves to the corrective and deterrent functions, is that all punishment to be justified must be based on retribution. Retribution may not be uppermost in mind, but it must be present; otherwise the infliction of any punishment is morally wrong.

1. Punishment may not be inflicted unless a crime has been committed. If punishment were merely corrective and/or deterrent, the government could inflict pain on any person, guilty or not, to improve that person or deter others from wrongdoing. When it is a question of improving someone or deterring people, the government may only threaten punishment, not inflict it. Only when a crime has been committed and guilt established may the government inflict punishment, for guilt calls for retribution and gives the government the right to inflict punishment. When inflicted on the basis of established guilt, punishment is not the use of an evil means to a good end but rather is the use of a good and necessary means to a good end, the restoring of the disrupted order of society for the common good of the citizens. Punishment may function as corrective and deterrent in addition to being retributive, but guilt, and nothing other than guilt, justifies the infliction of punishment. Even though guilt is the necessary and sufficient condition of punishment, this does not mean that punishment should in every case follow inexorably. There may arise cases in which extenuating circumstances would warrant clemency or even a pardon.

2. Punishment should be proportioned to the crime, but if the corrective and deterrent functions of punishment were the only ones, punishment should be proportioned to them. Not the offender's guilt but what is necessary to correct the offender or to protect society should measure the penalty. If criminals could be frightened from ever committing this crime again or be made such examples of as to deter many others from attempting it, we should be justified in punishing them beyond their deserts, but such punishment would reduce them to mere tools for their own or other's improvement. All admit that for good reasons punishment may be mitigated but never increased beyond what the guilt of the offender demands, no matter how much good it may do. Why? Because it is not deserved; just retribution does not call for it. Hence retribution is an essential element in punishment.

To sum up: It is immoral to punish unless the accused is guilty, no matter how much good the infliction of pain may do the accused or society. It is moral to punish the guilty even if there is no hope of correcting them or deterring others from crime. Therefore neither correction nor deterrence but retribution is the basis on which punishment is justified. However, the corrective and deterrent functions of punishment are very important, and human rulers should devise their punishments with these functions uppermost in mind, leaving full retribution to God, but they cannot overlook retribution entirely, for this alone makes punishment allowable.

Capital Punishment

The death penalty has been much discussed in recent years with arguments pro and con being presented in manners all the way from passionately hot to detachedly cool. The question is pertinent at this point not only in the context of punishment itself but also from the point of view of consistency. We have a philosophical need to be consistent in our approach to questions involving the taking of human life. If we are for abortion, for example, we can hardly be consistent if we argue against capital punishment. If no human authority has the right to take a human life for any reason, then we should all be against abortion, euthanasia, war, killing in self-defense, and capital punishment. We should be arguing that no crime could possibly be committed for which death would be a proportionate punishment. People are not always consistent in the moral positions they adopt on any of these questions and yet we find some, ourselves perhaps among them, demanding consistency of their adversaries while dispensing themselves from it.

From the beginning of recorded history the state has used capital punishment rather freely, often excessively. If the death penalty is out of all proportion to the crime, the state does wrong in using it. We are speaking of it here only as applied to very serious crimes, such as murder and treason, which all who approve of capital punishment acknowledge as its proper sphere.

The state exists to maintain equal justice for the common good of all the citizens, and one of its chief purposes is the prevention and punishment of crime. The contractualist theory has no way of explaining how the citizens who have no private right of taking others' lives can give this right to the state. Some natural law theorists have no such difficulty. They argue that in receiving its authority from God through the natural law, the state also receives from him the right to use the necessary means for attainment of its end. The death penalty, they argue, is such a necessary means, because it fulfills the retributive function of punishment. It reestablishes as far as possible the balance of outraged justice and is thought to be the only effectual deterrent against the most serious crimes.

Other natural law theorists argue that the natural law *allows* capital punishment in the sense of not positively forbidding it. We live in a world in which so many people are malicious and unjust that the state needs to use coercion to defend the rights of all its citizens against malefactors. Whenever some citizen acts like an animal, it is reasonable for the state to use force to counter that animal-like behavior in defense of the rights of the whole society. The use of capital punishment by the state is an exercise of the state's right to defend itself against unjust aggressors and to protect the juridic order of which it is the guardian. By using capital punishment the state sepa-

rates from society once and for all an evildoer whom it judges to be a menace to society. This is both an act of self-defense and an apportionment of deserved punishment (retribution). The state by its authority forbids the individual citizens the right to wreak vengeance on the person who commits a crime against them. The state authority reserves to itself alone the right of retribution for murder, manslaughter, treason, piracy, and terrorism to preserve the good of society as a whole. Retributive punishment is not a wrong; it is a good necessary for right order and to uphold the sanctity of the law.

Still other natural law theorists would argue for *allowing* the death penalty to be applied by the state when it is necessary in the particular circumstances in which a society finds itself. Since the purpose of having punitive authority is to safeguard and restore legal order, the death penalty may be justified when it is a necessary means to achieve this goal. For one and the same crime at different periods and circumstances different penalties may be necessary and so justified. The death penalty can, in certain circumstances, be necessary and so justifiable, but in other circumstances unnecessary and therefore unjustifiable. Even in circumstances in which capital punishment is justifiable, the state has an absolute duty to see that adequate measures are taken to preclude judicial error and hence judicial murder. For this reason alone there must be a constitutional provision for a right of reprieve and for the state authority to review the circumstances to see that they still justify the use of the death penalty. This version of natural law theory does not hold that the state simply has the right to use capital punishment in any and all times and circumstances. The state authority has the duty and responsibility to justify its use of the extreme penalty in each set of circumstances.

The natural law arguments may prove too much or too little. True, the state receives its authority from God through the natural law embedded in the very human nature of its citizens. The purpose of the state's authority is to order society under law for the attainment of the common good of the citizens. The state receives from God through the citizens the right to use the necessary means to attain the common good. The question still remains: Is capital punishment ever a *necessary* means to achieve this end? We shall examine the arguments against and then those counter-arguments for the death penalty.

Starting from the position that all taking of human life on human authority alone is morally wrong, opponents of capital punishment have produced the following arguments:

1. The *principle of totality,* sometimes called the principle of integrity, assures us that the removal of a part of the physical body is morally allowed when it is done for the sake of the whole body. This same principle applies analogously to society, the social organism. The government has the right to remove from the body of the citizenry a person whose actions are harmful to the social body. Since it is the duty of the government to foster the common good of the citizens and to protect them from harm, the government has the right to remove from membership in the group a person whose crime manifests his or her unfitness to live and move freely within the social group. Removal from society, however, does not necessarily mean capital punishment. Incarceration is just as effective a removal and adequately protects society from the harmdoer. The government has done its duty and has exercised its right with restraint and moderation. Justice has been done and retribution meted out. Life imprisonment without the possibility of parole together with loss of citizenship are completely adequate to safeguard society and foster the common good. The part has been removed for the sake of the whole.

2. The natural law arguments suffer from an inadequately articulated premise: that the state government has from God through the consent of its citizens the authority and therefore the right to exact the death penalty for murder and treason. No human being has the right as an individual to take either his or her own life or that of another. We regard both suicide and murder as wrong. The natural law arguments presume that the citizens as a group can give to the state the authority and the right to commit an act that each

as an individual has absolutely no right to perform, namely, to exact the death penalty. The contractual theory of government is just that, a theory. When it comes to the taking of someone's life, we ought to have clear and certain proof that God does indeed communicate this authority and right to the government through the consent of its citizens. Such proof appears to be lacking. In the absence of such proof the government would do well to avoid using the death penalty and look to other forms of punishment it can justifiably use.

3. Government exists for the sake of the common good of all and has the duty to preserve peace and order in society. Crimes such as murder and treason disrupt that peace and order because they violate the institutions necessary for the conduct of civic affairs and disrupt the daily occupations of the social group. Certainly no one denies the need to punish such crimes, but such a need does not supply a reason why that punishment should take the form of execution. To take the life of a person to restore the order of justice that has been violated is to do an evil to obtain a good. Here is the basic flaw in the arguments of those who defend the government's right to use capital punishment. No one, not even the government, is morally allowed to do evil that good may come of it.

4. The death penalty considered as retribution does not succeed, for a civilized society does not require the taking of human life for either its safety or welfare. A responsible society wants protection, not revenge; it has no need to avenge itself on a lawbreaker. Barbarity and brutality cannot masquerade as retributive justice, not in so-called civilized nations, for such punishment deserves to be called neither just nor retributive. Hatred of the crime easily passes over to hatred of the criminal. Retribution is based on guilt, and the punishment inflicted looks to the expiation of that guilt. The death penalty is of such a nature that it makes expiation impossible. Furthermore, to take another human life as punishment for the crime of taking a human life does not restore the balance of justice. Society collectively brutalizes itself by killing the person who has killed another.

The notion of retribution for its own sake as a justification for capital punishment cannot stand, for ultimately this simply means that the taking of the murderer's life is a morally good act, which it can never be.

5. In the past there have been gross inequities in the application of the death penalty. Those who receive the death penalty are usually the disadvantaged of society, the minorities, the poor, the mentally unstable and the retarded, the uneducated and friendless. The well-to-do, the influential, and those well represented in court are seldom executed. Black citizens have suffered the death penalty far out of proportion to their numbers in the general population In some states persons may be executed for crimes identical in degree and extenuating circumstances to those for which persons in other states would be given life sentences or lesser terms with the possibility of parole.

6. The innocent have been put to death through errors in human judgment. When convictions are obtained by forced confessions or other violations of due process and death is the penalty, the miscarriage of justice is final and irrevocable. There is no way to call a person back from the grave if the death penalty has been exacted for a crime not committed. Human life is too precious to be taken when there is the slightest possibility that it may be taken unjustly. Society cannot repair the damage done to the person executed nor can it offer help to rebuild his or her shattered life, but those who have suffered unjust penalities of other kinds can be given reparations and help to rebuild their lives.

7. The use of the death penalty is self-defeating, for it diminishes rather than enhances the value of human life. The spectacle of the state's deliberately snuffing out the life of one of its citizens for a so-called capital crime inevitably panders to those who have a taste for the sensational, but it is chilling, hideous, and appalling to persons with civilized sensibilities. The state degrades itself and exercises a corrupting influence on those who follow the bizarre event in the news media. Capital punishment can arouse violent and vicious dispositions in the hearts of some of the citizens and lead the mentally unstable to equal or even exceed the crimes of those made notorious by their long trials and extensive media coverage.

8. Capital punishment is not a deterrent as it was so long thought to be. Statistically, we have no evidence to show that it has a deterrent effect on others who might commit similar crimes. Where capital punishment has been abolished, there has been no increase of homicides. Studies show no pronounced difference in the rate of violent crimes between states that impose the death penalty and those bordering on them that do not.

9. Justice should be swift, certain, and fair. The death penalty perverts justice, because both judges and juries in trial courts and appellate courts want to be certain that an innocent person does not receive the death penalty. This makes the trial lengthy, involved, and costly. The time alone consumed makes swift justice impossible, and when an appeal is made, the time is further lengthened. Judges and juries are likely to strain the evidence and the law to acquit persons accused of capital crimes, because the death penalty is so repugnant to the moral consciences of people today. Juries may well be led to vote for acquittal even in the face of clear evidence that the person accused is guilty of a capital offense. Add to all of this the fact that the years of delay during the appeal process subject the accused to unreasonable torments.

The above arguments offered by those who oppose inflicting the death penalty do not persuade those who favor capital punishment. Even though the arguments offer much material for reflection and commend themselves to anyone who has genuine reverence for human life, the proponents find the arguments basically unsound.

1. The principle of totality does indeed justify removal of the criminal from society, and when it is a question of removing from the physical body a gangrenous limb, total removal is required. When, in the social body, one member murders another, the murderer deserves total removal, which is to say execution, not impris-

onment with or without loss of citizenship. The crime of murder clearly shows the murderer's unfitness to associate with others and his or her unwillingness to live and act in a manner befitting one endowed with a rational and free nature. The principle of totality must be maintained, for the common good of all the people is at stake and the very fabric of civilized life is in jeopardy when a murder is committed. The very common sense of humankind demands the total removal of such malefactors from society, and the government has not merely the right but the obligation to remove such evildoers by executing them.

2. That the government has the authority and the duty to exact the death penalty for certain crimes can be inferred from our rational free nature and the powers of reason God has given each of us. From God we have the powers to manage our personal lives as we live with and among our fellow humans. We have, for example, the right (moral power) to earn a living, protect ourselves from assault, safeguard our personal property, and use our ingenuity in any and every situation. The right to live together in peace and harmony also stems from the Creator, the Author of the universe and all that it contains. No great and difficult process of reasoning is required on our part to see that God is also the ultimate source of the government's power and authority. According to the *principle of subsidiarity,* which states that no higher organization should take over work that a lower organization can do satisfactorily, God leaves to us rational and free beings the direction of our personal lives and allows us to delegate to the government all that is necessary to protect our social existence. The government has the duty to care for the social community. Just as we have seen by the use of reason that each of us has the right to defend ourselves even to the point of allowing the loss of the attacker's life under certain conditions, so too the government, having the duty to care for the social body, has the right and the obligation to execute those whose actions threaten the common good and the safety of the people.

3. Clearly, if the application of the death pen-

alty were the use of an evil means to attain a good end, it would be immoral always and everywhere. Fortunately, the *double effect principle* dissipates such an objection. Consider the four conditions of the principle as it applies to capital punishment: (a) *one morally indifferent act* has two immediate effects, namely, the killing of the murderer or traitor simultaneously punishes the criminal and restores the order of justice that has been violated by the crime; (b) the good effect, the restoration of violated justice, and the foreseen and tolerated evil effect, the death of the criminal, both *result immediately from the one act* of executing the criminal; (c) one effect is *directly intended* by the government, the restoration of the violated order of justice, while the other effect, the death of the criminal, is foreseen and allowed; and (d) there is a *due proportion* between the good intended and the evil that is foreseen and tolerated.

4. Retribution is not the same as revenge. Neither does it necessarily follow that one is brutal and uncivilized because one accepts a retributive theory of justice. Of all justifications for punishment, retribution is the very one that allows for the human dignity of the criminal. It is true that hatred for the crime easily passes over to hatred of the criminal, but it need not do so and certainly ought not to do so in a civilized society. When a life has been deliberately taken by the offender, the death penalty is not invariably disproportionate to the crime. It is an extreme sanction, but it is indeed suitable to the most extreme crime of murder and expresses society's moral outrage at such offensive conduct. The retributive function of capital punishment may be repugnant to many people, but it is essential in an ordered society that asks its citizens to rely on the due process of law rather than self-help to vindicate their wrongs. Furthermore, when the death penalty is applied, it ought to be done in as swift and painless a manner as possible.

5. It is true that the poor, the blacks, the mentally unstable and retarded, the uneducated and friendless are executed more often than their numbers in the population would warrant. Neither death nor any other severe penalty is very

often imposed on the well-to-do and the influential. None of these facts constitutes an argument against the death penalty or against any other form of punishment. Rather, they provide the basis for an argument against the unjust and inequitable distribution of penalties in our society. If the trials of the rich are less likely to result in conviction than those of the poor and if the affluent are less likely to be charged with serious crimes than the less affluent, then the entire system of criminal justice is in need of reform.

6. To live without the risk of error is impossible for human beings. Mistakes can occur even when extreme care is taken to avoid them. Our judicial system is no exception. And any error that results in the loss of a human life is tragic; such error should be avoided as much as possible. This in itself does not constitute an argument against the death penalty. If there are good reasons to maintain the death penalty, then the risk of inflicting it when it is not deserved is one that society will have to bear. Death, we should note, is not the only irrevocable penalty. Time spent in prison unjustly can never be regained either. To think of life imprisonment as preferable to the death penalty or to think of it as "revocable" as opposed to "irrevocable" is to make a dubious assumption.

7. The bad effects of sensational publicity during the trials and executions of notorious criminals cannot be denied. This, however, is an argument calling for responsible reporting of the news and for a more responsible education of our citizens. It certainly is not a reasonable argument for the revision of the criminal code or an argument for the abolition of the death penalty. If this point is not admitted, the exploitation of sex by pornographers could be said to be an argument for the abolition of love. When the news media do their reporting responsibly, we have no reason to interfere with their freedom. Only through such publicity can a case deserving the death penalty have the deterrent effect that is desired. Capital punishment itself does not lead anyone to commit murder. The media coverage might act as a catalyst by setting off reactions in already mentally unbalanced persons who are disposed to commit crimes, but this is no reason to interfere with the freedom of the media.

8. No one has yet shown with certainty that capital punishment does *not* have a deterrent effect. Even though we have no clear proof that it does have a deterrent effect, we must be careful not to confuse this fact (the lack of proof) with proof that it does not have a deterrent effect. The evidence is inconclusive for either argument. Statistics alone prove nothing. Many factors enter into the crime rate such as economic, political, social, and psychological conditions. A significant decline in the number of murders following the abolition of the death penalty in some states does not necessarily mean that the abolition of the death penalty was the cause of the decline in murders.

9. The reluctance of judges and juries to impose the death penalty is no argument for the abolition of capital punishment. If the death penalty is retained by law, judges and juries must render judgments in keeping with the law as it is, not as they would like it to be. It is a perversion of justice not to proceed in accordance with the rules of the law. Granted that the long delay between judgment and execution is a dreadful experience for the person who must go through it, the nature of the death penalty itself does not require these long delays. The length of the appeal process again is not an argument against the death penalty but rather the basis for an argument against certain aspects of our criminal justice system. Justice should be swift, certain, and fair; it should be thorough as well.

Now that we have considered the principal arguments for and against capital punishment, we can better see our way to a position that is reasonable as well as consistent with the other positions we take on questions touching human life. In the view of this writer, none of the arguments in favor of capital punishment shows convincingly that its use by government is morally obligatory. Retribution for crimes such as murder and treason does not absolutely require the imposition of the death penalty. Loss of citizenship coupled with life imprisonment without the possibility of parole effectively removes the criminal from society and at the same time restores the violated order of justice *and* safeguards peace and order within society. The taking of human life as retribution for crime should be extremely restricted if not altogether abolished. Natural law theorists are not unanimous in holding that capital punishment is a necessary means that government must use to achieve its end. Some argue that capital punishment is not positively forbidden; others argue that it is allowed when the government finds it necessary in the particular circumstances in which society finds itself. In this latter view, given a change in those circumstances, capital punishment would no longer be allowed. The government must justify its use of the extreme penalty in each set of special circumstances.

Consider the present circumstances of our society. Human life is as seriously threatened in our time as it has ever been in human history. State power has been used and in some countries is still being used to wreak death on unprecedented numbers of persons; political terrorism and assassinations abound; abortion and euthanasia are widespread; starvation stalks millions; existing nuclear weapons are capable of destroying all human life. We live with these threats daily. Respect for human life is lessening. In these circumstances, reflection on the death penalty takes on new seriousness, depth, and urgency.

Given this set of circumstances and the need to be consistent in our approach to questions touching human life, we have to ask ourselves if advocacy of the death penalty is not one more manifestation of the too prevalent attitude that sees termination of life as the solution to the problem of undesired life. No human life is without value. The person who commits murder is certainly a criminal and has done a thoroughly reprehensible act. We do not minimize nor do we excuse such violent criminal acts; neither do we advocate the leaving of justice undone. We simply ask whether the use of the death penalty in this day and age does not further diminish the respect for human life, a respect that is sadly waning in so many countries, including our own, throughout the world.

Prison Reform

The prison, which is supposed to reform the prisoner, is itself in need of reform. Everyone knows that there are some classes of criminals that have to be locked up for the protection of the public, and therefore there is no question of abolishing all places of detention. However, we seem to have reduced all punishment down to fine, imprisonment, or both, and have not had the imagination to devise other suitable punishments that could be called neither cruel nor unusual. Years ago we abolished the debtors' prison, which made it impossible for one ever to pay off the debt. Now it seems time to divert from imprisonment to other forms of punishment those who have committed a crime but are no menace to the public safety.

The effect of prison life on those who are not yet habitual criminals is often to make criminals of them. Some prisoners are perverted by the criminals they have to associate with and embittered against society, which forced this condition on them and they often come out of prison far worse than when they entered. This effect is not the intention of the penal system, but it seems to happen too often for it to be dismissed as merely incidental. Hence arises the moral problem: Can we continue to use a method of punishment whose bad effects in so many instances outweigh its good effects? Not, surely, if we can find something better, and we are obliged to search for something better.

Just how to reform the penal system is a matter for penologists, criminologists, and other experts. The excellent work some of them have done so far only points to how much there is yet to be done. It is not the business of the ethician to try to do their job for them but only to point out the many moral inadequacies in the present system.

In discussing this matter, it is not well to put too much stress on the prisoner's rights. They retain, of course, their natural rights as human beings which no amount of waywardness can cause anyone to forfeit, such as the right to justice, decency, and respect as a person, and not to be brutalized, degraded, or treated cruelly. But prisoners do not necessarily retain their right to property or to liberty, since the punishment consists precisely in the privation of these things. What civil rights prisoners retain is decided by the civil state, which is the grantor of such rights. The prisoners by their crimes forfeit them, and the state can do as it pleases in applying the forfeit.

Any mode of prison reform will be enormously costly, but our present system is enormously costly without producing enough of the desired results. Any additional cost that would produce better results is worth the price.

SUMMARY

Government means the act of governing, the constitution of the state, or the persons holding political power. Government supposes authority. How does that authority become lodged in a particular ruler or ruling group?

1. The *divine right of kings* theory, holding that the ruler is directly appointed by God, is deservedly obsolete.

2. The *popular* consent theory of Bellarmine and Suarez holds that God gives authority to the whole people civilly united, who then transfer its exercise to an individual or group. The implied contract does not establish political society as such, but only the form of government and the ruler; all government exists by the consent, at least tacit, of the governed.

3. The *patriarchal* theory holds that one person or group can be so outstanding in qualities of leadership as to receive a grant of authority from God without the people's consent; authority dwells only in the ruler, not even basically in the people.

Of the last two theories the popular consent theory seems preferable. It alone can explain an interregnum and a justified revolution. Any government in which there is not at least tacit consent of the people must be a tyranny.

The functioning of government is more important than its structure. Monarchy, aristocracy, and democracy are all ethically acceptable in principle. Some think that democracy is absolutely best, but in practice we must consider the relatively best: which form is best *for a people* depends on their traditions and circumstances.

How far should government interfere with private life? Theories run from *anarchism,* no interference at all, to *totalitarianism,* total absorption of everything into the state. *Individualism* and *paternalism* are more moderate but still exaggerate the function either of the individual or of the state. The ideal is the middle position, one of giving positive assistance to private initiative, correcting its abuses while scrupulously respecting its rights.

Positive law, both *declarative* and *determinative,* is needed to supplement the natural law because:

1. The ignorant need instruction and control by the wise.
2. Definite penalties are required for the safety of society.
3. Concerted action demands teamwork and leadership.
4. Society must meet changed conditions harmoniously.

The *jus gentium,* or Roman *law of nations,* the source of most modern legal codes, was both a highest common factor among the positive laws of ancient civilized peoples and an approach to natural equity. The English *common law* is analogous to it in the latter function. They are both positive law embodying much of natural law.

There is a moral obligation to maintain the state and obey the civil law, because the state is demanded by our social nature and accomplishes its end by the civil law. Laws are binding on each individual citizen, whatever be the theoretical beliefs of the lawmaker. General disobedience does not nullify a law, and contrary customs require at least tacit approval of the authorities.

Are there *purely penal laws,* laws that do not oblige in conscience but have a penalty attached for violation? Some say that they are real laws imposing a disjunctive obligation, either to keep the law or to pay the penalty if caught. Others think that they are not real laws but merely directives for public order. Others discard the concept entirely.

The state has the right to *tax,* since it needs revenue, but not to overtax. It must distribute the tax load fairly. The citizens must pay taxes, but *some* particular tax laws seem to be either purely penal laws or mere directives.

Punishment has three functions: retribution, correction, and deterrence. It reestablishes the balance of outraged justice, rehabilitates the criminal, and prevents others from similar crimes. If we abolish the retributive function, we make all punishment unjust. It is immoral to punish unless the accused is guilty, no matter how much good the punishment may do the person or society. It is moral to punish the guilty even if there is no hope of correcting them or deterring others from crime.

Arguments *against capital punishment:* (1) the principle of totality justifies removal of criminals from society, but not necessarily execution; (2) natural law arguments do not prove conclusively that government has authority from God to mete out capital punishment; (3) to kill the criminal in order to restore violated justice is to do evil that good may come of it; (4) as a form of retribution it fails because expiation of guilt becomes impossible; it is mere revenge; (5) the poor and disadvantaged receive the death penalty more often than the well-to-do who are better represented in court; (6) applied erroneously, the death penalty is irrevocable and becomes a gross miscarriage of justice; (7) it diminishes rather than

enhances the value of human life, because media publicity provokes further violence and panders to the bloodthirsty in our midst; (8) it is not a proven deterrent to violent crimes; and (9) judges and juries are reluctant to convict and sentence a person to death.

Arguments *favoring capital punishment:* (1) the principle of totality applied to the social organism both justifies and requires the death penalty for certain criminals; (2) God, the Author of the universe and all it contains, has endowed humans with rationality and freedom to conduct their personal lives and to delegate to government all the power necessary to protect society; by the principle of subsidiarity, the government must put to death those whose actions threaten the common good and the safety of the people; (3) the principle of double effect (indirect effect) shows that one morally indifferent act, the killing of the criminal, has two immediate and simultaneous effects: (a) the restoration of the violated order of justice (good effect) and (b) the death of the criminal (evil effect), the good effect being directly intended and the evil effect being merely foreseen and tolerated because of the due proportion between the two effects; (4) retribution is the only justification for any punishment of crime; it is not at all revenge; (5) none of the facts about the poor and disadvantaged constitutes an argument against capital punishment; (6) the possibility of judicial error is no argument against capital punishment; (7) education as to the true nature of and the need for retribution is required, not abolition of the death penalty; (8) lack of proof that capital punishment is a deterrent does not constitute an argument against it; justice requires it; (9) judges and juries are sworn to uphold the law and must do so.

The penal system is in need of thorough overhaul. The obligation is moral, but only experts can devise and carry out proper reforms.

Questions for Discussion

1. The Constitution of the United States is two hundred years old. It is the supreme law of

the United States and has been interpreted for us by the Supreme Court in case after case throughout those two hundred years. In recent times, some critics of the Supreme Court have maintained that the Court has no power to interpret the Constitution but has the duty to hold to the original intent of the framers of the Constitution. Does the Constitution say anything about capital punishment? Can you justify the abolition of capital punishment on the basis of the Constitution?

2. The state itself continues year after year, but the government, in the sense of those holding and exercising the political power, changes every four years when a new president is elected. The political party together with the president then forms the government and proceeds to legislate the particular means to attain the common good. Imagine you are running for election as president of the United States. Put together a platform for furthering the common good of all and submit it to your classmates for discussion and adoption.

3. The citizens, we have maintained in this chapter, have a serious moral obligation to correct the defects in their government. Does this mean that we must correct the wielders of political power or correct how they exercise the political power we have given them by electing them? What defects do you detect and how would you work to correct them?

4. "The best government is the least government" could be the slogan of a candidate for president. From that statement alone can you label the candidate as either a proponent of the middle way or of reactionary conservatism? Explain your answer.

5. Conduct a debate in class on the merits of the position that all positive civil laws are purely penal laws.

Readings

On the philosophy of government in general see A.P. d'Entrèves's *Aquinas, Selected Political Writings,* containing a translation of *De Regimine Principum* and of other political passages in St. Thomas's works, together with d'Entrèves's introduction; Jacques Maritain's *Freedom in the Modern World,* pt. I and III, *True Humanism,* ch. 4–7, *Scholasticism and Politics,* ch. 1, 3–4; Yves Simon's *Philosophy of Democratic Government,* ch. 2–5; Heinrich Rommen's *The State in Catholic Thought,* ch. 13–14, 19–21; Frank Sheed's *Society and Sanity,* ch. 11–16; and Peter T. Mancias, *The Death of the State.*

On the recipient of authority, *The Political Works of James I,* edited by Charles McIlwain, and Sir Robert Filmer's *Patriarcha* are balanced by Robert Bellarmine's *De Laicis* (On the Laity), Francis Suarez's *De Legibus* (On Laws), bk. III, ch. 2–4, and John Locke's *Two Treatises of Government,* of which the first is a refutation of Filmer and the second (the important one) is an exposition of Locke's own views. John Figgis's *The Divine Right of Kings* is a standard work.

On forms of government, Plato's classification is found in his *Republic,* bk. VIII–IX; Aristotle's classification in his *Politics,* bk. III, ch. 6–9, 15–17, and bk. IV; and Cicero's observations in his *De Republica,* bk. I, ch. 22–47.

On state control and interference see Johannes Messner, *Social Ethics,* bk. III, pt. III; George Catlin, *The Story of Political Philosophers,* ch. 13, 20–22; as well as the works of Maritain, Simon, and Rommen mentioned previously. Walter Lippmann's *The Public Philosophy* is an interesting study of the natural law philosophy he considers inherent in the American form of government.

On human law read St. Thomas, *Summa Theologica,* I–II, qq. 95–97; q. 100, a. 2. Also read II–II, q. 57, a. 3, on *jus gentium;* q. 64, aa. 2–3, and q. 69, a. 4, on capital punishment; and q. 108, on vengeance, which he considers a virtue (retributive justice). Francis de Vitoria's *De Jure Gentium et Naturali* (On the Law of Nations and the Natural Law) is translated in J.B. Scott, *The Spanish Origin of International Law: Francisco de Vitoria and his Law of Nations,* appendix E. Francis Suarez's *De Legibus* (On Laws) is translated in part in J.B. Scott, *Classics of International Law: Suarez;* read bk. II, ch. 16–20; bk. III, ch. 1; bk. IV, ch. 9; and bk. VII, which is all on custom.

On punishment see Plato, *Protagoras,* §324, *Gorgias,* §525, and *Laws,* bk. XI, §934. Aristotle's *Nicomachean Ethics,* bk. V, on justice, contains much pertinent matter. Cesare Beccaria's *On Crimes and Punishments* did much to reduce the cruelty of punishments. J.D. Mabbott in his article "Punishment" in *Mind,* XLVIII (1939), and in his *Introduction to Ethics,* ch. 11, defends retributive punishment; this and opposing articles are printed in Joel Feinberg (ed.), *Reason and Responsibility.* The contemporary discussion of capital punishment is well argued by Burton M. Leiser in his *Liberty, Justice, and Morals: Contemporary Value Conflicts,* ch. 9; see also Raphael T. Waters's excellent article, "The Moral Justification of Capital Punishment," *Social Justice Review* (July-August, 1982), pp. 99–106; Franklin E. Zimring and Gordon Hawkins's *Capital Punishment and the American Agenda;* James Rachels (ed.), *Moral Problems,* ed. 3, Part IV; and Paul T. Jersild and Dale A. Johnson (eds.), *Moral Issues and Christain Response,* ed. 2, ch. 12. Johannes Messner in his *Social Ethics: Natural Law in the Western World,* revised ed., Book III, ch. iii, provides a brief but illuminating discussion of a natural law justification of capital punishment that depends on such punishment's being a *necessary* means at a particular time and set of circumstances to safeguard and restore legal order.

John Courtney Murray's *We Hold These Truths* interprets the ethics of America's pluralistic society. Paul Douglas's *Ethics in Government* and George A. Graham's *Morality in American Politics* discuss the practical aspects of ethics in political life.

27
Protest

PROBLEM

No government is ever perfect. Change from within is part of its life and necessary lest it suffer political death by stagnation. Change rarely comes from the top, where the ruling class is satisfied with its position and power. Growth in a state most often comes from groups within the body of citizens, who must have some way of redressing the grievances under which they labor and of initiating the improvements they feel to be desirable. Growth is a development from out of the past, not a putting to death of the past and a wholly new creation. Since not all persons see this lesson of history, in every state that is politically alive there will be tension between two extremes, the unbudging defenders of the status quo and the starryeyed visionaries of a new dream. How and where to find a reasonably progressive midpoint is the problem. Some observations on it from the ethical angle are now in order:

1. May the state limit freedom of speech?
2. Must the state respect the individual conscience?
3. What of the relations between church and state?
4. What are the rights of races and minorities?
5. Is there a right of civil disobedience?
6. Are rebellion and revolution ever morally justified?

CITIZENS' FREEDOMS

One of the ironies of history is the need for a Bill of Rights. The state, which exists to safeguard its citizens in the free exercise of their natural rights, has been a notorious violator of them. The history of the last few centuries portrays the victory of the people in their long struggle to get back from the state fundamental rights the state had usurped and liberties it had suppressed. Hardly had the victory been achieved when totalitarianism arose as the most ruthless destroyer of freedom yet to appear. The ferment of today is a continuation of the people's self-assertion. We can discuss only three of these rights, perhaps the last to be won and the first to be lost in a people's fight to be free.

Freedom of Speech

The fact that speech is a natural ability means that we have a right to use it. Speech is not merely repeating what one has been told to say but is the manifestation of one's own thoughts. Therefore a person has a natural right to say what he or she thinks. But no right is wholly unlimited. No one can have a moral right to say things that are untrue or injurious to another person or harmful to the public welfare.

The state has the right to limit freedom of speech and of the press (which is only an extension of the right of speech) insofar as is necessary for the welfare of the community. Libel, obscenity, and the active fomenting of rebellion are rightly suppressed, since each of us has a right to his or her good name, the public has a right not to be assaulted by the foul mouthings of dirty minds, and the state has a right to continued peaceful existence.

It is one thing to admit that the state has a *right* to limit freedom of speech, and quite a different thing to ask how far the state should go in the *prudent exercise* of its right. Obscenity and pornography pose well-nigh insoluble problems. The civil law has not even devised a workable definition, and the courts' judgments are arbitrarily discordant. Attempts of local communities to guard their public morals are made futile by nationwide communication. Filth will proliferate wherever it makes money, and it makes plenty. Its purveyors claim the right of free speech, but what they are asserting is a right to the abuse of speech. If the law acts leniently toward them, it is not because they have any right but because it is so difficult to control this kind of thing by law. There are two schools of thought. Zealots would move in and create what would amount to a police state governed by their own narrow prejudices. Permissivists would drop almost all legislation as ineffective and hope that, with the forbidden-fruit aspect gone, the evil would subside to a tolerable level. Neither side convinces the other.

In political matters, history has shown that an overactive censorship is an unwise policy, and that it is better to tolerate some abuses for the sake of liberty than to correct all abuses by suppressing liberty. A government afraid of criticism confesses its own weakness, and a government that stifles all criticism is tyrannical. Constructive criticism and free expression of opinion are the best way in which the government itself can find out how it stands with its people, what their needs are, and what reforms should be instituted for the common good.

A practically unrestricted right of free speech supposes an enlightened and responsible citizenry. If the government is not to restrict them, they must restrict themselves. A paradox occurs when a citizen abuses the right of free speech to advocate the overthrow of the government that guarantees free speech and the substitution of one that would abolish it. This behavior can be taken indulgently only as long as such persons are an uninfluential minority. Any government allowing it on a large scale is committing political suicide.

A sort of inverse of the right of speech is the right to listen. No government has the right to spy on what is said within the family, nor has it the right to censor its citizens' mail except during wartime, and then only within certain limits. The use of modern listening devices poses a very difficult problem. The right to privacy is too important to be trifled with, and yet a government must have some way of gathering information about criminals and protecting the people from them. If used at all, listening devices should be under the strictest supervision, and the public should know when and where they can find guaranteed privacy with sufficient opportunity to enjoy it. The right of the government does not take away the rights of the individual and the family.

Freedom of Conscience

Freedom of conscience is a natural and inalienable right. Just as citizens have a right to say what they think, so they have a right to do what they sincerely believe is required of them. No state has the right to force its citizens to perform acts that they consider immoral or to forbid them to carry out duties that they judge to be morally binding on them. The citizen's conscience concerning war will be considered when we come to that topic.

Each one's conscience is his or her own. In a sense, conscience has an inside but no outside. What goes on in a person's conscience can be known only from his or her own report, but actions dictated by conscience can have a social as well as an individual impact, and thus we can have a difficult situation. Every large society contains its quota of peculiar people, running all the way from mild cranks to wild lunatics, some of whom may feel driven by conscience to highly antisocial and destructive behavior. Society is obliged for its own protection to restrain them. Because antisocial speech can be tolerated more easily than antisocial action, there is a limit to freedom of conscience in its external expression. Where to draw the line between the normal and the abnormal, between the tolerable and the dangerous, takes a great deal of political prudence. The legal rule of "clear and present danger" is not always easy to apply.

Even within the compass of the normal there can be difficulties. Should genuine believers in polygamy be denied a right to follow their belief in a prevailingly monogamous country? Should those who would let their child die for want of a blood transfusion, because they consider transfusions immoral, be allowed to have their way, or should the state intervene for the sake of the child? Some help may be found in the principle that a negative duty of never doing anything wrong is stronger than an affirmative duty whose fulfillment may be excused or postponed; thus the people will more easily tolerate the forbidding of actions they think right than the command to do positive actions they think wrong. But this guideline does not cover all cases.

Freedom of Worship

The only way in which we can accept religious teaching is by being intellectually convinced of its truth. If we are convinced of its truth, we are morally bound to accept it; if we are convinced of its falsity, we are morally bound to reject it; if we are doubtful, we have the right to reserve judgment until further investigation convinces us one way or another. The state has no means at its command to enforce its will except the use or threat of physical coercion, which might produce a hypocritical conformity, but cannot beget conviction.

Religious persecution must be condemned as an immoral violation of a natural right. Religious tolerance came late in history, though it was advocated in theory long before it could be put into practice. What retarded its advent was the failure to distinguish between the belief and the believer, between error and the erring. Any religion that considers itself as the only true religion will consider contradictory religions to be false. This attitude is not confined to religion but includes any body of knowledge of which one is firmly convinced. But intolerance toward the belief does not justify intolerance toward the believer. As persons we have to find truth for ourselves; we have the right to make the search and to accept the results we sincerely arrive at. It is said that error has no rights. In a sense this is so, for only persons have rights, and error is not a person. In this sense neither has truth any rights. But the *person's* right must be respected. To grant it implies no approval of the beliefs held. There is nothing to prevent people of different faiths from living harmoniously side by side and agreeing to differ in religious belief, each respecting the other's moral and political right to follow his or her conscience. In reading the history of religious conflicts it is well to mark the distinction between the official teachings of a religious body and the behavior of some of its overzealous but misguided members.

Church and state are independent but related societies. The church is supreme in purely religious matters, the state in purely temporal matters. The church must not interfere in matters of a merely civic character, nor the state in the teaching and practice of religion. However, there will always be some relation between church and state because the same persons who are members of one society are also members of the other.

The two societies should harmoniously cooperate where their interests touch and should arrive at a working agreement.

The *separation of church and state* is a difficult problem because of the ambiguity in the word *separation*. How far does it go? If all citizens belonged to the same church, church and state would coincide in membership but differ in purpose and function, and be at least *distinct,* if not separate. Even here provision would be necessary for the freedom of possible dissenters and minority groups to follow their own conscience openly and peaceably. In a pluralistic society such as ours, where the people profess many different religions and are split into any number of sects, a practical separation of church and state seems to be the only workable arrangement. As the facts of history show, it has succeeded admirably.

It is well to note that the term *separation of church and state* is used in different senses in different parts of the world. In countries where anticlericalism is strong it often is only a euphemism for subordination of church to state and suppression of religious freedom. This is the same thing as persecution.

LIBERATION MOVEMENTS

Contemporary liberation movements have many faces—women seeking the freedom to be true feminists, Chicanos and blacks along with other racial minorities striving for the freedom to be themselves in a culture that is predominantly white, Anglo-Saxon, and Protestant, homosexuals of both sexes demanding the freedom to be "gay" or "lesbian" in a largely heterosexual or "straight" society. Before we discuss each of these liberation movements specifically, we would do well to ask ourselves what happens to people that makes them get involved in such movements? To become an activist in any liberation movement is to put one's very self "on the line" not only for one's own sake but for the sake of a whole group of other people as well. Something must happen to the person, within the person, that acts as a catalyst for that person's self-transformation. Some kind of transforming experience leads gradually to the person's changing his or her behavior. Becoming a feminist, a black or Chicano militant, or a gay liberationist does not happen overnight.

A profound personal transformation takes place gradually through the experience people have of themselves in terms of what is happening around them and to them in their social environment. They experience (become conscious of) the social situation as something to be negated and radically transformed or restructured. In the course of perceiving their situation this way, they change their behavior. They make new friends among people who share the same concerns; they respond differently to people and events; their habits of consumption change; and sometimes they alter their whole style of living. Along with these changes in behavior go changes in consciousness. They develop a radically altered and heightened consciousness of themselves, of others, and of their social environment. This altered and elevated consciousness in conjunction with their changed behavior requires an effort or struggle to maintain and clarify. New ways of being and acting require new ways of perceiving. They must keep their conscious awareness acute to sustain this newness. This is called "consciousness-raising" or "conscientization." The consciousness must be "raised" and kept at its new "height" and intensity.

Some liberationists adapt Marxist theory to their own purposes when they analyze consciousness in dialectical relation with the totality of social reality. They point to the existence of (1) "contradictions" in our society and (2) specific conditions that allow and even make for a significant alteration in the status of the group (women, Chicanos, blacks, "gays," and so on). The contradictory factors as they are lived and suffered by particular people must be identified and grasped in their full concreteness. The consciousness is aware of the "contradictions" and in anguish over them, but what raised the consciousness is the dawning of an awareness that "what is" need not be so. "What is" can be changed, moved, reshaped, or even destroyed to bring all of us closer to what ought to be. This is the consciousness of

possibility, new possibility, a consciousness that gradually emerges from the experience of undeserved victimization. The existing forms of social interaction come into conflict with the person's new awareness of what social relations might yet be and ought to be. The liberationist is aware of the same things that everyone else is aware of, but the liberationist is aware of them differently. The contradictory situation is perceived as unstable and intolerable, as rightfully bearing within itself the seeds of its own dissolution. To be aware of an existing situation as intolerable does not transform it. What is lacking? Power. The person with the raised consciousness needs power to effect the desired transformation. The liberation movement is born when people sharing a common concern have their consciousness sufficiently raised that they seek out and find their own personal power to effect the needed changes. When they find one another and share their concerns and awareness, they help raise one another's consciousness and begin to work together to develop the power to bring about those needed changes.

Women's Liberation

That half of the human race would accept a subordinate position, with denial of some of the most basic of human rights, and let this situation continue for many centuries is more than a curious fact of history. It is a tragedy. There were ancient matriarchies, and women were always able to exert a great deal of influence, especially in an indirect way, but for the most part men arrogated to themselves the work of government, gave women no place in it, and seriously curtailed women's rights. Plato[1] was one great exception, but even he, though he grants women full equality of opportunity, does not think women in general are quite as capable as men.

The emancipation of women, as it was called then, began in earnest in the last part of the nineteenth century with the campaign for the vote. It was the logical place to begin, for only

---

[1]Plato, *Republic,* especially bk. V, Stephenus nos. 451–458.

by the vote could they make their voice effective. Then, having achieved the vote, they went back to several decades of apathy. This was not true of all women, but enough were content to make the apathy seem general. Only recently has a rearoused women's liberation movement made itself felt. It did not start all at once; neither did it arise as a single phenomenon among others on the social scene. Social phenomena of this magnitude and importance are not born from a single book nor from a single event; they spring to life when their time has come.

The movement is not the product, at least not entirely, of the civil rights movement, the antiwar movement, the student activist movement, or any other movement. All of these, but none exclusively, created part of the climate for women's liberation. Some women saw the distinction made by theoreticians in the civil rights movement between *racism* and simple *bigotry*. Once the women saw this distinction and realized that racism is something built into our culture, they did not hesitate to draw the parallel distinction between *sexism* and *male chauvinism* or *masculinism*. Sexism is built right into our culture just as racism is. It took the feminist consciousness to make us aware of how deeply sexism is rooted in our culture and how women are victimized by it in so many subtle and not so subtle ways. What do women want? They want to be the persons each of them can be. They examine not only their personal lives and the obvious social discriminations and oppressions but the institutions of culture as well. Structural masculinism permeates the organizations and institutions of our culture. The women are trying to break up those masculinist cultural patterns and to set up new ones that will sustain human persons whether they are women or men.

The moral philosopher should applaud the general thrust of the women's liberation movement. Women are human beings with all the *natural* rights that belong to human beings. No moral justification could ever be made for denying these rights to fully human persons. *Civil* rights depend on the will of the citizens; yet only the most artificial arrangements of society could make women incapable of discharging the main functions of a citizen. If in earlier days citizenship was connected with military duty and political office with military leadership, there is no excuse in these times for perpetuating so obsolete a social structure. No woman should be excluded by reason of her gender from any of the rights that go with citizenship in the state. She should be eligible for the highest office in the land and should be able to compete with men on the sole basis of her ability.

Economic victimization of women is lessening as a result of the women's movement. The chief injustice done them was and still is not to pay them equally with men for the same kind and amount of work. The rationale for this injustice was that many women took jobs temporarily, never intending to be permanent members of the business but only waiting to acquire a husband. Note the masculinist approach to the rationale. It was thought equitable that men, who were to make their whole career in that business, should be encouraged by greater pay. Note again the masculinist approach. Thanks to the women's own liberation movement, this situation is no longer the prevalent one, and there are nearly as many women as men making a permanent career in some businesses. From the standpoint of justice, which is that of morals, women should have equal pay with men for equal work.

The question of careers for women still bothers some people of both genders. Some still maintain that woman's place is in the home, that she is supposed to find her fulfillment in bearing children, in taking care of the house, and in general acting as an unpaid servant. Some women find this a satisfactory life and defend it as woman's proper sphere. It may well be for some women, but there is an increasing revolt among women against the stultifying life of a household drudge. Educated women need something better to occupy their minds and cannot always find it in the trivia of suburban life. Each and every woman has a right to a career, to a form of life that is intellectually and emotionally satisfying. Why should a woman have a lesser right to a career than a man? Why less for a wife than for her husband? A woman is entitled to whatever a man is, and wives are entitled to whatever their husbands are entitled. Without the recognition of every human being as a person, there is no equal justice possible for all. As long as men refuse to face and to challenge the roles our culture teaches them to play, the women will have to do it for them. Ideally, men and women should work together to face and challenge the meanings and oppressions of those cultural roles. All of us together should assume that, unless proven otherwise, differences in temperament, interest, aptitude, and roles are a result of nurture, how people are raised in a particular culture, rather than nature. How girls and boys are brought up has a lot to do with their own self-image and the roles they accept as theirs in society.

Despite the fundamental equality of the two sexes, each sex has its own peculiar characteristics that cannot be denied unless we want to deny that there are two sexes. The women in the liberation movement realize this and do not try to deny it. And yet sex is an important question for the movement. The women have too long been regarded by men as sex objects. Men have defined the accepted sexual practices, and women have been expected to conform to that definition. But no longer. Women are revolting against any sexual relationship that is continually and inherently one of dominance by the man and submission by the woman. If the woman is expected to be continually submissive, she is being expected to repress her own personhood and individuality.

If the human race is to be propagated, women will still have to spend 9 months bearing the child, but the care and nurture of the child devolves equally on both parents. If wives and husbands want to go in for motherhood and fatherhood, they will have to discharge equally and together the responsibilities that go with parenthood. Our particular culture has not been equal to the sexes in specifying the amount of time and care that must be spent on the child that is the common fruit of their union. As things have been, nurture of the child has cut into the woman's career more often and to a greater degree than into the man's. Common state nurseries are not an answer. Cooperation between wife and husband in this whole matter is the only way that an equitable solution can be found when both parties want careers and a family.

The women's liberation movement has been hampered at times by the notoriety given it in the press over issues such as abortion, orgasm, lesbianism, and so on. As in any other movement, not everybody is in on all the acts. Neither are they approved by everybody in the movement. That all these matters need discussion by women is clear, but no one should jump to the conclusion that this is all that the women's liberation movement is about.

Finally, women's liberation means men's liberation too. Male is not normal; female is not semidumb, passive, dependent. Both men and women are equally persons with equal rights. For men to see women as persons will almost certainly bring with it the ability for men to see men as persons. It is a liberation when we open ourselves to others as the persons they are, and it is a reward to be able to meet and enjoy and like a whole person precisely as a person. The moral claims of justice and righting of a great historical wrong will be accomplished only with this total liberation.

Races and Minorities

The world in general and our country in particular have become more acutely conscious of the huge wrongs done to minorities. The horrors of the slave trade and the injustice of slavery as an institution came at last to be recognized for what they always were, the most enormous of social crimes. But the freeing of the slaves was only the first step in rectifying a gross evil. The hundred years' failure to integrate the freed slaves and their descendants into the nation's society on equal terms, as human beings with full human rights, was a culpable prolongation of the crime of the past. Now the minority racial groups have dramatized their plight by voice and deed and made it an ongoing issue.

The correction of these injustices is a moral

problem of the first magnitude, involving a vast social, economic, political, educational, and cultural task. However, the philosophical part of the problem is simple and clear, which may explain why philosophical ethicians have said so little about it. No philosopher of note has ever attempted to defend racial discrimination. Philosophers prefer arguable questions. This one has all the reasons on one side and none on the other.

All human beings have the rights that go with human nature. To differentiate people by their color, race, caste, or class, and not by their dignity and value as human persons, is to succumb to one of the grossest of irrational prejudices. To deprive others of equal rights because of racial or other accidental characteristics is to commit a serious injustice. There is a moral obligation on all, where such discrimination prevails, to cooperate in working for its removal. How to do it, especially where the prejudices are long ingrained, may tax the virtue of prudence to the limit, but the duty is there and must not be indefinitely postponed.

There are a number of rights involved in racial discrimination: the right to vote, to a fair trial, to equal application of the laws, to fair employment practices, to admission to labor unions, to desegregated schools, to nondiscrimination in housing, to the unhindered use of public facilities. One's private right to choose one's friends and company does not extend to denying others the public goods of the community. The supplying of *separate but equal* facilities is a fiction and an insulting one, since on the whole the facilities are not equal and the separateness is meant to be a stigma of inferiority.

What means may racial minorities use to obtain their rights? In any established society legal means must first be used and exhausted. What happens when courts are prejudiced, juries are loaded, state laws conflict with federal laws, and justice is constantly denied? Then the means of securing justice become the means of perpetuating and enforcing injustice. The right to vote can be denied by making registration impossible. The right of peaceful assembly and petition can be curtailed by the requiring of licenses for the use of meeting halls, public streets, and other places of assembly. The perpetual refusal of license renders nugatory the right the government itself is bound to protect. If such a situation were only temporary, the greater good might require that it be endured for a time, but when no legal remedy is in sight, there is no recourse except to extralegal methods.

The use of petition, assembly, and demonstration to obtain their constitutional and civil rights will not wholly relieve the plight of the black people in America. The law is conservative and does not usually initiate social change. All that the law could do, even if it were perfectly administered, would be to integrate the blacks into the mainstream of white culture. The whites are mostly under the illusion that, since this is what they have unjustly denied to the blacks in the past, granting it will rectify the evil and give them what they are protesting for. What the whites fail to see is that their own unjust use of the law has in the eyes of the blacks ruined the law as a means of justice. The law itself has been the means by which the whites have hitherto kept the blacks in subjection, reinforcing the negative self-image of inferiority, which the blacks have been taught by a predominantly white society, and producing a profound alienation and resentment against the whole notion of law and order, which to the blacks means only white law and order. Since they have received nothing from law and order but segregation, repression, and degradation, it is little wonder that they have no respect for it. Homogenization into the standard middle class may be an acceptable goal for some black people, but it is not at all what a great many of them want. They have seen this culture from the outside and have learned to despise it. The revulsion in its exaggerated form can be unjust, but the fact is there.

What, then, do they want? That they want self-respect, pride in their origin, recognition of their own culture, besides equality and nondiscrimination, goes without saying. How to reduce these abstractions to some concrete form is the problem. The answer will have to come from the black people themselves. Even the right answer would not be accepted from any other source. So far the voices of the black community are in conflict. Unless some outstanding leader can bring them into harmony, their efforts may remain a protest *against* rather than a program *for*. Even so, the negative part of the work is not yet finished. The removal of discrimination remains a worthwhile, if interim, goal.

The black people have learned by painful experience that nothing but blatant and persistent militancy will produce results. The whites immediately forget about the blacks' plight unless it is constantly and dramatically thrust before them, and the blacks slide back into apathy and resignation unless they are keyed up by ceaseless harping on the theme. The word *militancy* should not shock us. It need not be violent. It is organized and aggressive, of course, but it can be kept within legal limits. It can also step beyond legal limits to the extralegal or, as some prefer to call it, the supralegal.

Our concentration on the problems of the blacks in America has not been meant as neglect of other minorities, of the Mexican-American Chicanos or of the American Indians. Though neither has suffered the degradation of slavery, the Chicanos have a language difference with which to cope, and the Indians are slowly reviving from virtual extinction. We took the blacks because of their effectiveness in dramatizing their plight. The fact that race riots have quieted down does not mean that a moral investigation of the question is no longer pertinent.

America has no monopoly on problems arising from differences in race, language, religion, and culture. Glance at the world map and try to find a place wholly free from oppression by a dominant group. The same principles, arguments, and conclusions are applicable, with allowance for varied circumstances, to all oppressed and underprivileged peoples.

Gay Liberation Movement

The AIDS epidemic has aroused a great deal of antihomosexual sentiment around the country. Physical and verbal attacks on gay men are on the increase, fueled by fear that the disease is going to be spread from the initially infected gay community and intravenous drug users to the general population. This, of course, is not going to happen unless the majority of the population chooses to risk becoming infected. Nevertheless, the upsurge of scapegoating of gay people by members of the heterosexual majority is in some measure an indication of how threatened, frustrated, and helpless the majority feels in the face of the AIDS epidemic.

With such feelings abroad, gay people need their liberation movement even more than ever before. The heterosexual majority feels the urge to discriminate against the homosexual minority, little realizing not only that such discrimination is unjust but also places the very discriminators at risk of losing their own civil rights and having their own freedom restricted. Freedom and the rights that stem from that freedom are an all or nothing affair. No one can be free unless all are free. Unless all people are justly treated, no one can be sure that he or she will be justly treated by others.

Homosexuality, whenever it is discussed, generates a variety of reactions ranging from lurid curiosity to passionate hostility. For persons not quite secure in their own sexual identity, a discussion of justice for homosexuals becomes highly emotional with little possibility for being objective. Even people who are more secure in their heterosexual self-identity often have irrational fears concerning homosexual persons. The traditional stance of Judeo-Christian moralists and the Christian churches has contributed to much of the prejudice and discrimination that homosexuals suffer in society today.

Discrimination based on sexual orientation is unjust, for this gives an unfair advantage to the heterosexual majority. Some states have already decriminalized homosexual behavior between consenting adults in private. This is an important step in gaining civil rights for homosexuals, but it needs to be taken by every state before justice is truly achieved in this matter. The sanction of the civil law should not be used for the purpose of restraining sexual activity between consenting adults in private.

Discriminatory practices in both housing and employment on the basis of sexual orientation are also unjust. It is quite proper to use the sanction of the civil law to put an end to such unjust practices. While it seems inappropriate and misleading to describe a stable relationship between two homosexuals as a "marriage," it does seem reasonable to grant such persons the same kind of rights with regard to property and taxation that the law extends to the married. Homosexuals have the same rights to friendship, association, and community as heterosexuals.

If society continues to deny homosexuals their civil rights and to treat homosexuals as the objects of scorn, cruel jokes, and contempt, then the homosexuals have every right to protest just as any other minority group. The homosexual needs friendship and association with other homosexuals to share, like heterosexuals, their deepest feelings, fears, and emotions. They need friendship to construct their lives meaningfully, and so they need the kind of association that they cannot find except with one another. As long as they are alienated from the largest segment of society, they will need their protest movement.

Since discrimination and its remedies, including appeal to the extralegal, are not restricted to any one question, this is the place to take up the topic of protests in general and the militant means that may be used to obtain justified ends. They run from civil demonstrations through civil disobedience and rebellion to a complete political revolution.

CIVIL DISOBEDIENCE

Civil disobedience as *disobedience* is a deliberate breaking of a government law one is bound to obey, not a strike or boycott or some other form of private harassment. As *civil* disobedience, it must be nonviolent, nonrevolutionary, aimed not at overturning the state itself but at rectifying an evil or attaining a good within the existing political framework. It is used as a means of protest and therefore must be *public;* a mere breaking

of the law for personal advantage, such as robbing a bank, is disobedience but not civil disobedience. It may be a refusal to obey the very law against which protest is directed, as when such a law is thought unjust or otherwise immoral; or it may be a violation of other laws, just in themselves, such as trespassing, blocking streets, disturbing the peace, acting without a license, and similar troublesome but not permanently harmful acts, as a means of dramatizing the demands. This indirect method is the only way when a law is needed but does not exist, or when the breaking of the unjust law would cause too much disturbance.

It has been claimed that civil disobedience can never be moral:

1. Society requires order for its existence. The means that it uses to preserve order is law. To disobey the laws of society is to revolt against society itself. Whatever be the good intentions of the civilly disobedient, they are engaged in actual rebellion.

2. Any advanced society has means within it for the interpretation of its laws and for their just implementation. Since these means are within the legal structure itself, it is never necessary to resort to extralegal means. A higher authority can always be appealed to against an adverse decision of a lower authority.

3. There are as many consciences as there are people. Who is to decide that a certain law is unjust or that redress cannot be obtained by legal means? To set the private conscience up against the public conscience and let each one decide personally what laws to obey or not obey is to substitute anarchy for government.

4. The social consequences of disobedience are always worse than those of obedience. Civil disobedience always violates somebody's rights, at least those of the public to peace and order. Even if some immediate advantage is gained, the long-range result is always a lessening of respect for law and an increase of contempt for authority.

5. Experience shows that peaceful civil demonstrations easily degenerate into riots. The mob is notoriously a dangerous thing, gets out of hand, is swayed by demagogues, draws to itself irre-

sponsible agitators, ceases to be representative of the cause, and becomes demonstration for demonstration's sake. Riots, with the accompanying looting and destruction, are an inexcusable descent into barbarism and are morally indefensible.

6. Those who thus pass from extralegal to extramoral methods begin actually to defend their destructive behavior in principle. Nonviolent means of peaceful protests, they say, are too slow and ineffectual, whereas a few summers of rioting, looting, and burning made both the people and the government take notice and start acting. Some even defend looting and burning as involving mere property rights, which are not to be compared with the more important human rights.

Others claim that such arguments, drawn from theory, fail to face the actual facts of the situation:

1. Civil disobedience by its very nature is not an attack on society itself. No society is so perfect that it never needs reform. What is wanted is not an abolition of society but the correction of particular defects and injustices for society's own benefit. Not all protesters have such morally pure motives, but a good cause is not ruined by some immoral hangers-on.

2. Civil disobedience is to be used only when legal means have been tried and exhausted. It is not true that legal means are always available or that appeals will always be heard. What one has to look for here is the very purpose of law in general. Law does not exist for its own sake but for the sake of guaranteeing to the people their rights as human beings. Laws do not exist singly and independently but form a system of means for the common good. When observance of a single law produces the opposite effect, then it must yield, for it is irrational to insist on a means that makes the attainment of the end impossible.

3. Legality and morality do not always coincide, and there can be unjust laws. Except for the cumbrous process of judicial review, the law itself will not admit that it is unjust. Only the individual conscience can make that judgment. It should not do so lightly but only after a thorough investigation or a prolonged experience of frus-

tration. It can be confirmed in its judgment by the agreeing judgment of many other people, sometimes almost the whole people except the entrenched ruling clique.

4. The principle of proportion must be maintained. The cause agitated for must be worth the disturbance, and the means used must be kept within reasonable bounds. But it is absurd to think that some must continue forever to suffer gross injustices because the effort to remove them will cause others some inconvenience. The best way to lessen respect and produce contempt for the whole system of law and authority is to keep unjust laws on the books or to administer even just laws in an unjust manner.

5. No civil demonstration can be morally allowable unless it is under competent and responsible leadership, whose business it is to keep it within bounds and prevent it from turning into a riot. Otherwise the proportion of good to evil is violated and the rights of people in general are outraged. Experience shows that protests involving civil disobedience are quite possible without riot or violence, especially those in which the protesters willingly accept the penalty.

6. Extramoral methods can only mean immoral methods. Even justice cannot be obtained at the price of wreaking deliberate injustice on others. That property rights yield to human rights is a slogan with some truth to it, but it can be misapplied. It is not a question of comparing a person to a thing. Property rights are human rights in the sense that they are rights of human beings over their property. To destroy the property of innocent people, the ones usually hurt in a riot, is to attack the freedom of human beings to enjoy the fruits of their labor, and freedom is surely a human right. Destruction in a riot cannot be laughed off as if no one were responsible for it. They are responsible who did it or incited others to do it. It has no place in *civil* disobedience.

Civil disobedience strives to correct injustices and to seek redress within the existing structure of the state. It can also happen that the very structure of the state is the source of injustice, or the ruling power has become committed to exploitation. Then the stage is set for revolution.

REBELLION AND REVOLUTION

Rebellion is open, organized, and armed resistance to constituted authority. Revolt, insurrection, and sedition are more localized forms of the same thing. There will always be malcontents and disaffected groups even in the best of human societies. For the common good a government must try to keep them contented, which it can best do by scrupulous regard for minority rights, but no authority can allow itself to be openly defied. Since the state has the right to exist, it also has the right to put down rebellion by all efficient and legitimate means.

What if rebellion is provoked by abuse of power on the part of the ruler? Abuse of power does not by itself take away the right to power. A father unjustly punishing his son does not lose his paternal right, nor does a woman putting her money to unjust use lose the ownership of it. Small abuses of power are occurring constantly and serious ones occasionally in every state, because rulers are only human and fallible. Such causes cannot justify rebellion, though they call for protest and redress.

What may a private citizen do when unjustly oppressed? Unjust laws have only the appearance of laws and can impose no moral obligation. Injustice in a law must not lightly be presumed but clearly established.

1. Passive resistance or nonobedience is required if the citizen is ordered to do something evil in itself, for no human law can cancel the already existing obligation of the moral law. A so-called law that is unjust but does not order the doing of something evil in itself may be resisted or obeyed, as the subject thinks expedient. It is wrong to do injustice, but it is not wrong to suffer injustice. To prevent greater evils one may have an incidental obligation to obey, but there are some things one must refuse to do, no matter what the penalty.

2. Active resistance without physical force, by petitions, speeches, protests, books, pamphlets, editorials, and propaganda of all sorts, is always morally allowed against unjust laws and tyrannical rulers. But it is characteristic of tyrants to deny any opportunity for such peaceful methods.

3. Active resistance with physical force is allowed against a tyrant attempting to inflict grave personal injury, for the ruler in this case becomes an unjust aggressor. The rules of a blameless self-defense must be observed. If some citizens are unjustly attacked by a tyrannical ruler, others may come to their assistance against the ruler.

Despite occasional injustice, it is wrong to stir up and wage civil war against a *rightful* ruler, that is, one who retains the right to rule. The right referred to here is not so much legal right as moral right. The ruler may observe all legal and technical formalities and yet be a tyrant. Moral right means that the ruler has not acted in such a way as to forfeit the office justly held. No one may rightfully depose a just ruler.

How can a ruler lose the right to rule? There are two ways. First, abuse of power may destroy the title on which the right is held. If the ruler took office bound by certain conditions and breaks the contract, the people are not bound to the contract either; in feudal times subjects were released from their oath of allegiance, and modern republics have the machinery of impeachment. Second, no matter how absolute a ruler may be or how legitimate the title to office, such a ruler always loses the moral right to rule by certain, continued, and excessive tyranny. In this case rebellion against the tyrant becomes a justified revolution.

Revolution is a fundamental change in political organization or in a government or constitution: the overthrow or renunciation of one government or ruler and the substitution of another by the governed. Rebellion cannot be allowed unless it is the means for accomplishing a justified revolution. In a revolution a new kind of government may be established, or the same type may be retained with new personnel. The theory behind a justified revolution is that the ruler lost the right to rule by tyrannical behavior, and that sovereignty reverts to the people in whom it always dwells basically anyway (according to the theory of Bellarmine and Suarez). Consequently, it is not directed against a rightful ruler, since the ruler has lost the right, nor is it by private authority, but by the public authority of the whole people civilly united.

The following conditions for a justified revolution are set down not as absolute requirements, for historical contingencies are too diverse, but as useful norms:

1. The government has become habitually tyrannical and works for its own selfish aims to the harm of the people, with no prospect of a change for the better within a reasonable time.

2. All legal and peaceful means available to the citizens have been exhausted to recall the ruler to a sense of duty.

3. There is reasonable probability that resistance will be successful, or at least that it will secure a betterment proportional to the effort and suffering involved in a civil war.

4. The judgment that the government is tyrannical should be truly representative of the people as a whole. It should not be a movement of a single faction or party, of one geographical district, or of one social class or economic interest.

Nothing said here is intended to weaken the authority of legitimately established and functioning governments, whose laws the citizens are morally bound to obey. But the moral law, which condemns tyranny as one of the worst of crimes because it wreaks injustice on so many, cannot oblige people to submit meekly to being ground into the dust with no hope of relief. The power of a ruler is too sacred a trust to be used irresponsibly yet kept indefinitely.

SUMMARY

The state must be responsive to the people's need for change and development.

The state must acknowledge the citizens' right of *free speech* and not limit it more than the common good demands. It is better to allow more than less freedom of speech, but libel, obscenity, and incitement to rebellion need some curb.

The state must respect *freedom of conscience,* but it should protect the people against external antisocial behavior.

The state must allow *freedom of worship.* Religious persecution is morally wrong. We should distinguish the belief and the believer, condemning false beliefs while respecting the right of persons to profess what they sincerely believe. Separation of church and state is often the best working arrangement.

Women have equal human rights with men, especially to equal pay for equal work and to a career of their own.

The state is obliged in social justice to correct *racial prejudice* and any disabilities resulting from merely accidental differences of birth, race, color, or class. Minorities may seek their rights first by legal means and, these failing, even by extralegal but moral means.

It is argued that *civil disobedience* can never be moral, because it flouts law and order, bypasses the means within the legal structure, opposes private to public conscience, breeds contempt for law and authority, degenerates into riots, and results generally in more evil than good.

In answer it is said that civil disobedience wishes to correct injustice in society, may be used only when legal means have been exhausted, has to rely on individual judgment, must observe the principle of proportion, should be under responsible leadership, and can be kept from descending into anarchy.

The state's right to *suppress rebellion* is implied in its right to existence. Occasional injustice does not destroy a ruler's right to rule. A citizen may resist tyrannical acts by protest but may use violence only in self-defense against personal injury.

Citizens have the right of *revolution* only when the ruler has lost the right to rule. The conditions are habitual tyranny, no hope of improvement, the last resort, fair chance of success, and the backing of the people as a whole.

Questions for Discussion

1. In our pluralistic society we find many shades of opinion on questions such as abortion on demand or the buying and selling of explicitly sexual materials (books, magazines, videos, toys). We have agreed that error has no rights but that people do. You are running for a seat on your city's city council. In your city there is an abortion clinic operating openly, and there is also an adult theater showing X-rated films and two adult entertainment stores selling their wares to any adult who wishes to buy. Your constituency is composed in part by a couple of groups of Christian fundamentalists, a large Catholic parish, and two large Protestant church groups, Episcopalian and Methodist. All of these people are incensed that such businesses are allowed to operate in the city and they want to know what you are going to do about them if you are elected. What do you do?

2. White South Africa has institutionalized *apartheid* and it has now become a "ticking time bomb." Can you and your classmates create a program of reform that will defuse the "bomb" without an explosion? What needs to be done in South Africa and how does it need to be done?

3. The National Organization for Women (NOW) has consistently lobbied for an equal rights amendment to the Constitution. Do the federal and state governments have any moral obligations to ratify such an amendment? May the women of this country rebel if the amendment does not pass? Should the amendment be broadened to include homosexuals as well as other minorities? Why?

4. The House of Representatives in Washington, D.C., has a Subcommittee on Criminal Justice. Before the Subcommittee is a bill that would mandate the federal collection of statistics on crimes based on sexual orientation, race, religion, and ethnicity. Some members of the Subcommittee sponsored an amendment to remove the "sexual orientation" provision from the bill. That amendment failed to pass in a 4 to 3 vote. How would you have voted on that amendment if you were a member of the Subcommittee? Why?

5. Are those arrested while engaged in civil disobedience criminal offenders or political prisoners? Those engaged in nonviolent breaking of the law? Those engaged in violent destruction? Is destruction of property without hurting people basically nonviolent?

Readings

Plato's *Republic,* bk. VIII and IX, describes the degeneration of the state into tyranny. Aristotle's treatment of revolutions in the *Politics,* bk. V, is more factual than ethical. St. Thomas, *Summa Theologica,* II–II, q. 42, deals with sedition.

Famous works in defense of liberty are John Milton's *Areopagitica,* John Locke's *Letter Concerning Toleration,* and John Stuart Mill's essay *On Liberty.*

Locke's *Second Treatise on Government,* ch. 18–19, contains his idea of an appeal to heaven against tyranny.

Some well-known works on women's liberation are Simone de Beauvoir, *The Second Sex,* Betty Friedan, *The Feminine Mystique,* and Germaine Greer, *The Female Eunuch.* For a more extensive bibliography and for discussion of theoretical frameworks for women's liberation, see Sharon

Bishop and Marjorie Weinzweig (eds.), *Philosophy and Women.* A helpful book for men who have never looked into this question before is Gene Marine's *A Male Guide to Women's Liberation.* Jack Nichols's *Men's Liberation: A New Definition of Masculinity* can help men liberate themselves from contrived, socially fabricated prohibitions, cultural inhibitions, and mental stereotypes that control and restrain behavior through arbitrary definitions of masculinity.

The gay liberation movement has produced a great deal of literature. Peter Fisher's *The Gay Mystique* gives a good account of the beginnings of the movement and Joseph A. McCaffrey (ed.), *The Homosexual Dialectic* presents the movement from both the gay and straight perspectives.

Henry David Thoreau's article *Civil Disobedience* is dated but a classic. Martin Luther King's "Letter from Birmingham Jail" is on the way to becoming a classic statement. The *Autobiography of Malcolm X* is a vivid presentation of the blacks' case.

Daniel Stevick in *Civil Disobedience and the Christian* gives a well-balanced and constructive analysis of the problem.

See also Robert Drinan, *Democracy, Dissent, and Disorder;* Hugo Bedeau, *Civil Disobedience: Theory and Practice;* and Burton M. Leiser, *Liberty, Justice, and Morals: Contemporary Value Conflicts,* IV, ch. 15.

Bierman and Gould, *Philosophy for a New Generation,* is an unusual collection of articles, many of them most pertinent to the matter of this chapter.

PART VI
Socioeconomic Life

Having completed our survey of the state and its function in governing society, we turn now to examine some aspects of human socioeconomic life. That the state is intimately involved in many of our socioeconomic institutions should come as no surprise. Some people maintain that the whole business of government is the protection of private property and that government must keep its hands off the property it protects. Others hold that it is private property that has produced government and with it most of the world's miseries and inequities, that abolition of private property will eliminate the need for government, and

that meanwhile the government will work toward its happy demise by taking over and operating all productive property. In this section we examine the basis for the right of private ownership of property (Chapter 28), the nature and force of contracts (Chapter 29), earning one's livelihood through work (Chapter 30), and two forms an economy can take, namely, capitalism (Chapter 31) and Marxism (Chapter 32). We conclude this examination of our socioeconomic life with a consideration of some problems with our management, development, and distribution of the goods of the earth (Chapter 33).

28
Property

PROBLEM

The question of the private ownership of property is a nonquestion for most people because, of course, we humans have a need and a right to hold some things as our own with the assurance that no other person may rightfully deprive us of what we hold as our own. We take for granted that the private ownership of property is necessary for us to live a decent human life, and we rarely, if ever, ask ourselves how this idea ever got started. In the eighteenth and nineteenth centuries we experienced the revolutions from which emerged the present liberal states of western civilization. With the emergence of our own country as a free society came a new effort to define the boundary and limits of public and private. The people involved in the American revolution were responding to definite and actual historical circumstances, and so the domain of the private was understood and articulated in specifically historical terms. The domain of liberty and of human rights was concretely conceived as indissolubly linked with the institutions of private property. The Bill of Rights of the United States' Constitution was designed to protect the citizens against certain unwarranted incursions by government officials into their private lives, but from the very beginnings of this country no one doubted that property was the only basis for the security of life and liberty, that without the protection of property and the right to possess and to alienate one's own property no one could be free.

The connection between property and freedom was so clear from the very beginning that it has remained at the core of the institutions of our society even though we have passed beyond laissez-faire capitalistic industrialization to today's more socially responsible corporations. The institutional arrangements of today's society have emerged from this near identification of the domain of the private with private property. The blessing is clearly a mixed one because, while we are free from much coercion in our daily lives, we are easy prey for more extensive and impersonal forms of private and institutional coercion made possible by large corporations, the prevailing institutions of private property, which the government protects with many legal safeguards. The individual is in danger of being submerged in and/or by the massive impersonal corporations that are not real but only fictitious persons. The instrumentalities of government ensure the "rights" and the freedom of these large-scale corporations to exercise an immense power over our individual lives and our social environment. The liberal ideals of government and capitalism share a common genesis and development; they spring from an identification of the domain of the private with private property. We are so imbued with this inherited legacy that we find it difficult, if not well nigh impossible, to conceive of human freedom in any other terms.

The development of production and the acquisition of monetary wealth have become the highest goals of our world; all other goals take second place to these. Money is considered all-powerful. For its sake we have built a system of production that ravages nature and a kind of society that mutilates us as personal beings. At times we seem to have bought sheer materialism instead of the freedom we so deeply need and desire. Both our industrial civilization and the government that makes it possible must be scrutinized, seen for what they are, and brought under the control of the people they are meant to serve. And we, the people the institutions are meant to serve, must once again be clearheaded and farsighted about the good we want to achieve. Until we are clear about the good for us as personal beings, we cannot gear the forces of government, technology, and production to achieve that good. If we fail to do this, we shall have to put up with pollution, breakdown, and exhaustion.

People cannot live on this planet without using the material goods with which it abounds. In doing so, each person makes some of them *his or her own personal property*. The more recent challenges to the right of property we shall leave to a later chapter. But given these introductory remarks, we here limit ourselves to an investigation of the institution of private property as it has been accepted throughout most of our history and try to find what moral basis it has. We can discuss this question under the following headings:

1. What is ownership?
2. Why may we use material goods for sustenance?
3. What is theft and why is it wrong?
4. What are the chief economic systems?
5. How is the system of private property justified?
6. What are the main titles to property?

OWNERSHIP

The words *mine* and *thine* represent notions too elementary to be made simpler. The expression *one's own* universalizes the idea and makes it applicable to any person. A thing is said to be *one's own* when it is reserved to a certain person and all others are excluded from it. The one who holds a thing as *his* or *her own* is said to *own* it, to be its *owner,* to have the right of *ownership* over it. Things owned are said to *belong* to the owner and are called his or her *belongings*. So much any child knows. The English language feels more scientific when it dresses ideas in Latin derivatives; thus *one's own* is *proper* (in its old meaning as contrasted with *common*), an *owner* is a *proprietor, ownership* is *proprietorship,* and *belongings* are *property*.

Since we all know what ownership is, a definition may seem superfluous, but the following will help to clarify our ideas.

Ownership is the *right of exclusive control and disposal over a thing at will*. It is:

1. A *right*. Thus we distinguish between ownership and the mere holding of a thing in one's possession. A thief has possession of stolen goods, but does not own them, because a thief cannot acquire a right to another's property without the owner's free consent.

2. *Exclusive*. This term pertains to keeping others from the use of the thing owned. A thing over which everybody has equal rights is not owned at all. Several or many persons may own a thing together, either in joint ownership or as a corporation, but anyone outside the group is excluded from the property.

3. *Control and disposal*. This means doing anything possible with it: keeping, changing, giving away, selling, using, consuming, destroying. Of itself ownership is unlimited, though limitation may come from another source: from rights of a higher order, from love of the neighbor, or from the civil law.

4. *Over a thing*. The matter of the right cannot be further detailed except to say that whatever can be controlled or disposed of can be owned. We think of it first as a material object, but it can be actions, services, goodwill, or credit.

5. *At will*. The owner acts personally in his or her own name and need consult no one else as far as mere ownership is concerned. An agent or trustee may be given the right to control a thing or dispose of it, but only on behalf of and in the owner's name.

Property may be defined as *that which is owned* or that over which one has the exclusive right of control and disposal at will. Not everything can become property. The air, the sunlight, the ocean cannot be owned and can never be property; they must remain *common*. Wild beasts, fish in the sea, land in an unexplored wilderness are not actually owned but can be; they are potentially property but actually nobody's; they are *common* now but need not remain so.

There are various *kinds* of ownership, a few of which we can define briefly. Since a group can be an owner, and there is no limit to the size of this group, the whole community as such can own property: the federal government, the state, the county, the city. This is *public* as opposed to *private* ownership. In all ownership we must consider the substance of the thing owned as distinct from its use and fruits. *Full* ownership supposes right of control over all three; *limited* ownership denotes right of control over any one or two of these, but not over all three together. Lending, borrowing, renting, leasing, and the like render ownership limited. Only the one who retains control over the substance is properly called the *owner,* but it is obvious that the other has partial property rights in the matter and hence some sort of limited ownership. Ownership over the substance is called *direct* ownership; ownership over the use or fruits or both is referred to as *indirect* ownership.

PROPERTY AS SUSTENANCE

The right of ownership or the right to property in its simplest and most primitive form enables a person to take and use for his or her own sustenance, comfort, and development the goods that nature's bounty provides. That we have a right to act in this way is evident from our natural right to life. The material goods of this world are naturally fitted to become our property. In nature some beings are for the sake of others, for nature has so constructed them. Living things cannot maintain their lives except by the use and consumption of other beings, both living and inanimate. Since humans are personal beings, they are for nothing else, and all other things are for them to take and use. Nature does not portion out her goods to definite individuals. If no one else has already taken them, they are there for anyone to take. One who does so *appropriates* them, or makes them into his or her property. We have intellect and will, by which we can indicate the intention of keeping material goods for our own use and of excluding others from them. Intellect and will naturally equip us to become self-providers with ingenuity to control nature and make it supply our wants. Animals can only take what they find, as their instinct prompts them, but we humans, because of the control we can exert over nature, are naturally fitted for ownership.

The argument may be put as follows: Humans have a natural right to life, and not only to mere survival but also to the kind of life befitting personal beings: a decent life with opportunity for physical, mental and moral self-development. But the use of material goods is absolutely necessary for the maintenance of life and for proper self-development. Therefore humans have a natural right to use the material goods of this world.

THEFT

The violation of the right of property is called *theft* or *stealing.* Hence the proof that humans have a right to property is proof that theft is wrong. Theft is the *unjust taking of another's property,* and the taking is unjust when it goes against the owner's reasonable will. The word *reasonable* is put here because, though the owner may be unwilling to give me what I need, there are cases, as we shall see, in which refusal is unreasonable, and I may take it against the owner's will.

If nature were uniformly bountiful and no effort were needed to take and develop her products, there would be little motive for stealing. Its peculiar malice consists in the fact that one seizes the products another has gathered, labored on, and stored for his or her own use. No one reasonably wills to have this product taken without his or her consent. Thus the thief virtually reduces another person to the status of a slave working for the thief without recompense and, by disturbing the fundamental equality of all human persons, commits an act of injustice. Even an owner who has not worked to acquire the goods that the thief steals owns them by some other legitimate title, which does not cease without his or her consent. The wrong of theft is rectified first by restitution, the restoring of the stolen goods or their equivalent, and then by punishment, for theft is a crime upsetting the social order as well as an injury to the owner.

What happens when the right to life and the right to property come into apparent conflict? The general principle solving such conflicts is that the stronger right prevails. Obviously, property is for life, not life for property. Life is identified with the very person; property is but a means to support life and minister to its needs.

Life is indivisible, property divisible. A dead person has no use for property, but a live person who has lost his or her property can acquire new property and in the meantime be sustained by borrowing another's excess property. Natural rights, however, cannot be contradictory. It cannot be that every person has a natural right to life and to the means necessary for supporting life while at the same time some people have such rights over property as to nullify others' right to life. Therefore our right to use material goods for the maintenance of life prevails, as the stronger right, over any acquired right to property.

The argument as given refers to extreme need but is valid, with due proportion, for serious but less drastic emergencies. If I am attacked and have no weapon of my own, I may use another's weapon even against his or her will to defend myself, unless that person has equal need of it. If I am pursued by bandits, I may commandeer another's car or horse or any other means of escape. If the only way I can get out of a place in which my life is endangered lies through another's property, I need not worry about trespassing. In all such cases I must ask permission if time and circumstances permit, but if this is impossible or the permission refused, I may do these things anyway. I have no obligation to die or suffer very serious loss because some people are selfish. Of course, I must restore goods so taken as soon as the emergency is over. The owner is entitled to reimbursement for loss or damage done, to be paid eventually by the party at fault, if any. Civil law will have to decide disputes on indemnification.

If someone is starving, that person should first try to obtain food by every legitimate means. He or she must seek honest work and take the work found, even if it be of a menial character. He or she must contact public agencies of relief and not be too proud to accept their help. But if every effort has met with rebuff and it is practically impossible for the starving person to respect other people's property and at the same time to keep alive, then he or she has the right to seize what is needed, even though it is the property of another. This is not theft or stealing. Others have the duty to come to the starving person's relief, and if they do not, their lesser right to their property yields to the starving person's greater right to life.

We may sum up the points made so far. Humans have a right to use the goods of this world. They have a right not only to the goods absolutely necessary for subsistence but also to goods needed for a decent human life befitting their personal nature. Theft, or the unjust seizure of rightfully owned property, is morally wrong, but the right to property must yield to the right to life. It is not theft to seize goods needed for life or safety, even if they are someone else's property, unless that person is in equal need. Rather, there is an obligation to share goods with those in extreme need, since supplying human needs is the primary function of property.

DISTRIBUTION OF WEALTH

We come now to a more intricate question, that of the *economic system* that ought to prevail in society. Here we no longer deal with the basic form of property stemming out of basic human needs but with that more advanced form of property called *wealth*. Should nature's resources be left unowned for each to take what he or she needs, or be divided up among private owners, or be publicly owned and operated by the state? We can distinguish three primary systems for dividing the community's wealth:

1. Each one takes from nature's supply the goods that he or she needs for use at present or in the near future, without hoarding up goods for the far future. Land, especially, is left common as the hunting ground of the tribe. Property does not extend much beyond personal movable implements. This is the system of *primitive collectivism*.

2. Nearly all the resources of nature and goods of the community are divided among particular

owners. The land is marked off and distributed, with trespassing forbidden or restricted. Only that is left common that everybody judges worthless. What individuals do not own, the state owns, but the bulk of the property is in private hands. This is the system of *private ownership*.

3. The community or the state owns nearly everything, especially all the means of production, the farms and factories. The produce is distributed to the people in return for their work. Private property is allowed for use and consumption only. Here again hardly anything is left common as found in nature, though it may be called common in the sense of community-owned. This is the system of *socialism* or *communism*.

No enlightened person advocates a return to primitive collectivism. The system of private ownership has prevailed historically in almost all civilized countries up to the present century. Now some countries have substituted either socialism or communism for the system of private ownership. Because of its historical priority and former worldwide acceptance, the system of private ownership will be examined first, and then in a later chapter its possible replacement by socialism or communism.

PRIVATE OWNERSHIP OF WEALTH

What ethical justification has been offered for private ownership as the economic system of a community? There are three main opinions:

1. Private ownership of wealth rests on *convention*. It may be thought a good convention to be preserved or a bad convention causing most of our social woes. It is not a natural right.
2. Private ownership of wealth rests on the *jus gentium,* or law of nations. It agrees with natural law but is not demanded by it as a natural right. It is *a* morally acceptable system.
3. Private ownership of wealth rests on *natural law* as a natural right. It not only agrees

with natural law but is demanded by it. It is the *only* morally acceptable system.

The Conventional Basis for Private Ownership

Those who hold that humans are antisocial or extrasocial by nature and that society itself results from convention make the various appurtenances of society also conventional. Hobbes and Rousseau (but not Locke) make the right to property part of the social contract. People transferred all their liberties to the state and received some of them back in the form of rights, among which is the right to property. Logically, the state could take back from individual owners the property right it has allocated to them, could abolish all private property and institute some other system for the distribution of wealth. Hobbes and Rousseau, having no prevision of modern socialism or communism, accepted the private property system, but they had no reason for thinking it necessary or fixed for all time. It is not a natural but only a civil right.

This view of the moral and legal positivists should be adopted by utilitarians, pragmatists, and relativists, even though they may repudiate a contractual origin for human society, for they do not admit a natural law or any rights and duties stemming from human nature. The institution of private property is relative to the state of culture to which we have arrived and is to be judged by its practical effectiveness in promoting human welfare. It should be preserved in default of something better, but it is a human device, not a natural right.

The Marxists, because they put such stress on economic needs as the basic factor in every culture, are less severe on the institution of private property than one might think. For them it was an essential step in historical progress, and no civilization would have been possible without it. As the dialectic of history unfolds, however, it must give way to the superior system of socialism or communism. The private property system, therefore, is to be approved as an inevitable transitory arrangement. It becomes evil when, in its decadent capitalist form, it is perpetuated into the future, now that the time is ripe for the great economic and social revolution. Far from being natural or necessary, the system of private property must necessarily disappear. This view will be discussed at length in the chapter on Marxism.

The *Jus Gentium* Basis for Private Ownership

It might be thought that St. Thomas and other medieval defenders of natural law would make the system of private ownership a requirement of natural law. But such is not the case. St. Thomas, while approving the system of private ownership, bases it on the law of nations, or *jus gentium*. It may be well first to see his very cautious and enlightened treatment of this subject:

> Two things are competent to man in respect of exterior things. One is the power to procure and dispense them, and in this regard it is lawful for man to possess property. Moreover this is necessary for human life for three reasons. First, because every man is more careful to procure what is for himself alone than that which is common to many or to all: since each one would shirk the labor and leave to another that which concerns the community, as happens where there is a great number of servants. Secondly, because human affairs are conducted in more orderly fashion if each man is charged with taking care of some particular thing himself, whereas there would be confusion if everyone had to look after any one thing indeterminately. Thirdly, because a more peaceful state is ensured to man if each one is contented with his own. Hence it is to be observed that quarrels arise more frequently where there is no division of things possessed.
>
> The second thing that is competent to man with regard to external things is their use. In this respect man ought to possess external things, not as his own, but as common, so that, to wit, he is ready to communicate them to others in their need . . . .
>
> Community of goods is ascribed to the natural law, not that the natural law dictates that all things should be possessed in common, and that nothing should be possessed as one's own: but because the division of possessions is not according to the natural law, but rather arose from human agreement which belongs to positive law, as stated above (q. 57, aa. 2, 3). Hence the ownership of possessions is not contrary to the natural law, but an addition thereto devised by human reason.[1]

Several things are to be noted in this remarkable passage:

1. The first is that St. Thomas defends the institution of private property as a good thing, and by the usual arguments, suggested by Aristotle's[2] criticism of Plato's communistic ideas.

2. The second is St. Thomas's approval of Aristotle's theory that property should be privately owned but its use should be common. This arrangement was especially applicable to the ancient and medieval system of large landed estates, privately held but with definitely understood public obligations. The modern counterpart is the social function of private capital invested in industries and corporations serving public needs and supplying livelihood to thousands of employees.

3. The third point is that St. Thomas bases the division of goods into private hands on the law of nations, the *jus gentium,* which he discusses in question 57, to which he refers.

This third point is our present question. By his words St. Thomas seems to be making private ownership of wealth something allowed but not required by natural law, something coming from human agreement sanctioned by positive law and permitted by natural law, with an option for another arrangement equally in accord with natural law. This interpretation may be reading into St. Thomas more than is actually there, for he is not thinking of other possible economic systems as substitutes. He maintains that the institution of private property is a morally justified system, but he neither affirms nor denies that it is the only morally justified system. It is remarkable, however, that a man of his time should be so careful not to step beyond the bounds of his evidence and to leave room for future speculation. Many

[1]St. Thomas, *Summa Theologica,* II–II, q. 66, a. 2.
[2]Aristotle, *Politics,* bk. II, ch. 1–6, especially ch. 5, 1263a–1264b.

today agree with his view that the system of "ownership of possessions is not contrary to the natural law, but an addition thereto devised by human reason."

The Natural Law Basis for Private Ownership

Many natural law thinkers are convinced that we can go beyond St. Thomas's arguments and prove that the system of private ownership is the *only* method of managing the world's wealth consistent with the natural law. Such arguments do not form part of primary natural law but rather are supplementary natural law. The grounds for the argument are connected with the common experience of people down through the ages that personal self-realization is best served by each person's having the right to private ownership of some of the goods of the earth, and that the interest of all persons is best served by some system of private ownership. The grounds of the argument may be analyzed under two main headings: (1) the extension of the human person into the material world to achieve self-realization or self-fulfillment as a person; (2) the promotion and protection of the natural order of society and state for the sake of the freedom of the human person. Private ownership is demanded by the nature of the individual person and by the nature and purpose of society. We shall examine each part of the argument in turn.

1. The nature of the human person demands ownership of private property for the following reasons: (a) People have a natural desire for some property and achieve satisfaction in its possession; this desire belongs to and arises from the need each of us has to take reasonable care of himself or herself, a matter of ordered self-love. (b) Caring for others, especially for those we love, is a tendency we all have in some measure. We are able to care for and help them effectively only if we are in possession of some material goods. (c) Personal responsibility for our own well-being and self-development presupposes the right of private ownership, for we live our lives in the world of material goods and must make

some use of them. (d) The human person has an impulse for creative development that seeks satisfaction in the economic sphere both for its own sake and for development in the other spheres of life. (e) Humans have a tendency to provide for the needs of the future, because each person needs to be independent of chance and the power of others. (f) Parents have a natural tendency to provide for their children to ensure their children's future well-being, so the family presupposes private ownership to fulfill its present needs and to help in its future development.

2. The nature of society aiming as it does at the common good of the members demands ownership of private property for the following reasons: (a) Private ownership serves the basic social function of clearly delineating *mine* from *yours* and so serves to maintain the peace and obviate disputes. (b) Private ownership makes for a better utilization of available goods in the interest of all, since the individual owners have a personal interest in such utilization. People generally have less interest in what is common to all, treat it with less care, and are reluctant to devote time, effort and self-sacrifice to it. (c) Inability to be expert in everything brought about a division of labor. People specialize in certain kinds of work and exchange their products. Real commerce on the basis of division of labor promotes social cooperation among people and is a force for cohesiveness in society. (d) Within the bounds set by the common good, the members of society and groups within society work for one another in independence of the state. The individuals are free and have the control over and the responsibility for their own existence and labor. (e) Private ownership helps safeguard the person's social freedom against encroachments into the sphere of natural rights by the political authority of the state. When everyone is in complete material dependence on the state, the totalitarian claim of political authority has no further institutional obstacle to overcome. (f) The institution of private ownership serves to distribute power within a society, whereas common ownership concentrates immense power in the hands of the state with all the dangers of the

misuse of such power. When all economic and political power is in the hands of the ruling group, the individual citizen is in real danger of losing, or already has lost, both individual as well as social freedom.

Private ownership has a definite social function: to promote and protect individual freedom as well as the natural order of society and state. Since private ownership serves equally the common good and human freedom, it belongs essentially to natural law even though its concrete forms are governed by historical circumstances. The principle of private ownership, serving the common good as it does, is an essential and therefore permanent ordering principle in society; the form private ownership takes in any particular society depends on the socio-historical conditions prevailing at any particular time. The principle of private ownership is normative and can become a *principle of property reform*. As a normative principle, it can be used to judge existing forms and conditions of private ownership in terms of whether the social function of private property is being fulfilled in both its individual and social aspects. Only as a normative principle can the principle of private ownership be a principle of reform. If private ownership is made completely relative to the social order, it becomes simply a functional principle in the service of a particular social system. No form of private ownership is absolute; all forms of it are relative to historical circumstances. The principle of private ownership is inviolable and unalterable, demanded by natural law to serve the common good and human freedom. Natural law likewise demands the reform of the institution of private ownership whenever and wherever it has ceased to serve and promote both the common good and human freedom.

Marx was interested in reforming the system of private ownership of his day because he saw the social power wielded by private owners of the means of production as exploiting laborers and cheating them of the fruit of their labors. He advocated the overthrow of the capitalist system and the abolition of private ownership of the means of production. What he failed to see clearly is the distinction between private ownership and social power. Marx perceived private ownership of the means of production as social power. He thought this to be the case always and in all circumstances. Since private ownership and social power are clearly not the same but distinct realities, the real goal of social reform is *not* the elimination of private ownership but the elimination or limitation of its social power. To achieve this goal, we need a social system in which labor is an ordering principle along with but distinct from private ownership. This would put the two principles on an equal footing in directing the socioeconomic process. The further end of social reform must be to bring about a distribution of property that will allow the greatest possible number of society's members to enjoy private ownership and the income from their property. What we advocate here is not a mere redistribution of property. The goal of social reform is a socially just distribution of income out of the profits derived from socioeconomic cooperation so that those who do not own private property can acquire it.

Does the argument prove all that its backers ask of it? Does it prove that private ownership of wealth is so demanded by the natural law that there can be no substitute for it? Not without an examination of possible substitutes. This thesis must therefore remain incomplete until such substitutes as socialism and communism have been examined.

PROPERTY TITLES

The foregoing discussion was theoretical, asking whether there should be such a right as ownership and such a thing as property and on what moral grounds. Taking property as an existing fact, we now ask: How does someone come to own this or that piece of property? A person by the fact that he or she is human has the right of ownership in general, and yet may never exercise this right, may never actually own anything. Something must make this person acquire this piece of property, that person that piece, a function fulfilled by a title. A *title* to property is a historical fact that changes the abstract right of ownership in general into the concrete right of ownership over this particular piece of property. There are seven chief titles to property:

1. *Occupancy* is the original way of changing into property the objects that nature leaves common. It is defined as the taking of a thing that belongs to no one with manifest intent of holding it as one's own. It does not require dwelling or inhabiting, as the word *occupy* might suggest. There are three requirements: the thing taken must not actually be owned by anyone though capable of being owned, it must be effectively possessed with intent to hold it, and this intent must be made known to others by some suitable sign. The sign depends on custom: putting up a notice, fencing a field, staking a claim, recording the deed, keeping the thing on one's own person or in one's house. Some labor may be involved in securing possession, but the object itself is not the product of one's toil.

2. *Labor* cannot be the original title of ownership, because the raw materials must first be owned before one has the right to work on them. Labor, transforming raw materials into useful objects, creates new values that belong to the worker as products of his or her energy. Mental no less than physical labor is a natural title to its fruits. When the material belongs to one owner and the labor to another, the ownership of the finished product has already been determined by a contract of hire; the owner of the material keeps the product, and the worker is paid for his or her labor. Some think that labor is the only title to property; they can do so only by taking so broad a definition of labor as to include the act of occupancy, as John Locke[1] seems to do, or, like Karl Marx,[2] by restricting property to consumable goods distributed by the community to individuals in return for their labor.

3. *Gift* is a gratuitous transfer of ownership to

another and is implied in the owner's right of disposing of his or her property at will. In the making of a gift the property is alienated only on condition that it be accepted by the person to whom it is offered. Hence the title of gift is a variety of contract, though the benefit is all one way.

4. *Trade* is any form of exchange, running all the way from *barter,* through *buying and selling,* up to and including the intricate enterprises of world *commerce.* In fact, trade, whether money is used or not, is only mutual gifts, but it is better to class it as a separate title because of the different attitude we have toward gifts and purchases. Trade is the logical consequence of the division of labor and necessary for the good of all humans, resting on the mutual help demanded by our social nature, for each does help the other though personal gain be the motive.

5. *Inheritance* indicates that property on the death of the owner does not become common, to be occupied by the first comer, but passes to designated persons. If there is no will, the property goes to the natural heirs, the wife or husband and the children. Property is for the good not only of the individual but of the family, and after death it should continue to fulfill the function of supporting them. Civil law determines inheritance; it should be based on natural justice and protect the natural heirs. The goods of a person dying intestate, that is without having made a valid will, and without relatives or dependents would naturally become common if the state did not usually settle the matter by taking possession itself. *Bequest,* the disposing of property by a will, is a valid title, for a gift can be made to take effect at any time including the moment of death. In bequeathing his or her goods, the owner is in duty bound to provide for the natural heirs, but beyond this he or she may make any disposal of the property allowed while alive.

6. *Accession* is the title by which one gains ownership of the increment accruing to one's property. New trees in timberland, new births in a herd, new soil washed down on one's fields are examples of natural accession. The addition

[1]Locke, *Second Treatise on Government,* ch. 5.
[2]Marx, *Capital,* vol. I, pt. I, ch. I, sec. 1.

belongs to the owner of the property added to. Artificial accession, the inseparable mixing of two people's property without a previous agreement, such as painting a picture on another's canvas or building a house on another's land, can be settled by agreement or by the civil law. The property should go to the one who contributed the greater value, with compensation to the other.

7. *Prescription,* also called *adverse possession,* is the extinction of a previous owner's title and its transference to the present possessor through lapse of time. It concerns not only property itself but also such easements as passing across others' land and fishing or mining in certain areas. For occupancy the goods must have no actual owner; for prescription the goods must, unknown to the present holder, be actually owned by someone else. Prescription is a civil title with a basis in natural law. To be valid it must fulfill these conditions: the matter must not be protected against prescription by civil law; the possessor must have intended ownership, been in constant peaceful possession, and in good faith; the time determined by the civil law must have elapsed. Without prescription much modern ownership would be uncertain. Most property is obtained from former owners, who must transmit it with a clear title. Memories fail, witnesses die, documents perish. New claimants could constantly arise, basing their pretensions on forgotten transactions centuries old. Present owners would be in jeopardy of having to prove and re-prove their right against all comers. The only remedy is the extinction of all titles and claims that go back beyond the time set by the law. In all this the civil law is using the authority given to it by the natural law; it is an exercise of eminent domain.

Several of the seven titles to property (gift, trade, inheritance, and labor except labor for oneself) can be reduced to the general heading of *contract.* Not all contracts are about property, and not all property is acquired by contract, but all deliberate transfer of property from one owner to another implies offer and acceptance resulting in a mutual agreement, and hence a contract. Contracts in general and property contracts in particular form the topic of our next chapter.

CAUTIONARY REFLECTIONS

The natural law argument that the principle of private ownership of property is absolute and therefore inviolable and unalterable can be dangerous. Principles can be directed to unworthy or shortsighted ends. They can also enshrine what is in itself a moral good but become an obstacle to moral evolution by absolutizing that good. Principles containing absolutized values, such as the principle of private ownership of property, can be more dangerous than principles that enshrine exploitative possibilities such as slavery and the discrimination against women or races of people simply because the principle containing absolutized values looks more respectable.

Locke's theory of private property has enjoyed a considerable and enduring influence in the United States since the founding of the nation in the eighteenth century. The right to property seems for Locke to be the paradigmatic natural right and the fundamental right that is government's main purpose to protect. Both Locke and Jefferson claim that the natural right to property is self-evidently that kind of right. Claims of self-evidence demand our acceptance without our checking their credentials. Often such claims are presented in such a way as to make us feel obtuse if we too do not see the obvious. Any realistic ethics must challenge such claims, for without such challenge they can operate untested and contaminate all the ethics that is done using such a principle.

Locke's version of the principle of private property operates sometimes subliminally and often quite openly in the American defense of property rights and private enterprise. The principle operated in its purest and most absolute form during the riots of the 1960s when police were called on to shoot looters. Death was seen as a fitting penalty for violation of property rights. The civil rights boycotts and the foundation of private schools and academies to exclude blacks are instances in which property rights became weapons against black people. These examples are two instances when moral evolution was resisted on principle.

The point to remember here is that any right or principle, other than our inalienable natural rights, that is absolutized and given unqualified validity is in a disordered state. Rights and principles exist in relational tension with one another. In any particular situation we have to determine which right or principle, if any, applies. Principles, like ourselves, have a history. They do not just drop down from heaven or originate from pure intellectuality. We have to look at the historical and sociological roots of the principles we use or find embedded in our culture and its institutions. The natural law argument offered in this chapter is an effort to examine the principle of private ownership and to set it in relational tension with other natural rights precisely to avoid the problem we have been discussing.

SUMMARY

Ownership is the right of exclusive control and disposal over a thing at will. What is owned is *property.* Ownership is *public* if the property belongs to the community as such; otherwise it is *private. Full* ownership is control over the substance, use, and fruits, all three; otherwise it is *limited.* Ownership over the substance is *direct;* over the other two, *indirect.*

Every person has a natural right to use the material goods of this world. Nature leaves things common; humans are naturally self-providers with ingenuity to make nature supply their wants.

Theft, as the unjust seizure of rightfully owned property, is wrong, but life comes before property. Nature cannot allow anyone to acquire such a right to property as to extinguish the right to life that nature has already given to all at birth. In grave need a person can commandeer another's property without the guilt of theft.

There are three main *economic systems:* primitive collectivism, private ownership of wealth, and socialism or communism.

Many derive the system of private ownership of wealth wholly from human *convention.* Others, including St. Thomas, base it on the *jus gentium.*

Some modern natural law thinkers wish to base private ownership more directly on *natural law.* They argue: (1) the nature of *the individual person* demands it for the following reasons: (a) people have a natural desire for property, (b) people have a natural tendency to care for and help others, (c) personal responsibility presupposes it, (d) creative development demands it, (e) we need it to be able to provide for the future, and (f) the family presupposes it; and (2) the nature of society with its aim to promote the common good of the members demands it for the following reasons: (a) the clear delineation of *mine* and *yours* helps to maintain peace and obviates disputes, (b) it makes for a better utilization of the goods available in the interest of all, (c) it promotes social cooperation among people, (d) it preserves independence of existence and labor, (e) it ensures the social freedom of the human person, and (f) it makes for a distribution of power in society.

Only as a normative principle for society can the principle of private ownership be a principle of property reform. The principle is absolute; all concrete forms of private ownership are relative because they are governed by sociohistorical circumstances.

To be conclusive the natural law argument would have to show that there is no possible substitute for private ownership.

A title to property is a historical fact that changes the abstract right of ownership in general into the concrete right to this particular piece of property. There are seven titles:

1. *Occupancy:* appropriating what belongs to no one
2. *Labor:* adding new values to raw materials
3. *Gift:* gratuitous transfer of ownership to another
4. *Trade:* any kind of exchange including purchase
5. *Inheritance:* gift to take effect at one's death
6. *Accession:* increment accruing to one's property
7. *Prescription:* possession in good faith over a long time.

Questions for Discussion

1. The right to private ownership of property is not an absolute or unconditioned right. No one is justified in keeping for his or her exclusive use what he or she does not need when other persons lack even the necessities. Does this mean that the person who has more than he or she needs must give up or renounce the ownership of some of his or her property? If so, why? If not, why not?

2. The right to private ownership of property is an important element in forming a just economic policy, because that right enlarges our capacity for creativity and initiative. Think of the small and medium-sized farms, businesses, and enterprises operating in our economy. How are they important in the formulation of just economic policies on the national level? On the state level? Does this kind of ownership help diffuse excessive concentration of economic and political power in the hands of the few? Explain your answer.

3. Transnational corporations and banks help determine the justice or injustice of the world economy. They are not all-powerful but they have considerable power. A number of corporations and banks have stopped operating in South Africa because of that government's repressive racial policies. Should they have remained engaged in South Africa with a view to helping the South Africans improve their economy or were they justified in disengaging themselves? Explain your answer.

4. Owning one's own home is still the American dream. Does the right of every person to the private ownership of property mean that each person has a right to own his or her own home? Some people can afford to buy a home and some cannot. Is this the only limiting factor on that right? Or does the common good of all also require that some members of society be homeowners and some renters? Would our economy be a more just economy if more people owned their own homes? Explain your answer.

5. Businesses have a right to exist in a market framework that encourages them to act in a way that fosters the common good of all. Government must help by providing reasonable regulations and a system of taxation which encourages businesses to preserve the environment, employ disadvantaged workers, and create jobs in disadvantaged or depressed areas. Could any of this happen without private ownership of property? Explain your answer.

Readings

Plato describes the origin of property together with the origin of the state in the *Republic,* bk. II. Read Aristotle's *Politics,* bk. II, especially ch. 5–6, where he defends private ownership against Plato's theories. St. Thomas's *Summa Theologica,* II–II, q. 66, is based on Aristotle, and both are primary sources for the matter found here.

Read John Locke's *Second Treatise on Government,* especially ch. 5. Locke is a firm and even excessive defender of private property. Peter Manicas, *The Death of the State,* ch. 3, has a provocative discussion of the institution of private property as it is connected with the emergence of the liberal state in the early modern period. His discussions of the theories of Hobbes, Locke, Rousseau, and Marx are illuminating. See also Daniel C. Maguire, *The Moral Choice,* ch. 7.

Pope Leo XIII's *Rerum Novarum* (Condition of the Workingman), Pius XI's *Quadragesimo Anno* (Reconstruction of the Social Order), John XXIII's *Mater et Magistra* (Christianity and Social Progress), and the U.S. Bishops' Pastoral Message and Letter, "Economic Justice for All: Catholic Social Teaching and the U.S. Economy," can be found in many editions, some with excellent commentaries. They treat of many matters not pertinent to this chapter, but what they have to say on private ownership is much to the point.

John A. Ryan's *Distributive Justice,* ch. 4 and 18, though old, is still valuable. See Gottfried Dietz, *In Defense of Property.* Johannes Messner's *Social Ethics,* revised ed., bk. IV, pt. II, has supplied a good deal of material for this chapter, especially on the natural law basis for private ownership.

Walter Kaufmann, *Without Guilt and Justice: From Deci-dophobia to Autonomy,* ch. 3, mounts against distributive justice a strong attack that has implications for private ownership.

Pierre Prudhon's *What is property?* is an old and fiery attack; his answer to his question is "Theft!"

29
Contracts

PROBLEM

Why should there be justice among people? The question hardly needs to be asked. The notion of justice is too primitive to need proof. It is not innate but arises very early in our experience. Children and uneducated persons can tell fair from foul play. Even if they cannot define or explain justice, they know when they have been cheated. But reflective knowledge must go beyond inarticulate feelings and attempt a philosophical examination of justice.

Justice is derived from *equality*. Though unequal in many respects, all people have a certain basic equality. We all have the same rational and free nature and are personal beings. We all live under the same norm of morality and have the same moral obligations. To fulfill them we all have natural rights, which are the same for all and entitle all to what they need to achieve the purpose of life. To live fittingly as a human being, one needs not only life but food, clothing, shelter, liberty, education, property, recreation, companionship, and all that goes to make life tolerable as well as possible. To interfere with someone's use of these in such a way as to make his or her life a hardship and a burden, especially when we refuse to take the same ourselves, is to destroy that person's fundamental equality with us, to invade his or her rights, to be unjust.

Moral law and natural rights are thus the source from which justice flows. To protect ourselves in these rights we have instituted human law, the paramount expression of which is the civil law. The primary aim of the state and of civil law is to secure for its citizens the greatest benefits that can be derived from communal living and to distribute these benefits justly.

There are many transactions that are too personal in scope to be determined by the civil law. In these matters the parties concerned determine what they shall do by free agreement. Such mutual agreements, which concern the transfer of a right, are called *contracts*. In a typical contract two people agree to exchange goods, services, or whatever can be transferred. As far as this transaction is concerned, they start equal; then one carries out his or her side of the bargain and upsets the original equality, whereupon the other is now obliged to do his or her part and restore the equality. Until the second party does this, he or she is said to *owe* it, and it is said to be *due* the first party. What obliges each to do his or her part in view of the other's doing his or her part is commutative justice.

Thus we see three main sources of human rights, the preservation of which is justice and the violation injustice. To violate a *natural right* is to take from another person something that God has given, an act of injustice against both God and the person. To violate a *civil right* is to take from another person something the state owes that person in distributive justice, and our interference with the state's duty is a crime against social justice. To violate a *contractual right* (if we may use the term, for a contract does not originate rights but transfers them) is not only a breaking of one's given word but a violation of commutative justice. No one is obliged to make a contract, but commutative justice binds us to keep the contracts we make once we have made them. Both moral law and civil law protect the sanctity of contracts, each in its own sphere. The civil law can enforce only those contracts that fall within its jurisdiction, but the moral law is the guardian of all justice.

About these exchanges of goods and services, which are the embodiment of commutative justice and expressed in contracts, we ask:

1. What is meant by a contract?
2. When is a contract binding and when void?
3. What are the obligations of buyers and sellers?
4. Is there such a thing as a just price?
5. Is monopoly necessarily evil?
6. What are the duties of partners and stockholders?
7. Why is interest-taking allowable today?
8. Are gambling and speculation wrong?

NATURE OF A CONTRACT

Many moralists define a contract as a *mutual agreement concerning the transfer of a right*. The commonly accepted legal definition is that of Blackstone: "An agreement upon sufficient consideration to do or not to do a particular thing."[1] These definitions are not opposed but help to explain one another.

1. A contract is an *agreement* between two parties consenting to the same object; an offer that is made but not accepted cannot be a contract, for only one party consents.

2. It is a *mutual* agreement, for the consent on one side must be given in view of the consent on the other side; two people who accidentally happened to will the same thing without doing so in view of each other's consent would not form a contract.

3. The parties transfer a *right* and therefore bind themselves in *commutative justice;* pacts, promises, and engagements based on truthfulness, loyalty, friendship, or benevolence can impose serious obligations but are not strictly contracts. The transfer of a right produces a corresponding duty of doing or omitting something.

4. Apart from civil law a valuable *consideration* or recompense is not necessary in all contracts, and thus there can be gratuitous contracts such as gift or promise. Even here some intangible consideration in the form of affection, gratitude, or goodwill is normally to be expected.

5. Since the obligation in justice may be on both sides or only on one side, contracts may be bilateral or unilateral, onerous or gratuitous, but the *consent* must always be on both sides.

That there is a moral obligation to keep contracts hardly needs proof. One who makes a contract transfers a right to another. Then by breaking the contract he or she violates the right of another, the very right just transferred, and thus acts unjustly.

To be binding a contract must be valid, and to be morally allowable it should also be licit. Any alleged contract may be valid or licit, or both or neither. A *valid* contract is one that really is a contract, one that holds good and binds the parties to it. An *invalid* contract is null and void and therefore not a contract, though it may look like one. A *licit* contract is one that the contracting parties were morally or civilly allowed to make.

An *illicit* contract is one that is morally or civilly forbidden. Thus buying an article from its owner with my own money is valid and licit; buying extravagant articles with hardship to my dependents is valid but morally illicit; buying stolen articles without knowing that they are stolen is invalid but licit; buying an article that I know to be stolen is invalid and illicit. In the example given, the buyer of extravagant articles must pay for them if they cannot be returned, and thus the contract is valid, but he or she did wrong in making the contract, and thus it is illicit. Because it is always illicit to attempt a contract one knows to be invalid, it is only through invincible ignorance that a contract can be invalid but licit.

VALIDITY OF CONTRACTS

In every contract we can distinguish the contracting parties, the matter of the contract, and the mutual consent. These contribute the three main conditions for a valid contract:

1. The contracting parties must be competent persons.
2. The matter must be suitable for a contract.
3. The consent must be mutual, free, and in proper form.

Contracting Parties

That the contracting parties must be competent persons means that they must be able to understand the terms of the contract so that they can give voluntary consent to them. Because the making of a contract is a human act, one incapable of a human act is incapable of making a contract. The parties must have sufficient use of reason at least when agreeing to the contract. Infants and the insane are excluded, as are intoxicated, drugged, and hypnotized persons while in that condition.

The state, its purpose being to promote the common good, has as a natural society the authority to regulate contracts within the sphere of its jurisdiction. This authority it often exercises by decreeing that certain classes of persons are incompetent subjects with regard to certain con-

---

[1]Blackstone, *Commentaries,* bk. II, ch. 30, p. 442.

tracts, or by setting down conditions for their competence, thus invalidating contracts they may attempt to make to their own or others' harm.

Matter of a Contract

In a contract the matter is that which the contracting parties agree to do or not to do. A contract can concern goods, services, actions, or omissions. For a contract to be valid the matter must be something *possible* under the terms specified and not unduly difficult, something *definite* so that both parties know what they are agreeing to, something morally *permissible* and not contravening prior obligations; if the matter is a physical object, it must be *existing* either in fact or in prospect, and must *belong to* the contracting party so that he or she has the right to dispose of it. These conditions merely express the fact that a contract involves the transfer of a right and the assumption of an obligation. One must have a right to transfer it and must be capable of an obligation before assuming it.

A contract *to do evil* is invalid, that is, null and void, for a contract imposes obligation, and an obligation to do evil is canceled by a prior obligation not to do it. One who has agreed to do evil is not allowed to carry out the supposed contract. Such a person did wrong to begin with in entering into such an agreement and would do further wrong by attempting to fulfill it. If money has been paid in advance, he or she must return the price, for it cannot be claimed by any title. The whole is a bad bargain, and both must withdraw from it.

What if the evil is already done? It must be undone, if possible. If the act is irreversible, opinion is divided. The first opinion says that if the conditions for a valid contract are not met, the whole transaction is void; both agents ought to have known that neither is bound to anything. The second opinion makes a distinction, arguing that the promise to do evil was indeed invalid, but the act by which it was carried out was a real expenditure of physical effort or mental ingenuity worth a price—that here was a valid subsidiary contract attached to the main invalid

contract. Each of the parties may follow the probable opinion that is to his or her advantage, the one demanding and the other refusing payment. The doer of the evil deed may certainly ask for and accept the price, for even without a right to it by contract, he or she may always ask for and take a gift.

Bribery is the offering of money for evildoing, especially for the shirking of duty. If the money is offered or promised on condition that one do the evil act and this condition is accepted, there is an attempt to make a contract about illegitimate matter, and the principles just stated apply: the evil act must be avoided and the money returned, or if the act has been done, the money either must be returned, if one adopts the opinion that the whole transaction is void, or the money may be kept, if one follows the opinion that the payment of the price for service rendered is a valid contract attached to the invalid evil contract. But if the money is offered merely to persuade or allure someone to do wrong, there is no contract because there is no promise in return. Though it is understood why the money is given, the absence of mutual agreement makes it no more than a gift; if we regard only the purely contractual aspect of commutative justice, one could take the money and still refuse to do the evil act. But morality is not limited to strict justice. No self-respecting person will accept a bribe, and public officials particularly must not jeopardize their freedom to act impartially for the common good.

Much publicity has been given in the news media to companies that operate in foreign countries and engage in some form of bribery to do business. The corporate officials call this kind of payment to public officials of other countries a "gift" or simply refer to it as "part of the cost of doing business there." Ought such payments be made? Ought they be called a part of the ordinary cost of doing business in another country? Does each corporation operating in another country have some responsibility not to contribute further to a social problem in that country, namely, the problem of having corrupt public officials? Does such a practice interfere with free and open competition? If so, it is unjust and therefore immoral. Is it just for corporate officials to use the stockholders' money in this way? If the practice is immoral, then all the stockholders, the actual owners of the corporation, become cooperators in an immoral practice. When such practices become known, the stockholders have a moral obligation to see that they are stopped and to disengage the corporation from doing business in countries where it is impossible to operate morally.

Mutual Consent

The essence of the contract is the mutual consent of the parties. Consent implies offer and acceptance. The *offer* remains open as long as the offerer wishes. It may cease by withdrawal on the part of the offerer, by refusal on the part of the one to whom it was offered, or by lapse of time. *Acceptance* may not be revoked, for it seals the contract. Conditions attached to the offer or to the acceptance must be made known to and accepted by both parties. Regulation of contracts is a typical matter for human law and custom. In the absence of an agreement to the contrary, the prevailing conventions should be followed.

Mutual consent must be an external manifestation of a free internal act of will. It must be externally manifested, because a contract is between two persons and supposes communication between them. It must be internally given by a free act, because a contract is a *human act,* requiring an act of the will consequent on knowledge. Freedom of consent may be nullified by error or by fear.

Error voids a contract only insofar as it excludes consent. Any *substantial* error, whether involving deceit or not, invalidates the contract, for then the person consents to something quite different from the actual matter proposed, as when a person buys what he or she thinks is a live horse and gets a hobbyhorse. Errors about unimportant qualities do not affect the contract, as when a person finds that the horse bought is not the expected color. However, if such qualities were expressly stipulated so that the contract would not have been made except for them, the contract is invalid if the stipulations are not adhered to. Hence what is substantial to a contract may be determined not only by the nature of the matter concerned but also by the will of the contracting parties when they make a certain condition essential to the contract.

Fear voids a contract only if it destroys the use of reason, making voluntary consent impossible. This would be the strongly emotional, not the intellectual, type of fear. Since even grave fear does not normally destroy voluntariness, contracts made from the motive of fear are naturally valid. Fear may be artificially aroused in a person by the use of threats to extort his or her consent. Such unjust intimidation, though it leaves the contract valid, makes it voidable, that is, capable of being canceled without the intimidator's consent. It is valid because it is a human act but voidable because it is the result of injury that the intimidator is bound to repair. Positive law, for the sake of the common good, also has the authority to render invalid from the beginning contracts extorted under intimidation and duress. Whether it does so and under what conditions, the positive law itself would have to declare.

So much about contracts in general. They all deal with the transfer of rights and the consequent assumption of duties, to the observance of which each party binds himself or herself in justice. Implicit understandings may be sufficient among friends, but the public solemnity of the formal contract acts as a guarantee to each party concerned that the other party will respect the right transferred, fulfill the duty assumed, and thus maintain justice.

The remaining sections deal with various business and property contracts.

BUYING AND SELLING

The contract of *buying* and *selling,* or *purchase* and *sale,* is a contract whereby two persons agree to exchange a commodity for a certain price. It differs from *barter* by using money as the medium of exchange. The two are essentially the same sort of contract, but the idea of price brings up some special problems. The expression of consent to each other is normally enough to seal the contract, but the civil law may add certain formalities necessary for validity, as in the transfer of real estate, where it is important for the common good that the state know who owns the property.

The *seller* must own the object he or she sells, manifest its hidden defects, and deliver the actual article bought. Articles belonging to another, whether stolen or held by mistake, cannot be validly sold, and anyone who possesses them must return them to the real owner as soon as the real ownership becomes evident; a seller in bad faith must stand the loss, both refunding the price and seeing that the true owner receives the property, but no one need be disturbed about purchases made in good faith on the open market. The seller must manifest hidden substantial defects even without inquiry, for they touch the essence of the contract, but need not manifest hidden accidental defects except on inquiry, when he or she must tell the truth; in any case the seller must lower the price proportionately.

The *buyer* must accept on delivery the goods contracted for and pay in full within a reasonable time, either specified in the contract or dictated by custom. Precious objects should not be bought for a song from children or simpletons, and the law protects them by making consent of their guardians necessary. The buyer need not inform the seller how the property will be used or what profit is expected from it, but to have a meeting of the minds, both should know the *nature* of the goods even if they differ about their value.

Both buyer and seller, though neither need assist the other to make a good bargain, since each is out for his or her own advantage, must see to it that the contract is valid according to the norms set down for contracts in general. They are also bound to see that justice is done and therefore must agree on a just price.

The Just Price

In some economic circles the *just price* is regarded as a medieval notion inapplicable to the competitive methods of modern business. Since economics is not ethics, economists are privileged to ignore the idea of justice as being outside their field and to pursue their study in an ethical vacuum. In theory the two sciences must be kept distinct, but in practice life cannot be divided in that way. One does not cease to be human by operating a business. A business transaction has both a commercial and a moral aspect: commercial insofar as it involves a *price,* and moral insofar as it involves what is *just.* As it can be good or poor business, so it can be moral or immoral conduct, and these two spheres do not always coincide. To be viewed adequately as a piece of human endeavor, the act must be seen from both standpoints.

It solves nothing to say that the just price is that which gives the seller a fair profit after deducting his or her own expenses. This is only a rule of thumb, supposing an already existing price structure, prices for materials, machines, labor, and upkeep, besides prices for the commodities needed for a person's support and purchased with his or her profit. We want to know how this price structure itself arises and what can make it just.

Our discussion will begin with *staple* commodities bought and sold in the market by people *in business,* not with rare articles or occasional private transactions outside the usual realm of commerce. The former alone can give us a standard of value according to which prices can be scaled; the latter must also conform to the just price, but here it can be arrived at only by analogy and derivation from the former source.

The *price* of a thing is its value in terms of money. *Value* is the capacity of goods to satisfy human wants, and *money* is the accepted medium of exchange. The *just price,* then, is the true money value of the commodity, a price that can purchase other commodities having equal capacity for satisfying human wants as the commodity sold. The whole concept of commutative justice is based on the idea of equality, and trade itself with all its modern complexities is only a development of the same idea: that a person receives the equal of what he or she gives. The purpose of trade is social, to allow people to supply themselves with the commodities they need in exchange for those they have in surplus. Nor is this concept of equality contradictory to the idea of profit, for each one is entitled to the fruit of his or her superior industry and ingenuity and may make as good a bargain as possible without violating justice. There are limits set by justice, and human commerce is not allowed to have the antisocial purpose of prospering on the calamities and misfortune of others.

The problem is: How can the equal capacity of commodities for satisfying human wants be calculated? Two extreme views can be considered:

1. Each commodity has an exactly fixed money value.
2. Any price the buyer is willing to pay is just.

The first extreme is impossible. There is no way of determining what any individual will want, for human needs and desires differ too widely from person to person, vary too much from time to time in the same person, and depend on too many purely psychological factors such as taste and fashion. One will pay a king's ransom for an article that another would not take as a gift. Hence it is foolish to look for a just price as an absolutely fixed sum. It could only be a range within which prices fluctuate, and the whole range varies with the times.

The second extreme is immoral. A starving person would be willing to pay all he or she possesses for a bit of food, for a person in such a plight cannot eat money, but no one would be allowed to take such an advantage of a starving person. Were prices determined by what an individual is willing to pay, we should have the absurd situation that, as an individual's needs increase, the purchasing power of his or her money decreases, until in desperate straits it is practically worthless. The example given here is an extreme case, it is true, but it only goes to show how false the principle is. It would thwart the whole idea of money as a medium of exchange, of trade as a function of society, and of commutative justice as a moral virtue.

The just price, then, must be determined by the usefulness of the commodity not to this or that individual but to people generally. The price must represent the judgment of the buying public on the value of the article, eliminating the subjective conditions peculiar to the individual. This judgment is expressed in the open market, where buyers and sellers freely compete with one another and thus establish a true equation between the capacities of different commodities for satisfying human wants. The competitive price is the *natural* price that will drive out all other prices, and this is also the just price where there is pure competition.

There is not much pure competition remaining. Wants are artificially created by our huge advertising programs, and prices are monopolistically determined, but even an artificially induced want is a want and competes with other wants. Monopolistic prices can be judged outrageous or exorbitant, and the thing so priced will not sell, thus showing that the just price concept still obtains. Because there are conspiracies to boost or lower prices artificially, the government may step in and regulate prices; a price thus set by law is the *legal* price, and it is the just price if properly calculated to offset the distortion artificially induced. The government may also set legal prices to protect certain occupations, such as agriculture, that are essential to the public welfare.

The just price is elastic, a range between a *highest just price* and a *lowest just price*. Outside these limits justice is violated, but in between them any price is just. The reason for this elasticity is that the wants of the buying and selling public continually alter and take some time to make themselves felt, so that the market lags a bit behind these changes. To sell above the highest just price is to take an antisocial advantage of the buyer's needs and to make a profit out of human misery; to buy below the lowest just price is to take the opposite advantage of the seller's need to get rid of his or her goods in exchange for what the seller needs more. To act thus is to be guilty of injustice, and one who does so is morally bound to make restitution even without a legal decision.

Since possibility of loss or of long-deferred

payment may excuse from the market price, there is nothing wrong with the practice of a periodic "bargain sale" at reduced rates for the purpose of clearing out old stock or attracting new customers. The seller may raise the price if the article has personal or sentimental value, because he or she deserves compensation for this loss, but not if it has such value for the buyer only, because the seller does not possess this extra value and loses nothing on account of it.

The prices of rare articles, such as curios, museum pieces, collector's items, and objects of art and luxury, are determined by the narrow community that deals in such things. There is still a just price, but it is much more elastic. If the object is unique, the community may be narrowed down to one buyer and seller, and almost any price agreed on is just.

Auction is a sale in which the highest bidder becomes the purchaser. The highest bid determines the just price. Since no one is bound to buy in this manner, auctions work no injustice if the conventions are followed and free bidding is not interfered with.

Monopoly

Monopoly is exclusive control over a market. Monopolies may be state controlled or privately controlled; they may owe their existence to the nature of the marketable commodity or be granted by law.

Monopoly is *just* when it uses its control for the common welfare. Thus copyright and patent rights secure to people the fruits of their ingenuity and industry, large outlays of capital for railroads and toll bridges need protection, the state may establish a monopoly over a luxury as a source of revenue. The putting of so much economic power into the hands of one or a few is not wrong in itself. The whole question is how that power is used, for or against the common good. Once a monopoly over important commodities and services has been secured, it ceases to have a purely private interest and becomes a matter of public and social interest.

Monopoly is *unjust* when it uses its control against the common welfare. It is not unjust to undersell competitors, even though this act puts others out of business and tends to create a monopoly, provided one does not sell under the lowest just price. This is how competitive business works, though there are other obligations besides those of mere justice. The classic abuse of monopoly is to cut prices below the lowest just price for the purpose of driving out competitors and cornering the market, and then, when the monopolist has gained control, to raise the price above the highest just price. In such a process the monopolist ultimately aims at charging unjust prices and using economic dictatorship for personal profit contrary to the common good.

Partnership

Partnership is a contract by which several persons put together their money, labor, or skill into a business and share the profit and loss proportionately. We limit ourselves to a few remarks on its ethical aspects.

In the *firm* or company each partner is bound by a personal obligation and, in case of default, must make good out of his or her personal belongings for the total liability of the firm unless it is a "limited" firm. A *corporation* is a legal person having corporate rights and duties, each member being bound in proportion to the amount of capital subscribed. Besides limiting the members' liability, the corporation is endowed with a sort of immortality, continuing in existence indefinitely though all the members have changed.

The ethical disadvantage of the corporation is the diminished sense of responsibility on the part of the stockholders who leave the whole management of the corporation to the directors. Many stockholders never reflect that their money may be used by unscrupulous directors to perpetrate the grossest injustices. Securely shielded behind the impersonal front of the corporation, they may believe that they have sloughed off all personal responsibility onto the directors' shoulders. But it is impossible to avoid moral responsibility in this way, and the principles concerning *cooperation in evil* apply. As a rule people who have invested their money in reputable enterprises need not be disturbed, but if anything occurs to raise serious doubts, they have a moral obligation to investigate and take corrective action.

There is nothing wrong in principle with the more complex forms of business associations such as trusts, cartels, syndicates, holding companies, and conglomerates, but they are open to abuse and unjust monopolistic practices. They require supervision and control.

Interest and Usury

Loan of money generally carries with it a contract of interest. Formerly all interest was called *usury,* from the Latin *usura,* the price for the use of a thing; but now usury means only excessive interest. It is well to note this point in reading Aristotle's and St. Thomas's condemnation of *usury;* they do not mean excessive interest only, but any interest. Since they were only reflecting the common view of their day, we ask: Why was interest-taking formerly thought wrong and now is the accepted thing? According to Aristotle:

> The most hated sort [of wealth-getting], and with the greatest reason, is usury, which makes a gain out of money itself, and not from the natural object of it. For money was intended to be used in exchange, but not to increase at interest. And this term interest, which means the birth of money from money, is applied to the breeding of money because the offspring resembles the parent. Wherefore of all modes of getting wealth this is the most unnatural.[1]

St. Thomas accepts Aristotle's theory and works out the argument in greater detail. He says:

> To take usury for money lent is unjust in itself, because this is to sell what does not exist and this evidently leads to inequality which is contrary to justice.
>
> In order to make this evident, we must observe that there are certain things the use of which consists in their consumption: thus we consume wine when we use it for drink, and we consume wheat when we use it for food . . . .
>
> He commits injustice who lends wine or wheat,

and asks for double payment, viz., one, the return of the thing in equal measure, the other, the price of the use, which is called usury . . . .

> Now money, according to the philosopher was invented chiefly for the purpose of exchange: and consequently the proper and principal use of money is its consumption or alienation whereby it is sunk in exchange. Hence it is by its very nature unlawful to take payment for the use of money lent, which payment is known as usury: and just as a man is bound to restore other ill-gotten goods, so is he bound to restore the money which he has taken in usury.[2]

These views are no longer held, not because of any change in the moral principles of justice involved, but because of a change in the function of money. Interest was condemned as an attempt to get gain by no labor, expense, or risk from something that does not fructify (money) and hence can afford no just title for the gain.

In former ages Aristotle's statement that money is merely a medium of exchange was literally true. It could not be easily turned into capital. There were only handicrafts, no large factories. The only capital worth the name was land, and land, since it was owned by the nobility and was the title to their rank, was not generally on the market for sale. All that anyone could do with surplus money was to keep it locked in a chest or spend it on furnishings and luxuries.

The change in the function of money was brought about by the introduction of the capitalistic system, appearing first in the mercantile and later in the industrial form. When feudalism was breaking up and the new class of wealthy burghers was coming into prominence, the latter formed *joint stock companies* to finance projects greater than the wealth of any single person, the profit to be distributed in proportion to the amount contributed. Since the development of these enterprises and more so after the industrial revolution, money can always find profitable investments and can be readily turned into capital. By such investments money brings profit, breeds more money, and so does fructify.

Nowadays the person who lends money to an-

---

[1]Aristotle, *Politics,* bk. I, ch. 10, 1258b 2–8.

[2]St. Thomas, *Summa Theologica,* II–II, q. 78, a. 1.

other foregoes the opportunity of investing that money in profitable enterprises and is deserving of compensation for this loss. This is the modern function of interest. Now that anyone can readily invest money and turn it into capital, there is no reason why one person should ever lend money to another unless the lender can receive profit in the form of interest. To charge an excessive rate is unjust and has now become the crime of usury.

That this modern idea of interest does not rest on a change of moral principles, but only on a new interpretation of money, is confirmed by the fact that even the ancients admitted the right to compensation for the expenses of the transaction, the loss of the opportunity to seize good bargains, and the risk of not recovering the principal. In ancient times these were not always present or were negligible; now the reverse is true.

The foregoing refers to private loans only, in which the just rate of interest would be calculated to offset the loss of potential gain incurred in each case. How may we explain the uniform rates of interest prevailing in the money markets? And how is a person justified in taking interest on money loaned to the capitalistic enterprises themselves, in supporting those very institutions that make interest-taking on private loans almost an economic necessity? An investor in stocks is entitled to dividends, which are the investor's share in the profits, but why is the holder of bonds, who owns no share in the company, entitled to interest on his or her money?

The answer must be based on the function of credit in the modern financial world. The granting of credit is the placing of economic power at somebody's disposal. It is an economic service and as such is worth its price like any other service. Whoever makes personal property available for another's use charges rent for it. Whoever makes money or credit available for another's use can likewise charge for this use in the form of interest. Interest in this sense has changed radically from interest on private loans. It ceases to be the old contract of interest and becomes much like one of hire or lease. It is rendering a service to the enterprise and thereby to the whole community whose economic prosperity consists in the total complex of these enterprises. It sets up a market in money as in any other commodity, and the just price is determined in the same way as the price for any other service. The natural rate of interest is what people in general are willing to pay on the open market, and the legal rate is one that is fixed by law.

CONTRACTS OF CHANCE

Contracts of chance have to do with some uncertain event whose outcome results from luck, skill, or a combination of the two. Since a person may dispose of personal property as he or she pleases, gambling is not wrong in itself. However, contracts of chance, besides conforming to the requirements of contracts in general, must observe some special conditions of their own if they are to be conducted on a moral plane:

1. One must wager only what belongs to oneself and is not needed for satisfying other obligations, such as paying creditors or supporting one's family.

2. The matter of the contract must be something lawful in itself and understood in the same sense by all parties. Equality is not necessary, but inequalities should be made known. Odds and handicaps should be offered by the favored side but may be waived by the other side.

3. The outcome should be objectively uncertain and not a sure thing, if it is to be truly a contract of chance. Each may feel subjectively certain of winning but must not have so manipulated the matter beforehand as to cut down the other's chance. Anyone who insists on betting against another's protestation of certainty is making a gift, not placing a bet.

4. There must be no cheating, either by fixing the outcome beforehand or by engaging in an illegitimate style of play. What constitutes cheating depends on the conventions accepted in that kind of bet or game. Winnings through cheating are fraudulently acquired and must be refunded.

5. The loser must pay. This is evident from the whole supposition of the contract. Only those prepared to stand the losses have a right to the

winnings, because they impose this obligation on the other party and the obligation is mutual.

What if gambling is outlawed? If a civil law forbids gambling, it is either a purely penal law, leaving the contract valid and the obligation standing, or it is a law that binds morally, voiding the contract from the start, so that the principles on evil contracts apply. In the former case one does no moral wrong in gambling but must pay. In the latter case one probably need not pay but commits a wrong in the act of gambling.

Gambling, though not in itself morally wrong, is open to serious abuse. Some people get gambling in their blood and cannot stop until they have brought about their own and their family's ruin. For them gambling becomes a vice leading to many others. Just as some must practice total abstinence regarding drink, others must stay completely away from all forms of gambling, not because it is objectively wrong, but because of the subjective danger of excess in certain persons. Besides, professional gambling is conducted in such an atmosphere of general moral laxity as to provide many temptations beyond those of gambling itself. The civil law, instead of trying to forbid gambling, would spend its energies better in inspecting gambling facilities and seeing that they are run honestly.

Insurance has a purpose different from that of other contracts of chance, for it is not to make money quickly but to guard against loss. Gambling creates a risk where none existed before; insurance covers a risk that was already present. Insurance fills a definite need in modern society. Its contract, whose written form is called a *policy,* must follow the laws of contracts in general. Any fraudulent concealment or failure to live up to the terms of the contract is an act of injustice demanding restitution. Deliberately to cause damage to collect insurance money is the obvious crime here, removing the element of chance essential to the contract. Insurance companies must have the funds to pay indemnities for losses occurring at the normal rate, but not to cover all at once. Insurance has become so common and

has assumed such social significance that the civil law has the right and duty to regulate it strictly.

Insurance company practice is always something of a mystery to the average person. The language of the policies is practically incomprehensible to all but insurance lawyers, insurance company experts, and perhaps some students of insurance. Life insurance, health insurance, automobile insurance, and title insurance are the most common forms of insurance that the average person buys, often without understanding exactly what is being provided for the premiums paid. Already we have a moral problem, even if we do not face a legal one, because for a contract to be valid and moral, all the parties to the contract must understand fully the terms of the contract. Much of the insurance sold today is sold precisely to people who do not fully understand the terms of the contract. The government has a duty to protect its citizens from such practices, and it could fulfill that duty easily by requiring all insurance companies to write their policies in simple, straightforward language that is easily understood and to price their premiums justly in terms of the risk the company actually takes and the service it actually renders the insured person. Insurance companies also have a serious obligation not to sell people insurance they do not need or insurance that will do them little or no good. Given the enormous amount of money insurance companies amass from premiums paid by policyholders, they wield enormous monetary power and hence social power. The government has a serious duty to regulate the use of this power very strictly for the common good of all.

The practice of "red-lining" particular areas as high-risk areas especially for automobile insurance is morally questionable at best and completely immoral at worst. Who is hurt by this practice? Usually the people who can least afford the higher premiums and are the safest drivers. The insurance company collects its premiums, makes its profit, and refuses insurance to someone who lives in an area or is in an age group that has more than a specified number of accidents. How insurance companies can justify this practice of "red-lining" is difficult to comprehend. This practice is discriminatory and deserves to be outlawed.

Operations on the stock exchange and similar markets are in the first instance only buying and selling, though on a grand scale. The size of the transaction does not change its nature or the moral principles on which it rests. It becomes a contract of chance when it assumes the form of *speculation,* which consists of betting on future changes of price, and is thus a kind of gambling. In itself speculation is not morally wrong, and it follows the laws of betting. Those who engage in it, however, must consider not only themselves and their competitors, those willing to play the game, but also the producers of commodities and the vast horde of small investors whose interests are bound up with their own. Unscrupulous speculation on the market and its resulting artificial manipulation of prices can work serious harm to thousands of people and can wreck the economy of nations. To ruin others for one's own profit cannot be condoned by any law of justice or charity, and those who cause these evils bear a staggering load of moral guilt.

SUMMARY

Justice is derived from the fundamental *equality* of all people, based on their personhood and common human nature. To maintain this equality we are endowed with natural rights, define for ourselves civil rights, and transfer alienable rights by contract. Justice demands respect for all three kinds of rights; interference with any is injustice. Commutative justice guarantees the sanctity of contracts and obliges to their observance.

A *contract* is a mutual agreement by which two or more persons bind themselves to do or omit something. A *valid* contract holds good and really binds, and a *licit* contract is one lawfully entered into; a contract can be valid without being licit, and vice versa.

The *contracting parties* must be competent persons, with sufficient use of reason for a human act. Civil law may add further conditions.

The *matter* must be possible, existing, definite, transferable, and lawful. A contract to do evil is invalid, and one is forbidden to fulfill it; one who has done so may ask and accept the price, though the other probably need not pay it.

Mutual consent means that each party freely consents in view of the other's consent. Substantial error voids a contract, but not accidental error, unless it is about something expressly stipulated. Fear that destroys consent voids a contract; civil law may void naturally valid contracts made under duress.

The title to property is transferred by *contract.* The *seller* must own the object sold, manifest its hidden defects, and deliver the article bought; the *buyer* must accept the goods on delivery and pay within a reasonable time.

The *just price* is one that can purchase other commodities having equal capacity for satisfying human wants. It is neither an absolutely fixed money value nor any sum the buyer is willing to pay, but represents the judgment of the buying public in general, found by free competition on the open market. It is the *natural* price; if fixed by law, it is the *legal* price. The just price is elastic, a range between a *highest* and a *lowest* just price. To buy or sell outside these limits is unjust and demands restitution. Rare articles, bargain sales, and auctions are exceptions.

Monopoly, exclusive control over a market, is just when used for the common welfare, unjust when exploited for selfish ends.

Partnership is good in itself, though monopolistic forms need regulation. In a *firm* each partner has total liability. In a *corporation* liability is limited by the proportion of shares held. Stockholders cannot slough off onto the directors responsibility for immoral use of their capital.

Interest was formerly condemned as an attempt to get gain from what does not fructify. Capitalism, with unlimited opportunities for investment, changed the function of money so that it can fructify. Interest compensates the lender for the gain he or she might otherwise have made and for the service rendered. Now only excessive interest, *usury,* is wrong.

Contracts of chance deal with an uncertain event. Gambling, though not wrong in itself under proper conditions, is a great moral danger to certain people. Cheating demands restitution, and gambling debts must be paid. Insurance is a legitimate social necessity, but the industry needs careful control by the government for the common good of all. Market speculation, a complex form of betting, is capable of wreaking great harm unless kept within responsible control.

Questions for Discussion

1. We have said that the matter of a contract (what is actually exchanged) must be something possible, definite, permissible, and, if it is a physical object, belong to the party selling it. Surrogate mothers make a contract with the inseminator and his wife to be inseminated by the donor's sperm, carry the child, and after birth give up the child to the donor and his wife for a fee. Is the contract valid? Is the price just? Ought the government set some legal policy in regard to such contracts? Should we have a minimum fee, which would be automatically adjusted as the cost of living rises or falls?

2. On Monday, October 19, 1987, you are a small investor with holdings in blue-chip stocks. The market goes down and the Dow Jones industrial average loses 508.32 points. You are in the market along with the large mutual funds, pension funds, insurance companies, bank trust departments, and a host of foreign investors. The government regulates the stock market to some extent already. Do you see a need for further regulation? If so, what would be morally helpful? If not, explain the moral principles on which you base your answer.

3. Why do we place moral restrictions on contracts? If you own what you are selling and I am willing to pay the price you are asking, what more is needed? If I do not want to pay your price, I do not have to buy what you are selling. Is this sufficient for exchanges between individuals? What about the telephone company, the electric company, and the gas company? At present they are regulated, but are the regulations really necessary? Explain your answer.

4. People in their twenties, depending on where they live and the type of car they drive, usually pay more for automobile insurance than people ten years older who drive comparable automobiles. Is this fair (just)? Across the board women and smokers pay more than men and nonsmokers. The insurance companies calculate their risks and charge their premiums accordingly. Your state has a law that requires every automobile driver to carry liability insurance. Does the state have a moral obligation to protect its citizens from excessively high insurance rates? Explain your answer.

5. You are the mayor of a resort town of 25,000 people, some of whom depend heavily on tourism for their livelihood. An investor approaches you to discuss the possibility of opening a card parlor in which gambling would be allowed. How would you go about exploring with him the moral questions involved in his proposal? Would it be advisable to make the proposal public and invite public comment for a period of time? Do you have an obligation to follow the lead of the majority, no matter what your own views are?

Readings

On justice: Plato's treatise on justice takes up bk. I and the first part of bk. II of the *Republic*. Aristotle's *Nicomachean* *Ethics*, bk. V, is all on justice. St. Thomas writes on justice in the *Summa Theologica*, II–II, qq. 58–62. Of modern writers read Étienne Gilson's *Moral Values and Moral Life,* ch. 9, and his *Christian Philosophy of St. Thomas Aquinas,* pt. III, ch. 4; Heinrich Rommen's *The State in Catholic Thought,* pp. 184–192, 319–326; and Josef Pieper's little book *Justice* or the section on justice in his *The Four Cardinal Virtues.*

On economics: Aristotle, as the founder of economics as well as of so many other sciences, writes on household management and on wealth in his *Politics,* bk. I, ch. 8–11. St. Thomas discusses cheating and usury in the *Summa Theologica,* II–II, qq. 77–78. On usury, John T. Noonan's *Scholastic Analysis of Usury* is a thorough scholarly study. On the moral aspects of economics see John A. Ryan, *Distrib-* *utive Justice,* ch. 7, 10–11, 16; and Johannes Messner, *Social Ethics,* bk. IV, pt. I.

On the ethics of various particular business practices see Herbert Johnston's *Business Ethics,* Henry Wirtenberger's *Morality and Business,* Thomas M. Garrett's *Ethics in Business,* Marquis Childs and Douglas Cater's *Ethics in a Business Society,* Luther Hodges's *The Business Conscience,* Philip I. Blumberg, *The Megacorporation in American Society: The Scope of Corporate Power,* and W. L. La Croix, *Principles for Ethics in Business.* David Hapgood's *The Screwing of the Average Man* documents many questionable business practices, among them those of the insurance industry. The *Harvard Business Review* has an ethically oriented article in nearly every issue.

30
Work

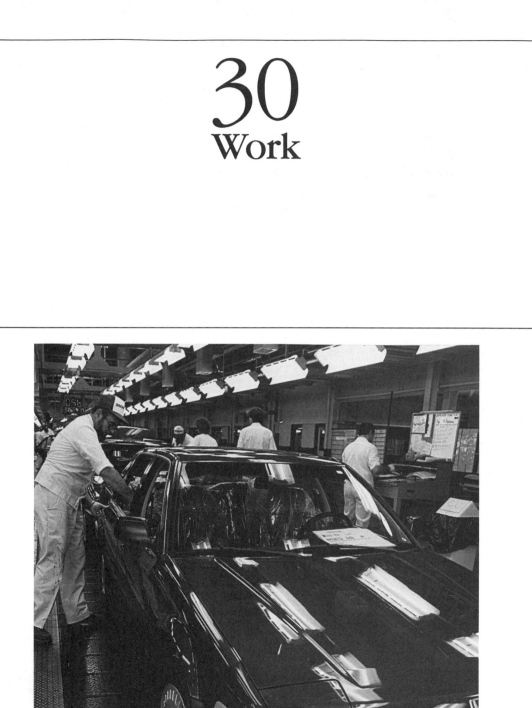

PROBLEM

Human beings are rational and free by nature; they are personal beings living in communion with one another. As persons, they are each subjects and can in no way be numbered among the objects of this world; their dignity is such that none can be used as a mere means to accomplish another's purpose. Each person is an end in himself or herself, and all persons together constitute a "kingdom of ends," as Kant reminds us. Sharing the same rational and free nature, the dignity of personhood, and a common world, all people can be said to be brothers and sisters. This much nontheists would admit. Theists go one step further and recognize God as the creator and father of the human family.

In relation with other persons sharing a common world for the common good of all, we work to supply our needs for food, shelter, and clothing and to satisfy our needs and desires for recreation, entertainment, communication, education, interpersonal intimacy and love, peace, and divine worship as well as many other material and spiritual goods. By "work" is meant any human activity in which physical strength and/or other powers are exerted to do or make something. Work may be physical or intellectual; it is important for the individual, for the family, and for society. Its significance may be seen from the mere fact that it occupies a considerable portion of each person's lifetime just to obtain a livelihood to secure the material basis for carrying out the tasks essential to the common good. What gives nobility to all work is that it is a form of interpersonal cooperation at a socially indispensable task.

Since most people get the income and/or property they need by working for it, we want to examine the person as worker, the kinds of work he or she does, and its impact on civilization and culture. Furthermore, we want to examine the relationship between employee and employer. By the wage contract, a person hires out his or her labor to another for a definite sum of money known as a wage or salary. The wage contract is singled out for special treatment because it raises the whole question of industrial relations, the relationship of management and labor, and the social responsibility of both these partners of industry. The following questions can guide our discussion:

1. Is work a fundamental dimension of personal existence?
2. What kinds of human activity count as work?
3. Is the wage system just?
4. How is the minimum just wage determined?
5. Has each person a right to work?
6. Has anyone a right to preferential treatment in competing with others for employment?
7. Are labor unions justified?
8. Why and when have employees a right to strike?
9. Are lockouts and boycotts justified?
10. What is the basis for social responsibility on the part of both labor and management?

THE PERSON AND WORK

In Chapter 15, *subjectivity* as the distinguishing mark of the person was discussed. The human being engaged in work is a personal subject capable of acting in a planned and rational way, capable of deciding about himself or herself and with a tendency to self-development. Work is therefore a personal activity that aims to do or make something, the *object* of the working. Abstract for the moment from the objective content of the work to focus on the subjective aspect. The personal subject's activity serves to realize (actualize) and develop that person precisely as a person. This constitutes the ethical value of work: the fact that the one who works is a person, a conscious and free subject, i.e., a subject who decides about himself or herself. The basis for determining the value of human work is not primarily the kind of work being done, but the fact that the one doing it is a person. The dignity of work lies first and foremost in this subjective dimension, and so work is "for the person" and the person is not merely "for work." Whatever work is done and whatever objective value it may have, it is always persons who are the purpose of the work that is done, no matter how tedious, monotonous, and alienating the work may be.

To recognize the primacy of the subjective dimension of work shows the error of treating humans as mere instruments of production. The true purpose of the whole process of production is to do or make something for persons, and the doer or maker is a person. Exploitation in the field of wages, working conditions, and Social Security is wrong precisely because it degrades the person who is working. Since human work is not merely an instrument of production, capital and its increase is objectively less important than the personal subjects who benefit from its increase, namely, the owners of capital and the workers. Focusing on the subjective dimension in the whole production process reveals the social dimension of the economic system more clearly and the basis and need for social justice.

The relation of the community of persons with regard to the nonpersonal world is one of caring and stewardship. People use the goods of nature to sustain personal life in various ways, and this use always involves all kinds of work. Much of that work is sheer physical labor, sometimes carried on under exceptionally strenuous conditions. Agricultural workers spend long days working the land so that they and others may have food. Miners work the mines and quarries to provide materials for construction and heating so they and others may have proper shelter for living and working. Steelworkers process the iron ore at blast furnaces to provide steel for all types of construction. Construction workers provide shelter for families, for businesses, and for many other organizations. Often the work is not only arduous, it is dangerous as well.

The stewardship and care of nature also involves much intellectual work. The scientists and engineers labor long and hard to help all of us understand our world and to put its goods to human use. The ultimate purpose of all the work is the person not only of the worker but those in the human community.

Work is good for people, even when it is difficult and taxing, and not just in the sense that it produces some good that people want or need. Work is good in the sense of being something worthy of the person, corresponding to personal dignity and increasing it. Through work, people transform the earth and its resources, adapting them to personal needs and desires, and they also fulfill themselves as persons, becoming more human, developing their humanity further. Because work is good for people, it is possible to understand the meaning of industriousness and why it is a moral virtue. Industriousness is a good moral habit whereby the person becomes good as a rational and free being cooperating in work with others for the common good of all.

Work makes it possible for people to start families, for the family needs the subsistence and sustenance which parents normally gain for themselves and their children from work. Work and industriousness have their impact on the whole process of education within the family, because everyone becomes more of a human being through work among other things and developing as a human being is the main purpose of the educational process. Work makes family life and its upkeep possible, and it also makes possible the achievement of other family purposes, one of which is education.

The working person, in addition to having his or her origin in the family, is also a member of a country where he or she lives and works together with others. Here the person belongs with others and shares with them a particular culture and history. Within the family and in the marketplace the person absorbs the contents and values that make up the particular culture and history. Each member of society inherits the fruits of the work of previous generations and by his or her own work carries on and increases the common good developed together with all the other members of society. The work that any person does serves to add to the heritage not only of the one society to which he or she belongs but to the heritage of the entire human family.

Such is the dignity of the person and the work that is done.

KINDS OF WORK

The economic aspect of society encompasses all phases of the process of producing the goods and services that people need and desire. In this process everything that people do counts as work—not just manual labor, but every activity people engage in to complete the process of production. The stewardship over and caring for the resources of the earth, the use of those resources, the creation of technology and machines to work those resources, the management of the capital, the direction of those who work on what they do not own—all count as work. The whole process of production is one vast interpersonal collaboration aimed at creating goods and services for the benefit of persons.

Every human being who shares in the production process is a personal subject and as such is the one for whom the work is ultimately being done. The machines, factories, laboratories, computers, capital, and whatever else is at the service of work is at the same time the result of work done by persons for persons.

Capital and labor cannot be separated from one another nor can they be opposed to one another. Since the person who works is primary, all else that is nonpersonal, including capital, is subordinate. If capital is taken as including all the means of production, it is still only a means. The end of the process, in the sense of the reason why the process goes on, is the common good of the community of persons. Note too that capital is being unceasingly created through the work that people do with the help of the means of production.

THE WAGE SYSTEM

A person who finds his or her business becoming too large to be run alone must either curtail its volume or engage the help of others. In the latter event, he or she may choose to take others into partnership and share with them the control of the business, or may wish to keep personal control and merely hire others to do part of the work. Partnership usually supposes an investment of capital in the business and is rewarded by a share in the profits. Employment does not suppose an investment in the business, and it is rewarded by the definite monetary return contracted for. The wage system seems to be as old as history and is accepted everywhere. Though perhaps not the only possible arrangement between employer and employee, it is in itself a valid and just form of contract.

Under the wage system the employee receives a fixed wage but has no share in the profits and losses, whereas the owner receives the profits and also sustains the losses. Thus the employee, who lacks capital, has the needed income security; the owner-employer, having a reserve of capital, takes the risks, is able to absorb the losses, and has the profits as fair compensation for those risks and losses. It is a fair bargain. Neither side can have it both ways. The *owner* may not take all the profits and then put off the losses on the employee when profits fail. The paying of a fixed wage is the employer's first obligation, taking precedence over all others. The *employee,* depending on the sale of his or her labor for immediate support, is assured of a steady income from that labor.

A fixed wage means that it is fixed over a certain period specified by contract, not that it is wholly static. The employee has no right to share in the immediate profits resulting from temporary fluctuations, but does have a right to share in the increasing wealth and prosperity of the community of which he or she forms a part, whether this community be the industry, the nation, or the whole world. Though the employee who is already being paid a just wage has no right to demand more merely because the employer happens at the moment to be making a temporary increase in profit, which a prudent owner will hold as a cushion against possible reverses, any really lasting increase in efficiency of productivity and therefore in profitability should be reflected in a higher wage scale.

The foregoing is an extremely simple view of the matter, but it is necessary to get down to fundamentals, or the problem cannot be seen at all. Our highly organized industrial society brings in a number of other factors, but the basic ones we have mentioned still remain. Many suggest a combination of the wage and partnership systems: that the employee be paid a fixed wage sufficient to support the employee and his or her family; and that over and above this wage he or she be given some shares in the business; and that these shares be not in the form of an occasional bonus but part of the employment contract. We have some discussion of such schemes later. Note here that they do not eliminate the wage contract, which remains the basic source of the employee's income.

MINIMUM JUST WAGE

The minimum just wage means the least amount any regular worker ought to be paid for his or her work. By *regular worker* is meant here an adult, competent, full-time employee who makes a living by giving the whole working day to the employer—not children, the physically or mentally handicapped, or those engaged part time or temporarily. These persons also must be paid justly, but they cannot furnish a standard; their pay will be a fair proportion of the regular worker's wage. The *minimum* just wage is not the minimum for a particular kind of work but for *any* work; it will apply chiefly to the unskilled worker, since skilled work will be worth so much more. We shall make no attempt to calculate the actual minimum wage in dollars and cents, for it will vary with the times, but only to find the *principle* that ought to govern any such calculation. How can it be determined?

1. Not by the length of time spent in work, for time itself has no definitely fixed and constant value; no one today could live on the wage given 50 years ago; the value of labor-time fluctuates, and time itself can form no standard.

2. Not by the value of the products of labor, for labor costs are included in the sale price of the product, thus supposing that the price of labor has already been set by some other standard.

3. Not by the usefulness of a certain laborer to the employer, for this is rewarded by wages above the minimum but cannot set a standard for the minimum itself; the minimum wage means the least wage any regular worker should be paid if employed at all.

4. Not by the law of supply and demand, for labor is no ordinary commodity on a par with the rest, since it involves the dignity of the human person; there is a point below which it cannot go without degrading the human person to a subhuman condition.

5. The only way in which the minimum just wage can be determined is from the function of human labor itself. *Why do people work?* Why are they willing to put in a day's labor for a sum of money? They work to make a living, to support themselves and their dependents. This is why a person will spend his or her life working, as an independent farmer, artisan, or shopkeeper. If people, instead of working for themselves, sell their labor to others, they do it for the same reason. If they cannot make a living by their work, there is no reason why they should work. The minimum just wage, therefore, is a wage capable of supplying the essentials of a human life.

What are these essentials? More than bare subsistence, for humans are not beasts of burden, and more than would satisfy the simple wants of primitives, for people have a right to share in the civilization of which they form a part and in the general progress of humanity. People have a right to the essentials of a human life precisely as *human,* a decent life befitting the rational and free kind of being each person is by nature. A minimum standard of living implies at least adequate housing, sufficient and wholesome food, time for sleep and relaxation, some inexpensive recreation, and a small surplus for emergency.

Is the minimum just wage a *personal* wage or a *family* wage, that is, must it be only enough for the worker alone or also enable him or her to support dependents? It must be a family wage.

The just price of labor, as of anything else, is determined in the open market by the common estimate of people, and the ordinary reason given by them for judging that a wage is too low is: "A person cannot support a family on such a wage." A wage sufficient only for the worker's personal support is not really sufficient even for this purpose, for since the worker is bound to share it with his or her family, not enough of it would be left even for personal support. The moral obligation is clear: an employer who monopolizes all the earning power of a family person is morally obliged to pay a wage that will enable the person to fulfill his or her natural duties to the family.

Should this family wage be *relative* or *absolute,* that is, should it be scaled to the size of the particular worker's family or be adjusted to the average family? The foregoing argument might seem to prove that it should be relative, for the worker must support the actual family he or she has, not some mathematical medium that may not be verified in his or her case. However, a relative wage would lead to untold confusion and conflict. The employer would be faced with an almost hopeless task of clerical work, would be unable to estimate labor costs for the coming year, and would have too strong a temptation to employ people with smaller families. There would be dissatisfaction among the employees paid differently for the same work, and those with the largest families, who most need work, would have the most difficulty finding and keeping it. Therefore the wage should be adjusted to the average family. Some sort of public subsidy might be necessary for very large families, but this is not strictly the employer's business; it devolves on society as a whole or on the state.

Have only married people a right to a family wage? No, this wage must be paid to all. Unmarried people have a right to marry or to save money for future marriage, and only a family wage will enable them to do so. It is one of the main motives driving young people to work industriously. Even an elderly unmarried person has the right to marry, though he or she may never exercise it and should not be penalized for not doing what he or she does not have to do. Besides, distinction in wages on this score would lead to trouble, for grasping employers would find pretexts to dismiss people when they marry and to hire unmarried people in their places.

A word of caution may be useful here. While stressing the obligation of the employer, we must not forget the other side of the picture. Our American standard of living is so high that we have come to confuse necessities with luxuries, and our habits of spending are eliminating all regard for thrift, a quality needed for survival in most parts of the world. If a person wants luxuries, he or she should earn them by developing into a skilled worker who will receive a wage far above the minimum.

EMPLOYMENT

Has a person a right to work, that is, to a steady job? The argument may be put very simply: If a person has a right to live, and can live only by work, then he or she has a right to work. The logic of the argument is perfect, but the second part of the hypothesis, that a person can live only by work, is normally and generally, but not universally and necessarily, true. The very rich are only an apparent exception because their capital works for them, but even outside this class there are always many who live by their wits and have no steady income. Some people turn green at the very mention of work and yet manage to stay alive. But work is the normal way of obtaining a living, and the economic structure of modern society is geared to it.

If the jobs do not exist, how can workers rightly demand them? In time of general calamity, such as widespread financial depression, workers will suffer as well as everyone else. Employers are obliged to tide over short periods of depression and not to lay people off too quickly, for to take the losses as well as the profits is part of their risk, but it is absurd to think that they can run private businesses indefinitely at a loss. By trying to employ too many people, they would soon be able to employ none. In such conditions the only one that can come to the worker's assistance is society itself and, as a last resort, the state. How to do it best is a matter of practical expediency and human ingenuity, but the duty itself is moral and binds in justice.

Under modern economic conditions society must see to it that there are enough jobs to go around for all who need them. Does this mean a planned economy? The phrase "planned economy" is often used to mean that the state should take over the work of private business, prescribing how much is to be produced and how many jobs are to be provided. Nothing of the kind is advocated here, but no enterprise can succeed without some planning. The state need not do the planning, but someone must; if private business cannot or will not, the state must either do it or see that it is done. Harmonious cooperation between them is the ideal.

The following groups are sore spots in the employment problem:

1. The first group is *temporarily unemployed* because of some financial crisis or industrial disturbance. The real cure is to remedy the financial or industrial situation and to take measures to prevent a recurrence. Until we find a way of reducing these troubles, a partial remedy can be found in employment bureaus, in a combination of periodic occupations, in social insurance, in temporary subsidy to private companies, and in the undertaking of public works.

2. The *"hard core" unemployable* are a difficult problem. Until recently many people thought that competitive business simply could not afford to hire such people. Some businesses in collaboration with government have undertaken the hiring and training of many economically underprivileged people. The results have been mixed. The efforts being made are not only commendable but really a matter of social justice. Both business and government should capitalize on the successes achieved and be alert to help further develop the skills necessary to train as many underprivileged people as possible. Society at large as well as the individuals benefit, for no self-respecting man or woman wants to be a burden on society if that can be avoided. Those

who are physically or mentally handicapped but not institutional cases should be given part-time employment, with the rest of their support made up by the state or by private foundations. They too have a right to professional training and work so that they can be productive in a way suited to them. The quarrelsome, the drunkards, and the drug addicts are the worst problems, but society cannot let them starve.

3. *Vagrants* deliberately put themselves outside the pale of human society and thus cut themselves off from any real right to social assistance. Begging is not in itself morally wrong, for anyone may ask another for help. We are speaking here of those professional beggars who could support themselves otherwise but refuse to do so. Since these persons often take to crime and are a menace to society, vagrancy laws are necessary. Compulsory labor is probably useless as a remedy. On the other hand, there seems to be no ethical reason why a person may not adopt a wandering life, especially if such a person has no dependents and is willing to do temporary work for his or her daily needs.

EQUAL OPPORTUNITY, AFFIRMATIVE ACTION, AND REVERSE DISCRIMINATION

Since 1960 the concept of "equal employment opportunity" has evolved and been made the rule rather than the exception in the employment sector of American society. The civil rights movement and the women's movement have been instrumental in the drive to eliminate discrimination from the economic side of society. At both the state and federal levels by means of executive order, legislative enactment, and judicial determination employers have been obliged not to consider race, color, religion, sex, or national origin in decisions affecting the employment relationship. Interestingly, there are two programs existing side by side as a result of all this activity: (1) Congress, by the Fair Employment Practices Law and the Civil Rights Act, both enacted in 1964, prohibits present and future discrimination; (2) the executive orders of John F. Kennedy and Lyndon B. Johnson require over and above equal employment opportunity, programs of "affirmative action" whereby certain racial minorities and women are given preferential treatment when they seek employment. The executive orders cover public schools, universities, civil services, the armed forces, construction and trade industries, unions, private corporations, businesses employing more than 25 people, and all organizations that either have government contracts or are regulated by governmental agencies. About 95% of the employment market is affected by these executive orders.

President Lyndon B. Johnson, in defending the policy of affirmative action, used the image of a shackled runner:

> Imagine a hundred yard dash in which one of the two runners has his legs shackled together. He has progressed 10 yards, while the unshackled runner has gone 50 yards. At that point the judges decide that the race is unfair. How do they rectify the situation? Do they merely remove the shackles and allow the race to proceed? Then they could say that "equal opportunity" now prevailed. But one of the runners would still be forty yards ahead of the other. Would it not be the better part of justice to allow the previously shackled runner to make up the forty yard gap; or to start the race all over again? That would be affirmative action towards equality.[1]

Since the proclamation of the policy of affirmative action, the executive branch of the federal government has interpreted the order to apply not only to Blacks, American Indians, and Mexican Americans but to women as well. Many employers advertise themselves as "an equal opportunity employer," meaning that they are nondiscriminatory and follow the affirmative action program of doing something positive to employ members of the specified racial minorities and women whenever it is possible to do so, giving them preference over other equally qualified applicants.

While all of this activity aims at equalizing employment opportunity for all citizens, the exec-

utive orders requiring programs of affirmative action have been criticized on two grounds: (1) that implementing special employment standards applicable only to special classes of employees is divisive and undesirable; and (2) that programs of affirmative action necessarily involve "reverse discrimination" and so violate the rights of the unfavored majority. We shall examine these criticisms as well as the equal opportunity principle.

The presupposition of the critics of affirmative action is that competition for jobs on the basis of ability is being eliminated and that this is bad because competition for jobs is essential to our democratic-capitalistic way of life. The critics are in agreement that job seekers must have an equal opportunity to compete with one another so that the best qualified person can be hired. To give preferential treatment to minority persons and women, the critics maintain, undermines genuine competition, fosters mediocrity and discourages excellence. We should note at this point that society ought to foster the kind of education and technical training that would enable everyone to find a specialty he or she could do well so that people would develop the greatest possible range of skills and abilities among themselves. Competition need not be the type that produces antagonism and isolation; it can be the friendly type in which everyone with the same specialty competes but the best qualified wins the job. To foster this friendly type of competition within reasonable limits would certainly not damage any social order that looks to the common good of all. Without such competition, we run the risk of fostering mediocrity and discouraging excellence, for without such competition people would have no incentive to develop their knowledge and skills as much as possible.

The second criticism of affirmative action is that it violates the rights of the unfavored majority and is racism and sexism in reverse. Nonminority people and men are penalized for their race and/ or sex just as much as the racial minorities and women were previously. Reverse discrimination is a violation of justice that is as bad as the injustice it is designed to overcome. Ultimately, this is destructive of what the civil rights movement and

---

[1] Johnson, Executive Order 11246, cited in John R. Burr and Milton Goldinger, editors: *Philosophy and Contemporary Issues,* ed. 2, p. 304.

the women's movement have tried to accomplish. The argument in favor of reverse discrimination is illogical, for its conclusion does not follow from its premises. The argument runs something like this: Justice requires that no one be excluded from employment because of color or sex, but blacks and some other minorities as well as women have been excluded in the past. Therefore, justice requires that minority persons and women be favored until the injustice has been remedied. The conclusion, say the critics, should be, if anything, not that minority persons and women be favored but that they not be excluded from employment.

Even if we grant the critics their point in this second criticism, the fact remains that past discrimination has hurt some minority persons and women. An injustice has been done these people and ought to be remedied. Some positive steps can be taken that will not violate the rights of anyone and yet redress the wrongs that have been done to the minority persons and women. The critics of affirmative action argue that such a program is superfluous, because the laws forbidding discrimination have already been passed and are being enforced. The past is over and done with; it cannot be changed. We should now be looking to the future to see that such discrimination does not happen again.

Some who favor affirmative action reply to the critics that looking to the future is not enough. Some reparation must be made for the past violations of justice, and the affirmative action program set forth by the government is a way for all the other members of our society who have benefited in the past from the discrimination practiced against blacks, other minorities, and women to make suitable reparation. Justice demands that reparation be made whenever an injustice has been done. The critics reply that the notion of reparation is nothing more than discrimination against people who have had no part in the discriminations of the past. Those who favor affirmative action counter this reply by arguing that the entire society shares a collective guilt for the past injustices and so all must make suitable reparation.

Collective guilt, we should note, is a notion that is difficult to justify and well nigh impossible to apply. A person is blameworthy only for evil for which he or she is responsible, responsibility being determined by voluntariness. Assessing the guilt or blameworthiness of an individual is in many cases difficult, especially in cases of many cooperating together in doing something evil. To assess the guilt of an entire society is well nigh impossible, since the cooperation of various people in the society probably runs the gamut from immediate and proximate through remote to no cooperation at all. To pursue this avenue of approach to the problem seems futile.

The problem, however, remains. Past discrimination is a fact; an injustice has been done. The ordinary citizens may well feel shame at the injustices of the past, but they need not blame themselves unless there was something they ought to have done and did not do to halt the injustice. Realistically, the only reparation that can and ought to be made is by those people who played a major role in perpetrating the injustice. To require society as a whole to make reparation makes no practical sense.

Given the fact of affirmative action as it is presently being enforced by the government, we still want to ask whether the goal itself is moral and, if so, whether the means being taken to achieve the goal are also moral. The goal, of course, is to guarantee each member of our society an equal opportunity to compete for the available jobs for which he or she is qualified. The means being taken is to give preferential treatment to those who have been discriminated against. The point of affirmative action is missed completely if unqualified minority persons and women are hired and/or promoted ahead of qualified persons, for equal opportunity has not been given everyone who competes for the job or promotion. The point the government has been insisting on is that employers make special efforts to consider qualified minority persons as well as qualified women for almost every job and promotion. Some agencies of the government have tried to set rigid quotas that compromise efficiency, overlook or dilute merit, and openly discriminate against whites and men. Such setting of quotas really works against the equal opportunity principle that the affirmative action program is trying to implement.

The equal opportunity principle has been criticized as being ultimately undemocratic and the institutionalization of inequality in society. The principle is undemocratic, say its critics, because a clear consequence of it is a hardening and deepening of the inequalities between the superior few and the average mass of people. Rather than being democratic, the principle nourishes a hierarchic, even oligarchic, mentality, and it does so in the name of democracy and justice. Furthermore, the critics maintain that virtually all the demand for the kind of equality expressed in the equal opportunity principle is really a demand for an equal right and opportunity to become unequal. As the ablest and most ambitious members of the disadvantaged rise to a more prosperous position and thus improve their condition, they surpass those who are also trying to raise themselves up. There is never enough for everybody, so one person's gain is usually another's loss.

Does the equal opportunity principle have to function as its critics say it does? It does not seem so. The critics seem to confuse two kinds of equality, namely (1) the *equality of being* a member of *and belonging* to a society and (2) the *equality of opportunity*. The one kind of equality is not the other. The equality that exists in the relations among the members of any genuine society is an *equality of being and belonging*. Each member of the society *is* as a person equal in dignity and worth to every other member and *belongs* to the society as fully as every other member. Certainly each member has a right to work, for each has a right to the average material provisions necessary for living together decently.

Despite the equality of being and belonging, we find inequalities among the members of any society, for not all have the same degree of knowledge and skill nor are all the people knowledgeable and skillful about the same things. In any society there is great variety of knowledges and skills and there are degrees of competence to be found among those who share any specialty. Every member of the society who is qualified in a specialty has an equal right to compete with every other qualified person for the job or promotion. Employers are obliged by law not to discriminate on the basis of race or sex among the qualified candidates, and by executive order they are further obliged to give preferential treatment to minority persons and women whenever such persons are among the qualified applicants. An employer, of course, is looking for the person best qualified for the job. When the minority person or woman is as qualified as any other applicant, then the employer hires or promotes the minority person or woman. Understood in this way, the affirmative action program does not appear to be grossly discriminatory against whites and men.

The goal of guaranteeing the equal right and opportunity to compete for jobs for which one is qualified is moral and is based on the equality of each person as being a member of and belonging to the same society. The means of affirmative action being taken to ensure the equal right and opportunity for minority persons and women is moral as long as the minority persons and women are as well qualified as the other applicants, otherwise the other applicants are being discriminated against and an injustice is being done them. To attempt to correct an injustice by means of a further injustice is simply to compound the injustice. The right of the specified minority persons and women to preferential treatment in their competition for jobs and promotions is a legal right, not a natural right. This legal right is moral as long as the imbalance created by past discrimination exists.

RETIREMENT

The idea of employment brings up that of retirement. We are much concerned today with our senior citizens, and the concern is most laudable. There is not much that can be said on the subject from the ethical standpoint, except that each community should do its best for its older people.

What it can do depends on its social structure and the means at its disposal, as well as what its people are willing to support.

We cannot expect business to keep employing those who have passed their time of usefulness. Since we grow old at varying rates, it is better not to have a fixed mandatory retirement age but to adjust retirement to the individual. In this way the talents of older persons are not sacrificed to a mathematical number but can be used for the benefit of both the individual and society. But some older people will not recognize that they are beyond their time, and the company must have some way of easing them out. Perhaps the largest industries can manage the problem only by having mandatory retirement at a fixed age.

How are these retired persons to spend the rest of their days? Not long ago the large patriarchal family supported its aged in honor and dignity in the ancestral home. Nothing seems to have taken the place of this tradition in our urbanized society. For the most part senior citizens live in apartments separated from their children and prefer it so. If ill or feeble, they are shunted off to rest homes, which in many instances are the only places equipped to care for them. The older person often has either a lonely or a semihospitalized existence, neither of which is satisfactory. The aged are supposed to have provided for their own old age by savings, pension, or insurance, or at least by social security. On the whole life is depersonalized and institutionalized at the very time when a person has leisure for more friendly personal relations. More efforts are now being made to bring senior citizens together and to provide them with meaningful activities.

Social justice requires that senior citizens partake in the benefits of social living in due proportion to their place in society and in regard for their contributions to society in their heyday. Just how to arrange the means to accomplish this end is a matter of social and political prudence. Ethics points out this obligation of society and counsels the community to be as generous as it can afford.

LABOR UNIONS

The individual worker is at a distinct disadvantage in bargaining with the employer for a suitable wage. The worker is without capital, power, or influence, is usually of lower educational attainments, is trained for only one kind of work, cannot travel but must take present opportunities, and needs a job immediately to live. The employer needs workers, but not any particular person, and thus can employ one who will work for the lowest wage. The workers would have to take any terms the employer wanted to give them unless they could band with their fellow workers for the purpose of *collective bargaining*. A large group of workers banded together can bargain with the employer on equal terms, since both parties are dependent on one another.

That the labor union is ethically justified is no longer in dispute. The labor union is the *only means* the workers have of obtaining the fair wages and fair treatment to which they as persons have a strict right. Unless the relation of management and labor is to be regimented by the state, the individual worker is at the mercy of the employer. The labor union is also a *legitimate means*. There is nothing contrary to justice or to good morals in an association of workers or in collective bargaining. What it is lawful to do separately, it is lawful to do together. If employers and producers can organize themselves into associations, so can the workers. If employers can agree among themselves on what wages they will pay, so can the workers on what wages they will take.

Like everything else, labor unions are open to abuse. They can make exorbitant demands, call unjustified strikes, ruin fair-dealing employers, operate in restraint of trade, become hotbeds of radicalism, and be betrayed by unscrupulous leaders. The remedy is not to disband the unions but to correct the abuses. Capital also has been seriously abused by unjust management, as history from the beginning of the industrial revolution to today amply testifies; yet the remedy lies not necessarily in the abolition of capitalism, supposing it to be a legitimate system, but in the correction of its abuses. When management failed to correct its own abuses, legislation became necessary; if labor will not be clear-sighted enough to put its own house in order, it must submit to the same remedy. In neither case does abuse preclude the use.

There is nothing wrong in principle with the *closed shop* or the *union shop,* but in practice both are open to abuse. No one should be forced to join a union, it is true, but if the situation is such that the union cannot achieve its end unless all the workers are organized, or if some are taking the benefits gained by union activity while evading the burdens of membership, it seems right that those who will not join should be denied jobs. No one has a right to this particular job, and anyone who wants it should take the conditions attached to it. But if a large part of the workers do not want unionization, it would be unjust to force it on them. The so-called "right-to-work laws," outlawing both the closed shop and the union shop, do not seem justified unless the abuses cannot be handled by less drastic measures, a controverted issue dependent on local conditions.

Likewise the *closed union* is not wrong in principle. Unions have a right to limit membership and form a closed union if otherwise their trade will be glutted with too many new people seeking to displace tried and reliable members who have given the union its strength. If limited membership is used, as sometimes happens, to create unduly high wages through artificial scarcity of workers, an unjust monopoly of labor is created against the public good.

STRIKES

The strike is the chief weapon in the hands of labor for enforcing its demands. Since the purpose of organized labor is to equalize the bargaining power between employer and employee, the only way to counteract refusal to pay fairly is by a concerted refusal to work.

A strike is an organized cessation of work by a number of workers to obtain their employer's assent to certain demands. In the strict sense a strike is of employees only, not of students or prisoners or other unpaid groups. A strike is a walkout of a large enough number to cripple the business. It is an organized movement; even a large, simultaneous quitting without organization is not a strike, unless the lack of organization is only pretended. The purpose of a strike is not to seek employment elsewhere but to regain the old jobs on better terms; therefore a mass movement from one employer to another who pays better is not a strike against the first.

Are strikes morally justifiable? To answer this question we must first distinguish the three main kinds of strike:

1. The *direct* strike, by workers actually laboring under the same industrial grievance
2. The *sympathetic* strike, by those who have no grievance of their own but act in support of others who have
3. The *general* strike, by all the workers of the community to support some political demand

The Direct Strike

The basic and original form of strike is the direct strike. Any worker has the right to quit a job provided he or she has fulfilled the contract, just as any employer who has fulfilled his or her contract need not rehire the worker. An *organized* cessation of work, especially in a large and essential industry, ceases to be a private affair and assumes a social significance. It brings about serious evils to:

1. The employer, through loss of profits
2. The worker, through loss of wages needed for support
3. The consumer, through lack of goods and services
4. The public, through general economic dislocation

Because it brings about these foreseen evils, which affect not only the persons concerned in the strike but the community at large, a direct strike involves among other principles that of double effect. It is quite possible and often happens that the four conditions are satisfied:

1. The direct strike is not wrong in itself. It contains four elements, none of which is essentially wrong. *Cessation of work* is not wrong in itself; otherwise, one could never quit work. *Organization* is not essentially wrong; if each may quit work separately, all may do it together and for their common benefit. *Just demands,* presented and refused, are the cause of the strike; no strike can be lawful unless these demands are just, but they can be and often are, such as insufficient pay or intolerable working conditions; the contract may have run its term, or been violated by the employers, or become null through an unforeseen change in the economic situation. *Circumstances* connected with a strike are not always and necessarily evil; violence and bloodshed have occurred in strikes, but there is nothing in the very idea of a strike that requires them.

2. The good effect is not obtained by means of the bad effect. The evils to the worker, to the consumer, and to the public are not means of rectifying the workers' condition, and they only accidentally put added pressure on the employer. But is not the good effect obtained through the evil to the employer? This is the crucial point. The strike is so designed as to hit the employer where it hurts, in the pocketbook; this financial loss is the strikers' means of moving the employer to yield at last to their demands. True, but the fact that a strike works in this way does not make it morally wrong. The principle of the *conflict of rights* comes in here to validate the double-effect principle. Financial loss is a physical evil that one can have a right to inflict; a judge does so when a fine is imposed as punishment. The strikers do no injustice to their unjust employer when they stop work for the purpose of stopping profits and thereby forcing the employer to stop being unjust toward them. To end the evil of loss to the business, all the employer need do is to behave justly toward the workers. Hence the evil done the employer is self-inflicted.

3. The strikers must not intend the evil in itself, but only the just wages and proper working conditions to which they have a right. The strike must not be aimed at fomenting hatred and class war, but only at getting back the old jobs on better terms. Personal hatred is morally wrong for individuals indulging in it, but it does not of itself invalidate an otherwise just cause.

4. There must be sufficient proportion between the good and the evil effect. The more painful and widespread the evil, the greater must be the cause required to balance it. A strike in a nationwide industry that would paralyze the country needs an overwhelmingly strong cause. This requirement does not put all the burden on the workers but emphasizes the duty of employers to anticipate trouble and to see that a really just cause for striking never arises. It would be out of proportion to call or continue a strike that had no hope of even partial success. The proportion depends on many factors that must be separately determined for each concrete case.

A strike among professional and vocational groups that provide essential services to society is almost never justifiable. Physicians, surgeons, nurses, paramedics, police, firefighters, and mass transit workers all provide services essential to the well-being of their communities. Under what conditions would the withdrawal of their services be justified? For any of these groups to go on strike, a significant part of their goals must be the improvement of the services rendered the public. The strike or job action must involve no serious risk to the lives of those served. In 1975 and 1976, for example, interns and residents in Los Angeles, Chicago, and New York organized significant mass strikes. They demanded that the 100- to 120-hour work week be reduced to 80 hours; they also had a variety of patient care demands. Such demands are clearly justified, for tired and overworked interns and residents can hardly be said to be capable of giving good care to their patients. An exhausted physician or surgeon is not likely a better one. Emergency services were provided, and in such situations this is requisite for the strike to be justifiable. Great care must be given to this provision of emergency services, otherwise the lives of the community are placed in disproportionate danger. Whenever people who provide essential services to the community contemplate a strike or serious job action, they must carefully balance their demands against the harms the strike will do to society. Finally, if it is ever a question of purely economic demands being made, the burden of the proof that such demands are just must fall clearly and squarely on those making the demands.

The sufficient proportion can be determined more in detail by considering the following four conditions of a justified strike:

1. *There must be a just cause.* Too little pay, too long hours, brutal treatment, and unsafe or unsanitary working conditions are certainly genuine grievances, whereas personal feuds, petty rivalries, and the ambitions of individual leaders are not. The workers may strike for the minimum just wage, and skilled workers may strike for the wage prevalent for the kind of work they do. When negotiating a new contract, they may refuse to work for the minimum just wage, even though it is a just wage, and may demand more. No law obliges people to take the least they have a right to, and the very idea of bargaining supposes the hope of getting more. But the proportion is upset if the workers strike for the very last cent of the highest just wage, though they may ask it, or if the owners stage a lockout because the workers refuse to accept the bare minimum. To stick adamantly to either extreme, unless some important principle is at stake, is really a refusal to bargain, and neither side has the right to be stubborn at the expense of the public.

2. *There should be proper authorization.* The decision to strike should come from the workers themselves by a free and unintimidated vote. Organized workers must have their strike backed by their union. If the employer can bargain with the workers only through the union, the workers must also use the same channel. Hence "wildcat" strikes are outlawed unless the circumstances are so unusual that the unions have really ceased to represent the workers and are repudiated by them.

3. *The strike must be the last resort.* Every other less painful means must have been exhausted. There is no need of trying plainly futile measures, but each side is morally bound to explore all avenues that offer any reasonable hope. This requirement is all the more important in strike

threats that would paralyze the community, in which case the state as protector of the common good may have a duty to intervene. Arbitration, mediation, cooling-off periods, and fact-finding boards may be disagreeable to either side, but they must be used if they have a reasonable chance of success.

4. *Only rightful means may be used.* These means are two: work stoppage and persuasion of other workers to keep the work stopped until the demands are met. Strikers have no right to injure the employer's person or property. There is no excuse for sabotage or violence. Peaceful picketing is a lawful means of persuasion, but strikers are not entitled to use physical force against those who try to cross the picket line, whether they be customers, nonstriking coworkers, or new workers genuinely seeking employment. Employers may hire peaceful workers to take the place of the strikers, but not professional strike-breakers, who, it is foreseen, will inevitably provoke violence. In a justified strike, the strikers have a right to be returned to their jobs, for it was merely in defense of their rights that they struck in the first place. Whoever begins the use of violence in a strike does wrong; once it has begun, each one has the right of self-defense. But violence is not a legitimate means of either winning or breaking a strike as such.

The Sympathetic Strike

There is great difference of opinion regarding the sympathetic strike. Some see red at the very mention of it, whereas others think it only a natural extension of the direct strike. The moderate view distinguishes two possible cases.

1. The first case involves several groups of workers belonging to different unions but hired by the same employer. One group strikes for a just demand, but because the members are too few to enforce it, they appeal to the other groups employed by the same company. This kind of sympathetic strike seems justified, provided all the other conditions for a just strike are fulfilled, because it is directed against the same unjust employer. Such a strike may even be directed

against several employers when they bind themselves into an employers' or producers' association to adopt a common policy toward their employees and this policy is unjust, or when one employer comes to the aid of another for the purpose of breaking a justified strike. Concerted effort on the part of management is met by concerted effort on the part of labor. A real grievance is spread among all strikers, who direct their efforts against actually unjust employers.

2. The second case involves groups of workers hired by different and unassociated employers. One group strikes because of a grievance, and to support them the other group goes out on strike against their own wholly blameless employer. The idea seems to be that solidarity among the forces of labor must be achieved at all costs. The second type of sympathetic strike seems unlawful for several reasons: *It is a violation of the wage contract*. These workers have no grievance against their own employer and yet refuse to do what they contracted to do, a breach of commutative justice. *The evil caused is out of proportion to the original demands*. If such a sympathetic strike spreads far enough, the public at large rather than the unjust employer of the original strikers is the chief one to suffer from it. *There is no logical place where such a sympathetic strike should stop*. All businesses are more or less connected. All use public utilities and, if these go out in sympathy, the whole city or country comes to a standstill.

The General Strike

The general strike is a political rather than an economic weapon and has the characteristics of rebellion or revolution. As a *mere strike,* it is out of all proportion. It aims not to remedy an evil but to inflict injury—not to bring pressure on unjust persons to make them fulfill the demands of justice, but to destroy their property and overthrow the order of society. A grave moral crime is thus perpetrated. As a *method of revolution,* its morality depends on the justifiability of the revolution, toward which it could be a legitimate means. We are talking here of a serious strike.

In some countries a general strike of a few hours or even of a whole day is used for political demonstration. This type of strike does not seem wrong if the people are willing to tolerate this sort of inconvenience and if no violence is used or permanent harm done.

LOCKOUTS AND BOYCOTTS

The *lockout* is the inverse of the strike. The employer, unwilling to grant the demands of the striking employees, shuts down the whole plant, thus putting out of work even those who are not striking. The lockout is the employer's weapon against the strike. As the workers are not obliged to submit to unjust treatment, neither is the employer. The plant cannot be kept running when key workers have quit and production is stalled, nor can the employer continue to pay wages without income. If the strike is justified, the lockout is not; but if the strike is unjustified, a lockout can be permissible so long as it conforms to the same conditions and restrictions that apply to the strike. The *sympathetic lockout,* the closing down of all the factories of the region to break a strike in one of them, causes a disproportionate amount of suffering. The employer has wealth and credit to ride out the strike, but the workers have not.

A *boycott* is a concerted refusal to patronize a certain business establishment and a persuading of others to join in this refusal. A boycott is justifiable for the same reasons and on the same conditions as a strike. No one is obliged to trade in one place rather than another, and a person may refuse to trade with unjust persons; there is no reason why he or she may not persuade others to do likewise, so long as these efforts are limited to persuasion and are not violent. The *secondary boycott* is directed against other firms that do business with the boycotted firm; if they do not join in the boycott, they will be boycotted themselves. The secondary boycott is much like the sympathetic strike and follows the same principles. These other firms are not unjust and should not be made to suffer for something they cannot help. Often they cannot obtain materials or services elsewhere to keep themselves going, or they have contracts with the boycotted firm that they are bound in justice to fulfill. If they cooperate with or connive at injustice, economic pressure can legitimately be brought against them.

INDUSTRIAL RESPONSIBILITY

The establishment and maintenance of good industrial relations is one of the most important problems of our age. Ethics is not called on to solve it but merely to point out some moral issues involved. It is not difficult to see in the abstract what ought to be done; the hard part is to get people to do what they know they ought. The ethical concept running through this whole discussion is that of justice. Justice itself never changes, but it must be applied to the new economic facts of the present day.

When our sense of social justice is outraged by the industrial unrest of today, we must not forget the enormous advances that social justice actually has made in the last hundred years. Capital, which formerly wielded its power with imperious recklessness, has been gradually brought to a better sense of the public welfare; it still has a long enough way to go in eliminating greed and selfishness. Labor, once so powerless, has by dogged persistence won for itself a position of impregnable strength; it is time for it to assume a larger share of social responsibility.

Union leaders have a delicate and difficult task. They must be upright and just, true leaders of their unions and jealous of their rights, but also must have a broad social vision embracing the welfare of the whole nation and not merely of the economic class they represent. The rank and file of labor have the obligation to attend meetings and vote, so as to make sure that the union will not fall prey to irresponsible leadership or adopt unjust policies. If a strike is to be called, workers have the duty to inform themselves on the justice of the strike, either by a direct study of the situation or, if they are incapable of this, by assuring themselves of the character and uprightness of their leaders.

Because it sets the pattern of industry, management's responsibility is inescapable. Despite its reforms hitherto, perhaps more of the vast wealth and energy devoted to expanding plants, developing new products, advertising its wares, opening up new markets, and attracting capital investment could be diverted to that extremely important but often forgotten cog in the whole machinery: the contented employee.

SUMMARY

Work is any human activity in which physical strength and/or other powers are exerted to do or to make something.

The *ethical value* of work is based on the fact that the one who works is a person, a conscious and free *subject*. The primary purpose of the process of production is to do or to make something for persons. It is wrong to treat persons as *mere* instruments of production.

Work is *good* in the sense of being something worthy of the person, corresponding to personal dignity and increasing it. *Industriousness* is the moral virtue whereby the person becomes good as a rational and free being cooperating in work with others for the common good of all. Work makes it possible for people to start and sustain a family; it also makes possible the further development of culture and civilization.

Capital and labor cannot be separated from one another, nor can they be opposed to one another.

By the *wage contract* people hire out their labor to another for a definite sum of money. Thus the workers have income security, which their lack of capital demands, whereas the employer takes the profits and losses, against which his or her capital acts as a cushion.

The *minimum just wage* is the least amount any regular unskilled worker should be paid. It is not determined like other commodities, because the dignity of the human person places a point below which it must not fall. It is determined by the reason a person works: to earn a livelihood. It must be a *family wage,* one sufficient to supply the essentials of a decent human life for an average-size family, whether the worker is married or not.

In our economy a person has a *right to work,* and society has the duty to provide jobs. If no one else will, the state must. Means must be taken to cure unemployment, care for the unemployable, regulate vagrancy, and eliminate discriminatory employment practices. Senior citizens must be provided for in any society.

Labor unions are morally justified as the only practical means of obtaining fair wages and fair treatment for the worker. By banding together for *collective bargaining,* workers can overcome their disadvantage and make the employer as dependent on them as they are on the employer.

The *strike,* an organized cessation of work to obtain certain demands, is labor's chief weapon. The *direct* strike can be justified by the two principles of double effect and conflict of rights; the strikers have the right to demand justice by inflicting on the employer a loss of profits that would otherwise be gained unjustly. There is sufficient proportion if the strike is for a just grievance, is backed by a recognized union, is the last resort, and limits itself to peacefully persuasive means. The *sympathetic* strike is justified if directed against unjust employers only; otherwise it is an injustice against innocent people. The *general* strike, if more than a demonstration, is out of proportion as a strike; it may be the means of a justified revolution. Lockouts and boycotts follow the same principles as the strike.

Great strides have been made toward *social justice,* but both management and labor need a still higher sense of social responsibility.

Questions for Discussion

1. In any office or shop in which a union is recognized as the bargaining agent by the employer, the individual employee most likely does not have a truly free choice about whether or not to join the union. Is this true? Ought everyone who benefits from collective bargaining have to join the union that does the bargaining? The government policy of affirmative action with regard to unions is designed to help correct union policies that are race-, color-, and/or sex-biased. Is it just for the government to force unions to take in applicants it does not want? Is it just for unions to force into membership workers who do not want to join?

2. Although there is a lot of talk about corporate social responsibility within the community in which a corporation operates, still the principal objective of any corporate business is to make profits. Individuals who are employed by corporations as executives, managers, and supervisors may well want to serve their neighborhoods and even larger social communities but, if they do, they do so as private individuals and not as representatives of their corporate employers. In a free enterprise, private property system, the corporate employee has only one responsibility and that is to make as much money as possible while conforming to the basic rules of society embodied in law and ethical custom. What do you think? Why?

3. The Catholic Worker Movement believes that our capitalist society fails to consider the whole of human nature but rather regards each human being as a factor in production. The worker is an item on the expense sheet of the employer. Profit determines what kind of work the employee shall do. Hence, the deadly routine of assembly lines and the whole mode of factory production. In a just social order (which we do not yet have) the question will be whether a certain type of work is in accord with human values, not whether it will bring a profit to the exploiters of labor. Is this view viable for our businesses to adopt? Why? Are there moral considerations underlying the Catholic Worker's position? What are they?

4. Liberty and equality are conflicting, not complementary goals. Liberty has to be restricted to achieve equality, but how much can we afford to restrict our liberty to achieve full equality of opportunity to work? How much

inequality is it reasonable for us to accept to preserve our liberty?

5. Suppose we, as a society, do manage to agree in general that women, blacks, American Indians, and Mexican Americans have some right to a privileged place in the structure of opportunities for a while, how will we know when that "while" is up? How much privilege is enough? When will the collective guilt be gone? When will the balance be restored? What criterion do we have to measure when we are done? What compensation is right for centuries of exclusion? Are we not engaged in an impossible task?

Readings

Pope John Paul II's *Laborem Exercens* (On Human Work), Pope Paul VI's *Populorum Progressio* (The Development of Peoples), Pope Leo XIII's *Rerum Novarum* (Condition of the Workingman), Pius XI's *Quadragesimo Anno* (Reconstruction of the Social Order), and John XXIII's *Mater et Magistra* (Christianity and Social Progress) are among the most important documents on the moral aspects of industrial relations. Their treatment of the subject is not primarily philosophical, but the ethical background is clearly brought out. There are numerous commentaries; outstanding among them is Oswald von Nell-Breuning's *Reorganization of Social Economy*.

See Johannes Messner's *Social Ethics*, revised ed., bk. II, pt. II, John F. Cronin's *Catholic Social Principles*, ch. 9–11; M.D. Chenu, *The Theology of Work*; and the U.S. Bishops' Pastoral Message and Letter, "Economic Justice for All: Catholic Social Teaching and the U.S. Economy."

On particular problems: William J. Smith, *Spotlight on Labor Unions*; Jerome Toner, *The Closed Shop*; Benjamin Selekman, *A Moral Philosophy for Management*; Frank Tannenbaum, *A Philosophy of Labor*; and Harwood Merrill, *Responsibilities of Business Leadership*. On equal employment opportunity, affirmative action, and reverse discrimination: Fred Luthans and Richard M. Hodgetts (eds.), *Readings on the Current Social Issues in Business: Poverty, Civil Rights, Ecology, and Consumerism*, pt. II B; James Rachels (ed.), *Moral Problems*, 3rd ed., pt. I; John R. Burr and Milton Goldinger (eds.), *Philosophy and Contemporary Issues*, 2nd ed., ch. 4; Walter Kaufmann, *Without Guilt and Justice: From Decidophobia to Autonomy*, ch. 3; Thomas A. Mappes and Jane S. Zembaty (eds.), *Social Ethics: Morality and Social Policy*, ch. 5; and Richard Wasserstrom (ed.), *Today's Moral Problems*, ch. 3.

31
Capitalism

PROBLEM

Ennobling as it is, earning a living is not our highest activity in point of dignity, but it consumes most of the ordinary person's time and effort. The economic side of human nature, unlike the domestic and political, is not taken care of by a corresponding natural society. There already is an economic aspect both to the family and to the state, the one extending up and the other down into the middle region between these two societies. Families and states are alike in having their essential functions prescribed for them by the natural law, but human nature does not incline us to one particular association that we must enter into for our economic support. That we must organize in some way for this purpose is evident, but *how* to do it is left to human ingenuity. As in most things human, people's efforts over the centuries in building up a socio-economic order have been only partially successful. Its remarkable complexity is balanced by haphazard performance, its astonishing fertility in production by its glaring inequity in distribution.

Must we give wholehearted approval to capitalism? No, neither in its present form nor in any form. The world existed for many centuries with private property, yet without that specific form of it called capitalism. We shall not enter into a dispute about the proper definition of modern capitalism but can take it loosely as the economic system characterized by four things: private ownership, free enterprise, the profit motive, and invested funds. The last element is important in distinguishing it from earlier forms of the private property system. Capitalism, both the system itself and the present form it has assumed, is a contingent historical occurrence. There are many details, adjuncts, and conditions not essential to the system of capitalism itself. It continues to develop, and there seems to be no final pattern into which it must necessarily congeal. When, if ever, it shall have changed so much as no longer to deserve the name of capitalism is a semantic question. Though capitalism in its practical working has not always been ideal, we are hard put to find another system of private property and free enterprise that could be substituted for it in an advanced society today.

We cannot turn back the clock of history and induce people to give up the comforts of modern living for the simple life. Nor was this life wholly desirable. One can romanticize the past by overlooking its disagreeable features, which for most people were far worse than anything we have today. The slave economy of ancient times made civilization possible by developing a leisured class, but only by the most hateful form of social injustice. The medieval knight could pursue his noble adventures only by the support of a horde of peasants and serfs who were excluded by birth from his privileges. Laissez-faire individualism, with its disregard for the dignity of the human person, proved its insufficiency within recent memory; the modern worker would embrace communism or some form of socialism rather than return to it.

On the other hand, no one has proposed a totally new economic system that can be taken with any seriousness. The working out of an ideal economy poses a challenging task for human ingenuity, but the finished blueprint would have to be highly practical as well as intellectually and emotionally satisfying. The slightest knowledge of history shows that human institutions develop gradually and that people are reluctant to adopt a system that has no strong link with the past. To be practical any such scheme would have to compromise with existing facts and thus could be no radical break with historical continuity.

One attitude toward capitalism is *conservative* and pessimistic. In itself conservatism is indifferent; it all depends on what one wants to conserve, whether it be good or bad. The conservatism that cherishes all that is valuable in the culture of the past is the very life of civilization. The conservatism that perpetuates the diseases of society is a force that makes for death. It is the latter form that is up for criticism, the attitude of wanting to maintain the economic status quo unchanged despite its acknowledged defects. We have arrived, they say, at an uneasy balance between private enterprise and statism.

To stop the state's constant encroachment on private rights we must fight hard for the retention of as much private enterprise as we can hold on to. Every suggestion for reform is branded as creeping socialism. If the present situation is bad, any other can only be worse. The best we can hope for in the losing battle is a stalemate. How should such an attitude be judged? It is natural that those whose economic situation is satisfactory should be loath to give up their advantages or compromise their position, but selfishness at the expense of others cannot be approved. The desire to preserve modes of conduct that are unjust is morally wrong. We are allowed to tolerate evils when they cannot be remedied, but the refusal even to seek a remedy for existing evils is not an ethically defensible position.

The other attitude is *progressive* and optimistic, recognizing the deficiencies of our present economic system and social order but seeking to remedy them gradually and peacefully. Utopia is impossible, and therefore optimism should be restrained; but though a perfect economy can never be achieved among fallible human beings, a better one is possible. The present arrangement manifests certain obvious defects that are not beyond improvement by human ingenuity. There has been constant progress in social and economic relations in the past, and there is no reason that the trend cannot be continued toward improvement. Violent agitation will accomplish nothing, but gradual pressure and persuasion can bring about more valuable if less spectacular results.

What are the areas in which improvement seems both desirable and possible, and what are the corrective measures most often proposed? This field is very controversial, and our remarks should be taken as tentative and suggestive. We ask:

1. What philosophical ideals underlie capitalism?
2. Can competition be mitigated by cooperation?
3. Is strife between management and labor inevitable?
4. Can business learn to regulate itself?
5. What, if anything, is wrong with bigness and centralization?
6. What is the "new property"?
7. How important is social responsibility for capitalism?
8. Are we being mastered by our own technology?

PHILOSOPHICAL IDEALS

A discussion of capitalism apart from the political and moral-cultural systems in which it operates is unsatisfactory, because it yields only a set of abstract ideas with little or no relation to reality. The experience of living in the United States, West Germany, or Japan, for example, shows that capitalism flourishes when it operates in a *political system* respectful of the rights of the individual to life, freedom, and the pursuit of happiness and in a *moral-cultural system* which sets the highest priority on freedom and justice for all the people. In this kind of context the economic, the political, and the moral-cultural systems, though separate and distinct, converge and function as one: (1) an economy based on markets and incentives, (2) a democratic form of government, and (3) a moral-cultural system which is pluralistic and dedicated to personal freedom and justice. Political democracy is compatible in practice only with a capitalistic economy and both the political and economic system can flourish only in a pluralistic culture that prizes personal freedom and justice for all. All three systems must be attended to. The work of this chapter is to bring one small part of the moral-cultural system to reflect on capitalism in its democratic political setting. This can best be done by examining the philosophical ideals of democratic capitalism.

1. **The community of persons.** Experience suggests that what is most real and of highest value in human life is a community of persons. This is the ideal of democratic capitalism. The problem is how to build human community without damaging or destroying human individuality. The differentiation between (a) the democratic government, (b) the free market economy, and

(c) the moral-cultural institutions (the churches, the universities, journalism, the communication media, the cinema, and so forth) makes for interaction in which each checks, corrects, and enhances the other two. This differentiation allows for many other sorts of smaller communities to flourish, such as families, neighborhoods, local agencies, special interest groups, voluntary associations, parishes, unions, corporations, guilds, societies, and schools. These various communities are intermediate between the individual and the state and are structured to accomplish more efficiently, less expensively, and with greater care and love what the state either cannot do at all or can do only poorly at prohibitive cost to the taxpayers. The individual is freer in this kind of system than in any politico-economic system ever devised by the human race. These intermediate communities multiply and thrive; they provide the individual a range of choice and afford enormous variety and possibility for personal enrichment. Each person living under democratic capitalism participates in many vital intermediate communities, with the result that the social life of each is neither exhausted by nor controlled by the state. The ideal of community and the freedom of the person to join those intermediate communities that suit his or her needs and desires oblige both the government and the economy to do better constantly.

2. **Practical realism.** Respect for and understanding of persons show that no one is either wholly good or wholly bad. The three systems operate not only to check and balance one another but to check and limit vice, especially the vice of tyranny. Practical realism teaches us to think concretely, face the facts as they are, respect the world as it is, acknowledging its limits, weaknesses, irrationalities, and evil forces without losing hope that people and the world can be improved. Such realism does not have time to indulge in utopian dreams, and yet it never ceases to strive for the ideal of justice with love. The realist knows that ideals are important and he or she also knows that ideals are never perfectly realizable this side of the grave.

3. **Competition is the natural play of the free person.** Competition is not in itself a vice, although it can be practiced viciously. To compete means to strive together as rivals for an objective. Sports, lotteries, and contests of every sort would make no sense if the competitive spirit were foreign to human nature. Most people rejoice in it. All human striving is based on measurement of the self by some ideal or standard. No individual could ever discover his or her potential without good friends and rivals whose exploits provide a measure or standard for the individual to measure up to or surpass. In a sense, competition is an indispensable element in natural and spiritual growth. Life among bright, alert, competitive people is a great gift and stimulus to one's own personal development. Under the spur of competition, each person strives along with others to become all he or she can become. The very soul of progress is the desire to do better. A noncompetitive world is one committed to the *status quo*.

Competition for money has been regarded as humankind's gravest moral danger. Money itself is neutral and may be used wisely or foolishly. It is impersonal, a mere means, an instrument which people use for good or ill. The natural interest of those who have money is to invest it well so as to have more of it than there was in the first place. If the investment succeeds, the possessor not only has more money, but the investment has created new opportunities for others. In a capitalist economy, it is in the interest of those who have money to see others prosper along with themselves. Money has value only within a system, and the soundness and health of the system is the only protection money has. If society at large is healthy and dynamic, the investments of money retain their value and increase.

4. **Human freedom is to be maximized and tyranny is to be inhibited.** Democratic capitalism is designed to encourage human freedom and to fragment and check power. The system is realistic; it was not designed to repress all moral evil. The realist knows that human freedom can be used for good or ill and that human intelligence is not only limited but at times biased and dis-

torted. When there is evil, the root of it is sought in persons, not in the system. A free society has confidence in the basic decency of people, even though not everyone is morally upright all the time. Given the checks and balances of the system, the vast majority of people respond to the challenges of everyday life with decency, generosity, common sense, and, at times, moral heroism.

5. **The separation of governmental, economic, and moral-cultural institutions.** The commitment to pluralism in the moral-cultural system safeguards the political and economic systems from becoming confessional systems. This is a check against possible tyranny in the name of morality or religion. The widest possible range of freedom for the community of persons is the aim. Economic liberty means that everyone must be permitted to establish his or her own set of values and priorities. The churches and other moral-cultural institutions may seek to persuade people to avoid some actions and to take others—for example, to repeal the laws legalizing abortions or to pass laws to control the publication and sale of pornography. Governmental authority also forbids some practices, regulates others, and commands still others. Nevertheless, the aim is to preserve as wide a range of freedom as possible, because this is the atmosphere most conducive to invention, creativity, and economic activism. The repression of freedom invites stagnation, and an economy based on the consciences of some would be offensive to the consciences of others and would create unnecessary tensions within the community of persons.

6. **Each member of the community of persons is to be respected as an individual person of intrinsic worth and dignity.** Without true individualism, there is no true community of persons but only some kind of collective. The individual person as a conscious and free subject is not isolated and atomic. He or she is, however, as an individual, *other* than all the rest of the community and has his or her own intrinsic worth and dignity. In order to create wealth, individuals must be free to be other and appreciated as other. Sympathy, cooperation, and association with oth-

ers are natural and necessary to the individual, for the fulfillment of the individual person lies in the community the individual loves. And any community worthy of that kind of love values the individuality and inviolability of each person. Such is the community that democratic capitalism aims to be in conjunction with its moral-cultural institutions.

This form of capitalism holds that economic activism creates wealth, and that the broader the stimulation of economic activism the greater the wealth created. This kind of activism benefits not only the individual but the entire community. By endeavoring to call forth the best efforts of each person, it reaches out, creates, invents, produces, distributes goods and services, and thereby raises the material base of the common good. Based on realism, it respects individuals as individuals and seeks to inspire each person to become all that he or she can become. Its ideal is that of a republic of independent, self-reliant, cooperative citizens, each of whose interests include the interest of all. Its realism demands of it continuous renewal, reform, and self-transformation in the light of the ideal.[1]

COMPETITION AND COOPERATION

A distinguishing mark of the capitalistic system is the principle of competition. At the close of the feudal period, aristocracy of birth gave way to aristocracy of wealth. Business ability is no greater guarantee of morality than noble birth was. Ability is determined by success, and success by competition, which crowns the winner and eliminates the loser, for whom it makes no provision. Many have succeeded in economic competition without descent into the unethical, but it takes an extra measure of ability to win from those who do not play the game honestly. In

---

[1]This attempt to outline the philosophical presuppostions underlying capitalism as we presently experience it was inspired by Michael Novak, *The Spirit of Democratic Capitalism,* Part III, in which he endeavors to provide the beginnings of a theological perspective on democratic capitalism.

unlimited competition there are no rules to the game, and the most ruthless has the best chance of winning. Thus the principle of unlimited competition puts a premium on self-interest and rugged individualism, as well as on intelligence and energy.

There is no way to eliminate all competition and maintain free enterprise. Only if the state were to set prices, fix wages, assign markets, allot quotas, and practically run all business would it be possible to do away with competition. The result would be full socialism, not free enterprise. Competition keeps the economy flexible, dynamic, progressive, resourceful, and efficient, but experience has also shown the need of putting a brake on unlimited individualism to protect the common good of the community.

There is no question of abolishing competition, for it is not contrary to human nature. However, competition is possible only because of the accidental differences we find among people. When two people, for example, compete for the same job which requires a certain skill, usually the better qualified person will get the job. Both are persons and essentially the same, but they differ accidentally in that one has a greater degree of skill than the other. Competition is always between persons, but the fact of competition is always based only on accidental differences. As persons, we all share in the essential sameness of personhood and belong equally to the same community of persons who share in the common good of all.

Competition must be supplemented by another principle, that of voluntary cooperation. Enterprise can remain free and private even while devoted to a common end as well as to an individual end. Self-interest is too powerful and insistent simply to be suppressed; it must be given some free rein for the simple reason that no one in the community is good or wise enough to decide how the individual's capabilities can best be used for the common good, how the individual's labor is to be rewarded, and how to anticipate the possibilities of useful work to which the individual's own initiative prompts him or her. The competitive spirit arising from self-interest can be harnessed to contribute to the common good as well as to the individual's good.

Citizens do not lose their freedom while voluntarily cooperating, and neither should business associations. Much cooperation actually goes on: against price slashing, against depletion of natural resources, against useless duplication of services, against false advertising, against a mad scramble for markets. Initiative for this cooperation had to come from legislation, but companies now recognize the value of most of this legislation and accept its protection. Now that the lesson has been learned, there is no reason that more cooperation cannot be initiated voluntarily without pressure from the law.

The population of the world is increasing so rapidly that it cannot be supported without a careful husbanding of the earth's resources. The earth can sustain a far larger population, but not by any haphazard methods of production and distribution. The answer of communism is to abolish private enterprise and establish a state-controlled economy. In a sparsely settled country such as America we can afford to brush this answer aside, but we cannot overlook the appeal it has to the teeming populations of Asia, the new nations of Africa, and the peoples of Central and South America, struggling to rise above their substandard living conditions. The capitalist economy must meet this problem and can do so only by a union of free enterprise with voluntary cooperation, the whole organized to work efficiently and for the common good of all people.

CLASS ANTAGONISM AND SOLIDARITY

At present, capital and management are lined up on one side and labor with its unions on the other. Because of the unfortunate history of long-standing hostility, it is assumed that these two groups are necessarily opposed. There is organization among employers, including the tightly knit organization of the company itself and the looser grouping of various companies into employers' associations. Workers are organized into unions and local unions into industrywide unions and nationwide federations. Between the two there is collective bargaining, each trying to obtain as much as possible for itself, often with little consideration for the long-term benefit of both or for the nation and society as a whole. Even when relations are amicable, the atmosphere is that of each side protecting and furthering its own interests against the other's encroachments.

There has been too much class conflict, but such conflict is not essential to capitalism. Collective bargaining cannot be eliminated in a free economy, but such negotiations need not be conducted in an antagonistic spirit of class against class. Two sides can vie with each other where their interests differ and yet unite where their interests agree. In the realm of sports we have each team striving its utmost to win the game, though both belong to the same league that scheduled the game and made common arrangements for the public's enjoyment. Economic rivalry is far more serious, but the analogy holds. Cooperation and competition are not mutually exclusive; there can be cooperation for the sake of legitimate competition. Just as more cooperation is needed between companies competing for the same market, so more cooperation is needed between management and labor engaged in the same field of production.

The proposal to unite both the management group and the labor group concerned in the same industry into a larger organization for the benefit of the whole industry seems eminently reasonable. There have been overtures toward labor-management cooperation, some of which have been successful, and this movement should be sedulously encouraged. But the effort has been partial and sporadic; it needs definite organization into recognized bodies for fact finding, policy making, standard setting, problem solving, and mediation service, in no way extinguishing or absorbing existing groups but setting the climate for individual enterprise. Human organizing genius is surely capable of filling this gaping hole in the social structure.

STATISM AND SUBSIDIARITY

Like it or not, business is now regulated to a great extent by the government. The economic order teeters precariously between the extremes of freedom and control. Conservatives stress the evils of statism and its bureaucracy and ask for a return to more individualism. Liberals note the failure of disorganized individualism and call for increased state intervention in economic life. Neither alternative is acceptable, and neither is necessary.

Government intervention came when and as it did because there was no mechanism in the business world for self-regulation. So huge and important a thing as our economic life cannot simply be let go undirected and uncontrolled. Individualism was mistaken in thinking that there are natural economic laws that, if left alone, will automatically bring about the best results for all concerned. Individualism failed, not only because it put a premium on waste, greed, and selfishness, but chiefly because it could not deal with the human person, who demanded respect for personal dignity and enough security to make personal freedom worth having. In the absence of any other power to help the citizens, the state gradually became conscious of its duty to protect their welfare, stepped into the vacuum and now finds itself burdened with functions that many think do not properly belong to it.

There is no question of eliminating all government influence from economic affairs. That would be neither desirable nor possible. The state is responsible for the welfare of its people and cannot be left out of any consideration of our economic life. There are fundamental laws regarding economic matters that any modern state must enact and enforce, but not everything should be the business of government. By the *principle of subsidiarity* a higher organization should not take over work that can be handled adequately by a lower organization. For example, the city or town should not do what the family can do for itself, nor the county what the city or town can do, nor the state what the county can do, and so forth. The principle of subsidiary function, as the principle of subsidiarity is sometimes called, is the natural law principle of the division of power in society, guaranteeing the particular rights of the smaller social units as distinct from the state. The subsidiarity principle can be described this way: "As much freedom and responsibility as possible, as much state intervention and control as necessary." An alternative wording would be: "As much self-help as possible, as much state help as necessary."

In the dilemma between no control offered by individualism and state control offered by complete socialism, there is a possible third alternative, that of self-control. With a proper degree of self-government of the industry by the industry, there could be a foreseeable limit to state regulation. Perhaps more governmental intervention than we now have may be necessary in our increasingly complex society. If we are to stop somewhere short of complete governmental control of the economy, a definite mechanism has to be set up to handle those problems that ought to be kept on a lower than governmental level.

BIGNESS AND DECENTRALIZATION

Concentration of wealth in the hands of the few has been one of the main criticisms of capitalist economy. The economy is said to be dominated by a few huge corporations, in each of which the directorship is lodged in a few persons. This centralization of economic power is not wrong in itself and often makes for greater efficiency. Government and the moral-cultural institutions provide a check on the use of this power, a use that should aim not only at profitability but also serve the common good of society. Only the test of experience can show how big is too big. How does this particular size work out in actual practice? Does it harm the common good? Does it work against the public interest? Perhaps another way to evaluate the matter of size is to ask whether society is better off, that is to say, are we as a society better able to develop the values we regard as important? Are we as a nation better able

to develop the kind of community of persons we want our country to be?

Unfortunately, business also has its bad side, just as one might expect, for business is operated by human beings. Big corporations have crowded small businesses out of the market and have tried at times to monopolize a particular market. Big business has also exerted undue pressure on government in pursuit of its own interests exclusively. It is not bigness as such that has caused these evils; it is people who have done these things to other people. The anti-trust laws were passed to prevent such evils from recurring and to penalize them when they do occur.

The concentration of power and the check on it by the anti-trust laws is not the chief ethical concern. More fundamentally, the ethical concern is the relation between corporate size and freedom. To what extent right now does the concentration of economic power and control actually harm either the political decision-making process of the government or the freedom of the citizens to exercise control over their own destiny?

The critics of bigness see *potential* for harm, but do they see *actual* harm? The government has far more coercive control over corporations than the corporations do over government. The corporations are said to have powerful lobbies, but so do other organizations like labor unions, medical associations, realtors, teachers, and many others. No matter how many lobbyists are heard, the government still sets the depreciation schedules, corporate tax rates, safety and health rules, Social Security benefits, and many other limits and restraints under which corporations operate. The experience of the automobile manufacturers and the steel companies in recent years seems to indicate that, even though they are large, they are finding it increasingly difficult to compete effectively with foreign producers.

Every increase of governmental control over the economic system has its costs as well as its benefits. The government ought not to be concerned about the size of a corporation just for the sake of size. Size ought rather to be determined by the task the corporation is trying to accomplish with a view to the common good of society. Some critics of bigness who see the large corporation as a threat to our socioeconomic order advocate a program of decentralization. It is true that, the more a corporation embodies the principle of subsidiarity in its organization, the closer it comes to the work force it employs. This is good management, for the workers on the line are usually very good at finding new and better ways to do things. When business decisions are made at the level closest to concrete reality, the business usually operates most intelligently and creatively. Higher management intervenes only when the lower levels cannot come to a decision. Every corporation, no matter how large, always has a real interest in finding better forms of organization for itself. It would be naive in the extreme to demand some form of organization that is inappropriate to the task of increasing the wealth not only of this nation but of the world.

Various proposals for decentralization have already been made. The large corporation is not the only form that free enterprise can take. Human imagination, ingenuity, and good will can accomplish a great deal, but the alternatives must be truly workable in the practical order. This means that society as such must benefit and the individual worker as a person must also benefit from whatever rearrangement is made. Some way of associating labor with the ownership of capital is the way to achieve that goal. Otherwise, what point is there to decentralization?

An older movement in this direction was *distributism*—a greater distribution of property, return to the land from the cities, benefits to rural areas, the making of farm life more attractive, tax favoritism to small farmers and businesses, more stringent antitrust laws, prohibition of large mergers and combines, and other modes of encouraging the "little man." Many think that any such regression to the past has long since ceased to be feasible without repressive governmental control.

The *cooperative movement* is a more promising scheme for decentralization. Its purpose is chiefly to eliminate the middleman by bringing producer in direct contact with consumer, thus saving money for both. There are thus both producers' cooperatives and consumers' cooperatives, and the two can form one larger cooperative. There is no giant corporation with directors and hired personnel; policies are determined in meetings of the members, in which each person has only one vote no matter how large his or her share. Thus there is diffused ownership and democratic control. The profit motive is played down, to be supplanted by the ideal of community service. The cooperative movement has met with considerable success, especially in agriculture, but not everywhere. A factory cannot be run on democratic principles; a cooperative factory would have to hire managers and supervisors with an unquestioned right to give orders; conditions of work would not differ much from the present factory owned by capital investors. Governing boards of cooperatives would differ little from those of our present corporations. Cooperatives deserve encouragement, but they are not a universal remedy.

A more modest approach is that of *profit sharing*. It is proposed as a supplement to the wage contract, not as a substitute for it. The worker's pay would be determined by collective bargaining and over and above this some share in the profits or even in the ownership of the business. Such schemes have been used successfully but by and large meet with resistance both from business and from labor. The purpose is to allay industrial unrest, to increase the worker's loyalty by making each one feel a part of the enterprise, and to make sustained production an advantage to the workers. But workers are suspicious that it is only a means of speeding up production, of tying them to the job, of giving them a poor substitute for increased wages, and of hamstringing their union's efforts at collective bargaining.

Profit sharing cannot be practiced universally, because some businesses are incapable of earning sufficiently high profits to justify paying the workers anything over and above the wages they earn. Furthermore, profit sharing could have just the reverse effect of increasing the size of those corporations which are in a position to achieve higher profits, because such corporations would attract more and better workers, increase their productivity and profitability, and so become even larger. Finally, it makes more sense in terms of social justice to give the workers a general increase in wages when profits remain high and to reduce prices for the benefit of all the members of society.

A still more controverted issue is that of *management sharing*. Most employers will not hear of it, and labor has been rather indifferent to it. To give ordinary laborers a place on the board of directors is thought to be unrealistic, but recent efforts toward labor-management cooperation may finally break down much existing prejudice. Intelligent workers often have good suggestions, if not about handling the company's finances, at least about efficient ways of running the factory. Contrariwise, management may obtain better results by explaining the reasons for its decisions instead of simply handing out flat orders. Companies have become acutely conscious of "human relations," and these efforts may work out into better labor-management teamwork, if not into actual management sharing. Since management and labor do have different functions, some would argue they had best be kept distinct, with emphasis put on increasing communication, cooperation, and integration between them.

Another alternative is *common ownership* or *commonwealth*, which has the advantage of being able to use industrial organization as a servant of the human beings who work within its structures rather than have the organization use the people simply as means to enrich the owners of capital. The common ownership is set up by transferring the assets of the corporation from the original owners to the collectivity of managers, supervisors, and workers in such a way that no one member of the collectivity can be said to own shares in the corporation but rather that the sole ownership of the corporation is vested in the community of people who operate the corporation, the commonwealth. While the members as individuals have no ownership, they have specific rights and responsibilities in the administration of the corporate assets.

Such a transfer of ownership could not happen without the original owners' being willing to effect the transfer either by sale or outright gift. No matter how generous this transfer may be, it is merely an enabling act, a necessary but not sufficient condition for the securing of higher aims. This kind of ownership makes it possible for the commonwealth to engage in other well-defined and commonly agreed on tasks over and above maximizing profits, growing and becoming powerful. The corporation engages in its economic task of securing orders that can be designed, made, and serviced in such a manner as to make a profit; it also engages in its technical task of enabling marketing to secure profitable orders by keeping that department supplied with up-to-date product design. This is not what makes the commonwealth idea attractive.

The possibility of a whole corporation embarking on social and political tasks of equal importance with the economic and technical tasks does provide us with an alluring picture. Possible examples include the social task of providing members of the commonwealth with opportunities for satisfaction and development through their participation in the working community, and the political task of encouraging other men and women to change society by offering them an example of an economically healthy and socially responsible corporation. The profit motive alone is not enough to galvanize a commonwealth into a community. Using some, even as much as 50%, of the profits to help others who need and cannot get such help otherwise can make operating a corporation in this manner a meaningful and worthwhile enterprise. For any of these ideas to take concrete shape at all, the commonwealth must remain limited in size so that every member can embrace it in his or her mind and imagination. Whenever circumstances seem to warrant growth beyond this limit, a new and fully independent unit should be organized along the same lines of the original common-wealth.[1]

The common good of the community of persons is best served when *each person, on the basis of his or her work, is actually a part owner of the means of production* on which he or she is working with everyone else. Each person is then working for himself or herself and, at the same time, for the common good of all. This truly joins the worker's self-interest to the common good, and also joins the employer's self-interest to the common good. The worker is not just a cog in a huge machine with brain divorced from brawn, a mere instrument of production; he or she is a personal subject receiving due remuneration for work done in the knowledge that he or she is working for himself or herself. That this is an idea "whose time has come" is clear from the fact that, by early 1982, more than six thousand firms and agencies had increased employee participation in ownership or management.

Employee ownership as producer cooperatives has a history that goes back to the eighteenth century, but it has never been very common in the United States. The development of the idea of employee ownership came from two directions: (1) the employee stock ownership plan (ESOP) movement, and (2) the efforts in the industrial Northeast to stave off plant closings and the flight of capital. The ESOP appeals as both a way of spreading wealth and of enjoying significant tax benefits. Employee buyouts were not always successful, but a body of information and skills to assess the problems and possibilities of employee ownership has been built up in recent years.

Currently there are four main sources of financing for employee participation in owner-ship: (1) individual employees, who use their savings to buy stock; (2) the company treasury, which pays part of the price per share; (3) pretax corporate profits used by the company to help employees buy stock in the company at little cost to themselves or to the company, for such income would normally be paid to the government in taxes anyway; and (4) the company's regular defined benefit pension plan, which is discontinued and the proceeds from the sale of assets used to buy back its own stock to fund what is now called a floor/offset ESOP pension, paying no excise or income taxes on the funds so generated as long as the asset recapture occurs before December 31, 1988. The Tax Reform Act of 1986 encourages the formation of floor/offset ESOP pensions. When the employees retire, they receive any and all gains from the stock appreciation. If the stock price falls, the company guarantees the same benefits the employee would have received if the old pension plan had remained in force.

Congress has made the floor/offset ESOP pension very attractive to corporate employers. Not only may the corporate employer convert an existing pension fund as described above, but if the company borrows money to buy back its stock to fund the floor/offset ESOP pension, both the principal and interest are tax-deductible, and the dividends on the stock in the ESOP that are used to repay the loan are likewise deductible. In addition, 50% of the interest payments to the lending institution are excluded from taxable income. The net result is that companies that borrow money to fund their floor/offset ESOP pension do so at 85% or less of the prime rate.

The benefits of employee ownership are both economic and human, for the corporation and the community as well as for the individual. Improved productivity and efficiency lead to work quality, improved quality of products and/or services, and increased profits. The material benefits are secondary to the human development that has taken place. People feel better about themselves. They enjoy going to work and have more self-esteem and self-confidence. They gain significant control over their lives and lose at least some of their sense of powerlessness. The ben-

---

[1]The Scott Bader & Co. Ltd. is a commonwealth that is alive and well in England at Wollaston in Northamptonshire. See E.F. Schumacher, *Small is Beautiful: Economics as if People Mattered*, pp. 258–266.

efits to the community come in the form of improved quality of products and services at lower prices.

ESOP is still relatively new to the economic landscape, as is the floor/offset ESOP pension. Both have generated a lot of interest, but neither can as yet be pronounced an unqualified success. The ESOP gives the employees as stockholders some power over management, a power that management does not universally regard as desirable. Unions, too, are not always supportive of the idea, because sharing in ownership seems to compromise the employees' position. Unions would rather see defined pension benefit plans guaranteed by the Pension Benefit Guarantee Corporation (PBGC) rather than ESOPs or floor/offset ESOP pensions, which currently have no federal guarantees.

Since 1974 Congress has passed a number of laws relating to employee ownership, the latest being the provisions in the Tax Reform Act of 1986. The government recognizes that employee ownership provides a way of preserving jobs and developing business activity, of keeping a small business small when it might otherwise be sold to a conglomerate, and of creating new small businesses from the sale of subsidiaries by large corporations. This kind of ownership can renew both the lives of people at their work and their business organizations. By working together with management they can make a difference in their personal lives and in the community.

The floor/offset ESOP pension is being put into place by a number of large corporations because of its tax incentives. Not all of these pensions are of the defined benefit type; they may have only the guarantee of the company but not that of the Pension Benefit Guarantee Corporation. Such pensions sound wonderful as long as the company does well, but suppose disaster should befall it and the employees lose their jobs. The company's stock has plummeted in value, and its finances are strained so that it is unable to make up the pension shortfall. The pension has either disappeared entirely or is so diminished in value as to be inconsequential.

The status of floor/offset ESOP pensions is vague. Congress has an obligation, now that it has encouraged the formation of such pensions, to do what is necessary to remove the risk. Pension plans should be as risk-free as possible. At present the floor/offset ESOP pension is laden with risk. Furthermore, ESOPs were never intended as pensions in the first place. The rush to form them now is due to the tax incentives Congress has provided.

Bigness need not be an inescapable feature of the modern world. We do not have to live with it if we do not want to. There are alternatives. Some have been suggested; others may yet be discovered if we can learn to think positively. The negative approach of trust-busting legislation has met with indifferent success. More can be accomplished by the positive approach of dispersing industries into outlying areas, giving the workers a chance to own at least their own homes, and demonstrating that everyone's prosperity depends on production of high quality products and services. After all, the goal is not an equal distribution of wealth but a standard of living that affords all a decent life befitting human dignity.

POWER WITHOUT PROPERTY

Capitalism as a way of organizing our economic life is among other things a system of power as it has always been. We expect good people to use power to further worthy causes; we insist that all use of power be guided by rules of fairness and moral sensitivity. We also fear power, because it can corrupt those who have it and destroy the freedom of those who are subject to it. The growth of large corporations in the last 60 years or so is also a growth in business power manifesting itself as power to determine when, where, and how to apply capital and resources, power to determine the product and its quality, power to give or withhold dividends, power to induce consumption and sales through advertising, power to set the goals of the majority of private research, power to influence public officials concerning legislation, power to sponsor entertainment on television, power to contribute needed funds to institutions of higher learning, and so on.

Sixty or so years ago business power was directly connected to ownership of the capital items used in the process of production. The owner who was the head of the corporation was very much like the owner-proprietor of any small business today. Either the owner was the manager or he selected the managers, and the entire management was ordered by and accountable to the owner. The justification of that corporate power rested on the prior justification of private property itself, that is, of the private ownership of the means of production. But this earlier world is no longer our world.

The situation we have today is one in which the owners, that is, the stockholders who supply the financial support for capital investment at least initially, are passive in respect to the decisions about the corporation's operations. Control is in the hands of managers who are more than likely either not stockholders at all or not owners of a controlling share of the outstanding stock. These managers belong to groups that are self-elective and self-perpetuating.

The large corporations are responsible for a substantial portion of our society's total economic activity, and their market power is not severely limited by competition. They also exercise decision control in other areas of society so that they are centers of private power that are significant to all of us and in many areas of our lives. Those managerial people who exercise this significant private power do so even though their acquisition and exercise of that power is not based on ownership and their accountability is vague. Corporate organizational operations give the tone to our society and control the major portion of our economic existence as well. That they do so is a fact; our question is, "Ought they to do so?" Society as a whole aims to achieve the common good of all. Insofar as the giant corporations are subsidiary structures within society, they should be judged in terms of how they contribute to the common good of all.

Clearly, those who manage the corporations make policy decisions that affect all of us. They are exercising power not based on the ownership of the means of production. This phenomenon is being spoken of now as the "new property." The corporation is legally owned by the stockholders, but how could the stockholders of American Telephone and Telegraph exercise any kind of significant control of AT&T? The purpose of stockholding has changed *from* ownership in order to control *to* investment seeking interest on money. The stockholders are divorced from any significant control of the corporation. The operating property is divorced from its owners, the stockholders, but remains in close relation to the experts who make it operate and to the socioeconomic system within which it operates. This operating property is significant social as well as economic power wielded not by the actual legal owners but by the managers. This "new property," this relationship to "operating property," functions today as wealth did in the past; it secures freedom, identity, and power.

Society today is in part composed of an interlaced network of large corporate organizations that interrelate not only among themselves but with governmental bodies and the social community itself. A person does not need vast holdings of private property to wield social power. All one needs to do is obtain a place in the interlaced socioeconomic system of organizations, and one then has power by having status in the organizational power systems. In earlier times, social status was a by-product of property possessed, ancestry, and/or profession. Status today is a place of socioeconomic power within the organizational power systems.

The upshot of this new kind of status is that those who work within an organizational power system tend to identify themselves in terms of the function they perform within the system. And not only this. One's identity is more and more dependent on the fate of one's immediate organization within the corporate society, on one's acceptance by functional peers, and on one's performance among functional inferiors. The primary concern of the person with "new property" has to be organizational, and his or her exercise of power determines some relations other people will have to the organization or its products and so to the corporate society.

The decisions made by the managers of corporations are not merely private decisions that affect the corporation in question and the employees who implement the decisions. What the corporation does is also a public matter affecting the citizens who use its products. For example, if all the major suppliers of certain foods modify their product in a certain respect and package it in a particular way, the ability of consumers to judge quality is denied them by what is in fact an exercise of public power. We are less and less a society of persons who enter into relationship with private organizations by invitation or privilege or who use the products of such organizations by free choice. When certain human values are determined for us by the corporate managers, then it is in the area of our human rights that we are being affected and so the power wielder is responsible ethically. And who is the power wielder? The managers of the corporations and their agents. Their power is exercised ethically as long as they use it to further the common good of all in the society and not just their own self-interest.

EMPLOYEE PENSION FUNDS

While employee pension funds go back at least to the Civil War, their tremendous growth has been a post-World War II phenomenon. Practically all early plans had invested in standard life insurance investments such as government bonds, mortgages, and other fixed-interest-bearing instruments. Since the end of World War II, however, most of these pension funds have been investing in common stock as a way of investing in America's productive assets and her capacity to produce and to grow. Some corporations and unions have administered these funds themselves, but for the most part they are administered by the trust departments of large banks or by insurance companies. These are the big institutional investors who, when they move in or out of the stock market, always influence the price of the stocks. They have enormous financial

power, which they exercise under government regulations, and it is all done in the name of the employees whose deferred wages they are administering. This is another way in which American workers share in the ownership of the means of production, but they have virtually no voice in the control and direction of those means of production. While the funds' managers invest the employees' contributions in order to increase the employees' retirement income, they nevertheless must also look to the common good of all in doing their investing and see to it that the employees are given some voice in the control and direction of the investing.

SOCIAL RESPONSIBILITY

Corporate social responsibility does not always mean the same thing to everyone. It is a condition in fact, not just a policy or response to some temporary situation that has occurred. The business community is the group of people who operate the economic side of our society. Any human society requires that each portion of it be responsible to that society in an acceptable way, in a way that enhances the common good of all the members of that society. During the late nineteenth and early twentieth centuries, the most powerful businessmen looked on the economy as though it were theirs, as though it belonged to them. They were self-seeking individuals and admitted it. *Laissez-faire* capitalism, economic individualism, and social Darwinism encouraged them in their view. More and more, today's leaders in business are recognizing that the economy is not theirs, even though they do operate it. They owe society certain responsibilities.

Society today no longer needs or wants unlimited economic growth. Production is no longer the primary goal, for it has been achieved. We live in a land of plenty, and in such a land economics is not king but merely another member of the court. The recognition of social responsibility is a recognition on the part of business that the economy is not the center of society. Society no longer shapes itself to the economy but now looks to the business leaders to shape the economy to it. Fouling the environment, polluting streams and lakes, contributing to social unrest by practicing discrimination in employment policies, promoting war, degrading the quality of life, perpetuating systems of privilege and injustice are no longer acceptable to society as a whole. Art and culture more than work are shaping the social structure of society. Production continues to be a goal but not the overriding one. Neither is society willing to accept profit as the sole measure of success in business.

Society as a whole expects business to operate in a way that enhances the quality of life throughout all of society. Business should not wait until there is a clear and present danger to life and health before it changes its policies and/or modes of operation. If business will not do this voluntarily, then society is prepared to make it mandatory. Social awareness must be made an integral part of the decision process at every level of a business organization. The penalities for lack of such awareness must be as severe as those for cost nonawareness. Provision must also be made to ensure a flow of environmental and social information to each corporation from other sectors of society.

One of the most important effects of business' adopting a socially responsible stance is the need to find new ways of handling technology. Technology itself is not a villain, but the people who use it can be. Research and development of technology are important and good; to conduct them with no concern for potential social and environmental impacts is clearly immoral and unconscionable today. Society as a whole has the obligation to set the goals (values) and policies if we are to stop technology from wandering aimlessly over the landscape to ravage it. Scientists and engineers must distinguish good uses of technology from bad and inform society and business about these uses.

A commitment to social responsibility means giving up the "side-effect" way of thinking.[1] Some business people like to talk about the results of

faulty forecasting, inadequate or sloppy research, and careless disregard for the impact on others as side effects of decisions and actions taken for some other purpose. Side effects are the effects of things we do when they come as a surprise. Labeling the death of peregrine falcons as a side effect of using DDT is actually an admission of failure, not an exoneration of conscience. It is no longer acceptable to market a technology or product of unknown consequences or to leave on the market a suspicious product just because it has not yet proved harmful.

Social responsibility on the part of business is necessary not only for the good of business itself but for society as a whole. Profound social changes are underway and business must adapt to them and fit itself into the newly emerging social patterns. Society is looking for responsible social action from business and is prepared to be the judge of whether business' social action has been responsible. As social responsibility on the part of business makes for better communication between the economy and society, changing goals and attitudes in society at large will be reflected more quickly in corporations and in their conduct.

TECHNOLOGY AND LEISURE

We turn our attention now to a consideration of the evils of technology and mass production, which would be a problem for socialism as well as for capitalism. It is said that the gain in productiveness, making available to nearly all a vast variety of comforts and luxuries formerly beyond the dreams of all but the most wealthy, is matched by the degradation of the worker, chained to the machine, condemned to a stultifying routine of uninteresting activity. The assembly line reduces workers to robotlike status, stunts their personalities, and starves their artistic spirit, leaving them with no pride of ownership, no joy in creativeness, no satisfaction except that of the pay.

What can be done about this state of affairs? No one, least of all the worker, will return to handicraft methods of manufacture. It takes too much effort to produce too little. Comparing the

---

[1]Votaw and Sethi, *The Corporate Dilemma: Traditional Values versus Contemporary Problems*, pp. 40–41; 45.

two economies, we see that in the handicraft system it was possible to work at what one liked with a sense of pride and creativeness, but one worked long hours for a pittance, whereas now one may work at a routine, noncreative task, it is true, but for shorter hours with good wages, making possible a style of living unthinkable for such workers a generation ago. Whenever was work free from drudgery? If the tedium of the factory were so much worse than the tedium of the farm, how explain the ceaseless movement from farm to factory? The creativeness of the workers was always limited by their ability to sell their products; not what they want but what the buyer will want must be their guide if they expect to make a living by their work.

Nevertheless, the problem exists. Many leading industries recognize it and take some steps to alleviate it by fitting workers into jobs for which they are best suited, rotating them from one job to another, determining optimum length of work and rest periods, and providing psychological counseling and social service facilities. However, there is no way of turning all work into play, so that the person on the job can do only what he or she finds personally interesting.

Automation is looked at fearfully by some as the final step in human degradation to the level of the machines humans have created, but machines can do only what they have been constructed and programmed to do. They are the best servants we have yet found, and their judicious use can be the most liberalizing influence history has afforded. Automation, far from being feared, should be welcomed as a marvelous blessing. It will take over more and more of the disagreeable side of mass production, freeing people from repetitive drudgery, presenting them with the challenge of intellectual effort in the use of machines, and giving them vastly increased leisure. The final effect will be to make work shorter, easier, safer, and pleasanter. The problem will be one of adjustment to a new society in which fewer workers will be needed out of a greatly increased population. There will be many initial dislocations, whose severity can be eased by the cooperative planning of manage-

ment and labor with the assistance of the government. People will have to be retrained to run the new machines, fitted for different jobs, or retired to pass an honorable old age at public expense. A moral obligation rests on management, labor, and government to initiate farsighted measures cooperatively and to begin doing so soon enough.

Work is good for people but it is nevertheless a mere means, not an end in itself. Leisure is the end, and leisure is not idleness but the freedom to do what one wants to do. We shall have to educate workers to make the best use of the many free hours technology will enable them to enjoy. The workers will still be economically bound to their jobs, but they will be bound for less and less of their time. With any creativeness in their makeup, they will at least have some opportunity to exercise it, if not on the job, then in their off time, whereas formerly most workers had no opportunity at all.

It is as foolish to paint too rosy a picture of the technological age as it is to overromanticize the preindustrial period. Socialism and communism have nothing more to offer here, except greater regimentation of the worker than need be feared under private enterprise. If this vexation cannot be eliminated from the capitalist economy, neither can it be eliminated from any workable economy in our modern age.

CONCLUSION

The preceding investigation has been an effort to examine capitalism in its concrete democratic political and pluralistic setting. The moral philosopher is not called on to solve the world's economic ills but merely to point out the moral obligation of society to seek a solution for those ills. By detailing a few of the suggested remedies, we have shown at least that some people are not standing by idly in smug complacency at the present or wringing their hands in futile fear of the future. Many things can be done, and those mentioned here may not be the only ones or the best.

The obligation bears on society, not on single companies or single unions, much less on single individuals, except that they must show a willingness to cooperate with others in working out a solution and in adopting measures to implement the solution. The larger the industry or union, the greater the obligation of the leaders to point the way and to take the first steps along it. The advance toward social justice is a serious moral obligation that stands squarely on the leaders of society who have the power and influence to do something about it. It will not happen automatically but requires the cooperative effort of all under the leadership of the most able.

SUMMARY

The philosophical examination of democratic capitalism in its present context of interaction with both government and the moral-cultural institutions of society seems to reveal it as committed to the following ideals: (1) a community of persons with the freedom to join intermediate communities of their choice for their personal and economic enrichment; (2) a practical realism that accepts the world as it is and yet strives for justice with love; (3) competition as the natural play of the free person; (4) human freedom to be maximized for all and tyranny to be inhibited for the sake of all; (5) the separation of governmental, economic, and moral-cultural institutions; and (6) each member of the community of persons to be respected as an individual person of intrinsic worth and dignity.

Capitalism is not an immoral economic system, but it should be revised to eliminate some of its worst defects:

1. For the exclusive use of *competition,* foster a spirit of *cooperation.* Competition is necessary to free enterprise, but unlimited competition was so greedy and wasteful that it had to be limited by law. Only greater cooperation can care for the increased population of the future.

2. For *strife* between management and labor, substitute *associations* or *councils* embracing both, representing the whole industry or field of occupational endeavor.

3. For too much *state control* and bureaucracy, substitute *self-control* by the industry itself on all levels of management and labor, and observe the principle of subsidiarity.

4. For *concentration* of economic control in the hands of too few, substitute a wider *distribution* of control. *Distributism* would prohibit mergers, break up combines, help small business, and promote rural life, all by means of state benefits and taxation. The *cooperative movement* eliminates the middleman, putting control in the owners rather than in boards of directors. *Profit sharing* would take the workers into the business as small owners, *management sharing* would give them some control in its operation, and *common ownership* or *commonwealth* would give the whole corporation as a community a chance to operate a profitable business to achieve important social and political goals. These schemes all have some advantages and some drawbacks.

The common good of the community of persons is best served when each person, on the basis of his or her work, is actually a part owner of the means of production on which he or she is working with everyone else. This is the idea behind the *employee stock ownership plan* (ESOP) movement.

5. The "new property" is corporate management's social power, which derives from their operating corporation property they do not own. Since exercise of such power affects the entire society, management must look to the common good of all in making decisions.

6. *Employee pension funds* administer workers' deferred wages and represent a significant share in the ownership of America's corporate assets by the workers. Those administering the funds have enormous economic power and can influence the movement of the stock market. The problem is that the employees whose funds are being so administered have virtually no voice in the control of the funds and the choice of investments made. The fund managers have an obligation not only to maximize the profits of the funds but also to look to the common good of all in doing their investing. They have the further obligation to give the employees an active voice in the operation of the funds.

7. Social responsibility is more than an ex-

pedient response by business to temporary social conditions; it is one of the important manifestations of profound social change occurring today. As the economy plays a less central role in structuring society, business must act more responsibly and be prepared to have society judge the appropriateness of corporate conduct.

8. For the stultifying effects of *mass production,* substitute training in the proper use of *leisure.* Since technology and automation are here

to stay and will increase, it would be better to adapt ourselves to them than to try to stop them. Education is faced with the great task of teaching the worker how to use vastly increased leisure profitably.

To remedy our economic ills and establish social justice is a serious moral obligation on society. No one can do it alone, but all are obliged to seek remedies and to cooperate in the use of those agreed on.

Questions for Discussion

1. The economy is measured not only by what it produces, but also by how it touches human life and whether it protects or undermines the dignity of the human person. Economic decisions have human consequences and moral content; they help or hurt people, strengthen or weaken family life, advance or diminish the quality of justice in this country. Consider the decision of the federal government to tolerate a 7% unemployment rate. Make a moral assessment of such a decision. Can anything be done to achieve full employment? Explain your answer.

2. More than 33 million Americans are poor; by any reasonable standard another 20 to 30 million are needy. These burdens fall most heavily on blacks, Hispanics, and native Amerians. What moral obligations do those who run the economy have to better this situation?

3. In recent years the military-industrial complex has absorbed almost $300 billion per year. Is

such a large expenditure of money justifiable in the light of the poverty mentioned in question #2? What values guided the choice to make such large expenditures? Is it possible to have both a strong military defense establishment and responsible social programs? If so, how? If not, why not?

4. Some social philosophers hold that everyone has a right to have a share of nature's goods sufficient for oneself and one's family. Does this mean that society as a whole has an obligation to help each one fulfill these basic needs? If not, what does it mean?

5. Does technology really dehumanize us? Is our urbanized civilization better or worse than the mainly rural life of our ancestors? Is more liberal education the answer to our greatly increased leisure? Do workers displaced by automation have a right to be taken care of and helped to develop another skill?

Readings

Thorstein Veblen, *The Theory of the Leisure Class;* Max Weber, *The Protestant Ethic and the Spirit of Capitalism;* Richard Tawney, *Religion and the Rise of Capitalism;* Milton Friedman, *Capitalism and Freedom* are well known works on capitalism.

The following discuss the issues raised or lay the background for them: Pope John Paul II, *Laborem Exercens* (On Human Work); U.S. Bishops' Pastoral Message and Letter, "Economic Justice for All: Catholic Social Teaching and the U.S. Economy;" Michael Novak, *The Spirit of Democratic Capitalism;* Michael Harrington, *Decade of Decision: The Crisis of the American System;* The Editors of "Fortune," *Working Smarter;* John Simmons and William Mares, *Working Together;* Peter F. Drucker, *The Unseen Revolution: How Pension Fund Socialism Came to America;* Ralph Nader and Mark J. Green (eds.), *Corporate Power in America;* Ralph Nader, Mark Green, and Joel Seligman, *Taming the Giant Corporation;* David E. Lilienthal, *Big Business: A New Era;* William Feree, *The Act of Social Justice;* William Drummond, *Social Justice;* Richard Mulcahy, *The Economics of Heinrich Pesch,* ch. 7; John F. Cronin, *Catholic Social Principles,* ch. 1, 7, 8, 13, 16; Johannes Messner, *Social Ethics,* revised ed., bk. I, pt. IV; bk. II, pt. II, bk. IV, pt. III; E.F. Schumacher, *Small is Beautiful: Economics as if People*

Mattered, pt. IV, ch. 4; W.L. La Croix, *Principles for Ethics in Business,* ch. 6; David Hapgood, *The Screwing of the Average Man,* passim; Peter T. Manicas, *The Death of the State,* ch. 3; and Dow Votaw and S. Prakash Sethi, *The Corporate Dilemma: Traditional Values versus Contemporary Problems,* pt. II. David Freudberg's *The Corporate Conscience: Money, Power, and Responsible Business* should be of interest to the student.

On the evils of technology read Gabriel Marcel, *Man Against Mass Society,* and his shorter statement of the same theme, *The Decline of Wisdom.* Friedrich Jünger, *The Failure of Technology,* and Jacques Ellul, *The Technological Society,* are strongly critical. Leon Bagrit, *The Age of Automation;* John Diebold, *Beyond Automation;* John Dunlop, *Automation and Technical Change;* and Walter Buckingham, *Automation: Its Impact on Business and People,* express a more hopeful view.

Francis X. Quinn edits a symposium, *The Ethical Aftermath of Automation,* now somewhat dated.

32
Marxism

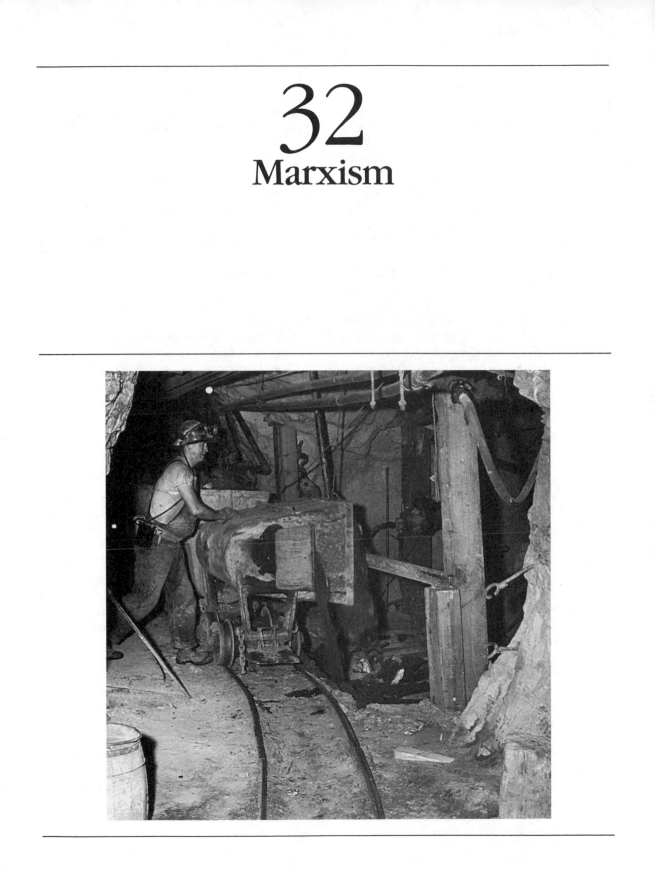

PROBLEM

Marxism, as a political-economic movement, is originally a product of nineteenth century Western social and philosophical thinking; with its international outlook and objectives, it exerts enormous influence today. The triumph of Marxism in Russia, spreading later to China and other places, was and still is considered to be a threat to the economic and political structure of the Western world. To the underdeveloped peoples of Southeast Asia, Africa, and many in Central and South America, however, Russia's gigantic strides and those of China in catching up with the Western capitalist nations in technology, production, and science are a source of inspiration and a model for many of these nations seeking methods to bring their people to economic and political maturity in the modern world.

The basic ideal of Marxism is humanistic both in focusing on the human beings in this world and in envisioning an ultimately classless society in which all people individually will achieve the full freedom of their humanity for the first time. The source of this ideal is the writings of Karl Marx himself. Under the inspiration of Marx, much has been written that departs in more or less significant ways from Marx's own thought. This is true of the writings of his friend and close collaborator, Friedrich Engels, as well as of Lenin, Stalin, Mao Tse-tung, and many other Marxist thinkers. To gain some appreciation of Marx's thought, we shall leave to others the study of modern Marxists and turn to two of Marx's early writings, the *Economic and Philosophical Manuscripts* of 1844 and *The German Ideology* of 1846, which were first published in English in 1959 and 1947, respectively. Until rather recently, Marx's chief claim to fame has been as the author of *Capital* and co-author with Engels of the *Communist Manifesto*. Now, largely as a result of the publication of his early writings, the philosophical aspects of his thought have caught the center of people's attention. His later writings cannot be effectively understood and interpreted unless they are seen as a development of these earlier writings. In these two early works Marx develops three basic themes: (1) the nature of human beings and their alienation, (2) the making of history by people who are at the same time developing themselves, and (3) the conscious participation of humans in the transformation of society. Our study of Marx's early thought will include the following:

1. Brief survey of his life and writings to orient ourselves to Marx's way of thinking
2. Analysis of his *Economic and Philosophical Manuscripts* and *The German Ideology* with special attention to
   a. Material aspects of history
   b. Division of labor as the source of alienation
   c. Notion of class struggles
   d. So-called stages of history
   e. Marx's new concept of history
   f. Reintegration of human labor by fostering the communist revolution and the establishment of communism
3. Assessment of Marx's Marxism

MARX'S LIFE AND WRITINGS

Karl Heinrich Marx, eldest son of Heinrich and Henrietta Marx, was born of Jewish parents in Trier in the Rhineland on May 5, 1818. His mother belonged to a family of Hungarian Jews who settled in Holland, where her father was a rabbi. Faced with anti-Semitism, Marx's father, whose own father and grandfather had also been rabbis in the Rhineland, not only changed his name from Levi to Marx but also joined the established Lutheran church, looking to a settled future as the head of a respectable German bourgeois family. The anti-Jewish laws of 1816 seem to have made his conversion to Lutheranism mandatory. The year before Karl was born, Heinrich was received into the church. Young Karl was baptized in 1824 along with the rest of the family.

Little is known about Marx's early years. He attended the local gymnasium in Trier where he was moderately successful in mathematics and theology. His main interests were literary and artistic, largely as a result of the influence of his father and their neighbor, Freiherr Ludwig von

Westphalen, a Prussian government official who befriended Karl, encouraged him to read, and lent him books and discussed them with him.

In 1837 Karl asked von Westphalen for the hand of his daughter, Jenny, in marriage; they were married in April, 1843. Although the greater part of her family objected to the marriage, Jenny was much in love and passionately loyal to Karl. He had revealed a new world to her, and she would devote her life to him and his work. He leaned on her in times of crisis and all his life remained proud of her beauty and intelligence as well as of her birth into the Prussian aristocracy. During their later years together they shared great poverty, but Jenny kept the family and household intact, enabling Karl to continue his work.

After he completed his course of studies at the gymnasium in Trier, Marx went on to study at the Universities of Bonn and Berlin. When he entered the university in Berlin in 1836, most of the faculty were disciples of Hegel. Marx's early works represent his long struggle to detach Hegel's dialectical method from his idealistic system. Since Marx cannot be understood without some knowledge of Hegel's approach to philosophy, we give here the barest outline of the dialectical method and system of Hegel.

The *Hegelian dialectic* is the process of development that pervades everything. For Hegel there is only one reality, which he calls the *Idea*. Only the rational is real, and the Idea is Thought itself thinking itself out. The process of thinking itself out is the *dialectic*. Thinking consists of contrasting each thought with its opposite, whereupon there arises a higher thought that is the union of the two. Thus the thought of *being* leads to the thought of its opposite, which is *nothing*; the union is *becoming*, or the passage from nothing to being. In every case the first stage is simply given or posited, the second stage is its negation, and the third stage, or the negation of the negation, is the union of the first two. What underlies this process is that reality itself is basically contradictory; thought first takes up one side of the contradiction (thesis), and then the other (antithesis), and finally succeeds in fusing

the two (synthesis). Any thought contains only part of the truth; there is some truth also in the opposite, and only when both are reconciled in a higher union does the whole truth appear. The process continues because each synthesis now becomes a thesis for further development.

In thinking itself out, thought arrives at the main antithesis to itself, which is inert matter. At this point the Idea objectifies itself in matter, turns into its opposite, contradicts its unity and totality, fractions itself into this manifold world of experience, and spreads itself out to become Nature. This, for Hegel, is the creation of the world. World evolution continues along dialectical lines. The first inkling of synthesis is life, in which thought reappears in matter, organizing plants, manifesting conscious instinct in animals, and arriving at self-consciousness in human beings, the spearhead of the process. The dialectic continues through human history, in which people have passed to higher and higher forms of social organization, culminating at present in the political state. Thus thought and matter, spirit and nature, are united in humans. The final synthesis will be a combination of the thesis (the Idea thinking itself out) with the antithesis (the Idea spread out into Nature) into the synthesis (Nature gathered back into the Idea in full self-consciousness as Absolute Spirit). The whole process can be looked on as the life of Spirit, whose evolution is the universe, of which human history forms a leading part.

Early in his student days in Berlin, Marx's attention was drawn to the revolutionary aspect of the Hegelian dialectic, namely, that no historical state of affairs can ever be considered final since further negation is always possible. He set himself to read Hegel's complete works, and joined the Berlin Club of Young Hegelians, a group of young men who had come to the conclusion that philosophy must be critical and seek to alter the world. In their company, Marx soon became convinced that philosophy alone was in no position to alter the real world. Philosophy needs the supplement of practical action.

In 1841 Marx completed his doctoral dissertation for the University of Jena but was not offered an academic appointment because he was considered too radical. He turned to socialistic journalism, taking an editorial position in 1842 on the *Rheinische Zeitung* (Rhineland Gazette), a newly founded revolutionary newspaper. This experience acquainted him with the social abuses of the day and encouraged him in the social orientation of his thought. In October, 1842, he became editor-in-chief of the newspaper, which under his direction took an even more radical turn in conducting a campaign against the Christian religion and the Christian state until the state censor finally suppressed the newspaper in March, 1843.

The banning of the *Rheinische Zeitung* marked a new period in Marx's intellectual development, for he began gradually to formulate his materialistic concept of history and eventually became a communist. His preoccupation with economic and social questions led him to be more and more critical of Hegel. Marx now occupied himself with a critical examination of Hegel's philosophy of the state. He worked at this critique throughout the summer of 1843 and moved to Paris in the autumn to collaborate in editing a periodical called *Deutsch-Französische Jahrbücher* (Franco-German Annals). Only one issue appeared but in it Marx published two articles: (1) "Introduction to the Critique of Hegel's Philosophy of Right," and (2) "On the Jewish Question," in which he begins to outline his philosophical analysis of social problems as well as a program of practical action to solve these problems.

In his critique of Hegel, Marx was influenced by the work of Ludwig Feuerbach who had already shown that Hegel's system and method were in contradiction with each other. Feuerbach claimed further that Hegel's entire philosophy, biased in favor of thought, simply eliminates physical reality. Feuerbach, on the other hand, maintains that philosophy is the science of reality and that the sum total of reality is physical nature. When philosophy pretends, as Hegel's does, to have a higher object than the human relation to physical nature, it becomes sheer illusion. Feuerbach showed Marx that dialectical philosophy can avoid (1) idealism by starting from human reality rather than from an ideal Absolute Spirit and (2) mechanistic materialism by taking the concrete nature of the human being, both spiritual and material, as its initial principle.

In his first article, "Introduction to the Critique of Hegel's Philosophy of Right," Marx poses the problem as to *why* humans create the illusory world of religion; he finds his explanation in the fact that society as it is at present is an inverted world. The world itself is upside down, alienated or estranged from its real nature. Religion is a spiritual mirror-image of that world and society; it is

> ... the general theory of this world, its encyclopedic compendium, its logic in popular form, its spiritual *point d' honneur,* its enthusiasm, its moral sanction, its solemn complement, its general basis of consolation and justification. It is *the fantastic realization* of the human being inasmuch as the human being possesses no true reality. The struggle against religion is, therefore, indirectly a struggle against *that world* whose spiritual *aroma* is religion.
>
> *Religious* suffering is at the same time an *expression* of real suffering and a *protest* against real suffering. Religion is the sigh of the oppressed creature, the sentiment of a heartless world, and the soul of soulless conditions. It is the *opium* of the people.
>
> The abolition of religion as the *illusory* happiness of men, is a demand for their *real* happiness. The call to abandon their illusions about their condition is a *call to abandon a condition which requires illusions.* The criticism of religion is, therefore, *the embryonic criticism of this vale of tears* of which religion is the *halo.*[1]

The campaign against religion must be enlarged, in Marx's view, into a campaign against the inverted world itself so that all men and women will be rid of illusions and come to be centered on their true being. The criticism of heaven must become the criticism of earth, the criticism of law and politics.

> It is the *task of history,* therefore, once the *otherworld of truth* has vanished, to establish the *truth of this world.* The immediate *task of philosophy,*

---

[1]Bottomore, *Karl Marx: Early Writings,* pp. 43–44.

which is in the service of history, is to unmask human self-alienation in its *secular form* now that it has been unmasked in its *sacred form*.[1]

In this same article, Marx reflects on the conditions in Germany and sees no way of gradually transforming and emancipating society except by a total revolution carried out by the mass of people who are uneducated and propertyless, the proletariat.[2] The proletariat will make the abolition of private property, which has been in fact forced upon it, into a principle for society. In this way, the proletariat will emancipate the whole of society so that egoism and social injustice are completely eliminated. In abolishing private property the proletariat undergoes a qualitative change; it ceases to be a proletariat. In emancipating itself, the proletariat ushers in the final and total emancipation of all people and so a complete transformation of the entire world.

> *Philosophy* is the *head* of this emancipation and the *proletariat* is its *heart*.[3]

The function of the future proletarian class will be to convert the German revolutionary philosophy into action. Philosophy becomes revolution as soon as it penetrates the proletariat, and in the revolution, philosophy will finally become ideas put into practice and so suppress itself because it will cease being mere ideas. Economic factors alone can never lead to revolution; philosophy is necessary to bring those who suffer under the economic conditions to a *consciousness* of their power. Marxism is then essentially a philosophy of action, because the revolutionary power of the proletariat depends on philosophy's penetrating the masses.

In his second article, "On the Jewish Question," Marx abandons the attempt to ascribe to philosophy a distinct and active role in social development. Religious radicalism and political liberalism are not enough; they must press on toward practical action, the transformation of society. The basic evil in society lies in the egoism generated by private property. Marx's ideal is of a communistic society in which private property is eliminated and the goals of the individual coincide with those of the community. He thinks of the transformation as occurring dialectically by means of a total revolution with the proletariat playing a decisive role, but philosophy no longer plays an independent part.

Marx continued his work in Paris, which would bring him even closer to the notion of the materialistic concept of history. In *Economic and Philosophical Manuscripts* of 1844, he examines the economic basis of law, morality, and the state and tries to show that the capitalist economy is the key to all moral, political, and social problems. To some extent this work is a logical continuation of the two articles discussed above.

During the Paris years (1843–1845), Marx studied the French Revolution exhaustively and delved into the works of the classical political economists, Adam Smith and David Ricardo. Along with these theoretical concerns, he worked as a revolutionary among the German emigrants, kept in contact with the secret French trade unions, and personally met Pierre-Joseph Proudhon, Mikhail Bakunin, Louis Blanc, Etienne Cabet, and became friendly with Georg Herwegh and Heinrich Heine. While in Paris he also worked on a German periodical published there called *Vorwärts* (Forward) and wrote a series of articles attacking Prussian absolutism and derisive of Frederick William IV. This was to lead the French government, at the request of the Prussian authorities, to expel Marx from France in January, 1845.

In August and September of 1844, Friedrich Engels on his way from London spent 10 days in Paris during which time he and Marx became acquainted. This marked the beginning of their intimate friendship and close personal collaboration that was to last the rest of their lives. They found themselves in complete agreement on all theoretical questions, although Engels was never to become Marx's equal as a philosopher. Engels was the son of a wealthy German textile manufacturer and had, while working in his father's factories in Manchester and observing first hand the actual conditions under which the working

---

[1]*Ibid.,* p. 44.
[2]*Ibid.,* p. 58.
[3]*Ibid.,* p. 59.

class in England labored and lived, arrived at a position very similar to Marx's. Marx now was able to give Engels a historical and philosophical framework for his ideas, and Engels provided Marx with a wealth of concrete data to support the philosophical theses of historical materialism.

Earlier in 1844 Engels had published an article in the *Deutsch-Französische Jahrbücher* entitled "Outlines of a Critique of Political Economy," which provided Marx with the notion that the laws that rule an economic system are impervious to all human control. Once people accept a particular economic system, they have no further control over its operation. Marx realized more and more clearly that efforts at social reform are vain since our social relations are determined by our economic conditions. Only a radical overthrow of the whole system can lead to social changes. The individual economic factors are not in need of criticism. The entire economic system of contemporary society must be criticized.

To do this, Marx needs a total philosophy of human nature. The economist cannot make the needed criticism, because the economic system, once accepted, encloses the economist. Only philosophy can criticize the system and show how it leads to our alienation rather than furthering our free development. Once people live in a certain economic system, they are subject to its laws, but they can reject the system in its totality since they are its makers.

Marx's concern is an ethical one, the good for people. Even though he moves now to concentrate on a study of the economy, his critique is philosophical. All the results of his previous studies are brought together in a single, powerful synthesis. He will remain basically faithful to this synthesis in all his later works.

Following his expulsion from France, Marx lived in Brussels for 3 years. He worked in conjunction with the trade unions and carried on intensive propaganda but was also anxious to put the finishing touches on his own philosophical development. First, he laid down eleven briefly stated theses against Feuerbach and later composed a more elaborate treatise, *The German Ideology* (1846), which makes the materialistic

concept of history its starting point. This work was never published in his lifetime, but is of enormous importance for understanding Marx's thought and work. In 1847, Marx published *The Poverty of Philosophy* as a rejoinder to Proudhon's *The Philosophy of Poverty*, which had appeared in 1846. Marx applies his materialistic theory of history in explaining social relationships, formulates the doctrine of the class struggle, and begins to develop the theory of "surplus-value."

In Brussels Marx found himself for the first time at the command of a truly revolutionary communist organization, the Communist League. Together with Engels, he became involved with many details of party organization and revolutionary activity, and tried to put his ideas into practice. Marx concluded that communism could be established only by a rising of the proletariat, so he devoted all his energies to the effort of organizing and disciplining the proletariat for this task. The second congress of the Communist League, held in London in November, 1847, asked Marx to draw up a complete theoretical and practical party program. In collaboration with Engels, Marx produced the famous *Communist Manifesto,* published in German in London in February, 1848.

There were many abortive revolutions in Europe in 1848, with Marx and Engels involved in most of them. Marx was in Paris during the French insurrection and hurried to Cologne with Engels in April after the revolution broke out in Germany. There he edited the radical daily newspaper, the *Neue Rheinische Zeitung,* which appeared from June 1, 1848 to May 19, 1849. After the revolution was put down in Germany, Marx was put on trial for treason and acquitted on February 9, 1849. While the Prussian government could not overturn his acquittal, it did succeed in having him expelled once again from Germany. Marx returned to Paris but, finding himself unwelcome there, emigrated to London where he was to live out the rest of his life.

His active revolutionary experience may have sobered Marx, for in London he kept relatively free of the conflicts between the socialist groups of German workers in London. He lived poorly with his wife, supported by Engels who was again working in his father's factory in Manchester. During the years of 1851–1862, Marx supplemented his income by writing as a European correspondent for Horace Greeley's *New York Tribune*. He concentrated his efforts in reading and writing daily in the library of the British Museum. In 1859 he published his *Contribution to the Critique of Political Economy,* the introduction of which is particularly important for Marx's sociology and philosophy of history and is the source of the "classical" formulation of historical materialism:

> It is not the consciousness of men that determines their existence, but, on the contrary, their social existence determines their consciousness.[1]

In the 1860s Marx became actively involved once again in the political scene. In 1864 he founded the International Working Men's Association and became the leader of the General Council of the Association, also called the First International. In his inaugural address he called for the working men of the world to unite, for in solidarity lies their only hope of becoming free from the oppression of capitalism. His intention was to combine in this organization the various forms of socialism that had emerged up to that time. The First International did not last very long, for it soon became involved in disputes chiefly concerned with the authority of the General Council. The "federalist" or "anarchist" faction was opposed to a "dictatorship" of the General Council, while the "centralists" like Marx favored a council with extensive powers so that it could lead the international workers' movement to victory. As its leader, Marx became a world-famous figure, but the First International did not survive its internal splits and expulsions.

During all this time of organizational and revolutionary activity, Marx continued his literary work at the British Museum. The first volume of his chief work, *Capital,* was published in 1867. The second and third volumes were published posthumously by Engels in 1885 and 1894. The strain of his practical activities on behalf of the First International, together with his research for and writing of *Capital,* took their toll on his health. Marx died on March 14, 1883, in London where he is also buried.

MATERIAL ASPECTS OF HUMAN HISTORY

Marx has been credited with giving the world "dialectical materialism," a theory of nature that separates nature from human history. Not only is Marx himself not responsible for the term "dialectical materialism," but the application of the so-called laws of "dialectical materialism" to human history is utterly foreign to Marx's thought. The concept of "dialectical materialism" arises from some of Engel's later writings, and the phrase itself was introduced by Georgi Plekhanov, a Russian Marxist (1856–1918).[2] The matrix of Marx's thought is a materialist concept of history, "historical materialism," which views nature and its transformations as belonging to human history.[3]

Marx, in the first part of *The German Ideology* entitled "Feuerbach," does not present an abstract theory of history but rather the drama of our historial existence. He writes:

> In direct contrast to German philosophy which descends from heaven to earth, here we ascend from earth to heaven .... We set out from real, active men, and on the basis of their real life-process we demonstrate the development of the ideological reflexes and echoes of this life-process. The phantoms formed in the human brain are also, necessarily, sublimates of their material life-process, which is empirically verifiable and bound to material premises. Morality, religion, metaphysics, all the rest of ideology and their corresponding forms of con-

[1]Marx, *Contribution to the Critique of Political Economy* as excerpted in *Reader in Marxist Philosophy: From the Writings of Marx, Engels, and Lenin,* selected and edited with introduction and notes by Howard Selsam and Harry Martel, p. 186.

[2]For a brief discussion of this matter, see Robert C. Tucker, *Philosophy and Myth in Karl Marx,* p. 23.
[3]The materialist theory of history is exclusively Marx's. Engels contributed nothing to it as a theory. On this point, see Tucker, *op. cit.,* p. 167 n.

sciousness, thus no longer retain the semblance of independence. They have no history, no development; but men, developing their material production and their material intercourse, alter, along with this their real existence, their thinking and the products of their thinking. Life is not determined by consciousness, but consciousness by life.[1]

Marx is opposing his own secular ideas to those of the Hegelians who had hoped that as a result of their critiques of the law, state, religion, and morality all abuses would automatically disappear from the world. But reality cannot be reformed by ideas. Marx wants to go the other way around and reform ideas through reality. His method is not without its premises.

> It starts out from the real premises and does not abandon them for a moment. Its premises are men, not in any fantastic isolation or abstract definition, but in their actual, empirically perceptible process of development under definite conditions. As soon as this active life-process is described, history ceases to be a collection of dead facts as it is with the empiricists (themselves still abstract), or an imagined activity of imagined subjects, as with the idealists.
>
> Where speculation ends—in real life—there real, positive science begins: the representation of the practical activity, of the practical process of development of men. Empty talk about consciousness ceases, and real knowledge has to take its place. When reality is depicted, philosophy as an independent branch of activity loses its medium of existence.[2]

History takes as its first and basic premise that people must be in a position to live to be able to "make history." Before everything else, life involves eating, drinking, housing, clothing, and many other things. Humans are physical beings living in relation to nature, and they have needs that they must satisfy just to exist. "The first historical act is thus the production of the means to satisfy these needs, the production of material life itself."[3] Unlike animals, humans actively trans-

form nature to produce their means of subsistence. This is what Marx means when he calls for the earthly or materialistic basis of history. Real history, the history that we human beings make in relationship to one another and to nature, has this material basis.

Marx's second basic premise is that as soon as the fundamental needs are satisfied, other needs arise that humans, with their newly acquired instruments, are equally able to satisfy. The first historical act thus has two moments: the creation of needs and their subsequent satisfaction. Because there is no limit to the needs we can generate and satisfy, we continually go beyond ourselves to become more and more human. We express ourselves in what we produce, and at the same time we develop ourselves further.

> As individuals express their life, so they are. What they are, therefore, coincides with their production, both with *what* they produce and with *how* they produce. The nature of individuals thus depends on the material conditions determining their production.[4]

Civilization develops, then, by the efforts of people to satisfy the needs they themselves create.

The third basic premise is that people not only produce their own lives from day to day, they also reproduce that life in their children. The process of begetting and rearing children, involving the cooperation of husband and wife, introduces the social factor into human history. Social relations soon pass beyond the merely reproductive one to productive functions and expand beyond the original familial relationship.

Marx's fourth and final basic premise is that this social expansion is entirely determined by our material needs and the state of our productive powers. Our social relations mark the extent to which our productive forces are developed. The opposite is also true, namely, that new social relations give rise to new forms of production. There is a mutuality between social life and production such that a change in one causes a change in the other.

---

[1]Marx and Engels, *The German Ideology: Parts I & III,* edited with an introduction by R. Pascal, pp. 14–15.
[2]*Ibid.,* p. 15.
[3]*Ibid.,* p. 16.

[4]*Ibid.,* p. 7.

ALIENATION RESULTING FROM DIVISION OF LABOR

Given the material aspects of human history, Marx is concerned to understand people as they are, as they find themselves engaged in this world making a living or at least trying to make a living. What does he find? People are alienated from their own personal selves, from one another, and from their own creative activity. What does he mean by alienation?

Alienation does not consist, as Hegel thought, of our estranging ourselves from ourselves in relating to physical nature, but in our estrangement from nature, in our inhuman relation to nature. This estrangement has three aspects: we are alienated from (1) the *products* we produce by our labor; (2) the very *act of producing;* and (3) our own *social nature.* In any society based on private property, and particularly in an industrialized capitalist society, the worker is merely an instrument in the process of producing material goods. As Marx puts it:

> The *alienation* of the worker in his product means not only that his labour becomes an object, assumes an *external* existence, but that it exists independently, *outside himself,* and alien to him, and that it stands opposed to him as an autonomous power. The life which he has given to the object sets itself against him as an alien and hostile force.[1]

Such labor enslaves rather than liberates the worker; it reduces the worker to an object.

> The worker becomes poorer the more wealth he produces and the more his production increases in power and extent. The worker becomes an ever cheaper commodity the more goods he creates. The *devaluation* of the human world increases in direct relation with the *increase in value* of the world of things. Labour does not only create goods; it also produces itself and the worker as a *commodity,* and indeed in the same proportion as it produces goods.[2]

We are natural beings, and nature provides us with our means of subsistence. The more the worker appropriates from nature, however, the less he or she receives from it.

> The needs of the worker are thus reduced to the need to maintain him *during work,* so that the race of workers does not die out. Consequently, wages have exactly the same significance as the *maintenance* of any other productive instrument, and as the *consumption of capital* in general so that it can reproduce itself with interest.[3]

To use anything more than is required to satisfy the worker's most immediate needs is to waste production capital. Political economy, in Marx's eyes, is the science of wealth, the science of renunciation; privation and saving, the science of asceticism. It actually succeeds in depriving us of fresh air and physical activity. Marx is most sarcastic in describing the ideal of this science:

> Its true ideal is the *ascetic* but *usurious* miser and the *ascetic* but *productive* slave. Its moral ideal is the *worker* who takes a part of his wages to the savings bank . . . . Its principal thesis is the renunciation of life and of human needs. The less you eat, drink, buy books, go to the theatre or to balls, or to the public house, and the less you think, love, theorize, sing, paint, fence, etc. the more you will be able to save and the *greater* will become your treasure which neither moth nor rust will corrupt— your *capital.* The less you *are,* the less you express your life, the more you *have,* the greater is your *alienated* life and the greater is the saving of your alienated being.[4]

The capitalist system alienates a person from the product made, but that first aspect of alienation is not the worst of it. This system estranges people even from their very activity of producing, and this is the second aspect of alienation. The work is external to the worker who is not fulfilled as a person in that work. The worker has to deny himself or herself, has a feeling of misery rather than well-being, and is physically exhausted and mentally debased. Instead of being the worker's self-creation or self-realization, work becomes self-negation.

The worker, therefore, feels himself at home only

---

[1]Bottomore, *op. cit.,* pp. 122–123.
[2]*Ibid.,* p. 121.
[3]*Ibid.,* p. 138.
[4]*Ibid.,* p. 171.

during his leisure time, whereas at work he feels homeless. His work is not voluntary but imposed, *forced labour*. It is not the satisfaction of a need, but only a *means* for satisfying other needs. Its alien character is clearly shown by the fact that as soon as there is no physical or other compulsion it is avoided like the plague. External labour, labour in which man alienates himself, is a labour of self-sacrifice, of mortification. Finally, the external character of work for the worker is shown by the fact that it is not his own work but work for someone else, that in work he does not belong to himself but to another person.[1]

The more a person works, the less human he or she becomes. The upshot of it all is that a person feels at home only in performing the mere animal functions of eating, drinking, and procreating. Labor has reduced the worker to animal status instead of liberating the worker's humanity.

The third aspect of alienation in a capitalist society is that we are estranged from our own social nature. The worker is estranged from his or her fellow human beings. As conscious beings, in our creative activity we go beyond satisfaction of our merely individual and physical needs.[2] Our consciousness, being peculiar to the human species, provides us with the perspective needed to see objects as useful or necessary in other than their immediate context. Consequently, we are capable of knowing and doing more than is needed for simple survival. The entire world is a possible object of our activity in art, science, and technology. The production of art, science, and technology is carried on with and for the whole human race. Any and all cultural production, no matter in what sphere, is a common enterprise, an enterprise whose product is to be shared by and with the whole human community. We, unlike the animals, produce as universal beings.

In a capitalist society, by contrast, the very labor by which we become universal and human is alienated from us and turned into animal-like labor. The productive impulse is deprived of its universal character and warped into a mere means

for satisfying individual physical needs. Human life is dehumanized, for in becoming fully determined by sheer physical necessity, the worker no longer molds the product to his or her own inspiration.[3]

To say that humans are alienated from their own human life means that each person precisely as human is alienated from all the others. In the alienated state, all people are strangers to me and competing with me as I seek to satisfy my own needs. "Thus in the relationship of alienated labour every man regards other men according to the standards and relationships in which he finds himself placed as a worker."[4]

In a capitalist society, division of labor means specialization, that is to say, the exploitation of the diversity of human talents for the sake of the production process. The work a laborer is employed to do is determined by the laborer's given physical or mental talents to produce something over which the worker has no claim. The capitalist uses the laborers according to their talents, but at the same time the laborer is made into just another means to satisfy the needs of the production process. Gradually, this division of labor deprives the workers of all human and social dignity, for social cooperation, essential for the production process, becomes inhuman as soon as the form of cooperation is determined by the product rather than by the workers. The product belongs not to the worker but to the owner of the materials and instruments of production. The original link between labor and product, between production and consumption, has been replaced by wages. Those who contribute the most to the production, the laborers, receive the least enjoyment from the product they produce. Division of labor, by depriving the laborer of the product of his or her work, alienates the laborer from his or her own activity. The laborers no longer freely determine their work for their own benefit.[5]

To state that *private property* is the basis of the

[1]*Ibid.*, p. 125.
[2]*Ibid.*, p. 126.

[3]*Ibid.*, p. 127.
[4]*Ibid.*, p. 129.
[5]Pascal, *op. cit.*, p. 22; Bottomore, *op. cit.*, p. 181.

division of labour and *exchange* is simply to assert that *labour* is the essence of private property; an assertion which the economist cannot prove and which we wish to prove for him. It is precisely in the fact that the *division of labour* and *exchange* are manifestations of private property that we find the proof, first that *human* life needed *private property* for its realization, and secondly, that it now requires the supersession of private property.

The *division of labour* and *exchange* are the two phenomena which lead the economist to vaunt the social character of his science, while in the same breath he unconsciously expresses the contradictory nature of his science—the establishment of society through unsocial, particular interests.[1]

Division of labor results from exchange. Marx quotes Adam Smith as admitting that exchange originates from motives of self-love.[2] No true society can ever be built on such a basis. Money, the means of exchange, takes the life out of all authentic human relations; it is a disruptive power for the individual and for social bonds, changing fidelity into infidelity, love into hate, hate into love, virtue into vice, vice into virtue, servant into master, stupidity into intelligence, and intelligence into stupidity. It is the confusion and transposition of all natural and human qualities. Money inverts the natural relationship between humans and the world; it secures the domination of the person by the object. People are reduced to what they can buy or sell. Their value is the value of their money; their power is their buying power.[3]

The capitalist system victimizes both the workers and the nonworkers, the holders of capital. Private property is an alienation of both their lives. The capitalist is the slave of his or her capital. The real god is the system itself. Capital is its own master; it alienates all people, not just the workers.

Marx's identification of human alienation with the alienation of labor as division of labor is new for him. His previous reflections had led him to regard private property as the cause of alienation, but now he sees that private property is the result of our alienation from our own labor.[4] He owes this new insight into the nature of alienation both to Hegel's *Phenomenology* and to the classical economists, Adam Smith and David Ricardo. With the help of these three men's works, Marx sees people alienated from their individual acts of self-realization as well as from the products of their acts. By declaring labor to be the ultimate economic value, Adam Smith interiorized the entire economic process. Property takes all its value from the amount of labor a person puts into it. Adam Smith sees the economic process as a human process that does away with wealth as something exterior to the person and makes property the person's own act of self-expression.[5]

The contradiction of the capitalist system is revealed in its making labor the subjective essence of all private property while leaving the worker without property. In such a system, based as it is on private property, the person is alienated from himself or herself, because the essence of labor is the person. The person has become simply an instrument to make things for others, not benefiting from the things made. The alienation is complete.

CLASS STRUGGLES

Since the class is the only real unit in an individualistic society and since the classes themselves stem from individualistic drives, the society will necessarily have class conflicts or struggles. One class will seek to dominate the others.[6]

Each class, struggling to dominate the other classes, must conquer for itself the political power it desires by gaining control of the state to represent its interests as the general interest of all. In actual fact, the general interest is nothing more than the special interest of the class that holds the political power. For this reason, every intervention of the state appears to the nonruling classes not as their own united power but as an alien force existing outside them[1] that enters their lives to manipulate them.

---

[1]Bottomore, *op. cit.,* p. 187.
[2]*Ibid.,* pp. 181–182.
[3]*Ibid.,* pp. 189–194.

[4]*Ibid.,* p. 131.
[5]*Ibid.,* pp. 147–148.
[6]Pascal, *op. cit.,* p. 23.

The state is an illusory community. Civil society itself is a group of classes stemming from the division of labor. The real interaction between individuals takes place in the economic sphere of life, not in the political. The politicians and military people may think they make history, but it is in civil society that the real struggles of history are fought.[2]

Summary: Division of labor leads to private property, which in turn creates social inequality, class struggles, and the formation of political structures. Marx now proceeds to illustrate this conclusion by an historical argument.

SO-CALLED STAGES OF HISTORY

Marx describes[3] each historical mode of production as a method of human productive self-expression conditioned by the nature of the available instruments of production. For example, modern industry is a mode of production conditioned by technology. Each historical mode of production has been accompanied by a particular form of intercourse or set of social relations of production. Each such form of intercourse is an expression of the division of labor in society, an expression of alienation. The form of intercourse is then a form of the relationship between non-owning producers and nonproducing owners of the materials and means of production. Changes in technology bring changes in the mode of production and with them changes in the concrete form of the division of labor in production. Marx sees the forms of property in the tribal, ancient, feudal, and bourgeois periods as different expressions of the division of labor determined by developments in the mode of production.

> It follows from this that a certain mode of production, or industrial stage, is always combined with a certain mode of co-operation, or social stage, and this mode of co-operation is itself a "productive

force." Further, that the multitude of productive forces accessible to men determines the nature of society, hence that the "history of humanity" must always be studied and treated in relation to the history of industry and exchange.[4]

NEW CONCEPT OF HISTORY

Marx's interpretation of history, of all his theories, is the one most widely misunderstood. He does not see history as proceeding in a predetermined course, a course determined only by economic factors. History as a whole, Marx does say, follows the course of human beings mastering the external environment to satisfy their needs, at first the basic needs of food and shelter and later broadening into all the cultural demands of civilization. Human beings make their own history and cannot but begin to do so in the economic sphere where they labor together to make their living and the wherewithal to create their civilization. This is a progressive process, but not a process driven by any natural necessity within the human beings. It is progressive, because people are continuously trying to improve their techniques of production and enrich their culture, seeking to overcome hunger, famine, deprivation, and discomfort. Nonhuman nature is wholly neutral in relation to human goals and desires except insofar as people themselves operate as living, conscious parts of nature.

The German idealists along with Hegel thought that human consciousness is the basic factor in the making of history. For Marx, the four basic factors—(1) the production of means of subsistence, (2) the creation of new needs, (3) the family as the basic unit of society, and (4) the division of labor extending beyond the family with the increase of production—shape the reality that makes history. Only on the basis of these factors or "moments" does consciousness enter into the process and, even then, not as a "pure" and independent factor. Consciousness is determined by language, and language arises out of social relations that are themselves dependent

---

[1]*Ibid.*, pp. 23–24.
[2]*Ibid.*, p. 26.
[3]*Ibid.*, pp. 43–78.

[4]*Ibid.*, p. 18.

on the material production. "The production of ideas, of conceptions, of consciousness, is at first directly interwoven with the material activity and the material intercourse of men, the language of real life."[1] "Consciousness is therefore from the very beginning a social product, and remains so as long as men exist at all."[2] Since social relations are determined by our relation to nature, consciousness is always consciousness of nature, conditioned by a definite development of our productive forces and of the social relations corresponding to these forces.

Consciousness also originates a relationship to oneself. This is the movement of reflection without which we would neither be aware that we are living in society at all nor be able to transform our passive relation to nature into an active one. By constituting this relationship to oneself, consciousness acquires a certain independence so that it can make a pretense at autonomy. This becomes apparent when society develops to the point when the division between physical (material) and mental labor appears.

> From this moment onwards consciousness *can* really flatter itself that it is something other than consciousness of existing practice, that it is *really* conceiving something without conceiving something *real;* from now on consciousness is in a position to emancipate itself from the world and to proceed to the formation of "pure" theory, theology, philosophy, ethics, etc. But even if this theory, theology, philosophy, ethics, etc. comes into contradiction with the existing relations, this can only occur as a result of the fact that existing social relations have come into contradiction with the existing forces of production . . . .[3]

The division between physical (material) and mental labor has cut consciousness off from the source of its life, the process of life production. The activity of intellectuals and speculative philosophers springs from this division, but no matter how much abstract speculation seems to rise above earthly concerns, it is still rooted in the material conditions of life. Speculation is nothing

more than the ideal expression of social relations underlying the rule of the dominating class. The class that gains control over the means of material production immediately inherits the means of "mental production" and begins to impose its own ideas on the whole society.

> The individuals composing the ruling class possess among other things consciousness, and therefore think. In so far, therefore, as they rule as a class and determine the extent and compass of an epoch, it is self-evident that they do this in their whole range, hence among other things rule also as thinkers, as producers of ideas, and regulate the production and distribution of the ideas of their age: thus their ideas are the ruling ideas of the epoch.[4]

Within the ruling class, the division of labor separates the thinkers from the active members, and this separation may lead to conflicts. Such collisions are harmless, because an ideology that endangers the dominance of the class automatically disappears. The ideas of the ruling class have no power distinct from the power of the class.[5] The error of historiographers and philosophers of history is that they abstract the ideas from the class in which the ideas originated and attribute an independent existence to the ideas. This gives the ideas of the ruling class a semblance of universality to make them palatable to the rest of society, presenting them as a universal and independent force that brought the class to power rather than the conceptual means to solidify their already acquired power.

The class concept provides us with an explanation of why the ideals of a new epoch are always more universal and abstract than those of the previous one. To rise to power, a class must rally round it all the other classes against the ruling class. This it can do successfully only by representing its own interests as the interests of the entire society. To appeal to more people, the ideological slogans had to become more universal.

> The class making a revolution appears . . . as the whole mass of society confronting the one ruling

---

[1]*Ibid.,* pp. 13–14.
[2]*Ibid.,* p. 19.
[3]*Ibid.,* p. 20.

[4]*Ibid.,* p. 39.
[5]*Ibid.,* p. 40.

class. It can do this because, to start with, its interest is really more connected with the common interest of all other nonruling classes, because under the pressure of conditions its interest has not yet been able to develop as the particular interest of a particular class. Its victory, therefore, benefits many individuals of the other classes which are not winning a dominant position, but only in so far as it now puts these individuals in a position to raise themselves into the ruling class. When the French bourgeoisie overthrew the power of the aristocracy, it thereby made it possible for many proletarians to raise themselves above the proletariat, but only in so far as they became bourgeois.[1]

As soon as society ceases to be organized in the form of class-rule, history will be written in terms of social realities instead of ideological abstractions. Class-rule will come to a natural end when the power is seized by the proletariat, the class that represents the interests of human beings precisely *as human* rather than of a particular class. History will be seen as the interaction between the production process and the social relations determined by this process. This, for Marx, is the only true historiography.[2]

This new concept of history implies a new concept of what it means to be a human being. To see history as the development toward self-consciousness as Hegel and his followers did is to view the human being as a purely mental being. Marx's human is a concrete reality who makes history by consciously interacting with productive forces and social patterns.

THE COMMUNIST REVOLUTION

In the final section of part one of the *Ideology,* Marx gives us his clearest and most complete analysis of the Communist revolution and its effects on society. The historical epoch of big industry shows the contradiction between the instruments of production and private property. Big industry itself produces the contradiction when it is highly developed. Only with big industry does the abolition of private property become possible.

> In big industry and competition the whole mass of conditions of existence, limitations, biases of individuals, are fused together into the two simplest forms: private property and labour. With money every form of intercourse, and intercourse itself, is considered fortuitous for the individuals. Thus money implies that all previous intercourse was only intercourse of individuals under particular conditions, not of individuals as individuals. These conditions are reduced to two: accumulated labour or private property, and actual labour.[3]

Big industry requires an accumulation of labor that, in turn, being private property, leads to an extreme division of labor. These factors cause an opposition between the instruments of labor and labor itself.

> The division of labour implies from the outset the division of the *conditions of labour,* of tools and materials, and thus the splitting up of accumulated capital among different owners, and thus, also, the division between capital and labour, and the different forms of property itself. The more the division of labour develops and accumulation grows, the sharper are the forms that this process of differentiation assumes. Labour itself can only exist on the premise of this fragmentation.[4]

The Dialectic

The opposition between capital and labor becomes an opposition within labor itself, because capital, like all private property, is nothing but accumulated labor. The opposition is between accumulated labor and actual labor. The productive forces (accumulated labor) become independent of the producing individuals (actual labor). This leads eventually to a fundamental opposition between productive forces and production relations.

Production relations are the social conditions, the forms of intercourse, under which the process of production is conducted. We have already seen that each way or mode of production has

---

[1]*Ibid.,* p. 41.
[2]*Ibid.,* p. 28.
[3]*Ibid.,* p. 64.
[4]*Ibid.,* p. 65.

its corresponding social structure. People are always looking for new methods of production, but the social relations do not keep pace with the new modes of production. From the lag or gap that develops between the two, an opposition arises between them. The social relations are no longer considered essential by the producing individuals, because now as they lag behind they hinder rather than further the production process from which they originated.

> These various conditions, which appear first as conditions of self-activity, later as fetters upon it, form in the whole evolution of history a coherent series of forms of intercourse, the coherence of which consists in this: that in the place of an earlier form of intercourse, which has become a fetter, a new one is put, corresponding to the more developed productive forces and, hence, to the advanced mode of the self-activity of individuals—a form which in its turn becomes a fetter and is then replaced by another. Since these conditions correspond at every stage to the simultaneous development of the productive forces, their history is at the same time the history of the evolving productive forces taken over by each new generation, and is therefore the history of the development of the forces of the individuals themselves.[1]

Since the evolution of social relations (forms of intercourse) is very slow and since they are maintained by a self-created political organism, the power of outmoded forms of intercourse can be broken only by a revolution. All revolutions in history have their origin in the contradiction between the productive forces and the forms of intercourse.[2] Up to the time of Marx, the mid-nineteenth century, revolutions merely readjusted the existing forms of intercourse to the state of the productive forces without making any adjustments in the basic relationship between productive forces and the producing individuals. This is no longer possible. The extreme division of labor has transformed the forces of production into independent material powers threatening the very existence of producing individuals. The present form of production is inhuman. The forms

of intercourse cannot be adapted to it. Neither can people just ignore it and put the production process on an entirely new basis, because the division of labor has made people so dependent on one another that they cannot survive without the complex machinery of the present production process. If the existing production powers were abolished, a similar complex system would immediately arise to take its place.

Inevitability of Revolution

The division of labor has put working people at the mercy of impersonal productive forces. Gradually the workers have become alienated from the very powers through which they were to create or develop themselves. In Marx's own words:

> ... we have a totality of productive forces, which have, as it were, taken on a material form and are for the individuals no longer the forces of the individuals but of private property, and hence of the individuals only in so far as they are owners of private property themselves. Never, in any earlier period, have the productive forces taken on a form so indifferent to the intercourse of individuals *as* individuals, because their intercourse itself was formerly a restricted one. On the other hand, standing over against these productive forces, we have the majority of the individuals from whom these forces have been wrested away, and who, robbed thus of all real life-content, have become abstract individuals, but who are, however, only by this fact put into a position to enter into relation with one another *as individuals*.[3]

As things are now, the productive forces fail to provide the majority of people with even a material subsistence, so the reappropriation of the forces of production by the people is no longer a matter only of achieving self-activity but also one of safeguarding their very existence.[4] Communism is thus a necessary and inevitable result of the present economic conditions.

All previous revolutions were restricted because, though caused by an opposition between productive forces and production relations, the

---

[1]*Ibid.*, pp. 71–72.
[2]*Ibid.*, p. 73.

[3]*Ibid.*, pp. 65–66.
[4]*Ibid.*, p. 66.

opposition was solved by the most important class in the production process bringing the existing social relations into proportion with the class's own importance. The advantages gained by the revolution were limited to this one class. This aggravated the division of labor and worsened the situation for all the other classes, because the one class acquired full control over that part of the productive forces that it directed. The one class accumulated more capital and thus worsened the division of labor.

The Communist revolution will be completely different, for it will do away with the division of labor and so bring to an end the inhuman opposition between actual labor and accumulated labor (private property). The proletarian revolution reappropriates all production powers to the whole society. This revolution will be accomplished in the present, for only now have the productive forces developed to their totality and only now has social intercourse become universal. The proletariat will carry out the revolution, because it is universal, not a particular class. The proletariat forms the majority of all members of society and epitomizes the total dehumanization of people. It is not merely national; it is international, for all people in distress are really partners, brothers and sisters, in distress.[1]

While the revolution of the proletariat is inevitable, it will not be accomplished by an economic process alone. A Communist consciousness must also be developed, which means that each proletarian must become conscious of his or her intolerable situation, which only complete revolution can remedy. This means that the proletarians must unite into a community based on the reality of the situation but knowing also that only in a community with others does each individual have the means of cultivating his or her gifts in all directions. This also means that only in community is personal freedom possible. This community of individuals knows it is dependent on economic conditions that affect the entire society. They, as individuals united, must found society anew by creating the forms of social

intercourse that are adequate to the community's control of the forces of production.[2] Communism is then not a stable state of affairs to be established any more than it is an ideal to which reality must adjust. It is the real movement that, through practical action, abolishes the present state of affairs,[3] and requires not only practical action but conscious reflection on what has been achieved so as to move on to do what can yet be achieved. The practical revolution requires an intellectual revolution too, for otherwise the result will be not progress but decline and disintegration.[4]

The Results

The success of the revolution requires the alteration of people on a mass scale, something only a revolution can accomplish. While Marx did not try to predict what the newly altered people would be like, he did describe the economic conditions under which people would live as a result of the inevitable revolution: (1) the limited social relations (forms of intercourse) determined by the *division of labor* will become an unlimited intercourse of *persons;* (2) labor will become self-activity (self-expression, self-realization); and (3) private property (accumulated labor) will be abolished.

The first result will make truly *personal* life possible for all by abolishing division of labor. People have been alienated from one another and from their true social life by the division of labor. The revolution overcomes the opposition between personal life and class life. The proletariat must abolish the very conditions of their present existence to preserve personal life, to live together in an interpersonal community. To restore the production powers to the community is to make such an interpersonal community possible.

With the reappropriation of the production powers, the work will become self-activity (second result), the free self-development of the

---

[1]*Ibid.,* pp. 66–69.

[2]*Ibid.,* pp. 69 and 74.
[3]*Ibid.,* p. 26.
[4]*Ibid.,* p. 69; see also John Lewis, *The Marxism of Marx,* pp. 198–211 but especially p. 210.

members of the community. The distribution of tasks will no longer be determined by impersonal productive forces but by the community members cultivating their own talents as they see fit.[1] Work becomes a creative act of the person instead of a self-alienating act of enslavement to inhuman powers.

Freedom and society will no longer be opposed to one another. Under Communism each individual will become free to develop as a person in relation to all other persons. To assert themselves as individual persons, the proletariat must overthrow the state,[2] which is based on class and division of labor.

The abolition of private property, the third result of the revolution, is hardly mentioned by Marx, since it is a natural consequence of the community's appropriating to itself all the productive forces. The creation of the proper social structures does away with the need for private property.

CONCLUSION

With *The German Ideology,* Marx ends the period of his strictly philosophical activity, begun in the *Economic and Philosophical Manuscripts.* He has tried to answer the following questions:

1. What determines the historical evolution of human beings?
2. What exactly is the relation between consciousness and nature?
3. What socioeconomic factors bring about alienation?

The philosophy of history stated in *The German Ideology* is Marx's answer to the question about human historical evolution. His socioeconomic theory on the division of labor (in both works) shows how alienation comes about.

The relation between consciousness and nature has been clarified, but it has also raised more questions for some students of Marx. Clearly, the products of consciousness have no independent value for Marx, because they are all conditioned by the development of the material production forces and the corresponding modes of social intercourse. Marx never discusses the nature or origin of consciousness itself. He developed his theory of historical materialism in opposition to both mechanistic materialism (all that exists is matter) and idealism (all that exists is thought or idea). Mental production (ideas) is conditioned by our socioeconomic relations, but this is not at all the same as saying that mental production is a kind of material production. The human being exists in relation to nature, but nature itself also exists in relation to human beings. The relationship is one of mutual conditioning. The same must be said for the relationship between consciousness and physical nature.

Our socioeconomic activity is at the basis of all our values, theoretical as well as practical. The process of production in any era together with its concomitant social relations determine the era's leading ideas, its moral and legal standards as well as its aesthetic creations. We look to philosophy and other speculative sciences in vain when we seek to understand our culture. We gain far more understanding of it from a historical study of our socioeconomic conditions, for here we find the roots and causes of all that we think, admire, hope for, and freely strive for.

Marx's historical materialism is a theory of action, based in human action, and returning, after reflection, to further action. It both expresses and participates in the active relationship between consciousness and nature, the relationship that constitutes human reality. Marx never intended his historical materialism to be a mere theory. It is exclusively based on and directed toward action.

The question of whether the ideas and the results of the early writings of Marx were abandoned by him later in his career is important. The answer appears to be that there is no fundamental break between the early and later writings of Marx.[3] Marx's work is all of a piece; its whole structure is built around social labor: (1)

---

[1]Pascal, *op. cit.,* p. 22.
[2]*Ibid.,* p. 78.

[3]See, on this point, Robert Tucker, *op. cit.,* and Louis Dupré, *The Philosophical Foundations of Marxism,* pp. 172–173.

producing the human being and the human world, (2) proceeding by exploitation and creating alienation, and (3) transcending class society to reappropriate the forces of production, overcome alienation, and achieve true social labor and fully developed human beings. To eliminate these three basic concepts from Marxist theory would be to reform it by abolishing it.

ASSESSMENT OF MARX'S MARXISM

For Marx, Communism is not a revolution against injustice and inequality, but a revolution that does away with the social relation between wage-labor and capital, between actual labor and accumulated labor. The revolution does away with both the material basis of domination of people by other people and the domination of all people by things. The productive force of all the people ceases to be a force that is alien and external to them and becomes subject to their own control. Production becomes self-activity, self-realization, and no longer the means to accumulate capital. The revolution is a radical transformation, for the means of production become what they should have been all along, namely, the multiplied power of associated, interdependent individuals fully emancipated to create themselves in and through their social labor and social relationships. A true Communist revolution would be a revolution of freedom.

"The philosophers," says Marx, "have only *interpreted* the world in various ways; the point, however, is to *change* it."[1] Marx's Marxism is not simply a theory about society but also a *method* of investigating society and its historical sequence of forms of order (forms of social intercourse). A method vindicates itself only in being successfully applied, in actually changing the world. Marx should be judged on the merits of his own case and not exclusively by what others have done. Certainly, the capitalist economic system is not

without its faults and failures. Even with government control and assistance, capitalism has failed to secure the satisfaction of all the human needs made possible by the immense resources presently available and the potentialities of industry to use those resources. This is the source of the great contradictions of modern capitalism.

Marx neither guarantees the success of the revolution nor does he take it for granted. Revolutionary consciousness is the *sine qua non* of social development. Without the intelligence and will of people to understand, appropriate, and implement ideas, no social transformation and certainly no social revolution will take place. Marx gives us no general formula for revolution; he provides no strategy or tactics. His advice is to look to the logic of the situation, find the contradictions, discover the structures of society where change is taking place, recognize the paradoxes and possibilities—and then make a move intelligently and with comprehension to bring about the good for all the people.

Marx's *dialectical method* successfully avoids both mechanistic materialism and idealism. By maintaining the human being's dialectical opposition to nature, Marx is able to avoid any completely deterministic interpretation of human nature. The dialectic is discovered empirically in the real relation between the human being and nature; it is a reality. The dialectical principle has an essentially ideal character, but this ideal character does not exist prior to or apart from reality. It is an aspect of human reality as humans exist in the world, and it is discovered through empirical analysis. This ideal character of the dialectical principle is what gives it its quality of necessity.

The human being is the unifier of the dialectical terms in that the human being is a part of nature from the very beginning of his or her existence and nature becomes humanized as soon as the human being begins to exist in the world. Humans, being both conscious and physical, unite consciousness with nature through their activity. Human activity, praxis, is the prereflective unity of nature and consciousness, the living unity of understanding an actual situation while we are

---

[1]Marx, "Theses on Feuerbach." In Marx and Engels, *Basic Writings on Politics and Philosophy,* ed. by Lewis S. Feuer, thesis XI, p. 245.

grappling with it. Praxis can be explicated in thought, but it cannot be initiated by thought. Being the living unity of nature and consciousness, human activity produces both a real freedom and a free reality. The dialectic is the conscious explication of the relationship between human consciousness and nature in such a way that neither is prior to the other. The practical dialectic of human activity provides the basis for the theoretical consciousness of the dialectic. In human activity, praxis, Marx's dialectical theory finds its final justification.

The dialectical method of Marx was discovered *in* history through careful analysis. Some interpreters of Marx have attempted to *impose* the dialectic *on* history and, in so doing, severed the principle from actual human activity where the principle alone holds true. The principle is thus made into a purely speculative principle, something Marx never intended, and of course this is self-contradictory because the dialectical principle states that no ideal value can be constituted independently of the human being's actual relation to nature.

Marx insisted that there is no idea, no theory, that is independent of our practical relation to nature. Many Marxists want to conclude from this that human activity itself contains no ideal element. This conclusion certainly cannot be justified on the basis of Marx's own writings. For Marx, the element of consciousness in human activity cannot be reduced to nature. Nevertheless, Marx himself must bear some of the responsibility for the inconsistencies into which some of his interpreters have fallen. At times he defines praxis (human activity) so exclusively in terms of a material life process that he seriously jeopardizes consciousness' ability to go beyond nature.

Marx never gives human praxis the careful analysis it deserves. He grossly oversimplifies praxis by identifying it with the fulfillment of physical needs. This is ultimately responsible for his disciples' later development toward mechanistic materialism. Marx himself was never a materialist in this sense, but his overemphasis on the economic interpretation of human praxis leads in this direction.

Marx rejected the absolute character of economic laws, and yet he accepts socioeconomic determinism, which leaves very little room for human freedom. His philosophy has no place for goals other than those prescribed by socioeconomic necessities. Human freedom is an essential part of Marx's thought, but he makes no attempt to reconcile it with the equally necessary socioeconomic determinism. The result is a permanent conflict in his philosophy between an authentically pragmatic humanism and an almost completely materialistic economism. After Marx's death, the economism trend began to predominate in the Marxist movement to the detriment of human freedom.

A final comment should be made on the social aspect of human existence, an essential part of Marx's philosophy. The humanization of nature and the self-creation of the human being is essentially a social task. By restricting the basic human activity to a satisfaction of physical needs, Marx has reduced its social character to cooperation for obtaining individuals' goals. Without economic cooperation, humans could not survive and develop; but to make human cooperation truly social, Marx should have described human praxis in terms of social as well as physical needs. The economistic limitations have converted Marx's humanism and profound theory of action into a system of oversimplifications that, in the hands of some of his followers, have led to terror and an almost complete disregard for human dignity.

SUMMARY

Marx developed three basic doctrines: (1) the nature of human beings and their alienation; (2) the making of history by people who at the same time are developing themselves; and (3) the conscious participation of humans in the transformation of society.

1. Human beings and their alienation

a. The human being is both a *conscious* (spiritual) and a *natural* (material) being and, as both conscious and natural, is a unique part of the natural world.

b. The *dialectical relationship* between humans and the natural world is mutual (reciprocal) in that humans shape the material world to their conscious purposes and are in turn shaped by the material world.

c. The *need to survive* is what initially causes human beings to engage in labor to satisfy those needs and, in so doing, to develop themselves.

d. Human beings also create further conscious needs and desires, and they unite with one another to satisfy those further needs and desires. This leads to the development of *culture and civilization*.

e. As conscious natural beings, humans are by their very nature *social*. They live and work together. Their consciousness is social from the very beginning of their existence just as their material being is social.

f. In a society based on private property, people are *alienated* (estranged) from nature. The alienation (our *inhuman* relation to nature) has three aspects: we are alienated from (1) the *products* we produce; (2) the very *act* of producing; and (3) our own *social nature*.

g. The capitalistic economic expression of the social character of labor within alienation is *division of labor* (specialization).

h. Labor is the essence of *private property,* the basis of division of labor and exchange.

i. The *contradiction* of the capitalist system is revealed in making labor the subjective essence of private property while leaving the worker without property.

j. Alienation can be overcome only by a *proletarian* (the uneducated, propertyless people) revolution that does away with private property and so is sufficient to abolish alienation within labor.

2. The social inequality created by the division of labor leads to the formation of *classes* in society, with the economically dominant class seeking to hold the political power in its hands to pursue its own interests. This leads to the *class struggle*.

a. In every *stage of history,* the mode of production is conditioned by the instruments available for production. Each mode of production has been accompanied by a particular form of intercourse or set of social relations.

b. The four basic factors in making history are: (1) the production of means of subsistence, (2) the creation of new needs, (3) the family as the basic unit of society, and (4) the division of labor extending beyond the family with the increase of production. Consciousness is also a factor, but only on the basis of the above four aspects.

c. *Human beings make history* and at the same time develop themselves by the interaction of productive forces and social patterns.

3. The Communist revolution arises from the *dialectic* of accumulated labor (private property) and actual labor (the producing individuals) in the capitalist system.

a. This dialectic leads to a fundamental *opposition* between productive forces and production relations (the social conditions or forms of intercourse).

b. The *power* of outmoded forms of intercourse (that is, those inadequate to the current mode of production) can be broken only by total revolution.

c. Revolution is *inevitable* because the proletariat cannot continue their inhuman existence created by capitalism's extreme division of labor.

d. The revolution will not be accomplished by an economic process alone (abolition of private property) but the proletariat *must become conscious* of their situation and see clearly that complete revolution is the only remedy for their situation.

e. The results of the revolution will be: (1) the limited social relations (forms of intercourse) determined by the *division of labor* will become an unlimited intercourse of *persons,* (2) labor will become *self-activity* (self-expression, self-realization), and (3) *private property* (accumulated labor) will be abolished. The means of production will be transformed into the multiplied power of associated, interdependent individuals fully free to create themselves in and through their social labor and social relationships.

Assessment of Marx's philosophy:

1. The *dialectical method* successfully avoids mechanistic materialism and idealism by begin-

ning from and staying rooted in human activity, praxis, the prereflective unity of nature *and* consciousness.

2. Interpreters and followers of Marx who have attempted to *impose* the dialectic on history sever the dialectical principle from actual human activity where the principle alone holds true.

3. Marx, at times, defines praxis so exclusively in terms of *a material life process* that he jeopardizes consciousness' ability to go beyond na-

ture. This has led some Marxists to deny any ideal element in human activity.

4. Because Marx never gave human praxis the careful analysis it deserves, he must be held ultimately responsible for the movement of his later disciples toward *mechanistic* materialism.

5. In his own philosophy, Marx never reconciled *human freedom* and *socioeconomic determinism*.

6. Marx should have described human praxis in terms of *social* as well as physical *needs*.

Questions for Discussion

1. Why bother with a discussion of Marx's philosophy in a course on ethics? Marx himself said that philosophy divorced from practical action is nothing but empty abstractions. Philosophers have interpreted the world, but they have not succeeded in changing it. Marx wants to *change* the world. What do you think of his goals for the world?

2. What do you think of Marx's historical materialism and his description of the material aspects of human history? Is Marx being true to human experience? What do you find in your own experience of the world and its history?

3. Does Marx's dialectical method have any validity and usefulness for us today? Could you use his method to analyze your own set of socioeconomic circumstances? Suppose you lived in an economically underdeveloped area

such as in Asia or Africa. Would Marx's method have any interest for you? Why?

4. Is alienation from nature still a problem for us today? Do you experience alienation in the terms in which Marx described it? In the social and political context of society, do we find any profound contradictions that reflect a person's estrangement from other people, from himself or herself, and from the values and institutions of society?

5. Marx was no defender of the *status quo*. Is the tenacity with which capitalist principles are maintained in the face of criticism and new ways of thinking related to "class interests" threatened by radical change? What vested interests does capitalism have to protect? Does communism have any to protect?

Readings

G.W.F. Hegel's dialectical process is described in his *Phenomenology of Mind*. There is an excellent exposition of it in Sidney Hook, *From Hegel to Marx*. Ludwig Feuerbach, *Essence of Christianity,* is readily available.

For general background on Marx, see Isaiah Berlin, *Karl Marx: His Life and Environment,* ed. 3.

Read Karl Marx and Friedrich Engels, *The Communist Manifesto,* in the light of the *Economic and Philosophical Manuscripts* and *The German Ideology*. It is a historical document of utmost significance in which Marx applies his historical materialism as both an interpretation of history and a theory of action. In *Karl Marx: Early Writings,* translated and edited by T.B. Bottomore, we find "On the Jewish Question," "Contribution to the Critique of Hegel's Phi-

losophy of Right. Introduction," and the *Economic and Philosophical Manuscripts. The German Ideology,* Parts I and III, is translated by R. Pascal. Marx's great work, *Capital,* should be looked at and the first few chapters read. Adoratsky (ed.), *Selected Works of Marx and Engels,* Emile Burns (ed.), *Handbook of Marxism,* and Howard Selsam and Harry Martel (eds.), *Reader in Marxist Philosophy: From the Writings of Marx, Engels, and Lenin,* contain what Marxists consider the most important works and documents. V.I. Lenin, *Materialism and Empirio-Criticism,* is his most theoretical work. Josef Stalin, *Dialectical and Historical Materialism,* is a short and readable exposition that was once authoritative. Mao Tse-tung's works are interesting, especially in the light of China's further development. Frederic L. Bender (ed.), *The Betrayal of Marx,* in his introduction to this book of selections from Marx's followers argues that one main obstacle to a clear understanding of Marx is the failure to distinguish the views of Marx from those who followed him and were inspired by his views.

Herbert Marcuse wrote a scholarly study, *Reason and Revolution: Hegel and the Rise of Social Theory,* before becoming the philosophical prophet of the New Left in *One Dimensional Man* and *An Essay on Liberation.*

Robert C. Tucker, *Philosophy and Myth in Karl Marx,* is an excellent study as is Louis Dupré, *The Philosophical Foundations of Marxism,* which follows Marx's philosophical development from his earliest writings through *The Communist Manifesto.* John Somerville, *The Philosophy of Marxism: An Exposition,* G.D.H. Cole, *Meaning of Marxism,* and John Lewis, *The Marxism of Marx,* represent the Marxist view. Peter T. Manicas, *The Death of the State,* has some interesting discussion of the democratic state, the liberal moral ideal, and the democratic community in the light of Marx's criticism of capitalism in his early writings. Charles McFadden, *Philosophy of Communism;* R.N. Carew Hunt, *Theory and Practice of Communism;* H.B. Mayo, *Democracy and Marxism;* Gustav A. Wetter, *Dialectical Materialism;* and William Barrett, *The Illusion of Technique,* ch. 16, are critical.

On the ethical impulse of Marx's work, see Eugene Kamenka, *Marxism and Ethics.*

On the other particular points, there are Benedetto Croce, *Historical Materialism and the Economics of Karl Marx,* and Nicholas Berdyaev, *Origin of Russian Communism.*

Edmund Wilson's *To the Finland Station* is a fascinating description of the development of Marxism.

33
Earth

PROBLEM

Both capitalistic and communistic economics, and indeed any other economic system one might imagine, suppose that there will be goods of the earth that can be managed, developed, and distributed. The resources and productivity of the earth have been taken for granted and used as if they were inexhaustible. Now we are shocked to find that some resources are nearly depleted and that nature's capacity for renewal is inadequate to cope with our capacity to pollute. We used to picture ourselves as small beings pitted against the vast forces of nature. Now we see the possibility of too many people swarming over a globe that can support only a limited number. *Ecology* has come to the fore as the science of the relation of living organisms to their environment. The place of humans in the general ecology of nature is being increasingly recognized. Not only can we upset the natural interdependence of animals and plants in a region by our interference, but we are as thoroughly dependent for survival on the environment as any other living being. We humans are an integral part of nature. We are beginning to see that unless a halt is called soon to our improvident exploitation of nature, we shall destroy ourselves by the excess of our own cleverness.

In such a wide-ranging subject, we shall have to restrict ourselves to the ethical issues involved. There is one ethical issue that we find running through most of the writings on this subject, that of intellectual honesty. The writers tend to become carried away by their emotional commitment to either one or the other side of the question, and to write in a strong vein of propaganda, so that it is difficult to derive from their statements a cool, objective, balanced, and honest appraisal of the question.

One school is that of the prophets of gloom, very vocal and strident, proclaiming that we have already destroyed ourselves, that we have carried the pollution of nature beyond the point of no return, that we have nothing to face but disease and starvation because of our foolish wasting of nature's goods, that the world is already much

overpopulated, and that doomsday awaits us in the near future unless we curtail our numbers. The opposite school cavalierly dismisses the problem, as if the resources of the earth were inexhaustible, as if the solution to the world's poverty were just around the corner, as if the cleaning up of our pollution were an easy and inexpensive task, and as if the earth could support an infinite number of people. In gathering the facts we shall have to go on the assumption that the truth probably lies somewhere between these extremes, and on that basis try to form a moral judgment. Here the chief enemies are apathy and hysteria.

There are several important ethical issues:
1. Exploitation: are we naturally and inevitably exploiters?
2. Resources: have we a moral obligation toward future generations?
3. Pollution: how much pollution of the environment is ethically tolerable?
4. Poverty: have rich nations a duty to help poor nations in their basic economic needs?
5. Population: are there ethical ways of controlling population growth?

EXPLOITATION

Some ecologists distinguish two attitudes toward nature. One is living in harmony with nature, adapting our lives to nature's cycle, integrating our activities into nature's rhythm, finding our equal place with all other natural objects, and subordinating ourselves as parts in the whole order of nature. The other attitude is to concentrate on our uniqueness, to celebrate our rationality as the only thinking beings in the world, to consider the other things in nature as objects to be used as means toward our own goals, and to exploit and dominate nature. Some connect the first attitude with primitive people, with a general pantheistic outlook, and with the contemplative character of Eastern thought, whereas they connect the second attitude with sophisticated society, with the activism of the West, and with the Judeo-Christian theism of a personal God. In particular they refer to the biblical command, "Be fertile and multiply; fill the earth and subdue it. Have dominion over the fish of the sea, the birds of the air, and all the living things that move on the earth."[1] Thus, they say, we have found divine approval for our reckless exploitation of the earth. Others answer that the passage must be taken in context, that the first person was put into the Garden of Eden to till it and keep it, and that our function is one of stewardship, of responsible management of things entrusted to us, for which we shall have to give an account to our Creator. Scripture is quoted here by both sides, not as an argument, but as representing the attitudes of two cultures, the one supposed to be gentle and natural, the other hostile and domineering.

It does not seem that we can draw a hard-and-fast line between these two attitudes: of submitting oneself to nature or of submitting nature to oneself. We do a bit of both, which is not contradictory, for we do it in different ways. Every living thing uses the environment for its own support, consuming other beings for food and thus subordinating them to itself. We do so more than any other beings and are more ingenious in manipulating nature to serve us, but there are limits beyond which nature cannot be bent, and in observing those limits we submit ourselves to nature's own structure. The practical result of ecology as a science is to define those limits and to keep human manipulation of nature within its proper bounds.

Rather than blame our exploitation of nature on the Judeo-Christian outlook, let us rather carry it back to the first major human interferences with nature: domestication of animals and development of agriculture. Here we freed ourselves from the food supply nature haphazardly offered by developing new strains of animals and plants whose whole purpose is to serve our needs. This legitimate use of human ingenuity is in accordance with our intelligent nature, which is capable of foresight, planning, and creativity. It is true that nature can get along without us, as it did for millions of years, but it is a mistake to think of ourselves simply as intruders into nature,

as if we were not continuous with our evolutionary forebears and as if there were something unnatural about a being that thinks and reasons. Humans also have a tendency toward greed, toward overdoing adaptation of nature, toward exhausting nature's fertility by stimulating it to overproduction. The remedy for our own greed we can find in reason, when we see that we have upset nature's balance too far and must pull back to more reasonable limits the demands we make on nature. Here is where the voice of ethics speaks. It must condemn greed, avarice, and cupidity as the excessive and unreasonable indulgence of human desires. Just where the desires become excessive must be judged by other criteria: by the quantity of nature's available stock, by the fairness of the distribution methods, and by the ease with which the goods can be replenished. Here ethics comes to ecology and allied sciences for a factual judgment. Thus ecology and ethics work hand in hand. The one determines when our use of nature is fair and proper, as well as when it is exploitative and destructive; the other insists on our obligation to use nature fairly and properly, with an eye to both present and future generations.

RESOURCES

Only the ethics of selfishness could say that we have no responsibility for future generations. If justice requires a fair distribution of nature's goods among people now living and love for one's neighbors requires a concern for their welfare, there is no reason that this justice and love should include all those living in various parts of space but exclude those living at different ages of time. It is true that only those who are existing are able to receive our benefit, but we should not make life intolerable for those whom we intend to bring into existence on this earth. A future generation does not yet exist to be the subject of a right, but the present generation does exist as the subject of duty. When we exercise the right of procreation, we undertake the accompanying duty of supplying our offspring with the conditions for a proper human life. As parents have

---

[1]Gen. 1:28.

such an obligation toward their future children, so in a wider sense the present generation of all humanity has such an obligation to future generations.

How far into the future? We have no notion of what life will be like a thousand years from now and are incapable of providing for it. With such problems we tend to use the phrase "foreseeable future." It is vague enough to fit almost anyone's interpretation and useless for providing any precise calculations; yet we may ask whether greater precision is possible or desirable. We can calculate, for example, the oil reserves in the earth, with their present rate of depletion, and can thus come to some fair idea of how much will be left for the next generation or two, and of when humans can no longer depend on this source of energy. It was thus that we calculated timber sources and after the reckless deforestation of the previous century have come to some measures of conservation and reforestation. In this matter of looking into the future, there seems to be a moderate position between saying that we cannot predict the future and therefore can do nothing about it, and trying to lay down a detailed blueprint for the future that the future is not going to follow. The future will have surprises and will solve some of our present problems in ways we cannot now imagine, besides bringing up new problems beyond our wildest imaginings. Some things are certain, and some conjectures have too much validity to be easily dismissed. We cannot continue to abuse certain aspects of nature in the way we are doing and command nature to come up with a remedy for our own folly.

Should we not let future generations solve their own problems? We had to solve ours. Why not let the next generation do as we had to do? But this is what is in question: was it moral of the last generation to have handed its unsolved problems on to us? No one can require that they solve insoluble problems, nor can that be expected of us. But was it moral for them to have refused to solve what they could have solved? Will it be moral for us to let the future generation do our job for us? Where we clearly see a trend in our

behavior now that will almost surely lead to disaster for future generations, are not we the ones who must desist from that behavior? Would it be according to the virtue of prudence to continue as we are doing and expect some unforeseen discovery to come to our assistance? Occasionally a stroke of good fortune rescues us from our stupidity, but to bank on such a rescue is stupidity squared.

It seems, then, that we do have the moral obligation of providing for future generations, of so using the resources of the earth as not to deprive our descendants of their use, and of acting as stewards or good managers of what has been put in our keeping. If we have not yet worked out the details of what we ought to do, we have the moral obligation of putting our effort into that work, of using the best scientific information available, and of alerting humanity in general to the problems that face us.

POLLUTION

How much pollution can nature tolerate? In a sense nature pollutes itself. Volcanoes spew ash and gases into the atmosphere, dust and sand storms blow over the world's deserts, lakes have a lifetime and then gradually silt up, the seas are the dumping ground for all nature's refuse. Nature maintains an equilibrium for a very long while, but that pattern of equilibrium breaks up and is succeeded by another pattern. Without any human interference, the fauna and flora of many an age passed away because nature itself made conditions of life impossible for them. Because such changes occurred so slowly, we do not call them pollution, and yet the essence of it is there: the environment is rendered unsuitable for the survival of some formerly thriving species of living things. Nature dirties itself and does not have to wait for us to do the job, but we reserve the words *dirt* and *pollution* for what we do to nature, because we can change nature so quickly and drastically, and because we are capable of controlling and avoiding our own action.

We cannot prevent the natural pollution that occurs within nature's own structure, nor can we stop the minimum pollution that follows from the very fact of keeping ourselves alive. There is no moral issue here. What does involve a moral issue is the voluntary indulgence in excess, the production of refuse that nature cannot recycle and that results in constantly growing piles of useless, indestructible, and even dangerous material.

The pollution of the air by smog resulting chiefly from the automobile; the pollution of the rivers by the dumping of raw sewage and industrial wastes; the near-death of lakes such as Lake Erie, which had lost its oxygen and its stock of fish by a humanly created imbalance; the poisoning of the land by an overuse of fertilizers, which are then washed off into the streams instead of forming part of nature's cycle; the overuse of DDT and other pesticides and herbicides that leave an indestructible residue; and even the fouling of nature's last repository, the ocean, which is even now giving notice that its power of recuperation is being taxed to the breaking point—all these facts testify that people do in fact pollute the environment, that advancing technology is enabling us to pollute it still more, that it is not enough even to hold to the present level, but that we are obliged to reverse our mode of behavior and repair as much as possible the damage done.

Nuclear waste is a particularly pressing problem, for it is a hazard not only for the earth itself but for all organic life. The fuel rods from nuclear power plants contain some unused uranium 235 (weapons-grade uranium) which can be extracted and put back to work in power plants; they also contain strontium 90 and caesium 137, and these must be isolated from all organic life for hundreds of years until they finally decay and lose their radioactivity. Some of the uranium 235 is converted into plutonium, which is so carcinogenic that the inhalation of the minutest particle can cause cancer. As time passes and nuclear power programs expand, the years needed for secure waste disposal will extend into the future further and further and the volume of deadly waste will increase steadily. Some of today's wastes will be safe only in the 25th century and still

others will be safe only around the year 4000. As of now, *no* safe technique for disposing of all this waste has been perfected. We are disposing of the waste but have no guarantee that we and future generations are secure from its dangers. In addition to all this high-level waste, we have a great deal of low-level waste that must also be safely stored, for it too is dangerous. Efforts are being made, but we must do more and do it quickly before we have tragedies rather than just accidents. Nuclear pollution is much worse than anything we have mentioned so far. The government has the direct responsibility to see that the needed technology is developed to handle this waste in a manner that does not endanger human life and, as far as possible, other organic life as well.

Much can be done about pollution. Unlike the depletion of natural resources, which when consumed cannot be restored, pollution is an ongoing human activity, and we can simply cease or be forced to cease our polluting activity. The difficulty is not physical but political. How do you persuade people to do what is necessary for their welfare?

Pollution is not leading to such swift and dire consequences as the prophets of gloom predict. All is not yet lost. Something, but not nearly enough, is being done about it. The moral obligation is to intensify the efforts toward pollution control up to but not beyond the point where the remedy would be worse than the disease. There may be need of more political control of the economy to make pollution control economically feasible. The cost of pollution control is considerable; it must either be absorbed by the government and paid for by increased taxes, or be imposed by the government and paid for by increased prices. Either way is a moral way, but neither way is palatable. Since the end is socially mandatory and since neither producer nor consumer is willing to contribute voluntarily to pollution control, there seems to be no other remedy than enforcement by the government.

Then there is the problem of making this control international. It seems to be almost beyond human ingenuity to persuade the nations of the world to agree on a matter that concerns them all if they can squeeze the slightest advantage out of independent action. Yet no individual country is excused from its moral duty because its neighbors fail to fulfill theirs. If a sufficient number of countries succeed in agreeing, they can exert pressure on the rest.

POVERTY

One of the ironies in this technologically advanced world of plenty is the claim that the earth can no longer feed even its present population. Right now, one third of the human race goes to bed hungry every night because they do not have sufficient food. Malnutrition is rampant in some areas of the world and, worst of all, some people are literally starving to death. The irony of the claim that the earth cannot produce enough food for all the people living here is that there is no such thing as an absolute scarcity of food. Every country in this world is capable of feeding its people! Hunger and poverty are not the problem; they are *symptoms* of a disorder in the societies of the world. The poor, who are hungry, malnourished, and even sometimes starving, are not a problem. They are people just like you and me who for various reasons do not have enough to eat, and it is not their fault nor is it the fault of the earth. The problem, of which the malnourished and starving poor are the symptom, is in the economic and political orders of the world's societies.

To speak of the world food crisis as a symptom of some basic disorders in society may sound strange, for we have been bombarded with rhetoric of another sort. We were told in the 1960s that world population growth is a "bomb" and later in the 1970s that it is a "human tidal wave." The finite resources of the earth are incapable of feeding the "exploding" population. The "human tidal wave" is beginning to inundate the earth, and all of us are going to suffer. We have to compete in the "race against hunger," but as in every race, some are going to lose. Such is the rhetoric of the prophets of gloom. They see at stake not only our diet but the very fabric of our

civilization, because the hungry are going to descend on us to take from us the food they need for themselves and thus destroy the very quality of our life.

On the other side are those who tell us that we, the rich nations, have a special responsibility to stave off the starvation of the world. We are made to feel guilty, because we have enough food while so many others do not. These prophets shift the food crisis out of the economic-political arena and try to place it on the shoulders of each individual consumer. Our consumption causes the hungry people's suffering. This message is as misguided as that of the gloomy prophets. We are made to feel shame at our own consumption as though that very consumption is some kind of moral failing. Eating one less hamburger this week does not mean that the meat and grain saved will necessarily get to some hungry person. We need to understand how hunger is actually created if we are to see all of this rhetoric from both sides for what it is, simply empty words.

The food crisis exists. This is a fact. The remedy is not to be found in panic nor in despair, not in some kind of triage nor in "lifeboat ethics," not in desensitizing ourselves to others' suffering nor in berating Judeo-Christian ethics as outmoded. We need to understand the fact of the food crisis, to seek out its underlying causes, and then to take action by eliminating the causes. This means that each nation of the world must reorder its priorities in such a way that food for its own people is placed first on its set of national goals. All other national problems are really insignificant until that nation's people are able to eat adequately. Until its people have fed themselves, no nation can afford to think of its food resources as a *means* to some other goal, for example, as a means to build up credit by exporting food to other nations. This applies to rich nations as much as it does to poor nations. No nation or group of nations can afford to look to a few nations of the world as suppliers of food to the whole world. Each nation can and must use and develop its own food resources to meet its own needs. Once this is accomplished, nations can trade with one another to expand choices for their people rather than deprive them of their rightful resources.

Once a nation puts food for its people first on its list of priorities and helps its own people to husband the nation's own food resources to feed themselves, that nation's very economic and political system, along with the accompanying social structures, are going to need to be reordered. The concentration of wealth and power in the hands of a few is intolerable when the nation sets out to feed all of its people adequately. If the vast majority of the people are hungry and undernourished, then not only is the system for distributing the food at fault but more fundamentally the control and participation in the production process are the cause of the unequal distribution of food. *If they are allowed to do so,* hungry people do, can, and will feed themselves. To allow them to do so means reordering the economic and political systems as well as the societal structures.

The goal of every nation should be food security for its people, and this goal can be realized only by giving all the people the control of the food economy. There is a connection between the way government works with the land monopolizers, both the traditional landed elite and corporate agribusiness, to undermine food security by cutting the vast majority of people out of the production process and therefore out of consumption. This is the *moral* problem that cries for solution, for the government that should be working for the good of all its people actually works only for the benefit of the wealthy land monopolizers, both local and foreign. These latter have proved themselves time and again to be the most inefficient, unreliable, and destructive users of food resources. The only way for a nation to guarantee long-term productivity and food security for its people is for the people themselves to take control of the food resources. If this means redistributing the land, then this is what is morally required.

The governments of both Cuba and China have succeeded in allowing their people to feed themselves. It can be done. Does this mean that rich nations have no obligations to the poorer nations of the world? Many of the poorer nations of the world are countries that were once colonies of the wealthier nations and are still suffering from some of the effects of the colonizing process. One of the effects of colonialism was that it actively prevented people from feeding themselves by (1) forcing the peasants to replace food crops with cash crops for which they were paid low prices, (2) taking over the best agricultural land for export crop plantations and then forcing the most ablebodied workers to leave the village fields to work for very low wages on the plantations, (3) encouraging a dependence on imported food, and (4) blocking native peasant cash crop production from competing with cash crops produced by settlers or foreign corporations. The continued dependence of these former colonies on export agriculture leaves the little people with less than adequate food, because most of the agricultural production is geared for export and not enough land is planted with crops for local consumption. The colonizing powers, in their desire to extract wealth from the colony, introduced a money economy and put their power behind the already wealthy. This promoted the increasing concentration of landholding by the few and the increasing landlessness of the many. This trend, set in motion centuries ago, forms the greatest obstacle to genuine agricultural development today. The rich nations now have a moral obligation to see to it that their own corporate agribusinesses do not continue the economic exploitation of poorer countries. They have a further obligation when they give economic aid to see to it that the aid reaches the hungry people. This means that aid must not be used for political purposes or for economic profit. Any aid given must have as its primary purpose the creation of the preconditions for local food self-reliance.

Social justice is not confined by the boundaries of political states, so that one has obligations to one's compatriots only, and to no one else. Our common humanity transcends any artificial grouping we may make, no matter how deeply these groupings are rooted in history and tradition. Other things being equal, our first obligation is to our own, but when we discuss the relation between rich and poor countries, other things are not equal. One country's basic requirements for survival are pitted against another country's luxuries and superfluities.

Just as the wealthy as a class of people have the moral obligation of contributing to the support of the needy, both for relieving immediate distress and for working toward a long-range solution of the poverty problem, so wealthy countries have the obligation of contributing toward the relief of needy countries, both in times of crisis from disaster and famine, and in the long-range plan of assisting such countries toward economic adequacy. Very few nations are willing publicly to repudiate such an obligation, but fulfillment of it is spotty. In too many instances, hungry people are fed rhetoric instead of food or are economically exploited under the guise of being helped. Economic and/or political advantage and power seem most often to be the rich nations' motives for "helping" underdeveloped countries. The food almost never reaches those who need it most, for the local profit-seekers siphon off the food to sell it at high prices to those who can afford to pay for it. Meanwhile the poor remain as hungry as before. Greed and other moral weaknesses of individuals are intensified in the behavior of nations. The moral obligation is clear. The difficulty here, as in so many areas of ethics, is in getting people to do what they know they ought to do.

POPULATION

Many think that the only remedy for our ecological ills lies in a restriction on the growth of the population. The trouble always comes down to "too many people." There is no doubt of the zooming population. It is doubling itself in increasingly shorter periods. The thesis of Malthus[1] may not be fulfilled in exactly the way Malthus proposed it, but in general lines his prophecy is coming true. Our efforts to stave off starvation and malnutrition are brought to nought by the fact that every increased food supply is met by

an even more greatly increased number of mouths to feed. Thus we are constantly falling behind in our attempt to feed humanity. It is true that the earth can produce much more food than it actually does, and therefore a short-term remedy may be possible. However, such a remedy is no answer to the fact that the population is exploding at an exponential rate, and the time must eventually come when there is no room on the earth for another human being. Before any such time arrives, the population explosion will have been contained by starvation and other disasters. The ethical problem is: Can we allow the population to increase at this alarming rate so as to make conditions of life impossible for a great part of the human race, or must we stop our rate of increase and contain it within reasonable limits? The problem is a new one. We had hitherto assumed that "the more the merrier" was a valid principle and that there was plenty of room for all. It is our own efficiency in controlling death that now requires us to control birth. Formerly nature eliminated the unfit; we have succeeded in enabling almost all to live.

There is an ethical obligation on the human race as a whole to limit its increase. Just as there was the ethical obligation to increase and multiply when there was a population shortage, so now there is the ethical obligation to keep reproduction within the bounds of the earth's finite capacity. If humans are fitted by their nature to live on this earth, their numbers must also be geared to what the earth can support. Though the earth can support, with human ingenuity, perhaps many times the number of people existing now, it cannot support the indefinite number toward which our exponential increase is rapidly leading. The time is growing short, and plans must be made now for setting a limit to our numbers.

How can this general obligation be applied to individual persons and families? Just as there is the general obligation on the human race to reproduce and continue itself, but no particular individual is obliged to marry and raise a family because enough will do so anyway, so a general obligation on the human race to limit its numbers

---

[1]Malthus, *Essay on the Principle of Population,* 1798.

would not fall on a particular individual or family, so long as enough were limiting their reproductive capacity to keep the size of the human race within proper bounds.

The best way to accomplish this limitation of births is by persuading people to limit their families voluntarily. A variety of methods has been suggested, some of them acceptable from a moral standpoint and others not. Infanticide would be the most objectionable, so much so that most people would simply refuse to do it or let it happen. Abortion is an acceptable method to those who see no moral wrong in abortion, but it is quite unacceptable to those who regard the fetus as a human being with a right to life; even those who do not condemn abortion think of it rather as a last resort for those for whom contraception has failed. Voluntary sterilization, of either the male or female, is another method advocated by those who see no moral obligation to preserve one's physical wholeness and who regard sterilization as a condition of permanent contraception, against which they have no moral scruples. Contraception is the favored method for those who do not consider contraception an unnatural or immoral act. Abstinence and the rhythm method are means that should be morally acceptable to all, but not all find them feasible. Late marriage is an efficient method of keeping down the birth rate in some parts of the world, but not all peoples would accept it, and it becomes useless if people indulge in premarital sex without contraceptives. Planning for the future, however, cannot bank on any marked reduction in extramarital sex, and one can only urge that if it is indulged in, it be with the use of efficient contraceptives.

Thus it is seen that the question of population control is bound up with most of the moral problems that concern the right to life and the use of sex. Most agree that the goal, population control, is good and is morally required in these times of actually existing or rapidly approaching overpopulation. The dispute is on the means, since a good end does not justify the use of immoral means.

Some advocate compulsory limitation of population. Not all the advocates of zero population growth (ZPG) favor compulsory methods, but some do. Their argument is that voluntary methods are insufficient, that people will practice them only half-heartedly, and that not enough people will practice them to make them effective. The governments of all the nations of the world will have to step in, to order the destruction of all children beyond the two who will replace their parents (to be more exact 2.2 children on an average to each married couple) and to sterilize those parents who exceed this number. Their reasoning is that otherwise the human race will not survive, and the obligation on the race toward survival is stronger than the right of any individual to survive and stronger than the right of parents to have as many children as they please. There is something very strange about this argument, as if the normal but undesirable controlling factors such as famine, war, and disease would become inoperative, that they would not serve to thin the population, but that the whole human race would arrive at the point of extinction at once. Thus, rather than let these factors thin the population for us, we should step in and kill those who would otherwise die. What is the purport of such an argument? Does it not come down to saying that since there is not enough to go around, we will make sure that we are the ones who will survive? How moral is this attitude? Hitherto it would have been called selfishness. Does it become different when done on global scale?

Most moralists would hold that only persuasive and voluntary methods can be used. Not only do these methods alone show the proper respect for individuals' rights, but they are the only ones that have a chance of succeeding. The surest way of producing worldwide revolution, and hence the destruction of humanity that the ZPG advocates want to avoid, would be the autocratic and forceful interference with the family necessary to implement compulsory population control.

But voluntary methods will reduce the population only slightly, not enough to save humanity! It seems, then, that we will have to live with continued population growth. Most of the developed countries have a fairly stable population. Runaway population growth is occurring chiefly in the developing countries. The aim today of both the developed and the developing countries is to turn the developing countries into developed countries. If this trend is followed, then when all the countries of the world are economically developed and have arrived at cultural and political maturity, all the countries of the world will also have arrived close to zero population growth. This will be a slower process and will allow for a larger world population than the more vehement ZPG advocates desire, but it seems to be the only way in which the absolute long-run evils of unlimited population growth can be avoided in a manner consistent with sound morals and a respect for the rights of the individual person.

The growth of urbanization, which is itself a kind of blight on the landscape, will help in lowering the population. Children are an asset on the farm but a liability in the city. More two- and three-children families will become the rule as the cities spread and set the fashion for the rural regions. Thus, although voluntary family limitation lacks that definite mathematical precision that a compulsory limitation would achieve, voluntary limitation seems to be the only way that is morally allowable, as well as being the only way that is politically and socially feasible. Whether it is enough to solve the problem, time alone will tell.

CONCLUSION

The moral questions involved in this chapter are fairly simple in principle but extremely difficult in practical application. No one has the right to use the gifts of nature in such a way as to produce widespread and intolerable harm to others. Few are going to do much about this social crime against humanity unless curbed by law, and lawmakers need more courage than they have so far shown to resist the pressure of vested interests. Legislation on the local level is usually not enough, nor even on the national level, and international cooperation is the most difficult thing in the world

to come by. What laws to enact and how to enforce them is the business of environmental experts and political agencies. The ordinary citizens can cooperate by disposing of their own refuse in a way that does not add to the general litter and by reinforcing the pressure of public opinion on their political representatives. That the public has become conscious of the problems is a great step forward but will mean little unless followed by continual resistance against greed and apathy.

SUMMARY

Ecology, the science of the relation of living organisms to their environment, has assumed increasing importance since we have come to experience the effects of our reckless exploitation of nature. We must guard against the exaggerations of the more hysterical environmentalists and the apathy counseled by the defenders of the status quo and vested interests. There are several ethical issues involved.

Exploitation. It is claimed that humans are by nature exploiters, that our natural greed is furthered by the Judeo-Christian ethic of dominating nature, and that the only remedy is to adopt the Eastern attitude of submission to nature, fostered by the pantheistic outlook of our continuity with all things. Many think that these attitudes are not incompatible and that we as stewards are meant to use and adapt nature to our purposes but always within the limits imposed by nature itself.

Resources. Nature has many nonrenewable resources that we are using up more and more swiftly as our technology develops. Do we have a moral obligation to future generations to save for them a proper share in nature's bounty? It would be difficult to deny such an obligation, though it is also difficult to give it exact limits. At least there can be no moral defense for sheer wastefulness. Now that we recognize our wastefulness, we have a moral obligation to correct it.

Pollution. People add to nature's own pollution of the environment. Nature's pollution cannot be corrected; ours can. The environment is not so hopelessly spoiled as some prophets of doom proclaim, but the trend toward humanly made pollution must be reversed. Our selfishness is such that this reversal will not be accomplished without strict government control, both on the national and international level. The cost will be great, but it must be faced because the alternative is not tolerable.

Poverty. Each nation has a moral obligation to put food for its own people first on the set of national goals. This will mean reordering the economic and political system to place the food economy in the hands of all the people. If achieving this goal means redistributing the land, the nation has a moral obligation to do so. Rich nations have a moral obligation to aid poorer nations in need. The purpose of food aid must not be political or economic gain, but rather to create the preconditions for local food self-reliance.

Population. The population explosion has been blamed for all these ecological ills. This is a gross exaggeration, for some of these ills are not tied to population, but the rapid multiplication of the population is itself a problem that will not go away by being ignored. Population growth must be curtailed, and moral methods must be used. Infanticide, abortion, sterilization, contraception, rhythm, abstinence, and late marriages are the most commonly suggested methods. The first three are morally disapproved by many, and the last three are morally acceptable to most but ineffectual in practice. Family limitation by contraception seems to be an effective method that most people would probably approve. To practice it morally, one should be convinced of the moral rightness of contraception. *Compulsory* population limitation goes against the fundamental rights of mankind and would be an immoral solution of a moral problem. Only persuasive and *voluntary* methods may be used. They already work in developed countries. When all developing countries have become developed, perhaps world population will be fairly well stabilized.

Questions for Discussion

1. Colonization has always been a way for a nation to accomplish at least two goals: (a) economic expansion and (b) relief of population pressure. In terms of relief of population pressure, now that there are no more empty lands to colonize on earth, is it not a logical extension of people's colonizing tendency to look for new homes among the stars and planets? Even when space travel becomes possible, will such colonizing relieve excess population on earth?

2. Getting the nations of the world to cooperate on supplying food, alleviating poverty, and controlling pollution is as difficult as getting them to prevent war. Is not the only realistic answer an acceptance of certain evils as inevitable?

3. Some people blame all our ecological ills on the advancing state of human technology. Everything has become so artificial that we have lost our sense of continuity with nature. What alternatives do we have but to declare a moratorium on technology, to halt our scientific advance until our human values have had a chance to catch up? Does Karl Marx offer us any guidance?

4. What would you do if ordered by the state to limit your children to two, the penalty for failure being the destruction of any other children you may have and sterilization for you and your spouse?

5. Today 5.5% of all farms in the U.S. control more than 50% of all farmland; six grain corporations control 85% of all grain exports; 50 out of almost 30,000 food manufacturers control half of all the industry's assets. The result of allowing our land, food processing, and distribution increasingly to be controlled by fewer and fewer people: almost $20 billion more spent each year for food, increasing poverty and malnutrition for many Americans, and the loss of livelihood for millions of rural

people. Do these facts not argue for land reform in the U.S.? Do Congress and the state legislatures have an obligation to protect us against the takeover of agriculture by corporations? Does the U.S. have a moral obligation to institute a program of land reform?

Readings

Interest in ecology and a warning on what we are doing to our environment was sparked by Rachel Carson's *Silent Spring.* She greatly overstates her case but is well worth reading.

Barry Commoner's *The Closing Circle* is one of the most influential books from the environmentalist standpoint. See also his *Science and Survival,* and his many articles. Ian McHarg's *Design With Nature* is an expensively produced work on nature and environment, with actual studies of Washington, Philadelphia, etc., and with reflections on man the exploiter. John Black puts out a small book, *The Dominion of Man: the Search for Ecological Responsibility;* he concentrates on the ethical and religious aspects: exploitation vs. stewardship. Ian Barbour edits a series of essays entitled *Earth Might be Fair.* Bruce Allsopp has a little book, *The Garden Earth: the Case for Ecological Morality,* that is rather far out. Joseph Margolis, *Negativities: The Limits of Life,* ch. 11, argues that any attempted resolution of the developing crisis of ecological imbalance requires a global ideology, something still to be developed to provide norms for ongoing human life extending into the indefinite future. John J. Berger's *Restoring the Earth: How Americans Are Working to Renew Our Damaged Environment* discusses what we can do to correct the pollution, destruction, and waste of our natural resources, and William Ashworth's *The Late Great Lakes: An Environmental History* is a powerful indictment of our callousness, apathy, and ignorance about our environment.

Nuclear Pollution: The results of the years of nuclear testing both in the atmosphere and underground by the federal government are being studied with a view to correcting past errors and preventing future tragedies. See Richard L. Miller's *Under The Cloud: The Decades of Nuclear Testing* and Howard Ball's *Justice Downwind: America's Atomic Testing Program in the 1950s.*

On the other side there is John Maddox, *The Doomsday Syndrome,* an interesting protest against such gloomy prophets as Carson, Commoner, and Ehrlich. Though antienvironmentalist, it seems to be fairly well balanced.

Who Speaks for Earth? is a small volume edited by Maurice F. Strong, containing speeches delivered at the International Institute for Environmental Affairs and the Population Institute, United Nations Conference on the Human Environment, Stockholm, June, 1972. The speakers are Barbara Ward, René Dubos, Thor Heyerdahl, Gunnar Myrdal, Carmen Miró, Lord Zuckerman, and Aurelio Peccei, an array certainly worth listening to.

Pope Paul VI's *Populorum Progressio* (The Development of Peoples) is an urgent call to all people of good will to work together to overcome poverty and injustice everywhere and to foster the solidarity of all peoples. Barbara Ward's *The Rich Nations and the Poor Nations,* though a bit old, is still a vital work from one of the world's best-known economists. Her later pamphlet, *A New Creation? Reflections on the Environmental Issue,* is very well done, environmentalist but restrained. Her *Progress for a Small Planet* argues for moderate and acceptable changes that can provide a stable basis for the earth's survival. She and René Dubos collaborated on *Only One Earth* in an effort to create in people an awareness of and an allegiance to the planet earth that we all occupy and call home. René Dubos, *Man Adapting,* explores the biological and social implications of our responses to the total environment. Michael Harrington's *The Other America: Poverty in the United States* sparked the war on poverty and is still relevant and so is Colin Clark's *Starvation or Plenty?*

The great beginner of population studies and demography is Thomas Malthus. The first edition (1798) of his *Essay on the Principle of Population* is worth reading. Here he announces his principle that population increases geometrically, whereas food production increases only arithmetically. He sees war, famine, and pestilence as the only ways of regulating the population. Francis Moore Lappé and Joseph Collins, *Food First: Beyond the Myth of Scarcity,* present a striking analysis of why there is hunger in a world of plenty and what the ordinary individual can do about it. See also Johannes Messner, *Social Ethics,* revised edition, bk. IV, pt. IV, on the international foodstuffs market and international social justice.

Paul Ehrlich's *The Population Bomb* exploded on the scene in 1968, together with the author's frequent speeches and the foundation of the Zero Population Growth movement. With his wife, Anne, he published *Population, Resources, Environment,* a more restrained version of the former. They are necessary reading on this subject, but beware of the strong propagandist presentation and test carefully every conclusion. Robert L. Sassone, *Handbook on Population,* 2nd ed., counters the prophets of doom with an array of facts about food, resources, energy, pollution, population, and the quality of life. This was first published as "Report to the California Legislature on Population at the Request of the Office of the Senate Majority Leader."

PART VII
International Society

We humans have created fairly efficient structures for our political life, although we often fail to use them. Peace on earth is what we long for and obviously need, but our international relations are still barbaric to a large extent. We have been through two major global conflicts and a large number of smaller wars in this century alone. Yet we allow ourselves to dream of total amity between nations, a world at peace without tragedy. How to move the heavy blocks of entrenched power from a jumbled, crushing heap into an intelligently planned order in which we can all live in peace has so far eluded the most gifted of the world's leaders. We cannot afford to live in splendid isolation from all the rest of humanity, and so we must learn to live in peaceful union with one another. This is the moral problem for all of us, but we have as yet no perfect solution to it. International relations (Chapter 34), war (Chapter 35), and peace (Chapter 36) form the final stage of our survey of the moral life.

34
Nations

PROBLEM

International relations are complicated by the fact that individual sovereign states have no superior to whom they can appeal and whose authority they respect. The state itself is a society of individuals and families, and one of its chief functions is to judge disputes between them, but when states themselves conflict they have nothing ultimately to appeal to but force, and that is war. There is no more inefficient way of settling disputes than war. To avoid its horrors, if possible, or at least to reduce them as far as can be, states have developed the instrument known as international law. We will discuss the following questions:

1. What is international law and how did it arise?
2. Is international law really law?
3. Are states bound by the natural law?
4. What duties in justice do states have to one another?
5. What duties in amity do states have to one another?

RISE OF INTERNATIONAL LAW

The ancients seem to have looked on foreign nations as enemies and their property as booty. Homer pictures the Greeks as supporting themselves by forays on other villages about Troy, and the custom was to kill or enslave the conquered. There was some unwritten code of honor among warriors, for they held sacred the person of heralds and had truces for burying the dead and exchanging prisoners. The Amphictyonic League was an attempt to bring harmony among the Greek city-states and to establish among them some common rules of action, but it met with little success.

The Romans, as we have seen, developed the *jus gentium,* which is not international law but what they found to be the common element in the internal laws of all their subjugated peoples. The *jus gentium,* because it was common to all peoples with whom the Romans came into contact, closely approached the natural law and became one of the sources from which international

law was later to be drawn, but the Romans felt no need for international law in the modern sense. Their final solution to the differences between nations was to absorb them all into their own vast Empire. Rome took on herself the task of keeping order in the civilized world, and her great achievement was the *Pax Romana.*

When the world emerged from the wreckage of the Roman Empire, there was one great international institution to which all Christian nations could turn for an adjudication of disputes, the Church. A common faith and a common code of morality did much to standardize the behavior of kings and princes into a common Christian pattern and to outlaw certain practices as unworthy of a Christian anywhere. The ideals of chivalry and knighthood, with their high sense of honor, exerted an enormous humanizing influence. Definite rules and customs, founded on the natural law, the *jus gentium,* and even the Church's Canon Law to some extent, governed the relations between states. Diplomatic negotiations, as we understand them now, seem to have originated among the medieval Italian city-states. Though without any force to impose her decisions and relying solely on her moral position, the Church arbitrated countless quarrels and did much to mitigate the horrors of war and conquest. Even so, the feudal period was all too barbarous, but at least between Christian peoples there was nothing like the wholesale enslavement of ancient times or the almost total war of today.

The breakdown of united Christendom in the sixteenth century and the ensuing lack of any common court of appeal acceptable to all Christian nations led to the formation of the concept of *international law* in the modern sense. Though it was prepared for by the work of Francis de Vitoria and Francis Suarez, who tried to codify existing customs and apply them to the rising nationalism of their day, the founding of international law is commonly attributed to Hugo Grotius, author of *The Rights of War and Peace.* He saw that henceforth, in the absence of a higher tribunal, relations between nations must be governed both by the natural law, which as the law of right reason is common to all people, and by voluntary agreement among states, based on their enlightened self-interest. His codification of existing customs, tested by these criteria, passed into the texture of modern international law.

International law is the result not of any definite enactment but of long custom and usage. Its rules can be found in recognized writers commenting on these customs, in treaties between civilized nations, in state papers and diplomatic correspondence, in decisions of international tribunals, and in court decisions of particular countries regarding citizenship, alien property, admiralty cases, and similar matters.

International law comprises the rules determining the conduct of political states in their dealings with each other. Which political organizations are *states*? In practice, a *state* is one so recognized by the nations of the world generally, and admitted to their circle. The theory on which this practice seems to be based is that a *state* is here taken in the strictest sense to mean one having the fullest degree of independent sovereignty.

This concept of the state supposes enough development and organization to make the state self-sufficient and capable of self-rule; it also supposes the actual possession of self-rule, full jurisdiction over the whole people in all departments of life, internal and external. Primitive and uncivilized tribes, though they have their natural rights, are not states because they lack the first requirement; the individual states of the United States, under the theory of divided sovereignty, have handed over control of foreign affairs to the federal government and thus fail in the second requirement.

The position of *client states,* whether they be called provinces, colonies, tributaries, dependencies, protectorates, or mandates, is a knotty question. Some of them retain a technical sovereignty and basic jurisdiction over all affairs, yet in practice have handed over to another state some of their affairs and especially their foreign relations. Those that are technically sovereign come under international law in theory, but foreign nations disregard this theoretical position in practice, since they cannot treat with them directly but only through the state that manages their foreign relations. Their position is somewhat like that of a minor, who has inherent personal rights equal to those of anyone else but is under a guardian's tutelage for the transaction of business. Some, especially colonies, gradually grow to a condition of full independence, and others show more or less initiative toward responsible self-rule.

MORAL ASPECTS OF INTERNATIONAL LAW

It may be argued that international law is not truly law because there is no one who has care of the community of nations, no common authoritative ruler over all states. In fact, the requirement that the states be fully sovereign makes it impossible for any real law to exist between states.

Natural law theorists answer this difficulty by distinguishing two parts of international law. Some parts of international law arise out of the very nature of the state and are merely reaffirmations of, or deductions from, the natural law, such as the right of a nation to defend itself when unjustly attacked, or its duty to fulfill just contracts freely made. Such rights and duties constitute *natural* international law. Other parts of international law are the result of express or tacit agreements made between nations and not directly deducible from the natural law, such as the diplomatic immunity accorded ambassadors, or the internment of warships by neutrals in war time. These areas of law constitute *conventional* or *contractual* international law.

Ethics is concerned with natural international law only, and this is truly law in the sense in which natural, or moral, law is said to be law, as embodying natural rights, natural justice, and natural morality. But contractual international law depends only on compact and agreement and relies for its enforcement only on the good faith of the contracting parties. There is nothing in the nature of things that demands the making of such contracts, and they are freely entered into for mutual benefit like contracts between private persons. Hence they are not laws in the strict sense.

We cannot conclude that such laws have no binding force. Contracts between individuals, though not themselves laws, impose obligation from the moral law, which prescribes that *just contracts must be kept*. The same is true of international agreements. Though they are entered into voluntarily and are not guaranteed by any higher authority on earth than the contracting parties, once made they bind nations and their rulers in conscience. Hence the distinction between natural and contractual international law, necessary for studying and formulating this law, is of less importance when there is the mere practical question of keeping its obligations. In both cases the obligation comes from the moral law, but in different ways: in natural international law, without any medium; and in contractual international law, through the intermediacy of a voluntary contract. In the first case the obligation cannot be avoided; in the second, it can be avoided by refusing to be a party to the contract.

The solution just given is based on the supposition that states are bound by morality and the moral law. It is a deplorable fact that many states have behaved as if they were not bound by any consideration of morality, but this observation does not mean that they approved this kind of action in theory. Nations most ruthless in violating the rights of others often shout loudest when their own rights are attacked, thus offering lip service, when it suits them, to the idea of international morality. But some philosophers and jurists insist that even in theory international law is outside the scope of morality.

Moral positivists, holding that all morality comes from the state, must logically accept this conclusion, but one need not be a moral positivist to do so. One may attempt a compromise, admitting individual morality but denying international morality on the grounds that the individual has a destiny beyond this world, whereas the state is merely a temporal affair; that morality deals with eternal ideals of conduct, whereas states are concerned with worldly needs and material wants; and that an individual can afford to be idealistic, but a state must be hardheadedly realistic.

History should provide a sufficient lesson to us about the horrendous results of conducting international affairs on the principle that might makes right. That states are bound by the moral law hardly needs any separate proof, but the following remarks will serve as a review:

1. The state is a natural institution, with a natural right to exist, based on human social nature. It cannot be exempt from the law that created it, maintains it, and gives it all its rights and authority.

2. The state is composed of human beings and is carried on by their activity. No human being can be exempt from the moral law, which governs every possible form of human conduct. It is absurd to think that a person can be rid of obligations merely by associating with others, or that anything is allowable as long as people do it together.

3. International law cannot be based entirely on agreement, for what would oblige the states to keep their agreements except some previous agreement? An infinite series of agreements is impossible. The source of all obligation is the natural moral law, which holds for states as well as for individuals.

4. That rights and duties exist between persons is as true of corporate persons (societies) as of physical persons (individuals). The state is a corporate person and, as a natural society, has a sort of natural incorporation. Business firms have obligations in natural justice; so likewise has the state.

5. The individual citizens of one state have natural rights and duties toward the citizens of other states. Justice does not end at the boundaries of states. Conflict of these rights and duties

often cannot be settled except through the intermediacy of the states concerned, and they will be governed by international law based on natural justice.

INTERNATIONAL JUSTICE

All people have equal rights because all are personal beings and have the same origin and goal. On this foundation the virtue of justice rests. They can be subordinated to one another only because of some other reason, when they are organized to achieve some lesser end, as when children are subordinated to parents, pupils to teachers, employees to employers, citizens to ruler. The family, the school, the business, and the state are organized each for a definite social function as well as for helping individual persons. Within these societies there is subordination, but between societies of the same kind there is equality of rights. Each is a corporate person and must be treated as an equal by its equals, not merely as a means for another's convenience.

Thus each state exercising full sovereignty has equal rights with every other state. They all have the same end, to promote the temporal welfare of their peoples, and derive their authority from their people and ultimately from God, not from any other state. No such state is subordinate to any other and may not be treated as subordinate. The rights of a sovereign state are not scaled to its political size or strength, any more than the individual's rights are dependent on physical size or strength. Whether or not states should curtail their sovereignty by becoming members of a world organization is a topic to be treated later, but even then the various states would be equal among themselves and not subordinate to one another, though they would come under the whole organization.

We must now discuss from the standpoint of morals some of the rights and duties states have in justice:

1. Independence
2. Entirety
3. Property
4. Colonization
5. Free action
6. Treaties

Independence

No state has the right wantonly to destroy the independent existence of another state. Independence is to a state what life is to an individual. As an individual has the right of self-defense against an unjust aggressor, so has a state. An individual may kill in self-defense under certain conditions; so also a state may deprive another of independence if its own independent existence is so seriously threatened as to leave no other remedy, but this is the only reason. These questions will be treated under war.

A state may be destroyed not only by attack from without but also from within by sedition and civil war. No state has the right to interfere in either way against its neighbor; a state has the right not only to bare existence but also to a peaceful and orderly existence.

We should note one difference between the life of an individual and of a state. An individual may not take his or her own life, since the individual is a physical person whose life is indivisible and incommunicable. A society, being a corporate person, does not have these attributes. Societies can merge or divide and even revive after extinction. A state can agree to unite with another or others in the formation of a larger state, as the original thirteen American states formed the United States. What was formerly one state may split up into several, as in the dissolution of the Austro-Hungarian Empire after World War I.

Entirety

Each sovereign state has a right to the whole of its territory and of its population. No state need submit to mutilation by its neighbors. Diseases of the kind that attack states are not cured by surgery; the principle that *the part is for the sake of the whole,* which justifies individual mutilation, cannot be applied to states, since the state exists for the benefit of the members. A state's right to expand is limited by its neighbor's right to all its land and all its people. We are not speaking here of border regions to which there are conflicting claims, but of the seizure of neighboring territory that certainly belongs to another state.

The *nationalist ideal,* that the state and the nation, the political unit and the ethnic unit, should be coterminous, would be a legitimate ambition if it could be accomplished without trampling on the rights of other states equally sovereign, but this ideal is rarely attainable. There is nothing in the nature of things that demands that all people of the same racial stock, language, and culture should be assimilated into the same political unit. Other things being equal, a homogeneous totality of population has certain advantages, but other things are hardly ever equal. The Swiss, for example, do not want to be divided among the neighboring states to which they have linguistic and cultural affinities. On the other hand, there is no reason why a number of small principalities should not voluntarily unite along nationalist lines, if they find it expedient and can do so without violating any rights.

Nor is it necessary, as the theory of *autarky,* or economic self-sufficiency, supposes, that the political unit be an economic unit. The self-sufficiency required for sovereignty does not mean that the country must produce all it consumes, but only that it be able to support itself adequately, either by produce, trade, or any other means. A state need not be both agricultural and industrial but can engage in a sort of economic symbiosis with another state. Remedy for surplus population, formerly found in emigration and colonization, must be sought in some other way and not in seizing the neighboring state's territory.

Property

The state, being a corporate person, can own property. The state's titles to property are about the same as those of individual ownership; the main difference is that the state has the additional title of legitimate conquest but lacks the title of inheritance as a natural heir, though it can accept bequests.

Property can come under the jurisdiction of the state in three ways. There is exclusively state-owned property, such as fortifications, highways, and public buildings. Then there is the private property of its citizens both at home and abroad, for which the state has a responsibility, since to protect its people's property is one of the reasons for the state's existence. Lastly, the very territory of the state, though most of it is divided among private owners, comes under the state's administration as far as foreign relations are concerned. Seizure of any of this territory by a foreign power is international theft, and culpable damage to it calls for indemnification.

Colonization

Colonization is obsolete, and we can now only judge the past actions of colonizing nations. Of itself there is nothing morally wrong in colonization, though it was subject to the most flagrant abuses. A state could take possession of territory not belonging to any other state and own it by title of occupancy. Mere discovery did not suffice, but annexation and settlement were necessary.

Land that was recognized as the territory of an existing state was not open to colonization, nor land that was adequately occupied by a people capable of statehood but with only incipient political organization. The territory could not be seized without violating the rights of those already in possession. These people either had a state of their own or were on the verge of forming one and could not rightfully be deprived of their independence. Instead of trying to annex this emergent state, more advanced nations had the obligation of recognizing it and assisting it in its transition to full political stature.

The only land that was legitimately open to colonization was land periodically overrun by nomadic hordes or very sparsely settled by primitive tribes. Nomads had no real possession of the soil and could not reserve for their exclusive use a whole wilderness that they only occasionally visited and did nothing to develop. Many settled tribes effectively occupied only their own villages and the immediate environs; over their vast hunting grounds they had no more definite control than nomads over the desert steppes. The world's teeming population could not be kept out of these regions forever. Any state might send in a colony, being careful meanwhile to respect the natives' genuine rights. The land was incorporated into the state's political territory and put under its government, but the natives retained the personal ownership of their private property and became citizens or at least wards of the state, which was now bound not only to respect but to defend their rights. These people were not deprived of political independence, for they have never had any political society. Great injustices have occurred in this type of colonization, not the least of them in our own country, but they are not essential to colonization as such.

Now that the colonial era is over, we are faced with a host of problems it left as its aftermath. Praise is due to those nations that prepared their colonies for future independence and responsible self-government, blame to those that were forced to turn them loose unprepared or still try to keep them in tutelage. The hates generated by colonialism did not just happen through nobody's fault, and we have to thank immoral colonizers for the moral problems they left us. These problems will not be solved by recriminations for the past but by cooperative effort toward the future.

Free Action

A state has the right to develop itself in any way it sees fit that does not conflict with the strict right of another state. It may adopt the form of government it wishes, change its constitution to suit itself, enter into commercial relations with others, trade with whom it likes, impose what tariffs it thinks just, and make treaties and carry on other negotiations. Some of these functions may be incidentally detrimental to other nations but are not unjust unless they violate others' rights. States may not prevent the development of other states on the mere plea that they are threatened with rivalry, any more than individuals are allowed forcibly to extinguish legitimate competitors. Free competition is not aggression and does not justify counteraggression.

Nations should have free access to the raw materials that nature provides and should be able to obtain them by trade. These goods are for all people, and no nation is allowed to monopolize them in such a way that the rest of the world must suffer. Here the rules of monopoly apply; a country has a right to a legitimate profit on its natural monopolies but should not raise the price beyond the reach of other nations in genuine need of these products.

What nations can do to one another in this respect has been dramatized for us recently by the action of the oil-producing states. Oil is a natural monopoly, and nations that have it, especially if they have little else, are entitled to profit by their one main resource. They enter into relationships with the customer nations, and inconsiderate unilateral action on either side goes counter to the dependence that has been established between them. The oil-buying nations have kept the price too long at an artificially low level by an abuse of their monopoly of capital, which they invested in the oil-producing country by developing the wells. The oil-producing nations should have been gradually brought more and more into the possession of their own natural resource, so that a proper balance of profit would accrue to both the owner and the developer. However, the answer to this abuse is not to engage in one or the other side. The way to adjust the grievance is by economic and political discussion and agreement, not by a sudden, world-upsetting use of monopolistic power. These remarks are not meant to suggest a simple solution to a complex problem but to reflect on the fact that the life of almost everybody in the world has been seriously interfered with by this action, on how enormous economic power can be, and on how important it is to use it responsibly.

Treaties

A treaty is a contract between sovereign states as states. It differs from a contract between a state and a private individual or corporation and also from a contract between states not acting in a strictly political capacity, as when one government purchases food or industrial equipment from another. To be binding, a treaty must be an act of the sovereign authority in this state, which must ratify the result of previous diplomatic negotiations. The conditions for a valid treaty are the same as those for any valid contract. Treaties, because they are contracts involving a transfer of rights and duties, bind in commutative justice and derive their binding force from the moral law.

Do unjust treaties bind? If the terms of the treaty are clearly and certainly unjust, there can be no contract, for no one can be bound in justice to do or suffer injustice. A state forcing such a treaty on another is morally bound to withdraw it and repair any damage caused. The injustice of a treaty is not to be lightly presumed, but proved with objectively certain reasons. Any nation can trump up dishonest reasons for repudiating perfectly valid treaties when they prove burdensome. The unilateral denunciation of a treaty as unjust before its fulfillment or expiration is very much to be suspected.

Do treaties made under duress bind? Ordinarily a contract made under duress is rendered null and void by positive law, but there is no positive law above states to regulate their actions or to set down conditions for the validity of their contracts. Hence treaties cannot become invalid for this reason. Moreover, the reason that positive law invalidates contracts made under duress is to protect the common good and discourage violence, but the invalidation of *treaties* made under duress would have the opposite effect. The typical treaty made under duress is the peace treaty at the end of a war. If an unjust aggressor is victorious, the treaty imposed is unjust and therefore invalid. We are speaking here only of just treaties; at the end of a war even they are imposed under duress. The defeated nation is driven by force of arms to accept unfavorable conditions, but it was for the very purpose of imposing such conditions that the war was fought. If such treaties were invalid, wars could never end. It is surely wrong for a nation to accept a treaty to secure cessation of hostilities and then to repudiate the treaty to avoid paying just reparations. The only case in which just treaties made under duress do not bind is when the signer of the treaty is subjected to *personal* threats or violence, for then the presumption is that the person signs solely from motives of personal safety and is not truly the representative of his or her government.

When do treaties cease to bind? A treaty becomes extinct in the same way as any other contract: when its object is completely fulfilled, by mutual consent of the parties, when one of the parties ceases to exist, when it becomes impossible of fulfillment, when an essential condition no longer holds good, or if it conflicts with a higher or more universal law. If a treaty is valid at the time it is made, there are as a rule only two reasons that can justify its repudiation: failure of the other party to fulfill an essential part of the assumed obligation, or extinction of the state resulting from fulfillment of the treaty unless that were part of the treaty itself. But the mere fact that a treaty becomes more burdensome to a state than was expected does not at all absolve a state from its obligation. It took this risk when it made the treaty, and such risks are involved in all contracts, private as well as international.

INTERNATIONAL AMITY

The term *amity* means friendly relations, especially between states. Call it benevolence, helpfulness, humanity, cooperation, friendliness, goodwill, or any other name you prefer. The duties of amity or friendship between states are about the same as the duties of love or charity between individuals. One state should come to the aid of another in distress, provided it can do so without serious hardship to itself, in the same way that an individual should help another in trouble. But there is one main difference between the state and the individual. An individual is allowed, though not obliged, to risk certain death to protect another; a state would not be allowed to do so because its first obligation is to its own people, whose rights it is not allowed to sacrifice. The state exists for its people.

Nationalism

Patriotism, or love of country, is a virtue akin to piety or love of parents and must be developed by every citizen. It can go so far as to demand the supreme sacrifice of life itself, as in national defense. True *patriotism,* however, must be distinguished from its caricature, *nationalism,* just as proper self-love differs from selfishness. To love self we need not hate others.

The state, even though self-sufficient and sovereign, is not superior to the common humanity that binds all people into the great human family. Political differences do not take away human likenesses, and the general welfare of the whole human race takes precedence over the welfare of any particular group. Each single state is organized for mutual helpfulness among its members, and this same principle that prevails within each state should also prevail between states. States exist for the sake of promoting for their people a full human life, and the full development of the people's social nature is not limited by any artificial political boundaries. Hence an exaggerated *nationalism,* which shows itself in hatred of all foreigners, is to some extent inhuman and therefore immoral, as contradicting people's essentially social nature. It is also poor service to one's own nation to seek its interests so exclusively as to make it a bad member among the family of nations. Selfishness can exist on a national as well as on an individual scale.

Intervention

The *principle of nonintervention,* defended especially by nineteenth century liberalism, is that no state may interfere in the internal affairs of another state for any reason, except where its own legitimate interests are involved. To do so is considered an infringement of sovereignty.

This opinion takes too narrow a view of sovereignty and violates the amity or helpfulness spoken of earlier. It is true that no state may meddle in the affairs of another except for the most serious of reasons, but such reasons can and do sometimes exist. A state can come to the aid of a weaker state unjustly attacked by a stronger, can help a state put down unjustified insurrection, can establish order in a state hopelessly harassed by continual anarchy, can help a people throw off the yoke of unbearable tyranny, and can enforce some policy absolutely necessary for the peace of the world. When one country appeals to another for assistance in such matters, there is no reason why the appeal must be rejected because of the fictitious principle of nonintervention. We may as well say that we have no right to interfere in a family when the husband is killing his wife or torturing his children. On the other hand, it would be wrong to try to run their family for them or to interfere when there is no call for it. Hence the principle of nonintervention is invalid as a sweeping generalization, but it has a validity within limits.

CONCLUSION

It is impossible for us to go deeper into the problem of international relations. Contractual international law is quite outside our scope, except insofar as it may conflict with morality. The complexity of international relations in the modern world raises many difficult questions, answers to which have not yet been thoroughly worked out. Students of ethics, law, and politics have here a promisingly fertile field for their efforts. However, it is one thing to devise a solution in theory and quite another to induce the nations of the world to adopt it.

The point that remains of prime importance to the moralist is that the political state is as thoroughly subject to the norms and demands of morality as the individual person. The acts of states are all the more important because they affect the lives of millions of people, and in our days even of the whole world. The rulers of states bear a responsibility proportionate to their power, and in a democracy this responsibility is partially shared by the people. In the course of history the world has paid a terrible price for international immorality, for injustice on a grand and global scale. Immoral conduct is inhuman conduct, and unless nations come to a better sense of justice and honor in their dealings with one another, we must be prepared to see more inhumanity on the international scene.

SUMMARY

International law, a gradual growth of custom and usage, comprises the rules determining the conduct of political states in their dealings with one another. A *state* here means one with full independent sovereignty, not client states whose foreign affairs are managed by others.

Since sovereign states have no superior, *is international law really law? Natural* international law, embodying natural right, justice, and morality, is law. *Contractual* international law, comprising free contracts between states, is not really law, though the contracts bind like any others.

States are bound by the moral law, for they derive their rights and authority from it, are composed of people subject to it in all their conduct, rely on it to give binding force to their contracts, are corporate persons with rights and duties based on it, and must see that natural justice is done between their own citizens and foreigners.

States have rights and duties to one another in *justice.* Every state has a right to:

1. *Independence.* This is a state's life; a state may defend itself against unjust attack and against undue interference by other states in its affairs.

2. *Entirety.* All its territory and population belong to it and must be free from encroachment by other states seeking to satisfy nationalistic or economic ambitions.

3. *Property.* The state, like any society, can own and administer property; it must also protect its citizens' property and maintain its territory, even the part of it that is privately owned.

4. *Colonization.* The state may annex and settle unclaimed and politically unorganized regions, with proper respect for the rights of nomads and aborigines, but the days of colonization are over.

5. *Free action.* Each state may develop itself in its own way, with access to the earth's raw materials, which other states may not withhold from it by unjust monopoly.

6. *Treaties.* These contracts between sovereign states as states bind in justice like any other contract. Unjust treaties cannot bind, but the injustice must be certain. Treaties made under duress, such as peace treaties, bind unless the negotiator signs under threat of personal violence. A valid treaty may be repudiated only if the other party fails to fulfill it or if it would mean the extinction of the state.

States also have duties in *amity* or friendship to one another, but their duty to their own people comes first. Exaggerated *nationalism* is immoral, against people's duty to fellow humans of whatever nation. *Intervention* in another nation's internal affairs is normally wrong, but there can be sufficient reasons to justify it.

Questions for Discussion

1. The social questions of poverty, pollution, the arms race, inequitable trade practices, immigrant workers, and so forth tie all peoples together in every part of the world. And yet the goal of any state is the temporal welfare of its own people. Does one state have the moral obligation to help another state with its social problems? Do the nations of the world have an obligation to cooperate together to help solve the world's ills? On what principle(s) do you base your answer?

2. The hungry nations of the world cry out to the peoples favored with abundance. The United States is certainly favored with an abundance of everything. Does it have a moral obligation to help nations in distress? If not,

why not? If so, what is the extent of that obligation and what form(s) should that help take?

3. Roughly speaking, the world is made up of developed nations and developing nations. The developing nations need help. Economic aid alone is not enough to assure proper development. What else might be done to assure the proper development of each individual person, each human group, and humanity as a whole? Do you as an individual have any obligation to help others in developing nations? What can you do?

4. Each person is individually the chief architect of his or her own success or failure as a human being. If this is so, why should anyone else be concerned? A healthy self-interest on the part of each one should be sufficient to achieve the self-development and self-fulfillment each one craves. What do you think? Why?

5. Pope Paul VI once recommended very strongly that each nation set aside part of its military expenditures for a world fund to relieve the needs of impoverished peoples. Imagine that you are President of the United States and that you already have the backing of the people and the Congress to do just that. What arguments would you use with the rest of the world's leaders to persuade them to do the same? If they went along with you, how would you set up the fund so that it would keep growing and enable enough relief to be given long enough to do away with poverty everywhere?

Readings

Francis de Vitoria faced the new moral problem of the Spanish conquest of the Americas. The translation of the text of his *De Indis* (On the Indians) and *De Jure Belli* (On the Right of War) is given in J.B. Scott, *Francisco de Vitoria and His Law of Nations,* together with Scott's comments. Francis Suarez's ideas on international law are gathered from his great work *De Legibus* (On Laws); the translation of bk. II, ch. 17–20, in J.B. Scott, *Classics of International Law: Suarez,* vol. II, shows how his thinking prepared the way for modern international law. See also J.B. Scott, *Catholic Conception of International Law,* treating of Vitoria, Suarez, and others.

Hugo Grotius, *Rights of War and Peace,* is a classic of international law.

From among the modern writers see: Pope Paul VI, *Populorum Progressio* (The Development of Peoples), argues that the human solidarity of all peoples demands cooperation among all nations to bring about the genuinely human development of each and every person on earth. See also John Eppstein, *The Catholic Tradition of the Law of Nations* and *Code of International Ethics,* with many quotations and documents; Don Luigi Sturzo, *Nationalism and Internationalism;* Alfred de Soras, *International Morality;* Robert Delavignette, *Christianity and Colonialism;* Heinrich Rommen, *The State in Catholic Thought,* ch. 28; Johannes Messner, *Social Ethics,* revised edition, bk. II, pt. IV and bk. IV, pt. IV; and Morris Ginsberg, *On Justice in Society,* ch. 11.

35
War

PROBLEM

If war can be said to be the ultimate in human social failure, the history of the human race is marked in every century with the blood of those failures. The twentieth century bears witness to our continuing failures, failures of which we can have no doubt because many of us have lived through a number of them: the German attack on Belgium in 1914 and on Poland and France in 1939, the Italian conquest of Ethiopia, the Japanese attack on China, the German and Italian interventions in the Spanish Civil War, the Russian invasion of Finland, the Nazi conquests of Czechoslovakia, Denmark, Belgium, and Holland, the Russian invasions of Hungary, Czechoslovakia, and Afghanistan, the Egyptian-Israeli war in 1967, and our own American wars in Korea and Vietnam. These are not the only armed conflicts we could mention, but they make the point clearly enough. War is the ultimate in human social failure. Unlike natural disasters, war is a wholly human affair, the result of greed, envy, hate, ambition, and passion, *and* apparently useless and unnecessary. No war taken as a whole can ever be justified, for it must start from some original injustice. Granted that the original injustice has been done, must it simply be suffered by the aggrieved nation, or is there a right to resistance and redress? Human behavior throughout history evidences a choice of the second alternative, but the mere fact that nations have acted in this way does not make it moral. Can any moral justification be made out, not for war itself as a whole, but for a nation to fight for its rights in a war not of its own making?

We shall first look at the traditional teaching on war and then discuss the more terrible forms of modern warfare. We cannot judge whether or not the old views still prevail until we know what they are. We ask the following questions:

1. Is there a middle ground between militarism and pacifism?
2. Is there a moral justification for war?
3. What is the just war theory and its conditions?
4. How do we distinguish aggression from defense?
5. How can we assess the morality of nuclear warfare?
6. To what extent is disarmament mandatory?
7. Is nuclear deterrence justifiable?

MILITARISM AND PACIFISM

There are two extreme attitudes on war between which most people try to find some intermediate position. *Militarists* look on war as inevitable, as a natural expression of human aggressive drives, as a necessary element in a nation's growth, and as the normal means by which it plays its role in history. *Pacifists* think that violence and bloodshed, whatever tendencies people may have to indulge in fighting, are so wrong in themselves that to use them even for defense is to use an evil means for a good end.

Militarism was tacitly assumed in practice by most of the world's empires, but it had almost no philosophical defenders until the nineteenth century, when Fichte identified morality with struggle, Hegel made war a necessary stage in the passage from peace to victory, and Nietzsche extolled master morality as the ethics of the will-to-power. Hitler's Nazism was doubtless inspired by views such as these. Revolutionary communism, inheriting Hegel's dialectic without his idealism, had its militaristic phase in the absorption of numerous satellite nations and in its behavior toward them at any stirring of independence.

While militarism is dismissed by most people as an untenable position from any moral standpoint, others insist that war lies beyond moral judgment. Neither morality nor law has any place in war, for war is a unique situation in which life (at least a nation's life) is at stake, where self-interest and necessity hold sway, where men and women do what they must to save themselves and their countries. "All's fair in love and war," so the proverb goes, and so any kind of deceit and violence is justifiable in war. To call war inhumane is unrealistic, and so to speak of cruelty, ruthlessness, atrocity, massacre, and terrorism as inhumanities is a mistake. They are simply manifestations of our common humanity under pressure. War, in this view, has stripped away our civility and revealed our nakedness as militarists.

Pacifism is not a simple movement; it exists on several levels. *Absolute pacifists* condemn all war and maintain that each of us has an absolute obligation to avoid the use of violence. No one, they say, is ever morally justified to raise a hand against another person even in defense of one's personal rights; neither is a nation ever justified in going to war to preserve or vindicate its rights. Pacifists have respect for the value of human life, the good of peace, the need for justice for all people, the value of human freedom, and the injustice of degrading poverty and political repression. Sometimes in the historical concrete situation, these various values are not simultaneously realizable. When that is the case, the absolute obligation to be nonviolent must take first place. No other value can be placed ahead of the value of human life, and so no injustice can be so grave as to justify the taking of another person's life.

Gandhi[1] in India made of pacifism a practical movement. War will be impossible, he argues, if people refuse to fight. Violence must be met by nonviolence, by the active nonviolent resistance of noncooperation. It is as wrong to run away as it is to fight. There must be no hatred toward the enemy and no show of cowardice, but simply a peaceful refusal to obey. If enough people can be persuaded to act this way, the enemy can achieve only a hollow victory, and force will cease to be a factor in history. The cost may be severe to the present generation, but nonviolence will ultimately triumph. Gandhi's critics think his views noble but impractical. They were not tested in a real war between sovereign states but only against an Empire that was already on the verge of dissolution.

Absolute pacifism is an attitude adopted usually on religious grounds, on the statements and example of Christ in the New Testament,[2] but some attempts have been made at giving it a philosophical justification. Human life, the pacifists argue, is an absolute value, and each human being has an unconditioned right to his or her life. Our right to life, being unconditioned, entails that this right must be respected in all circumstances. Even if someone denies my right to life, I must not deny that person's right to life. I must respect the life of even unjust aggressors, for they too have an unconditioned right to life. As we have seen earlier in the chapters on "rights" and "life," the right to life is an inalienable right, for life is given to us and we have no absolute control over it. Each of us is a person, an end in himself or herself to be respected unconditionally precisely as a person. We are not and never can be a mere means to some further end. This requires us to treat every human being—enemies, strangers, friends, relatives, and ourselves—with human dignity. The right each of us has to be treated with human dignity implies the right to life and thus implies pacifism.

Some absolute pacifists use an argument that turns on the nature of probability as used by utilitarian theorists when they tell us to look to the probable consequences of a particular act and, from those consequences, determine what is ethical. Such utilitarian proponents of the just war theory argue that we have a right and at times even a duty to go to war to defend ourselves and our country from unjust aggressors. We are justified in using violence to repel violence, they say, when our counterviolence is exercised under legitimate authority with just cause, with a right intention, and with the probability of success. When we consider not only the probabilities of success but also the probable consequences of failing to defend ourselves and our country, does not the greater good require us to defend ourselves and our country? Just as in the situation of individual self-defense it is the lesser of two

---

[1]Gandhi, *Non-Violence in Peace and War,* throughout.

[2]Matthew 5, 39–40; 26, 52.

evils to kill the person who unjustly attacks me in the attempt to kill me rather than let the aggressor have his or her way with me and perhaps others, is it not also the lesser of two evils for me to go to war and kill the enemy's soldiers who most probably will take my life and the lives of other of my fellow citizens if I do not defend myself and my country? The absolute pacifist answers a resolute "no" to both questions, basing that answer not so much on the consequences as on the very notion of probability. Probability cuts two ways simultaneously: if something probably *is* the case, it is at the same time also probably *not* the case. The probable consequence of my refusing to use violence or force in defense of myself and my country is my own probable loss of life and my country's probable loss of independence or territory, and so on. The consequences are probable, but not absolutely certain; they might not occur at all. If I act on the probability, take up arms against the aggressor, and kill on the assumption that I am going to be killed, then I become the murderer. I have murdered the probable murderer who then, although dead, remains innocent of murdering me. By acting as though a probability were a certainty, I have not only made a mistake about the nature of probability but I have done evil as well. The only moral attitude to take in such circumstances is that of absolute pacifism.

Critics of absolute pacifism, even those who admit that the use of force is regrettable and that peace among people is altogether desirable, deny the pacifist principle that the use of force to meet force is wrong as such. The reason for their denial is precisely the right each of us has to life. Having a right at all means having a right to defend oneself or to be defended from breaches of that right. The right to life is a moral power justifying preventive action to ward off an attacker who is trying to deprive me of my life. The reason that having a right to life involves having a right to defend oneself or to be defended from breaches of that right is because the prevention of infractions of that right is precisely what one has a right to

when one has a right at all. To say, as the absolute pacifists do, that each of us has a right to life but that none of us, singly or collectively, has any justification whatever to use force for preventing people from depriving us of our lives, is self-contradictory. If I claim a right to my life, then to describe some action as a violent act depriving me of my life, is logically to imply that the absence of such violent action is one of those things to which I have a strict right. Pacifists agree that we have the right not to have violence done to us, for they logically imply this in asserting it to be a duty on everyone's part to avoid violence. And this, the critics maintain, is why the pacifist's position is self-contradictory. If violence is wrong, then people have a right to its prevention, by force if necessary.

Relative pacifists are less extreme, objecting only to certain kinds of wars or certain uses of force. In particular there are *nuclear* pacifists, who admit that in principle there can be such a thing as a just war but that modern and especially thermonuclear war has grown so destructive as to be utterly unjustifiable. We shall see more about this view later.

MORAL JUSTIFICATION FOR WAR

Most people think the truth must lie somewhere between the extremes of militarism and absolute pacifism, that war is always an evil to be regretted and avoided as far as possible, but that occasions can arise in which it is not only inevitable but justifiable. A nation may have war thrust upon it against its will by an enemy's aggression and find no solution in pacifism. When a nation that refuses to fight for itself has been reduced to vassalage or slavery, it may then be forced to fight *for* its masters in their further conquests rather than against them. In such a world there will be no peace.

Why is the political state something people should defend with their lives? The reason is that human beings by nature are political, made to live not alone but in society, and not only in the basic society of the family but in the larger organization of the political state. Since one of the main motives for political organization is mutual defense against enemies from without, there is no sense or purpose to political society unless it can defend itself and its people.

As an individual is allowed to use force in self-defense and also to recover stolen property or redress violated rights when recourse to higher authority is impossible, so may the state, and for the same reasons. War in itself is a physical evil; it becomes a moral evil only when there is injustice on the part of the one using the force. A nation against which injustice is being committed justly defends itself, according to the principle of the unjust aggressor. It may likewise seek the recovery of goods it has been unjustly deprived of and the redress of violated rights, since there is no higher authority to which it can appeal. Though no war can be just on both sides (except subjectively, through mistaken judgment) and a war can be unjust on both sides (each nation violating the other's rights), it is possible for a war to be just on one side and unjust on the other.

The argument for the possibility of a just war can be stated thus: The state, since it is a natural society, has a natural right to use the means necessary for its preservation and proper functioning. However, conditions may be such that the only means by which a state can preserve itself in being, and can protect or recover its lawful rights, is by war. Therefore under such conditions the state has a natural right to wage war.

A state that would not wage war under any circumstances, however serious, would condemn itself to political death, to loss of independence, which is the very life of a state, and to servitude under the feet of its aggressive neighbors. If morality demanded this sacrifice, it would be giving only to immoral states a moral right to existence. It would impose on people the moral obligation to organize politically, and at the same time deny them the means necessary for attaining that goal. If a state cannot protect the lives and liberties of its citizens, it is failing in its chief function. If it cannot do so except through force, it must have the right to use force.

THE JUST WAR THEORY

The pacifist tradition in western civilization has its roots in very early Christianity. The commitment to the value of human life, peace, and nonviolence in the Christian community was so profound that the pacifist position was always a challenge to those Christians who would take up arms in war. Were such Christians betraying Jesus' example of a peaceful and nonviolent way of life? The violence of war was presumed to be morally unacceptable, and so the question kept recurring down through the years about whether a Christian may ever morally take part in war.

The *just war theory* is based on the conviction that nonviolence is the norm[1] and that the use of force can be moral only by way of exception if it is used at all. The theory provides a method for making moral judgments about the *reasons* states have for fighting and the *means* they adopt in fighting their wars. So war is always judged twice, first of all as to its justice or injustice and then as to how justly or unjustly it is fought. The moral reality of war cannot be comprehended without both forms of judgment, judgments about aggression and self-defense *and* judgments about the observance or violation of the customary and positive rules of engagement. Note too that the two sorts of judgment are logically independent of one another. This independence is revealed in the fact that a just war can be fought quite unjustly and an unjust war can be fought in strict accordance with customary and positive rules of battle. These two kinds of judgment point to the heart of all that is most problematic in the moral reality that is war.

---

[1]David Hollenbach, S.J., *Nuclear Ethics: A Christian Moral Argument* (New York/Ramsey, Paulist Press, 1983) calls our attention to this essential point for just war theory, namely, that nonviolence is the norm but that it is not absolute. See pp. 16–24.

The first noted writer to treat expressly of the morality of war was St. Augustine. He derived, seemingly from Cicero, certain conditions for a just war and is thus regarded as the founder of the just war theory. These conditions, scattered among St. Augustine's works, are gathered together and systematized by St. Thomas Aquinas:

> In order for a war to be just, three things are necessary. First, the authority of the sovereign by whose command the war is to be waged. For it is not the business of a private individual to declare war, because he can seek for redress of his rights from the tribunal of his superior. Moreover, it is not the business of a private individual to summon together the people, which has to be done in war time. And as the care of the common weal is committed to those who are in authority, it is their business to watch over the common weal of the city, kingdom or province subject to them. And just as it is lawful for them to have recourse to the sword in defending that common weal against internal disturbances, when they punish evildoers, . . . so too it is their business to have recourse to the sword of war in defending the common weal against external enemies . . . . And for this reason Augustine says:[1] The natural order conducive to peace among mortals demands that the power to declare and counsel war should be in the hands of those who hold supreme authority.
>
> Secondly, a just cause is required, namely that those who are attacked should be attacked because they deserve it on account of some fault. Wherefore Augustine says:[2] A just war is wont to be described as one that avenges wrongs, when a nation or state has to be punished, for refusing to make amends for the wrongs inflicted by its subjects, or to restore what it has seized unjustly.
>
> Thirdly, it is necessary that the belligerents should have a rightful intention, so that they intend the advancement of the good, or the avoidance of evil. Hence Augustine says:[3] True religion looks upon as peaceful those wars that are waged not for motives of aggrandizement or cruelty, but with the object of securing peace, of punishing evil-doers, and of

uplifting the good. For it may happen that the war is declared by the legitimate authority, and for a just cause, and yet be rendered unlawful through a wicked intention. Hence Augustine says:[4] The passion for inflicting harm, the cruel thirst for vengeance, an unpacific and relentless spirit, the fever of revolt, the lust for power, and suchlike things, all these are rightly condemned in war.[5]

St. Thomas recognized that a war could be fought for a just cause and yet become immoral because of the way it is fought. Hence, for a war to be morally allowable, besides the three conditions of lawful authority, just cause, and right intention, there is also to be considered the right use of means.

St. Thomas' opinions, stated so generally, needed further development. Among his many commentators, Vitoria, Suarez, and Bellarmine are outstanding in interpreting these conditions and applying them to the new nationalistic warfare of their day. Since these are the principles on which all prenuclear warfare was based, we must see them in greater detail.

Lawful Authority

War is an act of the political state as such. For this reason, only the person or body designated in the constitution of the state as having the authority to declare war can do so legitimately. Historically, this condition was invoked to limit the military activities of feudal lords, whereas in our world today it has the analogous function of limiting the military activities of independent nations for the good of the world. Since legitimate governments today act as surrogates for an unarticulated (except for the United Nations) international authority when they choose war or peace, they must in their decisions aim at a universal rather than an exclusively private good. The welfare of the world community is at stake when a nation deliberates about going to war, and a nation may sometimes have to sacrifice

---

[1] St. Augustine, *Contra Faustum Manichaeum*, bk. XXII, ch. 75.

[2] St. Augustine, *Quaestiones in Heptateuchum*, bk. VI, q. 10, on Josue viii.

[3] Not found in St. Augustine but in the *Decretum Gratiani* (Decree of Gratian, a medieval compilation of Canon Law), pt. II, causa 23, q. 1, canon 6.

[4] St. Augustine, *Contra Faustum Manichaeum*, bk. XXII, ch. 74.

[5] St. Thomas, *Summa Theologica,* II–II, q. 40, a. 1.

even a just claim for the sake of maintaining peace for the good of the world community.

Apart from the case of blameless self-defense, killing is always unjust when done by private authority, but killing is morally wrong only when it is unjust. The lawful authority of a nation is a public authority that has *both* the duty of caring for the welfare of the citizens *and* the authority to commit its armed forces to the defense of its citizens and the vindication of the nation's rights. Soldiers receive the right to kill by being legally and publicly designated as agents of their country in the prosecution of a just war. This formality, however, is not necessary in a purely defensive war, and the authority is rightly presumed. If the country is actually being overrun by the enemy, there is no need to wait for formal induction into the armed services.

Guerrilla warfare in the sense of raids unauthorized by any lawful government cannot be justified, but guerrilla tactics may be employed in a war declared by legitimate authority, especially in regions occupied by the enemy. Even the fact that a government has surrendered to an unjust invader does not mean that all underground resistance movements must cease for lack of proper authorization, for they began legitimately and may continue with hope of foreign assistance. When the government abdicated, sovereignty reverted to the people, who now tacitly acknowledge the leaders of the resistance as their temporary leaders. But after all possibility of success has been lost and the people have withdrawn their backing, guerrilla fighters would become outlaws. We shall discuss guerrilla warfare further when we take up the means used in fighting a war.

Just Cause

In every case just cause must be the real and certain violation, attempted or accomplished, of the nation's strict right to exist and carry out its duty of protecting the community of its citizens, maintaining the conditions necessary for decent human existence, and securing their basic human rights. Such violation might be the carrying off of part of its population, the seizing of its territory or resources or property, or such a serious blow to the nation's honor as to weaken its authority and jeopardize its control. Territorial aggrandizement, glory and renown, envy of a neighbor's possessions, apprehension of a growing rival, personal spites and jealousies between heads of state—these and the like are invalid reasons. The just cause implies several subordinate conditions:

1. There must be a *sufficient proportion* between the good (the values of justice) to be defended and the accompanying evil. War is so horrible an evil that only the most serious reasons can make it permissible. Nations must tolerate minor evils until changed times make their peaceful redress feasible. All the same, a nation need not be victimized by the Hitlerian technique of a series of small injuries and unjust demands, no one of which is worth fighting over, but adding up to a gradual loss of independence. Resistance is allowable as soon as the aggressive intent becomes morally certain.

2. War must be *the last resort*. Before a nation takes to war it must have exhausted every peaceful and nonviolent means consistent with its dignity: negotiation, mediation, arbitration, diplomatic pressure, economic sanctions, ultimatums, and every other means known to enlightened leadership. Once all nonviolent means have been exhausted, the aggrieved nation must formally declare war on the unjust aggressor nation. This declaration gives the adversary a final chance to redress the injustice without actual resort to violence *and* provides the opportunity for serious political debate and consent by the citizens and/or their representatives about the justice of their nation's cause. Otherwise there is no proof that war is unavoidable and hence no sufficient proportion.

3. There must also be *reasonable hope of success*. This hope need not amount to moral certainty, for the fortunes of war involve too many unpredictable elements, and moral certainty could occur only when the strongest nations are fighting the weakest. There is a reasonable hope when it is proportionate to the evils expected. We need *as a minimum* the reasonable assurance that the

outcome *will be* proportionate. To fight when there is no possible advantage is to impose evils on the nation to no purpose. However, a small nation may resist invasion as a protest against injustice and as a refusal to submit to conquest, with the hope that other nations may come to its aid.

Right Intention

A state may have objectively good grounds for war, or be subjectively convinced that it has, and yet fight it for other reasons. It may use a just cause as an excuse to seek wrong ends and thus spoil a good act by a bad intention. This intention may exist only in the minds of the rulers, whereas the people do no wrong in fighting because they have no such evil motives. Or an individual soldier fighting for his or her country in a just war kills for a motive of hatred and cruelty; the country's cause is good, but the soldier's own personal conduct is bad.

Note that a wrong intention will make the war subjectively immoral but not necessarily unjust. It is not morally allowed to continue an unjust war, and reparation must be made for the damage done; but in the prosecution of a just war an evil intention, if present at the beginning, can be corrected and the war continued for the worthy purpose.

That the war be fought with a right intention, the nation's cause must not only be just but *known to be just*. This can be presumed in a purely defensive war, but international relations have become so complex and affairs of state are kept so secret that the ordinary citizen is not always able to judge the justice of a war. Even the most bellicose nations refuse to admit that they are aggressors and put out reams of propaganda to deceive their own citizens as well as the rest of the world. After the war has been fought and all the documents are open to inspection, historians cannot always agree on war guilt.

This quandary can be handled in a practical way only by the rules for forming one's conscience. When the objective truth cannot be known, yet immediate action is imperative, there is no

other recourse but to use reflex principles and arrive at a prudentially certain subjective judgment of conscience. Not only private citizens but even statesmen themselves may be obliged to rely on their consciences when objective truth cannot be determined. Thus, though no war can be objectively just on both sides, the people and their leaders on both sides may be in a state of invincible ignorance, subjectively convinced of the justice of their cause, and acting with the right intention of saving their country. Bellarmine puts this clearly, as far as soldiers are concerned:

> The cause of war should be neither trivial nor doubtful, but weighty and certain, lest perchance the war bring about more harm than the hoped-for good; hence if there is any doubt a distinction must be made between the ruler and the soldiers, for the ruler himself sins, without doubt; for war is an act of retributive justice, but it is unjust to punish any one for a cause not yet proved; but the soldiers do not sin unless it is plainly evident that the war is unlawful, for subjects ought to obey their superior, nor should they criticize his commands, but they should rather suppose that their ruler has a good reason, unless they clearly know the contrary; just as when the offense of some particular individual is doubtful, the judge who condemns him sins, but not the executioner who carries out the sentence of death imposed on the condemned; for the executioner is not bound to criticize the sentence of the judge.[1]

Bellarmine hastens to add that he is speaking of the regular army (to which he would add conscripts and draftees, if he had heard of them), but not of volunteers and mercenaries. Since these latter are not obliged to fight but offer themselves for it, they must make certain that the cause is just.

This condition of having a right intention challenges governmental authorities to confront their purposes continually with the steadfast appraisal of their consciences. The ease with which nations rationalize their resort to war is a commonplace of diplomatic historians. The inhibitory influence of conscience may well have prevented more wars than we can possibly imagine. In addition,

---

[1]Bellarmine, *De Laicis,* ch. 15.

this requirement can help check vengeful dispositions like the demand for unconditional surrender when something as valuable could be achieved more quickly at less cost in lives and physical damage. And finally, a right intention in working out the peace settlement will prevent the imposition of harsh punitive measures that fester rather than heal the wounds of the defeated nation.

Conscientious objection is a painful problem in which the conscience of the individual clashes with that of the nation's leaders. The ethical principles involved are fairly simple and were explained in our chapter on conscience. No country has the right to force a citizen to do what he or she is firmly convinced is morally wrong. One drafted to fight in what seems a certainly unjust war, whether he or she has this attitude toward all war or only toward this particular war, is morally obliged to refuse to fight. Whether the person's judgment is objectively right or wrong is not the question here, for we are considering one who has done what is possible to settle his or her conscience and is convinced that participation in the war would be morally wrong. As we have seen, one is obliged to follow a certain conscience even when it is invincibly erroneous. Nations should have provisions for conscientious objection, and anyone whose conscience forbids fighting in a war is morally obliged to make use of those provisions. It seems reasonable to expect that conscientious objectors be required to substitute for military engagement some equivalent peaceful service to the country, because each citizen has a duty to contribute what is needed for the continued existence and well-being of the political community. If the political community has a right to place itself authoritatively on a war footing and also has the duty not to compel conscientious objectors to engage actively in combat, then the citizens also have a duty to serve according to the capacity their consciences allow unless and until they can clearly say it is unjust for them to serve.

The attitude that, to qualify as a conscientious objector, one must be a pacifist opposed to all war is logically indefensible. It supposes only two alternatives, both impossible for most: either all wars whatever are wrong, or all wars that my country fights are right merely because my country fights them. The whole idea behind the just war theory is that my country can fight a just war or an unjust war, and the judgment must be made about the particular war in question. Many judge that our response to Hitler's aggression was justified but our continued involvement in Vietnam was not. *Selective conscientious objection* is the only kind that makes sense. True, it may be difficult to administer so as to detect cowards and liars, and also the individual is opposing a personal judgment to that of the leaders of the country, but both these difficulties are inherent in any kind of conscientious objection, and draft boards are faced with a particular war anyway. Morally acceptable legislation on this subject is a crying need not obviated by the fact that a particular crisis like the Vietnam war is over.

Right Use of Means: The Conventions of War

Presupposing the justice of a war, we look now to the actual conduct of that war by the military and ask by what norms we can judge the moral character of their fighting. The whole set of articulated norms, customs, professional codes, legal precepts, religious and philosophical principles we call the *conventions of war*. We do not make an empirical examination of combat behavior to discover the conventions, but look rather to the expectations we have of how the military should behave in conducting the war. The moral arguments accompanying the practice of war are the basic source of the generally agreed on conventions that start from the principle that total war with its all-out violence is never justified. Even though combatants on both sides have an equal right to kill, they have an obligation to use restraint to keep the war from degenerating into murder and massacre. The conventions of war, based on that principle, provide guidelines of two sorts: (1) rules about *how* and *when* soldiers may kill, and (2) rules about *whom* they may kill. The conventions of war make for restraint in the use of force, for force is the essential means by which any war is fought. There is reason for restraint, because the use of force is always a brutal matter admitting of few finely drawn distinctions and delicate niceties. General William Tecumseh Sherman once said, "War is hell." What we are seeking then is restraint in the use of force to keep the hell of war from becoming simply an immoral nightmare in which "anything goes" as long as it succeeds and from which few, if any, emerge.

The first set of rules specifying how and when soldiers may be killed is important, because any rule that limits the intensity or duration of battle and the suffering of soldiers is to be welcomed. Such rules are always subject to the transformations brought about by social change, technological innovation, and reciprocal violation "legitimized" by the doctrine of reprisal. As long as combatants fight only with combatants, the rules about how and when they fight do not much alter the morality of war. One combatant kills another combatant. How and when the killing is done does not much change the hellish butchery that war is. To kill quickly and painlessly is clearly morally better than to do it slowly and as painfully as possible—even in hell.

The second set of rules specifying who may be killed in war is more closely connected with the moral notions of right and wrong. These rules aim to set certain classes of people beyond the permissible range of warfare, so that to kill any of them is not a legitimate act of war but a crime. People not engaged militarily in the war are immune from attack; they are not engaged currently in the business of the war. Killing such people deliberately is wanton, dishonorable, brutal, and murderous. This set of rules seeks to draw the line between *combatants* and *noncombatants* who are "innocent" of having done and of presently doing anything to warrant their being killed. Clearly this set of rules is of paramount importance, for it sets restraints on the license to kill and so obliges the combatants to respect the right to life, which noncombatants in a war zone clearly have.

Before we discuss the specifics of these two

sets of rules, we must be clear about the rights and duties of the soldiers and their officers. We expect each and every one of them to be moral agents, and we hold them responsible within the range of their own activity and authority. Today, especially, war cannot be fought without soldiers and their officers having to make decisions that affect the moral conduct of the war. Faced with decisions of this sort, they have clear obligations. They must fight to win, but they must fight morally. Most of the conflicts of conscience arise here, for whether they voluntarily enlist or are conscripted (drafted), they must accept personal risks for the sake of noncombatants. We expect them to risk their own lives rather than kill innocent people. The rights of noncombatants are what places the most effective restraint on military activity, because their rights establish hard and fast standards. This is clear for people who have voluntarily enlisted to fight the war; it may not seem so clear that conscripts have the same freedom since they come to the office of soldiering unwillingly. Even conscripts, however, are not mere instruments of their governments. So long as they have the freedom to kill or not to kill, they have the moral obligation not to kill noncombatants. Soldiers and their officers all must aim at victory, but they have at the same time a higher duty, the protection of the weak and unarmed. The officers control the means of death and destruction. The higher their rank, the greater the reach of their command, the more awesome their responsibilities. In planning their campaigns, the officers must take positive steps to limit even unintended civilian casualties and deaths and must also make sure that the numbers unavoidably killed are not disproportionate to the military benefits they expect. Further, in organizing their forces, officers must take positive steps to enforce the conventions of war and hold their own soldiers to its standards.

In terms of the rules specifying *who* may be killed in war, just war theorists are generally agreed on the following:

1. In the actual fighting of a just war, the terms *innocent* and *guilty* are not very helpful for determining who may be killed, for they amount

to the same as *noncombatants* and *combatants* when we consider the people on the unjust side. Noncombatants are to be presumed by both sides as innocent of cooperating in the waging of the war. In the simpler days of hand-to-hand fighting, the distinction was easy to apply. There was no excuse for deliberately chopping up defenseless women and children with the sword or shooting them down with muskets. In the more complex conditions of today, combatants are considered to be all those who belong to the armed forces of belligerent nations and all who actively and proximately cooperate in the military effort. Since cooperation ranges imperceptibly from proximate to remote, this norm is difficult to apply. Those who perform auxiliary military services, such as workers on arms, munitions, transport, communications, and the like, despite their technical civilian status, are regarded as combatants; their work is directly military in nature and can have no other purpose. The same is not true of farmers and shopkeepers, even though the military may need them; their cooperation is too remote. In between there will be many borderline cases.

2. The combatant-noncombatant distinction is based on the theory of natural rights. The combatants are authorized by their governments to kill other combatants, and so the combatants' right to life and to be protected by governmental authority from all infringements on this right is suspended on the field of battle. Noncombatants are men, women, and children with the right to life and the entitlement to be protected from being killed. They also have the right not to be used for any military purpose, even legitimate ones. Noncombatant immunity places the same restraints on both sides in any war. The rules of war apply with equal force to the aggressive and defensive sides. The rights of civilians must be upheld.

Noncombatants are often endangered not because anyone sets out to attack them, but because of their nearness to battle. Some degree of care must be taken not to harm the noncombatants. The military must recognize as best they can the rights of civilians within the context of the war.

The principle of *double effect* has been used, sometimes explicitly, by military commanders and their soldiers to reconcile the conflicts that do arise between the absolute prohibition against attacking civilians and the gaining of some military advantage in battle. It is permitted to do something that is likely to result in the killing of noncombatants provided the following four conditions are observed:

a. The act must be a legitimate act of war.
b. The direct effect of the act, for example, the destruction of military supplies or the killing of enemy soldiers, must not be obtained by means of killing noncombatants.
c. The killing of noncombatants must not be directly intended but only permitted as a by-product of accomplishing the legitimate military objective.
d. The military must have a proportionately grave reason for permitting the killing of noncombatants.

The third condition bears the burden of the argument. The good and bad effects proceed from a single action and ultimately from a single intention. The killing of the noncombatants must never be directly intended, but the problem is that the civilians die whether their deaths are directly intended or not. If I know ahead of time that I am going to kill some noncombatants in achieving my legitimate military objective of destroying the military supplies of the enemy and go ahead anyway, how can I be blameless? Their deaths are on my hands whether I intend them or merely permit them.

The use of the principle of the double effect may be defensible only when the two outcomes are actually the product of a double intention, namely, the legitimate military objective to be achieved *and* the reduction of the foreseeable deaths of noncombatants as far as possible letting the military accept the costs. Civilians have a right to be protected at some risk to the soldiers, for war necessarily places civilians in danger and the military has an obligation to minimize the dangers it imposes, even though it cannot always remove all danger.

In terms of the rules specifying *how* and *when*

soldiers may be killed, just war theorists are generally agreed on the following:

1. Since the purpose of a just war is to put the enemy's war machine out of commission to stop the enemy from using violence to wreak injustice, and since an effectively armed agent of an unjust government is an unjust aggressor, such persons may be killed *so long as they are effectively armed*. Once they are disarmed, if they are still alive, they may not be killed. A soldier who lays down his arms and offers to surrender may not be killed. The enemy soldiers or agents need not be personally guilty of their nation's unjust war nor need they be at the moment engaged in battle. As long as they are active members of an armed force seeking to inflict or maintain injustice, they may be killed. The soldier of a just government is commissioned by the country's public authority to eliminate this constant menace to its safety and rights. The soldier acts not as a private individual but as an agent of the state and with its authority. War is not between person and person but between state and state, not a matter of individual but of national defense. The attack on the nation continues as long as the war lasts, not merely as long as this particular soldier is in danger.

2. *Guerrilla warfare* carried on as resistance to military occupation after a government surrenders presents a number of difficulties. We shall consider only the matters that touch on (a) the rights of the guerrilla fighters, (b) the rights of the civilian population, and (c) the rights of regular soldiers fighting the guerrillas. The background of surrender is important, for surrender is an explicit exchange agreed on by the two sides. The surrendering government promises that its citizens will stop fighting in exchange for the restoration of regular peaceful public life; the surrendering soldier promises to stop fighting in exchange for benevolent detainment for the duration of the war. The captured soldiers may try to escape the prison camp, and the civilians may try to flee the occupied territory. If either or both succeed, they regain their right to fight in the war and so are free to fight again. Neither the soldiers nor the civilians may resist the occu-

pation authorities with force. If a prisoner of war attacks and kills a guard, the act is murder; if the civilians attack the occupation authorities, this has been considered treason or rebellion in time of war and punishable by death. Many theorists today tend to deny the term "treason" or "rebellion" as applicable to civilians, basing their denial on the experience of the guerrilla fighters of World War II who felt a moral commitment to defend their homelands even after the fighting was officially over. The tendency today is to deny that individuals are automatically bound by the decisions of their governments or by the fate of their armed forces. If, after surrender, there are still values worth defending, no one can defend them except the ordinary men and women who are citizens with no political or legal standing. The defense of the values seems to be the basis for the moral authority of people to resist.

This raises at least the following questions: If the citizens of a defeated state still have a right to fight, what is the meaning of surrender? What obligations do the occupying forces have? If the occupying authorities aim at restoring the everyday peacefulness of ordinary public life, they seem entitled to enjoy the security they provide and also to regard armed resistance as a criminal activity. If however the occupation authorities do not live up to their obligations under the surrender agreement, they lose their entitlements and the guerrilla struggle is moral.

Guerrilla warfare is subversive with reference to the occupation forces, the guerrillas' own government that surrendered, and the conventions of war. Guerrillas wear no distinctive uniform usually; they wear peasant clothes and hide among the civilian population. They are soldiers but do not give the appearance of being soldiers. This subverts the rules of warfare that try to specify a single identity for each individual. If the guerrillas do not maintain the distinction between soldier and civilian, why should the occupation forces?

The guerrilla fighters do not themselves attack civilians, but they invite the enemy to do so. By refusing to wear distinctive garb and fight openly, they try to make it impossible for the enemy to distinguish between combatants and noncombatants. In essence the political creed of the guerrillas is a defense of this refusal. Since the people are no longer being defended by an army, the only army in the field being that of the enemy, the people are defending themselves. Guerrilla war is a "people's war," authorized by the people. This was the rationale of the Vietcong during the Vietnamese war. The self-image of the guerrilla is not that of a solitary soldier hiding among the people, but rather that of one loyal citizen among an entire citizenry mobilized for war. The point is to place the enemy in the position of having to fight the entire civilian population, killing women and children, or to stop fighting and go back to its own homeland.

As a matter of fact, guerrillas at the outset of their resistance mobilize only a small part of the civilians; they depend on the enemies' counterattacks to mobilize the rest of the population. The strategy is to put the onus of indiscriminate warfare on the enemy. The guerrillas themselves have to discriminate if only to prove to the rest of the population that they are not the enemies of the people. The opposing soldiers do not have the same advantages the guerrillas have, for the soldiers wear uniforms that make them easy targets. The key moral issue is the guerrillas' use of civilian clothing as a political cover and a disguise. The problem is with the deceit involved— the guerrilla looks just like an ordinary, harmless civilian.

Guerrilla leaders claim war rights for all their followers, but the problem of the deceit of disguise remains. Perhaps it would be helpful to distinguish, if possible, between guerrillas who use civilian clothes as a ruse and those who merely depend on camouflage, surprise, the cover of darkness, and so on. If this were possible, we could treat those who depend on disguise as assassins if they are caught and treat all the others as conventional prisoners of war with the same war rights other soldiers have. This distinction, however, does not solve the problem because, if all the guerrillas have the popular support of the people or most of the people, then they have the same rights conventional soldiers have by reason of their being the political instruments of

their people. Whether they use the deceit of disguise or not makes no difference as long as their authority to make war stems from the consent of the people they are defending.

What rights do the guerrillas' civilian supporters have? Can they be truly described as noncombatants? The guerrillas do not merely fight *as* civilians, they fight *among* the civilians and depend on those same civilians for support and protection from discovery. Do the civilians lose their right to life and become fair game for the enemy soldiers to kill? There is no clear-cut answer to this question. To the degree that the vast majority of the civilians support the guerrillas, the antiguerrilla war can become a war against an entire people making all distinctions impossible. This is the limiting case. If the antiguerrilla forces cannot make the proper distinctions, they run the risk of killing older men and women as well as children simply because they do not know who the guerrillas are. If the war cannot be won without indiscriminately killing so many civilians that the people's society and culture is effectively destroyed, then that war should not be won. The degree of civilian support for the guerrillas that rules out any meaningful alternative strategies also makes the guerrillas the legitimate rulers of the country. The position of the antiguerrilla forces becomes untenable at that point, and the only moral action they can take is to withdraw.

3. The *siege* of a city has long been used by military commanders in fighting wars. The moral problem arises because the civilians are being attacked along with the soldiers or to get to the soldiers. With the enemy in place outside the city blocking effective entrance and exit, the civilians are exposed to the same risks as soldiers. During the siege of Leningrad during World War II, more civilians died than in the dreadful bombings of Hamburg, Dresden, Tokyo, Hiroshima, and Nagasaki combined. This seems to place the siege as a means of waging war as something the war convention ought to outlaw but does not. The principle of double effect really does not solve the sieging commander's moral problem, for morally is it not the same thing to lock the civilians in as to drive them in? If it is the same,

should not the civilians be let out so that the deaths of noncombatants can be minimized? If civilians have the opportunity to leave, then those who choose to remain and fight can be said to have chosen to share the risks. Without such an effort on the part of the sieging military commander, it is difficult to see how any siege can be justified. Soldiers are under an obligation to help civilians leave the scene of a battle.

4. *Economic blockade* is another questionable stratagem, for it subjects a whole country to siege conditions by cutting off vitally needed imports. Migration of the civilians from the besieged country is impossible, so they must be protected even while the siege commander is trying to cut off military supplies. To cut off food supplies from the military is legitimate, but how can this be done without at the same time cutting off food for the civilians? The naval blockade of Germany by the British in World War I is a good example of a military action that put immediate pressure on the civilian population and actually resulted in some starvation and mass malnutrition. Does the rule of double effect apply to this type of situation? It seems not, because the military were not taking direct aim at a military target but rather indirect aim through the civilians. Morally it is impossible to countenance any military action in which adequate provision is not made to minimize the risks to civilians.

5. *Reprisal* is doing something otherwise criminal in response to a crime previously committed by the enemy. The doctrine of reprisals gives harsh witness to the hell of war and to the need for the conventions of war. The purpose of reprisals is precisely to stop war crimes as soon as they occur. The problem with them is that the one taking reprisal on the enemy commits an act that is known to be immoral. Furthermore, reprisals can create a chain of wrongdoing that cannot be broken and leads to further atrocities on both sides. Some just war theorists argue that the threat of reprisal is the only thing that ever keeps both sides observing the war conventions as well as they do. If reprisal should become necessary, aim must be taken only and directly at military targets with every effort being made

to minimize risks to civilians. Other just war theorists argue that reprisal is never moral, because it is simply doing evil that good may come of it.

6. As far as the use of flame throwers, poison gas, napalm, defoliants, biological warfare, sinking ships without picking up survivors, and so on is concerned, natural morality can suggest some general principles when such means are used against soldiers. While each side in a war has the equal right to kill the soldiers of the opposing side, it seems inhumane and therefore immoral to kill one's enemy as painfully and slowly as possible. Since the war is between the sovereign states and not between one soldier and another, cruelty simply adds to the horror of the war and does not contribute to winning the war. All of the aforementioned means of killing or maiming have been used in the past, and we have always judged their use as a moral outrage. Any nation that goes to war using such horrible means runs the risk of reprisal by the other side. Perhaps it is the threat of reprisal that limits the use of such means.

7. On the treatment of prisoners and spies, the question of taking and using hostages, the commandeering and disposal of enemy property, the rights of neutral nations, and the reparations to be exacted after victory, again natural morality can suggest only general principles. The details have to be worked out by international agreement, with a view to reducing war's barbarism as far as possible. No civilized nation today could be morally justified in refusing to subscribe to such international agreements when the other nations of the world are willing to do so. States that are parties to such agreements are bound by the moral law to keep them.

AGGRESSION AND DEFENSE

Those who developed the just war theory seem to have had in mind chiefly offensive war and even punitive war. Defensive war appeared to them so eminently a just cause that it was either unnecessary to stipulate any conditions for it, or they were automatically fulfilled.[1] For the sake of clarity, we need to lay down a few definitions.

All know what war is, some by bitter experience, so that the word itself is clearer than any definition. If we must have one, we can take that of Karl von Clausewitz: "War is an act of violence intended to compel our opponent to fulfill our will."[2] The merit of this definition is the utterly stark way in which it lays bare the essence of war: the end is to impose our will on another, and the means is violence. This definition very properly leaves out any consideration of right or justice as not belonging to war as such.

War, in the strict sense in which it is taken here, is between one whole state, sovereign and independent, and another whole state, sovereign and independent; it is not between a state and some individuals, nor between a government and its people. Sedition, insurrection, rebellion, and revolution are often called civil war but are not war in the strict sense. People in a condition of revolution are virtually in a condition of war, and it becomes formal war if the insurgents succeed in establishing a working *de facto* government in the territory they control. War is *armed* hostility; commercial rivalry and diplomatic tilts are not strictly war, nor is the so-called "cold war." War is *active* hostility; mere preparation for future aggression or defense is not war, but there must be actual fighting, though it may be intermittent.

The older writers divided war into *defensive* and *aggressive* war. There seems to be a fairly common opinion that the nation that declares war or makes the first attack is waging aggressive war, whereas the nation against which war is declared or which is attacked first is waging defensive war. But this view is too superficial and formalistic. Hear Suarez on the subject:

> It remains for us to explain what constitutes an aggressive war, and what, on the other hand, constitutes a defensive war; for sometimes that which is merely an act of defence may present the appearance of an aggressive act. . . . We have to consider whether the injustice is, practically speaking, simply about to take place; or whether it has already done so, and redress is sought through war. In this second case, the war is aggressive. In the former case, war has the character of self-defence, provided that it is waged with a moderation which is blameless.[3]

Hence a nation is fighting a defensive war if its sole purpose is to protect itself against actual or imminent aggression, even if its defense assumes the appearance of attack. Just as individual persons need not wait until they have been shot at before taking defensive action, so a nation need not wait until it is actually invaded before using means of defense. Moral certainty of the enemy's intention seems sufficient. The formality of declaring war has been discarded by some states, and modern nations must be prepared to meet a surprise attack. The advantage of striking the first blow is so great in modern warfare that no nation, not even one merely defending itself, can afford to give this edge to the enemy. This seems to be what some modern writers call *preemptive* as opposed to *preventive* war.

Since the word *aggression* is now taken almost always in a bad sense, it is more consonant with modern usage to divide war into *offensive* and *defensive,* according to the nation responsible for provoking (not necessarily beginning) hostilities, and into *just* and *unjust,* according to the nation having moral right on its side. Aggression can then be reserved for unjust offensive war.

Punitive war, a war undertaken to punish a guilty nation, would come under the heading of a just offensive war. This is not understood to mean a war to force an unjust aggressor to give up ill-gotten gains, which is mere restitution, but to go farther and punish the unjust nation. And even if the war was not undertaken for the purpose of punishment as its chief aim, still the question of punishing those responsible for unjust aggression and barbarous conduct arises at the end of the war. The older writers, St. Augustine, St. Thomas, Vitoria, Bellarmine, and Suarez, for

---

[1]Vitoria, *De Jure Belli* (On the Right of War), no. 1, 3, and 13. Vanderpol, A., *Le droit de guerre d' après les théologiens et les canonistes du moyen àge,* pp. 42–43.
[2]Clausewitz, *On War,* vol. I, beginning.

[3]Suarez, *The Three Theological Virtues: On Charity,* disp. XIII, sec. I, no. 6.

example, think that a punitive war can be justified. Suarez is explicit:

> Just as within a state some lawful power to punish crime is necessary to the preservation of domestic peace; so in the world as a whole, there must exist, in order that the various states may dwell in concord, some power for the punishment of injuries inflicted by one state upon another; and this power is not to be found in any superior, for we assume that these states have no commonly acknowledged superior; therefore, the power in question must reside in the sovereign prince of the injured state, to whom, by reason of that injury, the opposing prince is made subject; and consequently, war of the kind in question has been instituted in place of a tribunal administering just punishment.[1]

This opinion is opposed by those who argue that punishment is an act of jurisdiction and must be inflicted by a superior on his or her inferior; since no state has jurisdiction over another, punishment of a guilty nation cannot be justified. This view seems too legalistic, as if there could be no law but positive law. Where there is a superior with jurisdiction, the superior and not the interested party is the one to pass sentence and administer punishment, but the mere fact that there happens to be no superior distinct from the parties concerned should not make the attainment of justice impossible. Here natural law, natural right, and natural justice take over.

Since the end of the war in Vietnam is so recent, we should consider the nature of *intervention* as one of the forms war can take. Normally, one nation should never intervene in the domestic affairs of another nation, but sometimes things are not normal. Intervention is not defined as a criminal activity of aggression even though it often threatens to violate the territorial integrity and political independence of the invaded nation. Some interventions are justifiable and *always* must be justified. The burden of proof falls on the government that intervenes to shape domestic arrangements or alter the conditions of life in another nation. The burden of proof is especially heavy when it is a case of military intervention, because the citizens of any sovereign state have the right not to be coerced or ravaged at the hands of foreigners.

Humanitarian intervention is called for and completely justifiable when it is a response to acts that shock the moral conscience of most people; for example, when a government turns its army loose on some of its own people in a systematic effort to massacre them, another nation is perfectly justified in using armed intervention to rescue those people. In fact, the community of nations would be justified in banding together to intervene for humanitarian reasons. India's intervention in Bangladesh (then East Pakistan) is a case in point. If within a nation the dominant forces are engaged in massive violations of human rights, there may well be no help for the people if help does not come from the outside.

Civil war is difficult to deal with because it often presents us with two or more parties or factions, each of which claims to speak for the entire nation, fighting with one another and drawing other nations into the struggle in secret or unacknowledged ways. Generally speaking, once a nation is effectively divided in civil war, other nations ought to maintain strict neutrality to allow those people the opportunity to work out their problems with one another and to establish the kind of government they want for themselves. Foreign intervention hardly serves the cause of self-determination, but when one nation does intervene, it opens the way for another nation to undertake what is called counterintervention to restrain the intervening state and maintain a balance of forces. The aim of counterintervention cannot be to win the war, but to maintain the balance so that self-determination becomes possible. When the character and the dimensions of the civil war are not respected by the intervening states, they may well lose sight of why they are there and try to take over the prosecution of the war themselves, and then it becomes a foreigners' war of at best dubious moral value fought in someone else's country.

---

[1]Suarez, *The Three Theological Virtues: On Charity,* disp. XIII, sec. IV, no. 5.

The same reasoning used for punitive war applies to the trial of *war criminals,* even though the whole war was not fought as a punitive war. It seems absurd to string someone on the gallows for a single peacetime murder and then to let those who have engaged in a set program of mass murder go scot-free, simply because nations have failed to enact a law providing for their punishment. Anyone who admits a morality independent of politics can well justify the punishment of war criminals. Whether it is expedient to punish them or not is a different question. It does set a dangerous precedent that future unjust aggressors who happen to be victorious can use with deadly ferocity against their blameless victims.

Who exactly are the war criminals? Aggression is first and foremost the work of the political leaders. The men and women who lead the nation into an unjust war are responsible for endangering their own people and the rest of us. We are right to hold them subject to moral judgment, for acts of state are the acts of particular persons, and if those acts are criminal acts, those persons are guilty. The head of state and the men and women immediately around the head of state are held accountable for the planning, preparation, initiation, and waging of the unjust war. Obviously a large number of people are required to do this. At what point does immediate and proximate cooperation become remote cooperation? Where to draw the line is not clear. Perhaps "significant contribution" is the criterion that would be most helpful, for it seems to signify a "major role" in the making and/or execution of the injustice.

What can be said about the moral accountability of the ordinary citizens of a nation engaged in an unjust war? Does it make sense to speak of some kind of collective responsibility? The citizens may well feel shame at what their country is doing, but they need not blame themselves unless there was something they ought to have done and did not do to halt the injustice. Clearly, the more a person can do, the more that person ought to do to stop the wrongdoing.

So much for the traditional theory of the just war. What war in history, we may well ask, ever observed all these rules? Probably none. They are not meant to be rules or laws that are authoritatively prescribed. Who has such authority and who could possibly enforce them? Rather, they are criteria for judging war. Some wars come closer to fulfilling more of them than others and can thus be said to be more just than others: to be more legitimately authorized, to have a better objective cause, to pursue it with nobler intent, and to be fought in a more humane way. We call someone good though he or she has some faults; we say, for example, that Joseph is a just man though he has committed some unjust acts. So we can call a war just if it approximates justice closely enough and rates high on most of the points detailed in the just war theory. War is too complex an affair to achieve a hundred percent score on all points.

NUCLEAR WAR

We distinguish between *conventional* warfare, which includes (except for the bombing of Hiroshima and Nagasaki) all the wars fought until now, and *nuclear* warfare, which threatens to be the war of the future. The atomic bombs dropped on Hiroshima and Nagasaki have already introduced us to nuclear war. The fateful year was 1945; we were ushered into the nuclear age and began living each day of our lives under the threat of annihilation. In the year following the destruction of those two Japanese cities, Bernard Brodie, one of the pioneer architects of U.S. nuclear strategy and diplomacy, wrote: "Everything about the bomb is overshadowed by the twin facts that it exists and that its destructive power is fantastically great."[1]

Brodie also warned at that time that no defense against the bomb exists and that the prospect of our having an adequate defense against it in the near future is exceedingly remote. And today, more than 45 years later, that adequate defense is still remote.

---

[1] Bernard Brodie, "War in the Atomic Age," in Brodie, ed., *The Absolute Weapon: Atomic Power and World Order* (New York, Harcourt, Brace, 1946), p. 52.

The reason for making such a sharp distinction between conventional and nuclear warfare is that we have here a difference not merely of degree but of kind. The new weapons developed since 1945 are so utterly destructive as to introduce a new element into warfare, absent from the wars of the past, so that the old principles seem no longer to apply. *Nuclear pacifists* argue that the *use* of nuclear weapons essentially violates the principles of the just war—in particular, the following principles:

1. The right use of means. The use of nuclear weapons is immoral in itself, because they cannot be directed at military targets only. Their sphere of destruction is so awesomely vast that they must by their very nature cause more damage to civilian life and property than to military personnel and installations. They cannot be used in such a way that civilian damage and death are merely regrettable by-products of efforts to destroy military personnel and installations. Wiping out whole cities involves the destruction of combatants and noncombatants indiscriminately. This is mass murder on a grand scale.

2. Reasonable hope of success. A nuclear war cannot be won. Both sides lose. The losses sustained by both parties would nullify any possible benefit derived from a nuclear exchange. Death and destruction, disease and suffering of pandemic proportions without the possibility of effective medical intervention or any other kind of help from the outside guarantee absolutely that neither side could claim a victory. Nuclear war is not just butchery of unimaginable magnitude, it is mutual mass suicide as well.

3. Just cause. The violation of a nation's strict rights is just cause for seeking redress, but not necessarily by means of war, much less by nuclear war. No nation's injured rights could be so precious as to justify the wiping out of another nation's population and the rendering of most or all of its territory uninhabitable for years to come. The nation that strikes first is itself subject to retaliation in kind. No just reason can be advanced for such mutual assured destruction.

4. The proportion of good to evil. Nuclear war cannot be contained within a limited locale;

it spreads to the whole world. Neither can the level of a nuclear exchange be kept limited. Once hostilities start, the holocaust is upon us. Neither party can achieve its war aims. The nature of the weapons makes this impossible. And even if one nation could achieve all its war aims, the good would be canceled by the evils inflicted on all humanity through the destruction of the earth's ecosphere, the poisoning of the atmosphere, raging epidemics, and mutating genes that would be passed on to future generations by the few who might by chance survive.

5. Legitimate authority. No individual or group has the authority to order a nation into nuclear war, for that would be tantamount to ordering the destruction of the whole human race. No person or group of persons has that authority. The complications of modern diplomacy and the efficiency of modern propaganda make it practically impossible for the ordinary citizen to determine whether the country's cause is just or not. How otherwise explain the millions who fought for Hitler? No longer can we blindly trust our leaders when the weight of evidence points to their probably being more wrong than right in having developed and stockpiled nuclear weapons *with the full and deliberate intention of using them* if they think it necessary to achieve some political purpose.

These and similar arguments cannot be taken lightly. They clearly call us to reexamine the traditional ethics of war. No one can reasonably deny that the world at large faces a very real problem, but is that problem basically insoluble? Absolute nuclear pacifists maintain that the only solution lies in nuclear disarmament. Others, apart from the out-and-out militarists, argue that by modifying the traditional principles of the just war and adding some new restrictions, a plausible case can be made for the theory of limited nuclear war.

Limited Nuclear War

The basic premise of the limited nuclear war theory is that the *use* of nuclear weapons is not in itself immoral. Furthermore, the theory of the just war can be made to fit the conditions of limited nuclear war if some further guidelines are adopted. We shall look carefully at this line of thinking now to be able to judge for ourselves whether such warfare is morally tolerable.

Bombing in itself is not intrinsically wrong. A bomb is simply a larger military weapon and, like any other, may be used against military targets; the killing of civilians, if any occurs, is incidental. Indiscriminate bombing of a city or area, with no attempt to distinguish military from non-military objectives, has been rightly considered in conventional war as mass murder. The phrase *military necessity,* which has its proper use, can be and has been misused and twisted to cover any act, however immoral. Nor is it excused by the desire to destroy the enemy's morale and terrorize him into submission, for terror can also be produced by the grossest and most bestial atrocities without in any way making these acts moral. Thus conventional bombing can be moral or immoral, depending on *how* it is used.

Since a nuclear bomb is merely a bigger and more destructive bomb, its use is governed by the same principles. A military target may be extensive enough to warrant the use of a nuclear bomb without disproportionate civilian damage; for example, a fleet at sea or an isolated munitions plant. The enemy cannot claim sanctuary by putting such a plant in a civilian sector and has the responsibility of evacuating the civilian population from the danger spot. If a nation is allowed to destroy a military target with a hundred ordinary bombs, why not with one nuclear bomb? Nor can it be said that the atom (fission) bomb has legitimate use but not the hydrogen (fusion) bomb. It is not the method but the extent and control of the destructiveness that have moral significance. These two types of bomb overlap, the largest fission bomb being considerably more destructive and emitting more fallout than the smallest fusion bomb.

Nuclear bombs pose the problem of radioactive contamination that is absent in conventional bombs. The point of strike and its environs are not only destroyed but rendered uninhabitable for some time. The radioactive cloud is blown to civilian sectors and even to neutral countries.

However, the amount reduces so rapidly as to come well within the limits of human tolerance, except near the center of the blast. Since there is natural radioactivity in the earth's crust and in cosmic rays, a nuclear explosion does not produce something entirely new but increases what is already there. Can an added susceptibility to bone cancer, leukemia, and mutational defects in the genetic pool be considered a byproduct of the war that can be permitted to occur in the civilian population by the principle of double effect? How much worse would this be than our peacetime pollution of the atmosphere by automobile exhausts and factory chimneys? In any war the civilians suffer greatly anyway, and in a world war even neutral nations are seriously affected, at least economically, by the possibility of malnutrition and other repercussions on their lives. To impose these effects on others is not out of proportion to a nation's right to its freedom. The hazard, however, must be reduced as far as possible, and the endeavor to develop cleaner bombs is a recognized moral requirement.

Guided missiles, whether intercontinental or of shorter range, cannot be considered wrong in themselves. What is important is the charge they carry and how accurately they are directed. If a nuclear bomb is justified, so also is this means of delivering it. It must be launched at military objectives only, and its accuracy must be such that civilian casualties caused by it are only incidental.

As bombs are legitimate weapons if used properly, so also are chemical and bacteriological weapons. The difficulty in these two types of warfare is one of control. Any means of waging war that is by its very nature uncontrollable cannot be condoned on any moral principle.

Despite what has been said, the terrible and extensive nature of the weapons used in a nuclear war even of a limited character imposes some restrictions not present in former wars. Some[1]

---

[1]This material is taken from John Courtney Murray, "Remarks on the Moral Problem of War," *Theological Studies,* March, 1959, reprinted in *We Hold These Truths,* ch. 11, and in *Morality and Modern Warfare,* ch. 5.

think that we must make the following additions to the theory of the just war. They can be formulated in two propositions:

1. *Any war of aggression, even a just offensive war, is morally forbidden*. No first use of nuclear weapons is morally allowable to any nation, no matter how grievously its rights are violated. The reason why this is so is that the horrendous character of nuclear war is such that no known reasons can possibly justify the first use of nuclear weapons.

2. *A defensive war to preserve a nation's rights and freedom by the use of effective means is morally admissible*. We can have no peace without justice, law, and order. Free field cannot be given to brutal violence and lack of conscience. Since we have entered the nuclear age, a nation's defense ought not to be restricted to conventional weapons, since to be adequate, its weapons must match the weapons of the attacker. Nuclear warfare of a limited character may be engaged in morally under the following conditions:

First, the war must be imposed on the nation by the enemy's obvious and grave injustice done in an act that can be met and stopped.

Second, nuclear weapons, if used, must be indispensable for defense and in response to an actual nuclear attack.

Third, the proportion of good to evil, including the prospect of success, must be maintained. This proportion is not to be estimated only in terms of deaths and physical damage but takes in such values as a nation's freedom and independence, for the preservation of such values has always been regarded as a valid cause for war.

Fourth, a new principle of limitation is introduced. While conventional warfare is naturally limited by the limited destructiveness of the weapons used, nuclear warfare cannot be limited in this way. Nuclear weapons have almost unlimited destructiveness. The limitation in nuclear warfare must be voluntarily self-imposed by all parties to the conflict. This principle of limitation bans a war of extermination and the unleashing of an evil that wholly escapes human control.

Critique of the theory: In the nuclear age, thinking about war and the use of moral restraint in war both need to be done in terms of the nuclear weapons we have at our disposal now and those in the planning (development) stage. We become hopelessly mired in all sorts of difficulties when we try to think our way through the problems of nuclear war in prenuclear terms. Nuclear weapons have changed the strategy, tactics, and politics of war. Conventional war and nuclear war are two different *kinds* of war. The strategy, tactics, and politics used in conventional warfare will simply not work in nuclear war. We need to break out of our prenuclear categories of thought and adjust our thinking to nuclear reality. We cannot afford to think about nuclear warfare only in theoretical terms which abstract from real life as we live it now. The theory of limited nuclear war is precisely such an abstraction.

To keep our thinking in touch with real life, we have to recall the collective experience we have and reflect critically on that experience. We already have some experience of nuclear detonations. The studies done on Hiroshima and Nagasaki and the people who did survive those detonations provide us with invaluable information to use in assessing "limited nuclear war." The United States engaged in atmospheric testing in Nevada, New Mexico, and on islands in the Pacific. Many servicemen present at those test sites were deliberately exposed to atomic radiation. We do have experience we can draw on if we choose to keep our thinking in touch with real life. Present weapons are thousands of times more powerful than any we experienced in the early stages of atomic testing. Robert Jay Lifton and Kai Erikson describe briefly what a limited nuclear exchange would entail:

A twenty-megaton bomb, for instance, if detonated over New York City, Chicago, or Leningrad, would vaporize, crush, incinerate, or burn to death almost every person within a radius of five or six miles from the center of the blast—two million people, perhaps. Within a radius of twenty miles, a million more or so would either die instantly or would suffer wounds from which they could not recover. If the bomb exploded on the ground, countless others who live miles away, far beyond the reach of the initial blast and searing heat wave, would be sentenced to a lingering death as radioactive fallout drifted quietly down onto people, buildings, water and food supplies, and the earth itself.

But that picture, harsh as it seems, is inadequate even for a limited nuclear war and certainly for a full-scale one. New York City, say, would be hit by many warheads, as would other cities, industrial centers, and military targets—hundreds of warheads, maybe thousands.

One has to try to imagine 100 million or more people dead, and lethal amounts of radioactivity scattered over huge areas.[1]

Such is the picture we contemplate when we think in realistic terms about "limited" nuclear war. Can any degree of nuclear warfare be fitted into the structure of the war convention? It seems not. First of all, the collateral damage caused by even a limited use of nuclear weapons would be so great that it would violate the proportionality limits fixed by the just war theory. The number of people killed would not be warranted by the goals of war, especially since the dead would include many or even most of the people for whose defense the war was being waged. Also, the number killed in individual nuclear exchanges would be all out of proportion to the value of the military targets destroyed. The principle of the double effect cannot be used to make even an individual nuclear exchange respectable.

Second, the limits voluntarily self-imposed in a "limited" nuclear war would almost certainly not be observed. We have no actual history of nuclear war and so no nuclear battles for moralists and strategists to study. We can only construct scenarios and imagine what might occur in different sets of circumstances. The proponents of the theory of limited nuclear war imagine that the limits might be maintained even after

nuclear weapons have been used in battle. However, the risks of escalation will be great no matter what limits are adopted because the weapons involved have such immense destructive power. Just imagine a nuclear warhead aimed at a military target. The warhead destroys the target and, as a side effect, destroys a city as well. The other side aims at and destroys one of the attacker's cities just to show its seriousness and maintain its credibility. While it is not necessarily the case that the war would become total war, the dangerous possibility is certainly there. The two belligerents, once a "limited" nuclear war is begun, have already started down the road to mutually assured destruction. Such a war is simply immoral.

In previous editions of this book we have included a discussion of total thermonuclear war from the point of view of those who argue that it can be made to fit the theory of the just war. The point of doing so was to help readers make up their minds about what they would do if some foreign power started dropping nuclear bombs and missiles on their country. We now see that, if that should come to pass, no one would be able to think further, for almost no one would be alive to do the thinking. Those who managed by chance to survive would resemble the dead so closely that there would be little or nothing to make up their minds about. They would have experienced hell and would have closed their minds to its horrors. Consequently, we shall forego entirely any discussion of arguments attempting to justify the morality of total thermonuclear war.

DISARMAMENT

Everything discussed in this chapter shows what an imperfect world we live in, but it is the only world we have. Here we have to live and live morally. The ultimate goal has to be the banishment of all war, both conventional and nuclear. Living as we do daily under the constant and ever-growing threat of extinction, we realize that we

---

[1]Robert Jay Lifton and Kai Erikson, "Nuclear War's Effect on the Mind," Copyright © 1982 by The New York Times Company. Reprinted by permission.

must make some changes. The very survival of the human race on this planet makes it imperative that we stop thinking in prenuclear terms about nationalistic aims and that we learn to adjust to the nuclear reality with which we live. The nuclear age demands new thoughts and patterns of thinking that are internationalistic.

To be realistic, however, we are still living in a world of sovereign nations, no one of which wants to give up any measure of its sovereignty. We do not have a world government to which all sovereign states submit and to which they are loyal. What we do have is international anarchy with some nations in possession of nuclear weapons held as a deterrent to other nations' initiating a nuclear attack. This is our world, a world in which one misstep can lead to Armageddon.

Every effort at disarmament must be made; but no nation can realistically be expected to disarm while its neighbors (potential enemies) remain armed. So long as some nations are unwilling to submit to a system of international inspection and control, mutual disarmament is an empty illusion. The only interim solution found thus far is a race to match nuclear arms for nuclear arms in the hope that neither side would dare use them first, knowing the price of retaliation. The nuclear arms race is the perpetuation of an irrational condition, and those who thrust it on the world by starting it and by their refusal to cooperate must bear the responsibility. Unilateral disarmament would be a government's abdication of its moral duty to protect its people. Hence we are faced with having to tolerate nuclear testing and the stockpiling of nuclear weapons until disarmament can actually be effected.

NUCLEAR DETERRENCE

We have concluded that the use of nuclear weapons can never be justified, and now we must face the further issue of how we can prevent their ever being used. This brings us to the discussion of deterrence theory. The United States and the Soviet Union both possess large numbers of nu-

clear weapons, a great mix of strategic and tactical nuclear weapons. Other countries also possess nuclear weapons, though not in such large numbers. So far, the United States is the only country ever to have used nuclear weapons in war. Once that was done, the world entered the nuclear age and began learning just how dangerous nuclear weapons are. Since the destruction of Hiroshima and Nagasaki, both superpowers have continued to refine and develop nuclear weapons systems designed to function as force to counterforce. Both have been maintaining a balance of terror in the hope that neither would ever use these weapons to attack the other. As the race has gone on, each superpower has built a formidable stockpile of nuclear weapons and threatens to use them in retaliation if attacked.

No one is exempt from the need to enter the debate about the morality of the deterrence theory. Absolute pacifists, nuclear pacifists, and just war theorists who think limited nuclear war to be morally justifiable must all be concerned with the prevention of nuclear war. The point of deterrence is precisely the prevention of nuclear war. That is the intention. How do we act out that intention? By preparing for and threatening to unleash nuclear war. Deterrence policy threatens what it seeks to avoid.

How can we assess the morality of this situation in which we find ourselves? We have to distinguish between physical and moral evil. Nuclear weapons are physical evils because of their enormous destructive capacity. Moral evil inheres only in the evil choices we make, not in the weapons as such. If we build and maintain the nuclear arsenal with the full and deliberate intention of using it, then we have chosen an evil. But if we build and maintain the nuclear arsenal as a credible and indispensable support for arms control and international stability *and* never intend to fire them, is that not perfectly moral? Is this not a situation which the principle of double effect can illuminate? The one act of building and maintaining a nuclear arsenal has two effects, one military and the other political, which are equally immediate: (1) the availability of immense destructive power, and (2) the credible and indispensable support for arms control and international stability. We intend the political end and merely tolerate the military end, but are we not really using the military might to achieve the political aim? Would any nuclear arsenal be able to function as a deterrent if the owner let it be known that the arsenal would never be used? Is it not immoral to *threaten* to do to another what would be immoral to do in actual fact? Realistically, is it possible at the present time to have a nuclear arsenal with no intention of ever using it?

We have an irrational situation, a clash of two irreconcilable purposes: (1) to permit the survival of the species by frightening everyone into not using nuclear weapons, and (2) to defend one's nation and serve its interests by threatening to use nuclear weapons. In actual fact, we have a contradiction and hence the irrationality. We are simultaneously intending to do something and not intending to do it. We try to avoid self-extinction by threatening to extinguish ourselves. The nuclear strategists have worked and worked to make nuclear weapons manageable, controllable, and conformable to human proportions. After some forty years of trying to impose order and rationality, the strategists have left us with the contradiction of deterrence and weapons which no one really has any idea how to control.

The logic of deterrence eludes satisfying analysis precisely because of the irrationality we find at the heart of it. Moral analysis also yields little satisfaction, for the circumstances surrounding deterrence are a complex of international political and military factors that cannot be ignored. We look for consistency and we do not find it, at least not complete consistency. Whether we regard deterrence as a paradox or a dilemma, we still have to deal with it. Both superpowers are engaged in shaping policies that aim at preventing nuclear war and that also make possible realistic arms control and reduction. The moral problem that faces us is one of assessing the various deterrence policies being proposed and those being implemented. At this point in time we cannot hope to eliminate the irrationality from our world, but we can contain and control it, keep it from going wild, and perhaps even reduce it. For this reason, no one can afford to exempt himself or herself from taking part in the deterrence debate.

Deterrence does not mean the same thing to everyone who uses the term and has a hand in fashioning nuclear policy and nuclear strategy. We need to distinguish between policies and strategies that *increase* the probability of nuclear war and those that *decrease* that probability. Some weapons systems deployed in a deterrent force will make war more probable and arms reduction agreement more difficult or even impossible to achieve. Deterrence policy that is morally tolerable will be such as to alter the current situation by making nuclear war less probable while at the same time increasing the possibility of arms reduction and disarmament. This is the best that we can do in the given current situation. Since unilateral disarmament is unrealistic, we have to adopt some kind of deterrent policy. We can make a moral judgment by asking: Is this policy in actual fact deterrent or not? If the policy decreases the probability of nuclear war and makes arms control and reduction more possible, it is a deterrent.

We build nuclear weapons to prevent war and conquest. We like to think we would never use nuclear weapons first, and yet we cultivate the appearance of being committed to the use of nuclear weapons if we or our allies are attacked with nuclear weapons. To rule out any first use for ourselves while cultivating the appearance of a commitment to use such weapons if we or our allies are attacked can only serve to make our potential adversaries cynical about our moral stance over all. Apart from our "no first use" policy, what we plan and intend if deterrence fails is incredible and monstrously immoral. We can never be sure we will never carry out the threats we make, and for the sake of our own mental health and that of the rest of the world we should acknowledge this and get on with realistic arms control and reduction with a view to ultimate disarmament. The just war theory simply cannot accommodate nuclear weapons, nor can it rehabilitate nuclear war.

CONCLUSION

Conventional warfare is one of the most regrettable things that has come to deface our fair world, a useless, wasteful, human evil. *Nuclear* war is and will remain morally unacceptable. But we must live with the people we find in this world, and if they make war on us, we must defend ourselves. Nuclear deterrence marks the outer limits to which we can go with nuclear weapons, forcing us to imagine wars that must never be waged. Short of those limits, however, there are wars that can, will, and maybe even should be waged, wars to which the just war theory and its rules apply with all their force. The possibility of a nuclear holocaust more than likely is the best incentive we have to wage conventional war as morally as possible. If attacked, we have the right to defend ourselves, for otherwise we must live as slaves of the wicked and leave them free for every kind of violence and tyranny. Conventional war is always an evil, but sometimes an unavoidable one. In a just war it is the duty of all citizens to support their country at the expense of fortune, liberty, and even of life itself if necessary, and their country has the right to call on them for such support. How to steer their country through the tangles of international complications without recourse to war's horrors is the virtue of the diplomatic leader.

SUMMARY

Militarism glorifies war; *pacifism* condemns it, either absolutely or relatively. Most think that war can sometimes be morally justified. It may be the only means a state has to protect or recover its lawful rights or even to preserve itself in being; it has a natural right to use the means necessary to achieve this end.

The just war theory has *three conditions for a just war:*

1. *Lawful authority.* War is an act of the state as such and must be properly authorized. This authorization gives soldiers the right to kill and use force. So long as there is hope, guerrilla fighting and underground resistance movements are lawful, even when the government that authorized them has fallen.

2. *Just cause.* This condition can be the result of either the attempted or the accomplished violation of a nation's strict rights. There must be *sufficient proportion* between the good intended and the evil permitted. War must be the *last resort* after the breakdown of all feasible forms of negotiation. There must be *reasonable hope of success,* or there can be no proportion.

3. *Right intention.* Objective grounds for war may exist, and yet the nation may fight it for the wrong motives. The cause must be *known to be just;* if it is doubtful, citizens can form their consciences and trust to the wisdom of their leaders. Nations must make proper provisions for *conscientious objectors,* even for those who object against a particular war only, and those who are firmly convinced of the wrongness of war must refuse to fight in it. The punishment of war criminals can be defended as an act of natural justice.

There is one added condition for a *morally allowable* war:

4. *Right use of means.* A war otherwise justifiable can become wrong by the way it is fought. The right way is the putting of the enemy's effective war machine out of commission without the undue killing of noncombatants. The treatment of prisoners, spies, and hostages; the use of siege and blockade; and the handling of enemy property and respect for the rights of neutrals—these and similar matters are regulated by general moral principles, but the specific details are determined by custom and international agreement. Such contracts must be kept unless they are substantially broken by the other side, but no nation may do what is inherently immoral because the other side does so.

Defensive war is *just* when fought to repel an unjust aggressor, even when the defense takes the appearance of attack. *Offensive* war is *just* when fought to vindicate seriously violated rights; otherwise it is *unjust* aggression.

Nuclear warfare is immoral because it essentially violates the principles of the just war: (1) the right use of means, for the destructiveness of nuclear weapons cannot be controlled; (2) reasonable hope of success, for both sides lose; (3) just cause, for no violated right could justify the death and destruction that would result; (4) the proportion of good to evil, for the evil far outweighs any possible benefit; (5) legitimate authority, for no government has the authority to order the destruction of the human race. If nuclear warfare is immoral, then *limited nuclear warfare* is also immoral.

Disarmament is to be promoted, but unilateral disarmament is unrealistic.

Nuclear deterrence as both strategy and policy does not lend itself to completely satisfactory analysis either logically or morally. The best we can do at present in terms of moral analysis is to ask whether the particular policy being examined decreases the probability of nuclear war *and* increases the possibility of agreement on arms control and reduction, with a view to eventual and total nuclear disarmament. If the answer is affirmative, then the policy or strategy is deterrent and morally tolerable.

Questions for Discussion

1. When we look at the irrational and inhuman thing war is, does absolute pacifism not become our only reasonable alternative to war? How can we deal with militaristic thinking?
2. Consider any war fought so far in this century. Does it satisfy the conditions of a just war?
3. Study the bombing of Hiroshima and/or Nagasaki. Was this "first use" of atomic weapons justified? For what reasons?
4. Can the notion of limited nuclear war be made to fit the conditions of the just war theory? Perhaps the argument given in this chapter is simply wrong-headed and deserves to be scrapped. What do you think? Why?
5. What can the ordinary citizen do to start the disarmament process? Should we press our political leaders to give up the strategy of deterrence? Do we have any realistic alternatives to offer?

Readings

The older writers who formed the theory of the just war, though they had no notion of modern war, still have something valuable to tell us. Read St. Augustine, *City of God,* bk. XIX, ch. 5–17; St. Thomas, *Summa Theologica,* II–II, qq. 40–42; Francis de Vitoria, *De Jure Belli* (On the Right of War) and *De Bello* (On War), both translated in J.B. Scott, *Francisco de Vitoria and His Law of Nations;* St. Robert Bellarmine, *De Laicis, or the Treatise on Civil Government,* ch. 14–15; Francis Suarez, *The Three Theological Virtues: On Charity,* disp. XIII (On War), translated in J.B. Scott, *Classics of International Law: Suarez,* vol. II, pp. 797–865; and Hugo Grotius, *Rights of War and Peace,* especially bk. I and III.

Perhaps the most useful and readable book on the just war theory is that of Michael Walzer, *Just and Unjust Wars: A Moral Argument with Historical Illustrations.* The following works on war in general will also be useful: Marshall Cohen, Thomas Nagel, and Thomas Scanlon (eds.), *War and Moral Responsibility;* Richard A. Wasserstrom (ed.), *War and Morality;* Rubin Gotesky and Ervin Laszlo (eds.),

Human Dignity This Century and the Next, pt. III; John K. Ryan, *Modern War and Basic Ethics;* John Eppstein, *Code of International Ethics* and *The Catholic Tradition of the Law of Nations;* and Heinrich Rommen, *The State in Catholic Thought,* ch. 19.

On pacifism: M.K. Gandhi, *Non-Violence in Peace and War,* reprints his numerous papers and authoritatively describes his position. Franziskus Stratmann, *War and Christianity Today,* is among the most forceful of pacifist literature. Roland Bainton, *Christian Attitudes Toward War and Peace,* is moderately pacifist with a good historical survey. John C. Ford's article, "The Morality of Obliteration Bombing," in *Theological Studies,* vol. V (1944), is an outstanding criticism of this phase of World War II. Ford's article is reprinted in Richard A. Wasserstrom (ed.), *War and Morality.* Jan Narveson's "Pacifism: A Philosophical Analysis," in James Rachels (ed.), *Moral Problems,* 3rd ed., argues against the absolute pacifist position as being basically inconsistent. Gene Sharp's *Exploring Nonviolent Alternatives* is a source book of basic information of the concept and technique of nonviolent action and civilian defense without armaments. Tom Regan's "A Defense of Pacifism" is an effort to reply to Jan Narveson's charge that the absolute pacifist is inconsistent. This article first appeared in *The Canadian Journal of Philosophy,* Vol. II, and is reprinted in Richard Wasserstrom (ed.), *Today's Moral Problems.*

Peter A. French (ed.), *Individual and Collective Responsibility: The Massacre at My Lai,* investigates the moral and legal questions of individual and collective responsibility in war.

James Finn edits *A Conflict of Loyalties: the Case for Selective Conscientious Objection.*

On nuclear war: David Hollenbach, S.J., *Nuclear Ethics: A Christian Moral Argument,* provides an excellent analysis of nuclear warfare in terms of just war theory; Lester Grinspoon (ed.), *The Long Darkness: Psychological and Moral Perspectives on Nuclear Winter;* Ulrich S. Allers and William V. O'Brien edit a discussion of *Christian Ethics and Nuclear Warfare;* Norman Cousins, *In Place of Folly,* argues for control of force; Raymond Aron's *On War* and *The Century of Total War* question the realism of Western military preparations; Herman Kahn, *On Thermonuclear War* and *Thinking about the Unthinkable,* though not treating of ethics, set the stage by analyzing what to expect in future wars. Peter Hodgson, *Nuclear Physics in Peace and War,* is a very clear short summary. Jonathan Schell, *The Fate of the Earth,* defines the shape and dimensions of our nuclear predicament, graphically describes a full-scale nuclear holocaust, and suggests some practical things each of us might do to help avoid the holocaust; Robert F. Drinan, S.J., *Beyond the Nuclear Freeze,* argues for working to establish a relationship of trust with the Soviet Union as the alternative to the arms race; Nigel Calder, *Nuclear Nightmares: An Investigation into Possible Wars,* argues that deterrence is giving way to a "first strike" mentality among strategists that may infect the thinking of our political leaders; Robert Jay Lifton and Richard Falk, *Indefensible Weapons: The Political and Psychological Case Against Nuclearism,* is particularly moving in the description of the mental breakdown that can be expected among those who might possibly survive a nuclear war; George F. Kennan, *The Nuclear Delusion: Soviet-American Relations in the Atomic Age;* Fred Kaplan, *The Wizards of Armageddon,* and Michael Mandelbaum, *The Nuclear Question: The United States and Nuclear Weapons, 1946–1976,* both discuss the development of nuclear strategy and nuclear diplomacy.

Nuclear deterrence: David Hollenbach, S.J., *Nuclear Ethics: A Christian Moral Argument,* ch. 6, gives a clear and penetrating analysis of deterrence theories; Michael Walzer, *Just and Unjust Wars,* Pt. IV, ch. 17 is excellent; Jonathan Schell, *The Fate of the Earth,* Pt. III, pp. 193–219, analyzes the irrationality of deterrence theory; Charles E. Curran, *Politics, Medicine, and Christian Ethics,* pp. 90–101; and Francis X. Winters, "Did the Bishops Ban the Bomb? Yes and No," *America* (Sept. 10, 1983), analyzes the qualified acceptance of nuclear deterrence by the United States Catholic Conference of Bishops in their pastoral letter on war and peace, "The Challenge of Peace: God's Promise and Our Response," which merits careful reading. Michael Nacht in *The Age of Vulnerability: Threats to the Nuclear Stalemate* argues that the nuclear stalemate, despite its inherent dangers, has served us well and we ought to try to preserve it rather than undermine it; Jonathan Schell in *The Abolition*

discusses deterrence and presents a rational plan for the abolition of nuclear weapons; Joseph S. Nye, Jr., *Nuclear Ethics;* Robert Ehrlich's *Waging Nuclear Peace: The Technology and Politics of Nuclear Weapons* views nuclear weapons as playing a vital role in deterring nuclear war; and William A. Au, *The Cross, The Flag, and The Bomb: American Catholics Debate War and Peace, 1960–1983.*

The nuclear arms race: The Harvard Nuclear Study Group, *Living With Nuclear Weapons,* puts all sides of the nuclear debate into perspective; Ground Zero, *Nuclear War: What's in It for You?,* and *What About The Russians—and Nuclear War?,* are both useful; Sidney Lens, *The Day Before Doomsday: An Anatomy of the Nuclear Arms Race,* thinks we need a defense against our political leaders more than we need a defense against foreign invasion; E.P. Thompson, *Beyond the Cold War: A New Approach to the Arms Race and Nuclear Annihilation,* advocates a nuclear-free Europe; and David Holloway, *The Soviet Union and The Arms Race,* helps to understand the Soviet thinking about nuclear power.

"No first use" policy: The United States Catholic Conference of Bishops, *The Challenge of Peace: God's Promise and Our Response,* is recommended for its argument against the first use of nuclear weapons; Daniel Ford, Henry Kendall, and Steven Nadis, *Beyond the Freeze: The Road to Nuclear Sanity,* argues for a "no first use" policy on the part of NATO; Lewis A. Dunn, *Controlling the Bomb: Nuclear Proliferation in the 1980's,* discusses the "no first use" policy and the problems entailed in such a policy.

The nuclear pacifist case is presented in Robert Ginsberg (ed.), *The Critique of War: Contemporary Philosophical Explorations;* Charles S. Thompson (ed.), *Morals and Missiles;* Walter Stein (ed.), *Nuclear Weapons, a Catholic Response;* Justus Lawler, *Nuclear War, the Ethic, the Rhetoric, the Reality;* Bertrand Russell, *Common Sense and Nuclear Warfare;* Ruth Adams and Susan Cullen (eds.), *The Final Epidemic: Physicians and Scientists on Nuclear War,* has particularly fine articles by R.J. Lifton, H.J. Geiger, and R. Fisher.

Disarmament: Roger Rapoport, *The Great American Bomb Machine,* advocates unilateral disarmament for the United States.

The Nuclear Freeze Movement: Christopher A. Kojm (ed.), *The Nuclear Freeze Debate* includes Robert C. Molander's "How I Learned to Start Worrying and Hate the Bomb," Peter H. Stone's "The Bomb: The Last Epidemic," and George F. Kennan's "World Peace through Law—Two Decades Later;" David P. Barash and Judith Eve Lipton, *Stop Nuclear War: A Handbook!* discusses what an individual can do to stop nuclear proliferation.

William Nagle (ed.), *Morality and Modern Warfare,* is a good symposium. Paul Ramsey, *War and the Christian Conscience,* is an excellent, well-balanced study. Charles Curran, *Politics, Medicine, & Christian Ethics, A Dialogue with Paul Ramsey,* ch. 2, presents Ramsey's position with some criticisms. Thomas E. Murray, *Nuclear Policy for War and Peace,* argues for limited war only, as does John Courtney Murray, "Remarks on the Moral Problems of War," in *Theological Studies,* vol. XX (1959), reprinted in his own book, *We hold These Truths,* ch. 11, in Nagle's symposium, ch. 5, and as a separate pamphlet by The Council on Religion and International Affairs entitled *Morality and Modern War.* A very pertinent short study is William V. O'Brien, *Nuclear*

War, Deterrence and Morality. Jeanne McDermott, *The Killing Winds: The Menace of Biological Warfare;* Desmond McForan, *The World Held Hostage: The War Waged By International Terrorism.*

On war crimes: Burton M. Leiser, *Liberty, Justice, and Morals: Contemporary Value Conflicts,* ch. 16, has a good discussion of the moral problems involved and provides an extensive bibliography on the topic; Michael Walzer, *Just and Unjust Wars,* pt. V, ch. 19, is excellent.

36
Peace

PROBLEM

If war is irrational and wars are not made by the common people but by the leaders of nations, and if the reason that nations have been unable to settle their differences without war is that there is no higher authority to which they can appeal and whose decisions they will respect, the question that immediately comes to mind is: Why do nations not establish such an authority?

The logic of the situation seems so reasonable that we may forget that human beings do not act on logic alone. Even when individuals see very clearly what they ought to do, often they do not do it. It is harder to get a group moving than an individual, and the larger and more complex the group, the harder it is. To move the whole human race, already caught up in a vast network of interlocking societies, has up to this point been impossible. But the point has been reached where, unless this problem is solved, the very survival of the human race is at stake. We ask these questions:

1. What is the normal human condition, peace or war?
2. What has been done to form an international organization?
3. Is international organization possible?
4. Is international organization necessary?
5. How do nationalism and internationalism argue their cases?
6. Can sovereignty be limited?

THE NORMAL HUMAN CONDITION

We must face the fact that throughout human history wars have been almost continual. Thomas Hobbes wrote:

Hereby it is manifest that during the time men live without a common power to keep them all in awe, they are in that condition which is called war; and such a war as is of every man against every man. For war consisteth not in battle only, or the act of fighting, but in a tract of time wherein the will to contend by battle is sufficiently known, and therefore the notion of time is to be considered in the nature of war, as it is in the nature of weather. For as the nature of foul weather lieth not in a shower or two of rain, but in an inclination thereto of many days together; so the nature of war consisteth not in actual fighting, but in the known disposition thereto, during all the time there is no assurance to the contrary. All other time is peace.[1]

If Hobbes could write this way in the seventeenth century, what would he say of our modern nations, which are permanently organized on a military basis? Each nation must live in constant fear of its neighbors, while the armament race, war of nerves, cold war, economic blockade, espionage, propaganda, and ideological warfare fill the interval between open hostilities. By Hobbes' definition there has been no peace within the memory of anyone now alive.

Despite the grain of truth in Hobbes' statement, we cannot accept his view that war is the normal and natural human condition, that war is the positive reality and peace is only its negation. Which one is the normal condition is not to be judged by the amount of time a nation spends in peace or war but by an analysis of the nature of each. The normal does not mean the most frequent, but the standard by which things are measured. There are probably only a few perfectly healthy persons in the world, but disease cannot be regarded as normal. International society is a chronic invalid indeed, but it is a fallacy to make its disease the very substance of its life.

St. Augustine's oft-quoted words containing his two famous definitions of peace as "well-ordered concord" and "tranquility of order" deserve to be read and pondered:

Whoever gives even moderate attention to human affairs and to our common nature, will recognize that if there is no man who does not wish to be joyful, neither is there any one who does not wish to have peace. For even they who make war desire nothing but victory—desire, that is to say, to attain peace with glory. For what else is victory than the conquest of those who resist us? and when this is done there is peace. It is therefore with the desire for peace that wars are waged, even by those who

---

[1]Hobbes, *Leviathan,* ch. 13.

take pleasure in exercising their warlike nature in command and battle. And hence it is obvious that peace is the end sought for by war. For every man seeks peace by waging war, but no man seeks war by making peace. For even they who intentionally interrupt the peace in which they are living have no hatred of peace, but only wish it changed into a peace that suits them better. They do not, therefore, wish to have no peace, but only one more to their mind . . . .[1]

The peace of the body then consists in the duly proportioned arrangement of the parts. The peace of the irrational soul is the harmonious repose of the appetites, and that of the rational soul the harmony of knowledge and action. The peace of body and soul is the well-ordered and harmonious life and health of the living creature. Peace between man and God is the well-ordered obedience of faith to eternal law. Domestic peace is the well-ordered concord between those of the family who rule and those who obey. Civil peace is a similar concord among the citizens. The peace of the celestial city is the perfectly ordered and harmonious enjoyment of God, and of one another in God. The peace of all things is the tranquility of order . . . . As, then, there may be life without pain, while there cannot be pain without some kind of life, so there may be peace without war, but there cannot be war without some kind of peace, because war supposes the existence of some natures to wage it, and these natures cannot exist without peace of one kind or another.[2]

The common philosophical tradition is that peace is the positive reality because it is the good, whereas war is the evil that consists in the absence or negation of this good. The state exists for the sake of preserving and promoting peace, both within itself and with other states; war is the result of some state's failure as a political and social entity. A state does not exist for the sake of waging war and of using peace only as a breathing space to prepare for more war; rather, it is supposed to go to war only for the sake of achieving a just and honorable peace. No cynical observations on how nations really do act can destroy the moral obligation placed on every nation to work for peace.

---

[1]St. Augustine, *City of God,* bk. XIX, ch. 12.
[2]*Ibid.* ch. 13.

HISTORY OF PEACE EFFORTS

The idea of a worldwide society embracing all nations is not new but has been prevalent throughout the ages. As imaginative writers have put forth many utopias portraying what they thought was the ideal structure of a single state, so there have been many idealistic schemes to bring about world union. The difference is that, although the ideal state has never existed, there do exist real states that function despite their defects; world union, on the other hand, has never yet even come near real accomplishment. However, there have been some more or less promising endeavors in that direction, roughly paralleling the development of international law.

In ancient times the Roman Empire took on itself the task of governing the then known world. Without consciously facing the problem, it solved it by the method of *one dominant nation,* and the solution was remarkably successful so long as the Empire preserved its vigor. Three main defects are apparent in this solution: the empire itself had to be built up by war and conquest before it could maintain world peace; it never did include the whole world, and its overextension contributed much to its downfall; and the solution was satisfactory to the dominant Romans but galling and irksome to their subjugated peoples. Militant dictatorships have tried this sort of solution in our time; free peoples will have none of it.

Medieval society naturally turned to the Church as a model of international organization. Why could not nations produce in the political sphere what the Church had successfully accomplished in the religious sphere? Feudalism, with its hierarchical arrangement of overlord and vassal, its limitation and subordination of powers, supplied the means for effecting this organization and logically tended toward a union of the whole world. Dante in his *De Monarchia* envisions the Pope and the Emperor side by side, one supreme in the spiritual and the other in temporal matters, with all other rulers owing them fealty. This arrangement never got far beyond the stage of an ideal, and as a political venture the Holy Roman

Empire was among the less successful, but the ideal colored the whole of medieval political thinking. This concept is past all hope of revival.

When the decline of feudalism and the breakup of united Christendom made the medieval ideal impossible, Renaissance writers such as Grotius turned to international law as the means for keeping the peace. Nations might retain full sovereignty yet cooperate by voluntary agreement. The Congress of Vienna, which assembled in 1815 after the French Revolution and the Napoleonic Wars, the Geneva Convention and the Court of Arbitration at The Hague, the League of Nations after World War I, and the United Nations of today are various attempts to mitigate or outlaw war and to maintain the peace of the world. They have had a moderate success in mediating small disputes but none at all in preventing the two world wars that have wracked our century. If we succeed in avoiding a third world war, the credit for doing so will hardly go to the United Nations as constituted at present.

The difficulty seems to be that, so long as each nation is unwilling to part with any of its sovereignty, there is no way of making any international organization authoritative and effective. World wars are not caused by small countries, which can easily be kept in line by threat of intervention, but by the great powers. If each sovereign great power can veto any decision it does not like, the only decisions that are of value are unanimous ones, and if there is unanimity, there is no dispute to settle. Hence a world organization along these lines seems to be either inadequate or superfluous, except as the expression of a hope that it will some day develop into an effective instrument.

POSSIBILITY OF INTERNATIONAL ORGANIZATION

Can we say that because efforts to create a workable international organization in the past have been unsuccessful, they must necessarily be so throughout all the future? Surely this conclusion would be unwarranted. Here a distinction must be made between the absolute perfectionists and those who are willing to limit themselves to human possibilities. The ideal of the absolute perfectionist can never be realized, for all human works are imperfect, and utopia in this world can never be more than a dream. This limitation affects single states as well as international organizations. We cannot hope that all threat of war will forever be abolished from the earth, any more than we can hope to see our own government functioning without the slightest snarl or hitch. But approximations to the ideal are possible, and we are able by our own efforts, aided by social cooperation, to improve our condition. That is how we have advanced this far, and who is to tell us we must stop? There is a midpoint between a foolish optimism and a paralyzing pessimism.

This problem is the concern of the moral philosopher and of the politicians. It can be phrased in two questions:

1. Are all people today morally obliged to work toward the establishment of an effective world organization?
2. How can we set up a world organization that will have sufficient authority to bring about world peace?

Only the first question concerns the moral philosopher; the second is for the politicians and outside our province. When we examined the theory of the state we did not try to draw up a constitution for any country, and when we studied industrial relations we merely suggested a few of the practical means to bring management and labor into accord; so now we merely point out to the people politically organized into separate nations with occasionally conflicting interests their international obligations and leave to their ingenuity the construction of the instruments.

One may immediately object that there can be no obligation to do the impossible, and thus until the second question is answered the first cannot be. This objection would be valid if we could prove that no effectual world organization is possible, neither now nor in the future. But how can this be proved? If I have an obligation to fulfill, but the means I am now using are futile, I am not thereby freed from seeking better means. We are not yet certain that better means can never be devised. If the refusal of even one great power to cooperate with the rest of the world makes useless all present effort toward international organization, we have no certainty that this situation must be perpetual. Does that nation not brand itself as guilty of immoral conduct, and so confirm the existence of the moral obligation?

The first question can therefore be answered independently of the second. If a thing can be proved impossible, there is no sense in trying to accomplish it. But if it cannot be proved possible except by actually doing it, we cannot wait for proof of possibility before starting to work at it. An international organization cannot be proved impossible, and positive proof of its possibility can come only from success in the effort.

NECESSITY OF INTERNATIONAL ORGANIZATION

The argument here is only a logical extension of the proof used to show that people are morally obliged to organize themselves into political society. There it was said that the state is the natural outgrowth of the family; that when a number of families in a region find it impossible to defend themselves or to supply their needs singly, they are morally obliged to cooperate for their common good; that when a simple tribal organization becomes inadequate, they are further obliged to form themselves into the society called the state and to set up governmental machinery with authority to carry on political functions. The formerly autonomous family was obliged to surrender part of its independence to create the sovereignty of the newly fashioned state.

Because of the diffusion of the human race across geographical barriers and the lack of contact between isolated sections, a number of political states sprang up in different parts of the world. Formerly it was quite possible for each state to be wholly or nearly self-sufficient. A state could defend itself against aggression from without and maintain law and order within, besides supplying its people with their comparatively simple needs. There were wars, all too fierce and frequent, but they were mostly localized. As yet there was no call for an international organization; travel was too difficult, and much of the world's surface was undiscovered.

Today advancing civilization and scientific discovery have broken through all geographical barriers and brought every part of the world into closest contact with every other part. No longer can any nation live in isolation, no matter how hard it tries. National economy is geared to world economy, and national peace is dependent on world peace. Overnight any nation can find its livelihood throttled or its territory the battleground of a world war through no action of its own. The self-sufficiency of the individual state has all but disappeared. Small states, though still technically sovereign, are caught up in the orbits of a few great powers, and these powers are at loggerheads, threatening to embroil the whole world in their clash. There is plainly a need of something larger than the state itself to curb international lawlessness.

As human society outgrew the family and, without destroying the family, required the formation of a larger organization, the state, so today human society is outgrowing the state and, without destroying it, is beginning to demand the formation of a still more extensive organization, a world society. Within each state the civil law can do efficiently enough its work of keeping order and making human life livable, but between states we find fear, suspicion, insecurity, deceit, disorder, and lawlessness, and the only court of appeal is force. We are morally obliged to do our best to eliminate such evils from international life. As now conducted, international life does not square with the norm of morality, for it is not rational.

NATIONALISM AND INTERNATIONALISM

In the debate between nationalism and internationalism, the nationalists argue that the dreams of the internationalists, as contained in the foregoing and similar arguments, are unrealistic;

1. The nations of the world are viable entities, for despite their imperfections they actually exist. But a union of all nations is unworkable. They are too diverse in location, race, resources, needs, language, and culture. They may communicate in words, but they do not understand each other. They cannot be made to agree or cooperate even for their mutual benefit.

2. A federation of nations on the analogy of the United States of America is impracticable. The thirteen colonies were alike in language and culture and occupied a single contiguous region. Even the union they created was unable to avoid a disastrous civil war. Thus a federation is not the answer to the problem of war nor an assurance of lasting peace between nations.

3. Our international efforts have succeeded in establishing only an international debating society. Hardly any accomplishment matches the enormous flood of words. No nation is willing to sacrifice even the least advantage and refuses to accept the decision of the majority. Votes of censure are cynically disregarded.

4. Every nation deserves representation in any international body, but the nations are so unequal in size and power that it is impossible to organize them equitably. Why should two tiny backward states have twice the vote of one large progressive state with twenty times their combined population? The large nations' veto power, designed to counterbalance this anomaly, is the most abused feature of the United Nations.

5. We see that no sooner are all nations united in one organization than they begin jockeying for position. Power blocs and splits are formed among them, negating the purpose for which they are united. What advantage is this over the alignment of nations by treaties and the workings of the balance of power?

6. To equip the world organization with legislative, executive, and judicial power is to make of it a superstate, whatever we call it. The tendency of a supergovernment is to absorb more and more power to itself, even if it is constituted on federal or confederated lines. The encroachment of the federal government in the United States should be a salutary warning. Ultimately the nations of the world, if they form a superstate, will have bartered away their sovereignty and independence.

7. There is the greater danger, not only of the world organization dominating the nations under it, but of one powerful nation seizing control of the world organization and using it as a means of making itself the world ruler. Thus a world organization could be perverted from its whole purpose. From being a protector of the rights of peoples, it would become their destroyer.

8. Contrary to its intent, the argument actually proves, not that nations can be organized to preserve peace among them, but that there can be no peace so long as there are nations. It would follow that the state is not a natural society but only a transitory one that history is outgrowing. By proving too much, it proves nothing.

The internationalists think they can meet objections of this sort. For instance:

1. Would a project such as the Roman Empire have seemed viable to anyone undertaking explicitly to organize it? True, it came into being on imperial and not on democratic lines, but it was so successful because it allowed much local autonomy to its constituent nations. We have now learned representative democracy and a better way of combining local autonomy with central control. No democratic body achieves full agreement, but it can come to a practical accommodation without war.

2. It would certainly be a much more difficult task to organize the nations of the world than to unite the American colonies, but there is more contact between even the remotest nations today than there was between neighboring colonies two centuries ago. Simultaneous translations make language no longer a barrier, and we know more about each other's customs and culture than ever before. We engage in international trade without difficulty; why should politics be an area of irresolvable conflict? The American Civil War was a disaster, but no one thinks it could be repeated.

3. The United Nations is ineffective precisely because nations are unwilling to sacrifice the least advantage and refuse to accept the decision of

the majority. The organization has no teeth, no power to enforce its decisions. No nation will take the lead in applying sanctions. The organization itself must have power above the separate nations.

4. Each nation deserves representation, but there should be some way of making the representation proportional. Why should there be more difficulty in doing this between nations than within a single nation made up of unequal regions and groups? Much ingenuity would be needed to devise the best scheme, but where is there a better use for human ingenuity?

5. Jockeying for position, blocs and alignments, lobbying and horsetrading characterize all human assemblies and should be expected in an assembly of nations. Let nations try to gain what advantage they can by talk, if only they will refrain from war, the sort of war that will destroy us all. Balance of power is one of the ways to curb power, especially if there is a superpower to keep it from getting out of balance.

6. There are those who find nothing repulsive in a worldwide superstate. If hundreds of millions of people can be united in one state, why not the several billion that make up the whole planet? Others prefer a federation or a confederacy, some with more, some with less national autonomy. Tendency toward encroachment by the world organization would have to be resisted, but would that be harder to cope with than the encroachment of nation against nation, as we have had to face in several world wars?

7. The ambition of one nation to dominate the world organization and use it as a means of world domination would have to be curbed by the other nations. They have to do this anyway, world organization or not. They would find in a world organization a ready-made means for acting together with a united front against encroachment, instead of being obliged to oppose it piecemeal, as now. Every effort should be made to build into the world organization checks and balances that would make the chance of a takeover as remote as possible. It would not be perfect, but it can be better than anything we have now.

8. If unlimited sovereignty is an absolute re-

quirement for a state, it would be impossible to organize states into any effective world organization without eliminating the states as distinct entities. But many challenge this concept of sovereignty, thinking it not only unnecessary but the very thing that will destroy all states if each one persists in claiming this fiction. The next section examines this point more fully.

LIMITATION OF SOVEREIGNTY

To be authoritative the world society, whatever form it may take at the dictation of political prudence, must have legislative, executive, and judicial power. To provide it with these powers individual states will have to consent to some limitation of their sovereignty. Any suggestion of this sort raises an agonized protest from outraged nationalism and a vigorous waving of the flag. But such protest is beside the point. Limitation of sovereignty is not in any way contrary to true patriotism, but only to that vicious sort of nationalism that is akin to racial and religious prejudice or is committed to a program of militaristic imperialism. Exaggerated nationalism has never been a virtue but a vice, the very vice from which most of our international chaos springs.

Limitation of sovereignty is only a recognition of the ethical fact that no human right can be absolutely unlimited. National freedom and independence must be maintained, but what right have we to make national *sovereignty* into such a fetish that we must wreck the world to preserve it? Sovereignty is only a means to an end, the common good; when it swells to such a size that it blocks the path to the goal, it must be trimmed down to its proper proportions. As the rights of the individual are limited by the rights of other individuals, as the rights of the family are limited by the rights of other families, so the rights of the state are limited by the rights of other states and of people generally.

Some say that the very concept of sovereignty requires that it be unlimited, that the notion of limited sovereignty is a contradiction in terms. There is good historical background for this interpretation, since the idea of sovereignty was developed to fit the claims of the newly emerged absolutist and autocratic monarchies of the sixteenth century. Jean Bodin,[1] originator of this concept, defines sovereignty as "the absolute and perpetual power of the commonwealth," and says that it "is not limited either in power, charge, or time," that the sovereign prince is "divided from the people," "is the image of God," and "need give account only to God." Democratic and other nonabsolutist states use the word *sovereignty* even in such a phrase as *sovereignty of the people,* but for them it can mean no more than independence, autonomy, nonsubjection to another state. There still remains about it some aura of its former meaning, some connotation of irresponsibility. If sovereignty must mean absolute and unlimited power it can belong to God alone, and never was or could be a real attribute of any state or prince. We have long ago repudiated any such fantastic claims of states and princes, and if the word *sovereignty* still has this meaning for us, we had better drop it.

Each state has the right to autonomy and independence, to full control over its domestic affairs, to *internal* sovereignty (if we wish to use that word). There is no reason why it must continue to insist on absolute *external* sovereignty, why it should not accept the guidance and submit to the authority of a world organization in the control of such of its international affairs as have worldwide repercussions and can lead to a worldwide disaster, engulfing that very state itself. Small states today, though clinging to the fiction of unlimited sovereignty, are practically obliged to accept the guidance of the great powers in their international behavior. The great powers are the ones that need curbing, and if this is not to be done by the system of the *one dominant nation,* it must be done by some organization superior to them all. Limitation of sovereignty is merely the acknowledgment of an existing fact, anyway. It would not destroy a nation's dignity but only its lawless irresponsibility. An individual does not lose personal dignity by becoming a citizen, nor should a state lose national dignity by becoming a member of an efficiently organized family of nations.

CONCLUSION

The very survival of the human race depends on our ability to solve this question of worldwide peace. The condition of international bumbling, with a world war breaking out every generation, never was a tolerable condition, and now that we have the nuclear capability to destroy ourselves and ruin our planet as a place to live in, the prospect of another world war is altogether too ghastly to face. If the human race succeeds in destroying itself, it will be our fault. We see the condition facing us and have the moral obligation to do something about it. World apathy in the presence of such destructive forces is an unreasonable attitude and not excusable because, by refusing to look at it, we foster a present moment of illusory safety. Will we continue sunk in the morass of unreason, or will we have the vision and courage to rise to the next step logically indicated in the social organization of humanity?

This is undoubtedly the main moral problem before the world today. We may never see it solved in our lifetime, but we cannot shirk the responsibility of seeking some solution and trying to lay the first stones in the edifice. The answer just suggested has been dismissed as visionary by tradition-directed minds still relying on a vanished isolation.

Meanwhile each nation as a whole and each citizen of each nation can do something positive about peace. Experience has already shown time and again that extreme disparity between nations in economic, social, and educational levels provokes jealousy, discontent, and discord, more often than not putting peace in jeopardy. All nations must learn to work together to fight poverty and oppose present unjust conditions, knowing that in doing so they are promoting the spiritual and moral development of the whole human race. Peace is not simply the absence of war; it is "the tranquility of order" created by human effort day after day to establish a more perfect form of jus-

---

[1]Bodin, *De la république,* bk. I, ch. 8. See Maritain, *Man and the State,* ch. 2.

tice among all people, precisely because all people share together in a common humanity.

Each nation is the architect of its own development and must bear the burden of this development, but no nation can do this in isolation from the others. Regional mutual aid agreements among the poorer nations, better and broader-based programs by the richer nations in support of the poorer, and major alliances between nations to coordinate and implement programs fostering genuine human development—these and other kinds of concerted action are steps toward international organization and world peace.

Knowing that development means peace, no one has to wait to begin to work for it in whatever way he or she can. Whatever be the social conditions in which our lot is cast, each must do what he or she can to contribute to the common betterment of the human race. Each person has a life to live and a personal character to develop in its uniqueness. In the ways open to each person, he or she can blaze the trails to mutual cooperation among people, to deeper knowledge, concern, and love for all people, and so to a human society based on mutual respect and harmony. Thus each one arrives at union with the highest good, which, for theists, is God, the father of the entire human family, and, for nontheists, is the good of living at peace in the family of nations with all our fellow humans who, like ourselves, are persons, to be respected as persons, and are in fact our brothers and sisters.

SUMMARY

Despite its frequency, war is the disease of our political life, peace its normal condition. Wars should be fought to secure peace; peace should not be used to prepare for more war. Peace is the good, war the evil that deprives us of peace.

Attempts to organize the nations of the world in the interest of international harmony have all been futile. This does not prove that the nations never can be organized, but only that we have not yet found successful means to do this. It is not for ethics to find these means, but to point out our obligation to search for them.

That an *international organization is necessary* is but a logical continuation of the argument that the state is necessary. The individual is insufficient and forms the family, the family is insufficient and forms the tribe, the tribe becomes insufficient and organizes itself into the political state. Today, because of the surmounting of geographical barriers, the state is no longer self-sufficient and must band with the other states of the world for their mutual safety and benefit.

Nationalists claim that a world organization is impossible because of the diversity of nations, the complexity of the organization, the wordy debates, the inequity of representation, the blocs and splits among the constituents, the tendency toward centralization, the danger of domination by a strong power, and the extinction of the states in a superstate.

Internationalists acknowledge the difficulties but think that they can be overcome. If the organization can offer some hope of eliminating world wars, it will be worth all the effort and will certainly be better than our present condition, which offers no such hope.

To be *authoritative and effective* a world society needs legislative, executive, and judicial power, so that states will have to consent to some *limitation of sovereignty*. Sovereignty cannot be absolute anyway but is limited by the rights of other states. A transfer of political sovereignty in matters that concern the peace of the world, provided all other states did the same, would not compromise a nation's dignity or independent equality with all other nations; it would only curb the lawless irresponsibility with which the great powers have pursued their selfish ambitions.

The present international chaos is immoral. If for good reasons the foregoing solution be unacceptable, right reason demands that some better one be sought.

Questions for Discussion

1. What seems to be the chief failure in the various peace ventures of the past? Can practical politicians be expected to bother about the ethical theories of philosophers? Is speculation on these matters doomed to futility?

2. What hope is there in the United Nations? Is there a moral obligation to support the United Nations, or is that optional? Should it be supported until something better can be devised?

3. What is your theory on national sovereignty? Must it be supreme, absolute? Can it be divided? Is the notion of limited sovereignty a contradiction? Has a nation the moral right to hand over part of its sovereignty to a more inclusive organization?

4. Is a world state inevitable? Would the formation of a world federation or confederation with real power tend to greater and greater centralization until it forms in effect one world empire? Is this too great a price to pay for peace? Is it the only price?

5. Is it moral for us to concentrate solely on the living of our individual moral lives and to avoid social, national, and international problems as something no one can do anything about? Is each person involved in these matters by the mere fact of being a person?

Readings

Read Immanuel Kant's famous little essay, *Perpetual Peace,* which is perhaps the first articulate call for world peace through world organization.

Two popes, Benedict XV in World War I and Pius XII in World War II, have expressed themselves on world organization; John XXIII in his encyclical letter, *Pacem in terris* (Peace on earth), and Paul VI in his address to the United Nations and in his encyclical, *Populorum Progressio* (The Development of Peoples) reinforce their statements. Though speaking as religious leaders, they base their views on the dictates of reason and political philosophy.

Robert M. Hutchins' lecture, *St. Thomas and the World State,* has some interesting speculations; so also has Mortimer Adler's *How to Think about War and Peace.* Read Jacques Maritain, *Man and the State,* ch. 1–2, 7, and Heinrich Rommen, *The State in Catholic Thought,* ch. 31–32. A hopeful sign is Charles Duryea Smith (ed.), *The Hundred Percent Challenge: Building a National Institute of Peace; A Platform for Planning and Programs.*

Don Luigi Sturzo, *Nationalism and Internationalism,* ch. 8–9, has pertinent material.

William Ebenstein, *Modern Political Thought,* and Robert Ginsberg (ed.), *The Critique of War: Contemporary Philosophical Explorations,* both reprint some provocative articles from prominent writers on the passage from nationalism to world order.

Bibliography

CLASSICAL PHILOSOPHERS AND MORALISTS

Plato, *Dialogues*. In Benjamin Jowett, *The Dialogues of Plato*, 5 vols., London, Oxford University Press, Inc., 1892. Other translations and editions.

Aristotle, *Nicomachean Ethics, Politics, Metaphysics, Categories, Posterior Analytics, Rhetoric, On the Generation of Animals*. In W.D. Ross (ed.), *The Works of Aristotle Translated into English*, 12 vols., Oxford, The Clarendon Press, 1908–1952. Other translations and editions.

Lucretius, *On the Nature of Things*, translated by Cyril Bailey, Oxford, The Clarendon Press, 1910. Other translations and editions.

Cicero, *Tusculan Disputations, On Duties, On the Republic, On Laws, Academics, Paradoxes of the Stoics, For Milo*. Loeb Classical Library, Cambridge, MA, Harvard University Press. Other translations and editions.

Seneca, *Letters* (Epistolae Morales), 3 vols., *Moral Essays* (Dialogi Morales), 3 vols., Loeb Classical Library, New York, NY, G.P. Putnam's Sons, 1917–1935.

Epictetus, *Discourses*, 2 vols., Boston, MA, Little, Brown & Co., 1891. Other editions.

Marcus Aurelius, *Meditations*, New York, NY, A.L. Burt Co., Inc., n.d. Other translations and editions.

Diogenes Laertius, *Lives and Opinions of Eminent Philosophers*, 2 vols., Loeb Classical Library, Cambridge, MA, Harvard University Press, 1925.

St. Augustine, *The City of God, On Free Will, Against Faustus the Manichaean, Questions on the Heptateuch, On Lying, Against Lying, The Happy Life, On the Morals of the Catholic Church, On Christian Doctrine*. English translations in the Fathers of the Church Series, New York, NY, Cima Publishing Co., and in the Ancient Christian Writers Series, Westminster, MD, The Newman Press. The English titles vary in different editions.

Boethius *The Theological Tractates* and *The Consolation of Philosophy*, Loeb Classical Library Cambridge, MA, Harvard University Press, 1918.

St. Isidore of Seville, *Etymologies*. In Migne, *Patres Latini*, vol. 82, Paris, 1850. No English translation available.

Abelard, Peter, *Ethics, or Know Thyself*. In J.R. McCallum, *Abelard's Ethics*, Oxford, Basil Blackwell & Mott, Ltd., 1935.

St. Thomas Aquinas, *Summa Theologica, Summa Contra Gentiles, In Libros Ethicorum, De Veritate, De Regimine Principium*. Commentary on the Nicomachean Ethics, Chicago, IL, Henry Regnery Co., 1964. *On Kingship to the King of Cyprus* (De Regimine Principum), Toronto, Pontifical Institute of Medieval Studies, 1949. *Summa Theologica*, 3 vols., New York, NY, Benziger Brothers, Inc., 1947. Older edition in 22 vols., Benziger Brothers, Inc., 1911–1929. Blackfriars Edition, Latin with English translation, New York, NY, McGraw-Hill Book Co., 1963–1965. *Truth* (De Veritate), 3 vols., Chicago, IL, Henry Regnery Co., 1953. *On the Truth of the Catholic Faith* (Summa Contra Gentiles), 6 vols., New York, NY, Doubleday & Co., Inc., 1954. Older edition in 5 vols., Benziger Brothers, Inc., 1923.

Cajetan, Thomas de Vio, *Commentaries on the Summa Theologica of St. Thomas*. In the Leonine Edition of St. Thomas' works. No English translation.

Machiavelli, Niccolò, *The Prince and Other Works*, New York, NY, Farrar, Straus, & Giroux, Inc., 1941.

Bodin, Jean, *On the Commonwealth* (De la république). An abridged translation by M.J. Tooley, New York, NY, The Macmillan Co., 1955.

James I. In Charles McIlwain (ed.), *The Political Works of James I*, Cambridge, MA, Harvard University Press, 1918.

Vitoria, Francisco de, *On the Indians, On the Right of War, On War*. In J.B. Scott, *The Spanish Origin of International Law: Francisco de Vitoria and His Law of Nations*, Oxford, The Clarendon Press, 1934.

Bellarmine, St. Robert, *On the Laity*. In *De Laicis, or the Treatise on Civil Government*, New York, NY, Fordham University Press, 1928.

Suarez, Francisco, *On Laws, Defense of the Catholic Faith, On the Theological Virtues: Charity*. In J.B. Scott, *The Classics of International Law: Selections from Three Works of Francisco Suárez*, Oxford, The Clarendon Press, 1944.

Grotius, Hugo, *The Rights of War and Peace*, New York, NY, Universal Classics Library, 1901.

De Lugo, John Cardinal, *On Justice and Right* (De Justitia et Jure), Venice, N. Pezzana, 1751. No English translation.

Hobbes, Thomas, *The Elements of Law, Natural and Politic*, New York, NY, Barnes & Noble Books, 1969. *Leviathan*, Oxford, The Clarendon Press, 1909. Many other editions.

Descartes, René, *Meditations, Objections and Replies*. In *The Philosophical Works of Descartes*, London, Cambridge University Press, 1931. Many other editions.

Spinoza, Baruch, *Ethics, Theologico-Political Treatise, Political Treatise*. In *Chief Works of Spinoza*, New York, NY, Dover Publications, Inc., 1951. Many other editions of the *Ethics*.

Leibniz, Gottfried, *Principles of Nature and Grace*. In *Leibniz Selections*, New York, NY, Charles Scribner's Sons, 1951.

Locke, John, *Letter Concerning Toleration*, New York, NY, Appleton-Century-Crofts, 1937. *Two Treatises of Government*, New York, NY, Hafner Publishing Co., Inc., 1947. Contains Sir Robert Filmer's *Patriarcha*.

Cudworth, Ralph, *Treatise Concerning Eternal and Immutable Morality*. In Selby-Bigge, in Raphael, and in Rand.

Mandeville, Bernard de, *An Inquiry into the Origin of Moral Virtue*. In *The Fable of the Bees*, etc. in Selby-Bigge, in Raphael, and in Rand.

Shaftesbury, Anthony, Earl of, *Characteristics of Men, Manners, Opinions and Times*. In Selby-Bigge, in Raphael, and in Rand.

Clarke, Samuel, *Discourse upon Natural Religion*. In Selby-Bigge and Raphael.

Hutcheson, Francis, *Essay on the Nature and Conduct of the Passions and Affections*, Delmar, NY, Scholars' Facsimiles & Reprints, 1969. *Illustrations on the Moral Sense*, ed. by Bernard Peach, Cambridge, MA, Belknap Press of Harvard University Press, 1971. *An Inquiry into the Original of Our Ideas of Beauty and Virtue*. In Selby-Bigge, in Raphael, and in Rand.

Butler, Joseph, *The Works of Joseph Butler*, vol. 2, *Sermons*, Oxford, The Clarendon Press, 1874. In Selby-Bigge, in Raphael, and in Rand.

Edwards, Jonathan, *Freedom of the Will*, ed. by Arnold S. Kaufman and William K. Frankena, Indianapolis, IN, The Bobbs-Merrill Co., Inc., 1969.

Hume, David, *Inquiry Concerning Human Understanding,*

Indianapolis, IN, The Bobbs-Merrill Co., Inc., 1955. *Inquiry Concerning the Principles of Morals,* Indianapolis, IN, The Bobbs-Merrill Co., Inc., 1957. *Treatise of Human Nature,* Oxford, The Clarendon Press, 1888.

Malthus, Thomas, *On Population,* ed. by Anthony Flew, Harmondsworth, UK, Penguin Books, Ltd., 1971.

Montesquieu, Charles Louis de Secondat, *The Spirit of the Laws,* translated by Thomas Nugent, introd. by Franz Neumann, New York, NY, Hafner Publishing Co., 1949.

Smith, Adam, *The Theory of Moral Sentiments.* In *Smith's Moral and Political Philosophy,* New York, NY, Hafner Publishing Co., Inc., 1948. In Selby-Bigge, in Raphael, and in Rand. *The Theory of Moral Sentiments,* New Rochelle, NY, Arlington House, Inc., 1969.

Reid, Thomas, *Essays on the Active Powers of Man.* In *The Philosophical Works of Thomas Reid,* vol. II, Edinburgh, James Thin, 1895.

Rousseau, Jean Jacques, *The Social Contract,* New York, NY, Hafner Publishing Co., Inc., 1947.

Kant, Immanuel, *Fundamental Principles of the Metaphysic of Morals, Critique of Practical Reason, The Metaphysics of Morals, Lectures on Ethics, Perpetual Peace.* Numerous translations and editions. All are in the Library of Liberal Arts, Indianapolis, IN, The Bobbs-Merrill Co., Inc., except *Lectures* (New York, NY, Harper & Row, Publishers). *Kant's Political Writings,* ed. by Hans Reiss, translated by H.B. Nisbet, Cambridge, Cambridge University Press, 1970.

Hegel, Georg W.F., *Encyclopaedia of the Philosophical Sciences,* Oxford, The Clarendon Press, 1892. *Phenomenology of Mind,* translated by J.B. Baillie, New York, NY, The Macmillan Co., 1931. *Philosophy of Right,* Oxford, The Clarendon Press, 1949. *Science of Logic,* New York, NY, The Macmillan Co., 1929.

Schopenhauer, Arthur, *The World as Will and Idea,* 3 vols., London, Trübner & Co., 1883–1886. *Complete Essays of Schopenhauer,* translated by T.B. Saunders, New York, NY, Wiley Book Co., 1942.

Kierkegaard, Søren, *Concluding Unscientific Postscript,* London, Oxford University Press, 1941. *Fear and Trembling, Sickness unto Death,* Princeton, NJ, Princeton University Press, 1941. *Philosophical Fragments,* Princeton, NJ, Princeton University Press, 1941.

Nietzsche, Friedrich, *Thus Spake Zarathustra, Beyond Good and Evil, Genealogy of Morals.* In Collected Works, New York, NY, Russell & Russell, Inc., Publishers, 1964.

Comte, Auguste, *The Positive Philosophy of Auguste Comte,* condensed by H. Martineau, 2 vols., London, Trübner & Co., 1853.

Bentham, Jeremy, *An Introduction to the Principles of Morals and Legislation,* New York, NY, Russell & Russell, Inc., Publishers, 1962. Other editions.

Huxley, Thomas H., *Evolution and Ethics,* New York, NY, Kraus Reprint Co., 1969. Reprint of 1897 ed.

Mill, John Stuart, *Essays on Economics and Society,* London, Routledge & Kegan Paul, Ltd., 1967. *Mill's Ethical Writings,* ed. by J B. Schneewind, New York, NY, The Macmillan Co., 1965. *Utilitarianism, On Liberty, Representative Government,* London, J.M. Dent & Sons, Ltd., Publishers (Everyman's Library), 1957.

Sedgwick, Henry, *The Methods of Ethics,* London, Macmillan & Co., Ltd., 1901, 1968.

Spencer, Herbert, *The Principles of Ethics,* 2 vols., New York, NY, D. Appleton & Co., 1896.

Marx, Karl, *Capital: a Critique of Political Economy,* New York, NY, The Modern Library, 1936. *Capital: a Critique of Political Economy,* ed. by Friedrick Engels, translated by Samuel Moore and Edward Aveling, 3 vols., New York, NY, International Publishers Co., Inc., 1967. *A Contribution to the Critique of Political Economy,* New York, NY, The International Library Publishing Co., 1904. *Critique of the Gotha Programme,* New York, NY, International Publishers Co., Inc., 1938. *Critique of Political Economy,* translated by S.W. Ryazanskaya, London, Lawrence & Wishart, Ltd., 1971. (Original, 1859). *Pre-Capitalist Economic Formations,* New York, NY, International Publishers Co., Inc., 1965. *Revolution and Counterrevolution,* ed. by E.M. Aveling, London, George Allen and Unwin, Ltd., 1971. *Selected Writings in Sociology and Social Philosophy,* translated by T.B. Bottomore, ed.; introd. and notes by T.B. Bottomore and Maximilien Rubel; foreword by Erich Fromm, New York, NY, McGraw-Hill Book Co., 1964.

Marx, Karl, *Early Writings,* trs. and ed. by T.B. Bottomore; foreword by Erich Fromm, New York, NY, McGraw-Hill Book Co., 1964.

Marx, Karl, and Engels, Friedrich, *The Communist Manifesto,* with selections from Marx, Karl, *The Eighteenth Brumaire of Louis Bonaparte* and *Capital,* ed. by Samuel H. Beer, New York, NY, Appleton-Century-Crofts, 1955.

Marx, Karl, and Engels, Friedrich, *The German Ideology,* New York, NY, International Publishers Co., Inc., 1947. *The Holy Family,* Moscow, Foreign Languages Publishing House, 1956.

Marx, Karl, Engels, Friedrich, and Lenin, Vladimir I., *Reader in Marxist Philosophy: From the Writings of Marx, Engels, and Lenin,* selected and ed. with introd. and notes by Howard Selsam and Harry Martel, New York, NY, International Publishers, 1963.

Engels, Friedrich, *Anti-Dühring; Herr Eugen Dühring's Revolution in Science,* Moscow, Foreign Languages Publishing House, 1962. *Dialectics of Nature,* New York, NY, International Publishing Co., Inc., 1960. *Ludwig Feuerbach and the Outcome of Classical German Philosophy,* New York, NY, International Publishers Co., Inc., 1941. *The Origin of the Family, Private Property and the State,* Moscow, Foreign Languages Publishing House, 1959. *Selected Writings,* ed. by W.O. Henderson, Baltimore, MD, Penguin Books, Inc., 1967. *Socialism, Utopian and Scientific,* Moscow, Foreign Languages Publishing House, 1958.

Lenin, Vladimir I., *Imperialism, the Highest Stage of Capitalism,* Moscow, Foreign Languages Publishing House, 1947. *The State and Revolution,* Moscow, Foreign Languages Publishing House, 1947; New York, NY, International Publishers Co., Inc., 1954 (copyright 1932).

Fromm, Erich (ed.), *Marx's Concept of Man,* New York, NY, Frederick Ungar Publishing Co., Inc., 1961.

Possony, Stefan T. (ed.), *Lenin Reader,* Chicago, IL, Henry Regnery, 1966.

Mao Tse-tung, *Papers: Anthology and Bibliography,* ed. by Ch'en Jerome, London, Oxford University Press, 1970. *Selected Works,* 5 vols., New York, NY, International Publishers Co., Inc., 1954.

Newman, John Henry, Cardinal, *Apologia pro Vita Sua,* New York, NY, D. Appleton & Co., 1865. *Grammar of Assent,*

London, Burns, Oates & Co., 1870. *The Idea of a University,* London, Longmans, Green & Co., 1885.

Bradley, Francis Herbert, *Ethical Studies,* London, P.S. King & Son, Ltd., 1876.

Moore, G.E., *Ethics,* 2nd rev. ed., New York, NY, Oxford University Press, 1966. *Principia Ethica,* London, Cambridge University Press, 1903.

James, William, *Pragmatism,* New York, NY, Longmans, Green & Co., Inc., 1907. *Principles of Psychology,* 2 vols., New York, NY, Henry Holt & Co., 1890. *The Will to Believe,* New York, NY, Longmans, Green & Co., 1932.

Dewey, John, *Human Nature and Conduct,* New York, NY, Henry Holt & Co., 1922. *The Quest for Certainty,* New York, NY, Minton, Balch & Co., 1929. *Reconstruction in Philosophy,* New York, NY, Henry Holt & Co., 1920. *Theory of the Moral Life,* with an introd. by Arnold Isenberg, New York, NY, Holt, Rinehart & Winston, Inc., 1960. *Theory of Valuation,* Chicago, IL, The University of Chicago Press, 1939.

Perry, Ralph Barton, *General Theory of Value,* Cambridge, MA, Harvard University Press, 1926. *Realms of Value,* Cambridge, MA, Harvard University Press, 1954.

Russell, Bertrand, *Authority and the Individual,* London, George Allen & Unwin, Ltd., 1966. *The Conquest of Happiness,* New York, NY, Liveright, 1958 (1930, 1st ed.). *Human Society in Ethics and Politics,* New York, NY, Simon & Schuster, Inc., 1955. *Marriage and Morals,* New York, NY, Liveright, 1957 (1929, 1st ed.). *Mysticism and Logic,* New York, NY, Longmans, Green & Co., Inc., 1918. *Road to Freedom: Socialism, Anarchism and Syndicalism,* New York, NY, Barnes & Noble Books, 1966. *Why Men Fight: A Method of Abolishing the International Duel,* New York, NY, Garland Publishing, Inc., 1972 (copyright 1916).

Brentano, Franz, *Foundation and Construction of Ethics,* translated by E.H. Schneewind, London, Routledge & Kegan Paul, Ltd., 1972; New York, NY, Humanities Press, 1973. *The Origin of Our Knowledge of Right and Wrong,* ed. by Oskar Kraus; Eng. ed. by R.M. Chisholm, translated by R.M. Chisholm and E.H. Schneewind, London, Routledge & Kegan Paul, Ltd.; New York, NY, Humanities Press, Inc., 1969.

Hartmann, Nicolai, *Ethics,* 3 vols., New York, NY, The Macmillan Co., 1932.

Heidegger, Martin, *Being and Time,* translated by J. Macquarrie and E. Robinson, New York, NY, Harper & Row, Publishers, 1962.

Sartre, Jean-Paul, *Being and Nothingness,* New York, NY, Philosophical Library, Inc., 1956. *Existentialism,* New York, NY, Philosophical Library, Inc., 1956.

Maritain, Jacques, *Essay on Christian Philosophy,* New York, NY, Philosophical Library, Inc., 1955. *Existence and the Existent,* New York, NY, Pantheon Books, Inc., 1948. *Freedom in the Modern World,* New York, NY, Charles Scribner's Sons, 1936. *Moral Philosophy: an Historical and Critical Survey of the Great Systems,* New York, NY, Charles Scribner's Sons, 1964. *The Person and the Common Good,* New York, NY, Charles Scribner's Sons, 1947. *The Range of Reason,* New York, NY, Charles Scribner's Sons, 1942. *The Rights of Man and Natural Law,* translated by Doris C. Anson, New York, NY, Gordian Press, Inc., 1971. *Science and Wisdom,* New York, NY, Charles Scribner's Sons, 1940.

True Humanism, New York, NY, Charles Scribner's Sons, 1938.

Gilson, Etienne, *Moral Values and Moral Life,* Hamden, CT, The Shoe String Press, Inc., 1961. *The Christian Philosophy of St. Thomas Aquinas,* New York, NY, Random House, Inc., 1956.

MODERN BOOKS ON ETHICS

Acton, Henry B., *Kant's Moral Philosophy,* London, Macmillan Publishers, Ltd., 1970.

Adler, Mortimer, *A Dialectic of Morals,* Notre Dame, IN, The Review of Politics, University of Notre Dame Press, 1941. *The Idea of Freedom,* Garden City, NY, Doubleday & Co. Inc., 1958. *The Time of Our Lives: the Ethics of Common Sense,* New York, NY, Holt, Rinehart & Winston, Inc., 1970.

Aiken, Lillian W., *Bertrand Russell's Philosophy of Morals,* New York, NY, Humanities Press, Inc., 1973.

Akrill, J.L., *Aristotle's Ethics,* London, Faber & Faber, 1973.

Allan, D.J., *The Philosophy of Aristotle,* London, Oxford University Press, 1952; revised ed., 1963.

Amato, Joseph A., *Ethics: Living or Dead? Themes in Contemporary Values,* Tuscaloosa, AL, Portals Press, 1982.

Aschenbrenner, K., *The Concept of Value, Foundations of Value Theory,* Dordrecht, the Netherlands, D. Reidel Publishing Co., 1971.

Atkinson, R.F., *Conduct: an Introduction to Moral Philosophy,* London, Macmillan Publishers, Ltd., 1969.

Ayer, A.J., *Language, Truth and Logic,* London, Victor Gollancz, Ltd., 1950. *Freedom and Morality and Other Essays,* New York, NY, Oxford University Press, 1984.

Baier, Kurt, *The Moral Point of View,* Ithaca, NY, Cornell University Press, 1958.

Barnes, Hazel E., *An Existentialist Ethics,* New York, NY, Alfred A. Knopf, 1967.

Barr, Stringfellow, *The Three Worlds of Man,* Columbia, MO., University of Missouri Press, 1963.

Barrett, William, *Irrational Man,* Garden City, NY, Doubleday & Co., Inc., 1958. *The Illusion of Technique: A Search for Meaning in a Technological Civilization,* Garden City, NY, Anchor Press, Doubleday, 1978.

Beardsmore, R.W., *Moral Reasoning,* London, Routledge & Kegan Paul, Ltd., 1969.

Beauchamp, Tom L., *Philosophical Ethics: An Introduction to Moral Philosophy,* Pace, Kaye (ed.), New York, NY, McGraw-Hill Book Co., 1982.

Beck, Lewis White, *A Commentary on Kant's Critique of Practical Reason,* Chicago, IL, The University of Chicago Press, 1960.

Becker, Lawrence C., *On Justifying Moral Judgments,* London, Routledge & Kegan Paul, Ltd.; Atlantic Highlands, NJ, Humanities Press, Inc., 1973.

Binkley, Luther J., *Conflict of Ideals: Changing Values in Western Society,* New York, NY, Van Nostrand Reinhold Co., 1969.

Bok, Sissela, *Lying: Moral Choice in Public and Private Life,* New York, NY, Pantheon Books, 1978. *Secrets: On the Ethics of Concealment and Revelation,* New York, NY, Pantheon Books, 1982.

Bond, E.J., *Reason and Value,* New York, NY, Cambridge University Press, 1983.

Bonhoeffer, Dietrich, *Ethics,* New York, NY, The Macmillan Co., 1955.

Borchert, Donald M., and Stewart, David, *Exploring Ethics,* New York, NY, The Macmillan Co., 1986.

Boulding, Kenneth E., *Human Betterment,* Newbury Park, CA, Sage Publications, Inc., 1985.

Bourke, Vernon, J., *Ethics,* 2nd ed., New York, NY, The Macmillan Co., 1966. *History of Ethics: a Comprehensive Survey of the History of Ideas from the Early Greeks to the Present Time,* New York, NY, Doubleday Publishing Co., 1968.

Boyle, Joseph M., Grisez, Germain, and Tollefson, Olaf, *Free Choice: A Self-Referential Argument,* Notre Dame, IN, and London, University of Notre Dame Press, 1976.

Brée, Germaine, *Camus and Sartre: Crisis and Commitment,* New York, NY, Dell Publishing Co., Inc., 1972.

Brennan, John M., *The Open Texture of Moral Concepts,* New York, NY, Barnes & Noble, 1977.

Broad, C.D., *Five Types of Ethical Theory,* London, Routledge & Kegan Paul Ltd., 1930.

Brody, Baruch, *Moral Rules and Particular Circumstances,* Englewood Cliffs, NJ, Prentice-Hall, Inc., 1970.

Brown, Robert, *The Nature of Social Laws: Machiavelli to Mill,* New York, NY, Cambridge University Press, 1986.

Buber, Martin, *I and Thou,* translated by Walter Kaufmann, New York, NY, Charles Scribner's Sons, 1970.

Camenish, Paul, *Grounding Professional Ethics in a Pluralistic Society,* New York, NY, Haven Publications, 1983.

Campbell, C.A., *In Defense of Free Will,* New York, NY, Humanities Press, Inc., 1967. *On Selfhood and Godhood,* New York, NY, The Macmillan Co., 1957.

Campbell, Keith, *A Stoic Philosophy of Life,* Lanham, MD, University Press of America, 1986.

Camus, Albert, *The Myth of Sisyphus,* New York, NY, Alfred A. Knopf, Inc., 1955. *The Rebel,* New York, NY, Alfred A. Knopf, Inc., 1954.

Castaneda, Hector-Neri, *The Structure of Morality,* Springfield, IL, Charles C. Thomas, Publisher, 1974.

Catalano, Joseph S., *A Commentary on Jean-Paul Sartre's "Being and Nothingness,"* New York, NY, Harper & Row, Publishers, 1974.

Cohen, Elliott D., *Making Value Judgments: Principles of Sound Reasoning,* Melbourne, FL, Robert E. Krieger Publishing Co., Inc., 1985.

Collins, James, *The Existentialists,* Chicago, IL, Henry Regnery Co., 1952.

Corbett, Patrick, *Ideologies,* London, The Hutchinson Publishing Group, Ltd., 1965.

Cranston, Maurice, *The Quintessence of Sartrism,* New York, NY, Harper & Row, Publishers, 1969.

Cronin, Michael, *The Science of Ethics,* 2 vols., New York, NY, Benziger Brothers, Inc., 1922.

Cua, A.S., *Dimensions of Moral Creativity: Paradigms, Principles, and Ideals,* University Park, PA, Pennsylvania State University Press, 1978.

Curran, Charles E., *Ongoing Revision: Studies in Moral Theology,* Notre Dame, IN, Fides Publishers, Inc., 1975.

Curran, Charles E., and McCormick, Richard (eds.), *Readings in Moral Theology:* No. 1, *Moral Norms and Catholic Tradition;* No. 2, *The Distinctiveness of Christian Ethics;* No. 3, *The Magisterium and Morality,* Ramsey, NJ, Paulist Press, 1979, 1980, 1981.

Danto, Arthur C., *Jean-Paul Sartre,* New York, NY, The Viking Press, 1975. *Nietzsche as Philosopher,* New York, NY, The Macmillan Co., 1965.

D'Arcy, Eric, *Conscience and its Right to Freedom,* New York, NY, Sheed & Ward, 1962. *Human Acts,* Oxford, The Clarendon Press, 1963.

D'Arcy, Martin, *The Mind and Heart of Love,* London, Faber & Faber, Ltd., 1945.

Darwall, Stephen L., *Impartial Reason,* Ithaca, NY, Cornell University Press, 1985.

Davitt, Thomas E., *Ethics in the Situation,* Milwaukee, WI, Marquette University Press, 1978.

Deeken, Alfons, *Process and Permanence in Ethics: Max Scheler's Moral Philosophy,* New York, NY, Paulist Press, 1974.

D'Entrèves, A.P., *Natural Law,* London, Hutchinson & Co. (Publishers), Ltd., 1951.

De Rougemont, Denis, *Love in the Western World,* New York, NY, Pantheon Books, Inc., 1956.

Desan, Wilfrid, *The Planetary Man,* 2 vols., New York, NY, The Macmillan Co., 1972. *Let the Future Come,* Washington, DC, Georgetown University Press, 1987.

Dilman, Ilham, and Phillips, D.Z., *Sense and Delusion,* New York, NY, Humanities Press, Inc., 1971.

Donagan, Alan, *The Theory of Morality,* Chicago, IL, University of Chicago Press, 1977.

Dorszynski, Julian A., *The Catholic Teaching about the Morality of Falsehood,* Washington, DC, The Catholic University of America Press, 1949.

Dunn, Robert, *The Possibility of Weakness of Will,* Indianapolis, IN, Hackett Publishing Co., Inc., 1986.

Dworkin, Gerald, *Determinism, Free Will, and Moral Responsibility,* Englewood Cliffs, NJ, Prentice-Hall Inc., 1970.

Dyck, Arthur J., *On Human Care: An Introduction to Ethics,* Nashville, TN, Abingdon Press, 1977.

Edel, Abraham, *Ethical Judgment: the Use of Science in Ethics,* New York, NY, The Free Press, 1964. *Method in Ethical Theory,* Indianapolis, IN, The Bobbs-Merrill Co., 1963.

Edgley, Roy, *Reason in Theory and Practice,* London, The Hutchinson Publishing Group, Ltd., 1969.

Edwards, Paul (editor-in-chief), *Encyclopedia of Philosophy,* 8 vols., New York, NY, The Macmillan Co. & The Free Press, 1967.

Edwards, Steven A., *Interior Acts: Teleology, Justice, and Friendship in the Religious Ethics of Thomas Aquinas,* Lanham, MD, University Press of America, 1986.

Ewing, A.C., *The Definition of Good,* new ed., London, Routledge & Kegan Paul, Ltd., 1966. *Ethics,* London, English Universities Press, Ltd., 1953. *The Morality of Punishment with some Suggestions for a General Theory of Ethics,* Montclair, NJ, Patterson Smith Publishing Corp., 1970 (reprint of 1929 ed., London, Kegan Paul).

Facione, Peter A., Scherer, Donald, and Attig, Thomas, *Values and Society: An Introduction to Ethics and Social Philosophy,* Englewood Cliffs, NJ, Prentice-Hall, Inc., 1978.

Farrell, Walter, *Companion to the Summa,* 4 vols., New York, NY, Sheed & Ward, 1938. Volumes II and III on ethical subjects.

Feinberg, Joel, *Doing and Deserving: Essays in the Theory of Responsibility,* Princeton, NJ, Princeton University Press, 1970. *Reason and Responsibility,* ed. 4, Encino, CA, Dickenson Publishing Co., Inc., 1978.

Field, G.C., *Moral Theory,* London, Methuen, 1966.

Findlay, J.N., *Axiological Ethics,* London, Macmillan Publishers, Ltd., 1970. *Values and Intentions: A Study in Value-Theory and Philosophy of Mind,* London, George Allen & Unwin Ltd. and New York, NY, The Macmillan Co., 1961.

Fingarette, Herbert, *On Responsibility,* New York, NY, Basic Books Inc., Publishers, 1967.

Finnis, John, *Fundamentals of Ethics,* Washington, DC, Georgetown University Press, 1983.

Fletcher, Joseph, *Moral Responsibility,* Philadelphia, PA, The Westminster Press, 1967. *Situation Ethics,* Philadelphia, PA, The Westminster Press, 1966.

Flew, A.G.N., *Evolutionary Ethics,* New York, NY, St. Martin's Press, 1967.

Foot, Philippa R., *Virtues and Vices and Other Essays in Moral Philosophy,* Berkeley, CA, University of California Press, 1979.

Fotion, N., *Moral Situations,* Yellow Springs, OH, Antioch Press, 1968.

Frankena, William K., *Ethics,* new ed., Englewood Cliffs, NJ, Prentice-Hall, Inc., 1974.

Franklin, R.L., *Freewill and Determinism,* New York, NY, Humanities Press, Inc., 1968.

Fried, Charles, *An Anatomy of Values: Problems of Personal and Social Choice,* Cambridge, MA, Harvard University Press, 1970.

Fromm, Erich, *The Art of Loving,* New York, NY, Harper & Row, Publishers, 1956.

Fuss, Peter, *The Moral Philosophy of Josiah Royce,* Cambridge, MA, Harvard University Press, 1965.

Gadamer, Hans-Georg, *The Idea of the Good in Platonic-Aristotelian Philosophy,* New Haven, CT, Yale University Press, 1986.

Garner, Richard T., and Rosen, Bernard, *Moral Philosophy: a Systematic Introduction to Normative Ethics and Meta-ethics,* New York, NY, The Macmillan Co., 1967.

Gauthier, David, *Morals by Agreement,* New York, NY, Oxford University Press, 1986.

Gauthier, David P., *The Logic of Leviathan: the Moral and Political Theory of Thomas Hobbes,* London, Oxford University Press, 1969. *Morality and Rational Self-Interest,* Englewood Cliffs, NJ, Prentice-Hall, Inc., 1970.

Gaylin, Willard, *Feelings: Our Vital Signs,* New York, NY, Harper & Row, Publishers, 1979.

Gelven, Michael, *Winter, Friendship, and Guilt: Sources of Self-Inquiry,* New York, NY, Harper & Row, Publishers, 1973.

Gert, Bernard, *The Moral Rules: A New Rational Foundation for Morality,* New York, NY, Harper & Row, Publishers, 1973.

Gerwith, Alan, *Reason and Morality* Chicago, IL, University of Chicago Press, 1978.

Girvetz, Harry K., *Beyond Right and Wrong,* New York, NY, The Free Press, 1973.

Glass, Bentley, *Science and Ethical Values,* Chapel Hill, NC, University of North Carolina Press, 1965.

Glover, Jonathan, *Responsibility,* London, Routledge & Kegan Paul, Ltd., 1970.

Gosling, J.C.B., *Pleasure and Desire: the Case for Hedonism Reviewed,* Oxford, The Clarendon Press, 1969.

Gotesky, Rubin, *Personality: the Need for Liberty and Rights,* New York, NY, Libra Publishers, Inc., 1967.

Greene, Norman, *Jean-Paul Sartre: the Existentialist Ethic,* Ann Arbor, MI, University of Michigan Press, 1960.

Grice, Godfrey Russell, *The Grounds of Moral Judgment,* New York, NY, Cambridge University Press, 1967.

Grisez, Germain, and Shaw, Russell, *Beyond the New Morality: The Responsibilities of Freedom,* rev. ed., Notre Dame, IN, University of Notre Dame Press, 1980.

Gula, Richard M., *What Are They Saying About Moral Norms?* Ramsey, NJ, Paulist Press, 1982.

Gustafson, James M., *Protestant and Roman Catholic Ethics: Prospects for a Rapprochement,* Chicago, IL, The University of Chicago Press, 1978.

Hampshire, Stuart, *Freedom of the Individual,* New York, NY, Harper & Row, Publishers, 1965. *Morality and Conflict,* Cambridge, MA, Harvard University Press, 1984. *Morality and Pessimism,* Cambridge, Cambridge University Press, 1972. *Thought and Action,* New York, NY, The Viking Press, Inc., 1960. *Two Theories of Morality,* New York, NY, Oxford University Press, 1977.

Hare, R.M., *Applications of Moral Philosophy,* London, Macmillan Publishers Ltd.; Berkeley, CA, University of California Press, 1972. *Essays on Moral Concepts,* London, Macmillan Publishers, Ltd., 1972. *Freedom and Reason,* New York, NY, Oxford University Press, Inc., 1965. *The Language of Morals,* new ed., London, Oxford University Press, 1973. *Moral Thinking: Its Levels, Methods, and Point,* New York, NY, Oxford University Press, Inc., 1982.

Häring, Bernard, *Free and Faithful in Christ,* vol. 1, "General Moral Theology," New York, NY, The Seabury Press, Inc., 1978.

Harrison, Jonathan, *Our Knowledge of Right and Wrong,* London, George Allen & Unwin, Ltd., 1971.

Harrod, Howard L., *The Human Center: Moral Agency in the Social World,* Philadelphia, PA, Fortress Press, 1981.

Hart, H.L.A., *The Morality of the Criminal Law,* London, Magnes Press; London, Oxford University Press, 1965.

Hartman, Robert S., *The Structure of Value: Foundations of Scientific Axiology,* Carbondale, IL, Southern Illinois University Press, 1967.

Hawkins, D.J.B., *Man and Morals,* New York, NY, Sheed & Ward, 1960.

Hazo, Robert, *The Idea of Love,* New York, NY, Praeger Publishers, Inc., 1967.

Heyd, David, *Supererogation: Its Status in Ethical Theory,* New York, NY, Cambridge University Press, Inc., 1982.

Hildebrand, Dietrich von, *Christian Ethics,* New York, NY, David McKay Co., Inc., 1953.

Hodgson, D.H., *Consequences of Utilitarianism: a Study in Normative Ethics and Legal Theory,* Oxford, The Clarendon Press, 1967.

Hook, Sidney, *Education and the Taming of Power,* LaSalle, IL, Open Court Publishing Co., 1973. *Reason, Social Myths and Democracy,* New York, NY, Harper & Row, Publishers, 1965.

Hooper, J. Leon, *The Ethics of Discourse: John Courtney Murray's Social Philosophy,* Washington, DC, Georgetown University Press, 1986.

Hospers, John, *Human Conduct,* 2nd ed., New York, NY, Harcourt Brace Jovanovich, 1982.

Howie, John, *Perspectives for Moral Decisions,* Washington, DC, University Press of America, 1981.

Hudson, W.D., *Ethical Intuitionism,* New York, NY, St. Martin's Press, 1967. *Modern Moral Philosophy,* London, Macmillan Publishers, Ltd., 1970.

Hughes, Gerard, *Authority in Morals,* Washington, DC, Georgetown University Press, 1904.

Inwood, Brad, *Ethics and Human Action in Early Stoicism,* New York, NY, Oxford University Press, 1985.

Johann, Robert O., *The Meaning of Love,* Westminster, MD., The Newman Press, 1955.

Johnson, Oliver, *Moral Knowledge,* The Hague, Martinus Nijhoff, 1966. *The Moral Life,* London, George Allen & Unwin, Ltd., 1969.

Jonas, Hans, *The Imperative of Responsibility: In Search of an Ethics for the Technological Age,* Chicago, IL, University of Chicago Press, 1985.

Jonsen, Albert R., *Responsibility in Modern Religious Ethics,* Washington, DC, Corpus Books, 1968.

Kaplan, Abraham, *American Ethics and Public Policy,* New York, NY, Oxford University Press, 1958, 1963.

Kattsoff, Luis O., *Making Moral Decisions: an Existential Analysis,* The Hague, Martinus Nijhoff, 1965.

Kaufman, A., *The Science of Decision Making; an Introduction to Praxeology,* translated by R. Audley, London, George Weidenfeld & Nicolson, Ltd., 1968.

Kaufmann, Walter, *Without Guilt and Justice, From Decidophobia to Autonomy,* New York, NY, Peter H. Wyden/Publishers, 1973.

Kaye, Michael, *Morals and Commitment,* London, Covent Garden Press, 1971.

Kemp, J., *Ethical Naturalism: Hobbes and Hume,* London, Macmillan Publishers, Ltd., 1970.

Kenner, George C., *The Revolution in Ethical Theory,* London, Oxford University Press, 1966.

Klubertanz, George, *Habits and Virtues,* New York, NY, Appleton-Century-Crofts, 1965. *Philosophy of Human Nature,* New York, NY, Appleton-Century-Crofts, 1953.

Knox, Sir Malcolm, *Action,* New York, NY, Humanities Press, Inc., 1968.

Kohlberg, L. and Hewer, A., *Moral Stages,* New York, NY, S. Karger, AG, 1983.

Kolenda, Konstantin, *The Freedom of Reason,* San Antonio, TX, The Princip Press of Trinity University, 1964.

Kovesi, Julius, *Moral Notions,* London, Routledge & Kegan Paul, Ltd., 1967.

Kupperman, Joel J., *The Foundations of Morality,* Winchester, MA, Allen & Unwin, Inc., 1983.

Kurtines, William M. and Gewirtz, Jacob L., *Morality, Moral Behavior, and Moral Development,* New York, NY, John Wiley & Sons, Inc., 1983.

Kurtz, Paul, *Decision and the Condition of Man,* Seattle, WA, University of Washington Press, 1965.

La Croix, W.L., *Principles for Ethics,* Washington, DC, University Press of America, 1978; rev. ed., 1979.

Lebacqz, Karen, *Professional Ethics: Power and Paradox,* Nashville, TN, Abingdon Press, 1985.

Lee, Keekok, *A New Basis for Moral Philosophy,* New York, NY, Methuen, Inc., 1985.

Lehmann, Paul, *Ethics in a Christian Context,* New York, NY, Harper & Row, Publishers, 1963.

Le Maire, H. Paul, *Personal Decisions,* Washington, DC, University Press of America, 1982.

Leiser, Burton M., *Liberty, Justice and Morals: Contemporary Value Conflicts,* 2nd ed., New York, NY, The Macmillan Co., 1979.

Lepp, Ignace, *The Authentic Morality,* New York, NY, The Macmillan Co., 1965.

Letwin, Oliver, *Ethics, Emotion, and the Unity of the Self,* New York, NY, Methuen, Inc., 1987.

Levinas, Emmanuel, *Ethics and Infinity,* tr. by Richard Cohen, Pittsburgh, PA, Duquesne University Press, 1985.

Lewis, C.I., *Analysis of Knowledge and Valuation,* LaSalle, IL, Open Court Publishing Co., 1946. *Values and Imperatives,* Stanford, CA, Stanford University Press, 1969.

Lewis, C.S., *The Four Loves,* London, Geoffrey Bles, Ltd., Publishers, 1960.

Lewy, Casimir, *G.E. Moore on the Naturalistic Fallacy,* from *Proceedings of British Academy,* vol. L (1964), London, Oxford University Press, 1965.

Llamzon, Benjamin S., *Reason, Experience and the Moral Life,* Washington, DC, University Press of America, 1978.

Loring, L.M., *Two Kinds of Values,* foreword by Karl Popper, London, Routledge & Kegan Paul, Ltd., 1966.

Luther, A.R., *Persons in Love: A Study of Max Scheler's "Wesen und Formen der Sympathie,"* The Hague, Martinus Nijhoff, 1972.

Lutzer, Erwin W., *The Necessity of Ethical Absolutes,* Grand Rapids, MI, Zondervan Publishing House, 1981.

Mabbott, J.D., *An Introduction to Ethics,* London, The Hutchinson Publishing Group, Ltd., 1966; New York, NY, Doubleday Publishing Co., 1969.

McCloskey, H.J., *Meta-Ethics and Normative Ethics,* The Hague, Martinus Nijhoff, 1969.

McCormick, Richard A., *Ambiguity in Moral Choice,* Milwaukee, WI, Marquette University Press, 1973. *Notes on Moral Theology,* Washington, DC, University Press of America, 1981.

McCormick, Richard, and Ramsey, Paul (eds.), *Doing Evil to Achieve Good: Moral Choice in Conflict Situations,* Chicago, IL, Loyola University Press, 1978.

McGann, Thomas F., *Ethics: Theory and Practice,* Chicago, IL, Loyola University Press, 1971.

McGrath, Patrick, *The Nature of Moral Judgment,* London, Sheed and Ward, Ltd., 1967.

McGill, V.J., *The Idea of Happiness,* New York, NY, Praeger Publishers, Inc., 1967.

MacIntyre, Alasdair, *Against the Self-Images of the Age, Essays on Ideology and Philosophy,* London, Gerald Duckworth & Co., Ltd., 1971; New York, NY, Schocken Books, Inc., 1971. *A Short History of Ethics,* New York, NY, The Macmillan Co., 1966. *After Virtue,* Notre Dame, IN, University of Notre Dame Press, 1982.

Mackay, Donald, *Freedom of Action in a Mechanistic Universe,* Cambridge, Cambridge University Press, 1967.

Mackie, J.L., *Ethics: Inventing Right and Wrong,* New York, NY, Penguin Books, Inc., 1977.

Macmurray, John, *Freedom in the Modern World,* London, Faber & Faber, Ltd., 1968. *Persons in Relation,* London, Faber & Faber, 1959; New York, NY, Humanities Press, Inc., 1962, 1970. *Reason and Emotion,* London, Faber & Faber, Ltd., 1935. *The Self as Agent,* London, Faber & Faber, 1957; New York, NY, Humanities Press, Inc., 1969.

Macquarrie, John, *Existentialism,* Baltimore, MD, Pelican Books, Penguin Books, Inc., 1972. *Three Issues in Ethics,* London, SCM Press, Ltd., 1970.

Maguire, Daniel C., *The Moral Choice,* Garden City, NY, Doubleday & Co., Inc., 1978. *The Moral Revolution,* New York, NY, Harper & Row Publishers, Inc., 1986.

Mandelbaum, Maurice H., *The Phenomenology of Moral Experience,* Baltimore, MD, The Johns Hopkins University Press, 1969.

Margenau, Henry, *Ethics and Science,* New York, NY, Van Nostrand Reinhold Co., 1964.

Margolis, Joseph, *Negativities: The Limits of Life,* Columbus, OH, Charles E. Merrill Publishing Co., 1975. *Psychotherapy and Morality; a Study of Two Concepts,* New York, NY, Random House, Inc., 1966.

Marx, Werner, *Is There a Measure on Earth? Foundations for a Non-Metaphysical Ethics,* tr. by Thomas J. Nenon and Reginald Lilly, Chicago, IL, University of Chicago Press, 1987.

Maslow, Abraham H., *Toward a Psychology of Being,* New York, NY, Van Nostrand Reinhold Co., 1962.

May, Rollo, *Love and Will,* New York, NY, W.W. Norton & Co., Inc., 1969.

Meilaender, Gilbert C., Jr., *The Theory and Practice of Virtue,* Notre Dame, IN, University of Notre Dame Press, 1984.

Meldin, A.I., *Rights and Persons,* Berkeley, CA, University of California Press, 1979.

Mercer, Philip, *Sympathy and Ethics: a Study of the Relationship Between Sympathy and Morality with Special Reference to Hume's Treatise,* Oxford, The Clarendon Press, 1972.

Meinong, Alexius, *On Emotional Presentation,* translated by Marie-Luise S. Kalsi, Evanston, IL, Northwestern University Press, 1972.

Messner, Johannes, *Social Ethics: Natural Law in the Western World,* revised ed., translated by J.J. Doherty, St. Louis, MO, B. Herder Book Co., 1965.

Miller, K. Bruce, *Ideology and Moral Philosophy,* New York, NY, Humanities Press, Inc., 1971.

Milo, Ronald D., *Immorality,* Princeton, NJ, Princeton University Press, 1984.

Minson, Jeffrey B., *Genealogies of Morals: Nietzsche, Foucault, Donzelot and the Eccentricity of Ethics,* New York, NY, St. Martin's Press, Inc., 1985.

Monan, J.D., *Moral Knowledge and its Methodology in Aristotle,* Oxford, 1968.

Monden, Louis, *Sin, Liberty and Law,* New York, NY, Sheed & Ward, 1965.

Monro, D.H., *Empiricism and Ethics,* Cambridge, Cambridge University Press, 1967.

Morano, Donald V., *Existential Guilt, a Phenomenological Study,* Assen, the Netherlands, Van Gorcum, B.V., 1973.

Mounier, Emmanuel, *Personalism,* London, Routledge & Kegan Paul, Ltd., 1952.

Munz, Peter, *Relationship and Solitude,* Middletown, CT, Wesleyan University Press, 1965.

Murdoch, Iris, *The Sovereignty of Good,* London, Routledge & Kegan Paul, Ltd., 1970. *The Sovereignty of Good over Other Concepts,* Cambridge, Cambridge University Press, 1967.

Nabert, Jean, *Elements for an Ethic,* translated by William J. Petrek, Evanston, IL, Northwestern University Press, 1969.

Narveson, Jan, *Morality and Utility,* Baltimore, MD, The Johns Hopkins University Press, 1967.

Nédoncelle, Maurice, *Love and the Person,* New York, NY, Sheed & Ward, 1966.

Neville, Robert C., *The Cosmology of Freedom,* New Haven, CT, Yale University Press, 1974.

Niebuhr, H. Richard, *The Responsible Self,* New York, NY, Harper & Row, Publishers, 1963.

Nolan, Richard T. and Kirkpatrick, Frank G., *Living Issues in Ethics,* Belmont, CA, Wadsworth Publishing Co., 1982.

Norman, Richard, *Reasons for Actions: a Critique of Utilitarian Rationality,* Oxford, Basil Blackwell & Mott, Ltd., 1971.

Nowell-Smith, P.H., *Ethics,* Baltimore, MD, Penguin Books, Inc., 1954.

Nygren, Anders, *Agape and Eros,* New York, NY, Harper & Row, Publishers, 1969.

O'Connor, D.J., *Aquinas and Natural Law,* London, Macmillan Publishers, Ltd., 1967. *Free Will,* New York, NY, Doubleday Publishing Co., 1971.

O'Connor, William R., *The Eternal Quest,* New York, NY, Longmans, Green & Co., Inc., 1947.

Olafson, Frederick A., *Principles and Persons,* Baltimore, MD, The Johns Hopkins University Press, 1967.

Olson, Robert, *The Morality of Self-Interest,* New York, NY, Harcourt, Brace & World Inc., 1965.

Olthuis, James H., *Facts, Values and Ethics,* Assen, the Netherlands, Van Gorcum, B.V., 1968.

O'Neil, Charles J., *Imprudence in St. Thomas,* Milwaukee, WI, Marquette University Press, 1955.

Outka, Gene, *Agape: An Ethical Analysis,* New Haven, CT, Yale University Press, 1972.

Packer, M.J., *The Structure of Moral Action: A Hermeneutic Study of Moral Conflict,* New York, NY, S. Karger, A.G., 1985.

Parfit, Derek, *Reasons and Persons,* New York, NY, Oxford University Press, 1985.

Paton, H.J., *The Categorical Imperative,* Chicago, IL, The University of Chicago Press, 1948.

Pepper, Stephen, *Sources of Value,* Berkeley, CA, University of California Press, 1959.

Perry, David L., *The Concept of Pleasure,* The Hague, Mouton Publishers, 1966.

Peters, Richard S., *Reason and Compassion,* London, Routledge & Kegan Paul, Ltd., 1973.

Pfänder, Alexander, *Phenomenology of Willing and Motivation,* translated by Herbert Spiegelberg, Evanston, IL, Northwestern University Press, 1967.

Phillips, D.Z., and Mounce, H.O., *Moral Practices,* London, Routledge & Kegan Paul, Ltd., 1970.

Pieper, Josef, *The Four Cardinal Virtues,* Notre Dame, IN, University of Notre Dame Press, 1967. *Leisure, the Basis of Culture,* New York, NY, Pantheon Books, Inc., 1952.

Pincoffs, Edmund L., *Quandaries and Virtues: Against Reductivism in Ethics,* Lawrence, KS, University Press of Kansas, 1986.

Poole, Roger, *Towards Deep Subjectivity,* New York, NY, Harper & Row, Publishers, 1972.

Prichard, H.A., *Moral Obligation,* Oxford, The Clarendon Press, 1949.

Purcell, Royal, *Ethics, Morality and Mores,* Bloomington, IN, Royal Purcell, Publisher, 1986.

Quinton, Anthony, *Utilitarian Ethics,* London, Macmillan Publishers, Ltd., 1973.

Rachels, James, *The Elements of Moral Philosophy,* Philadelphia, PA, Temple University Press, 1986. *Understanding Moral Philosophy,* Encino, CA, Dickenson Publishing Co., 1976.

Ramsey, Paul, *Deeds and Rules in Christian Ethics,* New York, NY, Charles Scribner's Sons, 1967.

Rand, Ayn, and Branden, Nathaniel, *The Virtue of Selfishness,* New York, NY, The New American Library, Inc., 1964.

Raphael, D.D., *Moral Philosophy,* New York, NY, Oxford University Press, 1981.

Reinhardt, Kurt, *The Existentialist Revolt,* Milwaukee, WI, The Bruce Publishing Co., 1952.

Rest, James R., *Development in Judging Moral Issues,* Minneapolis, MN, University of Minnesota Press, 1979.

Richman, Robert J., *Prolegomena to a Theory of Practical Reasoning,* Hingham, MA, Kluwer Academic Publishers, 1983.

Rickaby, Joseph, *Moral Philosophy,* Stonyhurst Series, London, Longmans, Green & Co., Ltd., 1910.

Riker, John H., *The Art of Ethical Thinking,* Washington, DC, University Press of America, 1978.

Ricoeur, Paul, *Fallible Man, Philosophy of the Will,* translated by Charles Kelbley, Chicago, IL, Henry Regnery Co., 1965. *Freedom and Nature: The Voluntary and Involuntary,* translated by Erazim V. Kohak, Evanston, IL, Northwestern University Press, 1966. *Freud and Philosophy: an Essay on Interpretation,* translated by Denis Savage, New Haven, CT, Yale University Press, 1970. *The Symbolism of Evil,* translated by Emerson Buchanan, New York, NY, Harper & Row, Publishers, 1967.

Roberts, Moira, *Responsibility and Practical Freedom,* New York, NY, Cambridge University Press, 1965.

Robins, Michael H., *Promising, Intending, and Moral Autonomy,* New York, NY, Cambridge University Press, 1984.

Robinson, Bishop John A.T., *Christian Morals Today,* Philadelphia, PA, The Westminster Press, 1964. *Honest to God,* Philadelphia, PA, The Westminster Press, 1963.

Rommen, Heinrich, *The Natural Law,* St. Louis, MO, B. Herder Book Co., 1948.

Rosen, Bernard, *Strategies of Ethics,* Boston, MA, Houghton Mifflin Co., 1978.

Ross, Stephen David, *The Nature of Moral Responsibility,* Detroit, MI, Wayne State University Press, 1972. *In Pursuit of Moral Value,* San Francisco, CA, Freeman, Cooper & Co., 1973.

Ross, W.D., *Foundations of Ethics,* Oxford, The Clarendon Press, 1939. *The Right and the Good,* Oxford, The Clarendon Press, 1930.

Rotenstreich, Nathan, *On the Human Subject,* Springfield, IL, Charles C. Thomas, Publishers, 1966. *Practice and Realization,* The Hague, Martinus Nijhoff, 1979.

Roubiczek, Paul, *Ethical Values in the Age of Science,* New York, NY, Cambridge University Press, 1969.

Rubenstein, Richard L., *Morality and Eros,* New York, NY, McGraw-Hill Book Co., 1970.

Ryle, Gilbert, *The Concept of Mind,* New York, NY, Hutchinson's University Library, 1949.

Sabini, Jon, and Silver, Maury, *Moralities of Everyday Life,* New York, NY, Oxford University Press, 1982.

Sanborn, Patricia F., *Existentialism,* Indianapolis, IN, Pegasus, 1968.

Scheler, Max, *Formalism in Ethics and Non-Formal Ethics of Values,* translated by Manfred S. Frings and Roger L. Funk, 5th rev. ed., Evanston, IL, Northwestern University Press, 1973.

Schlick, Moritz, *Problems of Ethics,* New York, NY, Dover Publications, Inc., 1939.

Schrag, Calvin O., *Existence and Freedom: Towards an Ontology of Human Finitude,* Evanston, IL, Northwestern University Press, 1961.

Sesonske, Alexander, *Value and Obligation: the Foundations of an Empiricist Ethical Theory,* New York, NY, Oxford University Press, 1964.

Sheriff, John K., *The Good Natured Man: The Evolution of a Moral Ideal,* Montgomery, AL, University of Alabama Press, 1982.

Shirk, Evelyn, *The Ethical Dimension: an Approach to the Philosophy of Values and Valuing,* New York, NY, Appleton-Century-Crofts, 1965.

Simon, Yves R., *Freedom of Choice,* ed. by Peter Wolff, New York, NY, Fordham University Press, 1969. *Freedom and Community,* ed. by Charles P. O'Donnell, New York, NY, Fordham University Press, 1968. *The Nature and Functions of Authority,* Aquinas Lecture, Milwaukee, WI, Marquette University Press, 1940. *The Tradition of Natural Law,* New York, NY, Fordham University Press, 1965.

Singer, Marcus George, *Generalization in Ethics: An Essay in the Logic of Ethics, with the Rudiments of a System of Moral Philosophy,* New York, NY, Atheneum Publishers, 1971.

Smart, J.J., *Ethics, Persuasion, and Truth,* New York, NY, Methuen, Inc., 1984.

Smart, J.J.C., and Williams, Bernard, *Utilitarianism: For and Against,* Cambridge, Cambridge University Press, 1973.

Solomon, Robert C., *The Passions: The Myth and Nature of Human Emotion,* Garden City, NY, Anchor Press, 1976. *Morality and the Good Life: An Introduction to Ethics*

Through Classical Sources, New York, NY, McGraw-Hill Book Co., 1984.

Sommers, Christina H., *Vice and Virtue in Everyday Life,* San Diego, CA, Harcourt Brace Jovanovich, Inc., 1985.

Spiegelberg, Herbert, *Stepping Stones Toward an Ethics for Fellow Existers,* Hingham, MA, Kluwer Academic Publishers, 1984.

Spitz, David, *The Liberal Idea of Freedom,* Tucson, AZ, University of Arizona Press, 1964.

Spong, John, and Haines, Denise, *Beyond Moralism,* New York, NY, Harper & Row Publishers, Inc., 1986.

Stein, Harry, *Ethics and Other Liabilities: Trying to Live Right in an Amoral World,* New York, NY, St. Martin's Press, 1983.

Stern, Alfred, *The Search for Meaning: Philosophical Vistas,* Memphis, TN, Memphis State University Press, 1971.

Stern, Axel, *The Science of Freedom: an Essay in Applied Philosophy,* translated by Christopher and Rosalind Strachan, foreword by Raymond Williams, Harlow, England, Longman Group, Ltd., 1969.

Stevenson, C.L., *Ethics and Language,* New Haven, CT, Yale University Press, 1946.

Stocks, John Leofric, *Morality and Purpose,* ed. by D.Z. Phillips, London, Routledge & Kegan Paul, Ltd., 1969; New York, NY, Schocken Books, Inc., 1969.

Stout, Jeffrey, *Flight from Authority: Religion, Morality, and the Quest for Autonomy,* Notre Dame, IN, University of Notre Dame Press, 1987.

Suter, Ronald, *Are You Moral?* Lanham, MD, University Press of America, 1985.

Taylor, Richard, *Good and Evil: a New Direction,* New York, NY, The Macmillan Co., 1970.

Thiroux, Jacques P., *Ethics: Theory and Practice,* 2nd ed., New York, NY, The Macmillan Co., 1980.

Toulmin, Stephen, *Examination of the Place of Reason in Ethics,* London, Cambridge University Press, 1950.

Urmson, J.O., *The Emotive Theory of Ethics,* London, The Hutchinson Publishing Group, Ltd., 1968.

Van Melsen, Andrew G., *Science and Responsibility,* translated by Henry J. Koren, Pittsburgh, PA, Duquesne University Press, 1970.

Varga, Andrew, *On Being Human,* New York, NY, Paulist Press, 1978.

Veatch, Henry, *Rational Man,* Bloomington, IN, Indiana University Press, 1964.

Vivas, Eliseo, *The Moral Life and the Ethical Life,* Lanham, MD, University Press of America, 1984.

Von Wright, Georg Henrik, *An Essay in Deontic Logic and the General Theory of Action,* with a bibliography of deontic and imperative logic, Amsterdam, North-Holland Publishing Co., 1969. *The Varieties of Goodness,* New York, NY, Humanities Press, Inc., 1963.

Walsh, W.H., *Hegelian Ethics,* London, Macmillan Publishers, Ltd., 1969.

Ward, Leo, *Christian Ethics,* St. Louis, MO, B. Herder Book Co., 1952. *Values and Reality,* New York, NY, Sheed & Ward, 1935.

Warnock, G.J., *Contemporary Moral Philosophy,* New York, NY, St. Martin's Press, 1967. *The Object of Morality,* New York, NY, Barnes & Noble Books, 1971.

Warnock, Mary, *Ethics Since 1900,* 2nd rev. ed., London, Oxford University Press, 1966. *Existentialist Ethics,* New York, NY, St. Martin's Press, 1967.

Werkmeister, W.H., *Man and His Values,* Lincoln, NB, University of Nebraska Press, 1967. *Theories of Ethics,* Lincoln, NB, Johnsen Publishing Co., 1961.

Wertheimer, Roger, *The Significance of Sense: Meaning, Modality and Morality,* Ithaca, NY, Cornell University Press, 1972.

Westermarck, Edward, *Ethical Relativity,* New York, NY, Harcourt, Brace & Co., 1932. *The Origin and Development of Moral Ideas,* 2 vols., New York, NY, The Macmillan Co., 1906–1908.

Weston, Michael, *Morality and the Self,* New York, NY, New York University Press, 1975.

Wild, John, *Plato's Modern Enemies and the Theory of Natural Law,* Chicago, IL, The University of Chicago Press, 1953.

Wilhelmsen, Frederick D., *The Metaphysics of Love,* New York, NY, Sheed & Ward, 1962.

Willey, Basil, *The English Moralists,* London, Chatto and Windus, Ltd., 1964; Methuen in "University Paperback Series," 1965.

Williams, Bernard A.O., *Ethics and the Limits of Philosophy,* Cambridge, MA, Harvard University Press, 1985. *Morality: an Introduction to Ethics,* New York, NY, Harper & Row, Publishers, 1972.

Winch, Peter, *Ethics and Action,* London, Routledge & Kegan Paul, Ltd., 1972.

Wolff, Robert Paul, *The Autonomy of Reason. A Commentary on Kant's Groundwork of the Metaphysic of Morals,* New York, NY, Harper & Row, Publishers, 1973.

Yezzi, Ron, *Directing Human Actions: Perspectives on Basic Ethical Issues,* Lanham, MD, University Press of America, 1986.

Zink, Sidney, *The Concepts of Ethics,* New York, NY, St. Martin's Press, 1962.

ANTHOLOGIES AND COLLECTIONS

Abelson, Raziel (ed.), *Ethics and Metaethics,* New York, NY, St. Martin's Press, Inc., 1963.

Anshen, Ruth Nanda, *Moral Principles of Action,* New York, NY, Harper & Row, Publishers, 1952.

Bayles, Michael D. (ed.), *Contemporary Utilitarianism,* New York, NY, Doubleday Publishing Co., 1968.

Berofski, Bernard (ed.), *Free Will and Determinism,* New York, NY, Harper & Row, Publishers, 1966.

Binkley, Robert, Bronaugh, Richard, and Marras, Ausonio (eds.), *Agent, Action, and Reason,* Toronto, University of Toronto Press, 1971.

Bowker, Gordon (ed.), *Freedom: Reason or Revolution?* London, Routledge & Kegan Paul, Ltd., 1970.

Burr, John R., and Goldinger, Milton (eds.), *Philosophy and Contemporary Issues,* 2nd ed., New York, NY, Macmillan Publishing Co., Inc., 1976.

Burtt, Edwin, *The English Philosophers from Bacon to Mill,* New York, NY, Modern Library, Inc., 1939.

Casey, John (ed.), *Morality and Moral Reasoning,* New York, NY, Barnes & Noble Books, 1971.

Castaneda, Hector-Neri, and Nahknikian, George (eds.), *Morality and the Language of Conduct,* Detroit, MI, Wayne State University Press, 1965.

Cheney, David R. (ed.), *Broad's Critical Essays in Moral Philosophy,* preface by C.D. Broad, London, George Allen & Unwin, Ltd.; New York, NY, Humanities Press, Inc., 1971.

Cox, Harvey, and Fletcher, Joseph (eds.), *The Situation Ethics Debate,* Philadelphia, PA, The Westminster Press, 1968.

Cunningham, Robert L., *Situationism and the New Morality,* New York, NY, Appleton-Century-Crofts, 1970.

Davies, Hugh Sykes, and Watson, George (eds.), *The English Mind: Studies in the English Moralists Presented to Basil Willey,* New York, NY, Cambridge University Press, 1964.

Davis, John William (ed.), *Value and Valuation: Axiological Studies in Honor of Robert S. Hartman,* Knoxville, TN, University of Tennessee Press, 1972.

Donnelly, John, and Lyons, Leonard (eds.), *Conscience,* New York, NY, Alba House, 1973.

Ebenstein, William, *Modern Political Thought,* New York, NY, Holt, Rinehart & Winston, Inc., 1954.

Enteman, Willard F. (ed.), *The Problem of Free Will,* New York, NY, Charles Scribner's Sons, 1967.

Fagothey, Austin, *Right and Reason—an Anthology,* St. Louis, MO, The C.V. Mosby Co., 1972.

Feinberg, Joel (ed.), *Moral Concepts,* London, Oxford University Press, 1969. *Reason and Responsibility,* Belmont, CA, Dickenson Publishing Co., Inc., 1965.

Finn, James (ed.), *A Conflict of Loyalties: the Case for Selective Conscientious Objection,* New York, NY, Pegasus, 1968.

Foot, Philippa (ed.), *Theories of Ethics,* London, Oxford University Press, 1967.

Gotesky, Rubin, and Laszlo, Ervin (eds.), *Human Dignity This Century and the Next: An Interdisciplinary Inquiry Into Human Rights, Technology, War, The Ideal Society,* New York, NY, Gordon and Breach, Science Publishers, Inc., 1970.

Gouinlock, James (ed.), *The Moral Writings of John Dewey: A Selection,* New York, NY, The Macmillan Co., 1976.

Hauerwas, Stanley, and MacIntyre, Alasdair (eds.), *Revisions: Changing Perspectives in Moral Philosophy,* Notre Dame, IN, University of Notre Dame Press, 1983.

Honderich, Tod (ed.), *Essays on Freedom of Action,* London, Routledge & Kegan Paul, Ltd., 1972.

Hook, Sidney (ed.), *Determinism and Freedom in the Age of Modern Science,* New York, NY, New York University Press, 1958. *Law and Philosophy, a Symposium,* New York, NY, New York University Press, 1964.

Hudson, W.D. (ed.), *The Is-Ought Question,* New York, NY, St. Martin's Press, 1969. *New Studies in Ethics, Vol. I, Classical Theories; Vol. II, Modern Theories,* London, Macmillan Publishers, Ltd., 1974.

In Quest of Value, Readings in Philosophy and Personal Values Selected by the San Jose State College Associates in Philosophy, San Francisco, CA, Chandler Publishing Co., 1964.

Jersild, Paul T., and Johnson, Dale A. (eds.), *Moral Issues and Christian Response,* 2nd ed., New York, NY, Holt, Rinehart & Winston, 1976.

Katope, C.G., and Zolbrod, P.G. (eds.), *Beyond Berkeley: a Source Book in Student Values,* New York, NY, World Publishing Co., 1966.

Kennedy, Eugene (ed.), *Human Rights and Psychological Research,* New York, NY, Thomas Y. Crowell Co., 1975.

Klausner, Samuel Z. (ed.), *The Quest for Self-Control, Classical Philosophies and Scientific Research,* New York, NY, The Free Press, 1965.

Körner, Stefan (ed.), *Practical Reason,* Oxford, Basil Blackwell & Mott, Ltd., 1974.

Laslett, P., Runciman, W.G., and Skinner, Q. (eds.), *Philosophy, Politics and Society,* Oxford, Basil Blackwell & Mott, Ltd., 1972.

Lawson, Douglas E., and Lean, Arthur E. (eds.), *John Dewey and the World View,* Carbondale, IL, Southern Illinois University Press, 1964.

Lepley, Ray (ed.), *The Language of Value,* New York, NY, Columbia University Press, 1957. *Value, a Cooperative Inquiry,* New York, NY, Columbia University Press, 1949.

Luthans, Fred, and Hodgetts, Richard M. (eds.), *Readings on the Current Social Issues in Business: Poverty, Civil Rights, Ecology, and Consumerism,* New York, NY, The Macmillan Co., 1972.

Mackinnon, Donald M. (ed.), *Making Moral Decisions,* London, S.P.C.K. (The Society for Promoting Christian Knowledge), 1969.

McLean, George F. (ed.), *New Dynamics in Ethical Thinking,* Lancaster, PA, Concorde Publishing Co., 1974.

Mandelbaum, M., Gramlich, F.W., Anderson, A.R., and Schneewind, J.B., *Philosophic Problems,* 2nd ed., New York, NY, The Macmillan Co., 1967.

Mappes, Thomas A., and Zembaty, Jane S. (eds.), *Social Ethics: Morality and Social Policy,* New York, NY, McGraw-Hill Book Co., 1977.

Mortimore, G.W. (ed.), *Weakness of Will,* London, Macmillan Publishers, Ltd., 1971.

Outka, Gene, and Ramsey, Paul (eds.), *Norm and Context in Christian Ethics,* New York, NY, Charles Scribner's Sons, 1968.

Quinn, Francis X. (ed.), *The Ethical Aftermath of Automation,* Westminster, MD, The Newman Press, 1962.

Rachels, James (ed.), *Moral Problems: A Collection of Philosophical Essays,* 3rd ed., New York, NY, Harper & Row, Publishers, 1979.

Radcliff, P. (ed.), *Limits of Liberty,* Belmont, CA, Wadsworth Publishing Co., Inc., 1966.

Rand, Benjamin (ed.), *The Classical Moralists,* Boston, MA, Houghton Mifflin Co., 1909.

Raphael, D.D. (ed.), *British Moralists,* 2 vols., Oxford, The Clarendon Press, 1969.

Regan, Tom, and Van De Veer, Donald (eds.), *And Justice For All: New Introductory Essays in Ethics and Public Policy,* Totowa, NJ, Rowman & Littlefield, Inc., 1982.

Schrader, George Alfred, Jr. (ed.), *Existential Philosophers: Kierkegaard to Merleau-Ponty,* New York, NY, McGraw-Hill Book Co., 1967.

Selby-Bigge, L.A., *British Moralists,* Indianapolis, IN, The Bobbs-Merrill Co., Inc., 1964.

Straus, Erwin W., and Griffith, Richard M. (eds.), *Phenomen-*

ology of Will and Action, Pittsburgh, PA, Duquesne University Press, 1967.

Thompson, Josiah (ed.), *Kierkegaard: A Collection of Critical Essays,* New York, NY, Doubleday & Co., Inc., 1972.

Thomson, J.J., and Dworkin, Gerald (eds.), *Ethics,* New York, NY, Harper & Row, Publishers, 1968.

Todd, Charles, and Blackwood, Russell T. (eds.), *Language and Value,* New York, NY, Greenwood Press, Inc., 1969.

Vesey, G.N.A. (ed.), *The Human Agent.* Royal Institute of Philosophy Lectures, 1966–67, vol. I, New York, NY, St. Martin's Press, 1968.

Wallace, G., and Walker, A.D.M. (eds.), *The Definition of Morality,* New York, NY, Barnes & Noble Books, 1970.

Walsh, James J., and Shapiro, Henry L. (eds.), *Aristotle's Ethics: Issues and Interpretations,* Belmont, CA, Wadsworth Publishing Co., Inc., 1967.

Warnock, Mary, (ed.), *Sartre: A Collection of Critical Essays,* New York, NY, Doubleday & Co., Inc., 1971.

Wasserstrom, Richard (ed.), *Today's Moral Problems,* 2nd ed., New York, NY, The Macmillan Co., 1979.

BOOKS ON APPLIED ETHICS AND ON TOPICS RELATED TO ETHICS

1. Legal Ethics: Rights, Law, Justice

Acton, H.B. (ed.), *The Philosophy of Punishment: a Collection of Papers,* London, Macmillan Publishers, Ltd., 1969.

Andelson, Robert V., *Imputed Rights,* Athens, GA, University of Georgia Press, 1972.

Armstrong, R.A., *Primary and Secondary Precepts in Thomistic Natural Law Teaching,* The Hague, Martinus Nijhoff, 1966.

Barry, Brian, *The Liberal Theory of Justice: a Critical Examination of the Principal Doctrines in 'A Theory of Justice' by John Rawls,* Oxford, The Clarendon Press, 1973.

Barth, Alan, *The Rights of Free Men: An Essential Guide to Civil Liberties,* Clayton, James E. (ed.), New York, NY, Alfred A. Knopf, Inc., 1984.

Battaglia, Anthony, *Toward a Reformulation of Natural Law,* New York, NY, Seabury Press, Inc., 1981.

Bayne, David C., *Conscience, Obligation and the Law: The Moral Binding Power of the Civil Law,* Chicago, IL, Loyola University Press, 1966.

Bedau, Hugo A., *Death Is Different: Studies in the Morality, Law, and Politics of Capital Punishment,* Boston, MA, Northeastern University Press, 1987.

Bellow, Gary, and Moulton, Bea, *The Lawyering Process: Ethics and Professional Responsibility,* St. Paul, MN, Foundation Press, Inc., 1981.

Berns, Walter, *For Capital Punishment: Crime and the Morality of the Death Penalty,* New York, NY, Basic Books, Inc., 1981.

Berry, Christopher J., *Human Nature,* Atlantic Highlands, NJ, Humanities Press International, Inc., 1986.

Bird, Otto A., *The Idea of Justice,* New York, NY, Frederick A. Praeger, 1967.

Blackstone, William, *Commentaries on the Laws of England,* San Francisco, CA, Bancroft-Whitney Co., 1915.

Block, Eugene B., *When Men Play God: The Fallacy of Capital Punishment,* Oakland, CA, Cragmont Publications, 1984.

Bodenheimer, Edgar, *Jurisprudence: The Philosophy and Method of Law,* Cambridge, MA, Harvard University Press, 1974. *Treatise on Justice,* New York, NY, Philosophical Library, 1967.

Bowie, Norman E., *Towards a New Theory of Distributive Justice,* Amherst, MA, University of Massachusetts Press, 1971.

Brownie, Ian (ed.), *Basic Documents on Human Rights,* London, Oxford University Press, 1971.

Burkoff, John M., *Criminal Defense Ethics: Law and Liability,* Nashville, TN, Broadman Press, 1986.

Cahn, Edmond, *The Moral Decision: Right and Wrong in the Light of American Law,* Bloomington, IN, Indiana University Press, 1981.

Caplan, Gerald (ed.), *ABSCAM Ethics: Moral Issues and Deception in Law Enforcement,* Cambridge, MA, Ballinger Publishing Co., 1983.

Care, Norman S., and Trelogan, Thomas K. (eds.), *Issues in Law and Morality,* Cleveland, OH, The Press of Case Western Reserve University, 1973.

Daniels, Norman, *Reading Rawls,* New York, NY, Basic Books, Inc., 1975.

Davis, Philip E., *Moral Duty and Legal Responsibility,* New York, NY, Appleton-Century-Crofts, 1966.

Elliston, Frederick A., and Bowie, Norman E. (eds.), *Ethics, Public Policy and Criminal Justice,* Cambridge, MA, Oelgeschlager, Gunn & Hain, Inc., 1982.

Endres, Michael E., *The Morality of Capital Punishment: Equal Justice Under the Law,* Mystic, CT, Twenty-Third Publications, 1985.

Erwin, R.E., *Liberty, Community, and Justice,* Totowa, NJ, Rowman & Allanheld, 1987.

Feibleman, James K., *Justice, Law and Culture,* Hingham, MA, Kluwer Academic Publishers, 1985.

Finnis, John, *Natural Law and Natural,* New York, NY, Oxford University Press, 1980.

Flew, Anthony, *Crime or Disease?* London, Macmillan Publishers, Ltd., 1973.

Friedrich, Carl Joachim, *The Philosophy of Law in Historical Perspective,* 2nd ed., Chicago, IL, University of Chicago Press, 1963.

Fuller, Lon L., *The Morality of Law,* rev. ed., New Haven, CT, Yale University Press, 1965.

Gerhart, Eugene C., *American Liberty and "Natural Law,"* reprint of 1953 ed., Littleton, CO, Fred B. Rothman & Co., 1986.

Ginsberg, Morris, *On Justice in Society,* Harmondsworth, UK, Penguin Books, 1971.

Goldinger, Milton (ed.), *Punishment and Human Rights,* Cambridge, MA, Schenkman Publishing Co., Inc., 1974.

Greenswalt, R. Kent, *Conficts of Law and Morality,* New York, NY, Oxford University Press, 1987.

Haines, Charles G., *Revival of Natural Law Concepts,* Cambridge, MA, Harvard University Press, 1930.

Harding, Arthur L. (ed.), *Natural Law and Natural Rights,* Dallas, TX, Southern Methodist University Press, 1955.

Hart, H.L.A., *The Concept of Law,* Oxford, The Clarendon

Press, 1961. *Punishment and Responsibility: Essays in the Philosophy of Law,* New York, NY, Oxford University Press, 1968.

Havelock, Eric A., *The Greek Concept of Justice: From Its Shadow in Homer to Its Substance in Plato,* Cambridge, MA, Harvard University Press, 1978.

Hodson, John D., *The Ethics of Legal Coercion,* Hingham, MA, Kluwer Academic Publishers, 1983.

Hollenbach, David, *Claims in Conflict: Retrieving and Renewing the Catholic Human Rights Tradition,* New York, NY, Paulist Press, 1979.

Holmes, Oliver Wendell, *Collected Legal Papers,* New York, NY, Harcourt, Brace & World, Inc., 1920. *Holmes-Pollock Letters,* Cambridge, MA, Harvard University Press, 1941.

Hook, Sidney (ed.), *Law and Philosophy,* New York, NY, New York University Press, 1964.

Jackson, Michael W., *Matters of Justice,* New York, NY, Basil Blackwell, Inc., 1987.

Jessup, Henry W., *The Professional Ideals of the Lawyer: A Study of Legal Ethics,* Littleton, CO, Fred B. Rothman & Co., 1986.

Kaplan, Morton A., *Justice, Human Nature and Political Obligation,* New York, NY, The Free Press, 1976.

Kelsen, Hans, *What Is Justice?* Berkeley, CA, University of California Press, 1957.

Kiefer, Howard, and Munitz, Milton (eds.), *Ethics and Social Justice,* Albany, NY, State University of New York Press, 1970.

Kindregan, Charles P., *Quality of Life: Reflections on the Moral Values of American Law,* New York, NY, Macmillan Publishers, Ltd., 1969.

Kinkead, Edgar B., *Jurisprudence, Law, and Ethics: Professional Ethics,* reprint of 1905 ed., Littleton, CO, Fred B. Rothman & Co., 1985.

Labadie, Laurance, *On Natural Law and Punishment,* Brooklyn, NY, Revisionist Press, 1979.

Lamont, W.D., *Law and the Moral Order,* Elmsford, NY, Pergamon Press, Inc., 1981.

Lebacqz, Karen, *Six Theories of Justice: Perspectives from Philosophical and Theological Ethics,* Minneapolis, MN, Augsburg Publishing House, 1986.

Le Buffe, Francis P., and Hayes, James V., *The American Philosophy of Law,* New York, NY, Jesuit Educational Association, 1953. Formerly entitled *Jurisprudence.*

Lee, Simon, *Law and Morals: Warnock, Gillick and Beyond,* New York, NY, Oxford University Press, 1986.

Leiser, Burton M., *Custom, Law, and Morality: Conflict and Continuity in Social Behavior,* New York, NY, Doubleday Publishing Co., 1969.

Leoni, Bruno, *Freedom and the Law,* Atlantic Highlands, NJ, Humanities Press, Inc., 1980.

Lindley, Richard, *Autonomy,* Atlantic Highlands, NJ, Humanities Press International, Inc., 1986.

Luijpen, Wilhelmus Antonius, *Phenomenology of Natural Law,* translated by Henry J. Koren, Pittsburgh, PA, Duquesne University Press, 1967.

Lyons, David, *Ethics and the Rule of Law,* New York, NY, Cambridge University Press, 1984.

Lyons, David (ed.), *Rights,* Belmont, CA, Wadsworth Publishing Co., Inc., 1979.

Madison, G.B., *The Logic of Liberty,* Westport, CT, Greenwood Press, 1986.

Malloy, Edward A., *The Ethics of Law Enforcement and Criminal Punishment,* Lanham, MD, University Press of America, 1983.

Meyers, Diana T., *Inalienable Rights: A Defense,* New York, NY, Columbia University Press, 1985.

Milne, A.J.M., *Freedom and Rights,* New York, NY, Humanities Press, Inc., 1968.

Mitchell, Basil, *Law, Morality and Religion in a Secular Society,* London, Oxford University Press, 1967.

Moberly, Sir Walter, *The Ethics of Punishment,* London, Faber & Faber, Ltd., 1968.

Nathan, N.M., *The Concept of Justice,* Atlantic Highlands, NJ, Humanities Press, Inc., 1972.

Natural Law and Modern Society, Center for the Study of Democratic Institutions, Cleveland, OH, World Publishing Co., 1962.

Natural Law Institute Proceedings, College of Law, University of Notre Dame, Indiana, 1947 ff.

O'Brien, David J., and Shannon, Thomas A. (eds.), *Renewing the Earth: Catholic Documents on Peace, Justice and Liberation,* New York, NY, Doubleday & Co., Inc., 1977.

Pattee, William S., *The Essential Nature of Law or the Ethical Basis of Jurisprudence,* reprint of 1909 ed., Littleton, CO, Fred B. Rothman & Co., 1982.

Pennock, J. Roland, and Chapman, John W. (eds.), *Equality,* New York, NY, Atherton Press, 1967.

Perelman, Chaim H., *Justice,* New York, NY, Random House, 1967.

Pollack, Ervin H., *Jurisprudence: Principles and Applications,* Athens, OH, Ohio State University Press, 1979.

Raphael, D.D. (ed.), *Political Theory and the Rights of Man,* London, Macmillan Publishers, Ltd., 1967.

Rawls, John, *A Theory of Justice,* Cambridge, MA, Belknap Press of Harvard University Press, 1972, copyright 1971.

Ritchie, David G., *Natural Rights,* London, George Allen & Unwin, Ltd., 1952.

St. John-Stevas, Norman, *Law and Morals,* New York, NY, Hawthorn Books, Inc., 1964. *Life, Death, and the Law,* Bloomington, IN, Indiana University Press, 1961. *The Right to Life,* New York, NY, Holt, Rinehart & Winston, Inc., 1963.

Schnabel, E.J., *Law and Wisdom from Ben Sira to Paul: A Traditional Historical Enquiry into the Relation of Law, Wisdom and Ethics,* Philadelphia, PA, Coronet Books, 1985.

Shapiro, Ian, *The Evolution of Rights in Liberal Theory: An Essay in Critical Anthropology,* New York, NY, Cambridge University Press, 1986.

Schwartz, Mortimer, and Wydick, Richard C., *Problems in Legal Ethics,* St. Paul, MN, West Publishing Co., 1983.

Shklar, Judith N., *Legalism,* Cambridge, MA, Harvard University Press, 1964.

Simpson, A.W.B. (ed.), *Oxford Essays in Jurisprudence,* Oxford, The Clarendon Press, 1972.

Snyder, Leslie, *Justice or Revolution,* New York, NY, Books in Focus, Inc., 1979.

Spurrier, William A., *Natural Law and The Ethics of Love: A New Synthesis,* Philadelphia, PA, Westminster Press, 1974.

Stoljar, S.J., *An Analysis of Rights,* New York, NY, St. Martin's Press, 1984.

Strauss, Leo, *Natural Rights and History,* Chicago, IL, The University of Chicago Press, 1953.

Stumpf, Samuel Enoch, *Morality and the Law,* Nashville, TN, Vanderbilt University Press, 1966.

Summer, L.W., *The Moral Foundation of Rights,* New York, NY, Oxford University Press, 1987.

Summers, Robert S. (ed.), *Essays in Legal Philosophy,* Oxford, Basil Blackwell & Mott, Ltd., 1968. *More Essays in Legal Philosophy, General Assessments of Legal Philosophies,* Berkeley, CA, University of California Press, 1971.

Tapp, June L., and Levine, Felice, *Law, Justice, and The Individual in Society,* New York, NY, Holt, Rinehart & Winston, Inc., 1977.

Tuck, R., *Natural Rights Theories: Their Origin and Development,* New York, NY, Cambridge University Press, 1980; 1982.

UNESCO (ed.), *Human Rights,* a symposium, Greenford, Middlesex, UK, Allan Wingate (Publishers), Ltd., n.d.

Veatch, Henry B., *Human Rights: Facts or Fancy,* Baton Rouge, LA, Louisiana State University Press, 1985.

Walzer, Michael, *The Spheres of Justice: A Defense of Pluralism and Equality,* New York, NY, Basic Books, Inc., 1983.

Weintraub, Lloyd L., *Natural Law and Justice,* Cambridge, MA, Harvard University Press, 1987.

Weiss, Paul, *Our Public Life,* Carbondale, IL, Southern Illinois University Press, 1966.

Wellman, Carl, *A Theory of Rights: Persons under Laws, Institutions and Morals,* Totowa, NJ, Rowman & Allanheld, 1985.

White, Alan R., *Rights,* New York, NY, Oxford University Press, 1984.

Wolff, Robert Paul, *In Defense of Anarchism,* New York, NY, Harper & Row, Publishers, 1970. *Understanding Rawls,* Princeton, NJ, Princeton University Press, 1977.

Wu, John C., *Fountain of Justice: A Study of the Natural Law,* Beaverton, OR, International Scholarly Book Services, Inc., 1980.

2. Medical Ethics: Life, Health, Safety

Abrams, Natalie, and Buckner, Michael D., *Medical Ethics: A Clinical Textbook and Reference for the Health Care Professions,* Cambridge, MA, MIT Press, 1982.

American Friends Service Committee, *Who Shall Live? Man's Control Over Birth and Death,* New York, NY, Hill & Wang, 1970.

Anderson, J.K., *Genetic Engineering: The Ethical Issues,* Grand Rapids, MI, Zondervan Publishing House, 1982.

Annas, George J., *The Rights of Hospital Patients: The Basic ACLU Guide to a Hospital Patient's Rights,* New York, NY, Avon Books, 1975.

Annas, George J., et al., *Informed Consent to Human Experimentation: The Subject's Dilemma,* Cambridge, MA, Ballinger Publishing Co., 1977.

Arras, John, and Hunt, Robert, *Ethical Issues in Modern Medicine,* 2nd ed., Palo Alto, CA, Mayfield Publishing Co., 1983.

Ashley, Benedict M., and O'Rourke, Kevin D., *Health Care Ethics: A Theological Analysis,* 2nd ed., St. Louis, MO, The Catholic Hospital Association, 1982. *The Ethics of Health Care,* St. Louis, MO, Catholic Health Association of the U.S., 1986.

Basson, Marc D. (ed.), *Ethics, Humanism, and Medicine,* New York, NY, Alan R. Liss, Inc., 1980.

Battin, Margaret, *Suicide and Ethics,* New York, NY, Human Sciences Press, Inc., 1983.

Beauchamp, Tom L., and Childress, James F., *Principles of Biomedical Ethics,* New York, NY, Oxford University Press, 1979; 2nd ed., 1983.

Beauchamp, Tom L., and McCullough, Laurence B., *Medical Ethics: The Moral Responsibilities of Physicians,* Englewood Cliffs, NJ, Prentice-Hall, Inc., 1984.

Beauchamp, Tom L., and Walters, LeRoy (eds.), *Contemporary Issues in Bioethics,* 2nd ed., Belmont, CA, Wadsworth Publishing Co., 1982.

Beecher, Henry K., *Research and the Individual: Human Studies,* Boston, MA, Little, Brown & Co., 1970.

Bell, Linda, (ed.), *Visions of Women,* Clifton, NJ, Humana Press, 1985.

Bier, William C. (ed.), *Human Life: Problems of Birth, of Living, and of Dying,* New York, NY, Fordham University Press, 1977.

Bliss, Brian P., and Johnson, Alan G., *Aims and Motives in Clinical Medicine: A Practical Approach to Medical Ethics,* London, Pitman Medical Publishing Co., Ltd., 1975.

Blum, Richard, and associates, *Utopiates,* New York, NY, Atherton Press, 1964.

Brody, Howard, *Ethical Decisions in Medicine,* Boston, MA, Little, Brown & Co., 1976; 2nd ed., 1981.

Burnette, Henlee H., *Exploring Medical Ethics,* Macon, GA, Mercer University Press, 1982.

Campbell, Alastair V., *Medicine, Health and Justice,* New York, NY, Churchill Livingstone, Inc., 1979. *Moral Dilemmas in Medicine,* 2nd ed., New York, NY, Churchill Livingstone, Inc., 1975.

Capron, Alexander M., et al. (eds.), *Genetic Counseling: Facts, Values, and Norms,* New York, NY, Alan R. Liss, Inc., 1979.

Carlton, Wendy, *In Our Professional Opinion . . . The Primacy of Clinical Judgment Over Moral Choice,* Notre Dame, IN, University of Notre Dame Press, 1978.

Childress, James F., *Priorities in Biomedical Ethics,* Philadelphia, PA, Westminster Press, 1981.

Christie, Ronald J. and Hoffmaster, C. Barry, *Ethical Issues in Family Medicine,* New York, NY, Oxford University Press, 1986.

Clark-Kennedy, A.E., *Man, Medicine, and Morality,* Hamden, CT, The Shoe String Press, Inc., 1970.

Claxton, Ernest, and McKay, H.A. (eds.), *Medicine, Morals and Man,* New York, NY, International Publications Service, 1969.

Cohen, Sidney, *The Beyond Within,* New York, NY, Atherton Press, 1964.

Curran, Charles E., *Issues in Sexual and Medical Ethics,* Notre Dame, IN, University of Notre Dame Press, 1978. *Politics, Medicine, and Christian Ethics,* Philadelphia, PA, Fortress Press, 1973.

Cutler, Donald R. (ed.), *Updating Life and Death,* Boston, MA, Beacon Press, 1969.

Darr, Kurt, *Ethics in Health Services Management,* New York, NY, Praeger Publishers, 1987.

Dawson, John, and Phillips, Melanie, *Doctors' Dilemmas: Medical Ethics and Contemporary Science,* New York, NY, Methuen, Inc., 1985.

Day, Stacey B. (ed.), *Ethics in Medicine in a Changing Society,* Minneapolis, MN, University of Minnesota, Bell Museum of Pathology, 1973.

Dedek, John F., *Contemporary Medical Ethics,* New York, NY, Sheed and Ward, Inc., 1975. *Human Life: Some Moral Issues,* New York, NY, Sheed & Ward, Inc., 1972.

Downie, R.S., and Calman, K.C., *Healthy Respect: Ethics in Health Care,* Winchester, MA, Faber & Faber, Inc., 1987.

Duncan, A.S., et al. (eds.), *Dictionary of Medical Ethics,* New York, NY, Crossroad Publishing Co., 1981.

Dyer, Allen, *Ethics and Psychiatry: Toward Professional Definition,* Washington, DC, American Psychiatric Press, Inc., 1987.

Edmunds, Vincent, and Scorer, C. Gordon, *Ethical Responsibility in Medicine: a Christian Approach,* New York, NY, Longman, Inc., 1967.

Edwards, Rem B. (ed.), *Psychiatry and Ethics: Insanity, Rational Autonomy, and Mental Health Care,* Buffalo, NY, Prometheus Books, 1982.

Ellison, David L., *The Bio-Medical Fix: Human Dimensions of Bio-Medical Technologies,* Westport, CT, Greenwood Press, Inc., 1978.

Engelhardt, H. Tristram, Jr., *The Foundations of Bioethics,* New York, NY and Oxford, UK, Oxford University Press, 1986.

Engelhardt, H. Tristram, Jr., and Callahan, Daniel (eds.), *The Foundations of Ethics and Its Relationship to Science:* Vol. I, "Science, Ethics and Medicine"; Vol. II, "Knowledge, Value and Belief"; Vol. III, "Morals, Science and Sociality"; Vol. IV, "Knowing and Valuing: The Search for Common Roots," Hastings-on-Hudson, NY, The Hastings Center, Institute of Society, Ethics and the Life Sciences, 1976, 1977, 1978, and 1980.

Entralgo, P.L., *Doctor and Patient,* New York, NY, McGraw-Hill Book Co., 1969.

Etziony, M.B. (ed.), *The Physician's Creed,* Springfield, IL, Charles C. Thomas, Publisher, 1973.

Faulder, Carolyn, *Whose Body Is It? The Troubling Issue of Informed Consent,* Topsfield, MA, Salem House Publishers, 1986.

Ficarra, Bernard, *Newer Ethical Problems in Medicine and Surgery,* Westminster, MD, The Newman Press, 1951.

Fletcher, Joseph, *Humanbood: Essays in Biomedical Ethics,* Buffalo, NY, Prometheus Books, 1979. *Morals and Medicine,* Princeton, NJ, Princeton University Press, 1954; Boston, MA, Beacon Press, 1960. *Morals and Medicine: The Moral Problems of the Patient's Right to Know the Truth,* Princeton, NJ, Princeton University Press, 1979.

Flood, Peter (ed.), *The Ethics of Brain Surgery,* Chicago, IL, Henry Regnery Co., 1955. *Medical Experimentation on Man,* Chicago, IL, Henry Regnery Co., 1955. *New Problems in Medical Ethics,* 2 vols., Westminster, MD, The Newman Press, 1953.

Francoeur, Robert T. *Biomedical Ethics: A Guide to Decision Making,* New York, NY, John Wiley & Sons, Inc., 1983.

Frazier, Claude, *Is it Moral to Modify Man?* Springfield, IL, Charles C. Thomas, Publisher, 1973.

Frazier, Claude A. (ed.), *Should Doctors Play God?* Nashville, TN, Broadman Press, 1971.

Freund, Paul A. (ed.), *Experimentation With Human Subjects,* New York, NY, George Braziller, Inc., 1970.

Frohock, Fred M., *Special Care: Medical Decisions at the Beginning of Life,* Chicago, IL, University of Chicago Press, 1986.

Fromer, Margot J., *Ethical Issues in Health Care,* St. Louis, MO, The C.V. Mosby Co., 1981.

Gelfand, Michael, *Philosophy and Ethics in Medicine,* New York, NY, Longman, Inc., 1968.

Giles, James E., *Medical Ethics: A Patient-Centered Approach,* Cambridge, MA, Schenkman Publishing Co., Inc., 1983.

Glaser, John W., *Caring for the Special Child,* Kansas City, MO, Sheed & Ward, 1985.

Glesnes-Anderson, Valerie A., and Anderson, Gary R., *Hospital Care Ethics: A Guide for Decision Makers,* Rockville, MD, Aspen Publishers, Inc., 1987.

Gorovitz, Samuel, *Doctors' Dilemmas: Moral Conflict and Medical Care,* New York, NY, Oxford University Press, 1985.

Gorovitz, Samuel, et al. (eds.), *Moral Problems in Medicine,* Englewood Cliffs, NJ, Prentice-Hall, Inc., 1976.

Gustafson, James M., *The Contributions of Theology to Medical Ethics,* Milwaukee, WI, Marquette University Press, 1975.

Gustaitis, Rasa, and Young, Ernle W.D., *A Time to be Born, A Time to Die: Conflicts and Ethics in an Intensive Care Nursery,* Reading, MA and Menlo Park, CA, Addison-Wesley Publishing Co., Inc., 1986.

Häring, Bernard, *Ethics of Manipulation: Issues in Medicine, Behavior Control and Genetics,* New York, NY, The Seabury Press, Inc., 1975. *Medical Ethics,* revised ed., Notre Dame, IN, Fides Publishers, Inc., 1975.

Harris, John, *The Value of Life: An Introduction to Medical Ethics,* New York, NY, Methuen, Inc., 1985.

Hauerwas, Stanley, Bondi, Richard, and Burrell, David B., *Truthfulness and Tragedy: Further Investigations into Christian Ethics,* Notre Dame, IN, University of Notre Dame Press, 1977.

Hayes, Donald M., *Between Doctor and Patient,* Valley Forge, PA, Judson Press, 1977.

Healey, Edwin, *Medical Ethics,* Chicago, IL, Loyola University Press, 1956.

Heyer, Robert, *Medical/Moral Problems,* New York, NY, Paulist Press, 1977.

Hiller, Marc D., *Ethics and Health Administration: Ethical Decision Making in Health Management,* Arlington, VA, AUPHA Press, 1986. *Medical Ethics and the Law: Implications For Public Policy,* Cambridge, MA, Ballinger Publishing Co., 1983.

Hsia, Y. Edward, et al. (eds.), *Counseling in Genetics,* New York, NY, Alan R. Liss, Inc., 1979.

Humber, James M., and Almeder, Robert F., *Biomedical Ethics and the Law,* New York, NY, Plenum Press, 1976; 2nd ed., 1979.

Huxley, Aldous, *Doors of Perception,* New York, NY, Harper & Row, Publishers, 1954.

Illich, Ivan, *Medical Nemesis: The Expropriation of Health,* New York, NY, Pantheon Books, Inc., 1976.

Ingle, Dwight J., *Who Should Have Children? An Environmental and Genetic Approach,* Indianapolis, IN, The Bobbs-Merrill Co., Inc., 1973.

Iserson, Kenneth V., *Ethics in Emergency Medicine,* Baltimore, MD, Williams & Wilkins, 1986.

Israel, Lucien, *Decision Making: The Modern Doctor's Dilemma,* New York, NY, Random House, 1982.

Jakobovits, Immanuel, *Jewish Medical Ethics,* New York, NY, Bloch Publishing Co., Inc., 1959.

Jonsen, Albert, and Siegler, Mark, *Clinical Ethics,* New York, NY, Macmillan Publishing Co., Inc., 1982.

Kantrowitz, Adrian, et al., *Who Shall Live and Who Shall Die: the Ethical Implications of the New Medical Technology,* New York, NY, Union of American Hebrew Congregations, 1968.

Kass, Leon R., *Toward a More Natural Science: Biology and Human Affairs,* New York, NY, Free Press, 1985.

Katz, Jay, *Experimentation With Human Beings: the Authority of Investigator, Subject, Professions and State in the Human Experimentation Process,* New York, NY, Russell Sage Foundation, 1972.

Kevorkian, Jack, *Medical Research and the Death Penalty,* Long Beach, CA, Penumbra, Inc., 1983.

Kieffer, George H., *Bioethics: A Textbook of Issues,* Reading, MA, Addison-Wesley Publishing Co., Inc., 1979.

Kelly, Gerald, *Medico-Moral Problems,* St. Louis, MO, Catholic Hospital Association, 1958.

Kuhse, Helga, *The Sanctity-of-Life Doctrine in Medicine: A Critique,* New York, NY, Oxford University Press, 1987.

Lamb, David, *Death, Brain Death and Ethics,* Albany, NY, State University of New York Press, 1985.

Lander, Louise, *Defective Medicine: Risk, Anger, and the Malpractice Crisis,* New York, NY, Farrar, Straus & Giroux, Inc., 1978.

Leach, Gerald, *The Biocrats,* Baltimore, MD, Penguin Books, Inc., 1972.

Levine, Howard, *Life Choices: Confronting the Life and Death Decisions Created by Modern Medicine,* New York, NY, Simon & Schuster, 1986.

Levine, Robert J., *Ethics and Regulation of Clinical Research,* Baltimore, MD, Urban & Schwarzenberg, 1986.

Levy, Charlotte, *The Human Body and the Law: Legal and Ethical Considerations in Human Experimentation,* 2nd ed., Dobbs Ferry, NY, Oceana Publications, 1983.

Lockwood, Michael, *Moral Dilemmas in Modern Medicine,* New York, NY, Oxford University Press, 1985.

Loewy, Erich H., *Ethical Dilemmas in Modern Medicine: A Physician's Viewpoint,* Lewiston, NY, The Edwin Mellen Press, 1986.

Lyons, Catherine, *Organ Transplants: the Moral Issues,* Philadelphia, PA, The Westminster Press, 1970.

Lucas, George R., Jr., *Triage in Medicine and Society. Inquiries into Medical Ethics,* III, Houston, TX, The Institute of Religion and Human Development, 1975.

McCormick, Richard, *How Brave a New World? Dilemmas in Bioethics,* Garden City, NY, Doubleday & Co., Inc., 1981.

McFadden, Charles, *Medical Ethics,* 6th ed., Philadelphia, PA, F.A. Davis Co., 1967.

MacKay, William, *Salesman Surgeon,* New York, NY, McGraw-Hill Book Co., 1978.

Macklin, Ruth, *Mortal Choices: Bioethics in Today's World,* New York, NY, Pantheon Books, 1987.

McLean, Sheila, *Consent to Medical Treatment,* Brookfield, VT, Gower Publishing Co., 1987.

Mahoney, John, *Bioethics and Belief,* Westminster, MD, Christian Classics, Inc., 1984.

Mann, Kenneth W., *Deadline for Survival: a Survey of Moral Issues in Science and Medicine,* New York, NY, The Seabury Press, Inc., 1970.

Mappes, Thomas, and Zembaty, Jane, *Biomedical Ethics,* New York, NY, McGraw-Hill Book Co., 1980.

Marshall, John, *Medicine and Morals,* New York, NY, Hawthorn Books, Inc., 1960.

Masters, N.C., and Shapiro, H.A., *Medical Secrecy and the Doctor-Patient Relationship,* New York, NY, International Publications Service, 1966.

May, William E., *Human Existence, Medicine and Ethics: Reflections on Human Life,* Chicago, IL, Franciscan Herald Press, 1977. *The Physician's Covenant: Images of the Healer in Medical Ethics,* Philadelphia, PA, Westminster Press, 1983.

Miller, George W., *Moral and Ethical Implications of Human Organ Transplants,* Springfield, IL, Charles C. Thomas, Publisher, 1971.

Munson, Ronald, *Invervention and Reflection: Basic Issues in Medical Ethics,* Belmont, CA, Wadsworth Publishing Co., Inc., 1979; 2nd ed., 1983.

Nelson, James B., *Human Medicine: Ethical Perspective on New Medical Issues,* Minneapolis, MN, Augsburg Publishing House, 1973. *Rediscovering the Person in Medical Care,* Minneapolis, MN, Augsburg Publishing House, 1976.

Oden, Thomas C., *Should Treatment Be Terminated,* New York, NY, Harper & Row, Publishers, 1977.

O'Donnell, Thomas J., *Medicine and Christian Morality,* New York, NY, Alba House, 1976.

O'Reilly, Sean, *Bioethics and the Limits of Science,* Front Royal, VA, Christendom Publications, 1980.

O'Rourke, Kevin, and Brodeur, Dennis, *Medical Ethics: Common Ground for Understanding,* St. Louis, MO, Catholic Health Association of the U.S., 1986.

Pappworth, Maurice H., *Human Guinea Pigs,* Boston, MA, Beacon Press, 1968.

Pellegrino, Edmund D., *Humanism and the Physician,* Knoxville, TN, University of Tennessee Press, 1979.

Pence, G., *Ethical Options in Medicine,* Oradel, NJ, Medical Economics Books, 1980.

Purtilo, Ruth B., and Cassel, Christine K., *Ethical Dimensions in the Health Professions,* Philadelphia, PA, W.B. Saunders Co., 1981.

Ramsey, Paul, *Ethics at the Edges of Life: Medical and Legal Intersections,* New Haven, CT, Yale University Press, 1978. *The Ethics of Fetal Research,* New Haven, CT, Yale University Press, 1975. *Fabricated Man: The Ethics of Genetic Control,* New Haven, CT, Yale University Press, 1970. *The Patient as Person: Exploration in Medical Ethics,* New Haven, CT, Yale University Press, 1974.

Reich, Warren T. (editor-in-chief), *Encyclopedia of Bioethics,* 4 vols., New York, NY, The Free Press, 1978.

Reidy, Maurice, *Foundations for a Medical Ethic,* New York, NY, Paulist Press, 1979.

Reiser, Joel, Dyck, Arthur, and Curran, William J. (eds.), *Ethics in Medicine: Historical Perspectives and Contemporary Concerns,* Cambridge, MA, The MIT Press, 1977.

Restak, Richard M., *Premeditated Man: Bioethics and the Control of Future Human Life,* New York, NY, Viking Press, 1975.

Robbins, Dennis A., *Legal and Ethical Issues in Cancer Care in the United States,* Springfield, IL, Charles C. Thomas, Publisher, 1983.

Schmeck, Harold M., *Semi-Artificial Man,* New York, NY, Walker & Co., 1965.

Shannon, Thomas A., *Twelve Problems in Health Care Ethics,* Lewiston, NY, The Edwin Mellen Press, 1985.

Shannon, Thomas A. (ed.), *Bioethics,* New York, NY, Paulist Press, 1976.

Shannon, Thomas, and DiGiacomo, James, *An Introduction to Bioethics,* Ramsey, NJ, Paulist Press, 1979.

Shannon, Thomas, and Manfra, JoAnn, *Law and Bioethics: Selected Cases,* Ramsey, NJ, Paulist Press, 1981.

Shapiro, Michael H., and Spece, Roy G., Jr., *Cases, Materials, and Problems on Bioethics and Law,* St. Paul, MN, West Publishing Co., 1981.

Shelp, Earl E., *Born to Die? Deciding the Fate of Critically Ill Newborns,* New York, NY, Free Press, 1986.

Sherlock, Richard, *Preserving Life: Public Policy and the Life Not Worth Living,* Chicago, IL, Loyola University Press, 1987.

Sigerist, Henry E., *Medicine and Human Welfare,* Washington, DC, McGrath Publishing Co., 1970.

Simmons, Paul D., *Birth and Death: Bioethical Decision Making,* Philadelphia, PA, Westminster Press, 1983.

Skegg, P.D., *Ethics and Medicine: Studies in Medical Law,* New York, NY, Oxford University Press, 1985.

Smith, Harmon L., *Ethics and the New Medicine,* Nashville, TN, Abingdon Press, 1970.

Smith, Harmon, and Churchill, Larry R., *Professional Ethics and Primary Care Medicine: Beyond Dilemmas and Decorum,* Durham, NC, Duke University Press, 1986.

Steele, Shirley M., and Harmon, Vera M., *Values Clarification in Nursing,* New York, NY, Appleton-Century-Crofts, 1979.

Stein, Jane J., *Making Medical Choices: Ethics and Medicine in a Technological Age,* Boston, MA, Houghton-Mifflin Co., 1978.

Stroman, Duane F., *The Medical Establishment and Social Responsibility,* Port Washington, NY, Kennikat Press Corp., 1976.

Szaz, Thomas, *The Theology of Medicine: The Political-Philosophical Foundations of Medical Ethics,* Baton Rouge, LA, Louisiana State University Press, 1977.

Tancredi, Lawrence P., and Slaby, Andrew E., *Ethical Policy in Mental Health Care: The Goals of Psychiatric Intervention,* New York, NY, Neale Watson Academic Publications, Inc., 1977.

Thomas, John E., *Matters of Life and Death: Crisis in Biomedical Ethics,* Sarasota, FL, Samuel Stevens & Co., 1978. *Medical Ethics and Human Life: Doctor, Patient and Family in the New Technology,* Sarasota, FL, Samuel Stevens & Co., 1983.

Thompson, Andrew, *Ethical Concerns in Psychotherapy and Their Legal Implications,* Washington, DC, University Press of America, 1983.

Torrey, E. Fuller, *Ethical Issues in Medicine: the Role of the Physician in Today's Society,* Boston, MA, Little, Brown & Co., 1968.

Van den Berg, Jan H., *Medical Ethics and Medical Power,* New York, NY, W.W. Norton and Co., Inc., 1978.

Vaux, Kenneth, *Biomedical Ethics,* New York, NY, Harper & Row, Publishers, 1974.

Veatch, Robert M., *Case Studies in Medical Ethics,* Cambridge, MA, Harvard University Press, 1977. *A Theory of Medical Ethics,* New York, NY, Basic Books, Inc., Publishers, 1981. *The Foundations of Justice: Why the Retarded and the Rest of Us Have Claims to Equality,* New York, NY, Oxford University Press, 1986.

Visscher, Maurice B., *Ethical Constraints and Imperatives in Medical Research,* Springfield, IL, Charles C. Thomas, Publisher, 1975.

Visscher, Maurice B. (ed.), *Humanistic Perspectives in Medical Ethics,* Buffalo, NY, Prometheus Books, 1972.

Wall, Thomas F., *Medical Ethics: Basic Moral Issues,* Washington, DC, University Press of America, 1980.

Walton, Douglas N., *Physician-Patient Decision-Making,* Westport, CT, Greenwood Press, 1985.

Weiss, Ann E., *Bioethics: Dilemmas in Modern Medicine,* Hillside, NJ, Enslow Publishers, 1985.

Wertz, Richard W. (ed.), *Readings on Ethical and Social Issues in Biomedicine,* Englewood Cliffs, NJ, Prentice-Hall, Inc., 1973.

Williams, Preston, *Ethical Issues in Biology and Medicine,* Morristown, NJ, General Learning Corp., 1973.

Winslow, Gerald R., *Triage and Justice: The Ethics of Rationing Life-Saving Medical Resources,* Berkeley, CA, University of California Press, 1982.

Wojcik, Jan, *Muted Consent: A Casebook in Modern Medical Ethics,* West Lafayette, IN, Purdue Research Foundation, 1978.

Yezzi, Ronald, *Medical Ethics,* New York, NY, Holt, Rinehart & Winston, Inc., 1980.

Zaner, Richard M., *Ethics and the Clinical Encounter,* Englewood Cliffs, NJ, Prentice-Hall, Inc., 1988.

A. Abortion

Arnstein, Helene S., *What Every Woman Needs to Know About Abortion,* New York, NY, Charles Scribner's Sons, 1973.

Baker, Don, *Beyond Choice: The Abortion Story No One is Telling,* Portland, OR, Multnomah Press, 1985.

Bajema, Clifford E., *Abortion and the Meaning of Personhood,* Grand Rapids, MI, Baker Book House, 1974.

Berger, Gary S., et al. (eds.), *Second Trimester Abortion: Perspectives After a Decade of Experience,* Littleton, MA, John Wright, PSG, Inc., 1981.

Bird, Lewis, *What You Should Know About Abortion,* ed. by William J. Petersen, New Canaan, CT, Keats Publishing, Inc., 1974.

Bluford, Robert, Jr., and Petres, Robert E., *Unwanted Pregnancy,* New York, NY, Harper & Row, Publishers, 1973.

Bondesor, William B., and Engelhardt, H. Tristram, *Abortion and the Status of the Fetus,* Hingham, MA, Kluwer Academic Publications, 1983.

Brennan, William, *The Abortion Holocaust: Today's Final Solution,* St. Louis, MO, Landmark Press, 1983.

Brody, Baruch, *Abortion and the Sanctity of Human Life: A Philosophical View,* Cambridge, MA, The MIT Press, 1976.

Brown, Harold O., *Death Before Birth,* Nashville, TN, Thomas Nelson, Inc., 1977.

Callahan, Daniel, *Abortion: Law, Choice and Morality,* New York, NY, The Macmillan Co., 1970.

Cohen, Marshall, Nagel, Thomas, and Scanlon, Thomas (eds.), *The Rights and Wrongs of Abortion,* Princeton, NJ, Princeton University Press, 1974.

Connery, John, *Abortion: The Development of the Roman Catholic Perspective,* Chicago, IL, Loyola University Press, 1977.

Davis, Nanette J., *From Crime to Choice: The Transformation of Abortion in America,* Westport, CT, Greenwood Press, 1985.

De Danois, Vivian, *Abortion and the Moral Degeneration of the American Medical Profession,* Albuquerque, NM, American Classical College Press, 1975.

DeMarco, Donald, *Abortion in Perspective,* Cincinnati, OH, Hiltz & Hayes, 1974.

Erdahl, Lowell O., *Pro-Life, Pro-Peace: Life Affirming Alternatives to Abortion, War, Mercy Killing and the Death Penalty,* Minneapolis, MN, Augsburg Publishing House, 1986.

Fleming, Alice, *Contraception, Abortion, Pregnancy,* Nashville, TN, Thomas Nelson, Inc., 1974.

Frohock, Fred M., *Abortion: A Case Study in Law and Morals,* Westport, CT, Greenwood Press, 1983.

Granfield, David, *The Abortion Decision,* New York, NY, Doubleday Publishing Co., 1969; 1971.

Grisez, Germain, *Abortion: the Myths, the Realities, and the Arguments,* New York, NY, Corpus Books, 1970.

Halimi, Gisele, *The Right to Choose,* Lawrence, ME, University of Queensland Press, 1977.

Hall, Robert E., *Abortion in a Changing World,* 2 vols., New York, NY, Columbia University Press, 1970. *Doctor's Guide to Having an Abortion,* New York, NY, New American Library, Inc., 1971.

Hardin, Garrett, *Stalking the Wild Taboo,* Los Altos, CA, William Kaufmann, 1973.

Harris, Harry, *Prenatal Diagnosis and Selective Abortion,* Cambridge, MA, Harvard University Press, 1975.

Harrison, Beverly W., *Our Right to Choose: Toward a New Ethic of Abortion,* Boston, MA, Beacon Press, 1983.

Hendin, David, *Everything You Need to Know About Abortion,* New York, NY, Pinnacle Books, 1971.

Hilgers, Thomas, and Horan, Dennis J. (eds.), *Abortion and Social Justice,* New York, NY, Sheed & Ward, Inc., 1973.

Horobin, G.W. (ed.), *Experience With Abortion,* New York, NY, Cambridge University Press, 1973.

Imber, Jonathan B., *Abortion and the Private Practice of Medicine,* New Haven, CT, Yale University Press, 1986.

Jenness, Linda, Lund, Carolina, and Jaquith, Cindy, *Abortion: Women's Fight for the Right to Choose,* New York, NY, Pathfinder Press, 1973.

Kalmar, Roberta, *Abortion: The Emotional Implications,* Dubuque, IA, Kendall/Hunt Publishing Co., 1977.

Keast, Laury, *The Abortion Controversy,* new ed., ed. by D. Steve Rahmas, Charlotteville, NY, Sam Har Press, 1973.

Kohl, Marvin, *The Morality of Killing: Euthanasia, Abortion and Transplants,* New York, NY, Humanities Press, Inc., 1974.

Legge, Jerome S., Jr., *Abortion Policy: An Evaluation of the Consequences for Maternal and Infant Health,* Albany, NY, State University of New York Press, 1985.

Lotstra, H., *Abortion: The Catholic Theological Debate in America,* New York, NY, Irvington Publishers, 1983.

Luker, Kristin, *Taking Chances: Abortion and the Decision Not to Contracept,* Berkeley, CA, University of California Press, 1976.

McCartney, James J., *Unborn Persons: Pope John Paul II and the Abortion Debate,* New York, NY, Peter Lang Publishing, 1987.

Mace, David R., *Abortion: the Agonizing Decision,* Nashville, TN, Abingdon Press, 1972.

McTaggart, Dan, *Abortion and the Outlaw: A Belated Dissent to Roe vs Wade,* Council Bluffs, IA, DeLago Press, 1987.

Mall, David, *In Good Conscience: Abortion and Moral Necessity,* Libertyville, IL, Kairos Books, Inc., 1982.

Mankekar, Kamla, *Abortion: a Social Dilemma,* Portland, OR, International Scholarly Book Service, 1974.

Martin, Walter, *Abortion—Is It Always Murder?,* Santa Ana, CA, Vision House Publishers, 1979.

McCarthy, John F., *In Defense of Human Life,* Houston, TX, Lumen Christi Press, 1970.

McEllhenney, John G., *Cutting the Monkey-Rope: Is the Taking of Life Ever Justified?* Valley Forge, PA, Judson Press, 1973.

Mohr, James C., *Abortion in America: The Origins and Evolution of National Policy,* New York, NY, Oxford University Press, Inc., 1978.

Newman, Sidney H., Beck, Mildred B., and Lewit, Sarah (eds.), *Abortion, Obtained and Denied: Research Approaches,* Bridgeport, CT, Key Book Service, 1971.

Noonan, John T. (ed.), *The Morality of Abortion: Legal and Historical Perspectives,* Cambridge, MA, Harvard University Press, 1970. *A Private Choice: Abortion in America in the Seventies,* New York, NY, The Free Press, 1979.

Osofsky, Howard J., and Osofsky, Joy D., *The Abortion Experience,* New York, NY, Harper & Row, Publishers, 1973.

Patterson, Janet, and Patterson, Robert C., *Abortion: the Trojan Horse,* Nashville, TN, Thomas Nelson, Inc., 1974.

Perkins, Robert L. (ed.), *Abortion: Pro and Con,* Cambridge, MA, Schenkman Publishing Co., Inc., 1974.

Reiterman, Carl (ed.), *California Committee on Therapeutic Abortion: Abortion and the Unwanted Child,* New York, NY, Springer Publishing Co., Inc., 1971.

Rudel, Harry W., Kincl, Fred A., and Henzl, Milan R. *Birth Control: Contraception and Abortion,* New York, NY, The Macmillan Co., 1973.

Saltman, Jules, and Zimering, Stanley, *Abortion Today,* Springfield, IL, Charles C. Thomas, Publisher, 1973.

Sarvis, Betty, and Rodman, Hyman, *The Abortion Controversy,* 2nd ed., New York, NY, Columbia University Press, 1974.

Shaw, Russell B., *Abortion on Trial,* New York, NY, International Publications Service, 1969.

Sloane, Bruce R. (ed.), *Abortion: Changing Views and Practice,* New York, NY, Grune & Stratton, Inc., 1971.

Storer, Horatio R., and Heard, Franklin F., *Criminal Abortion,* New York, NY, Arno Press, Inc., 1974.

Sumner, L.W., *Abortion and Moral Theory,* Princeton, NJ, Princeton University Press, 1981.

Tooley, Michael, *Abortion and Infanticide,* New York, NY, Oxford University Press, 1986.

Wennberg, Robert, *Life in the Balance: Exploring the Abortion Controversy,* Grand Rapids, MI, William B. Eerdmans Publishing Co., 1985.

Zimmerman, Mary K., *Passage Through Abortion: The Personal and Social Reality of Women's Experience,* New York, NY, Praeger Publishers, 1977.

B. Euthanasia

Barnard, Christiaan, *Good Life Good Death: A Doctor's Case for Euthanasia and Suicide,* Englewood Cliffs, NJ, Prentice-Hall, Inc., 1980.

Behnke, John A., and Bok, Sissela (eds.), *The Dilemmas of Euthanasia,* New York, NY, Doubleday & Co., Inc., 1975.

Cantor, Norman L., *Legal Frontiers of Death and Dying,* Bloomington, IN, Indiana University Press, 1987.

Downing A.B., *Euthanasia: Right to Death,* Plainview, NY, Nash Publishing Corp., 1970.

Downing, A.B., (ed.), *Euthanasia and the Right to Death: the Case for Voluntary Euthanasia,* New York, NY, Humanities Press, Inc., 1970.

Gervais, Karen G., *Redefining Death,* New Haven, CT, Yale University Press, 1987.

Gould, Jonathan, and Lord Craigmyle (eds.), *Your Death Warrant? The Implications of Euthanasia,* New Rochelle, NY, Arlington House, Inc., 1973.

Grisez, Germain, and Boyle, Joseph M., *Life and Death with Liberty and Justice: A Contribution to the Euthanasia Debate,* Notre Dame, IN, University of Notre Dame Press, 1979.

Gula, Richard S., *What Are They Saying About Euthanasia?,* Mahwah, NJ, Paulist Press, 1986.

Humphrey, Derek, and Wickett, Ann, *The Right to Die: Understanding Euthanasia,* New York, NY, Harper & Row Publishers, 1987.

Kluge, Eike-Henner W., *The Ethics of Deliberate Death,* Port Washington, NY, Associated Faculty Press, 1981.

Kohl, Marvin, *Beneficent Euthanasia,* Buffalo, NY, Prometheus Books, 1974.

Maguire, Daniel C., *Death by Choice,* New York, NY, Doubleday Publishing Co., 1974.

Mannes, Marya, *Last Rights,* New York, NY, William Morrow & Co., Inc., 1974.

May, William, and Westley, Richard, *The Right to Die,* Chicago, IL, Thomas More Press, 1980.

Rachels, James, *The End of Life: Euthanasia and Mortality,* New York, NY, Oxford University Press, 1986.

Robison, Wade L., and Pritchard, Michael S., *Medical Responsibility: Paternalism, Informed Consent, and Euthanasia,* Atlantic Highlands, NJ, Humanities Press, Inc., 1979.

Russell, O. Ruth, *Freedom to Die: Moral and Legal Aspects of Euthanasia,* New York, NY, Dell Publishing Co., Inc., 1975; rev. ed., New York, NY, Human Sciences Press, Inc., 1977.

Schaeffer, Francis A., and Koop, C. Everett, *Whatever Happened to the Human Race?,* Old Tappan, NJ, Fleming H. Revell Co., 1979.

Sobel, Lester, A., *Medical Science and the Law: The Life and Death Controversy,* New York, NY, Facts on File, Inc., 1977.

Steinbock, B., *Killing and Letting Die,* Englewood Cliffs, NJ, Prentice-Hall, Inc., 1980.

Steinfels, Peter, and Veatch, Robert M. (eds.), *Death Inside Out: The Hastings Center Report,* New York, NY, Harper & Row, Publishers, 1975.

Swinyard, Chester A., *Decision-Making and the Defective Newborn,* Springfield, IL, Charles C. Thomas, Publisher, 1978.

Trowell, Hugh, *The Unfinished Debate on Euthanasia,* Naperville, IL, Alec R. Allenson, Inc., 1973.

Trubo, Richard, *An Act of Mercy: Euthanasia Today,* Freeport, NY, Nash Publishing Co., 1973.

Veatch, Robert M., *Death, Dying, and the Biological Revolution: Our Last Quest for Responsibility,* New Haven, CT, Yale University Press, 1976.

Walton, Douglas N., *Ethics of Withdrawal of Life-Support Systems,* New York, NY, Praeger Publishers, 1987.

Weber, Leonard J., *Who Shall Live? The Dilemma of Severely Handicapped Children and Its Meaning for Other Moral Questions,* New York, NY, Paulist Press, 1976.

Wertenbaker, Lael T., *Death of a Man,* Boston, MA, Beacon Press, 1974.

Wilson, Jerry B., *Death by Decision: The Medical, Moral, and Legal Dilemmas of Euthanasia,* Philadelphia, PA, The Westminster Press, 1975.

3. Sociological Ethics: Society, Community, Education

Arendt, Hannah, *On Violence,* New York, NY, Harcourt, Brace & World, 1970.

Aron, Raymond, *Progress and Disillusion: Dialectics of Modern Society,* new ed., Harmondsworth, England, Penguin Books, Ltd., 1972.

Baier, Kurt, and Rescher, Nicholas (eds.), *Values and the Future: the Impact of Technological Change on American Values,* New York, NY, The Free Press, 1969.

Barry, Vincent, *Personal and Social Ethics,* Belmont, CA, Wadsworth Publishing Co., Inc., 1978.

Bay, Christian, *The Structure of Freedom,* New York, NY, Atheneum Publishers, 1965.

Beauchamp, Tom L., *Ethics and Public Policy,* Englewood Cliffs, NJ, Prentice-Hall, Inc., 1975.

Becker, Ernest, *Beyond Alienation: a Philosophy of Education for the Crisis of Democracy,* New York, NY, George Braziller, Inc., 1967.

Benjamin, A. Cornelius, *Science, Technology and Human Values,* Columbia, MO., University of Missouri Press, 1965.

Brandt, Richard B. (ed.), *Social Justice,* Englewood Cliffs, NJ, Prentice-Hall, Inc., 1962.

Brumbaugh, Robert S., and Lawrence, Nathaniel M., *Philosophers on Education: Six Essays on the Foundations of Western Thought,* Boston, MA, Houghton Mifflin Co., 1963.

Callahan, Daniel, and Jennings, Bruce (eds.), *Ethics, The Social Sciences, and Policy Analysis,* New York, NY, Plenum Publishing Co., 1983.

Cox, Harvey, *The Secular City,* New York, NY, The Macmillan Co., 1965.

Dewey, John, *Democracy and Education,* New York, NY, The Macmillan Co., 1916.

Danner, Peter L., *An Ethics for the Affluent,* Washington, DC, University Press of America, 1980.

Downie, R.S., *Roles and Values: an Introduction to Social Ethics,* New York, NY, Barnes & Noble Books, 1971.

Durkheim, Emile, *Suicide,* New York, NY, The Free Press of Glencoe, Inc., 1951.

Elliott, Deni, *Responsible Journalism,* Newbury Park, CA, Sage Publications, Inc., 1986.

Ellis, William W., *White Ethics and Black Power,* Chicago, IL, Aldine Publishing Co., 1969.

Emmet, Dorothy, *The Moral Prism,* New York, NY, St. Martin's Press, Inc., 1979. *Rules, Roles and Relations,* New York, NY, St. Martin's Press, 1966.

Feibleman, James K., *Moral Strategy: an Introduction to the Ethics of Confrontation,* The Hague, Martinus Nijhoff, 1967.

Feinberg, Joel, *Social Philosophy,* Englewood Cliffs, NJ, Prentice-Hall, Inc., 1973.

Fromm, Erich (ed.), *Socialist Humanism: an International Symposium,* New York, NY, Doubleday Publishing Co., 1965.

Gardner, John W., *Morale,* New York, NY, W.W. Norton and Co., Inc., 1978.

Goldstein, Tom, *The News At Any Cost: How Journalists Compromise Their Ethics to Shape the News,* New York, NY, Simon & Schuster, 1986.

Goodwin, H., *Groping for Ethics in Journalism,* 2nd ed., Ames, IA, Iowa State University Press, 1987.

Gotschalk, D.W., *Human Aims in Modern Perspective: Outlines of a General Theory of Value with Special References to Contemporary Social Life and Politics,* Yellow Springs, OH, Antioch Press, 1966.

Grimm, Robert H., and Mackay, Alfred F. (eds.), *Society: Revolution and Reform,* Cleveland, OH, The Press of Case Western Reserve University, 1971.

Hauerwas, Stanley, *A Community of Character: Toward a Constructive Christian Social Ethic,* Notre Dame, IN, University of Notre Dame Press, 1981.

Hill, Brian Victor, *Education and the Endangered Individual,* New York, NY, Teachers College Press, 1974.

Hoehn, Richard A., *Up From Apathy: A Study of Moral Awareness and Social Involvement,* Nashville, TN, Abingdon Press, 1983.

Jacobs, P., and Landau, S., *The New Radicals: a Report with Documents,* New York, NY, Random House, Inc., 1966.

Jünger, Friedrich, *The Failure of Technology,* Chicago, IL, Henry Regnery Co., 1956.

Keeling, Michael, *Morals in a Free Society,* London, SCM Press, Ltd., 1967.

Keniston, Kenneth, *The Uncommitted,* New York, NY, Harcourt, Brace & World, Inc., 1965. *Young Radicals,* New York, NY, Harcourt, Brace & World, Inc., 1968.

Kerans, Patrick, *Sinful Social Structures,* New York, NY, Paulist Press, 1974.

Kiefer, Howard E., and Munitz, Milton K. (eds.), *Ethics and Social Justice,* Albany, NY, State University of New York Press, 1970.

Kirk, Russell, *Academic Freedom,* Chicago, IL, Henry Regnery Co., 1955.

Koestler, Arthur, *Insight and Outlook: an Inquiry Into the Common Foundations of Science, Art, and Social Ethics,* Lincoln, NE, University of Nebraska Press, 1965.

Kurtz, Paul (ed.), *Moral Problems in Contemporary Society: Essays in Humanistic Ethics,* Englewood Cliffs, NJ, Prentice-Hall, Inc., 1969.

Kwant, Remy C., *Phenomenology of Social Existence,* Pittsburgh, PA, Duquesne University Press, 1965.

Lambeth, Edmund B., *Committed Journalism: An Ethic for the Profession,* Bloomington, IN, Indiana University Press, 1986.

Laszlo, Ervin, and Stulman, Julius (eds.), *Emergent Man: His Chances, Problems and Potentials,* New York, NY, Gordon & Breach, Science Publishers, Inc., 1973.

Lippmann, Walter, *The Good Society,* Boston, MA, Little, Brown & Co., 1937.

MacIver, Robert, *Academic Freedom in Our Time,* New York, NY, Columbia University Press, 1955.

Mappes, Thomas, and Zembaty, Jane, *Social Ethics: Morality and Social Policy,* New York, NY, McGraw-Hill Book Co., 1976; 2nd ed., 1982.

Marcel, Gabriel, *The Decline of Wisdom,* New York, NY, Philosophical Library, Inc., 1955. *Man Against Mass Society,* Chicago, IL, Henry Regnery Co., 1952.

Miller, David, *Individualism: Personal Achievement and the Open Society,* Austin, TX, University of Texas Press, 1967.

Natanson, Maurice, *The Journeying Self: a Study in Philosophy and Social Role,* Reading, MA, Addison-Wesley Publishing Co., 1970.

Niebuhr, Reinhold, *Man's Nature and His Communities: Essays on the Dynamics and Enigmas of Man's Personal and Social Existence,* New York, NY, Charles Scribner's Sons, 1965. *Moral Man and Immoral Society,* New York, NY, Charles Scribner's Sons, 1949.

Olen, Jeffrey, *Ethics in Journalism,* Englewood Cliffs, NJ, Prentice-Hall, Inc., 1988.

Ossowska, Maria, *Social Determinants of Moral Ideas,* Philadelphia, PA, The University of Pennsylvania Press, 1970; London, Routledge & Kegan Paul, Ltd., 1971.

Osterhoudt, Robert G. (ed.), *The Philosophy of Sport: a Collection of Original Essays,* Springfield, IL, Charles C. Thomas, Publisher, 1973.

Passmore, John, *The Perfectibility of Man,* London, Gerald Duckworth & Co., Ltd., 1970.

Peterson, Forrest H., *A Philosophy of Man and Society,* New York, NY, Philosophical Library, 1970.

Reamer, Frederic G., *Ethical Dilemmas in Social Service,* New York, NY, Columbia University Press, 1982.

Reeck, Darrell, *Ethics for the Professions,* Minneapolis, MN, Augsburg Publishing House, 1982.

Reisman, David, *The Lonely Crowd,* New Haven, CT, Yale University Press, 1950.

Rivers, William L., and Mathews, Cleve, *Ethics for the Media,* Englewood Cliffs, NJ, Prentice-Hall, Inc., 1988.

Ross, Ralph Gilbert, *Obligation: a Social Theory,* Ann Arbor, MI, University of Michigan Press, 1970.

Ryrie, Charles C., *What You Should Know About Social Responsibility,* Chicago, IL, Moody Press, 1982.

Schroyer, Trent, *The Critique of Domination*, New York, NY, George Braziller, Inc., 1973.

Sheed, Frank J., *Society and Sanity*, New York, NY, Sheed & Ward, 1953.

Sichel, Betty, *Moral Education: Character, Community and Ideals*, Philadelphia, PA, Temple University Press, 1988.

Snook, I.A. (ed.), *Concepts of Indoctrination: Philosophical Essays*, London, Routledge & Kegan Paul, Ltd., 1972. *Indoctrination and Education*, London, Routledge & Kegan Paul, Ltd., 1972.

Sorokin, Pitirim, *The Crisis of Our Age*, New York, NY, E.P. Dutton & Co., Inc., 1941.

Stone, Julius, *Social Dimensions of Law and Justice*, Stanford, CA, Stanford University Press, 1966.

Taylor, John F.A., *The Masks of Society: an Inquiry into the Covenants of Civilization*, New York, NY, Appleton-Century-Crofts, 1966.

Teodori, Massimo, *The New Left: a Documentary History*, Indianapolis, IN, The Bobbs-Merrill Co., Inc., 1969.

Thornhill, J., *The Person and the Group*, Milwaukee, WI, The Bruce Publishing Co., 1967.

Weinreich-Haste, Helen, and Locke, Don, *Morality in the Making: Thought, Action, and the Social Context*, New York, NY, John Wiley & Sons, Inc., 1983.

Weiss, Paul, *Sport: a Philosophic Inquiry*, Carbondale, IL, Southern Illinois University Press, 1969.

Van den Berghe, Pierre L., *The Ethnic Phenomenon*, New York, NY, Praeger Publishers, 1987.

Van Melsen, A.G., *Physical Science and Ethics: a Reflection on the Relationship between Nature and Morality*, Louvain, Belgium, N.V. Uitgeverij Nauwelaerts Edition S.A., 1969.

Wolff, Robert P., Moore, Barrington, Jr., and Marcuse, Herbert, *A Critique of Pure Tolerance*, London, Jonathan Cape, Ltd., 1969.

4. Domestic Ethics: Marriage, Family, Sex

Atkinson, Ronald, *Sexual Morality*, London, The Hutchinson Publishing Group, Ltd., 1965.

Atkinson, Ronald, et al., *Sexual Latitude: For and Against*, ed. by Harold H. Hart, New York, NY, Hart Publishing Co., Inc., 1971.

Baker, Robert, and Elliston, Frederick (eds.), *Philosophy and Sex*, Buffalo, NY, Prometheus Books, 1975.

Bayles, Michael, *Reproductive Ethics*, Englewood Cliffs, NJ, Prentice-Hall, Inc., 1984.

Bertocci, Peter, *Sex, Love, and the Person*, New York, NY, Sheed & Ward, 1967.

Bird, Joseph, and Bird, Lois, *The Freedom of Sexual Love*, New York, NY, Doubleday & Co., 1967.

Birmingham, William (ed.), *What Catholics Think About Birth Control*, New York, NY, Signet Book, 1964.

Block, Joel, *The Other Men, the Other Women*, New York, NY, Grosset and Dunlap, Inc., 1978.

Brenton, Myron, *The American Male*, New York, NY, Coward-McCann, 1966; Fawcett Premier Books, 1970.

Broderick, Carlfred B., *Marriage and the Family*, Englewood Cliffs, NJ, Prentice-Hall, Inc., 1979.

Bromley, Dorothy, *Catholics and Birth Control*, New York, NY, The Devin-Adair Co., 1965.

Buchanan, G. Sidney, *Morality, Sex and the Constitution: A Christian Perspective on the Power of Government to Regulate Private Sexual Conduct Between Consenting Adults*, Lanham, MD, University Press of America, 1985.

Burgess, Ernest, and Wallin, Paul, *Engagement and Marriage*, Philadelphia, PA, J.B. Lippincott Co., 1953.

Burr, Wesley R., et al. (ed.), *Contemporary Theories About the Family*, 2 vols., New York, NY, The Free Press, 1979.

Calderone, Mary S. (ed.), *Sexuality and Human Values*, New York, NY, Association Press, 1974.

Chadwick, Ruth F. (ed.), *Ethics, Reproduction and Genetic Control*, New York, NY, Methuen, Inc., 1987.

Comfort, Alex, *Barbarism and Sexual Freedom*, Brooklyn, New York, NY, Haskell House Publishers, Ltd., 1977.

Cooper, Boyd, *Sex Without Tears: a Guide for the Sexual Revolution*, ed. by Walter Schmidt, Los Angeles, CA, Charles Publishing Co., 1972; New York, NY, Bantam Books, Inc., 1974.

Crosby, John F., *Sexual Autonomy: Toward a Humanistic Ethic*, Springfield, IL, Charles C. Thomas, Publisher, 1981.

Dedek, John F., *Contemporary Sexual Morality*, New York, NY, Sheed & Ward, Inc., 1971.

Dupré, Louis, *Contraception and Catholics*, Baltimore, MD, Helicon Press, Inc., 1964.

Durkin, Mary, *Sexuality*, Chicago, IL, Thomas More Press, 1987.

Duvall, Evelyn Millis, *Why Wait Till Marriage?* New York, NY, Association Press, 1965.

Edwards, John N. (ed.), *Sex and Society*, Chicago, IL, Rand McNally & Co., 1972.

Ehrenberg, Miriam, and Ehrenberg, Otto, *The Intimate Circle: The Sexual Dynamics of Family Life*, New York, NY, Simon & Schuster, 1988.

Ford, John, and Kelly, Gerald, *Contemporary Moral Theology*, vol. II, *Marriage Questions*, Westminster, MD, The Newman Press, 1963.

Frankson, G., *Sex and Morality*, Great Neck, NY, Todd and Honeywell, Inc., 1987.

Fromer, Margot J., *Ethical Issues in Sexuality and Reproduction*, St. Louis, MO, The C.V. Mosby Co., 1983.

Grisez, Germain, *Contraception and the Natural Law*, Milwaukee, WI, The Bruce Publishing Co., 1964.

Guindon, Andre, *The Sexual Creators: An Ethical Proposal for Concerned Christians*, Lanham, MD, University Press of America, 1986.

Hanigan, James, *What Are They Saying About Sexual Morality?* Ramsey, NJ, Paulist Press, 1982.

Hildebrand, Dietrich von, *In Defense of Purity*, New York, NY, Sheed & Ward, 1938. *Marriage*, New York, NY, Longmans, Green & Co., Inc., 1942.

Hope, Wingfield, *Life Together*, New York, NY, Sheed & Ward, 1944.

Kennedy, Eugene C., *The New Sexuality: Myths, Fables and Hang-Ups*, New York, NY, Doubleday Publishing Co., 1973.

Kirkendall, Lester A., and Whitehurst, Robert N. (eds.), *The New Sexual Revolution*, New York, NY, Prometheus Press, 1974.

Kosnik, Anthony, et al., *Human Sexuality: New Directions in American Catholic Thought,* New York, NY, Paulist Press, 1977.

Lepp, Ignace, *The Psychology of Loving,* translated by B.B. Gilligan, Baltimore, MD, Helicon Press, Inc., 1963.

May, William E., *The Nature and Meaning of Chastity,* Chicago, IL, Franciscan Herald Press, 1977.

Meyners, Robert, and Wooster, Claire, *Sexual Style: Facing and Making Choices About Sex,* New York, NY, Harcourt Brace Jovanovich, Inc., 1979.

Morrison, Eleanor, and Borosage, Vera (eds.), *Human Sexuality: Contemporary Perspectives,* Palo Alto, CA, Mayfield Publishing Co., 1973.

Nelson, James B., *Embodiment: An Approach to Sexuality and Christian Theology,* Minneapolis, MN, Augsburg Publishing House, 1978.

Nichols, Jack, *Men's Liberation: A New Definition of Masculinity,* Baltimore, MD, Penguin Books Inc., 1975.

Nobile, Philip (ed.), *The New Eroticism: Theories, Vogues and Canons,* New York, NY, Random House, 1970.

Noonan, John T., *Contraception,* Cambridge, MA, Harvard University Press, 1965.

Novak, Michael (ed.), *The Experience of Marriage,* London, Darton, Longmans & Todd, Ltd., 1965.

Oakley, Anne, *Sex, Gender and Society,* New York, NY, Harper & Row, Publishers, 1973.

Oraison, Marc, *The Human Mystery of Sexuality,* New York, NY, Sheed & Ward, 1967.

Otto, Herbert A., *The New Sexuality,* Palo Alto, CA, Science and Behavior Books, Inc., 1971.

Paul, Leslie, *Eros Rediscovered: Restoring Sex to Humanity,* New York, NY, Association Press, 1970.

Provost, C. Antonio, *The Sexual Revolution,* New York, NY, Vantage Press, Inc., 1985.

Roberts, Archbishop T.D. (ed.), *Contraception and Holiness,* London, William Collins Sons & Co., Ltd., 1964.

Rock, John, *The Time Has Come,* New York, NY, Alfred A. Knopf, Inc., 1963.

Sacred Congregation of the Doctrine of the Faith Staff, *Instruction on Respect for Human Life in Its Origin and on the Dignity of Procreation,* Washington, DC, Origins, NC Documentary Service, 1987.

Sass, Lauren, *Sex Roles: Rights and Value in Conflict,* New York, NY, Facts on File, Inc., 1979.

Scruton, Roger, *Sexual Desire: A Moral Philosophy of the Erotic,* New York, NY, Free Press, 1986.

Suenens, Leon Joseph Cardinal, *Love and Control,* Westminster, MD, The Newman Press, 1961.

Thibon, Gustave, *What God Has Joined Together,* Chicago, IL, Henry Regnery Co., 1952.

Thielicke, Helmut, *The Ethics of Sex,* translated by J.W. Doberstein, New York, NY, Harper & Row, Publishers, 1964; Grand Rapids, MI, Baker Book House, 1975.

Wayne, T.G., *Morals and Marriage,* New York, NY, Longmans, Green & Co., Inc., 1936.

Wilson, John, *Logic and Sexual Morality,* Baltimore, MD, Penguin Books, Inc., 1965.

A. Women's Liberation

Adam, Ruth, *Woman's Place 1910–1975,* New York, NY, W.W. Norton & Co., Inc., 1977.

Andolsen, Barbara H., et al. (eds.), *Women's Consciousness, Women's Conscience: A Reader in Feminist Ethics,* New York, NY, Harper & Row, Publishers, 1985.

Altbach, Edith H. (ed.), *From Feminism to Liberation,* Cambridge, MA, Schenkman Publishing Co., 1980.

Andreas, Carol, *Sex and Caste in America,* Englewood Cliffs, NJ, Prentice-Hall, Inc., 1971.

Armundsen, Kristen, *The Silenced Majority,* Englewood Cliffs, NJ, Prentice-Hall, Inc., 1971.

Banks, Olive, *Faces of Feminism: A Study of Feminism as a Social Movement,* New York, NY, St. Martin's Press, 1981.

Barnett, Rosalind, and Baruch, Grace K., *The Competent Woman,* New York, NY, Halsted Press, 1978.

de Beauvoir, Simone, *The Second Sex,* translated by H.M. Parshley, New York, NY, Alfred A. Knopf, Inc., 1953; Bantam Books, Inc., 1971.

Benson, Betty, *The Autonomous Woman,* New York, NY, Vantage Press, Inc., 1978.

Bevan, Charles C., *Women's Liberation and Chaos,* New York, NY, Vantage Press, Inc., 1982.

Bird, Caroline, *What Women Want,* New York, NY, Simon & Schuster, Inc., 1979.

Bishop, Sharon, and Weinzweig, Marjorie (eds.), *Philosophy and Women,* Belmont, CA, Wadsworth Publishing Co., Inc., 1979.

Boulding, Elise, *Women in the Twentieth Century World,* New York, NY, Halsted Press, 1977.

Brownmiller, Susan, *Femininity,* New York, NY, Simon & Schuster, Inc., 1984.

Burghardt, Walter J. (ed.), *Woman: New Dimensions,* New York, NY, Paulist Press, 1977.

Burton, Clare, *Subordination: Feminism and Social Theory,* Winchester, MA, Allen & Unwin, Inc., 1985.

Chafe, William H., *Women and Equality: Changing Patterns in American Culture,* New York, NY, Oxford University Press, Inc., 1977.

Chafetz, Janet S., and Dworkin, Anthony G., *Female Revolt: The Rise of Women's Movements in World and Historical Perspective,* Totowa, NJ, Rowman & Allanheld, 1986.

Chapman, Jane R., and Gates, Margaret J. (eds.), *Economic Independence for Women: The Foundation for Equal Rights,* Beverly Hills, CA, Sage Publications, Inc., 1976.

Charvet, John, *Feminism,* London, J.M. Dent, 1982.

Conover, Pamela, and Gray, Virginia, *Feminism and the New Right: Conflict over the American Family,* New York, NY, Praeger Publishers, Inc., 1983.

Cooke, Joanne, Bunch-Weeks, Charlotte, and Morgan, Robin (eds.), *The New Women,* Indianapolis, IN, The Bobbs-Merrill Co., Inc., 1970; Fawcett World Library, 1971.

Cooper, John L., *The Seventh Decade: A Study of the Women's Liberation Movement,* Dubuque, IA, Kendall/Hunt Publishing Co., 1980.

Coote, Anna, and Campbell, Beatrix, *Sweet Freedom: The*

Struggle for Women's Liberation, Oxford, Basil Blackwell, 1982.

Corea, Gena, *The Mother Machine: From Artificial Insemination to Artificial Wombs,* New York, NY, Harper & Row Publishers, 1986.

Cott, Nancy F., *Grounding American Feminism,* New Haven, CT, Yale University Press, 1987.

Dahlstrom, Edmund (ed.), *Changing Roles of Men and Women,* rev. ed., Boston, MA, Beacon Press, 1971.

Daly, Mary, *Beyond God the Father: Toward a Philosophy of Women's Liberation,* Boston, MA, Beacon Press, 1973. *Gyn-Ecology: The Metaethics of Radical Feminism,* Boston, MA, Beacon Press, 1979. *Pure Lust: Elemental Feminist Philosophy,* Boston, MA, Beacon Press, 1984.

Davidson, Nicholas, *The Failure of Feminism,* Buffalo, NY, Prometheus Books, 1987.

Demetrakopoulos, Stephanie, *Listening to Our Bodies: The Rebirth of Feminine Wisdom,* Boston, MA, Beacon Press, 1983.

Dimen, Muriel, *Surviving Sexual Contradictions,* New York, NY, Macmillan Publishing Co., 1986.

Doane, Janice, and Hodges, Devon, *Nostalgia and Sexual Difference: The Resistance to Contemporary Feminism,* Frederick, MD, University Publications of America, 1983.

Douglas, Ann, *The Feminization of American Culture,* Garden City, NY, Doubleday & Co., Inc., 1988.

Eisenstein, Hester, *Contemporary Feminist Thought,* Boston, MA, G.K. Hall & Co., 1984.

Evans, Sara, *Personal Politics: The Roots of Liberation in the Civil Rights Movement and the New Left,* New York, NY, Alfred A. Knopf, Inc., 1978.

Feldman, Sylvia, *Rights of Women,* Rochelle Park, NJ, Hayden Book Co., Inc., 1974.

Ferguson, Kathy E., *Self, Society, and Womankind: The Dialectic of Liberation,* Westport, CT, Greenwood Press, 1980.

Figes, Eva, *Patriarchal Attitudes,* New York, NY, Stein & Day Publishers, 1970; Fawcett World Library, 1971.

Firestone, Shulamith, *The Dialectic of Sex,* New York, NY, William Morrow & Co., Inc., 1970; Bantam Books, Inc., 1971.

Friedan, Betty, *The Feminine Mystique,* new foreword and epilogue, New York, NY, Dell Publishing Co., 1975. *It Changed My Life: Writings on the Women's Movement,* New York, NY, Random House, Inc., 1976. *The Feminine Mystique: Twentieth Anniversary Edition,* New York, NY, W.W. Norton & Co., Inc., 1983. *The Second Stage,* New York, NY, Summit Books, 1982.

Fritz, Leah, *Dreamers and Dealers: An Intimate Appraisal of the Women's Movement,* Boston, MA, Beacon Press, Inc., 1979.

Gordon, Linda, *Woman's Body, Woman's Right: Birth Control in America,* New York, NY, Penguin Books, Inc., 1977.

Gould, Carol C., and Wartofsky, Marx W., *Women and Philosophy: Toward a Theory of Liberation,* New York, NY, G.P. Putnam's Sons, 1976.

Gould, E., *American Women Today: Free or Frustrated,* Englewood Cliffs, NJ, Prentice-Hall, Inc., 1977.

Greer, Germaine, *The Female Eunuch,* New York, NY, McGraw-Hill Book Co., 1971; Bantam Books, Inc., 1972.

Grimshaw, Jean, *Philosophy and Feminist Thinking,* Minneapolis, MN, University of Minnesota Press, 1986.

Hamilton, Roberta, *The Liberation of Women: A Study of Patriarchy and Capitalism,* Winchester, MA, Allen & Unwin, Inc., 1978.

Harbeson, Gladys, *Choice and Challenge for the American Woman,* 2nd ed., Cambridge, MA, Schenkman Publishing Co., 1972.

Hecker, E.A., *History of Women's Rights,* New York, NY, Gordon Press Publishers, 1977.

Heywood, Ezra H., *Uncivil Liberty: An Essay to Show the Injustice and Impolicy of Ruling Woman Without Her Consent,* Colorado Springs, CO, Ralph Myles, Publisher, Inc., 1978.

Jaggar, Alison M., *Feminist Politics and Human Nature,* Totowa, NJ, Rowman & Allanheld, 1982.

Janssen-Jurreit, Marielouise, *Sexism: The Male Monopoly on History and Thought,* trs. by Moberg, Verne, NY, Farrar, Straus & Giroux, Inc., 1982.

Justice, Betty, and Pore, Renate (eds.), *Toward the Second Decade: The Impact of the Women's Movement on American Institutions,* Westport, CT, Greenwood Press, 1981.

Komisar, Lucy, *The New Feminism,* New York, NY, Franklin Watts, Inc., 1971.

Levin, Michael, *Feminism and Freedom,* New Brunswick, NJ, Transaction Books, 1987.

Marine, Gene, *A Male Guide to Women's Liberation,* New York, NY, Avon Books, 1974.

Midgley, Mary, and Hughes, Judith, *Women's Choices: The Philosophical Problems of Feminism,* New York, NY, St. Martin's Press, 1983.

Mill, John Stuart, *Subjection of Women,* Cambridge, MA, The MIT Press, 1970.

Millet, Kate, *Sexual Politics,* New York, NY, Avon Books, 1973.

Mitchell, Juliet, *Women's Estate,* New York, NY, Pantheon Books, Inc., 1971.

Morgan, Robin (ed.), *Sisterhood is Powerful,* New York, NY, Random House, Inc., 1970.

Morgan, Robin, *Anatomy of Freedom,* Garden City, NY, Doubleday & Co., Inc., 1982.

O'Neill, William, *Everyone was Brave,* Chicago, IL, Quadrangle Books, 1969.

Overall, Christine, *Ethics and Human Reproduction: A Feminist Analysis,* Winchester, MA, Allen & Unwin, Inc., 1987.

Ozer, Jerome S. (ed.), *Women's Rights and Liberation,* 13 vols., New York, NY, Arno Press, Inc., 1969.

Richards, Janet R., *The Sceptical Feminist: A Philosophical Enquiry,* New York, NY, Methuen, Inc., 1980.

Rosenberg, Rosalind, *Beyond Separate Spheres: Intellectual Roots of Modern Feminism,* New Haven, CT, Yale University Press, 1982.

Roszak, Betty, and Roszak, Theodore (eds.), *Masculine/Feminine,* New York, NY, Harper & Row, Publishers, 1969.

Sabrosky, Judith A., *From Rationality to Liberation: The Evolution of Feminist Ideology,* Westport, CT, Greenwood Press, Inc., 1980.

Sacks, Karen, *Sisters and Wives: The Past and Future of Sexual Equality,* Champaign, IL, University of Illinois Press, 1982.

Schafly, Phyllis, *The End of an Era,* Chicago, IL, Regnery Gateway, Inc., 1982.

Snodgrass, Jon (ed.), *For Men Against Sexism: A Book of Readings,* Albion, CA, Times Change Press, 1977.

Storkey, Elaine, *What's Right With Feminism?,* Grand Rapids, MI, William B. Eerdmans Publishing Co., 1986.

Thomas, Claire S., *Sex Discrimination,* St. Paul, MN, West Publishing Co., 1982.

Vetterling-Braggin, Mary, et al. (eds.), *Feminism and Philosophy,* Totowa, NJ, Rowman & Littlefield, Inc., 1977.

Wolgast, Elizabeth H., *Equality and the Rights of Women,* Ithaca, NY, Cornell University Press, 1980.

B. Homosexuality

Abbott, Sidney, and Love, Barbara, *Sappho Was A Right-On Woman: a Liberated View of Lesbianism,* New York, NY, Stein & Day Publishers, 1972.

Baars, Conrad, *The Homosexual's Search for Happiness,* Chicago, IL, Franciscan Herald Press, 1977.

Baisden, Major J., Jr., *The Dynamics of Homosexuality,* Sacramento, CA, Allied Research Society, Inc., 1975.

Barnhouse, Ruth T., *Homosexuality: A Symbolic Confusion,* New York, NY, The Seabury Press, Inc., 1976.

Batchelor, Edward, Jr. (ed.), *Homosexuality and Ethics,* rev. ed., New York, NY, The Pilgrim Press, 1982.

Bayer, Ronald, *Homosexuality and American Psychiatry: The Politics of Diagnosis,* New York, NY, Basic Books, Inc., 1980; 2nd ed., Princeton, NJ, Princeton University Press, 1987.

Bell, Alan P., et al., *Sexual Preference: Its Development in Men and Women,* Bloomington, IN, Indiana University Press, 1981.

Bell, Alan P., and Weinberg, Martin S., *Homosexualities: A Study of Diversity Among Men and Women,* New York, NY, Simon & Schuster, Inc., 1978.

Boggan, E., et al., *The Rights of Gay People,* New York, NY, Avon Books, 1975.

Bronski, Michael, *Culture Clash: The Making of Gay Sensibility,* Boston, MA, South End Press, 1984.

Churchill, Wainwright, *Homosexual Behavior Among Males: a Cross Cultural and Cross Species Investigation,* Englewood Cliffs, NJ, Prentice-Hall, Inc., 1971.

Coleman, Gerald, *Homosexuality—An Appraisal,* Chicago, IL, Franciscan Herald Press, 1978.

Dannecker, Martin, *Theories of Homosexuality,* New York, NY, Gay Men's Press, 1981.

Davidson, Alex, *The Returns of Love: A Christian View of Homosexuality,* Downers Grove, IL, Inter-Varsity Press, 1977.

Day, Richard, *A General Ontology of Homophilia,* Boston, MA, IHI Press, 1977.

Drakeford, John W., *A Christian View of Homosexuality,* Nashville, TN, Broadman Press, 1977. *Forbidden Love: a Homosexual Looks for Understanding and Help,* Waco, TX, Word, Inc., 1971.

DuBay, William H., *Gay Identity: The Self Under Ban,* Jefferson, NC, McFarland & Co., 1987.

Dynes, Wayne R., *Homosexuality: A Research Guide,* New York, NY, Garland Publishing, Inc., 1987.

Edwards, George R., *Gay-Lesbian Liberation: A Biblical Perspective,* New York, NY, Pilgrim Press, 1984.

Fisher, Peter, *The Gay Mystique: the Myth and Reality of Male Homosexuality,* New York, NY, Stein & Day Publishers, 1972.

Green, Richard, *The "Sissy Syndrome" and the Development of Homosexuality,* New Haven, CT, Yale University Press, 1987.

Halloran, Joseph H., *Understanding Homosexual Persons: A Dialogue with Dignity,* Hicksville, NY, Exposition Press, Inc., 1979.

Karlen, Arno, *Sexuality and Homosexuality: a New View,* New York, NY, W.W. Norton & Co., Inc., 1971.

Kronemeyer, Robert, and Boe, Eugene, *Overcoming Homosexuality,* New York, NY, Macmillan Publishing Co., Inc., 1979.

Marmor, Judd, *Homosexual Behavior: A Modern Reappraisal,* New York, NY, Basic Books, Inc., 1979.

Martin, Del, and Lyon, Phyllis, *Lesbian-Woman,* New York, NY, Bantam Books, Inc., 1972.

McCaffrey, J. (ed.), *Homosexual Dialectic,* Englewood Cliffs, NJ, Prentice-Hall, Inc., 1972.

Oberholtzer, W. Dwight (ed.), *Is Gay Good? Ethics, Theology, and Homosexuality,* Philadelphia, PA, The Westminster Press, 1971.

Oraison, Marc, *The Homosexual Question,* New York, NY, Harper & Row, Publishers, 1977.

Pittenger, Norman, *Time for Consent: A Christian's Approach to Homosexuality,* Naperville, IL, Alec R. Allenson, Inc., 1976.

Richmond, Len, and Noguera, Gary (eds.), *The New Gay Liberation Book,* Palo Alto, CA, Ramparts Press, 1979.

Rosen, David H., *Lesbianism: A Study of Female Homosexuality,* Springfield, IL, Charles C. Thomas, Publisher, 1974.

Ruitenbeek, Hendrik M. (ed.), *Homosexuality, a Changing Picture: a Contemporary Study and Interpretation,* New York, NY, Humanities Press, 1974.

Ruitenbeek, Hendrik M., *Problem of Homosexuality in Modern Society,* New York, NY, E.P. Dutton & Co., Inc., 1963.

Sacred Congregation of the Doctrine of the Faith Staff, *Letter to the Bishops of the Catholic Church on the Pastoral Care of Homosexual Persons,* Washington, DC, National Catholic News Service, 1986.

Saghir, Marcel T., and Robins, Eli, *Male and Female Homosexuality: a Comprehensive Investigation,* Baltimore, MD, The Williams & Wilkins Co., 1975.

Tripp, C.A., *The Homosexual Matrix,* rev. ed., New York, NY, NAL Penguin, Inc., 1987.

Van Den Aardweg, Gerald J., *On the Origins and Treatment of Homosexuality: A Psychoanalytic Reinterpretation,* New York, NY, Praeger Publishers, Inc., 1985.

Weinberg, Martin S., and Williams, Colin J., *Male Homosexuals: Their Problems and Adaptations,* New York, NY, Oxford University Press, 1974.

Westwood, Gordon, *Society and the Homosexual,* Westport, CT, Greenwood Press, 1985.

Wysor, Bettie, *The Lesbian Myth,* New York, NY, Random House, Inc., 1974.

5. Political Ethics: State, Government, Protest

Barry, Brian, *Political Argument,* London, Routledge & Kegan Paul, Ltd., 1965.

Bedeau, Hugo, *Civil Disobedience: Theory and Practice,* New York, NY, Pegasus, 1969.

Berlin, Sir Isaiah, *Four Essays on Liberty,* London, Oxford University Press, 1969.

Berns, Walter, *For Capital Punishment: Crime and the Morality of the Death Penalty,* New York, NY, Basic Books, Inc., 1981.

Billingsley, Lloyd, *The Absence of Tyranny: Recovering Freedom in our Time,* Portland OR, Multnomah Press, 1986.

Black, Charles L., Jr., *Capital Punishment: The Inevitability of Caprice and Mistake,* rev. ed., New York, NY, W.W. Norton & Co., Inc., 1981.

Block, Eugene B., *When Men Play God: The Case Against Capital Punishment,* San Francisco, CA, Cragmont Publications, 1981.

Bonino, Jose M., *Toward a Christian Political Ethics,* Philadelphia, PA, Fortress Press, 1983.

Bosanquet, Bernard, *The Philosophical Theory of the State,* London, Macmillan Publishers, Ltd., 1966.

Bottomore, T.B., *Critics of Society: Radical Thought in North America,* 2nd revised ed., London, George Allen & Unwin, Ltd., 1969.

Bowie, Norman E., *Ethical Issues in Government,* Philadelphia, PA, Temple University Press, 1981.

Bowie, Norman E., and Simon, Robert L., *The Individual and Political Order: An Introduction to Social and Political Philosophy,* Englewood Cliffs, NJ, Prentice-Hall, Inc., 1986.

Braybrooke, David, *Three Tests for Democracy: Personal Rights, Human Welfare, Collective Preference,* New York, NY, Random House, Inc., 1968.

Bukovsky, Vladimir, *To Choose Freedom,* Stanford, CA, Hoover Institution Press, 1987.

Canavan, Francis S., and Cole, R.T. (eds.), *The Ethical Dimensions of Political Life: Essays in Honor of John H. Hollowell,* Durham, NC, Duke University Press, 1983.

Carter, April, *The Political Theory of Anarchism,* London, Routledge & Kegan Paul, Ltd., 1971.

Childress, James F., *Civil Disobedience and Political Obligation: a Study in Christian Ethics,* New Haven, CT, Yale University Press, 1971.

Cohen, Carl, *Democracy,* Athens, GA, University of Georgia Press, 1972.

Dahl, Robert A., *Democracy, Liberty, and Equality,* Philadelphia, PA, Coronet Books, 1986.

Dallmayr, Fred A., *Beyond Dogma and Despair: Toward a Critical Phenomenology of Politics,* Notre Dame, IN, University of Notre Dame Press, 1981.

Day, J.P., *Liberty and Justice,* Wolfeboro, NH, Longwood Publishing Group, 1986.

Deininger, Whitaker T., *Problems in Social and Political Thought, a Philosophical Introduction,* New York, NY, The Macmillan Co., 1965.

D'Entrèves, A.P., *Aquinas, Selected Political Writings,* Oxford, Basil Blackwell & Mott, Ltd., 1948.

Douglas, Paul H., *Ethics in Government,* Cambridge, MA, Harvard University Press, 1952.

Drew, P., *The Meaning of Freedom,* Elmsford, NY, Pergamon Press, Inc., 1985.

Drinan, Robert F., *Democracy, Dissent, and Disorder,* New York, NY, The Seabury Press, Inc., 1969.

Dunn, William N. (ed.), *Values, Ethics, and the Practice of Policy Analysis,* Lexington, MA, Lexington Books, 1982.

Ewin, R.E., *Liberty, Community, and Justice,* Totowa, NJ, Rowman & Allanheld, 1987.

Figgis, John, *The Divine Right of Kings,* London, Cambridge University Press, 1914.

Fishkin, James S., *Beyond Subjective Morality: Ethical Reasoning and Political Philosophy,* New Haven, CT, Yale University Press, 1986.

Flathman, Richard E., *The Philosophy and Politics of Freedom,* Chicago, IL, University of Chicago Press, 1987. *The Public Interest: an Essay Concerning the Normative Discourse of Politics,* New York, NY, John Wiley & Sons, Inc., 1966.

Fleishman, Joel L., et al. (eds.), *Public Duties: The Moral Obligation of Government Officials,* Cambridge, MA, Harvard University Press, 1981.

Frankel, Charles, *The Democratic Prospect,* New York, NY, Harper & Row, Publishers, 1964.

French, Peter A., *Ethics in Government,* Englewood Cliffs, NJ, Prentice-Hall, Inc., 1983.

Friedrich, Carl Joachim, *Tradition and Authority,* London, The Pall Mall Press, 1972.

Gewirth, Alan, *Political Philosophy,* New York, NY, The Macmillan Co., 1965.

Ginsberg, Morris, *On Justice and Society,* London, Heinemann Educational Books, Ltd., 1965.

Gorecki, Jan, *Capital Punishment: Criminal Law and Social Evolution,* New York, NY, Columbia University Press, 1983.

Graham, George A., *Morality in American Politics,* New York, NY, Random House, Inc., 1952.

Green, Thomas H., *Lectures on the Principles of Political Obligation,* introd. by Lord Lindsay of Birker, Ann Arbor, MI, University of Michigan Press, 1967.

Grigsby, Daryl R., *Reflections on Liberation,* San Diego, CA, Asante Publications, 1985.

Hall, Robert T., *The Morality of Civil Disobedience,* New York, NY, Harper & Row, Publishers, 1971.

Hamilton, Madison, and Jay, *The Federalist Papers,* New York, NY, The New American Library, 1961. Many other editions.

Hook, Sidney, *The Paradoxes of Freedom,* Berkeley, CA, University of California Press, 1962.

Horowitz, Robert H., *Moral Foundations of the American Republic,* 2nd ed., Charlottesville, VA, University Press of Virginia, 1982.

Humboldt, Wilhelm von, *The Limits of State Action,* ed. by J.W. Burrow, translated by editor and Joseph Coultard, Cambridge, MA, Cambridge University Press, 1969.

Kelly, John R., *Freedom to Be,* New York, NY, The Macmillan Publishing Co., 1986.

King, Martin Luther, Jr., *Why We Can't Wait,* New York, NY, Harper & Row, Publishers, 1964.

Lakoff, Sanford A., *Equality in Political Philosophy,* Cambridge, MA, Harvard University Press, 1964.

Letwin, Shirley Robin, *The Pursuit of Certainty,* Cambridge, Cambridge University Press, 1965.

Lindblom, Charles E., *The Intelligence of Democracy: Decision Making through Mutual Adjustment,* New York, NY, The Macmillan Co., 1965.

Lippmann, Walter, *The Public Philosophy,* Boston, MA, Little, Brown & Co., 1955.

Macfarlane, L.J., *Modern Political Theory,* London, Thomas Nelson & Sons, Ltd., 1970.

Malcolm X, *The Autobiography of Malcolm X,* New York, NY, Grove Press, 1964.

Maneli, Mieczyslaw, *Freedom and Tolerance,* New York, NY, Hippocrene Books, Inc., 1984.

Manicas, Peter T., *The Death of the State,* New York, NY, Capricorn Books, G.P. Putnam's Sons, 1974.

Maritain, Jacques, *Man and the State,* Chicago, IL, The University of Chicago Press, 1951. *Scholasticism and Politics,* New York, NY, The Macmillan Co., 1940.

Messner, Johannes, *Social Ethics: Natural Law in the Western World,* rev. ed., translated by J.J. Doherty, St. Louis, MO, B. Herder Book Co., 1949, 1965.

Monti, Joseph, *Ethics and Public Policy: The Conditions of Public Moral Discourse,* Washington, DC, University Press of America, 1982.

Moretti, Daniel, *Civil Liberty and Civil Rights,* 7th ed., Irving Sloan (ed.), Dobbs Ferry, NY, Oceana Publications, Inc., 1986.

Murray, John Courtney, *We Hold These Truths,* New York, NY, Sheed & Ward, 1960.

Nielson, Kai, *Equality and Liberty: A Defense of Radical Egalitarianism,* Totowa, NJ, Rowman & Allanheld, 1986.

Oliver, James H., *Demokratia, The Gods, and the Free World,* Baltimore, MD, The Johns Hopkins University Press, 1960.

Parekh, Bhikhu, and Berki, R.N. (eds.), *The Morality of Politics,* London, George Allen & Unwin, Ltd., 1972.

Pincoffs, Edmund L., *The Rationale of Legal Punishment,* New York, NY, The Humanities Press, 1966.

Plamenatz, J.P., *Consent, Freedom and Political Obligation,* 2nd ed., London, Oxford University Press, 1968.

Raphael, David Daiches, *Problems of Political Philosophy,* London, The Pall Mall Press, 1970.

Raz, Joseph, *The Morality of Freedom,* New York, NY, Oxford University Press, 1986.

Rees, John C., *Equality,* London, The Pall Mall Press, 1971.

Regan, Richard J., *The Moral Dimensions of Politics,* New York, NY, Oxford University Press, 1986.

Rommen, Heinrich, *The State in Catholic Thought,* St. Louis, MO, B. Herder Book Co., 1945.

Sanders, John T., *The Ethical Argument Against Government,* Washington, DC, University Press of America, 1980.

Sellin, Thorsten, *The Penalty of Death,* Beverly Hills, CA, Sage Publishing Co., 1980.

Shienbaum, Kim E. (ed.), *Legislating Morality: Private Choices on the Public Agenda,* Cambridge, MA, Schenkman Publishing Co., Inc., 1984.

Simon, Yves, *Philosophy of Democratic Government,* Chicago, IL, The University of Chicago Press, 1951.

Singer, Peter, *Democracy and Disobedience,* London, Oxford University Press, 1973.

Srisang, Koson, *Perspectives on Political Ethics: An Ecumenical Inquiry,* Washington, DC, Georgetown University Press, 1983.

Stevick, Daniel B., *Civil Disobedience and the Christian,* New York, NY, The Seabury Press, Inc., 1969.

Stewart, M.A., *Law, Morality, and Rights,* Hingham, MA, Kluwer Academic Publishers, 1983.

Stockdale, James B., and Hatfield, Mark O., *The Ethics of Citizenship,* Austin, TX, University of Texas Press, 1981.

Thompson, Dennis F., *Political Ethics and Public Office,* Cambridge, MA, Harvard University Press, 1987.

Thoreau, Henry David, *Civil Disobedience.* In *The Works of Thoreau,* Boston, MA, Houghton Mifflin Co., 1937.

Vaizey, John, *Social Democracy,* London, George Weidenfeld & Nicolson, Ltd., 1971.

Van den Haag, Ernest, and Conrad, John P., *The Death Penalty: A Debate,* New York, NY, Plenum Publishing Co., 1983.

Warner, Richard, *Freedom, Enjoyment, and Happiness: An Essay on Moral Psychology,* Ithaca, NY, Cornell University Press, 1987.

Wickum, Carl, *The Total State: a Philosophical Interpretation of Contemporary and Future Society,* Boston, MA, Forum Publications, 1964.

Willhoite, Fred H., Jr., *Beyond Nihilism: Albert Camus's Contribution to Political Thought,* Baton Rouge, LA, Louisiana State University Press, 1968.

Woetzel, Robert, *The Philosophy of Freedom,* Dobbs Ferry, NY, Oceana Publications, Inc., 1966.

Wolff, Robert Paul, *In Defense of Anarchism,* New York, NY, Harper & Row, Publishers, 1970.

Young, Robert, *Personal Autonomy: Beyond Negative and Positive Liberty,* New York, NY, St. Martin's Press, 1986.

6. Economic Ethics: Property, Business, Contracts

Acton, Henry B., *The Morals of Markets: an Ethical Exploration,* London, Longman in association with the Institution of Economic Affairs, 1971.

Anderson, James L., and Cohen, Martin, *The Competitive Edge,* New York, NY, Bantam Books, Inc., 1982.

Barry, Vincent, *Moral Issues in Business,* 2nd ed., Belmont, CA, Wadsworth Publishing Co., 1982.

Beauchamp, Tom L., and Bowie, Norman E., *Ethical Theory and Business,* Englewood Cliffs, NJ, Prentice-Hall, Inc., 1983.

Behrman, Jack N., *Essays on Ethics in Business and the Professions,* Englewood Cliffs, NJ, Prentice-Hall, Inc., 1988.

Bell, Robert, *The Crisis in Corporate Ethics,* New York, NY, Henry Holt & Co., 1987.

Benson, George C., *Business Ethics in America,* Lexington, MA, Lexington Books, 1982.

Boulding, Kenneth E., *The Organizational Revolution: a Study in the Ethics of Economic Organization,* New York, NY, Harper & Row, Publishers, 1953.

Bowie, Norman, *Business Ethics,* Englewood Cliffs, NJ, Prentice-Hall, Inc., 1982.

Braybrooke, David, *Ethics in the World of Business,* Totowa, NJ, Rowman & Allanheld, 1983.

Buchanan, Allen, *Ethics, Efficiency, and the Market,* Totowa, NJ, Rowman & Allanheld, 1985.

Cavanaugh, Gerald F., *American Business Values in Transition,* Englewood Cliffs, NJ, Prentice-Hall, Inc., 1976.

Cavanagh, Gerald F., and McGovern, Arthur F., *Ethical Dilemmas in the Modern Corporation,* Englewood Cliffs, NJ, Prentice-Hall, Inc., 1988.

Childs, Marquis, and Cater, Douglass, *Ethics in a Business Society,* New York, NY, Harper & Row, Publishers, 1954.

Christensen, C. Roland, Andrews, Kenneth R., and Bower, Joseph L., *Business Policy: Text and Cases,* 3rd ed., Homewood, IL, Richard D. Irwin, Inc., 1973.

Christian, Portia, and Hicks, Richard (eds.), *Ethics in Business Conduct: Selected References from the Record; Problems, Attempted Solutions, Ethics in Business Education,* Detroit, MI, Gale Research Co., 1971.

Coleman, Bruce P., and Bonge, John W., *Concepts for Corporate Strategy: Readings in Business Policy,* New York, NY, The Macmillan Co., 1972.

De George, Richard T., *Business Ethics,* New York, NY, The Macmillan Publishing Co., 1982.

Diamond, Sigmund, *The Reputation of the American Businessman,* Glouster, MA, Peter Smith, 1970.

Dietz, Gottfried, *In Defense of Property,* Chicago, IL, Henry Regnery Co., 1963.

Donaldson, Thomas, *Case Studies in Business Ethics,* Englewood Cliffs, NJ, Prentice-Hall, Inc., 1984.

Donaldson, Thomas, and Werhane, Patricia H., *Ethical Issues in Business,* Englewood Cliffs, NJ, Prentice-Hall, Inc., 1983.

The Editors of *Fortune, Working Smarter,* with introd. by Rukeyser, William S., New York, NY, Simon & Schuster, Inc., 1980.

Elbing, Alvar O., and Elbing, C.J., *Value Issues of Business,* New York, NY, McGraw-Hill Book Co., 1967.

Flubacher, Joseph Francis, *The Concept of Ethics in the History of Economics,* New York, NY, Vantage, 1950.

Fulton, R.B., *Adam Smith Speaks to Our Times; a Study of His Ethical Ideas,* Boston, MA, Christopher Publishing House, 1963.

Garrett, Thomas M., *Ethics in Business,* New York, NY, Sheed & Ward, 1963. *Business Ethics,* New York, NY, Appleton-Century-Crofts, 1966.

Garrett, Thomas M., Baumhart, R.C., Purcell, T.V., and Roets, P., *Cases in Business Ethics,* New York, NY, Appleton-Century-Crofts, 1968.

Garrett, Thomas M., and Klonoski, Richard J., *Business Ethics,* 2nd ed., Englewood Cliffs, NJ, Prentice-Hall, Inc., 1986.

Gelinier, Octave, *The Enterprise Ethic,* Levittown, NY, Transatlantic Arts, Inc., n.d.

Glenn, James R., *Ethics in Decision-Making,* New York, NY, John Wiley & Sons, Inc., 1986.

Hadley, Arthur T., *Standards of Public Morality,* reprint of 1907 ed., New York, NY, Arno Press, 1973.

Hanson, Solomon, *Above the Bottom Line: An Introduction to Business Ethics,* New York, NY, Harcourt Brace Jovanovich, Inc., 1983.

Hapgood, David, *The Screwing of the Average Man,* New York, NY, Bantam Books, Inc., 1975.

Hargreaves, John, and Dauman, Jan, *Business Survival and Social Change: A Practical Guide to Responsibility and Partnership,* New York, NY, Halsted Press, 1975.

Healy, James, S.J., *The Just Wage, 1750–1890, A Study of Moralists: From Saint Alphonsus to Leo XIII,* The Hague, Martinus Nijhoff, 1966.

Heilbroner, Robert L., *The Worldly Philosophers,* 4th ed., New York, NY, Simon & Schuster, Inc., 1972.

Heyne, Paul T., *Private Keepers of the Public Interest,* New York, NY, McGraw-Hill Book Co., 1968.

Hill, Ivan (ed.), *The Ethical Basis of Economic Freedom,* New York, NY, Praeger Publishers, Inc., 1980.

Hess, J. Daniel, *Ethics in Business and Labor,* Scottdale PA, Herald Press, 1977.

Hodges, Luther, *The Business Conscience,* Englewood Cliffs, NJ, Prentice-Hall, Inc., 1963.

James, Barrie G., *Business Wargames,* Cambridge, MA, Abacus Press, 1984.

Johnston, Herbert, *Business Ethics,* New York, NY, Pitman Publishing Corp., 1956.

Jones, Donald G. (ed.), *Business, Religion and Ethics: Inquiry and Encounter,* Cambridge, MA, Oelgeschlager, Gunn & Hain, Inc., 1982.

Kantrow, Alan M., *The Constraints of Corporate Tradition: Doing the Correct Thing, Not Just What the Past Dictates,* New York, NY, Harper & Row Publishers, Inc., 1987.

Kennedy, Tom, and Simon, Charles E., *An Examination of Questionable Payments and Practices,* New York, NY, Praeger Publishers, Inc., 1978.

Kugel, Yerachmiel, and Cohen, Neal P., *Government Regulation of Business Ethics,* 3 vols., Dobbs Ferry, NY, Oceana Publications, 1978.

Kugel, Yerachmiel, and Gruenberg, Gladys W., *Ethical Perspectives on Business and Society,* Lexington, MA, Lexington Books, 1977. *International Payoffs: A Dilemma for Business,* Lexington, MA,. Lexington Books, 1977.

La Croix, W.L., *Principles for Ethics in Business,* Washington, DC, University Press of America, 1976.

Laczniak, Gene R., and Murphy, Patrick E., *Marketing Ethics: Guidelines for Managers,* Lexington, MA, Lexington Books, 1986.

Lilienthal, David E., *Big Business: A New Era,* New York, NY, Arno Press, 1973.

Loeb, Stephen E., *Ethics in the Accounting Profession,* New York, NY, John Wiley & Sons, Inc., 1978.

Luthans, Fred, and Hodgetts, Richard M., *Social Issues in Business: A Text with Current Readings and Cases,* 2nd ed., New York, NY, The Macmillan Co., 1976.

McCoy, Charles S., *Management of Values: The Ethical Difference in Corporate Policy and Performance,* Cambridge, MA, Ballinger Publishing Co., 1985.

Masterson, Thomas, and Nunan, J. Carlton (eds.), *Ethics in Business,* New York, NY, Pitman Publishing Corp., 1968.

Matthews, J.B., and Goodpaster, K.E., *Policies and Persons: A Casebook in Business Ethics,* New York, NY, McGraw-Hill Book Co., 1985.

Merrill, Harwood, *Responsibilities of Business Leadership,* Cambridge, MA, Harvard University Press, 1948.

Milton, Charles R., *Ethics and Expediency in Personnel Management: a Critical History of Personnel Philosophy,* Columbia, SC, University of South Carolina Press, 1970.

Mulcahy, Richard, *Economics of Heinrich Pesch,* New York, NY, Holt, Rinehart & Winston, Inc., 1952.

Myrdal, Gunnar, *An American Dilemma,* New York, NY, Harper & Row, Publishers, 1944.

Nader, Ralph, and Green, Mark J. (eds.), *Corporate Power in America,* New York, NY, Grossman Publishers, 1973.

Nader, Ralph, Green, Mark, and Seligman, Joel, *Taming the Giant Corporation,* New York, NY, W.W. Norton & Co., Inc., 1976.

Nider, Johannes, *On the Contracts of Merchants,* ed. by R.B. Shuman, translated by C.H. Reeves, Norman, OK, University of Oklahoma Press, 1966.

Noonan, John T., *The Scholastic Analysis of Usury,* Cambridge, MA, Harvard University Press, 1957.

Passell, Peter, and Ross, Leonard, *Retreat from Riches: Affluence and Its Enemies,* New York, NY, The Viking Press, Inc., 1974.

Pastin, Mark, *The Hard Problems of Management: Gaining the Ethics Edge,* San Francisco, CA, Jossey-Bass, Inc., Publishers, 1986.

Pennock, J.R., and Chapman, John W. (eds.), *Ethics, Economics, and the Law,* New York, NY, New York University Press, 1982.

Powers, Charles W. (ed.), *People-Profits: the Ethics of Investment,* New York, NY, Council on Religion and International Affairs, 1972.

Preston, Lee E., *Social Issues in Marketing,* Glenview, IL, Scott, Foresman & Co., 1968.

Proudhon, P.J., *What is Property?,* translated by B.R. Tucker, New York, NY, The Humboldt Publishing Co., n.d.

Russon, Allen R., *Personality Development for Business,* 4th ed., Cincinnati, OH, South-Western Publishing Co., 1973.

Schumacher, E.F., *Good Work,* with a preface by George McRobie and an epilogue by Peter N. Gillingham, New York, NY, Harper & Row, Publishers, 1979. *Small is Beautiful: Economics As If People Mattered,* New York, NY, Harper & Row, Publishers, 1975.

Selekman, Benjamin, *A Moral Philosophy for Management,* New York, NY, McGraw-Hill Book Co., 1959.

Sen, Amartya, *On Ethics and Economics,* New York, NY, Basil Blackwell, Inc., 1987.

Sethi, S. Prakash, *Up Against the Corporate Wall: Modern Corporations and Social Issues of the Seventies,* 3rd ed., Englewood Cliffs, NJ, Prentice-Hall, Inc., 1977.

Sharp, Frank C., and Fox, Philip G., *Business Ethics: Studies in Fair Competition,* New York, NY, Appleton-Century-Crofts, 1969, copyright 1937.

Shenfield, Barbara, *Company Boards: Their Responsibilities to Shareholders, Employees, and the Community,* Mystic, CT, Lawrence Verry, 1971.

Silk, Leonard, and Vogel, David, *Ethics and Profit,* New York, NY, Simon & Schuster, Inc., 1976.

Simmons, John, and Mares, William, *Working Together,* New York, NY, Alfred A. Knopf, 1983.

Simon, John G., Powers, Charles W., and Gunnemann, Jon P., *The Ethical Investor: Universities and Corporate Responsibility,* New Haven, CT, Yale University Press, 1972.

Skurski, Roger, *New Directions in Economic Justice,* Notre Dame, IN, University of Notre Dame Press, 1983.

Smith, George A., Jr., and Matthews, John B., Jr., *Business, Society, and the Individual,* rev. ed., Homewood, IL, Richard D. Irwin, Inc., 1967.

Solomon, Robert C., and Hanson, Kristine, *It's Good Business,* New York, NY, Harper & Row Publishers, Inc., 1986.

Stevens, Edward, *Business Ethics,* New York, NY, Paulist Press, 1979.

Sufrin, Sidney C., *Management of Business Ethics,* Port Washington, NY, Kennikat Press Corp., 1979.

Tacusch, Carl F., *Policy and Ethics in Business,* reprint of 1931 ed., New York, NY, Arno Press, Inc., 1973.

Taylor, O.H., *Economics and Liberalism: Collected Papers,* Cambridge, MA, Harvard University Press, 1955.

Uris, Auren, *The Bluebook of Broadminded Business Behavior,* New York, NY, Thomas Y. Crowell Co., 1977.

Van Dam, Cees, and Stallaert, Luud M., *Trends in Business Ethics: Implications for Decision-Making,* Hingham, MA, Kluwer Boston, Inc., 1978.

Veblen, Thorstein, *The Theory of the Leisure Class,* New York, NY, The Macmillan Co., 1899.

Velasquez, Manuel G., *Business Ethics: Concepts and Cases,* Englewood Cliffs, NJ, Prentice-Hall, Inc., 1982.

Veri, Anthony, *The New Code of Action for the Large Corporation Executive,* Albuquerque, NM, American Classical College Press, 1977.

Votaw, Dow, and Sethi, S. Prakash, *The Corporate Dilemma: Traditional Values versus Contemporary Problems,* Englewood Cliffs, NJ, Prentice-Hall, Inc., 1973.

Walton, Clarence C., *Ethos and the Executive: Values in Managerial Decision Making,* Englewood Cliffs, NJ, Prentice-Hall, Inc., 1969.

Williams, Oliver F., and Houck, John M., *Full Value: Cases in Christian Business Ethics,* New York, NY, Harper & Row, Publishers, 1978.

Wirtenberger, Henry, *Morality and Business,* Chicago, IL, Loyola University Press, 1962.

7. Industrial Ethics: Management, Labor, Capitalism

Albus, James S., *People's Capitalism: The Economics of the Robot Revolution,* New York, NY, Gordon Press, Publishers, 1986.

Alford, Robert R., and Friedland, Roger, *Powers of Theory: Capitalism, the State, and Democracy,* New York, NY, Cambridge University Press, 1985.

Bagrit, Leon, *The Age of Automation,* New York, NY, The New American Library, 1965.

Baldwin, R.W., *Social Justice,* Elmsford, NY, Pergamon Press, Inc., 1966.

Bensman, Joseph, *Dollars and Sense: Ideology, Ethics, and the Meaning of Work in Profit and Nonprofit Organizations,* rev. ed., New York, NY, Schocken Books, Inc., 1983.

Berger, Peter L., *The Capitalist Revolution: Fifty Propositions about Prosperity, Equality, and Liberty,* New York, NY, Basic Books, Inc., 1986.

Bowie, Norman E., *Towards a New Theory of Distributive Justice,* Amherst, MA, University of Massachusetts Press, 1971.

Bowles, Samuel, and Gintis, Herbert, *Democracy and Capitalism: Property, Community, and the Contradictions of Modern Social Thought,* New York, NY, Basic Books, Inc., 1986.

Bradley, Keith, and Gelb, Alan, *Worker Capitalism: The New Industrial Relations,* Cambridge, MA, MIT Press, 1983.

Bradshaw, Thornton, and Vogel, David, *Corporations and Their Critics: Issues and Answers to the Problems of Corporate Social Responsibility,* New York, NY, McGraw-Hill Book Co., Inc., 1980.

Buckingham, Walter, *Automation: Its Impact on Business and People,* New York, NY, Harper & Row, Publishers, 1961.

Cecil, Andrew R., *The Third Way: Enlightened Capitalism and the Search for a New Social Order,* Austin, TX, University of Texas Press, 1980.

Chenu, M.D., *The Theology of Work: An Exploration,* tr. by Soiran, Lilian, Chicago, IL, Henry Regnery Co., 1963; 1966.

Clark, John Maurice, *Economic Institutions and Human Welfare,* New York, NY, Alfred A. Knopf, Inc., 1957.

Cooper, Terry L., *The Responsible Administrator: An Approach to Ethics for the Administrative Role,* Port Washington, NY, Associated Faculty Press, 1982.

Cronin, John F., *Catholic Social Principles,* Milwaukee, WI, The Bruce Publishing Co., 1950.

Davis, Annette, *Industrial Relations and New Technology,* New York, NY, Methuen, Inc., 1985.

Davis, Stanley M., *Managing Corporate Culture,* Cambridge, MA, Ballinger Publishing Co., 1985.

de Grazia, Sebastian, *Of Time, Work, and Leisure* New York, NY, The Twentieth Century Fund, Inc., 1962.

Diebold, John, *Beyond Automation,* New York, NY, McGraw-Hill Book Co., Inc., 1964.

Donaldson, Thomas, *Corporations and Morality,* Englewood Cliffs, NJ, Prentice-Hall, Inc., 1982.

Drucker, Peter F., *The Unseen Revolution: How Pension Fund Socialism Came to America,* New York, NY, Harper & Row, Publishers, 1976.

Drummond, William, *Social Justice,* Milwaukee, WI, The Bruce Publishing Co., 1955.

Dunlop, John T., *Automation and Technological Change,* Englewood Cliffs, NJ, Prentice-Hall, Inc., 1962.

Ellul, Jacques, *The Technological Society,* translated by John Wilkinson, New York, NY, Alfred A. Knopf, Inc., 1970.

Evans, William A., *Management Ethics: An Intercultural Perspective,* Hingham, MA, Kluwer-Nijhoff Publishing, 1981.

Forell, George W., and Lazareth, William H. (eds.), *Corporation Ethics: The Quest for Moral Authority,* rev. ed., Philadelphia, PA, Fortress Press, 1980.

Friedman, Milton, and Friedman, Rose, *Free to Choose: A Personal Statement,* New York, NY, Harcourt Brace Jovanovich, Inc., 1979, 1980.

Gibson, Mary, *Workers' Rights,* Totowa, NJ, Rowman & Allanheld, 1983.

Ginsberg, Eli, and Yohalem, Alice M., *Corporate Lib: Women's Challenge to Management,* Baltimore, MD, The Johns Hopkins University Press, 1973.

Harrington, Michael, *Decade of Decision: The Crisis of the American System,* New York, NY, Simon & Schuster, Inc., 1980.

Heilbroner, Robert L., *The Nature and Logic of Capitalism,* New York, NY, W.W. Norton & Co., Inc., 1985.

Hobson, John A., *Progressive Capitalism and the Need to Improve the Qualitative Essence of Life,* Albuquerque, NM, Institute for Economic & Financial Research, 1985.

Jansson, June, and Hellmark, Ann B., *Labor Owned Firms and Workers' Cooperatives,* Brookfield, VT, Gower Publishing Co., 1985.

Jones, Donald G. (ed.), *Doing Ethics in Business: New Ventures in Management Development,* Hingham, MA, Oelgeschlager, Gunn & Hain, Inc., 1982.

Logue, John, and Quilligan, James B., *Buyout! Employee Ownership as an Alternative to Plant Shutdowns: The Ohio Experience,* Kent, OH, Kent Popular Press, 1986.

Louthan, William C., *The Politics of Managerial Morality: A Value-Critical Approach to Political Corruption and Ethics Policy,* Washington, DC, University Press of America, 1981.

Mars, Gerald, *Cheats At Work,* London, George Allen & Unwin, Ltd., 1983.

Murchland, Bernard, *Humanism and Capitalism: A Survey of Thought on Morality and the Economic Order,* Washington, DC, American Enterprise Institute for Public Policy Research, 1984.

Nash, Roland H., *Poverty and Wealth: The Christian Debate over Capitalism,* Westchester, IL, Good News Publishers, 1986.

Nell-Breuning, Oswald von, *Reconstruction of Social Economy,* Milwaukee, WI, The Bruce Publishing Co., 1936.

Novak, Michael, *The Spirit of Democratic Capitalism,* New York, NY, An American Enterprise Institute/Simon & Schuster Publication, 1982. *Toward a Theology of the Corporation,* Washington, DC, American Enterprise Institute for Public Policy Research, 1981.

Owens, James, *Ethical Theory and Business Decisions,* Tantallon, MD, Management Education Ltd., 1982.

Rescher, Nicholas, *Distributive Justice: a Constructive Critique of the Utilitarian Theory of Distribution,* Indianapolis, IN, The Bobbs-Merrill Co., Inc., 1966.

Rojek, Chris, *Capitalism and Leisure Theory,* New York, NY, Methuen, Inc., 1985.

Ryan, John A., *Distributive Justice,* New York, NY, The Macmillan Co., 1942.

Schweikart, David, *Capitalism and Worker Control: An Ethical and Economic Appraisal,* New York, NY, Praeger Publishers, 1980.

Scott, John, *Corporations, Classes, and Capitalism,* 2nd ed., Wolfeboro, NH, Longwood Publishing Group, Inc., 1985.

Smith, William J., *Spotlight on Labor Unions,* New York, NY, Duell, Sloan & Pearce, Inc., 1946.

Smuts, Robert W., *Women and Work in America,* New York, NY, Columbia University Press, 1959.

Snoeyenobos, Milton, and Almeder, Robert (eds.), *Business Ethics: Corporate Values and Society,* Buffalo, NY, Prometheus Books, 1983.

Stern, Robert N., and Comstock, Philip, *Employee Stock Ownership Plans (ESOPs) Benefits for Whom?,* Ithaca, NY, ILR Press, 1978.

Tannenbaum, Frank, *A Philosophy of Labor,* New York, NY, Alfred A. Knopf, Inc., 1951.

Taub, Richard P., *Community Capitalism,* Boston, MA, Harvard Business School Press, 1988.

Tawney, R.H., *Religion and the Rise of Capitalism,* New York, NY, Harcourt, Brace & Co., Inc., 1926.

Toner, Jerome, *The Closed Shop,* Washington, DC, American Council on Public Affairs, 1944.

Weber, Max, *The Protestant Ethic and the Spirit of Capitalism,* London, George Allen & Unwin, Ltd., 1930.

8. Marxian Ethics: Communism, Socialism

Acton, H.B., *The Illusion of the Epoch: Marxism-Leninism as a Philosophical Creed,* London, Cohen & West, 1955.

Ash, William, *Marxism and Moral Concepts,* New York, NY, Monthly Review Press, 1964.

Avineri, Shlomo, *The Social and Political Thought of Karl Marx,* Cambridge, MA, Cambridge University Press, 1969.

Axelos, Kostas, *Alienation, Praxis, and Techne in the Thought of Karl Marx,* translated by Ronald Bruzina, Austin, TX, University of Texas Press, 1976.

Barton, William E., *The Moral Challenge of Communism: Some Ethical Aspects of Marxist-Leninist Society,* London, Friends Home Service Committee, 1966.

Bender, Frederic L. (ed.), *The Betrayal of Marx,* with an introduction by the editor, New York, NY, Harper & Row, Publishers, 1975.

Berdyaev, Nicholas, *The Origin of Russian Communism,* London, Geoffrey Bles, Ltd., Publishers, 1937.

Berlin, Isaiah, *Karl Marx: His Life and Environment,* 4th ed., New York, NY, Oxford University Press, 1978.

Bottomore, Tom, *Modern Interpretations of Marx,* Oxford, Basil Blackwell, 1981.

Bramann, Jorn K., *Capital as Power: A Concise Summary of the Marxist Analysis of Capitalism,* Rochester, NY, Adler Publishing Co., 1984.

Brenkert, George C., *Marx's Ethics of Freedom,* Boston, MA, Routledge & Kegan Paul Ltd., 1983.

Buchanan, Allen E., *Marx and Justice: The Radical Critique of Liberalism,* Totowa, NJ, Rowman & Littlefield, Inc., 1982.

Callinicos, Alex, *Marxism and Philosophy,* New York, NY, Oxford University Press, 1983.

Cameron, J.M., *A Scrutiny of Marxism,* London, SCM Press, Ltd., 1948.

Carver, Terrel, *Marx's Social Theory,* New York, NY, Oxford University Press, 1983.

Childs, David, *Marx and the Marxists: An Outline of Theory and Practice,* Atlantic Highlands, NJ, Humanities Press, Inc., 1973.

Chossudovsky, Michel, *Towards Capitalist Restoration? Chinese Socialism after Mao,* New York, NY, St. Martin's Press, 1986.

Cohen, G.A., *Karl Marx's Theory of History: A Defense,* Princeton, NJ, Princeton University Press, 1978.

Cohen, Jean L., *Class and Civil Society: The Limits of Marxian Critical Theory,* Amherst, MA, University of Massachusetts Press, 1983.

Cole, G.D.H., *Meaning of Marxism,* London, Victor Gollancz, Ltd., 1948.

Croce, Benedetto, *Historical Materialism and the Economics of Marx,* New York, NY, The Macmillan Co., 1914; London, Frank Cass & Co., Ltd., 1966.

Denno, Theodore, *The Communist Millenium: the Soviet View,* the Hague, Martinus Nijhoff, 1964.

Dunayevskaya, Raya, *Marxism and Freedom: From 1776 until Today,* preface by Herbert Marcuse, New York, NY, Twayne Publishers, Inc., 1964.

Dunn, John, *Modern Revolutions,* Cambridge, Cambridge University Press, 1972.

Dupré, Louis, *Marx's Social Critique of Culture,* New Haven, CT, Yale University Press, 1985. *Philosophical Foundations of Marxism,* New York, NY, Harcourt, Brace & World, Inc., 1966. *Marx's Critique of Modern Culture,* New Haven, CT, Yale University Press, 1983.

Fisk, Milton, *Ethics and Society: A Marxist Interpretation of Value,* New York, NY, New York University Press, 1980.

Foster, John B., *The Theory of Monopoly Capitalism: An Elaboration of Marxian Political Economy,* New York, NY, Monthly Review Press, 1986.

Friedrich, Carl J. (ed.), *Nomos VIII: Revolution,* New York, NY, Atherton Press, 1966.

Geras, Norman, *Marx and Human Nature: Refutation of a Legend,* New York, NY, Schocken Books, Inc., 1983.

Gottlieb, Roger S., *History and Subjectivity: The Transformation of Marxian Theory,* Philadelphia, PA, Temple University Press, 1987.

Hampsch, George H., *The Theory of Communism, an Introduction,* New York, NY, Philosophical Library, Inc., 1965.

Hansen, F.R., *The Breakdown of Capitalism: A History of the Idea in Western Marxism,* New York, NY, Methuen, Inc., 1985.

Hook, Sidney, *From Hegel to Marx,* New York, NY, Humanities Press, Inc., 1950.

Hunt, R.N. Carew, *Theory and Practice of Communism,* New York, NY, The Macmillan Co., 1951.

Kalin, Martin G., *The Utopian Flight from Unhappiness: Freud against Marx on Social Progress,* Chicago, IL, Nelson-Hall Co., 1974.

Kamenka, Eugene, *The Ethical Foundations of Marxism,* New York, NY, Praeger Publishers, Inc., 1962. *Marxism and Ethics,* New York, NY, St. Martin's Press, 1969.

Kautsky, Karl, *Ethics and the Materialist Conception of History,* Chicago, IL, Kerr, 1907.

Kropotkin, Peter A., *Ethics, Origin and Development,* New York, NY, Dial Press, 1924.

Krosch, Karl, *Marxism and Philosophy,* translated by F. Halliday, London, New Left Books, 1972.

Lewis, John, *Marxism and the Open Mind,* London, Routledge & Kegan Paul, Ltd., 1957. *The Marxism of Marx,* London, Lawrence & Wishart, 1972.

Lippi, Marco, *Value and Naturalism in Marx,* New York, NY, Schocken Books, Inc., 1980.

Lukes, Steven, *Marxism and Morality,* New York, Oxford University Press, 1985.

Lyon, David, *Karl Marx: A Christian Assessment of His Life and Thought,* Downers Grove, IL, Inter-Varsity Press, 1981.

MacIntyre, Alasdair, *Herbert Marcuse: an Exposition and a Polemic,* ed. by Frank Kermode, New York, NY, The Viking Press, Inc., 1970.

Marcuse, Herbert, *Counterrevolution and Revolt,* Boston, MA, Beacon Press, 1972. *An Essay on Liberation,* Boston, MA, Beacon Press, 1969. *One Dimensional Man,* Boston, MA, Beacon Press, 1964. *Reason and Revolution: Hegel and the Rise of Social Theory,* New York, NY, Humanities Press, Inc., 1954. *Soviet Marxism: a Critical Analysis,* New York, NY, Columbia University Press, 1958.

Marek, Franz, *Philosophy of World Revolution,* translated by D. Simon, London, Lawrence & Wishart, Ltd., 1969.

Mayo, H.B., *Democracy and Marxism,* New York, NY, Oxford University Press, Inc., 1955.

McFadden, Charles, *The Philosophy of Communism,* New York, NY, Benzinger Brothers, Inc., 1939.

Meyer, Alfred G., *Marxism: the Unity of Theory and Practice,* Cambridge, MA, Harvard University Press, 1970.

Mezaros, Istvan, *Marx's Theory of Alienation,* Atlantic Highlands, NJ, Humanities Press, Inc., 1973.

Niebuhr, Rienhold, *Moral Man and Immoral Society,* New York, NY, Charles Scribner's Sons, 1933.

Nivison, David S., *Communist Ethics and Chinese Tradition,* Cambridge, MA, The M.I.T. Press, 1954.

O'Brien, John C., *Karl Marx: The Social Theorist,* New York, NY, State Mutual Book, 1981.

Parsons, Howard L., *Ethics in the Soviet Union Today,* New York, NY, American Institute for Marxist Studies, 1965. *Humanism and Marx's Thought,* Springfield, IL, Charles C. Thomas, Publisher, 1971.

Petrazhitskii, Lev I., *Law and Morality,* Cambridge, MA, Harvard University Press, 1955.

Plamenatz, John, *Karl Marx's Philosophy of Man,* New York, NY, Oxford University Press, Inc., 1975. *Ideology,* London, The Pall Mall Press, 1970.

Przeworski, Adam, *Capitalism and Social Democracy,* New York, NY, Cambridge University Press, 1985.

Rader, Melvin, *Marx's Interpretation of History,* New York, NY, Oxford University Press, 1979.

Rattansi, A., *Marx and the Division of Labour,* Atlantic Highlands, NJ, Humanities Press, Inc., 1982.

Sanderson, John B., *An Interpretation of the Political Ideas of Marx and Engels,* London, Longman Group Ltd., 1969.

Schram, S.A., *The Political Thought of Mao-Tse-Tung,* Harmondsworth, UK, Penguin Books, Ltd., 1969.

Schumpeter, Joseph, *Capitalism, Socialism, and Democracy,* New York, NY, Harper & Row, Publishers, 1950.

Selsam, Howard, *Ethics and Progress: New Values in a Revolutionary World,* New York, NY, International Publishers Co., Inc., 1965. *Socialism and Ethics,* London, Lawrence & Wishart, Ltd., 1949.

Sheed, Frank, *Communism and Man,* New York, NY, Sheed & Ward, 1939.

Somerville, John, *The Philosophy of Marxism: An Exposition,* New York, NY, Random House, Inc., 1967.

Somerville, J., *Soviet Philosophy,* New York, NY, Philosophical Library, Inc., 1946.

Stalin, Joseph, *Dialectical and Historical Materialism,* New York, NY, International Publishers Co., Inc., 1940.

Stillman, Edmund O., *Bitter Harvest; the Intellectual Revolt Behind the Iron Curtain,* New York, NY, Praeger Publishers, Inc., 1959.

Suchting, Wallis A., *Marx: An Introduction,* New York, NY, New York University Press, 1983.

Sweezy, Paul, *Socialism,* New York, NY, McGraw-Hill Book Co., 1949.

Teeple, G., *Marx on Politics: The Development of His Critique 1842–1847,* Toronto, University of Toronto Press, 1984.

Titarenko, A.H., *Morality and Politics: Critical Essays on Contemporary Views about the Relationship between Morality and Politics in Bourgeois Sociology,* ed. by Jim Riordan, translated by Don Danemanis, London, Central Books, 1972.

Tucker, Robert C., *Philosophy and Myth in Karl Marx,* London, Cambridge University Press, 1961.

Venable, Vernon, *Human Nature: the Marxian View,* New York, NY, The World Publishing Co., 1966.

Von Mises, Ludwig, *Socialism,* New Haven, CT, Yale University Press, 1951.

Walliman, Isidor, *Estrangement: Marx's Conception of Human Nature and the Division of Labor,* Westport, CT, Greenwood Press, 1981.

Wetter, Gustav A., *Dialectical Materialism,* New York, NY, Frederick A. Praeger, Inc., 1958. *Soviet Ideology Today,* translated by Peter Heath, New York, NY, Frederick A. Praeger, 1966.

Wilson, Edmund, *To the Finland Station,* Garden City, NY, Doubleday & Co., Inc., 1940.

Wolfson, Murray, *Marx: Economist, Philosopher, Jew.* New York, NY, St. Martin's Press, Inc., 1982.

9. International Ethics: World Community, War, Peace

Abt, Clark C., *A Strategy for Terminating Nuclear War,* Boulder, CO, Westview Press, 1985.

Adams, Ruth, and Cullen, Susan (eds.), *The Final Epidemic: Physicians and Scientists on Nuclear War,* Chicago, IL, Educational Foundation for Nuclear Science, Inc., 1981.

Adler, Mortimer, *How to Think About War and Peace,* New York, NY, Simon & Schuster, Inc., 1944.

Aizenstat, A.J., *Survival for All: The Alternative to Nuclear War with a Practical Plan for Total Denuclearization,* New York, NY, Billner & Rouse, Inc., 1985.

Albert, Michael, and Dellinger, Dave (eds.), *Beyond Survival: New Directions for the Disarmament Movement,* Boston, MA, South End Press, 1983.

Alexander, Horace, *Everyman's Struggle for Peace,* Wallingford, PA, Pendle Hill Publications, 1983.

Allers, Ulrich S., and O'Brien, William V. (eds.), *Christian Ethics and Nuclear Warfare,* Washington, DC, Institute of World Polity, Georgetown University, 1961.

Aron, Raymond, *The Century of Total War,* Boston, MA, The Beacon Press, 1955. *On War,* translated by Terence Kilmartin, New York, NY, Doubleday & Co., Inc., 1958. *The Great Debate: Theories of Nuclear Strategy,* translated by Ernst Pawel, Lanham, MD, University Press of America, 1985.

Bainton, Roland, *Christian Attitudes Toward War and Peace,* Nashville, TN, Abingdon Press, 1960.

Baker, David, *Shape of Wars to Come,* Briarcliff Manor, NY, Stein and Day, 1982.

Barash, David P., and Lipton, Judith Eve, *Stop Nuclear War: A Handbook!,* foreword by Caldicott, Helen, New York, NY, Grove Press, Inc., 1982.

Barnaby, Frank, *Prospects for Peace,* Elmsford, NY, Pergamon Press, Inc., 1980.

Bartone, John C., *War: A Medical, Psychological and Scientific Subject Analysis with Research Index and Bibliography,* Annandale, VA, ABBE Publications Association of Washington, DC, 1983.

Beer, Francis A., *Peace Against War: The Ecology of International Violence*, New York, NY, W.H. Freeman & Co., 1981.

Beilenson, Laurence W., *Survival and Peace in the Nuclear Age*, Chicago, IL, Regnery Gateway, Inc., 1980.

Bender, David L. (ed.), *The Arms Race: Opposing Viewpoints*, St. Paul, MN, Greenhaven Press, 1982.

Beres, Louis R., *Apocalypse: Nuclear Catastrophe in World Politics*, Chicago, IL, University of Chicago Press, 1980.

Bertram, Christoph (ed.), *The Future of Strategic Deterrence*, Hamden, CT, Shoe String Press, Inc., 1981.

Betts, Richard K., *Nuclear Blackmail and Nuclear Balance*, Washington, DC, Brookings Institution, 1987.

Bobbitt, Philip, *Democracy and Deterrence: The History and Future of Nuclear Strategy*, New York, NY, St. Martin's Press, 1987.

Bottome, Edgar, *The Balance of Terror: Nuclear Weapons and the Illusion of Security in the Nuclear Age, 1945–1985*, Boston, MA, Beacon Press, 1986.

Brauch, Hans G., and Clarke, Duncan L. (eds.), *Decision Making for Arms Limitation in the 1980's: Assessments and Prospects*, Cambridge, MA, Ballinger Publishing Co., 1983.

Brembeck, Howard S., *The Alternative to Nuclear War*, Goshen, IN, Alternative World Foundation, Inc., 1985.

Brodie, Bernard, *War and Politics*, New York, NY, The Macmillan Co., 1973.

Bueno De Mesquita, Bruce, *The War Trap*, New Haven, CT, Yale University Press, 1983.

Bulkeley, Rip, and Spinardi, Graham, *Space Weapons: Deterrence or Delusion?*, Totowa, NJ, Barnes & Noble Books Imports, 1986.

Cadoux, C. John, *The Early Christian Attitude to War: A Contribution to the History of Christian Ethics*, New York, NY, The Seabury Press, 1982.

Calder, Nigel, *Nuclear Nightmares: An Investigation into Possible Wars*, New York, NY, The Viking Press, 1980.

Carlton, David, and Schaerf, Carlo (eds.), *The Arms Race in the Nineteen Eighties*, New York, NY, St. Martin's Press, 1982.

Cesaretti, Charles A., and Vitale, Joseph T. (eds.), *Rumors of War: A Moral and Theological Perspective on the Arms Race*, New York, NY, The Seabury Press, 1982.

Child, James, *Nuclear War: The Moral Dimension*, Bowling Green, OH, Social Philosophy & Policy Center, 1986.

Childress, James F., *Moral Responsibility in Conflicts: Essays on Nonviolence, War, and Conscience*, Baton Rouge, LA, Louisiana State University Press, 1982.

Clark, I.C., *Limited Nuclear War*, Princeton, NJ, Princeton University Press, 1982.

Clarke, Michael, and Mowlam, Marjoire (eds.), *Debate on Disarmament*, London, Routledge & Kegan Paul, 1982.

Clausewitz, Karl von, *On War*, translated by J.J. Graham, 3 vols., London, Routledge & Kegan Paul, Ltd., 1949. *On War*, ed. by Michael Howard and Peter Paret, Princeton, NJ, Princeton University Press, 1976.

Clouse, Robert G. (ed.), *War: Four Christian Views*, Downers Grove, IL, Inter-Varsity Press, 1981.

Cohen, Marshall, Nagel, Thomas, and Scanlon, Thomas (eds.), *War and Moral Responsibility*, Princeton, NJ, Princeton University Press, 1974.

Cohen, Sam, *The Truth About the Neutron Bomb: The Inventor of the Bomb Speaks Out*, New York, NY, William Morrow & Co., Inc., 1983.

Cookson, John, and Nottingham, Judith, *Survey of Chemical and Biological Warfare*, New York, NY, Monthly Review Press, n.d.

Cousins, Norman, *In Place of Folly*, New York, NY, Washington Square Press, Inc., 1962.

Crosser, Paul K., *War is Obsolete: the Dialectics of Military Technology and its Consequences*, Amsterdam, B.R. Grünner, 1972.

Delavignette, Robert, *Christianity and Colonialism*, New York, NY, Hawthorn Books, Inc., 1964.

De Soras, Alfred, *International Morality*, New York, NY, Hawthorn Books, Inc., 1963.

Doob, Leonard W., *The Pursuit of Peace*, Westport, CT, Greenwood Press, 1981.

Dotto, Lydia, *Planet Earth in Jeopardy: Environmental Consequences of Nuclear War*, New York, NY, John Wiley & Sons, Inc., 1986.

Dougherty, James E., *The Catholic Bishops and the Dilemmas of Nuclear Deterrence*, Cambridge, MA, Institute for Foreign Policy Analysis, 1983.

Dougherty, James E., et al., *Ethics, Deterrence, and National Security*, Elmsford, NY, Pergamon Press, Inc., 1985.

Douglass, James W., *Lightning East to West: Jesus, Gandhi, and the Nuclear Age*, New York, NY, Crossroad Publishing Co., 1983.

Douglass, Joseph D., and Livingstone, Neil C., *America the Vulnerable: The Threat of Chemical and Biological Warfare*, Lexington, MA, Lexington Books, 1987.

Drinan, Robert F., *Beyond the Nuclear Freeze*, New York, NY, The Seabury Press, 1983.

Dunn, Lewis A., *Controlling The Bomb: Nuclear Proliferation in the 1980's*, New Haven, CT, Yale University Press, 1982.

Ellison, Marvin M., *The Center Cannot Hold: The Search For a Global Economy of Justice*, Washington, DC, University Press of America, 1983.

Elshtain, Jean B., *Women and War*, New York, NY, Basic Books, Inc., 1987.

Eppstein, John, *The Catholic Tradition of the Law of Nations*, Washington, DC, Catholic Association for International Peace, 1935. *Code of International Ethics*, Westminister, MD, The Newman Press, 1953.

Ferguson, John, *Disarmament: The Unanswerable Case*, North Pomfret, VT, David & Charles, Inc., 1982.

Fisher, David, *Morality and the Bomb: An Ethical Assessment of Nuclear Deterrence*, New York, NY, St. Martin's Press, 1985.

Flynn, Eileen P., *My Country Right or Wrong? Selective Conscientious Objection in the Nuclear Age*, Chicago, IL, Loyola University Press, 1985.

Ford, Daniel, Kendall, Henry, and Nadis, Steven, *Beyond the Freeze: The Road to Nuclear Sanity*, Boston, MA, The Union of Concerned Scientists, Beacon Press, 1982.

Forsyth, M.G., Keens-Soper, H.M.A., and Savigear, P. (eds.), *The Theory of International Relations. Selected texts from Gentili to Treitschke*, London, George Allen & Unwin, Ltd., 1970.

Fotion, N., and Elfstrom, Gerard, *Military Ethics: Guidelines for Peace and War*, New York, NY, Methuen, Inc., 1986.

Fox, Michael, and Groarke, Leo, *Nuclear War: Philosophical Perspectives*, New York, NY, Peter Lang Publishing, 1985.

Freedman, Lawrence, *The Evolution of Nuclear Strategy*, New York, NY, St. Martin's Press, 1981. *The Price of Peace: Living with the Nuclear Dilemma*, New York, NY, Henry Holt & Co., 1986.

Frei, Daniel, and Catrina, Christian, *Risks of Unintentional Nuclear War*, Totowa, NJ, Allanheld, Osmun & Co., Publishers, Inc., 1983.

French, Peter A., *Individual and Collective Responsibility: Massacre at My Lai*, Cambridge, MA, Schenkmann Publishing Co., 1972.

Gabriel, Richard A., *To Serve With Honor: A Treatise on Military Ethics and the Way of the Soldier*, New York, NY, Praeger Publishers, Inc., 1987.

Gallie, W.B., *Philosophers of Peace and War*, New York, NY, Cambridge University Press, 1978.

Galtung, Johann, *Peace and World Structure*, Atlantic Highlands, NJ, Humanities Press, Inc., 1980.

Gandhi, M.K., *Non-Violence in Peace and War*, 2 vols., Ahmedabad, India, Navajivan Publishing House, 1942–1948.

Gara, Larry, *War Resistance in Historical Perspective*, Wallingford, PA, Pendle Hill Publications, 1983.

Garden, Timothy, *Can Deterrence Last? Peace Through a Nuclear Strategy*, Cincinnati, OH, Seven Hills Books, 1987.

Geyer, Alan, *The Idea of Disarmament: Rethinking the Unthinkable*, Aurora, IL, Caroline House, Inc., 1982.

Ginsberg, Robert (ed.), *The Critique of War: Contemporary Philosophical Explorations*, Chicago, IL, Henry Regnery Co., 1969.

Glossop, Ronald J., *Confronting War*, Jefferson, NC, McFarland & Co., Inc., 1983.

Goldman, Kjell, *International Norms and War Between States, Three Studies in International Politics*, Stockholm, Läromedelsförlagen, for The Swedish Institute of International Affairs, 1971.

Goddard, Harold C., *Atomic Peace*, Wallingford, PA, Pendle Hill Publications, 1983.

Goodwin, Geoffrey, *Ethics and Nuclear Deterrence*, New York, NY, St. Martin's Press, 1982.

Gorbachev, Mikhail S., *The Coming Century of Peace*, Stewart Richardson, ed., New York, NY, Richardson & Steirman, 1986.

Graham, Daniel, and Fossedal, Gregory A., *A Defense That Defends: Blocking Nuclear Attack*, Old Greenwich, CT, Devin-Adair Co., Inc., 1983.

Gray, Colin S., *Strategic Studies: A Critical Assessment*, Westport, CT, Greenwood Press, 1982.

Gray, J. Glenn, *The Warriors. Reflections on Men in Battle*, New York, NY, Harcourt Brace Jovanovich, Inc., 1959.

Gregg, Richard B., *Pacifist Program*, Wallingford, PA, Pendle Hill Publications, 1983.

Ground Zero, *What About the Russians—and Nuclear War?* New York, NY, Pocket Books, Inc., 1983.

Halevy, Elie, *The Era of Tyrannies: Essays on Socialism and War*, translated by R.K. Webb, note by Fritz Stern, New York, NY, Doubleday and Co., 1965.

Halperin, Morton H., *Defense Strategies for the Seventies*, Washington, DC, University Press of America, 1983. *Nuclear Fallacy: Dispelling the Myth of Nuclear Strategy*, Cambridge, MA, Ballinger Publishing Co., 1987.

Hardin, Russell, et al. (eds.), *Nuclear Deterrence: Ethics and Strategy*, Chicago, IL, University of Chicago Press, 1985.

Hauerwas, Stanley, *Should War Be Eliminated? Philosophical and Theological Investigations*, Milwaukee, WI, Marquette University Press, 1984.

Heller, Agnes, and Feher, Ferenc, *Doomsday or Deterrence? On the Antinuclear Issue*, Armonk, NY, M.E. Sharpe, Inc., 1986.

Herschberger, Guy F., *War, Peace, and Nonresistance*, rev. ed., Scottdale, PA, Herald Press, 1969.

Heyer, Robert (ed.), *Nuclear Disarmament: Key Statements of Popes, Bishops, Councils and Churches*, Ramsey, NJ, Paulist Press, 1982.

Hodgson, Peter, *Nuclear Physics in Peace and War*, New York, NY, Hawthorn Books, Inc., 1961.

Hoffman, Stanley, *Duties Beyond Borders: On the Limits and Possibilities of Ethical International Politics*, Syracuse, NY, Syracuse University Press, 1981.

Hollenbach, David, *Nuclear Ethics: A Christian Moral Argument*, New York/Ramsey, NJ, Paulist Press, 1983.

Holloway, David, *The Soviet Union and the Arms Race*, New Haven, CT, Yale University Press, 1983.

Hornus, Jean-Michel, *It Is Not Lawful For Me To Fight*, Scottdale, PA, Herald Press, 1980.

Horsburgh, H.J.N., *Non-Violence and Aggression: a Study of Gandhi's Moral Equivalent of War*, London, Oxford University Press, 1968.

Howard, Michael (ed.), *Restraints on War: Studies in the Limitation of Armed Conflict*, New York, NY, Oxford University Press, 1979.

Howard, Michael, *War and the Liberal Conscience*, New Brunswick, NJ, Rutgers University Press, 1978. *The Causes of War*, Cambridge, MA, Harvard University Press, 1983.

Huntziger, Alexander P., *The Metaphysics of Violence and the Theory of War*, Albuquerque, NM, Institute for Economic & Political World Strategic Studies, 1980.

Hutchins, Robert M., *St. Thomas and the World State*, Aquinas Lecture, Milwaukee, WI, Marquette University Press, 1949.

Jacobs, Dan, *The Brutality of Nations*, New York, NY, Alfred A. Knopf, Inc., 1987.

Johnson, James T., *Can Modern War Be Just?*, New Haven, CT, Yale University Press, 1984. *Just War Tradition and the Restraint of War: A Moral and Historical Inquiry*, Princeton, NJ, Princeton University Press, 1981.

Jones, John D., and Griesbach, Marc F., *Just War Theory in the Nuclear Age*, Lanham, MD, University Press of America, 1985.

Kahan, Jerome H., *Security in the Nuclear Age: Developing U.S. Strategic Arms Policy*, Washington, DC, Brookings Institution, 1975.

Kahn, Herman, *On Thermonuclear War*, Princeton, NJ, Princeton University Press, 1961. *Thinking about the Unthinkable*, New York, NY, Horizon Press, 1962.

Kaplan, Fred, *The Wizards of Armageddon*, New York, NY, Simon and Schuster, 1983.

Katz, Arthur M., *After Nuclear War: The Economic and Social Impacts of Nuclear Attacks on the United States,* Cambridge, MA, Ballinger Publishing Co., 1981.

Kennan, George F., *The Nuclear Delusion: Soviet-American Relations in the Atomic Age,* New York, NY, Pantheon Books, 1983.

Kennett, Lee, *A History of Strategic Bombing,* New York, NY, Charles Scribner's Sons, 1983.

Kernan, Thomas P., *The Future of Peace,* New York, NY, Philosophical Library, Inc., 1980.

Kojm, Christopher A. (ed.), *The Nuclear Freeze Debate,* New York, NY, The H.W. Wilson Co., 1983.

Kraybill, Donald B., *Facing Nuclear War,* Scottdale, PA, Herald Press, 1982.

Laarman, Edward J., *Nuclear Pacifism: "Just War" Thinking Today,* New York, NY, Peter Lang Publishing, Inc., 1984.

Lackey, Douglas P., *Moral Principles and Nuclear Weapons,* Totowa, NJ, Rowman & Allanheld, 1984.

Lawler, Justus, *Nuclear War, the Ethic, the Rhetoric, the Reality,* Westminster, MD, The Newman Press, 1965.

Lens, Sidney, *The Day Before Doomsday: An Anatomy of the Nuclear Arms Race,* Garden City, NY, Doubleday & Co., Inc., 1977.

Lifton, Robert Jay, and Falk, Richard, *Indefensible Weapons: The Political and Psychological Case Against Nuclearism,* New York, NY, Basic Books, Inc., Publishers, 1982.

Long, Edward L., *Peace Thinking in a Warring World,* Philadelphia, PA, Westminster Press, 1983.

McDermott, Jeanne, *The Killing Winds: The Menace of Biological Warfare,* New York, NY, Arbor House Publishing Co., 1987.

Macvey, John W., *Space Weapons—Space War,* Briarcliff Manor, NY, Stein & Day Publishers, 1979.

Mandelbaum, Michael, *The Nuclear Question: The United States and Nuclear Weapons, 1946–1976,* Cambridge, Cambridge University Press, 1979. *The Nuclear Revolution: International Politics Before and After Hiroshima,* Cambridge, Cambridge University Press, 1981.

Matheson, Peter, *A Just Peace,* New York, NY, Friendship Press, 1981.

Matty, Thomas, *Peace and Conscience Formation,* Winona, MN, St. Mary's Press, 1983.

Morgan, Patrick M., *Deterrence: A Conceptual Analysis,* 2nd ed., Newbury Park, CA, Sage Publications, Inc., 1983.

Mumford, Lewis, *The Human Way Out,* Wallingford, PA, Pendle Hill Publications, 1983.

Murnion, Philip (ed.), *The Challenge of Peace: A Commentary On the U.S. Catholic Bishops' Pastoral Letter on War and Peace,* New York, NY, Crossroad Publishing Co., 1983.

Murray, Thomas E., *Nuclear Policy for War and Peace,* Cleveland, OH, World Publishing Co., 1960.

Mushkat, Marion, *The Third World and Peace: Some Aspects of Problems of the Inter-Relationship of Interdevelopment and International Security,* New York, NY, St. Martin's Press, 1983.

Muste, A.J., *The World Task of Pacifism,* Wallingford, PA, Pendle Hill Publications, 1983.

Myers, Edward, *The Chosen Few: Surviving the Nuclear Holocaust,* San Francisco, CA, Sally Taylor and Friends, 1981.

Nagle, William, *Morality and Modern Warfare,* Baltimore, MD, Helicon Press, Inc., 1960.

Nye, Joseph S., Jr., *Ethics and Foreign Policy,* Lanham, MD, University Press of America, 1985.

O'Brien, William, *The Conduct of Just and Limited War,* New York, NY, Praeger Publishers, 1981.

O'Brien, William V., *Nuclear War, Deterrence and Morality,* Westminster, MD., The Newman Press, 1967.

O'Brien, William V., and Langan, John P., *The Nuclear Dilemma and the Just War Tradition,* Lexington, MA, Lexington Books, 1986.

Parsons, Howard, *Self, Global Issues and Ethics,* Atlantic Highlands, NJ, Humanities Press, Inc., 1980.

Paskins, B.A., and Dockrill, M.L., *The Ethics of War,* Minneapolis, MN, University of Minnesota Press, 1979.

Paxman, Jeremy, and Harris, Robert, *A Higher Form of Killing: The Secret Story of Gas and Germ Warfare,* New York, NY, Farrar, Straus, & Giroux, Inc., 1983.

Phillips, Robert L., *War and Justice,* Norman, OK, University of Oklahoma Press, 1984.

Pillar, Paul R., *Negotiating Peace: War Termination as a Bargaining Process,* Princeton, NJ, Princeton University Press, 1983.

Quester, George H., *The Future of Nuclear Deterrence,* Lexington, MA, Lexington Books, 1986.

Ramsey, Paul, *The Just War: Force and Political Responsibility,* Washington, DC, University Press of America, 1983. *War and the Christian Conscience: How Shall Modern War Be Conducted Justly?* Durham, NC, Duke University Press, 1961.

Rapoport, Anatol, *Strategy and Conscience,* introd. by Karl W. Deutsch, New York, NY, Harper & Row, Publishers, 1964.

Rapoport, Roger, *The Great American Bomb Machine,* New York, NY, E.P. Dutton & Co., Inc., 1971.

Reilly, Robert R., and Schall, James V., *Justice and War in the Nuclear Age,* Washington, DC, University Press of America, 1983.

Robinson, Julian P., *Chemical Warfare Arms Control: A Framework for Considering Policy Alternatives,* New York, NY, Taylor & Francis, Inc., 1985.

Rowe, Dorothy, *Living with the Bomb,* New York, NY, Methuen, Inc., 1985.

Rummel, R.J., *The Just Peace,* Beverly Hills, CA, Sage Publications, Inc., 1981.

Russell, Bertrand, *Common Sense and Nuclear Warfare,* New York, NY, Simon & Schuster, Inc., 1959.

Russell, Wilfred T., *The Role of Violence in History and the Metaphysics of War,* Albuquerque, NM, Institute for Economic & Political World Strategic Studies, 1979.

Ryan, John K., *Modern War and Basic Ethics,* Milwaukee, WI, The Bruce Publishing Co., 1940.

Saffer, Thomas H., and Kelly, Orville E., *Countdown Zero,* introd. by Stewart L. Udall, New York, NY, G.P. Putnam's Sons, 1982.

Schell, Jonathan, *Abolition,* New York, NY, Alfred A. Knopf, Inc., 1984. *The Fate of the Earth,* New York, NY, Alfred A. Knopf, Inc., 1982.

Scott, James B., *The Catholic Conception of International Law,* Washington, DC, Georgetown University Press, 1934.

Shannon, Thomas A. (ed.), *War or Peace? The Search For*

New Answers, Maryknoll, NY, Orbis Books, 1980. *What Are They Saying About Peace and War?* Ramsey, NJ, Paulist Press, 1983.

Sharp, Gene, *Exploring Nonviolent Alternatives,* Boston, MA, Porter Sargent Publisher, 1970.

Shrader-Frechette, K.S., *Nuclear Power and Public Policy: The Social and Ethical Problems of Fission Technology,* Hingham, MA, Kluwer Academic Publishers, 1980.

Snow, Donald M., *The Necessary Peace: Nuclear Weapons and Superpower Relations,* Lexington, MA, Lexington Books, 1987.

Snow, Michael, *Christian Pacifism,* Richmond, IN, Friends United Press, 1981.

Starr, Joyce R. (ed.), *Peace Through Economic Cooperation: Initiatives for the Near East,* New York, NY, Praeger Publishers, 1983.

Stockholm International Peace Research Institute, *The Arms Race and Arms Control, 1983,* New York, NY, International Publications Service, 1983.

Stratmann, F., *War and Christianity Today,* Westminster, MD, The Newman Press, 1956.

Stein, Walter, *Nuclear Weapons, a Catholic Response,* New York, NY, Sheed & Ward, 1961.

Sturzo, Luigi, *Nationalism and Internationalism,* New York, NY, Roy Publishers, Inc., 1946.

Sundberg, Gunnar, *Toward Pacifism,* Wallingford, PA, Pendle Hill Publications, 1983.

Taylor, Theodore B., *A World Without Nuclear Weapons,* Cambridge, MA, Ballinger Publishing Co., 1988.

Thompson, Charles S. (ed.), *Morals and Missiles,* London, James Clarke & Co., Ltd., Publishers, 1959.

Thompson, E.P., *Beyond the Cold War: A New Approach to the Arms Race and Nuclear Annihilation,* New York, NY, Pantheon Books, 1982.

Tooke, Joan D., *The Just War in Aquinas and Grotius,* London, SPCK (The Society for Promoting Christian Knowledge), 1965.

Tucker, Robert W., *Just War and Vatican Council 2: A Critique,* New York, NY, Council on Religion and International Affairs, 1966.

U.S. Catholic Bishops, *The Pastoral Letter on War and Peace,* "The Challenge of Peace: God's Promise and Our Response," Washington, DC, Origins, NC Documentary Service, 1983.

Uhl, Michael, and Ensign, Tod, *GI Guinea Pigs: How The Pentagon Exposed Our Troops to Dangers More Deadly Than War, Agent Orange and Atomic Radiation,* New York, NY, Playboy Press, 1983.

Walzer, Michael, *Just and Unjust Wars: A Moral Argument with Historical Illustrations,* New York, NY, Basic Books, 1977. *Obligations: Essays on Disobedience, War and Citizenship,* Cambridge, MA, Harvard University Press, 1982.

Wasserstrom, Richard A. (ed.), *War and Morality,* Belmont, CA, Wadsworth Publishing Co., Inc., 1970.

Wells, Donald A., *War Crimes and Laws of War,* Lanham, MD, University Press of America, 1984.

Woolsey, James (ed.), *Nuclear Arms: Ethics, Strategy, Politics,* San Francisco, CA, Institute for Contemporary Studies, 1983.

Wright, Quincy, *A Study of War,* abridged by Louise Leonard Wright, Chicago, IL, University of Chicago Press, 1964.

Yoder, John H., *When War is Unjust: Being Honest in Just-War Thinking,* Minneapolis, MN, Augsburg Publishing House, 1984.

Zagare, Frank C., *The Dynamics of Deterrence,* Chicago, IL, University of Chicago Press, 1986.

10. Earth: The Aged, Pollution, Population, Poverty, Resources

Allsop, Bruce, *The Garden Earth: the Case for Ecological Morality,* New York, NY, William Morrow & Co., Inc., 1972.

Armstrong, Terry R. (ed.), *Why Do We Still Have an Ecological Crisis?* Englewood Cliffs, NJ, Prentice-Hall, Inc., 1972.

Barbour, Ian, *Earth Might Be Fair: Reflections on Ethics, Religion and Ecology,* Englewood Cliffs, NJ, Prentice-Hall, Inc., 1972.

Barbour, Ian G. (ed.), *Western Man and Environmental Ethics,* Reading, MA, Addison-Wesley Publishing Co., Inc., 1973.

Barkley, Paul W., and Seckler, David, *Economic Growth and Environmental Decay: the Solution Becomes the Problem,* New York, NY, Harcourt Brace Jovanovich, 1972.

Baumol, William J., and Oates, Wallace E., *The Theory of Environmental Policy,* Englewood Cliffs, NJ, Prentice-Hall, Inc., 1975.

Bayles, Michael D. (ed.), *Ethics and Population,* Cambridge, MA, Schenkman Publishing Co., Inc., 1976.

Beatty, Ralph P., *Senior Citizen,* Springfield, IL, Charles C. Thomas, Publisher, 1962.

Benthall, Jonathan (ed.), *Ecology in Theory and Practice,* New York, NY, The Viking Press, Inc., 1973.

Black, John, *The Dominion of Man: the Search for Ecological Responsibility,* Chicago, IL, Aldine Publishing Co., 1970.

Blackstone, William T. (ed.), *Philosophy and Environmental Crisis,* Athens, GA, University of Georgia Press, 1974.

Borgstrom, Georg, *Too Many: an Ecological Overview of Earth's Limitations,* New York, NY, The Macmillan Co., 1971.

Boughey, Arthur S., *Ecology of Populations,* 2nd ed., ed. by Charles E. Stewart, New York, NY, The Macmillan Co., 1973.

Brantl, Virginia M., and Brown, Sr. Marie R. (eds.), *Readings in Gerontology,* St. Louis, MO, The C.V. Mosby Co., 1973.

Brewer, Richard, *Principles of Ecology,* Philadelphia, PA, W.B. Saunders Co., 1979.

Brubacker, Sterling, *To Live on Earth: Man and His Environment in Perspective,* Baltimore, MD, The Johns Hopkins University Press, 1972.

Bumagin, Victoria, and Hirn, Kathryn F., *Aging is a Family Affair,* New York, NY, Thomas Y. Crowell Co., 1979.

Callahan, Daniel, *Ethics and Population Limitation,* New York, NY, Population Council, Inc., 1971.

Carson, Rachel, *Edge of the Sea,* New York, NY, The New American Library, Inc., 1971. *Silent Spring,* Boston, MA, Houghton Mifflin Co., 1962.

Chen, Kan, and Lagler, Kurt (eds.), *Growth Policy: Population, Environment, and Beyond,* Ann Arbor, MI, University of Michigan Press, 1974.

Cobb, J.B., Jr., *Is It Too Late: a Theology of Ecology,* Milwaukee, WI, Bruce Publishing Co., 1971.

Commoner, Barry, *The Closing Circle,* New York, NY, Alfred

A. Knopf, Inc., 1971; Bantam Books, Inc., 1972. *Science and Survival,* New York, NY, Ballantine Books, Inc., 1970.

Cox, George W., and Atkins, Michael D., *Agricultural Ecology: An Analysis of World Food Production Systems,* San Francisco, CA, W.H. Freeman & Co., 1979.

Dangott, Lilliam, and Kalish, Richard, *A Time to Enjoy: the Pleasures of Aging,* Englewood Cliffs, NJ, Prentice-Hall, Inc., 1978.

Davis, Richard H. (ed.), *Aging: Prospects and Issues,* rev. ed., University Park, CA, University of Southern California, Andrus Gerontology Center, 1977.

De Beauvoir, Simone, *The Coming of Age: the Study of the Aging Process,* New York, NY, G.P. Putnam's Sons, 1972.

Deedy, John, and Nobile, Philip (eds.), *The Complete Ecology Fact Book,* New York, NY, Doubleday Publishing Co., 1972.

Degen, Charles, *Age Without Fear: How to Face the Later Years With Confidence,* Jericho, NY, Exposition Press, 1972.

Derr, Thomas S., *Ecology and Human Need,* Philadelphia, PA, Westminster Press, 1975.

Disch, Robert (ed.), *Ecological Conscience: Values for Survival,* Englewood Cliffs, NJ, Prentice-Hall, Inc., 1970.

Douglas, William O., *The Three Hundred Year War: a Chronicle of Ecological Disease,* New York, NY, Random House, Inc., 1972.

Dubos, René, *A God Within,* New York, NY, Charles Scribner's Sons, 1973. *Man Adapting,* New Haven, CT, Yale University Press, 1965. *So Human an Animal,* New York, NY, Charles Scribner's Sons, 1968. *The Wooing of Earth,* New York, NY, Charles Scribner's Sons, Inc., 1980.

Egler, Frank, *Way of Science: a Philosophy of Ecology for the Layman,* Riverside, NJ, Hafner Press, 1970.

Ehrenfeld, David *Conserving Life on Earth,* New York, NY, Oxford University Press, 1972.

Ehrlich, Paul, *The Machinery of Nature,* New York, NY, Simon & Schuster, 1987. *The Population Bomb,* new rev. ed., New York, NY, Ballantine Books, Inc., 1971.

Ehrlich, Anne H., and Ehrlich, Paul R., *Earth,* New York, NY, Franklin Watts, Inc., 1987.

Ehrlich, Paul, and Ehrlich, Anne, *Population, Resources, Environment,* 2nd ed., San Francisco, CA, W.H. Freeman & Co., Publishers, 1972.

Elliot, Robert, and Gare, Arran (eds.), *Environmental Philosophy,* University Park, PA, Pennsylvania State University Press, 1983.

Ellison, Jerome, *Life's Second Half: The Dynamics of Aging,* Greenwich, CT, Devin-Adair Co., Inc., 1978.

Emery, F.E., and Trist, E.L., *Towards a Social Ecology: Contextual Appreciation of the Future in the Present,* New York, NY, Plenum Publishing Corp., 1973.

Falk, Richard A., *This Endangered Planet: Prospects and Proposals for Human Survival,* New York, NY, Random House, Inc., 1972.

Foss, Philip O., *Politics and Ecology,* N. Scituate, MA, Duxbury Press, 1972.

Fraser, Dean, *The People Problem: What You Should Know About Growing Population and Vanishing Resources,* Bloomington, IN, Indiana University Press, 1973.

Frejka, Tomas, *The Future of Population Growth: Alternate Paths to Equilibrium,* New York, NY, John Wiley & Sons, Inc., 1973.

Graham, Frank, Jr., *Since Silent Spring,* New York, NY, Fawcett Book Group, 1977.

Green, Ronald M., *Population Growth and Justice: An Examination of Moral Issues Raised by Rapid Population Growth,* Missoula, MT, Scholars Press, 1976.

Hall, Judith, *The Problem That Cannot Be Resolved: Population and World Order,* New York, NY, Grossman Publishers, 1975.

Hardin, Garrett, *Exploring New Ethics for Survival: the Voyage of the Spaceship Beagle,* New York, NY, The Viking Press, Inc., 1972. *The Limits of Altruism: An Ecologist's View of Survival,* Bloomington, IN, Indiana University Press, 1977.

Harrington, Michael, *The Other America: Poverty in the United States,* Baltimore, MD, Penguin Books, Inc., 1963.

Hartman, Betsy, *Reproductive Rights and Wrongs: The Global Politics of Population Control and Contraceptive Choice,* New York, NY, Harper & Row Publishers, Inc., 1987.

Hartman, Robert H., ed., *Poverty and Economic Justice: A Philosophical Approach,* Mahwah, NJ, Paulist Press, 1984.

Hewitt, Ken, *Lifeboat: Man and a Habitable Earth,* New York, NY, John Wiley & Sons, Inc., 1976.

Holdgate, M.W., *A Perspective of Environmental Pollution,* New York, NY, Cambridge University Press, 1979.

Jackson, Barbara Ward, Lady, *A New Creation? Reflections on the Environmental Issue,* Vatican City, Pontifical Commission for Justice and Peace, 1973. *Progress for a Small Planet,* New York, NY, W.W. Norton & Co., 1979. *The Rich Nations and the Poor Nations,* New York, NY, W.W. Norton & Co., Inc., 1962.

Jackson, Barbara Ward, Lady and Dubos, René, *Only One Earth: the Care and Maintenance of a Small Planet,* New York, NY, W.W. Norton & Co., Inc., 1972.

Juzek, Charles, and Mehrtens, Susan, *Earthkeeping: Reading in Human Ecology,* Pacific Grove, CA, The Boxwood Press, 1974.

Kallen, Horace M., *Toward a Philosophy of the Seas,* Charlottesville, VA, University Press of Virginia, 1973.

Kaplan, S.J., and Kivy-Rosenberg, E., *Ecology and the Quality of Life,* Springfield, IL, Charles C. Thomas, Publisher, 1973.

Katz, Robert, *A Giant in the Earth: the Green Revolution and the Future With 100 Billion People,* New York, NY, Stein & Day, Publishers, 1972.

Kozlovsky, Daniel G. (ed.), *An Ecological and Evolutionary Ethic,* Englewood Cliffs, NJ, Prentice-Hall, Inc., 1974.

Lappé, Francis Moore, and Collins, Joseph, with Fowler, Cary, *Food First: Beyond the Myth of Scarcity,* Boston, MA, Houghton Mifflin Co., 1977.

Liang, Daniel S., *Facts About Aging,* Springfield, IL, Charles C. Thomas, Publisher, 1973.

Lippard, Vernon W. (ed.), *Family Planning, Demography, and Human Sexuality in Medical Education,* New York, NY, Josiah Macy, Jr., Foundation, 1974.

Livingston, John A., *One Cosmic Instant: Man's Fleeting Supremacy,* Boston, MA, Houghton Mifflin Co., 1973.

McCloskey, H.J., *Ecological Ethics and Politics,* Totowa, NJ, Rowman & Littlefield, Inc., 1983.

McHarg, Ian, *Design with Nature,* Garden City, NY, Natural History Press, 1971.

Maddox, John, *The Doomsday Syndrome,* New York, NY, McGraw-Hill Book Co., 1973.

Meeker, Joseph W., *The Spheres of Life: an Introduction to World Ecology,* New York, NY, Charles Scribner's Sons, 1974.

Passmore, John, *Man's Responsibility for Nature: Ecological Problems and Western Tradition,* New York, NY, Charles Scribner's Sons, 1974.

Percy, Charles H., and Mangel, Charles, *Growing Old in the Country of the Young,* New York, NY, McGraw-Hill Book Co., 1974.

Piburne, Michael, *The Environment: A Human Crisis,* Rochelle Park, NJ, Hayden Book Co., Inc., 1974.

Rozak, Theodore, *Person Planet: The Creative Disintegration of Industrial Society,* Garden City, NY, Doubleday & Co., 1979.

Sassone, Robert L., *Handbook on Population,* Santa Ana, CA, published by the author, 1972.

Scoby, Donald R. (ed.), *Environmental Ethics: Studies of Man's Self-Destruction,* Minneapolis, MN, Burgess Publishing Co., 1971.

Sloan, Irving J., *Environment and the Law;* Dobbs Ferry, NY, Oceana Publications, Inc., 1971.

Slusser, Gerald, and Slusser, Dorothy M., *Technology, the God That Failed: the Environmental Catastrophe,* Philadelphia, PA, The Westminster Press, 1971.

Smith, G., and Smyth, J.C., *Biology of Affluence,* New York, NY, Longman, Inc., 1973.

Soleri, Paolo, *The Bridge Between Matter and Spirit is Matter Becoming Spirit,* New York, NY, Doubleday Publishing Co., 1973.

Stanford, Quentin (ed.), *The World's Population: Problems of Growth,* New York, NY, Oxford University Press, 1972.

Stone, Glenn C. (ed.), *A New Ethic for a New Earth,* New York, NY, Friendship Press, 1971.

Strong, Maurice F. (ed.), *Who Speaks for Earth,?* New York, NY, W.W. Norton & Co., Inc., 1973.

Swift, Morrison I., *Can Mankind Survive?,* New York, NY, Gordon Press Publishers, 1977.

Taylor, Paul W., *Respect for Nature: A Theory of Environmental Ethics,* Princeton, NJ, Princeton University Press, 1986.

Vann, Anthony, and Rogers, Paul (eds.), *Human Ecology and World Development* New York, NY, Plenum Publishing Corp., 1974.

Vayda, Andrew P., *War in Ecological Perspective,* New York, NY, Plenum Publishing Corp., 1976.

Veatch, Robert M. (ed.), *Population Policy and Ethics: The American Experience,* New York, NY, Halsted Press, 1977.

11. Specialized Bibliographies

Bochenski, Joseph M. (ed.), *Guide to Marxist Philosophy: an Introductory Bibliography,* Chicago, IL, The Swallow Press, Inc., 1972.

Dollen, Charles J., *Abortion in Context: a Select Bibliography,* Metuchen, NJ, Scarecrow Press, Inc., 1970.

Elliston, Frederick A., and Van Schaick, Jane, *Legal Ethics: An Annotated Bibliography and Resource Guide,* Littleton, CO, Fred B. Rothman & Co., 1984.

Floyd, Mary K. (ed.), *Abortion Bibliography for 1970.* Troy, NY, Whitston Publishing Co., 1972. *Abortion Bibliography for 1971,* Troy, NY, Whitston Publishing Co., 1973. *Abortion Bibliography for 1972,* Troy, NY, Whitston Publishing Co., 1973. *Abortion Bibliography for 1973,* Troy, NY, Whitston Publishing Co., 1974. *Abortion Bibliography for 1974,* Troy, NY, Whitston Publishing Co., 1975. *Abortion Bibliography for 1975,* Troy, NY, Whitston Publishing Co., 1976. *Abortion Bibliography for 1976,* Troy, NY, Whitston Publishing Co., 1978. *Abortion Bibliography for 1977,* Troy, NY, Whitston Publishing Co., 1979. *Abortion Bibliography for 1978,* Troy, NY, Whitston Publishing Co., 1980. *Abortion Bibliography for 1979,* Troy, NY, Whitston Publishing Co., 1982. *Abortion Bibliography for 1980,* Troy, NY, Whitston Publishing Co., 1982.

Goode, Polly T. (ed.), *Abortion Bibliography for 1981,* Troy, NY, Whitston Publishing Co., 1984. *Abortion Bibliography for 1982,* Troy, NY, Whitston Publishing Co., 1985.

The Hastings Center Bibliography of Society, Ethics and the Life Sciences, published annually by the Institute of Society, Ethics and the Life Sciences, Hastings-on-Hudson, New York.

Hasting Center Staff, (ed.), *The Hastings Center's Bibliography of Ethics, Biomedicine and Professional Responsibility,* Frederick, MD, University Publications of America, 1984.

Israel, Stanley, *The Bibliography on Divorce,* New York, NY, Bloch Publishing Co., Inc., 1973.

Jones, Donald G., *A Bibliography of Business Ethics, 1971–1975,* Charlottesville, VA, University Press of Virginia, 1977.

Jones, Donald G., and Troy, Helen (eds.), *A Bibliography of Business Ethics, Nineteen Seventy-Six to Nineteen Eighty,* Charlottesville, VA, University Press of Virginia, 1982.

Jones, Donald G., and Bennett, Patricia (eds.), *Bibliography of Business Ethics 1981–1985,* Lewiston, NY, The Edwin Mellen Press, 1986.

Krichmar, Albert, et al., *The Women's Rights Movement in the United States 1848–1970: A Bibliography and Sourcebook,* Metuchen, NJ, Scarecrow Press, Inc., 1972. *The Women's Movement in the Seventies: An International English-Language Bibliography,* Metuchen, NJ, Scarecrow Press, Inc., 1977.

McLean, George F. (ed.), *An Annotated Bibliography of Philosophy in Catholic Thought, 1900–1964,* New York, NY, Frederick Ungar Publishing Co., Inc., 1967. *A Bibliography of Christian Philosophy and Contemporary Issues,* New York, NY, Frederick Ungar Publishing Co., Inc., 1967.

Matczak, Sebastian A., *Philosophy: A Select Classified Bibliography of Ethics, Economics, Law, Politics, Sociology,* Louvain, Belgium, N.V. Uitgeverij Nauwelaerts Edition S.A., 1969.

Nevins, Madeline M. (ed.), *Annotated Bibliography of Bioethics: Selected 1976 Titles,* Rockville, MD, Information Planning Associates, Inc., 1977.

Parker, William, *Homosexuality: a Selective Bibliography of Over Three Thousand Items,* Metuchen, NJ, Scarecrow Press, Inc., 1971. *Homosexuality Bibliography: Supplement, 1970–1975,* Metuchen, NJ, Scarecrow Press, Inc., 1977.

Pence, Terry, *Ethics in Nursing: An Annotated Bibliography,* 2nd ed., New York, NY, National League for Nursing, 1986.

Triche, Charles W., and Triche, Diane S., *Euthanasia Controversy, Eighteen Twelve to Nineteen Seventy-Four: A Bibliography with Select Annotations,* Troy, NY, Whitston Publishing Co., 1975.

Walters, LeRoy (ed.), *Bibliography of Bioethics,* 6 vols., Detroit, MI, Gale Research Co., 1975, 1976, 1977, 1978, 1979, 1980. *Bibliography of Bioethics,* vol. 7, New York, NY, Free Press, 1981. *Bibliography of Bioethics,* vol. 8, New York, NY, Macmillan Publishing Co., 1982. *Bibliography of Bioethics,* vol. 9, New York, NY, Macmillan Publishing Co., 1983.

Walters, LeRoy and Kahn, Tamar J. (eds.), *Bibliography of Bioethics,* vol. 10, Washington, DC, Georgetown University Press/Kennedy Institute, 1984. *Bibliography of Bioethics,* vol. 11, Washington, DC, Georgetown University Press/Kennedy Institute, 1985.

Weinberg, Martin, and Bell, Alan (eds.), *Homosexuality: an Annotated Bibliography,* New York, NY, Harper & Row, Publishers, 1972.

Index